MARKETING

MARKETING

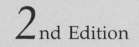

2nd Edition

STEVEN J. SKINNER
University of Kentucky

HOUGHTON MIFFLIN COMPANY
Boston Toronto
Geneva, Illinois   Palo Alto   Princeton, New Jersey

Sponsoring Editor: Diane McOscar
Project Editor: Mary Ann Carberry
Production/Design Coordinator: Jill Haber
Senior Manufacturing Coordinator: Marie Barnes
Marketing Manager: Robert D. Wolcott

Cover and Part Opening Illustrations: Paul Turnbaugh

Chapter opening photo credits:
Chapter 1 *5* Saatchi & Saatchi NYC—'92
Chapter 2 *35* The Gillette Company
Chapter 3 *71* Photo courtesy of Nautilus TM, The Multimedia magazine on CD-ROM.
(credits continue on page C1)

Printed in the U.S.A.
Library of Congress Catalog Card Number: 93-78653
Student Book ISBN: 0-395-62147-X
Examination Copy ISBN: 0-395-69243-1

123456789-DW-97 96 95 94 93

To Moira, Aaron, and Carrie Skinner

ABOUT THE AUTHOR

Steven J. Skinner is the Rosenthal Professor of Marketing in the College of Business and Economics at the University of Kentucky, where he has taught undergraduate and graduate courses in marketing for 13 years. He was previously on the faculty at Illinois State University, and was formerly a research administrator for State Farm Insurance Companies. His research interests include marketing ethics, channels of distribution, and sales management. His research has been published in a number of journals including *Journal of Marketing Research*, *Journal of Retailing*, *Academy of Management Journal*, *Journal of Business Research*, *Public Opinion Quarterly*, *Journal of the Academy of Marketing Science*, and *Journal of Personal Selling and Sales Management*. He has received the Mu Kappa Tau Award for the best article in the *Journal of Personal Selling and Sales Management*, is on the board of contributing advisors of the *Marketing Education Review*, and is on the editorial review board of the *Journal of Business Research*. He is also co-author of *The New Banker: Developing Leadership in a Dynamic Era*, a widely acclaimed professional book.

Brief Contents

Contents

Preface

When I wrote the first edition of *Marketing,* my objective was to involve students in the learning process by presenting traditional marketing concepts in a context that excites their imaginations. This was also my objective in revising the second edition. Marketing is ever-changing, making it a challenging and exciting field. Changes taking place in eastern Europe and the former republics of the Soviet Union, the emergence of the Pacific Rim and the European Community, and the North American Free Trade Agreement uniting the United States, Canada, and Mexico signify that barriers to trade are falling throughout the world. The Earth Summit in Rio has focused increasing attention on the environment. More and more firms throughout the world are adopting total quality management (TQM) programs, placing even more emphasis on customer satisfaction. Events like these will not only have an impact on a firms' marketing activities, they will also play a big role in our futures. Students seem to respond best and most imaginatively when they can see that the topics that illustrate the basic concepts of marketing are part of their future.

If we had a crystal ball, we might see that no event will have a greater impact on business and society in the 21st century than the end of the cold war. In a few short years, historically speaking, Japan has recovered from the devastation of World War II to become one of the leading economic powers in the world. They did it by investing in people, not weapons. The result was a nation bound together not by a common enemy, but by a common goal—to satisfy customers by making the best quality products in the world. As the United States, former republics of the Soviet Union, and others dismantle their military complex, it appears that economic strength, not military power, will determine which nations lead the world during the next century. Competition will be even tougher as Latin America, Viet Nam, China, and many other nations strive to make better goods and services that can be sold at lower prices.

Not every organization will survive in this competitive global environment, where products made anywhere compete with products made anywhere else. The common denominator will be a customer focus; successful firms will develop goods and services that satisfy customers. In everything they do, every individual in the organization will have a common aim—customer satisfaction. Thus, marketing activities will play a critical role in organizations as they fight for survival in the most competitive global environment in history.

ORGANIZATION OF THE BOOK

To accomplish the objective set forth above, *Marketing* is organized into eight parts that provide students with an integrated and strategic approach to the study of marketing concepts. Every chapter has a logical place in this framework that reflects the practice of marketing. Chapters that contain material that is critical to organizations in the 21st century—ethics and social responsibility issues, the global environment, and marketing for services and nonprofit organizations—appear early in the text. Part 1 introduces the foundations of strategic marketing planning, laying the groundwork for the remainder of the book. Part 2 describes the environment for strategic marketing, including ethical and social responsibility issues and the global environment. Part 3 presents the analysis for strategic marketing decisions, including segmentation and forecasting, consumer and business-to-business buying behavior, and information for marketing decision making. Parts 4 through 7 examine decisions relating to the marketing mix variables, including product strategy, price strategy, distribution strategy, and promotion strategy. Part 8 discusses organizing, implementing, and controlling marketing strategies, and illustrates the role of the marketing plan in strategic implementation.

Each of the eight parts of the book are built around the customer, the focus of marketing activities. Because there are no miscellaneous chapters at the end of the book, topics such as ethics and social responsibility and the global environment are integrated throughout the book. Four icons are used to help instructors and students identify these integrated themes and the topics.

 Close to the Customer   Ethics and Social Responsibility

 Marketing Strategy   Global Environment

CHANGES IN THE SECOND EDITION

Several changes have been made in the second edition to accommodate the needs of our customers—teachers and students. These changes reflect the practice of marketing and include the addition of significant new developments in the field. Every effort has been made to present the most current and comprehensive coverage of marketing concepts and practices.

- As noted earlier, the chapters called "Ethical and Social Issues in Marketing" and "The Global Marketing Environment" have been moved to Part 2, The Marketing Environment. Based on reviews of the book, it is felt that this better reflects the true nature of marketing.

- The chapter called "Products from Services and Nonprofit Organizations" has been moved to Part 4, Product Strategy. As services now account for over 70 percent of our GNP, many reviewers felt this chapter was an important part of the product section and should not be placed at the end of the book.

- A new chapter called "Developing the Marketing Plan" has been included. As the last chapter in the book, it discusses how the marketing plan details the activities necessary to implement marketing strategies.
- Four themes that mirror the issues of today's marketing environment are woven throughout the text. As noted above, these themes are called to the reader's attention by margin icons.

In addition to the new chapter, the changes in chapter sequence, and the integrated themes, text coverage has been completely revised and updated as follows:

- New opening vignettes introduce each chapter.
- A new feature has been added which illustrates how marketing activities bring organizations *Close to the Customer*.
- Each chapter once again contains two cases, with one featuring a global application. Over 90 percent of them are new, the remainder updated.
- New coverage of total quality management as it relates to marketing activities (see Chapter 1).
- New coverage of Porter's Generic Strategy Model has been incorporated into the topic strategic marketing planning (see Chapter 2).
- New coverage of the characteristics and values of society as they relate to the marketing environment and technology transfer (see Chapter 3).
- New coverage of ecology and green marketing and expanded coverage of consumerism (see Chapter 4).
- New coverage of the global marketplace, countertrading, and multinational trade groups (see Chapter 5).
- New coverage of international marketing research (see Chapter 9).
- Expanded coverage of product quality (see Chapter 10).
- New coverage of products from nonprofit organizations (see Chapter 11).
- Expanded coverage of products for global markets (see Chapter 12).
- Expanded coverage of pricing for global markets (see Chapter 14).
- New coverage of wholesaling in foreign countries and expanded coverage of trends in wholesaling (see Chapter 16).
- New coverage of retailing in foreign countries and expanded coverage of the changing retail environment (see Chapter 17).
- New coverage of integrated marketing communications and promotion and society (see Chapter 18).
- Expanded coverage of advertising for global markets and new coverage of infomercials (see Chapter 19).

- New coverage of sales positions in the future, managing the international selling effort, and sales promotion methods for international markets (Chapter 20).
- New coverage of empowerment, matrix organization, and teams (see Chapter 21).

FEATURES OF THE SECOND EDITION

Several features of *Marketing* increase students' involvement in learning. These features also make the book enjoyable to read and enjoyable to teach.

- *Objectives.* Each chapter begins with several learning objectives, guiding students to the most important concepts.
- *Outline.* An outline of the chapter follows the objectives, providing students with a chapter road map.
- *Opening Vignette.* The text for each chapter begins with a story that dramatizes a main concept of the chapter in concrete and contemporary terms. In this way students first see the topic in a real-world context.
- *Close to the Customer.* This feature illustrates how marketing practices bring firms close to the customer.
- *Marketing Close-up.* This feature describes in detail the actual business application of one of the chapter's topics.
- *Point/Counterpoint.* This feature presents a debate to stimulate student thought.
- *Margin Icons.* Four icons alert the reader to integrated coverage of four themes in this edition: close to the customer, marketing strategy, ethics and social responsibility, and global environment.
- *Examples.* Real-world examples of a wide variety of products, services, and organizations are used throughout the text.
- *Figures, Tables, and Photographs.* Numerous figures, tables, and photographs are integrated into the text. Photographs feature instructional captions.
- *Margin Notes.* Definitions of key terms are placed in the margin to facilitate student learning.
- *Chapter Summary.* Each chapter concludes with a summary of the major concepts discussed.
- *Key terms.* A list of the key terms highlighted in the text helps students review the material.
- *Questions for Discussion and Review.* Each chapter has ten or more discussion and review questions that enable students to evaluate their understanding of the material.
- *Two Cases.* Each chapter features two cases on current topics to help students sharpen their marketing skills; the second case is a global application.

- *Glossary*. Every key term in the text is also defined in the glossary.
- *Appendixes*. Career opportunities in marketing and financial analysis for marketing are discussed in the appendices.
- *Name and Subject Indexes*. Both a name index and a subject index help students find topics of interest.

INSTRUCTIONAL SUPPORT SYSTEM

A comprehensive instructional system accompanies *Marketing*. The system is coordinated with the text and is designed to provide instructional support for both students and professors.

Instructional Support for Students

- *Study Guide*. The Study Guide helps students review each chapter with matching, multiple choice, and fill-in-the-blank questions. In addition, challenging exercises based on actual marketing decision-making situations stretch students' imaginations.
- *Marketing Plan*. This allows students to construct their own marketing plan, giving them the kind of "real-world" practice needed to succeed in their careers. A template is accompanied with a sample plan and is available in both print and computerized IBM PC versions.
- *Marketer: A Simulation*. This marketing simulation for IBM-compatible microcomputers allows students to make marketing decisions through simulated real-world experiences. Acting as marketing teams, students encounter many factors as they make decisions. Additional support materials are provided for instructors.

Instructional Support for Professors

- *Marketing Videos*. Over six hours of high-quality videos give students a close-up look at marketing activities in real companies. This major program includes video illustration of important marketing concepts, a video case study, and one video per chapter developed around the themes of the text.
- *Laser Disc*. An exciting laser disc program illustrates key marketing concepts through video and includes transparency images.
- *Instructor's Manual*. The Instructor's Manual includes the chapter objectives, a perspective on the chapter, a detailed lecture outline, notes on the three in-text features, answers to discussion and review questions, comments on the cases and answers to case discussion questions, and involvement exercises.

- *Test Bank*. The Test Bank includes more than 3,300 essay, multiple choice, and true-false questions. The questions are labeled according to whether they test knowledge (KN), comprehension (CH), or application (AP).
- *Microcomputerized Test Bank*. The Test Bank is provided on microcomputer disk, and questions can be selected to provide a test master for duplication.
- *Call-in Test Service*. Questions can be selected from the Test Bank, and printed tests can be ordered by telephone.
- *Lecture Bank*. Lecture Bank includes the lecture outlines from the Instructor's Manual on microcomputer disk. The instructor's own notes can be incorporated into the outlines with a word processing program, and the combined lecture notes can be printed.
- *Color Transparencies*. A complete color transparency program that includes many figures from outside the text is included.

ACKNOWLEDGMENTS

I would like to acknowledge the many colleagues and students who have contributed much to this revision. The helpful suggestions of these reviewers are especially appreciated.

Madan M. Batra
Indiana University of
    Pennsylvania

Rudy Berdine
California State Poly
    University

Joseph Bonnice
Manhattan College

Thomas L. Burns
Metropolitan State
    University

Don Cappa
Chabot College

Anthony Cox
Indiana University

Bernice N. Dandridge
Diablo Valley College

Martin Decatur
Suffolk Community
    College

Suzanne B. Desai
Marshall University

Peter T. Doukas
Westchester Community
    College

Sam Dunbar
Delgado Community
    College

Brien Ellis
University of Kentucky

Audrey G. Federouch
Duquesne University

Linda Felicetti
Clarion University of
    Pennsylvania

Letty C. Fisher
Westchester Community
    College

Dennis E. Garrett
Marquette University

Jonathan Goodrich
Florida International
    University

Geoffrey Gordon
Northern Illinois
    University

Joyce Grahn
University of Minnesota/
    Duluth

Pola Gupta
University of Northern
    Iowa

Robert F. Gwinner
Arizona State University

Douglas K. Hawes
University of Wyoming

James Healey
Chabot College

Nancy P. Houston
Slippery Rock University
    of Pennsylvania

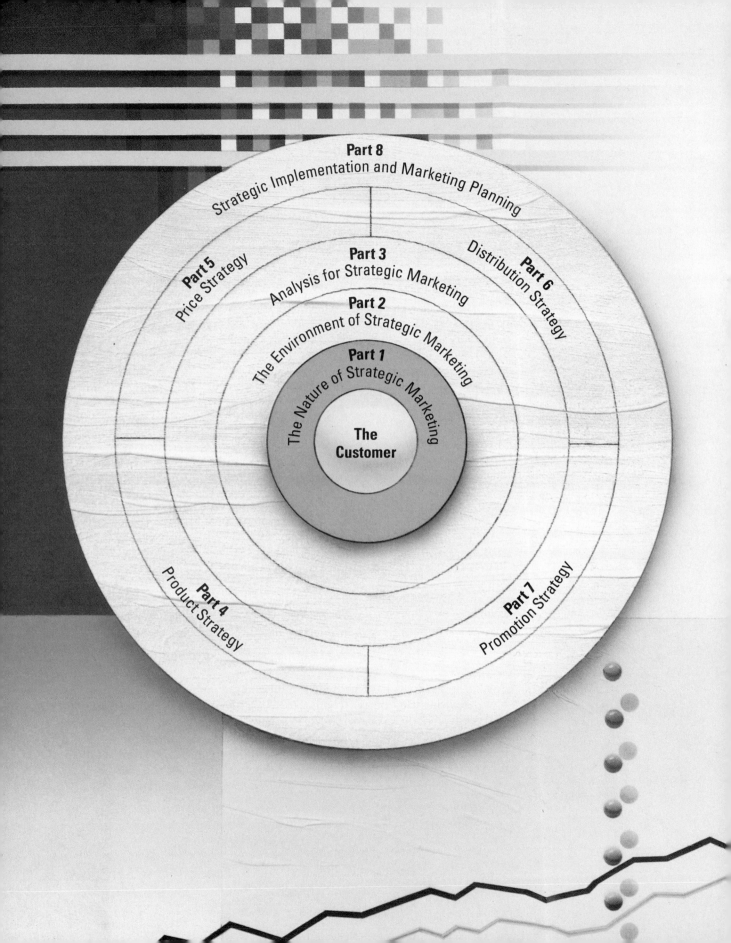

Part 8
Strategic Implementation and Marketing Planning

Part 5
Price Strategy

Part 3
Analysis for Strategic Marketing

Part 6
Distribution Strategy

Part 2
The Environment of Strategic Marketing

Part 1
The Nature of Strategic Marketing

The Customer

Part 4
Product Strategy

Part 7
Promotion Strategy

Sandra Hunter
University of
Nebraska–Omaha

Mary Joyce
Bryant College

James Kenderdine
University of Oklahoma

Maryon F. King
Southern Illinois
University, Carbondale

Duncan LaBay
University of
Massachusetts—Lowell

Kenneth J. Lacho
University of New
Orleans

Edward Laube
Macomb Community
College

Marilyn Lavin
University of
Wisconsin–Whitewater

Richard M. Lewis
Southern Arkansas
University

Patricia M. Manninan
North Shore Community
College

Suzanne McCall
East Texas State
University

Edward Menge
Franklin University

Mary Anne Milward
University of Arizona

William Motz
Lansing Community
College

Elaine Notarantonio
Bryant College

Nicholas Nugent
New Hampshire College

Eugene L. O'Conner
Cal Poly State University,
San Luis Obispo

Michael F. O'Neill
California State
University, Chico

Terry Paul
The Ohio State University

Raymond E. Polchow
Muskingum Area
Technical College

Kathy L. Pullins
Columbus State
Community College

Daniel Rajaratnam
Baylor University

Gary Rhoads
Idaho State University

Robert G. Roe
University of Wyoming

Robert H. Ross
Wichita State University

Harold Sekiguchi
University of
Nevada–Reno

Raj Sethuraman
University of Iowa

Alan Shao
University of North
Carolina–Charlotte

Rodger Singley
Illinois State University

Rawlie Sullivan
University of St. Thomas

James E. Swartz
California State
Polytechnic, Pomona

Ronald Taylor
Mississippi State
University

Kenneth Thompson
University of North Texas

Debbie M. Thorne
University of Tampa

C. Burk Tower
University of
Wisconsin–Oshkosh

Linnell H. Tunison
DeVry Institute of
Technology

Dennis White
Florida State University

Dena Winokur
Pace University

William R. Wynd
Eastern Washington
University

Several individuals have provided input and encouragement during the time I was revising this book. Thanks to Marty Meloche of Western Michigan University, Geoffrey Gordon of Northern Illinois University, and Theresa Bilitski of the University of Kentucky for their assistance. I am especially indebted to all the folks at Houghton Mifflin both in the forefront and behind the scenes, who provide inspiration and perspiration for their authors.

S.J.S.

The Nature of Strategic Marketing

Foundations of Strategic Marketing

OBJECTIVES

- *To define the term* marketing.

- *To explain how marketing activities facilitate satisfying exchanges.*

- *To discuss the evolution of marketing.*

- *To compare the marketing concept to the societal marketing concept.*

- *To explain the significance of marketing.*

- *To identify the major steps in developing a marketing strategy.*

- *To list the components of the marketing management process.*

- *To discuss the challenges regarding quality and competitiveness facing many organizations.*

OUTLINE

Many observers have labeled the 1990s as the decade of the customer. Managers have come to realize that the companies that are succeeding put their customers first. Books such as *Customer Satisfaction Guaranteed* and *The Service Advantage* can be found on managers' desks. Consulting firms report that customer-service work is on the rise. It almost seems as though paying attention to the customer is a new concept, but it isn't.

In the 1950s, General Motors gained a lead in customer satisfaction by designing cars to suit the needs of many different customers. In contrast to Henry Ford's policy in the early 1900's of providing a car in any color as long as it was black, GM produced a variety of models and soared to a 52 percent share of the U.S. automobile market in 1962. During the 1960s and 1970s, with a growing population and little foreign competition, GM assumed that customers were satisfied and concentrated on profits. Automobile manufacturers from Japan, Germany, Sweden, and other parts of the world realized that American consumers' needs were not being satisfied and moved quickly to do the job. By 1992, GM's market share was barely 35 percent.

The automobile industry is not the only one in which the United States has lost its dominance. As global competition intensified in the 1980s, the United States lost its preeminent position as a world leader in semiconductor, steel, and consumer electronics manufacturing. Foreign companies have also invested heavily in service industries such as banking, insurance, entertainment, and hotels. Today, firms are going back to the basics—customer satisfaction.

At MBNA, a Delaware-based credit card company, the words "THINK OF YOURSELF AS THE CUSTOMER" are woven into the carpet at all four entrances; above almost 1,000 doorways are signs saying, "THINK OF YOURSELF AS THE CUSTOMER." Phone service agents call customers who want to close an account and try to change their minds, even waiving annual fees at times. The senior vice president of the customer assistance department tells his 380 people that customers making late payments "need a hugging, not a mugging." This emphasis on the customer has helped MBNA retain 95 percent of its customers each year, while competitors keep about 88 percent.

Like MBNA, many firms try to find out what customers want and how to better serve them. Reliable Corp., an office supply house in Chicago, monitors its own performance with a regular questionnaire to customers. According to the firm's marketing manager, the survey is based on the belief that "we could be doing better." At Embassy Suites Hotels, at least five customers are interviewed each day and their comments posted for the entire staff to see. Technicians at Du

To some this glass is half full.
To our flight attendants it's definitely half empty.

On every British Airways flight our highly trained staff pays special attention to even the smallest detail. So you always arrive refreshed and ready. *It's the way we make you feel* that makes us the world's favourite airline.

The world's favourite airline.

Pont now spend significant time in customers' plants to figure out new applications for Du Pont products. A Du Pont salesman in Korea once asked managers at Reebok International Ltd. how his company could better serve them. As a result, the Du Pont flexible plastic tubes that were developed for the automobile industry are now built into the soles of Reebok's ERS sneakers to give them more bounce. At British Airways, service excellence, not operations, drives the business. As a result, the airline once nicknamed Bloody Awful now enjoys one of the best reputations in the industry.[1] ●

The examples used to start this book are meant to capture the views presented throughout this text. Many U.S. firms have steadily lost ground to foreign businesses over the last two decades. Although many factors have contributed to this problem, one is that U.S. firms often have lacked a customer orientation. Satisfying customers' needs and wants is the basis of effective marketing. Many firms now are fighting back by developing new products, modifying existing ones, and trying new ways to serve customers. These activities, which all come under the domain of marketing, are based on a fundamental, time-proven philosophy of providing customer satisfaction.

Every organization, large or small, profit or nonprofit, must have a purpose, a reason to exist. As we will see in Chapter 2, this is called the *organizational mission.* According to renowned management consultant Peter Drucker, the most fundamental mission of any organization is to satisfy its customers:

> There is only one valid definition of business purpose: to create a satisfied customer. It is the customer who determines what the business is. Because it is its purpose to create a customer, any business enterprise has two—and only these two—basic functions: marketing and innovation. . . . Actually marketing is so basic that it is not just enough to have a strong sales force and to entrust marketing to it. Marketing is not only much broader than selling, it is not a specialized activity at all. It is the whole business seen from the point of view of its final result, that is, from the customer's point of view.[2]

A new pattern in developing high-quality products and satisfying customers is emerging throughout the world. As you can see from Drucker's state-

---

[1] Based on information from Iris S. Rosenberg, "U.S. Industries Rethink the 'Role' of the Customer," *Quality Digest,* January 1993, pp. 41–47; "Satisfaction Action Is . . . ," *Marketing News,* January 20, 1992, p. 4; Stephen Phillips, Amy Dunkin, James B. Treece, and Keith Hammonds, "King Customer," *Business Week,* March 12, 1990, pp. 88–94; Patricia Sellers, "What Customers Really Want," *Fortune,* June 4, 1990, pp. 58–68; Sharyn Hunt and Ernest F. Cooke, "It's Basic But Necessary: Listen to the Customer," *Marketing News,* March 5, 1990, pp. 22–23; and Mark Maremont, "How British Airways Butters Up the Passenger," *Business Week,* March 12, 1990, p. 94.

[2] Peter F. Drucker, *The Practice of Management* (New York: Harper & Row, 1954), p. 37.

ment, marketing must be at the heart of this movement. Top-level executives from Diners' Club in Argentina were assigned the task of telephoning customers, searching for ways to improve service and delight customers. The results, according to the consultant who directed the project, were outstanding. Senior executives heard first-hand what was right and what was wrong with the company's services, giving an immediacy to customer concerns.[3] Organizations throughout the world have come to the realization that good things happen when you listen to customers. Chapter 1 introduces you to some of the foundations of strategic marketing and sets the stage for the remainder of the book. As you read, try your best to look at issues from the *customer's* point of view.

DEFINING MARKETING

One reason most students find the study of marketing interesting is that they already know something about it. You may not have thought about it, but you have performed many marketing activities. Whether it was opening a lemonade stand when you were a youngster or working part-time at a fast-food restaurant or retail store to help fund your education, you were engaged in marketing. The American Marketing Association, recognizing the wide range of marketing activities, offers the following definition of marketing:

> **Marketing** is the process of planning and executing the conception, pricing, promotion, and distribution of ideas, goods, and services to create exchanges that satisfy individual and organizational objectives.[4]

■ **marketing** the process of planning and executing the conception, pricing, promotion, and distribution of ideas, goods, and services to create exchanges that satisfy individual and organizational objectives

This definition of marketing is the one most widely accepted by marketing educators and practitioners.[5] It indicates that marketing involves a diverse set of activities directed at a wide range of products, and it stresses the importance of facilitating satisfying exchanges between buyers and sellers. In this view, the various marketing activities enable us to satisfy our needs and wants. A **need** is something that is required for basic human survival—water, food, shelter, or clothing. Human beings also need to belong, to be loved, and to express themselves. A **want** is something that is desired but not required for basic survival. People in our society want many things, such as sports cars, CD players, fashionable clothes, and quality entertainment. Without marketing, many of our needs and wants would remain unsatisfied because exchanges would be much more difficult to accomplish. To gain a full understanding of marketing, let's look at this definition more closely.

■ **need** something that is required for basic human survival—water, food, shelter, clothing, love, self-expression

■ **want** something that is desired but not required for basic survival

[3]Michael E. Raynor, "Fantastic Things Happen When You Talk to Customers," *Marketing News,* February 15, 1993, p. 8.
[4]"AMA Board Approves New Marketing Definition," *Marketing News,* March 1, 1985, p. 1. Reprinted by permission.
[5]O. C. Ferrell and George H. Lucas, "An Evaluation of Progress in the Development of a Definition of Marketing," *Journal of the Academy of Marketing Science,* Fall 1987, pp. 12–23.

FIGURE 1.1
Marketing Services
Marketing activities are not limited to companies that produce physical goods. Service organizations such as Sea World in Orlando, Florida also engage in marketing.

Marketing Involves a Diverse Set of Activities

When Playmates Ltd. (the Hong Kong firm of Teenage Mutant Ninja Turtles fame) introduced Water Babies, soft-bodied dolls that are filled with warm water, the company wasn't sure what to expect. Two million of the dolls sold the first year.[6] However, it took much more than a good product for Playmates' Water Babies to succeed. The following activities are just a few of the typical tasks that firms like Playmates Ltd. perform when marketing a product.

Determine if there is demand for the product.

Develop and test-market the product.

Name the product.

Design a package for the product.

Analyze competitors' products.

Determine the price of the product.

Develop advertisements for the product.

[6]Subrata N. Chakravarty, "The Water Babies Story: Persistence," *Forbes,* May 11, 1992, pp. 198–200.

Recruit and train salespeople.

Plan sales promotion activities such as displays and coupons.

Prepare and circulate news releases.

Develop procedures for shipping products.

Determine locations for plants and warehouses.

Decide where the product will be sold.

Collect feedback from customers.

As you can see, marketing is not simply selling or advertising or any single activity. The marketing process encompasses all of these diverse activities, each of which is then broken down into many more specific activities. For instance, product development entails dozens of activities, including researching and designing the product, analyzing competitors, naming the product, and packaging the product, to name a few.

Marketing Is Directed at a Wide Range of Products

Marketing activities are not limited to companies that produce physical goods or operate to make a profit. Financial institutions, hair stylists, accounting firms, and other service organizations such as Sea World (see Figure 1.1), conduct marketing activities. Nonprofit organizations such as universities, charities, hospitals, and military organizations perform marketing activities, too. For example, the Muscular Dystrophy Association uses a celebrity spokesperson (Jerry Lewis), the Labor Day telethon, and other marketing activities to raise money for its causes. Likewise, United Way relied on advertising and publicity to overcome a negative image that resulted when executives were accused of misusing funds.[7]

A wide range of individuals also use marketing activities. During the presidential campaign of 1992, Bill Clinton relied heavily on marketing research consultants in developing his campaign strategy. For years, members of professional associations have been reluctant to engage in marketing, but increased competition is changing that. Lawyers and dentists have added new services, expanded hours, and started to use television, radio, and newspaper advertisements to market their services. Although doctors still shy away from advertisements, many send their patients monthly newsletters that provide health information and discuss available services. The newsletters call public attention to the medical services the doctor is providing and serve as a more suitable form of advertising than a billboard.

We use the term *product* extensively throughout this text. For our purposes, a **product** is any good, service, or idea that satisfies a need or want and can be offered in an exchange. A **good** is a tangible object, something that can be seen and touched. The book you are reading is a good, as are automobiles, food, appliances, and clothing. A **service** is an intangible product that often

■ **product** any good, service, or idea that satisfies a need or want and can be offered in an exchange

■ **good** a tangible object, something that can be seen and touched

■ **service** an intangible product that often involves human or mechanical effort

[7]Pamela Sebastian, "Unemployment and Unforgotten Scandal Work Against United Way Campaigns," *Wall Street Journal,* October 21, 1992, pp. B1, B12.

■ **idea** a philosophy, concept, or image

involves human or mechanical effort. Examples of businesses that offer
services are airlines, dry cleaners, and day-care centers. Services are a very
important part of our economy; in fact, more people are employed in service
jobs than in jobs that produce goods.[8] An **idea** is a philosophy, concept, or
image. Organizations involved in crime prevention, personal nutrition, and
drug-abuse prevention are all marketing social ideas as products. *Social marketing* is the use of marketing activities to advance social ideas and causes.
For example, the Media-Advertising Partnership for a Drug-Free America
conducted a major advertising campaign to discourage illegal drug use. The
organization has reported higher awareness of the dangers of drugs and a 25
percent decrease in illicit drug use.[9]

Marketing Facilitates Satisfying Exchanges

■ **exchange** the process of
obtaining a desired product
from another party by giving that party something in
return

An **exchange** is the process of obtaining a desired product from another
party by giving that party something in return. For an exchange to take
place, five conditions must exist.

1. Two or more parties—individuals, groups, or organizations—must participate.
2. Each party must have something that is of value to the other party.
3. The parties to the exchange must be capable of communicating with each
other to make available their "something of value."
4. Each party must be free to give up its "something of value" to the other
party or to reject the offer.
5. The parties must feel it is appropriate and desirable to deal with each
other.[10]

The process of exchange is illustrated in Figure 1.2. The arrows indicate
that two parties communicate to make their "something of value" available
to each other. To be successful, the exchange must be satisfying to both
participating parties. For the buyer, satisfaction may be contentment with
the product. The seller's satisfaction may come from doing business with a
particular customer or customer group, making a profit through a particular
exchange relationship, or perhaps achieving some other organizational objective.

Marketing activities facilitate satisfying exchanges by creating place, time,
and possession utilities. Creating *place utility* is providing products at a location where consumers want to buy them. For instance, automobiles produced
in Japan are made available at convenient locations throughout America.
Creating *time utility* is making products available when consumers want to

---

[8]Karl Albrecht and Ron Zemke, *Service America* (Homewood, Ill.: Dow Jones-Irwin, 1985), p. 3.
[9]Thomas A. Hedrick, Jr., "Pro Bono Anti-Drug Ad Campaign Is Working," *Advertising Age,*
June 25, 1990, p. 22.
[10]Philip Kotler, *Marketing Management: Analysis, Planning, and Control,* 7th ed. (Englewood Cliffs,
N.J.: Prentice-Hall, 1991), p. 7.

FIGURE 1.2
Exchange Between Buyer and Seller

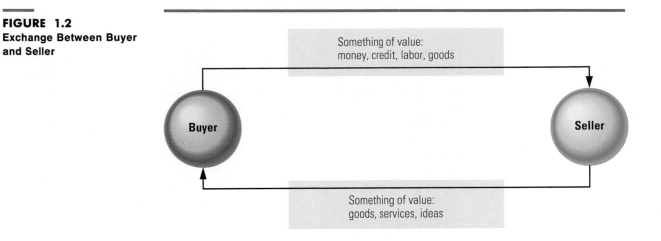

buy them. Most products we need are available with little or no waiting, through outlets such as 24-hour automatic tellers, walk-in health clinics, vending machines, and supermarkets open around the clock. Creating *possession utility* means facilitating the transfer of ownership or use of products to consumers. When purchasing a car, the buyer receives a title giving that person ownership of the car.

A marketer must ensure that customers receive levels of satisfaction that lead to future exchanges. Most organizations rely on repeat business, which requires developing a relationship with buyers. Leslie Otten, president of Sunday River Skiway in Maine, does everything he can to turn first-time customers into repeat buyers. Employees of the ski resort direct first-time visitors from the parking lot to an information center, give them an orientation, direct them to a separate entrance of the rental shop, and provide transportation to the slopes and free ski lessons. By teaching new customers how to ski for free, Otten encourages long-term relationships. Over 75 percent of the people who visit Sunday River for the first time return.[11]

Loyalty toward products, brands, or organizations results from a satisfying relationship between buyer and seller, and it can benefit both. The seller benefits from the security of knowing that customer expectations of product quality and performance are being fulfilled. If an organization fails to build satisfying relationships with buyers, its business eventually suffers. Organizations closest to their customers are most likely to succeed. In a 10-day period, sales representatives from United States Surgical visit each of 5,000 American hospitals where surgery is performed. They go into the operating rooms, explain to surgeons how to use complex instruments, and listen to doctors' likes and dislikes. It is this close connection to customers that led U.S. Surgical to pick up on the need for laparoscopic instruments, used to perform a variety of procedures through minute incisions. A woman working for the firm met a doctor who had rigged up a clip to remove gallbladders. She took

[11] Paul B. Brown, "Return Engagements," *Inc.*, July 1990, pp. 99–100.

FIGURE 1.3
Evolution of Marketing

FIGURE 1.3
Evolution of Marketing

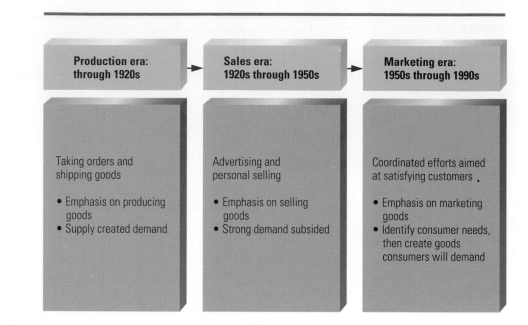

Production era: through 1920s	Sales era: 1920s through 1950s	Marketing era: 1950s through 1990s
Taking orders and shipping goods	Advertising and personal selling	Coordinated efforts aimed at satisfying customers .
• Emphasis on producing goods • Supply created demand	• Emphasis on selling goods • Strong demand subsided	• Emphasis on marketing goods • Identify consumer needs, then create goods consumers will demand

this information back to headquarters and the firm developed a laparoscopic stapler.[12] Today, U.S. Surgical is well ahead of the competition in developing laparoscopic instruments, one of the hottest trends in surgery.

THE EVOLUTION OF MARKETING

When did marketing begin? Historical accounts of trade practices have led some to conclude that marketing has always existed. As long as there have been people, some form of exchange has existed. Over 6,000 years of recorded history document that the roots of both Western and Eastern civilization included some form of trade. The term *marketing,* as we use it today, is thought to have originated in the United States between 1906 and 1911.[13] It was used to describe the different activities that took place in the distribution and sale of products.

Marketing did not always have the same thrust—that of facilitating satisfying exchanges—that it has today. As shown in Figure 1.3, the focus of marketing activities has changed dramatically since the late 1920s. This section explores the evolution of marketing.

The Production Era

production era the period of creating goods that began in the 1600s with the colonization of America and continued into the early part of the twentieth century

The **production era** began in the 1600s with the colonization of America and continued into the early part of the twentieth century. American business had its foundation in English mercantilism, a system in which public authority

[12]Jennifer Reese, "Getting Hot Ideas from Customers," *Fortune,* May 18, 1992, pp. 86–87.
[13]Robert Batel, *The History of Marketing Thought* (Columbus, Ohio: Grid, Inc., 1976), p. 3.

controlled and directed a nation's economic life. Prior to independence, the American colonies were largely dependent on England for both capital and commercial approval; mercantile practices discouraged American innovation. Early settlers arriving in the American colonies had to produce their own goods, such as food and clothing. Soon people began to perform production activities based on their specialized skills and to exchange their goods for those produced by neighbors. This marked the beginning of the separation of production and consumption. In 1776, Adam Smith wrote *The Wealth of Nations*, in which he criticized mercantilism and argued for free enterprise. These ideas led to more individual creativity and innovation.

The Industrial Revolution made its appearance in the United States in 1790 when a young mechanic named Samuel Slater developed America's first factory. The assembly line, mass production, and the division of labor made it possible to manufacture products more efficiently. After the Civil War ended in 1865, subsequent improvements in railroad and steamship transportation closed the gap between producer and consumer. As a result of new technology, new ways of using labor, and an increasing demand for goods, production became foremost in the U.S. economy. Companies were manufacturing-oriented, and marketing was limited to taking orders and shipping goods.

The Sales Era

As more and more firms became efficient in producing goods, competition among companies intensified. By the mid-1920s, mass production had provided sufficient products for consumers to satisfy many of their needs and wants, and the strong demand for products subsided. Managers began to realize that products would no longer sell themselves; they would have to be sold to consumers. This was the beginning of the **sales era,** the period from the mid-1920s to the early 1950s in which businesses looked on sales as the major means of increasing profits.

To help increase demand for products, companies began to advertise. The growth of radio in the 1920s and 1930s opened up new avenues for reaching large groups of people. Firms could now reach millions of people with their sales messages. Some firms also began to develop trained sales forces during this era. Salespeople personally reached thousands of people and, in some cases, used high-pressure tactics to convince consumers to buy products. Many industries, including automobile, insurance, tobacco, drug, and cosmetics industries, used advertising and sales to spur rapid growth.

The Marketing Era

During the sales era, many firms were still not considering the needs and wants of the marketplace. In fact, critics of the sales era believe that products were often sold without regard for the needs of consumers. But companies began to realize that many products were failing simply because they did not satisfy consumer needs.

By the early 1950s, companies moved into the **marketing era,** a customer-oriented period that continues today in which businesses try to make products

■ **sales era** the period from the mid-1920s to the early 1950s during which businesses looked on sales as the major means of increasing profits

■ **marketing era** a customer-oriented period beginning in the early 1950s and continuing today in which businesses determine customer needs first and then develop products that satisfy those needs; the era that gave rise to the marketing concept

that customers want. Businesses tried to determine customer needs first and then developed products to satisfy those needs. The marketing concept grew out of this era.

THE MARKETING CONCEPT

IBM dominated the market for automatic teller machines (ATMs) until an NCR plant in Scotland nearly put the giant out of the business. According to James Adamson, who runs ATM operations for NCR, the keys to success were constantly improving quality and staying close to the customer. Adamson traveled all over the world asking customers what they wanted in an automatic teller machine. In the meantime, IBM developed a new model that almost no one wanted. Today, NCR sells ATMs in more countries than anyone else.[14] NCR practices the marketing concept. The **marketing concept** is a management philosophy stating that an organization should strive to satisfy the needs of consumers through a coordinated set of activities that also allows the organization to achieve its objectives.[15] To be effective, the marketing concept must be embraced by all members of the organization, not only by those involved in marketing activities. For example, employees in the production department of NCR had to develop quality products that satisfied consumer needs and wants. Likewise, members of the credit department had to develop payment plans that satisfied customers. At every level of the organization and across all departments, employees must work toward customer satisfaction.

■ **marketing concept**
a management philosophy stating that an organization should strive to satisfy the needs of consumers through a coordinated set of activities that also allows the organization to achieve its objectives

Focus of the Marketing Concept

The marketing concept proposes that an organization focus on consumer needs and wants, coordinate its efforts, and strive to reach organizational goals. Satisfying the customer should be the major focus of all the organization's activities. To this end, firms must have a thorough understanding of customer needs and wants. A variety of factors affect customer satisfaction, including product quality, product availability, and after-sales support, such as warranties and service.[16] Organizations must determine what customers need and want and then develop products that satisfy those needs. If a firm can answer yes to the following questions, it is customer-oriented.

Are we easy for customers to do business with?

Do we keep our promises?

Do we meet the standards we set?

Are we responsive to customer needs?[17]

[14]Geoffrey Colvin, "The Wee Outfit That Decked IBM," *Fortune,* November 19, 1990, pp. 165–168.
[15]Lynn M. McGee and Rosann L. Spiro, "The Marketing Concept in Perspective," *Business Horizons,* May–June 1988, pp. 40–45.
[16]Milind M. Lele and Jagdish N. Sheth, "The Four Fundamentals of Customer Satisfaction," *Business Marketing,* June 1988, pp. 80–94.
[17]Benson P. Shapiro, "What the Hell Is 'Market-Oriented'?" *Harvard Business Review,* November–December 1988, pp. 119–124.

The marketing concept advocates that an organization coordinate its efforts to satisfy consumers. An organization is a group of people and departments performing different tasks. But the entire organization must be focused on the customer to effectively practice the marketing concept. This includes all departments—production, finance, research and development, personnel, marketing—and the individuals in these departments. At Whirlpool, the marketing department conducted a survey which showed that customers wanted a cooking range that was easy to clean. Engineers then designed a range with electronic touch pad controls, which can be cleaned with the sweep of a cloth or sponge. Industry wisdom suggested touch pads would fail, because earlier models with push buttons failed. Marketing, design, and engineering worked closely together to test consumer reactions every step of the way, and the new ranges succeeded where the old push-button design failed.[18]

Finally, the marketing concept recognizes that organizations have goals. In some instances, these goals may be profit-oriented; in others, they may be aimed at furthering a social cause. In any case, firms that adopt the marketing concept attempt to achieve their own goals by satisfying the needs of customers through coordinated organizational activities.

The nation's fastest-growing retailer, Wal-Mart Stores, practices the marketing concept. Reflected throughout the entire organization is the philosophy of Wal-Mart's founder, the late Sam Walton, that the business begins and ends with the customer. This applies not only to salespeople, but also to buyers, office workers, and all other employees. The company is also achieving its goal of making a profit; Wal-Mart sells nearly $45 billion worth of goods each year through its more than 1,850 stores.[19]

The Societal Marketing Concept

As our society moves through the 1990s, the marketing concept continues to evolve and take on new meanings. The traditional marketing concept has focused on satisfying consumer needs and wants to meet organizational goals. But the changing marketing concept now factors in a third consideration—the welfare of society. Emphasis is now being placed on how marketing affects society as a whole in an age of scarce resources, environmental destruction, and worldwide competition. This societal orientation questions whether satisfying customer needs serves the long-term interests of society. Thus the new concept, referred to as the **societal marketing concept,** is a management philosophy that considers the welfare of society as well as the interests of the firm and its customers.

■ **societal marketing concept** a management philosophy that considers the welfare of society as well as the interests of the firm and its customers

Firms adopting the societal marketing concept make marketing decisions in an ethical and socially responsible manner. They must consider not only the short-term needs of customers but also the well-being of everyone affected by their operations. For example, people want sufficient, economical energy to heat and cool their homes. Yet many people have felt the adverse effects of oil spills, toxic wastes, and acid rain. To meet both the short-term needs of consumers and the long-term welfare of society, a firm must balance

[18] Sally Solo, "How to Listen to Consumers," *Fortune,* January 11, 1993, pp. 77–79.
[19] Wendy Zellner, "Mr. Sam's Experiment Is Alive and Well," *Business Week,* April 20, 1992, p. 39.

the interests of its customers, the firm itself, and the society in which it operates. Saving the earth's environment will be one of the unifying principles of the post–Cold War world.

Many firms are adopting the societal marketing concept by preserving scarce resources or developing products that do not harm the environment, thus practicing *green marketing*. The societal marketing concept is difficult to implement because it requires firms to place the needs of society ahead of the goals of the organization. For example, building new factories that do not pollute or destroying toxic waste in a safe manner may decrease a firm's profits. But more and more firms are recognizing that in the long run they cannot survive if they ignore the welfare of society.

Organizations are responding to these environmental needs in several ways. Some use superficial green marketing techniques such as labeling plastic bags and diapers as degradable when in fact they may not be. Such techniques are neither ethical nor in the spirit of the societal marketing concept. Some businesses are responding with more substantive marketing activities. McDonald's changed from polystyrene boxes to a more environment-friendly paper wrapper for its sandwiches; 3M uses recycled paper for its Post-it note pads; Du Pont, Procter & Gamble, and other firms have tried to increase recycling of plastics and reduce package wastes. Such actions have a long-term benefit to society, the firm, and individual consumers.

To implement the societal marketing concept, some firms engage in **demarketing,** that is, using marketing activities to reduce the demand for a product. Anheuser-Busch used the "Susie Collins" advertisement shown in Figure 1.4 to promote the safe consumption of alcohol to retailers. Marketing activities also have been used to decrease the demand for tobacco products,

■ **demarketing** using marketing activities to reduce the demand for a product

FIGURE 1.4
Demarketing
Anheuser-Busch educates the public on alcohol awareness by providing videos and trained speakers to schools and financial support for alcohol-abuse programs. This advertisement is one way Anheuser-Busch practices the societal marketing concept by showing a concern for alcohol abuse.

POINT/COUNTERPOINT

Do Organizations Practice the Marketing Concept?

Without question, the marketing concept is an appealing philosophy. As consumers, we would certainly benefit if organizations strove to satisfy our needs. And organizations, by satisfying the needs of customers, can become more competitive. All organizations—colleges, religious groups, and civic associations, as well as business firms—can profit by adhering to the marketing concept. But can and do organizations actually put it into practice? Or is the marketing concept simply an idealistic philosophy that is easy to talk about but difficult or impractical to act on?

Point Most of today's firms practice the marketing concept. Companies have learned the importance of customer satisfaction and realize that anything less can result in failure. They also know that organizational objectives can be achieved by providing products that satisfy consumers. The days of making a quick profit without concern for the customer are gone.

Organizations are engaging in several activities that suggest they are practicing the marketing concept. Most firms rely heavily on marketing research to determine consumer needs and develop products that satisfy those needs. Many restaurants, hotels, and other firms are constantly asking customers if

they have any problems with the products they purchased. Some companies provide toll-free telephone numbers for customers to call with questions and complaints. Organizations of all types—hospitals, automobile manufacturers, banks, and substance-abuse clinics—are practicing the marketing concept.

Counterpoint The existence of dissatisfied consumers is simple proof that many organizations do not practice the marketing concept. Companies like the sound of the marketing concept and are certainly going to say they practice it. But the top priority of most companies is to make a profit, and this does not always mean satisfying the customer. True commitment to the customer is absent in many organizations.

Consumers frequently complain about the quality of products and say they cannot find good service when they need it. Products are developed that consumers do not need, and aggressive selling tactics are used to convince people to buy them. Other products are produced without concern for the environment or the safety of consumers. In some instances, firms charge extremely high prices that result in steep profits. Although the marketing concept is a logical way to operate a business, many firms have failed to put it into practice.

dangerous drugs, and scarce resources like energy. By decreasing the demand for harmful or dangerous products, business and nonprofit organizations are practicing the societal marketing concept.

The Marketing Concept in Practice

The marketing concept may sound simple, but it is not always easy to practice, and some organizations have difficulty gaining support for this concept at every level. It is the job of top-level management to sell other members of the organization on practicing the marketing concept. This requires incorporating the marketing concept into the policies used to operate the business so that all activities of the firm will be guided by this philosophy. At Federal Express, for example, all employees are routinely expected to take whatever actions are necessary to satisfy the customer.[20] Point/Counterpoint discusses the extent to which organizations practice the marketing concept.

Implementing the marketing concept may require restructuring the organization as well as enlisting the support of top-level management. Many organizations must be restructured to better coordinate activities and communication between departments and individuals. This restructuring may involve establishing an information system that enables the organization to ascertain customers' needs. It may also involve adding new departments, such as customer relations, and shifting the firm's emphasis from production to marketing. In order to be more responsive to the customer, Johnson & Johnson has restructured into 166 separate companies ranging in size from those drawing $100,000 in annual sales to those drawing $1 billion. Since this restructuring was begun in 1980, yearly profits have averaged over 19 percent.[21]

 Organizations encounter several barriers to adopting the marketing concept. Some firms simply do not understand the concept and therefore cannot implement it effectively. Other firms experience a conflict between short- and long-term goals; these firms are not willing to sacrifice short-term profits for long-term customer satisfaction, and thus fail to adopt the marketing concept. Finally, at times the customer is simply not the major priority of top-level management.[22]

THE SIGNIFICANCE OF MARKETING

As you began reading this book, you probably have some opinions and beliefs about marketing. Undeniably, marketing stirs a wide range of emotions. Critics contend that marketing activities stimulate the worst instincts and desires in people. In other words, marketing is inherently unethical. Advocates argue that marketing is driven by market forces that reflect the needs of society. Thus, marketing activities are not inherently unethical, because they satisfy consumer demands.[23] Perhaps it is difficult for you to come to grips with this issue, but we will touch on it several times throughout the book. In any event, marketing activities have become a significant part of our society for several reasons.

Marketing touches the lives of all members of society. Through the cost of what we purchase, each of us supports the costs of marketing. It is estimated that nearly half of every dollar spent on goods and services is used to

[20] Tom Peters, *Thriving on Chaos* (New York: Knopf, 1988), p. 292.
[21] Joseph Weber, "A Big Company That Works," *Business Week,* May 4, 1992, pp. 124–132.
[22] Frederick E. Webster, Jr., "The Rediscovery of the Marketing Concept," *Business Horizons,* May–June 1988, pp. 29–38.
[23] Robert E. Pitts and Robert Allan Cooke, "A Realistic View of Marketing Ethics," *Journal of Business Ethics,* April 1991, pp. 243–244.

pay the costs of marketing activities. Each time you make a purchase, large or small, a significant amount of the purchase price pays for marketing activities.

Roughly one out of every three students reading this book will work in a marketing-related field. Millions of people are employed in advertising, retailing, sales, distribution, product development, and marketing research jobs. These jobs can be found in a variety of manufacturing and service industries. Nonprofit organizations such as museums, churches, and clinics also employ individuals in marketing positions. Entire industries like advertising and transportation are supported by marketing activities. And the prospect for growth in marketing-related jobs, especially in large, international companies with operations in foreign countries, is bright.

Our highly complex world depends heavily on marketing activities: consider cars from Japan, microwaves from Korea, and oil from Saudi Arabia, not to mention the many American-made products exported to other parts of the world. Without a sophisticated system of communication and distribution, many of our needs and wants could not be satisfied. And by enabling organizations to operate more efficiently, marketing activities can help firms operate more profitably and at the same time increase customer satisfaction. For example, without marketing, the cost of automobiles would be prohibitive, companies would not make a profit, and we could not afford a trip to Detroit (or Japan) to pay a high price for a car. And United Way or other charitable organizations that rely on marketing activities to raise money would not be able to support their various causes.

AN OVERVIEW OF MARKETING STRATEGY

Marketing managers are responsible for developing and managing marketing strategies that facilitate satisfying exchanges between buyers and sellers. In Chapter 2 we discuss marketing strategy in much greater detail. In this section, we take a brief look at how organizations develop and manage marketing strategies.

Developing Marketing Strategies

A **marketing strategy** is a plan for selecting and analyzing a target market and developing and maintaining a marketing mix that will satisfy this target market. A **target market** is a group of consumers at whom an organization directs its marketing efforts. In a survey conducted for *Working Woman* magazine, 75 percent of the female executives polled indicated they purchased office computers. Subsequently, several computer firms, including IBM, Apple, and Hewlett-Packard, targeted their computers at women.[24]

■ **marketing strategy** a plan for selecting and analyzing a target market and developing and maintaining a marketing mix that will satisfy this target market

■ **target market** a group of consumers at whom an organization directs its marketing efforts

[24] Mark Lewyn, "PC Makers, Palms Sweating, Try Talking to Women," *Business Week,* January 15, 1990, p. 48.

■ **marketing mix** the combination of four elements: product, price, distribution, and promotion

Once a firm selects a target market, it must develop a marketing mix that satisfies the needs of this target. The **marketing mix** consists of four elements: product, price, distribution, and promotion.

A *product* is anything that satisfies a need or want and can be offered in an exchange. A product can be a good, service, or idea.

Price is the value placed on the "something of value" in an exchange. Consumers exchange something of value, normally purchasing power (money), for the satisfaction or utility they expect a product to provide.

Distribution refers to marketing activities that make products available to consumers at the right time and in a convenient location.

Promotion refers to marketing activities used to communicate positive, persuasive information about an organization, its products, and activities to directly or indirectly expedite exchanges in a target market.

■ **marketing environment** the forces of competition, regulation, politics, society, economic conditions, and technology surrounding the target market (customers) and the marketing mix

The marketing mix is built around the target market in a manner consistent with the marketing concept, as shown in Figure 1.5. The target market and marketing mix variables are surrounded by the **marketing environment,** which includes competition, regulation, politics, society, economic conditions, and technology. These forces influence marketing managers' decisions regarding the marketing mix. The variables in the marketing environment can fluctuate quickly, which is one reason that marketing is so challenging.

FIGURE 1.5
Components of the Marketing Mix and Marketing Environment

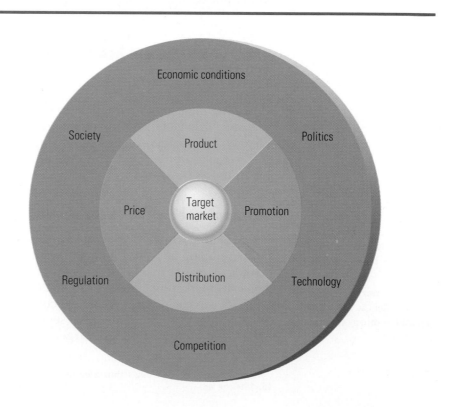

FIGURE 1.6
Global Marketing
Unisys markets information systems around the globe to thousands of companies and governments. Many firms are taking advantage of the global boom by targeting customers throughout the world, resulting in new marketing opportunities and greater customer satisfaction.

With permission, Unisys Corporation. Copyright Unisys Corp., 1992.

Global Marketing Strategies

The world is getting smaller. Transportation and telecommunications have linked nations around the globe. Just as foreign firms like Toyota and Sony market products in America, U.S. firms such as IBM and Coca-Cola as well as smaller firms market products throughout the world. As shown in Figure 1.6, Unisys markets its information systems in over 100 countries. This global boom is opening new opportunities, and many companies are developing global marketing strategies to capitalize on them. By developing marketing mixes for target markets throughout the world—or parts of the world—firms can satisfy more consumers and increase sales.

The global boom is also touching parts of the world previously closed to foreign countries. Only a few years ago it would have been hard to imagine a McDonald's or Pizza Hut restaurant in Moscow. But the former Soviet Union, Eastern Europe, Chile, and several Third World nations have abandoned communism. The democratizing of these nations is opening new markets with unlimited demand for quality goods and services. These markets also present new opportunities for firms developing global marketing strategies.

Managing Marketing Strategies

■ **marketing management** the process of planning, organizing, implementing, and controlling marketing strategies

Marketing management is the process of planning, organizing, implementing, and controlling marketing strategies.

Planning is necessary to help an organization define and attain its marketing objectives. Planning requires that marketing managers assess opportunities and available resources, establish marketing objectives, develop a marketing strategy, and determine how marketing strategies will be implemented and controlled. Planning also dictates how marketing activities will be performed and who will be responsible for performing them.

Organizing marketing activities entails structuring resources and activities to accomplish marketing objectives. The structure of the marketing department establishes the relationships among marketing personnel. It also specifies who is responsible for making certain decisions as well as who will perform specific activities. The structure of the marketing department can vary widely depending on the nature of the business and the philosophy of management.

Implementation is needed to put marketing strategies into action. To implement strategies, managers must first coordinate the actions of all marketing personnel. These actions must also be integrated with the activities of other units in the firm, such as production, finance, and personnel, and with organizations outside the firm, such as advertising agencies and shipping companies. Next, marketing personnel must be motivated to perform at a high level. Finally, effective communication lines must be established between marketing managers and top-level managers, managers of other departments, and other marketing personnel.

Controlling marketing strategies involves establishing desired (or standard) levels of performance, comparing actual performances with these standards, and taking the necessary actions to reduce the differences between desired and actual performances. Marketing control is needed to evaluate the effectiveness of marketing strategies. An organization should evaluate its marketing activities on a regular basis.

MARKETING, QUALITY, AND COMPETITIVENESS

One of the major challenges facing U.S. firms in the twenty-first century is developing quality products that can compete in the global economy. Throughout this chapter, we have noted the importance of satisfying customers. In their best-selling book *In Search of Excellence,* Tom Peters and Robert Waterman identify eight attributes that characterize the best-run companies in America. One of the attributes of excellent firms is that they remain "close to the customer."[25] In other words, these companies learn from the people they serve and provide outstanding quality, service, and reliability. In short, they are obsessed with customer satisfaction. Many of the best-run companies that Peters and Waterman identify—Caterpillar, Disney, McDonald's, and many more—share this obsession.

Because customer satisfaction is a critical element of quality and competitiveness, marketing activities have a predominant role in most companies' efforts to improve quality. Many American business leaders have yet to make the crucial link between quality improvement and customer satisfaction.[26]

---

[25] Thomas J. Peters and Robert H. Waterman, Jr., *In Search of Excellence* (New York: Warner Books, 1982), p. 1.
[26] Jerry Bowles, "Is American Management Really Committed to Quality?" *Management Review,* April 1992, pp. 42–45.

FIGURE 1.7
The Importance of
Customer Satisfaction
Percentage of businesses
that consider customer satisfaction a primary criterion
in the strategic planning
process

Source: Ernst & Young/American
Quality Foundation. For additional in-
formation about the International
Quality Study SM, contact Terrence R.
Oran, National Director, Performance
Improvement Services, Ernst &
Young, 1600 Huntington Building,
Cleveland, OH 44115.

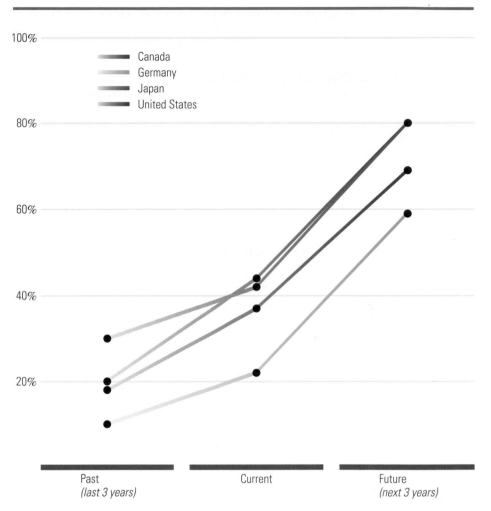

But this situation is changing rapidly. As you can see in Figure 1.7, roughly 40 percent of businesses in Canada, Japan, and the United States place primary emphasis on customer satisfaction in strategic planning. Figure 1.7 also indicates that over the next three years the emphasis on customer satisfaction will nearly double, a phenomenon that clearly substantiates the desire on the part of firms to get close to the customer. Quality and customer satisfaction will be recurring themes throughout the book. The remainder of this section examines the quality and competitiveness challenges facing organizations in the global economy. First, Close to the Customer illustrates the importance of customer satisfaction.

The Quality Challenge

Perhaps no greater challenge has grown out of the global economy than the challenge to produce quality goods and services. As you can see in Table 1.1, there are many different ways to define quality, but all the definitions say

CLOSE TO THE CUSTOMER

Take Me Out to the Ballgame

Just before old Comiskey Park closed, I was in Chicago with some friends. I wanted to see the White Sox play in the old park one last time. Just for the fun of it, I dragged my friends around to the back of the park to show them where I used to hang around for autographs when I was a kid. The fence and players' parking lot were still there, as were the young fans waiting for autographs. But one thing had changed: most players passed the children without looking at them, refusing to sign autographs. I guess it was understandable—lifelong .250 hitters making millions of dollars don't have time for kids. I couldn't help but remember how the Sox players years ago, not to mention Mickey Mantle and others from visiting teams, always had time for the kids.

Today the White Sox, like many major league baseball teams, play in a new stadium built by the city of Chicago after the owners threatened to move the team to another city. Most recently, the San Francisco Giants caused an uproar in that city when the owner announced they were moving from Candlestick Park to the Suncoast Dome in St. Petersburg, Florida. They eventually decided against the move, but will probably get a new stadium in San Francisco soon, away from the wind and the fog of the bay. Fans can go to these wonderful parks and enjoy some peanuts and Cracker Jack and a hot dog, plus shop in a mall or take in a waterfall. If they're lucky, they might see great baseball. But at $15 a ticket and $3 a hot dog, a family of four should be prepared to spend at least $100.

Adelanto, California, home of the High Desert Mavericks, is a long way from the major leagues. But this minor league baseball team, like many others, is prospering. The Mavericks draw more than 200,000 fans a year in this small community, and a night out at their stadium doesn't break a family bank account. In 1991, attendance at minor league games was nearly 27 million, a 10 percent increase over two years. During this same period, major league attendance increased 3 percent.

The growth in the popularity of minor league baseball is no accident. The owners have a deep respect for their customers that is missing in the major leagues. For example, nonsmoking sections have been added, low-priced specialty foods and souvenirs are offered, and changing tables are available in rest rooms for parents with babies. The night may be capped off with a fireworks display, a concert, or a contest in which fans participate. In Buffalo, home of the Bisons, Thursdays feature a contest in which fans try to catch pop-up fly balls; if someone catches all three, everyone in the stadium gets free pizza. Kids who go to see the Frederick Keys or the Hagerstown Suns in any kind of sports uniform get in free.

It's not surprising that many minor league franchises are doing well. Fifteen years ago, a Triple-A franchise (the closest team to the major leagues) sold for around $300,000. Today, it sells for around $5 million. Owners find local businesses anxious to advertise on outfield-fence billboard space and to sponsor promotional events. Even national advertisers like Procter & Gamble and Campbell Soup think minor league baseball is a good advertising buy and a way to build local loyalty. But in the end, with little or no television revenues, the owners worry most about satisfying the fans.

Based on information from Gretchen Morgenson, "Where the Fans Still Come First," *Forbes,* April 27, 1992, pp. 40–42; and Russell Mitchell, "Take Me Out to the Valley," *Business Week,* October 12, 1992, pp. 76–77.

TABLE 1.1
Different Ways
Organizations Define
Quality

Organization	Definition of Quality
IBM	". . . meeting the requirements of our customers, both inside and outside the organization, for defect-free products, services, and business processes."
Boeing	". . . it (quality) means providing a product that satisfies the needs of the customer; translated . . . 'conformance to requirements' . . . makes the customer's needs paramount. Now, the key to this? . . . 'Customer' means Boeing internal customer, also."
Corning	"Quality is knowing what needs to be done, having the tools to do it right, then doing it right—the first time."
Xerox	"At Xerox quality means meeting customer requirements. . . . You have to understand exactly what the customer requires for every bit of the work that you do for him."

Source: Quality definitions compiled from respective company publications.

■ **quality** the totality of features and characteristics of a good or service that bears on the ability to satisfy stated or implied needs

■ **total quality management (TQM)** a management approach to long-term success through customer satisfaction, based on the participation of all members of an organization in improving processes, products, services, and the culture in which they work

one thing: the customer is the focal point of quality requirements and standards. In the case of IBM and Boeing, "customer" refers to the individuals and organizations outside the firm that purchase or influence the firm's products, and also to "internal customers"—other employees or departments within the organization. (Internal customers will be discussed in greater detail in Chapter 21.) In essence, **quality** is the totality of features and characteristics of a good or service that bears on the ability to satisfy stated or implied needs. The challenge managers face in this environment is to manage in such a way that the outcome is a quality product. **Total quality management (TQM)** is a management approach to long-term success through customer satisfaction, based on the participation of all members of an organization in improving processes, products, services, and the culture in which they work.[27] TQM was initially used to describe the Japanese-style management approach to quality improvement, but the global marketplace has led companies throughout the world to adopt TQM. Continued focus on the customer is a major element of any successful quality program.

For TQM to work, managers must believe in quality for customers as a primary organizational aim, and they must act to achieve this aim.[28] Managers must create a pattern of shared values and beliefs throughout the organization so that all of its members work toward quality. Some quality experts have described TQM as a dream or a passion; unless *every* member of the

[27] "The Quality Glossary," *Quality Progress,* February 1992, pp. 20–29.
[28] Marshall Sashkin and Kenneth J. Kiser, *Total Quality Management* (Seabrook, Md.: Duchochon Press, 1991), p. 26.

FIGURE 1.8
Quality
Motorola's goal is to reach Six Sigma quality—perfection. This goal is a daily challenge for each Motorola employee throughout the world. This pursuit of perfection—making products better, faster, and at a lower cost—is a commitment to making customers happier.

Ad courtesy of Motorola, Inc.

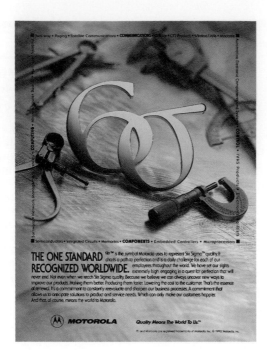

organization fully believes in quality for the customer, success through TQM is nearly impossible to achieve. The most important part of this system of total quality is the skills and talents of people and how they are managed. The challenge to managers is to develop an organization in which all the workers are committed to quality. Figure 1.8 illustrates how Motorola, winner of the prestigious Malcolm Baldrige Quality Award, places quality at the heart of the organization.

The Competitiveness Challenge

The quality of many products made in the United States has improved in a wide variety of industries ranging from computer chips to toilet paper made from recycled paper. Unfortunately, competitors throughout the world have also been improving product quality, in some cases at a faster pace than U.S. firms.[29] One outcome of the global economy is a change in the competitive structure within industries. Firms no longer compete on a local, regional, or national basis; they compete on a global basis. According to quality expert Philip Crosby, "We live in a boundaryless economy . . . where we're headed for is a place where you can compete with anybody."[30] Any product made anywhere has to compete with like products made anywhere else. Cars made in Kentucky must compete with cars made in Mexico; wine bottled in California must compete with wine bottled in France; flowers grown in Florida

---

[29] Andrew Kupfer, "How American Industry Stacks Up," *Fortune,* March 9, 1992, pp. 30–46.
[30] Lloyd Dobyns and Clare Crawford-Mason, *Quality or Else* (Boston: Houghton Mifflin Company, 1991), pp. 36–37.

must compete with flowers grown in Brazil. Remaining competitive in this environment is a major challenge facing managers.

Quality and competitiveness are closely related. To remain competitive, a firm must work toward continual improvement. Yet as American firms have experienced, competitors are also constantly improving quality. Such intense competition has increased interest in **benchmarking,** the continuous process of measuring a firm's goods, practices, and services against those of its toughest competitors.[31] Through benchmarking, a firm can find the best way to do something and implement it. For instance, Xerox found that competitors were selling their products for what it cost Xerox to manufacture them. Clearly, Xerox could not stay in business this way, so it began benchmarking. The effort produced tremendous results: Xerox copy quality is again recognized as the best in the world; copiers are 5 to 25 percent more reliable; customer satisfaction increased 38 percent; labor overhead was cut 50 percent; materials overhead was reduced 40 percent; and sales increased from $8.7 billion to $12.4 billion.[32]

The question facing many U.S. firms and organizations throughout the world is how to survive in the global economy. Consumers are demanding better products at lower prices, and the way to compete is through quality. Global competition has resulted in a better choice of products for less money. In the past decade, America's dominance in the world economy has faltered because of the decline in the competitiveness of American goods and services. As firms are responding to the quality and competitiveness challenge, the common goal of successful companies is customer satisfaction. This chapter has emphasized the importance of marketing activities in facilitating satisfying exchanges, and has laid the groundwork for the remainder of the book.

■ **benchmarking** the continuous process of measuring a firm's goods, practices, and services against those of its toughest competitors

THE ORGANIZATION OF THIS BOOK

Figure 1.9 shows the organization of the book, which is designed to follow a logical flow that parallels the development of a marketing strategy. Chapter 1 has presented the foundations of strategic marketing, and the remainder of Part 1 discusses the strategic marketing planning process. In Part 2, the environment for strategic marketing, including ethical and social issues and global markets, is presented. The environment must be considered first in developing a marketing strategy because the environment either directly or indirectly influences marketing strategy. Analysis for strategic marketing decisions is the subject of Part 3. These decisions regarding market segmentation and forecasting, consumer and organizational buying behavior, and marketing research are necessary for selecting a target market, and impact the marketing mix strategy. Remember, marketing strategy involves selecting and analyzing a target market and developing a marketing mix that will satisfy the target. Thus the marketing mix—product strategy, price strategy,

[31] "Conversations for the 90s: The Search for Superior Performance," Harris Trust and Savings Bank, 1992, pp. 1–19.
[32] "The Rebirthing of Xerox," *Marketing Insights,* Summer 1991, pp. 73–80.

FIGURE 1.9
Organization of This Book

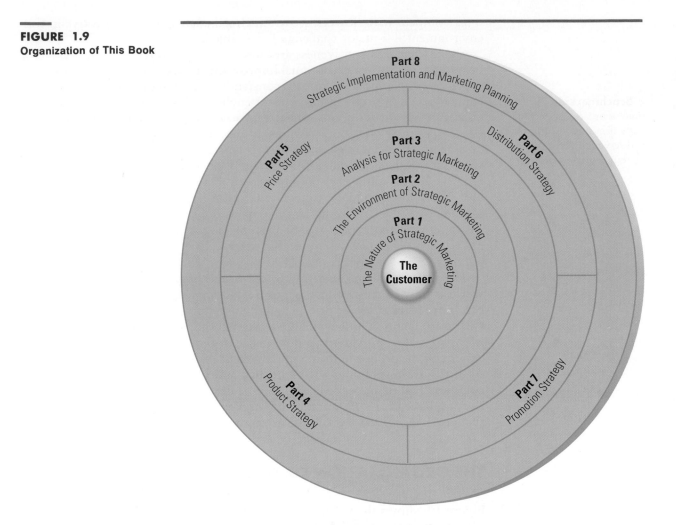

Part 8
Strategic Implementation and Marketing Planning

Part 5
Price Strategy

Part 3
Analysis for Strategic Marketing

Part 6
Distribution Strategy

Part 2
The Environment of Strategic Marketing

Part 1
The Nature of Strategic Marketing

The
Customer

Part 4
Product Strategy

Part 7
Promotion Strategy

distribution strategy, and promotion strategy—is presented in Parts 4, 5, 6, and 7, respectively. Part 8 discusses how organizations implement marketing strategies once they have been developed.

SUMMARY

Marketing is the process of planning and executing the conception, pricing, promotion, and distribution of ideas, goods, and services to create exchanges that satisfy individual and organizational objectives. Five conditions must exist for an exchange to occur: (1) two or more parties must participate, (2) each party must have something of value desired by the other, (3) the parties to the exchange must be able to communicate with each other to make their "something of value" available, (4) each party must be willing to give up its valued item to receive that held by the other, and (5) the parties must believe that dealing with each other is appropriate and desirable. Successful marketing creates place, time, and possession utilities.

Marketing has evolved through three periods: the production, sales, and marketing eras. The marketing concept, which grew out of the marketing era, is a management philosophy stating that an organization should try to satisfy consumers' needs through a coordinated set of activities that also allows the organization to achieve its objectives. Consumer satisfaction is the major objective of the marketing concept. The societal marketing concept proposes that firms must consider the well-being of everyone affected by their operations, not just the short-term needs of customers. This idea is expressed in green marketing.

The marketing concept cannot be implemented without the support of top-level management and an organizational structure that facilitates coordination among individuals and departments. Often organizations fail to adopt the marketing concept because they do not understand it, because they are not willing to sacrifice short-term profits for long-term customer satisfaction, or because their managements do not make the customer the top priority.

Marketing activities have become a significant part of our society. It is estimated that nearly half of every dollar spent on goods and services is used to pay the costs of marketing activities. About one-third of all jobs are in marketing-related fields. Without marketing, it would be difficult for our highly complex world to function as it does. Many of the improvements we wish to make in the quality of our lives can be achieved through an understanding of marketing activities.

Developing a marketing strategy involves two steps: (1) selecting and analyzing a target market and (2) creating and maintaining an appropriate marketing mix for the target market. A target market is a group of consumers at whom an organization focuses its marketing efforts. The four variables that make up the marketing mix are product, price, distribution, and promotion. These variables are built around the consumer in a manner consistent with the marketing concept. The mix variables are affected by forces in the marketing environment, which include economic conditions, society, technology, competition, regulation, and politics. Marketers must adapt the marketing mix to rapid changes in the environment. Many firms are developing marketing mixes for target markets throughout the world.

The marketing management process includes planning, organizing, implementing, and controlling marketing activities. Planning determines when, how, and who is to perform marketing activities. Organizing involves structuring resources and activities to achieve marketing objectives. Implementing marketing strategies requires coordinating marketing activities, integrating these activities with the activities in other units, motivating marketing personnel, and establishing an effective communication flow. To maintain control, performance standards must be set, and actual performances must be evaluated against these standards on a regular basis.

Two major challenges facing organizations in the global economy are quality and competitiveness. Because customer satisfaction is an important part of quality and competitiveness, marketing activities play a major role in efforts to improve quality.

KEY TERMS

marketing
need
want
product
good
service
idea
exchange
production era
sales era
marketing era
marketing concept

societal marketing concept
demarketing
marketing strategy
target market
marketing mix
marketing environment
marketing management
quality
total quality management
  (TQM)
benchmarking

QUESTIONS FOR DISCUSSION AND REVIEW

1. Now that you have read Chapter 1, how would you define marketing?
2. Give an example of a good, a service, and an idea. In what ways are they different?
3. Trace the history of the marketing concept by describing the production, sales, and marketing eras.
4. Name a business in your city that has adopted the marketing concept. If possible, name one that has not.
5. How can a firm adopt the societal marketing concept?
6. Why is the marketing concept difficult for some firms to implement?
7. Why is marketing a significant part of our society?
8. What are the two major components of a marketing strategy? Describe these two components in detail.
9. Why is target market selection so important?
10. Think of a product that you have purchased recently. Describe the features of the product, the price, the place or location where you bought it, and any advertisements or promotions that helped you learn about the product.
11. Why are global marketing strategies important to business firms?
12. What activities are involved in marketing management?
13. What is quality? What part does marketing play in total quality management?
14. Why do quality and competitiveness pose a major challenge to many organizations?

CASES

1.1 MARKETING CRIME PREVENTION

For over 50 years, the Advertising Council and its forerunner, the War Advertising Council, have marketed social issues such as stopping illegal drug use and preventing child abuse. The purposes of marketing social issues such as these are to open minds to new ideas, change attitudes, and—in some cases—to save lives. One of the Advertising Council's most successful efforts has been in marketing crime prevention.

Crime has long been a major social concern in the United States. The concern with crime became more formalized in 1970, when business, labor, and government leaders realized that crime was victimizing many Americans. Even more frightening, most people thought they couldn't do much about crime; it was something they had to live with. The Advertising Council, with the support of the Justice Department and the National Council on Crime and Delinquency, believed that an attempt had to be made to prevent crime. This resolution initiated a movement to implement an effective marketing strategy to get citizens to take an active part in crime prevention.

Many of the organizations involved, including law-enforcement establishments and the Justice Department, were skeptical about the willingness of citizens to get involved in crime prevention. The philosophy had always been that crime is fought by putting more police on the job. How could Americans be encouraged to protect their property and become involved in crime prevention? This was the marketing problem facing the Advertising Council.

The Advertising Council decided to develop an educational program that would teach Americans to protect themselves and their property. The Advertising Council knew the message they wanted to get across, but needed a spokesperson that Americans would listen to. The spokesperson selected wasn't a celebrity or a police officer; it was an animated dog named McGruff.

McGruff is a friendly looking character wearing a belted trenchcoat, plaid pants, and tennis shoes. He was developed to teach people they could actually do something about preventing crime, and to urge them to take what precautions they could.

To spread the message, McGruff appeared in radio and television commercials, in print advertisements, and on billboards. The canine detective provided tips on preventing burglaries, car theft, and employee theft, as well as information about starting Neighborhood Watch programs. Since McGruff first urged people to "take a bite out of crime" in 1978, he has become the "Smokey the Bear" of crime prevention. Both teachers and police use McGruff when making anticrime and antidrug presentations.

McGruff's message appears to be working. A study conducted by the University of Denver found that 25 percent of the people surveyed had taken preventive measures against crime after seeing an advertisement featuring McGruff. Another study found that more than half the adults surveyed have taken action to prevent crime as called for by McGruff. And a third study, conducted by the advertising agency Saatchi & Saatchi, reported that 97 percent of children aged 6 to 12 years follow McGruff's advice. One official of the National Crime Prevention Council said of McGruff: "Instead of preaching to the kids, he makes it cool."

As planned, the crime prevention theme is being replaced by a "help-each-other" message. The National Crime Prevention Council is using McGruff to recruit "block parents"—one house on each block that is designated as a place children can go in case of an emergency. A poster of McGruff is placed in a front window in the block parents' house. Children are instructed by their parents to use the "McGruff House" if they are bullied, followed by a stranger, or hurt while walking to school. The program is popular among families in which both parents work outside the home and children are home alone during part of the day. Some 137,000 McGruff Houses have now been established in 37 states.

Questions for Discussion

1. Is the Advertising Council marketing a good, a service, or an idea?

2. How do you think McGruff has helped the crime prevention education program to succeed?

3. What was the target market of the crime prevention program?

Based on information from Richard Scala, "Advertising to Our Hearts' Discontents," *Fund Raising Management,* August 1990, pp. 35–39, 58; Donald Dale Jackson, "Lead On, McGruff, and 'Take a Bite Out of Crime,'" *Smithsonian,* April 1988, pp. 120–131; Van Wallach, "Matters of Survival," *Advertising Age,* November 9, 1988, pp. 119–120; and Jeffrey Cohen, "Making Crime Pay," *Adweek's Marketing Week,* November 21, 1988, pp. HM8–HM9.

1.2   **KFC'S GLOBAL STRATEGY**

Since Harlan Sanders developed in 1939 a secret chicken recipe with eleven herbs and spices, KFC (formerly Kentucky Fried Chicken) has become known around the world. KFC's chicken is sold throughout North America, Europe, the Middle East, Africa, Asia, the South Pacific, Latin America, and the Caribbean. Worldwide sales in 1991 totaled $6.2 billion, with sales of $2.8 billion in markets outside the United States.

Colonel Sanders first became involved in international business in 1956 when he opened stores in Canada. Today, KFC has 3,434 international stores; 562 are owned by the company, 457 are joint ventures, and 2,405 are franchises. Worldwide, KFC has 8,480 stores. Its 70-restaurant operation in Mexico is expected to triple in five years. With 105 restaurants in Malaysia, KFC has 60 percent of the nation's fast-food market.

What is KFC's secret to global success? First and perhaps most important is the worldwide acceptance of chicken. In Malaysia, for instance, annual per capita consumption of chicken has doubled during the past decade. According to the president of KFC International, "Chicken is probably the most universally accepted source of protein. There is not a country in the world where you won't find chicken." And unlike other meats, chicken is not forbidden by religions or cultures, except among vegetarians. This acceptance presented an excellent opportunity for KFC, but it did not guarantee success.

KFC made some early mistakes in Latin America and Europe. The company learned that opening an American fast-food restaurant abroad is not simple. Cultural differences between countries result in different eating habits. For instance, people eat their main meal of the day at different times throughout the world. Different menus must also be developed for specific cultures while still maintaining the core product—fried chicken. You can always find original recipe chicken, cole slaw, and fries at every KFC outlet, but restaurants in China feature Chinese tea and French restaurants offer more desserts. Above all, KFC emphasizes consistency. Whether in Shanghai or Kentucky, the product basically tastes the same.

KFC usually enters a new market by opening a single store. The company locates the store in a large urban area on the most visible piece of real estate available. If the project fails, the land can be sold. Usually foreign stores are eat-in restaurants, not the take-out establishments generally found in the United States. Prices are usually high at first to appeal to an upscale market.

International markets offer many opportunities and challenges for KFC. The company is growing outside the United States at nearly five times the rate of domestic growth. While many businesses complain about the inability to compete in Japan, KFC has nearly 1,000 restaurants in Japan alone. The secret, according to Huston, is quality, such as using fresh chicken rather than frozen. Freezing chicken causes a discoloring of the bone, which bothers the Japanese. Eastern Europe also holds great promise for KFC. With two stores in Hungary, KFC is working on deals in Poland and the Czech Republic.

KFC also faces several challenges. In some areas of the world, such as Malaysia and Indonesia, it is illegal to import poultry, a situation that has led to product shortages. Another challenge facing KFC is to adapt to foreign cultures. The company has been most successful in foreign markets when stores are operated by people who understand the culture. The objective is to think like a local, not like an American company starting an American business in a foreign country.

Questions for Discussion

1. Why has KFC been successful globally?

2. What is KFC's strategy for entering a foreign market?

3. Why do you think Kentucky Fried Chicken changed its name to KFC? Does this name change have any global implications?

4. What challenges face KFC as it expands globally?

Based on information from Alan I. Kirschenbaum, "The 'Original Recipe' for International Success," *The Lane Report,* May 1992, pp. 17–24; Sid Astbury, "KFC Malaysia: By No Means Chickenfeed," *Asian Business,* August 1992, p. 8; and Heidi Dawley, "Franchising: Mexico's Arms Are Wide Open," *Restaurant Business,* March 20, 1992, pp. 74–77.

Strategic Marketing Planning

2

OBJECTIVES

- *To define strategic marketing planning.*

- *To explain how an organization determines its mission.*

- *To describe the meaning and importance of organizational objectives.*

- *To compare the different approaches used to develop organizational strategy.*

- *To discuss the meaning and importance of marketing objectives.*

- *To identify how organizations develop a marketing strategy.*

- *To list the steps involved in developing a marketing plan.*

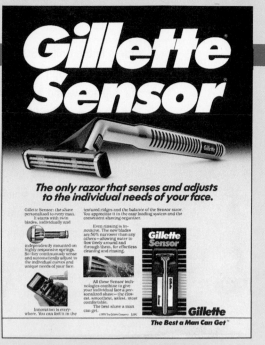

Gillette Sensor

The only razor that senses and adjusts to the individual needs of your face.

Gillette Sensor: the shave personalized to every man. It starts with twin blades, individually and independently mounted on highly responsive springs. So they continuously sense and automatically adjust to the individual curves and unique needs of your face.

Innovation is everywhere. You can feel it in the textured ridges and the balance of the Sensor razor. You appreciate it in the easy loading system and the convenient shaving organizer.

Even rinsing is innovative. The new blades are 50% narrower than any others—allowing water to flow freely around and through them, for effortless cleaning and rinsing.

All these Sensor technologies combine to give your individual face a personalized shave—the closest, smoothest, safest, most comfortable. The best shave a man can get.

Gillette
The Best a Man Can Get

A great product, a huge promotion budget, the right price—a sure formula for success. That's what Gillette Co. thought when it introduced the Sensor, its new high-tech razor with twin blades independently mounted on springs.

The Sensor is at the heart of Gillette's objective to regain market share lost to Bic and other companies that produce disposable blades. Gillette remains the industry leader, with 60 percent of the $2.6 billion worldwide blade-and-razor market. Since cartridge refills are much more profitable than disposable razors, Gillette hopes that the Sensor will help reverse a 15-year trend toward the inexpensive disposables.

Gillette took thirteen years and spent more than $200 million to develop the Sensor, making it the most expensive product in the firm's history. The cartridges contain 23 parts and require microlaser welding and complex assembly techniques involving 34 steps. The result is a thinner razor blade that provides a smoother, closer shave and makes the cartridges easier to clean. The complex manufacturing process also makes the Sensor cartridge difficult to copy, giving Gillette an advantage over competitors like Wilkinson Sword and Schick.

Gillette has used a single marketing strategy to sell the Sensor both in the United States and abroad, since company officials believe that shaving needs are similar around the world. But no matter what country, it is very hard to get consumers to change razors; those who already use cartridge systems like Gillette's Trac II keep their razors for seven to ten years. Gillette knew that getting customers to switch to the new system would be a challenge, but it believed that the Sensor's close shave would convince them.

Gillette established a $110 million advertising budget to launch the Sensor. The product was first introduced to the public with $3 million worth of commercials during the 1990 Super Bowl. The same spots played almost simultaneously in nineteen North American and European countries. Gillette distributed the Sensor to consumers through retailers at a price of $3.75 for a razor and three blades.

The Sensor's initial sales exceeded Gillette's wildest dreams. The firm shipped 4.5 million razors to U.S. retailers the first month. The product immediately became one of the hottest items in the industry, with some retailers selling out in three hours. Sales of the Sensor grew so fast that Gillette could not manufacture enough cartridges to meet demand. Many large drug store chains did not receive their orders in full or on time. Replacement cartridges were unavailable in many areas of the country for several months.

To resolve the problem, Gillette stopped advertising the Sensor for a few months, delayed introducing the product in Spain, Portugal, and Italy, and used razors intended for Europe to fill orders in the United States. Gillette also opened manufacturing facilities in West Berlin earlier than intended. Although some retailers were angry about shortages, Gillette anticipated that the advertising cutback would allow supply to catch up with demand. By the end of 1991, profits in blades and razors were up 20 percent from 1989 and Gillette had a 15 percent share of the $900 million market.

About a year after Gillette introduced the Sensor, Schick countered with a product of its own, the Tracer, a flexible cartridge that follows facial contours, and backed it with a $30 million promotion campaign. Gillette, in the meantime, developed the Sensor for Women and introduced it in 1992. Both companies now face a tough challenge with these new products. Schick's Tracer will have to compete against the successful Sensor, and Gillette will have to convince women to use shaving systems instead of disposable razors. With a radically different flat-handled design, Sensor for Women sold 7.6 million units in the first six months, more than Gillette expected to sell the entire first year.[1] ●

As the 1990s progress, experts are making several predictions. First, economic growth will be slower. This is not to say that there will not be a market that experiences rapid growth—perhaps some new technology will be introduced, for example. But markets for clothing, durable goods, banking services, and most other products will experience little or no growth. Market-share gains must come at the expense of competitors. Second, firms will face increased competition from U.S. and foreign firms. The quality of goods and services will improve as more firms implement total quality programs. Consumers will see better products at better prices, and firms will be faced with increased competition in markets that are not growing. These trends are placing increasing pressure on organizations to develop sound marketing strategies.

In Chapter 1, we said that marketing strategy involves selecting and analyzing a target market and developing a marketing mix for this target market. This chapter's opening story about Gillette's Sensor illustrates how important it is for an organization to develop a sound marketing strategy that fits its overall objectives. The Sensor took years to develop and cost millions of dollars. Without a carefully developed marketing strategy, the product may not have been so successful. But success is not guaranteed forever, because competitors like Schick introduce new products of their own. Gillette must then develop marketing strategies for other products, such as the Sensor for women, to maintain or increase its share of the market.

[1]Based on information from Mark Marement, "A New Equal Right: The Close Shave," *Business Week,* March 29, 1993, pp. 58–59; Pat Sloan, "Gillette to Launch Women's Sensor," *Advertising Age,* February 10, 1992, p. 36; Alison Fahey, "Schick Sharpens Razor Promotions," *Advertising Age,* February 25, 1991, p. 12; Keith H. Hammonds, "It's One Sharp Ad Campaign, But Where's the Blade?" *Business Week,* March 5, 1990, p. 30; Joshua Levine, "Global Lather," *Forbes,* February 5, 1990, pp. 146–148; Alison Fahey, "Sensor Sensation," *Advertising Age,* February 5, 1990, pp. 4, 49; and Keith H. Hammonds, "How a $4 Razor Ends Up Costing $300 Million," *Business Week,* January 29, 1990, pp. 62–63.

STRATEGIC MARKETING PLANNING DEFINED

The marketing concept states that an organization sh... needs of consumers through a coordinated set of ac... the organization to achieve its objectives. Most of today... ...ganiza-tions—both for-profit and nonprofit—continue to surv... ...e and grow because they have a competitive advantage. In other words, successful organizations do *something* better than their competitors do; it is the aim of strategic marketing planning to determine what that *something* will be. **Strategic marketing planning** is the continuous process of developing and implementing marketing strategies to achieve specific marketing objectives, which in turn lead to the achievement of an organization's overall objectives.

The process of strategic marketing planning includes six steps, as shown in Figure 2.1:

■ **strategic marketing planning** the continuous process of developing and implementing marketing strategies to achieve marketing objectives, which in turn lead to the achievement of overall organizational objectives

1. Defining the organizational mission

2. Establishing organizational objectives

3. Developing organizational strategy

4. Establishing marketing objectives

5. Designing marketing strategies

6. Developing a marketing plan

The first three steps are important not only for developing marketing strategies but also for guiding all departments in the organization, such as production, personnel, and finance. These steps enable top-level management to establish the direction for the entire organization. The mission, objectives, and strategy established at the top level then provide the foundation for planning activities in each department. The final three steps are necessary for developing and implementing marketing strategies. Thus the final three steps in the strategic marketing planning process must flow from the first three steps.

Today's managers face increased competition in both foreign and domestic markets as well as a constant stream of technological advances and changing market characteristics. To respond on a more timely basis and with a course of action in mind, marketing managers are increasingly turning to strategic marketing planning. By developing marketing plans—the output of the strategic marketing planning process—managers are forced to think ahead and anticipate events that will affect the firm's activities.

DEFINING THE ORGANIZATIONAL MISSION

What business is McDonald's in? Many organizations have failed, and continue to fail, because they don't understand what business they are in. Theodore Levitt, a professor at Harvard University, argued that organizations

FIGURE 2.1
The Strategic Marketing Planning Process

 must avoid taking a narrow view of their business.[2] He pointed out that railroad companies failed because they let other industries such as trucking and airlines fill consumer transportation needs. The railroads had defined their business as railroads instead of transportation; they focused their company mission on the product itself, and not the customer. Now, consider the question again: What business is McDonald's in?

Defining the organizational mission is the first step in the strategic planning process. The **organizational mission** is a formal statement describing what management wants the organization to be and what guidelines will be used for getting there. The organizational mission should answer three questions: What businesses are we in? What businesses should we be in? What do we do best? When defining the mission, an organization must consider its distinctive competencies and market opportunities. John Fluke Manufac-

■ **organizational mission** a formal statement describing what management wants the organization to be and what guidelines will be used for getting there

[2]Theodore Levitt, "Marketing Myopia," *Harvard Business Review,* July–August 1960, pp. 45–56.

FIGURE 2.2
Distinctive Competencies
Customer service has always been one of IBM's distinctive competencies. IBM continues to develop new services such as systems integration, network management, and user training.

Source: IBM is a registered trademark of IBM Corporation. © 1992.

turing, maker of voltmeters and other test and measurement devices, saw its markets fading fast. By taking advantage of its distinctive competencies and market opportunities, Fluke developed the following mission statement: to be the leader in compact professional electronic test tools. This mission led to a focus on customers; only products that meet market needs and use the firm's technological strength are manufactured by Fluke.[3] Table 2.1 presents organizational mission statements from several consumer, industrial, service, and nonprofit organizations. Notice that each mission statement takes a broad view of the organization's business; Morrison's Cafeterias, for example, refers to its mission as a "vision."

Distinctive Competencies

■ **distinctive competencies** an organization's skills and talents in areas such as production, finance, marketing, management, and use of resources (financial, human, technological, and material)

Distinctive competencies are an organization's skills and talents in areas such as production, finance, marketing, management, and utilization of resources (financial, human, technological, and material). One organization may have vast financial resources and the knowledge to use those resources efficiently and effectively; another firm might be more capable in the area of marketing or production. Figure 2.2 shows that one of IBM's distinctive competencies is service. An organization should base its mission on its distinctive competencies. Norfolk Southern (see Table 2.1) clearly builds on its resources, particularly its employees, to give the company a competitive advantage. Aluminum Co. of America (Alcoa) has achieved record profits the last few years by concentrating on the production of aluminum for such markets as

[3]Bill Saporito, "How to Revive a Fading Firm," *Fortune,* March 22, 1993, p. 80.

TABLE 2.1
Sample Organizational
Mission Statements

Norfolk Southern
Norfolk Southern's mission is to enhance the value of our stockholders' investment over time by providing quality freight transportation services and undertaking any other related businesses in which our resources, particularly our people, give the company an advantage.

IMC Fertilizer
We have a mission to make and keep IMC Fertilizer the world's most responsible and reliable supplier of quality crop nutrients to world agriculture. To achieve that mission or objective, the company has, since its creation, carried out a series of strategic measures to build the fertilizer industry's most effective combination of production, distribution and marketing capabilities. Technical advances, innovative financial and product management, market-specific agronomic and customer services, and an ongoing forward planning process that insures adequate in-the-ground reserves for future growth . . . all these things have supported the mission in the past, and will continue to do so in the years ahead.

Morrison's Cafeterias
Consistency. Quality. Stability. Performance. Four essentials for business success. Individually, each is impressive, but collectively they represent the entities, and more importantly, the vision of Morrison Incorporated. A vision that is founded on the premise of being the best in every market we serve, by providing superior service, outstanding food and excellent price/value.

Harsco Corporation
The Mission of Harsco Corporation is to be a world class competitor in the domestic and international manufacturing and marketing of diverse goods and industrial services, principally for defense, industrial, commercial and construction applications. The Corporation is committed to providing

(continued)

cars, trucks, and railcars.[4] By sticking with its distinctive competency for producing aluminum, Alcoa was able to take advantage of the strongest aluminum market in over a decade.

A sustainable competitive advantage can be based on either the assets or skills of the organization. Technical superiority, low-cost production, customer service and product support, location, financial resources, continuing product innovation, and overall marketing skills are all examples of distinctive competencies that can lead to a sustainable competitive advantage.[5] For example, Honda is known for providing quality automobiles at a reasonable price. Each succeeding generation of Honda cars has shown significant quality improvement over previous generations. This in turn made the Honda

[4]Tim Smart and Dean Foust, "Has Alcoa Found a Way to Foil the Aluminum Cycle?" *Business Week,* January 8, 1990, pp. 36–37.
[5]David Aaker, "Managing Assets and Skills: The Key to a Sustainable Competitive Advantage," *California Management Review,* Winter 1989, pp. 91–106.

innovative engineering solutions to specialized problems, emphasizing technology and close attention to customer service. In accomplishing its Mission, the Corporation will build upon the base of experience acquired during its long association with manufacturing and industrial services. Growth will be achieved through acquisition and internal development within a framework that balances risk of diversification against continued prudent management of current businesses.

Huntington Bancshares Incorporated
The mission of Huntington Bancshares Incorporated is to meet the financial services needs of individuals and businesses. We seek dominant position in the markets where we choose to compete by providing high quality, differentiated products and legendary customer service. Our thrust for business development is to penetrate existing markets, deliver products and services to new geographic markets, and strategically manage our business mix to achieve superior results.

Hilb, Rogal and Hamilton Company
Hilb, Rogal and Hamilton Company is in the business of assisting its clients to manage and transfer risk. We serve our clients through our expanding American insurance system, which now extends to nearly 50 U.S. cities and the District of Columbia, as well as by placing business overseas through HRH International. Our goal is to be the strongest professional insurance service organization in every community where HRH is represented. We are finding new and better ways to do this every year.

United Way of the Bluegrass
Increasing the organized capacity for people to care for one another.

Sources: Norfolk Southern, 1991 Annual Report; IMC Fertilizer Group, Inc., 1991 Annual Report; Morrison Incorporated, 1991 Annual Report; Harsco Corporation, 1991 Annual Report; Huntington Bancshares, 1991 Annual Report; Hilb, Rogal and Hamilton Company, 1991 Annual Report; and United Way of the Bluegrass, 1991 Annual Report.

Accord the leading selling car in the United States, with a 5 percent market share in 1991. This share fell to 4.5 percent in early 1992 when the Ford Taurus gained a 4.3 percent share by closing the quality gap.[6] Companies can also gain a competitive edge through patent protection, low costs, innovative products, a favorable brand image, or a strong sales force.[7] Rally's has built a competitive advantage in the fast-food industry by cutting costs. Rally's costs as a percentage of sales fell from 39 percent in 1990 to 35 percent in 1992.[8] The key to sustaining a competitive advantage is to focus and build upon the assets and skills that will lead to long-term performance gains. Close to the Customer illustrates how Disney's quality service gives the firm a competitive edge.

[6] Krystal Miller, "Slowing Sales of Honda Accord May Signal a Changing Market," *Wall Street Journal,* June 11, 1992, pp. B1–B2.
[7] David W. Cravens, "Gaining Strategic Marketing Advantage," *Business Horizons,* September–October 1988, pp. 44–54.
[8] Claire Poole, "Easy on the Beef!" *Forbes,* March 15, 1993, p. 74.

CLOSE TO THE CUSTOMER

Disney Delivers Service

Service through people is the theme at Disney, and its people make the difference at Disney theme parks. Each day "cast members," not employees, provide outstanding service to thousands of "guests," not customers. The term *overkill* has been used by many to describe Disney's approach to quality service. Perhaps no firm in the world stays closer to its customers than does Disney.

Inspired by the vision and spirit of founder Walt Disney, The Walt Disney Company was a leader in the family entertainment industry for years. The studio brought fantasy to life through animated movie classics like *Fantasia* and *Mary Poppins,* adventure films like *Treasure Island,* cartoon characters like Mickey Mouse and Donald Duck, and innovative amusement parks like Disneyland and Walt Disney World. But after Disney's death in 1966, the company stagnated. Its movies failed, its weekly television series "The Wonderful World of Disney" was canceled, and stock prices dropped. The "magic kingdom" became dependent on theme parks and hotels for over half its revenues.

In 1984, with only 3 percent of domestic box office receipts, Disney ranked eighth among Hollywood's top studios and was facing threats by corporate raiders. Then Michael D. Eisner became chairman and CEO. Determined to revitalize Disney, Eisner developed a multipronged marketing strategy that targets every segment of the entertainment business and every age group.

First, Disney upgraded its theme parks and raised admission prices. New attractions were added at Walt Disney World to compete with newer and more thrilling rides at other parks. Disney opened the MGM Studios theme park in Florida and created

Tokyo Disneyland. Euro Disney, which opened in April 1992 outside of Paris, is a $3.9 billion theme park and resort complex and one of Europe's largest construction projects. The French government assumed the bulk of the risk; Disney put up only $160 million of its own capital.

Eisner has led Disney back to the top of the movie industry with hits like *The Little Mermaid* and *Beauty and the Beast.* Disney has released films with adult themes under two different labels, Touchstone Films (*Pretty Woman*) and Hollywood Pictures (*Arachnophobia*). To tap the huge home video market, the studio began releasing videocassette versions of its animated classics, including *101 Dalmatians* and *Fantasia*—the greatest-selling video of all time. Disney also returned to television with eleven shows on the networks—more than any other studio.

The service quality theme at Disney starts at the top, and filters down to every individual in the firm, even those on cleanup duty in the theme parks. In fact, the parks are where the company's reputation for quality is earned daily. Disney's secret is a training program that turns out a legion of followers dedicated to serving customers. Ask any ticket taker or attendant where to find the nearest restaurant or rest rooms or when the next parade begins and you will get the answer. That's why it takes four days for employees to learn how to take tickets at a Disney park.

Sources: Richard Turner and Peter Gumbel, "As Euro Disney Braces for Its Grand Opening, the French Go Goofy," *Wall Street Journal,* April 10, 1992, pp. A1, A8; Thomas J. Peters and Robert H. Waterman, Jr., *In Search of Excellence* (New York: Warner Books, 1982), pp. 167–168; and "Marketing Achievement Awards," *Sales & Marketing Management,* August 1991, pp. 33–39.

Market Opportunities

When defining the organization's mission, management must carefully match the firm's capabilities with opportunities in the market—that is, what customers need and want. **Market opportunities** arise when the right combination of circumstances and timing allows an organization to take action to reach a particular market. Many factors, such as changing consumer values and preferences, growth rate, and technological innovations, can create market opportunities. The factors that determine how attractive a market is vary because products and industries differ. Concerns about heart disease and cancer provide a market opportunity for firms producing foods high in fiber or low in cholesterol. The microwave oven gave birth to microwaveable frozen dinners, vegetables, soups, and snacks. The popularity of certain movies and television programs creates market opportunities for producers of many products. For instance, the "Beverly Hills 90210" logo can be found on more than forty products, including clothing, jewelry, school supplies, and posters.[9]

Marketers sometimes use the term **strategic window** to describe the often limited periods of time during which market opportunities match the particular capabilities of a firm competing in a particular market.[10] As firms move in to take advantage of these opportunities, the window is said to close, meaning that the market opportunities no longer exist because of some change in the marketing environment. For example, Bill Gates built the software firm Microsoft into a billion-dollar business by capitalizing on the growing need for software to run personal computers (PCs). By doing a better job of developing software, Microsoft has captured 90 percent of the market for PC operating systems, largely through the success of its Windows program.[11] Firms ranging from IBM to Apple are trying to reduce Microsoft's dominance in PC operating systems but are finding that opportunities are limited because of Microsoft's market strength. Many factors can result in a market opportunity for an organization. For example, for a limited time following a recession, firms have taken advantage of low interest rates, lower cost of location, and an abundance of qualified workers.

When defining the organization's mission, management must carefully match the capabilities of the firm with opportunities in the market. The mission of Morrison's Cafeterias, presented in Table 2.1, matches its capabilities of consistency, quality, stability, and performance with customers' needs for superior service and outstanding food at an excellent price.

ESTABLISHING ORGANIZATIONAL OBJECTIVES

The second step in the strategic marketing planning process is establishing organizational objectives. **Organizational objectives,** derived from the

---

[9]Cyndee Miller, "Backlash Brewing Against '90210,'" *Marketing News,* January 20, 1992, pp. 1, 11.
[10]Derek F. Abell, "Strategic Windows," *Journal of Marketing,* July 1978, p. 21.
[11]Kathy Rebello and Evan I. Schwartz, "Microsoft," *Business Week,* February 24, 1992, pp. 60–65.

TABLE 2.2
Typical Organizational
Objectives

Objective	Desired Result	Time Frame
Increase profits	By $5 million	1 year
Increase percentage of market share	By 5 percent	1 year
Increase sales	By $100 million	2 years
Reduce defective parts	To less than 1 percent	1 year
Reduce consumer complaints	By 10 percent	1 year

organizational mission, specify what the organization wants to accomplish. Table 2.2 illustrates some typical organizational objectives. Each objective in the table answers these questions: What is to be accomplished? How much is to be accomplished? When is it to be accomplished? The first objective, for example, states that the company wants to increase its profits by $5 million within one year. By stating exactly what is to be accomplished and providing specific targets and a time frame, managers can realistically evaluate the organization's performance toward achieving that objective.

Organizational objectives vary, in terms of both the objective itself and the time frame for accomplishing it. A firm in serious financial trouble may be concerned solely with the short-term objectives needed to stay in business. In such a case, the firm's organizational objectives probably relate to surviving and increasing its cash flow. If the firm has losses of $25 million, its organizational objective might be to reduce its costs by $15 million and increase its revenue by $10 million within one year to remain in business for the long term. A more successful company, however, may want to sacrifice this year's profits for long-term objectives, such as finding new customers or growth. Recognizing that the amusement industry has limited growth potential, Disney has purchased several family magazines, including *Discover* and *Family Fun*. Although the bulk of the company's sales will continue to come from theme parks and movies, Disney hopes that in the long run the sales from magazines will increase profits.[12]

DEVELOPING ORGANIZATIONAL STRATEGY

■ **organizational strategy** a plan that defines the means by which an organization will achieve its organizational objectives

Developing organizational strategy is the third step in strategic marketing planning. An **organizational strategy** defines the means by which an organization will achieve its organizational objectives. It specifies how an organization will match its financial, production, marketing, and other capabilities with market opportunities to achieve its objectives. It also provides the key

[12]Scott Donaton, "Disney to Buy Magazine," *Advertising Age,* February 3, 1992, pp. 1, 48.

ideas and concepts that will be used to reach the organization's objectives. In a nonprofit organization with the objective of increasing contributions by $100,000 within one year, management will develop organizational strategies that specify how the company will accomplish this objective. This organizational strategy might specify that the company increase marketing expenditures by 10 percent or implement some other strategy or combination of several strategies.

 business-portfolio analysis evaluating an organization's current mix of products and businesses

Business-portfolio analysis—evaluating an organization's current mix of products and businesses—is useful in developing organizational strategy, especially in large companies. As you can see in Figure 2.3, some firms have a wide variety of products, and developing strategies for all of them can be very complex. Business-portfolio analysis helps organizations identify those businesses or units that have an opportunity to grow, those that should be sold or eliminated, and those that need extra attention and resources. Managers using this analysis generally examine the competitive position of a product or product line and the potential for improving the product's profitability.

strategic business unit (SBU) a division, product line in a division, or other profit center within a parent company

The concept of a **strategic business unit (SBU)**—a division, product line in a division, or other profit center within a parent company—is important in business-portfolio analysis. In some cases, a single product may be an SBU. Each strategic business unit is a single business with its own mission of marketing distinct goods or services to an identifiable group of customers. Each SBU has its own manager and is in competition with a well-defined group of competitors. For example, Parker Hannifin Corporation is composed of operating groups for aerospace systems, fluid connectors, fluid power, automotive and refrigeration components, sealing devices, rotary fluid transfer components, and motion-control systems.

FIGURE 2.3
Business-Portfolio Analysis
Dial's portfolio of products includes soaps, shampoos, detergents, bleach, cleansers, food items, financial services, and even cruises. Business-Portfolio Analysis can help organizations like Dial evaluate each product and allocate resources among them.

Source: Courtesy the Dial Corp.

FIGURE 2.4
Organizational Strategies of the Boston Consulting Group

Source: Adapted by permission, from *Perspectives*, No. 66, "The Product Portfolio." Copyright © 1970 The Boston Consulting Group, Boston, MA.

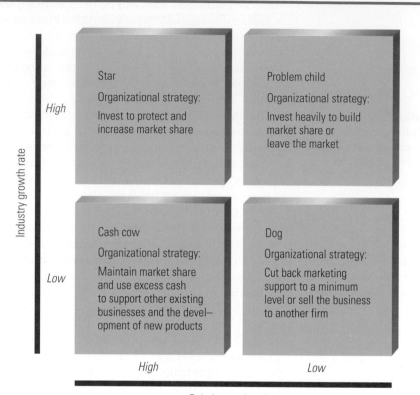

Business-portfolio analysis allows an organization to assess the status of each of its strategic business units. By examining the profitability and growth rates of the various SBUs, management can decide how to allocate resources among them. The company can strengthen successful units with additional resources and sell off or eliminate units that are not profitable or do not fit organizational objectives. General Electric Co., for example, sold its small-appliance division to Black & Decker Mfg. Co. because the division no longer fit the company's overall objectives.

Boston Consulting Group (BCG) Approach

■ **Boston Consulting Group (BCG) approach**
a method developed by a management consulting company that evaluates strategic business units on the basis of market growth rate and relative market share

The **Boston Consulting Group approach,** which was developed by a management consulting company, evaluates strategic business units on the basis of market growth rate and relative market share. Market growth rate is the annual rate of sales increase in the SBU's industry. Relative market share is the percentage of sales an SBU has in a particular market relative to its competitors. The BCG approach is also called product-portfolio analysis.

In the Boston Consulting Group approach, all of a firm's businesses are integrated to determine organizational strategies for individual SBUs and for the entire organization. The BCG approach enables the organization to classify its business units into four basic types: stars, cash cows, problem children, and dogs. Figure 2.4 summarizes the organizational strategies based on these classifications.[13]

Stars are businesses that have a leadership position in the industry or market, good prospects for growth, and substantial profits. Organizations with stars should invest financial resources to improve their product, price, promotion, and distribution to protect and increase the stars' position in the market. Coca-Cola's Diet Coke is an example of a product that would be considered a star.

Cash cows are businesses that have a dominant share of the market and earn more profits than are needed to maintain their market position. However, cash cows have limited prospects for growth. Organizations with cash cows should strive to maintain market share and use extra profits to support growth in other parts of the organization, such as research and development of new products. Classic Coke is an example of a cash cow.

Problem children are businesses that have a subordinate share of a growing market, earn low profits, and require a large amount of cash to build market share. Organizations with problem children might choose to invest heavily in the market, focus on a particular niche in the market, or acquire a competitor in order to increase market share. Alternatively, the organization might choose to sell the business to another firm or eliminate it altogether. Coca-Cola's Tab has a low market share in the growing diet cola market.

Dogs are businesses that have a subordinate share of the market and few prospects for growth; they are usually found in markets that are no longer growing. Organizations with dogs may choose to specialize in a segment of the market in which they can achieve dominance, cut back all expenses associated with the business to a minimum level that will sustain it for the rest of its life, sell the business to another firm, or eliminate the business entirely. The beverage Fresca, also made by Coca-Cola, is an example of a dog.

Market Attractiveness–Business Position Model

■ **market attractive-ness–business position model** a two-dimensional matrix that extends the BCG approach to include market attractiveness and business strength

The **market attractiveness–business position model** is a two-dimensional matrix pioneered by General Electric that extends the Boston Consulting Group approach to include market attractiveness and business strength. In this approach, illustrated in Figure 2.5, management assesses each strategic business unit according to its placement on the matrix. The vertical dimension, industry attractiveness, includes factors that relate to the strengths and weaknesses of the market, such as seasonality, intensity of competition, market sales, and the overall cost and feasibility of entering the market. The horizontal dimension, business position, includes factors that relate to the business's strengths and weaknesses, such as sales, relative market share, research and development, price competitiveness, product quality, and market knowledge.

[13]George S. Day, "Diagnosing the Product Portfolio," *Journal of Marketing,* April 1977, pp. 30–31.

The best situation is for a firm to have a strong business position in a highly attractive market—represented by the upper left area (area 1) of the matrix in Figure 2.5. This area calls for a strategy of investment for growth, although the matrix does not indicate how to implement such a strategy.

The diagonal area of the matrix (area 2) is characterized by medium overall attractiveness. The strategy for businesses in this area is to maintain their position and strive for growth and earnings.

The lower right area of the matrix (area 3) is an area of weak business position and low market attractiveness. The best strategy for businesses that fall in this area is harvesting or divesting. Harvesting is gradual withdrawal of marketing resources on the assumption that sales will slowly decline but profits will still be significant at a lower sales volume. Divesting is immediate disposal, usually a sale, of an SBU.

Porter's Generic Strategy Model

Michael Porter of Harvard University developed a model for determining organizational strategy that is appropriate for a wide variety of organizations

FIGURE 2.5
**Market Attractiveness–
Business Position Model**

Source: Derek F. Abell and John S. Hammond, *Strategic Market Planning: Problems and Analytical Approaches,* © 1979, p. 213. Adapted by permission of Prentice-Hall, Inc., Englewood Cliffs, N.J.

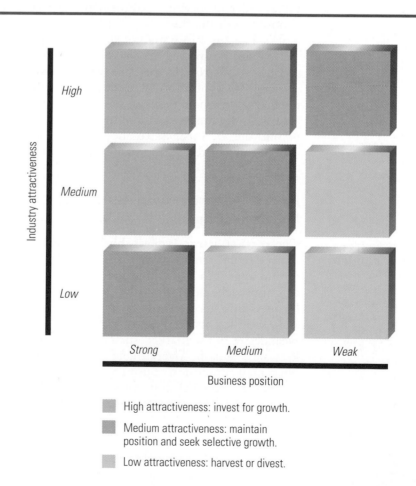

High attractiveness: invest for growth.

Medium attractiveness: maintain position and seek selective growth.

Low attractiveness: harvest or divest.

FIGURE 2.6
Porter's Generic Strategy Model

Source: Adapted with permission of The Free Press, a Division of Macmillan, Inc. from *Competitive Advantage: Creating and Sustaining Superior Performance* by Michael E. Porter. Copyright © by Michael E. Porter.

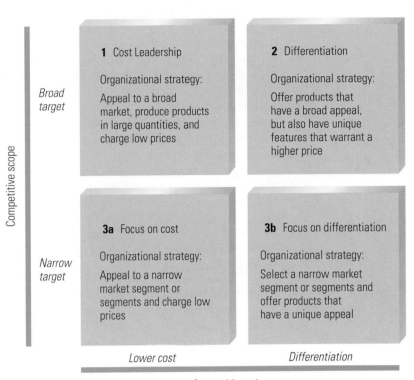

■ **Porter's Generic Strategy Model** a model developed by Michael Porter which suggests that organizations should analyze their industry and then define a competitive niche using one of three generic strategies: cost leadership, differentiation, and focus

across diverse industries. **Porter's Generic Strategy Model** suggests that firms should first analyze their industry, then define a competitive niche using one of three generic strategies: cost leadership, differentiation, and focus.[14] Porter's model is based on the concepts of competitive scope and competitive advantage. *Competitive scope* refers to the range of a firm's activities, which can be broad target or narrow target. *Competitive advantage* is created by offering value to customers that is not offered by competitors, either through lower cost or through unique benefits that differentiate the product. The Porter model combines the two concepts of competitive scope and competitive advantage to create three generic strategies, shown in Figure 2.6.

With the *cost leadership strategy,* the firm appeals to a broad market and attempts to become the lowest-cost producer in the industry. A firm can accomplish this through efficiencies in production, product design, technology, distribution, or some other means. By minimizing costs and producing large quantities, a firm is able to gain a competitive advantage by charging lower prices than competitors. Firms such as Kmart Corp., Timex Group Ltd., and Motel 6 have used the cost leadership strategy.

[14] Michael E. Porter, *Competitive Advantage: Creating and Sustaining Superior Performance* (New York: The Free Press, 1985), pp. 11–26.

The *differentiation strategy* involves gaining a competitive advantage by offering products with a broad appeal but also with unique characteristics that buyers consider important. These unique characteristics might pertain to design, quality, service, or some other factor. Because the product has a unique appeal that is valued by customers, the organization can charge a higher price for it. The makers of Rolex watches and Mercedes automobiles have differentiated their products on the basis of high quality.

The *focus strategy* differs from the first two strategies because it involves achieving a competitive advantage in a target segment through either cost leadership or differentiation. Thus the focus strategy suggests a tradeoff between market share and profitability. For instance, Ale-8-One is a profitable beverage manufacturer that targets its soft drink at a small geographic region—central and eastern Kentucky. The beverage, which has a high sugar and caffeine content, is differentiated through a regional appeal.

Profit Impact of Market Strategy (PIMS) Program

■ **Profit Impact of Market Strategy (PIMS) program** a research program—developed by the Strategic Planning Institute (SPI), a nonprofit think tank—that assists member firms in analyzing marketing performance and formulating marketing strategies

The **Profit Impact of Market Strategy (PIMS) program** is a research program developed by the Strategic Planning Institute (SPI), a nonprofit think tank of member firms. The institute maintains a database of confidential operating and competitive data on more than 2,800 businesses for a minimum of four years. It collects a variety of data on the strategic business units of each member firm, including industry characteristics, competitive position, resource allocation, strategies, and results. The SPI analyzes the data and prepares reports for member organizations to help them evaluate their current strategies and assess alternatives. Unlike the other approaches to developing organizational strategy, the PIMS program provides both diagnostic and prescriptive information. For example, a large, diversified European corporation was considering a proposal to acquire an American company. The European firm's managers used the PIMS database and models to simulate the performance of the combined business units; this analysis was a key piece of evidence in the final decision to go ahead with the acquisition of the American firm.[15]

The PIMS program has identified many factors that affect the performance of firms. These factors can be grouped into three categories: (1) those relating to the structure of the marketplace; (2) those describing the firm's competitive position in the industry; and (3) those relating to the firm's strategy. The PIMS database has indicated a strong relationship between market share and profitability. The data have also suggested that organizations offering higher quality tend to be more profitable than their competitors. Product quality, as the Porter model suggests, can justify higher prices. The PIMS data also suggest that lower costs increase profitability, whereas high investment demands reduce profitability.

---

[15] Robert Buzzell and Bradley T. Gale, *PIMS Principles: Linking Strategy to Performance*, 1987.

FIGURE 2.7
Organizational Growth Strategies

Source: Adapted from H. I. Ansoff, *New Corporate Strategy*, John Wiley, New York, 1988. Reprinted by permission of the author.

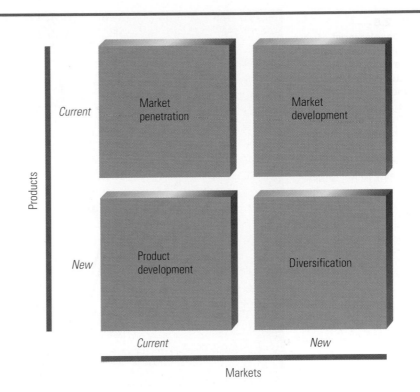

The Product/Market Growth Matrix

Managers must plan for long-run survival by developing organizational strategies that will help the organization to continue to grow. As shown in Figure 2.7, organizational growth strategies can be classified into four broad categories: market penetration, product development, market development, and diversification.[16]

When a firm sees an opportunity to increase sales in one of its current markets, it is likely to use market penetration or product development. **Market penetration** is a strategy of increasing sales of existing products in current markets. An automobile manufacturer, for instance, might try to increase its market share by increasing its advertising efforts and the size of its sales staff. This is the strategy that Burger King, the number two hamburger chain, used when it introduced "The Best Food for Fast Times" campaign to chase number one McDonald's.

Product development is a strategy of increasing sales by improving existing products or developing new products for current markets. For example, electronics manufacturer Sony Corp. developed a new, lightweight, long-lasting rechargeable battery that is one-fourth the weight of a typical battery and lasts more than twice as long. PepsiCo has introduced several

■ **market penetration**
a strategy of increasing sales of existing products in current markets

■ **product development**
a strategy of increasing sales by improving existing products or developing new products for current markets

---

[16] H. I. Ansoff, "Strategies for Diversification," *Harvard Business Review,* September–October 1957, pp. 113–124.

FIGURE 2.8
Product Development
Tandy Corporation is constantly developing new audio equipment that makes the customer ask, "Is it live, or is it Memorex?" This strategy enables Memorex to increase sales for its current market and to communicate the image of quality to the target market.

Source: © Tandy Corporation, reprinted with permission. Memorex and the Shattering Glass logo are registered trdemarks of Memorex Telex, N.V., licensed to Tandy Corporation.

[MEMOREX AUDIO EQUIPMENT.   JUST BREAKING.]

new beverages, including Crystal Pepsi and All Sport H20H, transforming PepsiCo into a total beverage company.[17] In the same vein, General Foods Corporation expanded its Bird's Eye frozen vegetable line with a new potato product. Figure 2.8 illustrates how Tandy Corporation uses this strategy.

When a business sees that a current market has little potential for growth, it may decide to enter new markets, using either a market development strategy or a diversification strategy. **Market development** is a strategy of increasing sales by introducing current products into new markets. This strategy often involves expansion into new geographic areas. Reebok International Ltd.'s expansion into the athletic shoe markets in Canada and France is an example of market development.

Diversification is a strategy of developing new products to sell in new markets. Through diversification, a firm with adequate resources can move into new, expanding markets, reduce risk by investing in different businesses, and increase its chances of surviving in the long run. Diversification can be accomplished through internal development or acquisition of other firms. Tyson Foods acquired Holly Farms Corp. and Arctic Alaska Fisheries Corp. in an effort to expand its chicken market and move into new, global markets.[18] Many companies diversify because their current sales are stagnating.

■ **market development**
a strategy of increasing sales by introducing current products into new markets

■ **diversification** a strategy of developing new products to sell in new markets

[17]Laura Zinn, "Pepsi's Future Becomes Clearer," *Business Week,* February 1, 1993, pp. 74–75.
[18]Bob Ortega, "Tyson Has Global Appetite That Goes Beyond Fish," *Wall Street Journal,* June 24, 1992, p. B4.

For instance, the Procter & Gamble Co. has diversified from orange juice such as Citrus Hill into juice drinks like Hawaiian Punch in an effort to increase its share of the juice market.[19] Unfortunately, diversification, especially unrelated diversification (into markets that are not related to the firm's current products), has led to problems for some firms. One study of diversification strategies undertaken by thirty-three large U.S. corporations found that the vast majority of the diversifications were mistakes. In nearly 20 percent of the cases, firms that followed diversification strategies were taken over.[20] Diversification generally requires a large amount of resources, and is often the most risky of the organizational growth strategies. Some firms may be better off using their resources to improve current products and to develop a specialty or distinctive competency in a single area.

The Significance of Organizational Strategy Approaches

The approaches discussed in this section are useful planning tools to help managers develop an organizational strategy. However, they are meant to be supplements to and not substitutes for a manager's own judgment. These approaches do not serve as formulas for success or quick-fix solutions to an organization's problems. Rather, they are used to help managers diagnose a firm's strengths and weaknesses and prescribe strategies for achieving the firm's objectives.

A word of caution regarding business-portfolio analysis is necessary. The classification of an SBU into a specific cell of a portfolio matrix (such as the BCG approach) depends upon several factors: the dimensions used to define the matrix, the rules used to divide the dimensions into high and low groups, and the specific approach used. Changes in any of these factors could result in a different classification for a single SBU. Moreover, some of the strategies suggested may be difficult to implement. For instance, harvesting or divesting an unprofitable SBU may not be possible in a stagnant industry. Other strategies may limit future growth opportunities; for instance, a firm might eliminate a dog that it could have turned around and made profitable. Victor Kiam bought failing Remington Products from Sperry Rand Corp. in 1980 for $25 million. Within ten years, he turned Remington into a $250-million-a-year company.[21]

Perhaps the greatest strength of business-portfolio analysis is its emphasis on managing a portfolio of businesses and products, each with different opportunities and risks. Portfolio analysis suggests that the long-term success of an organization depends on having some businesses and products that generate cash and others that use cash for growth opportunities. Thus business-portfolio analysis suggests that an organization's long-term performance depends on an organizational strategy that focuses not only on

[19] Laurie Freeman, "P&G Shifts Strategy in Juices," *Advertising Age,* June 18, 1990, p. 33.
[20] Michael E. Porter, "From Competitive Advantage to Corporate Strategy," *Harvard Business Review,* May–June 1987, pp. 43–60.
[21] Geoffrey Smith and Lisa Driscoll, "Victor Kiam, the Self-Sacking Quarterback," *Business Week,* February 25, 1991, p. 46.

maintaining successful businesses but also on developing businesses for future successes. And despite recent criticisms that portfolio models are no longer useful in strategic planning, many organizations continue to use these tools which have been integral to their success.[22]

ESTABLISHING MARKETING OBJECTIVES

■ **marketing objective**
an objective that specifies what is to be accomplished through marketing activities

Once the organization has analyzed its current business situation and developed organizational strategies, its managers can establish marketing objectives. A **marketing objective** asks what is to be accomplished through marketing activities. Establishing marketing objectives is the fourth step in strategic marketing planning. As with organizational objectives, marketing objectives should be expressed in clear, simple terms so that everyone involved understands exactly what they are trying to achieve and so that their accomplishments can be measured accurately.

Suppose a firm has an organizational objective to increase profits by 10 percent within a year. Although the firm could choose other organizational strategies to achieve this objective, in this case, the firm decides to pursue a market development strategy. One of the firm's subsequent marketing objectives might then be to increase market share by 5 percent within a year by finding new customers for existing products. Notice how this marketing objective is consistent with the organizational objective:

Organizational objective:	Increase profits by 10 percent within a year.
Organizational strategy:	Market development (find new customers for current products).
Marketing objective:	Increase market share by 5 percent within a year by finding new customers for current products.

Marketing objectives are typically stated in terms of sales volume or market share. If a company has a marketing objective to increase market share by 10 percent, the firm should be able to accurately measure changes in its market share. A marketing objective should also indicate the time frame for accomplishing the objective. For example, a firm that sets an objective of introducing three new products should state the time period in which this is to be accomplished.

Transamerica Corporation is one of the world's largest financial services companies, providing specialized financial and insurance products and services to individuals and organizations. The finance group includes four companies: Transamerica Financial Services, Transamerica Commercial Finance, Transamerica Leasing, and Transamerica Real Estate Services. The insurance group consists of three firms: Transamerica Life Companies, Transamerica

[22]Donald L. McCabe and V. K. Narayanan, "The Life Cycle of the PIMS and BCG Models," *Industrial Marketing Management,* 1991, pp. 347–352.

Insurance Group, and Transamerica Asset Management Group. The firm's organizational objective is to increase earnings by 10 to 15 percent a year. To accomplish this goal, Transamerica's marketing objectives have focused on increasing market share. For example, Transamerica Insurance Group has specialized within carefully selected property and casualty markets where it has maintained prices and become a market leader. Emphasis has been placed on quality products and services and timely customer support. Thus achieving the Insurance Group's marketing goal of becoming a market leader has helped Transamerica achieve its organizational goal of increasing earnings.[23]

DESIGNING MARKETING STRATEGIES

The fifth step in strategic marketing planning is designing marketing strategies. As explained in Chapter 1, a *marketing strategy* entails selecting and analyzing a target market and developing a marketing mix for this target market. A marketing strategy determines the means for achieving marketing objectives. It is critical to an organization because it is used to assess customer needs and the firm's potential for gaining a competitive advantage.[24] When a marketing strategy is implemented properly, it achieves the organization's marketing objectives; these, in turn, contribute to accomplishing the organization's overall objectives. Thus a degree of overlap exists between organizational strategy and marketing strategy.

Marketing strategy is critical in gaining a competitive advantage, and it should be based on a firm's strengths and weaknesses. For instance, Japanese automobile manufacturers knew they could not compete head-on with General Motors—they did not have the resources. So companies like Toyota and Honda initially developed small cars built better than GM's and gained a competitive advantage. Industry leaders must also develop competitive marketing strategies to maintain their dominance. Marketing Close-Up examines how McDonald's remained competitive by changing its marketing strategy.

Selecting and Analyzing a Target Market

A *target market* is a group of customers—consumers or other businesses—for whom a business tailors a marketing mix. The organization focuses its marketing efforts on this group and tries to meet its specific needs and preferences. The state of Rhode Island, for instance, has targeted Europe in an effort to develop international trade. Rhode Island, known for its jewelry, is promoting the state as the "jewelry capital of the world."[25] When analyzing potential target markets, marketing managers must determine whether the organization has the resources to produce a marketing mix that meets the

---

[23] Transamerica Corporation, 1992 Annual Report.
[24] Yoram Wind and Thomas S. Robertson, "Marketing Strategy: New Directions for Theory and Research," *Journal of Marketing,* Spring 1983, p. 12.
[25] "Rhode Island Targets Europe," *Marketing News,* January 15, 1993, p. 19.

MARKETING CLOSE-UP

McDonald's Alters Its Marketing Strategy

McDonald's became the number one restaurant chain by developing a marketing strategy based on the philosophy of founder Ray Kroc. He envisioned a chain of restaurants that provided speedy service, a simple menu, consistent quality, and good value. Kroc's dream has resulted in more than 11,000 restaurants, steady growth for over two decades, and annual revenues of $6.1 billion. But in recent years growth has slowed and has been coming mostly from overseas outlets; the average number of customers in U.S. restaurants has remained constant for over five years.

Executives at McDonald's believe that the major reasons for the slowdown are competition and changing eating habits. McDonald's faces fierce competition from other chains such as Burger King, Arby's, and Kentucky Fried Chicken. Additionally, small independent restaurants and delis, convenience foods, and the microwave are taking business from the restaurant chains. Consumer tastes are moving away from red meat, fried foods, cholesterol, and salt.

To compete in the 1990s, McDonald's is altering its marketing strategy. The changes run deep, cutting at the very heart of the strategy that made McDonald's famous and successful. The one-time simple menu that reflected Kroc's devotion to the hamburger now consists of more than forty items, with more to come. A typical McDonald's now serves salads, chicken, and sausage on a biscuit.

McDonald's is also targeting a new market—dinner customers. A similar strategy worked for the chain in the 1980s when it increased sales by introducing a breakfast menu. McDonald's hopes to attract couples, families, and teenagers for dinner with new menu items like fried fish and chicken. One new item McDonald's hopes will boost sales is pizza, which has passed hamburgers as the most popular evening meal eaten in restaurants.

McDonald's tested pizza in a 24-store market in Kentucky and Indiana in 1989. The 14-inch pie, which is available after 4:00 P.M., comes in four varieties—cheese, sausage, pepperoni, and deluxe—and is priced between $5.84 and $9.49. Baked in special ovens designed by McDonald's engineers working with oven manufacturers, the pizzas take about five and a half minutes to prepare—longer than traditional fast food but faster than an average pizza, which takes about twenty minutes.

McDonald's also continues to develop its foreign restaurants. In 1992, Canada was the first country in McDonald's 59-nation network to serve pizza in all 633 restaurants. And in Switzerland, two McDonald's dining cars are offering passengers the usual menu and more. The railroad cars run on two routes, from Geneva to Brig and Geneva to Barel. According to McDonald's marketing manager in Switzerland, the Swiss enjoy the menu, but several items have been added to appeal to local tastes. Red or white wine and beer are available, and the national breakfast of croissants, marmalade, butter, and hard cheese has replaced the Egg McMuffin.

Sources: Ronald Henkoff, "Big Mac Attacks with Pizza," *Fortune*, February 26, 1990, pp. 87–89; Scott Hume, "McDonald's Fred Turner: Making All the Right Moves," *Advertising Age*, January 1, 1990, pp. 6, 17; Carla Rapoport, "Big Mac Attacks Swiss Tracks," *Fortune*, June 1, 1992, p. 13; and "McDonald's Serves Pizza in Canada," *Advertising Age*, March 23, 1992, p. 8.

needs of the target market and whether satisfying those needs is consistent with the firm's overall objectives. Managers must also evaluate possible markets to see how entering them would affect the firm's sales, costs, and profits. Finally, managers must consider the size and number of competitors already in that market.

Careful selection of a target market is necessary for an organization to achieve its marketing objectives. Many businesses have floundered or failed because they did not adequately identify the target group at which they were aiming their products and marketing efforts. Sears' attempt to switch to everyday low prices to compete with Wal-Mart and Kmart actually clashed with customers' image of Sears. Within a year, Sears returned to the former strategy of frequent sales on selected merchandise, further confusing customers. Today, Sears has fallen from the position of the top retailer to third, behind Wal-Mart and Kmart.[26]

Businesses that try to satisfy all customers generally do not satisfy the needs of any particular customer group very well. When IBM experienced several years of disappointing profits beginning in 1985, some company officials thought the firm might be trying to be all things to all people. IBM was producing typewriters, personal computers, and software as well as traditional mainframe computers. IBM salespeople were concentrating on selling products and lost sight of the problems facing diverse groups of customers. Finally in August of 1990, IBM sold its typewriter division following a decision by management to concentrate on computer systems.[27] Thus it is important for an organization's management to specify which customers the firm is trying to serve and to have adequate information about those customers. Changes in the population also necessitate changes in target market strategies. As baby boomers (those born between 1946 and 1964) are aging, companies are targeting younger consumers who purchase more homes, packaged goods, travel, home furnishings and beauty, fashion, and fragrance products.[28] Likewise, companies must respond to other shifts in the population. Within 20 years, Hispanics will become the nation's largest minority group, with a population of about 39 million.[29] This market will represent a much larger piece of the American consumer pie, posing new challenges and new opportunities for businesses.

Developing a Marketing Mix

The selection and analysis of a target market provides a foundation on which a marketing mix—product, price, distribution, and promotion—can be developed. These elements are called marketing mix *variables* because marketing managers vary the type and amount of each element according to the needs of the target market. An organization's marketing strategy should enable the

[26] Kate Fitzgerald, "Brennan Will Have to Answer to Upset Sears Shareholders," *Advertising Age,* April 20, 1992, pp. 3, 42.
[27] Tom Daykin, "IBM to Keep Small Stake in New Firm," Lexington, Ky. *Herald-Leader,* August 2, 1990, pp. A1, A10.
[28] Karen Ritchie, "Get Ready for 'Generation X,'" *Advertising Age,* November 9, 1992, p. 21.
[29] Thomas G. Exter, "The Largest Minority," *American Demographics,* February 1993, p. 39.

firm to create and maintain a marketing mix that satisfies customers' needs for a particular product.

The marketing mix must be developed to precisely match the needs of the target market. By collecting information about the target, marketers are in a better position to develop a mix that satisfies the people in the target market. Such information might include demographic data like age, income, sex, and education level; preferences for product designs and features; attitude toward price and advertising; or extent of product usage. The marketing mix should also be altered to reflect changing market conditions and changes in competitors' marketing strategies. For example, prices may need to be reduced in response to lower prices of competitors. Now let us examine the decisions and activities related to each marketing mix variable.

Product Variable   As noted in Chapter 1, a product can be a good, a service, or an idea. The *product variable* is important in marketing strategy decisions because it relates directly to satisfying the needs and wants of the target market. Businesses must find out what customers need and want (through marketing research) and create products with characteristics that fulfill those needs and wants. Businesses may also develop other aspects of the product to meet customers' needs, such as packaging, labeling, warranties, and service.

To satisfy customers and achieve organizational objectives, a marketer must continue to develop new products, modify and improve existing ones, and eliminate those that no longer satisfy buyers and yield acceptable profits. Fast-food chains have added new items to their menus—McDonald's, the McLean Deluxe; and KFC, skinless chicken—in response to consumers' nutritional concerns. Automobile manufacturers are constantly making product improvements, such as air bags, to increase safety, quality, and customer satisfaction.

Price Variable   Marketing managers are usually involved in establishing pricing policies and determining product prices. The *price variable* is important in the design of marketing strategy because customers are concerned about the value obtained in a purchase, and price is the easiest of the marketing mix variables to alter. Price is often used as a competitive tool; in fact, extremely intense price competition sometimes leads to price wars. In 1992, for example, intense competition between airlines led United, Delta, American, and other carriers to engage in fierce airfare price wars, with the result that the lowest advance purchase fares were cut by 50 percent.[30]

Price also helps to establish a product's image. Liz Claiborne's designer clothing and Calvin Klein's Obsession perfume probably would not have the same image if they were sold at lower prices. Image is critical in establishing a brand in the minds of consumers.

---

[30]Wendy Zellner, "The Airlines Are Killing Each Other Again," *Business Week,* June 8, 1992, p. 32.

Distribution Variable   In dealing with the *distribution variable,* a marketing manager attempts to make products available in the quantities desired to as many customers as possible and to keep physical distribution costs (inventory, transportation, and storage) as low as possible. The distribution variable also involves selecting intermediaries (wholesalers and retailers), establishing and maintaining inventory control procedures, and developing and managing transportation and storage systems.

Products can be distributed in numerous ways, and innovations in distribution can dramatically improve a firm's sales. Goodyear Tire & Rubber Co. expanded its distribution capacity by selling its brands to Sears. Goodyear's share of the U.S. tire market had dropped from 15 to 12 percent as consumers began purchasing tires at multibrand discount stores and warehouse clubs. By distributing tires through Sears, Goodyear puts its tires where consumers shop. Sears sells 9.5 million tires each year, and Goodyear hopes that 2.5 million of those will be its brand.[31]

Promotion Variable   The *promotion variable* is important in marketing strategy because it facilitates exchanges by informing consumers about an organization and its products. The promotion variable includes advertising, sales promotion, publicity, and personal selling. Promotion is used to increase public awareness of an organization, a new product, or a new brand. It may also be used to enhance a firm's image. In addition, promotion is used to educate consumers about product features or to urge people to adopt a particular position on a political or social issue.

Large and small, profit and nonprofit organizations alike, as well as individuals and trade associations, rely heavily on promotion (see Figure 2.9). In 1992, thousands of billboards appeared across the country with the message "Buck the recession. Spend a buck today, end the recession tomorrow." This public service message was sponsored by the outdoor advertising industry in the midst of a major slump. Advertising Suppliers Association, a trade group, spent $27,000 creating and producing the signs; space was donated by billboard companies. Although industry officials said there was no way to measure the signs' effectiveness, merchants followed suit in beginning promotional campaigns to get shoppers into stores.[32]

It is critical that marketing managers develop a strong marketing mix. One weak variable can greatly reduce a product's success. A solid product with a good price and an efficient distribution network may fail because of ineffective advertising. Thus the marketing mix variables are related to each other. The product, for example, will influence the method of distribution. Fresh produce might be shipped in refrigerated trucks, whereas a critical computer component can be distributed via overnight mail.

---

[31] Zachary Schiller, "Goodyear Is Gunning Its Marketing Engine," *Business Week,* March 16, 1992, p. 42.

[32] Richard Gibson, "Billboard Industry Urges Consumers to Spend," *Wall Street Journal,* July 1, 1992, p. B1.

DEVELOPING THE MARKETING PLAN

■ **marketing plan** a formally prepared and written
document detailing the activities necessary to implement
the marketing strategies

The final step in strategic marketing planning is developing the marketing
plan. A **marketing plan** is a formally prepared and written document detailing the activities necessary to implement the marketing strategies. The marketing plan serves as a subset of organizational strategy in that it specifies
those marketing activities needed to achieve the goals of the organization.
Some organizations develop several marketing plans, one for each product. A
marketing plan examines the current marketing situation of the organization,
assesses the opportunities and problems facing the organization, establishes
the marketing objectives, defines the marketing strategies and action programs needed to achieve those objectives, and specifies the controls needed
to monitor the plan. The contents of a typical marketing plan are summarized
in Table 2.3.

   Developing marketing plans is not a one-time exercise. Plans must be
changed as forces in the organization or the marketing environment change.
As new competitors enter the market, a firm may need to alter some of its
marketing activities. In the telecommunications industry, AT&T had to
make adjustments in price and product offerings when faced with competition from firms like MCI and US Sprint. The best marketing plans are those

FIGURE 2.9
Promotion
Organizations large and
small, profit and nonprofit,
use promotion to communi-
cate their message to the
target market.

Source: Courtesy The Advertising
Council Inc.

TABLE 2.3
Contents of a Typical Marketing Plan

I. **Executive Summary**
A brief summary of the marketing plan

II. **Current Marketing Situation**
An analysis of trends and changes in the marketing environment, the market situation, customers, and competitors

III. **Opportunities and Problems**
The major opportunities and threats (both inside and outside the organization) facing the product for which the plan is being developed

IV. **Marketing Objectives**
The goals to be achieved through the marketing plan in such areas as customer satisfaction, sales volume, or market share

V. **Marketing Strategies**
The overall marketing strategies—market segmentation and product, price, promotion, and distribution activities—that will be used to achieve the objectives

VI. **Action Programs**
Programs that pinpoint who is responsible for the marketing activities and that establish budgets and timetables for executing the marketing strategies

VII. **Controls**
The procedures for monitoring the plan over time and for taking corrective action if needed

that are updated continuously to reflect changing conditions in the marketing environment.

Marketing plans may vary in duration. Short-range plans cover a period of one year or less; medium-range plans usually encompass two to five years; long-range marketing plans generally extend for more than five years. Long-range plans are relatively rare because the marketing environment changes so quickly. However, as the marketing environment continues to change and business decisions grow in complexity, profitability and survival will be more and more dependent on the development of long-range plans.[33]

SUMMARY

Strategic marketing planning is a continuous process of developing marketing strategies to achieve marketing objectives and overall organizational

[33] Ronald D. Michman, "Linking Futuristics with Marketing Planning, Forecasting, and Strategy," *Journal of Consumer Marketing,* Summer 1984, pp. 17–23.

objectives. First, an organization must define its mission. Second, it establishes organizational objectives and develops an organizational strategy to achieve those objectives. Next, a firm sets marketing objectives and designs marketing strategies to achieve those objectives. Finally, the organization develops a marketing plan for implementing its strategies.

The organizational mission is a formal statement that indicates what business the organization wants to be in and the guidelines for getting there. A firm's mission depends largely on its capabilities and market opportunities. Capabilities are the distinctive competencies a company has developed—skills and talents at which it excels. Market opportunities exist when circumstances and timing allow an organization to reach a target market. A strategic window is a limited period of time during which market opportunities match a firm's capabilities to reach a particular market.

Organizational objectives specify what the organization wants to accomplish. These specifically state what is to be accomplished, how much is to be accomplished, and when it is to be accomplished.

Organizational strategy defines the means by which an organization will achieve its organizational objectives. This strategy specifies how the firm will match its capabilities with market opportunities to achieve its objectives. In developing an organizational strategy, an organization must assess the status of its products and businesses and plan for future growth.

Business-portfolio analysis allows an organization to evaluate each of its strategic business units. A strategic business unit (SBU) is a division, product line or some other profit center within an organization. Business-portfolio analysis is a diagnostic tool that helps organizations identify those SBUs that have growth potential and those that should be eliminated.

The Boston Consulting Group (BCG) approach to developing organizational strategy evaluates strategic business units on the basis of market growth rate and relative market share. It classifies business units as stars, cash cows, dogs, or problem children. The market attractiveness–business position model evaluates strategic business units on a two-dimensional matrix based on industry attractiveness and business position. Porter's Generic Strategy Model suggests that firms should first analyze their industry, then define a competitive niche using one of three generic strategies: cost leadership, differentiation, and focus. The Profit Impact of Market Strategy (PIMS) program, used by the Strategic Planning Institute, evaluates the strategic business units of member organizations according to a number of factors, such as industry characteristics, competitive position, and resource allocation.

Management must plan for future growth by developing organizational strategies that will help the organization continue to grow. Current market strategies include market penetration (increasing sales of existing products in current markets) and product development (improving existing products or developing new products for current markets). Strategies for new markets are market development (introducing current products into new markets) and diversification (developing new products to sell in new markets).

Marketing objectives specify what is to be accomplished through marketing activities. These objectives are generally stated in terms of sales volume or market share. They should be expressed in clear, understandable, and measurable terms, and must be consistent with an organization's overall goals.

Designing a marketing strategy involves selecting and analyzing a target market and developing a marketing mix for that market. In developing a marketing strategy, an organization must carefully select a target market to achieve its marketing objectives. It must also determine what types of marketing mix variables and how much of each (product, price, distribution, and promotion) will satisfy the needs and wants of that target market. A firm must determine whether it has the resources to produce a marketing mix to satisfy a particular target market and whether satisfying those needs is consistent with the firm's objectives. When a marketing strategy is implemented properly, it achieves the organization's marketing objectives, which in turn contribute to the achievement of the organization's overall objectives.

A marketing plan details the activities necessary to implement the marketing strategies. Developing marketing plans is a continuous process. Short-range plans cover one year or less; medium-range plans usually encompass two to five years; and long-range plans last for more than five years.

KEY TERMS

strategic marketing planning
organizational mission
distinctive competencies
market opportunities
strategic window
organizational objectives
organizational strategy
business-portfolio analysis
strategic business unit (SBU)
Boston Consulting Group
   (BCG) approach
market attractiveness–business
   position model

Porter's Generic Strategy
   Model
Profit Impact of Market
   Strategy (PIMS) program
market penetration
product development
market development
diversification
marketing objective
marketing plan

QUESTIONS FOR DISCUSSION AND REVIEW

1. What is the purpose of strategic marketing planning?
2. Name the steps of the strategic marketing planning process, and explain how they are interrelated.
3. What is an organizational mission? What factors should be considered in determining an organization's mission?
4. What business is each of the following organizations in: Avis, Toyota, Commerce Bank, the university you attend?
5. How can a company develop a sustainable competitive advantage? Give three examples of organizations that you think have a sustainable competitive advantage and state the advantage each has.

6. What is a market opportunity? What is a strategic window? How do market opportunities relate to the organizational mission?

7. Why is it important to develop an organizational strategy? How is business-portfolio analysis used in developing organizational strategies?

8. Define the four classifications of business units in the Boston Consulting Group approach to business-portfolio analysis. What are the organizational strategies for each?

9. Explain Porter's Generic Strategy Model. For each of the four strategies in Porter's matrix (Figure 2.6), identify a firm that you think has a competitive advantage based on this strategy.

10. According to the PIMS program findings, what are some of the factors that influence a firm's performance?

11. How can a firm increase sales in current markets? How can it increase sales in new markets?

12. What is a marketing objective? How are marketing objectives related to a firm's organizational objectives?

13. Why should an organization develop a marketing plan?

14. Distinguish between short-range, medium-range, and long-range marketing plans.

CASES

| 2.1 | **APPLE'S PLAN FOR THE FUTURE** |

When Steve Jobs and Stephen Wazniak invented a computer in a garage in 1976, they wanted to make a machine that was easy and fun to use. With this modest and perhaps naive mission, the two young upstarts founded Apple Computer and developed the billion-dollar personal computer (PC) market. Today, Apple continues to be a viable force in the industry but faces intense competition from a host of firms, including IBM, Compaq, and Dell. With growth slowing, current chairman John Sculley questioned Apple's long-standing strategy of high prices and huge product differentiation. Apple lost much of its differentiation with the introduction of Microsoft's Windows, and industry price wars have made PCs a commodity product.

The challenge facing Apple is to develop a viable strategy for the 21st century. Sculley is staking Apple's future on new markets and new products, including a trillion-dollar megamarket that takes electronics and computers even deeper into the lives of consumers. As part of this strategy, Apple wants to become the industry leader in Japan. Sales of the Macintosh have grown in Japan from a few thousand units in 1988 to an estimated 180,000 in 1992; market share has grown from 1 to 6 percent of the $7 billion Japanese market.

A new distribution agreement with major Japanese companies (Mitsubishi, Sharp, Brother Industries, Kokuyo, and Minolta) could move Apple into Japan's lucrative corporate market. Some experts predict that Apple will eventually control about 13 percent of all PC sales in Japan.

In addition to the large customer base in Japan, Apple is also developing relationships with Japanese manufacturers. Working with these firms, Apple plans to link its software with a new generation of consumer electronics products. To execute this strategy, Sculley has Sony Corp. building Apple's smallest laptop, the PowerBook 100, Sharp Electronics making Apple's new electronic organizer, and Toshiba manufacturing a new Mac that combines video, text, and sound. By moving toward new markets, Apple hopes to pull away from U.S. PC manufacturers fighting for modest profits and small growth potential. Apple also plans to develop a number of digital technology gadgets for what could be a $3 trillion market in the year 2000. As the borders between telecommunications, office equipment, computers, consumer electronics, and media and publishing dissolve, the demand for personal electronic devices is expected to grow substantially. Software will be a key to making these digital products useful and easy to use, and software is Apple's forte.

Selling $2,000 machines has brought Apple success over the years, and now marketing products that sell for $250 or less is quite a change. Sculley believes that the core business in ten years still will be the Macintosh, but Richard Shaffer, editor of *Computer Letter,* thinks the personal electronic devices could help Apple double its revenues. The problem, he says, will not be manufacturing, because Apple can farm out that part and indeed plans to do so, nor will it be software, Apple's strength. The major problem will be marketing—developing and delivering quality Macintosh computers for under $1,000. Apple's objective is to strengthen its position in the consumer market with a lower-priced PC that will come with the software already loaded. Then the new digital devices should be ready for the marketplace. Products being developed include an electronic Rolodex, an electronic scratchpad with a built-in cellular phone that can record handwriting and transmit to any fax machine, and a multimedia reader the size of a compact tape recorder and weighing only a few pounds.

The strategy is risky. By taking on so many new ventures, Apple could find itself overloaded. And by making its distinctive software widely available, the firm could lose some of its appeal. Finally, Apple may have to relinquish some control to those firms manufacturing its new electronic devices. But Sculley thinks Apple would face even greater risks by avoiding change. If the strategy works, Apple could gain a large share of the growing personal electronic devices market by making machines that are easy and fun to use.

Questions for Discussion

1. What is Apple's mission? How has this mission served Apple over the years?

2. What is Apple's organizational strategy for growth?

3. What is Apple's marketing strategy, and how is it consistent with the organizational strategy?

4. Why is growth so important to Apple? What risk does the firm face with its plan for the future?

Based on information from Neil Gross and Kathy Rebello, "Apple? Japan Can't Say No," *Business Week,* June 29, 1992, pp. 32–33; Andrew Kupfer, "Apple's Plan to Survive and Grow," *Fortune,* May 4, 1992, pp. 68–72; and G. Pascal Zachary and Stephen Kreider Yoder, "Apple Moves Its Microsoft Battle to the Marketplace," *Wall Street Journal,* April 16, 1992, p. B4.

2.2   NISSAN CHANGES ITS STRATEGY

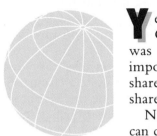

Yes, Japanese automakers can make mistakes, and Nissan is living proof. Only fifteen years ago it looked as though Nissan, with its sporty 240Z, was headed for greatness. In 1975, the firm passed Volkswagen as the top importer to the United States. But from 1980 to 1991, Nissan's U.S. market share fell from 5.5 to 4.7 percent; during this time, Japan's overall market share grew from 17.7 to 26.5 percent.

Nissan's troubles come as a shock to those who think Japanese automakers can do no wrong. Much like U.S. automakers, Nissan failed to listen to its customers, thus missing changes in their needs and losing sight of important market segments like family sedans and minivans. Although its quality remains on the same level as that of major competitors, Nissan's productivity lags and its costs are higher than those of other Japanese automakers. Nissan's location in Tokyo increases overhead and puts the firm at a 10 percent cost disadvantage relative to Toyota. Higher labor costs (8 percent of Nissan's operating costs compared with 5 percent of Toyota's) add to the problem. And many observers think that Nissan's main manufacturing plants are too old to compete with newer and more efficient plants built by competitors.

Nissan broke into the U.S. market in 1958 when it began exporting the Bluebird. But it wasn't until 1968 and 1969, with the Datsun 510 and the Datsun 240Z, that the firm made a big impact in the U.S. market. Then the 1973 oil crisis put Nissan in the right place at the right time as panicked Americans abandoned their gas-guzzling vehicles. In 1983, the name Datsun was changed to Nissan to match the name of the parent company. By trading on the image of its Z cars, the firm tried to move upscale. Advertising themes turned over rapidly: "We are driven"; "The name is Nissan"; "Built for the human race." But none of these messages conveyed a distinctive image. Sales peaked out in 1985 at 831,000; by 1992, sales had dropped to 583,000.

Managers at Nissan know it will take a sound marketing strategy to get the firm back to where it once was. Perhaps their biggest challenge is to reestablish their mission and focus. What was once their distinctive competency, building quality economy cars, was lost when the car maker rolled out a steady stream of new models in the late 1980s. According to Earl

Hesterburg, head of the U.S. Nissan division: "We haven't been successful in the market where our competitors make their bread and butter. We have to drive traffic into dealers at the middle of the market for Altima and then let them go up to the Maxima if they choose, or down to the Sentra." The Altima, introduced in 1992, is a mid-sized family sedan built to compete with Toyota's Camry and Honda's Accord.

It won't be easy for Nissan. John Schnapp of Boston's Mercer Management Consulting says of the challenge of introducing the Altima: "It's like trying to break into the lineup against Babe Ruth and Lou Gehrig. You've got to come up with something sensational."

Questions for Discussion

1. What factors contributed to Nissan's loss of market share?

2. Does Nissan have a distinctive competency?

3. What do you think is the greatest challenge Nissan will face as the firm changes its marketing strategy?

Based on information from Karen Lowry Miller, Larry Armstrong, and James B. Treece, "Will Nissan Get It Right This Time?" *Business Week,* April 20, 1992, pp. 82–87; Alex Taylor, "Driving for the Market's Heart," *Fortune,* June 15, 1992, pp. 120–121; and Clay Chandler, "Weary Nissan Now Seeks to Cooperate, Rather Than Compete, with Toyota," *Wall Street Journal,* May 19, 1992, p. A8.

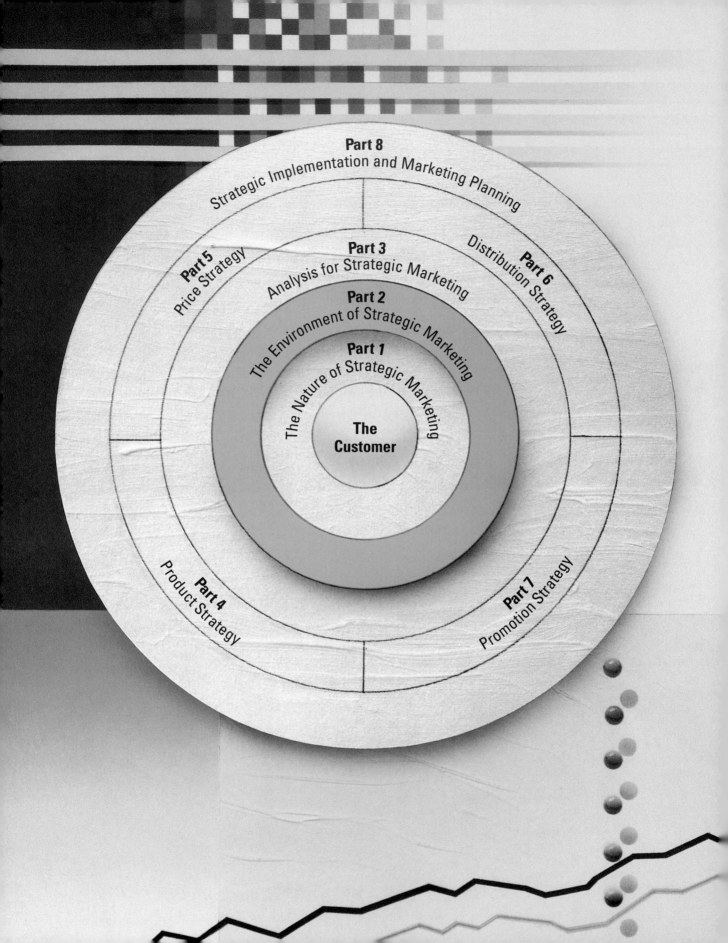

The Environment of Strategic Marketing

The Marketing Environment

OBJECTIVES

- To describe how forces in the marketing environment affect an organization's marketing activities.

- To compare the various types of competition and understand how an organization assesses competitors.

- To identify the laws and regulatory agencies that influence marketing activities.

- To explain how politics affects a firm's marketing activities.

- To discuss how the changing characteristics and values of society affect marketing activities.

- To determine how economic conditions influence competition and consumer purchasing patterns.

- To explain how technology is changing the way we do business.

- To discuss the importance of monitoring the marketing environment.

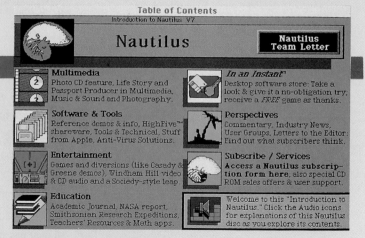

Thanks to technology, music buffs now are enjoying dramatically different and better sound systems, especially compact disk (CD) players and rack systems. Technology is also changing the music industry itself, with computers telling who the top-selling artists are and consumers shopping in the comfort of their homes.

For years, the record industry relied on store clerks and managers to determine what was selling. Not anymore. Now, in an industry long accustomed to hype, a new computer system provides a source of hard data. The record charts published by *Billboard* magazine are measured by an information-gathering system developed by Soundscan, of Westchester County, New York. Soundscan pays record stores for exclusive access to their sales information and then sells its information services to *Billboard* and to record companies. Soundscan measures more than 60 percent of all record, tape, CD, and music video sales and returns in the United States on a daily basis, for every musical genre. Record companies like the David Geffen Co. use the Soundscan data to boost airplay for their records that are reported to be selling well in record stores.

Compact disc technology now allows buyers to skip record stores altogether. Music lovers who subscribe to *Nautilus,* an electronic monthly magazine issued on compact disk, can listen to sixty-second samples of records from Windham Hill, a small company featuring New Age music. If they like what they hear, they can order the entire CD simply by using a modem command. The CD is conveniently delivered by mail to their door.

With a new software system from Metatec Corp., *Nautilus* subscribers won't even have to wait for their CDs to arrive in the mail. Subscribers will receive disks with a whole album of Windham Hill music. They will be able to listen to a sample and, if they like it, "buy" the full disk immediately with a mere modem command. The command triggers a response from a host computer that unlocks the rest of the music, and the customer's credit card is charged automatically. An instant purchase, all without leaving the room. "The information is already on the disk," explains Mary Vaughn, Metatec's vice president of marketing, "but you cannot get at it until you pay for it."

Small record companies especially have welcomed the new direct-to-consumer methods that technology has brought. Dozens of small independent labels have been bought out by giant record companies in the last several years; one result is less shelf space available to the remaining independents. Meanwhile, record store chains have been getting bigger and fewer. The big retailers are less likely to carry products that do not have high turnover, a category often applicable to the offerings of small music companies.

Digital radio technology also may provide ways for music buyers to bypass stores and for companies to aim at precise groups of customers. Two major digital radio suppliers in the United States each transmit up to thirty channels of finely targeted digital music programming over existing television cable networks. They are having some success with pay-per-listen events. The introduction of digital tape and recordable CDs makes it possible for listeners to lift recorded music directly off cable, and makes record companies anxious. Says Jay Berman, president of the Recording Industry Association of America, "You may have a celestial jukebox, putting all recorded music in digital format on a satellite, permitting people to listen to what they want when they want, thereby avoiding having to go to a store to buy the product." The notion is not all that far-fetched; GTE Spacenet Corp. already has nine satellites orbiting the earth, all capable of delivering digital information to homes. Syracuse University's Belfer Audio Laboratory & Archive has developed a digitized archive that will contain hundreds of thousands of recordings that can be loaded by computer onto blank digital tape or recordable CDs. The archive is linked to the U.S. Copyright Office so that performers will automatically get any royalties due them.

Not to be left behind by the technology that is changing music marketing, some record stores, are forging new delivery systems. Tower Records/Video, one of the country's bigger chains with seventy-seven U.S. stores, has aligned with Digital Cable Radio. Listeners can call an 800 number, obtain song information, and be put through to a Tower order line to order tapes and CDs at a discount. Musicland, the nation's largest music retailer with 8 percent of the market, joined with the Prodigy computer network owned by Sears and IBM. Prodigy users can order from the Musicland catalogue of over twenty thousand music titles and eight thousand video titles. Although the Musicland-Prodigy experiment hasn't had a big response, Musicland plans to continue it.[1] ●

As the opening feature illustrates, marketing does not take place in a vacuum. Successful companies are sensitive to the market forces that create change. They look beyond what customers need and want today and the current limits technology places on satisfying them. When developing marketing strategies, organizations must take into consideration the environment in which they operate.

When a business is prospering and growing, customers are satisfied, and no threat of competition is apparent, owners and managers often find it difficult to realize that changes in the marketing environment can become a threat. But history has shown that such threats are real and dangerous. From Santa Fe Railroad in the mid-1900s, which failed to see the competitive threat

---

[1] Based on information from Christopher Palmeri, "Media Merchant to the Baby Boomers," *Forbes,* March 15, 1993, pp. 66–70; Peter Newcomb, "Endangered Species?" *Forbes,* July 20, 1992, pp. 52–54, 58; and Robert G. Woletz, "Scan System Changes Record-Chart Rules," Lexington, Ky. *Herald-Leader,* January 26, 1992, p. B8.

FIGURE 3.1
The Marketing
Environment

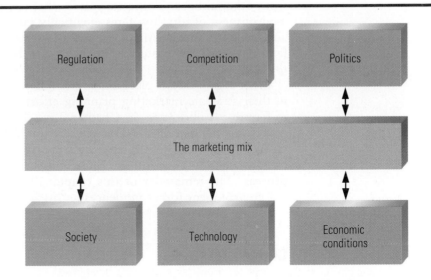

posed by airlines, to Pan Am in the late 1900s, which failed to recognize the impact of deregulation on the airline industry, firms continue to fail largely because they do not respond to changes in the marketing environment.

Waste Management illustrates how one company is dealing with changes in the marketing environment. About half of the firm's revenues come from landfills and the handling of solid wastes. Society, however, has developed a negative view of landfills, and the increase in recycling has cut down the amount of trash dumped into landfills. Waste Management has already adapted to these changes by going to the source of waste and providing in-house waste management services, such as the disposal of hazardous waste, recycling, environmental engineering, and water and air treatment.[2] Waste Management is one of many companies that are changing their marketing strategies in response to changes in the marketing environment. Thousands of other firms face similar challenges from forces in the marketing environment, and risk failure unless they adapt to these forces.

DEFINING THE MARKETING ENVIRONMENT

■ **marketing environment** all the forces outside an organization that directly or indirectly influence its marketing activities; includes competition, regulation, politics, society, economic conditions, and technology

The **marketing environment** includes all the forces outside an organization that directly or indirectly influence its marketing activities. These forces include competition, regulation, politics, society, economic conditions, and technology (see Figure 3.1). Any one of these forces can dramatically change the course of an organization. For example, deregulation had a profound effect on the airline industry, particularly in terms of prices. The industry became price competitive as carriers reduced fares to lure passengers away

---

[2]"Change with the Market or Die," *Fortune,* January 13, 1992, pp. 62–63.

from other airlines. Those companies that could not maintain profits in this environment of ultralow fares eventually failed or were purchased by other airlines, as in the USAir purchase of Piedmont. We already mentioned the failure of Pan Am; Eastern, Allegheny, and Midway airlines can be added to the list.

Most organizations place a major emphasis on the marketing environment in their strategic marketing planning efforts, as the Chrysler advertisement in Figure 3.2 illustrates. In Chapter 2 we discussed the marketing plan; the section on the current marketing situation deals specifically with trends and changes in the marketing environment. Thus an analysis of the marketing environment is a critical component of the strategic marketing planning process. The remainder of this chapter discusses how each of the marketing environment forces influences an organization's marketing activities.

COMPETITION

■ **competition** firms that market similar or substitutable products in the same geographic area; in general, the rivalry among businesses for consumer dollars

To a particular organization, competition usually means others that market similar or substitutable products in the same geographic area. In general, the term **competition** refers to the rivalry among businesses for consumer dollars. For example, the manager of a university bookstore views all bookstores near the university as competition but probably does not think of university bookstores in other geographic areas as competition. In general, all the bookstores near the university, as well as other stores that sell clothes and various products with the university logo, compete for students' dollars. Some organizations take a very broad view of competition because they see a wide

FIGURE 3.2
The Marketing Environment
Analysis of the marketing environment is a critical part of strategic marketing planning. Notice how this Chrysler advertisement stresses most of the environmental forces that influence marketing.

Source: Chrysler Corporation.

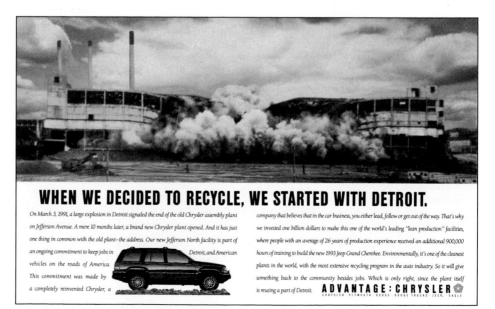

WHEN WE DECIDED TO RECYCLE, WE STARTED WITH DETROIT.

On March 3, 1991, a large explosion in Detroit signaled the end of the old Chrysler assembly plant on Jefferson Avenue. A mere 10 months later, a brand new Chrysler plant opened. And it has just one thing in common with the old plant—the address. Our new Jefferson North facility is part of an ongoing commitment to keep jobs in Detroit, and American vehicles on the roads of America. This commitment was made by a completely reinvented Chrysler, a company that believes that in the car business, you either lead, follow or get out of the way. That's why we invested one billion dollars to make this one of the world's leading "lean production" facilities, where people with an average of 26 years of production experience received an additional 900,000 hours of training to build the new 1993 Jeep Grand Cherokee. Environmentally, it's one of the cleanest plants in the world, with the most extensive recycling program in the auto industry. So it will give something back to the community besides jobs. Which is only right, since the plant itself is reusing a part of Detroit. **ADVANTAGE : CHRYSLER**

CHRYSLER · PLYMOUTH · DODGE · DODGE TRUCKS · JEEP · EAGLE

TABLE 3.1
Characteristics of Competitive Market Structures

Type of Structure	Number of Competitors	Product	Example
Monopoly	One	Almost no substitutes	Commonwealth Edison Co.
Oligopoly	Few	Homogeneous or differentiated (real or perceived differences in) products	General Motors Corp.
Monopolistic competition	Many	Product differentiation with many substitutes	Apple Computer, Inc.
Perfect competition	Unlimited	Homogeneous products	Farmers' market

variety of products as substitutable. For instance, a company that owns movie theaters may consider restaurants, night clubs, sporting events, and videotape rentals as competition for consumers' entertainment dollars.

Failing to know its competitors can be disastrous for an organization. No one knows this better than U.S. automakers, who were late acknowledging the mid-sized Honda Accord as the best-selling car in America. Since mid-sized cars make up 34 percent of the U.S. market and return a high profit, a loss in market share is very damaging. By 1992, Ford rebounded with the mid-sized Taurus, thereby moving back into the number one spot, outselling the Accord by 16,274 vehicles.[3] But as the other U.S. automakers are producing mid-sized cars of their own, Honda is fighting back and Toyota is pushing its restyled Camry. If Ford has learned its lesson, it is closely watching the actions of its competitors. In developing and implementing a strategic marketing program, an organization must consider the types of competition in its markets and assess the actions of its competitors.

Types of Competition

The number of organizations that sell a product may affect the strength of competition. When there are many businesses selling a particular product, for example, price considerations and product differences are more important than when only one business is selling that product. The number of firms selling a similar product determines the structure of the market. Table 3.1 compares some characteristics of the four general types of competitive market structures.

[3]Jacqueline Mitchell and Neil Templin, "Ford's Taurus Passes Honda's Accord as Bestselling Car in Lackluster Year," *Wall Street Journal,* January 7, 1993, p. B1.

monopoly a market structure in which only one firm is marketing a product for which there are no close substitutes

oligopoly a market structure in which few firms are marketing a product and they control much of the supply of the product

monopolistic competition a market structure in which many firms are marketing a product, and each firm attempts to differentiate its product to convince consumers that its product is the one to buy

A **monopoly** exists when only one firm is marketing a product for which there are no close substitutes. The firm has complete control over the supply of the product. Although monopolies are generally discouraged, the U.S. government allows utility companies, such as Commonwealth Edison Co. and Cooke Cablevision, to have monopolies in providing electricity, cable television, and other utilities because the costs of operating such businesses are too high for most organizations to enter those markets. A monopoly can change into a competitive market when regulations are changed, however. For example, the government is considering whether to allow telephone companies to offer cable television services. If this occurs, consumers may see a competitive cable market. Without regulation, a firm with a monopoly can charge unreasonably high prices and offer inferior service if the product is in high demand and there is no substitute available. The former Soviet Union finds itself in that exact situation as it moves toward a market economy. Under communist rule, product quality and service were poor because government-run businesses in effect had monopolies.

An **oligopoly** exists when few firms are marketing a product and they control much of the supply of the product. Products in oligopolistic competition may be *homogeneous* (similar or uniform in nature), such as coal or steel, or *differentiated* (having real or perceived differences), such as cigarettes or airline services. The market for batteries is an example of an oligopoly; Duracell has a 41.5 percent market share and Eveready's Energizer has a 35.9 percent share.[4] In an oligopoly, each seller must consider the reactions of other sellers to changes in marketing activities. During the airlines' price wars of the 1980s, for example, whenever Continental Airlines, Inc. reduced its fares, other air carriers had to follow suit to remain competitive. However, barriers may prevent a business from entering an oligopolistic market and competing with other organizations. For instance, few companies have the financial and engineering resources necessary to enter the automobile or airplane manufacturing industries. Thus organizations like Toyota and The Boeing Co. have relatively few competitors in their respective markets.

Monopolistic competition exists when many firms are marketing the same or similar products; each firm attempts to differentiate its product to convince consumers that its product is the one to buy. For example, American Telephone & Telegraph Co. (AT&T) has established a differential advantage for its new Universal credit card by offering lower interest rates on its VISA and MasterCard credit cards.[5] Although many other firms issue credit cards, AT&T has carved out its share of the market by using a differential marketing strategy. At times it is difficult to differentiate a product in a competitive market. Dr Pepper/Seven-Up Cos. attempted to differentiate 7UP by introducing 7UP Gold and Cherry 7UP, but 7UP's share of the market for lemon-lime sodas fell from 46 percent in 1985 to 37 percent in 1990. 7UP Gold had an unmemorable taste and disappeared quickly. Any

[4]Julie Liesse, "Duracell Ups Lead over Energizer," *Marketing News,* April 16, 1990, p. 4.
[5]Peter Pae, "Success of AT&T's Universal Card Puts Pressure on Big Banks to Reduce Rates," *Wall Street Journal,* February 4, 1992, pp. B1, B8.

■ **perfect competition**
an ideal market with a large number of sellers, no one of which can significantly influence the price or supply of the products

gains from Cherry 7UP were lost as Coca-Cola Co. heavily promoted its Sprite and increased its market share from 36 to 42 percent.[6]

Perfect competition, if it existed, would be a market with a large number of sellers, no one of which could significantly influence the price or supply of the products. Products would be homogeneous, and potential sellers of the products would have full knowledge of the market and easy entry into it. There is no market with perfect competition because social and economic factors make it impossible for all buyers and sellers to have complete information about the products. The closest example of perfect competition is the market for agricultural products such as corn, cotton, and soybeans.

Assessing Competition

Organizations must carefully and continually assess their competition and develop strategies that differentiate themselves from their competitors. A firm can differentiate itself by adjusting the elements of its marketing mix or by providing a product that is superior in some way to those of competitors.[7] For example, a consumer may purchase a Maytag washing machine because it has a reputation for dependability. On the other hand, a Sears washer may be priced lower and some buyers may consider this factor more important than dependability. In Japan, where consumers traditionally have not been as calorie conscious as Americans, PepsiCo's Japanese subsidiary introduced a Diet Pepsi advertised to have one-twelfth the calories of Coke's Light brand. PepsiCo believes that young women in Japan are becoming more concerned with calories and hopes to take advantage of this trend. Coke immediately responded by introducing another diet drink, Caffeine-Free Diet Coke.[8]

Businesses also need to monitor the changes their competitors are making. For example, a marketing manager should determine if, and why, major competitors are changing prices, product designs, warranties and service policies, packaging, distribution methods, or promotional factors such as sales force size and advertising. Knowledge of such changes helps the marketing manager decide what adjustments to make to current marketing strategies and how to plan new ones. Thomson Consumer Electronics Inc.'s RCA and GE television businesses, after losing market share to Sony and other companies, are offering more competitive prices and stressing styling features such as round edges and black and gray colors.[9] Marketers can obtain information about changes their competitors are making from direct observation, salespeople, customers, trade journals, marketing research, and distributors.

[6]Kevin Kelly and Walecia Konrad, "Seven-Up: Where Have All the Bubbles Gone?" *Business Week,* January 29, 1990, p. 95.
[7]George S. Day, "Deciding How to Compete," *Planning Review,* September–October 1989, pp. 18–23.
[8]Yumiko Ono, "Cola Makers Lighten Up in Market-Share Fight," *Wall Street Journal,* April 21, 1992, p. B1.
[9]Lois Therrien and Jonathan B. Levine, "Thomson Needs a Hit, and It's Up to Nipper to Go Fetch," *Business Week,* July 6, 1992, p. 80.

Act	Purposes
Sherman Act (1890)	Prohibits contracts, combinations, or conspiracies to restrain trade; establishes as a misdemeanor monopolizing or attempting to monopolize
Clayton Act (1914)	Prohibits specific practices such as price discrimination, exclusive dealer arrangements, and stock acquisitions which may substantially lessen competition or tend to create a monopoly
Federal Trade Commission Act (1914)	Created the Federal Trade Commission; gives the FTC investigatory powers to be used in preventing unfair methods of competition
Robinson–Patman Act (1936)	Prohibits price discrimination that lessens competition among wholesalers or retailers; prohibits producers from giving disproportionate services or facilities to large buyers
Wheeler–Lea Act (1938)	Prohibits unfair and deceptive acts and practices regardless of whether competition is injured; places advertising of foods and drugs under the jurisdiction of the FTC
Lanham Act (1946)	Prohibits false description or representation of goods and services
Celler–Kefauver Act (1950)	Prohibits any corporation engaged in commerce from acquiring the whole or any part of the stock or other share of the capital or assets of another corporation when the effect substantially lessens competition or tends to create a monopoly
Consumer Goods Pricing Act (1975)	Prohibits the use of price maintenance agreements among manufacturers and resellers in interstate commerce
Trademark Counterfeiting Act (1980)	Provides civil and criminal penalties against those who deal in counterfeit consumer goods or any counterfeit goods that can threaten health or safety

TABLE 3.2
Federal Laws That
Preserve Competition

Many firms also gain valuable information about competitors by hiring employees who formerly worked in key positions for competitors. Many industries follow this practice of acquiring *competitive intelligence,* as it is sometimes called. Although the practice has raised some ethical questions, its use has been on the increase for some time and is likely to continue. One group that aims to make the area of competitive intelligence more formalized and ethical is the Society of Competitive Intelligence Professionals (SCIP) in Washington, D.C. SCIP emphasizes that competitive intelligence is more than only hiring workers away from competitors. It also includes gathering competitive information from overlooked sources such as local newspapers, tax assessors, libraries, labor unions, and security analysts.[10]

[10]Howard Schlossberg, "Competitive Intelligence Pros Seek Formal Role in Marketing," *Marketing News,* March 5, 1990, pp. 2, 28.

REGULATION

regulation laws and regulatory agencies that influence the conduct of business

Regulation consists of laws and regulatory agencies that influence the conduct of business. Regulatory forces in the marketing environment exert a significant influence on marketing activities because violations of laws and regulations may result in penalties. (Chapter 5 discusses how laws and regulatory agencies influence the conduct of global marketing activities.)

Laws

In the United States, Congress has enacted a number of laws that influence marketing decisions about pricing, advertising, personal selling, distribution, product development, product warranty and repair policies, and other marketing activities. These laws can be broken down into two categories: (1) laws designed to preserve competition and (2) laws designed to protect consumers.

Laws Designed to Preserve Competition   Several major laws have been enacted to prohibit unfair trade practices and deceptive actions. Table 3.2 presents a summary of these laws. Beginning with the Sherman Act in 1890, these laws have gradually focused more directly on specific marketing practices. Because the Sherman Act was written in vague terms, the courts have interpreted its provisions in ways that have sometimes been harmful to competition. Subsequent legislation—including the Clayton Act, the Federal Trade Commission Act, the Robinson-Patman Act, and the Wheeler-Lea Act—has been directed more toward specific practices.

Laws have a profound impact on marketing activities. For instance, the Lanham Act has been used recently to regulate advertisements that compare alternative brands. In one case, American Home Products, which manufactures Advil, claimed that Johnson & Johnson was engaging in false and misleading advertising with its claim about Tylenol that "you can't buy a more potent pain reliever without a prescription." A New York federal judge ruled that a number of Tylenol advertisements were false and misleading and that certain Advil advertisements also were misleading. The judge issued an injunction preventing the use of several specific claims by both firms.[11] Thus businesses must constantly evaluate their marketing activities to ensure that they do not violate laws designed to preserve competition.

Laws Designed to Protect Consumers   Although many states passed laws in the mid-1800s to prohibit the adulteration of food and drugs, the first federal consumer protection laws were not passed until the early 1900s. Consumer protection laws mushroomed in the mid-1960s and early 1970s in response to consumer concerns about environmental protection and product safety. Table 3.3 summarizes a number of federal laws designed to ensure consumer safety. For example, the Pure Food and Drug Act, the Flammable

[11] Michael B. Bixby and Douglas J. Lincoln, "Legal Issues Surrounding the Use of Comparative Advertising: What the Non-Prescription Drug Industry Has Taught Us," *Journal of Public Policy & Marketing*, 1989, pp. 143–160.

Act	Purposes
Pure Food and Drug Act (1906)	Regulates labeling of food and drugs and prohibits manufacture or marketing of adulterated food or drugs; amended in 1938 by Food, Drug and Cosmetics Act
Meat Inspection Act (1906)	Regulates meat-packing houses and provides for federal inspection of meats
Textile Labeling Laws: Wool Products Labeling Act (1939) Fur Products Labeling Act (1951) Flammable Fabrics Act (1953) Textile Fiber Products Identification Act (1958)	Require the manufacturer to indicate what the product is made of
Automobile Information Disclosure Act (1958)	Requires manufacturers to post suggested retail prices on new passenger vehicles
Kefauver-Harris Drug Amendments (1962)	Requires that new drugs be labeled with their generic names, that new drugs be pretested, and that new drugs get approval of the Food and Drug Administration before being marketed
National Traffic and Motor Vehicle Safety Act (1966)	Provides for safety standards for tires and automobiles
Fair Packaging and Labeling Act (1966)	The "truth in packaging" law that regulates packaging and labeling
Cigarette Labeling and Advertising Acts (1966, 1969)	Require manufacturers to label cigarettes as being hazardous to health and prohibits television advertising of cigarettes
Consumer Credit Protection Act (1968)	The "truth in lending" law that requires full disclosure of interest rates and other financing charges on loans and credit purchases
Fair Credit Reporting Act (1970)	Regulates the reporting and use of credit information
Consumer Product Safety Act (1972)	Establishes the Consumer Product Safety Commission with broad powers to regulate the marketing of products ruled unsafe by the commission
Consumer Product Warranty Act (1975)	Increases consumers' rights and sellers' responsibilities under product warranties
FTC Improvement Act (1980)	Limits the power of the Federal Trade Commission to set and enforce industry trade regulations; in effect, reverses the trend toward more FTC protection of consumers

TABLE 3.3
Federal Laws that Protect Consumers

Fabrics Act, and the Consumer Product Safety Act were enacted to protect people from actual and potential physical injuries.

Most firms realize that product safety violations not only break laws but also lead to customer dissatisfaction. Consumers perceive quality violations that reduce product safety as serious problems. In fact, research has shown that consumers believe violations in most product classes are so serious that they would consider not buying the brand again.[12] And it generally costs a firm much more to find new customers than to keep existing ones satisfied. In the case of the Audi 5000, sales were decimated by consumer perceptions based on a *60 Minutes* report that the car was prone to sudden, uncontrollable acceleration. By the time scientific evidence proved that the cause of the acceleration was accidentally placing a foot on the wrong pedal, sales had fallen roughly fifty thousand units a year.[13]

To ensure that consumers are better informed, Congress has enacted several laws requiring the disclosure of certain information. These laws deal with information about specific products such as prescription drugs, textiles, furs, cigarettes, and automobiles and focus on specific marketing activities, including product development and testing, packaging, labeling, advertising, and consumer financing. Marion Merrell Dow Inc., manufacturer of Seldane, the world's best-selling prescription antihistamine, was ordered to strengthen the warning on the product labels. Seldane has been linked to life-threatening cardiac problems when mixed with certain drugs or used improperly.[14] Refer to Table 3.3 for a description of the various laws that regulate such practices. Marketing Close-Up examines some prominent tobacco product liability cases and how they may affect marketing in the tobacco industry.

One area of consumer protection that has received a great deal of attention in recent years is package tampering. No package is tamper-proof; packages can be made tamper-resistant, but a determined criminal can still get into a package to cause harm. Businesses must design packages that comply with regulations developed by the Food and Drug Administration (FDA). Some of these regulations were passed in response to several deaths in Chicago in 1982 that were traced to cyanide-laced Tylenol capsules. FDA regulations state that firms should develop packages that minimize the possibility of unnoticed tampering. Firms should also educate consumers about how to identify packages that have been tampered with.[15]

Regulatory Agencies

The effectiveness of laws is greatly influenced by the extent to which they are enforced. Both government and nongovernment agencies have been created to enforce specific laws.

---

[12] Jacques C. Bourgeois and Michael Laroche, "The Measurement of the Seriousness of Product Violations," *Journal of Public Policy & Marketing*, 1987, pp. 1–15.

[13] Peter Huber, "Junk Science in the Courtroom," *Forbes*, July 8, 1991, pp. 68–72.

[14] John Cloud and Kathleen Deveny, "FDA Orders Strong Warning on Seldane Use," *Wall Street Journal*, July 8, 1992, pp. B1, B5.

[15] Fred W. Morgan, "Tampered Goods: Legal Developments and Marketing Guidelines," *Journal of Marketing*, April 1988, pp. 86–96.

MARKETING CLOSE-UP

Tobacco Liability Cases Heating Up

The tobacco industry says it has never paid a dime on a suit from a smoker claiming health damage from cigarettes. In fact, few tobacco product liability cases have ever gone to trial, and only a handful have reached juries since the 1960s. But a case that reached the U.S. Supreme Court may have far-reaching effects on tobacco product liability.

The case began when Rose Cipollone, a smoker for forty years, sued Liggett, Philip Morris, and Lorillard after having a cancerous lung removed. After her death in 1984, her family pursued the lawsuit, blaming the three companies for her death. The suit claimed that the cigarette companies failed to properly warn of health risks, that they made false statements, and that they intentionally committed fraud and conspired to hide the truth about smoking. In 1988, a federal jury in New Jersey found that Mrs. Cipollone was 80 percent responsible for her illness, but ordered Liggett to pay her husband $400,000, on the basis of many years of smoking (between 1942 and 1965) before warning labels were required on cigarette packages. The other two firms were absolved. In 1990, an appeals court overturned the verdict and ordered a new trial. Thomas Cipollone, Rose's son, appealed to the U.S. Supreme Court, and in an unusual move, the tobacco companies agreed that the high court should hear the case, since so many similar lawsuits were pending.

In June of 1992, the Supreme Court ruled that smokers may not file lawsuits charging tobacco companies with failing to provide adequate warnings. However, they may file lawsuits alleging that cigarette makers hid or distorted the health dangers of tobacco. The court gave the Cipollone family the option of retrying their suit.

Both tobacco companies and antismoking groups claimed the Supreme Court ruling as a victory. Plaintiffs gained a way to persuade juries that cigarette makers committed fraud or misrepresentation, and a chance to obtain punitive damages. Says Matt Myers, counsel to the Coalition on Smoking OR Health, "The decision focuses attention on what truly is the potential Achilles' heel of the tobacco industry: whether their own research showed that smoking causes disease and whether they consciously sought to conceal that fact."

But that's why the tobacco companies hailed the decision. They say they are off the hook unless someone can prove they lied to the public, and they insist they did not. Industry representatives say that smokers will have to prove that misconduct by companies led them to start or continue to smoke. "There was so much information in the public realm about the dangers of smoking that it will be very difficult to find plaintiffs who are able to persuade a jury that they either began to smoke or continued to smoke because of misleading statements from the tobacco industry," says Victor Schwartz, a product liability expert who has consulted for tobacco companies.

Antismoking forces already claim that they have information that proves cigarette corporations have been deliberately covering up information for decades. In another suit, a federal judge in New York City ruled in early 1992 that tobacco companies must hand over 1,500 pages of evidence concerning the Council for Tobacco Research, an industry trade group formed in 1954 to study the health risks of smoking. The plaintiff says that cigarette makers and the council withheld important research that showed the dangers of smoking. Worse, the suit says the industry's claim that it was sponsoring independent research was a fraud, and the judge agreed. Federal prosecutors who are conducting a criminal probe of tobacco companies and the research council are watching the case. *(Continued on next page)*

Tobacco companies may really feel the heat as the secondhand smoke controversy intensifies. One class-action suit filed by seven flight attendants in Miami seeks $5 billion against six major tobacco companies. The suit, on behalf of sixty thousand flight attendants, says that the plaintiffs suffer from lung cancer and other diseases as a result of their exposure to secondhand cigarette smoke before Congress banned smoking on flights in 1989. In June 1992, the U.S. Environmental Protection Agency issued a report reinforcing findings that environmental smoke is a known human carcinogen and is particularly dangerous to children. Antismoking lawyers predict that secondhand-smoke liability cases will proliferate if lawyers find any evidence that cigarette makers knew about and concealed the dangers. On November 5, 1992, lawyers for the estate of Rose Cipollone dropped the most prominent damage case filed against a tobacco company. With the exception of the $400,000 awarded in the case, no jury has assessed damages against a tobacco company. But evidence collected in the Cipollone case is expected to lead to even more lawsuits. And the Supreme Court's decision to permit damage suits alleging the industry hid the risks of smoking may signal more problems for the tobacco industry.

Sources: Michael Galen, "When the Smoke Clears, Cigarette Makers May Get Burned," *Business Week*, November 23, 1992, p. 89; Walecia Konrad and Catherine Yang, "This Decision May Be Hazardous to Tobacco's Health," *Business Week*, July 6, 1992, p. 33; Joanne Lipman, "Marketers Say Ruling Spares Tobacco Ads," *Wall Street Journal*, June 26, 1992, p. B3; Milo Geyelin, "Liability Suits, While Rising, May Not Prevail," *Wall Street Journal*, June 26, 1992, p. B1; Paul Barrett, "Surprise Court Ruling Could Have Big Impact Far Beyond Cigarettes," *Wall Street Journal*, June 25, 1992, pp. A1, A10; and Maxine S. Lans, "Ruling on Cigarette Ads: What Does It Really Mean?" *Marketing News*, August 17, 1992, p. 15.

Federal Regulatory Agencies Federal regulatory agencies oversee many marketing activities, including product development, pricing, packaging, advertising, personal selling, distribution, and storage. Regulatory agencies usually have the power to enforce specific laws and some discretion in establishing operating rules and drawing up regulations to guide certain types of industry practices. As a result of this discretion and overlapping areas of responsibility, there is frequently confusion, and even conflict, as to which agencies have jurisdiction over specific activities. Two different agencies, the Federal Trade Commission and the Food and Drug Administration, have become involved in allegations with weight loss chains. The Federal Trade Commission is concerned with advertising claims about weight loss, and the Food and Drug Administration wants to ban some of the drugs used to treat obesity.[16]

Table 3.4 outlines the major areas of responsibility of several federal regulatory agencies. Of these agencies, the Federal Trade Commission has the greatest influence on marketing activities. The **Federal Trade Commission (FTC)** has many administrative duties, but its basic function is "to prevent the free enterprise system from being stifled by monopoly or anticompetitive practices and to provide the direct protection of consumers from unfair or

■ **Federal Trade Commission (FTC)** a federal regulatory agency whose basic function is "to prevent the free enterprise system from being stifled by monopoly or anticompetitive practices and to provide the direct protection of consumers from unfair or deceptive trade practices"

[16]Larry Armstrong and Maria Mallory, "The Diet Business Starts Sweating," *Business Week*, June 22, 1992, pp. 32–33.

Agency	Major Areas of Responsibility
Federal Trade Commission (FTC)	Enforces laws and guidelines regarding business practices; takes action to stop false and deceptive advertising and labeling
Food and Drug Administration (FDA)	Enforces laws and regulations to prevent distribution of adulterated or misbranded foods, drugs, medical devices, cosmetics, veterinary products, and particularly hazardous consumer products
Consumer Product Safety Commission	Ensures compliance with the Consumer Product Safety Act; protects the public from unreasonable risk of injury from any consumer product not covered by other regulatory agencies
Interstate Commerce Commission (ICC)	Regulates franchises, rates, and finances of interstate rail, bus, truck, and water carriers
Federal Communications Commission (FCC)	Regulates communication by wire, radio, and television in interstate and foreign commerce
Environmental Protection Agency (EPA)	Develops and enforces environmental protection standards and conducts research into the adverse effects of pollution
Federal Power Commission (FPC)	Regulates rates and sales of natural gas producers, thereby affecting the supply and price of gas available to consumers; also regulates wholesale rates for electricity and gas, pipeline construction, and U.S. imports and exports of natural gas and electricity

TABLE 3.4
Major Federal Regulatory Agencies

deceptive trade practices."[17] Fraud is one of the more common deceptive practices that the FTC regulates. In recent years the FTC has made a major effort to crack down on products, sold through catalogs or the mail, that do not perform as claimed.[18] Much of the effort is devoted to cutting off the marketing channels of fly-by-night companies. The FTC is composed of five commissioners who are appointed to seven-year terms by the president of the United States with the consent of the Senate.

Several industries have been deregulated by the federal government in the last few years, including the airline, telecommunications, railroad, trucking, and banking industries (see Table 3.5). The intent of deregulation is to foster more competitive industries, but this goal is not always achieved. Some

[17]"Your Federal Trade Commission" (Washington, D.C.: Federal Trade Commission, 1977), pp. 8–9.
[18]Stephan Barlas, "FTC Steps Up Battle Against Fraud," *Marketing News,* June 25, 1990, pp. 1, 13.

Act	Purpose
Natural Gas Policy Act (1978)	Requires pipelines to accept gas that they do not own
Airline Deregulation Act (1978)	Eliminates the regulation of airline rates and schedules
Motor Carrier Act (1980)	Allows trucks to travel more freely and change prices more quickly
Staggers Rail Act (1980)	Gives railroads more flexibility to raise and lower rates without government approval
Depository Institutions Deregulatory Committee Act (1981) Depository Institutions Act (1982)	Permit financial institutions to compete on a more even basis for deposit accounts (by paying higher interest rates) and to broaden investments beyond homes and small commercial mortgages
Drug Price Competition and Patent Term Restoration Act (1984)	Allows generic drugs to reach the market more quickly by giving patents for shorter periods of time

TABLE 3.5
Federal Laws Deregulating Various Industries

■ **Better Business Bureau** a local nongovernment regulatory agency (supported by local businesses) that settles problems between consumers and specific business firms and also acts to preserve good business practices in a community

critics point to the savings and loan crisis, the collapsing airline, bus, and trucking industries, and higher telephone and cable television rates as evidence of the failure of deregulation.[19]

State and Local Regulatory Agencies   All states and most communities have agencies that enforce laws and rules regarding marketing practices. These regulatory agencies try to avoid establishing and enforcing regulations that conflict with those of national agencies. State and local agencies typically enforce specific laws dealing with the production or sale of particular goods and services. A New Jersey law, for example, prohibits stores from selling milk below a specified price.[20] Industries that are commonly regulated by state agencies include financial services, utilities, and liquor.

Nongovernment Regulatory Programs   The **Better Business Bureau,** perhaps the best-known nongovernment regulatory group, is a local regulatory agency supported by local businesses. There are currently more than 140 such bureaus that help settle problems between consumers and specific business firms. The bureaus also act to preserve good business practices in a community, although they do not have strong enforcement tools to deal with businesses that engage in questionable practices. When a firm continues

[19]Paul Stephen Dempsey, "Has Deregulation Derailed American Industry?" *Business and Society Review,* Spring 1991, pp. 53–55.
[20]Carolyn Lochhead, "Soured on New Jersey's Milk Law," *Insight,* January 8, 1990, pp. 42–43.

POINT/COUNTERPOINT

Are Self-Regulatory Programs Effective?

For many years, federal, state, and local governments have regulated nearly every aspect of the business world. During the eight years of the Reagan administration, however, the government greatly decreased the extent to which it regulated the activities of business organizations. This trend is expected to continue into the 1990s. The logic behind the move toward self-regulation is that the government cannot afford to police each and every activity of businesses. Government regulation costs billions of dollars each year in paperwork, legal fees, employee salaries, and so on. These costs are passed on to business firms and consumers in the form of higher taxes and higher prices. Self-regulatory programs, therefore, have great appeal and can benefit business firms and consumers alike. But do they work?

Point Self-regulatory programs are an effective way to preserve good business practices. They usually are less expensive to establish and implement than government programs, and their guidelines generally are more realistic and operational. Because of these advantages, firms are motivated to comply with self-regulatory programs. Organizations usually realize that if self-regulation fails, government programs probably will be instituted. Most firms prefer self-regulation to government regulation.

In addition, organizations such as the Better Business Bureau and the National Advertising Review Board have developed their own self-regulatory programs. These programs allow industries to establish their own standards of business conduct and reduce the need to expand government bureaucracy. Such programs enable firms to build good will by demonstrating to society that the participating firms are concerned with business conduct and social welfare.

Counterpoint Self-regulatory programs have several drawbacks that hamper their effectiveness. When a trade association creates a set of industry guidelines, nonmember firms are not required to follow them. Many self-regulatory programs also lack the tools or authority to enforce such guidelines. Often guidelines set through self-regulation are less strict in the first place than are those established by government agencies.

Industry self-regulatory programs are similar to the fox guarding the henhouse. If firms are not regulated by the government, the temptation to ignore industry-established guidelines often is overwhelming. Without strictly enforced guidelines and stiff penalties for firms found in violation, industry self-regulation programs are of little value.

■ **National Advertising Review Board (NARB)** an agency created by the Council of Better Business Bureaus and three advertising trade organizations; screens ads for honesty and processes complaints about deceptive ads

to violate what the Better Business Bureau believes to be good business practices, it warns consumers through local newspapers that the firm is operating unfairly.

The Council of Better Business Bureaus and three advertising trade organizations have created a self-regulatory agency called the **National Advertising Review Board (NARB).** In addition to screening national advertisements for honesty, the NARB processes complaints about deceptive advertisements. The NARB has no official enforcement powers. If a firm refuses to comply with its decision, however, the NARB publicizes the questionable practice and files a complaint with the Federal Trade Commission.

In addition, individual businesses and industry trade associations may establish their own self-regulatory programs. Self-regulatory programs are generally less expensive to administer than government programs and their guidelines more realistic. However, since such programs have no mechanism or authority to enforce the guidelines, they may be less effective than government-administered regulatory programs. A recent study published in the *Annals of Internal Medicine* concluded that many pharmaceutical ads were misleading. Government regulators may use this study to call for new legislation regulating pharmaceutical advertising. Some industry sources have suggested that the advertising agencies and their clients could avoid costly government intervention by creating a self-regulating system which prevents abuses of pharmaceutical advertising before they occur.[21] Point/Counterpoint discusses the pros and cons of individual self-regulatory programs.

POLITICS

■ **politics** the policies and goals of the government and its elected officials

Politics, the policies and goals of the government and its elected officials, and regulation are closely related forces of the marketing environment. Businesses should try to maintain good relations with political officials for several reasons. When political officials have positive attitudes toward specific companies or industries, they are less likely to create and enforce laws or regulations that might be unfavorable to those organizations. One of the first actions taken by the Clinton administration was to initiate procedures to raise tariffs on foreign minivans and sport utility vehicles, which is good news for the Big Three U.S. auto companies.[22] Governments are also big consumers, and elected officials have the ability to influence how much a government purchases and for what purpose. As the Cold War has drawn to an end, most companies in the defense industry have attempted to commercialize their technologies. However, even after cutbacks in defense spending, the proposed military budget for 1993—$280 billion—is huge.[23] A third reason for seeking political favor is that political officials can help open foreign markets to American businesses. When officials from the United States, Canada, and Mexico finalized the North American Free Trade Agreement, many new opportunities opened up, especially in Mexico, for American firms specializing in motor vehicles and parts, apparel, telecommunications, financial services, and agriculture, to name a few.[24] The agreement is discussed further in Chapter 5.

[21] Ted Klein and Eugene Secunda, "Rx for Pharmaceutical Ads," *Advertising Age,* August 17, 1992, p. 20.
[22] Douglas Lavin and Bob Davis, "Auto Industry May Get Boost from Clinton," *Wall Street Journal,* January 27, 1993, pp. A2, A8.
[23] Rick Wartzman, "Lockheed Navigates the Transition to More Civilian Work," *Wall Street Journal,* February 10, 1992, pp. A1, A5.
[24] Kenneth H. Bacon, "Trade Pact Is Likely to Step Up Business Even Before Approval," *Wall Street Journal,* August 13, 1992, pp. A1, A10.

All organizations are affected by decisions made by political officials. Some companies simply try to adjust to conditions that result from these decisions. Other companies, however, try to build political advantage by lobbying against unfavorable legislation and endorsing candidates who can help them achieve their organizational objectives. Today, more than 150 companies have offices in Washington, D.C., and another 2,500 companies have some other form of representation in the nation's capital. In addition, more than fifteen thousand lobbyists can be found working with Congress and various regulatory agencies.

The semiconductor industry illustrates the advantage of establishing strong political allies in Washington. In 1985, the Semiconductor Industry Association (SIA) lobbied Washington officials for fair access to foreign markets, particularly Japan. Fourteen months later, the Japanese signed an agreement to open their markets to foreign semiconductors and to stop selling chips below cost. In 1987, however, Japanese firms violated that agreement by selling chips below cost, capturing market share, driving U.S. firms out of business, and then setting their own prices because there was less competition. The SIA lobbied political officials to punish Japan, and Japan was ultimately fined $300 million for violating the agreement. Why did the semiconductor industry succeed in getting what it wanted from Washington when many larger industries have failed? The companies in the semiconductor industry, including manufacturers, suppliers, and customers, presented a united front. Top executives of semiconductor firms got involved and traveled to Washington to meet with key political officials. Thus, in less than ten years, the semiconductor industry has built a constructive relationship with the government.[25]

Many organizations try to influence politics by using campaign contributions, get-out-and-vote efforts, endorsements, and advertisements to support political candidates. Although there are laws that restrict corporate contributions to campaign funds, many organizations channel corporate money into campaign funds as personal contributions from executives and stockholders. Such actions violate the spirit of laws governing corporate campaign contributions. These actions are also unethical: A large contribution may carry with it an unwritten understanding that the elected official will make decisions favoring the contributor.

SOCIETY

■ **society** all of the individuals that make up a nation's population and their characteristics and values

Society, another force of the marketing environment, includes all of the individuals that make up the population of a country and their characteristics and values. As members of our society, we seek many different goods and services that will enrich our lives. However, we expect businesses to produce these products without jeopardizing the safety of our society. When companies pollute the environment, manufacture products that injure consumers, or use lies and deception to persuade consumers to buy their products, the

---

[25]David B. Yoffie, "How an Industry Builds Political Advantage," *Harvard Business Review,* May–June 1988, pp. 82–89.

public raises questions about the marketing activities of these firms. By making ethical decisions and behaving in a socially responsible manner, businesses can satisfy the needs of consumers without placing society in danger.

The characteristics and values of society are constantly changing. These changes influence the types of products that consumers want. For instance, by the year 2060 the majority of Americans will belong to minority groups.[26] This will mean not only changing demographics, but changing social values, which are reflected in fashions, eating habits, and leisure activities. Consumers change their preferences for various products quickly. Foreign automobile manufacturers began marketing small cars in the United States at a time when large cars were popular. American consumers switched to the smaller cars when the cost of gasoline increased and the quality of American cars came into question. Current preferences among young adults (high school seniors) for later marriages, smaller families, greater wealth, and more leisure time away from home will have an impact on the types of products that will be most successful in future years.[27] The changing characteristics and preferences of society present both opportunities and threats for marketers.

Characteristics of Society

The 1990 census identified several significant changes taking place in the United States. Some of these changes, such as the fact that the population is older, better educated, and more diverse, are exerting a profound impact on the marketing activities of many firms.[28] The age distribution of the 250 million people who live in the United States is changing dramatically. In 1990, 43 percent of family members were 35 to 54 years old; by the year 2000, half of all family members will fall in this age category.[29]

Although *yuppies*—young, urban professionals—have received a great deal of attention from marketing professionals because of their affluence and materialism, Americans in the over-50 age group outnumber the much-publicized yuppies four to one. Firms are beginning to fully comprehend the significance of this so-called mature market, the fastest-growing segment in the United States and other countries. By the year 2010, 13.8 percent of the U.S. population will be over 65; for Germany, that figure will be 20.7 percent; for Japan, 18.2 percent.[30]

The "graying of America" will influence the marketing activities of many firms (see Figure 3.3). Businesses need to create, adapt, or improve products that satisfy the needs and wants of this mature market, including housing for the elderly, health care, drugs, entertainment, and recreation. Individuals in the over-50 age group also have needs for products that provide security

[26] Brad Edmondson, "American Diversity," *American Demographics Desk Reference,* July 1991, pp. 20–21.

[27] Eileen M. Crimmins, Richard A. Easterlin, and Yasuhiko Saito, "What Young Adults Want," *American Demographics,* July 1991, pp. 24–33.

[28] Judith Waldrop and Thomas Exter, "What the 1990 Census Will Show," *American Demographics,* January 1990, pp. 20–30.

[29] Thomas G. Exter, "Middle-Aging Households," *American Demographics,* July 1991, p. 63.

[30] Japan Economic Institute, "Projected Demographic Changes in the Major Industrial Countries," *Japan Economic Report,* March 27, 1987, p. 5.

FIGURE 3.3
Characteristics of Society
As the U.S. population ages, many firms are responding to this opportunity by creating, adapting, or improving products for the mature market.

Source: Reprinted with permission of the Pharmaceutical Manufacturers Association.

How we help grand dads be grand dads longer.

With each passing decade, people have been able to hold onto more of life's rich moments.

In 1950, the average life span of men was 65. Today it's approaching 80, due in many ways to advances in medicine. At the forefront are pharmaceutical companies who are making America's largest investment in drug research.

We now have 329 medicines in test for 45 diseases of aging that affect so many families. These efforts hold hope for breakthroughs that will lead to longer, more enjoyable, independent lives.

Yet the process is slow and difficult, with only a few of the thousands of compounds developed ever achieving success.

This exhaustive, high risk research increases the industry's cost of doing business, and in turn the price of drugs. But it also contributes to saving lives, shortening hospital stays and eliminating the need for surgery.

To learn more about the latest research developments for diseases of aging like cancer, Alzheimer's and osteoporosis, and what it means to you, call or write for our free booklet, "Good Medicine."

The Pharmaceutical Manufacturers Association, 1100 15th St, NW, Box R, Wash., DC 20005. 1-800-221-2157.

PHARMACEUTICALS
Good Medicine For A Better Life.

(electronic security systems), comfort (clothing), convenience (appliances and transportation), and a sense of purpose (travel programs).[31] Identifying the needs of this segment of the population will be critical to businesses in the years ahead.

The U.S. population is also more educated; the leading edge of the baby boom, now aged 37 to 46, is the most educated generation ever. Individuals with higher levels of education spend more on learning, travel, and entertainment.[32] They also demand higher levels of product quality and service. Other nations with high levels of education include Canada, Australia, the Netherlands, Spain, and Japan.

American society is also becoming more diverse in many ways. More than 2.6 million Hispanics in the United States have household incomes of $50,000 or more, a 234 percent increase since 1972.[33] Of America's 7 million black families, 13 percent have incomes of $50,000 or more.[34] In the next century, blacks, Hispanics, and Asians will outnumber whites in the United States. Marketers who target these groups may find this strategy rewarding, and firms that ignore them may miss an excellent opportunity.

Values of Society

Members of a society hold certain values in common, and marketers have the social responsibility to provide products consistent with these values. Among the values our society considers important are the rights of consum-

[31] Charles D. Schewe, "Get in Position for the Older Market," *American Demographics,* June 1990, pp. 38–41, 61–63.
[32] Judith Waldrop, "Spending by Degree," *American Demographics,* February 1990, pp. 22–26.
[33] William O'Hare, "The Rise of Hispanic Influence," *American Demographics,* August 1990, pp. 40–43.
[34] Judith Waldrop, "Shades of Black," *American Demographics,* September 1990, pp. 30–34.

■ **consumer movement**
individuals and organizations that attempt to protect the rights of consumers

ers. The **consumer movement** involves individuals and organizations that attempt to protect the rights of consumers. When an organization's activities violate consumers' rights or society's values, such as with products that are unsafe or harm the environment, consumer movement forces may organize boycotts or pressure legislators to enact consumer protection laws.

Consumers are becoming more concerned about what they as well as business firms can do to protect the environment. Concerns for such issues as pollution, waste disposal, the destruction of rain forests and the depletion of the sun's ozone layer have been growing in recent years. Over 75 percent of the adults in the United States consider themselves to be environmentalists.[35] This majority of society wants to help firms clean up the air, water, and land, find alternative ways to dispose of garbage, and recycle and reuse packages. Many firms are thus practicing what has become known as *green marketing,* developing products less harmful to the environment. By the year 2000, nearly one-third of the nation's landfill capacity will be depleted.[36] Recycling and reusing packages can help solve this problem. Americans are currently recycling over 60 percent of all aluminum beverage cans.[37] Materials such as paper, glass, plastics, and cardboard are also being recycled by manufacturers with greater frequency. The Procter & Gamble Co. sells liquid Tide, Cheer, and other products in containers made of recycled plastic. Of course, many environmentally sound products cost more than the alternatives, and consumers are sometimes reluctant to pay this premium.[38] These and many other issues regarding ethics and social responsibility are discussed in Chapter 4.

Consumers in the United States are also placing greater value on health and safety. People are more closely monitoring their diets, exercise routines, and safety habits. When making purchase decisions, consumers are more concerned with issues such as product safety and ingredients than ever before. This trend is influencing purchase decisions for many products. Sales of sun care products have increased from $280 million a year in 1985 to the current level of $530 million a year.[39] Consumers are reducing their purchases of products such as alcoholic beverages, cigarettes, and other tobacco products, as well as foods containing high levels of salt, fats, and cholesterol, and are increasing their purchases of "natural" foods, exercise equipment, and sportswear.

Successful marketers know that every changing consumer attitude or lifestyle leads to a market opportunity. Many firms have developed products to satisfy the needs of a health-conscious society. Products such as cars with air bags, low-salt canned foods, alcohol-free wines and low-alcohol beers, cholesterol-free baked goods, and low-fat dairy items are a few examples. Figure 3.4 shows how cable television capitalizes on a changing society.

[35]Joe Schwartz, "Earth Day Today," *American Demographics,* April 1990, pp. 40–41.
[36]Lee Clark and Tara Clark, "Waste Disposal in the 21st Century," *Your Business,* April 1990, p. 4.
[37]"Americans Push Aluminum Can Recycling Rate to Record 61%," *USA Today,* August 7, 1990, p. 5D.
[38]Jacquelyn Ottman, "Sometimes, Consumers Will Pay More to Go Green," *Marketing News,* July 6, 1992, p. 16.
[39]Todd Gutner, "Protection Racket," *Forbes,* August 17, 1992, p. 90.

FIGURE 3.4
Values of Society
As the values of society change and become more diverse, marketers must develop strategies that appeal to this diversity. Cable television offers a variety of channels that appeal to a more diverse society.

Source: Courtesy of National Cable Television Association.

ECONOMIC CONDITIONS

▪ **economic conditions** the various forces in the economy that influence organizations' abilities to compete and consumers' willingness and ability to purchase goods and services

Economic conditions are those forces in the economy, such as consumer buying power, consumer spending behavior, and the business cycle, that influence organizations' abilities to compete and consumers' willingness and ability to purchase goods and services. For example, as consumer buying power decreased during the recent recession, hundreds of consignment (resale) shops thrived as consumers tightened their budgets.[40]

Consumer Buying Power

▪ **buying power** the ability to make purchases, which depends on the extent of one's personal resources (goods, services, financial holdings) and the state of the economy

A person's **buying power** is his or her ability to make purchases. Buying power depends on the extent of the person's resources (goods, services, financial holdings) and the state of the economy. Economic conditions affect buying power. When prices are rising during inflationary periods, consumers have less buying power because they need more dollars to buy products. Products today, for instance, cost more than three times as much as they did in 1967. Conversely, in periods of declining prices, consumers have greater buying power because their resources go farther. The major financial resources that make up buying power are income, credit, and wealth.

▪ **income** the amount of money a person or organization receives from wages, sales, rents, investments, pensions, and subsidy payments in a given period, usually one year

Income   **Income** is the amount of money a person or organization receives from wages, sales, rents, investments, pensions, and subsidy payments in a

---

[40]Lawrence G. Budgar, "Consignment Shops Thrive in Thrifty Era, *Wall Street Journal,* June 15, 1992, p. B2.

given period, usually one year. Consumers normally use this money to pay taxes, purchase goods and services, and save for the future. The greater a person's income, the greater his or her buying power. Because of differences in educational levels, abilities, occupations, and wealth, income is not equally distributed.

■ **disposable income** after-tax income left for spending or saving

Marketing professionals are interested in **disposable income,** which is the income left for spending or saving after taxes have been paid. Because disposable income is a ready source of buying power, marketers want to know the total amount available in our country. American consumers currently save less than 5 percent of their disposable income. One factor that affects the amount of total disposable income is the amount of total national income. Total national income is affected by wage levels, unemployment rates, and interest rates. Taxes are another factor affecting disposable income. When taxes rise, disposable income declines; when taxes fall, disposable income increases.

■ **discretionary income** disposable income left for spending and saving after an individual has purchased basic necessities such as food, clothing, and shelter

Discretionary income is disposable income left for spending and saving after an individual has purchased basic necessities such as food, clothing, and shelter. People use discretionary income to purchase a variety of goods and services: compact disks (CDs), automobiles, education, books, pets, plants, furniture, personal computers, stereos, televisions, appliances, vacations, entertainment, and so on. Changes in total discretionary income affect the sales of these products, especially the more expensive items such as automobiles, furniture, and large appliances.

■ **credit** a buyer's ability to purchase something now and pay for it later

Credit   **Credit** is a buyer's ability to purchase something now and pay for it later. Consumers may obtain credit through personal loans from banks, store credit cards, and bank credit cards. Credit transactions allow consumers to acquire goods and services immediately and pay for them out of income that will be earned in the future. Credit increases current buying power at the expense of future buying power.

Several factors determine whether consumers use credit or wait until they have cash to make a purchase. First, consumers must apply and qualify for credit by having a specified minimum income and a good history of meeting financial obligations such as rent and loans. Even if individuals and organizations qualify for credit, lending institutions may not be willing to make loans. After the savings and loan crisis and the failure of over 124 banks in 1991, commercial lending by U.S. banks fell 8 percent over a one-year period.[41] Interest rates also affect consumers' decisions to use credit because these rates determine the cost of using credit. When interest rates are high, consumers tend to delay purchases of expensive items such as homes, appliances, and automobiles. Credit usage is also affected by the terms of the credit agreement, such as the size of the down payment, the amount and number of monthly payments, and late fees.

■ **wealth** the accumulation of past income, natural resources, and financial resources

Wealth   **Wealth** is the accumulation of past income, natural resources, and financial resources. It is possible for a person to have a high income and very

---

[41]Gary Hector, "Victims of the Credit Crunch," *Fortune,* January 27, 1992, pp. 100–102.

METRO AREA County City	Total EBI ($000)	Median Household EBI	Percent of Households by EBI Group (A) $10,000–$19,999 (B) $20,000–$34,999 (C) $35,000–$49,999 (D) $50,000+				Buying Power Index
			A	B	C	D	
Manchester–Nashua	6,350,280	43,623	10.1	19.6	22.2	40.6	.1666
Hillsborough	6,350,280	43,623	10.1	19.6	22.2	40.6	.1666
Manchester	1,655,113	35,070	14.5	24.1	22.6	27.5	.0490
Nashua	1,558,455	43,604	10.1	19.4	22.4	40.3	.0472
Suburban total	3,136,712	50,426	6.7	16.3	22.0	50.6	.0704
Portsmouth–Dover–Rochester	6,230,070	41,644	10.9	21.9	23.0	37.4	.1700
Rockingham	4,615,665	44,346	9.6	20.3	22.4	41.6	.1274
Portsmouth	434,998	32,827	15.1	29.8	19.8	26.4	.0181
Strafford	1,614,405	35,969	14.1	26.0	24.0	27.6	.0426
Dover	426,641	34,731	15.3	26.4	23.7	25.9	.0126
Rochester	398,814	33,792	15.9	27.5	24.6	23.3	.0118
Suburban total	4,969,617	44,388	9.5	20.1	22.9	41.4	.1275
Other counties							
Belknap	740,081	33,493	16.0	27.7	22.4	25.0	.0234
Carroll	543,444	30,355	19.5	29.0	19.6	21.8	.0180
Cheshire	1,055,688	34,227	15.5	26.4	21.7	26.9	.0314
Coos	429,873	27,483	20.5	26.8	21.3	15.8	.0131
Grafton	1,068,554	31,963	18.0	25.8	20.8	24.0	.0328
Merrimack	2,101,615	39,037	12.8	23.2	23.3	33.3	.0568
Sullivan	535,389	31,204	17.6	27.7	22.8	19.9	.0149
Total metro counties	12,580,350	42,619	10.5	20.8	22.6	39.0	.3366
Total state	19,054,994	39,040	12.7	22.8	22.3	34.0	.5270

Source: Reprinted by permission of *Sales & Marketing Management*. Copyright: Survey of Buying Power, August 24, 1992.

TABLE 3.6
Sample Data from the
Survey of Buying Power:
Effective Buying Income
(EBI) for New Hampshire
(1991)

little wealth; it is also possible, but not likely, for a person to have great wealth but not much income. Wealth can exist in many forms, including cash, stocks and bonds, checking and savings accounts, art, jewelry, antiques, real estate, minerals, machinery, and even animals. Like income, wealth is unevenly distributed among people in this country. The significance of wealth to marketers is that, as people become more wealthy, they gain more buying power. They can use their wealth to make current purchases, to generate more income, and to acquire large amounts of credit.

Marketers need to analyze buying power because it has a tremendous impact on consumers' reactions to firms' marketing strategies. Marketing managers can use buying power analysis for many purposes, such as evaluating sales quotas and budgeting marketing expenditures. Buying power information is available from government sources, trade associations, and research agencies. The *Survey of Buying Power,* published each year by *Sales & Marketing Management* magazine, is one of the best sources of buying power data. Table 3.6 shows sample data from the *Survey of Buying Power.* As you can see, data are presented for geographic areas, including states (in this case, New Hampshire), counties, and cities (with populations of more than forty thousand).

The *Survey of Buying Power* uses two direct indicators of buying power: effective buying income and the buying power index. **Effective buying income (EBI)** is similar to disposable income; it includes salaries, wages, dividends, interest, profits, and rents, less federal, state, and local taxes. The **buying power index (BPI)** is a weighted index that consists of population, effective buying income, and retail sales data. A high BPI indicates great buying power. This index is useful when comparing the buying power of one region with that of another.

Marketing managers should monitor current levels of and forecast changes in consumer buying power in their own markets because buying power directly affects the types and quantities of goods and services that consumers purchase. However, just because consumers have buying power does not ensure that they will buy; they must also be willing to use their buying power.

Consumer Spending Behavior

A person's **willingness to spend** is related to his or her ability to buy. Of course, a person who has more buying power will generally be more willing to buy. A product's absolute price and its price relative to the price of substitutable products influence a person's willingness to spend. Other factors that affect willingness to spend are expectations about future satisfaction from a product, employment, income levels, prices, household size, and general economic conditions. Perceptions of future economic conditions also have an impact on a person's willingness to spend. When the economy was recovering from the recent recession, consumers were reluctant to spend, expecting the weak economy to continue for some time.[42]

Businesses are particularly interested in how consumers spend their disposable income. **Consumer spending patterns** indicate how much money households actually spend on certain kinds of goods and services each year. Households are usually categorized on the basis of several characteristics, such as income, number of persons in the household, age of the household head, geographic area, and number and ages of children in the household. Marketers analyze consumer spending patterns to identify general trends in the ways that households spend their money on various kinds of products. Analyses of spending patterns help marketers gain both a perspective and a background for decision making. There are two types of spending patterns: comprehensive spending patterns and product-specific spending patterns.

■ **effective buying income (EBI)** disposable income, including salaries, wages, dividends, interest, profits, and rents, less federal, state, and local taxes

■ **buying power index (BPI)** a weighted index that consists of population, effective buying income, and retail sales data

■ **willingness to spend** a disposition toward buying, which is influenced by a person's ability to buy, absolute and relative product prices, expected satisfaction from a product, and numerous psychological and social forces

■ **consumer spending patterns** the amount of household money annually spent on certain kinds of goods and services

[42] Dana Milbank, "Consumers Agree Economy Is Improving But Aren't Persuaded to Part with Cash," *Wall Street Journal,* June 12, 1992, pp. B1, B5.

■ **comprehensive spend-ing patterns** the amount of household income allotted to annual expenditures for general classes of goods and services

■ **product-specific spending patterns** the amount of annual household income spent on specific products within a general product class

■ **business cycle** a general pattern of fluctuations in the U.S. economy consisting of four phases: prosperity, recession, depression, and recovery

■ **prosperity** a phase of the business cycle in which unemployment is low and the total national income is relatively high

■ **recession** a phase of the business cycle in which total production, employment rates, income, and buying power decline

■ **depression** a phase of the business cycle in which unemployment is extremely high, income is very low, to-tal disposable income is at a minimum, and consum-ers lack confidence in the economy

Comprehensive spending patterns indicate the amount of income that households allot to annual expenditures for general classes of goods and services. Marketing managers can obtain data to identify specific comprehen-sive spending patterns from government publications and private trade asso-ciations. **Product-specific spending patterns** indicate the annual amount of income households spend for specific products within a general product class. Sources such as government publications, trade publications, and consumer surveys can provide marketing managers with information to construct prod-uct-specific spending patterns.

The Business Cycle

Fluctuations in the economy follow a general pattern, which is often referred to as the **business cycle.** Economic conditions fluctuate in all countries. These fluctuations affect (and are affected by) supply and demand, consumer buying power and willingness to buy, consumer spending levels, and the intensity of competitive behavior. The business cycle consists of four phases: prosperity, recession, depression, and recovery.

Prosperity is a phase of the business cycle in which unemployment is low and the total national income is relatively high. As long as inflation remains low, consumers have a great deal of buying power in prosperous times, and they continue to spend as long as the economic outlook remains prosperous. Businesses often expand their product offerings to take advantage of this increased buying power. In prosperous times, businesses may be able to capture larger shares of their markets by intensifying distribution and promo-tion efforts.

A **recession** is a phase of the business cycle in which total production, employment rates, income, and buying power decline. According to an *Inc.* magazine survey of 960 growth companies, the three major indicators of a recession are high interest rates, high unemployment rates, and a volatile stock market.[43] Recessions typically generate a pessimism that stifles spend-ing by both consumers and businesses. Marketing managers should therefore revise their marketing activities to satisfy consumers' desire for value and utility. They must focus their marketing research on determining precisely what product functions consumers want and then must build these functions into their products. Promotional efforts should stress value and utility. Firms can profit during a recession by selling products that save customers money, repackaging goods to lower costs, pressing suppliers for better terms, refi-nancing to take advantage of lower interest rates, and exploiting competitors' weaknesses such as high prices or poor service.[44]

A **depression** is a phase in which unemployment is extremely high, in-come is very low, total disposable income is at a minimum, and consumers lack confidence in the economy. The federal government tries to counter the effects of recession, depression, and inflation with monetary and fiscal poli-

[43]Jay Finegan, "Do You See What I See?" *Inc.,* April 1990, pp. 52–56.
[44]Joseph Weber, Wendy Zellner, and Zachary Schiller, "Seizing the Dark Day," *Business Week,* Jan-uary 13, 1992, pp. 26–28.

cies. Monetary policies are employed to control interest rates and the supply of money available in the economy, which in turn influence spending, saving, and investment by individuals and businesses. The government tries to influence how much consumers and businesses spend or save by using fiscal policies, which change the levels of government expenditures and income. Some experts believe that effective use of monetary and fiscal policies can eliminate depressions from the business cycle.

■ **recovery** a transition phase in the business cycle during which the economy moves from recession to prosperity

Recovery is a transition phase during which the economy moves from recession to prosperity. During this period, the high unemployment rate begins to decline, total disposable income increases, and consumer buying power and willingness to spend rise. During recovery, marketing managers should try to develop flexible marketing strategies so that they can make adjustments as the economy moves from recession to prosperity. American Airlines surveys passengers to get a feeling for consumer confidence in the recovery. When confidence is high, both pleasure travelers and businesses tend to increase expenditures on travel.[45] Chicago's Brunswick Corp. finds that sales of its boats are tied very closely to the business cycle. Boats tend to be a luxury item, and sales peaked in 1988 and decreased during the recession that followed. But 1993 sales were predicted to increase by 15 percent as the economy showed signs of improvement.[46]

TECHNOLOGY

Advances in technology—robotics, computer chips, satellites—are changing the way we do business. Marketers are using technology to gain an edge over competitors by using software and databases to monitor inventory levels and market share, segment markets, link electronically to customers, and automate the sales force.[47] In the 1990s, the success or failure of businesses will depend largely on whether they bring sophisticated technology-based products to market faster than the competition.[48] Wang Laboratories Inc., pioneer of word-processing computers, filed for bankruptcy in 1992. The rapid downfall of this industry giant illustrates what can happen when a firm fails to keep pace with technological trends.[49]

■ **technology** the knowledge—often acquired from scientific research—of how to accomplish tasks and goals

Technology is the knowledge of how to accomplish tasks and goals.[50] This knowledge is often acquired from scientific research. Technology enables people to develop machines, materials, and processes that allow societies to have a higher standard of living. Within a few years, for instance, you will be able to make and take calls anywhere in the world with a universal

[45] Brian O'Reilly, "How to Manage the Recovery," *Fortune,* March 23, 1992, pp. 62–64.
[46] Gary Slutsker, "Toss in the Water," *Forbes,* March 15, 1993, pp. 70–72.
[47] Betsy Spethman, "Marketers Tap into Tech," *Advertising Age,* January 25, 1993, p. 30.
[48] T. Michael Nevens, Gregory L. Summe, and Bro Uttal, "Commercializing Technology: What the Best Companies Do," *Harvard Business Review,* May–June 1990, pp. 154–163.
[49] William M. Bulkeley and John R. Wilke, "Filing in Chapter 11, Wang Sends Warning Signal to High-Tech Circles," *Wall Street Journal,* August 19, 1992, pp. A1–A4.
[50] Herbert Simon, "Technology and Environment," *Management Science,* June 1973, p. 1110.

FIGURE 3.5
Technology
Many firms use technology to gain a competitive edge. This advertisement illustrates how technology is a major aspect of Toshiba's marketing strategy.

Source: Courtesy Toshiba America, Inc.

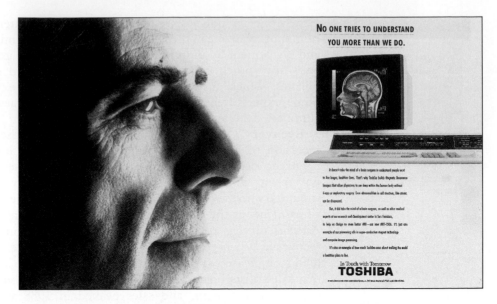

wireless phone that fits in your shirt pocket.[51] Technology lets workers be more productive, do less physical labor, and earn larger incomes with which to purchase a vast number of technologically improved goods and services. Nevertheless, technology can detract from the quality of life by contributing to such undesirable side effects as unemployment, pollution, crime, and other social and environmental problems. In some instances, consumers purchase high-tech products that rarely get used because they are too complicated to operate.[52] Few people, for instance, know how to use all the functions on their VCRs. Whether the effects of technology are positive or negative is determined largely by how it is applied. For example, technology has been used to improve health care so that people can live longer, and to allow humans to explore space; however, it also has been used to develop nuclear weapons that are capable of destroying the world.

The rapid technological growth of the last several decades is expected to continue through the 1990s. The United States has fallen behind other nations in manufacturing semiconductors, memory chips, and consumer electronics, but many U.S. executives are optimistic about regaining ground. A resurgence in American-made products is already taking place, with new products such as AT&T's 1337 telephone-answering device and new VideoPhone; Motorola's latest phone, the MicroTac Lite Digital Personal Communicator; and U.S.-pioneered high-definition television.[53] Researchers also are working on new developments in technology and applying them to such areas as medicine, waste disposal and recycling, extraction of precious metals, communications, recreation, computers, and robotics (see Figure 3.5). Ultimately, this research will lead to the development of many new products to

[51] Andrew Kupfer, "Phones That Will Work Anywhere," *Fortune,* August 24, 1992, pp. 100–112.
[52] William Mullen, "High-Tech Headaches," Lexington, Ky. *Herald-Leader,* March 18, 1990, pp. K1–K6.
[53] Gene Bylinsky, "A U.S. Comeback in Electronics," *Fortune,* April 20, 1992, pp. 77–86.

satisfy consumers' needs for information, health, convenience, and recreation. Such technological developments will have a definite impact on buyers and on marketers' decisions.

Technology affects marketing decisions in many ways. It determines how people satisfy their physiological needs. Eating and drinking habits, sleeping patterns, and health care are all influenced both by existing technology and changes in technology. Low-calorie and low-sodium foods, new methods of packaging foods, and home blood-sugar test kits and blood-pressure monitors have had a definite impact on how people satisfy physiological requirements. Recent advances in catalysts—substances that form new chemical bonds in other materials to make a desired product, then emerge unchanged and ready to start over—could lead to miraculous new drugs, smaller computer circuits, and innovative ways to reduce pollution.[54]

Technology also affects the types of products that businesses can offer. Technological improvements in production processes and materials sometimes result in more durable, less expensive products. Japanese firms, with the world's most productive factories, have become major competitors in the automobile industry. They are known as high-quality, low-cost automobile producers both in Japan and the United States. A study conducted in 1989 by Eastor Consultants reported that American-made cars required the replacement of 42 percent more critical parts than did imports.[55] But this gap has been closed rapidly. According to a 1992 survey by J. D. Power, a research firm specializing in the auto industry, U.S. car owners reported 136 problems per 100 cars, compared with the industry average of 125.[56]

Technology has also altered the ways in which organizations inform consumers about goods and services. Companies can now reach large numbers of people through direct mail and television home shopping. This capability has led to a rapid growth in mail-order businesses like Lands' End and L.L. Bean, and televised home shopping services such as Home Shopping Network. Interactive television, still in its infancy, enables advertisers and consumers to interact with each other. Consumers can travel farther and more often than ever before, and therefore have access to a larger number of stores for a greater selection of goods and services. In addition, technological changes in transportation have improved producers' ability to distribute products to consumers. Generally, manufacturers of small and relatively lightweight products can ship their goods to any of their dealers within twenty-four hours.

■ **technology transfer**
the process by which an organization transforms new technologies into successful products

How a firm uses and adapts technology is important for its long-term survival. **Technology transfer** is the process by which a firm transforms new technologies into successful products. A firm that decides not to transform a new technology to its products may lose sales to a competitor that does use that technology. For example, Sony Corp. continued to promote its Betamax videosystem, keeping its VHS technology proprietary, but JVC licensed its VHS technology to many companies. Betamax quickly became obsolete, costing Sony millions of dollars.[57] Also, poor decisions may affect a firm's

[54]Pamela J. Black, "Better Living Through Catalysts?" *Business Week,* March 23, 1992, pp. 84–85.
[55]Alex Taylor III, "Can American Cars Come Back?" *Fortune,* February 26, 1990, pp. 62–65.
[56]Anthony J. Michels, "Mercedes Skids in Quality Race," *Fortune,* June 29, 1992, p. 12.
[57]Andrew Tanzer, "Sharing," *Forbes,* January 20, 1992, p. 82.

FIGURE 3.6
Monitoring the Marketing Environment
Attention to the marketing environment enables Digital to help firms like John Deere succeed. Digital's total solutions approach to manufacturing and software makes it quicker and easier for managers to make decisions that ensure product quality.

Source: Courtesy of Digital Equipment Corporation.

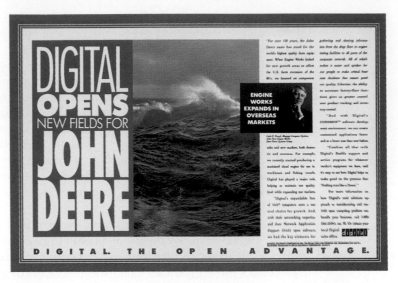

profits by requiring expensive corrective actions. Texas Instruments spent seven years developing an innovative computer chip called "magnetic bubble memory." But by the time the technology was transferred to the marketplace, ordinary computer chips had become so advanced that computer manufacturers refused to switch to the new product, and Texas Instruments lost millions of dollars.[58]

MONITORING THE MARKETING ENVIRONMENT

The marketing environment is dynamic. Whether the forces of that environment change slowly or rapidly, they create uncertainty, obstacles, and opportunities (see Figure 3.6). Marketers must constantly monitor the marketing environment to capitalize on opportunities and minimize adverse conditions. Each element should be monitored, with special emphasis on those forces most likely to have an impact on the organization. To monitor changes in the marketing environment effectively, marketing managers engage in environmental scanning and analysis.

Environmental Scanning

■ **environmental scanning** the process of collecting information concerning forces in the marketing environment

Environmental scanning is the process of collecting information concerning forces in the marketing environment. Scanning involves gathering information through observation; reviewing business, trade, and government publications; and engaging in marketing research efforts. Although this information is very important to marketing managers, they must be careful not to acquire so much information that sheer volume makes analysis impossible.

Useful information about *competition* can be obtained through newspapers and trade publications. Firms can read about the activities of competitors in

---

[58]Gene Bylinsky, "Turning R&D into Real Products," *Fortune,* July 2, 1990, pp. 72–77.

the *Wall Street Journal, Business Week,* and other business publications. Marketers also talk to store managers and monitor the purchases of customers to spot trends in the competitive environment. Large organizations may take a more sophisticated approach to monitoring competition. In some cases, engineers disassemble competitors' products and closely examine them. Additionally, firms may conduct research studies for the specific purpose of obtaining information about the activities of competitors. Domino's Pizza drivers in some Florida locations followed Pizza Hut drivers to their delivery destinations and offered free pizzas to Pizza Hut customers so they could compare the two brands.[59] There have also been allegations that many industrial nations engage in industrial espionage against U.S. firms. Targets are technology and trade secrets of high-tech firms—everything from aerospace technology to law research.[60]

Organizations also monitor changes in *regulation* and *politics.* New laws and new political leaders may have a profound effect on a firm's products and marketing practices. Sometimes laws that have existed for many years are more heavily enforced because of repeated abuses by businesses. Changes in laws and politics in foreign countries may open new markets to U.S. firms. Political leaders can also influence marketing activities. For instance, during the eight years of the Reagan administration, with its hands-off policy toward business, marketers were somewhat insulated from regulation. Immediately following George Bush's election, more than thirty proposals calling for stricter regulation of advertising appeared in the U.S. Senate and House of Representatives.[61]

Organizations must also scan the marketing environment for changes and trends taking place in *society.* Useful information is available through the Bureau of Labor, the Census Bureau, and publications such as *American Demographics.* Some firms conduct special research studies that track social changes. For instance, it is important for marketers to know that on average the population is growing older and more conservative, or that new social trends will influence the purchase of clothing, cars, and entertainment.

Many sources provide information regarding *economic conditions.* The government publishes economic indicators quarterly and annually, including figures on consumer spending, business investment, construction, debt, and output. In 1990, when the government indicated that the national debt had passed $10 trillion and national output was weak for the second quarter in a row, firms knew that the country was probably entering a recession.[62] This recession lasted well into 1992, and recovery has been very slow. Other useful information can be obtained from sales records and inventory levels.

Some data regarding economic conditions is suspect, making it somewhat difficult to understand what is really happening to the economy. For example, studies have shown that over the past decade, annual consumer price inflation may have been overstated by as much as 1.8 percent. Likewise, measures of unemployment are usually distorted; it's impossible to say ex-

[59]John P. Cortez, "Pizza Pie Spies Heat Up Florida," *Advertising Age,* April 20, 1992, pp. 1, 48.
[60]Norm Alster, "The Valley of the Spies," *Forbes,* October 26, 1992, pp. 200–204.
[61]Steven W. Colford, "Ad-bashing Is Back in Style," *Advertising Age,* April 30, 1990, pp. 4, 58.
[62]Karen Pennar, Christopher Farrell, Chuck Hawkins, Ty Holland, and Barbara Buell, "Are We in a Recession?" *Business Week,* August 13, 1990, pp. 28–32.

actly what the unemployment rate is.[63] Many data collection and analysis techniques are designed to measure yesterday's economy and do not accurately portray current economic activity.

To keep up with changing *technology,* marketing managers can scan magazines that publish technological innovations, attend new product trade shows, and participate in industry conferences on new product development. Many organizations also employ individuals responsible for monitoring new technologies. The results from scanning the technological environment, along with the information from scanning the other environmental forces, must be analyzed and incorporated into a firm's marketing strategy.

Environmental Analysis

■ **environmental analysis** the process of assessing and interpreting the information gathered through environmental scanning

Environmental analysis is the process of assessing and interpreting the information gathered through environmental scanning. A manager reviews the information for accuracy, tries to reconcile inconsistencies in the data, and interprets the findings. Analysis allows a marketing manager to discern changes in the environment and, if possible, to predict trends and changes. By evaluating these changes, a manager should be able to determine possible threats and opportunities associated with environmental fluctuations.

Knowledge of current and predicted environmental changes helps a marketing manager assess the performance of current marketing efforts and develop marketing strategies for the future. Organizations specifically address this topic in their marketing plans. As noted in Chapter 2, a typical marketing plan has a section on the current marketing situation, which includes an analysis of trends and changes in the marketing environment. Changes in the marketing environment can spell both opportunities and threats for the organization. For instance, new laws regulating product safety, the entry of new competitors, or an innovative technology can pose a threat. On the other hand, increased consumer spending or changing social trends can result in an opportunity. Organizations must be prepared to respond quickly to threats or to seize opportunities arising from changes in the marketing environment. The major opportunities and threats both inside and outside the organization are also addressed in the marketing plan.

Responding to Environmental Forces

Organizations should have a plan in place for responding to environmental forces. Marketers use one of two general approaches. In the traditional approach, marketing managers view the forces of the marketing environment as uncontrollable. Thus they assume that an organization can do little to alter the influence of the various forces in the marketing environment. A well-managed organization taking this *reactive* approach tries to prepare itself to respond quickly to changes in the environment. For example, although an organization has little power to alter economic conditions, or the actions of competitors, it can monitor the environment closely and adjust its marketing strategy to counter the effects of inflation, or product improvements by competitors.

[63]Louis S. Richman, "Why the Economic Data Mislead Us," *Fortune,* March 8, 1993, pp. 108–114.

A second response to the marketing environment is to take a *proactive,* or aggressive, stance toward environmental forces.[64] A growing number of marketing professionals argue that the forces of the marketing environment can be controlled, at least to some extent. They believe that marketing itself represents a significant force that can be used to create change and extend its influence over the environment. Through lobbying, legal action, advertising of key issues, and public relations, organizations can alter some environmental forces.[65] For instance, a firm can control its competitive environment by using aggressive pricing or competitive advertising strategies to influence the decisions of rival firms. It can lobby political officials to repeal legislation that it believes will restrict its business. Likewise, a firm can use its political skills and public relations activities to create opportunities by opening foreign markets to American businesses.

Neither response to environmental forces is superior. For some organizations, the reactive approach is more appropriate; for others, the proactive approach leads to better performance. Many organizations find it most efficient to employ both reactive and proactive responses. The selection of a particular approach is determined by an organization's managerial philosophies, objectives, financial resources, markets, and human skills, and by the composition of the set of environmental forces in which the organization operates.

SUMMARY

The marketing environment includes the forces of competition, regulation, politics, society, economic conditions, and technology. These external forces directly or indirectly influence an organization's marketing activities.

To a particular company, *competition* refers to businesses in the same geographic area that market products that are similar to its own products; it also refers to the rivalry among businesses for consumer dollars. Several factors influence the intensity of competition in a firm's environment, including the type of competitive structure (monopoly, oligopoly, monopolistic competition, or perfect competition) in which a firm operates and the kinds of competitive tools employed by the organizations in that industry.

Regulation consists of laws and regulatory agencies that influence the conduct of business. Laws pertain to all major areas of marketing and can be divided into two categories: those designed to preserve competition and those designed to protect consumers. Businesses must be aware of state and local laws, and must be concerned with the courts' interpretation of these laws. Businesses must also concern themselves with federal and state regulatory agencies. Regulatory agencies have the power to enforce specific laws and have discretion to establish operating rules and regulatory guidelines that carry considerable weight in the marketplace. Nongovernment self-regulation programs are another source of controls. Such programs generally cannot enforce compliance as effectively as government agencies can.

[64] Carl P. Zeithaml and Valarie A. Zeithaml, "Environmental Management: Revising the Marketing Perspective," *Journal of Marketing,* Spring 1984, pp. 46–53.
[65] Philip Kotler, "Megamarketing," *Harvard Business Review,* March–April 1986, pp. 117–124.

Politics is the policies and goals of the government and the elected officials within it. Businesses should try to maintain good relations with political officials for several reasons: Those officials have the power to create and enforce laws or regulations that might be unfavorable to business, the government is a major consumer, and political officials can help open foreign markets to American businesses. All companies are affected by decisions made by government officials; some businesses attempt to influence the decisions of political officials through lobbying and campaign contributions.

Society, which is all of the individuals that make up a nation's population and their characteristics and values, also affects marketing activities. In the United States and many developed parts of the world, society expects business organizations to help satisfy its needs for goods and services without jeopardizing the environment. The characteristics and values of society are changing constantly. Recent changes of particular interest to marketing professionals are the aging of the American population and the trend toward a more health-conscious lifestyle.

Economic conditions also influence marketing activities. Consumer demand is affected by consumers' buying power and their willingness to spend. A person's buying power, or ability to make purchases, depends on the extent of his or her financial resources (income, credit, wealth) and the state of the economy. Factors that affect consumers' willingness to spend are product price; the level of satisfaction that is obtained from currently used products; family size; and expectations about future employment, income, prices, and general economic conditions. Businesses analyze consumer spending patterns, which indicate how much money households actually spend on certain kinds of goods and services, to identify trends in household spending.

General economic conditions affect supply and demand, buying power, the willingness to spend, consumer expenditure levels, and the intensity of competitive behavior. The overall state of the economy fluctuates in a general pattern known as the business cycle. The four stages of the business cycle are prosperity, recession, depression, and recovery.

Technology is the knowledge of how to accomplish tasks and goals. It determines how people satisfy their physiological needs, the types of products that businesses can offer, and how businesses inform consumers about products and services. Technology influences marketing decisions such as product research and development, packaging, promotion, and distribution. How a firm chooses to use and adapt technology is important for its long-term survival. Businesses that choose not to use new technology may lose sales to competitors that do use technology.

The marketing environment is constantly changing, and marketing managers must monitor these changes to ensure organizational survival. To monitor the changes, marketing managers engage in environmental scanning (collecting information about forces in the marketing environment) and environmental analysis (assessing and interpreting the information gathered from environmental scanning). Scanning and analysis help marketing managers predict opportunities and threats associated with environmental fluctuations. Marketing management may assume either a reactive or a proactive approach in responding to these environmental fluctuations. There is no superior method of response.

KEY TERMS

marketing environment
competition
monopoly
oligopoly
monopolistic competition
perfect competition
regulation
Federal Trade Commission (FTC)
Better Business Bureau
National Advertising Review
  Board (NARB)
politics
society
consumer movement
economic conditions
buying power
income
disposable income
discretionary income

credit
wealth
effective buying income (EBI)
buying power index (BPI)
willingness to spend
consumer spending patterns
comprehensive spending
  patterns
product-specific spending
  patterns
business cycle
prosperity
recession
depression
recovery
technology
technology transfer
environmental scanning
environmental analysis

QUESTIONS FOR DISCUSSION AND REVIEW

1. Explain how various forces in the marketing environment interact to influence a firm's marketing mix.

2. Distinguish between monopoly, oligopoly, monopolistic competition, and perfect competition. Why is competition a concern to marketers?

3. What laws designed to preserve competition affect marketing practices?

4. What government and nongovernment agencies are involved in regulation? How do government agencies help enforce laws?

5. What is the purpose of deregulation? What industries have been deregulated in recent years? What are the results?

6. Why might businesses prefer self-regulatory programs over government regulation?

7. Explain how politics and regulation are closely interrelated in the marketing environment.

8. How do societal forces influence a firm's marketing activities?

9. What are some changing characteristics and values of society that may present threats and opportunities to organizations?

10. Why should marketers be concerned with consumer spending behavior?

11. Describe how technology affects society. How does it affect marketing decisions?

12. How can marketing managers effectively monitor changes in the marketing environment?

3.1   OVERCHARGING AT AUTOMOBILE CENTERS STALLS SEARS

Over the decades Sears, Roebuck and Co. has built a reputation for reliability and value and established itself as a premier store where middle America shops, not only for clothes, appliances, and other goods, but also for insurance (Allstate) and automobile repairs. "You can count on Sears" has been one of the company's well-publicized advertising slogans.

But on June 11, 1992, Sears customers and indeed all of America found out that perhaps consumers cannot always count on Sears. On that day the California Department of Consumer Affairs accused Sears of systematically overcharging automobile repair customers at its seventy-two Sears Tire & Auto Centers in that state and proposed revoking the company's license to operate the centers.

A growing number of consumer complaints had spurred the consumer affairs department to conduct a yearlong undercover investigation. It found that its agents were overcharged nearly 90 percent of the time, by an average of $223. "This is a flagrant breach of trust and confidence the people of California have placed in Sears for generations," said Jim Conran, the department's director. "Sears has used trust as a marketing tool, and we don't believe they've lived up to that trust."

Law enforcement officials, consumer groups, and consumers themselves believe that automobile repair fraud is common. But most cases involve individual garages. The Sears case may be the biggest fraud action yet against an automobile repair operator. On June 15, four days after California's charges, New Jersey accused six Sears automobile centers, along with five unrelated repair shops, of doing unneeded work. Other states, including Florida, Illinois, New York, and Alabama, began studying California's action.

Sears emphatically denied any wrongdoing and said it would appeal California's delicensing action before an administrative judge and in the courts, if necessary. The attorney who represents Sears in the California case, Dirk Schenkkan, accused the consumer affairs department of beating up on Sears to boost its own standing at a time when its funding was threatened by California budget cuts. A statement by Sears said the California investigation was "very seriously flawed and simply does not support the allegations. The service we recommend and the work we perform are in accordance with the highest industry standards."

The investigation took place in two phases. In the first, undercover agents took thirty-eight cars with worn brakes but no other defects to twenty-seven Sears automobile centers throughout California from December 1990 to December 1991. In thirty-four instances, or 89 percent, agents were told that additional and more expensive repairs were needed. A Sears automobile center in a San Francisco suburb overcharged an agent $585 to have the front brake pads, front and rear springs, and control-arm bushings replaced. The consumer affairs department said that in some instances cars were returned damaged or unsafe, with loose brake parts or improperly installed coil springs. In the second phase, the department told Sears about the investigation in December 1991, then conducted ten more tests in January; seven resulted in unnecessary repairs. The department found that the centers stopped selling unnecessary springs and shocks but continued to overcharge the agents by an average of $100.

What caused one of the nation's most respected retailers to wind up in such a mess? Critics believe the trouble started in 1990 when Sears had a 40 percent drop in earnings and a 60 percent drop in net income for its merchandise group (including the automobile centers and appliances). Chairman Edward A. Brennan started a shakeup, slashing costs by $600 million, renovating the company's 868 stores, and pushing new everyday low prices. In 1990 Sears standardized compensation for automobile service employees nationwide, introducing commissions and by-the-job pay rates in some areas. Conran of the California consumer affairs department said that complaints began soon after Sears established a quota of parts and repair sales for every eight-hour shift. Those who failed to meet the quotas had work hours reduced or were transferred.

Similar pressures apparently existed in other Sears ventures. Several major-appliance salespeople say they were pushed extremely hard to sell maintenance agreements on big-ticket appliances. Such agreements can generate up to 50 percent of annual store earnings and can cost more than 35 percent of the appliance's value. Meanwhile, Allstate Insurance agents nationwide are concerned about reports of agents who have received warnings that if they don't bring in a certain amount of premiums they'll lose their jobs. Although Allstate got rid of production quotas years ago, some agents say they've been fired for not meeting sales quotas. One agent has filed a complaint with Maryland regulators, and a former automobile center employee, claiming he was fired for not meeting his quota of sixteen oil changes a day, has filed a wrongful discharge suit.

Sears chairman Brennan has insisted that, based on a twelve-day internal investigation, no systemic problem led to cheating in the automobile centers. "Isolated errors? Yes," he conceded. "But a pattern of misconduct? Absolutely not." However, Brennan did abolish commissions and product-specific sales goals for automobile center employees nationwide.

Sears settled charges with New Jersey on June 21, 1992 by agreeing to pay $200,000 to the National Association of Attorneys General for a study of automobile repair standards and an additional $3,000 in penalties. But the big blow came a few months later on September 2, when Sears agreed to pay an estimated $15 million to settle charges in California and forty-one other states, as well as to settle nineteen related class-action lawsuits. Denying any charges, Sears agreed to refund $50 to affected consumers for up to five repair services. Sears also agreed to pay the state of California $3.5 million for reimbursement of legal fees, and $1.5 million to establish an automobile repair training program. Sears could potentially pay over $46 million, but officials do not expect all eligible customers to apply for refunds. The damage to Sears's reputation and loss of good will is impossible to measure.

Questions for Discussion

1. What marketing environment forces probably influenced Sears in its reported practices of systematically overcharging automobile repair customers? Explain the influence of each of these forces.

2. In what type of competitive market structure does Sears operate? Explain.

3. What did Sears do in response to the action by the California consumer affairs department? To New Jersey's action? What approach did Sears use in responding?

4. Business leaders, elected officials, politicians, economists, and others frequently argue about the need for more or less regulation of business in the United States. How does this case reflect the benefits or drawbacks of regulation of U.S. firms?

Based on information from Julia Flynn, Christina Del Valle, and Russell Mitchell, "Did Sears Take Other Customers for a Ride?" *Business Week,* August 3, 1992, pp. 24–25; Gregory A. Patterson, "Sears Will Pay $15 Million Settling Cases," *Wall Street Journal,* September 3, 1992, p. A4; Kevin Kelly and Eric Schine, "How Did Sears Blow This Gasket?" *Business Week,* June 29, 1992, p. 38; and Tung Yin, "Sears Is Accused of Billing Fraud at Auto Centers," *Wall Street Journal,* June 12, 1992, pp. B1, B6.

3.2   HONDA FACES CHANGING MARKETING ENVIRONMENT

In the 1970s Honda's motorcycle division dominated the U.S. market. Honda's formula for success was fairly simple: Offer consumers a high-quality product at a low price. Honda was also very creative with its advertising program. The "You meet the nicest people on a Honda" campaign successfully convinced many people to become first-time motorcycle buyers. Honda found itself at the top of the motorcycle industry.

But today, Honda's motorcycle division is fighting a sharp decline in sales. In 1985, Honda led the industry with a 58.5 percent share of the U.S. market; Yamaha was a distant second with a 10.2 percent share. By 1990, Honda's share had dropped to 28.9 percent, and Yamaha's share had increased to 15.6 percent. Sales fell from $1.1 billion in 1985 to $230 million in 1990. What went wrong for Honda?

Honda fell victim to its own failure to adapt its marketing strategy to a changing marketing environment. First, consumer values have changed. Motorcycles seem to have regained the black-leather-jacket image that Honda fought so hard and so successfully to change in earlier decades. According to the motorcycle industry, sales of motorcycles and all-terrain vehicles (ATVs) have dropped 45.6 percent since 1984. The tastes and preferences of society have moved upscale, and the demand for motorcycles has fallen sharply.

Realizing that society was changing, Honda changed its marketing strategy. The company thought Americans would be willing to pay higher prices for the latest in technology, so it attempted to introduce bikes for the upscale market. Unfortunately, the yen was rising sharply against the dollar at the time, and Kawasaki and Suzuki held firm on prices. The result: About six hundred Honda motorcycle dealers went out of business and Honda's move upscale was a failure.

Honda made several other costly errors. In 1985, the Consumer Product Safety Commission began a campaign to outlaw three-wheel all-terrain vehicles, which accounted for nearly 40 percent of Honda's North American sales. Honda failed to step up production of four-wheel ATVs even while competitors boosted production and advertising. As a result, Yamaha soon replaced Honda as the largest producer of ATVs in America.

Honda also placed too much emphasis on technology. Its philosophy has been to design technologically superior products and hope that consumer demand will follow. But two of Honda's most innovative bikes—the 1988 version of the Gold Wing and the Pacific Coast, introduced in 1989—met with little success. The price of the Pacific Coast has been dropped from $7,698 to $6,500. Honda discovered that consumers were not willing to pay that price for motorcycles, no matter how superior the bike.

Honda is working hard to correct its mistakes. The company is using promotion heavily, including offering free rides in shopping malls, sponsoring races, and offering free training at rider safety education centers throughout the country. The company is also going back to the strategy that once worked so well: quality products at low prices. Honda has reduced prices on several of its models. It hopes that its fresh advertising campaign "Come ride with us," which is quite similar to "You meet the nicest people on a Honda," will attract a new group of bikers. And for the first time in many years, the political and economic environment may be in Honda's favor because of rising fuel costs, increased traffic jams, and growing concerns over pollution.

Questions for Discussion

1. Which environmental variables had the greatest impact on Honda's motorcycle division?

2. Did Honda practice the marketing concept in designing new motorcycles?

3. Why do you think Honda's strategy to attract upscale consumers failed?

4. How do you evaluate Honda's chances of recapturing its lost market share?

Based on information from Stephen Phillips, "That 'Vroom' You Hear Is Honda Motorcycles," *Business Week,* September 3, 1990, pp. 74–76; Thomas R. King, "Honda Revs Up a Hip Cycle Campaign," *Wall Street Journal,* July 31, 1989, p. B1; and Michael Flagg, "Low Gear for Honda," *Los Angeles Times,* March 19, 1989, p. 1.

Ethical and Social Issues in Marketing

OBJECTIVES

● *To discuss the meaning and importance of marketing ethics.*

● *To identify the factors influencing marketers' ethical or unethical decisions.*

● *To describe how ethical behavior can be encouraged.*

● *To explain how social responsibility relates to market- ing organizations.*

● *To define the terms* consumerism, ecology, *and* green marketing.

● *To discuss how firms evaluate social responsibility activities.*

Donella and Dennis Meadows sparked intense debate in 1972 with the release of their book *Limits to Growth*. Through the use of computer models, the authors predicted that population growth would collide with the earth's ability to absorb pollution and regenerate itself. Some saw this as a serious warning of a potential global catastrophe; others passed it off as a false alarm. Twenty years later, leaders and negotiators from 170 countries met in Rio de Janeiro for the U.N. Conference on Environment and Development (UNCED). The major topic was a controversial agenda to protect the earth's atmosphere and inhabitants, attack poverty, and foster less destructive industrialization. The problems are far from simple:

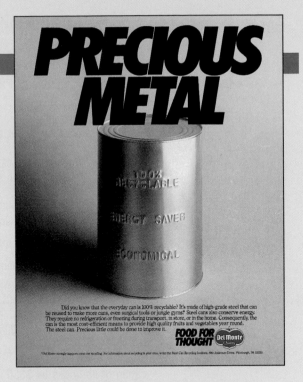

- World population is expected to double, reaching 11 billion within forty years. Industrial output would have to quintuple to meet the needs of all these people.

- Industrialized nations make up only 25 percent of the world's population, yet they consume 70 percent of the resources. As more nations become developed and boost economic growth, resources will be scarce.

- Seven industrial countries, including the United States, are responsible for 45 percent of human-caused greenhouse gas emissions. As developing nations industrialize, worldwide pollution will skyrocket.

- Human activities are destroying the earth's soils, forests, wetlands, and grasslands. Over 40 million acres of tropical forests are destroyed each year, and the ozone layer is thinning, increasing the potential for global warming.

- Damage to the environment costs industrialized nations 1 to 5 percent of their GNP (gross national product). Forest damage in Western Europe is cutting GNP by $30 billion a year.

- In places like Mexico City and Eastern Europe, millions breathe toxic air. China will soon deplete all its harvestable forests. The Baltic Sea is dying from sewage and other pollution.

A different yet related crisis also grips many parts of the world. As the economic slowdown lingers, more managers are cutting ethical corners. These actions are often motivated by the most basic of instincts, fear of losing their jobs. According to Gary Edwards, president of the Ethics

Resource Center, "The message out there is, reaching objectives is what matters and how you get there isn't that important." Perhaps this attitude provides at least a partial explanation for the following:

- Citicorp fires the president and senior executives of a credit card processing division for overstating revenues.

- Alamo Rent A Car agrees to refund $3 million to customers who were overcharged for repair costs to damaged vehicles.

- Toys "R" Us managers sent employees to competitor Child World stores throughout the country to buy up heavily discounted products, only to resell them at their own stores.

- Products such as toxic chemicals that have been outlawed in the United States are sold in underdeveloped nations, where regulations are much more lenient.

- Scandals have plagued the savings and loan and banking industries, with bailouts costing investors and taxpayers billions of dollars.

- Drug chain Phar-Mor filed for bankruptcy after a massive fraud scheme, including the falsification of its books by $350 million.

- After twelve years and $11 billion, only 84 of the 1,245 sites on the Superfund list have been cleaned up, while some of the government cleanup money has been used for dancing lessons, Christmas parties, and legal squabbles.[1] ●

U nfortunately, some of the predictions made over twenty years ago by Donella and Dennis Meadows have come true. To blame industry for all the social and ethical problems confronting society would be unfair. The opening examples illustrate the delicate balance between the forces of nature and the individuals inhabiting the earth. Individuals and organizations have a responsibility to maintain this balance; sometimes we fail for one reason or another. Most of us know right from wrong, work hard every day, value our family and friends, and want a better life for future generations. We also understand our responsibility to society. But a strong catalyst—like financial pressure—can result in an ethical dilemma.

The consequences of social conduct and business decisions are far-reaching. Because of the demand for beef in America, forests are being cut

---

[1] Based on information from Zachary Schiller, "Wait a Minute—Phar-Mor is Still Kicking," *Business Week,* March 8, 1993, pp. 60–61; Emily T. Smith, "Growth vs. Environment," *Business Week,* May 11, 1992, pp. 66–75; Kenneth Labich, "The New Crisis in Business Ethics," *Fortune,* April 20, 1992, pp. 167–176; and Peter Hong and Michele Galen, "The Toxic Mess Called Superfund," *Business Week,* May 11, 1992, pp. 32–34.

down in Argentina to make pastures for grazing cattle. The oil fires in Kuwait during and after the 1991 Persian Gulf war created perhaps the worst man-made disaster ever and resulted in black rain thousands of miles away. Firms are relocating factories to foreign countries not only because of cheaper labor but also because of more relaxed regulation. We may not agree on whether these firms are behaving in an ethical and socially responsible way, but we can agree on one point: Decisions made by individuals and organizations have outcomes we do not anticipate or plan for.

This chapter examines ethical and social issues in marketing. The objective is to open our minds to the issues confronting organizations conducting marketing activities and to understand, at least to some extent, how decisions are made. By gaining an understanding of what constitutes ethical and socially responsible behavior, each of you will be in a better position to make the best decision when confronted with an ethical dilemma.

THE NATURE AND IMPORTANCE OF MARKETING ETHICS

■ **marketing ethics** the moral evaluation of marketing activities and decisions as right or wrong on the basis of commonly accepted principles of behavior

The term *ethics* refers to principles of behavior that distinguish between good and bad, right and wrong.[2] In simple terms, **marketing ethics** is the moral evaluation of marketing activities and decisions as right or wrong. Marketing behavior is judged as ethical or unethical on the basis of commonly accepted principles of behavior established by the expectations of society, various interest groups, competitors, the organization's management, and individuals' personal moral values. Individuals decide how to behave on the basis of these principles, and the general public and various interest groups evaluate whether the actions are ethical.

Marketing ethics is ultimately a function of mutual trust among individuals and organizations. Although marketers often act in their own self-interest, the relationships among marketers, employees, and consumers must be grounded in trust—mutual confidence and reliance. An ethical violation makes continued trust in marketing exchanges difficult, if not impossible.[3] There are also significant costs resulting from unethical behavior in the form of reduced sales and loss of good will.[4] But despite the importance of ethics, several studies suggest that ethics is declining further. Surveys of Americans 18 to 30 years of age show that between 70 and 80 percent included false information on résumés.[5] Another study of college students reported that nearly 80 percent of the students surveyed thought that business ethics has

[2]Vern E. Henderson, "The Ethical Side of Enterprise," *Sloan Management Review*, Summer 1982, p. 8.
[3]Vernon R. Loucks, Jr., "A CEO Looks at Ethics," *Business Horizons*, March–April 1987, p. 4.
[4]Gene R. Laczniak and Patrick E. Murphy, "Fostering Ethical Marketing Decisions," *Journal of Business Ethics*, April 1991, pp. 259–271.
[5]Kenneth Labich, "The New Crisis in Business Ethics," *Fortune*, April 20, 1992, pp. 167–176.

MARKETING CLOSE-UP

An Ethical Dilemma at Bath Iron Works

Suppose you are a sales manager in charge of closing a big deal. If you make the sale, a raise and a promotion are guaranteed. If you fail, the promotion will go to a coworker who has had a better year. After meeting with the customer to make your sales presentation, you notice that a file folder has inadvertently been left in your office. Upon closer inspection, you find the folder contains a confidential report about your major competitor for this sale. At your fingertips is information that could help you put a final bid together that would beat the competition. What would you do?

William E. Haggett, CEO of Bath Iron Works in Maine, was confronted with this dilemma. After meeting with the navy in bidding for the Aegis destroyer, a vice president told Haggett that a confidential navy report had been found by a janitor in the firm's conference center. The report contained proprietary information, including cost data, about Bath Iron's chief competitor, Ingalls Shipyard.

Haggett ordered two vice presidents to photocopy the report and read it thoroughly. According to Haggett, "Later the same day we reflected upon our actions and concluded that it had been inappropriate for us to copy, retain, or even scan the document."

The report was returned to the navy that afternoon, and Haggett submitted a full report of his actions. He also gave a full report to the CEO of Ingalls. Admitting he had made a mistake, Haggett also resigned from day-to-day responsibility at the shipyard.

Many business ethicists applauded Haggett's behavior but said he had made an inexcusable ethical mistake. According to W. Michael Hoffman, director of the Center for Business Ethics at Bentley College, "Opening and reading the document was the same as opening and looking in someone's briefcase." And, Hoffman continues, "business ethics starts at the top and it is damaging to an entire company's morale when a leader does such a thing."

In the midst of an intensive bidding battle in the shrinking shipbuilding market, what Haggett did was clearly human. Few people, having looked at the report, would have admitted to error. Upon reflection, he knew he had made a mistake. Unfortunately, the man once considered a potential candidate for governor in 1994 will be remembered most for his breach of ethics.

Sources: Doug Bailey, "A Breach of . . . Ethics," *Boston Globe*, September 17, 1991, pp. 39, 49; and Paul Hemp, "What Would You Do?" *Boston Globe*, September 19, 1992, pp. 37, 39.

deteriorated over the years, and over 82 percent think the situation will get worse.[6]

Ethical considerations continue to capture the spotlight because of well-publicized cases of unethical practices in business, politics, sports, and even religion. These cases place individuals and organizations in a bad light and overshadow the many positive contributions that businesses make to society;

[6]Robert A. Peterson, Richard F. Beltramini, and George Kozmetsky, "Concerns of College Students Regarding Business Ethics: A Replication," *Journal of Business Ethics*, Volume 10, 1991, pp. 733–738.

ethical behavior often goes unnoticed, while unethical conduct receives a great deal of media attention. This is not to say that the media are unfair. Reporting on the thousands of ethical decisions individuals make daily is difficult if not impossible. The unethical decisions ultimately lead to negative consequences and thus are made public. Put another way, in all your years of school, have you ever been complimented for taking a test *without* cheating? Probably not. But the subject of cheating receives a lot of attention, despite the fact that most students refrain from cheating. Marketing Close-Up looks at how bad conduct often overshadows the good.

Although unethical behavior may seem to be proliferating, this is not the first period of time in which the ethical conduct of business firms has been highly criticized, and it's not likely to be the last. Unethical behavior on the part of bankers, industrialists, and others is documented throughout history. Adam Smith, in his famous book, *The Wealth of Nations,* wrote the following often-quoted lines: "It is not from the benevolence of the butcher, the brewer, or the banker, that we expect our dinner, but from their regard to their own self-interest. We address ourselves, not to their humanity but to their self-love, and never talk to them of our own necessities but of their advantages."[7] This quote expresses the moral contradiction of capitalism, in which morally questionable intentions combine to produce morally beneficial results.[8] In other words, businesses are not altruistic and are actually self-serving, but they provide needed goods and services that have improved our lives. We are perhaps no closer to resolving this moral contradiction today than Adam Smith was over two hundred years ago. But as Figure 4.1 illustrates, many companies such as Ford are concerned with the impact of their products on the environment.

UNDERSTANDING ETHICAL BEHAVIOR

One reason behind the numerous instances of unethical behavior is that businesses do not understand how people make decisions when faced with ethical dilemmas. Understanding how people form their ethical standards and what causes them to engage in unethical behavior may help businesses reduce unethical activities. Figure 4.2 presents a framework for understanding ethical behavior. As you can see, the marketing environment, personal moral philosophies, and organizational factors influence a person's ethical behavior.

The Marketing Environment

Every day, marketing managers face ethical issues arising from pressures of the marketing environment. In fact, more than two-thirds of corporate decision makers face constant pressure to compromise ethics in order to

---

[7] Adam Smith, *The Wealth of Nations* (New York: The Modern Library, 1937).
[8] David Vogel, "It's Not Nice to Fool Business Ethicists," *Business and Society Review,* Summer 1991, pp. 23–32.

FIGURE 4.1
Environmental Concerns
Although unethical decisions may receive more attention, many firms make decisions that show concern for society. For example, Ford is developing new products—such as cars with CFC-free air conditioning and electric vehicles—that are less harmful to the environment.

Source: Courtesy of Ford Motor Company.

"Environmental responsibility fuels our research."

Roberta J. Nichols, Ph.D
Ford Environmental Engineer

At Ford Motor Company, responsibility for the environment goes hand in hand with building quality cars and trucks. That's why we're already building vehicles that meet California's strict emission standards for the late 90's. It's also why we're the first U.S. manufacturer to build a car with CFC-free air conditioning and why we'll soon have a fleet of electric vehicles on the road. At Ford Motor Company, we take our responsibilities seriously.

QUALITY IS JOB 1. IT'S WORKING.

achieve organizational and personal goals.[9] To be a contender in today's fiercely competitive marketplace, marketing managers sometimes feel they need to lie or deceive. *Plagiarism,* the taking of someone else's work and representing it as one's own without the originator's consent, is one example. Chase Manhattan, a large New York bank, sued advertising agency J. Walter Thompson for copying an advertisement. The suit charged that J. Walter Thompson got ideas when competing with other agencies for Chase's $35 million global campaign and used them to develop advertisements for Northwestern Mutual Life Insurance Co.[10]

Another common ethical problem facing marketers is conflict of interest. A conflict of interest arises when an individual acts to further his or her own selfish concerns rather than the long-term interest of the organization or society. Although situations may differ across organizations, opportunities often arise to maximize personal welfare in a way that hurts others or the organization. For instance, when bribes—in the form of payments, gifts, or special favors—are offered to obtain new customers or satisfy existing customers, a conflict of interest occurs. Both the offerer of the bribe and the receiver of the bribe are placing their own selfish interests ahead of those of the organization and consumers. Even though bribes may benefit the

[9]Daniel E. Maltby, "The One-Minute Ethicist," *Christianity Today,* February 19, 1988, pp. 26–29.
[10]Laura Bird, "Thompson Is Named in Copycat Lawsuit," *Wall Street Journal,* July 13, 1992, p. B3.

FIGURE 4.2
Framework for Understanding Ethical Behavior

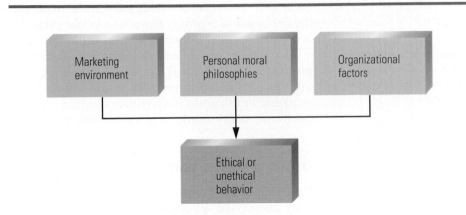

organization in the short run, they are generally illegal and may damage the firm in the long run. Bribes are often encountered by firms marketing products in foreign countries, and will be discussed further in the next chapter.

Communications, particularly in the form of advertising, may pose ethical problems in the marketing environment. False and deceptive advertising and personal selling tactics are unethical and result in consumer dissatisfaction. Manipulating communications and withholding information about the safety of products and pollution control are other examples of unethical communications activities. According to *Consumer Reports,* for instance, drug companies often engage journalists and spokespersons in unethical behavior by paying them to misinform consumers about the healing powers of certain drugs.[11]

To bring integrity and fairness into marketing exchanges, limit conflicts of interest, and eliminate deceptive communications, marketers must obey all applicable laws and regulations. Beyond complying with laws, however, marketing organizations are expected to not knowingly harm others through deception, misrepresentation, or coercion.

Personal Moral Philosophies

■ **moral philosophy** a set of principles that dictates the right and moral way to behave

■ **utilitarian philosophy** a moral philosophy that seeks the greatest satisfaction for the largest number of individuals

Along with pressures from the marketing environment, a person's moral philosophy also influences ethical behavior. A **moral philosophy** is a set of principles that dictates the right and moral way to behave. People learn these principles through their family, social groups, and formal education. Moral philosophies can be divided into two categories: utilitarian and humanistic.

People and organizations that adhere to the **utilitarian philosophy** seek the greatest satisfaction for the largest number of individuals. Whether a particular activity achieves the greatest good for the greatest number can be determined through a social cost-benefit analysis, in which the sum of all the

[11] "Miracle Drugs or Media Drugs?" *Consumer Reports,* March 1992, pp. 142–146.

costs of a particular action is subtracted from the sum of all the benefits. If the net result is positive, the action under consideration is considered ethical; if the net result is negative, the action is unethical.[12]

■ **humanistic philosophy** a moral philosophy that focuses on individual rights and values

In contrast, people and organizations following the **humanistic philosophy** focus on individual rights and values. A marketing organization adopting this philosophy honors its moral obligations to support customers' and workers' health and safety without regard for cost. If a product poses potential harm to any workers or customers, it is taken off the market.

Organizational Factors

Fundamentally, ethics is a series of individual decisions on how to react to daily issues. To an organization success is determined by achieving objectives, such as increased profits, market share, or safe products (see Figure 4.3). Whether a person achieves these objectives in an ethical or unethical manner is influenced by two organizational factors: interactions with significant others in the organization and opportunities to engage in unethical behavior.

Interaction with Others   Ethical behavior is often learned in the process of interacting with family, friends, and other social groups at work, church, school, and so on. Each of these groups has its own norms, values, and attitudes. The more that individuals witness ethical behavior in each of these groups, the greater the likelihood that they will behave ethically. Conversely, the more individuals are exposed to unethical behavior in these groups, the more likely they will be to behave unethically. In fact, an employee's perception of the ethics of peers and superiors in the organization is often a stronger predictor of behavior than is the individual's own system of moral and ethical values.[13] Thus, if an employee sees a coworker manipulate research data to generate a more favorable result, the employee is more likely to follow suit, even if he or she believes this action to be unethical.

■ **opportunity** a set of conditions that either limits unfavorable behavior or rewards favorable behavior

Opportunity   **Opportunity** is a set of conditions that either limits unfavorable behavior or rewards favorable behavior. Rewards may be internal (intangible feelings of goodness and worth derived from doing a favor for no reason) or external (tangible compensation received in exchange for providing a good, service, or idea). Humanistic philosophy focuses on rights and values relating to internal rewards; utilitarian philosophy emphasizes external rewards from peers or top management.

Many managers who behave unethically do so to gain power and money. When a person is rewarded, either internally or externally, or is not punished for acting unethically, he or she will probably repeat the behavior. But if the person receives no rewards or is punished for behaving unethically, he

---

[12]R. Eric Reidenbach and Donald P. Robin, *Ethics and Profits* (Englewood Cliffs, N.J.: Prentice-Hall, 1989), p. 69.
[13]O. C. Ferrell and Larry Gresham, "A Contingency Framework for Ethical Decision Making in Marketing," *Journal of Marketing*, Summer 1985, pp. 87–96.

FIGURE 4.3
Organizational Factors
Organizations can have many marketing objectives, including safety. As shown in this advertisement, a major focus of Saturn's marketing strategy is the safety of its automobiles.

Source: Courtesy of Saturn Corporation.

or she probably won't repeat the action. Thus the greater the rewards and the smaller the punishment for unethical behavior, the greater is the likelihood that unethical behavior will occur. The severity of the punishment for unethical behavior sends a message about the acceptability of such activities. The penalties received by individuals like Michael Milken and Ivan Boesky in highly publicized Wall Street trading scandals are often lenient, given the scope of the crimes. Such lenient sentences may not discourage other financial traders from behaving unethically.

ENCOURAGING ETHICAL BEHAVIOR

How can an organization encourage ethical behavior? Many businesses and universities are now offering courses and seminars in ethics. In addition to ethics education, codes of ethics and ethics-related corporate policies can be used to reduce unethical behavior in the workplace.[14] **Codes of ethics** are organization rules and policies that provide members with formal guidelines for professional conduct. By establishing corporate policies and codes of ethics, employers help employees to better understand what is expected of them. The enforcement of codes of ethics through rewards and punishments limits the opportunities to engage in unethical behavior, and thus should result in greater acceptance of ethical standards. Table 4.1 presents the American Marketing Association's (AMA) Code of Ethics, which AMA members

■ **codes of ethics** organization rules and policies that provide members with formal guidelines for professional conduct

[14] O. C. Ferrell and Steven J. Skinner, "Ethical Behavior and Bureaucratic Structure in Marketing Research Organizations," *Journal of Marketing Research*, February 1988, pp. 103–109.

TABLE 4.1
American Marketing
Association's Code
of Ethics

Members of the American Marketing Association (AMA) are committed to ethical professional conduct. They have joined together in subscribing to this Code of Ethics embracing the following topics:

Responsibilities of the Marketer
Marketers must accept responsibility for the consequences of their activities and make every effort to ensure that their decisions, recommendations, and actions function to identify, serve, and satisfy all relevant publics: consumers, organizations, and society.

Marketer's professional conduct must be guided by:

1. The basic rule of professional ethics: not knowingly to do harm
2. The adherence to all applicable laws and regulations
3. The accurate representation of their education, training, and experience
4. The active support, practice, and promotion of this Code of Ethics

Honesty and Fairness
Marketers shall uphold and advance the integrity, honor, and dignity of the marketing profession by:

1. Being honest in serving consumers, clients, employees, suppliers, distributors, and the public
2. Not knowlingly participating in conflict of interest without prior notice of all parties involved
3. Establishing equitable fee schedules including the payment or receipt of usual, customary, and/or legal compensation for marketing exchanges

Rights and Duties of Parties
Participation in the marketing exchange process should be able to expect that:

1. Products and services offered are safe and fit for their intended uses
2. Communications about offered products and services are not deceptive
3. All parties intend to discharge their obligations, financial and otherwise, in good faith
4. Appropriate internal methods exist for equitable adjustment and/or redress of grievances concerning purchase

It is understood that the above would include, *but is not limited to,* the following responsibilities of the marketer:

In an area of product development and management:
Disclosure of all substantial risks associated with product or service usage
Identification of any product component substitution that might materially change the product or impact on the buyer's purchase decision
Identification of extra-cost added features

(continued)

In the area of promotions:
Avoidance of false and misleading advertising
Rejection of high-pressure manipulations or misleading sales tactics
Avoidance of sales promotions that use deception or manipulation

In the area of distribution:
Not manipulating the availability of a product for purpose of exploitation
Not using coercion in the marketing channel
Not exerting undue influence over the resellers' choice to handle a product

In the area of pricing:
Not engaging in price fixing
Not practicing predatory pricing
Disclosing the full price associated with any purchase

In the area of marketing research:
Prohibiting selling or fund raising under the guise of conducting research
Maintaining research integrity by avoiding misrepresentation and omission
    of pertinent research data
Treating outside clients and suppliers fairly

Organizational Relationships
Marketers should be aware of how their behavior may influence or impact
on the behavior of others in organizational relationships. They should not
encourage or apply coercion to obtain unethical behavior in their relationships with others, such as employees, supplies, or customers

1. Apply confidentiality and anonymity in professional relationships with regard to privileged information
2. Meet their obligations and responsibilities in contracts and mutual agreements in a timely manner
3. Avoid taking the work of others, in whole or in part, and represent this
   work as their own or directly benefit from it without compensation or
   consent of the originator or owner
4. Avoid manipulation to take advantage of situations to maximize personal
   welfare in a way that unfairly deprives or damages the organization or
   others

Any AMA members found to be in violation of any provision of this Code
of Ethics may have his or her Association membership suspended or re-
voked.

Source: Reprinted by permission of the American Marketing Association.

agree to follow. Notice how responsibilities are outlined in the areas of product, promotion, distribution, pricing, and marketing research. The value of teaching ethics is the subject of Point/Counterpoint.

Recognizing the role of ethics codes and corporate policies in decision making, many organizations are establishing codes and policies to foster ethical decision making. But these codes must be enforced to be effective. Ninety percent of the firms in the financial services industry have a code of ethics, but only 30 percent have any ethics training in place.[15] Ethics codes, even with the support of top-level management, do not always guarantee ethical behavior.

Codes of ethics often stress certain issues, such as conflicts of interest and accurate record keeping, but place less emphasis on issues like product safety and personal character.[16] CILCORP, a public utility company in central Illinois, for example, includes the following statement in its code of ethics: "We must neither accept nor solicit any gifts, loans, advances, payments, finder's or agent's fees, services, kickbacks, rebates, privileges, or other favors from any business organization that sells or buys, or seeks to sell or buy, products or services to or from the company." The company's code of ethics says, among other things, "No employee ever helps the Company by acting unethically to achieve a desired result. There is no place in the Company for thinking that 'the end justifies the means.' Equally important, our actions should be perceived as ethical, adhering to both the spirit and letter of the law."[17]

Ethical behavior is also encouraged by *whistle-blowers,* individuals that disclose unethical activities within the organization. In some cases, whistle-blowers have been subject to harassment, demotion, and even being fired. On the other hand, some firms provide ethics hot lines so that employees can report unethical behavior without fear of punishment. It is estimated that more than one hundred companies have such hot lines. Raytheon Co., with 68,000 employees, says it fires about two people a month and disciplines several others based on tips from its hot line.[18] Under the False Claims Act, whistle-blowers can receive up to 25 percent of the fine that results from their tips.[19] Some critics say that the use of hot lines to encourage whistle-blowing at times results in a damaging investigation of the caller.

A person can evaluate a specific behavior by asking others in the organization or industry if they approve of it or by checking to see if there is a specific company policy on the activity. The practice of an activity by members of an organization, however, does not in itself make the activity ethical. During the Oliver North trial, Judge Gerhard Gesell told the jury, "A person's general impression that a type of conduct was expected, that it was proper

[15] Gary Edwards, "Banking Ethics Today," *Ethics Journal,* September–October 1991, pp. 1, 4.

[16] M. Cash Matthews, "Codes of Ethics: Organizational Behavior and Misbehavior," in *Research in Corporate Social Performance and Policy,* ed. William C. Frederick (Greenwich, Conn.: JAI Press, 1987), pp. 107–130.

[17] *CILCORP Code of Ethics,* CILCORP Inc.

[18] Joan E. Rigdon, "Tipsters Telephoning Ethics Hotlines Can End Up Sabotaging Their Own Jobs," *Wall Street Journal,* August 27, 1992, pp. B1, B4.

[19] Lisa Driscoll, "A Better Way to Handle Whistle-Blowers: Let Them Speak," *Business Week,* July 27, 1992, p. 36.

POINT/COUNTERPOINT

Can Ethics Be Taught?

Long before they graduate and take jobs, students are faced with ethical dilemmas. Should I copy answers to the test from the student in front of me? Others in the class are cheating and the instructor isn't paying close attention. Once individuals are working for an organization, the choices get even tougher. Should I take credit for that terrific idea I got from a coworker? My boss pads the expense account, so why shouldn't I? In some organizations, it may seem as though behaving unethically is the only way to get ahead. Many organizations realize this problem and are trying to instill ethical values in their employees.

Point Many companies are adding ethics to training programs. At Boeing, for instance, line managers lead ethics training seminars. Colleges and universities also are adding ethics courses to their curriculum. In 1987, former Securities and Exchange Commission chairman John Shad gave the Harvard Business School $20 million to develop and teach courses in ethics. Today Harvard requires all MBAs to take a nine-session course on ethics and offers three ethics electives.

The primary function of courses on business ethics is to teach students how to analyze managerial dilemmas. Emphasis is placed on understanding why decision makers behave as they do, not on teaching ethical principles or morals. By looking at the various factors that influence marketing decisions—individual beliefs and values, pressure from peers and managers, and opportunity—students can understand why a person becomes involved in an insider trader scandal, for example. Once they are out in the working world, students can apply this understanding if they face similar ethical dilemmas.

Counterpoint Ethics is not something that can be taught. The moral standards of individuals have been developed long before they enter school or begin a career. Families, friends, schools, churches, and other social experiences shape a person's moral fiber. Values are tested when a person begins a job and is faced with ethical dilemmas. It would be difficult for a course in ethics to change deep-rooted, long-held values. People with a strong moral foundation are more likely to behave ethically; people without such values are more inclined to behave unethically.

Many signs point to changing moral values in America. Increases in crime, drug abuse, alcoholism, as well as the growing number of scandals in business and government, indicate a shift in fundamental values in our society. What is needed is a new direction in the lives of individuals. A course in ethics cannot be expected to accomplish such a task.

because others were doing the same, or that the . . . act would help someone avoid political consequences, does not satisfy the defense of authorization."[20] In other words, the conduct of others does not authorize a person to act in the same way. Ultimately, each individual is responsible for his or her actions. Table 4.2 presents a short test that can help a person determine whether decisions are ethical.

[20]Fred Kaplan, "North Trial Goes to Jury; Bush Silent on His Role," *Boston Globe*, April 21, 1989, pp. 1, 12.

TABLE 4.2
A Short Test to Determine
if Decisions Are Ethical

1. **Is the decision legal?**
   If the answer is no, stop here.

2. **Is the decision fair?**
   If the decision is not fair to all parties involved, it could be unethical.

3. **How will the decision make me feel about myself?**
   Unethical decisions generally induce feelings of uneasiness or guilt, and when they are made public, bring about shame and humiliation.

SOCIAL RESPONSIBILITY

■ **social responsibility**
the conscious effort by an organization to maximize its positive impact and minimize its negative impact on society

Society expects businesses to act as responsible members of the social community as well as to provide goods and services efficiently.[21] **Social responsibility** is the conscious effort by an organization to maximize its positive impact and minimize its negative impact on society as a whole and on various groups and individuals within society. Although social responsibility may sound like an abstract ideal, it is an important part of the relationship between business organizations and society. Society expects businesses to make a profit. But society also expects businesses to obey laws, to be ethical, and to be good corporate citizens.[22] This pyramid of social responsibility is shown in Figure 4.4.

Most companies today consider the costs incurred for social responsibility as investments that require planning. They try to anticipate what actions will be perceived by society as socially responsible and direct current resources toward meeting those expectations.[23] For instance, Stone Container Corp., for over a decade, has been involved in forest preservation. The firm's experimental farm in Costa Rica, where tropical forests have shrunk by 80 percent during the past fifty years, will be producing 600,000 tons of pulpwood annually by 1995. These young forests absorb more carbon dioxide than older forests, emit more oxygen into the atmosphere, and provide jobs and opportunity for the Costa Rican economy.[24] After Hurricane Andrew left parts of Florida devastated, dozens of businesses pledged financial aid and

[21] Keith Davis and William C. Frederick, *Business and Society: Management, Public Policy, and Ethics,* 5th ed. (New York: McGraw-Hill, 1984), pp. 41–42.
[22] Archie B. Carroll, "The Pyramid of Corporate Responsibility: Toward the Moral Management of Organizational Stakeholders," *Business Horizons,* July–August 1991, pp. 39–48.
[23] Margaret A. Stroup and Ralph L. Neubert, "The Evolution of Societal Responsibility," *Business Horizons,* March–April 1987, pp. 22–24.
[24] James Cook, "New Growth," *Forbes,* June 8, 1992, pp. 109–110.

FIGURE 4.4
The Pyramid of Social Responsibility

Source: Adapted from Archie B. Carroll, "The Pyramid of Corporate Social Responsibility: Toward the Moral Management of Organizational Stakeholders." Reprinted from *Business Horizons,* July–August 1991, p. 42. Copyright 1991 by the Foundation for the School of Business at Indiana University. Used with permission.

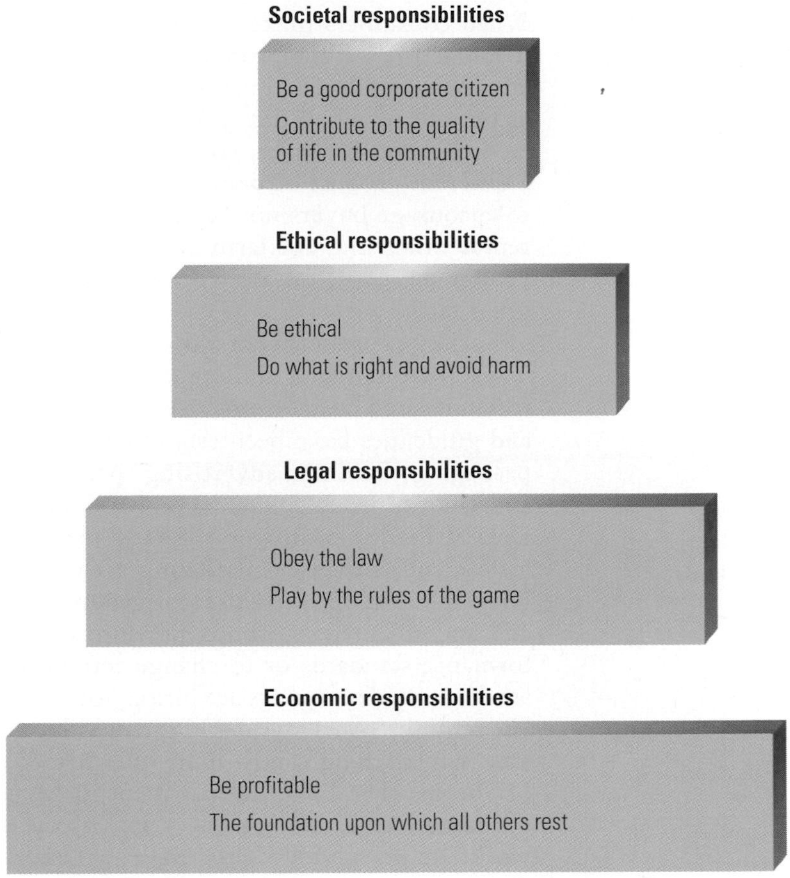

Societal responsibilities

Be a good corporate citizen
Contribute to the quality of life in the community

Ethical responsibilities

Be ethical
Do what is right and avoid harm

Legal responsibilities

Obey the law
Play by the rules of the game

Economic responsibilities

Be profitable
The foundation upon which all others rest

donations of food and supplies to victims. Some firms also helped employees get back on their feet by paying them even as the stores they worked in were closed for repairs.[25]

To be successful, an organization must determine what customers, employees, government regulators, and competitors, as well as society in general, want in terms of social responsibility. It must also monitor changes in these expectations. Today, consumers are asking retailers for car-care products that do not harm the environment. This has meant a boom for Turtle Wax, Inc., which has been selling only biodegradable products packaged in recyclable containers for over twenty years.[26] As consumers' expectations changed, Turtle Wax was already in a position to give them what they were looking for in a product.

[25] Jeffrey Trachtenberg and Laurie M. Grossman, "Firms Offer More than Tea and Sympathy After Andrew," *Wall Street Journal,* September 4, 1992, p. B1.
[26] Joe Schwartz, "Turtle Wax Shines Water, Too," *American Demographics,* April 1992, p. 14.

Societal Expectations

When consumers make a purchase, they cast a vote for the product and its manufacturer. If the product is priced fairly, satisfies their needs, and has no adverse side effects, consumers will continue to vote for it by purchasing it again and again. If the product is of low quality or harms them or the environment, however, consumers will probably vote against it by selecting a different product or brand. In some cases, groups have organized boycotts to encourage buyers not to purchase a certain product. For instance, groups representing migrant farm workers have organized boycotts of produce to protest the poor, unsafe working conditions and low wages offered to migrant farm workers.

Society expresses what it does not want from marketers in several different ways. Through laws and regulatory groups, it attempts to prohibit and control undesired business practices. As discussed in Chapter 3, a number of laws and guidelines have been established to regulate product safety, warranties, packaging, labeling, advertising, personal selling, pricing, and competitive and environmental issues. The Food and Drug Administration (FDA), the Federal Trade Commission (FTC), and other federal, state, and local regulatory agencies oversee marketing activities and enforce the laws and guidelines. In addition to these legal groups, nongovernmental regulatory forces and special interest groups pressure organizations to achieve desired performance standards or to change certain ongoing activities. In many states, small candy distributors are hiring young children to sell candy door-to-door late at night. An 11-year-old girl was hit and killed by a car in Washington state while selling candy alone on a school night at 10 P.M., 160 miles from her home. The Labor Department in Miami fined Burger King $500,000, the largest child labor penalty in history, for letting 14- and 15-year-olds work late on school nights; the Fair Labor Standards Act of 1938 prohibits children this age from working after 7 P.M.[27]

Many companies operate within legal guidelines established for the safety of our society. However, minimum compliance with laws and regulations is not always enough. Firms that are truly concerned with social responsibility often voluntarily engage in activities that maintain or improve the well-being of society. Such organizations benefit in the long run by building a relationship of trust and respect with their employees, customers, and society in general. Several organizations, including Adolf Coors, Exxon, General Motors, GTE, and Motorola, have developed corporate literacy programs to help individuals prepare for jobs that require greater skills benefitting the individual, the company, and society at large.[28]

Corporations throughout the world meet society's needs in many ways, thereby adopting the societal marketing concept. Large and small firms alike contribute to the arts, support public television, build parks, provide comput-

---

[27] Brian Dumaine, "Illegal Child Labor Comes Back," *Fortune,* April 5, 1993, pp. 86–95.
[28] Troy Segal, Karen Thurston, and Lynn Haessly, "When Johnny's Whole Family Can't Read," *Business Week,* July 20, 1992, pp. 68–70.

ers for schools, and sponsor social programs to help the disadvantaged. Mobil Corporation, for example, provides a grant that supports *Masterpiece Theatre* on the Public Broadcasting System. Kroger has provided free computers to schools that have saved $250,000 worth of grocery receipts. Lederle Laboratories, a pharmaceutical manufacturer, has established an $11 million program to provide antibiotics for homeless people and to fund the development of health care programs. The McDonald's Ronald McDonald House has developed learning centers for the handicapped. Martin Marietta helps to support the Academy for Teachers of Science and Math at the University of Tennessee, as shown in Figure 4.5. Many other companies meet the needs of society by contributing to charities, by participating in local organizations like Rotary and Kiwanis, and by encouraging employees to share their knowledge with their communities.

Consumerism

■ **consumerism** all the activities undertaken by independent individuals, groups, and organizations to protect their rights as consumers

Consumerism consists of all the activities undertaken by independent individuals, groups, and organizations to protect their rights as consumers. Consumerism originated as a force in the United States and has evolved through several phases. The rapid industrial growth between 1870 and 1900 gave rise to many undesirable conditions, such as long working hours, low pay, false advertising, and the sale of unsafe food and drugs. Books like Upton Sinclair's *The Jungle,* an exposé of the meat-packing industry, documented shocking conditions in many industries. As a result, the Consumers' League was formed in New York City, and other groups were soon organized

FIGURE 4.5
Societal Expectations
Martin Marietta, through its support of the Academy for Teachers of Science and Math, helps teachers to master their craft. By helping teachers, Martin Marietta is meeting society's need for quality education, thus adopting the societal marketing concept.

Source: Martin Marietta Corporation.

throughout the United States. The consumer movement grew rapidly during the 1920s and 1930s and product safety once again came under fire. Consumer groups such as the Better Business Bureau became more effective, and independent testing firms like Consumer's Research were created. Courses in high school, such as home economics, began to emphasize consumer rights. In the 1960s, interest in consumer issues was renewed as product safety and environmental concerns fueled the growth of consumerism. Consumer advocates like Ralph Nader pointed out many abuses by "big business." During this period, President John F. Kennedy declared that consumers have basic rights that must be protected.

Many goals of those involved in the consumer movement today have a foundation in John F. Kennedy's consumer "bill of rights." Kennedy's bill covered four areas: the right to safety, the right to be informed, the right to choose, and the right to be heard. These four rights became the basis of much of the consumer legislation passed over the last three decades.

The Right to Safety   The right to safety means that a product must be safe for its intended use, include thorough and explicit directions for use, and have been tested properly to ensure reliability and quality. Society expects marketing organizations to not knowingly sell any product that could result in personal injury or harm, and it wants unsafe products modified or removed from the market. Products that are defective or dangerous damage public confidence in a company's ability to serve society. For instance, consumers have become concerned with electromagnetic fields and their possible link to cancer, reducing the public's confidence in utility companies and certain products such as cellular phones and electric blankets.[29] Although the evidence linking electromagnetic fields to cancer is not conclusive, many industries have yet to address public fear in a convincing manner. The cellular phone industry is spending over $1 million on research, but only to validate the findings of existing studies which have found cellular phones to be safe.[30] Companies have made great strides in providing safer products. Automobiles, appliances, children's toys, and many other products are safer today than they once were. Product packages have also been made more tamper-resistant. But instances of chemicals found in foods, such as apples treated with Alar (a chemical linked to cancer) or Perrier water with traces of benzene (a dangerous chemical used in cleaning fluids), illustrates that even more progress is needed to ensure safe products.

The Right to Be Informed   The right to be informed gives consumers the freedom to review all information about a product before purchasing it. Consumers today are able to make more informed decisions than ever before. Society expects manufacturers to print detailed information about ingredients

[29] Bill Richards, "Electric Utilities Brace for Cancer Lawsuits Though Risk Is Unclear," *Wall Street Journal,* February 5, 1993, pp. A1, A8.
[30] David Kirkpatrick, "Do Cellular Phones Cause Cancer?" *Fortune,* March 8, 1993, pp. 82–89.

and instructions for use on labels and packages so that consumers know how to use the product and what it is made of. This right to be informed extends to services. Financial services, for example, must clearly state in a contract the true cost of borrowing money or repayment terms so that consumers can understand the credit purchase. Prudential–Bache Securities Inc. has been sued by hundreds of investors for failing to disclose potential conflicts of interest and the risk involved in the sale of limited partnerships. The firm has already lost millions of dollars and is being investigated by the Securities and Exchange Commission.[31]

The Right to Choose   The right to choose means that consumers have the opportunity to purchase a variety of products and services at competitive prices. Consumers also expect satisfactory quality and service at a fair price. Competition should be free to thrive without one company becoming so powerful that consumers do not have the opportunity to seek out new, improved products that provide better value. Many people fear that the increasing number of mergers of major companies may jeopardize consumers' right to choose. As a result of recent mergers in the consumer food products industry, for example, consumers may end up having fewer alternatives, paying higher prices, and receiving lower-quality service than they would if more competitors were available to serve them.

The Right to Be Heard   The right to be heard guarantees that consumer interests will be fully considered in the formation of government policy and in the fair treatment of consumers who have complaints about a purchased product. Consumer advocates like Ralph Nader apprise lawmakers and regulators about consumer concerns and problems. Many trade groups have been organized to process consumer grievances so that consumers can take an appeal beyond a company if they are unable to resolve a complaint through internal action. Most marketers recognize that one highly dissatisfied customer can have a significant negative impact on their reputations in the community. Therefore, they try to resolve consumer dissatisfaction and complaints. Many manufacturers provide a toll-free telephone number, often printed on the package or product, to help consumers resolve problems.

Ecology

■ **ecology** the study of the relationship between living things and their environment

Consumers are not the only ones with rights. Unfortunately, many individuals and businesses alike have yet to come to an understanding of the delicate balance between the earth's inhabitants and our natural surroundings. **Ecology** is the study of the relationship between living things and their environment.[32] More than sixty years ago, in his classic book *Economic Control of*

---

[31] Chuck Hawkins and Leah Nathan Spino, "Pru Securities Isn't Secure Yet," *Business Week,* September 7, 1992, pp. 82–84.
[32] Frederick D. Sturdivant, *Business and Society* (Homewood, Ill.: Richard D. Irwin, 1981), p. 119.

■ **pollution** the contamination of water, air, and land

Quality Manufactured Product, Walter Shewhart stressed concern for the environment in the design of new products. Managers, he pointed out, must attempt to make decisions that minimize the negative impact of business operations on the natural environment.[33] Table 4.3 shows how the public perceives environmental problems in the United States.

One vital concern we are faced with today is **pollution,** the contamination of water, air, and land. Water pollution is caused by the dumping of toxic chemicals, sewage, and garbage into rivers and streams. Toxins and pollutants can also find their way into underground water supplies. Environmental laws such as the Water Quality Improvement Act of 1970 and the Water Pollution Control Act Amendment of 1972 regulate pesticides, but prosecutions have been rare. Although the earth's water is in abundance, millions of Americans have unsafe water supplies; by the year 2000, water supplies will be severely inadequate in 17 of 106 U.S. water supply regions.[34] Many areas of the world, including Japan, Russia and the other states of the former Soviet Union, Brazil, and India, are experiencing water pollution.

Air pollution is caused by carbon monoxide and hydrocarbons that come from motor vehicles and by smoke and other pollutants from manufacturing plants. The Clean Air Act of 1970 and the Clean Air Act Amendment of 1977 provide stringent emission standards for automobiles, airplanes, and factories. But even though much progress has been made in fighting air pollution, the majority of the world's inhabitants breathe contaminated air. In addition, many scientists fear that the earth's ozone layer, which shields the planet from the sun's deadly ultraviolet rays, is being destroyed. Evidence of this threat is stronger than ever. The National Aeronautics and Space Administration, along with scientists from several institutions, recently completed a study of the earth's atmosphere. They reported that the ozone layer over some regions, including the northernmost parts of the United States, Canada, Europe, and Russia, is temporarily depleted by as much as 50 percent.[35]

Land pollution results from strip-mining of coal and minerals, forest fires, garbage disposal, and dumping of industrial wastes. Congress created the Superfund in 1980 to help clean up polluted land. The Resource Conservation and Recovery Act of 1984 requires federal regulation of potentially dangerous solid waste disposal. But land pollution remains a major problem. Landfills are filling up at an ever-increasing rate. Land pollution also leads to water pollution because toxic wastes drain into water supplies. Sulphur dioxide pumped into the air by manufacturing and power plants mixes with air, creating rain with a high acid content (or *acid rain*), which also damages forests and lakes. Of the 6,750,000 square miles of the earth's original forests, only about 40 percent remains. Global forest destruction extends from the

---

[33] Walter A. Shewhart, *Economic Control of Quality Manufactured Product* (New York: D. Van Nostrand, 1931).
[34] Jeanne McDowell and Richard Woodbury, "A Fight over Liquid Gold," *Time,* July 22, 1991, p. 26.
[35] Michael D. Lemonick, "The Ozone Vanishes," *Time,* February 17, 1992, pp. 60–63.

TABLE 4.3
How the Public Ranks the United States's Environmental Problems

Problem	Percent of Respondents Ranking Problem as Serious
Water pollution from waste products of manufacturing plants	77
Oil spillage from tankers	77
Environmental contamination from chemical waste disposal	75
Air pollution from industrial plants and factories	74
Destruction of the ozone layer	69
Contaminated drinking water	67
Environmental contamination from nuclear waste disposal	67
Air pollution from auto exhaust	62
Acid rain	60
Landfills for garbage disposal from household and industry	58
Worker exposure to toxic chemicals	56
Water pollution caused by sewage from homes and offices	53
Radiation from nuclear power plants	52
Pesticide residues on food eaten by humans	51
The "greenhouse effect"	49
Litter of streets, parks, highways, and the countryside	44
Indoor air pollution	32
Strip mining of coal, iron, copper	30
Radiation from X-rays, microwave ovens, etc.	26

Source: "The Environment: Public Attitudes and Individual Behavior," a public opinion study by the Roper Organization, commissioned by S.C. Johnson & Son Inc., 1990. Reprinted by permission.

U.S. Pacific Northwest to the tropical forests of Brazil and Malaysia.[36] If forests are not managed properly, commercial timber harvesting, fuel source use, and cattle ranching threaten to destroy forests even further. In addition, deforestation contributes to soil loss, which exceeds new soil formation by over 25 billion tons annually.

Individuals, business firms, the government, and special interest groups are trying to solve these problems. Many products and containers can be

[36] Nancy C. Morey and Robert V. Morey, "Business and the Environment in the 21st Century," *Business Forum,* Winter 1992, pp. 51–55.

recycled, slowing the need for more and bigger landfills. Some firms, in addition to making products that can be recycled, educate consumers and encourage them to recycle. Figure 4.6 shows how Amway supports environmental education. A major refiner in Houston, Lyondell Petrochemical, has started making gasoline from used motor oil.[37] The U.S. and Mexican governments are working together on the pollution problem inside Mexico's border with the United States, where some factories burn tires for fuel; the region has been described by the American Medical Association as a "virtual cesspool."[38] Economists working for the United Nations and the Environmental Defense Fund are trying to link countries with vastly different economies and environmental laws into a single pollution-control system.[39] These are just a few examples, and the results may seem small in comparison to the size of the problem, but they represent steps in the right direction. It will take the ongoing participation of every individual and firm and cooperation from the governments of all nations to reverse the current threats to the environment.

Green Marketing

More than 100 million people took part in Earth Day 1990 on April 22, kicking off what many have called "the decade of the environment." Although many firms openly embrace environmentalism, they are learning that to be considered an environmentalist requires moving beyond the law and ahead of the industry.[40] Danger exists at two levels: (1) damage to local environments, such as from toxic waste dumping, which leaves the earth unable to support living organisms, and (2) damage to global systems of climate, atmosphere protection, and food resources that are breaking down as a result of pollution.[41] As the previous section pointed out, global systems already in danger include the ozone layer, the rain forests, and topsoil.

■ **green marketing** developing products and packages that are less harmful to the environment

As noted in Chapter 3, **green marketing** involves developing products and packages that are less harmful to the environment. Green marketing includes many areas ranging from conservation to control of pollution. For example, Pacific Gas & Electric has joined with environmental groups to develop energy conservation programs. Du Pont pulled out of a $750-million-a-year business because it might have harmed the environment. Many companies, like McDonald's, have become proponents of recycling. And large companies, such as Procter & Gamble Co., are developing product

[37]Caleb Solomon, "Refiner Begins Making Gasoline from Used Oil," *Wall Street Journal,* February 11, 1992, pp. B1–B2.

[38]Dianna Solis and Sonia L. Nazario, "U.S., Mexico Take on Border Pollution, *Wall Street Journal,* February 25, 1992, pp. B1, B8.

[39]Jeffrey Taylor, "New Rules Harness Power of Free Markets to Curb Air Pollution," *Wall Street Journal,* April 14, 1992, pp. A1, A4.

[40]Art Kleiner, "What Does It Mean to Be Green?" *Harvard Business Review,* July–August 1991, pp. 38–47.

[41]James E. Post, "Managing As If the Earth Mattered," *Business Horizons,* July–August 1991, pp. 32–38.

FIGURE 4.6

Environmental Education
In this advertisement Amway promotes the fact that many of its distributors are involved in activities that help the environment, Amway is one of many organizations that support environmental conservation.

Source: Courtesy of Creative Resources, a division of Amway Corporation.

containers that are less damaging to the environment. As Figure 4.7 shows, many consumers look specifically for products with green labeling, and this trend is expected to increase.

Corporations that excel in green marketing will benefit from better relations with customers, regulators, suppliers, and other firms in their industry.[42] Firms that choose to ignore the environment face loss of profits and market share. Although this is difficult to prove, most experts agree that as environmental regulations are tightened, forward thinking today will pay off tomorrow. That is why 3M decided to comply with a new federal regulation for underground storage tanks by 1992, when compliance was not required until 1998. Many firms are finding that the longer they wait to deal with current—or future—regulations, the more it costs. In short, firms are realizing that green marketing adds to the bottom line.

To have a successful green marketing program, a company must have the commitment of top management, as well as an internal environment that encourages employees to act as environmentalists. Some companies have established new positions, such as vice president of environment, health, and safety. Others reward employees for reducing waste or developing new products that are less harmful to the environment. But green marketing can

[42]Todd L. Hooper and Bart T. Rocca, "Environmental Affairs: Now on the Strategic Agenda," *Journal of Business Strategy,* May–June 1991, pp. 26–30.

FIGURE 4.7
Do Consumers Look for Green Labeling?

Source: *Marketing News,* September 16, 1991, p. 8. Reprinted by permission.

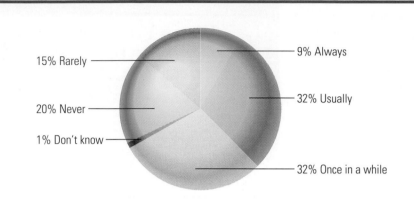

15% Rarely

9% Always

20% Never

32% Usually

1% Don't know

32% Once in a while

also be abused by firms that are not socially responsible. The popularity of environmentally sound products has led to concerns that firms may make exaggerated claims about products to show their concern for the environment. Thus some firms are learning that rhetoric is not enough. California, New York, and Rhode Island, for instance, recently passed laws limiting what marketers can say about the environmental benefits of their products.[43]

As individuals become more committed to the environment, green products will gain a competitive edge. But because environmental claims have been used to mislead consumers, some firms are finding it difficult to successfully launch a green marketing program. In addition, in some cases consumers have not responded well to green products because of the confusing language that surrounds the products.[44] Terms such as *recyclable, recycled, degradable, biodegradable, environmentally friendly,* and *ozone safe* are examples of claims that are confusing. Successful green marketing requires being as precise as possible to enable consumers to understand the claims made in the message.[45] Phrases like "this product contains 60 percent recycled material" should be used rather than "friendly to the environment." And if a package cannot be recycled, manufacturers should not call it recyclable.

As a result of all this, some firms have retreated from making environmental claims about their products, even though they continue to develop products and packages that are better for the environment. Part of the reason is that firms do not know which claims violate which state laws; to date, there are no federal standards regulating green marketing.[46] Price is also a big concern, since green products typically cost more than competing brands, sometimes considerably more.[47] Consumers prefer green products when they are readily available and their price and quality are similar to that of other products. But even environmentally conscious people will balk at paying

[43] Mark Landler, Zachary Schiller, and Tim Smart, "Suddenly Green Marketers Are Seeing Red Flags," *Business Week,* February 25, 1991, pp. 74–76.
[44] Carl Frankel, "Blueprint for Green Marketing," *American Demographics,* April 1992, pp. 34–38.
[45] Debra Aho, "Be Precise; Don't Overstate Claims," *Advertising Age,* June 29, 1992, pp. 5–6.
[46] Jennifer Lawrence, "Marketers Drop 'Recycled,'" *Advertising Age,* March 9, 1992, pp. 1, 48.
[47] Valerie Reitman, "'Green' Product Sales Seem to Be Wilting," *Wall Street Journal,* May 18, 1992, p. B1.

quite a bit more for green products. Despite these problems, many believe that in the long run companies that demonstrate concern for the environment will be rewarded.

EVALUATING SOCIAL RESPONSIBILITY

Marketing practices are generally evaluated in terms of effective results and socially acceptable consequences. They are judged by diverse special interest groups, each of which has its own set of criteria. Figure 4.8 lists the concerns of various groups that evaluate marketing activities. A socially responsible marketer acknowledges that feedback from all these public and private groups should be carefully considered. Because these groups can and do speak out against organizations, their actions can have a strong impact on a firm's future. For instance, if a marketer engages in unfair trade practices, its competitors may complain to the Federal Trade Commission, which has the power to bring charges against the marketer for violating the provisions of the Sherman, Clayton, and Federal Trade Commission acts. If special interest groups believe that a marketer's activities are not socially responsible, they may organize a boycott of the firm's products. When some consumers became unhappy with Nestlé's aggressive marketing practices in promoting infant formulas in Third World nations, they organized a worldwide boycott

FIGURE 4.8
Concerns of Groups That Evaluate Marketing Decisions

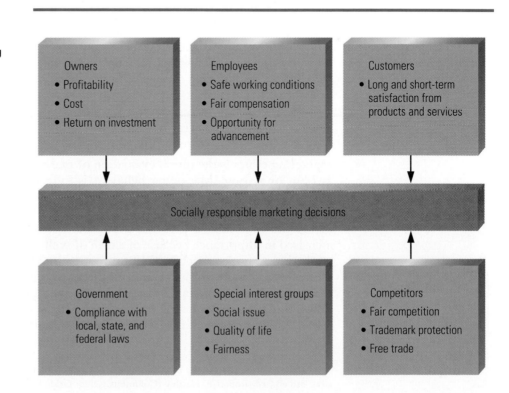

of all products made by Nestlé and its subsidiaries. Only when Nestlé agreed to halt its aggressive tactics did the boycott come to an end.[48]

Many organizations evaluate their social responsibility activities through the use of a **social audit**—a systematic examination of the firm's objectives, strategies, and performance of social responsibility activities. The social audit looks at the company's long- and short-term contributions to society. Much like a marketing audit helps marketers evaluate whether marketing strategies and plans are working effectively, the social audit helps firms determine whether social responsibility activities and strategies are leading to the achievement of organizational and marketing objectives. An audit can also help marketing managers determine future social responsibility activities. Socially responsible organizations should conduct social audits on a regular basis to show where the company has been and to develop a plan to direct its activities in the future.

■ **social audit** the systematic examination of a firm's objectives, strategies, and performance of social responsibility activities

The social audit consists of five steps:

1. Identify current and new programs that support social responsibility causes or issues.
2. Determine the resources required to support the programs and the benefits achieved to date.
3. Identify organizational objectives and make certain that the social responsibility activities support them.
4. Define the reasons for undertaking particular programs or for supporting certain causes.
5. Evaluate the success of each social responsibility program undertaken, and establish goals for future involvement.

Social audits are designed to occur somewhat informally. Few black-and-white standards are available for evaluating social responsibility actions.

SUMMARY

Marketing ethics is the moral evaluation of marketing activities and decisions as right or wrong. Marketing behavior is judged to be ethical or unethical on the basis of commonly accepted principles established by the expectations of society, various interest groups, competitors, the organization's management, and individual's personal moral values. Ethical considerations have increased in importance because of a rash of well-publicized cases of unethical marketing activities. Such behavior can often be attributed to a lack of understanding of how people develop moral philosophies.

Ethical decision making is influenced by the marketing environment, personal moral philosophies, and organizational factors. Marketing managers face ethical issues arising from pressures of the marketing environment. Some

---

[48]"Nestlé's Infant Formula: The Consequences of Spurning the Public Image," in *Marketing Mistakes,* 3rd ed., ed. Robert F. Hartley (Columbus, Ohio: Grid, 1986), pp. 47–61.

of these issues relate to maintaining honesty and fairness in marketing activities, avoiding conflicts of interest, and ensuring that all communications are complete and accurate. A moral philosophy is a set of principles that dictates the right and moral way to behave. The utilitarian philosophy seeks the greatest satisfaction for the largest number of people; the humanistic philosophy focuses on individual rights and values. Organizational factors such as interactions with significant others and opportunities to engage in unethical behavior also influence ethical behavior. The more that people witness unethical behavior in their closest social groups, and the greater the rewards and the smaller the punishment for such behavior, the greater is the likelihood that they will behave unethically.

Organizations can encourage ethical behavior by incorporating formal codes of ethics into the organizational structure. By establishing corporate policies and codes of ethics, employers can help employees better understand what is expected of them. Through rewards and punishments, employers can limit employees' opportunities to engage in unethical behavior.

Social responsibility is the conscious effort by a firm to maximize its positive impact and minimize its negative impact on society. Companies today view the costs of social responsibility as investments. They try to anticipate what actions will be perceived as socially responsible and direct resources toward meeting the expectations of society.

Society expects businesses to act as responsible members of the social community as well as to provide goods and services efficiently. Consumerism is all the activities undertaken by independent individuals, groups, and organizations to protect their rights as consumers. It includes the rights specified in John F. Kennedy's consumer "bill of rights": the right to safety, the right to be informed, the right to choose, and the right to be heard. Ecology is the study of the relationship between living things and their environment. One of the major ecological problems today is the pollution of water, air, and land. Socially responsible firms and individuals attempt to minimize pollution, and they take remedies to correct existing problems. Green marketing, developing products that are less harmful to the environment, is another way in which firms can demonstrate social responsibility. Marketing practices are generally evaluated by diverse special interest groups in terms of effective results and socially acceptable consequences.

Many organizations evaluate their social responsibility activities through the use of a social audit—a systematic examination of the firm's objectives, strategies, and performance of social responsibility activities.

KEY TERMS

marketing ethics	social responsibility
moral philosophy	consumerism
utilitarian philosophy	ecology
humanistic philosophy	pollution
opportunity	green marketing
codes of ethics	social audit

QUESTIONS FOR DISCUSSION AND REVIEW

1. What is marketing ethics? Why is it important?

2. How might the marketing environment influence a marketing manager to behave unethically?

3. Where do individuals develop moral philosophies? Distinguish between the utilitarian and humanistic moral philosophies.

4. How do interaction with others and opportunity influence individuals to behave unethically?

5. How can codes of ethics be used to increase ethical behavior?

6. What is social responsibility? What types of actions demonstrate that a firm is socially responsible?

7. Describe the relationship between marketers and society. How can marketers meet the needs of society?

8. What rights are included in the consumer "bill of rights"? Explain each.

9. What is ecology? What are some of the current dangers to our environment?

10. Who is responsible for protecting and preserving the environment? Can the current trend of environmental damage be reversed?

11. How can green marketing help the environment? What are some of the barriers to a successful green marketing program?

12. How can the social audit be used to evaluate a firm's contribution to social responsibility?

CASES

4.1 DOW CORNING'S PRODUCT LIABILITY NIGHTMARE

Until early 1992, breast implants represented a $90 million market. Dow Corning Corp., of Midland, Michigan, was a major manufacturer of silicone breast implants. Since the mid-1970s, 600,000 women have received silicone implants made by Dow Corning. Although some recipients chose implantation as part of reconstruction after breast cancer surgery, about 80 percent opted to enlarge their breasts for purely cosmetic reasons.

But questions about the safety of silicone gel implants began to arise as women reported that implants erupted or leaked inside the body and caused health damage. Lawsuits bombarded implant makers, especially Dow Corning. In December 1991, a San Francisco jury agreed with an implant recipient that Dow Corning knowingly sold her a defective implant. The woman, whose suit said that leaking silicone had damaged her immune system, was awarded $7.3 million. Although the only previous verdict against the company was in 1984, for $1.7 million, Dow Corning has been quietly settling several cases. Considering the number of outstanding suits claiming that the manufacturer hid the health risks of its silicone gel implants, the damages could cost Dow Corning hundreds of millions of dollars—against a business that contributed less than 1 percent of the company's $1.84 billion in 1991 revenues.

The firm's legal risks are staggering:

- Hundreds of women who received implants and later suffered health problems have filed suits; damages could exceed $500 million.
- Stockholders have filed about ten suits charging that the company failed to disclose the implants' risks; the suits seek hundreds of millions in damages.
- Dow Corning risks civil liability under food and drug laws for selling or shipping adulterated products; government action could result in fines reaching $1 million.
- Under federal criminal statutes and food and drug laws, company executives could be charged with rigging or hiding data.

Many critics believed the manufacturer was slow to respond to safety concerns. Dow Corning continued to maintain that the implants were safe. Yet officials in government probes said they had reviewed documents which seemed to show that the company had been misrepresenting its safety data on implants for more than fifteen years. A figure highly visible in the media coverage of the controversy was a former Dow Corning engineer, Thomas D. Talcott, who said that for years the company sold silicone implants that could rupture and leak, posing a serious health risk. One of the developers of the original silicone gel used in implants, Talcott quit in 1976 in protest when Dow Corning switched to a more liquid gel designed to make the implants softer. He said he feared the thinner gel could migrate through the body.

As the Food and Drug Administration began hearings on whether silicone implants should be banned, Dow Corning's CEO, Keith R. McKennon, promised to cooperate fully. He also discussed funding research and paying the medical bills of poor women whose implants must be removed. In early March 1992, the FDA's advisory committee decided that implants could remain on the market in limited use but would be tested for safety in clinical trials. On March 19, Dow Corning Corp. announced that it would stop making breast implants altogether.

How, some observers asked, could such a debacle occur at Dow Corning, long recognized as a pioneer in corporate ethics? The company was one of the first to establish an ethics program, one which many believe to be the most elaborate of any in American corporations. In 1976, Dow Corning's chairman started a Business Conduct Committee. Six managers serve for three years and devote up to six weeks a year to committee business. Two committee members audit every business operation every three years, hold reviews with employees, and report results to an Audit and Social Responsibility Committee of the board of directors. Company training programs include segments on ethics, and semiannual surveys ask employees about ethics issues.

Since 1983, four audits failed to turn up any questions on the safety of breast implants. Nor did a three-hour audit in October 1990 with nine employees at the unit that makes silicone implants. Yet some evidence of controversy apparently existed. Talcott, the whistle-blowing engineer, quit Dow Corning in protest in 1976, the same year the ethics program was launched. A 1977 memo by another employee, Frank Lewis, noted reports by four doctors that 52 of 400 implant procedures had resulted in ruptures.

Why didn't an audit turn up such internal documents? Ethics experts point out that programs are not designed to deal directly with complex problems, but rather to help build an overall environment of ethical conduct. At Dow Corning, product safety issues are channeled through managers and the company's Medical Device Business Board, which had decided to conduct further safety studies on the implants. Also, ethics programs are constrained because few managers or employees are likely to discuss moral issues openly in meetings with several other employees or managers, including the boss. And employees are not likely to raise concerns about safety when top managers believe such concerns are not justified. In fact, Dow Corning maintained throughout the controversy and litigation that breast implants do not pose unreasonable risks.

Questions for Discussion

1. What consumer rights were involved in the silicone breast implant controversy? Explain.

2. To what extent do you believe a manufacturer like Dow Corning should be responsible for product safety? To what extent is the old adage "let the buyer beware" applicable to product safety?

3. Dow Corning's ethics program and periodic audits failed to prevent serious product liability problems. What else could the company have done to make sure product safety concerns were addressed internally?

Based on information from John A. Byrne, "The Best-Laid Ethics Programs," *Business Week,* March 9, 1992, pp. 67–69; Michele Galen, "Debacle at Dow Corning: How Bad Will It Get?" *Business Week,* March 2, 1992, pp. 36, 38; Tim Smart, "This Man Sounded the Silicone Alarm—in 1976," *Business Week,* January 27, 1992, p. 34; and Joseph Weber, "'I Guess the Price of Salt Water Is Going Up," *Business Week,* April 6, 1992, p. 28.

4.2 AN ENVIRONMENTAL MENACE TO THE WORLD

The old Soviet Union is gone, but it won't be forgotten anytime soon. Through seventy-four years of mismanagement, its Communist regime left behind a legacy of environmental damage that threatens neighboring Europe and Asia and requires billions of dollars for cleanup.

The Soviet empire once spanned one-sixth of the earth, and the environmental problems it left equal it in magnitude. Says a spokeswoman for the Washington, D.C.–based Natural Resources Defense Council, "If we don't deal with [Commonwealth of Independent States] environmental problems now, we won't have to worry about dealing with economic problems." Germany and France are pushing the world's leading industrial nations to pledge billions of dollars in environmental aid besides the $24 billion in economic assistance they have already promised.

Russia and the other former Soviet republics need help not only with cleanup but also in stopping ongoing environmental destruction. A Western diplomat in Moscow describes the Commonwealth of Independent States (CIS) as a "big polluting machine." Cars pollute the air with leaded gasoline and their lack of catalytic converters. Hundreds of factories pour waste into the Gulf of Finland and the Neva River, from which the Russian city of St. Petersburg gets its drinking water—contaminated by untreated sewage. CIS households, with smaller houses and fewer appliances, use 90 percent less energy than do Western households, but factories and the oil and gas industries produce vast wastefulness and environmental nightmares. Manufacturing, designed without the environment in mind, uses more than four times as much energy per unit of GNP as in the United States. Malfunctioning and old equipment, the lack of spare parts, poor workmanship, and shabby repairs regularly produce immense blowouts, leaks, and spills in the oil and gas industry throughout the former Soviet Union.

A horrendous disaster occurred in March 1992 near Tashkent, the capital of Uzbekistan, when drillers struck oil at a well in the Fergana Valley oil fields but could not control the flow. Oil shot hundreds of feet into the air, filling the sky with black slime and smoke, for sixty-two days. After a month, Uzbek officials called in Oklahoma-based Cudd Pressure Control, Inc., to seal off the well. Before it was finally controlled in early May, the well had thrown out as much as 6.2 million barrels of oil, which soaked into nearby cotton fields or burned off in the air. Uzbekistan officials never said how severe the damage was, and neither did the U.S. Environmental Protection Agency, which sent a technical team to the site at the Uzbekistan government's request. Experts estimate the oil spill to be some twenty-four times the amount spilled by the *Exxon Valdez* in Alaska. The loss from this well alone cost the Uzbeks around $130 million, as well as untold environmental damage.

The Fergana Valley spill, although the worst reported, is but one of many disastrous incidents in recent years. One blowout near the Caspian Sea blazed for a year before it was controlled. A gas pipeline explosion several hundred miles south of Moscow resulted in the deaths of 607 people when sparks from passing trains ignited the leak. In western Siberia, a break in a rusted oil line leaked three million barrels of oil into the ground and caused twenty-seven wells to be shut down. Moscow officials have admitted that in 1989, 26,000 ruptures occurred, spilling 4.3 million barrels of oil.

Over 370,000 miles of oil and gas pipelines cross through the former Soviet Union. Many stretches of pipeline, as well as compressors, need to be repaired or replaced. Some German consultants estimate that principal gas lines are leaking almost 10 percent of their annual production, and local connecting networks are losing up to 40 percent of their load; the loss far exceeds Germany's entire yearly gas requirement. Leaking pipelines are said to have cost the former Soviet republics some $8 billion in oil and gas revenues in 1991.

The biggest danger to the outside world lies in the CIS nuclear energy program. Of the thirty-seven reactors, which provide 12 percent of the commonwealth's energy, at least fifteen are poorly designed and should be taken out of operation. Their slowness to cool during emergencies can cause the core to explode, which is what happened at the Chernobyl plant in 1986. The aftermath was felt throughout Europe. Nearly $180 million of agricultural products had to be destroyed in Poland, Germany, Austria, and Hungary; herds of reindeer were destroyed in Finland, Sweden, and Norway; and in Britain, some 1,350 miles away, the sale of sheep was banned until radioactive isotopes they may have consumed while grazing had dissipated. The radioactive contamination that fell on Europe is expected to cause about six thousand more cancer deaths in the next fifty years. More than 2.5 million acres of farmland in the Ukraine and Belarus was never properly cleaned up, and radioactive food occasionally shows up in markets.

"Radioactive contamination is our number one problem," says Alexei Yablokov, a scientist and advisor to president Boris Yeltsin. The problem sites are numerous. Around Chelyabinsk, the Soviet Union's top-secret nuclear weapons production site, scientists have been dumping radioactive wastes in local lakes and rivers since 1950. The *Bulletin of Atomic Scientists* estimates that you could get a lethal dose of radiation in under an hour just by standing on the bank of the once-beautiful Karachai Lake. Officials tried to seal off the Techa River by surrounding it with a barbed-wire fence, but radioactive waste has been found where the river empties into the Arctic Ocean one hundred miles away. For thirty years, the Soviet navy dumped nuclear waste in the Barents Sea in a known fishing area several hundred miles from the Norwegian coast; because the protective barrels floated, the Soviets punctured them so they would fill with water and sink.

If other nations do provide emergency assistance, companies that can help with environmental cleanup and restructuring will have many opportunities. U.S. companies make the gas turbine power plants that should replace the deficient Russian nuclear reactors. Conoco, in bidding to develop a 100-million-barrel oil field, sent environmentalists to recommend ways to drill without harming forests. Other Western companies are offering help in disposing of nuclear and other hazardous wastes, controlling air and water pollution, and bringing nuclear reactors up to global safety standards. The Ukrainian government will be taking bids for a contract to finally bury the still hot Chernobyl plant, now encased in a giant tomb which was never fully sealed.

Questions for Discussion

1. Did the concept of social responsibility exist in the Soviet Union, a socialist state?

2. How does a nation's system of government, general economic condition, and cultural traditions affect the degree of social responsibility its organizations display? Cite examples of various countries.

3. Why must governments, business organizations, and citizens of other countries of the world be concerned with changing the dreadful environmental situation in the CIS? Should other countries pay to clean up the huge mess and get industries there on the right track?

Based on information from Richard C. Morais, P. Pietsch, and Christoph von Schoeller, "Blowout," *Forbes*, July 20, 1992, pp. 65, 68; Paul Hofheinz, "The New Soviet Threat: Pollution," *Fortune*, July 27, 1992, pp. 110–114; and Associated Press, "Sewage Is Found Pouring into River Used for Russian City's Drinking Water," Lexington, Ky. *Herald-Leader*, September 17, 1992, p. A8.

The Global Marketing Environment

OBJECTIVES

● *To explain the nature and importance of the global marketplace.*

● *To discuss the levels of U.S. involvement in international marketing.*

● *To compare the approaches to international marketing.*

● *To describe the role of primary and secondary data in the analysis of foreign markets.*

● *To identify the environmental forces in foreign markets.*

● *To determine the significance of multinational market groups.*

OUTLINE

Over the past few years a lot of noise has been made about Americans purchasing foreign-made goods. The United States has always been home to democracy, free enterprise, and a spirit of confidence. Why then are some American executives pleading with fellow citizens to "buy American"? According to General Motors Corp.'s former chairman Robert Stempel, the Japanese are not interested in a portion of the U.S. automobile market; rather, they want it all, the same as with radios, cameras, and video cameras. Said Stempel, "I'm not asking for sympathy. I just want to compete fair and square." But even if this competitiveness problem can be resolved through the sale of U.S. cars, "buy American" is easier said than done.

According to Harvard University political economist and Secretary of Labor Robert B. Reich, "it's more difficult than ever to find out what is an American product." For instance, you can't be truly American and drive a Chevrolet Lumina (assembled in Canada), eat at Burger King (British owned), or watch a movie from Columbia Pictures (a Japanese company). Trying to buy American-made clothes can be especially confusing. Van Heusen shirts are made in Thailand, London Fog coats in South Korea, and Nike's garments in Malaysia; Fruit of the Loom underwear is truly American. And what constitutes an American product? Toyota Camrys are made in Kentucky, by American workers, have 75 percent American parts, and are exported to Japan. Does the U.S. economy benefit more from Toyotas made in Kentucky or Fords made in Mexico? Reich argues that where the product is made is important, because this translates into jobs.

The "buy American" argument is emotional and difficult to resolve. But facts can be separated from emotions. The competitiveness of American-owned corporations is not the same as American competitiveness. Take IBM, often considered the model competitive U.S. corporation. Forty percent of IBM's employees are non-American, and the percentage is growing. IBM Japan employs 18,200 Japanese, and with sales exceeding $6 billion, is one of Japan's leading exporters of computers. Whirlpool, after cutting its American work force by 10 percent, employs 43,500 people in forty-five countries; most are non-American. Texas Instruments employs 5,000 people in Japan making semiconductors, many of which are exported to the United States. Thus American *ownership* of the corporation is less critical to America's economic future than the skills and knowledge of American *workers,* who are increasingly employed in the U.S. by foreign-owned firms.[1] ●

[1] Based on information from James S. Hirsch, "'Buy American' Is Easier Said Than Done," *Wall Street Journal,* January 28, 1992, pp. B1, B6; Jerry Flint, "One More Chance?" *Forbes,* August 17, 1992, p. 94; Robert B. Reich, "Who Is Us?" *Harvard Business Review,* January–February 1990, pp. 53–64; and Stephen Koepp and William McWhirter, "I'm Not Asking for Sympathy," *Time,* January 27, 1992, pp. 45–46.

As you can see, the global environment is very complex. Products are designed in one country, assembled in another with materials from several others, and sold throughout the world. This situation presents many challenges for a firm and influences its marketing activities. As global competition intensifies, firms that do not acknowledge the changes taking place or do not adapt to them risk failure.

THE GLOBAL MARKETPLACE

After World War II, Japan decided to invest in its people. Today, Japan has one of the leading economies in the world. Changes taking place in Eastern Europe, South Korea, and Taiwan also suggest that market power, not military strength, will dominate the world. Learning how to do business in this new environment will be critical to America and to U.S. firms with operations around the globe.

More than ever before, people throughout the world want the same things—modern appliances, the latest in fashions, fast-food restaurants, high-quality services, even candy (see Figure 5.1). As larger portions of the world desire modern conveniences, corporations must be prepared to compete in an increasingly interdependent global environment. Even if firms choose not to compete directly in this environment, they will be affected by other U.S. and foreign competitors that do. In reality, whether a firm manufactures microwave ovens or automobiles, it cannot avoid competing in the global marketplace.

Telecommunications will also grow in its ability to link nations, people, and business. Not only are we becoming a global marketplace, but we are moving toward a single worldwide information network. Fiberoptic calls are much clearer and faster than calls using copper wire. In 1991, 150,416 miles of fiberoptic cable were laid throughout the world.[2] The United States and Japan are now linked by a fiberoptic cable, and North America, Europe, Asia, and Australia are stringing fiberoptic cable. In the near future, businesses will be able to communicate throughout the world in any form—voice, data, text, or image—at the speed of sound.

A shift in the world's economic power is another aspect of the global marketplace. The world's trade center, which gravitated from the Mediterranean to the Atlantic more than five hundred years ago, is now moving toward the Pacific. Large trade centers can now be found in Los Angeles, Tokyo, Sydney, and Hong Kong. The Pacific Rim includes all countries touched by the Pacific Ocean. Although Japan is the economic power of the Pacific Rim today, the four tigers—South Korea, Taiwan, Hong Kong, and Singapore—will challenge Japan's economic strength in the future.

Countries in Eastern Europe, the former Soviet Union, Chile, and other Third World nations are also becoming part of the global marketplace. People

[2]Harper's Index, May 1992, Kessler Marketing Intelligence, Newport, R.I.

FIGURE 5.1
Global Marketplace Changes
Only a few years ago, it would have been hard to imagine something as American as M & M's being promoted in Russia. But the fall of communism has opened doors to American goods in the former Soviet Union and Eastern Europe.

Source: Jeffrey Aaronson/Network Aspen.

in these countries want more and better goods and services and realize that free enterprise and private ownership will be needed to supply them effectively. The failed coup attempt in the Soviet Union, when Communist hardliners tried to overthrow the government of Mikhail Gorbachev in 1991, illustrates the momentum democracy has gained in some parts of the world. Perhaps no country has experienced a faster and more successful process of privatization than Argentina. The state-owned oil company, railroads, telephones, airline, and utilities have been privatized, as have the television and radio stations. Inflation has fallen to 17.5 percent, from over 4,000 percent in the late 1980s, and growth is exceeding 6 percent a year.[3]

These changes are having a profound impact on business firms. As global competition intensifies, the number of firms operating solely in domestic markets is decreasing rapidly. The challenge marketers face is to develop marketing strategies that will be competitive in this global marketplace.

INTERNATIONAL MARKETING

■ **international marketing** the performance of marketing activities across national boundaries

International marketing is the performance of marketing activities across national boundaries.[4] The difference between *marketing* and *international marketing* is not the activities performed but the manner in which they are

---

[3]"Argentina Starts to Count Again," *Fortune,* February 22, 1993, pp. 102–104.
[4]Vern Terpstra, *International Marketing,* 4th ed. (Hinsdale, Ill.: Dryden Press, 1987), p. 4.

Rank	Company	Export Sales (in millions)	Total Sales (in millions)	Exports as Percent of Sales
1	Boeing	$17,856	$ 29,314	60.9
2	General Motors	11,285	123,780	9.1
3	General Electric	8,614	60,236	14.3
4	IBM	7,668	64,792	11.8
5	Ford Motor	7,340	88,963	8.3
6	Chrysler	6,168	29,370	21.0
7	McDonnell Douglas	6,160	18,718	32.9
8	Du Pont	3,812	38,031	10.0
9	Caterpillar	3,710	10,182	36.4
10	United Technologies	3,587	21,262	16.9
11	Hewlett-Packard	3,223	14,541	22.2
12	Philip Morris	3,061	48,109	6.4
13	Eastman Kodak	3,020	19,649	15.4
14	Motorola	2,928	11,341	25.8
15	Archer-Daniels-Midland	2,600	8,568	30.3
16	Digital Equipment	2,200	14,024	15.7
17	Intel	1,929	4,779	40.4
18	Allied-Signal	1,729	11,882	14.6
19	Sun Microsystems	1,606	3,260	49.3
20	Unisys	1,598	8,696	18.4

Source: "Top 50 Leading U.S. Exporters," *Fortune,* June 29, 1992, p. 95. © 1992 Time Inc. All rights reserved.

TABLE 5.1
Twenty Largest U.S. Exporters

■ **multinational corporations** corporations that have assets committed to operations or subsidiaries in foreign countries

performed. Because of the increasingly interdependent global environment, firms are involved in international marketing more than ever before; increased foreign competition and new growth opportunities in foreign markets leave firms little choice but to become involved in international marketing. As more and more nations develop economically, foreign competition will increase, as will market opportunities for American firms in foreign countries.

American businesses can be involved in international marketing in a number of ways. Many firms, called **multinational corporations,** have assets committed to operations or subsidiaries in foreign countries. Multinational companies include large *Fortune* 500 firms such as ITT, Exxon, and IBM, as well as smaller firms with operations in various countries. But multinationals are not the only companies engaged in international marketing. Many U.S. firms market products abroad by exporting them to foreign countries but have no assets committed to foreign operations. For instance, American farmers produce crops in the United States and export them to numerous foreign countries. The twenty largest U.S. exporters are shown in Table 5.1. Boeing is about the size of Chrysler in terms of total sales but exports 60.9 percent of its products, which makes it the leading exporter based on percentage of sales. The next sections look more closely at the various levels of U.S. involvement in international marketing, global marketing, and approaches to international marketing.

FIGURE 5.2
Levels of Involvement in International Marketing

① No international marketing
- No active involvement in international marketing
- Unsolicited foreign orders are filled

② Infrequent international marketing
- Temporary production surpluses may be marketed overseas
- As domestic demand increases, international marketing activities are reduced

③ Regular international marketing
- Permanent production capacity is devoted to goods marketed abroad continuously
- International marketing activities and overseas operations typically begin

④ Global marketing operations
- Full commitment to and involvement in international marketing activities
- World is viewed as market for product
- Production is planned for entire globe

FIGURE 5.2
Levels of Involvement in International Marketing

Levels of International Marketing Involvement

Companies that enter foreign markets must decide on the degree to which they will be involved. Some companies prefer a limited amount of involvement; others may become totally involved. In general, an organization can commit to one of four distinct levels of international marketing: (1) none, (2) infrequent, (3) regular, or (4) global.[5] Figure 5.2 illustrates how involvement increases at each subsequent level.

Organizations at the first level of involvement make no active commitment to international marketing. Sales are made only to foreign companies that come directly to the firm. At the second, or infrequent, level of involvement, companies may sell surplus goods caused by production variations or demand fluctuations to foreign markets. However, there is very little change in the operations of the firm. Companies at the third, or regular, level of involvement develop international marketing strategies to achieve the firm's goals. In global marketing operations, the fourth level, firms make a total commitment to international marketing.

Global Marketing

■ **global marketing** the development of marketing strategies as if the entire world (or regions thereof) were one large market

Global marketing is the development of marketing strategies as if the entire world (or regions thereof) were one large market.[6] At the global level of

[5]Philip R. Cateora, *International Marketing*, 6th ed. (Homewood, Ill.: Richard D. Irwin, 1987), pp. 18–19.
[6]Theodore Levitt, "The Globalization of Markets," *Harvard Business Review*, May–June 1983, pp. 92–102.

Rank	Company	Country	Market Value (in billions of U.S. dollars)
1	Royal Dutch/Shell Group	Netherlands	77.82
2	Nippon Telegraph & Telephone	Japan	77.52
3	Exxon	United States	75.30
4	Philip Morris	United States	71.29
5	General Electric	United States	66.00
6	Wal-Mart Stores	United States	60.82
7	Coca-Cola	United States	58.47
8	Merck	United States	58.41
9	American Telephone & Telegraph	United States	55.85
10	IBM	United States	51.82
11	Toyota Motor	Japan	43.97
12	Glaxo Holdings	Britain	42.64
13	British Telecommunications	Britain	40.65
14	Mitsubishi Bank	Japan	39.84
15	Bristol-Myers-Squibb	United States	37.60
16	Sumitomo Bank	Japan	37.12
17	Du Pont	United States	35.41
18	Procter & Gamble	United States	34.74
19	Dai-Ichi Kangyo Bank	Japan	34.68
20	Industrial Bank of Japan	Japan	34.04

Source: "The Global 1000—The Leaders," *Business Week,* July 13, 1992, p. 53. Reprinted from the July 13, 1992 issue of *Business Week* by special permission, copyright © 1992 by McGraw-Hill, Inc.

TABLE 5.2
Twenty Largest Global Firms

marketing, companies generally develop a standardized marketing mix for the product. The Coca-Cola Company, for instance, pursues the same basic marketing strategy in most of the world.[7] Products most suitable for global marketing include movies, automobiles, heavy equipment, machine tools, computer hardware, major appliances, paper products, soft drinks, and cosmetics.[8]

As consumers everywhere begin to want the same things, more and more firms are being drawn into global marketing.[9] When Volupte, a women's fragrance by designer Oscar de la Renta, was introduced worldwide, every aspect of the launch, including the name and the advertisements, was designed to appeal to a global audience.[10] The increased globalization of markets has resulted in greater competition among corporations throughout the world and an erosion in the world dominance of U.S. firms, a trend that is expected to continue.[11] Table 5.2 lists the twenty largest global corporations;

[7]"How Coke Markets to the World," *Journal of Business Strategy,* September–October 1988, pp. 4–7.
[8]"Global Marketing: How Executives Really Feel," *Ad Forum,* April 1985, p. 30.
[9]Robert T. Green and Trina L. Larsen, "Changing Patterns of U.S. Trade: 1985–1989," *Business Horizons,* November–December 1991, pp. 7–13.
[10]Pat Sloan, "Vividly Volupte," *Advertising Age,* February 10, 1992, p. 36.
[11]Lawrence G. Franko, "Global Competition II: Is the Large American Firm an Endangered Species?" *Business Horizons,* November–December 1991, pp. 14–22.

the top two are non-U.S. firms, and the next eight are U.S. firms; seven of the ten remaining are non-U.S. firms. Over half of the top one hundred global firms are from foreign countries.[12]

The trend toward globalization does not mean that all markets are global. Although Toyota, Levi Strauss, and KFC sell relatively standardized products throughout the world, marketing strategies must often be adapted or customized to accommodate differences among nations in cultures, values, and languages. KFC has 8,480 stores worldwide, and chicken is one of the most universally accepted foods. Nonetheless, some adaptation has been necessary. Fundamentally, every KFC outlet offers the same mainstay product— original recipe chicken, cole slaw, and fries. KFC then customizes the menu to specific cultures. For instance, more desserts are included on the menu in France, and restaurants in China feature Chinese tea.[13]

Developing a standardized marketing mix for the entire world is obviously extremely difficult. Global markets do exist for some products, but for other products, marketing mixes must be adapted to the cultural needs of different countries and regions. The issue of global marketing versus customized marketing is not easily resolved, as Point/Counterpoint illustrates.

APPROACHES TO INTERNATIONAL MARKETING

After choosing a level of involvement, a company must decide on the approach for becoming involved in international marketing. A firm's options range from occasional exporting to expanding overall operations (production and marketing) into other countries. Possible approaches include exporting, licensing, trading companies, countertrading, joint ventures, and direct ownership.

Exporting

■ **exporting** the sale of products to a foreign country, which represents the lowest level of commitment to international marketing

Exporting, the sale of products to a foreign country, represents the lowest level of commitment to international marketing. More than half of all businesses entering foreign markets first do so by exporting.[14] Exporting is often handled through an export agency, which performs most marketing functions associated with selling to customers in other countries. Such agencies can provide low-cost assistance to firms with limited resources, thereby enabling the firms to avoid significant upfront investment.[15] Thus exporting requires only minimum expenditures of effort, personnel, and money, although some product modifications in packaging, labeling, style, or color

---

[12]"The Global 1000—The Leaders," *Business Week,* July 13, 1992, p. 53.
[13]Alan I. Kirschenbaum, "The 'Original Recipe' for International Success," *The Lane Report,* May 1992, pp. 17–24.
[14]John S. McClenahen, "How U.S. Entrepreneurs Succeed in World Markets," *Industry Week,* May 2, 1988, pp. 47–49.
[15]Joseph V. McCabe, "Outside Managers Offer Packaged Export Expertise," *Journal of Business Strategy,* March–April 1990, pp. 20–23.

POINT/COUNTERPOINT

Can Marketing Strategies Be Standardized for International Marketing?

Many firms recognize that the world is getting smaller. Competition is no longer defined by regions of the country or even the entire nation. Competition for many American firms includes not only other U.S. firms but also companies from Japan, Germany, Korea, and so on. As global competition intensifies, firms are scrambling to increase their commitment to international marketing. As they do so, a great temptation exists to market products in foreign countries using the same strategies that have proven successful in the United States.

Point The people of the world are becoming more similar in their product wants. Because of modern communication and transportation technologies, people of all nations are aware of—and desire—the latest products available. The result is a global market for standardized consumer products. Coca-Cola and Pepsi-Cola, for instance, are standardized products sold almost everywhere. Marketing strategies for many services, such as hotels and air travel, can be standardized for international marketing.

The economic and competitive payoffs for standardized marketing strategies are enormous. Global marketing can be implemented more quickly than a customized approach. By selling the same product in the same manner everywhere, the firm operates at a relatively low cost. Costs of production and marketing are minimized by standardizing the marketing mix. These cost savings can be translated into lower worldwide prices, giving the firm a strong competitive edge.

Counterpoint When marketing internationally, firms must customize most products and marketing strategies to the cultural needs of different countries. Although different countries may contain market segments with similar product demands, a firm nevertheless must be concerned with cultural differences from country to country. Some products that are successful in one culture do not achieve success in another. McDonald's, for example, was not successful in Germany until it began selling beer.

Although the cost of customizing marketing strategies is high, the cost of *not* customizing may be higher. Marketers must strive to offer products that meet the needs of consumers. By standardizing marketing strategies, firms often sacrifice consumer satisfaction. Products should be adapted to the specific needs of the target market, consistent with the marketing concept.

---

may be required. German wine producers make little or no modification in products exported to the United States, as shown in Figure 5.3.

American exports are on the rise and have dramatically reduced the *trade deficit*, which results when a country imports more than it exports. In 1987, the United States had a record deficit of $146 billion. By 1992, the trade deficit had fallen to $99 billion.[16] Most of the growth is coming in Canada,

[16] Howard Banks, "Many Ways to Look at U.S. Trade," *Forbes*, April 12, 1993, p. 39.

FIGURE 5.3
Exporting
A variety of fine German wines are exported to the United States. Since little or no modification of the product is needed, German wine manufacturers make relatively small expenditures to export their products.

Source: German Wine Information Bureau.

■ **licensing** an international marketing arrangement in which the licensee (a foreign company) pays the licensor (an international marketing firm) commissions or royalties for the right to use its name, products, patents, brands and trademarks, raw materials, production processes, or managerial and technical assistance

Japan, Mexico, Korea, Taiwan, and Germany, in such items as medical products, computers and semiconductors, scientific instruments, telecommunications equipment, and consumer goods. As exports continue to grow, the United States should see a *trade surplus* shortly, whereby exports exceed imports. Exports are a key to growth, especially when domestic markets are saturated. The United States, for instance, is the number one exporter of food to Japan, with sales exceeding $10 billion.[17] General Motors is developing a minivan that will be manufactured in the United States and sold in Europe under the Opel name. GM expects to export about $750 million worth of vans starting in 1996.[18] Many small companies also rely on exports as a source of sales and growth. Midwest Tropical exports $5.5 million in aquariums, Treatment Products exports $5 million in automobile wax, and Sharper Finish exports $3 million in laundry and ironing equipment.[19]

Licensing

An alternative to exporting is **licensing**—an international marketing arrangement in which the *licensee* (the owner of a foreign company) pays the *licensor*

[17]"Japan's Big Appetite for American Foods," *Parade,* June 7, 1992, p. 8.
[18]Jerry Flint, "Baby Steps," *Forbes,* April 13, 1992, p. 92.
[19]William J. Holstein and Kevin Kelly, "Little Companies, Big Exports," *Business Week,* April 13, 1992, pp. 70–72.

(the international firm) commissions or royalties for the right to use its name, products, patents, brands and trademarks, raw materials, production processes, or managerial and technical assistance. The licensor may charge an initial down payment or fee when the licensing agreement is signed. Licensing is a practical approach to international marketing when production, technical assistance, or marketing expertise is required to market products across national boundaries. Licensing may also be an attractive alternative to more direct involvement in international trade when the political stability of a foreign country is in doubt or when resources are unavailable for more direct involvement. Playboy Enterprises has licensed foreign editions of *Playboy* magazine in fifteen countries, the most recent being Czechoslovakia, Hungary, and Taiwan. Playboy has also licensed twenty sportswear boutiques in mainland China, operated by the Chinese government. The boutiques sell outerwear, jogging suits, jeans, and other products, all with the rabbit logo.[20]

Licensing offers benefits to both parties. The licensee gains products or technology that would be costly to develop. The licensor gains entry to international markets with a minimal investment. However, the payoff to the licensor is relatively low, generally about 5 percent of sales. In addition, licensing agreements typically expire in less than ten years, at which time the licensee may continue to market the product without paying the licensor. Many American marketing executives argue that licensing agreements result in giving away the best American technology for 5 percent of sales, only to have foreign countries use this technology to beat American businesses in their own markets.

Trading Companies

■ **trading company**
a company that serves as a link between buyers and sellers in different countries

Businesses wishing to sell their products overseas may choose to sell through a **trading company,** which serves as a link between buyers and sellers in different countries. Trading companies are not involved in manufacturing products. They are marketing intermediaries that take title to products and undertake all the activities required to move products from the domestic country to customers in a foreign country. In addition, they provide marketers with information about markets, product quality and price expectations, distribution, and foreign exchange in domestic or international markets. Trading companies assume much of the manufacturers' risk in international marketing.

Because they are usually favored by their own (domestic) governments, trading companies can facilitate entrance into foreign markets. Some countries, such as Brazil, have passed laws that give trading companies various tax advantages. The Export Trading Company Act, passed in 1982, encourages the efficient operation of trading companies in the United States. The act also improves the availability of financing for international trade and provides limited protection from antitrust laws when conducting export activities. After the act was passed, many major companies, such as Sears, General Electric, and Kmart, developed their own export trading companies.

[20]Joshua Levine, "The Rabbit Grows Up," *Forbes,* February 17, 1992, pp. 122–127.

Countertrading

■ **countertrading** a form of international trade involving bartering agreements between two or more countries; allows nations with limited cash to participate in international trade

Complex bartering agreements between two or more countries are involved in **countertrading.** (*Bartering* refers to the exchange of merchandise between countries.) Countertrading allows a nation with limited cash to participate in international trade. The country wishing to trade requires the exporting country to purchase products from it before allowing its products to be sold there. For instance, McDonnell Douglas sold $25 million worth of helicopters to Uganda and took in return a plant that catches and processes Nile perch and a factory that turns pineapples into concentrate; the factories were sold to buyers in Europe. It is estimated that agreements like this account for 20 percent of U.S. exports, or $110 billion.[21]

The use of countertrade agreements is expected to grow during the 1990s. Countertrading provides an established trading vehicle for countries in Eastern Europe and the former Soviet Union and developing and Third World countries that want U.S. goods but lack the currency to pay for them.[22] Although many U.S. companies still do not use countertrading, firms will find they have no choice if they wish to compete in global markets.

Countertrading has several drawbacks. First, it is often difficult to determine the true value of goods offered in a countertrade agreement. Second, it may be difficult to dispose of the bartered goods after they are accepted. These problems can be reduced or eliminated through market analysis and negotiation. Companies have been developed to assist firms in handling countertrade agreements. Despite the drawbacks, companies that choose not to become involved in countertrading will risk missing significant opportunities.

Joint Ventures

■ **joint venture** a partnership between a domestic firm and a foreign firm or government

A **joint venture** is a partnership between a domestic firm and a foreign firm or government. For instance, General Motors was able to enter the world's largest market by forming a joint venture with China's Jinbei Automobile to build light trucks. GM owns 30 percent of the new venture, which plans to produce 50,000 trucks by 1998.[23]

Joint ventures are becoming more common because of cost advantages and the number of inexperienced firms entering foreign markets. Sometimes joint ventures are a political necessity because of nationalism and governmental restrictions on foreign ownership of property or industry. In environments with scarce resources, rapid technological changes, or massive capital requirements, joint ventures may be the best way for smaller firms with limited resources to attain better positions in global industries. Joint ventures may also be created to gain access to marketing channels, suppliers, and technology.

Not all organizations are willing to accept the terms required by a foreign government to establish a joint venture. The Coca-Cola Company pulled

[21] Shelley Neumeier, "Why Countertrade Is Getting Hotter," *Fortune,* June 29, 1992, p. 25.
[22] Matt Schaffer, "Countertrade as an Export Strategy," *Journal of Business Strategy,* May–June 1990, pp. 33–38.
[23] Harris Collingwood, "GM Goes Trucking to China," *Business Week,* January 27, 1992, p. 41.

out of India rather than give up majority ownership and risk revealing its secret formula. As a result, Double-Cola, a small soda maker from Chattanooga, Tennessee, beat PepsiCo to become the first American bottler to bring cola back to India. Despite some of the problems with joint ventures, they are expected to grow in the future, since they are the only way to enter many foreign markets.

A recent mechanism for entering foreign markets is a strategic alliance. A **strategic alliance** occurs when two firms pool their resources in a partnership that goes beyond the limits of a joint venture. IBM has established over four hundred strategic alliances with firms in the United States and abroad. In the highly competitive global marketplace, strategic alliances have been growing at an annual rate of 27 percent since 1985.[24] Through a strategic alliance, firms hope to gain access to a new market or technology and beat competitors to market with a new product.

■ **strategic alliance** an agreement between two firms who pool their resources in a partnership more extensive than a joint venture; allows firms to gain access to new markets or technology

The major requirement for an effective strategic alliance is *trust*. If a firm cannot trust its prospective partner, it should not enter into an agreement. Without mutual trust, greed and self-serving behavior dominate the relationship. But trust cannot be written into a partnership; rather, it must come voluntarily and requires time to develop. Thus firms must often expand their time frame in forming alliances. Ford Motor Co. and Mazda Motor Corporation have been involved in strategic alliances for thirteen years. The two firms cooperate on new vehicles and exchange expertise. As a result, Ford is the best-selling foreign automaker in Japan.[25] Building trust over many years contributed greatly to this success.

Direct Ownership

■ **direct ownership** a long-term commitment to international marketing in which a business owns a foreign subsidiary or division

Direct ownership is a long-term commitment to international marketing in which an organization owns a foreign subsidiary or division. Multinational companies like IBM, Procter & Gamble, Nestlé, and Toyota use this approach to international marketing. Direct ownership represents the highest level of commitment to international marketing. A firm does not have to compromise any aspect of its marketing program when it owns 100 percent of its foreign interests because the foreign subsidiary and the parent company have the same objectives. Thus direct ownership means greater control and flexibility.

Some well-known firms operating in the United States are actually subsidiaries owned by foreign firms. Magnavox, Pillsbury, Saks Fifth Avenue, and Baskin-Robbins are wholly owned subsidiaries of foreign multinational companies. Nonprofit organizations such as the Red Cross and the U.S. Army also own foreign subsidiaries or divisions.

Firms invest in foreign subsidiaries for a number of reasons. Direct ownership can reduce manufacturing costs because of lower labor and overhead costs. Direct ownership also enables a firm to avoid paying tariffs and other costs associated with exporting. Additionally, by paying taxes in the

---

[24] Stratford Sherman, "Are Strategic Alliances Working?" *Fortune,* September 21, 1992, pp. 77–78.
[25] James B. Treece, Karen Lowry Miller, and Richard A. Melcher, "The Partners," *Business Week,* February 10, 1992, pp. 102–107.

host country and providing employment for local residents, a foreign company can build good relations with the host government. The greatest danger of direct ownership is that a firm may lose a sizable investment because of market failure or nationalization of its interests by a foreign government. When problems do arise in a foreign country, it is often very difficult and expensive to move operations out of the country.

ANALYZING INTERNATIONAL MARKETS

The growth of foreign competition and the increased involvement of U.S. firms in international marketing have created new marketing challenges. Because of the uncertainty and risk involved in developing international marketing strategies, it is even more important to analyze foreign markets than domestic markets.[26] Many firms have failed because they entered international markets without an adequate understanding of the markets, competition, consumers, environment, or geography.

Exactly what should a company know before it makes the decision to engage in international marketing? Information is needed to make specific marketing decisions, such as what price to charge, what advertising theme to use, what product features to modify, and how to design distribution channels. Information also is needed about differences in culture, economic conditions, and demographic variations. Table 5.3 lists several questions that should be answered when analyzing international markets. Companies like IBM, Procter & Gamble, and Toyota asked and answered these questions—and many more—before they achieved success internationally.

The first step in analyzing a foreign market should be to collect *secondary data* (data that already exist). Businesses may refer to sources such as U.S. government publications, international organizations such as the United Nations, governments of foreign countries, and international trade organizations. Data from such sources are useful for selecting countries that might be feasible international targets, for estimating the marketing potential of a particular country, and for monitoring changes in the environment.

Collecting secondary data about international markets is a difficult task. Although there is normally an abundance of secondary data on domestic markets, secondary data on international markets may be scarce. Moreover, the accuracy and reliability of data from some foreign countries often are suspect. Census data from foreign countries, for example, are often open to question because they are reported on the basis of estimates from village priests or elders.[27]

Because of the questionable nature of secondary data from foreign sources, *primary data* may be required to analyze international markets. (Primary data are data collected for the first time, such as from a survey.) The advantage

[26] S. Tamer Cavusgil, "Guidelines for Expert Market Research," *Business Horizons,* November–December 1985, pp. 27–33.
[27] Susan P. Douglas and C. Samuel Craig, *International Marketing Research* (Englewood Cliffs, N.J.: Prentice-Hall, 1983), p. 17.

of primary data is that the data can be tailored to meet the needs of a specific situation. For example, information about buying behavior, such as attitudes toward a product, the role of the family in decision making, or the position of men and women in society, may be important in certain situations. Such information is not likely to be readily available through secondary data sources.

Collecting primary data about international markets is complex. The design of the questionnaire has to be adjusted for different languages, cultural values, and social environments. In some countries, collecting primary data is difficult because the residents view questionnaires and surveys as an invasion of their privacy. Low literacy rates may also create problems in the collection of primary data. Finally, questionnaire respondents are often impossible to locate. These problems are compounded when firms use outside international research suppliers. Locating and evaluating qualified overseas suppliers is difficult, and maintaining quality control over the data collection at such distances is even more problematic.

Nevertheless, the advantages of collecting information about foreign markets outweigh the limitations. The cost of making marketing decisions without sufficient information is higher than the cost of collecting data. The analysis of carefully obtained information from both secondary and primary

TABLE 5.3
Questions to Ask When Analyzing International Markets

About Markets
How large is the market?
How many consumers use the product?
What is our expected market share?
Is the market growing?

About Competitors
Who are our major competitors?
What is the market share of each competitor?
What are the trends in market share among competitors?

About Culture
What is the distribution of the population by education, occupation, and
   religion?
Does our product fit the cultural values of the foreign country?
Can our marketing program be adapted to these cultural values?

About Consumers
What types of consumers buy this product?
What are the characteristics of the consumers in terms of demographics, life-
   style, and attitudes?
How and when do consumers use the product?
What are their motives for buying the product?

About Geography
What is the climate, elevation, and terrain of the nation?
Is there access to the country or region by water, air, railroads, or
   highways?
Can we get our products to the customer at a reasonable cost?

FIGURE 5.4
International Marketing Environment
Global firms such as AIG Companies must have a deep understanding of laws, regulations, customs, and business practices of the countries in which they operate.

Source: Courtesy of American International Group, Inc.

WE COVER THE WATERFRONT. ALL 223,000 MILES OF IT.

World trade in goods and services now surpasses $4 trillion annually, and the importers and exporters for whom the AIG Companies provide insurance coverages touch virtually every coastline in the world. Our global network consists of people with deep understanding of the laws, regulations, customs and business practices of the countries in which they work. As well as local insurance markets and needs. That's why multinational businesses can rely on our people and our services. In the seven decades since our founding, we've built a global network in 130 countries and jurisdictions that could not be duplicated today. At any cost.

AIG WORLD LEADERS IN INSURANCE AND FINANCIAL SERVICES.
American International Group, Inc., Dept. A, 70 Pine Street, New York, NY 10270.

sources can reduce the uncertainty and risk involved in entering international markets. Collecting information about foreign markets is discussed in greater detail in Chapter 9.

THE ENVIRONMENT FOR INTERNATIONAL MARKETING

There are usually significant differences in the marketing environments of domestic and foreign markets. As Figure 5.4 illustrates, a detailed analysis of these differences is critical in determining whether to enter a foreign market. If a marketing strategy is to be effective across national boundaries, differences in cultural, social, economic, political, legal, and technological environments must be understood.

Cultural Environment

Culture is all the learned values, behaviors, and other meaningful symbols, including tools, buildings, foods, clothing, literature, and art, shared by a society. Appreciating the differences in cultures is a basic requirement for successful international marketing.[28] **Cultural diversity** refers to the differences that exist both within and between cultures.[29] Meanings attached to body language, time, greetings, and spatial patterns and other symbols differ significantly across cultures.

■ **cultural diversity** the differences that exist both within and between cultures

---

[28] Kazuo Nukazawa, "Japan and the USA: Wrangling Toward Reciprocity," *Harvard Business Review,* May–June 1988, pp. 42–52.
[29] Nancy J. Adler, *International Dimensions of Organizational Behavior* (Boston: Kent, 1986), pp. 10–11.

When products are introduced into one nation from another, acceptance is far more likely if differences between cultures are recognized and accommodated. For example, the executives of McDonald's realized that when they opened restaurants in Japan, they would have to adapt to Japanese culture. The first McDonald's restaurant was therefore located in a prestigious area in Tokyo to impress the Japanese. Had the restaurant been opened in the suburbs, the Japanese would have considered it a second-class enterprise. Understanding how Japanese consumers view location helped make the efforts of McDonald's in Japan successful.[30] On the other hand, Tokyo-based Yokohama Rubber Co. had to recall automobile tires with a tread pattern that resembled the Arabic word for Allah after receiving protests from Islamic customers. The company apologized for its lack of knowledge of Islam, stopped producing the tires, and replaced them free of charge in Islamic nations.[31]

For international marketers, cultural differences have implications that relate to product development, personal selling, advertising, packaging, and pricing—virtually every aspect of the marketing program. Sometimes cultural differences are small enough that the same marketing mix variable—such as promotion or advertising—can be used in multiple markets. For example, coffee drinking is such a universal habit, if not a ritual, that Colombian coffee growers use the same advertisements in American and foreign markets. More frequently, however, marketing mix elements must be adjusted. Personal selling offers numerous examples. Foreign salespeople doing business in Japan know that saving face and achieving harmony are more important than a sale to the Japanese. Thus, to be successful, salespeople never put a Japanese businessperson in a position where he or she must admit failure. They also approach a Japanese prospect at the highest level possible in the organization (the first person approached will be involved throughout the negotiation). Direct communication about money is avoided if feasible. Finally, and perhaps most difficult of all, American salespeople must wait patiently for Japanese meetings to move forward to the purchase stage.[32]

A growing number of U.S. firms provide cross-cultural training to help managers adjust to differences in foreign countries. Such programs offer a variety of services, including foreign language lessons; lessons on the culture, history, and background of the foreign country; and instructions on how to do business in the foreign country. Many companies also screen employees carefully before giving them international assignments. For instance, some firms require that candidates for international positions speak at least one language other than their native one, have lived outside the United States, and have had some prior international work experience. American Express Company's global management exchange program enables junior managers with at least two years' experience to transfer abroad for eighteen months.[33]

[30]Philip R. Harris and Robert T. Moran, *Managing Cultural Differences* (Houston: Gulf, 1987), p. 189.
[31]"Tires Recalled So They Don't Tread on Allah," Lexington, Ky. *Herald-Leader,* July 25, 1992, p. A3.
[32]Harris and Moran, p. 391.
[33]Joann S. Lublin, "Younger Managers Learn Global Skills," *Wall Street Journal,* March 31, 1992, p. B2.

Social Environment

Social forces such as family, education, religion, and customs directly influence marketing activities. These institutions are identifiable and change from country to country. By finding major deviations in institutions among countries, marketers can gain insights into the adaptation of marketing strategy.

Although the family is the basic unit in all societies, the roles of family members vary. Swiss homemakers, for example, generally consider cleaning the house as one of their primary roles. They will therefore reject advertisements for household products that emphasize saving time and effort.[34]

Education also affects marketing activities. Printed promotions cannot be used sucessfully in countries with low literacy rates.

In some countries, religion exerts a major influence on consumer purchasing behavior, and products may be rejected because of religious beliefs. For instance, Buddhists stress the absence of desire, and Muslims are somewhat reluctant to accept products from Western cultures. Acceptance of certain types of food and clothing are also influenced by religion. International marketers cannot underestimate the impact of religion on the value system of a society and how this impact, in turn, affects consumer behavior.

Business customs play a major role in international marketing. In some countries, one of the major goals in business is to be accepted by others. Japanese workers, for instance, are more concerned with being accepted by their fellow employees than with making a profit. In the Middle Eastern oil markets, companies frequently have to do business via a "connector" who has access to the oil producers and receives a commission for this role. Differences in ethical standards also influence marketing activities. Price fixing, payoffs, and bribes are considered acceptable behavior in some countries. In Mexico, bribes and payoffs are a way of doing business. The Foreign Corrupt Practices Act (FCPA) of 1977 makes it illegal for a U.S. corporation to bribe officials of foreign governments. The FCPA was enacted in the wake of foreign bribery scandals involving U.S. companies and the governments of Belgium, the Netherlands, Honduras, Italy, and Japan.[35]

Economic Environment

In designing international marketing strategies, marketers must examine each country's economic environment. Foreign economies are unfamiliar and often fluctuate even when the domestic economy is stable. Thus marketers must determine the stability of a nation's economy before they can assess the market potential for their products.

The size of the foreign market is another economic factor that must be understood before marketers engage in international marketing. A firm should verify that a market is large enough to justify the costs of marketing products there. Two factors are used to assess the size of a foreign market—population and income. The population of a country must be large enough to attract a firm's interest. The acceptable size varies considerably from one

---

[34]Cateora, pp. 102–103.
[35]Andrew W. Singer, "The Murky Land of the FCPA," *Across the Board,* September 1991, p. 33.

TABLE 5.4
Twenty-five Largest Countries

Rank	Country	Population (in millions)
1	China	1,151.5
2	India	869.5
3	United States	252.5
4	Indonesia	193.5
5	Brazil	155.3
6	Russia	148.3
7	Japan	124.0
8	Nigeria	122.5
9	Pakistan	117.5
10	Bangladesh	116.6
11	Mexico	90.0
12	Germany	79.5
13	Viet Nam	67.6
14	Philippines	65.7
15	Iran	59.0
16	Turkey	58.0
17	Italy	57.8
18	United Kingdom	57.5
19	Thailand	56.8
20	France	56.6
21	Egypt	54.4
22	Ethiopia	53.2
23	South Korea	43.1
24	Spain	39.4
25	Poland	37.8

Source: *Statistical Abstract of the United States,* 1992, pp. 820–822.

company to another. Some firms market only to the largest nations, which are listed in Table 5.4. Other firms market products in countries where the population is less than one million. Marketers must also investigate population trends to determine if the country is growing.

Next, businesses must examine the prospective market's income as measured by output. A nation's **gross national product** is an overall measure of its economic standing in terms of the value of all goods and services produced by that nation for a given period of time, usually a year. The United States has a GNP of more than $5,400 billion, the largest in the world. Gross national product per capita, which takes into account a nation's GNP in relation to its population, measures a nation's standard of living. The per capita GNP of the United States is $20,910. Japan's GNP is $2,910 billion, but the per capita GNP is $22,900.[36] Thus, the average Japanese citizen has as high a standard of living as an American.

Gross domestic product (GDP) measures the purely domestic output of a country. The difference between GNP and GDP is net factor income from abroad, or income received from other nations by domestic residents less

■ **gross national product (GNP)** an overall measure of a nation's economic standing in terms of the value of all products produced by that nation for a given period of time

■ **gross domestic product (GDP)** a measure of the purely domestic output of a country

[36] *Statistical Abstract of the United States,* 1992, pp. 830–831.

TABLE 5.5
GNP and GDP for
Selected Countries

Country (currency units)	GNP (billions)	GDP (billions)
Australia	294	240
Canada	558	507
France	1,188	818
Ireland	37	32
Japan	2,910	1,908
Netherlands	276	204
Spain	487	402
Turkey	110	248
United Kingdom	975	821
United States	5,465	5,132

Source: *Statistical Abstract of the United States,* 1992, pp. 830, 833.

income payments made to foreign residents. In other words, GDP equals GNP minus net income from abroad, and represents the market value of the final goods and services produced by factors of production in the domestic country. Some countries report only GDP data, and international organizations often use it as a comparison of output between nations. Table 5.5 lists GNP and GDP for several countries. In many countries, GNP exceeds GDP because the factor income received from abroad exceeds the factor income paid out to foreign countries. If GDP exceeds GNP, more is paid to foreign factor owners than is received from abroad by domestic factor owners.

If a foreign market is large enough to capture marketers' interest, that nation's economic condition should be examined more closely. Developed countries such as the United States, Canada, and Japan have high literacy rates, modern technology, and high GNP per capita. These nations often provide the greatest marketing opportunities. In developing countries, especially in Latin America, education and technology are improving, but GNP per capita is fairly low. Many less developed countries in Africa and Southeast Asia have lower education levels, limited technology, and very low GNP per capita. But although current marketing opportunities are limited in developing and less developed countries, long-term opportunities may be extremely favorable as these nations progress.

■ **infrastructure** the communications, transportation, and energy facilities that mobilize a nation

The **infrastructure** of a nation—the communications, transportation, and energy facilities that mobilize the country—also provides an indication of its economic condition.[37] The extent to which a firm can successfully promote a product in different countries partially depends on the communications media available. Similarly, the quantity and quality of transportation facilities affect a firm's ability to distribute its products. In a developed country like Italy, marketers use sophisticated telecommunications systems to conduct business and marketing activities. AT&T has established a joint venture in China to help modernize the country's phone system. It is the largest foreign venture ever for the phone giant.[38] In sharp contrast, many less developed

[37] Terpstra (1987), p. 31.
[38] Bart Ziegler, "AT&T Reaches Way Out for This One," *Business Week,* March 8, 1993, p. 83.

nations have neither a sizable newspaper circulation nor an adequate road or railway system. Another good measure of economic conditions is a country's energy consumption: the higher the level of energy consumption, the greater the market potential. Energy is needed to power machinery and transform resources into usable products.

Political and Legal Environment

Political and legal forces also shape a firm's international marketing activities. A government's policies toward public and private enterprise, consumers, and foreign firms influence marketing across national boundaries. Some countries encourage and seek out foreign investors. Other countries develop barriers to prevent companies from doing business there.

One of the major factors international marketers must be concerned with is the political stability of foreign nations. Countries experiencing intense political unrest may change their policies toward outside firms at any time. This creates an unfavorable environment for international marketing. In some political power struggles, production facilities have been destroyed, corporate assets seized, and personal security of employees and their families jeopardized; such situations existed in Iran and Libya in the 1980s and in Yugoslavia in the 1990s.

How government regulations restrict business can influence a firm's decision to enter a foreign market. Some nations are relatively open to international marketing, and others use trade barriers to discourage entry of products or operations. A **quota** limits the amount of a product that can leave or enter a country. Europe has placed a quota on the number of Japanese cars that can be sold in the European market. Some quotas are established on a voluntary basis and tend to foster good will between nations. Japan has agreed to set a target to buy 20 percent of its computer chips from U.S. firms; imported chips accounted for over 17 percent of Japan's market in 1992.[39] An **embargo** prohibits the import or export of certain goods. Embargoes often are politically motivated, such as the United Nations' embargo of goods to Iraq after that nation invaded Kuwait. An **import tariff** is a tax or duty levied against goods brought into a country. Tourists traveling to a foreign country must pay a duty on goods they purchase and bring back to their home country. Likewise, duties are placed on a variety of goods such as watches or cameras brought into one country from another. Within days of taking office, President Clinton used tariffs to double the price of European steel, touching off talk about possible retaliation from Europe.[40] An **exchange control** limits how much profit a foreign-based firm can return to its home country. Exchange controls can be used to limit the amount of goods that importers can purchase with a particular currency.

Many countries rely on customs and entry procedures to restrict the entry of foreign products. **Customs and entry procedures** govern the inspection, documentation, and licensing of goods entering a country. The documents governments require are often extensive and complex. Japan requires six

■ **quota** a limit on the amount of a product that can leave or enter a country

■ **embargo** a government restriction that prohibits the import or export of certain goods

■ **import tariff** a tax or duty levied against goods brought into a country

■ **exchange control** a government restriction that limits how much profit a foreign-based firm can return to its home country

■ **customs and entry procedures** rules and procedures governing the inspection, documentation, and licensing of goods entering a country

---

[39] Douglas Harbrecht, Neil Gross, and Peter Burrows, "Suppose They Gave a Trade War and Nobody Came," *Business Week,* March 29, 1993, p. 30.
[40] Richard C. Morais, "Saber Rattling," *Forbes,* March 1, 1993, p. 49.

TABLE 5.6
U.S. Laws Affecting
International Marketing

Law	Purpose
Webb-Pomerene Export Trade Act (1918)	Exempts U.S. firms from antitrust laws if they are acting together to develop international trade
Foreign Corrupt Practices Act (1977)	Makes bribing foreign officials to obtain sales illegal for U.S. firms
Export Trading Companies Act (1982)	Encourages the formation of export trading companies by eliminating antitrust barriers and allowing banks to participate in such ventures

volumes of standards for each automobile that enters the country. Without proper documentation, products do not clear Japanese customs. In France, customs documentation must be in French, a requirement that often slows product clearance. Beer cannot be imported into Mexico without a license. To obtain a license, the importer must prove that domestic demand cannot be met by Mexican brewers alone. India requires licenses for all imported goods.[41]

The major U.S. laws affecting American firms engaged in international marketing are summarized in Table 5.6. The *Webb-Pomerene Export Trade Act* of 1918 exempts U.S. firms from certain antitrust laws if they are working together to develop export markets. The Webb-Pomerene Act does not allow companies to reduce competition in the United States or to use unfair methods of competition. As mentioned earlier, the *Foreign Corrupt Practices Act* of 1977 prohibits American firms from making bribes to foreign officials. This law spells out the penalties for companies and individuals who are in violation: Companies may be fined up to $1 million, and individuals may receive a fine of up to $10,000 and a prison sentence of up to five years. The *Export Trading Companies Act* of 1982 eliminates some antitrust barriers and allows banks to participate in joint ventures. (An export trading company is an organization that attempts to create exports).

The highest risks for international firms are found in countries such as El Salvador, Afghanistan, and Iran, which are politically unstable and place many restrictions on business. On the other hand, countries such as the United States, Japan, Australia, and South Korea are considered attractive because they are politically stable and place fewer restrictions on business.

Technological Environment

Technology is also a major consideration when becoming involved in international marketing. Not all countries are at the same level of technological

[41] Sak Onkvisit and John J. Shaw, "Marketing Barriers in International Trade," *Business Horizons,* May–June 1988, pp. 64–72.

development. For instance, electricity is not readily available in some parts of the world, and thus demand is not high for products requiring electricity to operate. Communications systems also differ throughout the world. Some countries lack modern broadcasting and postal services; therefore, much of the marketing technology used for advertising cannot be used in these nations. Firms engaged in international marketing must determine how the levels of technology in foreign countries might affect their decisions. Close to the Customer illustrates how production technology gives Toyota a competitive edge.

MULTINATIONAL MARKET GROUPS

■ **multinational market group** a group of two or more countries that agree to reduce trade and tariff barriers between one another

Companies operating in the global marketing environment must recognize that economic cooperation among nations is increasing. A **multinational market group** is created when two or more countries agree to reduce trade and tariff barriers between one another. Several current and emerging markets are discussed in this section, including North America, the European Community, the Pacific Rim, and Eastern Europe and the Commonwealth of Independent States (former Soviet Union).

North America

In 1989 the United States and Canada signed the Free Trade Agreement (FTA) providing for the eventual elimination of tariffs and other trade barriers. Trade between the United States and Canada was nearly $170 billion annually before the FTA was signed.[42] The agreement essentially merged the U.S. and Canadian markets and made them the largest free trade zone in the world. The FTA calls for most trade restrictions to be removed in stages over a ten-year period. Tariffs were removed immediately on some products. Trade barriers for business personnel and restrictions on financial services are being phased out as quickly as possible.[43] This agreement is intended to help both U.S. and Canadian firms compete more effectively with companies in Europe and Asia.

An even more far-reaching proposal than the FTA is the North American Free Trade Agreement (NAFTA), a three-nation alliance of the United States, Canada, and Mexico. The agreement makes sense to many, since the United States needs resources and a source of new labor, Canada is resource-rich but has a small population, and Mexico has oil and an abundance of workers but desperately needs exports to help its economy. Together, the three nations would constitute a $6 trillion market of about 360 million consumers.[44]

[42] Ann H. Hughes, "United States and Canada Form World's Largest Free Trade Area," *Business America,* January 3, 1989, pp. 2–5.
[43] Robin Gaines, "FTA Provides Vehicle for Driving into the Future," *Business America,* January 30, 1989, p. 5.
[44] Blayne Cutler, "North American Demographics," *American Demographics,* March 1992, pp. 38–42.

CLOSE TO THE CUSTOMER

No Foreign Language at Toyota

In order to produce world-class, quality automobiles at competitive price levels, Toyota Motor Manufacturing, U.S.A. has developed an integrated approach to production which manages equipment, materials, and people in the most efficient manner. The Toyota production system is built on two main principles: just-in-time production and *jidoka.* Underlying this management philosophy and the entire production process is the concept that "good thinking means good product."

Just-in-Time The *just-in-time* production philosophy is the foundation of the Toyota process. This concept refers to the manufacturing and conveyance of only what is needed, when it is needed, and in the amount needed. In addition, a minimum amount of inventory is kept on hand. This enhances efficiency and enables quick response to change.

Jidoka Top quality for Toyota's automobiles is ensured through *jidoka.* This defect detection system automatically or manually stops the production operation and/or equipment whenever an abnormal or defective condition arises. Any necessary improvements can then be made by directing attention to the stopped equipment and the worker who stopped the operation. The jidoka system puts faith in the worker as a thinker and allows all workers the right to stop the line on which they are working.

Kanban Toyota's use of *kanban,* a unique information-carrying device, ensures that every operation produces only the amount of a product that will actually be used in the next step of the production process.

Heijunka The *heijunka* method of leveling production at the final assembly line makes just-in-time production possible. This involves averaging both the volume and sequence of different model types on a mixed-model production line.

Kaizen *Kaizen,* or continuous improvement, is the hallmark of the Toyota production system. The primary objectives are to identify and eliminate *muda* or waste in all areas, including the production process, and to ensure quality and safety. The key elements of kaizen emphasize making a task simpler and easier to perform, increasing the speed and efficiency of the work process, maintaining a safe work environment, and constantly improving the product quality.

Standardized Work The Toyota production system organizes all jobs around human motion and creates an efficient production sequence without *muda.* Work organized in such a way is called standardized work. It is made up of three elements: takt-time, working sequence, and standard in-process stock.

Takt-Time *Takt-time* is the time which should be taken to produce a component or one vehicle. This timing mechanism is based on the monthly production schedule. Daily total operating time is figured on the basis of all machinery operating at 100 percent efficiency during regular working hours.

Working Sequence This refers to the sequence of operations in a single process through which a floor worker produces quality goods in the most efficient way.

Standard In-Process Stock This is the minimum quantity of parts always on hand for processing in and between subprocesses. It allows the worker to do his or her job continuously in a set sequence of subprocesses, repeating the same operation over and over in the same order.

Source: Alan I. Kirschenbaum, "Revving Up the American Auto Industry—the Toyota Way," *The Lane Report*, November 1991, p. 12.

On August 12, 1992, representatives of the United States, Canada, and Mexico consented to the historic agreement, which awaits the approval of the respective governments. Combined trade among the three nations, which was $237 billion before NAFTA, could soar once trade barriers between the nations are removed.[45] But many are concerned that the agreement will mean more U.S. jobs lost to Mexico, where wages are about 10 percent of those in the United States.[46] Some economists argue that over the long run NAFTA should benefit the American economy. By cutting labor costs, U.S. firms would be in a better position to take on European and Japanese competitors.[47] They also contend that the treaty will keep U.S. exports to Mexico booming, and create more good jobs in three key sectors of the U.S. economy: motor vehicles and parts, textiles and apparel, and telecommunications.[48]

The European Community

The twelve-nation European Community (EC), created by the Treaty of Rome in 1957, agreed to eliminate most trade barriers between its members (Germany, France, Italy, the United Kingdom, Spain, the Netherlands, Belgium, Denmark, Greece, Portugal, Ireland, and Luxembourg) by 1992. Historically, the member nations have primarily been separate markets and could not compete with the giant resources of Japan and the United States. When the barriers are dissolved, however, it is expected that more competitive European companies will be tapping the unified European market. Consisting of more than 340 million consumers, unified Europe will be one of the largest markets in the world.[49]

Although unification has cost more than expected, Europe's economy has already benefited. The elimination of trade barriers has meant big gains in several industries, including airlines, telecommunications, and financial services (see Figure 5.5). Travelers no longer need passports to travel between borders, and shippers have seen red tape cut significantly. Although single market reform has generally been successful, the critical second phase of unification—monetary union—has been less successful. The Maastrict Treaty, an amendment to the original Treaty of Rome, mandates a single European currency by 1999 and a framework for coordinating defense and foreign policies. Denmark rejected the treaty early in 1992; France nearly rejected it several months later. Establishing one currency would eliminate expensive currency transactions that cost firms billions of dollars and would make it easier for companies to sell products across borders and for consumers to compare prices.[50] Failure to establish a single currency would be a major setback to unification.

---

[45] Gaylon White, "Run for the Border," *Express Magazine,* Summer 1991, pp. 10–13.
[46] Kenneth H. Bacon, "With Free-Trade Pact About Wrapped Up, the Real Battle Begins," *Wall Street Journal,* August 7, 1992, pp. A1, A14.
[47] Amy Borrus, "A Free-Trade Milestone, with Many More Miles to Go," *Business Week,* August 24, 1992, pp. 30–31.
[48] Louis S. Richman, "How NAFTA Will Help America," *Fortune,* April 10, 1993, pp. 95–102.
[49] Phil Davies, "Europe Unbound," *Express Magazine,* Spring 1992, pp. 16–19.
[50] Shawn Tully, "Europe 1992," *Fortune,* August 24, 1992, pp. 136–142.

FIGURE 5.5
The European Community
The unification of Europe means new opportunities for companies in many industries, such as France Telecom, which ran this ad in 1991 and 1992 to advertise its ability to connect firms around the world with firms located in the European Community.

Source: Courtesy France Telecom, Inc.

A unified Europe will be prepared to fight for a larger share of the global market. Prior to unity, European industry was inefficient, with 22 airlines, 12 automobile manufacturers, and 225 brands of home appliances. Firms are redesigning themselves to take advantage of the large European market. Dutch manufacturer Phillips Electronics has cut 20 percent of its work force and is closing plants to concentrate production at its most efficient sites. British Telecommunications PLC has cut 170,000 jobs and invested $17 billion in new technology, and is taking business from U.S. firms. French steel maker Usinon-Sacilor, near bankruptcy ten years ago, has eliminated half of its jobs and invested in new technology to become the world's second largest steel maker.[51] Many U.S. companies that already had a presence in Europe, including IBM, GM, and Coca-Cola, should also benefit from a unified Europe.

The Pacific Rim

The Pacific Rim nations include Japan, China, Taiwan, South Korea, Singapore, Hong Kong, the Philippines, Malaysia, Indonesia, Australia, and Indochina. Firms from these nations, especially Japan, have become increasingly

[51] Stewart Toy, John Templeman, Richard A. Melcher, John Rossant, and Stanley Reed, "Europe's Shakeout," *Business Week*, September 14, 1992, pp. 44–51.

competitive with U.S. firms. Names like Toyota, Sony, and Canon are not only household words, but they also represent firms that have eroded the market share of their U.S. counterparts—General Motors, Zenith, and Kodak. Firms from Taiwan, South Korea, Hong Kong, and Singapore are expected to be even more competitive in the future. The Pearl River Delta region of southern China is the fastest-growing economy in the world and demonstrates the economic potential of China. U.S. and other Western firms, including Procter & Gamble, Pabst Brewing Co., Lockheed, and GEC Alsthom of France, are doing business in this region.[52] In mid-1997, China takes over the British colony of Hong Kong, and promises to let capitalism flourish. This could make Hong Kong an open international business hub in China.[53]

Although no formal alliances exist among nations in the Pacific Rim, there has been much speculation about future alliances. Some have noted the possibility of an alliance between the United States, Japan, Taiwan, China, and Hong Kong. Although there has been some talk of a U.S.-Japanese free trade agreement, any such arrangement is years away. The lack of such an agreement has led many U.S. leaders to criticize Japan's trade restrictions on products from the United States and other nations. Although many formal trade barriers have been removed by the Japanese government, firms trying to do business in Japan are still confronted with other barriers, such as the high cost of doing business there, which includes long delays in receiving patents, during which time Japanese companies examine patent applications and duplicate new technologies; corruption, including collusion among Japanese bidders; and purchasing agents who, as part of old-boy networks, refuse to buy foreign goods.[54]

Eastern Europe and the Commonwealth of Independent States

In 1985, Communist party secretary Mikhail Gorbachev began a new program called *perestroika,* or economic restructuring. This program promoted reduced government control and fewer regulations. Under *perestroika,* the Soviet Union and the Eastern European nations of Poland, Hungary, Yugoslavia, Czechoslovakia, Romania, and Bulgaria have undergone great changes. In December of 1991, Russian president Boris Yeltsin organized the Commonwealth of Independent States to replace the staggering Soviet Union and bring together the former Soviet republics in a loose economic and political alliance. Borders between the states are open, but there is no central government. The commonwealth agreement does commit the republics to coordinate economic policies. Barely twelve months after launching his bid to create a market-oriented democracy, Yeltsin faced many setbacks, includ-

[52]Ford S. Worthy, "Where Capitalism Thrives in China," *Fortune,* March 9, 1992, pp. 71–75.
[53]Louis Kraar, "Storm Over Hong Kong," *Fortune,* March 8, 1993, pp. 98–104.
[54]Edmund Faltermayer, "Does Japan Play Fair?" *Fortune,* September 7, 1992, pp. 38–52.

ing a deep recession and large numbers of layoffs.[55] On March 12, 1993, Yeltsin's opponents in the parliament slashed his presidential powers, but Yeltsin may yet prevail as the public seems to remain committed to economic and political unity.[56]

Most of the rationale behind the dramatic changes in Eastern Europe and the Commonwealth of Independent States is the desire to improve the economic conditions of these nations. The result is a more market-oriented society in which businesses formerly owned by the government have been granted independence. Economic and political restructuring also means marketing opportunities for American and other foreign firms, either through joint ventures or through direct ownership. GM's Trinity Motors, a Russia–United States–United Kingdom joint venture, opened its first dealership in downtown Moscow to sell GM cars to customers from all over the former Soviet Union. The showroom is across the street from McDonald's.[57] Consumers are also adjusting, making Eastern Europe a hot market. U.S. exports to Poland, Czechoslovakia, and Bulgaria rose 25 percent in 1992, to about $1.5 billion.[58]

The former Soviet Union is also a potential gold mine for oil. The states of the commonwealth, especially Russia, have about 25 percent of the world's undiscovered oil, as much as the Middle East. They also have more natural gas than Saudi Arabia. If all this energy were developed and marketed, it could help balance the world's supply of oil for years to come and greatly reduce Western dependence on the Middle East for oil.[59] This opportunity has many large Western oil companies, including Chevron, British Petroleum, Elf Aquitaine, Texaco, Royal Dutch/Shell, Exxon, Mobil, Amoco, Gulf Canada/British Gas, and many others, rushing to help develop these resources.[60] By the end of the century, exports from this part of the world could reach six million barrels a day.

Several of the reforming nations, including Russia and Poland, want to reduce trade restrictions to encourage trade with other countries. The Russians have found that joint ventures, such as the one between the Moscow City Council's division of food service and McDonald's, can be rewarding. For example, McDonald's is helping the Russians learn new agricultural and food-processing systems and a new appreciation for capitalism. These sweeping changes will also lead to more opportunities for Eastern European nations. Many already are speculating that some of these nations will join the European Community or eventually will form their own multinational market group. The reunification of East and West Germany, for example, has resulted in a single Germany that is a major force in the European Community.

[55] Paul Hofheinz, "Russia 1993," *Fortune,* January 25, 1993, pp. 106–108.
[56] Rose Brady, Deborah Stead, Richard A. Melcher, Gail E. Schares, and David Greising, "Why Yeltsin May Prevail," *Business Week,* April 5, 1993, pp. 34–35.
[57] Betsy McKay, "Caddies Supplant Communism as GM Sells Autos in Moscow," *Advertising Age,* June 15, 1992, p. 10.
[58] Rick Tetzeli, "Eastern Europe is One Hot Market," *Fortune,* January 25, 1993, p. 14.
[59] Peter Nulty, "The Black Gold Rush in Russia," *Fortune,* June 15, 1992, pp. 126–130.
[60] Toni Mack, "The Last Frontier," *Forbes,* May 11, 1992, pp. 54–58.

SUMMARY

International marketing is the performance of marketing activities across national boundaries. The primary difference between marketing and international marketing is the manner in which these activities are performed. Learning how to do business in other countries is critical to U.S. firms. More than ever before, people throughout the world have similar wants and needs. As competition in this global marketing environment intensifies, the number of firms operating solely in domestic markets is decreasing.

In general, an organization can commit to one of four distinct levels of international marketing: (1) none, (2) infrequent, (3) regular, or (4) global. Global marketing involves developing marketing strategies as if the entire world were one large market. Some firms develop a standardized marketing mix for their products; other firms believe the marketing mix should be customized to take into account differences among nations in cultures, values, and languages.

There are several approaches to international marketing. Exporting, the lowest level of commitment to international marketing, is the sale of products to a foreign country. Licensing is an arrangement in which the licensee (a foreign company) pays the licensor (an international firm) commissions or royalties for the right to use its name, products, patents, brands and trademarks, raw materials, production processes, or managerial and technical assistance. Businesses may enter international markets through trading companies, which buy products in the domestic market and sell them in foreign markets. Countertrading, involving bartering agreements between two or more countries, allows nations with limited cash to participate in international trade. Other approaches to international marketing include the joint venture and direct ownership. A joint venture is a partnership between a domestic firm and a foreign firm or government. Direct ownership of foreign divisions or subsidiaries represents the highest level of commitment to international marketing and involves the greatest risk.

Because of the uncertainty involved in international marketing, marketers must analyze international markets. Both secondary and primary data are needed to analyze the potential of foreign markets. Marketers need information to make specific marketing decisions such as what price to charge, what advertising theme to use, what product features to modify, and how to design distribution channels. Information is also needed about differences in culture, economic conditions, and demographic variations.

There are usually significant differences in the marketing environments of domestic and foreign markets. A detailed analysis of the foreign environment is critical in making international marketing decisions. Environmental aspects of special importance include cultural, social, economic, political, and legal forces. Cultural aspects of the environment that are most important to international marketers include countries' values, behaviors, and meaningful symbols. Social forces such as family, education, and religion also influence marketing activities.

Marketers must examine each country's economic environment. Population and income are often used to measure the size of a market. A nation's gross national product (GNP) is an overall measure of its economic standing in terms of the value of all products produced by that nation for a given period of time. Gross national product per capita, which takes into account a nation's GNP in relation to its population, is a measure of a nation's standard of living. Gross domestic product (GDP) is a measure of a nation's domestic output. The nation's stage of development and infrastructure are also used to assess its economic condition.

Political and legal institutions influence a firm's international marketing activities. Firms must be concerned with government policies; the political stability of foreign nations; and government regulations used to restrict foreign business, such as quotas, embargoes, import tariffs, exchange controls, and customs and entry procedures. Firms engaged in international marketing must also determine how different levels of technology in foreign countries might affect their decisions.

A multinational marketing group is created when two or more countries agree to reduce trade and tariff barriers between one another. The United States and Canada, through the Free Trade Agreement (FTA) signed in 1989, are eliminating tariffs and other trade barriers. Trade between Mexico and the United States has been growing, and the North American Free Trade Agreement (NAFTA) between the United States, Canada, and Mexico has been finalized. The twelve members of the European Community (EC) agreed to eliminate most trade barriers between members by 1992. A market group is emerging in the Pacific Rim, although no formal trade agreements exist among nations. The Commonwealth of Independent States and other Eastern European nations are reducing government control of trade, which could lead to new market groups.

KEY TERMS

international marketing	cultural diversity
multinational corporations	gross national product (GNP)
global marketing	gross domestic product (GDP)
exporting	infrastructure
licensing	quota
trading company	embargo
countertrading	import tariff
joint venture	exchange control
strategic alliance	customs and entry procedures
direct ownership	multinational market group

QUESTIONS FOR DISCUSSION AND REVIEW

1. What is the difference between marketing and international marketing?
2. What is meant by the global marketplace? What is the significance of the global marketplace?
3. Why should American firms become involved in international marketing?

4. What is the difference between standardizing the marketing mix and customizing the marketing mix? Under which conditions can a firm effectively standardize the marketing mix?

5. What are the critical factors a firm must consider in determining an approach to international marketing?

6. Describe the direct ownership approach to international marketing. Why do firms invest in foreign subsidiaries?

7. What are some of the problems encountered in obtaining secondary data about international markets? Primary data?

8. Why is it important to examine the environment of a foreign market before engaging in international marketing activities?

9. Name some social forces that might influence international marketing activities.

10. What is the difference between GNP and GDP? Which is more useful in comparing the output of different nations? Explain.

11. How can government regulations be used to restrict a firm from entering a foreign market?

12. What is a multinational market group? Discuss two such groups that will mean greater competition for the United States.

CASES

5.1 COCA-COLA LOOKS TO EASTERN EUROPE

It's "You Can't Beat the Feeling" in America; "I Feel Coca-Cola" in Japan; "A Unique Sensation" in Italy; and in Chile, "The Feeling of Life." The subtle differences in these slogans reflect Coca-Cola's philosophy regarding global marketing: Plan globally and act locally. In other words, Coca-Cola has developed a fairly standardized marketing strategy and views the entire world as a single market, but it is also sensitive to local cultures. The formula has succeeded. International sales account for about 80 percent of Coca-Cola's profits.

But Coca-Cola, like many firms, is finding growth difficult. Coca-Cola's share of the grocery store soft drink market fell from 61.8 to 60.4 percent in 1991. One point of market share is worth about $460 million in sales. Some cola drinkers are changing to cheaper store brands like Wal-Mart's Sam's American Choice. Noncolas like Dr Pepper and Barq's root beer have also grown in popularity, along with flavored seltzers, juice drinks, and "natural" sodas.

Changing tastes and falling market share have Coca-Cola looking to Eastern Europe for new market opportunities. Since 1989, Coca-Cola has invested $450 million in eastern Germany. Former East Germans, who watched

Coca-Cola commercials on West German television for years, are crazy about Coca-Cola. Germany is Coca-Cola's largest market among European Community nations, which contributed $767 million in 1991 profits, more than the United States did. And in Moscow, Coca-Cola is building a $15 million production plant and training facility. At 177 rubles a can (27 cents), not many Russians can afford it yet, but Coca-Cola has plans to stay in Russia for the long haul. They are planning to build a $50 million production plant in St. Petersburg.

Horst Muller, the head of Coca-Cola's operations in eastern Germany, encountered one major difficulty—finding sales representatives. Muller needed sales representatives to handle orders, deliveries, and sales promotions. But the people of eastern Germany come from a culture where selling is a foreign idea. So he turned to his 2,100 employees, many of whom came from former East German plants that Coca-Cola bought from the state. The friendliest technicians, factory workers, and clerks were sent to the West for sales training. The result was an enthusiastic team of sales representatives hustling for new business. Coca-Cola sold 74 million cases of soda in eastern Germany in 1991, up from zero cases the previous year.

With this level of success, Coca-Cola expects to take on PepsiCo, Inc., which has had a stronghold in most of Eastern Europe and the former Soviet Union for years. Pepsi has always been weaker than Coca-Cola in Germany, and Coca-Cola's dominance in Western Europe (where it outsells Pepsi 6 to 1) has helped bring Coca-Cola closer to lucrative markets in Eastern Europe dominated by Pepsi. Industry analysts expect Coca-Cola to start shipping to Poland from its eastern German plants. Coca-Cola also has facilities planned for Bulgaria, Romania, Czechoslovakia, and Russia.

Success will not come easy for Coca-Cola in Eastern Europe. PepsiCo already has sixty-five bottling plants in Eastern Europe and the former Soviet Union. Awareness of the Pepsi brand is higher than of any other brand. Pepsi sold 45 million cases in the former Soviet Union alone in 1991, and has allocated $1 billion for global expansion. But as the cola wars are staged on new ground in the future, many expect Coca-Cola's superior global resources to neutralize PepsiCo's advantage in Eastern Europe.

Questions for Discussion

1. Does Coca-Cola have a global marketing strategy? Explain.
2. What cultural barriers did Coca-Cola encounter in eastern Germany?
3. Why does Coca-Cola consider Europe (member nations of the EC) and Eastern Europe so important?
4. Will competitors be able to follow Coca-Cola into Eastern Europe with the same degree of success?

Based on information from Laurie Hays, "Amid Russian Turmoil, Coca-Cola Is Placing a Bet on the Future," *Wall Street Journal,* April 6, 1993, pp. A1, A5; Walecia Konrad and Igor Reichlin, "The Real Thing Is Thundering Eastward," *Business Week,* April 13, 1992, pp. 96–98; Walecia Konrad, "The Cola Kings Are Feeling a Bit Jumpy," *Business Week,* July 13, 1992, p. 112; and Jim Wagner, "A Brand Name Ball Game," *Food Processing,* September 1991, pp. 65–80.

5.2   AIRBUS BECOMES A MAJOR GLOBAL PLAYER

Aircraft manufacturer Airbus Industrie has taken the industry by storm. Airbus has gained about 30 percent of new orders in the world market, while Boeing, long dominant in the commercial aircraft business, has seen its percentage of new orders drop from nearly 80 to around 70 percent and McDonnell Douglas has been virtually shut out. By offering the latest in technology, a wide range of planes, and customer service, Airbus has persuaded fifteen of the seventeen largest airlines in the world to fly its jets.

Airbus is a consortium of four European partners—France's Aerospatiale, Germany's Deutsche Airbus, Britain's Aerospace, and Spain's CASA—and is supported by their respective governments. When the consortium came together in 1970, many people questioned whether experts from four distinct and sometimes hostile cultures could build and sell a product as complex as aircraft. Airbus has become a model of multinational cooperation, although the partners still face the major problem of having four different currencies in the dollar-based global aircraft market, and bitter battles still arise over where manufacturing will be done.

Airbus brought out its first plane, the A-300, a twin-engine wide body, in 1974 and made its first U.S. sales in 1977, to Eastern Air Lines. It practically gave the planes away to enter the North American market, which accounts for 45 percent of the world market. But at the time Airbus offered few service guarantees and lacked experience with the aircraft buying and selling network, in which financial help and service are paramount.

It took a revamped marketing strategy for the consortium to gain credibility in the crucial North American market. Responding to customer needs, Airbus added longer-range, more powerful, and fuel-efficient planes to its product line. It took chances on new technology and started from scratch to design its jets for maximum efficiency, with everything planned to work as a whole, from the galley to the lavatory.

To spur sales, the North American operation hired as its head a veteran airline leasing executive, plus salespeople experienced in the U.S. market. Then came a service overhaul. Airbus had trailed competitors on delivery times of parts and on quality and prices of material. In 1988 Airbus opened a mechanics' and pilots' training center in Miami and in 1991 a parts distribution center at Washington's Dulles Airport, with $125 million of parts in stock.

A break came for Airbus when American Airlines, searching for new, fuel-efficient aircraft with plenty of cargo space, bought thirty-five stretched A300s. Says the head of Airbus's North American operation, "That was the deal that required everyone in the industry to look at what we had to offer." Air Canada, Federal Express, America West, and TWA followed American in buying Airbus planes. In 1991, Delta ordered nine narrow-body A310s. Then, in July of 1992, United Air Lines agreed to lease fifty narrow-body A320s and took options on fifty more. The United deal means that nearly every major U.S. airline now flies Airbus jets (USAir Inc. is the exception).

United's agreement to lease the Airbus A320s came after fourteen years of ordering only Boeing planes. Compared to Boeing's 737-400, the Airbus jet has a 15 to 20 percent advantage in range, an ability to fly further out of high-altitude airports, advanced fly-by-wire electronic controls, and a heavily computerized cockpit. Boeing had considered an innovative design but instead added technical improvements to the existing 737, in the belief that airlines would still want the plane for "commonality" savings, such as not having to retrain flight and maintenance crews. Yet Airbus offered an advantage there, too; it will train United's pilots and mechanics.

The European consortium also offered tremendous financial incentives to obtain the lease with United, a deal worth $3 billion. Some industry observers estimate that Airbus knocked the price per plane from about $41 million down to about $30 million. It also gave United a "walkaway" deal: United can get out of the lease on eleven months' notice. Boeing, although offering generous customer financing, could not meet similar terms. A U.S. government official said the United States will take action if the Airbus-United transaction involved government subsidies that are illegal under GATT.

Airbus's subsidies from European governments have been controversial from the beginning. Boeing and McDonnell Douglas have long sought an end to the subsidies on the grounds that the payments violate international trade agreements. A U.S. House of Representatives committee report has called Airbus's success a "direct assault" on U.S. competitors. Says Congressman Robert Walker, "When you consider that sales of U.S.-manufactured aircraft abroad have been the only consistently positive area in the balance of trade since World War II, you realize how important it is that this industry be treated fairly."

Airbus insists that the billions of dollars it has received are long-term loans that eventually will be repaid. Its officials say that Europe had to provide subsidies to build an airline industry from the ground up, and they contend that U.S. commercial aircraft manufacturers have benefited from defense and NASA contracts and tax incentives, to the tune of around $40 billion. After six years of talks, U.S. and European negotiators reached a tentative agreement that would limit direct European government subsidies to 33 percent of new development costs and limit indirect benefits, such as new technology developed for the military that can be applied to commercial planes.

Questions for Discussion

1. Which approach to international marketing does Airbus represent?

2. Observers would classify Airbus as a European company, and Boeing and McDonnell Douglas as American companies. How accurate are these classifications?

3. In marketing planes to North America, what environmental aspects did Airbus have to consider?

Based on information from Jeff Cole, "Airbus Is Said to Step Up Duel with Boeing," *Wall Street Journal*, January 21, 1993, p. A3; Jeff Cole, "Boeing's Dominance of Aircraft Industry Is Beginning to Erode," *Wall Street Journal*, July 10, 1992, pp. A1, A6; Dori Jones Yang, "Now, Airbus Is Cruising Comfortably," *Business Week*, July 27, 1992, p. 33; and Kenneth Labich, "Airbus Takes Off," *Fortune*, June 1, 1992, pp. 102–104, 108.

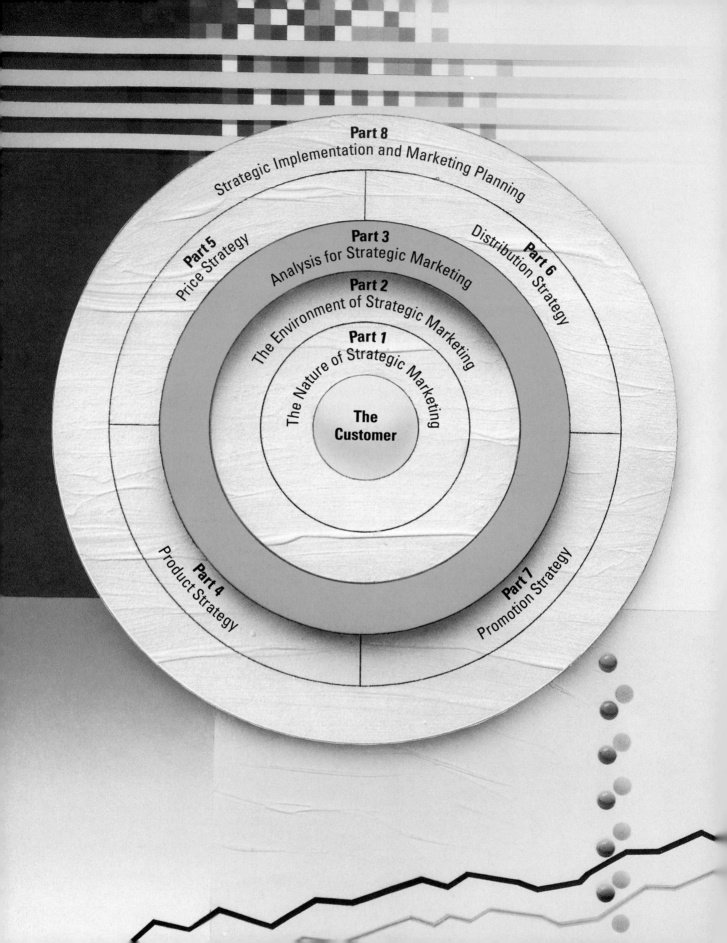

Part 8
Strategic Implementation and Marketing Planning

Part 5
Price Strategy

Part 3
Analysis for Strategic Marketing

Part 6
Distribution Strategy

Part 2
The Environment of Strategic Marketing

Part 1
The Nature of Strategic Marketing

The Customer

Part 4
Product Strategy

Part 7
Promotion Strategy

Analysis for Strategic Marketing

Market Segmentation and Forecasting

6

OBJECTIVES

- *To discuss the nature of markets.*

- *To contrast consumer markets and organizational or business markets.*

- *To define the term* market segmentation.

- *To identify the different bases used to segment markets.*

- *To explain the approaches for selecting target markets.*

- *To discuss sales potentials and sales forecasts.*

It's not too late to run away.

first came baby boomers, then yuppies. Now there are RUBs, rich urban bikers. Apparently the number of aging baby boomers buying motorcycles to reclaim lost youth is increasing rapidly. This unique segment of the market includes people like Stuart Kirk, a Columbia University professor, and Michael Fitzgibbons, a Rensselaer County, New York, high school teacher. The two friends, both 46, began reminiscing about the motorcycles they rode when they were younger. A few weeks later, each paid over $7,000 to buy red BMW 750cc sports bikes. According to Stuart Kirk, "We didn't want to end up 70 and regretting not having ridden again."

The growing market of older bikers is bringing hope and excitement to the motorcycle industry, which has been declining for years. Sales peaked in 1984 at 525,000 bikes; 1991 sales totaled 156,000. Even though sales of motorcycles fell by 7,000 units in 1991, demand exceeded supply. Most companies had cut production, anticipating a prolonged slump in sales, and underestimated the strong demand for bikes in 1991. Harley Davidson executives estimate that RUBs accounted for an increase in sales of 2,000 motorcycles; the firm would have sold more had it not been for a strike and problems on the plant's paint line. Honda also fell short on supply when demand picked up, as did Kawasaki. Yamaha dealers were angered when the company couldn't produce bikes fast enough to meet demand.

Not too much is known yet about this new breed of biker, but nearly all companies are studying this phenomenon carefully. According to a Harley Davidson spokesperson, RUBs are buying lifestyle, not transportation. The bike is a way of making a statement, in much the same way a Rolex watch or Rolls-Royce automobile makes a statement. They are older baby boomers, in their mid-forties to early fifties, and they can afford the product. They are not all males, but include women like Martha Liebmann, a 53-year-old Manhattan psychotherapist who rides a 700cc Honda.

Most motorcycle manufacturers, encouraged by the increase in the number of older bikers, have increased production rates. They anticipate that the most popular bikes will be the big touring bikes and sports bikes, which are also the most expensive bikes. Harley Davidson has about 60 percent of this market. Japanese producers are hoping to cut into this share, but in a market where image and nostalgia mean almost everything, Harley Davidson is hard to beat.[1] ●

[1] Based on information from Richard L. Stern, "The Graying Wild Ones," *Forbes,* January 6, 1992, p. 40.

Earlier we said that designing a marketing strategy entails selecting and analyzing a target market and developing a marketing mix for that market. In selecting target markets, a company identifies specific groups of customers and directs its marketing activities at those groups. By targeting motorcycles at older customers who purchase more expensive bikes, Harley Davidson and other firms hope to rebound from an industrywide slump that began a decade ago.

Different consumers have different wants and needs. Henry Ford introduced the Model T in 1909; it sold for $850 and was available in one color, black. For seventeen years, Ford made no significant changes except to lower prices as economies of scale were realized. By the 1920s, Americans wanted something different, and GM introduced Chevrolet, featuring color, comfort, style, and new safety features. This competition was the beginning of the end of the Model T. Ford developed the Model A, and although it was successful, the company never regained all of the market share it lost to GM. Much later, Toyota and other companies built higher-quality and more fuel-efficient cars and took market share from the U.S. manufacturers, who are fighting to recapture it.

The wants and needs of individuals and groups constituting a market can be very diverse. A car or motorcycle can satisfy the fairly universal need for transportation. But as we learned in the opening feature, a motorcycle may be purchased to recapture lost youth, just as a specific watch may be purchased to make a statement. By understanding the nature of markets, firms are better able to develop marketing activities that satisfy their customers.

THE NATURE OF MARKETS

The term *market* is used in many different contexts. Fresh produce is purchased at the "farmers' market." Investors "play the stock market." Perhaps you have an idea about something you would like to "market." In this book, a **market** will be defined as a group of people who

■ **market** a group of people who need and want a particular product, and have the buying power, willingness, and authority to purchase the product

1. Need or want a particular product
2. Have the ability (buying power) to purchase the product
3. Are willing to spend resources to obtain the product
4. Have the authority to buy the product

A group of people who lack any of these four conditions is not a market. For instance, young children may not have the buying power to purchase the latest toy even though they want the product and are willing to spend their resources to obtain it.

There are many markets in our society. Based on the characteristics of the individuals and groups that make up a specific market and the purposes for which they buy products, markets can be divided into two broad categories: consumer markets and organizational or business markets.

FIGURE 6.1
Organizational Markets
Organizational markets include companies such as Hoechst Celanase, which sells a stretch fiber for fabric to Lee, the world's largest manufacturer of jeans.

Source: Courtesy Hoechst Celanese Corporation.

You May Not Know Us, But Lee® Thinks We're A Perfect Fit.

Not long ago, Lee, one of the world's largest manufacturers of jeans, wanted a fabric that would make their jeans fit and feel great. Naturally, they came to the one company with the flexibility to help them do it: Hoechst Celanese. And now, using ESP, a remarkable stretch fiber created by Hoechst Celanese, Lee truly has become "the brand that fits."

It's no wonder that blue chip companies all over the world trust Hoechst Celanese for new and inventive solutions to their problems. For whether it's creating the medicines that keep you well, or the fibers that simply fit your needs, we take our responsibilities very seriously. With a partner like that, what company wouldn't feel comfortable?

Hoechst Celanese   **Hoechst** 🔲

The Name Behind The Names You Know

■ **consumer market** purchasers or persons in their households who plan to consume or benefit from the purchased products and who do not buy products for the purpose of making a profit

A **consumer market** includes purchasers or persons in households who plan to consume or benefit from the purchased products and who do not buy products for the purpose of making a profit. The multitude of people who have the need and desire, ability, willingness, and authority to purchase such products as housing, clothes, automobiles, food, appliances, books, musical recordings, and personal services constitute the consumer markets for those products. Consumer markets are discussed in greater detail in Chapter 7.

■ **organizational** (or **business**) **market** individuals or groups that purchase a specific kind of product for resale, direct use in the production of other products, or use in general daily operations

An **organizational** or **business market** includes individuals or groups that purchase a specific kind of product for resale, direct use in the production of other products, or use in general daily operations. For example, a computer manufacturer that buys chips to use in the production of computers is part of the organizational market for chips. The computer maker also purchases brooms, glass cleaner, and other supplies to clean its office and production areas. Although the cleaning supplies are not used in the direct production of computers, they are used in the operations of the firm. Thus, the manufacturer is part of the organizational market for cleaning supplies. Similarly, a hospital that purchases beds and other furniture to accommodate patients and workers is part of the organizational market for furniture. And a jeans manufacturer that purchases fabric for its products is part of the organizational market for stretch fiber (see Figure 6.1). Organizational markets are discussed further in Chapter 8.

MARKET SEGMENTATION

If you asked ten friends, "What's your favorite kind of music?" you might get ten different answers. Some prefer rock; others prefer jazz. Some people listen only to country and western music; others listen to classical. These tastes and preferences will change over time with lifestyle changes—new jobs, marriage, children, new hobbies, and so on. Just as music listeners have different needs and wants, markets are made up of many consumers who have different needs and wants. By dividing markets into segments of consumers with similar characteristics and needs, businesses can better satisfy consumers' needs and wants with their marketing activities. In other words, segmentation enables organizations to increase quality by getting closer to the customer.

Market Segmentation Defined

■ **heterogeneous market** a market that consists of individuals with dissimilar product needs

■ **market segmentation** the process of dividing a total market into groups of consumers who have relatively similar product needs

■ **market segment** a group of individuals, groups, or organizations that share one or more characteristics that cause them to have relatively similar product needs

■ **market niche** a small, unique part of a market segment

A market that consists of individuals with dissimilar product needs is called a **heterogeneous market.** The market for music, as just illustrated, or the markets for homes, clothing, food, and automobiles are heterogeneous. As you can see in Figure 6.2, the market for tennis shoes is also heterogeneous. **Market segmentation** is the process of dividing a total market into groups of consumers who have relatively similar product needs. A **market segment** is a group of individuals, groups, or organizations that share one or more characteristics that cause them to have relatively similar product needs. For example, Book-of-the-Month Club produces catalogs for four different market segments: history and biography; women's fiction; self-help and leisure interests; and general fiction.[2] Organizations divide markets into market segments to facilitate the development of a marketing mix (or mixes) that more precisely matches the needs of individuals in the target market, the segment (or segments) at whom the organization directs its marketing effort. Designers like Albert Nipon and Adrienne Vittadini target their clothes at larger women, an estimated 40 percent of the market for women age 40 and over.[3]

A more recent approach to market segmentation is targeting market niches. A **market niche** is a small, somewhat unique part of a market segment. By targeting marketing activities at a market niche, referred to as *niche marketing,* organizations can even more precisely match customer needs. After the 1989 earthquake in California, with working telephones in short supply, long lines formed at pay phones. One entrepreneur decided to rent his cellular phones to people who didn't want to wait in line, and his idea eventually became Action Cellular Rent a Phone Inc. In less than five years, this unique market niche for cellular phone rentals grew to $500 million.[4] The 1990 U.S. census shows that racial and ethnic minority groups are growing more than

---

[2]Meg Cox, "For the Nation's Troubled Book Clubs, Main Selection of This Year Is Change," *Wall Street Journal,* July 24, 1992, pp. B1–B2.
[3]Amy Feldman, "Hello, Oprah, Good-bye, Iman," *Forbes,* March 16, 1992, pp. 116–117.
[4]Gautam Naik, "Cellular-Phone Rental Firms Mine a Neglected Market," *Wall Street Journal,* September 1, 1992, p. B2.

FIGURE 6.2

Heterogeneous Markets

Since the market for tennis shoes is heterogeneous, Reebok divides the market into segments of consumers with similar tastes and preferences. In this advertisement, Reebok promotes two different shoe styles to two market segments.

Source: Courtesy Reebok International Ltd.

seven times as fast as the non–Hispanic white majority.[5] Because of the increasingly diverse U.S. population, many firms are attempting to identify market niches with needs and wants that are not being satisfied. Close to the Customer illustrates how firms are targeting customers in the age of diversity.

Segmenting a heterogeneous market into groups of people with similar needs enables an organization to design a marketing mix that meets the needs of a relatively homogeneous group. A computer manufacturer, for instance, would find it difficult to design a single marketing mix for the entire personal computer (PC) market because this market has many diverse needs. PC customers have different needs in terms of prices, capabilities of the computer, and service, to name a few. Thus Apple designs several PCs to meet the needs of these different segments. Likewise, a telephone company could not address the needs of all its home customers by offering only one telephone model. Southwestern Bell Corporation tries to satisfy its customers with different colors, styles, and features of telephone equipment, as well as with a variety of long-distance plans and other services.

Requirements for Effective Market Segmentation

Five conditions must exist for market segmentation to be effective. First, a firm must determine whether the market is heterogeneous. If consumers' needs for the product are homogeneous, then there is no reason to segment the market. Second, the market segments must be identifiable and divisible.

[5] Brad Edmondson, "The Big Picture," *American Demographics,* July 1991, pp. 4–5.

CLOSE TO THE CUSTOMER

Niche Marketing in the Age of Diversity

In the age of diversity, many firms are looking for smaller, unique niches in the market. When Art Vuolo was a college student, he marked road maps showing the best rock stations all the way from Michigan to Florida. Today, Vuolo publishes *RadioGuide,* a brochure that lists radio stations and their formats for markets across the country. A variety of brochures are published, such as *Rock RadioGuide,* listing rock stations and formats nationwide. Even a *Rush RadioGuide* is available, detailing stations that carry the "Rush Limbaugh Show." About five million *RadioGuide*s are published annually, generating $250,000 in revenue.

Bennett's MicroFridge Inc. makes a product of the same name, a miniature microwave/refrigerator/freezer. The product is targeted at the college dormitory market; next will be senior citizen facilities, no-frills motels, and military barracks. Some expect MicroFridge to become the largest-selling small appliance for the institutional market. Robert Bennett, who developed the product, said it was simply a matter of coming up with an innovative concept out of the mainstream. Although MicroFridge does not appeal to everyone, the product makes good sense for consumers such as college students who live or work in small quarters.

Niche marketing has helped smaller firms compete with giants. Preferred Physicians Mutual Risk Retention Group is an insurance company founded in 1987 to insure anesthesiologists. By avoiding brokers' and agents' fees, Preferred Physicians offers premiums considerably lower than those of competing firms, and it is the number one firm in its specialty.

Octel Communications Corp. is another upstart firm that has dominated a market that includes giant competitors like IBM and AT&T. Octel did it by finding a niche where the large firms had failed and filled it through the use of leading technology. Only ten years old, Octel is the leading firm in a new area of telecommunications called voice information services, technology that electronically links voice, data, and image processing over the telephone network. At any time of the day, anyone in the world with a touch-tone phone can use the technology to access computerized information sources such as corporate databases, voice mail, and E-mail. Octel's equipment is more compact and more versatile than that of its competitors.

Firms also look for niches in crowded markets. Evian is aiming its bottled water at folks who want to be different and want to carry a bottle in their gym bags or even their pockets. In this crowded market, Evian doubled its sales in a single year. Giants Coca-Cola and Pepsi are also looking for niches in the beverage market as cola sales level off. Both firms are trying to reach noncola drinkers with beverages ranging from iced tea to colorless cola.

Sources: John P. Cortez, "Radio Fanatic Finds Marketing Niche," *Advertising Age,* August 10, 1992, p. 12; Seth Lubove, "Perched Between Perrier and Tap," *Forbes,* May 14, 1990, p. 120; Gene Bylinsky, "How to Shoulder Aside the Titans," *Fortune,* May 18, 1992, pp. 87–88; Brent Bowers, "Finding a Niche Based on Experience," *Wall Street Journal,* February 6, 1992, p. B2; and Howard Schlossberg, "No 'Me Too' for These Two," *Marketing News,* May 14, 1990, pp. 1, 10.

There must be some logical basis for effectively dividing in[...] total market into segments, each of which has a relatively hom[...] for the product. Third, the total market should be divided so t[...] [...] [...] ing manager can compare the estimated sales potential, costs, and profits of each segment. Fourth, one or more of the segments must have enough profit potential to warrant developing and maintaining a special marketing mix. Finally, it must be possible to reach the chosen segment with a particular marketing mix.

It may be difficult or impossible to reach some market segments because of environmental constraints. For example, until the last few years, laws and nationalism prevented American businesses from reaching market segments in the former Soviet Union, except through the illegal black market. However, the Commonwealth of Independent States is opening many Russian markets for consumer and organizational goods, such as agricultural and industrial machinery, computers, clothing, food, and other products. Many American businesses, including Pizza Hut, McDonald's, and Combustion Engineering, are attempting to develop marketing mixes to satisfy the needs and wants of diverse market segments in the commonwealth.

BASES FOR MARKET SEGMENTATION

■ **segmentation base** (or **variable**) a characteristic of individuals, groups, or organizations that marketing managers use to divide a total market into segments

A **segmentation base** (or **variable**) is a characteristic of individuals, groups, or organizations that marketing managers use to divide a total market into segments. Age, sex, location, personality characteristics, and rate of product usage are used frequently to segment markets. The choice of segmentation bases is critical because segmenting on the basis of an unsuitable variable reduces an organization's chances of satisfying its consumers' needs and desires.

Marketers should consider several factors when selecting the bases for market segmentation. Consumers' needs, uses, attitudes, and actions should vary according to the chosen segmentation characteristic. Automobile producers, for example, might segment the automobile market on the basis of income, but they probably would not segment it on the basis of politics because political beliefs do not normally influence people's automobile needs. Also, the segmentation variable must be measurable if the marketing manager is to segment the market accurately. Marketing researchers often segment markets on the basis of age, race, income, and sex because these characteristics can be measured through observation or questioning; segmenting a market on the basis of intelligence would be difficult because this characteristic cannot be measured accurately.

Segmenting Consumer Markets

A marketing manager can use a single variable or a combination of several variables to segment a consumer market. As shown in Figure 6.3, segmentation bases for consumer markets can be grouped into four categories: demographic, geographic, psychographic, and product-related.

FIGURE 6.3
Segmentation Bases for Consumer Markets

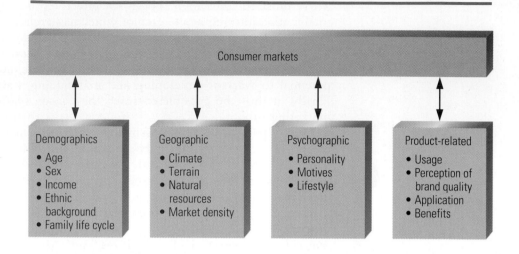

Demographic Bases Demographers study the characteristics of total populations, such as the distribution of age and sex, fertility rates, migration patterns, and mortality rates. Marketing professionals use these demographic characteristics to segment markets because they can be easily measured and they are closely related to customers' product needs and purchasing behavior. The broad range of demographic variables used as a basis for segmenting markets also includes income, ethnic background, education, occupation, household size, and family life cycle.

Age is one of the most common demographic variables used to segment markets. The distribution of age groups in the United States is changing, and marketers need to understand how these changes will influence various markets. The median age of the U.S. population will be 35.7 years in 2000, up from 32.8 in 1990; over 37 million people will fall in the 45- to 54-year-old age group.[6] Demographers project that the population will increase steadily from 225 million in 1992 to about 383 million by 2050.[7] As baby boomers born between 1946 and 1964 age over this period, more than 43 percent of the population will be over 45 years old; more than 20 percent will be over 65.[8] This increase will present some major opportunities for organizations that market products for this age group. People in their forties and fifties tend to focus on personal finances, which provides opportunities for financial services firms.

Many markets are segmented according to age. Some companies target their marketing efforts at teenagers, who spend about $55 billion of their

[6]Christy Fisher, "Boomers Scatter in Middle Ages," *Advertising Age,* January 11, 1993, p. 23.
[7]Judith Waldrop, "New Projections Show Faster Growth, More Diversity," *American Demographics,* February 1993, pp. 9–10.
[8]Lucinda Harper, "Census Bureau Lifts Population Forecast, Citing Fertility, Immigration, Longevity," *Wall Street Journal,* December 4, 1992, pp. B1, B14.

own money and $27 billion of their families' money each year.[9] Another age group that is targeted by marketers is the lucrative senior citizen segment. By about 2010, people aged 65 and older will account for roughly 20 percent of the population.[10] Toy giant F.A.O. Schwarz has added a Grandma's Shop in its largest stores and trains its sales force to help grandparents select gifts for their grandchildren.[11] Markets that are commonly segmented by age include clothing, toys, music, automobiles, soaps and shampoos, and foods.

Another commonly used segmentation variable is sex. Markets that are generally segmented on the basis of sex include clothes, cosmetics and toiletries, magazines, and cigarettes. Mattel Inc., which has successfully targeted the Barbie line of toys at girls, has been weak when it comes to boys' toys.[12] Many toy manufacturers segment the market on the basis of both sex and age. Changing roles among men and women continue to influence the marketing strategies of many firms. Today, men dominate shopping in only one category—large, durable goods. Most married men do some of the food shopping for their households, as well as some of the housework.[13] These trends represent opportunities for businesses to develop marketing mixes that satisfy consumers' changing needs. As a result, some companies are now targeting advertisements for grocery products and household cleaners and appliances at men as well as women.

Markets are also segmented on the basis of income. The median family income in the United States rose from $9,867 in 1970 to $31,600 in 1991.[14] American families, especially married couples, are becoming more affluent. Married couples with children have a median income of about $42,500. Families headed by single women have a median income of $14,500.[15]

Income is used to divide markets because it influences people's product needs. It affects consumers' buying power (discussed in Chapter 3) and their aspirations for a certain style of living. Markets segmented by income include housing, furniture, automobiles, clothing, alcoholic beverages, food, sporting goods, and luxury items such as china, crystal, and art. For example, Campbell Soup Company's Le Menu frozen dinner line is aimed at consumers with higher incomes, whereas Budget Gourmet frozen dinners are targeted at consumers who are more price conscious.

Ethnic background is another variable used to segment markets for goods such as food, clothing, and music and for services such as banking and insur-

[9] William Dunn, "Hanging Out with American Teenagers," *American Demographics,* February 1992, pp. 24–35.
[10] Warren A. French and Richard Fox, "Segmenting the Senior Citizen Market," *Journal of Consumer Marketing,* Winter 1988, pp. 61–72.
[11] Dody Tsiantar and Annetta Miller, "Dipping into Granny's Wallet," *Newsweek,* April 1, 1991, p. 43.
[12] Eric Schine and Gary McWilliams, "Mattel: Looking for a Few Good Boy Toys," *Business Week,* February 17, 1992, pp. 116–118.
[13] Diane Crispell, "The Brave New World of Men," *American Demographics,* January 1992, pp. 38–43.
[14] Margaret K. Ambry, "Receipts from a Marriage," *American Demographics,* February 1993, pp. 30–37.
[15] Judith Waldrop, "Choose the Income That's Right for You," *American Demographics,* December 1992, pp. 9–10.

TABLE 6.1
The Largest Hispanic Markets

Rank	Metro Area	Hispanic Population
1	Los Angeles–Long Beach, CA	3,351,242
2	New York, NY	1,889,662
3	Miami–Hialeah, FL	953,407
4	Chicago, IL	734,827
5	Houston, TX	707,536
6	Riverside–San Bernardino, CA	686,096
7	San Antonio, TX	620,290
8	Anaheim–Santa Ana, CA	564,828
9	San Diego, CA	510,781
10	El Paso, TX	411,619
11	Dallas, TX	368,884
12	Phoenix, AZ	345,498
13	McAllen–Edinburg–Mission, TX	326,972
14	San Jose, CA	314,564
15	Oakland, CA	273,087
16	Fresno, CA	236,634
17	San Francisco, CA	233,274
18	Washington, DC–MD–VA	224,786
19	Brownville–Harlingen, TX	212,995
20	Denver, CO	211,005
21	Newark, NJ	188,299
22	Boston–Lawrence–Salem–Lowell–Brockton, MA	186,652
23	Jersey City, NJ	183,465
24	Corpus Christi, TX	181,860
25	Albuquerque, NM	178,310

Source: *American Demographics Desk Reference,* July 1991, p. 15.

ance. The United States is becoming an increasingly diverse nation. Non-Hispanic whites' share of the U.S. population is expected to decline from 75 percent in 1990 to 72 percent in 2000, and 68 percent in 2010.[16] One of the fastest-growing ethnic groups as a market segment is the American Hispanic population. Composed of Americans of Mexican, Cuban, Puerto Rican, and Central and South American heritage, this ethnic group is growing five times faster than the general population. If the Hispanic population continues to grow at its current rate, it will be the largest ethnic group in the United States by the year 2020. Businesses are beginning to tailor marketing strategies to satisfy the needs of this growing market. McDonald's, for instance, added chicken fajitas to its menu to target this segment. Miami-based Market Seg-

[16]Thomas G. Exter, "The Declining Majority," *American Demographics,* January 1993, p. 59.

ment Research reported that Hispanic brand loyalty is high. Most Hispanics (62 percent) buy the same brands of food, beverage, and household items on a regular basis, and only 35 percent are lured away by sales.[17] The largest Hispanic markets are listed in Table 6.1. It is estimated that $600 million is spent annually to advertise to this segment.[18]

The African-American population grew by 13.2 percent during the 1980s, faster than the national average but not as fast as the growth rate for Hispanics.[19] Blacks currently represent the largest ethnic group in America. Since this segment has built economic clout—$263 billion in income in 1990— more firms are targeting black consumers.[20] Pillsbury, for instance, has geared its advertisements for Hungry Jack pancake mix directly to blacks. J.C. Penney opened "Authentic African" boutiques in several of its stores where black customers frequently shop. And black-oriented radio stations in Chicago banded together to promote the African-American market to advertisers.[21]

Household product needs vary according to age, number of persons in the household, marital status, and the presence and ages of children. These characteristics can be combined into a single variable called the *family life cycle*. The family life cycle has been broken down in many different ways. Table 6.2 shows the typical stages in the life cycle of today's nuclear family. Housing, furniture, appliances, food, and automobiles are a few of the numerous product markets sometimes segmented by family life cycle stages.

Individuals in a particular life cycle stage may have very specific needs that can be satisfied by precisely designed marketing mixes. For instance, insurance companies find it useful to segment the life insurance market for women by life cycles, as shown in Figure 6.4. Each life cycle stage has different needs for life insurance.

Geographic Bases   Geographic variables such as climate, terrain, natural resources, and population density also influence consumer product needs. Businesses may divide product markets into regions because differences in geographic variables can cause consumer needs and wants to differ from one region to another. Climate, for instance, has an impact on segmenting markets for heating and cooling systems, tires, clothing, even automobiles. Subaru has historically targeted the rural snowbelt, where consumers need inexpensive cars they can drive on bad roads. The number one Subaru dealer in the United States is in Anchorage, Alaska; numbers two and three are in Colorado.[22] National markets might be divided into regions, such as the

---

[17] Christy Fisher, "Poll: Hispanics Stick to Brands," *Advertising Age,* February 15, 1993, p. 6.

[18] Howard Schlossberg, "Hispanic Market Strong, but Often Ignored," *Marketing News,* February 19, 1990, pp. 1, 12.

[19] Kathy Bodovitz, "Black America," *American Demographics,* July 1991, pp. 8–10.

[20] Maria Mallory and Stephanie Anderson, "Waking Up to a Major Market," *Business Week,* March 23, 1992, pp. 70–73.

[21] Cyndee Miller, "Black Radio Stations Join Forces to Woo Advertisers," *Advertising Age,* May 1, 1992, pp. 3, 12.

[22] Joe Schwartz, "Climate-Controlled Customers," *American Demographics,* March 1992, pp. 24–32.

TABLE 6.2
Stages in the Family Life Cycle

1. Young single

2. Young married without children

3. Other young
   a. Young divorced without children
   b. Young married with children
   c. Young divorced with children

4. Middle-aged
   a. Middle-aged married without children
   b. Middle-aged divorced without children
   c. Middle-aged married with dependent children
   d. Middle-aged divorced with dependent children
   e. Middle-aged married without dependent children
   f. Middle-aged divorced without dependent children

5. Older
   a. Older married
   b. Older unmarried

Source: Patrick E. Murphy and William A. Staples, "A Modernized Family Life Cycle," *Journal of Consumer Research*, June 1979, p. 16. Copyright © *The Journal of Consumer Research*, Inc., 1979. Reprinted by permission.

Pacific, Southwest, Central, Midwest, Southeast, Middle Atlantic, and New England regions. Smaller markets or areas might be regionalized by counties, cities, zip code areas, or other units.

■ **market density** the number of potential customers within a unit of land area, such as a square mile

Market density refers to the number of potential customers within a unit of land area, such as a square mile. Although market density is related to population density, the relationship is not exact. For example, in two different geographic markets of approximately equal size and population, the market density for pens, paper, and notebooks might be much higher in one area than in another if one area includes a university and thus a significantly greater proportion of students.

Psychographic Bases   Psychographic variables pertain to personality characteristics, motives, and lifestyles. A psychographic variable can be used by itself to segment a market, or it can be combined with other types of segmentation variables.

Personality characteristics are a person's individual character traits, attitudes, and habits. Markets may be segmented according to characteristics such as compulsiveness, thriftiness, competitiveness, extroversion, introversion, ambitiousness, and aggressiveness. Segmenting by personality characteristics is practical when a product is similar to many competing products and consumers' needs for the product are not affected significantly by other segmentation variables.

When segmenting by a personality characteristic, marketing managers try to select a trait that is valued positively by many people so that individuals

FIGURE 6.4
The Life Insurance Market for Women

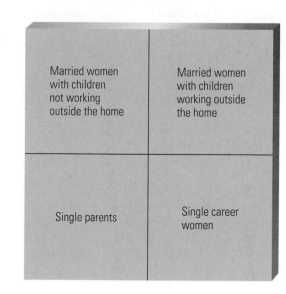

Married women with children not working outside the home

Married women with children working outside the home

Single parents

Single career women

who have this characteristic, as well as those who would like to have it, may be influenced to buy that marketer's brand. For example, Cherry 7Up is aimed at "cool" teenagers and those who aspire to be "cool," with the slogan "Isn't it cool in pink?" and advertisements that show "cool" young people coping with everyday situations. Marketing managers are not concerned about measuring how many people have the characteristic because they assume that most of the people in the target market either have the characteristic or want to have it.

A motive is an internal energizing force or reason that moves a person toward a goal. Although motives are difficult to measure, marketing managers occasionally use them to segment markets. Product durability, economy, convenience, and status are motives that may affect the types of products consumers purchase and where they purchase them. For example, one motive for purchasing a family-sized product is economy. Or a person might buy a Mercedes-Benz automobile because of its high-class, luxury image.

Lifestyle is the manner in which people live and spend time and money.[23] Lifestyle analysis provides marketers with a broad view of consumers because it segments markets into groups on the basis of how consumers spend their time (activities), the importance of things in their surroundings (interests), and their beliefs about themselves and broad issues (opinions).[24] Demographic variables are also used in lifestyle segmentation. Table 6.3 provides sample dimensions from the major categories of lifestyle. Each of these life-

---

[23]James F. Engel, Roger D. Blackwell, and Paul W. Miniard, *Consumer Behavior* (Chicago: Dryden Press, 1986), p. 252.
[24]Joseph T. Plummer, "The Concept and Application of Lifestyle Segmentation," *Journal of Marketing,* January 1974, p. 33.

TABLE 6.3
Lifestyle Categories and Examples

Activities	Interests	Opinions	Demographics
Work	Family	Themselves	Age
Hobbies	Home	Social issues	Education
Social events	Job	Politics	Income
Vacation	Community	Business	Occupation
Entertainment	Recreation	Economics	Family size
Club membership	Fashion	Education	Dwelling
Community	Food	Products	Geography
Shopping	Media	Future	City size
Sports	Achievements	Culture	Stage in life cycle

Source: Reprinted from "The Concept and Application of Life Style Segmentation," by Joseph T. Plummer, *Journal of Marketing*, January 1974, p. 34, published by the American Marketing Association.

style factors offers organizations a potential basis for identifying a market segment.[25]

■ **VALS (Values and Lifestyles) program**
a popular approach to consumer market segmentation that divides American lifestyles into nine categories: survivors, sustainers, belongers, emulators, achievers, I-am-me, experiential, societally conscious, and integrated

One popular approach to lifestyle segmentation is the **VALS (Values and Lifestyles) program.**[26] This program surveys American consumers and divides them into groups with similar values and lifestyles. The VALS 2 classification divides American consumers into eight lifestyle categories, as shown in Table 6.4. These eight lifestyles are valuable in segmenting markets for a variety of products. For instance, achievers favor established products that show off their success, believers prefer American products and established brands, and experiencers spend heavily on clothing, fast food, and music.[27]

The use of psychographic segmentation bases by marketers has been limited for several reasons. First, psychographic variables are more difficult to measure accurately than are other types of segmentation variables. Second, the relationships between psychographic variables and consumer needs and desires are sometimes vague and difficult to document. Third, segments that result from psychographic segmentation may not be reachable. For example, a marketing manager may determine that introverted individuals desire a certain type of furniture; however, it may be very difficult to develop a marketing mix to reach this segment at a reasonable cost.

Product-related Bases   Organizations may also segment a market on the basis of a product-related characteristic, such as use, application, or expected benefits. For example, a total market may be divided into users and nonusers. Users may then be classified as heavy, moderate, or light. To encourage a

---

[25] Chester A. Swensen, "How to Sell to a Segmented Market," *Journal of Business Strategy,* January–February 1988, pp. 18–22.
[26] Arnold Mitchell, *The Nine American Lifestyles: Who We Are & Where We Are Going* (New York: Macmillan, 1983), p. 165.
[27] Martha Farnsworth Riche, "Psychographics for the 1990s," *American Demographics,* July 1989, pp. 24–31, 53.

specific group, such as heavy users, to purchase its product, a firm may have to develop a distinctive product, set special prices, and initiate special promotion and distribution activities. Hotels, airlines, and car rental companies have devised special programs to reward frequent users with lower prices or free rooms, flights, or cars, as well as free upgrades.

Perception of brand quality is another product-related segmentation base. As shown in Table 6.5, seven brand quality segments have been identified: intellects, conformists, popularity seekers, pragmatists, actives, relief seekers, and sentimentalists.[28] Each segment includes 11 to 17 percent of the consumer population aged 15 and older, and has a unique pattern in brand quality perception. For instance, popularity seekers prefer brands that they perceive as trendy. Consumers tend to use this perception of quality in selecting brands and media, making quality segments as easy to target as demographic segments.

The way customers use or apply a product may also be a basis for segmenting the market. To satisfy customers who use a product in a certain way, the packaging, size, texture, or color of the product may have to be designed precisely to make the product easier to use, safer, or more convenient. For instance, business organizations have different lighting needs than consumers. Therefore, General Electric, Sylvania, and other companies make a variety of incandescent and fluorescent light bulbs for different consumer and organizational needs. In addition, businesses may have to develop special distribution, promotion, or pricing strategies to satisfy different product needs.

■ **benefit segmentation**
the division of a consumer market according to the benefits that customers want from the product

The benefit that consumers expect from a product is another product-related characteristic. **Benefit segmentation** is the division of a market according to the benefits that customers want from the product. For instance, banking consumers may be segmented into loan seekers, one-stop bankers, value seekers, and front-runners.[29]

The effectiveness of benefit segmentation depends on several factors. First, a business must be able to identify the benefits consumers expect from the product. Second, the firm must be able to group people seeking certain benefits into recognizable segments. Third, it must be able to reach one or more of the resulting segments with its marketing efforts. Finally, the benefits sought by consumers must be similar over time. If the benefits change, the company has to alter its market segmentation strategies. The utility of benefit segments is addressed in Point/Counterpoint.

Segmenting Organizational or Business Markets

Businesses also segment organizational markets to satisfy organizations' product needs. A business may segment organizational markets on the basis

[28]John Morton, "Brand Quality Segments: Potent Way to Predict Preference," *Marketing News,* September 14, 1992, pp. 8, 14.
[29]Roger J. Calantone and Alan G. Sawyer, "The Stability of Benefit Segments," *Journal of Marketing Research,* August 1978, p. 398.

Segments	Description	Percent of Population	Percent with Some College	Median Age
Actualizers	Highest incomes, high self-esteem, and abundant resources. Image is important to them as an expression of their taste, independence, and character. Their consumer choices are directed toward the finer things in life.	8	95	43
Fulfilleds	Abundant resources and principle-oriented. Mature, responsible, well-educated professionals. Leisure activities center on their homes, but they are well-informed about what goes on in the world and they are open to new ideas and social change. They have high incomes but are practical consumers.	11	81	48
Believers	Lower resources and principle-oriented. Conservative and predictable consumers who favor American products and established brands. Lives are centered on family, church, community, and the nation. They have modest incomes.	16	6	58
Achievers	Abundant resources and status-oriented. Successful, work-oriented people who get their satisfaction from their jobs and families. Politically conservative and respect authority and the status quo. Favor established products and services that show off their success to their peers.	13	77	36

TABLE 6.4
VALS 2 American Lifestyles

of geographic location, type of organization, customer size, and product use (see Figure 6.5).

Geographic Location Like consumer products, the demand for some organizational products varies considerably from one geographic area to another as a result of differences in climate, terrain, natural resources, or similar factors. Paper mills, for instance, tend to be located in regions with vast forests because trees are the primary resource used in making paper. Geographic segmentation may be especially appropriate for reaching industries that are concentrated in certain locations. For example, many producers of computer software and other computer products are concentrated in the Silicon Valley region of California.

Segments	Description	Percent of Population	Percent with Some College	Median Age
Strivers	Lower resources and status-oriented. Values very similar to Achievers but have fewer economic, social, and psychological resources. Style is extremely important as they strive to emulate people they admire and wish to be like.	13	23	34
Experiencers	Abundant resources and action-oriented. Youngest of all the segments with a median age of 25. Have a lot of energy, which they pour into physical exercise and social activities. Avid consumers, spending heavily on clothing, fast foods, music, and other youthful favorites—with particular emphasis on new products and services.	12	41	26
Makers	Lower resources and action-oriented. Practical people who value self-sufficiency. Focused on the familiar—family, work, and physical recreation—and have little interest in the broader world. Appreciate practical and functional products.	13	24	30
Strugglers	Lowest incomes. They are the oldest of all the segments with a median age of 61. Within their limited means, they tend to be brand-loyal consumers.	14	3	61

Source: Martha Farnsworth Riche, "Psychographics for the 1990's." Reprinted with permission © *American Demographics,* July 1989. For subscription information, please call (800) 828-1133.

Type of Organization   Another basis for segmenting organizational markets is the types of organizations in that market. Different types of organizations often require different product features, distribution systems, and price structures. Because of these variations in needs, a marketer may decide to concentrate on a single segment with one marketing mix or may focus on several segments with multiple mixes. A producer of pet supplies might segment potential customers into several groups, including veterinarians, breeders, boarding kennels, pet stores, and grocery and discount stores. Similarly, a producer of report binders and folders may divide its customers into school and college students, business professionals, and stationery and paper suppliers. Figure 6.6 illustrates how a firm targets producers of plastics, who need specific additives for their products.

Name of Segment	Brand Quality Perception	Quality Attribute Example	Quality Celebrity Example	Brand Example	Favored Media Example
Intellects	Super-premium	Sophisticated	Luciano Pavarotti	Volvo	*Wall Street Journal*
Conformists	Dominant	Not sophis-ticated	Mickey Mouse	Campbell's	*Sports Illus-trated*
Popularity seekers	Trendy	Youthful	Bart Simpson	Nike	MTV
Pragmatists	Functional	Hard-working	Merle Haggard	Lee	*Prevention*
Actives	Service	Not sedentary	Barbara Walters	American Express	*Travel & Leisure*
Relief seekers	Fantasy/escape	Not domestic	Madonna	Nyquil	HBO
Sentimentalists	Humble	Caring	Bob Hope	One-A-Day	*Family Circle*

Source: *Marketing News,* September 14, 1992, p. 8. Reprinted by permission.

TABLE 6.5
Brand Quality Segments

Buying procedures in various types of organizations also dictate marketing activities. Businesses that sell to the federal government must know how to prepare proposals, bids, and contracts, and their products must meet certain standards. For example, organizations that manufacture radar components for U.S. Air Force fighter planes must meet exact specifications so that the planes' radar systems work correctly. A marketing manager may need to direct marketing efforts at a specific person (the chief executive officer) or a committee of individuals (purchasing agents or engineers) who have a say in

FIGURE 6.5
Segmentation Bases for Organizational Markets

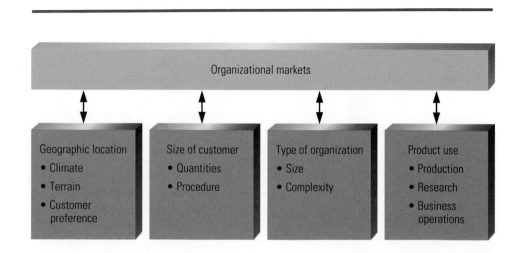

FIGURE 6.6
Segmenting Organizational Markets
Some firms target types of organizations that have different product needs. This advertisement from Witco Corporation, producers of additives that aid in processing, targets organizations that manufacture plastics.

Source: Courtesy Witco Corporation.

the purchasing decisions of a manufacturing organization. Marketing to a committee is quite different from selling to an individual.

Size of Customer   An organization's size may affect its purchasing procedures and the types and quantities of products it needs. Westin Hotel Company, for example, needs different types and larger quantities of light bulbs, linens, paper products, and the like than does a single bed-and-breakfast inn. To reach a particular-sized segment, a business may have to adjust its marketing activities. For instance, a company may offer discounts to customers that buy in extremely large quantities. Personal selling is often crucial to serving the needs of larger organizational buyers effectively. Because the needs of large and small buyers differ, marketing managers frequently employ different marketing practices to reach various customer groups.

Product Use   The way a firm uses products affects the types and amounts of the products purchased as well as the method of making the purchase. Some products, particularly raw materials such as iron, steel, petroleum, and lumber, are used in many different ways. For example, paper is used for such purposes as correspondence, record keeping, taking notes, presentations, books and other products, and packaging. A paper manufacturer such as Mead Corporation segments organizational markets for paper by types of use because an organization's paper needs depend on the purpose for which the paper is purchased.

Selecting the appropriate bases for segmentation is critical because the specific variable used is the major factor in defining the target market. In some cases, several variables are used in segmenting the market to help create and maintain a more precise and satisfying marketing mix.

POINT/COUNTERPOINT

Is Benefit Segmentation Useful?

As more companies turn to national brands, geographic segmentation can no longer be used by many large consumer goods companies. Other segmentation bases, such as demographics, are descriptive; these variables are useful, but they do not take into account the reasons *why* consumers purchase a product. Benefit segmentation provides a powerful approach to dividing consumer markets according to why consumers purchase a product—for the benefits they are seeking. Although benefit segmentation was first pioneered in the early 1950s, some marketing managers still question whether this approach is useful.

Point   Benefit segmentation is a useful approach to identifying market segments. Many segmentation bases are traits describing customers, such as age, income, or frequency of product use. However, benefits sought by consumers are more likely to determine purchase behavior than are descriptive characteristics. For instance, it is the need to mow the yard—a benefit—that prompts a consumer to buy a lawn mower, not age or income.

The fundamental reason markets exist is to provide benefits consumers are seeking. By segmenting on the basis of benefits, marketers can concentrate their efforts on satisfying consumers' wants and needs. Once marketers identify benefit segments, they can examine each segment in terms of demographic, psychographic, and geographic bases. Thus they are able to gain the deepest possible understanding of market segments.

Counterpoint   The concept of benefit segmentation has several serious drawbacks. Many of the benefits consumers perceive to be important in a purchase decision are constantly changing. With new technologies, changing social values, and competitive offerings, marketers must constantly reassess benefit segments. For example, when a new personal computer that is faster, smaller, and capable of performing better graphics than those already available is introduced, the benefits desired by consumers also change. The original benefit segments may no longer exist, and market segmentation strategies have to be changed.

Even if the benefits sought by consumers remain similar over time, the size of the segment might change. If a segment becomes much smaller, it may no longer be profitable to target this segment. The demographic make-up of the benefit segment also changes over time. Though the desired benefits remain the same, consumers in a benefit segment may grow older or less affluent. Once again, such changes will require corrections in market segmentation strategies.

APPROACHES FOR SELECTING TARGET MARKETS

Once a firm understands its markets and the appropriate bases for segmenting those markets, it must choose an approach for selecting its target markets. There are three different approaches for selecting target markets: the total market approach, the concentration approach, and the multisegment approach. Figure 6.7 illustrates each of these three approaches.

Total Market Approach

■ **total market** (or **undif-ferentiated**) **approach**
a market segmentation approach in which a company develops a single marketing mix and directs it at the entire market for a particular product

In the **total market** (or **undifferentiated**) **approach,** a company develops a single marketing mix and directs it at the entire market for a particular product. This approach is used when an organization defines the total market for a particular product as its target market. Dole uses this approach in marketing its bananas.

A company using the total market approach assumes that individual customers in the target market for a specific type of product have similar needs. Therefore, the firm creates a single marketing mix that it hopes will satisfy most of those customers. The company makes one type of product with little or no variation, sets one price, designs one promotional program aimed at everyone, and establishes one distribution system to reach all customers in

FIGURE 6.7
Approaches for Selecting Target Markets

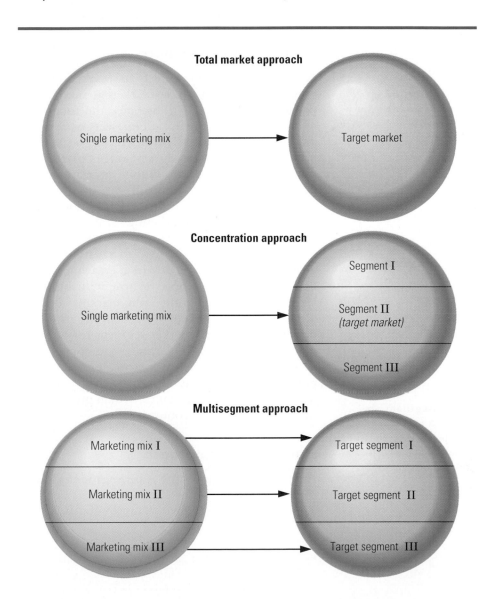

the total market. Products that can be marketed successfully with this approach include staple food items such as sugar and salt, certain kinds of farm produce, and other goods that most customers think of as identical to competing products. Argo Cornstarch, for instance, is aimed at the total market. A single marketing mix can satisfy most consumers of cornstarch.

Two conditions must exist for the total market approach to be effective. A large proportion of customers in the total market must have similar needs for the product, and the organization must be able to develop and maintain a single marketing mix that satisfies customers' needs. In other words, the company must be able to identify a set of product needs that are common to most customers in the total market, and it must have the resources and skills to reach that market. If customers' needs are dissimilar or if the organization is unable to develop and maintain a satisfying marketing mix, then this approach will not be effective in satisfying the market.

Concentration Approach

■ **concentration approach** a market segmentation approach in which an organization directs its marketing efforts toward a single market segment through a single marketing mix

When an organization directs its marketing efforts toward a single market segment through a single marketing mix, it is using a **concentration approach.** As Figure 6.7 illustrates, the total market may consist of several segments, but the organization selects only one of the segments as its target market. For example, *Baseball Weekly,* a sports magazine published by Gannett Co., concentrates on a segment of readers who want a great deal of statistics. The magazine, with a circulation of over 300,000, includes nine pages consisting of columns of statistics.[30]

A major advantage of the concentration approach is that it allows a company to focus all its marketing efforts on a single segment. The company can analyze the characteristics and needs of a distinct customer group and then direct all its efforts toward satisfying that group's needs. A firm can generate a large volume of sales by reaching a single segment. The concentration approach also enables a firm with limited resources to compete with larger organizations in the same market.

A major disadvantage of the concentration approach is that, if a company depends on a single market segment for all its sales and that segment's demand for the product declines, the company's sales and profits will also decline. Moreover, when a firm dominates one segment of a market, its popularity and reputation may keep it from moving into other segments. Jaguar Cars Ltd., for instance, would probably find it difficult to successfully market minivans or economy cars.

Multisegment Approach

■ **multisegment approach** a market segmentation approach in which an organization directs its marketing efforts at two or more segments by developing a marketing mix for each segment

An organization using the **multisegment approach** (refer to Figure 6.7) directs its marketing efforts at two or more segments by developing a marketing mix for each segment. This approach is used by Coca-Cola, Procter &

---

[30]Norm Alster, "Just the Stats, Sir," *Forbes,* July 20, 1992, pp. 42–43.

FIGURE 6.8
Multisegment Approach
Chrysler not only makes a variety of cars, it makes several different minivans. As shown here, Chrysler makes four different minivans, each targeted at a different segment, depending on customers' needs for length, seating options, and luxury.

Source: Chrysler Corporation.

Gamble, Toyota, General Foods, and Sony as well as by many others (see Figure 6.8). L'Oréal's Niosôme face cream is sold in exclusive, upscale beauty shops, while its Plénitude face cream sells for one-sixth as much in supermarkets and discount stores.[31] A firm may use the multisegment approach after successfully using the concentration approach in one market segment and expanding to other segments. Because of the costs involved, few firms begin with a multisegment approach; Ford started out offering one car, Coca-Cola with one beverage, and State Farm Life Insurance with one policy.

A business using the multisegment approach can usually increase its sales in the total market by focusing on more than one segment because the firm's mixes are reaching more people. Thor-Lo Inc. designs socks for eighteen different sports and has captured 50 percent of the market for athletic socks. The firm's executives believe there is still potential to expand sales into other segments, such as preventive health care and treatments for foot problems.[32] A firm with excess production capacity may find the multisegment approach practical because the development of products for additional market segments may use up the excess capacity. However, production and marketing costs may be higher with the multisegment approach because it often requires a greater number of production processes, materials, and skills, as well as several different promotion, pricing, and distribution methods. When General Motors began to downsize cars after the 1973 oil crisis, the models began

[31] William Echikson, "Aiming at High and Low Markets," *Fortune,* March 22, 1993, p. 89.
[32] Gretchen Morgenson, "The Foot's Friend," *Forbes,* April 13, 1992, pp. 60–62.

to look the same. The result is a number of different cars that appeal to the same segments. But each of these models has its own design crew, engineers, and factories, a situation resulting in cost problems for GM.[33]

MEASURING SALES POTENTIAL AND FORECASTING SALES

Having selected a target market or markets, an organization must next measure the sales potential of the market(s) and forecast sales. The target market or markets selected must have enough sales potential to justify the cost of developing and maintaining one or more marketing mixes. Several techniques are used to measure sales potential and to forecast sales.

Sales Potential

■ **market sales potential**
the amount of a product that specific customer groups are likely to purchase within a specifiec period at a specific level of industrywide marketing activity

Market sales potential is the amount of a product that specific customer groups are likely to purchase within a specified period at a specific level of industrywide marketing activity. Market sales potential is usually stated in terms of dollars or units and can refer to a total market or to a market segment. For instance, a creamery might estimate that, given a stable rate of industrywide marketing activity, all the segments of its target market are likely to buy 150,000 units of ice cream products in the coming year. When estimating market sales potential, it is important to specify a time frame and to indicate the relevant level of industry marketing activities; market sales potential changes over time and with increases or decreases in industry marketing effort.

■ **company sales potential** the amount of a product that an organization is likely to sell during a particular time period

Company sales potential is the amount of a product that an organization is likely to sell during a particular time period. The creamery, for example, might estimate that it will sell 30,000 units of ice cream in the coming year. Company sales potential is influenced by the market sales potential, industrywide competition, and the intensity of a firm's marketing efforts relative to its competitors.

■ **breakdown approach**
an approach for measuring company sales potential based on a general economic forecast for a specific time period and the market sales potential derived from it

The breakdown approach and the buildup approach can be used to measure company sales potential. In the **breakdown approach,** the marketing manager first develops a general economic forecast for a specific time period and then estimates the market sales potential on the basis of this economic forecast. From the economic forecast and the market sales potential, the manager derives the company sales potential. This approach is called the breakdown approach because the marketing manager starts with broad, comprehensive estimates of general economic activity and ends up with an estimate of the firm's sales of a specific product.

■ **buildup approach** an approach for measuring company sales potential based on projections of market sales potential for individual geographic areas

In the **buildup approach,** the marketing manager begins by estimating how much of a product a potential buyer in a specific geographic area, such as a sales territory, will purchase in a given period. Next, the manager multiplies that amount by the total number of potential buyers in the area. For

[33]Jerry Flint, "Platform Madness," *Forbes,* January 20, 1992, pp. 40–41.

each geographic area in which the firm sells products, this calculation is made. Then the marketer adds the totals for each area to calculate the market sales potential. Finally, on the basis of a specific level of marketing activity, the manager estimates the company sales potential, or the proportion of the total market potential that the business can obtain. The marketing manager may calculate several company sales potentials on the basis of different levels of marketing activities. Both the breakdown and the buildup approaches rely heavily on sales forecasts.

Sales Forecasts

■ **company sales forecast** the amount of a product a company actually expects to sell during a specific period at a specified level of marketing acitivities

A **company sales forecast** is the amount of a product that a company actually expects to sell during a specific period at a specified level of marketing activities. To elaborate on the creamery example, after considering economic conditions, its marketing resources, and the strength of its competition, the creamery forecasts that it will actually sell 60,000 units of ice cream in the coming year. Recall that when analyzing sales *potential,* marketing managers consider what sales amounts are possible at various levels of marketing activities, assuming that certain environmental conditions exist. However, when developing a sales *forecast,* marketing managers concentrate on what the actual sales are expected to be at a certain level of marketing effort.

A sales forecast should apply to a specific period of time. Sales estimates can cover periods of less than a year (short range), one to five years (medium range), or more than five years (long range). The length of time chosen for the sales forecast depends on the purpose of the forecast, the stability of the market, and the firm's objectives and resources. For instance, an organization that has an objective to increase its share of a particular market within one year will want a short- or medium-range forecast.

Marketing managers rely on a number of forecasting methods, including executive judgment, surveys, time series analysis, correlation methods, market tests, and various combinations of methods.

■ **executive judgment** the intuition and experience of one or more company managers

Executive Judgment   A company may sometimes forecast sales on the basis of **executive judgment**—the intuition and experience of one or more company managers. Although this approach is quick and inexpensive, it is not scientific. Executive judgment may be satisfactory when product demand is relatively stable and the forecaster has years of market-related experience. However, intuition tends to be swayed most heavily by recent experience, and the forecast may be overly optimistic or pessimistic as a result. Another drawback to executive judgment is that the forecaster has only past experience as a guide for deciding where to go in the future.

■ **customer forecasting survey** a technique of predicting sales by asking customers what types and quantities of products they intend to buy during a specific period

Surveys   A second way to forecast sales is to question customers, sales personnel, or experts regarding their expectations about future purchases. Businesses can ask customers what types and quantities of products they intend to buy during a specific period. This technique is called a **customer forecasting survey.** However, it is limited in usefulness to businesses that have relatively few customers who purchase fairly large ticket items. For example, a company such as RJR Nabisco, with its many diversified products

■ **sales-force forecasting survey** a technique of predicting sales by asking members of a firm's sales force to estimate the anticipated sales in their territories for a specified time period

■ **expert forecasting survey** a technique of predicting sales that uses experts to help prepare the sales forecast

■ **time series analysis** a method in which the forecaster studies the firm's historical sales data to discover patterns in the firm's sales volume over time

■ **trend analysis** an analysis that focuses on aggregate sales data, such as annual sales figures over a period of many years, to determine whether annual sales are rising, falling, or stable

■ **cycle analysis** an analysis that examines sales figures over a period of three to five years to determine whether sales fluctuate in a consistent, periodic manner

■ **seasonal analysis** a technique in which the forecaster studies daily, weekly, or monthly sales figures to evaluate the degree to which seasonal factors such as climate and holiday activities influence the firm's sales

■ **random factor analysis** an analysis that attributes irregular sales variations to random, non-recurrent events such as regional power failures or natural disasters

and millions of customers, would find it highly impractical to survey its customers about their future purchases.

Customer surveys have several disadvantages. Customers must be able and willing to make accurate estimates of future product requirements. Some customers cannot make such estimates, or simply may not wish to participate in a survey. Sometimes respondents give answers that they know are incorrect, making survey results inaccurate. Moreover, customer surveys reflect buying intentions, not actual purchases. Customer surveys also consume a great deal of time and money.

In a **sales-force forecasting survey,** a firm asks members of its sales force to estimate the anticipated sales in their territories for a specified time period. The sales forecaster combines these territorial estimates to arrive at a tentative forecast. A sales-force forecasting survey can be effective because the sales staff members are closer to customers on a daily basis than are other company personnel and therefore should know more about customers' future product needs. Furthermore, when sales representatives assist in developing the forecast, they are more motivated to work toward its achievement.

Sales force surveys have several drawbacks. Salespeople may be too optimistic or pessimistic because of recent experiences, resulting in estimates that are too high or low. Salespeople also tend to underestimate the sales potential of their territories when they believe that their sales goals will be determined by their forecasts. Finally, salespeople generally dislike paperwork because it consumes time that could be spent selling.

In an **expert forecasting survey,** businesses call on experts to help prepare the sales forecast. These experts may be economists, management consultants, advertising executives, college professors, or other persons outside the firm who have a large amount of experience in a specific market. The use of experts is quick and relatively inexpensive. However, experts may not be as motivated as company personnel to do an effective job because they work outside the firm.

Time Series Analysis   **Time series analysis** is a method in which the forecaster studies the firm's historical sales data to try to discover patterns in the firm's sales volume over time. If the forecaster discovers a pattern, it can be used to forecast sales. Time series analysis assumes that the past sales pattern will continue in the future. The accuracy and usefulness of this analysis depends heavily on the validity of this assumption.

Time series analysis generally involves four types of analysis: trend, cycle, seasonal, and random factor.[34] In **trend analysis,** a forecaster studies aggregate sales data, such as annual sales figures over a period of many years, to determine whether annual sales are generally rising, falling, or stable. In **cycle analysis,** the forecaster examines sales figures over a period of three to five years to determine whether sales fluctuate in a consistent, periodic manner. In **seasonal analysis,** the forecaster studies daily, weekly, or monthly sales figures to evaluate the degree to which seasonal factors such as climate and holiday activities influence the firm's sales. **Random factor analysis** is

[34] Norbert L. Enrick, *Market and Sales Forecasting: A Quantitative Approach* (San Francisco: Chandler, 1969), pp. 39–40.

an attempt to attribute irregular sales variations to random, nonrecurrent events such as regional power failures and natural disasters. Before Hurricane Andrew in 1992, for example, sales of bottled water, canned food, batteries, and other emergency goods rose dramatically along the Florida coast because residents feared they would be without power and water during the storm. And the sales of plywood, shingles, and other building materials increased afterwards as residents tried to repair homes and businesses. After performing each of these analyses, the forecaster combines the results to develop the sales forecast.

Time series analysis is an effective forecasting method for products that have reasonably stable demand, such as appliances, but it is not very practical for products that have highly erratic demand, such as snow blowers.[35]

■ **correlation method**
a technique of sales forecasting in which the forecaster tries to detect a relationship between past sales and one or more variables such as population, per capita income, or gross national product

Correlation Methods   In a **correlation method** of sales forecasting, the forecaster tries to detect a relationship between past sales and one or more variables such as population, per capita income, or gross national product. A correlation method requires the use of regression analysis, which studies the statistical relationships among changes in past sales and changes in one or more variables. Using regression analysis, the forecaster attempts to develop a mathematical formula that accurately describes a relationship between the firm's sales and one or more variables. However, the formula indicates only an associational relationship, not a causal one. Once an accurate formula has been developed, the forecaster inserts the necessary information into the formula to derive the sales forecast.

A correlation method is practical when a precise relationship can be established, but forecasters seldom find a perfect correlation. Performance of salespeople may be correlated with compensation, but many other factors such as job satisfaction and satisfaction with one's supervisor are also related. In addition, this method can be used only when the available historical sales data are extensive. Thus a correlation technique is generally useless for forecasting the sales of new products.

■ **market test** a means of forecasting the sales of new or existing products by making the product available to consumers in one or more test areas and measuring consumer purchases and responses to distribution, promotion, and price

Market Tests   In a **market test,** a business makes a product available to consumers in one or more test areas and measures consumer purchases and responses to distribution, promotion, and price. Test areas vary in size but generally are cities with populations of 200,000 to 500,000. A market test permits the evaluation of sales volume in relation to the intensity of other marketing activities such as advertising, in-store promotions, pricing, packaging, and distribution. On the basis of consumer response in test areas, marketers can forecast product sales for larger geographic units.

The market test has advantages and disadvantages. Because it does not require historical sales data, it is a practical method of forecasting the sales of new or existing products in new geographic areas. A market test provides the forecaster with information about customers' real actions rather than their intended or approximate behaviors. It also provides an opportunity to test various elements of the marketing mix. However, a market test can be time

---

[35] David Hurwood, Elliot S. Grossman, and Earl Bailey, *Sales Forecasting* (New York: Conference Board, 1978), p. 2.

consuming and expensive. In addition, a marketing manager cannot be certain that the consumer response during a market test represents the total market response or that such a response will continue in the future.

Combination Methods   Although many businesses rely on a single sales forecasting method, most firms use more than one technique. A firm may be forced to use several methods when it markets diverse product lines. However, even for a single product line, several forecasts may be needed, especially when the product is sold in different market segments. For example, a producer of fuel injection systems may employ one technique for forecasting sales of new fuel injectors and another technique to forecast the sales of replacement fuel injectors. Variation in the length of the sales forecast may dictate the use of several different methods. For instance, a firm that employs the sales-force forecasting survey method for a short-range forecast may find it necessary to use a different method, such as a time series analysis, for long-range forecasting. Occasionally, a marketing manager may use another method or methods to confirm the results of a favored forecasting method.

SUMMARY

A market is a group of people who, as individuals or as organizations, have a need for a product and the ability, willingness, and authority to purchase the product. A consumer market includes purchasers and persons in households who intend to consume or benefit from the purchased product and who do not buy products with the intention of making a profit. An organizational or business market includes individuals and groups that purchase a specific kind of product for resale, for use in producing other products, or for use in day-to-day operations.

Heterogeneous markets consist of individuals with different product needs. Market segmentation is the process of dividing a total market into groups of people with similar product needs. A market segment is a group of individuals, groups, or organizations that share similar characteristics that cause them to have relatively similar product needs.

Five conditions are necessary for market segmentation to be effective. First, consumers' needs for the product should be heterogeneous. Second, the market segments should be identifiable and divisible, and each should have a relatively homogeneous need for the product. Third, the total market should be divided so that the segments can be compared with respect to estimated sales potential, costs, and profits. Fourth, at least one segment must have enough profit potential to justify the development of a special marketing mix for that segment. Fifth, the firm must be able to reach the chosen segment with a particular marketing mix.

Segmentation bases (or variables) are characteristics of individuals, groups, or organizations that marketing managers use to divide a total market into segments. The bases for segmentation should be related to consumers' needs for, uses of, or behaviors toward the product; and the segmentation variables must be measurable. There are four categories of segmentation bases for consumer markets: demographic (age, sex, income, ethnic background, family life cycle); geographic (climate, terrain, natural resources, market density); psychographic (personality characteristics, motives, lifestyle); and product-related (degree of use, perception of brand quality, application, expected benefits). Segmentation bases for organizational or business markets include geographic factors, type of organization, customer size, and product use.

Businesses can use one of three approaches to selecting target markets. A firm using a total market approach designs a single marketing mix and directs it at an entire market for a particular product. A company using the concentration approach directs its marketing efforts toward a single market segment through one marketing mix. This approach allows a firm to analyze the characteristics and needs of a particular market segment and focus all its marketing efforts toward satisfying that segment. In the multisegment approach for selecting target markets, an organization develops different marketing mixes for two or more segments. This is a costly approach because it requires different promotion and distribution methods, but it can enable a firm to increase its sales by reaching more consumers.

A business must be able to evaluate the sales potential of possible target markets as well as target markets that it currently serves. Market sales potential is the amount of a product that specific groups of customers are likely to purchase in a specified time period at a specific level of industrywide marketing activity. Company sales potential is the amount of a product that a business is likely to sell in a specific time period. There are two general approaches to measuring company sales potential: the breakdown approach and the buildup approach.

A company sales forecast is the amount of a product that the company actually expects to sell during a specific period at a specified level of marketing activities. Businesses can use one or more methods to forecast company sales: executive judgment; surveys of customers, the sales force, or experts; time series analysis, which includes trend, cycle, seasonal, and random factor analyses; correlation methods; market tests; and combination methods.

KEY TERMS

market
consumer market
organizational or business
   market
heterogeneous market
market segmentation
market segment
market niche
segmentation base (variable)
market density

VALS (Values and Lifestyles)
   program
benefit segmentation
total market (undifferentiated)
   approach
concentration approach
multisegment approach
market sales potential
company sales potential
breakdown approach

buildup approach	trend analysis
company sales forecast	cycle analysis
executive judgment	seasonal analysis
customer forecasting survey	random factor analysis
sales-force forecasting survey	correlation method
expert forecasting survey	market test
time series analysis	

QUESTIONS FOR DISCUSSION AND REVIEW

1. What is a market? Distinguish between a consumer market and an organizational or business market.

2. Why would a firm want to segment a market?

3. What are the requirements for effective market segmentation?

4. Discuss the four major bases for segmenting consumer markets. Provide an example of each.

5. Give examples of the bases that automobile companies use to segment markets. Also, give examples for appliance manufacturers and banks.

6. How are organizational or business markets segmented?

7. What is the total market (undifferentiated) approach for selecting a target market? When should this approach be used? Give an example of a company that is using this approach.

8. Why would an organization decide to use the concentration approach as its market segmentation strategy?

9. What is the multisegment approach to market segmentation? What are the advantages of this strategy?

10. What is the difference between market sales potential and company sales potential?

11. Discuss five ways a company might go about forecasting sales. What are the advantages and disadvantages of each method?

CASES

6.1 CAMPBELL SEGMENTS THE SOUP MARKET

For many years, from one end of the United States to the other, shoppers looking for soup have automatically picked Campbell's. The product with the familiar red and white label seemed to own the soup market. H.J. Heinz Company tried to enter the market in the late 1960s but failed because of Campbell Soup Company's domination; Heinz no longer makes soup under its own name. By the early 1970s, Campbell's market share had grown to over 80 percent. One survey found that Campbell is the second most recognized brand name in America; only Coca-Cola ranks higher. But times are changing at Campbell Soup Company, and so is its marketing strategy.

A growing number of competitors are eating away at Campbell's market share, which dropped to 60 percent in 1988. Progresso of St. Louis, the Anglo-Dutch firm Thomas J. Lipton, and Maruchan and Nissin Foods of Japan have emerged as the major competition. Unit sales of Campbell's condensed soup (red and white label) dropped 5 percent in 1987 for the second year in a row; Chunky ready-to-eat soup fell 6 percent. Financial performance has also been under par for Campbell during this period. Return on investment has been around 15 percent, compared with an industry average of 20 percent. Campbell stock has also performed modestly. Between 1980 and 1988, share price increased by 252 percent, compared with an average food index gain of 402 percent and a 444 percent increase for Heinz.

To help maintain its position in the food industry, Campbell is changing the way it markets soup. Campbell has always sold the same products in the same way throughout the country. The company began advertising on New York City streetcars in 1899, and by 1911 it was marketing soup across the country. In the late 1950s, Campbell reached half of America by sponsoring the television show *Lassie*. But treating the entire country as though it were a single market is no longer effective. Consumers have developed a more sophisticated taste for foreign-flavored soups like Progresso's Italian-style soups and Maruchan and Nissin's Japanese noodle soup. In response to consumers' changing preferences, Campbell has pioneered a regional segmentation approach.

Campbell is targeting its products and promotions to fit specific regions of the country, right down to neighborhoods within a city. In Texas and California, the company sells a nacho cheese soup that is spicier than that sold in the rest of the country. Creole soups are marketed in southern states, and a red bean soup in Hispanic areas. Even when the product is not changed to reflect taste differences across regions, the promotion is. Campbell now relies less on national advertising and more on local advertising and coupons. As one consultant said, "The day of a single ad campaign mass-marketed across the country is in its twilight."

To facilitate regional segmentation, company executives divided the United States into twenty-two regions. Each region has its own sales and marketing staff, and a promotion budget to be spent in any way the regional staff decides is appropriate. For instance, in Nevada's Sierra Mountains, skiers were treated to samples of Campbell's soup of the day. In New York, with the Giants going to the 1987 Super Bowl, a sales manager used part of her budget for a football-related radio promotion. And in California, advertisements have run on Spanish radio stations.

CEO David Johnson also believes that growth in this industry can come only by matching product offerings with diverse and changing consumer needs. Consumers are demanding increased convenience, sophistication, and variety in foods. As a result, Campbell has released new soup lines targeted at the growing markets, such as single servings of Chunky soups for the convenience market, Home Cookin' soups for the premium market, and low-salt Special Request soups for the health-conscious. Campbell is also perfecting an inexpensive, easy-open microwaveable container that can double as a soup bowl. Frozen, microwaveable soups and sandwiches are also being developed. And since most growth potential is abroad, Johnson wants no less than half of Campbell's revenues ($6.3 billion in 1992) to come from outside the United States by 2000. This will require developing more new products that appeal to regional tastes, like fiery cream of chile poblano soup sold in Mexico or watercress and duck-gizzard soup sold in China.

Questions for Discussion

1. What approach did Campbell originally use to segment the soup market? Why was it successful?

2. What are the strengths and weaknesses of using regions of the country to segment the soup market?

3. What are some market segments Campbell may want to consider in the future?

Based on information from Joseph Weber, Gail Schares, Stephen Hutcheon, and Ian Katz, "Campbell: Now It's M–M–Global," *Business Week,* March 15, 1993, pp. 53–56; Janet Novack, "We're Not Running the Company for the Stock Price," *Forbes,* September 19, 1988, pp. 41–52; Bill Saporito, "The Fly in Campbell's Soup," *Fortune,* May 9, 1988, pp. 67–70; and Christine Dugas, Mark N. Vamos, Jonathan B. Levine, and Matt Rothman, "Marketing's New Look," *Business Week,* January 26, 1987, pp. 64–69.

6.2   FIRMS COURT HISPANIC CUSTOMERS

Hispanics represent the fastest-growing ethnic group in the United States. The 1990 census counted more than 22 million Hispanic Americans, a 53 percent increase since 1980. Hispanics will contribute 47 percent of the U.S. population growth during the 1990s.

With its population growth and a combined household income of $134 billion, the Hispanic market has caught the attention of many firms. Hispanics have distinct spending habits. For example, Hispanic consumers are far more likely than other Americans to buy fruit juice but are less likely to buy wine. The "Hispanic market," however, is actually at least five markets, each with cultural variations and a different economic profile.

The Census Bureau divides Hispanic Americans into five ethnic subgroups: Mexicans, who constitute 60 pecent of U.S. Hispanics and are highly concentrated in the Southwest; Puerto Ricans, the second largest group at just 12 percent, who dominate the Hispanic population of New York City; Cubans, who are 5 percent of the U.S. Hispanics and the majority of Hispanics in southern Florida; Central and South Americans; and Hispanics who trace their lineage to Spain.

Of the U.S. Hispanics, Cuban Americans are the oldest, with a median age of 39; the best educated, since 20 percent of those age 25 and older have attended at least four years of college; and the most affluent, with a median income of $25,900. Mexicans are the youngest Hispanic subgroup, with a median age of just 24. Only 6 percent of Mexican-Americans have completed four or more years of college, and their median income is $22,439. The median income of U.S. Puerto Rican households is $16,169. Overall, Hispanics in the United States are younger and earn less money than the overall population. Hispanic median age is 26.2 and income is $22,330, compared with the overall U.S. median age of 33 and income of $29,943.

Despite their lower median income, their growing numbers make Hispanics an important target for marketers. But U.S. companies may not be successful in reaching Hispanics if they stick with traditional methods. First, all firms that target Hispanics must deal with the language question: whether to use Spanish or English in advertisement. It's not an easy choice. Researchers disagree on which language is appropriate for different kinds of advertising. Most Hispanics speak both English and Spanish. More and more upwardly mobile, assimilated Hispanics use English in their business and professional lives. Glossy English-language magazines like *Hispanic Business, Nuestro,* and *Hispanic Review of Business* appeal to this group. English-language media can reach large numbers of young Hispanics. But for many Hispanics, especially recent immigrants to the United States, the Spanish-language media are a primary source of information. One study found that in common situations—at home, with friends, watching television—the majority of Hispanics think and speak in Spanish.

Hispanics are critical of advertising and other marketing activities that do not truly portray Hispanics or an understanding of their culture. Many would like to see more Hispanics and Hispanic products in advertisements, and trust Spanish-language advertisements more than those in English.

Companies wishing to reach Hispanics through Spanish-language media outlets have more options than ever before. Such outlets proliferated in the United States in the last decade and include more than a hundred television stations broadcasting Spanish programs, 158 newspapers, and about 660 radio stations. Univision Holdings, owned by Hallmark Cards Inc., is the number one U.S. Spanish-language television network and produces 45 percent of its programming.

But translating advertisements into Spanish is no guarantee of reaching the diverse Hispanic market because each subgroup has its own cultural, racial, and linguistic differences. Half of Mexican-Americans say they cannot easily understand Cubans, Puerto Ricans, or Central Americans. Miami-based Telemundo, the second largest Hispanic-language television network in the United States, received protests from West Coast viewers who said the programming had too much of a Cuban slant. Telemundo responded with more focus on Mexican and general Hispanic programming and hired more purely Spanish and Mexican news anchors.

Telemundo, as much as possible, programs for the total Hispanic market. The network's marketing director points out that although marketers always have to be sensitive to differences between Puerto Ricans, Cubans, Mexicans, and others, those differences are similar to differentiating between "a person from Georgia and one from Maine." Like Americans in general, Hispanics as a group have basic concerns and similarities regardless of ancestry.

Many companies have discovered a highly effective way to market to Hispanics: linking advertising to strong promotional efforts. Many activities are linked to church activities. Some 70 percent of Hispanics are Roman Catholic, and their churches are not only places of worship but also centers for social activity, charitable events, and holiday celebrations. Thirty food and beverage companies joined together to sponsor more than one hundred celebrations and fund-raising activities in Texas and California. The program, called "Friends of the Community," is anchored by H. E. Butt Grocery Company in Texas and Ralph's Grocery Company in California. The "Friends" donate products and gift certificates to churches and nonprofit groups for their events; in return, the companies get recognition and product exposure. In California, "Caramba!" soft drinks sponsors Olivera Street festivals and other community events. In Florida, Anheuser-Busch, Campbell Soup Company, and Coca-Cola are major sponsors of the nine-day Carnival Miami.

Soccer is another unifying element among Hispanics, since many of them grew up playing soccer in Mexico and South America and still love the sport. Several years ago, Ford began sponsoring amateur soccer in the United States, with world-famous Pelé as the celebrity spokesman. Ford will reap a bounty of publicity when the United States hosts the World Cup of Soccer in 1994. Other cross-cultural ties among Hispanics are art and music. McDonald's sponsored the Hispanic Heritage Art contest. Coors is sponsoring a two-year tour of Hispanic art throughout the country. PepsiCo and Coca-Cola have sponsored Hispanic music awards, and Pepsi commercials have featured the well-known group Miami Sound Machine. Many firms have found that Hispanic communities respond when sponsorship involves genuine interest and commitment: sponsoring festivals, arts events, or sports teams year after year, with company representatives attending.

Many advertisers believe that marketing to Hispanics—and Spanish-language advertising—will expand dramatically as the North American Free Trade Agreement brings about a common North American market. Univision is moving to the international market and distributes shows to eighteen countries in Latin America. Already some companies have run U.S.-produced advertisements in Latin America and Latin American–produced advertisements in the United States. Coca-Cola has run television commercials starring Mexican singer Luis Miguel in the United States, Mexico, Costa Rica, and Puerto Rico. Rival Pepsi has run commercials starring the Mexican actor Chayanne in the United States and Latin America. Mexican companies are eyeing the United States to target not only Hispanics but also the general population.

Other firms have found that targeting Hispanics can have broad results. In 1991, McDonald's added chicken fajitas to its menu for Cinco de Mayo,

Mexico's biggest spring holiday, which is one of the most popular festivals in the American Southwest. Although the new product was aimed at Mexican-Americans, it became a hit and proved that some Hispanic products hold appeal for the rest of the population. About 33.5 million women serve Mexican food at home; that's about three times the number of Mexican-American homemakers.

Questions for Discussion

1. Is the U.S. Hispanic market heterogeneous?

2. What bases could a national consumer products company use to segment the U.S. Hispanic market? Explain.

3. An investment firm would like to target the Hispanic market in the United States. Which approach would you recommend? Why? Which approach would you recommend for a food manufacturer?

4. How do you think a common U.S.-Mexican market would affect the approaches firms use to select target markets among Hispanics?

Based on information from Judith Waldrop, "The Mexican Way," *American Demographics,* May 1992, p. 4; Christy Fisher, "Shops Look Covetously on Mexico," *Advertising Age,* February 3, 1992, pp. 25, 27; Joe Schwartz, "Hispanic Affluence Has a Cuban Accent," *American Demographics,* March 1992, p. 18; Kathy Bodovitz, "Hispanic America," *American Demographics Desk Reference,* July 1991, pp. 14–15; and Howard Schlossberg, "Hispanic Market Strong, but Often Ignored," *Marketing News,* February 19, 1990, pp. 1, 12.

Understanding Consumer Behavior

OBJECTIVES

● *To define the term* consumer behavior.

● *To identify the stages consumers go through in making purchasing decisions.*

● *To discuss the different types of consumer decision making.*

● *To describe the social influences on consumer decision making.*

● *To explain how psychological factors influence consumer purchasing decisions.*

● *To discuss the personal factors that affect consumer decisions.*

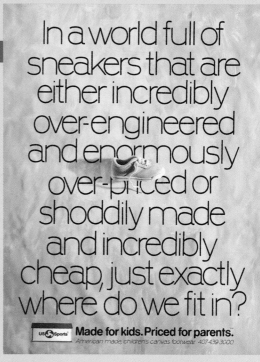

In a world full of sneakers that are either incredibly over-engineered and enormously over-priced or shoddily made and incredibly cheap, just exactly where do we fit in?

us Sports **Made for kids. Priced for parents.**
American made, children's canvas footwear. 407-439-3000

Whatever happened to the good old-fashioned, all-purpose sneaker—the kind made of canvas with rubber bottoms that came in white and black? For $15, you could buy a pair of U.S. Keds, Converse All Stars, or P.F. Flyers.

Prosperous consumers from the baby boom generation and the hawking of athletic shoes by sports superstars have changed all that. Today, 93 percent of Americans own at least two pairs of sneakers. More than 150 million pairs of brand-name sneakers are sold in the United States each year. There are dozens of brands from which to choose, and they come in every color imaginable and in some unimaginable. Reebok offers 175 different models in 450 colors and patterns. Nike has an even larger selection—300 models and 900 styles. Sneakers are designed for everything from walking to sailboarding. The Athletic Footware Association estimates that, because of the myriad of choices, only 12 percent of consumers know what brand they are going to purchase before they enter the store.

Sneakers used to serve a strictly practical purpose, as footwear. Now people buy them to "make a statement" or express an "attitude." Members of a Los Angeles street gang all wear the same kind of shoes as part of their identification. In a poor neighborhood in Chicago, a teenager does not think he can get a date without a $90 pair of shoes. Even children wear sneakers designed from the hit movie *Batman*. That's attitude.

Consumers aren't especially loyal to sneakers any longer. When a model is introduced, many are quick to abandon their old one. To some, sneakers represent a fantasy. As Byron Scott of the L.A. Lakers says, "A lot of people are into BMWs. I'm into gym shoes." And most kids cannot buy BMWs.

The footwear industry has been criticized for exploiting youngsters, especially inner-city kids, who cannot afford the high prices. But children and teens are willing to buy a dream, such as being able to leap as high as Michael Jordan. The industry estimates that the consumer market for sneakers is about $5.8 billion a year. In Cincinnati, a store manager says that the number of Nike Air Jordans he can sell is limited only by the price.[1] ●

[1]Based on information from Joseph Pereira, "New Balance Disproves Myths About Urban Workers," *Wall Street Journal*, June 9, 1992, p. B4; "Marketing Achievement Awards," *Sales & Marketing Management*, August 1991, p. 36; Paul Daugherty, "Sneakers," *Cincinnati*, June 1990, pp. 33–35; and E.M. Swift, "Farewell My Lovely," *Sports Illustrated*, February 19, 1990, pp. 74–80.

n Chapter 1, we explained that the major thrust of the marketing concept is satisfying customer needs. Without understanding consumers, it would be difficult, if not impossible, to develop a marketing mix that brings the organization closer to the customer. Vans shoes, for instance, appeal to consumers who want to pay between $29 and $54 for a pair of shoes, rather than from $50 to $130 for Nike or Reebok.[2] Many factors, such as cultural values or attitudes toward a brand, influence consumer behavior. Just as sneakers serve a variety of needs, so do many products we purchase. And the decision-making process used to decide which products or brands to buy can be fairly complex. Thus understanding consumers, their needs, and how they make buying decisions is critical to developing a successful marketing strategy.

CONSUMER DECISION MAKING

■ **consumer behavior** the actions and decision processes of people who purchase goods and services for personal consumption

■ **consumer decision making** the five-stage process people go through when deciding what products to buy; includes problem recognition, information search, evaluation of alternatives, purchase decision, and postpurchase evaluation

Before businesses can develop marketing strategies to satisfy consumers, they must understand *how* consumers make purchasing decisions. **Consumer behavior** refers to the actions and decision processes of people who purchase goods and services for personal consumption.[3] Consumer behavior is of particular interest to marketers, who wish to influence or change the behavior of others. **Consumer decision making** is the process people go through to decide what products to buy and is shaped by many factors, such as internal motivations, social pressures, and marketing activities. Some decisions are made by carefully weighing all alternatives and evaluating the functional attributes of a product. This is often called *rational* decision making. On the other hand, buying decisions can be influenced by *hedonic benefits*—emotional responses, aesthetic pleasures, or other factors that are pleasing to the senses.[4] Functional attributes of a car purchase might include gas mileage, legroom, size of engine, trunk space, and so on; hedonic benefits include style and the statement the car makes. Both functional attributes and hedonic benefits can influence consumer decision making.

Consumer decision making generally consists of five stages: problem recognition, information search, evaluation of alternatives, purchase decision, and postpurchase evaluation (see Figure 7.1).

As you can see in Figure 7.1, the actual act of purchasing is only one step in the consumer decision-making process. Purchases are important, of course, but the process is initiated several steps prior to the actual purchase. You may be thinking about purchasing a new car because your old one is running poorly, but it may take some time before you make the actual purchase. A person may also terminate the process at any time. You may go shopping for a new suit or dress, but decide not to buy one.

[2]Shelley Neumeier, "Vans," *Fortune,* March 9, 1992, p. 3.
[3]James F. Engel, Roger D. Blackwell, and Paul W. Miniard, *Consumer Behavior* (Hinsdale, Ill.: Dryden Press, 1990), p. 3.
[4]Elizabeth C. Hirschman and Morris B. Holbrook, "Hedonic Consumption: Emerging Concepts, Methods, and Propositions," *Journal of Marketing,* Summer 1982, pp. 92–101.

| Problem recognition | → | Information search | → | Evaluation of alternatives | → | Purchase decision | → | Postpurchase evaluation |

FIGURE 7.1
Five Stages in Consumer Decision Making

Problem Recognition

The consumer decision-making process begins when a buyer recognizes a problem or an unsatisfied need or desire. For example, a consumer might think it is time to buy a new car when his current one has to be repaired four times in one month. Or a student might have the desire for a compact disk (CD) player because some of her friends own them. Since consumers may not always recognize that they have a problem or a need, businesses use products, advertising, packaging, and sales personnel to help trigger consumer awareness of needs and desires. For example, a person may not realize that he or she is hungry until seeing a television commercial for home-delivered pizza. Consumers may experience problem recognition rather slowly or quite quickly.

Problem recognition is a critical stage in the consumer decision-making process because a consumer will not move to the next stage of the process—information search—unless he or she recognizes a problem, a need, or a desire. Marketers must study the target market to distinguish whether consumer inaction is the result of a lack of problem recognition or a lack of movement after problem recognition has taken place. They can then adjust their marketing strategies to either trigger and stimulate problem recognition or to identify and overcome resistance on the part of reluctant consumers. The end goal is to initiate some buying action that will bring about a solution. For example, suppose that a consumer is lonely. Marketing efforts could focus on making the consumer aware of existing but unknown goods or services that offer a solution—such as dating services, classified advertisements for singles, or public dances. If no such products exist, marketers could develop products to address the need. Choosing an effective strategy means clearly defining the consumer problem and selecting products, media, and promotional appeals that fit the target market.[5]

Information Search

After recognizing a problem or need, the consumer seeks out information on how to satisfy it. An information search can focus on product features, prices, availability of brands, seller characteristics, warranties, and other factors. Businesses can expedite the information search by supplying consumers with useful, accurate, timely, and readily available product information.

[5]Gordon C. Bruner II and Richard J. Pomazal, "Problem Recognition: The Crucial First Stage of the Consumer Decision Process," *Journal of Consumer Marketing,* Winter 1988, pp. 53–63.

Consumers usually begin the search process with an *internal search* into their memory. Usually, a person had some previous experience satisfying a particular need and has stored information in his or her mind for dealing with that need. In this case, a decision can be made with little or no additional information search. However, if more information is needed, consumers engage in an *external search*.[6] In this case, additional information is obtained from a variety of external sources. One source of information is communication with other people, including friends, family, and associates. Although it is difficult to gauge which of these sources are actually used, they are considered a powerful influence on buying decisions. Marketing sources of information include advertising, salespeople, dealers, and product packages. Buyers can also obtain information from public sources such as independent product ratings and newspaper articles. These sources, such as *Consumer Reports,* are important because they are thought to be objective and provide information on quality and value. Finally, examining the product or actually using the product may provide additional information.

How consumers process this information depends on a number of factors, including amount of information, availability, method of presentation, quality, and confidence. One danger firms face is the situation in which a consumer reaches an information overload. A person may collect so much information that it becomes difficult to evaluate the alternatives.[7] Although firms cannot eliminate this possibility, they should provide only information based on the criteria that are most important to target customers. The way in which the information is transmitted also influences how it is processed. For many products, pictures are recalled with greater accuracy than are words, and the combination of pictures and words is most effective.[8] The quality and availability of the information also influence how consumers process information.

After the information is processed, it should yield a group of brands from which the buyer can choose. This group of brands is sometimes called the buyer's **evoked set.** For example, the student's search for a CD player might yield an evoked set of Sony, Jensen, Sanyo, Pioneer, Alpine, Denon, and Magnavox machines. The consumer must then evaluate each of the alternatives in the evoked set.

■ **evoked set** a group of brands from which the buyer can choose

Evaluation of Alternatives

To evaluate the products in the evoked set, the consumer develops a set of criteria against which he or she can compare the features of each product. These criteria include the features that the buyer desires, as well as those that are not desired. For example, the student evaluating CD players may want one that can be programmed to play selections at random from several com-

---

[6] Sharon E. Beatty and Scott M. Smith, "External Search Effort: An Investigation Across Several Categories," *Journal of Consumer Research,* June 1987, pp. 83–95.
[7] Kevin L. Keller and Richard Staelin, "Effects of Quality and Quantity of Information on Decision Effectiveness," *Journal of Consumer Research,* September 1987, pp. 200–213.
[8] Michael J. Houston, Terry L. Childers, and Susan E. Heckler, "Picture-Word Consistency and the Elaborative Processing of Advertisements," *Journal of Marketing Research,* November 1987, pp. 359–369.

pact disks. However, she may not want to pay $500 for a CD player. The consumer assigns a level of importance to each criterion; some features and characteristics are valued more than others. The student may value price, reliability, and compatibility with a current stereo system more than color or style in a CD player.

Some consumers try to simplify the evaluation process by developing some procedure for evaluating the different alternatives. For instance, some consumers may weigh price very heavily or make the evaluation on the basis of a recognized brand name. Other consumers may make the evaluation process fairly complex by collecting information for several brands and comparing them on different features such as price, quality ratings, guarantees, and so on. This process can be described through attitude modeling as follows:

1. The consumer has information about a number of brands.
2. The consumer perceives that some of the brands can satisfy a recognized problem or need.
3. Each brand has product attributes such as color, price, quality, and so on.
4. Some of these attributes are important to the consumer, who perceives that different brands vary in the extent to which they possess these attributes.
5. The consumer prefers the brand that offers the desired amounts of the important attributes.
6. The consumer intends to purchase the preferred brand.[9]

Sales personnel can play an important role in this stage by helping consumers evaluate alternatives and moving them closer to a purchase decision. Because of their close relationship with customers, salespeople can answer questions about the specific criteria used to evaluate brands and also provide persuasive evidence about a particular brand. A salesperson, for instance, could explain the features of the various brands of CDs, discuss why some are priced higher than others, and perhaps make a recommendation according to the customer's needs.

Purchase Decision

The consumer decides what product or brand to buy in the purchase decision stage. The consumer also decides where to buy the product in this stage because the choice of seller may influence the final product selection. The sale terms, if they are negotiable, are determined during the purchase decision stage. Other issues of concern to the consumer, such as price, delivery, warranty, maintenance, installation, and credit arrangement, are discussed and agreed on in this stage. The student, for example, may decide to purchase her CD player from a discount store because the store has the widest selection of CD players in stock at the most reasonable prices.

[9]Blair H. Sheppard, Jon Hartwick, and Paul R. Warshaw, "The Theory of Reasoned Action: A Meta-Analysis of Past Research with Recommendations for Modification and Future Research," *Journal of Consumer Research,* December 1988, pp. 325–343.

The actual purchase also takes place during this stage. However, the consumer may terminate the buying process prior to the purchase if one or more of the terms is unacceptable. For example, the student may decide to buy a compact disk player from a specific retail store. If the CD players at that store cost more than $500 or do not have the desired features, she may decide not to buy a CD player at all.

Postpurchase Evaluation

After making a purchase, the buyer evaluates the product to determine if it satisfies the need for which it was purchased. Generally, this involves comparing expectations to actual product performance.[10] The outcome of this evaluation is satisfaction or dissatisfaction. A $200 ceiling fan with a lifetime warranty may not satisfy the buyer if the motor hums too loudly. On the other hand, a hamburger at a fast-food restaurant may satisfy the buyer if it meets or exceeds expectations. Consumer satisfaction or dissatisfaction influences future purchase decisions. Firms must be cautious not to establish unrealistic expectations that can't be met, since this will only result in dissatisfied consumers and failed marketing strategy.[11] By advertising its hotels as no-frills, Motel 6 is establishing realistic expectations which, if they are met or exceeded, should lead to customer satisfaction.

■ **cognitive dissonance**
the conflict buyers experience when they have doubts about a purchase, such as whether the product should have been purchased at all or whether a different brand or type of product should have been purchased

After purchasing an expensive product, consumers may worry that they have purchased the wrong product. **Cognitive dissonance** is the conflict consumers experience when they have doubts about a purchase, such as whether the product should have been purchased at all or whether a different brand or type of product should have been purchased. The student who purchased the CD player, for example, may worry that she should have bought a less expensive brand. A consumer experiencing cognitive dissonance may try to return the product or seek positive information about it to rationalize the choice.

Marketers can help reduce cognitive dissonance by reassuring consumers that they have made the best choice. Some organizations use advertising to do this. In Figure 7.2, notice how the advertisement states, "It's definitely not a car that years from now you'll say, 'What was I thinking?'" Infiniti is helping consumers reduce cognitive dissonance. For large purchases such as a car or appliance, many firms write to customers reinforcing their choice and offering to help with any problems. Cognitive dissonance can also be reduced by providing toll-free lines for problems and follow-up sales calls to customers.

After purchasing the product, the consumer evaluates it to determine whether it is performing as expected. The criteria developed in the evaluation-of-alternatives stage are frequently used during postpurchase evaluation. The outcome of this stage is either satisfaction or dissatisfaction, which influ-

---

[10] Richard L. Oliver and John E. Swan, "Consumer Perceptions of Interpersonal Equity and Satisfaction in Transactions: A Field Survey Approach," *Journal of Marketing,* April 1989, pp. 21–35.
[11] Robert A. Westbrook, "Product/Consumption-Based Affective Responses and Postpurchase Processes," *Journal of Marketing Research,* August 1987, pp. 258–270.

FIGURE 7.2
Cognitive Dissonance
By reassuring that they
won't second guess their
decision years later, Infiniti
helps consumers reduce
cognitive dissonance.

Source: Courtesy of Infiniti Division
of Nissan Motor Corporation U.S.A.

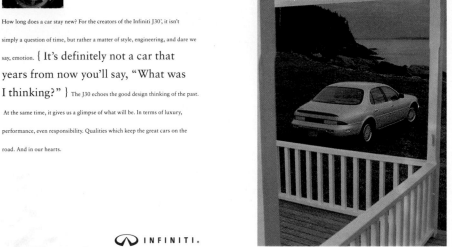

ences subsequent purchases. If the student who purchased the CD player is
satisfied with its performance, she will consider buying other stereo components from the same company when it is time to upgrade her stereo system
again. On the other hand, dissatisfied customers not only do not return, but
they also tell others about the problems they encountered.

TYPES OF CONSUMER DECISION MAKING

Consumers make many purchasing decisions to satisfy their current and future needs and desires. The extent to which they follow the five-step decision
process we just discussed can vary from one decision to another. Consumer
decision making can be represented by a continuum with routine decision
making and extensive decision making at the extremes and limited decision
making in the middle (see Figure 7.3).[12]

■ **routine decision mak-
ing** the type of decision
making a consumer uses
when purchasing frequently
purchased, low-cost items
that do not require much
thought

Many consumer purchases are made on a repeat basis. For such purchases,
consumers develop buying routines which simplify the decision-making
process. **Routine decision making** is used for frequently purchased, low-
cost items that do not require much thought. For instance, most consumers
don't spend much time evaluating the alternatives when purchasing products
such as pens, sugar, salt, and socks.

[12]John A. Howard and Jagdish N. Sheth, *The Theory of Buyer Behavior* (New York: Wiley, 1969),
pp. 27–28.

FIGURE 7.3
A Continuum of Consumer Decision Making

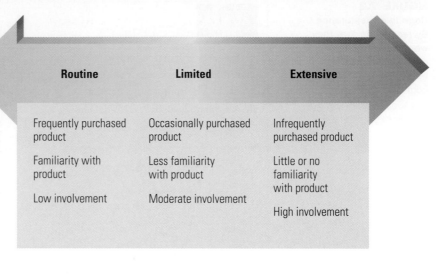

Routine	Limited	Extensive
Frequently purchased product	Occasionally purchased product	Infrequently purchased product
Familiarity with product	Less familiarity with product	Little or no familiarity with product
Low involvement	Moderate involvement	High involvement

■ **involvement** the degree of perceived relevance and personal interest a buyer has in a product or brand in a particular situation

■ **impulse purchase** the most routine decision, in which there is no decision-making process prior to the purchase

■ **limited decision making** the type of decision making employed for products that are purchased occasionally or when a buyer needs to acquire information about an unfamiliar brand in a familiar product category

■ **extensive decision making** the type of decision making a consumer uses when purchasing an unfamiliar expensive product or an infrequently bought item

The degree of involvement influences the extent to which consumers engage in decision making. **Involvement** refers to the degree of perceived relevance and personal interest a buyer has in a product or brand in a particular situation.[13] When involvement is low, consumers are much more likely to engage in routine decision making. Low-involvement buyers spend much less time and effort deciding which product or brand to purchase. Buyers may either skip some of the stages in the consumer decision-making process or simplify the process dramatically. For instance, toilet paper may be a low-involvement item for some consumers, who may simplify the decision-making process by purchasing the cheapest brand.

The most routine decision is called an **impulse purchase,** in which there is no decision-making process prior to the purchase. Consumers make spur-of-the-moment purchases based on instinct or impulse, and the product evaluation takes place after the purchase. Marketing activities like point-of-purchase displays or in-store coupons can trigger impulse purchases.

Limited decision making is used for products that are purchased only occasionally or when a buyer needs to acquire information about an unfamiliar brand in a familiar product category. For instance, although decisions about fabric softener generally fall into the category of routine decision making, a consumer learning about a new product with added features needs more information before deciding to select the new brand over a preferred brand. This type of decision making requires a moderate amount of time to search for information and evaluate the alternatives.

Extensive decision making is used when a consumer purchases an unfamiliar expensive product or an infrequently bought item. This type of decision making is the most complex of the consumer decision-making

[13]John Antil, "Conceptualization and Operationalization of Involvement," in *Advances in Consumer Research,* ed. Thomas Kinnear (Provo, Utah: Association for Consumer Research, 1984), p. 204.

behaviors. A buyer uses a large number of criteria to evaluate alternative brands and spends a great deal of time seeking information and deciding on the purchase. Consumers do not have the time or resources to frequently engage in extensive decision making. Most consumers probably use extensive decision making when buying a home or an automobile.

Extensive decision making is generally used in the purchase of high-involvement items. Involvement is highest when choices reflect one's self-image (jewelry), when the risk of negative consequences is high (a house), when social acceptance is influenced by the choice of product (club membership), or when the item purchased provides significant pleasure (vacation).[14] Because it is important to make the right choice, consumers closely follow the stages in the decision-making process, although not necessarily in the exact order.

The type of decision making used varies from person to person and from product to product. For instance, people might use extensive decision making the first time they buy a certain product, and then use limited decision making for subsequent purchases of that product. Likewise, a men's suit purchase may be a limited decision for a high-paid professional but an extensive decision for a student preparing for a major job interview.

SOCIAL INFLUENCES ON CONSUMER DECISION MAKING

■ **social factor** a force that other people exert on consumer behavior

A **social factor** is a force exerted by other people that affects consumer behavior. As shown in Figure 7.4, four social factors can influence the consumer decision-making process: social class, reference groups, roles and family, and culture and subculture.

Social Class

■ **social class** a relatively homogeneous and stable group of people with similar values, interests, lifestyles, and behaviors

A **social class** is a relatively homogeneous and stable group of people with similar values, interests, lifestyles, and behaviors.[15] The criteria used to classify individuals into social classes vary from one society to another. In American society, many factors are used to classify people, including income, wealth, occupation, education, religion, race, ethnic background, and possessions. For example, as more Americans receive college educations and earn higher incomes, they move into higher social classes.[16]

Social class influences many aspects of a person's life: religion, educational attainment, and occupation, as well as attitudes, desires, and lifestyles. People within a social class may develop and take on common patterns of behavior. They may have similar attitudes, language patterns, and possessions. Because

---

[14] Gilles Laurent and Jean-Noel Kapferer, "Measuring Consumer Involvement Profiles," *Journal of Marketing Research,* February 1985, pp. 41–53.
[15] Engel, Blackwell, and Miniard, p. 329.
[16] Brian O'Reilly, "How Much Does Class Matter?" *Fortune,* July 30, 1990, pp. 123–128.

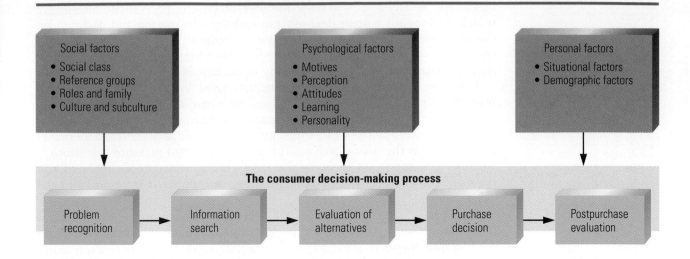

FIGURE 7.4
**Factors Influencing
Consumer Decision
Making**

social class affects so many aspects of a person's life, it also influences buying decisions as the advertisement in Figure 7.5 illustrates.

Analysts of social class often divide people in the United States into four classes, which are outlined in Table 7.1. As you can see, social class determines to some extent the type, quality, and quantity of products that people in a particular class buy and consume. Social class even affects a person's shopping patterns. People in the upper class, for example, are likely to shop in upscale retail stores such as Saks Fifth Avenue and Neiman-Marcus, whereas persons in the working class are more likely to shop in stores like Kmart and Sears.

Reference Groups

■ **reference group**
a group with whom an individual identifies to the extent that he or she takes on many of the values, attitudes, or behaviors of group members

A **reference group** is a group of people with whom an individual identifies to the extent that he or she assumes many of the values, attitudes, or behaviors of group members. Most people have several reference groups—family, friends, church, civic groups, and professional organizations.

Some reference groups may be viewed negatively by a person. Someone may be a part of a specific reference group at one time but later reject the group's values and members. For example, a person may be associated with a particular religion or church as a child but reject that religious affiliation as an adult and seek out a new one more in keeping with his or her changed values and ideas. A person can also take specific actions to avoid a particular group.[17] For purposes of this discussion, however, reference groups are those viewed positively by the person involved.

Reference groups may serve as points of comparison and as sources of information for a person. Consumers may change their behavior to be more

[17]Henry Assael, *Consumer Behavior and Marketing Action* (Boston: Kent, 1987), p. 369.

FIGURE 7.5
Social Class
Social class influences many consumer buying decisions. This advertisement from Apple Canada is aimed at consumers who belong to a class that is attaining a college education.

Source: Apple and the Apple logo are registered trademarks of Apple Computer, Inc.

in line with the actions and beliefs of group members. For example, teenagers often switch brands of clothing in an effort to dress more like their peers—another reference group. Likewise, a person may ask members of the reference group for information about factors affecting a purchase decision, such as where to buy a certain product. A member of a business association may ask other members for advice on what type of business computer to buy and where to buy it.

Some members of groups are highly respected by others because of their status, skills, or knowledge. These individuals are referred to as *opinion leaders*. In some cases, opinion leaders serve as role models and are often sought out for information and advice about products. By identifying opinion leaders, marketers can target this group with information or feature them in advertisements. The Roper Organization has studied opinion leaders for nearly fifty years and has found them to be a good predictor of marketplace developments. Opinion leaders are found to have advanced education, are highly active members of their communities, are likely to have high incomes, and are heavy users of print media.[18]

How much a reference group affects a person's decision to purchase depends on the person's strength of involvement with the group and susceptibility to the influence of the reference group. Reference groups may influence the purchase decision, brand decision, or both. Generally, the more prominent a product is, the more likely reference groups will influence a consumer's brand decision. Typical products for which the brand decision is influenced by reference groups include sailboats, wristwatches, and golf clubs.

Roles and Family

■ **role** a set of functions and activities that a person in a particular position is expected to perform

A **role** is a set of functions and activities that a person in a particular position is expected to perform. Because people occupy many positions within groups, organizations, institutions, and society at large, they have many roles. For example, your roles may include student, daughter or son, friend,

[18] Rebecca Piirto, "The Influentials," *American Demographics,* October 1992, pp. 30–38.

Class (percentage of population)	Behavioral Traits	Patterns of Buying Behavior
Upper (14) includes upper-upper, lower-upper, upper-middle	Socially prominent; may possess inherited wealth; may live in large homes in exclusive neighborhoods; investors, merchants, professionals, and middle management; well educated; college degrees from major institutions; socially at ease; high expectations for their children	Purchase or inherit large homes that indicate social position; value quality merchandise and prestigious brands; products purchased show good taste; patronize exclusive shops; invest in art; spend money on travel, theater, books, and sports clubs
Middle (32)	Respectability is a major objective; white-collar workers, managers, owners of small businesses; want attractive homes in well-maintained neighborhoods, often in suburban tracts; enjoy travel and physical activities; involved in children's school and sports activities	Own rather than rent houses; maintain their houses well, often with do-it-yourself products; buy attractive home furnishings, usually moderately priced and of standard design; consult experts through books or magazines before buying; make socially acceptable purchases; will spend for experiences they think worthwhile for their children (college, trips); enjoy travel
Working (38)	Blue collar, semiskilled; earn adequate incomes; seek job security; reside in older, less expensive neighborhoods; depend on family, especially for economic and emotional support (information about jobs, help in times of trouble); enjoy leisure time and recreational activities; enjoy mechanical items	Live in small houses or apartments; spend less than other classes on housing and more on household items such as kitchen appliances; strong sense of value; shop for bargains; favor national brands and are brand loyal; buy vehicles and equipment for recreation and sports; enjoy local travel and recreational parks
Lower (16) includes upper-lower, lower-lower	Poorly educated, unskilled workers plagued by high unemployment; often unemployed through situations beyond their control, such as layoffs or factory closings; live in less desirable neighborhoods; may be welfare recipients or the homeless; often have strong religious beliefs	Products purchased are for survival; purchases are impulsive rather than planned; often pay high prices and interest rates; are able to turn good discards into usable items; prefer to shop in local stores where they know the owner

Source: Adapted from Richard P. Coleman, "The Continuing Significance of Social Class," *Journal of Consumer Research*, December 1983, pp. 265–280. Copyright © *The Journal of Consumer Research*, Inc., 1983. Reprinted by permission.

TABLE 7.1
U.S. Social Classes

employee, fraternity or sorority member, and perhaps spouse and parent. In some cases, individuals can be portrayed in roles that are insulting or stereotypical. Stereotypes, especially of women and minorities, are often pervasive in our society. For example, even though *Ms.* magazine had a stated advertising policy precluding advertisements insulting to women, a study reported that over time, advertising in *Ms.* increasingly portrayed women as alluring or as sex objects.[19] A person's various roles influence buying behavior as well as general behavior. Parents buy clothing for children, students buy books for classes, and executives buy clothing and jewelry appropriate for their roles. Although you may never have purchased baby food, one of your future roles may lead you to this buying behavior.

Family roles also influence buying behavior. Although women's roles are changing, research shows that women still make most buying decisions related to household items such as health care products, laundry supplies, paper goods, and foods.[20] Husbands and wives make joint decisions pertaining to a variety of products, particularly durable goods such as furniture, appliances, and other expensive items. In addition, children now play a bigger role in family purchasing decisions. Children ages 4 to 12 spend roughly $9 billion of their own money each year.[21] When several family members participate in buying decisions, their roles may dictate that each is responsible for carrying out certain tasks, such as initiating the idea, searching for information, evaluating alternatives, selecting a specific brand, or deciding whether to buy at all.

To develop a marketing mix that precisely satisfies the needs and desires of a target market, marketing managers need to know not only who does the actual buying but what roles influence the purchase. Additionally, because roles are changing rapidly, particularly the roles of women and children, marketing managers must verify that their information about roles is current and accurate.

Culture and Subculture

■ **culture** all the learned values, behaviors, and other meaningful symbols shared by a society

Culture is all the learned values, behaviors, and other meaningful symbols shared by a society.[22] Culture includes tangible items such as food, furniture, buildings, clothing, tools, and art, as well as intangible concepts such as education, welfare, and laws. Cultural factors influence buying behavior because they are such a large part of our daily lives. Culture determines what people wear, what and how they eat, where they live, and where they travel. It broadly affects how they buy and use products, and their satisfaction with them. For example, in cultures where laundry is done by hand, Procter & Gamble markets a laundry soap in bar form to satisfy the needs of those consumers.

Because culture determines to some extent how products are purchased and used, it also affects the development, promotion, distribution, and pricing of products. Americans, for example, tend to buy groceries in large, full-service supermarkets only once or twice a week. Europeans, on the other hand, are more likely to shop for groceries in small, more specialized

[19]Jill Hicks Ferguson, Peggy J. Kreshel, and Spencer F. Tinkham, "In the Pages of *Ms.*: Sex Role Portrayals of Women in Advertising," *Journal of Advertising,* 1990, pp. 40–51.

[20]Harry L. Davis, "Decision Making Within the Household," *Journal of Consumer Research,* March 1976, pp. 241–260.

[21]James McNeal, "Children as Customers," *American Demographics,* September 1990, pp. 36–39.

[22]J. Paul Peter and Jerry C. Olson, *Consumer Behavior: Marketing Strategy Perspectives* (Homewood, Ill.: Richard D. Irwin, 1990), p. 334.

shops—bakery, dairy, and butcher shops—and they tend to buy in smaller quantities more frequently. American businesses that market products in other countries have to adjust their marketing mixes to accommodate the different attitudes, values, desires, and needs of other cultures. Some international businesses attempting to market their products in other countries fail because they do not or cannot adjust to cultural differences.

■ **subculture** a subdivision of a culture in which people share similar attitudes, values, and actions that are different from those of the broader culture

A **subculture** shares similar attitudes, values, and actions that deviate from those of the broader culture. A culture can be divided into subcultures on the basis of such factors as geographic regions (the South, the East); demographic characteristics such as age (adolescence, old age); political beliefs (conservatism, liberalism); or ethnic background (black, Hispanic). People in different subcultures often exhibit product preferences different from those in the broader culture. For example, one study reported that upwardly mobile blacks—college graduates earning more than $30,000 a year—buy many of the same products as upwardly mobile whites, but also that they respond more to products and messages that appeal to their black pride and address their ethnic diversity.[23]

Subcultural differences may result in considerable variations in what, how, when, and where people buy. For example, a firm that markets products that have a high consumption rate among Hispanics may need to advertise in Spanish and use bilingual labeling to ensure that its products appeal to and satisfy this rapidly growing market segment. Similarly, a U.S. firm marketing products only in this country may have to make product modifications from state to state, or even from city to city, to satisfy members of particular subcultures.

PSYCHOLOGICAL INFLUENCES ON CONSUMER DECISION MAKING

■ **psychological factor** a force within an individual that affects purchasing behavior

A force within an individual that affects his or her purchasing behavior is called a **psychological factor.** As shown in Figure 7.4, five major psychological factors affect the consumer decision-making process: motives, perception, attitudes, learning, and personality.

Motives

■ **motive** an internal energizing force or reason that moves a person toward a goal

A **motive** is an internal energizing force or reason that moves a person toward a goal. Consumers usually are affected by a set of motives rather than just one motive. The strength of a person's motives may vary from one time to another, and at a single point in time some motives may be stronger than others. For example, a person's motives for eating are much stronger after fasting all day than after eating a meal only a few hours earlier. Some typical motives are shown in Table 7.2.

[23] Cyndee Miller, "Upwardly Mobile Blacks Keep Strong Sense of Identity," *Marketing News,* February 10, 1990, pp. 10, 11, 14.

TABLE 7.2
Examples of Typical Motives

Love of offspring	Taste	Courtesy
Appetite/hunger	Cleanliness	Amusement
Comfort	Pleasure	Warmth
Health	Competition	Style
Safety	Social distinction	Cooperation
Rest/sleep	Sympathy	Efficiency
Possession	Imitation	Manipulation
Approval of others	Curiosity	Hospitality
Ambition	Play	Coolness
Parental affection	Cooperation	Shyness
Personal appearance	Humor	Revenge
Home comfort	Physical activity	Teasing
Economy	Fear	Urgency

■ **patronage motive**
a motive that influences where a person purchases products on a regular basis

■ **motivation research**
research that lets marketers analyze the major motives that influence consumer buying behavior

■ **depth interview** an interview in which the researcher tries to get the subject to talk freely about several subjects to create an informal atmosphere

■ **group interview** an interview in which the researcher—through informal, unstructured questions—tries to generate discussion about one or several topics among six to twelve people

Many different motives influence buying behavior at the same time. For instance, a person who is purchasing a refrigerator might be motivated by several characteristics, such as social distinction, home comfort, and economy. A company that emphasizes only one of those characteristics will probably fail to generate a satisfactory sales level.

A motive that relates to where a person chooses to shop on a regular basis is called a **patronage motive.** Consumers may purchase products at a specific store because of such patronage motives as price, service, location, product variety, or honesty and friendliness of salespeople. For example, a person might patronize a particular automobile repair shop because its owners and employees are honest, knowledgeable, and fast workers. Or a consumer may buy jewelry, fine china, and crystal only at a store like Tiffany & Company because of its image and exclusiveness. To profit from patronage motives, businesses must determine why regular customers patronize a store and then emphasize those characteristics in the store's marketing mix.

Marketing professionals analyze the major motives that influence consumer buying behavior through **motivation research.** However, motives are difficult to measure because they often operate at a subconscious level. Since people generally do not know what motivates them, marketing researchers cannot simply ask them about their motives. Therefore, most motivation research relies on interviews or projective techniques.

Marketing researchers may study motives through depth interviews, group interviews, or a combination of both. In a **depth interview,** the researcher attempts to create an informal atmosphere by encouraging a single subject to talk freely about several topics. The researcher asks the subject general, unstructured questions and then asks the subject to clarify the responses. Depth interviews may last for several hours. In a **group interview,** the researcher, using informal, unstructured questions, tries to generate discussion about one or several topics among six to twelve people. The interviewer uses the issues discussed to try to discover people's motives relating to some issue, such as the use of a product.

■ **projective technique**
a test in which subjects are asked to perform specific tasks for particular purposes while, in fact, they are being evaluated for other purposes

By contrast, subjects in a **projective technique** are asked to perform specific tasks for particular purposes while in fact they are being evaluated for other purposes. Because projective techniques by-pass consumers' built-in sensoring devices, these tests are especially useful in obtaining honest information about sensitive subjects.[24] Using techniques such as sentence-completion tests, word-association tests, and fantasy tasks, researchers try to make predictions about a person's subconscious motives. For instance, in a study of major hotel chains, consumers were shown different symbols, such as a sun, globe, beef, and so on. The top-rated hotel was associated with the trees, sun, globe, diamond, and lady; that hotel was perceived as expensive and luxurious.[25] Thus researchers use projective techniques in an attempt to understand why a person is motivated to purchase a particular good or service.

Perception

■ **perception** the process through which people select, organize, and interpret information inputs and give them meaning

■ **information input**
a sensation people receive through the sense of sight, taste, hearing, smell, or touch

■ **selection** the first step of the perception process, in which people select some inputs and ignore others

■ **selective exposure** the phenomenon of selecting some inputs (to be exposed to our awareness) and ignoring others because of the inability to be conscious of all inputs at one time

Two people often hold quite different views about the same thing, whether it be a movie, a class, a teacher, an event they both witness, or an experience they share, because they perceive it differently. **Perception,** as illustrated in Figure 7.6, is a three-step process through which people select, organize, and interpret information inputs and give them meaning. An **information input** is a sensation that people receive through the sense of sight, taste, hearing, smell, or touch. When a person hears an advertisement, sees a friend, smells polluted air or water, or touches a product, he or she is receiving information inputs.

The first step in the perception process is called **selection** because people select some inputs and ignore others. People are bombarded by many information inputs at one time but are aware of only a few of them. Some inputs are selected, and others are ignored because people simply cannot be conscious of all the inputs they receive at one time. People select the inputs that will be exposed to their awareness in a phenomenon sometimes called **selective exposure.** As you are studying, for example, you probably are not aware that it is sunny or cloudy outside, that people and animals are making noise outside, or even that you are touching a book. Although you are receiving these inputs, you ignore them until they are brought to your attention.

There are several reasons why people become conscious of some information inputs but not others. People are more likely to be aware of an input if

[24] Sharon L. Hollander, "Projective Techniques Uncover Real Consumer Attitudes," *Marketing News,* January 4, 1988, p. 34.
[25] Sidney J. Levy, "Interpretation Is the Essence of Projective Research Techniques," *Marketing News,* September 28, 1984, p. 1.

FIGURE 7.6
The Perception Process

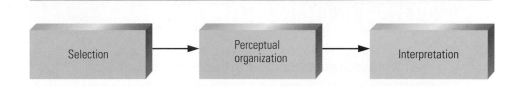

Selection → Perceptual organization → Interpretation

it relates to an anticipated event. For example, South of the Border, a roadside amusement park on the border of North and South Carolina, uses a series of billboards to encourage travelers to anticipate the now-famous spot. Even though not all motorists stop, most notice this tourist attraction because of the billboards. People are also more likely to become aware of an input if the information helps to satisfy current needs. For example, you are more likely to notice a General Electric advertisement for kitchen appliances if you are planning to buy a new house. But if you live in a furnished apartment, there is a good chance that the advertisement will not reach your awareness. Changes in the intensity of inputs also affect whether or not people become conscious of them. When the price of gasoline increases slightly, most drivers do not notice because the change is not significant. In the fall of 1990, however, consumers certainly noticed and complained when gasoline prices increased by 20 cents or more per gallon during the crises in the Persian Gulf. Point/Counterpoint explores whether consumers can be influenced by inputs that do not reach their conscious awareness.

The selective nature of perception directly relates to two other conditions: selective distortion and selective retention. **Selective distortion** is the changing or twisting of currently received information. Selective distortion may occur when a person receives information that contradicts his or her feelings or beliefs. For example, if a person sees an advertisement that says a particular brand "tastes better than all the rest" but the person knows from past experience that it tastes terrible, the person may distort the information received to make it more consistent with prior views. This distortion notably lessens the effect of the advertisement on the person. **Selective retention** occurs when a person remembers information inputs that support personal feelings and beliefs and forgets inputs that do not. After hearing a political campaign speech, for example, a voter may forget many of the points if they contradict that person's political beliefs.

Even when a person does become conscious of information inputs, they are not received in an organized form. Inputs are organized and take on meaning through **perceptual organization,** the second step of the perception process. Ordinarily, this organizing is done rapidly. How a person organizes information affects the meaning obtained. For example, two students might organize the information from a teacher's lecture differently, each obtaining different meanings.

People make sense out of information inputs in the third step of the perceptual process, **interpretation.** This step is necessary to reduce confusion. People base their interpretations of information inputs on what is familiar to them. This may create problems for companies that modify the packaging of a product, alter the product itself, or change its name as a result of a

■ **selective distortion** the changing or twisting of currently received information

■ **selective retention** a phenomenon in which a person remembers information inputs that support personal feelings and beliefs and forgets inputs that do not

■ **perceptual organization** the second step of the perception process, in which information inputs are organized and take on meaning

■ **interpretation** the third step of the perceptual process, in which people make sense out of information inputs

POINT/COUNTERPOINT

Can Subliminal Messages Influence Consumers?

An interesting yet controversial issue in the field of marketing is subliminal perception, a person's ability to perceive and respond to inputs that are below the level of consciousness. By their very nature, subliminal messages generate a great deal of interest. People are intrigued with the idea of invisible commercials on television and movie screens and of background music in stores encouraging consumers to buy products. Interesting, yes, but can subliminal messages influence consumers?

Point   Messages aimed at the subconscious can influence consumers. If an individual has a basic desire to act in a certain way, a subliminal message that reinforces the behavior can be effective. This concept was first supported in 1957, when the messages "Eat popcorn" and "Drink Coca-Cola" were flashed on the screen of a drive-in theater in New Jersey. The messages flashed so quickly that viewers were not consciously aware of them. The drive-in theater experienced a dramatic increase in the sales of popcorn and Coke.

Since its conception, the subliminal message has been used in several ways. Antitheft messages such as "Do not steal," played in the background of department stores' music, were reported to reduce

thefts. Some firms also have embedded hidden words or symbols in advertisements for various products such as shampoo, alcohol, and food. Although these symbols cannot be seen under normal viewing conditions, they appeal to the consumer's subconscious attention.

Counterpoint   Although the subliminal message is an appealing concept, little scientific evidence supports its existence. It has come under question from the first time the concept was employed in the drive-in theater in 1957. Other possible explanations for the increase in the sales of Coke and popcorn could be the weather or the movie being shown. Additionally, numerous attempts to repeat the original study and obtain the same results have failed. The failure to duplicate the experiment has led some to conclude that the original data were fabricated.

Subliminal messages also are criticized because of the weak nature of the stimuli or message. A message so weak that it does not reach consciousness is not likely to change a person's behavior. Even subliminal messages that are perceived by individuals are probably drowned out by stronger stimuli. And since people have the power to screen out unwanted messages, the concept of a subliminal message is not plausible.

 merger or acquisition. When L'eggs modified the packaging of its pantyhose products, the manufacturer decided to use in-store displays to alert consumers to the change and the reasons for it. Because people look for the familiar and may not recognize something in a new form, businesses must notify consumers about changes or possibly lose sales.

Organizations often find it difficult to successfully influence consumers' perceptions. A buyer might perceive a seller's information differently than it was intended. When a pharmaceutical firm advertises that "more doctors recommend this pain reliever than any other," a customer may erroneously interpret this claim to mean that the product is available only with a prescription. Additionally, a buyer who receives information inputs that are inconsistent with prior beliefs will probably not remember the information for long. Thus, if a prospective buyer is told about the benefits of life insurance but does not believe the salesperson's pitch, the customer probably will not retain the information for very long.

Attitudes

attitude a person's overall feeling toward some object

An **attitude** is a person's overall feeling toward some object. Attitudes can be favorable, unfavorable, or neutral. People hold attitudes about almost anything, such as products, stores, religion, politics, friends, and teachers. A person acquires attitudes through experience and interaction with others. Although attitudes can be altered, they generally remain stable and do not change from moment to moment. Likewise, all of a person's attitudes do not have equal impact; some may be stronger than others at any one time.

Consumer attitudes toward a company and its products certainly affect the success or failure of the firm's marketing strategy. Consumers with strong negative attitudes about one or more aspects of a firm's marketing practices may not only stop buying the firm's product but also appeal to their family and friends to do the same. For example, when the oil tanker *Exxon Valdez* spilled nearly eleven million gallons of oil in Alaska's Prince William Sound, many Exxon customers cut up their credit cards in protest; some mailed oil-soaked cards to Exxon's corporate headquarters. Because attitudes exert such a tremendous influence, businesses should gauge consumer attitudes toward product features, prices, package designs, brand names, advertisements and promotions, salespeople, repair services, and store locations of existing or potential products. Some components of the marketing mix may need to be adjusted to counter negative attitudes toward a product.

Marketing managers can use several methods to measure consumer attitudes. One of the simplest is to ask people directly. A researcher for a consumer products company, for example, might ask respondents what they think about the taste and packaging of the firm's new frozen dinner. Marketing researchers can also employ the projective techniques used in motivation research to measure attitudes. Attitude scales are a third method sometimes used to evaluate consumer attitudes. An **attitude scale** is typically a series of adjectives, phrases, or sentences about an object that subjects are asked to respond to. For instance, the statements in Table 7.3 might be used to measure consumer attitudes toward Wendy's hamburgers. By asking subjects to state the degree to which they agree or disagree with the statements, a marketer can assess the intensity of the respondents' feelings toward the product.

attitude scale a method used to measure consumer attitudes; usually consists of a series of adjectives, phrases, or sentences about an object that subjects respond to indicating the intensity of their feelings toward the object

Attitudes can also be a useful basis for segmenting markets. For instance, The Goodyear Tire & Rubber Company asked consumers about their attitudes toward its brand of tires, the tire outlet or store, and the price. On the basis of this information, Goodyear identified six attitude segments:

	Strongly Disagree	Disagree	Neutral	Agree	Strongly Agree
1. I think Wendy's hamburgers are greasy.	1	2	3	4	5
2. I think Wendy's hamburgers are tasty.	1	2	3	4	5
3. The price of a Wendy's hamburger is too high.	1	2	3	4	5
4. I really like Wendy's hamburgers.	1	2	3	4	5
5. I would rather eat a Wendy's hamburger than any other.	1	2	3	4	5

TABLE 7.3
Attitude Scale for Wendy's Hamburgers

1. The *prestige buyer* makes the brand decision first and the store decision second.

2. The *comfortable conservative* looks for the store first and the brand second.

3. The *value shopper* considers brand first and price second.

4. The *pretender* wants a major brand, but the price ultimately determines the choice.

5. The *trusting patron* chooses the store first and the price second.

6. The *bargain hunter* shops for the price first and the store second, but price is the major consideration.[26]

When a business discovers that a significant number of consumers have strong negative attitudes toward an aspect of its marketing mix, it may try to change consumer attitudes to make them more favorable. Changing negative consumer attitudes to positive ones is generally a long, expensive, and difficult task that may require extensive promotional efforts. Marketing Close-up illustrates how one industry went about trying to change unfavorable consumer attitudes.

■ **learning** changes in a person's behavior that are caused by information and experience

Learning

Learning refers to changes in a person's behavior that are caused by information and experience, both direct and indirect. Variations in behavior resulting

[26]"Attitude Research Assesses Global Market Potential," *Marketing News,* August 1, 1988, pp. 10, 13. Reprinted by permission.

MARKETING CLOSE-UP

Beef for Dinner

For the last two decades, nutrition- and health-conscious consumers have been trying to reduce fat and cholesterol in their diets, by eating less red meat and more fish and poultry. Feeling the impact of this trend, the beef and pork industries have tried to convince consumers to put more of their meats on the table.

The Beef Industry Council (BIC) sponsored a $42 million, seventeen-month campaign to curb falling consumption. With the theme "Beef. It's what's for dinner," print and television advertisements showed mouth-watering shots of beef kebabs, stir fry, and steaks. It was the most extensive marketing campaign the BIC has ever done to promote beef consumption and included in-store tie-ins with Lea & Perrins Steak Sauce and an 800 number people can call for recipe booklets or grilling tips. So far the campaign is working, but the advertisement budget is expected to go down to about $20 million as the BIC says it cannot support this program indefinitely.

Unlike former advertising efforts, the "It's what's for dinner" campaign avoids talking about nutrition, focusing on taste and different ways to prepare beef. Consumers are using chicken in more creative ways, whereas they think of beef as only steaks and burgers, according to Donna Schmidt, a spokeswoman for the Chicago-based BIC. Research with consumers showed that when they were selecting foods and meats, they were "looking for variety and things that are easy to use," Schmidt said. "When we came right down to it, people wanted more information on ways to prepare beef."

Thus, the BIC chose to focus on contemporary dishes and convenience, with the main target women 25 to 54 years old who have convenience-oriented families. To help consumers prepare beef and to think of the product in new ways, the council developed a collection of "30 beef meals in 30 minutes." Print advertisements in women's magazines and general interest publications featured a variety of recipes that require a half hour or less.

But the biggest problem is probably beef's image. U.S. government tests show that the leanest cuts of cooked beef are almost identical in terms of fat, cholesterol, and calories to skinless, roasted chicken. However, people often eat fattier cuts of red meat and larger portions than the 3 or 4 ounces recommended. Thus, for several years health experts have urged people to cut down on red meat to reduce their intake of fat and cholesterol.

Environmental concerns and animal rights issues have also added to the controversy about beef. At the same time the beef council launched its promotional campaign, a coalition of 35 environmental, food policy, and animal rights groups started delivering a contrasting message. The "Beyond Beef" coalition ran advertisements in the *New York Times* and other newspapers urging consumers to cut their beef consumption in half by 2002. The ads encouraged consumers to replace beef with grains, fruits, and vegetables and listed eight reasons for doing so, including helping restore the global environment, freeing up arable land to grow food for hungry people, protecting health, and reducing the suffering of cattle. The coalition suggested that consumers sign petitions pledging to cut their beef intake in half. To address the accusations against the cattle industry, the BIC joined with twelve meat and farming organizations to form the Food Facts coalition. Food Facts, saying its rival coalition relies on scare tactics and unsubstantiated claims, plans to focus on "the positive beliefs consumers already have."

Sources: "Beef Ads Work, but Money Scarce," *Marketing News,* March 15, 1993, p. 1; Carrie Goerne, "'Don't Blame the Cows,'" *Marketing News,* June 22, 1992, pp. 1–2; "For the Record," *Advertising Age,* March 30, 1992, p. 57; and Steve Weiner, "Beef Is a Four-Letter Word," *Forbes,* February 19, 1990, pp. 124, 128.

from physiological conditions such as hunger, fatigue, physical growth, and deterioration are not considered to be learning.

■ **knowledge** the outcome of learning; consists of information stored in a person's memory

Knowledge is the outcome of learning and consists of information stored in a person's memory. Consumers store a variety of information regarding products and brands, including where to buy them, how to use them, and which ones best satisfy their needs. Knowledge influences the behavior of consumers, including the search, recall, and use of information.[27]

The consequences of a person's behavior have a strong influence on the learning process. When a person's actions bring about rewarding or satisfying consequences, the person will probably behave in the same way in future, similar situations. However, when behavior has negative consequences, the person will probably behave differently in future situations. For example, when a consumer buys a new brand of shampoo and likes the results, that person is more likely to buy the same brand the next time. In fact, he or she will probably continue to purchase that brand until it no longer provides satisfaction.

To market products successfully, a firm must help consumers learn about them. Consumers learn about products directly by experiencing them. Many companies try to provide consumers with direct experiences by offering free samples of food, detergent, shampoos, and other consumer products. Automobile dealers permit potential buyers to testdrive new models to allow them to experience the automobiles directly. Consumers also learn about and experience products indirectly through information from salespeople, advertisements, friends, and relatives. Sales personnel and advertisements allow organizations to provide information before and even after purchases to influence what consumers learn and to create a more favorable attitude toward the products.

Although marketers do try to influence what a consumer learns, their attempts are seldom completely successful. Marketers face problems in attracting and holding consumers' attention, providing consumers with the kinds of information they need for making purchase decisions, and convincing them to try the product.

Personality

■ **personality** the total of all the traits, experiences, and behaviors that make up a person

Personality is the total of all the traits, experiences, and behaviors that make up a person. The manner in which these elements are organized within each individual makes each person unique. Personalities typically are described as having one or more characteristics, such as compulsiveness, dogmatism, ambitiousness, gregariousness, authoritarianism, introversion, extroversion, and competitiveness. Although marketing researchers have tried to find relationships between personality characteristics and buying behavior, few such

[27] Akshay R. Rao and Kent B. Monroe, "The Moderating Effect of Prior Knowledge on Cue Utilization in Product Evaluations," *Journal of Consumer Research,* September 1988, pp. 253–264.

relationships have been established. Nevertheless, some marketing professionals maintain that personality does influence the types and brands of products a person purchases. For example, the style of clothing, jewelry, or automobile that a person buys may reflect one or more personality traits.

Marketers sometimes aim their promotional efforts at general types of personalities. When they do, they usually focus on positively valued personality characteristics such as individualism or competitiveness. Products that are promoted in this way include soft drinks, beer, cigarettes, and clothing. Figure 7.7 illustrates how a firm targets a specific personality type.

PERSONAL INFLUENCES ON CONSUMER DECISION MAKING

■ **personal factor** a factor unique to a person that affects buying behavior

A **personal factor** is a factor unique to a person that affects buying behavior. Personal factors that may influence consumer decision making include situational factors and demographic factors (see Figure 7.4).

FIGURE 7.7
Personality
Hot Spring Spa uses personality to communicate their message: Hot Spring's portable spas can help an intense person unwind and relax.

Source: Watkins Manufacturing Corporation. Sacks/Fuller Advertising.

FIGURE 7.8
Situational Factors
Travelers may unexpectedly find they need a product like Dramamine II to prevent motion sickness.

Source: Courtesy the Upjohn Company.

Situational Factors

■ **situational factor** a circumstance or condition that exists when a consumer is making a purchase decision

A **situational factor** is a condition or circumstance that exists when a consumer is making a purchase decision (see Figure 7.8). Sometimes a consumer must make a buying decision because of an unexpected situation. A homeowner may have to purchase a new furnace when the old one breaks down and repairing it is not cost-effective. Circumstances may cause a person to lengthen or terminate the buying decision process. A homeowner who is considering the purchase of a new home but is laid off during the evaluation-of-alternatives stage would probably reject the new purchase entirely.

Situational factors can influence a consumer's actions during the buying decision process in a variety of ways. If a consumer has little time for selecting and purchasing a product, he or she may make a quick choice and purchase a brand that is readily available. Uncertainty about future employment status may cause a person to delay the purchase of an expensive item. A single person contemplating marriage might delay the purchase of durable goods such as appliances and furniture. Finally, consumers who believe the supply of certain goods will become sharply limited are likely to buy them. People purchased a variety of products, including batteries, lanterns, food and plywood, before Hurricane Andrew hit Florida and Louisiana in 1992.

The atmosphere surrounding a purchasing situation can also influence consumer behavior. Spectators at a baseball game may find themselves eating a hot dog even though they usually do not eat that type of food. Likewise, people who rarely purchase popcorn may be inclined to buy some at a movie.

Demographic Factors

■ **demographic factor**
a personal characteristic—
such as age, race, sex, income, education, marital
status, family size, or occupation—that affects buying
behavior

As discussed in Chapter 6, a **demographic factor** is a personal characteristic such as age, race, sex, income, education, marital status, family size, or occupation. Such factors influence consumer buying decisions and divide the consumer population into subcultures. Product, price, promotion, and distribution strategies must be tailored to the purchasing patterns of these various subcultures.

A person's age strongly affects purchase decisions. Elderly consumers spend more of their income on food, housing, and health care than do younger people.[28] On the other hand, the demand for rental housing peaks during the ages of 25 to 34, when few young people can afford their own homes, and then drops sharply as they begin to buy their first houses. Spending for food away from home is highest among those aged 35 to 54; young people eat outside of the home frequently, but they do not spend as much as the middle-aged group does.[29]

Consumers' decisions are influenced by the composition of their households. Single-parent households and married couples with dependent children spend the majority of their incomes on the basics—shelter, food consumed in the home, and clothing. Married couples with adult children spend much less on basics and more on education and transportation.[30] The family unit can also influence the particular type of products purchased. For instance, a married couple with children is more likely to buy a small van or station wagon than is a single person. Household composition can affect who makes a purchasing decision as well. Husbands and wives without children are more likely to share decision-making responsibility than those with children.[31]

Income certainly influences purchasing decisions because it determines how much people can afford. For example, families with incomes below $30,000 find it very difficult to buy a home.[32] On the other hand, families in the higher-income categories are buying luxury automobiles and vacation homes in record numbers.

Occupation and education influence purchasing behavior in several ways. Education has been associated with the purchase of books, healthier foods, and entertainment. Education also influences how decisions are made. Educated consumers seek more information and demand better-quality products. Occupations can affect the type of clothing a person buys, transportation choice, food purchases, and the need for timesaving products. For example, a product manager (a marketing professional) at Pillsbury Company would probably purchase business suits to wear on the job, but a residential painter would most likely buy blue jeans and T-shirts for work.

[28] Beth J. Soldo and Emily M. Agree, "American's Elderly," *Population Bulletin,* September 1988, pp. 5–45.
[29] Thomas W. Merrick and Stephen J. Tordella, "Demographics: People and Markets," *Population Bulletin,* February 1988, pp. 3–46.
[30] Ibid., pp. 3–46.
[31] Pierre Filiatrault and J. R. Brent Ritchie, "Joint Purchase Decisions: A Comparison of Influence Structure in Family and Couple Decision-Making Units," *Journal of Consumer Research,* September 1980, pp. 131–140.
[32] Courtenay Slater, "The Working Rich," *American Demographics,* July 1988, pp. 4–7.

SUMMARY

Consumer behavior is the actions and decision processes of people who purchase goods and services for personal consumption. Consumer decision making is the process consumers go through when deciding what products to buy. Understanding consumer behavior is essential to creating a marketing mix that satisfies customer needs.

The consumer buying decision process consists of five stages: problem recognition, information search, evaluation of alternatives, purchase decision, and postpurchase evaluation. Problem recognition occurs when a buyer recognizes a problem, need, or desire. Information search involves the consumer seeking information about factors such as availability of brands, product features, seller characteristics, warranties, and prices. In the evaluation of alternatives, the consumer establishes criteria based on the information search and uses them to compare product characteristics. The consumer buys the product in the purchase decision stage. In the postpurchase evaluation, the buyer assesses the product. Some buyers experience cognitive dissonance—conflict and doubts about the purchase, including whether the purchase should have been made at all.

The three types of consumer decision making are routine, limited, and extensive. Routine decision making is used for frequently purchased, low-cost items that require very little search and decision effort. Limited decision making is used for products that are purchased occasionally or when a buyer needs to acquire information about an unfamiliar brand in a familiar product category. Extensive decision making is used for unfamiliar, expensive products or infrequently bought items.

Consumer decision making is influenced by social, psychological, and personal factors. Social factors are the forces exerted by other people that affect consumer behavior. Four social factors that influence consumer decision making are social class, reference groups, roles and family, and culture and subculture. A social class is a relatively homogeneous and stable group of people with similar values, interests, lifestyles, and behaviors. A reference group is a group with which an individual identifies to the extent that he or she assumes its values, attitudes, and behaviors. A role is a set of functions and activities that a person in a particular position is expected to perform. Culture is all the learned values, behaviors, and meaningful symbols shared by a society. A culture can be divided into several subcultures.

Psychological factors are internal forces within people that affect buying decisions. Psychological factors are motives, perception, attitudes, learning, and personality. Motives are internal energizing forces or reasons that direct a person toward a goal. Motivation research involves analyzing the major motives that influence buying behavior; it includes depth interviews, group interviews, and projective techniques. Perception is the process through which an individual selects, organizes, and interprets information inputs to create meaning. Information inputs are the sensations people receive through their senses. An attitude is a person's overall feeling toward some object. Learning refers to changes in one's behavior caused by information and experiences. Personality is the total of all the traits, experiences, and behaviors that make up a person.

Personal factors, which include situational and demographic factors, are unique to each person. Situational factors are the conditions or circumstances that exist when a consumer is making a purchase decision. Demographic factors are personal characteristics such as age, sex, race, and ethnic background.

KEY TERMS

consumer behavior
consumer decision making
evoked set
cognitive dissonance
routine decision making
involvement
impulse purchase
limited decision making
extensive decision making
social factor
social class
reference group
role
culture
subculture
psychological factor
motive
patronage motive
motivation research

depth interview
group interview
projective technique
perception
information input
selection
selective exposure
selective distortion
selective retention
perceptual organization
interpretation
attitude
attitude scale
learning
knowledge
personality
personal factor
situational factor
demographic factor

QUESTIONS FOR DISCUSSION AND REVIEW

1. What are the five stages of the consumer decision-making process? Do consumers ever skip some of these stages?

2. How can a marketer help a consumer reduce cognitive dissonance?

3. What types of decision making are used by consumers?

4. Describe how reference groups can affect the consumer decision-making process. Has one of your own purchasing decisions ever been influenced by a reference group?

5. In what ways do roles and family affect purchase decisions?

6. What is a motive? How do researchers study motives?

7. How do attitudes influence a person's buying decisions? Can attitudes be changed?

8. How can businesses help consumers learn about products?

9. What are some situational factors that might affect buying decisions?

10. Explain how demographic factors can influence the buying decision process.

C A S E S

7.1 SINGLE-USE CAMERAS GAIN POPULARITY AND RECYCLABILITY

Ever since the turn of the century, when Eastman Kodak Company made photography a hobby accessible to everyone, manufacturers have been developing increasingly complex cameras. In nine decades the camera evolved from the simple box camera to the ultrasophisticated cameras used by professionals. But a new trend began in the early 1980s and continues today. Consumers wanted the quality pictures produced by the expensive state-of-the-art, professional cameras, but they did not want to bother learning how to use the sophisticated equipment. They also wanted portable cameras without a variety of lenses and other bulky add-ons. Thus were born the auto-focus "point-and-shoot" cameras.

Taking this idea one step further, camera makers came up with the ultimate in convenience: an extremely portable and simple-to-use camera that is used only once. It's essentially a roll of film encased in molded plastic or paperboard boxes. The aperture and shutter speed are factory set; the only controls are the film advance and the shutter release. The consumer takes the pictures, then delivers or mails the entire unit for processing. Both Kodak and Fuji Photo Film USA introduced one-use cameras in 1987. Kodak's Fling contained a single lens and a 24-exposure roll of 200-speed 110mm film. Fuji's QuickSnap was similar but with 35mm film.

The concept behind single-use cameras actually goes back to the early days of photography, since Kodak founder George Eastman's original cameras were preloaded with film. Single-use cameras are not intended to replace more sophisticated equipment but rather to be used where a larger or more expensive camera is not advisable. They are ideal for beachgoers, campers, skiers who would be worried about taking a $400 camera up on a mountain, or travelers who forgot to pack their cameras. Kodak first sold its disposable cameras at its Disney World concession.

But the convenience of the one-use camera that was so appealing to consumers also led to controversy. Growing awareness of environmental problems led to protests that the companies marketing one-use cameras were promoting disposal of unrecyclable products with extremely brief life spans. In response, both Eastman Kodak and Fuji, the two biggest marketers in the category, started recycling programs in 1990. The cameras are collected at the photofinisher, where consumers already take or send cameras for processing. Participating photofinishers are reimbursed for shipping and handling and earn 5 cents credit per camera. Kodak also dropped the name Fling, which consumers associated with discarding the camera, to FunSaver. Consumers were alerted that the Kodak and Fuji cameras were recyclable in the companies' advertisements and at point of purchase. Both camera makers changed their packaging to include the fact that the products can be recycled.

The cameras have improved over their short life span. Some have a flash to overcome a major limitation of the original ones, which produced proper exposures only in daylight, with the subject no closer than 4 feet away and not moving faster than a trot. Kodak's FunSaver line now offers five types of cameras, including models using 35mm film. Fuji also offers five QuickSnap versions.

With their ease and convenience, single-use cameras are now one of the photographic industry's bright spots. A total of 9.3 million were sold in 1991 in the United States, more than triple the number sold in 1989. Kodak is the U.S. leader. The firm's research shows that more than half of the pictures taken with single-use cameras would not have been taken otherwise, according to the Kodak executive who handles marketing for the FunSaver cameras. Kodak spends $7.4 million to advertise them and plans to increase that amount, especially for television advertising.

Questions for Discussion

1. What types of consumer motives is Kodak trying to target with the Fun-Saver camera?

2. Discuss the concept of problem recognition and how it applies in the case of the disposable camera.

3. What perceptions of a disposable camera have Kodak and other manufacturers had to contend with?

Based on information from "Kodak FunSaver," *Advertising Age,* July 6, 1992, p. S22; Alison Fahey, "Reaching a Flashpoint," *Advertising Age,* July 8, 1991, p. 17; Andy Grundberg, "This Newcomer Is Disposable," *New York Times,* March 20, 1988, p. 64L; and Mason Resnick, "Showdown on South Street: The Great Disposable Shoot-Out," *Modern Photography,* February 1988, p. 30.

7.2 LOOKING FOR THE INTERNATIONAL CONSUMER

With the immense global marketplace opening further each year, many firms no doubt wish that selling the same product in the same way all over the world were as easy as it sounds. Marketers familiar with consumer behavior in the West find that consumers elsewhere have different experiences, needs, and buying patterns.

As the twelve member nations of Europe's Economic Community (EC) work to unite politically and economically, companies are looking for the picture of a prototypical consumer to emerge from the new, single market.

Many businesses believe that besides common political hopes, Europeans share common needs, desires, and buying behavior. But the "Euroconsumer" is proving to be an elusive idea. Take fabric softener, for example. Lever Europe has found that Germans want a product that is gentle on lakes and rivers and are willing to pay a premium for it. The same goes for the people in Sweden, where adopting an environmentally friendly formula is required by law. But Spaniards want cheaper products that get shirts white and soft, rather than the more advanced and more costly environmentally friendly softeners. Greeks want smaller packages that let them hold down the cost of each store visit. In the past Lever was heavily decentralized in Europe and left marketing decisions to managers in various countries. As a result, Lever has many versions of the same product, with names that sound appealing in local languages, packages that fit local tastes, and sometimes even different formulas. To cut production and marketing costs, Lever is trying to combine its various fabric softeners into one formula, one brand, and one package (like rival Procter & Gamble), but it is changing slowly so as not to alienate consumers. In the Netherlands, for example, Lever switched in stages from the popular orange bottle for one of its cleaners to the white bottle used elsewhere. The company announced the change with a television advertisement showing an orange bottle doing the striptease. Then for a while it sold the white bottle in an orange wrapper for the consumer to peel off, before going totally to white bottles.

In Eastern Europe, where the former Soviet manufacturing system failed to supply consumer products considered basic by Westerners, Western companies are rushing to fill the gaps. In the Ukraine, S.C. Johnson & Son, Inc. has set up production of detergents, household cleaners, and shampoo; Tambrands, Inc. is making feminine hygiene products there. The two companies use local labor and suppliers so they can keep prices in line with what consumers can pay. In Russia, Gillette Co. has a joint venture to make blades and razors. Firms introducing Western consumer products to the area have been lauded almost as early explorers bringing wonders from other worlds. One woman wrote to Johnson about a cleaning liquid: "Please produce more of this product and bring some happiness to women at this difficult time."

These firms and others are tapping into a market that offers huge consumer buying power but no information about those consumers. In fact, the population is unfamiliar with market concepts. Buying habits have most often been shaped by what products were available. No consumer data exist for firms investigating the potential of the market, and those trying to gather data find a primitive communications system. Yet organizations are taking polls, holding discussion groups, and doing media and lifestyle studies in Eastern Europe to watch and understand consumer behavior there.

New buyers for Western products may also be found in Asia. Japan and the "four dragons"—South Korea, Taiwan, Hong Kong, and Singapore—together have 200 million people, and their incomes compare to those of West Europeans. In recent years, for example, South Korea's consumers have had much more money to spend. Since 1986, disposable income has increased 141 percent as manufacturing wages there have risen an average of 18 percent a year. Korea is the largest consumer market in Asia after Japan. The average

Korean urban household income is about $12,400. People are educated, and about 10 percent have college degrees. More and more families have two incomes, which is increasing the popularity of convenience foods and high-quality products—long popular in the West.

Because Asia's populations are so vast, even the poorest parts of the continent are home to fairly large numbers of relatively well off consumers, even if they represent a small proportion of the population. In a poor country like Indonesia, where the per capita gross national product (GNP) is $550 a year, it would seem at first glance that consumers would be unable to buy non-necessities such as detergents, cosmetics, and packaged food. But in the Indonesian capital of Jakarta, with 14 million people, the gross domestic product (GDP, the value of all goods and services produced by an economy) is about $2,000 per person a year—the same as Mexico's and nearly half that of Portugal. Thus large numbers of Indonesians are able to buy many household and personal goods.

The challenge for companies is to find the appropriate consumers and market products to them in ways that fit their lifestyles, culture, and incomes. Sometimes that means packaging products in small lots, distributing to remote outlets, and charging competitive prices. British- and Dutch-owned Unilever (parent company of Lever), which markets food, detergents, and personal products, sells 1-ounce packets of its concentrated detergent Rinso Ultra for about 7 cents in Indonesia. It sells shampoo and detergent to farmers from mobile shops which make their way down India's rural roads. Unilever has experience in Asia dating back to the 1890s. Although Europe and the United States are Unilever's most important markets, Asian sales are growing more than twice as fast as sales in either of those regions and are expected to double in the next five years. Because Asia is so huge, Unilever has decentralized as much as possible to meet local conditions and differing consumer tastes. Unilever found, for example, that Filipinos like different qualities in a bar of soap than do Thais.

Questions for Discussion

1. How feasible is it for firms to try to define and market to the typical European consumer, or Euroconsumer?

2. What kind of decision-making process have Eastern European consumers generally used over the last few decades?

3. To what degree does culture influence consumer behavior? Explain your answer and include examples.

Based on information from Damon Darlin, "U.S. Firms Take Chances in South Korea," *Wall Street Journal,* June 24, 1992, pp. B1, B5; "Poor Countries Rich in Wealthy People," *The Economist,* August 15, 1992, pp. 56–57; E.S. Browning, "In Pursuit of the Elusive Euroconsumer," *Wall Street Journal,* April 23, 1992, pp. B1, B3; Lourdes Lee Valeriano, "Western Firms Poll Eastern Europeans to Discern Tastes of Nascent Consumers," *Wall Street Journal,* April 27, 1992, pp. B1, B10; and Tim Carrington, "Ukraine Women Love These Two Firms," *Wall Street Journal,* February 6, 1992, p. A11.

Business-to-Business Buying Behavior

OBJECTIVES

- To describe the different types of organizational customers.

- To discuss the unique aspects of organizational transactions.

- To explain what is meant by organizational buying behavior.

- To list the stages of the organizational buying decision process.

- To identify the ways in which business-to-business marketers analyze organizational markets.

OUTLINE

Raytheon Co. develops a wide range of sophisticated electronic products for the U.S. defense industry, including missiles, radar, electronic jammers, and communications systems. The number-five defense contractor also manufactures air-to-air

missiles such as the Sidewinder, ground-to-air missiles like the Stinger, Maverick air-to-ground missiles, and the Standard, a ship-launched missile. During the Persian Gulf crisis, the U.S. military relied on the Raytheon Patriot air defense system's ability to intercept Iraq's Scud missiles. The Patriot is Raytheon's biggest product, accounting for nearly $1.5 billion in 1990 sales. Its success in the Gulf could have a big impact on the firm's future prospects. In 1992, Raytheon's backlog of government orders amounted to $6.9 billion. A Patriot order by Saudi Arabia could increase the backlog significantly.

Raytheon did not start out as a military equipment company. At the beginning of World War II, it produced vacuum tubes for radios. During the war, the company grew by producing microwave tubes for radio. Raytheon stagnated after the war as demand for vacuum tubes fell, but as the Cold War began, it seized the opportunity to cash in on its military experience and became a major producer of missiles.

Just as Raytheon moved beyond vacuum tubes, so the company has also set its sights beyond the defense industry as the Cold War comes to an end. Nongovernment sales make up about 40 percent of Raytheon's $95 billion in revenues. In response to decreased U.S. defense spending, the company cut its work force by 10 percent in 1992 and is investigating other ways to bring the firm into the twenty-first century. One of the areas in which Raytheon has succeeded is the light aircraft industry. The company purchased Beech Aircraft in 1980 and began developing new models of the popular King Air corporate aircraft. Raytheon also got into the regional commuter market by developing its 1900 series. And even though Raytheon still earns 70 percent of its profits from defense, its appliance division includes the brands Amana, Caloric, and Speed Queen.

Most recently, Raytheon has invested $300 million to develop the Starship corporate aircraft, the first civilian aircraft made of all-composite materials (graphite, epoxy, and carbon) instead of metal. The design of the Starship is a radical departure from the typical turboprop: Its two turboprop engines face backwards and push the plane rather than pull it, resulting in a faster, quieter, and more fuel-efficient plane. The plane also costs more than other turboprop aircraft.[1] ●

[1] Based on information from Geoffrey Smith, "Raytheon's Strategy: Guns and Lots More Butter," *Business Week,* November 16, 1992, p. 96; "Raytheon Net Rose 5.2% for 3rd Period," *Wall Street Journal,* October 8, 1992, p. B3; Kenneth Labich, "No Scudbuster T-Shirts Here," *Fortune,* February 25, 1991, pp. 60–64; Subrata N. Chakravarty, "The Limits of Synergy," *Forbes,* October 15, 1991, pp. 38–40; Harlan S. Byrne, "Raytheon Co.," *Barron's,* April 2, 1989, pp. 61–62; and Bill Travis, "Steady Improvements in Small-Signal Microwave Discretes," *EDN,* July 12, 1990, pp. 8–9.

ompanies like Raytheon market their products to businesses, the government, and other institutions rather than to ultimate consumers. A single organizational customer like Sony or the federal government spends billions of dollars each year on products and services to support its operations. All organizations, both large and small, profit and nonprofit, exchange goods and services in organizational markets.

Exchanges between businesses differ from exchanges between businesses and consumers. In organizational markets, organizations buy goods and services for their operations; in consumer markets, individuals buy goods and services for personal or family care. Thus, business-to-business marketing involves all organizations that buy goods and services needed to support their operations. These organizations have different motives for buying than do consumers. Therefore, business-to-business buying behavior is somewhat different than consumer buying behavior. Marketers must understand these differences to develop successful business-to-business marketing strategies.

THE NATURE OF BUSINESS-TO-BUSINESS MARKETING

■ **business-to-business marketing** marketing of products to organizations rather than to consumers

In Chapter 6, an *organizational* or *business market* was defined as a market that includes individuals or groups that purchase products for resale, direct use in the production of other products, or use in daily operations. Transactions in organizational markets have more than twice the total dollar value of consumer purchases.[2] **Business-to-business marketing** refers to the marketing of products to organizations rather than consumers.[3] One example is Bekaert NV, a Belgian firm that sells steel cord to tire companies and wire to companies making springs, staples, concrete, fences, and hundreds of other products.[4] Business-to-business marketing serves many different types of organizational customers, including producers, resellers, government organizations, institutions, and international customers.

Producers

■ **producers** individuals and business organizations that purchase products to use in the production of other products or in their daily operations for the purpose of making a profit

Producers include individuals and business organizations that purchase products to use in the production of other products or in their daily operations for the purpose of making a profit. Electrical connectors used in a variety of products ranging from circuit boards to automobiles constitute a $17 billion

---

[2]Robert W. Eckles, *Business Marketing Management* (Englewood Cliffs, N.J.: Prentice-Hall, 1990), p. 5.
[3]Frank G. Bingham, Jr., and Barney T. Raffield III, *Business to Business Marketing Management* (Homewood, Ill.: Richard D. Irwin, 1990), p. 4.
[4]Bob Hagerty, "Bekaert of Belgium Bets $1 Billion on Becoming Best," *Wall Street Journal,* May 5, 1992, p. B4.

TABLE 8.1
Number of Firms by Industry Groups

Industry	Number of Firms
Agriculture, forestry, fishing	593,000
Mining	229,000
Construction	2,152,000
Manufacturing	680,000
Transportation, public utilities	768,000
Wholesale and retail trade	3,578,000
Finance, insurance, real estate	2,673,000
Services	7,748,000

Source: *Statistical Abstract of the United States,* 1992, p. 519.

world market. Amp Inc. has about 18 percent of this market, with customers such as Apple, the big three U.S. automakers and all Japanese automakers, and DEC.[5] Producer markets include buyers of tools, machinery, and raw materials, as well as finished and semifinished items used to produce other products. Automobile producers are part of the producer market for computers and machinery, steel, aluminum, plastic, fiber glass, glass, tires, and other components of automobiles. A variety of industries makes up producer markets, including agriculture, mining, construction, manufacturing, transportation, retail, and services. As indicated by Table 8.1, large numbers of businesses are involved in producer markets. Plastics producers are part of the producer market for a variety of goods, including air bags (see Figure 8.1).

Producers make up a very significant part of the U.S. economy. More dollars are spent by producers than by consumers of goods and services. The largest dollar volume of producer purchases is accounted for by manufacturing firms. There are roughly 680,000 manufacturing firms in the United States, responsible for $3,182 billion in sales.[6] The output of these organizations is the foundation of our economic system. And perhaps more important to you, more than half of today's college graduates take jobs with firms that operate in producer markets.

Resellers

■ **resellers** intermediaries, such as wholesalers and retailers, that buy finished goods and resell them to make a profit

Resellers include intermediaries—such as wholesalers and retailers—that buy finished products and resell them to make a profit. Wholesalers buy products and resell them to other resellers and to producers, governments, and institutions; retailers purchase products to sell to ultimate consumers. For example, a wholesale restaurant supply company buys products such as salt, tomato sauce, cooking oil, plates, utensils, and pots and pans from the manufacturers of these goods and sells them to various restaurants. Subway Sandwiches

[5]Andrew Erdman, "Staying Ahead of 800 Customers," *Fortune,* June 1, 1992, pp. 111–112.
[6]*Statistical Abstract of the United States,* 1992, p. 519.

and Salads is a retailer that buys goods to make into sandwiches for sale to ultimate consumers. (Wholesalers and retailers are discussed in Chapters 16 and 17.) In general, resellers do not change the physical characteristics of the products they handle, except, perhaps, for minor alterations. All consumer products are first sold to reseller markets, with the exception of items that consumers buy directly from producers.

Resellers consider several factors when making purchase decisions. They assess the level of demand for a product to determine in what quantity and at what prices they should resell the product. They also assess the amount of space required to store and handle a product relative to its potential profit. Resellers are concerned about a producer's ability to supply adequate quantities of a product because resellers' customers expect them to be able to supply a product when it is needed. Resellers are also concerned about the ease of placing orders and the availability of technical assistance from the producer. When considering the purchase of a new product, resellers must determine whether the product will compete with or complement the products they currently handle. These concerns set reseller markets apart from other types of markets; thus businesses must recognize and address these concerns when selling to wholesalers and retailers.

Government Organizations

■ **government organizations** includes federal, state, county, and local governments

Government organizations include thousands of federal, state, county, or local government buying units. Governments spend billions of dollars annually for a variety of goods and services to support internal operations and to provide citizens with education, roads and highways, national defense, police

---

FIGURE 8.1
Producers
Firms that produce plastics are part of the producer market for air bags, packaging materials, protective clothing, bicycle helmets, and other products that help make the world safer.

Source: American Plastics Council.

Some Benefits Of Plastic Last For Only Half A Second.

FIGURE 8.2
Government Organizations
Governments spend billions of dollars each year to support internal operations and to provide services to citizens. Products purchased by the government can be as complex as a space shuttle, or as simple as the batteries to power it.

Source: Reprinted with permission of Rayovac Corporation.

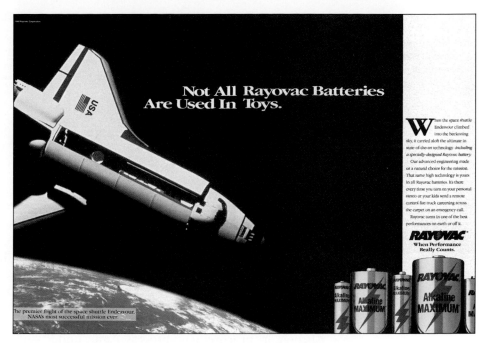

and fire protection, clean water, trash disposal, energy, and other products that meet social needs (see Figure 8.2). Annually, the federal government spends more than $300 billion on defense, about $45 billion on education, and over $100 billion on medical care.[7] In fact, annual expenditures by government units account for about 25 percent of the U.S. gross national product.

In the United States, there are 83,186 local governments and 3,042 county governments in addition to the federal government and 50 state governments.[8] Spending by local, county, state, and federal governments has increased tremendously over the last thirty years because the number of services they provide and the costs of providing these services have increased. According to Table 8.2, the federal government spends more than half of the total amount spent by all governments.

Governments select organizations from which they will buy goods and services through bids or negotiated contracts. To make a sale under the bid system, a company must appear on a list of qualified bidders. When a government needs to make a purchase, it sends out a detailed description of its product needs to qualified bidders. Businesses that wish to sell such products submit bids (offers of prices for which they are willing to sell the products). The government generally buys the products from the organization with the lowest acceptable bid. This process is frequently used for highway construction and repairs.

[7] *Statistical Abstract of the United States,* 1992, p. 317.
[8] *Statistical Abstract of the United States,* 1992, p. 278.

TABLE 8.2
Annual Expenditures
by Government Units
(in billions of dollars)

Year	Federal Government Expenditures	State and Local Expenditures	Total Government Expenditures
1960	90	61	151
1970	185	148	333
1975	292	268	560
1980	526	432	959
1985	1,032	658	1,581
1990	1,393	976	2,219

Source: *Statistical Abstract of the United States*, 1992, p. 279.

Governments prefer to purchase nonstandard or highly complex products through negotiated contracts. Under this procedure, the government selects only a few firms with which it negotiates specifications and terms. It eventually awards the contract to one of the negotiating firms. Defense-related purchases have traditionally been made through negotiated contracts, but the Pentagon procurement process came under review in 1988 as a result of abuses and fraud within the system. Other products purchased through negotiated contracts include vehicles and services.

Institutions

■ **institutions** nonbusiness or nonprofit organizations that seek to advance nonbusiness goals; includes churches, hospitals, museums, universities, and charitable organizations

Institutions are nonbusiness or nonprofit organizations that seek to advance nonbusiness goals. This market is made up of a variety of organizations, including churches, hospitals, museums, universities, and charitable organizations. These organizations, which also use marketing activities to facilitate exchanges, spend billions of dollars each year to purchase goods and services for their operations or to resell to raise additional revenue. Hospitals, for instance, purchase drugs, beds, emergency room equipment, and the like. The Girl Scouts purchase cookies to be resold for fund raising. Nonprofit organizations are discussed in greater detail in Chapter 11.

International Customers

Many business-to-business marketers are pursuing international customers. U.S. businesses export millions of dollars worth of goods to organizational customers in foreign countries. As more countries strive for development and industrial self-sufficiency, organizational markets will continue to grow in many parts of the globe. Because of increased global competition and the threat to domestic sales, firms cannot ignore organizational customers in foreign markets. Many other factors, including better transportation, improved communication, reduced trade barriers, and changing political and economic climates, are causing an increasing number of business-to-business firms to enter international markets. Paxar Corp., manufacturer of tags and labels for clothing, is the dominant firm in the $400 million U.S. label and tag market. One of Paxar's strengths is its aggressive development of accounts overseas; 25 percent of its business comes from international customers.[9]

UNDERSTANDING ORGANIZATIONAL TRANSACTIONS

To understand organizational transactions, it is important to examine the differences between organizational purchases and consumer purchases, the factors that influence organizational customers, the different types of organizational purchases, and the demand for products sold to organizational customers.

Characteristics of Organizational Transactions

As shown in Table 8.3, organizational transactions differ from consumer transactions in several ways. Organizational purchases tend to be much larger than individual consumer purchases. One reason is that organizations that buy in large quantities often get discounts from suppliers. Another reason is that, generally, organizational suppliers must sell their products in large quantities to make profits. As a result, they may not want to sell to consumer markets, in which orders are smaller.

Organizations generally make purchases less frequently than do consumers. Companies may buy capital equipment (large, expensive items such as robots, cranes, and lathes) that will be used directly in production processes for a number of years. Or they may purchase accessory equipment for such internal purposes as operations documentation, record keeping, and office activities. Other products, such as raw materials and component parts (items that become part of the finished product), are used continuously in production and replaced frequently, but contracts for the sale and supply of these items are likely to be long-term agreements that are renegotiated every few years. Negotiations tend to be a cooperative process between buyers and suppliers.[10]

reciprocity an arrangement unique to organizational sales in which two organizations agree to buy from each other

Organizational transactions sometimes involve **reciprocity**, an arrangement in which two organizations agree to buy from each other. For example, a computer software manufacturer might agree to purchase computer hardware from a company that is buying its software and computer supplies. Reciprocal agreements that threaten fair competition are illegal, and the Federal Trade Commission and the Justice Department have the authority to stop them. However, informal reciprocal agreements do occur in small businesses, especially in the service industries, and to a lesser extent in some larger

---

[9]Jerry Flint, "Who Would Want to Be in Their Business?" *Forbes*, July 6, 1992, p. 90.
[10]Paul A. Dion and Peter M. Banting, "Industrial Supplies–Buyer Negotiations," *Industrial Marketing Management*, February 1988, pp. 43–47.

TABLE 8.3
Comparing Organizational and Consumer Markets

Characteristic	Organizational Markets	Consumer Markets
Purchases	Tend to be larger	Tend to be smaller
Frequency of purchases	Less frequent	More frequent
Reciprocity	Frequently used	Infrequently used
Product	More complex, customized; product support is critical	Less complex, standardized; product support is important
Price	Competitive bidding and negotiation; list prices on standard products	List prices
Distribution	More direct (shorter)	Less direct (longer)
Promotion	Emphasis on personal selling	Emphasis on advertising

corporations.[11] Because reciprocity restricts organizations to only a few suppliers, its use can reduce organizations' chances of getting the most optimal purchases.

Finally, the marketing mixes for organizational and consumer products are different. First, organizational products like the one shown in Figure 8.3 tend to be more complex. In many instances, products must be customized for a specific organizational buyer. Product support activities, such as service, installation, technical assistance, and spare parts, are also critical. Morton International, which produces automotive air bags for customers like Mercedes-Benz and Chrysler, has 55 percent of the world market and a reputation for quality and service. Air bags are a complex product and a liability nightmare because they are made of highly volatile explosives and are difficult to build.[12] Morton marketers must therefore consider a variety of factors in developing their marketing mix.

Second, price generally plays a different role in organizational transactions. Competitive bidding is very common, and prices are often negotiated, whereas bidding and negotiation are rarely used in buying consumer products. In addition, distribution is more direct in organizational settings.

[11] E. Robert Finney, "Reciprocity: Gone but Not Forgotten," *Journal of Marketing,* January 1978, p. 55.
[12] Jessica Skelly von Brachel, "A High-Stakes Bet That Paid Off," *Fortune,* June 15, 1992, pp. 121–122.

FIGURE 8.3
Organizational Products
Organizational products tend to be more complex, requiring many products to be customized for specific markets or customers. In this advertisement, Eaton promotes its broad selection of electronic sensors.

Source: Courtesy Eaton Corporation.

Whereas most consumer goods are purchased through retailers, organizational buyers typically purchase directly from representatives of the manufacturer. Finally, to promote products, business-to-business marketers rely more heavily on personal selling than on advertising.

Factors Influencing Organizational Buyers

Organizational buyers consider a variety of factors when they make purchasing decisions, particularly quality level, service, and price.

To ensure a specific level of quality, organizational customers establish a set of technical specifications that they expect the products they buy to meet. In turn, most business-to-business marketers try to conform to such standard specifications and to maintain an acceptable level of quality in the products they offer.

If a raw material or component part does not meet specifications and is used to manufacture a final product that fails to work for the ultimate consumer, both the organizational customer and the ultimate consumer will be unhappy. The organizational customer may decide to switch to a different supplier as a result. On the other hand, organizational customers do not ordinarily purchase products that exceed specifications because such products frequently cost more and result in increased production costs.

Service is another concern of organizational buyers. Organizational customers commonly desire such services as market information, inventory maintenance, on-time delivery, availability of repair services and replacement parts, and credit. The services offered by suppliers directly and indirectly affect organizational customers' sales and profits. Thus many firms view customer service as a strategic weapon in organizational markets. When goods are the same or very similar (as are most raw materials), different suppliers may sell the goods at the same price, with the same specifications, and even in the same kinds of containers. In such cases, the services offered by a supplier can be the best means by which to differentiate itself and gain a competitive advantage.[13] For example, although all aluminum is basically the same, an aluminum processor willing to deliver its product directly to a manufacturer's shop floor in two days may allow that manufacturer to get its own products to the market faster than if it purchased its aluminum from another processor that delivered the aluminum in a week. Reynolds Metals Co. has successfully targeted many products once dominated by Bethlehem Steel Corp. and other large steel producers. It pioneered many aluminum products such as grain bins, baseball bats, siding, and appliance parts. And Reynolds has provided exceptional service. For instance, when automakers needed cheaper aluminum for parts, Reynolds leased them space at its plants and delivered molten metal to their doors.[14] Marketing Close-up illustrates the importance of service in organizational transactions.

Obviously, price is important to organizational customers because it influences operating costs as well as the costs of the final products. These costs in turn affect the customers' selling prices and profit margins. When purchasing capital equipment, organizational buyers generally perceive the price as the amount of investment necessary to obtain a certain level of return or savings. Thus an organizational purchaser will probably compare the price of a machine with the value of the benefits that the machine is expected to provide. However, an organizational buyer does not compare alternative products strictly on the basis of price; product quality, supplier services, and other factors are equally important considerations in the purchase decision. In fact, organizational buyers generally are reluctant to compromise quality and service for a reduced price.[15]

In summary, organizational buying can be traced to a single need—to solve a problem.[16] The problem may be a one-time event like a machine breakdown or a continuous problem such as a requirement to improve quality and increase profitability. Organizational customers are often concerned with how purchasing products from a specific supplier will add value to the bottom line. They often ask suppliers this question: "How will purchasing from you help me be more profitable?" Greater profitability can be accomplished when products meet desired specifications and service levels and when prices are competitive. In this market, competition between suppliers is usually intense, and organizational buyers will select the supplier that can help them solve a problem.

[13] M.P. Singh, "Service as a Marketing Strategy: A Case Study at Reliance Electric," *Industrial Marketing Management,* August 1990, pp. 193–200.
[14] Dana Milbank, "Aluminum Producers, Aggressive and Agile, Outfight Steelmakers," *Wall Street Journal,* July 1, 1992, pp. A1, A6.
[15] Michael D. Hutt and Thomas W. Speh, *Business Marketing Management* (Fort Worth, Tex.: Dryden Press, 1992), p. 80.
[16] Herbert E. Brown and Roger W. Brucker, "Charting the Industrial Buying Stream," *Industrial Marketing Management,* February 1990, pp. 55–61.

MARKETING CLOSE-UP

Service at Harnischfeger Industries

Harnischfeger Industries, a Milwaukee-based manufacturer of materials handling equipment, is the industry leader in the sales of overhead cranes. The firm drifted into complacency and lost money in 1988 despite its industry leadership. Since it has recovered, it is again the talk of the industry. In 1991, operating income jumped 44 percent to $12 million.

To accomplish this turnaround, Harnischfeger decided to concentrate on service. Although the firm had a solid reputation for quality, it had always left installation of its cranes to the customer and provided little in the way of follow-up service. Thomas C. Caughey, director of marketing communication, recalls that customers never associated Hernischfeger with parts and service. He says, "Their attitude was, 'Don't talk to Harnischfeger until you need a new crane.'" Since the products are made to last, the sales and marketing executives analyzed the market to come up with a way to exploit overlooked niches and increase product and service awareness.

To improve service at the customer's plant, Harnischfeger developed a special group to oversee installation. After finding out that many cost-conscious manufacturers hesitated to buy new cranes and hoists, marketers identified two profitable service operations. One buys and sells used cranes, and the other modernizes the customer's equipment, even if it was made by a competitor. Trained service personnel are also sent to customers directly from the factory.

Harnischfeger also exploited a niche it had long overlooked by introducing lower-margin products and giving them different distribution and promotion. Smaller hoists are sold over the telephone using an 800 number that is promoted in trade publications and through direct mail. Marketers also began using trade shows to reach maintenance superintendents and other new prospects. After attending twenty-five trade shows, Harnischfeger's share of the small-hoist market jumped from 2 percent to 18 percent.

Source: "Marketing Achievement Awards," *Sales & Marketing Management,* August 1991, p. 38.

Types of Organizational Purchases

Organizational transactions fall into one of three purchase categories: new-task, modified rebuy, or straight rebuy.

A **new-task purchase** is one in which an organization is purchasing an item for the first time to perform a new job or to solve a new problem. For example, a food manufacturer may want to buy fish products for its new line of microwaveable frozen foods. New-task purchases may require the development of product specifications, vendor specifications, and procedures for future purchases of the product. In all such purchases, the organizational buyer needs a great deal of information. This kind of purchase is significant to a supplier because, if the organizational buyer is satisfied with the new product and the supplier's service, the organization may buy large quantities of the product from the supplier over a period of years.

■ **new-task purchase**
a type of organizational purchase in which an organization is purchasing an item for the first time to perform a new job or to solve a new problem

■ **modified rebuy purchase** a type of organizational purchase in which a new-task purchase is changed the second or third time it is ordered or the requirements associated with a routine purchase are modified

A **modified rebuy purchase** is one in which a new-task purchase is modified the second or third time it is ordered or the requirements associated with a routine purchase are revised. For example, the food manufacturer in the previous example might seek faster delivery, lower prices, or a higher-quality fish to meet its customers' changing needs. A modified rebuy situation may cause regular suppliers to become more aggressive and competitive to keep a customer's business. Other competing suppliers may see an opportunity to obtain the company's business.

■ **straight rebuy purchase** a type of organizational purchase in which a buyer purchases the same products routinely under approximately the same terms of sale

A **straight rebuy purchase** is a routine purchase of the same products under approximately the same terms of sale. Buyers require little information for straight rebuy purchase decisions. For example, the frozen-food manufacturer will continue to purchase fish under the same terms of sale as long as it is satisfied with the quality and price of the fish and as long as the frozen-food line continues to sell. Organizational buyers tend to purchase from familiar suppliers that have provided satisfactory service and products in the past. These suppliers try to set up automatic reordering systems to facilitate reordering for organizational buyers. Some suppliers even monitor the organizational buyer's inventory and let the buyer know what needs to be ordered and when.

Purchase decisions are extremely important to organizational buyers. It is critical that organizations purchase quality materials and components for their operations. Business-to-business marketers should continue to make contacts with buyers who are doing business with other suppliers, because at some point in time these buyers may become dissatisfied with their current suppliers.

Demand for Organizational Products

Demand for products sold to organizational customers is called organizational demand. Organizational demand differs from consumer demand in that it is derived, inelastic, joint, and more subject to fluctuation.

■ **derived demand** organizational demand derived from consumer demand; a demand for products that arises because organizations purchase them to be used directly or indirectly in the production of goods and services to satisfy consumers' demand

Derived Demand   The demand for organizational products is called **derived demand** because organizations purchase products to be used directly or indirectly in the production of goods and services to satisfy consumers' demand. Consequently, the demand for organizational products is *derived* from the demand for consumer products. For example, as long as consumers continue to purchase pencils, there will be an organizational demand for graphite and wood to manufacture pencils. If there were no consumer demand for pencils, there would be no demand for wood and graphite to make pencils.

Figure 8.4 illustrates how the demand for wool is derived from the demand for wool sports coats. As a result, organizations like wool manufacturers often target marketing efforts at the ultimate consumers even though the firms do not sell to them directly. For instance, wool producers create advertisements that encourage consumers to buy wool products. Because organizational demand is derived, it is important that business-to-business marketers forecast both the demand for organizational products and the demand for consumer products.

FIGURE 8.4
Derived Demand for Wool

inelastic demand
a type of demand in which
a price increase or decrease
will not significantly affect
the quantity demanded

Inelastic Demand The demand for many organizational products is inelastic. **Inelastic demand** means that an increase or decrease in the price of a product will not significantly affect demand for the product. Elastic demand, common in consumer markets, means that a change in price will cause an opposite change in demand; if the price of a product goes up, demand for that product will decline. (Elasticity of demand is also discussed in Chapter 13.) Since the demand for most organizational products is inelastic and since most products contain many parts, an increase in the price of one or two parts of a product will result in only a slightly higher per-unit production cost. However, a sizable price increase for a component that represents a large proportion of a product's cost may cause demand to become more elastic if the price increase of the component part causes the price of the consumer product to rise sharply. For example, if the price of wood rises sharply, paper manufacturers are likely to pass this increase on to consumers, who may in turn cut back on their paper consumption because of the greatly increased price.

Inelastic demand for an organizational product applies only to market or industry demand, not to the demand for an individual supplier's product. Suppose, for example, that a specific bread producer increases the price of its hamburger buns sold to small restaurants but that its competitors continue to maintain their same lower prices. The bread producer that raises its prices will probably experience reduced sales because most small restaurants will switch to lower-priced hamburger buns. A specific firm is quite vulnerable to elastic demand, even though industry demand for a particular product may be inelastic.

joint demand a type
of organizational demand in
which the sale of one product is dependent on the sale
of another

Joint Demand In many instances, organizational products can be used only in conjunction with other products. **Joint demand** exists when the sale of one product is dependent on the sale of another. For example, producers of gasoline require additive products like boron and octane. If a gasoline producer cannot obtain any one of these products, it does not need the others.

Business-to-business marketers need to recognize products that are subject to joint demand. When a customer begins purchasing one of the jointly demanded items, a supplier has a good opportunity to sell that customer other related products. Moreover, when customers buy several jointly demanded products, the producer must be careful to avoid shortages of any of the items because such shortages threaten the sales of all the jointly demanded products. For example, the demand for microcomputer floppy-disk drives may be affected by shortages of memory chips.

Demand Fluctuations   Because the demand for organizational products is derived from consumer demand, it may fluctuate enormously. In general, when the demand for particular consumer products is high, producers of those products purchase large quantities of raw materials and component parts to guarantee that they can meet long-term production requirements. For example, if the demand for nutritious, high-fiber cereals is high, producers of those products will probably purchase large quantities of wheat, corn, oats, flour, sugar, and other ingredients to process the cereal, as well as paper for packaging the products. Producers may also increase their production capacity and purchase capital equipment for new or expanded plants.

Conversely, a decline in the demand for certain consumer goods significantly reduces the demand for the products used to produce those goods. Under such conditions, sales of certain organizational products may actually come to a brief stop. When consumer demand is low, organizational customers reduce their purchases of raw materials and component parts and stop purchasing equipment and machinery, even for replacement purposes. For example, should the sales of telephones drop sharply, telephone manufacturers like AT&T would cut back or stop their purchases of plastic and electrical wire used in manufacturing telephones. They also might delay plans for purchasing new equipment until demand rises again.

ORGANIZATIONAL BUYING BEHAVIOR

■ **organizational buying behavior** the actions and decision processes used by producers, resellers, governments, and institutions in deciding what products to buy

Organizational buying behavior refers to the actions and decision processes used by producers, resellers, and governments in deciding what products to buy. Although some of the factors that influence consumer behavior (discussed in Chapter 7) also influence organizational purchasing decisions, organizational buying behavior is characterized by several unique factors. The next sections discuss the participants in organizational purchase decisions, specifically the buying centers, and the process they go through in making purchasing decisions.

The Buying Center

■ **buying center** all the individuals in an organization who participate in the purchase decision process, including users, influencers, buyers, deciders, and gatekeepers

Organizational purchase decisions are seldom made by only one person. Instead, most organizations make purchase decisions through a **buying center,** which consists of all the individuals in an organization who participate in the purchase decision process, including users, influencers, buyers, deciders, and gatekeepers.[17]

Users are the individuals in the organization who actually use the product being purchased. They frequently initiate the purchase process; establish the criteria, or specifications, for the purchase; and evaluate the product's performance relative to those criteria. *Influencers* are technical personnel, such

[17]Philip W. Mahir, *Business-to-Business Marketing* (Boston: Allyn and Bacon, 1991), pp. 116–117.

FIGURE 8.5
Organizational Buyers
Buyers play an important role in a variety of organizations, including retail chains such as Kmart, because they decide what stores will need.

Source: Kmart Corporation. Photo: Rashakoor Studio.

as engineers, who help develop the specifications and evaluate alternative products. Influencers are critical when the product being purchased involves a new technology. *Buyers,* also called purchasing agents, actually select suppliers and negotiate the terms of purchase. They may also be involved in developing specifications. In reseller organizations, buyers play a critical role in determining what products will be sold to customers (see Figure 8.5). Buyers' decisions are heavily influenced by other individuals in the buying center. *Deciders* are the individuals who actually choose the products and suppliers. For routinely purchased items, deciders and buyers may be the same; for purchases that exceed a certain dollar limit, however, higher-level management personnel generally make the decisions. *Gatekeepers* are individuals, often secretaries and technical personnel, who control the flow of information to and among the persons in the buying center. Gatekeepers also bring new information into the organization through ties with people at other companies and attendance at trade shows.

Although most organizations make purchase decisions through a buying center, one member of the buying center may exert more influence than others in the final decision.[18] Often, it is assumed that buyers (or purchasing

[18]Donald W. Jackson, Jr., Janet E. Keith, and Richard K. Burdick, "Purchasing Agents' Perceptions of Industrial Buying Center Influence: A Situational Approach," *Journal of Marketing,* Fall 1984, pp. 75–83.

FIGURE 8.6
The Organizational Buying
Decision Process

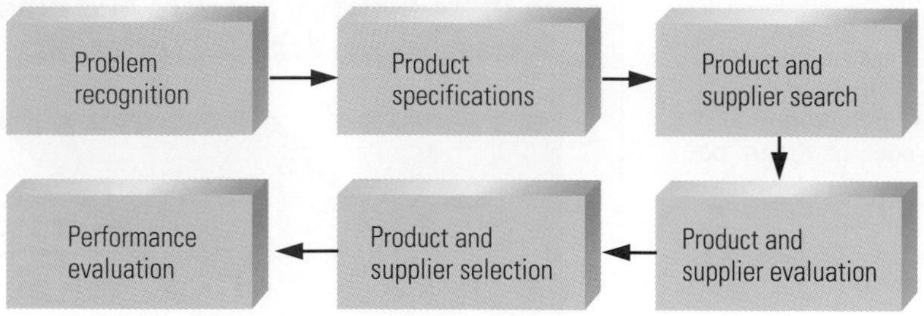

agents) have the most influence in organizational purchase decisions because they are responsible for selecting vendors or suppliers. In some situations, however, other members of the buying center may exert more influence than the buyers. For instance, influencers such as engineers possess a greater level of technical expertise than do buyers. Thus engineers may be in a more influential position than buyers, especially if the product being purchased is fairly technical in nature.

The Organizational Buying Decision Process

As shown in Figure 8.6, the organizational buying decision process consists of six stages.[19] Like the consumer decision-making process, the first stage of the organizational buying decision process involves problem recognition, whereby one or more persons recognize a problem or a need. Problem recognition may occur under a variety of circumstances—for example, when an old machine breaks down. It might also occur as a result of modifications to a currently manufactured product or the development of a new one. Users, influencers, buyers, or others in the buying center may be involved in problem recognition, but it may also be prompted by external sources, such as members of the sales force.

In the product specifications stage, organizational participants assess the problem or need and determine what is required to resolve or satisfy it. During this second stage, users and influencers often provide information and advice used in developing product specifications. Specifications may pertain to quality, durability, availability, warranty, and other product requirements. For example, in an automobile manufacturing plant with a broken paint-spraying machine, engineers, technicians, and machine operators assess the situation and determine that the organization needs to replace the machine. They develop a set of necessary features for a replacement machine, specifying that it must be able to paint ten cars per hour, change colors of paint quickly, require only one operator, and take up a small amount of space. The financial managers then establish a price range for the machine.

---

[19] Michael H. Morris, *Industrial and Organizational Marketing* (Columbus, Ohio: Merrill, 1988), pp. 33–37.

The third stage of the organizational buying decision process entails searching for possible products to solve the problem and locating suppliers of those products. In this stage, members of the buying center may look in company files and trade directories, contact suppliers for information, solicit proposals from known suppliers, and examine catalogs and trade publications. Hundreds of trade magazines are published regularly containing news, developments, and advertisements relating to particular industries. Search efforts should result in a list of several alternative products and suppliers. In the search phase, for example, members of the automobile maker's buying center look for paint-spraying products that meet the specifications established in the second phase. The buying center develops a list of paint-spraying machines and robots available from various suppliers.

In the fourth stage, product and supplier evaluation, the buying center evaluates the products on the list to determine which one (if any) meet the product specifications developed in the second stage. Various suppliers are also evaluated on the basis of multiple criteria such as price, service, accessibility, and ability to deliver. At Joy Technologies' mining machinery division, five general categories are used in a criteria check list: human resources, capabilities, quality, financial and pricing, and responsiveness.[20] In the example of the automobile manufacturer, members of the buying center evaluate the paint-spraying machines and robots on their list according to the criteria established by the engineers and technicians who will operate the new machine. They also evaluate the suppliers of these products to determine their ability to supply and service the product.

Information compiled during the evaluation stage is used in the fifth stage to select the product to be purchased and the supplier from which to buy it. The buyer(s) actually orders the product and works out the specific details of the sale, including terms, credit arrangements, delivery dates and methods, and technical assistance. At this stage, the deciders and buyers from the automobile maker's buying center decide to purchase a paint-spraying robot from the ACME Robot Manufacturing Company because it paints ten vehicles per hour, changes colors quickly, and requires only periodic supervision by one person. In addition, the company offers credit, training, and a service contract, and the robot can be delivered within a week.

In the final stage of the organizational buying decision process, the new product's performance is evaluated. The product's actual performance is compared to specifications, and any necessary adjustments are made. For example, had the automobile maker's new paint-spraying robot not functioned as expected, the organization would have asked the supplier to fix or replace it. At this time, the supplier's performance is also evaluated. If it is found to be unacceptable, the purchaser will seek corrective action from the supplier or search for a new supplier.

The organizational buying decision process can be influenced by the selling firm. For example, the selling firm may use its own sales force to help organizational buyers recognize problems, and can assist buyers in developing product specifications. Suppliers also attempt to influence the evalua-

---

[20] Somerby Dowst, "Define What You Want to Get What You Need," *Purchasing,* March 8, 1990, pp. 84–85.

CLOSE TO THE CUSTOMER

Building Partnerships Between Buyers and Suppliers

Buyer-supplier relationships have changed dramatically in recent years as more firms are emulating Japanese manufacturing systems. Contracts were once short term, suppliers were numerous, and competition was based primarily on price. Now new contracts are increasingly long term; only a single supplier is involved; and competition is based on quality, delivery, and engineering as well as price. The result is a long-term partnership between suppliers and their customers. This means working with buyers to obtain the information needed to deliver materials of the quality the organization requires.

It is very common for an organization committed to total quality management (TQM) to work with its suppliers to design parts and materials that the organization needs. In some instances, engineers and technicians employed by the buyer may work with the supplier to identify problems using TQM tools. Some quality-driven organizations like Motorola, Inc. will work only with suppliers who adopt TQM.

Quality expert W. Edwards Deming advocates working with a single supplier in a long-term relationship. How can a supplier be innovative and quality-conscious if the relationship is short term? Deming advises against selecting suppliers on the basis of price alone. Rather, organizations should base such decisions on the supplier's record of quality, responsiveness to customer needs, and willingness to become part of the organization's team.

Perhaps buyer-supplier partnerships are most evident in the automobile industry. In this highly competitive, global industry, the success of a manufacturer depends on the effectiveness of relationships with suppliers. Over 50 percent of parts and assemblies for cars are purchased from vendors outside the firm; these components are the major cost items

in car manufacturing. Thus buyer-supplier relationships have a significant impact on the efficiency and competitiveness of the automobile companies. As part of a massive restructuring effort, GM is pushing suppliers to reduce their costs. A study conducted in the automobile industry found that suppliers today are more likely to provide detailed information to customers, to have long-term contracts, to believe that their customers are serious about product quality, and to have defect prevention systems in place.

Firms in other industries are also developing buyer-supplier relationships. When Wal-Mart founder Sam Walton realized that poor supplier relations were hurting his company, he began working with suppliers to build long-term relationships. The partners worked to develop new products that customers wanted and to improve the quality of production and delivery processes. The strategy paid off: Wal-Mart has become the nation's largest retailer, in large part because of the strength of its relationships with suppliers. Procter & Gamble, one of Wal-Mart's suppliers, liked the relationship so well that it began to develop similar partnerships with other retail customers and its own suppliers. With Kmart, P&G created teams consisting of sales, purchasing, and data-processing experts working together as partners. P&G now has 120 teams working with different customers. Kraft uses a similar concept and has four hundred partnership teams.

Sources: Peter Turnbull, Nick Oliver, and Barry Wilkinson, "Buyer–Supplier Relations in the UK Automotive Industry," *Strategic Management Journal*, February 1992, pp. 159–168; Deidre A. Depke, "GM Puts Its Parts Suppliers on Notice," *Business Week*, June 15, 1992, p. 47; Susan Helper, "How Much Has Really Changed Between U.S. Automakers and Their Suppliers?" *Sloan Management Review*, Summer 1991, pp. 15–28; and Marshall Sashkin and Kenneth J. Kiser, *Total Quality Management* (Seabrook, Md.: Ducochon Press, 1991), pp. 53–54.

TABLE 8.4
Example of the Standard Industrial Classification System

Level	SIC Code	Description
Basic industry	19–39	Manufacturing
Major group	34	Fabricated metal products
Industry group	342	Cutlery, hand tools, general hardware
Specific industry	3423	Hand and edge tools
Product class	34231	Mechanics' hand service tools
Product	3423111	Pliers

Source: *1987 Standard Industrial Classification Manual*, U.S. Office of Management and Budget.

tion and selection process by developing goods and services that meet the specifications established by the buyer. Close to the Customer examines how partnerships between buyers and suppliers improve purchase decisions.

ANALYZING ORGANIZATIONAL MARKETS

Organizational marketers are fortunate to have access to considerable information about potential customers, much of which appears in government and industry publications. Comparable data are not available for organizations that market to ultimate consumers. Even though marketing managers may use different procedures to analyze organizational markets, most follow a similar pattern of (1) identifying potential customers, (2) locating where they are, and (3) estimating their purchase potential.[21]

Identifying Potential Customers

■ **Standard Industrial Classification (SIC) system** a system developed by the federal government to classify selected economic characteristics of industrial, commercial, financial, and service organizations

Much of the information about organizational customers is based on the **Standard Industrial Classification (SIC) system,** which was developed by the federal government to classify selected economic characteristics of industrial, commercial, financial, and service organizations. This system is administered by the Statistical Policy Division of the Office of Management and Budget. Table 8.4 shows how the SIC system can be used to identify potential customers. Various types of businesses are separated into ten basic industries, each with a two-digit code. Codes 19 to 39, for instance, represent manufacturing. Each industry is then divided into numbered, two-digit major groups. Thus group 34 includes all firms that manufacture fabricated metal products. Each major group is divided into subgroups with three-digit

[21] Edward F. Fern and James R. Brown, "The Industrial/Consumer Marketing Dichotomy: A Case of Insufficient Justification," *Journal of Marketing,* Spring 1984, pp. 168–177.

TABLE 8.5
Types of Organizational Market Data Available from Government Sources

Value of industry shipments
Number of establishments
Number of employees
Exports as a percentage of shipments
Imports as a percentage of apparent consumption
Compound annual average rate of growth
Major producing areas

codes, and each subgroup is separated into detailed industry categories that have four-digit numbers. The most recent SIC manual contains 83 major groups, 596 subgroups, and 1,005 detailed industry categories.[22]

A large amount of data is available for each SIC category through various government publications, such as the *Census of Business, Census of Manufacturers,* and *County Business Patterns.* Table 8.5 shows some types of information that can be obtained from government sources. Some data are available by state, county, and metropolitan area. Organizational market data also appear in nongovernment sources, such as Dun & Bradstreet's *Market Identifiers, Sales & Marketing Management's Survey of Industrial Purchasing Power,* and other trade publications.

After determining the SIC numbers of the industry categories that buy the kinds of products the firm makes, the marketing manager can ascertain the number of firms that are potential buyers nationally, by state, and by county. Government publications such as the *Census of Business, Census of Manufacturers,* and *County Business Patterns* report the number of establishments within SIC classifications, along with other types of data such as those shown in Table 8.5. For manufacturing industries, *Sales & Marketing Management's Survey of Industrial Purchasing Power* contains state and county SIC information regarding the number and size of plants and shipment sizes. The *Survey of Industrial Purchasing Power,* unlike most government sources, is updated annually.

Locating Customers

At this point, a business-to-business marketer has identified what types of industries purchase his or her firm's products, as well as the number of organizations in those industries and certain other information. Now the marketing manager must find out the names and addresses of potential customers to establish contact with them.

One approach to identifying and locating potential customers is to use state or commercial industrial directories such as *Standard & Poor's Register,* Dun & Bradstreet's *Middle Market Directory,* and *Million Dollar Directory.*

---

[22] *1987 Standard Industrial Classification Manual,* U.S. Office of Management and Budget.

FIGURE 8.7

Locating Customers

Once business-to-business marketers identify potential customers, they must locate them. As illustrated here, some organizations use response cards in advertisements to locate customers.

Source: Thomas Register of America Manufacturers.

These sources contain such information about a firm as its name, SIC number, address, telephone number, and annual sales. By referring to one or more of these sources, a business–to–business marketer can isolate customers by SIC numbers, determine their locations, and thus develop lists of potential customers by city, county, and state.

Another approach, which is more expedient but also more expensive, is to use a commercial data company. Dun & Bradstreet, for example, can provide a list of firms that fall into a particular four-digit SIC group. For each firm on the list, Dun & Bradstreet identifies the name, location, sales volume, number of employees, type of products handled, names of chief executives, and other information.

Firms use several other methods to identify organizational customers. Some firms rely heavily on trade shows to locate customers. Response cards that accompany advertisements in trade magazines or inserted in direct mail advertisements are also useful (see Figure 8.7). Toll-free (800) numbers are often provided to encourage organizational customers to contact a certain supplier. Finally, business–to–business marketers rely heavily on referrals from the sales force to locate customers. Information from the sales force is also useful in establishing desired levels of customer service, determining selling prices, and designing new products.[23]

---

[23] Douglas M. Lambert, Howard Marmorstein, and Arun Sharma, "Industrial Salespeople as a Source of Market Information," *Industrial Marketing Management,* May 1990, pp. 141–148.

Any of these approaches can be used effectively to identify and locate a group of potential organizational customers. However, a business probably cannot pursue all the firms on its list. Because some organizations are more likely to purchase the firm's products than others, the marketer must determine which ones to pursue.

Estimating Purchase Potential

To estimate how much organizational customers or groups of customers are likely to purchase, a business-to-business marketer must find a relationship between the size of potential customers' purchases and a variable available in SIC data, such as number of employees. For example, a paint manufacturer might attempt to determine the average number of gallons purchased by a specific type of organization relative to the number of persons employed. If the business-to-business marketer has no previous experience in this market segment, it will probably be necessary to survey a random sample of potential customers to establish a relationship between purchase sizes and numbers of persons employed. Once such a relationship has been established, it can be applied to potential customer segments to estimate their purchases. After deriving these estimates, the business-to-business marketer selects the customers to be included in the target market.

SUMMARY

Organizational customers—producers, resellers, government organizations, institutions, and international customers—purchase products for resale, direct use in the production of other products, or use in daily operations. Producers include individuals and organizations that purchase products for use in the production of other products or in their daily operations for the purpose of making a profit. Resellers consist of intermediaries that buy finished products and resell them to make a profit. Government organizations include federal, state, county, and local governments. Institutions are non-business or nonprofit organizations.

Organizational transactions differ from consumer transactions in several ways. Organizations tend to make considerably larger orders but negotiate less frequently. Organizational transactions sometimes involve reciprocity, an agreement in which two organizations agree to buy from each other. Finally, these transactions involve different marketing mixes than do consumer transactions.

When purchasing products, organizational customers are concerned about quality, service, and price. Quality is important because it directly affects the quality of products the buyer's firm produces. Because services can have such a direct influence on a firm's costs, sales, and profits, such things as market information, on-time delivery, availability of parts, and credit can be crucial to an organizational buyer. Price is a prime concern because it directly influences a firm's profitability.

Organizational purchases are usually one of three types. A new-task purchase is one in which an organization purchases an item for the first time to perform a new job or to solve a new problem. A modified rebuy purchase is one in which a new-task purchase is modified the second or third time it is ordered or the requirements associated with a routine purchase are revised. A straight rebuy purchase is a routine purchase of the same products under approximately the same terms of sale.

Organizational demand differs from consumer demand in several ways. Organizational demand derives from the demand for consumer products. Organizational demand is inelastic; if the price of an organizational item changes, demand for the product will not be greatly affected. In many instances, organizational products can be used only in conjunction with other products. The demand for these products can fluctuate widely.

Organizational buying behavior includes the actions and decision processes of producers, resellers, and governments in deciding what products to buy. Organizational purchase decisions are often made through a buying center—a group of individuals who participate in the purchase decision process. Users are the individuals in the organization who actually use the product. Influencers help develop product specifications and evaluate alternative products for possible use. Buyers are responsible for selecting the suppliers and negotiating the terms of the purchases. Deciders choose the products and vendors. Gatekeepers control the flow of information to and among persons who occupy the other roles in the buying center.

The six stages of the organizational buying decision process are recognizing a problem, establishing product specifications, searching for products and suppliers, evaluating products and suppliers, selecting and ordering the most appropriate product, and evaluating the product's and the supplier's performance.

Business-to-business marketers generally follow a pattern when analyzing organizational markets. First, potential customers are identified through Standard Industrial Classification (SIC) codes and government and industry publications. Once potential customers are identified, they must be located through industrial directories or commercial data companies. Finally, business-to-business marketers must determine which buyers have the greatest purchase potential.

KEY TERMS

business-to-business marketing
producers
resellers
government organizations
institutions
reciprocity
new-task purchase
modified rebuy purchase

straight rebuy purchase
derived demand
inelastic demand
joint demand
organizational buying behavior
buying center
Standard Industrial
    Classification (SIC) system

QUESTIONS FOR DISCUSSION AND REVIEW

1. What are some of the differences between organizational markets and consumer markets?

2. Describe the major types of organizational customers.

3. Name some factors that influence organizational buyers' decisions.

4. How do the marketing mixes for organizational and consumer products differ?

5. Compare the three different types of organizational transactions. How do they differ?

6. What is meant by derived demand? Give an example of a product for which demand is derived.

7. Demand for organizational products generally fluctuates widely. Why?

8. Who are the individuals that typically make up a buying center? Describe their functions.

9. What are the stages of the organizational buying decision process?

10. How can the Standard Industrial Classification system be used by business-to-business marketers?

11. Describe the approaches commonly used to locate potential customers.

CASES

8.1   PURCHASING AT BOEING

In a single year, The Boeing Co.'s Commercial Airplane Group's Material Division negotiates contracts to purchase over $6 billion in parts from some 3,500 suppliers. (For most planes, Boeing makes only the wings.) For many years, Boeing played the tough negotiator, demanding the lowest prices from suppliers. That emphasis has changed. Today, Boeing is more interested in quality, cost, and on-time delivery. To accomplish this goal, Boeing is developing better relationships with its suppliers.

Before 1984, purchasing at Boeing was performed by each individual airliner program. In other words, the group in charge of building 747s would handle its purchasing needs, as would the 757 team, the 767 team, and so on. This method became cumbersome as Boeing's commercial airplane business began to grow. For instance, the 747 is made from roughly six million parts obtained from more than 1,500 suppliers. Boeing created one division—the

Material Division—to keep track of parts and suppliers for all the commercial planes. Additionally, by combining similar parts orders for different jets, Boeing's buyers could get better prices than if they purchased the items separately.

In 1987, Boeing began awarding longer-term contracts and involving suppliers very early in the actual design, engineering, and specifications of parts for all new planes. By working closely with suppliers, Boeing has been able to hold costs down on projects such as the new 767-X. Last-minute changes and special orders from Boeing can dramatically increase the cost of producing a plane. By having eighteen major suppliers consult with engineers and designers on the 767-X, Boeing eliminated about 60 percent of such changes.

Boeing has also designed a catalogue that offers different options to customers such as Delta and United. For instance, the catalogue may provide the various options in lavatories or location of galleys. Before the catalogue was used, customers commonly made six hundred or more requests for changes in an original order. Since the catalogue has been introduced, the number of requests for changes on the 747-400 has dropped below fifty.

Boeing's improved relationships with suppliers has resulted in another benefit. By awarding longer-term contracts, it can avoid shipping delays and supply shortages. For example, when Boeing realized that a shortage of seats and lavatories was developing, it contacted suppliers in Germany and Japan to get them to increase capacity. These suppliers increased capacity by 50 percent within a year, thus helping Boeing avoid a parts shortage.

Good relationships with suppliers will be even more important in the future. Boeing's current backlog is $9 billion in orders. The company dominates the commercial aircraft industry with a 54 percent market share. And the company has plans for a new long-distance plane, the 777, which will target customers all over the world. With enough business to keep factories buying throughout this decade, good relationships with its suppliers could mean more profits for Boeing in the years ahead.

Questions for Discussion

1. What type of organizational purchase is Boeing's purchase of parts from its suppliers?

2. Why is it critical for Boeing to establish good relationships with its suppliers?

3. How did Boeing benefit by combining all purchases under one division?

4. Why did establishing long-term relationships with suppliers reduce costs for Boeing?

Based on information from Dori Jones Yang, Micheal Oneal, Steward Toy, Mark Maremont, and Robert Neff, "How Boeing Does It," *Business Week,* July 9, 1990, pp. 46–50; Marc Beauchamp, "No More Weekend Stands," *Forbes,* September 17, 1990, pp. 191–192; and Gene G. Marcial, "A Beleaguered Boeing May Be on Lockheed's Tail," *Business Week,* March 13, 1989, p. 130.

8.2   U.S. FORK LIFT PRODUCERS LOSE THEIR STRENGTH

Until the late 1970s, U.S. producers dominated the fork lift market in North America. Clark Equipment Co. of South Bend, Indiana, the biggest manufacturer, and rivals Allis-Chalmers, Caterpillar, Yale, and Hyster produced durable machines that commanded the domestic market, which accounts for about 25 percent of the $5 billion in world truck lift sales. Clark alone had 27 percent of the North American market for its leading product, gas-powered, heavy-duty lift trucks used in factories and warehouses. In those days, Nissan, Toyota, Komatsu, and other Japanese companies had only a 17 percent share at the low end of the American market.

But the Japanese companies emerged as a major threat in the early 1980s. Their lift trucks lacked the array of features of U.S.-made trucks and were less durable, but they were reliable and less expensive. Customers found that the Japanese models met their needs.

The Japanese price advantage widened to as much as 30 percent when the value of the dollar rose in the early 1980s. One former Clark executive said that his company couldn't buy components, let alone assemble a machine, for what it cost Toyota to build and export one. The Japanese companies also had better economies of scale than the U.S. producers, which enabled them to obtain parts at a considerable cost advantage. By 1984, Japanese companies had tripled their share of gas-powered lifts, which account for two-thirds of U.S. sales versus one-third for electric models.

U.S. giants Clark and Caterpillar tried to fight back but were too slow in adapting to market shifts. Clark invested $25 million to upgrade its fork lifts with new technology. In 1982, the company introduced a new electric model that contained several costly features, such as oil-cooled brakes and a transaxle more durable than most customers needed. But buyers decided to save money. The new fork lift was such a failure that the company scrapped it before it could introduce a gas-powered version. Clark finally introduced a lower-cost product in 1985, but it could not stop its market share slide until 1990, at 20 percent. Caterpillar also did not respond quickly enough with the simpler, cheaper machines customers wanted. It began competing with the Japanese manufacturers on the basis of price in 1990 and managed to keep its market share in the low teens, but only at the expense of profits.

Only Hyster, which makes larger fork lifts and faces less Japanese competition than other U.S. manufacturers, had a workable strategy to become a competitive, low-cost producer. To improve quality and reduce development time from five to four years, the U.S. firm began engineering—Japanese-style—with teams of employees from marketing, design, and manufacturing. Hyster persuaded the British government to pay for a new plant in Northern Ireland and moved production there to cut costs. It also cut jobs. In 1989, when NACCO Industries bought the company, Hyster was making as many trucks as it had ten years earlier with half as many employees. As a result, Hyster maintained its 17 percent market share.

Clark and Caterpillar also searched for inexpensive manufacturing sites and settled on Korea. In 1983 Caterpillar signed an agreement with Daewoo to assemble fork lifts there and subsequently closed a plant in Ohio. But the move created very complex logistics. Caterpillar closed its Ohio plant too soon and left dealers without some of its best-selling models for as long as nine months. The new supply chain was lengthy and resulted in big inventories and occasional shipping delays. At one point, Caterpillar had to ship key parts by air from Korea to meet changing customer demand. Clark, which signed a ten-year production accord with Samsung in 1986, encountered other problems. Because the quality of the Samsung-made fork lifts was poor, Clark incurred costs to re-engineer the trucks and pay warranty claims. In addition, the cost savings for the American manufacturers in Korea were less than expected as wages there tripled during the 1980s. When the value of the dollar fell against the Korean won, costs rose even more.

After battling quality problems, industry overcapacity, Japanese competition, and deeply discounted prices, Clark was losing money on its fork lifts, once the guts of its operation. In the summer of 1992, Clark sold its fork lift unit to Terex Corp. At the same time, Caterpillar turned over its fork lift operations to an 80 percent–20 percent joint venture controlled by Japan's Mitsubishi Heavy Industries Ltd. NACCO's Hyster-Yale is the only remaining strong U.S. producer in the field.

Ironically, fork lift production has been moving back to the United States. In the late 1980s, the Japanese began opening assembly plants in the United States to avoid paying import duties imposed by the International Trade Commission. The commission slapped duties of up to 51.3 percent on Japanese fork lifts as the result of a complaint filed by Hyster that the Japanese companies were dumping (selling products in foreign countries for a lower price than in the country of origin). Caterpillar's new venture with Mitsubishi will produce fork lifts in Houston; some observers say that Mitsubishi's production strength combined with Caterpillar's distribution and service will help the venture thrive. Terex is expected to bring production of Clark's gas-powered machines back to the United States, but some wonder whether the parent company, strapped with hefty long-term debt, will make the necessary investments in new Clark products to meet customers' needs as the market evolves.

Questions for Discussion

1. What were the major reasons for the decline of Clark and Caterpillar in the market they long dominated?

2. Why did Clark's new, state-of-the-art electric lift truck fail so miserably? What does that incident reveal about the factors influencing organizational buyers?

3. Which organizational customers did Caterpillar have trouble serving after it moved production to Korea? Explain what these customers want in organizational transactions.

Based on information from Kevin Kelley and Zachary Schiller, "How U.S. Forklift Makers Dropped the Goods," *Business Week,* June 15, 1992, pp. 105, 107; Marcia Berss, "Crying Uncle," *Forbes,* December 9, 1991, p. 186; and Thomas Jaffe, "Clark's Cash," *Forbes,* July 6, 1992, p. 128.

Information for Marketing Decision Making

OBJECTIVES

- To discuss the importance of marketing information systems and marketing research.

- To describe the five stages in conducting marketing research projects.

- To explain the difficulty involved in conducting international marketing research.

- To identify ethical issues in marketing research.

ost marketers realize the importance of customer satisfaction, but how do you measure it? Since 1981, J.D. Power has been surveying car buyers and publishing the Customer Satisfaction Index (CSI). Since then, customer satisfaction and product quality have become the major goals of automakers and dealers as well as many other businesses throughout the world. Power has helped to make the words *customer satisfaction* part of the everyday language of organizations throughout the world.

Firms scoring high on the CSI reap many rewards—good publicity, national advertising campaigns that brag about quality, and often higher sales and profits. When the Buick LeSabre jumped from 44th to 2nd (behind Nissan Maxima) in one of Power's rankings, Buick began advertising that the LeSabre was the U.S. car with the fewest reported problems. Sales took off, increasing 5.7 percent over the previous year in the first month of the campaign, and 9.3 percent, 32 percent, 91 percent, and 99 percent in subsequent months. Buick's success led many other automakers to concentrate on improving quality.

Power uses mail surveys to conduct his studies. He purchases a list of registered owners from Detroit-based R.L. Polk and typically surveys seventy thousand car owners. The questionnaire is generally six to eight pages long and has about ninety questions. It takes around thirty to forty minutes to complete, and a dollar bill is often enclosed to encourage participation. Approximately 150 completed questionnaires per model are needed to yield accurate results. Anywhere from 38 to 50 percent of those receiving questionnaires respond—a high response rate for mail survey research. Power attributes the high response to name recognition and Americans' interest in quality cars.

Once the questionnaires are returned, a team of workers begins to process the results. Information must be taken from the surveys, loaded on the computer, and analyzed. A two-step analysis is used. First, consumers' main concerns are identified. For example, in the three-year Vehicle Performance Index (VPI), the concerns were reliable operation, interior space, and clear instruments and handy controls. Second, each issue is given a weight depending on how important it is to consumers. For the VPI, reliable operation was weighted most heavily, 54 percent. The result is a ranking of models based on these issues. For instance, Lexus was the top-ranked car in the 1992 Customer Satisfaction Index, followed by Infiniti and Saturn.

Power uses twelve studies to measure the performance of automakers and their dealers. Toyota's Lexus claimed first place on three of the studies after establishing rigorous industry benchmarks for satisfying luxury car buyers, who are already accustomed to quality. Other firms are also establishing programs to increase quality and service in the hope of improving their score on one of Power's surveys. Power, in the meantime, is looking for growth in other industries. He wants to expand customer satisfaction surveys to products and services such as airlines, heavy-duty trucks, recreational vehicles, and personal computers.[1] ●

Just as research helped automobile manufacturers create better cars, so marketing research helps businesses create more satisfying products for consumers. Customer satisfaction measurement is at the heart of most firms' quality improvement programs.[2] Marketing research and information systems are the means through which businesses acquire the knowledge and facts they need to carry out the marketing concept. Some analysts have suggested that the increasing inability of American products to compete successfully with products from other nations may have its roots in American businesses' lack of understanding and application of the marketing concept.[3] Without understanding what consumers need and want, a company cannot create products that satisfy them; understanding exactly what consumers need can be best accomplished through marketing research.[4] J.D. Power surveys have motivated automobile companies to listen to customers before designing and manufacturing cars.

Businesses have access to more information today than ever before, which leads many commentators to label this the Age of Information. The main catalyst for growth in the current global economy will be information.[5] But the sheer volume of information, as well as the increasingly diverse population, presents a real challenge to marketing managers. In the 1990s, a continued 80 percent or higher failure rate for new products will mean more stress on a rebounding economy and could spell disaster for some manufacturers and retailers. Kathleen MacDonnell, vice president of Campbell Soup Company, argues that marketing research must be conducted on the front end of product development so that product refinement and introduction are conducted on a customer-oriented foundation.[6]

[1] Based on information from Alex Taylor III, "More Power to J.D. Power," *Fortune,* May 18, 1992, pp. 103–106; Raymond Serafin and Cleveland Horton, "Automakers Focus on Service," *Advertising Age,* July 6, 1992, pp. 3, 33; and Rahul Jacob, "Saturn in Orbit," *Fortune,* July 27, 1992, p. 12.

[2] Gail Gilbert, "Customer Satisfaction Measurement Is Core of Firm's Quality Improvement," *Marketing News,* January 4, 1993, p. 18.

[3] A. Parasuraman, "Hang on to the Marketing Concept," *Business Horizons,* September–October 1981, p. 40.

[4] John R. Hauser and Robert L. Klein, "Without Good Research, Quality Is Shot in Dark," *Marketing News,* January 4, 1988, p. 1.

[5] Floyd Kemske, "Brains Will Replace BTUs," *Information Age,* June 1990, pp. 22–24.

[6] Bickley Townsend, "Market Research That Matters," *American Demographics,* August 1992, pp. 58–60.

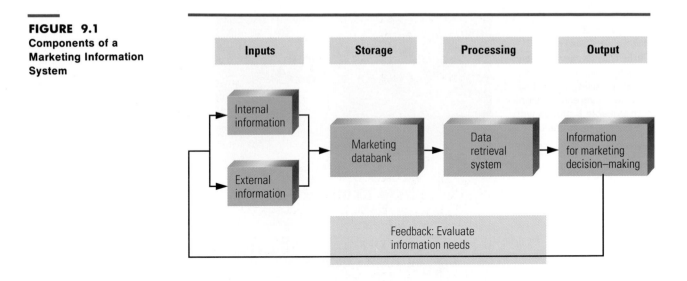

FIGURE 9.1
Components of a Marketing Information System

MARKETING INFORMATION SYSTEMS AND MARKETING RESEARCH

■ **marketing information system (MIS)** a program for managing and organizing information gathered from inside and outside an organization

A **marketing information system (MIS)** is a program for managing and organizing information gathered from inside and outside an organization; most marketing information systems are computerized. An MIS allows a business to store, retrieve, and classify the information it collects about customers, prices, advertising expenditures, sales, competition, and distribution expenses. It incorporates both data collected routinely and data collected for special research projects. Figure 9.1 presents the chief components of an MIS.

Internal information inputs include regular sales reports, data on costs and inventory levels, and records of salespersons' activities. External sources of data consist of economic forecasts, annual reports, competitor analyses, and data from customers. Data are then stored in the MIS databank for later processing and analysis.

■ **marketing research** the collection, analysis, and interpretation of data for guiding marketing decisions

Marketing research is the collection, analysis, and interpretation of data for guiding marketing decisions. It is conducted on a special-project basis and involves investigation of specific problems. For example, Kmart conducted research to determine how baby boomers will spend their money when they reach their 50s. Group and in-store interviews were used to collect a variety of information ranging from how consumers react to certain types of advertising to why they buy what they do at Kmart.[7] This information is helping Kmart decide what type of merchandise to carry and how to face competitors as the firm plans for the years ahead. Figure 9.2 illustrates the importance of using research to develop products based on customer needs.

---

[7]John P. Cortez, "Kmart Studies Boomers to Glean Spending Insights," *Advertising Age,* October 12, 1992, p. 2.

FIGURE 9.2
Marketing Research
Marketing research enables firms to focus on the customer. By using marketing research, Eveready designs rechargeable batteries with the customers in mind.

Source: Eveready Battery Company, Inc. Eveready® and Energizer® are registered trademarks of Eveready Battery Company.

Often a business needs information that can be obtained only from sources outside its formal channels. For example, an organization may want to gain an objective understanding of its customers or its perceived reputation among those customers. Such information needs can be addressed by an independent study conducted by a marketing research firm. Table 9.1 presents the top ten U.S. marketing research organizations and the top ten international organizations.

An organization stores routinely collected information and data acquired through marketing research in its **marketing databank.** Data can be retrieved for future use from the firm's databank, which is generally a complex computer storage and retrieval system. Through its Friends & Family program, MCI Communications Corp. created a databank which contains a list of existing, new, and potential customers. Participants receive a 20 percent discount on frequently called numbers as long as both parties are members of the program.[8] The output of the MIS is relevant information for marketing decision making. MCI, for instance, used its databank to develop advertising and telemarketing programs; MCI's share of the $55 billion long-distance market increased by 2 points to 15 percent within a year.[9]

■ **marketing databank** files (often computerized) of routinely collected information and data acquired by an organization through marketing research

[8] Kate Fitzgerald, "Circle of 'Friends' Rounds Out MCI Base," *Advertising Age,* January 13, 1992, p. 26.
[9] Ibid., p. 26.

Rank	U.S. Firms	U.S. Revenues (millions)	International Firms	International Revenues (millions)
1	A.C. Nielsen Co.	$492.0	A.C. Nielsen Co.	$708.0
2	Arbitron Co.	201.7	IMS International	344.0
3	Information Resources, Inc.	183.9	Research International	102.3
4	IMS International	165.0	MRB Group	59.1
5	Westat	86.9	Millward Brown	40.3
6	Maritz Marketing Research	59.6	Information Resources, Inc.	23.8
7	M/A/R/C Group	56.1	Louis Harris & Associates	13.7
8	Abt Associates	55.3	Gallup Organization	4.5
9	NFO Research	45.6	Harte-Hankes Marketing Services	2.0
10	Gallop Organization	43.5	Walker Group	1.6

Source: *Advertising Age,* June 22, 1992, pp. 52–54. Reprinted by permission.

TABLE 9.1
Top Ten U.S. and International Marketing Research Firms by Revenues

Marketing research and marketing information systems are quite valuable because they enhance a marketer's ability to make decisions. Research and marketing information systems provide an organization with feedback on how customers feel about the organization and its products. Without this feedback, a marketer cannot create products that satisfy consumers. Thus the use of research in marketing decision making is increasing as managers recognize its benefits. Marketing Close-up shows how a high-tech shopping cart helps stores collect data for their MIS.

STAGES IN THE MARKETING RESEARCH PROCESS

Organizations approach marketing research in a systematic manner to maintain the control necessary to obtain accurate data. The success of marketing research depends on the quality of the input. Therefore, effective control over a research project is crucial. Marketers design research projects using practical and understandable procedures so that the results provide useful information to decision makers.

As Figure 9.3 shows, the five steps used in conducting marketing research projects are as follows:

1. Problem definition
2. Research design
3. Data collection
4. Data analysis and interpretation
5. Research report

Problem definition → Research design → Data collection → Data analysis and interpretation → Research report

FIGURE 9.3
Stages in the Marketing Research Process

■ **problem definition** the first step toward solving a marketing problem through a research study; involves identifying the nature and boundaries of a problem

Problem Definition

Problem definition, in which marketers try to identify the nature and boundaries of a problem, is the first step toward solving a marketing problem through a research study. The first sign of a problem is usually a deviation from normal operations, such as a failure to attain objectives. For example, if an organization's objective is to increase its share of a particular market to 15 percent but it has captured only 10 percent of the market, the organization should recognize that a problem exists. Decision makers should realize that something inside or outside the organization has blocked the achievement of the desired objective or that the objective may be unrealistic. Decreasing sales, increasing expenses, and decreasing profits are all broad indications of problems. Whatever the problem, researchers and decision makers should remain in the problem definition stage until they have established precisely what they want from the research and how they will use it.[10]

Unfortunately, conducting marketing research after a serious problem has been recognized does not guarantee that the problem can be resolved. By the time many firms realize that their customers are unhappy, they have lost a significant share of the market; research and subsequent changes may not be able to bring all the customers back. As a result, marketing research is a continuous function in many firms. Consumer product and service firms and business-to-business marketers constantly monitor buyer attitudes and try to detect potential problems before they actually occur.

Whether research is conducted on an ongoing basis or after a problem occurs, it is critical that the marketing researcher work closely with the marketing manager in the problem definition stage. If together they can clearly define a problem, the researcher can conduct research that will provide information the manager requires to make marketing decisions.

Research Design

■ **research design** the overall plan for conducting a research investigation

Once the problem has been defined, researchers must obtain the information needed to resolve it. The **research design** is the overall plan for conducting the research investigation. Marketing research projects must be designed so that the results are reliable and valid. *Reliability* means that similar results can be obtained if the research is repeated. A college entrance exam is reliable if

---

[10]Bruce R. Dreisbach, "Marketing: The Key to Research Management," *Marketing News,* January 4, 1985, p. 3.

MARKETING CLOSE-UP

VideOcart Gives Information to Shoppers and Stores

For supermarkets, VideOcart must seem like a godsend. This innovation—a grocery cart with a video screen mounted on the handle and a battery pack underneath—gives shoppers all sorts of information and advertises to them while it collects market research data for the store's MIS.

Information Resources Incorporated (IRI), a marketing research company which pioneered the use of check-out scanner data, developed VideOcart as a very direct marketing tool. While customers are shopping, the screen shows advertisements from national companies and lists store specials. Several major firms, including Nabisco, Procter & Gamble, Pepsi, Ralston Purina, and Kraft, have signed up. Advertisers pay about $4 to reach one thousand shoppers, compared with about $7 for a newspaper coupon insert and $10 to $12 for an evening television network commercial. Early results suggest that VideOcart actually works. Shoppers using VideOcarts spend an average $1 more per visit than those who don't. A study at one Midwest supermarket chain showed that sales of some items promoted by VideOcart were 5 to 60 percent ahead of usual levels.

Here's how VideOcart works. As a shopper pushes the cart down the aisles, sensors in the screen pick up infrared signals from control units throughout the store. As the cart passes a control unit on the store shelf, it triggers an advertisement for a specific brand stocked there. When the cart is near the cereal, for example, an advertisement for a brand of cereal appears on the screen.

To help shoppers, VideOcart provides a detailed map of the store and an index of where every item is located—a useful feature in large modern super-

markets stocked with 22,000 or more products. Shoppers can call up information seen in a previous aisle. By pushing buttons on a simple keyboard, they can also get recipes with specific product ingredients, nutritional information, sale-item information, and "paperless coupons" redeemable at the check-out line. And at the check-out, local news and weather reports are triggered automatically.

Besides displaying information, the VideOcart collects information from shoppers. The screen is a transmitter that tracks the cart's movement through the store and reports to a series of electronic sensors in the store's ceiling. It can report how much time shoppers spend in various parts of the store—knowledge that store owners and marketers find extremely valuable. One survey showed that customers spend an average of forty-two seconds in the bread section and more than two minutes in the baby-products section. The VideOcart can also interact with shoppers. The unit can gather information about shoppers' opinions of various products and displays and then dump the information at the check-out counter, where it is stored for later analysis.

Data obtained from the carts will allow grocery marketers to analyze shopping patterns. They will be able to determine whether some areas are more congested than others and plan for the optimal placement of products. The information can also be used to gauge the success of displays and special promotions. All this information will be useful in designing grocery stores that facilitate traffic patterns.

Sources: Joshua Levine, "The Ultimate Sell," *Forbes,* May 13, 1991, pp. 108, 110; Otis Port, "Video Gizmos Do Everything but Bag the Groceries," *Business Week,* September 16, 1991, p. 97; and Tibbett Speer, "The Grocery Cart That Got Smart," *American Demographics,* July 1992, p. 9.

you score similar results after taking it a second time. *Validity* means the research must actually measure what is being investigated. If the objective of a college entrance exam is to measure potential for success in college, the test is valid if it predicts success. Depending on the specific problem being investigated, several different types of studies can be employed, including exploratory, descriptive, and experimental studies.

Exploratory Studies   When marketers need more information about a problem, they conduct an **exploratory study,** in which they review existing information on the topic or informally investigate the problem. For instance, marketers may gain insight into the nature of a problem by reviewing information in the organization's databank or publicly available data. They may also question knowledgeable people inside and outside the organization. For example, to discover some of the reasons behind a sales decline for one of its products, a company might question members of its sales force and the product manager before doing any further study. One benefit of using the exploratory approach is that it enables marketers to conduct small studies with a very limited database.

Exploratory studies are especially useful in taking broad problems and developing more specific hypotheses. A **hypothesis** is an educated guess or a conjectural statement that specifies how two or more variables are related. The term *variable* is used often in marketing research and refers to a measurable phenomenon that takes on different values, such as age, attitude, or purchase behavior. A researcher studying the sales force may hypothesize as follows: Salespeople with the highest job satisfaction are the most productive. Once hypotheses are established, information is gathered to test them. Hypotheses are often tested using descriptive or exploratory studies. The acceptance or rejection of hypotheses becomes the main outcome or conclusion of the research.

Descriptive Studies   A **descriptive study** is used when marketers want to understand the characteristics of certain phenomena underlying a particular problem. A great deal of marketing research involves descriptive studies. Marketing researchers may conduct surveys of consumers' education, occupation, or age; they may find out how many consumers buy a certain magazine in a given month; or they may determine how many teenage girls do the grocery shopping for their families. A company wanting to open a new restaurant near a university might conduct a descriptive study to identify what kinds of food students like, how often they eat out, how much they spend when they eat out, and whether they are willing to try a new restaurant. The information obtained from the survey could be used to develop a restaurant that would satisfy the students.

Descriptive studies are very rigid. They assume that the problem is clearly defined and require prior knowledge of the problem so that hypotheses can be developed. These hypotheses specify clearly who, what, where, when, and so on, since descriptive studies seek to answer such questions. Accuracy is critical in this type of research because errors can yield results that are

■ **exploratory study** the type of research conducted by marketers when more information is needed about a problem; a review of existing information on a topic or informal investigation of a problem

■ **hypothesis** an educated guess or a conjectural statement that specifies how two or more variables are related

■ **descriptive study** the type of study undertaken when marketers recognize that they must understand the characteristics of certain phenomena underlying a particular problem

FIGURE 9.4
How Independent and
Dependent Variables Are
Related

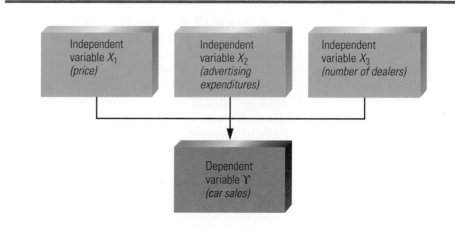

experimental study
a research study that in-
vestigates the relationship
between different varia-
bles—the data collected
proves or disproves that a
particular variable X is the
cause of the variable Y

experimentation re-
search that controls those factors that are related to or
may affect the variables under investigation so that the
effects of the experimental
variables may be measured

independent variable
the variable that is manipulated in an experimental
study; a variable free from
the influence of, or not dependent on, other variables

dependent variable in
an experimental study, the
variable that is contingent
on, or affected by, the value
of the independent variable

misleading to managers. However, accuracy is difficult to achieve in descriptive studies because errors often occur in sampling, questionnaire design, and
information reported by respondents. These issues will be discussed later in
the chapter.

Experimental Studies   An **experimental study** investigates the relationship between different variables. In an experimental study, marketing researchers hypothesize that one thing, the variable X, is the cause of something
else, the variable Y. The research must be planned so that the data collected
prove or disprove that X causes Y. For example, one study hypothesized
that the use of brand extensions—extending brand names into new product
areas—increases new product market share. In other words, a recognizable
brand name should cause increased market share when a company expands
into a new product area. Researchers found that brand extensions do in fact
contribute positively to market share.[11]

Experimental studies differ from other research methods because the research setting is controlled. **Experimentation** involves controlling those factors that are related to or may affect the variables under investigation so that
the effects of the experimental variables may be measured. One variable—the
independent variable—is manipulated, and its effect on another variable—
the **dependent variable**—is measured; meanwhile, all the other variables not
in the experiment are controlled. Figure 9.4 illustrates the relationship between these variables. For example, when an automobile manufacturer sets
the price of a new model, the firm may want to estimate the number of
automobiles that consumers would buy at various prices. The dependent
variable would be sales, and the independent variable would be price. Researchers would design the experiment so that other independent variables

[11]Daniel C. Smith and C. Whan Park, "The Effects of Brand Extensions on Market Share and Advertising Efficiency," *Journal of Marketing Research,* August 1992, pp. 296–313.

that might influence sales, such as advertising expenditures and number of dealers, would be controlled.

Experimental studies may be conducted in the laboratory or in the field. Both research settings, however, have advantages and disadvantages.

■ **laboratory experiment** an experimental study in which participants are invited to a central location to react or respond to experimental stimuli

A **laboratory experiment** is an experimental study in which participants are invited to a central location to react or respond to experimental stimuli. In such an isolated setting, researchers can control independent variables that might influence the outcome of an experiment. Laboratory settings might include interview rooms, one-way mirrors, taste kitchens, video equipment, slide projectors, tape recorders, or central telephone banks. For example, in an experiment to determine the effect of various types of sweeteners (independent variables) on the taste (dependent variable) of a new reduced-calorie cookie, consumers would be invited to a taste kitchen. Researchers would ask subjects to taste cookies made from each of the sweeteners. Subjects might then be asked to say whether they liked or disliked the taste, or to rank the taste, of each kind of cookie.

One disadvantage of laboratory experiments is that they are isolated from the real world. Laboratory settings simply cannot duplicate all the conditions that affect choices in the marketplace. On the other hand, laboratory settings allow researchers to control variables that cannot be controlled in the real world so that the experiment can focus on variables that may be significant for the success of a marketing strategy.

■ **field experiment** an experimental study conducted in a natural setting; allows a marketer to obtain a more direct test of marketing decisions than does a laboratory setting

A **field experiment** is an experimental study conducted in a natural setting, such as a supermarket or shopping center. This type of setting allows a marketer to obtain a more direct test of marketing decisions than does a laboratory setting. Although field experiments also involve manipulation of one or more independent variables under controlled conditions, researchers do not attempt to set up special conditions as they do in laboratory experiments.

Field experiments pose several limitations. They can be influenced by inadvertent events such as weather or major economic news. Additionally, carry-over effects of field experiments are impossible to avoid. That is, what participants have been asked to do in one time period will bias what they do in another time period. For example, respondents who are asked to evaluate new proposals for an organization's future advertisements may be prejudiced by their prior evaluation of competing advertisements. Respondents also may be unwilling to cooperate because they don't understand what role they play in an experiment. Finally, researchers can control only a small number of variables in field experiments. For example, they cannot control competitors' advertising or limit competitors' attempts to influence the results of an experiment. Competitors may use a number of tactics to foil field test marketing efforts, including increased advertising and special sales.

■ **secondary data** data from inside or outside an organization previously collected for some purpose other than the current investigation

Data Collection

The third step in the marketing research process involves collecting the data needed to solve the problem. Marketing researchers can use either of two types of data, secondary or primary. **Secondary data** are information from

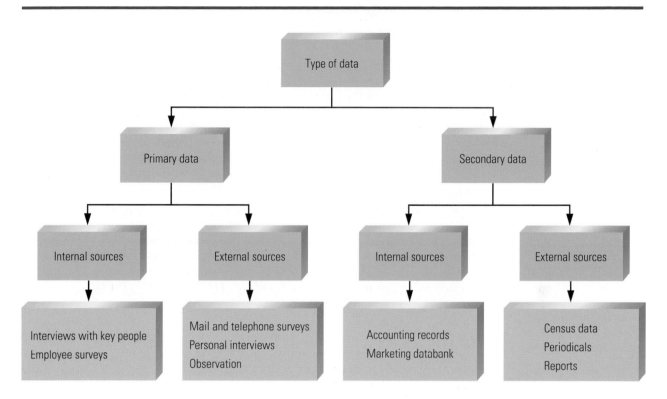

FIGURE 9.5
Sources of Primary and Secondary Data

inside or outside the organization previously collected for some purpose other than the current investigation. Usually such data are already available in private or public reports or have been collected and stored by the organization itself. Secondary data might include general market-share statistics provided by various data services, retail inventory levels, and consumers' purchasing behavior. Secondary data can be collected quickly and are usually less costly to obtain than primary data. In some cases, they can be used to solve the problem, which eliminates the need for primary data. In many cases, however, secondary data are not relevant to the information needs of the study, and their accuracy is sometimes questionable.

■ **primary data** data collected for a specific project

Primary data are collected for a specific project. These data must be gathered by observing phenomena or by surveying respondents directly. Consumer attitudes measured through a telephone survey are an example, as are responses to a courtesy card in a store or restaurant. Primary data are expensive and require technical knowledge to collect, but they may be the most relevant data for the information needs of the study. Figure 9.5 illustrates different sources of primary and secondary data. Most marketing researchers use a combination of both kinds.

Obtaining Secondary Data To study a marketing problem, a business may use data available in its marketing databank (such as sales records and research reports) as well as information from external sources. Table 9.2 lists several internal and external sources of secondary data.

TABLE 9.2
Examples of Secondary Data Sources

Internal Sources	External Sources
Company reports	**Government Publications**
Sales and cost data from accounting records	County, city, and state statistics
	Economic indicators
Cash-register data/scanner data	*Statistical Abstract of the United States*
	Survey of Current Business
Sales staff reports	**Census Data**
Previous research reports	Population statistics
VideOcarts	Retail trade statistics
	Service industry statistics
	Private Publications
	Moody's manuals
	Banks and Finance
	Municipals and Governments
	Public Utilities
	Transportation
	Standard & Poor's Registers
	Sales & Marketing Management's Survey of Buying Power (annual supplement)
	A Guide to Consumer Markets
	Editor and Publisher Market Guide

Businesses should begin all research efforts by collecting internal secondary data, which are the most readily available and least expensive data to obtain. Accounting records are an excellent source of secondary data. However, because the large volume of data collected by the accounting department does not automatically flow to the marketing area, accounting records are often overlooked. Such information, when collected systematically and continuously through a carefully planned marketing information system, is vital to the success of marketing efforts.

Secondary data are also found outside the organization in journals and government publications. Marketers may consult business publications such as *Business Week, Advertising Age, American Demographics, Sales & Marketing Management,* and *Industrial Marketing Management* for general information that is helpful in defining problems and developing hypotheses. *Survey of Buying Power* (the annual supplement to *Sales & Marketing Management*) contains sales data for major industries on a county-by-county basis. Federal government publications such as the *Census of Business, Census of Agriculture,* and *Current Population Reports* are other helpful sources of secondary data. There are literally hundreds of research firms that collect and sell data on consumer markets and trends. Market Development, Inc., for instance, specializes in research for the U.S. Hispanic market.

On-line computer searches can also be used to locate secondary data. There are currently hundreds of computerized databases that can be used to obtain marketing information. Many companies compile databases and sell access to them. A typical database may contain specific information about companies, industries, the economy, legislation, people patterns, products and brands, and many other types of information. The user pays for access to the data as well as for the information obtained. There are also charges for use of phone lines from the user's computer to the database, in addition to connecting charges and printing charges. Popular databases include Infotrack, Data-Star, and Dialog.

Obtaining Primary Data   Although secondary data are extremely useful for marketing researchers, such data are often insufficient to resolve marketing problems. For many research projects, primary data must be collected in addition to or instead of secondary data. Table 9.3 provides some examples of internal and external primary data. Primary data can be collected through surveys and observation. As shown in Figure 9.6, marketing research organizations such as Quality Controlled Services specialize in collecting primary data.

A **survey** is an interview conducted by mail, telephone, or in person. It is commonly used to collect data. The selection of a survey method depends on the nature of the problem, the data required to test the hypotheses, and the resources (such as finances and personnel) available to the researcher. Table 9.4 summarizes and compares the advantages and disadvantages of the three basic survey methods.

In a **mail survey,** researchers send questionnaires to respondents, who are encouraged to complete and return them. Mail surveys are used most often when the individuals selected for questioning are distributed over a wide area

■ **survey** an interview conducted by mail, telephone, or in person; commonly used to collect data

■ **mail survey** a survey in which questionnaires are sent to respondents, who are encouraged to complete and return them

TABLE 9.3
Examples of Primary Data

Internal Primary Data	External Primary Data
Employee job satisfaction	Product usage rates
Employee motivation	Brand loyalty
Employee performance	Media patterns
Employee turnover	Store loyalty
Employee absenteeism	Consumer attitudes toward spending, shopping, family, products
Employee job security	
Employee attitudes toward work, subordinates, superiors, customers	Consumer need for adventure
	Consumer lifestyles

FIGURE 9.6
Obtaining Primary Data
Quality Controlled Services uses a variety of techniques to collect primary data, including focus groups, mall intercepts, telephone interviews, and test kitchens.

Source: Quality Controlled Services. Photo: Dave Sucsy/FPG.

America's Data Collection Authority Lets You See What's Down The Road.

How do you avoid those potholes? Is that a fork in the road ahead, or a dead end?
When you need to anticipate what's down the road, you need accurate research data. QCS gives you a road map of consistent, dependable information.
And now, QCS offers complete project management services, to make your job even easier!

With nearly 40 focus group suites, over 15 mall intercept locations, 500+ telephone interviewing stations, and more than 25 test kitchens, QCS is national in scope, but neighborhood-friendly when it comes to personal service.
At QCS, you won't get lost—and you'll get where you're going a lot faster. Call QCS today for a bid on your next project.

800-325-3338

Quality Controlled Services®

ADFAX INQUIRY #1110

and funds for the survey are limited. For example, each year Whirlpool mails its Standardized Appliance Measurement Satisfaction (SAMS) survey to 180,000 households, asking them to rate all their appliances on many different characteristics. If a competitor's product ranks higher, Whirlpool engineers examine it to find out why.[12] A mail survey is the least expensive survey method as long as the rate of response (percentage of people completing and returning the survey) is high enough to produce reliable results. The main drawbacks of this method are the possibility that the response rate may be low and the possibility that the results may be inaccurate if respondents differ significantly from the population being surveyed.

Researchers can ensure a high response rate by offering respondents some motivation to return the questionnaires. The three techniques that have been most successful in achieving a good response rate include (1) getting a "foot in the door" by involving respondents in some small task (like a short telephone interview) before presenting them with the questionnaire, (2) sending a follow-up letter two or three weeks after mailing the questionnaire, and (3) offering a monetary incentive.[13]

---

[12] Sally Solo, "How to Listen to Consumers," *Fortune,* January 11, 1993, pp. 77–78.
[13] Francis J. Yammarino, Steven J. Skinner, and Terry L. Childers, "Understanding Mail Survey Response Behavior: A Meta-Analysis," *Public Opinion Quarterly,* Winter 1991.

Survey Characteristic	Mail Survey	Telephone Survey	Personal Interview Survey
Cost	Lowest	Moderate	Highest
Geographic distribution	Wide	Wide	Narrow
Flexibility of questioning	Lowest	Moderate	Highest
Interviewer bias	None (no interviewer)	Moderate	High
Speed of data collection	Slowest	Fastest	Moderate
Control over data	Lowest	Moderate	Highest
Response rate	Poor	Good	Excellent
Anonymity of respondent	High	Moderate	Low
Capacity for follow-up	High	High	Low
Length of questionnaire	Short	Moderate	Long

TABLE 9.4
Comparison of the Three Basic Survey Methods

■ **telephone survey** a survey in which interviewers solicit respondents' answers to a questionnaire over the telephone and record their answers

Although these techniques help boost response rates, they may introduce sample-composition bias. Sample-composition bias occurs when those responding to a survey differ in some important respect from those who do not respond to the survey. In other words, the techniques used to increase response rates may appeal to some members of the sample and alienate others, causing the results to be nonrepresentative of the population of interest.[14]

In a **telephone survey,** researchers call respondents to ask them questions from a questionnaire and record their answers. A telephone survey has some advantages over a mail survey. Generally, the rate of response is higher because it takes less effort to answer the telephone and talk than to fill out a questionnaire and return it. Also, a telephone survey can be conducted quickly if there are enough interviewers. Thus political candidates and businesses can use a telephone survey to get an immediate measurement of public reaction to an event. Additionally, the use of WATS (Wide Area Telecommunications Service) lines can reduce the cost of long-distance calling. Because of their speed and economy, telephone surveys have become a very popular method for collecting primary data.

The introduction and growth in the use of personal computers have led to an increase in computer-assisted telephone interviewing. This technique

[14]Charles D. Parker and Kevin F. McCrohan, "Increasing Mail Survey Response Rates: A Discussion of Methods and Induced Bias," in *Marketing: Theories and Concepts for an Era of Change,* ed. John Summey, R. Viswanathan, Ronald Taylor, and Karen Glynn (Southern Marketing Association, 1983), pp. 254–256.

combines questionnaires, data collection, and tabulations, and thus speeds up the data collection process. The printed questionnaire is replaced by the computer screen, and interviewers can enter the data into the computer while conducting the interview. Preliminary tabulations of the data can be calculated instantly.

Telephone interviews also have disadvantages. Researchers cannot use visual aids or observe respondents over the telephone. Telephone surveys are further limited because potential respondents may not be at home or may not have telephones. Many households are excluded from surveys because they have unlisted numbers or because the residents moved after the directory was published. If households with unlisted numbers are systematically excluded from the survey, the resulting sample will be somewhat older, more rural, more white, more educated, more retired, and more white collar than the universe of households with telephone service.[15] One firm, Walker: Research & Analysis, recently conducted an image study of telephone surveys and reported that time-strapped consumers are becoming tougher to reach because of inconvenient timing of calls and telephone answering machines. Difficulty in finding willing survey participants increases the cost of telephone interviews.[16]

Because of these disadvantages, researchers must make some adjustment for groups of respondents that may be undersampled because of a smaller-than-average percentage of telephone listings. Researchers may use random-digit dialing (adding random numbers to a certain telephone prefix) and plus-1 telephone sampling (adding the number 1 to the last digit of a number in the directory). These methods make it possible to dial any working number, even if it is not listed in a directory.

■ **personal interview survey** a face-to-face interview; the most flexible method for collecting primary data

The most flexible method of collecting primary data is the **personal interview survey,** a face-to-face interview. Researchers can incorporate audiovisual aids—such as pictures, products, diagrams, or prerecorded advertising copy—into a personal interview. For example, a researcher might ask a subject to respond to a demonstration of a new product along with possible packaging and advertising. The rapport established in a personal interview survey permits more in-depth interviewing, including probes, follow-up questions, or psychological tests. In addition, face-to-face interviews can yield more information because they are generally longer than other types of surveys. Finally, researchers can select respondents for a personal interview survey more carefully and explore the reasons for their failure to respond to certain questions.

There are three types of personal interviews. In a *shopping mall intercept interview,* researchers interview people passing by "intercept" points in a mall. This method of interviewing is a suitable substitute for telephone inter-

---

[15] Patricia E. Moberg, "Biases in Unlisted Phone Numbers," *Journal of Advertising Research,* August–September 1982, p. 55.
[16] Howard Schlossberg, "Latest Image Study Finds Mixed Results for Researchers," *Marketing News,* September 14, 1992, pp. 8–9.

viewing, given a comparable sample of respondents.[17] Survey questionnaires can also be displayed and completed on a personal computer once respondents are intercepted in the mall. In a *focus-group interview,* researchers observe a group interaction when participants are exposed to an idea or concept.[18] This type of interview is generally informal and conducted without a structured questionnaire. Focus-group interviews are useful in spotting consumer trends, which are good predictors of a new product's failure or success.[19] Marketers often use focus groups to help determine the tone and direction of their advertisements.[20] *In-home interviews* allow researchers to probe subjects to discover their true motivations and feelings. The in-depth nature of these interviews helps researchers discover "hot buttons" that elicit emotional responses in consumers.[21] Close to the Customer shows how focus groups can help firms get closer to children.

Careful construction of the questionnaire is crucial to the success of a survey. Survey questions must be designed to evoke answers that meet the data requirements of the study. The questions must be clear, easy to understand, and directed toward a specific objective. Researchers should not attempt to develop a questionnaire until the research problem has been defined because the composition of the questions depends on the nature of the problem and the level of detail required. Maintaining an unbiased, objective approach in constructing questions is very important.

Questionnaires can include open-ended, dichotomous (two choices), or multiple-choice questions. Examples of each are shown in Table 9.5. Most questionnaires use a combination of different types of questions. Table 9.6 is a sample questionnaire used to ask customers of an insurance company about their experience with drive-in claim centers.

■ **observation** a method of collecting primary data in which researchers record the overt behavior of respondents, taking note of physical conditions and events

In addition to surveys, primary data can be collected by observation. **Observation** involves recording the overt behavior of individuals and taking note of physical conditions and events. Researchers avoid direct contact with subjects; instead, they systematically observe their actions. For example, makers of children's toys, such as Hasbro and Fisher-Price, often bring children into "play labs" to observe which toys the children play with and how they play with them. Table 9.7 lists other ways in which firms might use observation to collect primary data.

Data gathered through observation may be biased if subjects are aware that they are being observed. Observers can sometimes be placed in a natural market environment, such as a grocery store, without prejudicing the actions of shoppers. However, when the presence of an observer is likely to bias the

[17] Alan J. Bush and A. Parasuraman, "Mall Intercept Versus Telephone-Interviewing Environment," *Journal of Advertising Research,* April–May 1985, p. 42.
[18] William D. Wells, "Group Interviewing," in *Handbook of Marketing Research,* ed. Robert Ferber (New York: McGraw-Hill, 1977), pp. 2–133.
[19] Judith Langer, "Researcher: Focus Groups Are the Best Way to Spot Trends," *Marketing News,* March 28, 1988, p. 16.
[20] Richard Grinchunas and Tony Siciliano, "Focus Groups Produce Verbatims, not Facts," *Marketing News,* January 4, 1993, p. FG-19.
[21] Hal Sokolow, "In-Depth Interviews Increasing in Importance," *Marketing News,* September 13, 1985, p. 26.

CLOSE TO THE CUSTOMER

Using Focus Groups to Get Opinions from Children

Many researchers agree that during the 1980s focus groups became one of the most widely used means of collecting primary data. The use of focus groups expanded from packaged goods companies to financial services, durable goods, and industrial products. As nonprofit organizations, the government, and industries that have been manufacturing-oriented recognize the need to emphasize the customer, continued growth in the use of focus groups is expected. The cost of conducting focus groups is also growing—today's average is $3,000 to $4,000 per group—as organizations using them demand more professionalism and the cost of obtaining group participants increases.

Nonetheless, organizations continue to use focus groups because they are an excellent means of obtaining valuable information from customers, including children. Cindy Clark, owner of C.D. Clark Ltd., a company that researches children, uses focus groups to get information from kids. According to Clark, "the biggest problem in marketing to children is that adults want easy answers and stereotypes, rather than to really understand kids." Unlike adults, children provide information not so much by what they say, but by how they say it. Focus groups enable the moderator to talk to children, get them involved, and learn about their likes and dislikes in products, brands, commercials, and so on.

The research industry has been influenced by changing family patterns. During the last ten years, children have become more independent at a younger age and are more involved in family purchase decisions. But getting them to give their opinions is not always easy. Nine- and 10-year-olds are most open with their opinions, whereas younger children are tied to their families and older children can be cynical and susceptible to peer pressure. Interviewing kids individually avoids this problem completely but also eliminates group interactions. Focus-group moderators often keep kids within a two-year age span and separate girls from boys.

Nickelodeon, the children's cable television network, has found one way to get opinions from children. The firm has set up one of the first consumer-product focus groups established over a computer network. The children—75 of them ages eight to 12 and living in areas from Boston to Los Angeles—can go online and chat informally with each other or Nickelodeon researchers. Though the system is not perfect, the children feel less peer pressure in this format and provide the network with valuable insights, something they might not do in person.

A lot can be learned from children. Most are aware of brand names and can explain commercials clearly. They like humor and they dislike numerous commercials. And since children do not always have the final say in purchasing decisions, NCM International, a premiums company, also conducts focus groups with mothers, who, after all, are people, too.

Sources: William M. Bulkeley, "Nickelodeon Sets Up Online Focus Group," *Wall Street Journal*, March 29, 1993, p. B4; Betsy Spethman, "Focus Groups Key to Reaching Kids," *Advertising Age*, February 10, 1992, pp. S-1, S-24; Thomas L. Greenbaum, "What the '90s Will Hold for Focus Group Research," *Advertising Age*, January 22, 1990, p. 26; and Betsy Spethman, "Researchers Report: Moms are People Too," *Advertising Age*, February 10, 1992, p. S-24.

TABLE 9.5
Sample Survey Questions

Type of Question	Example
Open-ended	How do you feel about lowering the legal age for alcoholic beverage consumption?
Dichotomous	What is your sex?
	Male _____ Female _____
Multiple-choice	To what age group do you belong?
	Below 18 _____
	18–20 _____
	21 and above _____

■ **mechanical observation device** a camera, recorder, counting machine, or equipment that records physiological changes in individuals

outcome or when human observation abilities are inadequate, a mechanical means of observation must be used. A **mechanical observation device** refers to a camera, recorder, counting machine, or other piece of equipment that records physiological changes in individuals. A check-out scanner, for instance, can record data on sales and consumers' purchase patterns.[22] Some marketing researchers are now purchasing such scanner data.

Sampling Investigating all members of a population is virtually impossible because the time and resources available for research are limited. Thus researchers obtain the needed amount of data through **sampling,** selecting a limited number of units to represent the characteristics of a total population. Sampling procedures are used to study human behavior as well as to estimate the likelihood of events not directly connected with an activity. Marketers can use the reactions of the representative sample to project the reactions of the total population. Of course, a poor sampling (of the wrong people or not enough of the right people) can lead to costly marketing mistakes, such as a product that won't sell.

■ **sampling** selecting a limited number of units to represent the characteristics of a total population

■ **population** all the elements, units, or individuals that are of interest to researchers for a specific study

A **population** is composed of all the elements, units, or individuals that are of interest to researchers for a specific study. If a survey is designed to determine the percentage of Americans that has purchased a specific brand of VCR, all consumers in the United States would constitute the population. A representative national sample of several thousand consumers would be selected in the survey to determine the percentage of buyers of the specified brand.

There are two broad types of sampling techniques: probability samples and nonprobability samples. With *probability samples,* each population element has

[22]Fitzhugh L. Carr, "Scanners in Marketing Research: Paradise (Almost)," *Marketing News,* January 4, 1985, pp. 1, 15.

TABLE 9.6
Sample Insurance-Claim Questionnaire

1. Did you recently visit one of our drive-in claim centers?

   Yes _____ (Please continue.)

   No _____ (Thank you.)

2. What sum did the insurance company estimate to be the approximate

   cost to repair your car? _____

3. Were you satisfied with the estimate?

   Yes _____

   No _____

   Why do you feel this way?

   _____

   _____

   _____

4. Which of the following methods of handling claims do you consider more fair?

   _____ One estimate at a drive-in center

   _____ Getting multiple estimates at repair shops

   _____ Don't know

■ **random sampling** basic probability sampling in which all units in a population have an equal and known chance of being selected

■ **stratified sampling** sampling in which researchers divide the population of interest into groups, or strata, according to a common characteristic and then conduct a random sample within each group

■ **area sampling** a variation of stratified sampling involving two stages: (1) dividing the population into geographic areas, such as blocks or census tracts, and (2) selecting units or individuals within the selected geographic areas for a random sample

a known chance of being selected. **Random sampling** is basic probability sampling; that is, all units in a population have a known and equal chance of being selected. In a game that uses dice, for example, a specific side of a die has a 1 in 6 probability of being thrown at any one time. Similarly, in a lottery, when all the ticket numbers are mixed up, each number should have an equal probability of being selected. Sample units are usually selected from a list of the population using a computer program that generates random samples.

In **stratified sampling,** researchers divide the population of interest into groups, or strata, according to a common characteristic, and then conduct a random sample within each group. Normally, samples are stratified when researchers believe that there may be variations among different types of respondents. For example, many political opinion surveys are stratified by sex, race, and age. Stratified sampling may reduce some of the errors that could occur in a simple random sample. By ensuring that each major group of the population receives its proportionate share of sample units, investigators avoid including too many or too few sample units from each stratum.

A variation of stratified sampling is **area sampling,** in which researchers (1) divide the population into geographic areas, such as blocks or census

TABLE 9.7
Behaviors That Can Be Observed to Provide Primary Data

Behavior	Observation
Physical actions	A large retailer observes the shopping patterns of customers.
Verbal behavior	An airline observes how customer service personnel handle complaints.
Expressive behavior	A sales organization evaluates salespeople's performance by observing facial expressions and noting tones of voice.
Location-specific activity	A fast-food franchise investigates the attractiveness of a new location by recording automobile and pedestrian traffic counts.
Time patterns	A supermarket observes how long customers have to wait in check-out lines.

■ **convenience sampling** a method of nonprobability sampling in which the researcher uses respondents who are readily available

■ **judgment sampling** a method of nonprobability sampling in which the researcher hand-picks participants for the study

■ **quota sampling** a form of nonprobability sampling in which the researcher selects a certain number or quota of respondents

tracts, and (2) select units or individuals within the selected geographic areas for a random sample. Researchers may choose every *n*th house or unit, or randomly select a given number of units or individuals from a total listing within the selected geographic areas. Area sampling may be used when a complete list of the population is not available.

Nonprobability samples involve the researcher's personal judgment; elements of the population do not have a known chance of being selected. **Convenience sampling** is a nonprobability sampling technique in which the researcher samples those elements of a population that are available. A researcher on the street questioning passers-by is an example of a convenience sample. With **judgment sampling** the researcher hand-picks participants for the study. This sampling technique is useful in exploratory research or when people with some unusual characteristic must be sampled. In testing a new allergy medication, a researcher might employ a judgment sample to select people with a certain allergy. Finally, **quota sampling** is nonprobability sampling in which the researcher selects a certain number or quota of respondents. For instance, a researcher may stand in a mall parking lot and interview owners of BMWs until he or she reaches a certain quota. Each of these sampling techniques involves personal judgment on the researcher's part.

Data Analysis and Interpretation

The fourth step in the marketing research process involves analyzing the collected data and interpreting the results (see Figure 9.7). First, the data must be tabulated. Simple frequency counts or percentages are often used in this step. If the researcher intends to apply the results to individual categories of the people or phenomena being studied, then cross-tabulation may be

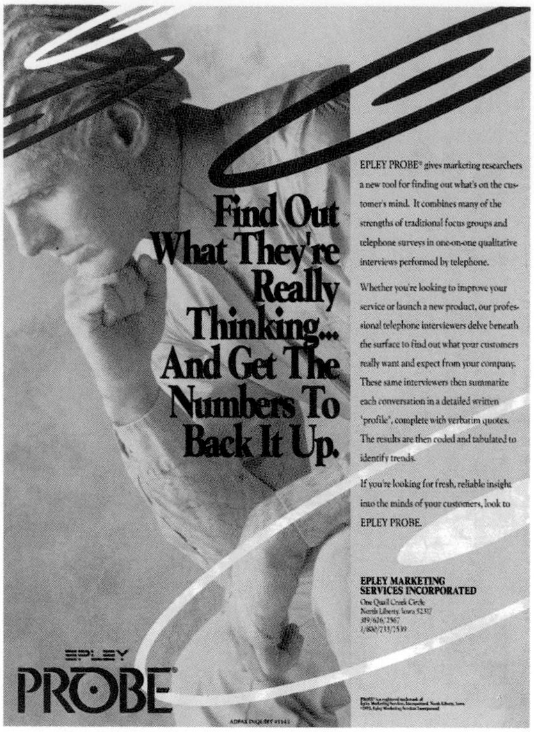

FIGURE 9.7
Data Analysis and Interpretation
Analyzing and interpreting data requires technical skills that may not be available in all organizations. Some companies, such as Epley Marketing Services, provide data analysis and interpretation services, in addition to data collection.

Source: Epley Marketing Services, Inc.

EPLEY PROBE® gives marketing researchers a new tool for finding out what's on the customer's mind. It combines many of the strengths of traditional focus groups and telephone surveys in one-on-one qualitative interviews performed by telephone.

Whether you're looking to improve your service or launch a new product, our professional telephone interviewers delve beneath the surface to find out what your customers really want and expect from your company. These same interviewers then summarize each conversation in a detailed written 'profile', complete with verbatim quotes. The results are then coded and tabulated to identify trends.

If you're looking for fresh, reliable insight into the minds of your customers, look to EPLEY PROBE.

Find Out What They're Really Thinking... And Get The Numbers To Back It Up.

EPLEY MARKETING SERVICES INCORPORATED

■ statistical interpretation analysis that focuses on what is average or what deviates from the average; shows how widely responses vary and how they are distributed in relation to the variable being measured

quite useful. For example, a cross-tabulation could show how men and women differ in some behavior, such as purchasing clothing.

After tabulation, the data must be analyzed. Researchers often use **statistical interpretation,** which concentrates on what is average or what deviates from the average. Statistical interpretation shows how widely responses vary and how they are distributed in relation to the variable being measured. When interpreting statistics, marketers rely on estimates of expected error or deviation from the true values of the population. The analysis and interpretation of data may lead researchers to accept or reject the hypothesis being studied. Like quota sampling, interpretation is an aspect of marketing research that calls for judgment or intuition.

Research Report

The last step in the marketing research process is reporting the research findings. Before writing the report, the marketer must take a clear, objective look at the findings to see how well the facts collected resolve the fundamental research problem defined in the first stage. In most cases, it is extremely unlikely that the research will provide everything needed to solve the research problem. This lack of completeness, together with the reasons for it, will probably have to be pointed out in the report.[23]

[23] George E. Breen and Albert B. Blankenship, "How to Present a Research Report That Gets Action," *Marketing Times,* March–April 1983, p. 33.

Research results are usually communicated in a formal written report. Because the purpose of the report is to enlighten the decision makers who will use the research findings, researchers must decide how much detail and supporting data to include in the report. Often the summary and recommendations are presented first, especially if decision makers may not have time to study how the results were obtained. A more detailed report does allow readers to analyze data and interpret recommendations because it describes the most important data gathered and the research methods employed.

When marketing decision makers have a basic understanding of research methods and procedures, they can integrate reported findings with their own personal experience. If marketers spot limitations in the research from reading the report, then personal experience may weigh more heavily in their decisions. However, the inability of some marketers to understand basic statistical assumptions and data-gathering procedures may cause them to misuse research findings. Thus report writers should consider the backgrounds and research abilities of those who will use the report to make decisions.

Most research studies follow a sequence of steps similar to those discussed in this chapter. However, researchers and managers sometimes have different views of their responsibilities in the marketing research process. Managers may think that they should define the problem and interpret the results and that researchers should be concerned only with research design and data collection. Many researchers believe that they should have a primary role in all stages.

INTERNATIONAL MARKETING RESEARCH

 When organizations operate in foreign markets, the need for marketing research is as important as it is in domestic markets. The tools and techniques we have discussed in this chapter also apply to research conducted in foreign markets. However, the complexity and diversity of some foreign environments make it difficult to conduct this kind of research. Several factors must be considered, including the broad scope of international marketing research, the availability of secondary data, and the problems of gathering primary data.

Scope of International Marketing Research

In many cases, the activities of international marketing researchers are much broader than those conducted in domestic markets. Researchers are responsible for obtaining data about consumer preferences, market potential, and other areas that domestic researchers examine. But much information specific to foreign market environments must also be obtained. In Chapter 5, we discussed various elements of the international marketing environments, including cultural, social, economic, political, legal, and technological forces, and how they impact international marketing decisions. We also noted the likelihood that the marketing mix may have to be adapted to foreign markets,

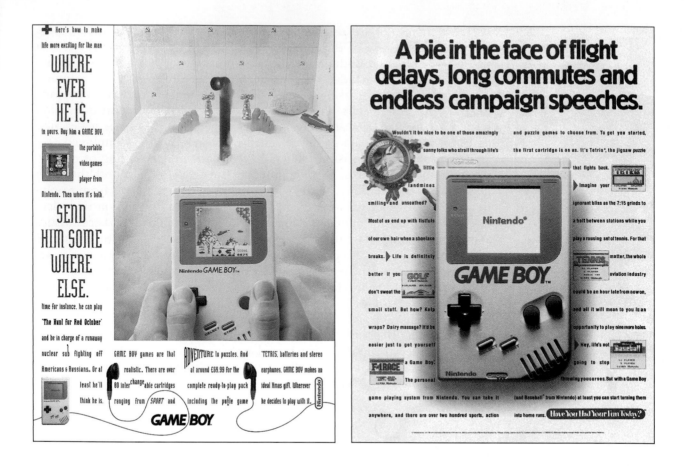

FIGURE 9.8
International Marketing Research
International marketing research can help companies tailor their product promotion to markets in different countries. These two advertisements show how Nintendo uses different types of advertisements to promote their Game Boy in Britain (left) and the United States (right).

Source: Courtesy of Nintendo of America, Inc. and Nintendo of Europe GmbH.

as shown in Figure 9.8. Researchers are expected to provide the information needed to analyze these issues.

The breadth of information needs influences international marketing research activities in several ways. Because of the large amount of information needed, the research is likely to cost more than domestic research. Very often, new studies have to be conducted for each market (or country) because data from one market are of little value in assessing opportunities in another. The research design may also have to be modified for different countries. For example, telephone surveys cannot be used in countries in which many consumers do not have phones or in cultures where such interviews are unacceptable. Also, firms may not be able to obtain accurate results when questioning people about goods or services that have never been available to them.

Secondary Data

Although a great amount of secondary data exists for domestic markets, such data are not readily available in foreign markets. This is especially true in less developed countries, where secondary data are either nonexistent or inaccurate or incomplete. For instance, economic data from some foreign countries often present an overly optimistic picture, reflecting national pride or political motivation to make the country look good. Finally, the secondary data may not be available in a relevant form. For example, a domestic firm may be interested in data pertaining to a certain market or region, but the data are available only for an entire country.

Despite these limitations, several sources of secondary data for international markets are available. The U.S. government publishes a variety of reports and data on international markets, primarily through the Department of Commerce and one of its branches, the International Trade Association. Reports include data on exports, international economic indicators, market share, and foreign market opportunities. International organizations such as the United Nations and multinational market groups such as the European Community also publish information about international markets. A number of research agencies also specialize in collecting and selling information about foreign markets.

Primary Data

Given the limitations of secondary data on foreign markets, international marketing researchers are often faced with collecting primary data. The cost of collecting these data is especially high. In many cases, there are no research firms or data collection vendors in foreign countries. This means the domestic firm must invest large sums of money training interviewers or hiring a research consulting firm to collect data.

Cultural differences between domestic and foreign markets also influence the collection of primary data. Businesses and residents of some countries are simply not willing to respond to questionnaires, nor will they agree to be interviewed. Some foreign businesses may actually fear that responding to a questionnaire from a U.S. firm may be bad business. In some instances, respondents find it difficult to respond to questions about products they have never seen or experienced. And in some cases, observation may be more useful than questionnaires. In Japan, where the population is more homogeneous than in many countries, many firms prefer to observe people to determine their shopping patterns, what goods they possess, and how they use them; the Japanese tend to mistrust hard data.[24] Researchers must take these differences into consideration when collecting primary data.

The most common problem in collecting primary data on foreign markets is the language difference. Because of differences in culture and idiom, direct translations are not equivalent. But researchers can use a bilingual translator who is aware of these differences and can make the necessary changes. In countries with low literacy rates, written questionnaires cannot be used.

Sampling also poses problems when collecting primary data. The researcher may not have access to adequate lists and characteristics of the population. Furthermore, various data collection techniques may be limited. For

[24]Jeff Shear, "Japanese Marketing Strategy Makes 'the Customer King,'" *Insight,* March 5, 1990, pp. 38–39.

instance, lack of mailing lists and inferior postal services make it impossible to conduct mail surveys. When lists are not available, the only alternative may be to use a nonprobability sampling technique.

ETHICS IN MARKETING RESEARCH

An important issue in marketing research is ethics. Acceptable standards of marketing research are essential for maintaining the professional image of marketing researchers. Common examples of unethical research practices include deception, invasion of privacy, disguising sales efforts as marketing research, and reporting faulty conclusions.

Several controversies have turned the spotlight on marketing research ethics. Beecham Products sued the research company Yankelovich Clancy Shulman for $24 million, the sum Beecham claimed it lost in launching the laundry product Delicare, because of "significant errors" in the research company's forecasts.[25] Although Beecham settled this malpractice suit out of court (details of the settlement were not released), experts fear such lawsuits will increase in the future.[26] Midwest Communications, Inc., parent company of WCCO-TV in Minneapolis, sued a marketing research firm and another television station. It charged that a survey conducted during a Nielsen rating period was an attempt to manipulate the ratings.[27] (A.C. Nielsen Co. rates television programs.) And consider this: A recent poll reported that 32 percent of the scientists surveyed believe that researchers they know falsify data.[28]

Several other ethical problems confront the research industry. One is invasion of privacy. Because firms have shared customer information with one another, and because consumers have been bombarded with surveys and telephone solicitations, many new privacy laws have been introduced.[29] Typical lists offered for rent or sale include the following:

- 2.4 million people who ordered by phone using a credit card
- 11 million people who recently moved
- 140,426 grandparents who bought Johnson & Johnson child development toys
- 95,293 people who visited the Basketball Hall of Fame and bought a souvenir at the novelty shop[30]

[25]"The Cost of Research 'Malpractice,'" *Advertising Age,* July 20, 1987, p. 16.
[26]Ted Knutson, "Marketing Malpractice Causes Concern," *Marketing News,* Oct. 10, 1988, pp. 1, 7.
[27]Gregg Cebrzynski, "TV Stations Sues over Alleged 'Phony' Survey," *Marketing News,* August 28, 1987, p. 1.
[28]"Poll: 32% of Scientists Think Others Falsify Data," Lexington, Ky. *Herald-Leader,* August 30, 1987, p. A7.
[29]Jack Honomichl, "It Wasn't a Very Good Year, but Luckily We Don't Sell Cars," *Marketing News,* January 6, 1992, pp. 16, 29.
[30]Robert S. Boyd, "Deprived of Privacy," Lexington, Ky. *Herald-Leader,* July 8, 1990, pp. F1, F6.

Almost anything consumers do today lands their names on some organization's list. This situation threatens legitimate organizations that are developing databases to better serve their customers. It also encourages consumers to request unlisted telephone numbers and ignore mail, and could eventually diminish an organization's ability to develop useful databases. According to Pat Heinzman, director of marketing and information services for Lord Sullivan & Yodes, Columbus, Ohio, "It doesn't bother me that people know I live in a suburb of Columbus, Ohio, and have X number of kids. It bothers me that these people know the names of my wife and kids and where they go to school."[31] This statement illustrates the fine line between collecting information and invading privacy.

Another problem is that a growing number of studies described as "independent" are actually sponsored by companies or groups with an interest—usually financial—in the outcome. And some of the research used to support products and positions in advertisements has also been called into question. At times study questions are asked in such a way that the response is predictable. For example, when Levi Strauss asked college students which clothes would be most popular during one school year, 90 percent said Levi's 501 jeans—the only jeans on the list. Black Flag put the following question on a survey: "A roach disk . . . poisons a roach slowly. The dying roach returns to the nest and after it dies is eaten by other roaches. In turn, these roaches become poisoned and die. How effective do you think this type of product would be in killing roaches?"[32] Of course, the vast majority—79 percent—of respondents said it would be effective. A flawed questionnaire does not yield valid and reliable results.

Controversies such as these underlie the importance of emphasizing marketing research ethics. Most studies of ethics in marketing research have focused on either defining the responsibilities of researchers to clients and respondents or exploring whether certain marketing research practices are perceived as ethical or unethical. For example, one study revealed that 61 percent of the marketing researchers surveyed said they have many opportunities to engage in unethical behavior.[33] Another study found that opportunity and the perceived behavior of peers and superiors are major determinants of ethical behavior.[34]

Enforcing ethical standards is not easy. However, codes of ethics can lay the foundation for ethical conduct. A recent study reported that the existence and enforcement of codes of ethics are associated with higher levels of ethical behavior on the part of marketing researchers.[35] The American Marketing Association and the Marketing Research Association both have codes to promote marketing research ethics.

[31] Melanie Rigney, "Too Close for Comfort, Execs Warn," *Advertising Age,* Jan. 13, 1992, p. 31.
[32] Cynthia Crossen, "Studies Galore Support Products and Positions, but Are They Reliable?" *Wall Street Journal,* November 14, 1991, pp. A1, A7.
[33] Shelby D. Hunt, Lawrence B. Chonko, and James B. Wilcox, "Ethical Problems of Marketing Researchers," *Journal of Marketing Research,* August 1984, pp. 309–324.
[34] O.C. Ferrell and Larry Gresham, "A Contingency Framework of Ethical Decision Making," *Journal of Marketing,* Summer 1985, p. 89.
[35] O.C. Ferrell and Steven J. Skinner, "Ethical Behavior and Bureaucratic Structure in Marketing Research Organizations," *Journal of Marketing Research,* February 1988, pp. 103–109.

SUMMARY

Marketing research and information systems are essential for implementing the marketing concept. The marketing information system (MIS) is a program for managing and organizing information gathered from inside and outside the organization. Marketing research is the collection, analysis, and interpretation of data for guiding marketing decisions. MIS focuses on data storage, retrieval, and classification; marketing research is characterized by in-depth analysis of major problems or issues. Organizations store data in their marketing databanks. Marketing research and information systems help improve a marketer's ability to make decisions.

The five steps used in conducting marketing research are problem definition, research design, data collection, data analysis and interpretation, and the research report.

Problem definition involves recognizing a problem, usually a deviation from normal operations. However, conducting research after a problem is detected does not guarantee that the problem can be resolved. Research, therefore, is a continuous function in many firms.

Research design is an overall plan for conducting the research study. In exploratory studies, marketers review existing information on the problem or investigate it informally. Descriptive studies are used to understand the characteristics of certain phenomena underlying a particular problem. Experimental studies are used to investigate relationships. Experimentation involves manipulating an independent variable and measuring its effect on a dependent variable while controlling all other variables. Experiments can be conducted in the laboratory or in the field.

Data collection is the process of obtaining the information needed to solve the research problem. Secondary data already exist in the organization's databanks or in sources outside the organization; primary data are collected specifically for the research study. Data collection generally begins by obtaining internal secondary data. Primary data can be collected through surveys and observation. Surveys are interviews conducted by mail, by telephone, or in person. Observation involves recording the overt behavior of respondents.

Sampling is the selection of a limited number of units to represent the characteristics of a total population. Sampling procedures are used to study human behavior as well as to estimate the likelihood of events not directly connected with an activity. With probability samples, each population element has a known chance of being selected. Nonprobability samples involve personal judgment on the part of the researcher.

Once the data have been collected, marketers must tabulate and analyze the data and interpret the results. Statistical interpretation focuses on what is average or what deviates from the average.

The final stage of the marketing research process is reporting the findings. A report must present a clear, objective discussion of the results of the study.

Marketing research is needed by firms operating in foreign markets. The complexity and diversity of some foreign environments makes it difficult to conduct international marketing research. In many cases, international marketing research is much broader than research conducted in domestic markets, which makes it more expensive. Secondary data are less readily available in many foreign markets. Finally, the cost of collecting primary data in foreign markets is usually quite high, and data collection is heavily influenced by cultural differences, sampling problems, and language differences.

Acceptable standards of marketing research are essential for maintaining the professional image of marketing researchers. Enforcing ethical standards is not easy. However, codes of ethics, especially when enforced, appear to be effective in encouraging ethical behavior in marketing researchers.

KEY TERMS

marketing information system
  (MIS)
marketing research
marketing databank
problem definition
research design
exploratory study
hypothesis
descriptive study
experimental study
experimentation
independent variable
dependent variable
laboratory experiment
field experiment
secondary data

primary data
survey
mail survey
telephone survey
personal interview survey
observation
mechanical observation device
sampling
population
random sampling
stratified sampling
area sampling
convenience sampling
judgment sampling
quota sampling
statistical interpretation

QUESTIONS FOR DISCUSSION AND REVIEW

1. Why should firms conduct marketing research?
2. What is the relationship between an organization's MIS and its marketing research activities?
3. What is an example of a research problem?
4. Under what conditions would a firm employ an exploratory study? A descriptive study?
5. In what ways do experimental studies differ from exploratory and descriptive studies?
6. Distinguish between secondary and primary data. Give some examples of each.
7. How can a researcher encourage response to a mail survey?

8. What are some of the limitations of telephone surveys?

9. In what situations would observations be used to collect information for a research study?

10. What is the major benefit of a random sample? Give an example of a situation in which a researcher would want to use stratified sampling.

11. How does international marketing research differ from marketing research?

12. Discess the problems associated with obtaining secondary and primary data in foreign markets.

13. What is the role of ethics in marketing research? How can ethical standards be enforced?

CASES

9.1   THE JACKSONVILLE SYMPHONY ORCHESTRA

All types of organizations rely on marketing research to make decisions, even some that you might not expect. After conducting a large-scale marketing survey, the Jacksonville (Florida) Symphony Orchestra recently undertook a marketing program to attract younger audiences to performances.

Historically, symphony orchestras have not relied heavily on marketing. The little marketing they have done has been aimed at a fairly narrow market segment. The Jacksonville Symphony Orchestra decided to market itself like a packaged good, and thus undertook a marketing research program to broaden its base of support and increase ticket sales.

The orchestra conducted a two-phased research study. The first phase consisted of three focus-group interviews: one with current subscribers, one with former subscribers, and one with future prospects. The interviews were designed to reveal attitudes and lifestyle activities of the three focus groups. The orchestra hoped that this information would help explore entertainment alternatives and find out what future audiences want.

The second phase of the research involved a telephone survey of 502 Jacksonville consumers: 101 randomly selected from the current subscriber list, 101 randomly selected from the lapsed subscriber list, and 300 randomly selected from the telephone directory and screened to include those who listen to classical music or pops-style music. Developed from issues identified through the focus-group interviews, the telephone survey asked respondents about programming, location of events, and appearances by guest artists. It also asked them why they subscribe to the symphony, why they failed to renew their subscription, or what would encourage them to become subscribers.

The results of the survey indicated that the new subscribers the orchestra wanted to attract were younger and had lower median incomes than current subscribers. About 70 percent of the current subscribers were 45 or older, whereas 45 percent of the future prospects were younger than 45. Approximately 40 percent of the current subscribers had median family incomes of $75,000 or more, but only 24 percent of the prospects were in that income range.

Accordingly, the orchestra launched a new marketing program aimed at younger audiences. To increase awareness of its activities, it used aggressive promotion methods, such as billboards, mail flyers, and television advertisements, emphasizing that going to the symphony can be fun, romantic, and sensual. To attract new customers, the orchestra scheduled special events, including guest appearances by artists such as Luciano Pavarotti and Itzhak Perlman.

From all indications, the marketing program was a success. Awareness of the Jacksonville Symphony Orchestra increased dramatically; more important, ticket sales nearly doubled the following season.

Questions for Discussion

1. Evaluate the design of the research study conducted by the Jacksonville Symphony Orchestra.

2. What type of sample was used?

3. Are you surprised that an organization like an orchestra relies on marketing research? Can you think of some similar organizations in your community that could benefit from marketing research?

Based on information from Tracy A. LaFlamme, "Symphony Strikes a Note for Research as It Prepares to Launch a New Season," *Marketing News,* August 29, 1988, p. 12; Monica Gonzales, "Beethoven for Boomers," *American Demographics,* June 1988, p. 19; Ann Hyman, "JSO Tailors Its Season to Patrons," *Florida Times-Union,* July 31, 1988, pp. E1–E2; and correspondence with Lynda Erwin, Development Director, Jacksonville Symphony Orchestra.

9.2   INTERNATIONAL QUALITY STUDY OF CUSTOMER FOCUS

Quality improvement is a fundamental business strategy of the 1990s. No business will survive in the global marketplace without it. The American Quality Foundation and Ernst & Young conducted the International Quality Study (IQS) to provide a global benchmark for quality progress. The IQS addressed many different aspects of quality, including customer focus.

Over five hundred companies in three continents participated in the IQS. Data were collected through surveys mailed to executives and managers; 84 percent of the firms invited to participate in the study chose to do so. The surveys took a team of up to five executives and managers from each participating business about 16 hours to complete. Management practices were examined in four countries (Canada, Germany, Japan, and the United States) within four industries (automotive, banking, computers, and health care). Initially, focus groups were conducted with representatives from each industry, which formed the international basis for developing the questionnaire.

A major aspect of the IQS was customer focus—a specific process for gathering customer information and responding to customer needs. Customers seek one another out, talk to each other, and share information. Businesses that talk to customers are better able to respond to their needs for service and quality. Without a customer focus, there is a major gap in a business's ability to build quality into its offerings.

To measure customer focus, study participants were asked several questions, including:

- How important are customer satisfaction measures in your business's strategic planning process?
- How often are customer expectations translated into the design of new products or services by the department developing them?
- How important is the use of technology for meeting customer expectations?

The results suggest that about 40 percent of the businesses in Canada, Japan, and the United States place primary emphasis on customer satisfaction in the strategic planning process; in Germany, roughly half as many do. Between 20 and 30 percent of businesses in Canada, the United States, and Germany feel customer satisfaction should play a minor role in the planning process; only 5 percent of the businesses in Japan feel the role is minor. Thus, despite claims of the importance of customer satisfaction, the findings suggest that current planning practices in countries other than Japan do not support those claims.

German businesses are twice as likely (40 percent of the time) as businesses in Canada (14 percent) and the United States (22 percent) to include customer expectations over 90 percent of the time in developing new goods and services. Japanese businesses are three times as likely (58 percent of the time) to do so. Incorporating customer expectations into new product development can give firms a significant competitive advantage. Currently, Japan and Germany have strongly adopted this practice.

Businesses in all four countries are increasingly using technology in meeting customer expectations. About half of the Japanese businesses place primary emphasis on using technology to meet customer expectations; roughly one third for Canada and Germany; and about one fifth for the United States. However, the United States is planning the largest increase of the four countries (from 22 percent to 53 percent) in the use of technology to meet customer expectations.

Questions for Discussion

1. What is the research problem being addressed in the International Quality Study (IQS)?
2. What type of research design was used for the IQS?
3. How was customer focus measured? Do you feel this was a valid and reliable measure?
4. What are some of the implications from the results of the study?

Based on information from American Quality Foundation and Ernst & Young, *International Quality Study* (Cleveland, Ohio: American Quality Foundation and Ernst & Young, 1991).

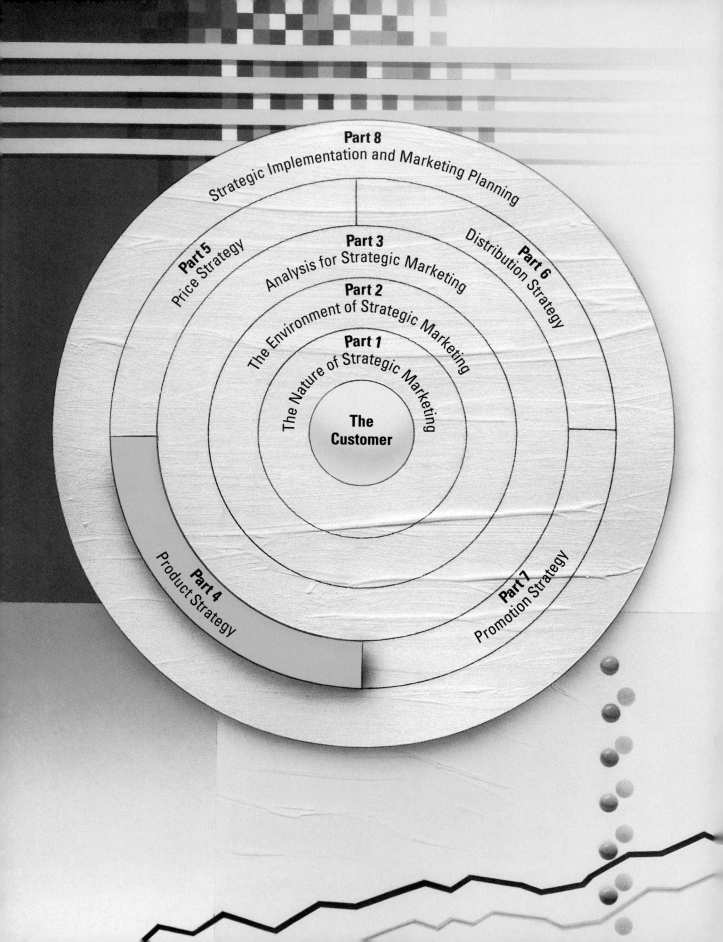

Part 8
Strategic Implementation and Marketing Planning

Part 5
Price Strategy

Part 3
Analysis for Strategic Marketing

Distribution Strategy
Part 6

Part 2
The Environment of Strategic Marketing

Part 1
The Nature of Strategic Marketing

The Customer

Part 4
Product Strategy

Part 7
Promotion Strategy

Product Strategy

Product Concepts

OBJECTIVES

● To identify the different tangible and intangible attributes that make up a product.

● To describe how products are classified.

● To discuss how product mix and product line decisions influence a firm's product offerings.

● To explain the concept of the product life cycle and how it can be used by organizations.

● To define the terms brand, brand name, brand mark, and trademark, and discuss how branding is used.

● To evaluate the importance of a product's packaging.

● To explain how labeling is used to help market products and meet legal requirements.

● To discuss the importance of product quality and supportive services.

● To describe the unique characteristics of products for organizational markets.

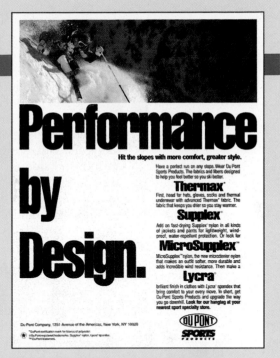

In 1926, when pure research was a rare phenomenon, Du Pont, an explosives and gunpowder manufacturer, decided to open a chemistry laboratory. At the time, General Electric Co. had one of the only pure research laboratories in the United States. To head the laboratory, Du Pont hired Wallace Hume Carothers, a Harvard University chemist.

Through his experimental work with complex molecules known as polymers, Carothers created the first synthetic rubber, Neoprene, which today is employed in industry because of its resistance to chemicals. In 1930, Carothers invented another substance—made entirely from chemicals found in coal, water, and air— that could be formed into fibers characterized by elasticity and strength. The substance, which later came to be known as nylon, took Carothers and his assistants seven more years to perfect. In April 1937, Du Pont patented the miracle synthetic. Carothers, however, never lived to see its success. Despite his pioneering work in the polymer sciences, he was convinced he was a failure and committed suicide three weeks later.

Carothers was obviously no failure. When it was introduced to the market, nylon hosiery immediately displaced baggy cotton and pricey silk stockings—the only choices women had. It created chaos in department stores, where women lined up and fought over it, and spurred other manufacturers to set up their own research laboratories. After two years of brainstorming, Du Pont officials came up with the name *nylon* (from "no run"), but they didn't choose to register it as a trademark. As a result, more than 50 years later, *nylon* is still used as a generic term.

Today, Du Pont is trying to reinvent itself. The firm is striving to create a new culture driven by profits, not just research. Sales and earnings fell in 1991; revenues dropped $1.35 billion, to $38.7 billion; and earnings plunged 39 percent, to $1.4 billion—the lowest since 1985. CEO Edgar Woolard, Jr., believes that improvements in the way Du Pont develops new products and the way it makes mainstays like nylon could result in huge savings. Woolard thinks the major problem is that the company takes too long to "convert research into products that can benefit our customers." Mounting competition is forcing Du Pont to deliver both new and existing products faster and more efficiently. So Woolard has shifted 30 percent of the firm's research budget, about $400 million a year, toward speeding products to customers.[1] ●

[1] Based on information from Joseph Weber, "DuPont's Trailblazer Wants to Get out of the Woods," *Business Week,* August 31, 1992, pp. 70–71; Scott McMurray, "DuPont Tries to Make Its Research Wizardry Serve the Bottom Line," *Wall Street Journal,* March 27, 1992, pp. A1, A4; and Kevin Maney, "Nylon: 'The Fabric of Everyday Life,'" *USA Today,* January 12, 1988, pp. 1B–2B.

Many products never reach their fiftieth anniversary. If Du Pont were still producing nylon for the sole purpose of making women's stockings, the firm would probably be defunct today. By exploring new markets and developing new products, the nylon industry has grown over the years. But as the opening feature illustrates, even a history of dominating an industry doesn't make a firm immune from competition. Now Du Pont aims to grow by introducing new products faster and more efficiently. Such successful product development and growth require an understanding of basic marketing and product concepts.

PRODUCT DEFINED

In Chapter 1, we define *product* as any good, service, or idea that satisfies a need or want and can be offered in an exchange. Figure 10.1 provides examples of both profit-oriented and nonprofit-oriented products. A *good* is a tangible object, such as this textbook. For many years, the United States has had a goods-oriented economy, mass-producing various products for worldwide consumption. A *service* is intangible yet provides direct benefits to customers. Haircuts, health care, copy services, and overnight mail delivery are examples. Services are critical as the United States moves from a product economy to a service economy. Today, more people are employed in the service sector than in any other sector of our economy.[2] An *idea* is a philosophy or concept, such as the DARE drug education program for children or a politician's campaign platform. Nonprofit organizations often market ideas. Chapter 11 discusses services and nonprofit organizations in greater detail.

When consumers purchase a product, they buy not only its tangible features but also its intangible attributes, including its functional, social, and psychological benefits.[3] For example, although an automobile is a tangible good, it also includes such intangible attributes as the warranty, customer service, or perception of the vehicle's quality. Credit is another intangible product, but tangible cues, such as American Express Company's use of famous card members in its advertisements, can make credit more tangible to the consumer.

Products are often a firm's most important links with consumers. They are critical to the achievement of organizational objectives.[4] The product is a key variable in the marketing mix—promotion, distribution, and price decisions must be coordinated with product decisions. If a company's products do not meet the desires and needs of its customers, the company will fail. If it identifies customer needs and wants and develops products that

---

[2]Howard Banks, "What's Ahead for Business," *Forbes,* May 25, 1992, p. 37.
[3]Leonard L. Berry, "Services Marketing Is Different," *Business,* May–June 1980, pp. 26–27.
[4]Glen L. Urban, John R. Hauser, and Nikhilesh Dholakia, *Essentials of New Product Management* (Englewood Cliffs, N.J.: Prentice-Hall, 1987), p. 1.

FIGURE 10.1
Examples of Products

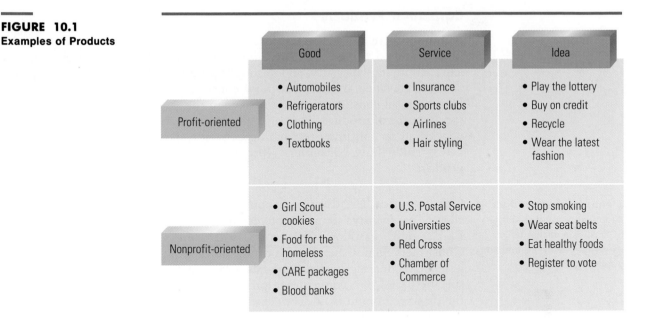

	Good	Service	Idea
Profit-oriented	• Automobiles • Refrigerators • Clothing • Textbooks	• Insurance • Sports clubs • Airlines • Hair styling	• Play the lottery • Buy on credit • Recycle • Wear the latest fashion
Nonprofit-oriented	• Girl Scout cookies • Food for the homeless • CARE packages • Blood banks	• U.S. Postal Service • Universities • Red Cross • Chamber of Commerce	• Stop smoking • Wear seat belts • Eat healthy foods • Register to vote

satisfy them, it is more likely to succeed. For instance, CPC International manufactures Hellmann's mayonnaise, Mazola corn oil, and Skippy peanut butter, all high in fat. The firm recently introduced a line of "wholesome" foods like Roasted Honey Nut Skippy, a blend of high-fat peanut butter and naturally sweet honey. The line was designed to appeal to people who want healthy foods but who are turned off by the taste of existing "lite" brands.[5] New products must continually be developed to satisfy and even to anticipate consumers' changing needs.

PRODUCT CLASSIFICATIONS

■ **consumer product**
a product purchased for personal and family consumption

■ **industrial product**
a product bought for use in the production of other products or in an organization's operations

Products are generally classified into two broad categories on the basis of consumers' intentions.[6] A product purchased for personal and family consumption is a **consumer product;** a product bought for use in the production of other products or in an organization's operations is an **industrial product.** Businesses buy products to satisfy the needs of their organizations; consumers buy products to satisfy personal needs. Thus the intended or ultimate use of the product determines whether a product is classified as a consumer or an industrial product. Both consumer and industrial products are broken down into additional classifications.

[5] Suein L. Hwang, "Its Big Brands Long Taunted as Fatty, CPC Tries a More 'Wholesome' Approach," *Wall Street Journal,* April 2, 1992, pp. B1, B3.
[6] Yorum J. Wind, *Product Policy: Concepts, Methods and Strategy* (Reading, Mass.: Addison-Wesley, 1982), p. 67.

Consumer Products

Although there are several approaches to classifying consumer products, the most widely accepted approach divides them into four categories: convenience, shopping, specialty, and unsought products. With this approach, products are classified according to how consumers go about purchasing them. However, all consumers do not behave in the same way when purchasing a specific type of product. Thus a single product can fit into all four categories, depending on consumer purchasing behavior. To reduce this problem, marketers study how consumers *generally* behave when purchasing a specific product.

■ **convenience product**
a frequently purchased, inexpensive item that buyers spend little effort to find and purchase

Convenience Products   A **convenience product** is a frequently purchased, inexpensive item that buyers spend little effort to find and purchase. Bread, milk, gasoline, newspapers, soft drinks, and candy are examples. Consumers do not spend much time planning the purchase of a convenience item or comparing available brands and sellers. A consumer who prefers a specific brand of a convenience product will willingly accept a substitute if the preferred brand is not conveniently available.

Classifying a product as a convenience product influences the marketing strategy for the product. Convenience products are sold in many retail outlets. Because sellers experience rapid turnover of these products, their gross margins per unit can be relatively low. As a result, sellers are reluctant to promote convenience products such as Dr Pepper and Wonder Bread. Therefore, producers of those products must promote them in the form of product advertising or packaging. Packaging is an important form of promotion for convenience products because most of them are available only on a self-service basis at the retail level or through vending machines.

■ **shopping product**
a product (such as an appliance, furniture, or clothing) that consumers are willing to spend more effort to plan for and purchase

Shopping Products   Consumers are willing to spend more effort to plan for and purchase a **shopping product,** such as an appliance, furniture, clothing, a bicycle, or a stereo. Buyers spend considerable time comparing brands and sellers with respect to price, product features, quality, service, and warranty. Although shopping products are more expensive than convenience products, most buyers of shopping products are not particularly brand loyal.

Producers of shopping products should consider several things when devising a marketing strategy. Shopping products are sold in fewer retail outlets than are convenience products. They generally last longer and are purchased less frequently. Thus sellers experience lower inventory turnover and expect to earn higher gross margins. Shopping products may require large sums of money to be spent for personal selling and advertising (see Figure 10.2). The producer and intermediaries (resellers) usually cooperate with one another in providing parts and repair services and in performing promotional activities.

■ **specialty product**
a product with one or more unique characteristics that buyers are willing to spend considerable time and effort to purchase

Specialty Products   A **specialty product** is a product with one or more unique characteristics that a group of buyers is willing to spend considerable time and effort to purchase. Consumers carefully plan the purchase of a specialty product because they know exactly what they want and will not accept a substitute. An original painting, a designer evening dress, and a

FIGURE 10.2
Shopping Products
Consumers spend more effort to purchase shopping products and firms allocate more resources to market them. Samsung spends a great deal of money to promote the features as well as the price of its portable CD player.

Source: Courtesy Samsung Electronics (UK) Ltd.

luxury yacht are examples of specialty products. Consumers do not evaluate alternatives when searching for specialty products. They are extremely brand loyal and are concerned primarily with finding an outlet that has the preselected product available.

Specialty products affect marketing decisions in several ways. They are often distributed through a limited number of outlets or sometimes through just one outlet. Also, since specialty products are purchased infrequently, they result in lower inventory turnover and thus require relatively high gross margins and consequently high prices.

■ **unsought product**
a product purchased as a result of the sudden occurrence of a problem or in response to aggressive selling tactics that result in a sale that otherwise would not take place

Unsought Products   An **unsought product** is purchased as a result of the sudden occurrence of a problem or in response to aggressive selling tactics that result in a sale that otherwise would not take place. Consumers generally do not think of buying unsought products on a regular basis. Some classic examples of these products include emergency automobile repairs, replacement appliances, and cemetery plots. Marketers should stress advertising and personal selling in marketing unsought products.

Industrial Products

Organizational buyers are more concerned with the functional characteristics of industrial products than with the psychological rewards associated with consumer products. On the basis of their characteristics and intended uses, industrial products can be classified into seven categories: raw materials, capital equipment, accessory equipment, component parts, process materials, supplies, and services.[7]

[7]Frederick E. Webster, Jr., *Industrial Marketing Strategy,* 2nd ed. (New York: John Wiley, 1984), pp. 5–8.

■ **raw material** a basic good that actually becomes part of a physical product

■ **capital equipment** the large tools and machines used in a production process

■ **accessory equipment** equipment that is used in production or office activities but does not become part of the final physical product being manufactured

■ **component part** a finished item or an item that needs little processing before becoming part of the physical product being manufactured

■ **process material** material that is used directly in the production of other products; unlike a component part, is not readily distinguishable from the product

■ **supply** something that does not become part of a finished product but does expedite production and operations

Raw Materials   A **raw material** is a basic good that actually becomes part of a physical product. Examples include minerals, plastics, fabrics, chemicals, and agricultural products. Organizations typically purchase raw materials in large quantities according to grades and specifications. The raw material Unitane is a chemical pigment used as a whitening agent in such products as paint coatings, paper, textiles, cosmetics, and plastics.

Capital Equipment   **Capital equipment** refers to the large tools and machines used in a production process. Bulldozers, lathes, robots, cranes, and stamping machines are typical examples. Capital equipment is normally expensive and is intended to be used for a long period of time. Because it is expensive, purchase decisions are often made by high-level management. Manufacturers of capital equipment frequently offer a variety of services, such as installation, training, repair and maintenance assistance, and aid in financing a purchase. Caterpillar Inc., for example, prides itself on its excellent reputation for servicing its heavy earth-moving equipment.

Accessory Equipment   **Accessory equipment** is used in production or office activities but does not become part of the final physical product. For instance, motors, hand tools, meters, word processors, calculators, and office furniture are used in production and daily operations. Accessory items are usually much less expensive than capital equipment and are purchased more routinely. They are sold through more outlets than capital equipment, and sellers do not have to offer the many services expected of capital equipment makers.

Component Parts   A **component part** is a finished item or an item that needs little processing before becoming part of the physical product. Although component parts are used in the manufacture of larger products, they are easily distinguishable from those products. Microchips, hard and floppy disk drives, graphics cards, monitors, and cases are all component parts of the personal computer. Organizations purchase such parts according to their own specifications or industry standards. They expect the parts to be of a specified quality and delivered on time so that production does not have to slow down or stop. Producers that are basically assemblers, including most computer manufacturers, rely heavily on the suppliers of component parts.

Process Materials   Like a component part, a **process material** is used directly in the production of another product; however, it is not readily distinguishable from the finished product. For example, a company that manufactures cosmetics might purchase alcohol for use in make-up or perfume. Process materials are purchased according to industry standards or the purchaser's specifications.

Supplies   A **supply** does not become part of the finished product, but it does expedite production and operations. Paints, fuses, cleaning materials, paper, pens and pencils, and computer disks are examples. Supplies are usually sold through numerous outlets and are purchased routinely. They are also referred to as *MRO items* because they can be divided into three categories: *maintenance* items (brooms and cleaners); *repair* items (replacement parts); and *operating* items (electricity and office supplies). To ensure that supplies are available when needed, buyers frequently deal with several suppliers.

Industrial Services   An **industrial service** is an intangible product that many organizations require in their operations. Financial, legal, janitorial, and marketing·research services are necessary for most organizations. As shown in Figure 10.3, some organizations even require a temporary workforce. Organizations must decide whether to purchase services from outside the organization or provide their own internally. They generally base this decision on the costs associated with each alternative and the frequency of their need for the services.

■ **industrial service** an intangible product that many organizations require in their operations, such as financial, legal, or janitorial services

PRODUCT MIX AND PRODUCT LINE

Marketers must determine the assortment of products they are going to offer consumers. Some firms sell a single product; others sell a variety of products. A **product item** refers to a unique version of a product that is distinct from the organization's other products. For example, Jell-O Instant Pudding is a product item offered by General Foods Corporation. An organization's **product line** is a group of closely related products that are considered a unit because of marketing, technical, or end-use considerations. General Foods's various desserts together constitute a product line; each product item in the product line is packaged and promoted in a similar manner.

■ **product item** a unique version of a product that is distinct from the organization's other products

■ **product line** a group of closely related products that are considered a unit because of marketing, technical, or end-use considerations

FIGURE 10.3
Industrial Services
Olsten Staffing Services offers organizations skilled assignment employees, eliminating unproductive overstaffing or under-staffing at any particular time.

Source: © 1993 The Olsten Corporation.

■ **product mix** the total group of products offered by a firm, or all of the firm's product lines

■ **product mix width** the number of product lines offered by a firm

■ **product line depth** the number of products offered in a given product line

A **product mix** is the total group of products offered by a firm or all of its product lines. General Foods has several product lines, including desserts, coffees, cereals, pet foods, beverages, and household products (see Figure 10.4). These different lines make up the firm's product mix. **Product mix width** is the number of product lines offered by a firm. General Foods has a fairly wide product mix. **Product line depth** is the number of products offered in a given product line. Figure 10.4 illustrates the concepts of product mix width and product line depth applied to selected General Foods products. General Foods has a deep dessert line and a relatively shallow household products line.

To develop the ideal product line, marketers must understand consumers' needs. Each item in a product line usually reflects the needs of different target markets. Figure 10.5 illustrates Purina's deep line of dog foods, each of which provides different kinds of nutrition depending on the activity level of the dog. Hi-Pro, for instance, helps active dogs maintain their optimum energy level, and is especially high in protein and calories, while Fit & Trim is for the less active dog. Although these products share the same manufacturing facilities and distribution channels, each is promoted as a distinct product targeted at a specific market segment.

FIGURE 10.4
Product Mix and Product Lines of General Foods Corporation

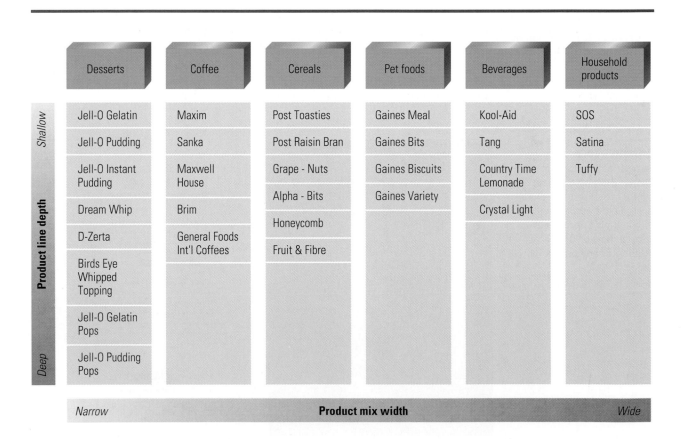

Desserts	Coffee	Cereals	Pet foods	Beverages	Household products
Jell-O Gelatin	Maxim	Post Toasties	Gaines Meal	Kool-Aid	SOS
Jell-O Pudding	Sanka	Post Raisin Bran	Gaines Bits	Tang	Satina
Jell-O Instant Pudding	Maxwell House	Grape - Nuts	Gaines Biscuits	Country Time Lemonade	Tuffy
Dream Whip	Brim	Alpha - Bits	Gaines Variety	Crystal Light	
D-Zerta	General Foods Int'l Coffees	Honeycomb			
Birds Eye Whipped Topping		Fruit & Fibre			
Jell-O Gelatin Pops					
Jell-O Pudding Pops					

Product line depth: *Shallow* → *Deep*

Product mix width: *Narrow* → *Wide*

FIGURE 10.5
Product Line Depth
In developing a product line, marketers must consider the needs of the customer. Purina makes a variety of dog foods for different types of dogs. Though each product is packaged and promoted in a similar manner, each reflects the needs of a different target market.

Source: © 1991, Ralston Purina Company. Used with permission.

Business-to-business marketers also develop a product mix. Raytheon, for instance, is a diversified, international, technology-based company with eight divisions. Its product mix includes five lines: electronics, aircraft products, energy services, major appliances, and other lines. Each line is fairly deep. The electronics line alone includes missile programs, shipboard systems, sonar systems, air traffic control and air safety systems, surveillance radar, military communications, electronic combat systems, military computers, electronic components/research and development, and commercial electronics and international business.

THE PRODUCT LIFE CYCLE

A product has a life cycle in much the same way a living organism does. A new product is introduced to consumers, it grows, and when it loses appeal, it declines and eventually is taken off the market. Product life cycles can be modified and extended by marketers. (Chapter 12 discusses the marketing strategies for modifying and extending product life cycles.)

As Figure 10.6 demonstrates, a **product life cycle** has four stages: (1) introduction, (2) growth, (3) maturity, and (4) decline. Understanding the typical life cycle pattern helps businesses to manage profitable products and

■ **product life cycle**
the course of product development, consisting of four stages: introduction, growth, maturity, and decline

FIGURE 10.6
Four Stages of the Product Life Cycle

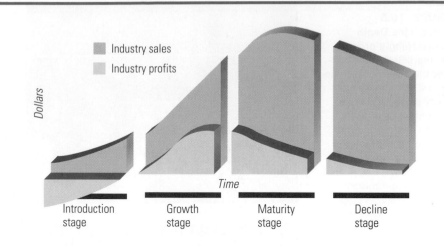

to know when it is time to terminate unprofitable ones. As a product moves through its life cycle, the strategies for promotion, pricing, distribution, and competition must be regularly evaluated and adjusted. Perceptive marketing managers try to ensure that the introduction, modification, and termination of a product are timed and executed properly.

Introduction Stage

■ **introduction stage** the stage in a product's life cycle when the product first appears in the marketplace, sales are zero, and profits are negative

In the **introduction stage** of the life cycle, the product is first presented to consumers. For example, Kodak Company's new line of 35mm Ektar films is in the introductory stage. As seen in Figure 10.6, profits for a newly introduced product are negative because initial sales are low during this stage and the firm must recover its research and development expenses while it is spending large sums for promotion and distribution. Notice in Figure 10.6 that sales move upward from zero, but profits move from below zero. Few new products represent major innovations. Most product introductions involve a newly packaged convenience food, a new automobile model, or a new fashion in clothing.

In the introduction stage, the company must communicate the product's features, uses, and advantages to potential buyers, often through advertisements. The advertisement in Figure 10.7 does just that. Introducing a product is difficult for two reasons. First, not all businesses have the resources, technological knowledge, and understanding of marketing to launch a product successfully. Second, the initial price of a new product may have to be high to recover research and development costs. Many products, such as Listerine Toothpaste and Campbell's Red Kettle Soups, never get beyond the introduction stage.

Growth Stage

■ **growth stage** the product life cycle period in which sales rise rapidly and profits peak and then start to decline

Sales rise rapidly during the **growth stage,** while profits peak and then start to decline. Competitors' reactions to the product's success in this stage will

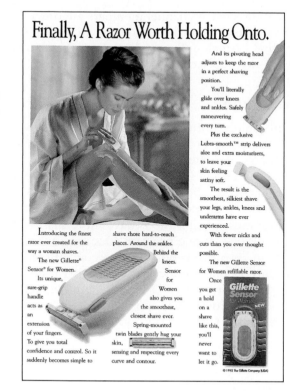

FIGURE 10.7
Introduction Stage
This advertisement for Gillette Sensor for Women communicates that it is a new product with a unique feature: a sure-grip handle.

Source: The Gillette Company.

affect its life expectancy. Profits decline late in the growth stage as other firms enter the market, forcing the company to lower prices and spend heavily on promotion. At this point, the typical marketing strategy focuses on encouraging strong brand loyalty and competing with aggressive imitators of the product. The company tries to develop a competitive niche in the growth stage by emphasizing the product's benefits.

Organizations typically resort to aggressive promotional pricing, including price reductions, during the growth stage. The compact disk (CD) player industry in the United States is currently in the growth stage. There are many competitors in the market with products that have different features. By adjusting their prices competitively, firms like Sony and Magnavox can maintain their share of the market during the growth stage.

Maturity Stage

maturity stage the product life cycle period during which the sales curve peaks and begins to decline and profits continue to decline

The sales curve peaks and begins to decline during the **maturity stage,** and profits continue to decline. Competition is fierce at this stage as many brands enter the market. Each competitor highlights differences and improvements in its versions of the product, and weaker competitors are squeezed out or lose interest in the product.

A product in the maturity phase begins to lose its distinctiveness. Organizations with mature products must therefore develop new promotional and distribution efforts. A fresh advertising campaign, new packaging, or incentives directed at channel members are often employed. Hasbro boosted the sales of the G.I. Joe line of toys by increasing advertising and relaunching the original 12-inch doll, which is about 8 inches taller than the second G.I. Joe figure that replaced it.[8]

Decline Stage

■ **decline stage** the stage in the product life cycle in which sales fall rapidly and profits decrease

Sales fall rapidly during the **decline stage.** New technology or new social trends may cause product sales to decline dramatically. At this time, the producer considers eliminating items from the product line that are not earning a profit. The business may eliminate distributors with poor sales, cut promotion efforts, and ultimately plan to phase out the product. The rotary-dial telephone is an example of a product in the decline stage.

Because most organizations have more than one product in their product mix, the decline of one product does not cause a company to fail. Various products in an organization's mix are at different stages in the product life cycle. Thus, as one product declines, other products are in the introduction, growth, or maturity stage. Therefore, businesses must simultaneously handle new product introductions and manage existing products in their various life cycle stages (see Chapter 12).

■ **brand** a name, term, design, symbol, or any other feature that identifies one seller's good or service as distinct from those of other sellers

BRANDING

■ **brand name** the part of a brand that can be verbalized; includes letters, words, and numbers, such as 7Up or Colgate

Branding refers to decisions about product names, including brands, brand names, brand marks, and trademarks. A **brand** is a name, term, design, symbol, or any other feature that identifies one seller's good or service as distinct from those of other sellers. A brand may identify one item, a family of items, or all items of that seller. If used for the firm as a whole, the preferred name is trade name.[9] A **brand name** is the part of a brand that can be verbalized; it includes letters, words, and numbers, such as 7Up or Colgate. A brand name is sometimes a product's only distinguishing characteristic, as is the case with gasoline products. A brand name helps a product develop an identity, simplifies shopping, and connotes quality to consumers.[10] Table 10.1 lists the ten strongest brand names based on a consumer survey of quality perceptions.

■ **brand mark** a symbol, design, or other element of a brand that cannot be spoken

The **brand mark** is a symbol, design, or other element of a brand that cannot be spoken. The inscribed polo player on Ralph Lauren Polo shirts and the golden arches of McDonald's are examples. A **trademark,** which is

■ **trademark** a legal designation, registered with the U.S. Patent and Trademark Office, that gives the owner exclusive use of a brand name, brand mark, or part of a brand and prohibits others from using it

---

[8]Joseph Pereira, "Hasbro Enjoys Life off the Toy-Market Roller Coaster," *Wall Street Journal,* May 5, 1992, p. B6.

[9]Reprinted from *Dictionary of Marketing Terms* by Peter D. Bennett, 1988 edition, published by the American Marketing Association.

[10]James U. McNeal and Linda Zeren, "Brand Name Selection for Consumer Products," *MSU Business Topics,* Spring 1981, p. 35.

TABLE 10.1
Ten Strongest U.S. Brand Names*

1. Disney	(Disneyland/Disney World)
2. Kodak	(film)
3. Hallmark	(greeting cards)
4. UPS	(delivery service)
5. Fisher-Price	(toys)
6. Levi's	(jeans)
7. Mercedes-Benz	(cars)
8. Arm & Hammer	(baking soda)
9. AT&T	(long-distance telephone service)
10. IBM	(computers)

*Based on a national telephone survey of 2,000 men and women over the age of 15 who were asked to rate goods or services according to quality perceptions.

Source: Carrie Goerne, "Disney Rated Top U.S. Brand," *Advertising Age,* April 27, 1992, pp. 1, 5. Reprinted by permission.

registered with the U.S. Patent and Trademark Office, is a legal designation giving the owner exclusive use of a brand name, brand mark, or part of a brand and prohibiting others from using it. Nearly seventy thousand new product names are registered as trademarks each year.[11] Marketing Close-up shows how some organizations go to great lengths to protect a name.

Reasons for Branding

Branding helps consumers identify the specific products they like or dislike so that they can purchase the products that satisfy their needs. Branding also helps consumers evaluate the quality of products, especially when they cannot judge a product's characteristics. In addition, a brand that symbolizes status can provide a psychological reward to consumers. For example, BMW automobiles, Gucci leather goods, Rolex watches, and Godiva chocolates (see Figure 10.8) are sought by some consumers for their status and prestige.

Branding also benefits sellers because brands identify their products, which encourages repeat purchases by consumers. For this reason, BP America Inc., the American subsidiary of British Petroleum Co., gave all its American gas stations—which sold gasoline under many names, including Gulf, Boron, and Sohio—the same brand name and brand mark to facilitate consumer recognition. When consumers become loyal to a specific brand, the producer's share of that product market achieves a certain level of stability. Moreover, brands that have some degree of customer loyalty can command premium prices.

[11] Robert Johnson, "Naming a Product Is Tough When the Best Names Are Taken," *Wall Street Journal,* January 19, 1988, p. 33.

SPEND YOUR BIRTHDAY WITH THE ONES YOU LOVE.
Whether it's luscious hazelnut praline, butterscotch caramel or mocha buttercream enveloped in milk chocolate, a gift of Godiva is a true surprise party for your taste buds. To send Godiva, call 1-800-643-1579.

GODIVA
Chocolatier

Branding can facilitate the introduction of a new product that carries the name of an organization's existing products because buyers are already familiar with the firm's existing brands. For example, when Hershey Foods Corp., maker of Reese's peanut butter cups, introduced Reese's peanut butter with the familiar orange and yellow label on the jars, the Reese's name gave the new product quicker recognition and trial in the marketplace than an unfamiliar brand name would have.[12] Reese's grabbed a 3.5 percent share of the market the first year, with sales exceeding \$32 million.[13] Finally, branding expedites promotional efforts because the promotion of each branded product indirectly promotes all other products with a similar brand name.

Selecting an Effective Brand

Because the brand affects customers' perceptions of and attitudes toward a product and sometimes toward the firm, it ultimately affects purchase decisions. Consequently, selection of an appropriate brand is a critical decision for organizations. Manufacturers, who may risk as much as \$20 million to

---

[12]Judann Dagnoli, "Reese's Brand Spreads," *Advertising Age,* February 27, 1992, p. 56.
[13]Valerie Reitman, "Hershey Stirs Up Peanut-Butter Market," *Wall Street Journal,* October 27, 1992, pp. B1, B6.

MARKETING CLOSE-UP

Trademark Wars

Consumers commonly identify a product with its trademark, and companies consider it a critical element in projecting a corporate image. For this reason, companies spend millions of dollars to develop their trademarks—and to protect them. Recent court battles show how fiercely companies will defend their trademarks and guard against consumer confusion.

Economy Lodging recently filed a lawsuit charging Motel 6 with violation of the Trademark Act of 1946. Economy claims that Motel 6 used signs and architectural designs that Economy has the sole right to use. In response, Motel 6 argues that architectural trademarks are not capable of legal protection and that they are not inherently distinctive, recognized by the consuming public, and associated in the minds of consumers as exclusive to Economy Lodging. As many as seventy-three lawsuits may be filed.

Two Pesos Inc., a drive-through restaurant chain, has been accused of intentionally and deliberately copying the concept of rival Taco Cabana International. Both restaurants are 24-hour patio concepts that specialize in Mexican food and margaritas. The U.S. Supreme Court has agreed to review the case to determine whether the appearance of something comes under trademark law, and if so, what conditions must be met. What is of particular interest is whether, over time, the public associates the appearance of a restaurant or other concept with the source of its goods and services. The attorney for Two Pesos argues that Taco Cabana's appearance is too generic in a Mexican context to be considered a protectable trademark and is not recognized by the public as an identifying symbol.

McDonald's has waged more than fifty battles to protect its *Mc* prefix. The fast-food giant has filed lawsuits against McDharma (a vegetarian fast-food restaurant), McSleep (an economy hotel chain), Molly McButter (a butter substitute), and McTravel (a travel agency). Following the legal doctrine of "use it—and protect it—or you lose it," McDonald's claims that the *Mc* prefix will lead people to believe that a given business is owned by McDonald's, and that "policing" its trademark is the only means McDonald's has to keep it from becoming a generic term. The companies being sued say the burger chain does not *own* the prefix. Nonetheless, the courts have barred Quality Inns from using McSleep, and a bakery from using the name McBagel.

The Goodyear Tire & Rubber Company sued Fuji Photo Film Co., Ltd., because the latter used the blimp shape in its promotion. Fuji now cannot use the blimp shape to sell or promote tires and other rubber products. Although Fuji does not make rubber goods, Goodyear thinks it has sent a message to competitors who might infringe on its trademark rights to the blimp shape.

Sources: Marilyn Alva, "High Noon in the Court," *Restaurant Business*, March 20, 1992, p. 41; Timothy N. Troy, "Knights Parent Sues Motel 6," *Hotel & Management Journal*, April 6, 1992, pp. 1, 26; Rick Wartzman, "Now All They Have to Do Is Stop Folks from Thinking of Goodrich," *Wall Street Journal*, August 13, 1988, p. 23; and Julie Amparano, "Not to Court Trouble, but We'd Like You to Read This McStory," *Wall Street Journal*, November 17, 1987, p. 41.

introduce a new consumer product, often turn to consultants to find the perfect name.[14] Some firms spend as much as $75,000 to develop a name for a product, with no guarantee of the product's success, of course.

In selecting a brand name, marketers should consider a number of issues. A brand name should be easy for consumers to say, spell, and remember. This includes foreign customers if the product is to be marketed in other countries. A short, one-syllable name such as *Bounce* is easy to say, spell, and recall. The brand name should also suggest a product's uses and special characteristics in a positive way. A perfume's name, for example, might suggest fragrance and magnetism. Calvin Klein's Obsession and Elizabeth Taylor's Passion sound seductive and luxurious because of their names and their association with famous producers. A name shouldn't bring unpleasant thoughts to mind or have negative meanings in other languages. The name should describe the product's major benefits. A survey of large consumer-goods producers found that almost 60 percent identified descriptiveness as a major criterion in brand name selection.[15]

An effective brand must be compatible with other products in the line. The manufacturer of KitchenAid appliances, for example, might have some doubts about putting the KitchenAid name on a household drill or vacuum cleaner. Finally, a brand should be designed so that it can be used and recognized in newspapers, magazines, and billboards, and on television and radio.

A brand name should also convey the desired product image. For instance, A-1 Steak Sauce suggests a high-quality product. Sporting goods made by Everlast have an image of strength and durability. On the other hand, a bank named Fifth Third Bank may convey an image of an unsuccessful bank or a bank that is not the leader.

A company should be certain that its selected brand name is not likely to be considered an infringement on an existing brand already registered with the U.S. Patent Office. This requirement may be difficult to achieve because infringement is determined by the courts, which base their decisions on whether a brand name causes consumers to become confused, mistaken, or deceived about the source of the product.[16]

Another consideration is designing a brand that can be easily protected. Some brands can be legally infringed on more easily than others. Generic words cannot be protected as exclusive brand names. Brand names that are difficult to protect include surnames, descriptive terms or geographic names, and those that relate to a product feature.[17] Businesses must attempt to prevent their brand names from becoming generic terms used to refer to a general product category. For example, names such as *cellophane, linoleum,* and *shredded wheat* were brand names at one time. Eventually, however, they became generic terms that refer to general product classes and thus could no longer be protected by their originators.

[14]Johnson, p. 33.
[15]McNeal and Zeren, p. 37.
[16]George Miaoulis and Nancy D'Amato, "Consumer Confusion and Trademark Infringement," *Journal of Marketing,* April 1978, pp. 48–49.
[17]Dorothy Cohen, "Trademark Strategy," *Journal of Marketing,* January 1986, p. 63.

Categories of Brands

■ **manufacturer brand**
a brand developed and
owned by its producer, who
is usually involved with distribution, promotion, and to
some extent pricing deci-
sions for the brand

Brands fall into three categories: manufacturer, private distributor, and generic brands. A **manufacturer brand** is developed and owned by its producer, who is usually involved with distribution, promotion, and to some
extent pricing decisions for the brand. IBM, Sony, Pepperidge Farm, Kraft,
and Levi's are manufacturer brands. Manufacturer brands make it possible
for consumers to identify products with their manufacturers at the point of
purchase. Manufacturers try to stimulate demand for their brands and create
brand loyalty through promotion, quality control, and guarantees. Stimulating demand for the product also encourages sellers and resellers to carry the
product.

■ **private distributor (**or
private) brand a brand developed and owned by a reseller, such as a wholesaler
or retailer

A **private distributor** (or **private**) **brand** is developed and owned by a
reseller, such as a wholesaler or retailer. The manufacturer of a private brand
is not identified on the product. Resellers employ private distributor brands
to develop more efficient promotion, generate higher gross margins, and
improve store image. Private brands are rapidly gaining market share in
several product categories, including cigarettes, frozen chicken, hot cereal,
cold and allergy medicines, and disposable diapers.[18] In 1992, Kraft cheese
lost 3 points of market share and Gerber baby food lost 2 points, mostly to
private brands.[19] Familiar retailer brand names include Thrifty Maid (Winn-
Dixie Stores) and Die-hard and Kenmore (Sears, Roebuck and Co.). Wholesaler brands include IGA (Independent Grocers' Alliance) and Topmost (General Grocer). Discounted private brand soft drinks, such as Wegman's W
Cola, Kroger's Big K Cola, and Wal-Mart's Sam's American Choice, have
an 8 percent share of supermarket drink sales.[20]

■ **generic brand** a brand
that identifies only the product type (peanut butter, tomato sauce), but not the
manufacturer or any other
distinguishing information

A **generic brand** does not list the manufacturer or any other distinguishing
information on its label; only the product type (such as peanut butter, tomato
sauce, cigarettes, paper towels) is identified. Because generic brands are rarely
advertised, many grocery stores sell them at lower prices than they sell comparable branded items. Much of the growth in generic grocery brand sales has
been at the expense of private distributor brands.[21] In recent years, however,
generic brands have fallen as a percentage of retail grocery sales, and now
represent less than 1 percent.[22]

Branding Strategies

When deciding on branding strategies, the first decision an organization must
make is whether to brand its products at all. When products are homogeneous

[18]Kathleen Deveny, "More Shoppers Bypass Big-Name Brands and Steer Costs to Private-Label
Products," *Wall Street Journal,* October 20, 1992, pp. B1, B8.
[19]Lois Therrien, Maria Mallory, and Zachary Schiller, "Brands on the Run," *Business Week,* April
19, 1993, pp. 26–29.
[20]Michael J. McCarthy, "Soft-Drink Giants Sit Up and Take Notice As Sales of Store Brands
Show More Fizz," *Wall Street Journal,* March 16, 1992, pp. B1, B3.
[21]Martha R. McEnally and Jon M. Hawes, "The Market for Generic Brand Grocery Products: A
Review and Extension," *Journal of Marketing,* Winter 1984, pp. 75–83.
[22]Alan Miller, "Gains Share in Dollars and Units During 1990 Third Quarter," *Private Label,* January–February 1991, pp. 85–89.

and similar to competing products, they may be difficult to brand. Raw materials, such as farm produce, chemicals, coal, and gravel, are not easily branded because they are homogeneous and difficult to differentiate.

A firm may choose to brand its products using one or more of the following strategies for branding: individual, overall family, line family, and brand-extension branding. Brand licensing is a fifth option.

Individual branding is a strategy of using a different brand name for each product. This strategy allows an organization to develop products for different segments of the same product market. Each product is given a separate, unrelated name and can be aimed at a specific segment. General Foods, for example, employs an individual branding strategy for its line of coffees, including Maxwell House, Maxim, Brim, Sanka, and General Foods International Coffees. Another advantage of individual branding is that a brand that acquires a negative image does not affect the company's other products.

A strategy of giving all of a company's products the same name or part of the name is called **overall family branding.** For years, Dr. Scholl's has used family branding to promote its various products. With overall family branding, the promotion of one item with the family brand promotes the firm's other products.

Line family branding occurs when an organization uses family branding only for products within a particular line rather than for all its products; that is, the same brand is used for all products within a line but not for products in different lines. Ralston Purina Company, for example, markets its line of pet foods—including Purina Dog Chow, Purina Cat Chow, Tender Vittles, and Happy Cat—under the Purina brand name and symbol. However, the company markets many other products, including Chex cereals, under a variety of different brands.

Brand-extension branding is a strategy of using an existing brand name as part of a brand for an improved or new product that is usually in the same product category as the existing brand. For example, General Mills, the maker of Kix cereal, extended the name Kix to Berry Berry Kix, a sweet ready-to-eat cereal that competes with Quaker Oats's Cap'n Crunch.[23]

In another branding strategy, called **brand licensing,** a company allows approved manufacturers to use its trademark on other products for a licensing fee. The licensor—the company permitting the use of its trademark—generally charges a royalty fee ranging from 2 to 10 percent of wholesale revenues. Many well-known companies such as The Coca-Cola Company, Playboy Enterprises, Inc., and Harley-Davidson Motor Co., Inc., have licensed their trademarks. Sears has a licensing agreement with McDonald's to sell McKids children's clothing. In this arrangement, Sears is responsible for all manufacturing, selling, and promotional functions.

For the licensor, brand licensing provides trademark protection and can give a firm free publicity. It is inexpensive and relatively safe. If the venture fails, the licensee is responsible for the costs. But licensing does have several drawbacks. The licensor has little control over the manufacturing process

---

■ **individual branding** a branding strategy of using a different brand name for each product

■ **overall family branding** a branding strategy of giving all of a company's products the same name or part of the name

■ **line family branding** a branding strategy in which an organization uses family branding only for products within a particular line rather than for all its products

■ **brand-extension branding** a branding strategy of using an existing brand name as part of a brand for an improved or new product that is usually in the same product category as the existing brand

■ **brand licensing** a branding strategy in which a company allows approved manufacturers to use its trademark on other products for a licensing fee

---

[23]Julie Liesse, "New Kix Gets Boost," *Advertising Age,* March 30, 1992, p. 13.

and could become associated with a product failure. Moreover, licensing sometimes results in consumers being overexposed to the same name, which may reduce the effectiveness of the brand.

Organizations can use more than one branding strategy. Branding strategy decisions are affected by the number of products and product lines produced by the firm, the characteristics of its target markets, the number and types of competing products available, and the firm's resources. The Campbell Soup Company, for example, employs both individual and line family branding. The company uses individual branding for V8 vegetable juice but line family branding for LeMenu and Swanson's frozen dinners and for Pepperidge Farm cookies and crackers.

PACKAGING

■ **packaging** the development of a container and a graphic design for a product

Packaging is the development of a container and a graphic design for a product. Packaging can make a product easier to use, safer, and more versatile. It can also affect consumers' attitudes toward a product, which in turn affect their purchase decisions. The trend toward clear bottles illustrates the many benefits of packaging (see Figure 10.9). Clear bottles can create an image of a product that is purer, milder, and lighter; they can be made of recycled plastic and can contain less material than thicker, opaque bottles; and they let customers see how much the package contains. A host of products are packaged in clear packages, including beverages, dish detergents, and deodorants.[24]

Because consumers' impressions of a product are significantly influenced by its packaging, marketers try to develop innovative packages that satisfy the needs of the target market. For instance, when a scientific study reported that taking one aspirin daily can help prevent heart attacks, the makers of Bayer aspirin quickly designed "calendar paks" to help buyers make sure they take their daily tablet. Innovative packages can also give a brand an edge over competing brands.

Functions of Packaging

Packaging serves a number of purposes. First, it protects the product and maintains its functional form. Fluids such as milk, soft drinks, and hair spray need packages that preserve and protect them. The package should protect the product to reduce the possibility of damage that could affect its usefulness and increase costs. With the threat of product tampering for many types of products, companies have developed several tamper-resistant packaging techniques to counter the problem. Organizations are also experimenting with packages that extend the shelf life of fresh fruit and vegetables.

---

[24]Cyndee Miller, "Trendy Marketers Want Consumers to See Right Through Their Products," *Marketing News,* February 1, 1993, pp. 1–2.

FIGURE 10.9
Packaging
Clear packaging is necessary for the new Crystal Pepsi. A big hit for PepsiCo, clear cola creates an image of a milder and lighter product.

Source: Courtesy Pepsi-Cola Company.

Another function of packaging is convenience. The size or shape of a package may affect the product's storage, convenience of use, or replacement rate. Small, single-serving cans of soup and vegetables, for instance, can prevent waste, facilitate storage, and offer convenience for consumers. Size can be critical for industrial products because of the standard sizes required for pallets, fork lifts, and storage facilities. Yet another function of packaging is promotion—communicating a product's features, uses, benefits, and image.

Major Packaging Issues

Organizations consider many issues as they design packages. One of the most important considerations is cost. Although companies can choose from a variety of packaging materials, processes, and designs, some are quite costly. Consumers in recent years have shown a willingness to pay more for improved packaging, but only within reason. Businesses should conduct research to determine just how much consumers are willing to pay for packaging.

Another issue is whether to package the product singly or in multiple units. Multiple packaging may boost demand for a product because it increases the amount of the product available at the point of consumption. Multiple packaging can also make products easier to handle and store, as with six-packs of soft drinks and four-packs of yogurt and pudding. Moreover, special price offers, such as a two-for-one sale, are facilitated by multiple packaging. Finally, multiple packaging may increase consumer acceptance of a product by giving consumers the opportunity to try it several times. On the other hand, consumers may hesitate to try a product in the first place if they must buy several units. Single packaging generally is best for infrequently used products because buyers do not like to tie up their dollars or store these products for a long time.

The impact of packaging on the environment has also become a major issue. Packages from a variety of consumer and industrial products result in tons of waste dumped into landfills each day in the United States. As noted in Chapter 4, some firms practicing green marketing design packages that are more friendly to the environment. For example, Kellogg Co. puts its cereals into boxes made from recycled paper.[25] Many beverage producers use recycled aluminum cans; more than 60 percent of all aluminum cans are recycled.[26] Other products, including newspapers, office paper, tin cans, glass, and plastic containers, can be recycled to reduce the costs of producing new products and packages and to slow the filling of landfills. Concentrated Ultra Downy fabric softener comes in a smaller bottle than original Downy; the container is made with 50 percent postconsumer recycled plastic and 35 percent less packaging by weight. And Ultra Downy Refill is sold in a paper-based carton. Eventually everything from dish detergents to laundry detergents will be sold in concentrated form.[27] In spite of these efforts, however, many companies continue to develop wasteful packages.

Package designers must also consider the promotional role of packaging. A package can grab consumers' attention and encourage them to examine the product. With so many brands available, a drab package can be lost in the clutter. Using verbal and nonverbal symbols, a package can communicate to potential buyers information about the product's content, features, uses, advantages, and hazards. With advertising budgets tightening, firms are increasingly viewing packaging as a selling tool. Close to the Customer illustrates the importance of designing a customer-friendly package.

A package designer can create desirable images and associations through the choice of size, color, design, shape, and texture. Perfume bottles are a particularly good example of how packaging can be used to create a certain image. Different sizes, shapes, and exterior containers, such as velvet string bags, are used to convey a desired image to the target market. The choice of color for a package also affects consumers' perception of the product because colors are often associated with certain feelings or connotations. Red, for example, suggests danger, anger, fire, or blood; yellow is linked with

[25] Susan Dillingham, "Hawking Consumer Goods with the Environmental Pitch," *Insight*, March 26, 1990, pp. 40–42.

[26] "Americans Push Aluminum Can Recycling Rate to Record 61%," *USA Today*, August 7, 1990, p. 50.

[27] Jennifer Lawrence, "P&G's Downy Goes Ultra," *Advertising Age*, June 15, 1992, p. 2.

CLOSE TO THE CUSTOMER

Freshening Up the Package

Kaytee Products had a small share of the $500 million U.S. market for wild birdseed. With annual revenues around $10 million, Kaytee could not afford an elaborate advertising campaign. Willian Engler, Jr., CEO of the Chilton, Wisconsin–based bird and pet food company, decided to give the birdseed package a new look. He hired a Chicago firm to transform Kaytee's dull package into something more artsy and exciting. Engler thought a new package would enable him to expand his distribution from hardware stores to pet food shops and supermarkets.

The designers asked what motivates people who feed birds. They decided that people consider birds their guests and want to feed them only the best. Feeding birds brings people closer to nature. What was needed was a classy package that would convey this idea. The result, brightly colored birds placed against a forest background, brought Kaytee's package to life. Today Kaytee is the country's top-selling wild birdseed. Sales increased from $10 million to approximately $90 million, and Engler credits the new package for much of the growth.

Freshening up a package may not always lead to such dramatic results. But as the cost of advertising continues to increase, more firms are trying this option. The cost of updating a package is relatively low: about $100,000 to $200,000 for a small brand and generally below $500,000 for a national brand. On the other hand, a $10 million to $20 million advertising budget is standard for a national brand. And since consumers are confronted with so much clutter when they enter a store—the typical chain store stocks roughly forty thousand items—the package has to stand out on crowded shelves.

Colgate-Palmolive Co. developed its new Stand-Up tube to stand out in stores and in consumers' minds. The nation's number two toothpaste marketer hopes that consumers will switch to the new plastic upside-down tube because it prevents the messy toothpaste spills of tubes; it also uses less packaging and costs less than pumps. "Packaging innovations can quickly allow you to take huge chunks of the market," says Nigel Burton, general manager of oral care for Colgate. He expects Colgate's Stand-Up to account for as much as 15 percent of the toothpaste market and to be followed by similar packages from competitors.

Procter & Gamble replaced its Ivory Liquid, formerly a white liquid in a white bottle, with a clear liquid in a clear bottle to highlight the product. The clear package also reinforces the message that Ivory Liquid is pure and gentle. Rayovac faced the clutter problem with its batteries, and redesigned its package to make it stand out. Since then, market share has jumped from 12.7 to 17.8 percent. Charles Finkel, head of Merchant du Vin, sells quality beer and ale. Drawing from his college studies in fine arts and marketing, Finkel set out to design a distinctive package to help his beers stand out on supermarket and liquor store shelves. Says Finkel, "That's where the importance of distinctive packaging comes in; it gets consumers to try your products. And if they like them—if their quality is a justification of the price—then they'll continue to buy them based on their tastes. That's how the marketing of quality beers works."

Sources: Kathleen Deveny, "Toothpaste Makers Tout New Packaging," *Wall Street Journal,* November 10, 1992, p. B1; Gretchen Morgenson, "Is Your Product Your Advocate?" *Forbes,* September 14, 1992, pp. 468–474; Richard Szathmary, "Charles Finkel Brews a Taste for Beer," *Sales & Marketing Management,* August 1992, pp. 32–33; and Valerie Reitman, "Transparent Brands Are Clearly Trendy," *Wall Street Journal,* May 21, 1992, p. B1.

sunlight, caution, warmth, and vitality; and blue can imply coldness, sky, water, and sadness.[28] Thus marketers must decide whether a particular color will create a positive or negative response in consumers. Colors are also chosen to attract attention. For its new line of Cajun foods, Luzianne Blue Plate Foods developed a package with a green background, a yellow logo, and an illustration of a southern plantation house. Because green is an unusual and unexpected color for packaged dinners, the cartons stand out from other packaged dinner products on the shelves.[29]

A final issue in packaging decisions is the degree of continuity among an organization's package designs. **Family packaging** is a strategy of using similar packages or one major element of the design in the packaging of all products. This approach is used for lines of products, such as Progresso soup and Jhirmack hair care products.

Packaging can be a powerful competitive tool as well as a major component of a marketing strategy.[30] A better box or wrapper, a more convenient container size, or a unique closure may give a firm a competitive advantage. For example, in 1988, Procter & Gamble created a new spill-proof closure for its Tide powdered detergent. Manufacturers of packaged foods, detergents, beer, and other products spend large sums of money to research consumers' reactions to packages. To provide the desired benefits to consumers, organizations must often make tradeoffs between packaging and cost.

■ **family packaging**
a packaging strategy of using similar packages or one major element of the design in the packaging of all products

LABELING

■ **labeling** the display of important information on a product package

Labeling is the display of important information on a product package. Marketers can use labels to promote other products or to encourage proper use of products and therefore greater satisfaction with them. Labeling is an important marketing decision for legal reasons as well. Consumer interest in food labeling has increased as an aging and health-conscious population tries to avoid toxic substances, fats, and sodium. The Food and Drug Administration and the Consumer Product Safety Commission can require that certain products be labeled or marked with warnings, instructions, ingredients, certifications, and manufacturer's identifications. The Bush administration, during its final days, announced a package of nutrition-labeling rules that will require food makers to adopt uniform labels for hundreds of thousands of products. The rules, which take effect in 1994, will cost the food industry $2 billion, but will also give consumers much more information about nutrition content, limit health claims that can be made, and reduce health costs by improving nutrition.[31]

[28]James U. McNeal, *Consumer Behavior: An Integrative Approach* (Boston: Little, Brown, 1982), pp. 221–222.
[29]"Something Unexpected Adds Spice to Cajun Packaging," *Marketing News,* February 29, 1988, p. 20.
[30]Sue Bassin, "Innovative Packaging Strategies," *Journal of Business Strategy,* January–February 1988, pp. 28–32.
[31]Rose Gutfield, "Food Label 'Babel' to Fall as Uniform System is Cleared," *Wall Street Journal,* December 3, 1992, pp. B1, B7.

Color and sophisticated graphics can be used to overcome the clutter of words—called "mouse print" by designers—that government regulations require on most labels. Front labels now contain more direct information about what a product is and does and, in many cases, an eye-catching picture of the product. Because so many similar products are available, an attention-getting device is necessary to attract consumer interest.

The *Universal Product Code (UPC)* is another important part of the label. The UPC is read by an optical scanner that generates the price of the item on the cash register. Nearly all grocery stores have installed UPC scanners at check-out lines. The scanners save time and labor costs and result in greater inventory control.

OTHER PRODUCT-RELATED ISSUES

When researching and developing products, organizations make decisions about many issues. Some relate to the physical characteristics of the product; others relate to less tangible supportive services that are very much a part of the total product.

Product Quality

In response to intense foreign competition, American manufacturers have improved product quality dramatically in recent years. Yet some managers still believe that product quality detracts from the bottom line. In other words, improving quality calls for better materials and more expensive processing, which increase production costs and ultimately the product's price. In his book *Quality Is Free*, quality expert Philip Crosby challenged the notion that quality reduces the bottom line. The quality program he established at ITT was based on the belief that the real costs detracting from the bottom line are the costs of inspection and fixing problems, and all others associated with not doing the job right the first time. One of the "other costs" is that of winning back lost customers.[32]

Many firms have adopted Crosby's program, shown in Table 10.2. The underlying premise addresses the attitude that mistakes are human and acceptable. By committing themselves to avoiding errors—*zero defects*—workers build quality into a product and eliminate costly inspections. Product quality is an ongoing process, as firms constantly improve, striving for zero defects. The result is products that conform to customers' expectations.

Quality is becoming a given, a ticket into the ballpark. Without durability, conformance to customer specifications, and on-time delivery, a firm cannot survive in today's environment. The future focus must be on more and better product features, flexible factories that can respond quickly to customer preferences, expanded customer service, and new product introductions.

---

[32] Philip B. Crosby, *Quality Is Free* (New York: McGraw-Hill, 1979), pp. 101–107.

TABLE 10.2
Crosby's Quality Improvement Program

1. **Management Commitment.** To make it clear where management stands on quality.

2. **Quality Improvement Team.** To run the Quality Improvement Process.

3. **Measurement.** To provide a display of current and potential nonconformance problems in a manner that permits objective evaluation and corrective action.

4. **Cost of Quality.** To define the ingredients of the Cost of Quality (COQ) and explain its use as a management tool.

5. **Quality Awareness.** To provide a method of raising the personal concern felt by all employees toward the conformance of the product or service and the quality reputation of the company.

6. **Corrective Action.** To provide a systematic method of resolving forever the problems that are identified through the previous action steps.

7. **Zero Defects Planning.** To establish a committee to investigate the zero defects concept and ways to implement a zero defects program.

8. **Employee Education.** To define the type of training all employees need in order to actively carry out their role in the Quality Improvement Process.

9. **Zero Defects Day.** To create an event that will let all employees realize, through a personal experience, that there has been a change.

10. **Goal Setting.** To turn pledges and commitments into action by encouraging individuals to establish improvement goals for themselves and their groups.

11. **Error Cause Removal.** To give the individual employee a method of communicating to management the situations that make it difficult for the employee to meet the pledge to improve.

12. **Regulation.** To appreciate those who participate.

13. **Quality Councils.** To bring together the appropriate people to share quality management information on a regular basis.

14. **Do It All Over Again.** To emphasize that the Quality Improvement Process is continuous.

Source: Philip B. Crosby, *Quality Is Free* (New York: McGraw-Hill, Inc.), pp. 112–119. Reprinted with permission of McGraw-Hill, Inc.

Supportive Services

All products possess intangible qualities, whether they are goods or services. When consumers cannot experience a product before buying it, they are asked to buy what essentially are promises of satisfaction. Even when products are tangible, testable, and can be seen, touched, or smelled, they are still only promises before they are purchased.[33] Supportive product-related services such as warranties, repairs and replacements, and credit help fulfill promises of satisfaction.

■ **warranty** a document that stipulates what the manufacturer will do if a product does not work properly

A **warranty** stipulates what the manufacturer will do if a product does not work properly. The type of warranty offered with a product can be a critical issue for consumers, especially for expensive, technically complex products such as appliances and automobiles. Government actions in recent years have required companies to state more simply and specifically the terms and conditions under which they will take action in a warranty. Because warranties must be so precise today, businesses are using them more aggressively as tools to give their brands a competitive advantage.

Manufacturers often need to establish a system to provide replacement parts and repair services. This support service is especially important for expensive, complex products that buyers expect to last a long time. Although some manufacturers offer these services directly to consumers, it is more common for such services to be provided through regional service centers or intermediaries. For example, repairs of General Electric VCRs are generally handled through regional service centers. Regardless of how services are provided, it is important to customers that they be performed quickly and correctly the first time.

Credit services are another important support service. Although offering credit to consumers may place financial burdens on an organization, it can yield several benefits. Offering credit services can help a firm obtain and maintain a stable share of its market. Many department stores, for example, offer revolving credit accounts as a means of competing with discount stores and other retail outlets. For expensive items, credit enables a larger number of people to buy the product, thus enlarging the market for the item. Credit services also earn interest income from customers.

PRODUCTS FOR ORGANIZATIONAL MARKETS

Chapter 8 explains that organizational or business markets consist of products sold for resale, direct use in producing other products, or use in day-to-day operations by organizations and institutions. Compared with consumer products, organizational products often require a greater emphasis on services, both before and after sales.

Before a sale, business-to-business marketers provide potential customers with technical advice regarding product specifications, installation, and application. Many business-to-business marketers depend heavily on long-term customer relationships that foster sizable repeat purchases. Therefore, business-to-business marketers make a considerable effort to provide services after the sale. Because organizational customers must have products when needed, on-time delivery is an important aspect of the product component

---

[33] Theodore Levitt, "Marketing Intangible Products and Product Intangibles," *Harvard Business Review,* May–June 1981, pp. 94–102.

of many organizational marketing mixes. Availability of parts is also very important because a lack of parts can result in costly production delays. Since customers that make large purchases on a regular basis often desire credit, some business-to-business marketers include credit services in their product mixes.

Technical product characteristics generally have a greater impact on the purchases of organizational products than any other factor.[34] Thus business-to-business marketers tend to concentrate on product research directed at functional features rather than on marketing research. Because organizational products are often sold on the basis of specifications and are rarely sold through self-service outlets, the major consideration in the package design is protection. Less emphasis is placed on the package as a promotional device.

Research on organizational customer complaints indicates that buyers usually complain when problems are encountered with product quality or delivery time. Consumers, on the other hand, exhibit more varying complaint behavior. This type of feedback from buyers allows marketers to gauge marketing performance and to provide satisfaction whenever possible. It is important that businesses respond to valid complaints because the success of most organizational products depends on repeat purchases. Buyer complaints serve a useful purpose, and many business-to-business firms facilitate this feedback by providing customer service departments.[35]

SUMMARY

A product is anything that satisfies a need or want and can be offered in exchange. A product can be a good, service, idea, or combination of these three. When consumers purchase a product, they buy not only the tangible features but also the intangible attributes, including functional, social, and psychological benefits.

Products fall into one of two general categories: consumer or industrial products. Consumer products satisfy personal and family needs; industrial products are purchased for use in a firm's operations or to make other products. Consumer products can be subdivided into convenience, shopping, specialty, and unsought products. Industrial products include raw materials, capital equipment, accessory equipment, component parts, process materials, supplies, and industrial services.

A product item is a unique version of a product that is distinct from an organization's other products. A product line is a group of closely related products that are considered a unit because of marketing, technical, or end-use considerations. The product mix is the total group of products offered by a firm, or all of the firm's product lines. Product mix width is the number of product lines offered by a firm; product line depth is the number of product items in a product line.

---

[34] Michael H. Morris, *Industrial and Organizational Marketing* (Columbus, Ohio: Merrill, 1988), pp. 78–79.
[35] Hiram C. Barksdale, Jr., Terry E. Powell, and Earnestine Hargrove, "Complaint Voicing by Industrial Buyers," *Industrial Marketing Management*, May 1984, pp. 93–99.

The product life cycle describes how products move through the stages of (1) introduction, (2) growth, (3) maturity, and (4) decline. The life cycle concept is used to evaluate and adjust marketing strategies. Sales start at zero in the introduction stage, rise during the growth stage, peak and begin to decline during the maturity stage, and then decline. Profits start from below zero in the introduction stage and peak near the end of the growth stage. Most firms have many products moving through various stages of the product life cycle.

Branding refers to decisions about product names. A brand is a name, term, symbol, design, or combination thereof that identifies a seller's products and differentiates them from competitors' products. A brand name is the part of a brand that can be verbalized; a brand mark is a symbol or design that cannot be spoken. A trademark gives the owner exclusive use of a brand name, brand mark, or some part of a brand and legally prohibits others from using it. When selecting a brand, a marketer should choose one that is easy to say, spell, and remember; the brand name should also suggest the product's uses, benefits, or special features. Brands fall into three categories: manufacturer, private distributor, and generic brands. A manufacturer brand is developed and owned by the producer; a private distributor brand is owned by a reseller; and a generic brand identifies only the product type, not the manufacturer or any other information. Major branding strategies are individual, overall family, line family, and brand-extension branding. Brand licensing is a fifth option.

Packaging serves the functions of protection, economy, convenience, and promotion. When developing a package marketers must consider packaging costs relative to the needs of target market members, whether to employ single or multiple packaging, how to design the package so that it is an effective promotional tool, and the impact of the package on the environment.

Labeling is used on packages to provide instructions, content information, certifications, and manufacturer identifications. Labels can perform both informational and promotional functions.

Businesses must consider other product-related issues such as physical characteristics and less tangible supportive services. Marketers must make decisions regarding product quality, product features, and supportive services such as warranties, repairs and replacements, and credit services.

Organizational marketers generally place a greater emphasis on services than do consumer marketers. Functional features, on-time delivery, and availability of parts are also important aspects of organizational products, and the major consideration in the package design is protection.

KEY TERMS

consumer product
industrial product
convenience product
shopping product

specialty product
unsought product
raw material
capital equipment

accessory equipment
component part
process material
supply
industrial service
product item
product line
product mix
product mix width
product line depth
product life cycle
introduction stage
growth stage
maturity stage
decline stage
brand

brand name
brand mark
trademark
manufacturer brand
private distributor (or private)
   brand
generic brand
individual branding
overall family branding
line family branding
brand-extension branding
brand licensing
packaging
family packaging
labeling
warranty

QUESTIONS FOR DISCUSSION AND REVIEW

1. Distinguish between a good, a service, and an idea. What are some goods that you have purchased recently? Some services? Have you ever purchased an idea?

2. When you purchase a new automobile, what are some of the tangible and intangible attributes you are buying?

3. Suppose an accountant buys a box of paper to be used in his or her accounting practice. Is this a consumer good or an industrial good? Explain.

4. What is the difference between a convenience product, a shopping product, a specialty product, and an unsought product? Give examples of each.

5. Would a VCR that sells for $429 be a convenience, shopping, specialty, or unsought product? Why?

6. What is the difference between accessory equipment and component parts?

7. Differentiate between product mix and product line. Give an example of a firm with a shallow product line and one with a wide product mix.

8. Why is the concept of the product life cycle important to marketers?

9. Describe each of the four stages of the product life cycle. For each stage, give an example of a product you think is currently in that stage. Justify your choices.

10. What is the difference between a brand, a brand name, and a brand mark?

11. What are some considerations in selecting a brand name?

12. Distinguish between a manufacturer brand, a private distributor brand, and a generic brand. Give an example of each.

13. What is the benefit of individual branding in comparison to overall family branding?

14. Why is packaging critical to the success of most products?

15. Why is labeling an important marketing decision?

16. What is the significance of quality and supportive services when developing and marketing products?

17. Which type of market, consumer or organizational, places a greater emphasis on service? Why?

CASES

10.1 BORDEN CHANGES ITS PRODUCT LINE

The milk business founded by Gail Borden in 1857 became one of the most profitable in the dairy industry. The name Borden became synonymous with milk. But the dairy business that made "Elsie the cow" a familiar character expanded into many other businesses, ranging from sugar to fertilizer. By 1979, less than 30 percent of Borden's sales came from dairy products.

Although dairy products accounted for more sales than any other line of products in 1979, Borden's product mix included more than a dozen different product lines, including chemicals. This strategy worked for Borden (sales in 1979 were $4.3 billion), but some of the product lines were not very profitable. Additionally, an increase in prices signaled that the chemical business was reaching maturity. Borden had built chemicals into a $340-million-a-year business.

Borden realized it had too many product lines and was not paying enough attention to each. Accordingly, the firm decided to focus its marketing efforts on consumer products, especially dairy products, salty snack foods, and pasta. By 1987, Borden had sold or dropped its fertilizer, sugar, commodity chemicals, bulk cheese, and beverage lines, and had placed more emphasis on the remaining products, including grocery, dairy, and snack products.

Between 1979 and 1987, annual sales increased from $4.3 billion to $6.5 billion. Borden also increased its hold on the dairy business. With the purchase of Meadow Gold, Borden's top share in the liquid milk market jumped to 10 percent. Dairy products accounted for 36.8 percent of 1987 sales. Borden continues to reinforce its brand name through advertising, portraying itself as the farm down the road that rushes the product from the cow to the market before the cream rises. This strong brand image is known in the industry as the "Borden difference." When asked exactly what this difference is, a dairy industry veteran said, "About a buck a gallon."

Between 1986 and 1991, Borden spent $1.9 billion on ninety-one acquisitions. Current brands include Creamette and Prince pastas and Aunt Millie's pasta sauces, Eagle condensed milk, ReaLemon lemon juice, Wise potato chips, Cheez Doodles, Cracker Jack, Creamora coffee creamer, and Elmer's glue. In total, Borden's brands add up to $7.2 billion in annual revenues. Borden is number one or two in market share in over a dozen product lines, ranging from pasta to plastic wrap.

But fierce price wars in processed cheese, snacks, and dairy products have forced CEO Anthony D'Amato to confront the problems facing Borden: ineffective marketing, poor earnings, slumping sales, and market-share losses to Frito-Lay, Eagle Snacks, and Kraft. A major problem is that with all the acquisitions, Borden failed to integrate the various brands into a single, cohesive network. Whereas Borden makes 2,800 snack products alone, industry leader Frito-Lay offers only 445. One supermarket executive said, "It's really difficult to understand what business Borden is in today when you look at the number of items they have." In simple terms, Borden could not take advantage of the economies inherent in selling the same or similar products, which put the firm at a huge cost disadvantage.

In October 1992, D'Amato announced a major overhaul of the company. The plan includes closing ten plants, reducing the work force by three thousand, folding four divisions into one, and eliminating the weakest parts of the snack division. The objective is to build the parts into an efficient whole. In the past big customers like Wal-Mart had to call five different divisions to place orders. The new integration process should serve customers better. The snack food group has already been cut from twelve regional profit centers to three. Some Wall Street analysts predict that Borden will have to sell one or more divisions, but D'Amato says he has no plans to sell anything yet, and maintains that Borden will be back on track in a year. In an attempt to rebuild its image and stimulate sales of its dairy products, Borden decided to bring back its symbol of Elsie the cow, out of use for twenty years. Critics claim that Elsie's appearance in print and television advertisements may remind the over-40 audience about Borden but will do nothing to attract younger consumers. D'Amato believes that Elsie recalls a simpler time of wholesomeness and quality that even the younger generation can relate to and says it is worth the money and effort to find out.

Questions for Discussion

1. Evaluate the width of Borden's product mix and the depth of its product lines.
2. Do Borden products have life cycles? Explain.

3. What type of branding strategy does Borden use? Is Borden a strong brand name?

4. Why did acquisitions lead to a major problem for Borden? Do you think the firm is on the right track to resolve this problem?

Based on information from Seth Lubove, "Pulling It All Together," *Forbes,* March 2, 1992, pp. 94–96; Judann Dagnoli, "Borden Joins Snack Price War," *Advertising Age,* March 23, 1992, p. 20; Elizabeth A. Lesley, "Borden Faces Facts: It's Time to Shed the Flab," *Business Week,* November 9, 1992, p. 44; Walter Guzzardi, "Big Can Still Be Beautiful," *Fortune,* April 25, 1988, pp. 50–64; and Kevin Goldman, "Experts Say Borden Has Milked Elsie the Cow for All She's Worth," *Wall Street Journal,* November 12, 1992, p. B9.

10.2   NESTLÉ FLEXES ITS MUSCLE

The Switzerland-based Nestlé corporation, once a Swiss chocolate maker, now is the world's largest food company and the largest producer of coffee, powdered milk, and frozen dinners. With the purchase of Perrier for $20.7 billion, Nestlé became the world's largest producer of mineral water, with 20 percent of the world market. After passing Mars, the company also became number one in candy. Nestlé achieved its success through intensive global expansion. Only 2 percent of Nestlé's sales come from Switzerland; the other 98 percent come from foreign countries.

One of the first multinational corporations, Nestlé now has production facilities in more than sixty countries. Its products can be found almost everywhere around the globe. In Europe, where Nestlé has experienced the greatest success, sales of instant coffee, mineral water, yogurt, frozen foods, cold cuts, candy, and cereal bars are roughly $10.2 billion. The company's sales in North America are approximately $6.7 billion, for products such as Nescafé instant coffee, Carnation Coffee-mate nondairy creamer, Friskies pet food, Nestlé Crunch chocolates, and Stouffer frozen foods. Other big markets for Nestlé have been Asia ($3.1 billion in sales), Latin America ($2.4 billion in sales), and Australia, New Zealand, and other islands of the Pacific ($.6 billion in sales). Annually, Nestlé spends approximately $1.2 billion in advertising.

One secret to Nestlé's success is that many of its products, especially instant coffee, chocolates, and frozen foods, appeal to consumers all over the world. For example, coffee is closing in on tea as the favorite drink in Japan. Frozen dinners, long a hit in the United States, are catching on in Europe. And of course chocolate tastes the same in any language. Although these products have to be adapted slightly to local tastes, they can be generally sold worldwide. Because of the high research and development costs, as well as the high costs of marketing, Nestlé benefits greatly by offering products with global appeal. After making large investments in its products, the company has been able to move brands from one country to another with relative ease.

Nestlé's Lean Cuisine dinners provide a good illustration of how the company expands internationally. Lean Cuisine was introduced in the United

States in 1981 and became a huge success. In 1985, Nestlé chief executive Helmut Maucher endorsed a plan to sell Lean Cuisine in Britain. In the beginning, before the company's British frozen-food plant reached full production, products were imported from a plant in Canada. The cost of shipping frozen dinners in refrigerated ships, in addition to paying customs taxes, was extremely high. But Maucher was patient and the venture paid off. In 1989, sales of frozen dinners in Britain reached $100 million and Nestlé achieved a 33 percent share of the market. Lean Cuisine has also been successfully introduced in France.

Because of its tremendous brand awareness, Nestlé has successfully launched several new products. Coca-Cola Nestlé Refreshment Company (CCNR), a joint venture between Coca-Cola and Nestlé, dominates the ready-to-drink iced tea market with its Nestea. Distribution, handled by the Coke bottling system, is through all channels, although a heavy emphasis is being placed on vending machines in New York. Nestlé also purchased U.K. confectioner Rowntree Mackintosh. Rowntree has high recognition throughout Europe and should help Nestlé build brand awareness in national markets. In Thailand, Nestlé manages its own marketing and distribution operation without the assistance of a local agent. Nestlé has cracked the tight Bangkok business community and media circles, achieving an 80 percent share of Thailand's instant coffee market, and has launched an iced coffee drink.

Now Nestlé is looking to what Maucher thinks is the market of the future, the Third World. Currently, 20 percent of the world's population consumes 80 percent of Nestlé's products. Maucher thinks his company's products will soon be seen in more parts of the world. The company also will look to what Maucher considers the food of the future—pasta. As he puts it, "We can't feed the world on beefsteak. So noodles will conquer the world."

Most industry experts agree that Nestlé is in the best position of any food company to expand internationally. Most of its competitors, which have been concentrating on their domestic markets, are scrambling to become involved in the profitable international trade.

Questions for Discussion

1. Why has Nestlé had so much global success with its products?

2. Why is it so expensive for Nestlé to sell a product like Lean Cuisine in other countries?

3. Will competitors be able to follow Nestlé into foreign markets with the same degree of success?

4. Does Nestlé have to change its products for foreign markets? Explain.

Based on information from Bruce Crumley, "Nestlé Muscle May Pump Perrier," *Advertising Age,* March 30, 1992, p. 59; John Parry, "Nestlé's Name Plan," *International Management,* December 1991, pp. 54–55; Greg W. Prince, "Coke-Nestlé Venture Finally Bears Tea," *Beverage World,* January 31, 1992, pp. 1, 4; Joyce Rainat, "In Thailand, Nestlé Goes Direct to the People," *Asian Finance,* September 15, 1991, p. 14; and Shawn Tully, "Nestlé Shows How to Gobble Markets," *Fortune,* January 16, 1989, pp. 74–78.

Products from Services and Nonprofit Organizations

OBJECTIVES

- *To describe the nature and importance of services.*

- *To discuss the characteristics that distinguish services from goods.*

- *To classify services.*

- *To identify marketing strategies for services.*

- *To discuss the concept of service quality.*

- *To identify marketing strategies for nonprofit organizations.*

OUTLINE

Delivering its product better than anyone else in the business has put Carnival Cruise Lines into the number one spot in the cruise industry. Carnival was not the first cruise line to advertise on network television or the first to use the theme that cruises are great fun. But the firm became successful by providing a consistent product and message.

Carnival's founder, Ted Arison, came up with the brainstorm that has become his company's underlying principle: Make the ship itself one of the destinations. While most major cruise lines were emphasizing the ports of call, Arison focused on the shipboard experience. He turned Carnival's ships into floating resorts equipped with pools, casinos, entertainment, and plenty of food. Passengers enjoy being on the ship as much as landing at some exotic Caribbean port. The ships' names, like *Mardi Gras* and *Fantasy,* as well as everything else about Carnival, suggest fun. Even a major competitor has acknowledged that "Carnival's marketing approach has been brilliant. Nobody has been able to truly compete in their niche."

Carnival's superior service on board reinforces the idea that the ship is a primary destination. Whereas some competitors provide room service sixteen hours a day, Carnival provides it around the clock. Each day, passengers are treated to three full meals and a midnight buffet; snacks are available regularly beginning at 6:30 A.M. Room stewards constantly make rounds to keep the cabins clean, to help with luggage, and to even turn down beds. Waiters who serve passengers on the pool deck learn beverage preferences and offer refills before being asked.

Carnival prices its cruises competitively, and the all-inclusive cruise package is less expensive than comparable land-based vacations. This pricing has allowed Carnival to target cruises at people who previously could not afford them. Typical Carnival passengers have a median income of $56,300. The popular seven-day Caribbean cruise on the *Celebration* costs about $1,000, including airfare to Miami, the port of departure.

Carnival has also made the most of possible distribution outlets. Using travel agents to help facilitate the transaction has enabled Carnival to establish a highly effective sales mechanism. The firm encourages travel agents to present cruises as an alternative to other trips, or combine a vacation stay with a theme park like Disney World. Carnival employees visit travel agents to develop a relationship and to build cooperation. Another incentive for agents to recommend Carnival cruises is the cash awards the firm sometimes provides for bookings. The cruise line's strategy works, since the majority of Carnival passengers say a travel agent recommended it.

Promotion is also a critical part of Carnival's marketing strategy. Carnival's promotion and marketing budget is geared to attracting the first-time cruiser, with a significant allotment of its marketing budget to network television and over 200 major metropolitan newspapers. The company's marketing strategy has gained it a significant percent share of the North American cruise market and industry dominance.

A huge potential market exists for the cruise industry. Although cruises have become more popular among vacationers, only 6 percent of Americans have taken one. The entire cruise industry generated 4.3 million people in 1992 and research shows the potential market to be between 40 to 100 million people per year. Carnival hopes to lure more passengers with its new Super Liners—*Fantasy, Ecstasy,* and *Sensation,* three of the world's largest passenger ships, and will be taking delivery of the *Fascination* and *Imagination* in 1994 and 1995.[1] ●

As the opening feature illustrates, producing a service is much different than producing goods. Carnival Cruise Lines is selling something that isn't tangible like a compact disk or a cheeseburger. Call a cruise fun, adventure, romance, or whatever you like, it is a service. And the success of a service firm, like that of any organization, depends on its ability to satisfy customers. To succeed, Carnival must identify a target market and develop a product, price, distribution, and promotion strategy; provide superior service; and develop new ventures.

Marketing services has become a critical issue as service firms face many of the same challenges manufacturing firms have experienced, including increased competition and consumer demand for higher quality. Some experts have noted that some of the current challenges facing service firms are similar to those contributing to the U.S. decline in manufacturing.[2] The future of service organizations depends upon their ability to deliver quality services.[3]

THE NATURE AND IMPORTANCE OF SERVICES

■ **service** an intangible product that provides benefits to consumers and often involves human or mechanical effort

In Chapter 10, a *product* is defined as a good, service, or an idea. A good is a tangible product that consumers can physically possess. A **service** is an intangible product that provides benefits to consumers and often involves

[1] Based on information from Bradley Johnson, "Carnival," *Advertising Age,* July 6, 1992, pp. 5, 22; Michael J. McCarthy, "Carnival Plans Europe Venture with Club Med," *Wall Street Journal,* May 19, 1992, pp. B1, B12; Faye Rice, "How Carnival Stacks the Decks," *Fortune,* January 16, 1989, pp. 108–116; Fran Durbin, "Carnival Plans to Use Fantasy on Short Trips," *Travel Weekly,* October 27, 1988, pp. 1–2; and Stephen Koepp, "All the Fun Is Getting There," *Time,* January 11, 1988, pp. 54–56.
[2] James Brian Quinn and Christopher E. Gagnan, "Will Services Follow Manufacturing into Decline?" *Harvard Business Review,* November–December 1987, pp. 95–103.
[3] James L. Heskett, W. Earl Sasser, Jr., and Christopher W.L. Hart, *Service Breakthroughs* (New York: The Free Press, 1990), p. 1.

TABLE 11.1
Ten Largest Service Firms
in the United States

Rank	Name	Industry	Sales (millions)
1	American Telephone & Telegraph	Telecommunications	$63,314
2	Cargill	Commodity sales	49,148
3	Exxon	Fuels	13,522
4	Fleming	Wholesale	12,902
5	Time Warner	Entertainment	12,021
6	Super Value Stores	Wholesale	11,638
7	Sprint	Telecommunications	8,780
8	Marriott	Hotels	8,729
9	MCI Communications	Telecommunications	8,439
10	McKesson	Wholesale	8,421

Source: *Fortune*, June 1, 1992, p. 174. *Fortune Service 500,* © 1992 Time Inc. All rights reserved.

human or mechanical effort. A service cannot be physically possessed. Banks, hotels, and insurance companies, for example, provide services to their customers. Table 11.1 lists the top service firms in the United States.

Few products can be classified as a pure good or a pure service. For example, when consumers purchase a VCR, they assume ownership of a physical item that provides entertainment, but the warranty associated with the purchase is a service. When consumers rent a VCR, they are purchasing an entertainment service provided through temporary use of the recorder. Thus, most products contain both tangible and intangible elements. However, one element usually predominates, and this dominant element is the basis for classifying products as goods or services. A Carnival cruise is a service, but it has tangible elements such as ships, employees, furnishings, and food. Figure 11.1 shows how United Airlines advertises its services.

Figure 11.2 demonstrates the concept of tangibility by placing a variety of goods and services on a continuum of tangibility and intangibility. Products in which tangible elements predominate (sugar, clothing, automobiles) are arranged on the left side according to their degree of tangibility. Intangible-dominant products (health care, education, financial consulting) are arranged on the right side of the continuum. The products falling in the middle of the continuum (fast food, haircuts, air travel) have a strong mix of both tangible and intangible elements. For example, a haircut can be seen and felt, but the satisfaction derived from the haircut comes from the service rendered by the hair stylist.

FIGURE 11.1
Services
Services such as airline travel are intangible products because they cannot be physically possessed by customers. In this advertisement, United Airlines emphasizes comfort and speed to help consumers evaluate the service.

Source: United Airlines.

The service sector of the American economy is becoming increasingly important. Service industries now account for nearly 70 percent of the U.S. gross national product.[4] More people are employed in the service sector than in any other sector of the economy. The number of service jobs increased from 65 million in 1980 to about 86 million in 1992. At its peak in the late 1980s, 220,000 new service jobs were added each month, far outpacing manufacturing.[5] This growth has leveled off in recent years as service industries have experienced intense competition, some from foreign firms. Nonetheless, service jobs are expected to grow faster than jobs in other sectors of the economy. Two-thirds of Americans aged 75 or older are women, and the number of men and women in this age group is expected to increase from 13.2 million in 1990 to 18.3 million in 2010. This means a growth in a variety of services, especially those targeted at elderly widows, such as estate planning, home delivery, health care, or simply someone to take care of daily activities such as paying bills.[6] This is also resulting in increased competition among domestic and foreign firms' marketing services. Marketing Close-up looks at foreign competition in service industries.

[4] *Statistical Abstract of the United States,* 1992, p. 429.
[5] Howard Banks, "What's Ahead for Business," *Forbes,* May 25, 1992, p. 37.
[6] "Where the Boys Aren't," *American Demographics Desk Reference,* No. 4, 1992, pp. 8–14.

CHARACTERISTICS OF SERVICES

Four basic characteristics distinguish services from goods: intangibility, in-separability of production and consumption, perishability, and heterogene-ity. These characteristics are important because they pose several unique marketing problems.

Intangibility

■ **intangibility** the charac-teristic of not being capable of assessment by customers' sense of taste, touch, sight, smell, or hearing

The primary characteristic that distinguishes services from other products is **intangibility,** the quality of not being able to be assessed by customers' sense of taste, touch, sight, smell, or hearing. The other three characteristics unique to services all derive from their intangibility. Services such as banking, insur-ance, and education cannot be physically possessed like a tangible good.

FIGURE 11.2
A Continuum of Product Tangibility and Intangibility

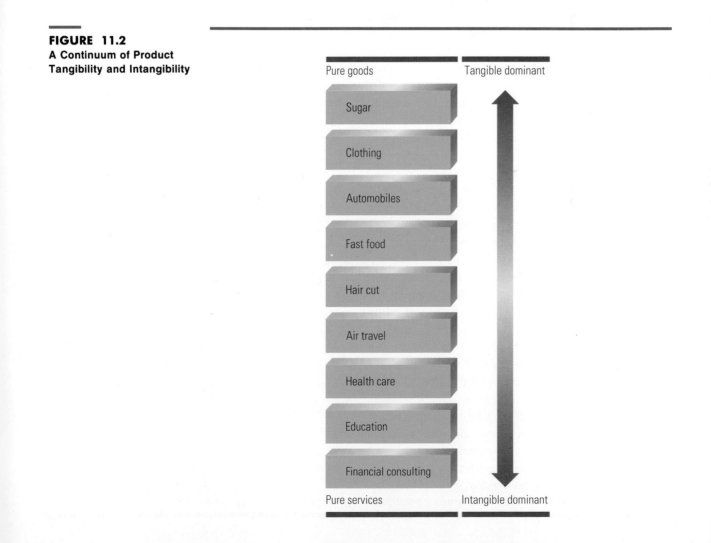

MARKETING CLOSE-UP

The Service Industry Sees Global Competition

In the U.S., nearly eight out of ten workers are employed by service companies. That fact wouldn't surprise many people, but this one might: Services also dominate the world economy. They now account for nearly 70 percent of the gross domestic product and most of the new jobs created in the world's industrial nations.

The United States is the world leader, with 150 companies in the *Fortune* Global Service 500. But with the global economy slowing and foreign competition increasing, America is undergoing a wave of restructuring in the service sector just as it did in manufacturing. Mergers and downsizing in service industries such as banking, insurance, retail trade, and airlines have cut out jobs in the last few years. Until recently, services had little threat from competition and little incentive to increase efficiency. Many companies let white-collar ranks swell, invested too heavily in information technology, and let productivity stagnate. But deregulation and foreign investment are challenging business as usual in many service industries. Some experts are warning U.S. service companies to get ready for a dramatic change.

Just as the smokestack industries remade themselves in the 1980s, so service industries will strive for increased productivity in the 1990s. Although the creation of new jobs was hailed as a strength of the service economy, in fact it is a symptom of inefficiency: Many service firms have hired new workers but haven't used new technology to its potential or achieved economic efficiency. The result: a bloated and vulnerable service economy. Service workers hold nearly 80 percent of the jobs in private industry, and their companies must make them more productive to remain competitive. An increased standard of living depends on improved productivity.

Americans used to believe that services were immune to foreign competition. Whereas cars, televi-sions, and microwaves could flow freely across national borders, insurance, hotels, and banking could not. We have found out differently. The United States is the world's richest market for services and represents great opportunities for multinational firms looking to expand. Many foreign companies are investing directly in U.S. service industries. Foreigners have roughly a $20 billion ownership stake in U.S. banks. But most foreign investment has been in non-financial services such as retail and wholesale trade, business services, hotels, and entertainment. Notable foreign acquisitions include the following:

- MCA by Matsushita (Japan) for $7.9 billion
- Columbia Pictures by Sony (Japan) for $4.7 billion
- Motel 6 by Accor (France) for $2.2 billion
- Holiday Inn by Bass PLC (Great Britain) for $2.2 billion
- Saks Fifth Avenue by Investcorp Bank (Bahrain) for $1.5 billion
- First Maryland Bancorp by Allied Irish Banks (Ireland) for $1.1 billion

Foreign buyers are not likely to run off with the assets of U.S. service companies. But as foreign firms gain ground in American markets, U.S. service firms will need to respond to heightened competition through quality and productivity. So far, companies have cut costs by slashing payrolls, eliminating business units, and consolidating operations—much of it long overdue. But the challenge now facing U.S. services is to expand to maintain market share in a world economy.

Sources: Adapted from Stephen S. Roach, "Services Under Siege—The Restructuring Imperative," *Harvard Business Review*, September–October 1991, pp. 82–91; Nora E. Field and Ricardo Sookdeo, "Introducing a New List," *Fortune*, August 26, 1991, pp. 166–170; and Michael Mandel, "There's a Silver Lining in the Service Sector," *Business Week*, March 4, 1992, pp. 60–61.

Intangible services are more difficult for consumers to evaluate than are tangible goods. For instance, it is more difficult to evaluate services provided by a physician than to evaluate an automobile. A person can look at the car, take it for a test drive, and form an opinion. A physical examination cannot be assessed in the same manner.

Of course, although it is difficult to walk into a store and evaluate a service, it is not impossible for consumers to make some judgment about services. For instance, before selecting a health club, you could visit the facilities, look at the condition and quality of the equipment, examine the credentials of the instructors, and observe the atmosphere at the facility. Such criteria would provide some tangible means of evaluating different health clubs. This once again illustrates that just as most tangible goods have some intangible element, so most intangible services have some tangible element. The tangible element of services is very important because it may be used by consumers to evaluate and compare alternative services or service providers. We talk about this issue more throughout the chapter.

Inseparability of Production and Consumption

■ **inseparability** the characteristic of having simultaneous and indivisible production and consumption of services

Another characteristic of services is the **inseparability,** or indivisible nature, of production and consumption: Services, such as education, are generally produced and consumed at the same time. Because of this characteristic, the service provider plays a very important role in the delivery of services. In many cases, the service provider *is* the service. For instance, a hair stylist is the actual service, and must be present when the service is produced and consumed.

Because production and consumption occur simultaneously, the *customer* also has an important role in the delivery of services.[7] In most cases, the service cannot be performed unless the customer is present or directly involved in the production process. For instance, many service-station customers fill their own gasoline tanks, bank customers operate automatic teller machines (ATMs), and as you can see in Figure 11.3, a traveler who sightsees and interacts with local residents is involved in the production and consumption of a city's tourism services. Because customers often play an active role in the production and delivery of services, the service customer must have the ability, skill, training, and motivation needed to engage in the production process. The service encounter cannot be completed successfully unless customers have the skills needed to participate in the transaction. By encouraging customers to share the responsibility for delivering services, organizations can reduce the number of consumer complaints.[8]

[7]Peter K. Mills and James H. Morris, "Clients as 'Partial' Employees of Service Organizations: Role Development in Client Participation," *Academy of Management Journal,* December 1986, pp. 726–735.
[8]Cathy Goodwin, "I Can Do It Myself: Training the Service Customer to Contribute to Service Productivity," *Journal of Services Marketing,* Fall 1988, pp. 71–78.

FIGURE 11.3
Inseparability
The production and con-
sumption of a city's tourism
services cannot be sepa-
rated, so travelers must be
in Quebec to consume the
many delights the city has
to offer.

Source: BCP Strategy Creativity.

Perishability

■ **perishability** the characteristic that service capacity
unused in one time period
cannot be stored for use in
the future

A result of the inseparability of production and consumption is that services
are characterized by **perishability**—that is, service capacity unused in one
time period cannot be stored for use in the future. The key issue is that
supply does not always equal demand. A company selling goods would deal
with this problem through inventory control. But service marketing cannot
handle this problem in the same way. Consider the movie theater's seating
capacity dilemma. At a matinee showing of a movie, the theater is more
than half empty. However, that evening, so many people want to get into
the 8 o'clock feature that many must be turned away because of a lack of
seating. Unfortunately, the extra seats from the matinee cannot be stored for
use in the evening. Other types of services, such as air-conditioning repair
and tax preparation, are time-sensitive in other ways. The bulk of these
service activities must be performed at one point in time or close to the time
the customer demands the service. Because services cannot be stored, such
fluctuations in demand for services cause serious problems for marketing
managers.

Heterogeneity

Most services are performed by people, and people are not always consistent
in their performance. This inconsistency or variation in performance is re-

■ **heterogeneity** the characteristic of inconsistency or variation in performance of services

ferred to as the **heterogeneity** of services. Performance may vary from one individual or service to another within the same organization, or in the service one individual provides from day to day and from customer to customer. For instance, many people take their automobiles to a favorite automobile mechanic at a certain service station because they think this mechanic provides better service than others. But even a favorite automobile mechanic may provide inferior service once in a while. Thus services are much more difficult to standardize than tangible goods.

Although the lack of standardization in services is a problem, it also provides opportunities in the marketing of services. By customizing services to meet the specific needs of consumers, service marketers can be in a better position to satisfy their customers. For example, airlines provide alternative levels of service by offering flights in first, business, and coach class. Likewise, a consulting firm can provide customized services to various clients.

CLASSIFYING SERVICES

It is important to develop a classification scheme for services. Not only do such schemes help managers gain a better understanding of customer needs, but they also provide insights into the marketing of services.[9] A categorization scheme for services answers questions such as the following:

- Does the customer have to be present to initiate or terminate the service transaction?
- Does the customer have to be present for the service to be delivered?
- Does the customer participate in the service transaction?
- Is the customer or target of the service changed in some way after the service transaction is completed?
- Is there a high degree of labor intensiveness?
- How much skill is required of the service provider?

Answers to questions like these help marketing managers enhance the quality of the service. Consider taking a car to an automobile repair shop. If customers have to drop off the car to initiate the service, their satisfaction will be determined to some extent by their interactions with the personnel, their success in explaining the problem, and whether they get satisfactory results. On the other hand, using an ATM card requires little contact with the bank. It is important that the automatic teller works, that it is simple to use, and that the transaction be satisfactory, but how the money gets into the machine—the process—is of little interest to customers.

---

[9]Leonard L. Berry, David R. Bennett, and Carter W. Brown, *Service Quality: A Profit Strategy for Financial Institutions* (Homewood, Ill.: Dow Jones-Irwin, 1989), p. 26.

Services are a very diverse group of products encompassing such industries as automobile rentals, repairs, health care, barbershops and beauty salons, health clubs and gyms, amusement parks, day care, domestic services, legal counsel, banking, insurance, air travel, education, business consulting, dry cleaning, and accounting. Despite this diversity, services can be classified on the basis of the following criteria: (1) type of market, (2) degree of labor intensiveness, (3) degree of customer contact, (4) skill of the service provider, and (5) goal of the service provider. Figure 11.4 illustrates this classification scheme.

Services are classified according to the type of market, or customer, they serve—consumer or organizational. This distinction is important because, as discussed in Chapters 7 and 8, the buying decision process differs between organizations and consumers. In addition, the type of market generally dictates the design of the marketing mix for a service. For instance, a janitorial firm that cleans both residential homes and office buildings or factories will have different marketing mixes for each type of customer because home owners have different needs and expectations regarding cleaning services than do organizations.

Services are also classified by degree of labor intensiveness. Many services, including repairs, education, and hair styling, depend heavily on the knowledge and skills of the service providers. Others, such as telecommunications, gyms, and public transportation, rely more on equipment. Labor-intensive (people-based) services are generally more heterogeneous than are equipment-based services. Consumers tend to view the providers of people-based services as the service itself. Flight attendants, for instance, represent an airline to many people. Consequently, service providers must pay special attention to the selection, training, motivation, and control of employees.

 A third criterion for classifying services is degree of customer contact. Health care, hotels, real estate agencies, and restaurants are examples of high-contact services (see Figure 11.5). With high-contact services, actions are generally directed toward individuals. The consumer must be present during production; in fact, the consumer must often go to the production facility. The physical appearance of the service facility may therefore be a major factor in the consumer's overall evaluation of a high-contact service. With low-contact services, such as repairs, dry cleaning, and mail services, customers generally do not need to be present during service delivery. For example, consumers do not wait at dry cleaners while their clothes are being laundered. As a result, physical appearance is not so important for low-contact facilities.[10]

A fourth way to classify services is the level of skill of the service provider. Professional services tend to be more complex and more highly regulated than nonprofessional services. In the case of a physical examination by a doctor to diagnose a medical problem, consumers often do not know what the actual service or its cost will be until the service is completed because the

---

[10]Christopher H. Lovelock, "Classifying Services to Gain Strategic Marketing Insights," *Journal of Marketing,* Summer 1983, p. 15.

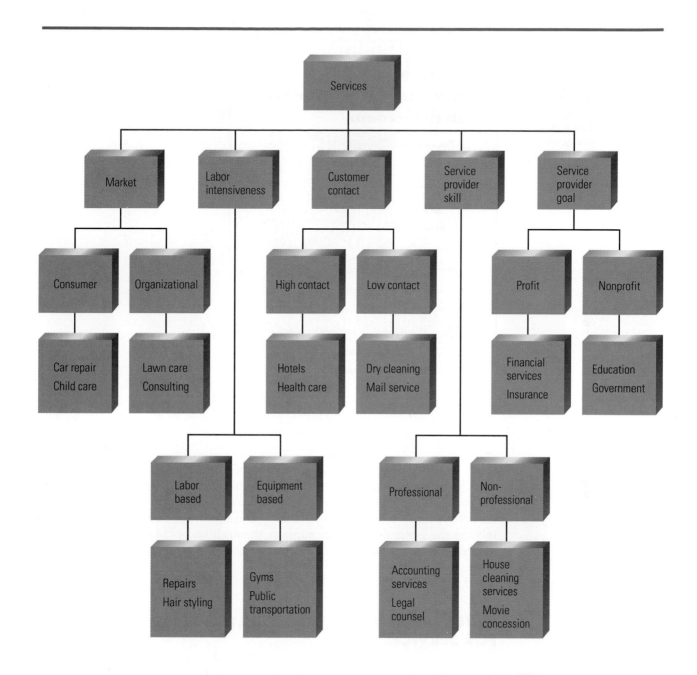

FIGURE 11.4
Classification of Services

final product is situation-specific. Also, doctors and surgeons are regulated by laws and by professional associations. Even less skilled service providers, such as airline pilots, undergo extensive training and retraining and must comply with a host of regulations and policies. However, clerks in movie theater concession stands need few skills to carry out their jobs.

Finally, services can be classified according to the goal of the service provider—profit or nonprofit. There are several differences in marketing profit

FIGURE 11.5

High-contact Services
Hotels are high-contact services. The customer must be present at the hotel to consume the service and the physical appearance of the facility and the services provided are major factors in the consumer's evaluation of the hotel.

Source: Westin Hotels and Resorts.

and nonprofit services. The objectives of nonprofit organizations are not stated in financial terms, and the benefits of nonprofit services are not measured by profit or return on investment. In addition, organizations marketing nonprofit services usually have two audiences—clients and donors. A public school system is marketed to families with school-age children but must also rely on the general public for support through taxes. Many nonprofit services, such as legal aid, are marketed to low-income segments.

DEVELOPING MARKETING STRATEGIES FOR SERVICES

Like marketers of tangible goods, service marketers must strive to satisfy consumers through the application of the marketing concept. Service organizations must therefore develop strategies that satisfy the needs of consumers in the target market. As you recall, developing a marketing strategy involves identifying a target market and developing a marketing mix for this target market. The unique characteristics of services should be considered in developing marketing strategies. The next sections discuss some of the unique aspects of developing marketing strategies for services.

Product Strategy

As noted earlier, services cannot be defined in terms of their physical attributes because they are intangible. It is often difficult, then, for consumers to understand service offerings and to evaluate possible service alternatives. Tangible elements—facilities, employees, communications—associated with a service help to form the product and are often the only features of a service that can be viewed or evaluated prior to purchase. That is why marketers should pay close attention to these tangible elements and ensure that they are consistent with the selected image of the service product. Marketers should also focus on the benefits the customer is buying rather than on the service itself.[11] For instance, airline advertisements often focus on the food, service, personnel, and travel experience that the airline provides.

As we have noted, consumers often equate service products with the provider of the service; this is especially true for labor-based services. Consider a bank, for instance. Money, a tangible good of the bank, is an undifferentiated product—it is the same at all banks. But a teller—who may be competent and accommodating or slow and irritable—is the service provided by the bank. Because service personnel like tellers are perceived as the service and because they are inconsistent in their behavior, it is essential that marketers carefully select, train, motivate, and control these contact people. Service providers are selling long-term relationships as well as providing a service.

 Selecting a name for a service organization can be critical because, in services, the company name *is* the service. A well-chosen name can give a company a decided marketing edge over competitors by providing strong brand identity and giving the service some degree of tangibility. For instance, the name Federal Express is appropriate for an overnight delivery service. *Federal* suggests a far-ranging enterprise, and *express* implies speedy service.[12] Good service names should be distinctive, relevant, memorable, and flexible. Table 11.2 provides examples of good and bad names, based on these criteria.

Promotion Strategy

Because services are intangible-dominant products, they are difficult to advertise. Something intangible is not easily depicted in advertising, whether the medium is print, television, or radio. Therefore, advertising of services should emphasize tangible cues, or symbols, of the services that are more easily perceived and understood by consumers. For instance, advertising might focus on the physical facilities in which the service is performed or some other relevant tangible aspect that symbolizes the service itself.[13] The cues should also be associated with the benefits the customer is seeking from the service. For instance, Express Mail uses a powerful eagle with widespread

[11] Betsy D. Gelb, "How Marketers of Intangibles Can Raise the Odds for Customer Satisfaction," *Journal of Services Marketing,* Summer 1987, pp. 11–18.
[12] Leonard L. Berry, Edwin F. Lefkowith, and Terry Clark, "In Services, What's in a Name?" *Harvard Business Review,* September–October 1988, pp. 28–30.
[13] William R. George and Leonard L. Berry, "Guidelines for the Advertising of Services," *Business Horizons,* July–August 1981, pp. 52–56.

TABLE 11.2
Examples of Names for Services

Criterion	Good Name	Bad Name
Distinctive	Chase Marriott	Allied United
Relevant	Humana VISA	Joe's Service Station
Memorable	NYNEX	Grand Union U.S. West
Flexible	Delta Sentry	First Nation Air South

Source: Leonard L. Berry, Edwin F. Lefkowith, and Terry Clark, "In Services, What's in a Name?" *Harvard Business Review*, September–October 1988, pp. 28–30.

wings to represent the courier of overnight letters. Although the eagle has nothing to do with how the mail gets transported, the symbol makes it easier for consumers to grasp the intangible concept of speedily delivered, airborne mail. Figure 11.6 shows how Traveler's Insurance uses the image of an umbrella as a tangible cue in its advertising.

As pointed out earlier, the variability in the performance of service contact personnel, which arises from the labor-intensive nature of many services, poses problems for service marketers. Advertising can have a positive effect on service contact personnel; it can shape employees' perceptions of the company, their jobs, and how management expects them to perform. It can also serve as a tool for motivating, educating, and communicating with employees. When an Avis employee sees an advertisement portraying a worker at an airport rental counter providing friendly service, it sends a clear message about performance expectations at Avis. When good relationships exist between employers and employees and between customers and employees, the buyer–seller relationship can be the focal point of marketing efforts rather than the service itself.[14]

Personal selling can play a powerful role in promoting service because it enables consumers and salespeople to interact. If properly trained, salespeople can use this interaction to reduce customer uncertainty, give reassurance, reduce dissonance, and promote the reputation of the organization. Once again, careful training and management of customer contact personnel is crucial to the success of a service provider, since sales personnel provide a close link to service customers.

Sales promotions are more difficult to implement for services than for goods. Promotion methods such as point-of-purchase displays and free

[14]James H. Donnelly, Jr., "Intangibility and Marketing Strategies for Retail Bank Services," *Journal of Retail Banking*, June 1980, pp. 39–43.

FIGURE 11.6
Tangible Cues
In advertising their insurance services, The Travelers Companies use the image of an umbrella as a tangible cue to convey the idea of security and protection.

Source: © 1992 The Travelers Corporation.

samples are generally impossible to use. Intangible products like health care and accounting services cannot be displayed, and if free samples are used, the firm has to give away the entire product. Coupons, rebates, contests, and free first-time visits to service facilities are feasible sales promotion tools for some service firms and can be used to smooth out demand.

Finally, service firms usually rely more heavily on publicity than do firms marketing goods. This is especially true of nonprofit organizations, which cannot afford extensive advertising; publicity is often easier for nonprofit organizations to obtain because they provide services that benefit the community. Service firms also rely on publicity because it is viewed as being more objective than advertising.

Price Strategy

The intangible nature of services makes establishing prices difficult. The price of physical goods can be based on the cost of production (materials, labor, and overhead). However, determining the cost of producing a service for the purpose of setting a price is more complicated.

For services, price may function as an important cue to consumers. When services—particularly labor-based services—are equivalent, price may be important in selecting a service provider. For instance, if all airline companies are perceived as being similar, the airline with the lowest price may be selected. Southwest Airlines' strategy is to keep costs as low as possible, and offer a bargain price. By using fuel-efficient planes, flying large numbers of passengers on high-frequency, one-hour routes, and cutting amenities, Southwest's fares average around $58 one-way, much lower than its larger rivals.[15] When services are perceived as being dissimilar, price may still weigh heavily in a consumer's selection decision. A consumer seeking help with financial planning, for example, may believe that a full-service financial counselor who charges more than a discount broker is more qualified and thus may choose the financial adviser rather than the discount broker.

■ **bundling** the marketing of two or more services together as a single package for a special price

Marketing two or more services together as a single package for a special price is a practice called **bundling.** The use of bundling to stimulate demand for services has been expanding in recent years.[16] Many airlines bundle vacation packages combining air travel, car rentals, and hotel accommodations. Likewise, banks offer special programs in which customers receive credit cards, traveler's checks, and other financial services.

Pricing can also be used to smooth fluctuations in demand for services. A service provider may lower prices to help stimulate demand during slow periods and raise prices during peak periods to discourage demand. Airlines, vacation resorts, movie theaters, restaurants, and hotels rely heavily on price to help smooth their demand.

Distribution Strategy

Because of the inseparability of production and consumption, most services are limited to direct channels of distribution. However, some types of services can and do make use of marketing intermediaries. Low-contact services, for example, can be offered through retail outlets. Consumers often drop off film at a supermarket or drug store for developing, but the film is generally sent somewhere else for actual developing—the retailers are simply drop-off centers. This separation of service provider and retailer is possible because the service is directed toward the consumer's physical possessions and the consumer need not be present during service delivery.

Other service industries make use of different types of marketing intermediaries. Travel agencies, for instance, help facilitate exchanges between consumers and airlines, car rental companies, and hotels. ATMs serve as electronic intermediaries for financial services. MasterCard and VISA credit cards have enabled banks to extend their credit services to consumers in widely dispersed geographic areas. Some examples of marketing intermediaries for services in various industries are shown in Table 11.3.

The distribution of services is closely linked to product development. To provide tangibility, a marketer may develop a physical symbol of the service. If a physical symbol can be created, then the service can be separated from the provider, and direct sale is not the only distribution alternative. For

---

[15] Richard Woodbury, "Prince of Midair," *Time,* January 25, 1993, p. 55.
[16] Joseph P. Guiltinan, "The Price Bundling of Services: A Normative Framework," *Journal of Marketing,* April 1987, pp. 74–85.

TABLE 11.3
Marketing Intermediaries for Services

Industry	Marketing Intermediary
Health care	Health maintenance organization (HMO)
Insurance	Vending machine
Communications	Walk-up telephone
Financial	Direct deposit of paycheck

instance, bank credit cards, which are physical symbols of credit, enable retailers to act as *indirect* intermediaries in the distribution of an intangible service—credit. Additionally, extending a line of credit to a consumer allows him or her to *store* the intangible service of credit.

Since customers must be present when services are produced, location is an important issue in the marketing of services. Service facilities or outlets should be located in close proximity to the target market. Many banks that are located in downtown districts have opened branches for this reason. Location can also be used to give the service a desired image such as prestige or economy.

SERVICE QUALITY

One aspect of service marketing that is receiving increasing attention from marketers is the quality of the services. Many service organizations have recognized that, when competing services are similar, customers are won and lost based on the quality of service. We are moving into a time when service organizations do not merely produce, they perform; customer value is a focus for competitive advantage.[17] For instance, many airline companies have several daily flights between Chicago and New York. In most cases, the fares for the flights are identical. Why then does a traveler select one airline over another? The quality of the service may be a major factor. The next sections define service quality and explore ways to improve the quality of services.

Defining Service Quality

■ **service quality** the conformance of service(s) to customer specifications and expectations

Only the customer can judge the quality of services. Thus, **service quality** is the conformance of service(s) to customer specifications and expectations.[18] To the administrators of a medical clinic, service quality is often viewed as

[17] Karl Albrecht, "Total Quality Service," *Quality Digest,* January 1993, pp. 18–19.
[18] Berry, Bennett, and Brown, p. 26.

the credentials of the physicians; consumers, however, are more concerned with waiting time and interactions with doctors and staff members than with where the doctors obtained their degrees.[19] Service organizations must determine what benefits customers expect to receive and must then develop service products that meet or exceed those expectations. Performing the wrong functions for customers is not service quality. Only by meeting consumer expectations on a consistent basis can an organization deliver service quality.

True service quality rarely goes unnoticed. Providing service quality is easier said than done, however. The evidence of poor service is readily available: planes are late, restaurants provide slow or inefficient service, sales clerks are rude. Such occurrences—and many others—have led poor service to be labeled as a growth industry.[20] Close to the Customer examines how several firms avoid the high cost of poor service.

Improving Service Quality

To improve the quality of its services, a service provider must first understand how consumers judge service quality. Because the service itself is intangible, consumers generally make quality judgments based on *how* the service is performed. Table 11.4 lists five criteria consumers use to judge service quality. These criteria are basically the same regardless of the type of service.[21] Once a firm has an understanding of consumers' criteria for evaluating services, it can take steps to improve its service product.

Service quality is difficult to improve. In some cases, companies simply do not recognize that service quality problems exist. Many dissatisfied customers never complain to the company. For example, in a recent survey of airline passengers, a consumer group of 100,000 frequent fliers ranked airline food lowest among fourteen airline services. But passengers usually do not complain to airlines about the food.[22] Service quality is also difficult to manage. One airline employee may interact with hundreds of customers every day. It is impossible for managers to observe each of these encounters and evaluate the quality of services, especially if unhappy customers do not complain.[23] Nonetheless, studies have shown that customers tell twice as many people about bad service experiences as they do about good ones.[24] Customers left unhappy, whether they complain or not, may destroy a service organization.

Service quality is not an accident. It can be improved through total organizational commitment. First, managers must take quality seriously. Without

[19] Berry, Bennett, and Brown, p. 26.
[20] Gregg Fields and Joan Chrissos, "Service Without a Smile a Growth Industry," Lexington, Ky. *Herald-Leader,* October 4, 1987, pp. A1, A14.
[21] A. Parasuraman, Valarie A. Zeithaml, and Leonard L. Berry, "A Conceptual Model of Service Quality and Its Implications for Future Research," *Journal of Marketing,* Fall 1985, pp. 41–50.
[22] Monci Jo Williams, "Why Is Airline Food So Terrible?" *Fortune,* December 19, 1988, pp. 169–172.
[23] Thomas C. Keiser, "Strategies for Enhancing Service Quality," *Journal of Services Marketing,* Summer 1988, pp. 65–70.
[24] Patricia Sellers, "How to Handle Customers' Gripes," *Fortune,* October 24, 1988, pp. 88–100.

CLOSE TO THE CUSTOMER

Quality Service

The United States economy has been labeled a "service" economy, and indeed the evidence points that way. Service industries have grown faster than manufacturing. McDonald's has more employees than U.S. Steel. White-collar workers outnumbered blue-collar workers for the first time in 1956, and the trend toward greater job growth in the service sector has continued ever since. In recent years, jobs have emerged in industries such as the following:

- Transportation, communication, and public utilities
- Insurance, real estate, and financial institutions
- Wholesale and retail trade
- Service business
- Medical and progressional services
- Nonprofit organizations

The boom in *services* has brought with it a growing interest in *service*—customer service, that is. Since services are products that involve human effort, quality services often require quality efforts from people. Quality efforts result in excellent customer service—which is essential to success. One quality consultant says it costs five times as much to get a new customer as to keep an old one. Thus many firms have turned their attention to service quality.

Southwest Airlines always spells the word *customer* with a capital *C* in ads, brochures, and the annual report to show employees and the public that the Customer matters. As CEO Herbert Kelleher explains, "The bigger we get, the smaller I want our employees to think and act." Frequent fliers get birthday cards, and passengers get personal responses to letters, sometimes several pages long. It's time consuming and expensive for employees to spend many hours each week answering letters, but Kelleher thinks that letters are the best way to keep track of his airline's performance. Because treating customers right is easier when employees are treated right, each division at Southwest also identifies its internal customers—employees—and focuses on their needs. For instance, mechanics target pilots and marketing personnel target reservation agents. Providing quality services to one another makes it easier to provide quality services to customers.

Quality service is also a top priority at McDonald's. A recent advertisement pledges that if customers are not satisfied, "We'll make it right or the next meal's on us. What you want is what you get. Guaranteed." Other fast-food chains are also trying to improve service. Domino's Pizza is testing a customer satisfaction guarantee to replace its 30-minute delivery guarantee. Bennigan's dinnerhouse chain claims in advertisements that "you don't have to be a celebrity to be treated special." Burger King provides a toll-free number consumers can call with complaints or suggestions, and it takes calls seriously. The number of complaints is entered into an index compiled on each store, along with comments from "mystery shoppers" who visit stores to check service, food quality, and cleanliness. Rax Restaurants has had a satisfaction guarantee policy for years. "Customer service has been the backbone of this industry since day one," says Bill Welter, Rax's executive vice president for marketing. "Value messages are important, but they're not worth anything if the customer is served inattentively."

Sources: Adapted from Raymond Serafin and Cleveland Horton, "Automakers Focus on Service," *Advertising Age*, July 6, 1992, pp. 3, 33; Richard S. Teitelbaum, "Where Service Flies Right," *Fortune*, August 24, 1992, pp. 115–116; and Scott Hume, "Fast-Food Chains Look Up Ways to Improve Service," *Advertising Age*, June 8, 1992, pp. 3, 46.

TABLE 11.4
Criteria Used to Judge
Service Quality

Criteria	Examples
Reliability: Consistency in performance and dependability	Accuracy in billing Keeping records correctly Performing the service at the designated time
Tangibles: Physical evidence of the service	Physical facilities Appearance of personnel Tools or equipment used to provide the service
Responsiveness: Willingness or readiness of employees to provide service	Mailing a transaction slip immediately Calling the customer back quickly Giving prompt service (e.g., setting up appointments quickly)
Assurance: Knowledge of employees and ability to convey trust and confidence	Knowledge and skill of contact personnel Company name or reputation Personal characteristics of contact personnel
Empathy: Caring and individualized attention to customer	Learning customers' specific requirements Providing specialized individual attention Consideration for the customer

Sources: Adapted from Leonard L. Berry and A. Parasuraman, *Marketing Services: Competing Through Quality* (New York: The Free Press, 1991), p. 16; A. Parasuraman, Valerie A. Zeithaml, and Leonard L. Berry, "A Conceptual Model of Service Quality and Its Implications for Future Research," *Journal of Marketing,* Fall 1985, p. 47; and A. Parasuraman, Valerie A. Zeithaml, and Leonard L. Berry, "SERVQUAL: A Multiple-Item Scale for Measuring Consumer Perceptions of Service Quality," *Journal of Retailing,* Spring 1988, p. 23.

commitment to quality at the highest levels of the organization, lower-level employees cannot be expected to follow suit. Next, all employees must be committed to quality. Organizations must develop specific service guidelines that are communicated to employees and enforced by management. Finally, it is important that high-quality service be recognized and rewarded. At the Washington, D.C.–based travel business Travelogue, Inc., owner Osman Siddigue and her people are polite and accommodating, above all else. By providing highly personalized service at no extra cost, Travelogue generates $40 million a year in revenues while competing against travel industry giants like American Express and Carlson Travel.[25]

In any service organization, the front-line workers—bank tellers, flight attendants, receptionists—are the most critical resource. Part of what a

[25] Tatiana Pouschine, "In the Shadows of American Express," *Forbes,* October 26, 1992, pp. 154–159.

service firm sells is its employees.[26] A rude flight attendant is a rude airline, and an incompetent receptionist is an incompetent doctor's office. Unfortunately, these front-line employees are often the least trained and lowest-paid members of the organization. A firm must realize that its employees are the critical link to the service customer before it can improve service quality.

PRODUCTS FROM NONPROFIT ORGANIZATIONS

■ **nonprofit marketing**
all marketing activities conducted by individuals or organizations to accomplish goals other than financial profit

In Chapter 10, we state that nonprofit organizations also market products. **Nonprofit marketing** includes all marketing activities conducted by individuals or organizations to accomplish goals other than financial profits. Organizations like the Girl Scouts, United Way of America, and the American Cancer Society provide goods (cookies), services (help for victims of spousal abuse), and ideas (giving up smoking) to the target groups they serve. In most cases, nonprofit organizations have some basic social mission—a service or idea—and the sale of tangible goods is secondary to that mission. For example, the sale of calendars and posters by an art museum is secondary to its mission of broadening and enhancing the cultural values of the community; the sale of gift items serves this purpose and is nonprofit.

Nonprofit organizations are a significant part of the U.S. economy. There are over 1,000,000 nonprofit organizations in the United States. This sector of the economy is growing fast; it has approximately 8 million employees, 80 million volunteers, and accounts for 2 to 3 percent of the U.S. gross national product.[27] Nonprofit organizations include many hospitals, educational institutions, religious organizations, charities, social service organizations, museums and orchestras, and various government agencies. The remainder of this chapter examines the ways nonprofit marketing differs from that of profit-seeking organizations, the types of nonprofit marketing, and marketing strategies for nonprofit organizations.

How Nonprofit Marketing Is Different

Several years ago, you might have raised some eyebrows if you suggested that religious organizations could make effective use of marketing activities. But in recent years, churches and many other nonprofit organizations have been using marketing activities to facilitate satisfying exchanges. St. Vincent de Paul Village, a shelter for the homeless in San Diego, raised $30 million using a variety of fund-raising tactics, including videos on tax breaks, an annual golf tournament sponsored by Merrill Lynch, and television commercials.[28] Thus marketing in nonprofit organizations can be somewhat similar

---

[26] A. Parasuraman, "Customer Oriented Corporate Cultures Are Crucial to Services Marketing Success," *Journal of Services Marketing,* Summer 1987, pp. 39–46.
[27] Peter F. Drucker, *Managing the Nonprofit Organization* (New York: HarperCollins Publishers, 1990), pp. xvii, xviii.
[28] Jonathon Dahl, "A San Diego Shelter Feeds the Homeless with an Uneven Hand," *Wall Street Journal,* February 18, 1992, pp. A1, A6.

to marketing in profit-oriented organizations. However, there are a number of differences between nonprofit marketing and marketing in profit-oriented organizations.

The objectives of nonprofit organizations are generally different than the objectives of profit-oriented firms. Since the success or failure of a nonprofit organization cannot be determined solely in financial terms, the objectives are somewhat more complex. For example, the major objective of the American Cancer Society may be to reduce and eventually eliminate a deadly disease; but they may also have other objectives, such as creating awareness of the disease, educating the public, encouraging people to stop smoking, and so on. In many cases, the objective of a nonprofit organization is concerned with people (a political candidate), ideas (wearing seat belts), or places (discovering Missouri), in addition to goods and services. An organization's success in achieving this objective will to a large extent depend on its ability to generate resources. For example, the success of a political candidate is largely dependent on fund raising, as is the success of United Way.

Because nonprofit organizations are not striving to achieve financial objectives, the exchange process is also somewhat different. In many cases nonprofit organizations must satisfy two entirely different parties in an exchange, clients and donors. *Clients* are the recipients of the product. For instance, clients of the Muscular Dystrophy Association (MDA) are individuals with the disease who make use of the services provided. *Donors* are those individuals who provide financial resources and volunteer work to nonprofit organizations. Donors to the MDA include corporations and individuals who give money to the organization, and people who work as volunteers for various MDA functions. Thus the group making payment to the nonprofit organization does not always receive the benefits provided. Clients receive the product provided by the organization, and donors receive the satisfaction of helping to further a social cause.

The medium of exchange in nonprofit marketing also takes many forms. In marketing a political candidate, votes are exchanged for a politician's platform, and in return a candidate gains an elected office. In a stop-smoking campaign, a smoker gives up a habit he or she enjoys for better health and can expect to live longer. Nonsmokers also benefit from better health and a cleaner environment.

Although nonprofit organizations do not have profitability as a goal, raising money is a very important activity. In addition to donations from individuals and corporations, nonprofit organizations also rely on government grants for operating budgets. If the government cuts back on funding and private donations drop, nonprofit organizations can face failure just as profit-oriented firms do. Many corporations, for instance, have cut back on donations to charities as they restructure and downsize. As a result, many nonprofit organizations have had to cut staff and programs.[29] Since there is a

---

[29]Lois Therrien, "Corporate Generosity Is Greatly Depreciated," *Business Week,* November 2, 1992, pp. 118–120.

limited amount of money given by donors and government grants, nonprofit organizations compete with each other to obtain resources. Marketing plays an important role in determining which organization raises the money needed to sustain operations. Several nonprofit cultural groups like the Philadelphia Ballet have avoided financial disaster by obtaining corporate sponsorships. While cash donations are down, companies are increasing budgets for marketing sponsorships.[30] As its older patrons diminish in number, the New York City Ballet established the Fourth Ring Society, named after the less-expensive balcony seats that traditionally attracted younger people. By educating them about ballet and getting them involved, the organization hopes to turn the younger MTV crowd into regular patrons as they grow older.[31]

Evaluating the performance of nonprofit organizations is also different than evaluating profit-oriented firms. A successful year may be measured by the amount of money raised or the number of new donors attracted. But the manner in which the money is used is also a measure of performance. The Red Cross helped a large number of victims of Hurricane Andrew in Florida and Hurricane Iniki in Hawaii and was strained financially in the process.[32] Some nonprofit organizations have come under fire for the way they spend the money they raise. Motivating employees toward performance is also difficult for nonprofit organizations, because employees are not judged in financial terms. If a corporation is not profitable, changes may take place and people may even lose their jobs. But employees in some public and private agencies may realize they will never go out of business because of financial problems and will begin to lose sight of the organization's goals.

Types of Nonprofit Marketing

As we said earlier, there are thousands of nonprofit organizations that offer both tangible and intangible products to their target markets. Table 11.5 lists the major types of nonprofit marketing: idea marketing, person marketing, place marketing, and organization marketing. An example of each type, its objective, and its target market is also provided.

■ **idea marketing** using marketing activities to increase the acceptance of a social cause or social idea within a target market

Idea Marketing   **Idea marketing** involves using marketing activities to increase the acceptance of a social cause or social idea within a target market. For example, the American Heart Association promotes exercise and a healthy diet to reduce the risk of heart disease. The Partnership for a Drug Free America uses advertisements to communicate the dangers of drugs (see Figure 11.7). In many cases, organizations marketing ideas must change consumer attitudes toward a cause or behavior. Nonprofit organizations have found it extremely difficult to increase the acceptance of their ideas. Even as

---

[30] Pamela Sebastian, "As Corporate Gifts Shrink, Arts Groups Are Soliciting Promotional Sponsorships," *Wall Street Journal,* February 19, 1992, pp. B1, B6.
[31] Elizabeth Comte, "Hey, Dig That Swan," *Forbes,* December 21, 1992, p. 254.
[32] Pamela Sebastian, "Red Cross Is Strained by Disasters Even As It Revamps Its Programs," *Wall Street Journal,* September 15, 1992, pp. A1, A5.

Type	Example	Marketing Objective	Target Market
Idea marketing	"Recycle"	To inform people about recycling and to preserve the environment	Anyone purchasing materials that can be recycled
Person marketing	"Vote for Bush"	To encourage voters to re-elect George Bush	Republicans, Democrats who may change parties, and voters not affiliated with a party
Place marketing	"Kentucky open for business"	To stimulate business activity and investment in the state of Kentucky	Business firms considering relocating or new businesses looking for a location
Organization marketing	"Be all that you can be"	To increase enlistment in the army	Men and women ages 19 to 23

TABLE 11.5
Types of Nonprofit Marketing

the evidence began to build supporting the danger of cigarette smoking, the American Cancer Society found it difficult to change attitudes toward smoking. But by using marketing activities over a long period of time, it has seen much more encouraging results.

Person Marketing

person marketing the use of marketing activities to increase the visibility of and preference for an individual among a target market

Person Marketing   **Person marketing** refers to the use of marketing activities to increase the visibility of and preference for an individual among a target market. Many politicians and celebrities rely on marketing activities to advance their own causes or goals. During his 1992 presidential campaign, Governor Clinton's campaign advisors relied heavily on feedback from the "consumer" to stay in touch and get their candidate close to the voters and to remain focused.[33] Most successful sports figures use public relations specialists to develop a desirable image. This often leads to greater opportunities in terms of endorsements, guest spots on television and radio programs, and even higher pay. In this case, the enhancement of image, a nonfinancial goal, leads to the achievement of other, financial goals.

place marketing marketing activities used to attract members of a target market to a particular area

Place Marketing   **Place marketing** is the use of marketing activities to attract members of a target market to a particular area. Many state government tourism bureaus are using marketing activities to encourage tourists to visit their states. Increased tourism, of course, has a positive impact on the economy of the state in terms of revenues and jobs. Many cities and states also attempt to market their location to business enterprises. Several cities, including Louisville, Denver, and Indianapolis, attempted to influence

[33] "A New Team: Clinton and Marketing," *Advertising Age,* November 9, 1992, p. 18.

United Air Lines to select their city for the location of a new repair facility. The facility meant thousands of jobs to the city selected—Indianapolis.

Organization Marketing **Organization marketing** is the marketing effort designed to persuade members of a target market to identify with or become members of an organization. Many organizations, such as public libraries, parks, or museums, simply want to make people aware of their existence and the services they offer. Other organizations want to encourage a target market to contribute to the organization in some way. For instance, colleges and universities target their alumni with fund-raising efforts of some kind, whether it be joining the alumni association or contributing to a phonathon.

■ **organization marketing** marketing effort designed to persuade members of a target market to identify with or become members of an organization

Developing Marketing Strategies for Nonprofit Organizations

Like profit-oriented firms, nonprofit organizations must develop marketing strategies to satisfy the needs of their target markets. Developing a market strategy involves selecting a target market and developing a market mix that meets the needs of this target. As we noted previously, nonprofit organizations may attempt to facilitate exchanges with diverse groups, both clients and donors. For instance, the target market may be individuals who have concern for a cause such as convincing people to stop smoking, and can

FIGURE 11.7
Nonprofit Marketing
Partnership for a Drug Free America uses advertisements such as this to raise awareness about drug use and to influence people's thinking.

Source: Courtesy of Partnership for a Drug-Free America.

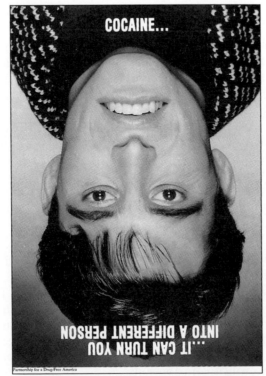

include both smokers who won't quit and concerned nonsmokers who make donations. Developing a marketing mix for this situation requires some creativity on the part of marketers.

Product Strategy   Nonprofit organizations typically market ideas and services rather than goods. Because of the intangible nature of these products, it is important to establish something with which the target market can identify. The Muscular Dystrophy Association (MDA) has been successful in doing this with Jerry Lewis. Although the MDA and Lewis have their critics, few dispute the success of MDA in raising funds. Both clients and donors alike identify with "Jerry's Kids." Many charity and nonprofit organizations fail because the target market does not recognize or identify with the ideas and services offered.

Promotion Strategy   Advertising and publicity are used by nonprofit organizations to communicate with clients and donors. Clients must be made aware of the product offered, where it is available, and how it can be obtained. For instance, colleges, symphony orchestras, and drug rehabilitation clinics all use advertising and publicity to encourage people to use their services. Direct mail advertising is the most popular way for nonprofit organizations to solicit contributions from donors. Telephone solicitation and television advertising are also used. Personal-selling activities are used to obtain donations from larger donors such as wealthy individuals and corporations. Some charities like the American Heart Association also use volunteers who go door to door to solicit contributions in person.

Price Strategy   Because nonprofit organizations do not attempt to make a financial profit, pricing strategies often stress the welfare of clients over costs and revenues. The emphasis is on a fair price that clients or customers can afford; in some cases, there is no charge. For example, the Salvation Army provides free meals and beds for the night; donations, grants, and fund-raising activities pay for these services. The price charged by some nonprofit organizations can be viewed as an **opportunity cost,** the value that a client or donor gives up in an exchange. For instance, clients who use a stop-smoking clinic give up the habit of smoking and suffer through the difficulty of quitting. Donors who volunteer their time or make financial contributions give up the time or money they could have used in another way.

■ **opportunity cost** the value that a client or donor gives up in an exchange

Distribution Strategy   Because production and consumption of most of their services and ideas take place simultaneously, nonprofit organizations generally distribute directly to clients and donors. To distribute information about a political candidate, parties open local campaign headquarters. By opening more locations, nonprofit organizations can serve their clients better. Likewise, charitable organizations attempt to increase donations by opening more locations where contributions can be made or by recruiting more volunteers to solicit contributions.

SUMMARY

Services are intangible products involving human or mechanical efforts that cannot be physically possessed. Services are increasingly important in the American economy, accounting for nearly 70 percent of the American gross national product, more jobs than any other sector of the economy, and more than 50 percent of consumer expenditures.

Several characteristics distinguish services from goods: (1) intangibility (services cannot be tested, touched, seen, smelled, or heard); (2) inseparability of production and consumption (services are generally produced and consumed at the same time); (3) perishability (services cannot be stored); and (4) heterogeneity (services are not always consistent).

Services can be classified according to the type of market, the degree of labor intensiveness, the degree of customer contact, the skill of the service provider, and the goal of the service provider.

In developing marketing strategies for services, the marketer must consider several factors. In terms of the product, services are often difficult for consumers to understand and evaluate. The tangible elements associated with a service may be the only visible aspects of the service. Thus marketers must carefully manage these tangible elements. Since services are often viewed in terms of the providers, service firms must carefully select, train, motivate, and control employees. Name selection is also critical because the company name is the service.

Because services are intangible-dominant products, they are difficult to advertise. Advertising should focus on the tangible cues, or symbols, associated with the services. Advertising can also be used in internal marketing to motivate and educate employees. Personal selling can be a very powerful tool in promoting services because it lets consumers and salespeople interact. Sales promotions are more difficult to implement for services than for goods. The final component of the promotion mix, publicity, is vital to many service firms.

Setting prices, which serve as important cues to consumers, is sometimes difficult because of the intangible nature of services. Sometimes two or more services are bundled together in a single package for a special price. Pricing can be used to help smooth fluctuations in demand.

Most services are limited to direct channels of distribution because of the inseparability of production and consumption. However, some types of services do make use of indirect channels such as retailers (drop-off centers), intermediaries (travel agents), and electronic distribution (ATMs). Physical symbols of a service, such as bank credit cards, enable retailers to act as indirect intermediaries in the distribution of intangible services.

Service quality is the conformance of service(s) to customer specifications and expectations, which only the customer can judge. To improve the quality of its services, a service provider must understand that consumers judge service quality on the basis of how the service is performed. Service quality can be improved with the total commitment of the organization and the recognition that front-line employees are extremely important.

Nonprofit marketing includes all marketing activities conducted by individuals or organizations to accomplish goals other than financial profits. There are a number of differences between nonprofit marketing and marketing in profit-oriented organizations. The objectives of nonprofit organizations are somewhat complex. Nonprofit organizations often engage in exchanges with two different groups, clients and donors, and the medium of exchange is not always money. Evaluating and controlling the activities in nonprofit marketing is also different, because performance is not measured by profit.

There are several different types of nonprofit marketing. Idea marketing is the use of marketing activities to increase the acceptance of a social cause or idea. Person marketing is the use of marketing activities to increase the visibility of an individual and a target group's preference for him or her. Place marketing is the attempt to attract people to a particular place. Organization marketing is used to enhance the image of an organization or increase its membership.

Nonprofit organizations must develop marketing strategies. Because most nonprofit products are services or ideas, it is important to establish something tangible that the target market can identify with. Promotion is important to communicate the organization's message with clients and donors. Price strategies often stress the welfare of clients over costs and revenue. Nonprofit organizations generally distribute directly to clients and donors.

KEY TERMS

service   nonprofit marketing
intangibility   idea marketing
inseparability   person marketing
perishability   place marketing
heterogeneity   organization marketing
bundling   opportunity cost
service quality

QUESTIONS FOR DISCUSSION AND REVIEW

1. What is a service? Name five different services.
2. What are the characteristics that distinguish services from goods?
3. How can tangible elements be associated with a service?
4. What are high-contact services? Describe some important issues in marketing high-contact services.
5. Why is the name of a service important? Give an example of a name that you think was well chosen.

6. Why are services difficult to advertise?

7. What is price bundling? How can services be bundled?

8. Why are services generally limited to direct channels of distribution?

9. How do consumers judge service quality?

10. If the president of an airline asked you how service quality could be improved, how would you respond?

11. What is nonprofit marketing? Give an example of a nonprofit organization that markets a good, one that markets a service, and one that markets an idea.

12. What are the major differences between marketing activities conducted by profit-oriented organizations and those conducted by nonprofit organizations?

13. What are the four types of nonprofit marketing? Give an example of each.

CASES

11.1 SCANDAL HAMPERS FUND RAISING AT UNITED WAY OF AMERICA

Give the United Way has been a familiar slogan to generations of Americans. Through payroll deductions, millions of workers donate to local charities under the umbrella of United Way of America. But a controversy over excessive spending by an official at United Way has threatened its fund-raising efforts and raised questions about charities in general.

In February 1992, media reports of lavish spending and mismanagement by United Way of America president William Aramony began to appear. Aramony received an annual compensation package of $463,000, flew first class, rode in limousines, and routinely hired family and friends for jobs at United Way affiliates. On February 28, 1992, Aramony resigned. Even though the unethical behavior may have been limited to Aramony himself, the affair tarnished the image of the long-time charity. The problem pointed to a serious lapse in accountability; many observers wondered why the national board or outside auditors failed to detect the indiscretions sooner. Robert O. Bothwell, executive director of the National Committee for Responsive Philanthropy, claimed that the scandal had "tarred and feathered United Way's motherhood-and-apple-pie image."

United Way of America, which grew from the Community Chests of the 1920s, was the first to take charity campaigns to the workplace and to use the payroll deduction system. It has worked closely with the business community, with corporate executives serving terms on local United Way boards. United Way raises funds for several charities under one campaign. Recipients include popular mainstream causes such as the American Red Cross, the Boy Scouts, and the YMCA, as well as drug-abuse clinics, spousal-abuse shelters, and child development centers. The 2,100 local United Ways throughout the country pay dues to the national organization.

Since the scandal, United Way has tried desperately to restore public trust. New president Elaine L. Chao, former deputy secretary of transportation and former director of the Peace Corps, declared, "The old way of doing things has got to change—the old-boy network and the whole culture." The national board added representatives from United Way affiliates and initiated new financial controls to reassure local affiliates, who protested the national organization's mismanagement by withholding dues.

Whether trust has been restored remains to be seen. In 1991, the 2,100 local United Way organizations raised $3.17 billion, an increase of 1.9 percent from 1990. In some locations, United Way contributions dropped as much as 10 percent in 1992. Local affiliates attribute reductions to the weak economy, corporate downsizing, and unemployment.

The United Way scandal has raised serious questions about fund raising. Is there adequate oversight of charity organizations by boards of directors and outside auditors? Should corporate America continue with office fund drives? Nonprofit executives say that discontinuing workplace campaigns would be a mistake, since such campaigns relieve corporations of having to deal with thousands of solicitations. Besides, fundraising through an umbrella group, such as United Way, provides an efficient way for charities to raise money with relatively little overhead.

The United Way controversy has helped push open corporate America's door to other federated charities. Some large firms, like Citibank and Nike have included Earth Share, an umbrella organization for forty-three environmental groups, as an option in giving through payroll deduction. At American Telephone & Telegraph, employees in New York can use payroll deductions for Black United Funds. In Boston, Polaroid and Lotus Development let workers donate to Community Works. And almost everyone agrees that firms that permit charity drives should eliminate arm-twisting, which most employees resent.

In the meantime, many local United Ways are investigating their accounting procedures and perks for executives. More United Way affiliates are providing ways for donors to direct their contributions to specific causes and groups. Some of the largest United Way organizations in New York and Los Angeles are rethinking the way funds are distributed.

Charity organizations are at a critical juncture. Government cuts and rising unemployment place a heavy burden on charities. In addition, Americans are now more worried about having enough money in the future, a concern that means less giving to charity. Charitable organizations today need to go back to the basics and ask the following questions: What is our mission? Who are our customers? Are we meeting their expectations? Public trust in charities in general has declined, according to a survey conducted by Independent Sector. If this trend continues, United Way and other charity organizations face a difficult future.

Questions for Discussion

1. In what type of nonprofit marketing is United Way engaged?

2. How would you compare the goals of United Way to the goals of IBM or McDonald's?

3. Why is fund raising so important to United Way? Why is a positive image so important to a charitable organization?

4. How can marketing be used to restore the public trust in United Way?

Based on information from Ron Stodghill II, Christina Del Valle, Greg Sandler, and Lois Therrien, "United They Stand?" *Business Week,* October 19, 1992, p. 40; Pamela Sebastian, "Unemployment and Unforgotten Scandal Work Against United Way Campaigns," *Wall Street Journal,* October 21, 1992, pp. B1, B12; and Susan B. Garland, "Keeping a Sharper Eye on Those Who Pass the Hat," *Business Week,* March 16, 1992, p. 39.

11.2 BRITISH AIRWAYS IMPROVES SERVICE TO BECOME INDUSTRY LEADER

In the intense competition of the airline industry in the 1990s, providing service will no doubt be the key to success. Carriers have lost billions of dollars in recent years and desperately need to raise fares. Some airline executives believe that improved service will make higher fares more acceptable to customers. So rather than competing on price, airline companies are focusing on service. Nobody does that better than British Airways, named in an annual *Euromoney* magazine poll of business travelers as the airline providing the best service.

British Airways has come a long way. In 1982 it lost $1 billion, an industry record. When Colin Marshall took over as CEO in early 1983, the airline was an industry laughingstock. Comedians referred to it, known by its initials BA, as "Bloody Awful." Employee morale had hit rock bottom; thousands of employees had been laid off, and those remaining were embarrassed to work for the world's worst airline. Marshall's first challenge was to restore pride. To send a clear message to both employees and potential customers, he ordered newly designed uniforms for all personnel. The planes were repainted with bright stripes and the motto "To fly, to serve."

To make sure the airline lived up to its new motto, Marshall launched a major campaign to change employees' attitudes toward service. He surmised that many passengers, especially business travelers, wanted better service. He therefore required all employees to participate in a two-day seminar, "Putting People First," which put the airline employees in the role of customers. In the seminar, employees discussed some of their own experiences with poor service.

Immediately, British Airways worked to overcome obvious problems, such as uninteresting food, poor cabin service, and insufficient legroom. But

Marshall also scrutinized the less obvious. For example, because research had shown that passengers like to be called by name, BA employees spent several months observing passengers on flights from London to Glasgow and Manchester. The airline's customer satisfaction scores went up approximately 60 percent when ticket agents addressed passengers by name. From then on, BA agents were expected to call customers by name whenever they could. Employees fluent in several languages were placed at London's Heathrow Airport to help passengers. BA set up booths at JFK Airport in New York City so that passengers could videotape comments about BA service. Finally, the airline changed flight schedules according to customers' convenience.

British Airways also revamped its Concorde flights. Marshall decided to use BA's seven Concordes, which were losing money, to symbolize a revitalized airline. The firm redecorated the planes and raised fares substantially, to levels 30 percent higher than first-class fares on conventional jets. Since the Concorde can cross the Atlantic Ocean in half the time it takes other jets, BA focused its advertising on the importance of time to business travelers. As a result, BA's Concorde flights achieved over 60 percent occupancy—the breakeven point—on transatlantic routes.

Next, British Airways invested $40 million to improve first-class service. The airline redesigned cabin interiors and put a video terminal at each seat. A new wine cellar offers an improved selection; menus allow first-class passengers to eat when they wish.

In discussing service, British Airways CEO Marshall recalls the famous Twentieth Century Limited, the train that ran from New York to Chicago. Conductors would pay passengers $1 for every minute the train was late, no matter who or what was to blame. Air traffic delays and weather problems would make it next to impossible for airlines to make the same offer. But, as Marshall says, "We could promise to make the delays completely painless with concentrated service attention. Think how many customers you could acquire for life if and when the guarantee is cheerfully, quickly and easily paid."

The improvements at British Airways have drawn the attention of managers from other airlines and other service industries. The changes have also turned the company around. In 1991, profits at British Airways were at an industry high of $496 million. Its average revenue per passenger, $396, was among the best in the industry. In terms of passengers carried and passenger miles flown, British Airways has become the largest international airline in the world.

British Airways would like to provide its much-lauded service to passengers throughout the world. In July 1992, it finalized an agreement with USAir to form a transatlantic alliance. But it withdrew its $750 million bid for 44 percent of USAir as it became clear that the U.S. government would not approve the deal. The proposed deal resulted in protests from major U.S. airlines, which claimed the British would have a huge head start to becoming the first global airline. British Airways' second bid of $300 million for 19.9 percent of USAir was approved in March 1993. Together, the two carriers will serve 339 cities in 71 countries.

Questions for Discussion

1. Why was it critical for CEO Colin Marshall to change employees' attitudes toward service?

2. How did British Airways use research to help serve customers better?

3. Why would a passenger pay 30 percent more to fly the Concorde than what it costs to fly first class on a conventional jet?

4. What effect would a British Airways/USAir alliance have on the service offered by other U.S. airlines?

Based on information from Paula Dwyer, "British Air: Not Cricket," *Business Week,* January 25, 1993, pp. 50–51; "British Investment in USAir Approved," *Lexington* (KY) *Herald-Leader,* 1993, p. B3; Stewart Toy, Andrea Rothman, and Paul Dwyer, "Air Raid," *Business Week,* August 24, 1992, pp. 54–61; Richard D. Hylton, "United to BA: Take Off," *Fortune,* September 7, 1992, p. 9; "Best and Worst in the Air," *Parade Magazine,* June 7, 1992, p. 8; and Kenneth Labich, "The Big Comeback at British Airways," *Fortune,* December 5, 1988, pp. 163–174.

Developing and Managing Products

OBJECTIVES

- To identify the organizational alternatives for managing products.

- To describe the phases of new product development.

- To discuss how firms position new products.

- To identify the strategies for managing products after commercialization.

- To discuss product strategies for global markets.

OUTLINE

The production techniques Henry Ford developed in 1913 were revolutionary, efficient, and effective; Ford succeeded in bringing affordable cars to American buyers. U.S. automobile manufacturers were still using those same basic production techniques in the 1970s and 1980s. But by that time, the techniques were outmoded and U.S. automobile manufacturing was bloated with inefficiency, unlike the Japanese firms. *The Machine That Changed the World,* written by researchers at Massachusetts Institute of Technology's (MIT's) International Motor Vehicle Program and published in 1990, showed stark differences between the two nations in automobile manufacturing. The MIT group pointed to the new Japanese system of lean production, which involved using less inventory, labor, factory space, and investment. U.S. executives claimed that Japanese firms rode to success because of lower labor costs. But Honda disproved that notion after it opened the first Japanese plant in the United States in 1982; even paying American wages, Honda maintained its lower labor costs.

In the last several years, U.S. companies who make automobiles and many other products have improved quality dramatically, often by imitating ideas pioneered by the Japanese. Using Honda's example, Chrysler cut $1 billion in annual costs. Many U.S. firms are manufacturing better products in less time with fewer workers and reduced inventory. In many industries, U.S. companies have bridged the quality gap and are catching up to their Japanese counterparts. According to the 1992 *Car Book,* an annual consumer guide, U.S. automakers have gained ground on quality measures and have moved ahead of Japanese rivals in producing safe cars.

Now the world's best companies are gearing up for the next challenge—flexible manufacturing. Many firms recognize that quality is only the beginning. Manufacturing has progressed from product quality (doing it right) to reliability (always doing it right) and now to flexibility (adding variety and speed) through a flexible manufacturing system (FMS).

A single factory with FMS uses computer-controlled robots to turn out a wide variety of products. By reading the market quickly, manufacturing several different products on the same line, and switching from one to another instantly and at lower cost, a firm can respond to customers quickly and economically. Manufacturers get new products to markets faster, make product improvements faster, and leave competitors to catch up. Many experts believe that competitiveness will hinge on flexibility in the decade ahead. Japan is ahead of the United States in this new race. According to Aleda Roth, a Duke University manufacturing expert, "Most American companies are a generation behind—as far behind as they were on quality."

Many leading U.S. companies, including General Electric, Figgie International, and Motorola, are working hard to develop FMS. Baxter Healthcare is testing an intravenous solutions factory that can be shipped anywhere, set up in a week, and moved anytime. Baxter can make working prototypes of complex medical instruments and ship them only twenty-four hours after receiving the specifications. General Motors put flexible manufacturing to work in its Lordstown, Ohio, plant. Robots and other machinery can easily be reprogrammed to build a wide mix of cars to meet changing demand. Workers have been retrained to handle a variety of tasks instead of repeating a few over and over. More cars—450,000—can be built on one assembly line there than at any other plant in the world.

Despite these shining examples, American manufacturers as a whole lag behind their Japanese rivals, who have been investing in flexible manufacturing for over a decade. Toyota, Toshiba, Kao Corporation (Japan's largest soap and cosmetics company), and other firms are finding that flexibility saves money while it enables a factory to turn out many products. U.S. firms can catch up, but they must start immediately.[1] ●

I n the decade ahead, the customer will truly be king. Firms will continue their struggle to find new ways to make better products faster and at less cost. New products will be brought to the market much more quickly and prices will be highly competitive. The world of product development will change rapidly. As the opening feature illustrates, new technologies will enable firms to read markets quickly and change production processes economically to respond to customer needs. One objective of the downsizing at large firms like General Motors and IBM is to become more efficient in bringing products to market and responding to customers' needs.

Figure 12.1 shows the percentage of businesses whose departments always or almost always (meaning 91 to 100 percent of the time) translate customer expectations into the design of new products or service. These figures, based on a two-year global study conducted by the American Quality Foundation and Ernst & Young, include data from five hundred firms throughout the world.[2] As you can see in Figure 12.1, Japanese and German companies are well ahead of the U.S. and Canadian companies in responding to consumer expectations in the development of new products.

Quality products are critical to the success of an organization. Incorporating customer expectations into the design of new products and services can

[1] Based on information from Thomas A. Stewart, "Brace for Japan's Hot New Strategy," *Fortune,* September 21, 1992, pp. 62–74; Bradley A. Steitz, "Detroit's New Strategy to Beat Back Japanese Is to Copy Their Ideas," *Wall Street Journal,* October 1, 1992, pp. A1, A10; James B. Treece and Patrick Oster, "General Motors: Open All Night," *Business Week,* June 1, 1992, pp. 82–83; and "U.S. Making Safer Cars Than Japan, Guide Says," Lexington, Ky. *Herald-Leader,* December 2, 1992, p. B5.

[2] American Quality Foundation and Ernst & Young, "International Quality Study," 1991, pp. 1–52.

FIGURE 12.1
Percentage of Businesses Whose Departments Always or Almost Always Translate Customer Expectations into the Design of New Products and Services

Source: American Quality Foundation and Ernst & Young, "International Quality Study," 1991, p. 21. For additional information about the International Quality Study^{SM}, contact Terrence Oran, National Director, Performance Improvement Services, Ernst & Young, 1600 Huntington Building, Cleveland, OH 44115.

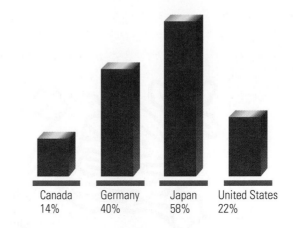

Canada	Germany	Japan	United States
14%	40%	58%	22%

give a firm a substantial edge over competitors. Japan and Germany have currently adapted this practice to a much greater extent than has North America. But global competition will mandate that all firms incorporate customer expectations into the design, modification, and elimination of products. These actions and the way a firm is organized to implement them are important aspects of product management.

ORGANIZING FOR PRODUCT MANAGEMENT

Businesses frequently discover that the functional structure of organization traditionally used to manage products does not fit their needs. In the functional structure, managers specialize in such business functions as advertising, sales, and distribution. Instead of using this approach, businesses may elect to use the product-manager, market-manager, or venture-team approach.

A **product manager** is responsible for managing a product, product line, or several distinct products that make up an interrelated group. A product manager who is responsible for a single brand is called a **brand manager.** Procter & Gamble, for example, has one brand manager for Tide detergent and another for Cheer. To achieve marketing objectives, product or brand managers coordinate marketing mix decisions such as distribution, promotion, pricing, packaging, and branding for their products or brands. They also coordinate research and development, engineering, and production. Marketing research helps product managers not only identify target markets but also understand what consumers need and want. The product-manager approach is used by many large consumer-goods companies that market considerable numbers of products (see Figure 12.2).[3]

■ **product manager** a person responsible for managing a product, product line, or several distinct products that make up an interrelated group

■ **brand manager** a type of product manager who is responsible for a single brand

[3]Thomas J. Cosse and John E. Swan, "Strategic Marketing Planning by Product Managers— Room for Improvement?" *Journal of Marketing,* Summer 1983, pp. 92–102.

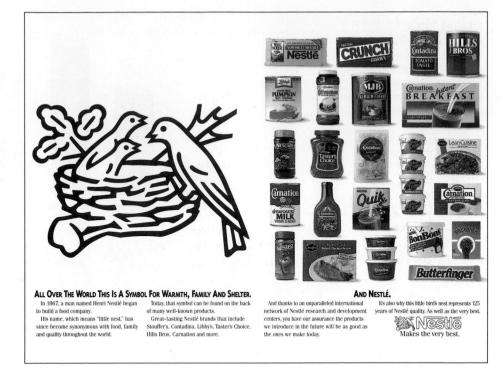

ALL OVER THE WORLD THIS IS A SYMBOL FOR WARMTH, FAMILY AND SHELTER.

In 1867, a man named Henri Nestlé began to build a food company.

His name, which means "little nest," has since become synonymous with food, family and quality throughout the world.

Today, that symbol can be found on the back of many well-known products.

Great-tasting Nestlé brands that include Stouffer's, Contadina, Libby's, Taster's Choice, Hills Bros, Carnation and more.

AND NESTLÉ.

And thanks to an unparalleled international network of Nestlé research and development centers, you have our assurance the products we introduce in the future will be as good as the ones we make today.

It's also why this little bird's nest represents 125 years of Nestlé quality. As well as the very best.

Nestlé
Makes the very best.

market manager a person responsible for overseeing the marketing activities that serve a particular group or class of customers

venture team an organizational unit responsible for creating entirely new products aimed at new markets

In the market–manager approach, a **market manager** is charged with overseeing the marketing activities that serve a particular group or class of customers. This approach is especially effective when a firm employs different types of marketing activities for diverse customer groups. For instance, a lighting manufacturer might have one market manager for organizational markets and another for consumer markets.

Unlike the product manager and market manager, the **venture team** is an organizational unit responsible for creating entirely new products aimed at new markets. The venture team handles every facet of a product's development: research and development, engineering, production, finance and accounting, and marketing. Team members generally come from different functional areas of an organization. Because they work outside established divisions, venture teams can develop innovative approaches to new products and markets and take advantage of opportunities in highly segmented markets. When their new product has proved successful, venture team members may return to their functional areas or join a new or existing division to manage the product. Management of the new product may be turned over to an existing division, a market manager, or a product manager.[4]

 Many companies, including IBM (personal computers), Boeing (757 airplanes), and Xerox (nonxerography products), have successfully used the venture-team approach. One of the major benefits of using venture teams is

[4]Richard M. Hill and James D. Hlavacek, "The Venture Team: A New Concept in Marketing Organization," *Journal of Marketing*, July 1972, p. 49.

that the number of products can be rapidly expanded. Another benefit is that the status and importance of new products are boosted because the teams operate in a separate structure within the organization.[5]

DEVELOPING NEW PRODUCTS

Firms spend billions of dollars each year developing new products. Boeing alone will spend over $5 billion designing a new jet, the 777. If successful, the 777, like the 747, will be a profitable machine for years to come.[6] But many of the more than ten thousand new products introduced each year fail.[7] According to a recent survey of new product managers conducted by Group EFO Ltd., a Connecticut-based consulting firm, 8 percent of their new products survived to reach the market. Once there, 83 percent of these new products failed, which overall results in a 99 percent failure rate.[8] Many reasons account for the high failure rate of new products. The most common reasons are lack of research, design problems, and poor timing of the products' introduction.[9] The most successful new products are superior to competitors' offerings, have been developed to meet well-defined consumer wants and needs, and enable customers to perform a unique task.[10] Close to the Customer examines the importance of packing products with value.

Although it is risky to introduce new products, an organization cannot afford *not* to do so. New products are critical to a firm's growth for several reasons. As products age, profits decrease and their expected life span becomes shorter.[11] About 15 percent of corporations' sales are based on new products.[12] Without new product development, even the best of organizations risk decline. For instance, the railroad industry, in recent years, has experienced an unanticipated rapid decline. By failing to explore new transportation alternatives that would better satisfy customer needs, it became vulnerable to competition from trucking and air transportation. One study reported that internationally developed new products and services are expected to increase dramatically in the next five years.[13] Companies that fail to introduce new products risk even greater losses than those firms that do. In fact, as numerous firms are cutting staff and reducing operating costs, they

---

[5]Christopher K. Bart, "Organizing for New Product Development," *Journal of Business Strategy,* July–August 1988, pp. 34–38.

[6]Jeremy Main, "Betting on the 21st Century Jet," *Fortune,* April 20, 1992, pp. 102–117.

[7]Jim Betts, *The Million Dollar Idea* (Point Pleasant, N.J.: Point, 1985), p. 7.

[8]Cyndee Miller, "Survey: New Product Failure Is Management's Fault," *Marketing News,* February 1, 1993, p. 2.

[9]Robert G. Cooper, *Winning at New Products* (Agincourt, Ontario: Gage, 1987), p. 14.

[10]R. G. Cooper and E. J. Kleinschmidt, "Success Factors in Product Innovation," *Industrial Marketing Management,* August 1987, pp. 215–223.

[11]Thomas S. Robertson, *Innovative Behavior and Communication* (New York: Holt, Rinehart and Winston, 1971), p. 11.

[12]D. S. Hopkins, "New Product Winners and Losers," Report No. 773 (New York: The Conference Board, 1980), p. 1.

[13]"Study: Launching New Products Is Worth the Risk," *Marketing News,* January 20, 1992, p. 2.

CLOSE TO THE CUSTOMER

Product Value

According to Jack Welch, CEO of General Electric, "The value decade is upon us. If you can't sell a top-quality product at the world's lowest price, you're going to be out of the game." This global challenge is affecting markets for both consumer and organizational products. Customers throughout the world want the same thing—better value for the price—and global competition means they are going to get it.

Companies throughout the world like Monsanto, Gillette, Nissan, and Apple Computer, to name a few, are looking for ways to load their products with value. Global competition alone does not account for the emphasis that value is receiving. Industrial capacity is down worldwide; U.S. plants are operating at about 80 percent capacity. Much of this underutilization of capacity arises from new technology which has increased the capacity of many factories. Competition will force capacity to continue to grow faster than demand. Additionally, buyers' expectations for value have skyrocketed as the quality of many products has improved dramatically over the past decade. As a result, high-quality manufactured goods are available in an abundance the world has never before known. To survive, firms must develop new products—and modify existing ones—that offer value to customers.

Understandably, value is not a simple concept for organizations to grasp. Consumers are complex; each buyer assesses value in a different way. As IBM's corporate director of brand management put it, "It's not as simple as price, or we'd all be driving Hyundais." In short, value is giving customers what they want at a fair price. As basic as that sounds, today you have to provide *top* value, better than any competitor does. And you cannot determine what customers want unless you ask them. Is it durability, better service, a particular feature, a guarantee, or lower price? Lexus and Infiniti, by providing higher performance at lower prices, have hurt high-priced German automobile manufacturers. Now BMW and Mercedes-Benz are responding with competitively priced cars of their own.

Firms must also provide value to organizational customers. Monsanto, in an effort to nurture existing products and develop new ones, has rediscovered the importance of corporate customers. When NutraSweet, a division of Monsanto, introduced fat substitute Simplesse, the product was pushed at major food producers, who balked at buying it. Now scientists are working jointly with organizational customers to develop foods low in calories, cholesterol, and fat, which is exactly what food producers want.

The only point of view that matters in this issue is the customer's. Many organizations have added features or facilities that increase cost without adding value, a true formula for failure. Delivering value to customers requires a clear understanding of customer needs, superior product design, the application of the newest technologies, and a relentless focus on quality and costs. The formula becomes a simple one: Offer products that customers want at a competitive price and deliver them in a manner that consistently beats the competition.

Sources: Stratford Sherman, "How to Prosper in the Value Decade," *Fortune*, November 30, 1992, pp. 90–103; Peter C. Yesawich, "The Marketplace: Value Provides Competitive Edge," *Lodging Hospitality*, August 1992, p. 22; and Ronald Henkoff, "Learning from Its Mistakes?" *Fortune*, January 27, 1992, pp. 81–84.

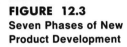

FIGURE 12.3
Seven Phases of New Product Development

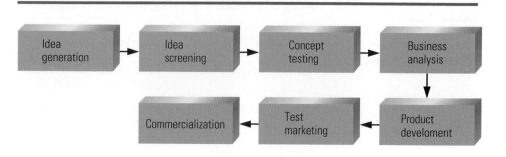

are at the same time increasing budgets to launch new products.[14] Investing in new products during an economic downturn is a good opportunity to get ahead of competitors who are cutting back on new products.

The term *new product* has many connotations. Most definitions of the term have a common element: New products offer innovative benefits. An electronic component that offers features not previously available to consumers, such as an erasable compact disk, is considered a new product. But products that are different from and better than existing products are also viewed as new. The following product innovations have made news in recent years: high-tech telephones, Lycra bicycle shorts, desktop publishing equipment, laptop computers, microwaveable foods, health maintenance organizations (HMOs), disposable contact lenses, and miniature TV-VCRs. For our purposes, a **new product** is one that a specific organization has not marketed previously, although other organizations may offer similar products. Smart Ones, a line of frozen entrees from H.J. Heinz that contain 1 gram of fat or less, is considered a new product even though ConAgra offers a similar line of frozen dinners called Healthy Choice.[15]

Before a product is introduced to consumers, it goes through the phases of **new product development** shown in Figure 12.3: (1) idea generation, (2) idea screening, (3) concept testing, (4) business analysis, (5) product development, (6) test marketing, and (7) commercialization. Products can be, and often are, abandoned at any stage of development. Following the new product development process does not guarantee success, but it does reduce the likelihood of failure.[16] Table 12.1 presents some of the major marketing activities at each stage of new product development; these stages will now be discussed in greater detail.

■ **new product** a product that a specific organization has not marketed previously, although other organizations may offer similar products

■ **new product development** a seven-phase process consisting of idea generation, idea screening, concept testing, business analysis, product development, test marketing, and commercialization

■ **idea generation** searching for new product ideas that will help firms achieve their objectives

Phase 1: Idea Generation

Searching for new product ideas that will help firms achieve their objectives is called **idea generation.** Few ideas generated in this phase are good enough

[14]Gabriella Stern, "To Outpace Rivals, More Firms Step Up Spending on New-Product Development," *Wall Street Journal,* October 28, 1992, pp. B1, B7.
[15]Gabriella Stern, "Heinz to Introduce Line of Low-Fat Frozen Entrees," *Wall Street Journal,* June 2, 1992, p. B4.
[16]John Stephen Davis, "New Product Success & Failure: Three Case Studies," *Industrial Marketing Management,* May 1988, pp. 103–109.

TABLE 12.1
Marketing Activities at Each Phase of New Product Development

Phase of New Product Development	Marketing Activities
Idea generation	Search for new product ideas from both inside and outside the firm.
Idea screening	Select ideas with the greatest potential. Reject ideas that have limited potential. Analyze the needs and wants of buyers, the environment, and competitors.
Concept testing	Describe or show product concepts and their benefits to potential customers to determine their reactions. Identify and eliminate poor product concepts. Obtain useful information for product development and marketing personnel.
Business analysis	Assess the new product's potential profitability and compatibility with the marketplace. Examine the organization's research, development, and production capabilities. Ensure that financial requirements for development and commercialization are available. Project economic returns.
Product development	Determine whether it is technically and economically feasible to produce the product. Convert the product idea into a working model. Develop and test various elements of the marketing mix.
Test marketing	Launch the product in small regions. Determine the reactions of consumers in the target market. Measure the new product's sales performance. Identify weaknesses in the product or the marketing mix.
Commercialization	Make the necessary cash outlays for production facilities. Manufacture and market the product in the entire target market. Communicate the product's benefits.

to be commercially successful. Some organizations acquire their ideas virtually by chance, but most firms develop systematic approaches for generating new product ideas. Purposeful, focused efforts are necessary to identify new ways to serve consumers. Unexpected events, incongruities, new needs, industry and market changes, and demographic changes represent new opportunities for astute marketers.[17] Sam Farber got the idea of making user-friendly kitchen gadgets from his wife, who has arthritis and was having

---

[17] Peter F. Drucker, "The Discipline of Innovation," *Harvard Business Review,* May–June 1985, pp. 67–68.

FIGURE 12.4
Idea Generation
New product ideas that become commercially successful, like the Kodak Photo CD System, help firms achieve their objectives.

Source: Photo courtesy of Eastman Kodak Company. Kodak and Photo CD symbol are registered trademarks.

 trouble working in the kitchen. Farber developed an attractive, easy-to-grip gadget handle, founded Oxo International, and sold $3.4 million (wholesale) worth of its garlic presses, potato peelers, and pizza cutters in the first full year of business.[18] The advent of the compact disk enabled Kodak to develop a way for people to put their favorite pictures on television, as shown in Figure 12.4.

New product ideas can originate from several sources. They may come from internal sources, such as marketing managers, salespersons, researchers, engineers, and other organizational personnel. One of the most successful products in Black & Decker's history, the Piranha circular saw blade, was invented by one of the firm's engineers, a former automobile mechanic. He also developed the Bullet, a powerful drill bit that Black & Decker expected would revolutionize the market. Many organizations rely on employees to generate new ideas. Colgate Venture Co., a division of Colgate-Palmolive Co., is shielded from Colgate's rigid bureaucracy to spark creative new product ideas. Similar units have been established by General Foods Corp., Scott Paper Limited, and S.C. Johnson & Son, Inc. (maker of Johnson's Wax).[19] At 3M, engineers are encouraged to "bootleg," or borrow time, energy, and funds from other assignments to explore new product ideas.[20]

---

[18]Christopher Palmeri, "I Need to Be Making and Selling Things," *Forbes,* February 17, 1992, p. 97.
[19]Ronald Alsop, "Consumer-Product Giants Relying on 'Intrapreneurs' in New Ventures," *Wall Street Journal,* April 19, 1988, p. 19.
[20]Thomas J. Peters and Robert H. Waterman, Jr., *In Search of Excellence* (New York: Harper & Row, 1982), p. 144.

TABLE 12.2
Check List for Screening New Products

Requirement	Score (1–5)	Weight (percent)	Weighted Score
Relationship to current product line	3	.10	.30
Profit potential	4	.20	.80
Exclusive design	5	.10	.50
Production knowledge	4	.15	.60
Production capabilities	4	.15	.60
Compatibility with present distribution channels	3	.10	.30
Investment required	3	.20	.60
Product rating			3.70

Ideas for new products may also originate from sources outside the firm—competitors, suppliers or vendors, advertising agencies, government agencies, management consultants, private research organizations, universities, and even customers. In making its innovations, Procter & Gamble used customer panels to generate ideas regarding product improvements and modifications for consumer products.[21]

Phase 2: Idea Screening

■ **idea screening** selecting ideas with the greatest potential for further development

Selecting ideas with the greatest potential for further development is referred to as **idea screening.** Ideas that have limited commercial potential or that do not match a firm's objectives are rejected in this phase. It is extremely important that the firm analyze the needs and wants of buyers, the competition, and environmental factors at this time. The firm's overall ability to produce and market the product must also be analyzed. Most new product ideas are rejected during the idea screening phase.

Sometimes marketing managers use a check list of new product requirements when screening new product ideas. The list encourages them to be systematic and reduces the likelihood that they might neglect an important detail. Table 12.2 provides a sample of a typical check list used to screen new products. Note how each requirement is scored on a scale of 1 (poor) to 5 (excellent). Requirements are also weighted because some are more important than others; the weights add up to 100 percent. Thus a firm may establish an acceptable product rating, such as 3.7. The requirements can change from one product to another. Marketing research (as discussed in Chapter 9) may be necessary to clarify details and answer unresolved questions about the

[21] Cooper, p. 72.

FIGURE 12.5
Concept Test for
Textbooks on Disk

Product Description

A publishing company is considering producing textbooks
on computer disk. The product would be much like
textbooks you already use, except that you would purchase
a disk rather than a bound book. Disks compatible with
any type of personal computer would be available and
would cost about 50 percent less than the book version.
You could read the text on a computer screen and be able to
print out copies of pages or sections as desired. Of course,
photographs and artwork would no longer be in color.
Selling or copying your disk would be prohibited by law.

Questions

1. What do you think in general about this type of a text?

2. What do you like the most about this product, compared
   with bound textbooks?

3. What do you like least?

4. Would you be likely to buy this product at a 50 percent
   saving over traditional hardbound texts?

5. If not, is there anything that could be done to change
   your mind?

viability of a product. A survey of 173 CEOs found that current customers
are the best source of marketing research for new products.[22]

Phase 3: Concept Testing

■ **concept testing** presenting product concepts
and benefits to potential customers in order to identify
and eliminate poor product
concepts

After screening ideas, organizations test product concepts. **Concept testing**
involves describing or showing product concepts and their benefits to potential customers to determine their initial reactions. First and foremost, the
objective of concept testing is to identify poor product concepts so they can
be eliminated. If, for instance, students reject the idea of textbooks on disk
instead of bound paper, the concept should probably be rejected. A concept
test also proves useful for product development and marketing personnel. If
students react favorably to the idea of textbooks on disk, they may also
provide information about design, packaging, price, and so on. Figure 12.5
shows a concept test for the proposed textbook. Most major firms would
use some form of concept testing in the new product development process.

[22] "What's the Best Source of Market Research?" *Inc.*, June 1992, p. 108.

Although concept testing is useful in most cases, it is not always appropriate. Concept testing often fails when a project's major benefit is something personal or intangible. In such cases, it is difficult to communicate the concept in a way that potential customers can visualize the product. A new service—intangible by nature—is especially difficult to test, short of actually demonstrating the service. A concept test for fax machines, for example, would have been difficult simply because potential customers could not visualize or comprehend fax technology. The product itself, of course, was a huge success. Because of this difficulty, concepts that may have the potential to become successful products are sometimes rejected.

Phase 4: Business Analysis

■ **business analysis** an assessment of a new product's potential profitability and compatibility with the marketplace

Business analysis is an assessment of a new product's potential profitability and compatibility with the marketplace. Compatibility factors of interest to marketers include the company's manufacturing and marketing capabilities, its financial resources, and its management's attitude toward the product. During the business analysis phase, marketing managers must determine if the product is compatible with the firm's current product mix. If it is, demand must be strong enough to justify entering the market. The potential impact of environmental factors—political, legal, societal, competitive, and economic—on the product's sales, costs, and profits must be assessed. The organization also has to examine the organization's current research, development, and production capabilities. For instance, if new production facilities need to be constructed, the firm must determine if they can be built on an economical and timely basis. Marketers should also ensure that the financing required for development and commercialization is available at terms that yield a favorable return on investment. At this time, the organization makes early projections of economic returns for the product using forecasting techniques.

Marketing managers seek information about the market during this phase. Customer surveys and secondary data provide information for estimating potential sales, costs, and profits. The firm also considers its financial objectives and related financial issues.

Phase 5: Product Development

■ **product development** the phase in which a new product is moved from concept to test stage and other elements of the marketing mix (promotion, price, and distribution) are developed

Product development is the phase in which the product is moved from concept to test stage and other elements of the marketing mix (promotion, price, and distribution) are developed. During the product development phase, the company determines whether it is technically feasible to produce the product and whether the product can be produced at costs low enough to sell it at a reasonable price. In this phase, the product idea is converted into a working model, or prototype. The prototype should reveal tangible and intangible characteristics that consumers might associate with the product. Its design, mechanical features, and intangible aspects must be linked to consumer needs and wants. This phase of new product development is generally lengthy and expensive. As a result, only a relatively small number of product ideas reach this phase.

Perceptions of quality that are formed in early stages of product development are critical. From the customer's perspective, quality is what a person requires from a good or service. Thus quality is the conformance to customer requirements. Firms must find out what the customer wants, record it, train everyone to accomplish it, and then deliver it to the customer on time.[23] The perception of quality generally depends on how well the product meets the evaluator's specifications and requirements. In judging the quality of a Sony or a Zenith, for example, a television buyer will compare the two products on performance, features, reliability, aesthetics, and other requirements before purchasing. These issues must be considered during product development; once the product is put on the market, sales will depend to a great extent on quality. Whether a buyer purchases another Sony or Zenith television years later will depend on how well the first television meets his or her expectations.

As we note in the opening feature, pressure from competitors increases the importance of high quality in product development. Foreign competitors—Volvo, Toyota, BMW—have stimulated the improvements in quality now taking place in the American automobile industry. Meanwhile, the Japanese are again defining and expanding the notion of quality in the development of new products. Their newest concept is called *miryokuteki hindshitsu,* making cars that are not only reliable but that fascinate, bewitch, and delight.[24] This notion, referred to as "the second phase of quality," will give each car a special look, sound, and feel. Competition, customer expectations, and good marketing practices motivate all companies to focus on quality. Thus quality is an increasingly important consideration in the product development phase.

In addition to working out the mechanical and production aspects of the product, marketing management must test the various elements of the marketing mix, including preliminary advertising copy, packaging, labeling, and copyrights, to discover any legal problems. Plans for personal selling and distribution must be made at this time. The ultimate purpose is to ensure the effective integration of all marketing mix elements.

Phase 6: Test Marketing

■ **test marketing** a trial launch of a product and its marketing mix in small regions chosen to represent the target market

Test marketing is essentially a trial launch of the product and the marketing mix in small regions chosen to represent the target market. The purpose of test marketing is to determine the reactions of consumers in the target market. The test marketing phase should be conducted only after the product has gone through the earlier stages of new product development and after initial decisions about the other marketing mix variables have been made. Firms then look for cities that closely match the income, age, and racial mix of the country as a whole in which to test new products.[25] Figure 12.6 locates some popular test markets for new products.

[23]Philip B. Crosby, *Completeness: Quality for the 21st Century* (New York: Dutton, 1992), p. 116.
[24]David Woodruff, "A New Era for Auto Quality," *Business Week,* October 23, 1990, pp. 84–96.
[25]"Looking for Norman Normal," *The Economist,* April 25, 1992, p. 76.

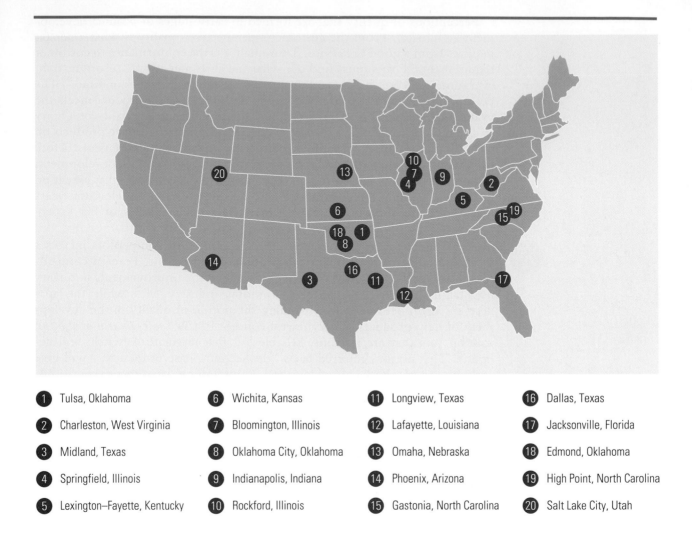

1 Tulsa, Oklahoma

2 Charleston, West Virginia

3 Midland, Texas

4 Springfield, Illinois

5 Lexington–Fayette, Kentucky

6 Wichita, Kansas

7 Bloomington, Illinois

8 Oklahoma City, Oklahoma

9 Indianapolis, Indiana

10 Rockford, Illinois

11 Longview, Texas

12 Lafayette, Louisiana

13 Omaha, Nebraska

14 Phoenix, Arizona

15 Gastonia, North Carolina

16 Dallas, Texas

17 Jacksonville, Florida

18 Edmond, Oklahoma

19 High Point, North Carolina

20 Salt Lake City, Utah

FIGURE 12.6
Twenty Most Popular Test Markets in the United States

Source: Reprinted with the permission of Donnelley Marketing Information Services (DMIS), Stamford, CT.

Test marketing is important for several reasons. It enables the organization to obtain a measure of a new product's sales performance under natural marketing conditions. It also allows marketers to identify weaknesses in the product or in other parts of the marketing mix. Because it can be extremely expensive to correct product weaknesses discovered after nationwide introduction, it is more practical to make adjustments after test marketing. Test marketing may show that an organization needs to make alterations in product line extensions, spending and distribution levels, pricing strategy, product formulation, advertising copy and strategy, package design, or shelf location.

Of course, test marketing is risky; the cost is high and competitors may try to interfere. To combat the recognition and purchase of a new brand, for example, a competitor may try to "jam" the test program by increasing its advertising or promotions, lowering prices, and offering special incentives. Such tactics can lead to inaccurate test results. Competitors may also rush to develop their own version of the product for introduction to the market. Thus it is important to move quickly and commercialize as soon as possible after testing. Resources such as *Hispanic Media and Markets* provide demographic and lifestyle information, which is useful in test market evaluation.

Because of the high costs of test marketing and the risk of giving competitors a chance to seize the same opportunity, some firms have developed newer, faster, and less expensive ways to test-market their products. One alternative is to skip test marketing altogether, which R.J. Reynolds did when it introduced its Camel Wides brand. This strategy is extremely risky because managers have no way of estimating a product's potential. Alternatives to omitting test marketing include pretesting the product and advertisements for it with a small group of consumers, or using computer models and historical data on similar products to develop sales projections. Colgate-Palmolive used a "lead country" strategy by launching Optims shampoo in the Philippines, Australia, Mexico, and Hong Kong after pretesting, then rolling out the product in Europe, Asia, Latin America, and Africa.[26]

Phase 7: Commercialization

■ **commercialization** the full-scale manufacturing and marketing of a new product

Commercialization is the full-scale manufacturing and marketing of the new product. In the initial stages of commercialization, marketing management analyzes the results of test marketing to determine what changes in the marketing mix are required before the product is introduced nationally. For example, the test market results may tell the marketers to change one or more of the product's physical attributes, alter the promotion program, change the product's price, or modify the distribution plans. At this time, the organization gears up for full production. This step may require considerable capital expenditures for plants, equipment, and additional personnel.

The product is introduced to all members of the target market during the commercialization stage. Organizations often spend exorbitant sums of money at this time to communicate a product's attributes to the target market. Of the $5 billion General Motors invested to develop and launch Saturn, advertising consumed $100 million.[27] Such promotional and capital expenditures make commercialization quite costly and may not be recovered for several years.

■ **product adoption process** the five-stage process that buyers go through in accepting a product; includes awareness, interest, evaluation, trial, and adoption

Commercialization is significantly easier when the new product is quickly accepted by customers. Understanding the process by which consumers accept products helps marketers foster product acceptance. Marketers generally acknowledge that buyers go through a five-stage process, called the **product adoption process,** in accepting a new product. These five stages are as follows:

1. *Awareness.* The buyer becomes aware of the product.

2. *Interest.* The buyer seeks information and is interested in learning about the product.

---

[26] Christopher Power, "Will It Sell in Podunk? Hard to Say," *Business Week,* August 10, 1992, pp. 46–47.

[27] Raymond Serafin, "The Saturn Story," *Advertising Age,* November 16, 1992, pp. 1, 13.

3. *Evaluation.* The buyer evaluates the product's benefits and decides whether to try it.

4. *Trial.* The buyer examines, tests, or tries the product to determine its usefulness.

5. *Adoption.* The buyer purchases the product and can be expected to use it to solve problems.[28]

The stages of product adoption have several implications for marketers. Promotion should be used to generate widespread *awareness* of the product. During the *interest* stage, consumers should be provided with information that helps them learn how the product is used and the benefits it provides. Product fact sheets or comparative advertisements can help consumers make a product *evaluation*. Salespeople can also provide customers with information about competitors' products and answer any questions they may have while making an evaluation. Free samples, show room displays, and demonstrations can help buyers in the *trial* of the product. Finally, production and distribution must be linked to patterns of *adoption,* and promotional activities are used to stimulate repeat purchases.

Not all consumers begin the product adoption process at the same time, nor do they move through the process at the same speed. Of those who eventually purchase a product, some are satisfied and adopt it immediately. Others are not satisfied and do not purchase the product again. For them, adoption never takes place.[29]

Marketers sometimes classify consumers into adopter categories based on the length of time they take to adopt a new product. The five major adopter categories are innovators, early adopters, early majority, late majority, and laggards.[30] Figure 12.7 shows each adopter category and the percentage of total adopters that it typically represents.

Innovators are the first people to adopt a new product. They are eager to try new products and ideas and tend to be rash, daring, and self-confident. Innovators generally are better educated and have higher incomes than members of the other groups. **Early adopters** select new products more carefully and may be viewed by persons in the remaining adopter categories as opinion leaders. The **early majority** are deliberate and cautious about trying new products. The **late majority** are quite skeptical of new products but eventually adopt them because of economic necessity or social pressure. **Laggards,** the last consumers to adopt a new product, are oriented toward the past. They are so suspicious of new products that when they finally adopt one it may already have been replaced by a newer product. Laggards generally tend to be of the lowest socioeconomic class. When developing promotional efforts, a marketer should recognize that persons in different adopter categories often need different types of information. Marketers should therefore vary their means of communication.

■ **innovators** the first people to adopt a new product

■ **early adopters** people who select new products carefully; may be viewed by people in the early majority, late majority, and laggard categories as opinion leaders

■ **early majority** people who are deliberate and cautious about trying new products

■ **late majority** people who are quite skeptical of new products but eventually adopt them because of economic necessity or social pressure

■ **laggards** the last consumers to adopt a new product; are oriented toward the past and suspicious of new products

[28] Everett M. Rogers, *Communication of Innovations* (New York: The Free Press, 1971), pp. 99–104.
[29] John H. Antil, "New Product or Service Adoption: When Does It Happen?" *Journal of Consumer Marketing,* Spring 1988, pp. 5–16.
[30] Rogers, pp. 180–182.

FIGURE 12.7
Classification of Adopter Groups

Source: Reprinted with permission of The Free Press, a division of Macmillan, Inc., from *Diffusion of Innovations,* Third Edition, by Everett M. Rogers. Copyright © 1962, 1971, 1983 by The Free Press.

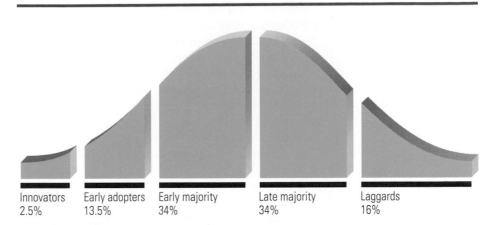

| Innovators 2.5% | Early adopters 13.5% | Early majority 34% | Late majority 34% | Laggards 16% |

POSITIONING THE PRODUCT

■ **product positioning**
a firm's decisions and activities aimed at shaping and maintaining a product concept in consumers' minds

When marketers introduce a product, they attempt to characterize it as possessing the attributes most desired by the target market. **Product positioning** refers to a firm's decisions and activities aimed at shaping and maintaining a product concept in consumers' minds. Dutch Boy, for example, has attempted to differentiate itself from competitors by positioning its paint as a fashion-oriented product for the young consumer. Consumers' perceptions of a product's attributes relative to those of competitive brands is the *product position*.

Many organizations use a *perceptual map* such as the one shown in Figure 12.8 to position a product. The figure shows that sportiness and degree of luxury are two important attributes in customers' choice of automobiles. These attributes are identified through marketing research. Consumers are asked which product attributes are most important in their decision to purchase a product, in this case cars, and how they perceive various brands according to each of the attributes identified. In this hypothetical example, a Corvette is perceived as a luxurious sports car and a Camry as an economy sedan.

Product positioning is crucial when market segmentation is used. Segmentation enables the company to target a given brand at a specific portion of the total market. Product positioning helps a company serve a specific market segment by establishing a favorable perception of the product in the minds of customers in that segment. For instance, Pontiac automobiles are positioned as sporty performance vehicles for younger consumers, whereas Cadillacs, also made by General Motors, are positioned as luxurious, high-class vehicles that appeal to older, more affluent consumers. If not properly positioned, these brands would not be separated from other brands in consumers' minds.

Products can be positioned to compete head-on with rival products or to avoid competition. For example, the U.S. Postal Service has positioned its Express Mail to compete directly with Federal Express in the overnight delivery market, whereas 7Up has avoided head-to-head competition with Coca-

Cola and Pepsi by positioning itself as an alternative to colas. Head-to-head positioning may be the best strategy if the product's attributes are at least equal to those of competitive brands and if the product has a lower price. This strategy may be appropriate even when the price is higher if the product is superior to competing products. By contrast, positioning to avoid competition may be best when the product's characteristics are not significantly different from those of competing brands. In addition, positioning a brand to avoid competition may be beneficial when that brand has unique characteristics that are important to buyers.

Positioning to avoid competition is critical when a firm introduces a brand into a market where it already has one or more brands. In this situation, the organization tries to avoid obtaining sales at the expense of its existing brands, unless, of course, the new brand will earn substantially larger profits. For example, when Procter & Gamble introduces a new detergent product, it must position the new product carefully to avoid damaging its other detergents such as Dreft, Bold 3, and Cheer. Each of its products is positioned to appeal to a different target market: Dreft is for washing infants' clothing; Bold 3 is for color washes; and Cheer is for use in all temperatures.

It is important to evaluate a product's position over time. Because of changes in customer preferences, technology, and competing products, it may be necessary to reposition a product. Perhaps the classic example is Marlboro cigarettes, which nearly failed when they were introduced as a

FIGURE 12.8
Perceptual Map of Automobiles

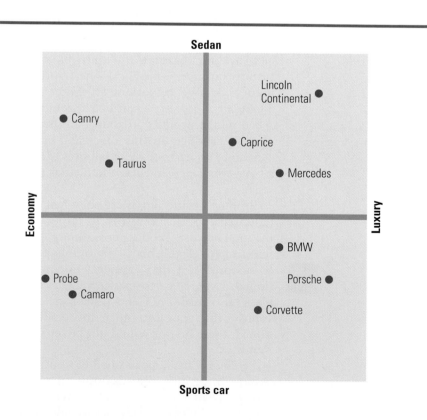

FIGURE 12.9
Repositioning
Holiday Inn repositions itself from a family hotel to a worldwide collection of fine business hotels with boardrooms and special executive floors.

Source: Courtesy Holiday Inns, Inc. A Bass Company.

cigarette for women many years ago. After the cigarette was repositioned to appeal to men, with the rugged Marlboro Man created as its image, it became a number one seller. More recently, Dial Corp. repositioned Breck as a premium brand shampoo against such top brands as Vidal Sassoon and Finesse.[31] And TWA repositioned by abandoning its low-price image in favor of a quality service approach, with the new advertising theme, "The most comfortable way to fly."[32] Figure 12.9 illustrates how Holiday Inn repositioned itself as a fine business hotel.

PRODUCT MANAGEMENT DURING THE LIFE CYCLE STAGES

Table 12.3 summarizes marketing strategies for managing products after commercialization. Most new products do not generate enough sales initially to produce profits. While consumers are learning about the product, marketers should watch for product weaknesses. Any necessary corrections or adjustments must be made quickly to sustain demand and prevent the early death of a product. An organization should design a marketing strategy to attract the market segment that is most interested in the product and that has the fewest objections.

[31] Carrie Goerne, "Dial Repositions Breck as a Premium Brand," *Marketing News,* May 11, 1992, p. 6.
[32] Jennifer Lawrence, "TWA Embraces Quality, Drops Low-Price Image," *Advertising Age,* March 1, 1993, p. 8.

	Growth Stage	**Maturity Stage**	**Decline Stage**
Product Strategy	Expand to appeal to more specialized markets Correct weak or omitted product features	Make product modifications Offer quality enhancements Find new uses for product Increase number of users Increase frequency of usage	Changes are unlikely Deletion is considered
Price Strategy	Lower price as costs fall Stabilize price if demand is strong and there are few competitors	Flexibility is important Markdowns and price incentives are common Price increases are possible if costs increase	Maintain price Squeeze out all remaining profits
Distribution Strategy	Fine tune distribution system Make sure physical distribution system is efficient Provide service adjustments and credit for defective parts	Encourage dealers to support product Provide dealers with incentives for selling manufacturer's brand	Maintain profitable outlets Close unprofitable outlets Consider liquidating remaining inventory
Promotion Strategy	Stress brand loyalty Lower promotion costs as sales increase	Spend heavily to maintain market share Increase usage of sales promotion and personal selling	Promotion loses its importance Sales incentives such as coupons are useful Spend less on promotion

TABLE 12.3
Marketing Strategies for Managing Products after Commercialization

Marketing Strategy in the Growth Stage

As the product's sales increase, the marketing manager must evaluate and, if necessary, adjust the marketing strategy to stimulate growth and brand loyalty. In this stage, the organization might expand the product to appeal to more specialized markets. Marketers should analyze the product's position relative to competing products and correct any major weaknesses.

A company may be able to reduce prices after recovering its research and development costs. The prices of video cameras, for example, have declined as producers have recouped their development expenses. Also, as sales volume increases, efficiencies in production can result in lower costs. These savings may be passed on to buyers. As long as demand remains strong and there are few competitive threats, prices tend to remain constant. By providing price cuts, a company can encourage price competition and discourage new competitors from entering the market.

The distribution system should also be fine tuned during the growth period. Sometimes marketers expand their distribution coverage to include more distributors. Marketers must also ensure that the physical distribution system is working efficiently and gets the products to wholesalers and retailers before their inventories are exhausted. Because competitors introduce their own versions of the product during the growth period, service adjustments and prompt credit for defective products are important marketing tools.

Promotion should be used to emphasize brand loyalty during the growth stage. Advertising and sales promotions—such as coupons, refunds, free samples, and trial-size versions of the product—give consumers incentives to try the product. As sales increase, promotion costs should decline as a percentage of total sales, contributing significantly to increased profits.

Marketing Strategy in the Maturity Stage

As a product reaches the maturity stage of its life cycle, the competitive environment stabilizes and weaker competitors may drop out of the market. At this time, new marketing strategies may be needed. Some researchers have suggested that as a product matures its customers (particularly organizational customers) become more experienced and specialized. These customers then seek different or additional product benefits.[33] Table 12.3 lists marketing strategies that can be used to respond to changing customer demands.

■ **product modification**
the changing of one or more of a product's characteristics

Marketers may need to modify mature products to give them a competitive edge. **Product modification** entails changing one or more of a product's characteristics. Modification is not as risky as developing a new product. For example, Whirlpool Corporation modified its dishwashers by making them quieter.

Product modification can be effective under three conditions. First, it must be possible to modify the product. Second, current customers (if they are still the target market) must be able to recognize that the product has been modified. Third, the modification should make the product better satisfy customers' desires. Firms can make three types of modifications to existing products: quality, functional, and style modifications.

■ **quality modification**
a change that relates to a product's dependability and durability and that usually involves an alteration in the materials or production process employed

A **quality modification** is a change that relates to a product's dependability and durability. Such modifications usually alter the materials or production process employed. Reducing the quality of a product may allow the organization to lower its price and aim it at a larger target market. On the other hand, raising the quality level may foster customer loyalty and lower customer sensitivity to price, therefore allowing the company to charge a higher price for the product. Some experts suggest that improving product quality is a major means of successfully competing with foreign producers.[34] However, increasing quality may require the use of more expensive components, fewer

[33] F. Stewart DeBruicker and Gregory L. Summe, "Make Sure Your Customers Keep Coming Back," *Harvard Business Review,* January–February 1985, pp. 92–98.

[34] Frank S. Leonard and W. Earl Sasser, "The Incline of Quality," *Harvard Business Review,* September–October 1982, p. 171.

■ functional modification a change that affects a product's versatility, effectiveness, convenience, or safety; it usually requires that the product be redesigned

standardized production processes, and other manufacturing and management techniques that result in higher prices.[35]

A **functional modification** affects a product's versatility, effectiveness, convenience, or safety; it usually requires that the product be redesigned. Considerable functional modifications have been made in products such as automobiles, appliances, and office and farm equipment. Functional modifications can make a product satisfy the needs of more people, enlarging its market. For instance, since The Boeing Co. introduced the 747 jet in 1970, its flying range has nearly doubled and its fuel efficiency has increased dramatically. Other modifications to the 747 include a simplified instruction panel and digital electronics, which have reduced the number of pilots required to fly the plane from three to two.[36] Such changes can position a product favorably by providing benefits not offered by competing products. Functional modifications can also help an organization achieve and maintain a progressive image.

■ style modification an alteration in taste, texture, sound, smell, or visual characteristics that affects the sensory appeal of a product

A **style modification** is an alteration in taste, texture, sound, smell, or visual characteristics that affects the sensory appeal of a product. Figure 12.10 shows how Playskool modified Tinkertoys during the maturity stage of the product's life cycle. Style modifications help a firm differentiate its product from competing brands and thus gain increased market share. For example, Del Monte Corp.'s fruit cocktail packed in light syrup and made with natural ingredients was modified to appeal to health-conscious consumers and to win market share from competitive brands that use artificial sweeteners and flavoring. Frito-Lay spent $50 million to develop Doritos Tortilla Thins, and an additional $50 million to promote the thinner and lighter-flavored version of its famous Doritos Corn Chips. Sales of the traditional Doritos had declined for two consecutive years.[37] The biggest disadvantage of style modifications is that their value is determined subjectively. Although a firm may seek to differentiate a product through style modifications, consumers may actually find the modified product less appealing, a situation Coca-Cola experienced when it introduced New Coke.

During the maturity stage, some firms attempt to extend the product life cycle by finding new uses for the product. Connecticut Energy Corp., based in Bridgeport, is developing new uses for natural gas, including motor vehicles and air conditioners.[38] Marketing Close-up shows how the maker of Arm & Hammer baking soda has found new uses for the product over the years.

In addition to modifying the product, marketers may make adjustments in the product's pricing during the maturity stage. Price flexibility is often

---

[35] Lynn W. Phillips, Dae R. Chang, and Robert D. Buzzell, "Product Quality, Cost Position and Business Performance: A Test of Some Key Hypotheses," *Journal of Marketing,* Spring 1983, pp. 26–43.

[36] Stephen S. Cohen, "Inspiration: U.S. Manufacturers That Are Doing It Right," *Boardroom Reports,* September 15, 1988, p. 9.

[37] Caroline E. Mayer, "New Doritos Lighten Up to Satisfy Boomers," *Lexington* (KY) *Leader,* April 14, 1993, pp. D1, D10.

[38] Allanna Sullivan, "Connecticut Energy Targets New Natural Gas Markets," *Wall Street Journal,* June 29, 1992, p. B4.

FIGURE 12.10
Product Modification
Tinkertoys were modified by developing bigger, brighter, and easier to use plastic pieces, extending the life cycle of a mature product.

Source: © 1993 Playskool, Inc.

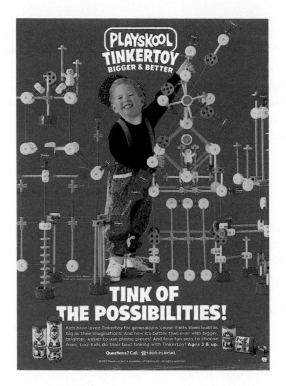

used to differentiate items in product lines. Price increases may be necessary if production and distribution costs increase, but price cuts and incentives are more common for mature products.

Businesses actively encourage distributors to support maturing products. A firm, for example, may offer dealers promotional assistance by sharing the cost of advertising. In general, an organization goes to great lengths to serve dealers and to offer incentives for selling its brand, in part because private distributor brands are a threat at this time.

Products in the maturity stage often require large advertising expenditures to maintain market share. Sales promotion and aggressive personal selling may be formidable marketing tools to combat increasing competition. At this time, buyers are often informed about new uses for the product or encouraged to use it more frequently. Mott's now uses their advertisements to promote the use of their applesauce as a healthy substitute for oil in baking (see Figure 12.11).

Marketing Strategy in the Decline Stage

When a product's sales peak and then decline, profits decline as well. As long as the product contributes to profits or enhances the overall effectiveness of a product mix, the company can justify keeping it on the market. However, when the product is no longer profitable, marketers reduce production and plan for the product's eventual elimination. Strategies for managing declining products are listed in Table 12.3.

MARKETING CLOSE-UP

Church & Dwight Make NaHCO₃ a Growth Industry

D o you remember from high school chemistry class what NaHCO₃ is? Bicarbonate of soda. Church & Dwight Co. of Princeton, New Jersey, has been making the white powder for nearly 150 years. We recognize it as Arm & Hammer baking soda. Surprisingly, annual sales and income have more than tripled over the last decade. Are that many more people baking?

Church & Dwight have always known the value of finding new uses for an old product. From the start, NaHCO₃ was sold in bulk (it would be $300 a ton in today's market) to other firms for a variety of uses ranging from fire extinguishers to cake mixes. When Church & Dwight began advertising a new use for Arm & Hammer baking soda—placing it in the refrigerator to eliminate odors—half the households in America began purchasing the product. In the 1980s, the company added consumer products like air fresheners, carpet deodorizers, toothpaste, and laundry detergent. In 1992, new products included a cat litter deodorizer and a nonaerosol pump air freshener.

Dwight Church Minton, the CEO and fifth-generation descendent of the founders, is moving into industrial markets. Sales of the firm's industrial products have passed $100 million a year and long-term growth opportunities look excellent. Some of the new industrial uses include the following:

- Armakleen, an industrial cleanser for printed circuit boards. The product does not use CFCs (which deplete the ozone) as other cleaners do. The market for this product is an estimated $1 billion.

- Armex, baking soda combined with other ingredients to blast walls and buildings. It is said to be safer than sandblasting, which can contribute to lung disease, and gentler on buildings.

- Good old baking soda, which is being sold as an additive to municipal water supplies. Experiments have shown that it neutralizes acids that can leach lead from old pipes.

Sources: Peter Nulty, "No Product Is Too Dull to Shine," *Fortune*, July 27, 1992, pp. 95–96; Riccardo A. Davis, "Arm & Hammer Seeks Growth Abroad," *Advertising Age*, August 17, 1992, pp. 3, 42; and Gerald Schoenfeld, "Treat Old Products like New," *Marketing News*, July 31, 1989, p. 15.

Usually, declining products have lost their distinctiveness because similar competing products have entered the market. Intense competition reduces buyer sensitivity to minor product differences, resulting in increased substitution and brand switching. As a result, marketers generally make few changes in style, design, or other attributes of a product during its decline.

Maintaining a declining product's profitability may be more important to a firm than maintaining a certain market share. Thus, despite declining sales and competitive pressures, marketers may maintain the product's price to squeeze out all possible remaining profits. Marketers may even increase prices as costs rise if there is still demand for the product. Conversely, the price may be cut to reduce existing inventory so that the product can be terminated. Some firms also relaunch the product in foreign markets.

FIGURE 12.11
New Uses for a Product
Mott's attempts to extend the life cycle of its natural applesauce by advertising it as a healthy substitute for oil in baking recipes.

Source: Mott's is a registered trademark of Cadbury Beverages Inc. Reprinted with permission. © Cadbury Beverages Inc.

During a product's decline, its producer is likely to maintain outlets with loyal buyers and eliminate unprofitable outlets. Distributors of the product that do not make sufficient contribution to profits may be eliminated at this stage. Sometimes a factory outlet may be established to sell off the remaining inventory of an obsolete product. As sales decline, the product tends to become a specialty item, and loyal buyers may seek out dealers that carry it.

During the decline stage, promotion loses its importance, and emphasis is generally shifted to more profitable products. Advertising may be used to retard the rate of decline; and sales incentives, such as coupons and premiums, may temporarily recapture buyers' attention. However, declining sales may signal that the time has come to delete the product.

■ **product deletion** the elimination of a product that no longer satisfies consumers or contributes to the achievement of organizational objectives

Product deletion is the elimination of a product that no longer satisfies consumers or contributes to the achievement of organizational objectives. Product deletion is just as important to the maintenance of an effective product mix as are modification of existing products and new product introductions. Declining products require too much of a marketer's time and resources that could be otherwise directed toward modifying thriving products and developing new ones. Moreover, the negative image associated with a weak product may rub off onto some of the firm's successful products.

Organizations are generally reluctant to delete products because of the cost and effort involved in establishing a successful product. If you pick up a marketing textbook from 1970, black-and-white televisions are probably used as an example of a product in its decline stage. This same example could be used today. So why haven't back-and-white televisions been deleted? As long as a product provides satisfaction for a sufficient number of customers and contributes in some way to an organization's objectives, the firm will avoid deleting it.

Several different strategies can be used to delete products. A phase-out strategy involves letting the product gradually decline, with little or no change in marketing efforts. A run-out strategy is used to exploit any strength left in the product. Increasing marketing efforts—perhaps more advertising or a decrease in price—causes a sudden increase in sales and profits. Finally, unprofitable products that have become a severe financial burden may be dropped immediately. Products should be deleted so that problems for the company and its distributors are minimized and so that replacement parts are available to customers.

PRODUCT STRATEGIES FOR GLOBAL MARKETS

In Chapter 5, we discuss the global marketing environment. Firms that are willing to market their products in foreign countries have many opportunities for growth. Any company deciding to become involved in international marketing must determine which product strategy to use when developing products for global markets. In this section, we examine three product strategies for global markets: global marketing, product modification, and new product development.

Global Marketing

The standardization of products versus product modification or new product development has been the subject of much debate. Some firms attempt to market the same product in a foreign country that has been successful in the U.S. market. This global marketing approach is appealing because it eliminates the expenses of marketing research and product redevelopment. Firms like the Coca-Cola Company and PepsiCo have successfully marketed their products in foreign markets with no product modifications. However, this strategy may not work for all products. For instance, when General Electric Co. marketed refrigerators in Japan, customers reported two major problems: The refrigerators were too noisy and they were too large to fit in most Japanese homes.[39] In some instances, the same product can be marketed in a foreign country but the communicating message must be changed. Bicycle and motorcycle manufacturers, for instance, must adapt communication in countries such as Asia and Latin America, where these products are used primarily as a means of transportation rather than recreation.

Global marketing is most successful when the needs for the product are similar across cultures. If the tastes, values, and other social and psychological

[39] Mauricio Lorence, "They're Cheap, They're Late . . . They're American Products," *Business Marketing,* September 1987, pp. 94, 96.

factors are similar in domestic and foreign markets, a global marketing strategy is advisable. This is especially true for organizational products, such as plant machinery, which are purchased for the same reasons throughout the world. However, as global competition intensifies, it is becoming increasingly difficult to sell the same product to foreign markets that is produced for domestic markets. In some cases, products must be modified or new products developed to suit the needs of the market. Thus although global marketing is desirable because of its considerable cost effectiveness, it can rarely be achieved for consumer goods and is the exception even for organizational products.

Product Modification

Often, products must be modified to meet different conditions of use in foreign countries. Soap and detergent manufacturers have adapted their products to local water conditions and washing appliances. Household appliances often are adapted to the different voltage requirements in foreign countries. Even jets, like the Boeing 737, have been adapted to different runways and other landing conditions in different countries. Some countries also have laws or other restrictions that make it necessary to modify a product. For example, only nonalcoholic versions of beer may be sold in Saudi Arabia because alcoholic beverages are illegal there.

Products may also have to be adjusted to overcome cultural or social obstacles. Ore-Ida Foods Co. makes frozen French fries in Tokyo with less salt than those sold in the United States because the Japanese prefer to add the seasoning themselves. Maggi, a Hispanic producer of ethnic foods, sells a narrower line of products in the United States to satisfy Americans' needs and tastes. Firms marketing books, magazines, and movies must translate them to overcome language barriers between people of different countries and cultures. General Mills adapted its cake mix so that it could be baked in an electric rice cooker, which in Japan is much more common than the electric oven. The product failed, however, because customers feared that making cake in the same cooker might affect the rice flavor.

New Product Development

When existing products cannot be modified to meet the needs of consumers in a foreign market, marketers may develop new products to satisfy those needs. This is especially true when one country is more developed or less developed than another. Thus a product sold in a developed country may not satisfy the needs of consumers in a less developed country; an entirely new product may be needed. General Motors, for example, developed an all-purpose, Jeep-like motor vehicle that can be assembled in underdeveloped nations by mechanics who have no special training. Colgate-Palmolive developed an inexpensive, all-plastic, hand-powered washing machine for households that have no electricity. Strategies that involve the invention of products may be quite costly, but the payoffs can be great. In many cases, if an original product can be redesigned to a lower level of complexity, it is less costly to produce and results in a less expensive product and greater sales.

SUMMARY

Developing and managing products is critical to an organization's survival and growth. Three approaches to organization help firms effectively manage products. In the product-manager approach, a product or brand manager coordinates all marketing activities for a single product, product line, or group of related products. In the market-manager approach, a market manager manages products for a specific market. In the venture-team structure of organization, venture teams, whose members come from different functional areas within the organization, are responsible for developing new products for new markets.

New product development is a seven-phase process: (1) idea generation—searching for new product ideas; (2) idea screening—selecting ideas with the greatest potential; (3) concept testing—presenting product concepts and benefits to potential customers to determine their reactions in order to identify and eliminate poor product concepts; (4) business analysis—assessing a new product's potential profitability and compatibility with the marketplace; (5) product development—moving the product from concept to test stage and developing other elements of the marketing mix; (6) test marketing—launching the product on a trial basis; and (7) commercialization—producing and marketing the product on a full-scale basis.

The process that buyers go through in adopting a new product includes the five stages of awareness, interest, evaluation, trial, and adoption. The five major categories of adopters are innovators, early adopters, early majority, late majority, and laggards.

Marketers use product positioning to shape and maintain a product concept in consumers' minds. Products can be positioned to compete head-on with rival products or to avoid competition.

As a product moves through its life cycle, marketing strategies may require continual adaptation. In the growth stage, it is important to develop brand loyalty by correcting weaknesses in the product, filling holes in the distribution system, and reducing prices. In the maturity stage, a product may be modified or new market segments may be targeted to rejuvenate its sales. Product modification is changing one or more of a product's characteristics. Products can undergo modifications in quality, function, or style. Marketers of mature products may reduce prices, encourage distributors to support the products, and spend large sums on advertising. A declining product is usually maintained as long as it contributes to profits or organizational objectives. To maintain an effective product mix, a firm has to eliminate, or delete, some products.

Many opportunities for growth exist in global markets. Firms involved in international marketing can use several product strategies. Some firms attempt to market the same product in a foreign market that has been successful in a domestic market. Products can also be modified to meet the needs of consumers in a different country. Finally, new products can be developed if existing products cannot be modified to meet the needs of consumers in a foreign market.

KEY TERMS

product manager
brand manager
market manager
venture team
new product
new product development
idea generation
idea screening
concept testing
business analysis
product development
test marketing
commercialization

product adoption process
innovators
early adopters
early majority
late majority
laggards
product positioning
product modification
quality modification
functional modification
style modification
product deletion

QUESTIONS FOR DISCUSSION AND REVIEW

1. Distinguish between the product-manager approach and the market-manager approach used to manage products.

2. Under what circumstances should an organization consider using a venture team?

3. Why are new products so important to firms?

4. How do you define *new product*? Give examples of three products that you consider new.

5. How would you go about generating new product ideas for a medium-sized printing company?

6. What is the purpose of test marketing? Do you think test marketing is essential, or could most firms skip this phase of new product development?

7. Trace one of your recent purchases (preferably a higher-priced item like a durable good) through the product adoption process. How did you become aware of the product, get interested in it, and so on?

8. How should marketing strategies change as a product goes through the stages of its life cycle?

9. What is product modification, and why is it used during the maturity stage of the product life cycle? Can you name a product that has been modified recently?

10. When would a firm consider deleting a product?

11. Discuss the different strategies that can be used to delete a product.

12. Under what conditions could a firm successfully use a global marketing strategy?

13. Why must firms modify existing products or develop new products for foreign markets?

C A S E S

12.1   BOEING DESIGNS HIGH-TECH 777 TO BEAT THE COMPETITION

United States aircraft manufacturer Boeing holds a 60 percent share of the global market for commercial aircraft and has a $92 billion order backlog representing about 1,605 planes. Its 737, 747, 757, and 767 all are profitable. Boeing is the nation's largest exporter, accounting for about 70 percent of new orders worldwide in 1992. Perhaps more than any American manufacturer, Boeing has dominated its industry. But tough times for airline companies have forced them to cut orders, eating deeply into Boeing's sales and profits. Boeing's revenues will drop as low as $20 billion in 1994, down from $30.2 billion in 1992. This has caused the firm to cut thousands of jobs—nearly 20 percent of its payroll.

Boeing is also facing increased competition. Its vulnerability was made clear when United Air Lines placed a large order with European aircraft manufacturer Airbus Industries in 1992. United ordered 50 narrow-body A320s from Airbus and took options on 50 more. The A320s will replace United's aging Boeing 727s. Airbus has now signed up fourteen of the seventeen largest airlines in the world. United's purchase gives Airbus even more credibility in the aircraft industry, which will be asked to provide an estimated 8,500 new jets to the world's airlines in the next fourteen years. Most experts expect orders to be slow in the near future, but to pick up by the end of the decade. The manufacturer offering the best products will emerge on top.

United chose the A320 because of its range, speed, fuel efficiency, comfort, and leading edge technology. Stewart Iddles, chief marketing officer of Airbus, says, "We like to say we are offering a BMW, not a Ford." Pilots seated in the cockpit of the A320 use joysticks at the side of their seats rather than steering wheels. Commands are transmitted by computers rather than manually. This "fly-by-wire" technology keeps the plane on course and takes much of the decision making out of pilots' hands.

Boeing also hopes to ensure its future with technologically advanced aircraft. In the works is the 777, a twin-engine, medium-range to long-range wide-body that will be Boeing's jet for the twenty-first century. The firm will spend billions designing this new jet, scheduled to go into service in May 1995. The 777 will be Boeing's first plane to be designed entirely on computer. Boeing is relying on a computer-assisted design (CAD) system to build an efficient, economic plane with fewer of the problems that usually plague new planes. The manufacturer hopes to save millions usually spent on fixing problems during production and after planes have been delivered to airlines. The system also enables Boeing to skip the many paper drawings and full-scale markups usually required by going straight from paper images to the actual plane. Rather than having only designers develop the jet's design, the CAD process considers the views of airline personnel, mechanics, and the people who will build and market the plane.

Boeing is using a digital system called Catio for computer-aided, three-dimensional, interactive application. The system uses the largest cluster of mainframe computers in the world, eight IBM 3090s. Since Catio is three-dimensional and capable of displaying solid objects, the digital system shows how all pieces fit together. If two parts clash, the problem shows up on the screen. For instance, if a tube cannot get around a spar, Catio detects the problem. Catio-man, a computer-simulated human, can climb inside the three-dimensional images and show how difficult it would be for a real human to reach a problem area or make a repair. Catio-man discovered that a human mechanic would not be able to reach the red navigation light on the roof of the plane to change the bulb.

CAD is not intended to speed up delivery of the 777 but rather to make a better plane from the start. In the past, engineers were still designing when manufacturing started. Changes were made as problems showed up in the factories, or worse, after the planes were built. Tools and dies and maintenance manuals had to be reworked and unusable parts were wasted. When the 747–400 went into use, Boeing had to assign three hundred engineers to eliminate bugs.

No doubt everyone at Boeing feels the pressure of the 777 project. If successful, it could mean a beautiful, profitable machine that travels the globe long into the future. If it fails, it could deeply hurt a company even Boeing's size. But Phil Condit, executive vice president in charge of the 777 project, knows Boeing has no choice. "My strong feeling is that you retain your competitive position by continuously improving what you do. Our job is to make sure we keep turning out the best planes in the world."

Questions for Discussion

1. Why is Airbus a threat to Boeing, the world's leading aircraft manufacturer?

2. How does the CAD system used by Boeing cut costs?

3. What does Boeing hope to accomplish with CAD? What are some of the benefits of Catio-man?

Based on information from Dori Jones Yang and Andrea Rothman, "Boeing Cuts its Altitude as the Clouds Roll In," *Business Week,* February 8, 1993, p. 25; Jeff Cole, "Boeing's Bid to Avoid Swings in its Business Falls Short of Hopes," *Wall Street Journal,* February 16, 1993, pp. A1, A5; "Betting on the 21st Century Jet," *Fortune,* April 20, 1992, pp. 102–117; Jeff Cole, "Boeing's Dominance of Aircraft Industry Is Beginning to Erode," *Wall Street Journal,* July 10, 1992, pp. A1, A6; and Doris Jones Yang, Seth Payne, and Stewart Toy, "Now Airbus Is Cruising Comfortably," *Business Week,* July 27, 1992, p. 33.

12.2 CIBA-GEIGY ADDS NEW PRODUCTS, EXTENDS OLD ONES

Switzerland-based Ciba-Geigy CA is the world's number five drug company, with sales of around $4.28 billion in the $200-billion-a-year pharmaceutical industry. It is an industry in which the major firms spend millions on research and development in hopes of finding new drugs that will become blockbusters. But since blockbuster medicines are rare—only about twenty now reach sales above $750 million each—Ciba-Geigy depends on effective product management rather than huge breakthroughs to secure its future.

Ciba-Geigy's best-known new product in recent years is the nicotine patch, a smoking-cessation device available with a doctor's prescription. The patch, which looks like a big round Band-Aid, releases small, controlled doses of nicotine through the skin into the bloodstream over a three-month period. Ciba-Geigy received U.S. Food and Drug Administration (FDA) approval for its Habitrol patch in December 1991 and introduced it in early 1992 to immediate competition. Marion Merrell Dow had received FDA approval for its Nicoderm a few weeks ahead of Ciba-Geigy; American Cyanamid Co.'s Lederle division got approval for ProStep several weeks later. Warner-Lambert Company trailed the others by a few months with its Nicotrol patch. In 1992, worldwide sales of patches were about $900 million, more than double initial estimates.

A new product introduction could hardly be more intense than that of the nicotine patches. Essentially, three firms released three brands of a new prescription product within a few weeks of each other. The patches are remarkably similar, differing somewhat in the amount of nicotine contained and the services accompanying them. To gain an edge on the competition, Ciba-Geigy includes "The Habitrol Smoking Cessation Program." It consists of two brochures—one with tips for smokers and one to help their relatives and friends deal with them during withdrawal—and an audiotape prepared by the American Lung Association that explains relaxation techniques and gives motivational messages.

Although only doctors can actually prescribe patches for patients, Ciba-Geigy and the other manufacturers ran aggressive advertising campaigns to get their names out to the target audience in hopes that consumers would ask for a patch by name. "It's important for pharmaceuticals to have a brand image, but with something like this, more so than most," said Doug Arbesfeld, spokesman for Ciba-Geigy in Summit, New Jersey. His company—and rival Marion Merrell Dow—sponsored television and radio commercials and advertisements in newspapers and leading consumer magazines such as *Time, Newsweek, U.S. News and World Report, People, Sports Illustrated, Business Week,* and *Parade.* During Habitrol's first few months on the market, Ciba-Geigy spent $9.9 million for magazine advertisements alone. Industry observers estimated the company's cost for marketing Habitrol in the first year to be as much as $35 million.

With the nicotine patches, Ciba-Geigy and its competitors are fighting for shares of a huge potential market. According to the American Lung Association, more than 51 million Americans smoke; about 18 million try to quit each year, but only about 1.3 million succeed. Wall Street analysts estimate that the patch market will eventually exceed $1 billion. Immediately after the patches were put on the market, smokers flocked to them. In some areas of the country, the enormous demand caused shortages, especially of Nicoderm, the first patch to hit the market. Within the first few months, Ciba-Geigy saw sales of Habitrol reach $110 million. The company later emerged from the pack as the leading seller with 60 percent of the market.

Ciba-Geigy expects to launch at least a dozen new medicines during the 1990s. Yet while its labs have worked to develop new products, its marketers have worked to keep existing products going strong. Even if the firm's new drugs reach their market potential, a core group of older products still will account for its pharmaceutical sales for many more years. "We kept our major drugs going over an amazingly long period of time with consistent growth rates—even some products that were old or off patent," says Stephen Leventhal, chief of international product development. For example, the company has formulated several new versions of its extremely successful anti-arthritis drug Voltaren. Along with the original tablets, Voltaren now comes as eyedrops, as an intravenous solution, as time-release pills, and as "emulgel," a cross between cream and ointment for which Ciba-Geigy has been awarded a 20-year patent. In 1991, Voltaren, with sales of $1.2 billion, was the world's fourth best-selling pharmaceutical. Nearly one-third of Voltaren sales come from the United States, where it was not even introduced until 1989, when many original European patents had already expired. Ciba-Geigy obtained U.S. "market exclusivity" status through June 1993, which kept generic-drug producers from developing a nonpatented version. The firm expects to see generic rivals to Voltaren on the market in early 1995 and estimates that they will take about half of its Voltaren sales. Ciba-Geigy is preparing to meet the challenge head-on by moving into the generic segment, too, both in the United States and in Europe.

Questions for Discussion

1. Describe how Ciba-Geigy positioned its Habitrol nicotine patch.

2. Do you think Ciba-Geigy or the other manufacturers of the nicotine patch test-marketed these products? Why or why not?

3. What has Ciba-Geigy's marketing strategy been for products in the maturity stage?

4. Explain Ciba-Geigy's strategy for marketing Voltaren internationally.

Based on information from Patricia Winters, "Sales Spark May Be Out for Nicotine Patches," *Advertising Age,* January 18, 1993, pp. 3, 51; Stephen D. Moore, "Ciba Finds Marketing Is Its Own Kind of Blockbuster," *Wall Street Journal,* July 14, 1992, p. B4; Kathleen Deveny,"Heated, if Smokeless, Competition Rages Among Makers of Nicotine Skin Patches," *Wall Street Journal,* March 4, 1992, p. B1; Scott Donaton, "Nicotine Patch Eases Cig Ad Retreat," *Advertising Age,* June 29, 1992, p. 12; Pat Sloan, "Consumers Craving Nicotine Patches," *Advertising Age,* March 23, 1992, p. 3; and Carrie Goerne, "Pharmaceutical Companies Compete Aggressively to Help Smokers Quit Habit," *Marketing News,* March 30, 1992, p. 8.

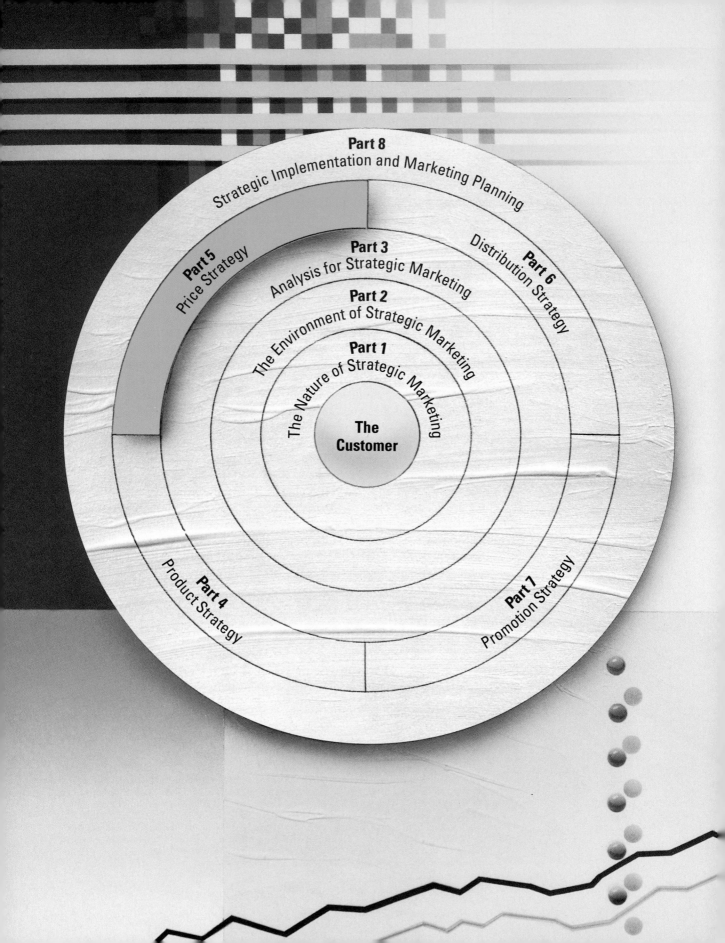

PART

5

Price Strategy

Price Concepts

OBJECTIVES

- To discuss the importance of price in an organization's marketing mix.

- To explain the difference between price and nonprice competition.

- To identify different pricing objectives.

- To discuss the issues that affect pricing decisions.

- To describe the factors that influence pricing decisions in organizational markets.

At the Sotheby's Holdings, Inc. auction house in New York, speculators have paid $2.1 million for baseball cards and other sports memorabilia. The most sought after item was the uniform Roger Maris wore during the 1961 baseball season, when he broke Babe Ruth's home run record. Sports Heroes Inc., a sports card brokerage firm that bought the highest-priced items and spent $480,095, gave the winning bid of $120,000. Although the purchases were made partly to generate publicity, a representative of Sports Heroes said that the "primary motive was return on investment."

Baseball cards in particular are in high demand among collectors. At Sotheby's, a 1952 Topps card of rookie Yankee slugger Mickey Mantle went for $46,750; the card had sold for $49,500 the previous year. A card of Jackie Robinson, the first black major league player, sold for $4,675. And a Honus Wagner card, one of only forty known to exist, sold for $220,000, compared with $451,000 the previous year.

Of course, not all sports collectibles sell at the lofty prices owners would like. Lou Gehrig's 1937 Yankee jersey still sits on a table at Christie's International PLC. The auction house values the jersey at $375,000 to $425,000, perhaps the highest price ever set on one piece of clothing. Gehrig is a true baseball legend. Known as "the Iron Horse," he played 2,130 consecutive games, a record even today. He died from the muscle disease that now bears his name and left behind only a limited amount of memorabilia. It is estimated that fewer than a dozen authentic Gehrig jerseys still exist. Yet no buyers have come forward at the current price.

Collecting trading cards remains popular today, and the card business has become a billion-dollar industry. During the 1980s, sales increased annually at a rate of 20 percent, and they continue to rise in the 1990s. The card-collecting market is still dominated by 12-year-old boys, but more and more adults are becoming speculators, and for good reason. Rookie cards of some of today's stars have increased rapidly in value. A rookie card of Cal Ripken, Jr., sold at Sotheby's for $65, an increase of 117 percent from the previous year. Dave Justice's rookie card sold for $4, a 167 percent increase. It's hard to beat that kind of return on investment.[1] ●

[1] Based on information from Alexandra Peers, "Speculators Take the Field at Sotheby's Baseball Card Auction," *Wall Street Journal,* March 2, 1992, pp. C1, C18; Jennifer Pellet, "It's in the Cards," *Discount Merchandiser,* March 1992, pp. 32–39, 71; and "Gehrig Baseball Jersey Fails to Sell at Auction," *Wall Street Journal,* October 19, 1992, p. A6.

C ollecting sports memorabilia has become big business. As we discuss in this chapter, the prices customers pay for products reflect the value they receive in return. Many of us cannot see paying thousands of dollars for a baseball card, even if we had the money. But each of us is willing to purchase something of value relative to our ability to pay the going price.

THE MEANING AND IMPORTANCE OF PRICE

■ **price** the value placed on what is exchanged

From a buyer's perspective, **price** is the "something of value" that a buyer gives up in an exchange. Although most prices are not set through an auction, the consumer has a major influence on the price of products. If the value received is not worth the value given up, consumers may purchase a substitute product or decide not to purchase the product at all. Consumers exchange something of value, normally buying power, for the satisfaction or utility they expect from a product. As Chapter 3 points out, buying power depends on a buyer's income, credit, and wealth. However, price does not always involve money or some other financial consideration offered in exchange. The trading of products, or **barter,** is the oldest form of exchange.

■ **barter** the trading of products

Consumers still use barter for a variety of products today, such as records, baseball cards, and books. Small companies sometimes barter services with other small companies. A small law firm, for instance, may barter legal services with an accounting firm in return for bookkeeping and tax services.

As the opening feature shows, the price consumers are willing to pay depends on the amount of satisfaction or utility they expect to receive from a product. A complete set of the original edition of *The Birds of America,* John James Audubon's 435 hand-colored engravings, sold in 1992 for $4.07 million, the highest price ever paid for a piece of printed Americana.[2] A buyer purchased Van Gogh's *Portrait of Dr. Gachet* in 1990 for $82.5 million.[3] And at a 1992 auction, the blue-and-white gingham dress worn by Judy Garland in *The Wizard of Oz* was sold for $48,400; an original Beatles drumskin cover brought $17,600.[4] The price of these products reflects the value consumers place on them.

Price is expressed in many different terms. For instance, insurance companies charge a *premium;* lawyers who represent you charge a *fee;* a taxi or airline charges a *fare;* and apartment complexes charge *rent.* Sometimes a *toll* is charged when you use a bridge or turnpike. Organizations and clubs charge *dues* to permit membership. Regardless of how price is described, its purpose is to communicate to consumers the value of products offered in the market.

[2] Christie Brown, "Petrels in a Storm," *Forbes,* August 31, 1992, pp. 79–82.
[3] Harris Collingwood, "Van Gogh, Gogh, Goghing, Gone," *Business Week,* May 28, 1990, p. 34.
[4] Marcy Rivinius, "Oz Auction," *Lexington* (KY) *Herald Leader,* December 20, 1992, p. A14.

Of all the marketing mix variables, price is probably the most flexible. Organizations can adjust prices much more easily than they can modify the product, change the promotional program, or redesign the distribution system. Product development and promotional campaign planning are quite time consuming. Establishing a distribution system usually requires long-term relationships with intermediaries that will handle the product. Thus price is often the only marketing mix variable that can be adjusted quickly in response to competitors' actions or changes in demand. On successive trips to the supermarket, you may have noticed how quickly prices can be changed. One drawback, however, is that price changes can easily be matched by competitors.

Price is also the marketing mix variable that relates most directly to revenue.[5] Whereas product, promotion, and distribution efforts require expenditures by a firm, the price of a product determines how much money comes into an organization. Thus prices affect an organization's profits, which are vital for long-term survival.

Price also has a psychological impact on customers. By setting a high price, a company can highlight the quality of a product and try to increase the status associated with owning it. An automaker like Porsche A.G., for example, uses high prices to connote quality and prestige in its vehicles. The base price of a 1993 XJS dropped $10,750, but the car still costs customers $49,750.[6] By contrast, cars such as Toyota Motor Corp.'s Lexus, which are as sophisticated as European luxury cars but sell for thousands less, suggest a bargain and attract customers who have budgeted less money to the purchase of a luxury car.[7] The advertisement shown in Figure 13.1 uses price to attract buyers.

PRICE VERSUS NONPRICE COMPETITION

Firms can choose to compete on a price or nonprice basis. The choice affects decisions and activities not only for pricing but also for other marketing mix variables.

Price Competition

■ **price competition**
a policy whereby a firm focuses on price as a means of differentiating its products from others and attempts to match or beat its competitors' prices

An organization that uses **price competition** focuses on price as a means of differentiating its products from others and attempts to match or beat its competitors' prices. A company using price competition must be willing and

5 S. Tamer Cavusgil, "Unraveling the Mystique of Export Pricing," *Business Horizons,* May–June 1988, pp. 54–63.
6 Krystal Miller, "Jaguar Pulls In Its Car-Pricing Claws," *Wall Street Journal,* October 14, 1992, pp. B1, B8.
7 Krystal Miller, "Sideswiped by Texas and Frugal Buyers, Luxury-Car Makers Take Discount Route," *Wall Street Journal,* June 29, 1992, pp. B1, B8.

FIGURE 13.1

The Importance of Price
This advertisement for the Jeep Cherokee has a psychological impact on customers by emphasizing that its $17,492 price is a good bargain.

Source: Chrysler Corporation.

able to change prices frequently and should be the low-cost producer of the product. To make this strategy work, the firm must respond quickly and aggressively to competitors' price changes. Figure 13.2 shows how Hit or Miss Stores compete on the basis of price.

Price competition affords flexibility; a marketer can adjust prices to counter changes in the firm's costs or in demand for the product. Additionally, an organization using price competition can respond quickly when competing firms try to gain market share by cutting their prices. A major disadvantage of price competition is that competitors also have the ability to adjust their prices. Moreover, if an organization using price competition is forced to raise its prices, competing firms not under the same pressures may choose not to follow suit. Another disadvantage of price competition is that a firm's cost advantage could be eliminated by a new technology.

Price competition is practiced by a number of firms in many different industries. Nintendo Co. and Sega Enterprises Ltd. have steadily lowered the prices of their basic video game systems from $199.95 to $99.[8] Jan Bell Marketing Inc., a jewelry distributor, sells private label jewelry—gold chains, earrings, tennis bracelets, and rings—wholesale for about one-third

[8]Joseph Pereira, "Strategy of Slashing Prices Helps to Lift Video-Game Makers out of Sales Slump," *Wall Street Journal,* October 14, 1992, pp. B1, B8.

FIGURE 13.2
Price Competition
Hit or Miss Stores advertise a complete outfit for under $125, telling prospective customers that you don't have to outspend others to outdress them.

Source: Courtesy Hit or Miss Inc.

OUTDRESS THEM, DON'T OUTSPEND THEM.

Hit or Miss
S T O R E S

1-800-94-STYLE

Complete outfit under $125.

of what other manufacturers charge.[9] Taco Bell added a Value Menu of 59-cent items aimed at the frequent customer who dines at fast-food restaurants an average of seventeen times a month. The strategy has helped Taco Bell grow faster than the average company in the Mexican fast-food industry.[10] And a small company in Plano, Texas, called PageNet, became the number one firm in the paging industry by pricing its pagers lower than those of competitors. While the average monthly cost of a pager is $15, PageNet's average cost is $12.[11]

Nonprice Competition

■ **nonprice competition** a policy in which a seller focuses on aspects other than price—such as distinctive product features, service, product quality, promotion, and packaging— to differentiate its products from competing brands

Nonprice competition occurs when a seller focuses on aspects other than price—such as distinctive product features, service, product quality, promotion, and packaging—to differentiate its products from competing brands. When using nonprice competition, firms focus on aspects of the product that offer value to the target market. For example, manufacturers of nearly every major brand of toothbrush have increased sales by almost 25 percent while

[9]Paul B. Brown, "How to Compete on Price," *Inc.,* May 1990, pp. 105–107.
[10]Cleveland Horton, "Taco Bell Expands Price Strategy," *Advertising Age,* November 5, 1990, p. 20.
[11]Gretchen Morgenson, "A Pager in Every Pocket?" *Forbes,* December 21, 1992, pp. 210–214.

raising prices. Rather than selling the brushes on the basis of price, which was once a common practice, companies are emphasizing how their brushes with tiny shock absorbers and rippled bristles benefit teeth and gums.[12]

One advantage of using nonprice competition is that it enables a seller to increase sales by some means other than adjusting price. Sales may be increased by product quality or a unique product feature. Another advantage is that a firm can build customer loyalty to a brand by stressing features other than price. When customers prefer a brand because of its features, quality, or associated services rather than its price, they are less likely to be attracted to competing firms and brands. But when price is the primary reason that customers buy a particular brand, the competition can capture such customers by cutting prices.

Nonprice competition is most effective when several conditions exist. First, it must be possible to distinguish the product from competing products on the basis of some feature other than price, such as quality, promotion, or service. For example, a new light bulb has been developed that is said to last 20,000 hours and use 75 percent less electricity than conventional bulbs, which makes it easily distinguishable from other bulbs.[13] Second, the feature used to differentiate the product must be important and meaningful to consumers. Manufacturers of heating systems, for instance, often advertise that their systems are energy-efficient because this characteristic is usually important to consumers. Finally, the feature used to distinguish a product from competitors' offerings should not be easily emulated. Pop-top cans initially set one beverage company apart from the others, but soon all beverages became available in pop-top cans.

Firms in a variety of industries compete on the basis of nonprice competition. In the athletic shoe industry, Nike uses the "Bo Knows" advertising campaign to create images that differentiate its products from competitors' shoes.[14] Sony sells televisions and stereo equipment by emphasizing high product quality. Sony is successful in charging higher prices in a very competitive market. Robinson Brick Co., the largest maker of residential brick in Colorado, uses nonprice competition to make its bricks something more than just a commodity. Knowing that quality, choice of color, and speed of delivery are more important to his customers than price, owner George Robinson emphasizes these aspects of his products while charging higher prices than competitors.[15]

It is important to note that a seller attempting to compete on a nonprice basis cannot ignore competitors' prices. The firm must know what price competitors are charging for their products and will probably set its product's price near or slightly above that of competing brands. Thus price remains a significant component of the marketing mix, even in situations that call for nonprice competition.

---

[12]Kathleen Deveny, "Today's Toothbrushes: 'Improved' and Pricey," *Wall Street Journal,* November 10, 1992, pp. B1, B10.
[13]"New Bulb Said to Last 20,000 Hours," *Lexington* (KY) *Herald-Leader,* May 31, 1992, p. A9.
[14]James Buckley, Jr., "Bo Knows Business," *Sports Illustrated,* November 5, 1990, p. 52.
[15]Paul B. Brown, "The Product Is the Message," *Inc.,* June 1990, pp. 104–105.

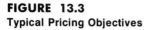

FIGURE 13.3
Typical Pricing Objectives

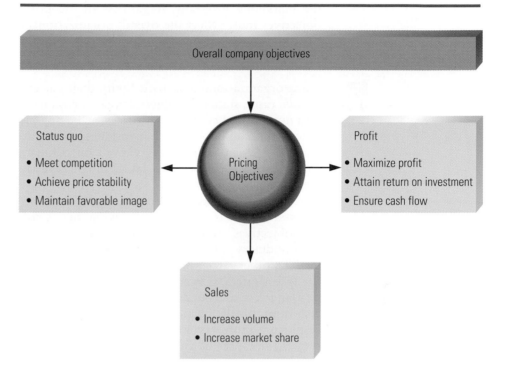

DETERMINING PRICING OBJECTIVES

■ **pricing objective**
a general goal that describes
what an organization hopes
to achieve through its pricing activities

Before a firm can determine the right price for a product, it must determine the role of price in the marketing mix. A **pricing objective** is a general goal that describes what an organization hopes to achieve through its pricing activities. Pricing objectives should be measurable so that they can be evaluated. Since they affect decisions in other functional areas, such as finance and production, they must be consistent with the organizational mission and objectives. For example, if an organization wants to provide the highest-quality product in the industry, its pricing objectives must be consistent with this objective.

Survival is the broadest and most fundamental pricing objective. Organizations can endure short-run losses, internal restructuring, and other difficulties if they are necessary for survival. Because price is flexible and relatively easy to adjust, companies sometimes cut prices in order to increase sales volumes to levels that match the organization's expenses. For instance, several years ago Continental Airlines discounted its airfares to a level lower than competitors' fares rather than go out of business. Many steel companies have been faced with a similar situation.

Beyond the obvious objective of survival, there are three major categories of pricing objectives: status quo, profit, and sales. The various objectives that fall under each category are summarized in Figure 13.3. Some firms use a combination of these objectives when determining the role of price in the marketing program. Regardless of the pricing objectives pursued, the objectives must reflect the overall organizational objectives.

Status Quo Objectives

Some organizations are satisfied with their current market position and sales. In such cases, status quo objectives can focus on several dimensions—meeting (but not beating) competitors' prices, achieving price stability, or maintaining a favorable public image. For instance, when gasoline prices soared in the late 1970s, many consumers viewed oil companies negatively. Since then, gasoline prices have become stable, and oil companies have generally regained a more positive image.

By pursuing status quo objectives, a firm can help stabilize demand for its products. This, in turn, reduces the firm's risk. Conversely, when status quo objectives are not pursued, a climate of price competition can develop in an industry. For example, when several airlines drastically lowered fares in 1992, other carriers cut fares a step further; most competitors then matched the lower prices. The lack of price stability resulted in severe price competition and lost revenues for all the airlines. Status quo pricing objectives can also diminish the chances of government intervention because stable prices result in a more favorable public image (unfavorable public image is often one of the causes of government intervention).

Profit Objectives

Many firms establish the profit objective of maximizing profits. The major problem with this specific objective is that it is difficult to measure whether profit maximization has been achieved and almost impossible to determine the maximum possible profit. Because of this difficulty, profit objectives are generally set at levels that owners and top-level decision makers view as "satisfactory." Profit objectives may be stated in terms of actual dollar amounts or in terms of the percentage of change relative to the profits of a previous period. Some pharmaceutical firms, for instance, have established the pricing objective of increasing quarterly profits by 20 percent.[16]

Another profit objective used by industry leaders is the attainment of a specific rate of return on the firm's investment. Because large firms such as IBM and General Motors establish their pricing objectives more independently of competition than do smaller firms, they are in a better position to set target returns. Most pricing objectives that are based on return on investment (ROI) are achieved by trial and error because all cost and revenue data required to forecast the return on investment may not be available at the time prices are set. A major disadvantage of ROI objectives is that they do not reflect prices of competitive products or customer perceptions of price.

Some organizations set prices to recover cash as quickly as possible to keep cash flowing throughout the organization. Understandably, financial

---

[16] Elyse Tanouye, "Price Rises for Drugs Cool, Manufacturer Profits Chill," *Wall Street Journal,* April 9, 1992, p. B4.

managers want to quickly recover money spent on product development. This is especially true when the marketer anticipates that a product will have a short life cycle, as is often the case with fad products like "stuck-ons"—stuffed animals with suction cups that attach to glass panes. Cash flow objectives do not realistically portray the role of price in determining profits. If prices are set too low, they may lead to lower profits; if prices are too high, competitors with lower prices may gain a large share of the market.

Sales Objectives

The pricing objective of some companies is to increase sales volume. This objective is typically expressed as a percentage of sales over a specified time period. For instance, a firm's pricing objective might be to boost sales by 10 percent over a one-year period.

Another sales objective relates to market share, which is a firm's sales in relation to total industry sales.[17] Many businesses establish pricing objectives to maintain or increase market share. For example, a company's pricing objective might be to increase its market share for a particular product from 15 to 20 percent within the coming year. In some cases, market-share objectives lead to dramatic price cutting. Winn-Dixie, the largest grocery chain in the Southeast, has continued to cut prices on thousands of items in an effort to increase its market share.[18]

Maintaining or increasing market share does not always depend on industry growth. Sometimes market-share gains come at the expense of other organizations.[19] During a battle that raged for years, MCI and Sprint tried to increase their market share by taking share from AT&T. The result has become a bitter war for larger chunks of the $55-billion-a-year long-distance market, in which the three firms spend more than $4 billion annually on marketing. MCI has raised its share of the market to 17 percent, mostly at the expense of AT&T, whose share is 65 percent; Sprint struggles to maintain a 10 percent share.[20]

FACTORS TO CONSIDER IN THE PRICING DECISION

Marketers must consider many factors in making their pricing decision. Figure 13.4 shows how buyers' expectations, the marketing mix variables, competitive structure, costs, and government action all have an impact on pricing

---

[17]J. Joseph Cronin and Steven J. Skinner, "Marketing Outcomes, Financial Conditions, and Retail Profit Performance," *Journal of Retailing,* Winter 1984, pp. 9–22.

[18]Kathleen Madigan, Joseph Weber, and Geoffrey Smith, "The Latest Mad Plunge of the Price Slashers," *Business Week,* May 11, 1992, p. 36.

[19]Al Ries and Jack Trout, *Marketing Warfare* (New York: McGraw-Hill, 1986), p. 32.

[20]John B. Keller, "AT&T, MCI, Sprint Raise the Intensity of Their Endless War," *Wall Street Journal,* October 20, 1992, pp. A1, A6.

FIGURE 13.4
Factors Influencing Pricing Decisions

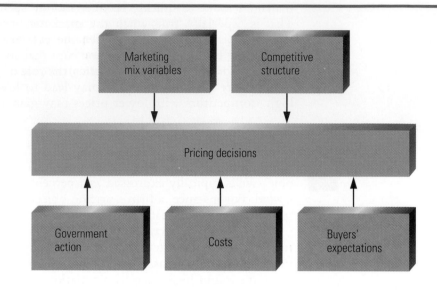

decisions. Before determining a price, a firm should carefully analyze each of these factors. (Determining actual prices is the subject of Chapter 14.)

Buyers' Expectations

When setting prices, an organization should consider consumers' expectations and concerns. Some consumers are more concerned about the price of a product than are other consumers. Business fell 30 percent at the Moscow McDonald's when the price of a Big Mac was raised from 3.75 rubles to 6.95 rubles—the equivalent of $12.64 at the official exchange rate. But even though a Big Mac, fries, and Coca-Cola cost 20 percent of the average weekly salary in Moscow, a high rate of customers keeps going back.[21] Members of one market segment may be more price sensitive than members of a different target market. Also, the importance of price to buyers will vary across different product categories.[22] For example, price may be a more important factor in the purchase of clothing than in the purchase of over-the-counter medicines, because consumers may be more price sensitive to clothing than they are to medicines.

For most products, consumers have a range of acceptable prices. In some cases, the range is fairly narrow, but for other product categories there is a wider range. A marketing manager should try to determine the acceptable range of prices in the relevant product category and set prices accordingly. When its sales in the United States fell 24 percent, Mercedes-Benz found that

---

[21]Joel M. Ostrow, "Prices Soar at McD's," *Advertising Age,* November 12, 1990, p. 16.
[22]Kent B. Monroe, "Buyers' Subjective Perceptions of Price," *Journal of Marketing Research,* February 1973, p. 70.

$70,000 was simply out of the acceptable range of prices buyers were willing to pay.[23] Marketing managers should also recognize that frequent price changes may cause buyers to postpone purchases in hopes of a lower price. Furthermore, lowering prices may lead buyers to have unrealistic expectations; it is generally more difficult to raise prices once they have been lowered.

Marketing Mix Variables

Because the marketing mix variables are highly interrelated, pricing decisions must be made in conjunction with product, promotion, and distribution decisions.

Product Activities A product's price generally influences consumer demand for it. A high price, for instance, may result in low sales, which in turn may lead to higher production costs per unit. Conversely, low prices may generate higher demand and result in lower per-unit production costs. For many types of products, consumers associate a high price with better product quality and a low price with lower product quality.[24] This perceived price-quality reltionship influences the overall image customers have of products or brands. For instance, dressmaker Leslie Fay Cos. found its dresses were too low-priced for the upscale image of several retail stores. After Leslie Fay raised dress prices to the $100 range, sales of its dresses doubled in most retail stores.[25] However, the association of higher prices with quality may weaken as prices fall over time in a competitive market.[26]

The price-quality relationship does not apply to all products.[27] Products with high ticket prices that are not purchased frequently tend to display a stronger price-quality relationship than products that are purchased frequently. Additionally, high prices sometimes signal noneconomical packaging rather than high quality. And in some cases there is little difference in the price of alternative brands. Point/Counterpoint takes a closer look at the price-quality relationship.

Promotion Activities Promotion is also affected by price. Advertisements often display bargain prices, whereas premium prices are less likely to appear in advertising messages. Nevertheless, advertisements for upscale products such as luxury cars or fine jewelry may highlight a premium price to set the products apart from other products. In addition, higher-priced products are more likely to require personal-selling efforts than lower-priced

---

[23] Mark Landler, "Mercedes Finds Out How Much Is Too Much," *Business Week,* January 20, 1992, pp. 92–96.

[24] Robert A. Petersen, "The Price-Perceived Quality Relationship: Experimental Evidence," *Journal of Marketing,* November 1970, p. 525.

[25] Monica Roman, "Why Leslie Fay's Duds Aren't Duds Anymore," *Business Week,* June 4, 1990, p. 86.

[26] David J. Curry and Peter C. Riesz, "Prices and Price/Quality Relationships: A Longitudinal Analysis," *Journal of Marketing,* January 1988, pp. 36–51.

[27] Eitan Gerstner, "Do Higher Prices Signal Higher Quality?" *Journal of Marketing Research,* May 1985, pp. 209–215.

POINT/COUNTERPOINT

Does Price Really Signify Quality?

Buyers use many factors when making quality judgments about products. Some brand names have a reputation of being high in quality, and this reputation is reinforced through advertisements and service. When a new item is added to the product line, consumers then assume that it is a high-quality product. Previous experience with a product also influences perception of quality. If a product performs satisfactorily, consumers may perceive the product to be high in quality. If the product fails, it will be perceived as low in quality. Price has also been seen as a factor in quality judgments. But to what extent do buyers use price to evaluate the quality of a product?

Point   Consumers often use price to assess the quality of products. When they come across a product that is priced higher than a competitor's version, they assume that the product is also higher in quality. Firms can therefore use price strategically to signal quality to buyers. Stores like Neiman Marcus are perceived as having higher-quality merchandise than other department stores because they charge higher prices. Likewise, the high prices of certain perfumes and brands of clothing signify quality to buyers.

Studies have shown that price influences consumers' perceptions of quality for such products as shirts and towels. When consumers are uncertain about a purchase decision, they rely heavily on price as an indicator of quality. When other tangible cues are not available, as with a service like hair styling, price may be the primary measure used by consumers to assess quality.

Counterpoint   Consumers may use price as an indicator of quality when no other information is available. But in most purchase situations, consumers also consider brand names, information about the product itself, and recommendations from other users. Furthermore, some people tend to rely on price more than others in making purchases. Their perception of the price-quality relationship depends on personal characteristics such as attitudes and motives.

Higher prices do not suggest higher quality for many products. Instead, they may reflect higher costs associated with production, distribution, advertising, or some other expense. Foreign automobile manufacturers initially gained large market shares in the United States by offering higher quality products at competitive prices. In general, the price-quality relationship tends to be product specific and is fairly weak for frequently purchased products.

ones. For example, a customer might be willing to purchase a Panasonic all-in-one stereo unit in a self-service outlet, such as Target, yet that same person would expect knowledgeable and personal help from a salesperson if a $5,000 Bang & Olufsen stereo system were the product being purchased.

Distribution Activities   The price of a product is also related to its distribution. Premium-priced products such as the one advertised in Figure 13.5 are often sold in a limited number of stores, whereas lower-priced products

FIGURE 13.5
Limited Distribution
This Lasalle watch, a premium-priced product, is sold in a limited number of stores, such as Borsheim's, Marshall Field's, and Fortunoff.

Source: © Seiko Time 1992.

in the same or similar product categories may be sold in numerous stores. Godiva and other premium-priced chocolates are distributed through selected specialty stores, but Hershey's chocolates are distributed through many outlets, including grocery and discount stores and vending machines. Low-priced products may also suffer from periodic stockouts or capacity problems. For example, US Sprint initially had to turn away long-distance customers because its low prices led to consumer demand that could not be met.

Competitive Structure

The competitive structure that characterizes a particular industry affects a firm's flexibility in setting prices. Knowledge of the competitive structure does not suggest what price an organization should charge for a product, but it does provide a feasible range of prices that might be established. Firms must also recognize that too high a price may encourage other firms to enter the market. (Chapter 3 discusses several types of competitive market structures.)

When a company operates under a *monopoly* and without government regulation, it can set prices at whatever level it chooses. Of course, it must take into consideration what consumers will pay, or what the market will bear. A regulated monopoly has less pricing flexibility, but the government generally permits the organization to set prices that generate a reasonable profit. In an *oligopolistic* market structure (see Chapter 3), a business may raise its price in the hope that the few other sellers in the industry will follow suit. A firm in an oligopolistic market achieves little by lowering its price and could cause a *price war,* in which competing firms struggle to undercut each other's prices. A bitter price war started by Chicago-based Keebler, the cookie manufacturer, wounded rival RJR Nabisco slightly; Keebler's earnings dropped 60 percent.[28] And profits in the pet food industry, along with advertising spending, fell dramatically when the top pet food marketers used every tactic available to lower prices.[29] In a market characterized by *monopolistic competition,* the many sellers often practice nonprice competition and focus instead on differentiating their products along other lines. Finally, in a market characterized by *perfect competition*—where there is a large number of sellers and buyers view all sellers' products to be the same—a marketer has no flexibility in setting prices. Marketing Close-up examines the price war in the airline industry.

Costs

Costs are certainly a key concern when establishing prices. A company may sell its products below cost for a brief period of time to match competition, to improve cash flow, or even to increase market share, but in the long run, no organization can survive by selling products below cost. Even firms that have a high-volume business cannot survive if they sell their products slightly below cost. Thus it is critical that the marketing manager analyze all costs so that they can be included in the total cost of a product. Most marketing managers regard a product's cost as the minimum below which the product cannot be priced. Limited-service hotel chains like Hampton Inn have thrived by holding the biggest cost—labor—to a minimum. A staff of 20 to 24 can run a typical Hampton.[30] Shaw Industries became the largest carpet manufacturer in the United States by cutting costs and reducing prices. For instance, to bypass wholesalers, who add costs and slow deliveries, Shaw installed a communications system that enabled the company to take orders directly from 37,000 retailers.[31]

Marketers must also consider the costs that a product shares with others in the product line. Many products share the cost of research and development, production, and distribution. In this case, total revenues from the products must be greater than costs. Firms will often raise prices to cover increasing costs. For example, the cost of raw silk has jumped by about 65 percent, causing the price of silk neckties to increase by 45 percent.[32]

---

[28] Marcia R. Berss, "Biscuit Wars," *Forbes,* April 26, 1993, p. 47.

[29] Julie Liesse, "Price War Bites at Pet Food Ad $," *Advertising Age,* April 5, 1993, p. 12.

[30] Pauline Yoshihashi, "Limited-Service Chains Offer Enough to Thrive," *Wall Street Journal,* July 27, 1992, p. B1.

[31] Brian O'Reilly, "Know When to Embrace Change," *Fortune,* February 22, 1993, p. 40.

[32] Seth Lubove, "As the Worm Turns," *Forbes,* March 19, 1990, pp. 76–83.

MARKETING CLOSE-UP

Price Wars in the Airline Industry

Since airline deregulation, the industry has been characterized by deep price cutting. Prior to deregulation, the Civil Aeronautics Board established airfares. Travelers were charged according to the distance they traveled—the longer the trip, the higher the fare. After deregulation, pricing became much more competitive, resulting in ridiculously low prices for certain routes and bankruptcy for several carriers.

In April 1992, American Airlines led a move by the industry to simplify fares and eliminate steep discounts. American's plan called for a fare structure which cut the highest fares by 38 percent and established only four fares for any route. All other carriers, with the exception of TWA, followed American's lead and established similar plans. TWA was operating under bankruptcy court protection and had been offering fares 20 percent below its competitors. It was TWA's only hope of emerging from bankruptcy.

A month later, Northwest Airlines introduced a new promotion: a free ticket to anyone over 12 accompanied by a paying passenger between the ages of 2 and 17. Even though Northwest called this a promotion rather than a change from the new fare structure it had so recently adopted, American responded by slashing its lowest advance purchase fares by 50 percent. A one-way fare between New York and Los Angeles, for example, was a mere $100. The result was the most severe price war in the history of the industry. From May 28, when American announced its cut, until June 5, the date by which tickets had to be purchased, airline companies and travel agents were deluged by travelers buying half-price tickets.

Whereas hotels, resorts, and car rental companies reaped a windfall, the fare war was a disaster for airlines and travel agents. The airlines lost an estimated $500 million. Travel agents found that with fares so low, the cost of writing a ticket was more than they could earn on commissions. To make matters worse, the agents had to reissue old tickets at the new prices and were asked to return commissions on the rebookings at lower rates. Many travel agencies saw any chance of a profitable summer wiped out. Some experts say it will take years to fully assess the impact of this drastic fare war. While the major airlines lose billions, only smaller commuter airlines, like Delta Connection, Comair, and Skywest are prospering.

Sources: Eric Schine and Andrea Rothman, "The Big Time Beckons the Small Birds," *Business Week*, March 29, 1993, pp. 57–58; Maria Mallory and Greg Bowers, "Oh, What a Lovely Fare War," *Business Week*, June 29, 1992, p. 37; Bridget O'Brien and Brett Pulley, "American Airlines Slashes Its Fares Yet Again," *Wall Street Journal*, May 28, 1992, pp. B1, B6; Andrea Rothman and Seth Payne, "The Superlosers in the Supersaver War," *Business Week*, June 15, 1992, p. 44; and Bridget O'Brien and James S. Hirsch, "Simplifying Their Fares Proves More Difficult Than Airlines Expected," *Wall Street Journal*, June 4, 1992, pp. A1, A6.

Government Action

Pricing decisions can also be strongly influenced by government action. In response to economic conditions, such as inflation, the federal government may establish price controls, "freeze" prices at certain levels, or determine the rates at which prices can be increased. In many states, a regulatory agency determines at what prices products such as insurance, liquor, dairy goods, and electricity can be sold.

Many laws and regulations govern pricing decisions and activities. The Sherman Act forbids agreements to control prices, and various court interpretations of the act have confirmed that price fixing among firms in an industry is inherently illegal. Consequently, organizations must develop independent pricing policies and set prices in ways that do not even suggest collusion with competitors. The Federal Trade Commission charged the three largest infant formula makers with conspiring to set prices of infant formula. The companies—Abbott Laboratories, Mead Johnson, and American Home Products—admitted no wrongdoing, although Mead Johnson and American Home Products agreed to a settlement.[33] The Federal Trade Commission Act and the Wheeler-Lea Act prohibit deceptive pricing.

The Robinson-Patman Act also addresses pricing decisions. Businesses may want to sell the same type of product at different prices for various reasons. However, provisions of the Robinson-Patman Act, as well as those in the Clayton Act, limit the practice of charging different prices to different customers. Price differentials that tend to diminish or harm competition are considered discriminatory and are prohibited by the Robinson-Patman Act.

Resellers in states that have effective unfair trade practices acts are limited in their use of pricing as a competitive tool. Because such acts set lower limits on prices that retailers and wholesalers can regularly charge, organizations that employ price competition must be familiar with the laws regarding pricing policies. Over half of the states have passed unfair trade practices acts. Firms can generally charge high prices as long as they do not engage in collusion or discrimination.

PRICING IN ORGANIZATIONAL MARKETS

Organizational markets (discussed in Chapter 8) are individuals and organizations that purchase products for use in the production of other products or in daily operations. Business-to-business marketers are especially concerned with prices as they try to control the cost of doing business (see Figure 13.6). Business-to-business marketers face several additional issues, including how policies that pertain to geographic factors, price discounting, and price discrimination influence pricing decisions.

Geographic Pricing

Geographic pricing involves reductions for transportation and other costs associated with the physical distance between the buyer and the seller. Organizations may specify that a price is **F.O.B. (free-on-board) factory**—

■ geographic pricing
a form of pricing that involves reductions for transportation and other costs associated with the physical distance between the buyer and the seller

■ F.O.B. (free-on-board) factory a price that excludes transportation charges and indicates a shipping point; F.O.B. factory is the price of merchandise at the factory, before it is loaded for shipment—therefore, the buyer must pay for shipping

---

[33]Kevin G. Salwen, "Infant-Formula Firms Rigged Bids, U.S. Says," *Wall Street Journal,* June 12, 1992, pp. A3, A14.

FIGURE 13.6
Organizational Markets
Business-to-business marketers try to hold down price by controlling costs, and UPS uses this advertisement to appeal to cost-conscious businesses.

Source: Courtesy of United Parcel Service.

Costlier than a corporate jet.

The company mail cart has quietly become a vehicle of runaway abuse. According to a *Wall Street Journal* report, the impulse to "overnight it" needlessly cost American businesses over $3 billion last year.

No one is more alarmed by this than UPS, because no one is more qualified to prevent it. After all, we offer you a broad array of cost-effective shipping options. Including ground, two-day air, and international air. As well as overnight air delivery Monday to Saturday for far less than our competitors charge.

If that kind of cost control appeals to you, just call UPS. We consider every package to be a priority. We just don't price them that way. We run the tightest ship in the shipping business.

■ **uniform geographic pricing** a form of pricing that results in a fixed average cost of transportation; sometimes referred to as postage-stamp pricing

■ **zone price** a regional price that takes advantage of a uniform pricing system; adjusts prices according to transportation costs by region

■ **freight absorption pricing** a form of pricing whereby organizations absorb all or part of their customers' actual shipment costs

that is, it excludes transportation charges and indicates a shipping point. F.O.B. factory is the price of the merchandise at the factory, before it is loaded for shipment. Thus the buyer must pay for shipping and is responsible for any loss or damage claims against the shipper.

To avoid the difficulties of setting different prices for each customer, a business-to-business marketer may employ uniform geographic pricing. **Uniform geographic pricing** (sometimes referred to as postage-stamp pricing) results in a fixed average cost of transportation. A packing company in Wisconsin, for example, would pay the same price for paper products as would a manufacturer in Florida.

A regional price that takes advantage of a uniform pricing system is called a **zone price.** This pricing policy adjusts prices according to primary geographic regions; as the transportation cost increases, the price increases. For example, a Texas computer maker's prices may be higher for buyers in New England and Canada than for buyers in the South.

Organizations that absorb all or part of their customers' actual shipment costs are using **freight absorption pricing.** This method might be used when a seller wants to do business with a certain customer or to obtain more business. Sellers using freight absorption pricing assume that the increased business will cause the average cost to fall and offset the extra freight cost. This strategy is used to improve market penetration and to maintain a hold in an increasingly competitive market.

Price Discounting

Discounts are commonly employed in organizational markets to provide intermediaries with a reduction in the list, or manufacturer's suggested, price. The six common types of discounts are quantity, trade, cash, allowances, rebates, and seasonal discounts.

Quantity Discounts A **quantity discount** is a price reduction that reflects the economy of purchasing in large quantities. As the size of a customer's order increases, some of the costs of serving the customer, such as billing and sales contracts, may remain the same or even go down. Larger orders result in cost savings because of greater production efficiency and because the seller does not have to hold inventory.[34] Large-quantity purchases also reduce per-unit selling costs and may shift some of the costs associated with storage, finance, and risk taking to the customer. Thus quantity discounts usually reflect legitimate reductions in costs.

Quantity discounts can be cumulative or noncumulative. A **cumulative discount** is a quantity discount accumulated over a specified period of time. For instance, an organization might get a 1 percent discount for ordering more than five thousand units of merchandise over a six-month period. A **noncumulative discount** is a one-time price reduction based on the dollar amount of the order, the number of units purchased, or the product mix purchased.

Trade Discounts A **trade** (or **functional**) **discount** is a reduction off the list price that a manufacturer gives to an intermediary for performing certain functions. Such discounts are usually expressed in terms of a percentage off the list price. Intermediaries are given trade discounts as reimbursement for performing activities such as selling, transporting, storing, doing final processing, and perhaps providing credit services.

Cash Discounts Business-to-business marketers often offer a price reduction known as a **cash discount** to buyers that make prompt or cash payments. Such discounts are a common practice and are sometimes a major concern in setting prices. Cash discounts are based on cash payments or cash paid within a stated period of time. For instance, "2/10 net 30" means that the customer will be allowed a 2 percent discount if the account is paid within 10 days; if the payment is made between 11 and 30 days, the customer does not get a cash discount. Such discounts are generally effective in speeding up payment and increasing cash flow.

Allowances Another type of discount is an **allowance**—a concession in price offered by a seller to a buyer, usually to boost sales. Trade-in allow-

■ **quantity discount** a price reduction that reflects the economy of purchasing in large quantities

■ **cumulative discount** a quantity discount accumulated over a specified period of time

■ **noncumulative discount** a one-time price reduction based on the dollar amount of the order, the number of units purchased, or the product mix purchased

■ **trade** (or **functional**) **discount** a reduction off the list price that a manufacturer gives to an intermediary for performing certain functions

■ **cash discount** a price reduction that business-to-business marketers offer to buyers that make prompt or cash payments

■ **allowance** a concession in price offered by a seller to a buyer, usually to boost sales

[34]James B. Wilcox, Ray D. Howell, Paul Kuzdrall, and Robert Britney, "Price Quantity Discounts: Some Implications for Buyers and Sellers," *Journal of Marketing,* July 1987, pp. 60–70.

ances, for example, are price reductions given for turning in a used item when purchasing a new one. Such concessions help buyers afford new purchases that they might not otherwise make. This type of discount is popular in the computer and automobile industries.

■ **rebate** a refund of part of the purchase price given by the seller to the buyer

Rebates   A **rebate** is a refund or part of the purchase price given by the seller to the buyer. Rebates are commonly used to increase the sales of durable goods during slow periods. This method has been used often by automobile manufacturers to provide dealers with a means of increasing car sales. Rebates also have been used in many other industries, including clothing, grocery, and sporting goods.

■ **seasonal discount** a price reduction offered to buyers that buy goods or services out of season

Seasonal Discounts   A **seasonal discount** is a price reduction offered to buyers that buy goods or services out of season. These discounts allow the seller to maintain steadier production during the year. Manufacturers of heating and cooling equipment, for example, might offer seasonal discounts to retailers that purchase out-of-season products.

Price Discrimination

■ **price discrimination** a policy of charging different prices to different groups of customers to give those paying less a competitive advantage

Price discrimination is a policy of charging different prices to different groups of customers to give those paying less a competitive advantage. This practice becomes illegal when an intermediary or organizational customer gains an advantage over competitors because it can purchase products at a price lower than other similar customers can obtain. However, if customers are not in competition with each other, the producer can legally charge different prices. For example, a railroad might charge a mining company one price to haul coal and charge an automaker another price to haul automobiles, even when the two products are going the same distance.

Price differentials are lawful only when they can be justified on the basis of cost savings, are used to compete in good faith, and do not injure competition. The Robinson-Patman Act outlaws price discrimination that lessens competition among wholesalers and retailers, and it prohibits sellers from offering disproportionate services to large buyers. The vast majority of the cases—85.5 percent—prosecuted under the Robinson-Patman Act have dealt with price discrimination. Firms in the food and tobacco industries have been prosecuted more often than firms in any other industry, and nearly half the firms prosecuted have sales revenues exceeding $1 billion.[35]

SUMMARY

Price is the "something of value" in an exchange. A buyer exchanges buying power for satisfaction or utility from a product. Price does not always involve the payment of money; barter is the trading of products. Price is the only

---

[35] Norton E. Marks and Neely S. Inlow, "Price Discrimination and Its Impact on Small Business," *Journal of Consumer Marketing,* Winter 1988, pp. 31–38.

variable in the marketing mix that can quickly and easily be adjusted to respond to changes in the external environment. It is also the only marketing mix variable that relates directly to revenue.

Price competition focuses on price as a means of differentiating products from those offered by competitors. Nonprice competition focuses on aspects other than price, such as distinctive product features, service, product quality, or other factors.

Pricing objectives are general goals that describe what an organization hopes to achieve through its pricing activities. The broadest and most fundamental pricing objective is survival. Other pricing objectives are maintaining the status quo, maximizing profits, and increasing sales and market share. Market share is a firm's sales in relation to total industry sales.

When making pricing decisions, marketers consider several factors, including buyers' expectations, marketing mix variables, competitive structure, costs, and government action. Buyers' expectations of price vary. Some consumer segments are price sensitive; others are not. Because the marketing mix variables are interrelated, pricing decisions must be made in conjunction with product, promotion, and distribution decisions. The competitive structure that characterizes an industry affects a firm's flexibility in setting prices. An organization should analyze all costs and include them in the total cost of the product; the product's cost is generally the minimum below which the product cannot be priced. Government actions and laws also strongly dictate pricing decisions.

When setting prices, organizational marketers take into consideration geographic factors and purchase characteristics. Geographic pricing involves reductions for transportation and other costs associated with the physical distance between the buyer and the seller. An F.O.B. factory price means the buyer pays for shipping. Uniform geographic pricing occurs when the seller charges a fixed average cost for transportation. Zone prices take advantage of a uniform pricing system adjusted for major geographic regions; as transportation costs increase, prices increase. A seller that absorbs all or part of its customers' shipping costs is employing freight absorption pricing.

Producers commonly provide discounts off list prices to intermediaries. The six common types of discounts employed are quantity, trade (or functional), cash, allowances, rebates, and seasonal discounts.

Price discrimination is a policy of charging different prices to certain groups of customers to give those paying less a competitive advantage. Such policies are legal only when they can be justified on the basis of cost savings, are used to compete in good faith, and when they do not injure competition.

KEY TERMS

price
barter
price competition

nonprice competition
pricing objective
geographic pricing

F.O.B. (free-on-board) factory
uniform geographic pricing
zone price
freight absorption pricing
quantity discount
cumulative discount
noncumulative discount

trade (or functional) discount
cash discount
allowance
rebate
seasonal discount
price discrimination

QUESTIONS FOR DISCUSSION AND REVIEW

1. State three reasons why pricing decisions are important to organizations.

2. Distinguish between price and nonprice competition. Give an example of a firm that uses price competition and one that uses nonprice competition.

3. What is a pricing objective? Under what conditions would a firm establish a status quo objective?

4. How do pricing decisions relate to the other marketing mix variables—product, promotion, and distribution?

5. What impact does the competitive structure of an industry have on pricing decisions?

6. Name several products that you purchase whose price is an important factor. Name some products that you purchase whose price is relatively unimportant to you.

7. How do government actions influence pricing decisions?

8. What is geographic pricing? What does *F.O.B. factory* mean?

9. Compare the different types of price discounts.

10. Under what circumstances is price discrimination legal?

CASES

13.1 ALAMO COMPETES ON PRICE

Vacation travelers who rent cars want low prices, and that's exactly what Alamo Rent A Car promises. Competing on price helped Alamo—with revenues of more than $500 million a year—become one of the fastest-growing and most profitable firms in the highly competitive rental car industry.

Alamo, based in Fort Lauderdale, Florida, started in 1974. The name was chosen so it would be the first company listed among rental car firms in the telephone directory. Its founders decided to use low prices to compete with the larger, established rental car companies. Alamo advertises rental prices as much as 20 percent lower than competitors and does not add extra charges for mileage.

Alamo aims for a specific but large market segment—leisure travelers who typically value low prices more than they do convenience. With airline deregulation in the early 1980s bringing more competition and lower fares, Alamo chairman Michael Egan assumed correctly that more travelers would fly to vacation destinations and would need an inexpensive rental car when they arrived. In fact, the leisure rental car market has grown 10 to 15 percent, compared with about 5 percent for the commercial market. The leisure rental car market is estimated to be worth about $2.3 billion.

To keep prices down, Alamo tries to keep costs down. It selects rental locations based on cost and limits the number and types of cars offered. Instead of locating most facilities in airport terminals, where space is very expensive, Alamo puts rental offices outside airport gates and transports customers by bus from the airport to the Alamo office. It keeps about 75,000 cars at 90 of the most highly trafficked locations in the United States and the United Kingdom, far fewer than the approximately 300,000 cars Hertz leases from 5,400 sites.

Alamo's low price strategy helped increase its sales by an average of 20 percent a year in the 1980s. The firm is number five in the industry, behind the big four rental agencies of Hertz, Avis, National, and Budget. Targeting leisure travelers proved so effective for Alamo that competitors also started to target that segment, which was believed to offer the most growth potential for the 1990s. To compete with Alamo, Avis and Hertz also began to advertise unlimited mileage, with certain restrictions. Alamo, which spends about $20 million yearly for advertising, replied with its own advertisements promising free mileage for "every car, every day, everywhere" with no restrictions. Said the Alamo print advertisements: "No wonder the other car rental companies are trying to copy our style."

Maintaining a low-cost, low-price strategy throughout the 1990s may prove difficult for Alamo. The major rental car firms have begun increasing their prices, and customers are finding that rental cars are sometimes scarce. Available cars often are older and less spic-and-span than they used to be. Cost-cutting measures have also resulted from new policies by automakers. First, they have discontinued generous discounts to rental car companies. For years, cars had been discounted from $400 to $2,000, a practice that cost automobile manufacturers millions of dollars. Costs for 1993 models increased from 25 to 35 percent from the previous year. Hertz expects rising costs to result in a 10 to 15 percent increase in the prices it charges customers; average rates rose about 12 percent in 1992 when the airfare wars and the resulting increase in travelers dramatically increased the demand for rental cars.

Alamo already is feeling the impact of the car makers' new policies. For years, rental companies sold their cars back to the manufacturers after four months. But the sale of nearly new rental cars was reducing the sales of new cars. Now the Big Three automakers have decided they will wait six to nine months to buy back their 1993 models, hoping a longer wait will help new car sales. Car rental firms also are being forced to examine cars more carefully because they are under increasing pressure to return them to automakers in top condition. Alamo, which gets most of its models from General Motors, must either repair dents or sell dented vehicles back for less money. As a result, Alamo's costs are going up and forcing the firm to raise its prices.

Questions for Discussion

1. How does Alamo compete with much larger firms like Hertz and Avis?

2. What market segment is Alamo targeting with its pricing strategy?

3. What is the key for Alamo to keep its prices low?

4. How could changes in the prices charged by the automakers affect Alamo?

Based on information from James S. Hirsch, "Rental Car Firms Jack Up Their Prices," *Wall Street Journal,* November 4, 1992, pp. B1, B7; Claire Poole, "Born to Hustle," *Forbes,* May 28, 1990, pp. 190, 194; Ira Teinowitz, "Alamo's Fighting Mad on Mileage," *Advertising Age,* March 26, 1990, p. 46; and Melinda Grenier Guiles, "Auto Renters Sell Off New Cars Quickly, Stir Complaints by Dealers," *Wall Street Journal,* June 29, 1989, pp. A1, A5.

13.2 RISING PRICES PLAGUE FRENCH WINE MAKERS

Many wine importers were shocked when the price of Côte-Rotie, a red wine from France, rose to $250 for a twelve-bottle case. Eighteen months earlier, the same case had sold for $140. But many restaurateurs and importers on this side of the Atlantic refused to pay the price; instead, they started buying California wines to replace the pricey French wines. They want to buy wines their customers can afford.

When American customers start switching from French to American wines, that spells trouble for France's $10 billion wine industry, which employs 700,000 people. The United States is one of the largest importers of French wines. But steady price hikes since 1985 and a slumping economy have contributed to a dramatic drop in exports of French table wine to the United States. Meanwhile, sales of California wines have doubled in the last two decades. While sales of jug wines and wine coolers are dropping, sales of mid-priced and expensive California wines (costing $5 and up) continue to climb. These better vintages, called "varietals" because they are identified by the main variety of grape they contain, are the wines competing with the French imports. Many wine retailers believe that California wines offer good value for the money, but fewer see French wines that way. Sparkling wine is also becoming a more affordable alternative to high-priced French wines. Spain's champagne producers, for instance, have succeeded by improving quality while keeping prices down.

Prices for French wines rose through the 1980s and are continuing to rise. One factor is the exchange rate. Compared with the dollar, the franc has been strong, a situation which boosts the price U.S. customers pay for French wine. But some industry analysts say that the French vintners want to take advantage of outstanding grape crops and make as much profit as possible from the resulting wines, which are in demand. Price increases for especially good vintages have been as high as 62 percent from the previous year.

Some U.S. wine merchants say such sharp price increases are the result of greed on the part of growers, wine makers, and distributors. While some growers have taken 10 percent increases, others have raised prices 18 percent and as high as 25 percent. Added to that increase is the 2 to 3 percent for middlemen who represent these growers to the distributors. Then the distributors mark up prices another 10 to 25 percent. For superior vintages in much demand, distributors have marked up prices 30 to 50 percent. To avoid paying top prices yet still trade in French wines, some U.S. buyers look for bargains and lesser-known wines of good quality.

Some French wine makers have reluctantly cut prices. Chateau Talbot, a top wine maker from Bordeaux's St. Julien region, discounted by 30 to 40 percent some 800,000 bottles of fine 1983 to 1990 wines on the wholesale market. Chateau d'Yquem sold the 1987 vintage of its fine, sweet white wine at about 50 percent less than its 1986 vintage, which sold for $133 to traders and much more in retail stores. But even after steep discounts, high-priced wine does not sell easily. The less expensive California wines, sold to consumers at $7 or less a bottle, are in great demand.

To make matters worse, a trade war between the United States and Europe could push the prices of white wines exported from France even higher. In 1992, President Bush proposed increasing tariffs to 200 percent on $300 million worth of white wine and other exports from France, Germany, and Italy. Bush declared his intentions after negotiators failed to settle a long-standing dispute over agricultural subsidies. Such a tariff would increase the average price of a bottle of white wine from France from $6 to $10. A tariff would have even more effect on the price of more expensive wines. Such disputes between sellers on one continent and buyers on another could spell disaster for French wine makers.

Questions for Discussion

1. What benefits do consumers receive when they purchase an expensive French wine?

2. Is the wine industry characterized by price competition or nonprice competition?

3. Is there a price-quality relationship for wine? If so, why are the French wine makers losing their maket share?

4. How will a tariff affect French wine makers?

Based on information from Bill Javetski, Patrick Oster, and John Templeman,"Bush's First Shot May Avert a Trade War," *Business Week,* November 23, 1992, p. 34; E.S. Browning, "Fine French Vintages Become a Hard Sell in Slumping Economy," *Wall Street Journal,* October 20, 1992, pp. A1, A12; Christopher Elias, "No Whines over '89's Great Grapes," *Insight,* May 28, 1990, p. 38; and John Rossant, "For French Winemakers the Glass Is Half Empty," *Business Week,* February 15, 1988, p. 50.

Determining Prices

OBJECTIVES

- *To determine how the demand for products influences pricing decisions.*

- *To describe the relationship between demand, costs, and profits.*

- *To explain the impact of competitors' prices on pricing decisions.*

- *To identify various pricing policies.*

- *To compare the major pricing methods.*

- *To discuss the practical aspects of determining a final price.*

- *To explain why the prices of domestic and foreign products are usually different.*

OUTLINE

hen The Walt Disney Company released its hit movie *Beauty and the Beast* on videocassette in October 1992, the firm expected to break all records. After all, the film had been the highest-grossing animated film ever. *Beauty* was sold through video and record stores, supermarkets, and discount stores at a suggested retail price of $24.99. Many stores sold it for less than $20. Within six weeks of its release on videocassette, *Beauty* became the top-selling home video of all time. It quickly outpaced the previous best-seller, Disney's *Fantasia*, released the year before and similarly priced.

The success of home videos geared to family viewing can be attributed to good timing—huge numbers of baby boomers are buying cassettes for their children—and to smart pricing. Making videos of popular films available to consumers at affordable prices has created a booming market for home videos. The trend started with *E.T.*, the biggest-selling movie of all time, with gross receipts of nearly $700 million worldwide. Released in 1982, *E.T.* immediately jumped to the top of the box office charts. MCA Home Entertainment officials estimated that more than 240 million people have seen the picture in theaters around the globe.

The *E.T.* success story continued when MCA released it on videocassette in October 1988. At a time when many major motion pictures on video were selling for $89.95, MCA executives decided to price *E.T.* at $24.95, the lowest price ever for a major movie in its first video release. A $25 million promotion venture with PepsiCo, Inc. lowered the video's price even further, since consumers who bought certain Pepsi products received a $5 rebate on the video purchase.

Several reasons prompted the decision to release the *E.T.* video at this low price. MCA executives predicted that 500,000 copies would sell easily at $89.95; but at $24.95, they estimated sales at six million. Moreover, offering the cassette at $25 or less ensured that the film would be available to most people, and thus reduced the likelihood that poorly prepared pirated copies would circulate. MCA's strategy was successful; a month before *E.T.*'s video release in October, advance orders exceeded 10 million copies. Thirteen million copies had sold by the time MCA removed the video from the market after Christmas that year.

The success of the *E.T.* video ushered in a new era in videocassette pricing. The Disney studio adopted the $24.99 price for its video releases and began making and breaking sales records. *The Little Mermaid* in 1990 set a Disney record at 9.8 million copies, *Fantasia* surpassed it with 13.5 million copies sold in a 50-day limited release in 1991, and *Beauty and the Beast* topped that with 14.2 million copies sold in its 100-day release in the fall of 1992. Disney and other entertainment companies also began using product tie-ins with consumer-goods marketers, including Nabisco Brands Inc.

Some videocassettes of hit movies have been made available at dramatically low prices. At the same time *Beauty* was making its way to the top, MCA re-released *E.T.* in a promotion with Sears and AT&T. Consumers could purchase the video, an E.T. poster, and 15 minutes of AT&T long-distance time for $7.99, exclusively at Sears. And at McDonald's, customers who purchased food or drinks could buy videos from the financially troubled Orion studio—the hit *Dances with Wolves* for $7.99, or *Babes in Toyland* and *Dirty Rotten Scoundrels* for $5.99.[1] ●

The success of *E.T., Fantasia, Beauty and the Beast,* and other videocassettes illustrates the importance of pricing decisions. At the price of $89.95, MCA or Disney probably would not have sold as many copies so quickly. Marketing managers must consider many issues when determining what price to charge for products. First, they must evaluate demand for the product. Next, the relationship among the product's demand, cost, and profit should be examined. Competitors' prices must then be evaluated, and a pricing policy selected. Finally, marketers must choose a method for setting prices and determine the final price.

EVALUATING DEMAND

Marketing managers, with the assistance of marketing researchers, are responsible for evaluating the demand for a product. This involves establishing the relationship between a product's price and the quantity demanded, as well as determining the product's price elasticity of demand.

The Relationship Between Price and Quantity Demanded

■ **demand curve**
a graphic representation showing the quantity of products that consumers are willing to buy at different prices

For most products, an inverse relationship exists between price and quantity demanded. In other words, the quantity demanded goes up as the price goes down, and vice versa. Figure 14.1 illustrates the effect of price on the quantity demanded. A **demand curve** (D_1 in Figure 14.1) shows the quantity of prod-

[1]Based on information from David Tobenkin, "Disney's 'Beauty' Becomes Top-Selling Video of All Time," Lexington, Ky. *Herald-Leader,* December 6, 1992, p. K5; Thomas R. King, "Walt Disney Plans Oct. 30 Release of 'Beast' on Video," *Wall Street Journal,* April 7, 1992, p. B5; "Marketing & Media: Disney's 'Fantasia' Posts Record Home Video Sales," *Wall Street Journal,* January 16, 1992, p. B1; and Jefferson Graham, "*E.T.* Video's Down-to-Earth Price," *USA Today,* May 6, 1988, p. 1A.

FIGURE 14.1
Demand Curve Illustrating Price-Quantity Relationship and an Increase in Demand

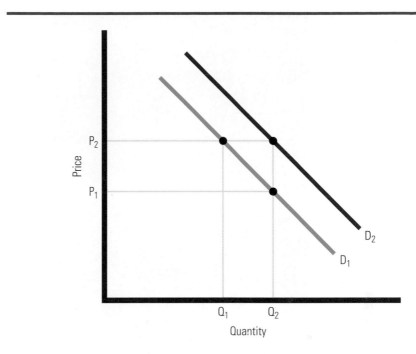

ucts that consumers are willing to buy at different prices. The classic demand curve is a line that slopes downward to the right, demonstrating that as the price of a product decreases (from P_2 to P_1), the quantity demanded increases (from Q_1 to Q_2). Demand is also dependent on other elements of the marketing mix—product, promotion, and distribution. An improvement in any of these elements, such as product quality, may cause the demand curve to shift to a new position, for instance, D_2. That is, an increased quantity (Q_2) of the product will be demanded at the same price (P_2).

Demand varies from product to product, and not all demand curves are represented by the one shown in Figure 14.1. Prestige products such as selected clothing, perfumes, jewelry, and liquors often sell better at high prices than at low ones. If the price of the crystal shown in Figure 14.2 fell sharply so that many consumers could afford to buy it, it would lose some of its appeal.

The demand curve for prestige products is presented in Figure 14.3. Demand for such products increases as the price increases, but only up to a point. As Figure 14.3 illustrates, when the price is increased from P_1 to P_2, the quantity demanded increases from Q_1 to Q_2. If the price of the product is raised too high, however, the quantity demanded declines. Thus, in Figure 14.3, when the price is raised to P_3, the quantity demanded declines to its earlier level of Q_1.

■ **price elasticity of demand** the relative responsiveness of changes in quantity demanded to changes in price

Price Elasticity of Demand

After examining the demand curve for a product, marketing managers must determine its **price elasticity of demand,** or the responsiveness of changes

FIGURE 14.2
Prestige Products
Not all products sell better at lower prices. The appeal of prestige products, such as fine crystal, is based partly on their high price.

Source: Durand International/Cristal d'Arques.

elastic demand the type of demand for a product in which a change in price causes an opposite change in total revenue—that is, an increase in price decreases total revenue, and a decrease in price increases total revenue

inelastic demand the type of demand for a product in which a change in price results in a parallel change in total revenue—that is, an increase in price increases total revenue, and a decrease in price decreases total revenue

unitary demand the type of demand for a product in which the product's revenue does not vary with price changes

in quantity demanded to changes in price (see Figure 14.4). A marketing manager determines price elasticity of demand by analyzing the changes in total revenue that result from changes in a product's price. Total revenue is calculated by multiplying price times quantity. Thus, 50,000 compact disks sold in one year at a price of $12 per disk equals $600,000 of total revenue.

With **elastic demand,** a change in price causes an opposite change in total revenue—in other words, an increase in price decreases total revenue, and a decrease in price increases total revenue. Demand for products such as compact cars is relatively elastic. Thus, in Figure 14.4, as the price of compact cars rises from P_1 to P_2, the quantity demanded decreases sharply, from Q_1 to Q_2; in addition, the automaker's total revenue declines. By contrast, an **inelastic demand** results in a parallel change in total revenue—that is, an increase in price will increase total revenue, and a decrease in price will decrease total revenue. For necessity products such as table salt, demand is *relatively* inelastic. When the price of table salt is increased from P_1 to P_2 (as shown in Figure 14.4), the quantity demanded decreases only a little, from Q_1 to Q_2, and the producer's total revenue declines slightly. **Unitary demand** occurs when a product's revenue does not vary with price changes.

The following formula is used to determine the price elasticity of demand:[2]

$$\text{Price elasticity of demand} = \frac{\%\text{ change in quantity demanded}}{\%\text{ change in price}}$$

[2] Willis L. Peterson, *Principles of Economics: Micro,* rev. ed. (Homewood, Ill.: Irwin, 1974), p. 67.

FIGURE 14.3
**Demand Curve Illustrating
the Price-Quantity Relationship for Prestige Products**

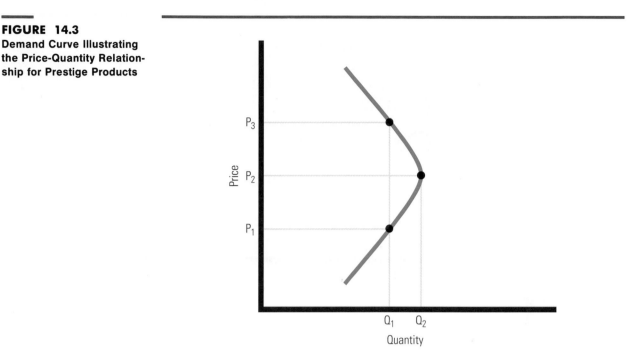

For example, if a price increase of 3 percent results in a 9 percent decline in demand for a particular product, its price elasticity of demand is −3. (The negative sign reflects the inverse relationship between price and demand and is usually dropped for interpretation.) If demand increases by 4 percent when a product's price is decreased by 8 percent, then the product's elasticity is −1/2. A price elasticity less than 1 reflects inelastic demand, and a price elasticity greater than 1 indicates elastic demand. If price elasticity equals 1, demand is unitary.

The less elastic the demand for a product, the more beneficial it is for the seller to raise its price. Generally speaking, demand is more inelastic for products that

- Have unique characteristics distinguishing them from competitors' products.
- Are a necessity for consumers.
- Have few available substitutes.
- Require only a small amount of the customer's budget.[3]

Price elasticity of demand can change over the life of a product.[4] In the maturity and decline stages of a product's life, consumers have more information about price and more alternative products from which to choose. For

---

[3] Michael H. Morris and Mary L. Joyce, "How Marketers Evaluate Price Sensitivity," *Industrial Marketing Management,* May 1988, pp. 169–176.
[4] Gerald J. Tellis, "The Price Elasticity of Selective Demand: A Meta-Analysis of Econometric Models of Sales," *Journal of Marketing Research,* November 1988, pp. 331–342.

FIGURE 14.4
Price Elasticity of Demand

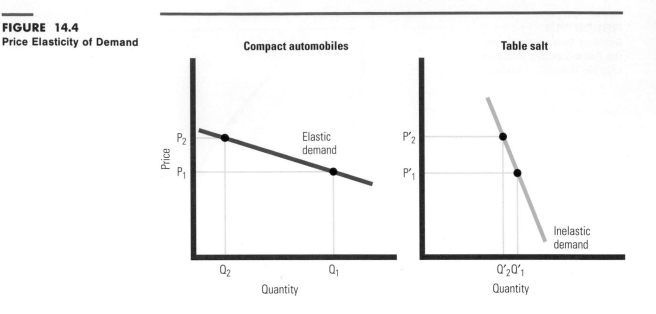

example, when televisions were first introduced, consumers were fairly in-sensitive to price (inelastic demand). Today, the demand for black-and-white televisions is elastic; any increase in price would reduce the demand for black-and-white televisions.

EXAMINING DEMAND, COST, AND PROFIT RELATIONSHIPS

The relationship between price and demand is not the only consideration in setting prices. Marketing managers must also examine the relationships be-tween demand, cost, and profit. To survive, a business must charge prices that cover all of its costs; prices must exceed costs for a business to be profitable. There are two approaches to understanding demand, cost, and profit relationships: marginal analysis and breakeven analysis. The next sec-tions explore these two approaches after identifying several different types of costs.

■ **fixed cost** a cost that does not change when the number of units produced or sold changes

■ **average fixed cost** the fixed cost per unit produced; calculated by dividing the to-tal fixed costs by the num-ber of units produced

Types of Costs

An organization incurs costs in the production of products. A **fixed cost** does not change when the number of units produced or sold changes. For instance, a cassette-deck manufacturer's costs for rent or property taxes do not change when the manufacturer increases production from one shift to two shifts a day or because it sells twice as many cassette decks. The **average fixed cost**—the fixed costs per unit produced—is calculated by dividing the total fixed costs by the number of units produced.

■ **variable cost** a cost that varies directly with changes in the number of units manufactured or sold

■ **average variable cost** the variable cost per unit produced; calculated by dividing the total variable costs by the number of units produced

■ **average total cost** the sum of the average fixed cost and the average variable cost

■ **total cost** the sum of total fixed costs and total variable costs

■ **marginal cost (MC)** the additional cost incurred when a firm produces one more unit of a product

---

TABLE 14.1
Various Costs and Their Relationships (for production of cassette decks)

By contrast, a **variable cost,** such as wages, electricity, freight, and materials, varies directly with changes in the number of units manufactured or sold. The costs of wages, shipping, electronic components, and other materials used in the production of cassette decks increase when the manufacturer increases the number of shifts or the number of cassette decks produced. The **average variable cost**—the variable cost per unit produced—is calculated by dividing the total variable cost by the number of units produced. The average variable cost typically starts out at a high level and declines as efficiencies in production and purchasing are achieved. At some point, however, the average variable cost goes back up as more workers are hired and more materials are purchased to produce additional units.

The **average total cost** is the sum of the average fixed cost and the average variable cost. **Total cost** is the sum of total fixed costs and total variable costs. **Marginal cost (MC)** is the additional cost incurred when a firm produces one more unit of a product. Table 14.1 illustrates the relationships among various costs for the cassette-deck manufacturer. As the number of cassette decks produced increases, the average fixed cost falls. If charted on a graph, the average variable cost and average total cost would each form a U shape; they would fall to a point and then increase. From the table you can see that the lowest average variable cost is $50, when the manufacturer produces three cassette-deck units. The lowest average total cost is $80, at four cassette-deck units. The manufacturer's marginal cost equals its average total cost between three and four units of production, when the average total cost is at its lowest level. As long as the marginal cost is less than the average total cost, the average total cost decreases; it increases when the marginal cost rises above the average total cost.

The marketing manager must be able to calculate average total cost, marginal cost, and other types of costs to determine a price that results in the maximum profit.

1 Quantity Produced	2 Total Fixed Cost	3 Average Fixed Cost (2) ÷ (1)	4 Total Variable Cost	5 Average Variable Cost (4) ÷ (1)	6 Average Total Cost (3) + (5)	7 Total Cost (2) + (4)	8 Marginal Cost
1	$110.00	$110.00	$ 60.00	$ 60.00	$170.00	$ 170	
2	110.00	55.00	110.00	55.00	110.00	220	$ 50
3	110.00	36.67	150.00	50.00	86.67	260	40
4	110.00	27.50	210.00	52.50	80.00	320	60
5	110.00	22.00	310.00	62.00	84.00	420	100
6	110.00	18.33	450.00	75.00	93.33	560	140
7	110.00	15.71	630.00	90.00	105.71	740	180
8	110.00	13.75	850.00	106.25	120.00	960	220
9	110.00	12.22	1,110.00	123.33	135.55	1,220	260
10	110.00	11.00	1,410.00	141.00	152.00	1,520	300

FIGURE 14.5
Typical Relationship
Between Marginal
Revenue (MR) and
Average Revenue (AR)

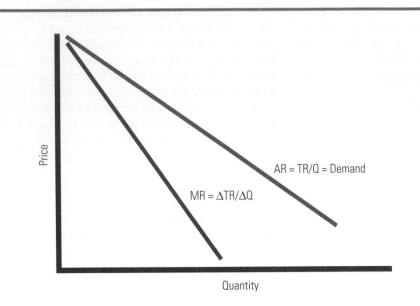

Marginal Analysis

**marginal revenue
(MR)** the change in total
revenue that results from the
sale of an additional unit of
a product

average revenue (AR)
the total revenue divided by
the quantity produced

Marginal analysis means investigating what happens when one more unit is produced by an organization. **Marginal revenue (MR)** is the change in total revenue (ΔTR) that results from the sale of an additional unit of a product. **Average revenue (AR)** is total revenue (TR) divided by the quantity (Q) produced. These concepts and their relationship are illustrated in Figure 14.5. Figure 14.6 shows the relationship between marginal cost and average cost.

Most products have downward-sloping demand curves. In other words, to sell additional units of a product, the manufacturers must lower their prices. In this situation, each additional unit sold generates less revenue than the previous unit. Consequently, marginal revenue is less than average revenue, as shown in Figure 14.5. Eventually, MR will reach zero, and additional sales will only hurt the company.

Because profit equals total revenue minus total cost, a firm must know both the costs of producing a product and its revenue before it can determine if the product is profitable. If marginal revenue is one unit's contribution to revenue and marginal cost is one unit's addition to cost, then MR minus MC indicates whether the unit is profitable. Table 14.2 illustrates the relationships between price, quantity sold, total revenue, marginal revenue, marginal cost, and total cost for the manufacturer of cassette decks. It indicates what maximum profits are possible at various combinations of price and cost.

Table 14.2 shows that at one unit of sales, total revenue equals marginal revenue. This means that the first revenue earned by the cassette-deck manufacturer is the marginal revenue. When two cassette decks are sold, the marginal revenue is computed by subtracting the total revenue at one unit from the total revenue at two units: $380 minus $200 equals marginal revenue of $180. The other values for marginal revenue are calculated the same way.

FIGURE 14.6
Typical Relationship
Between Marginal
Cost (MC) and Average
Cost (AC)

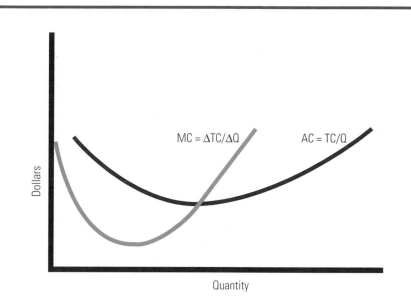

The product makes the largest profit at the point where the marginal cost equals marginal revenue. In Table 14.2, this occurs at the sale of five cassette-deck units. At this point, a price of $160 yields a profit of $380. Up to this point, the additional revenue generated from the sale of an extra cassette deck exceeds the additional total cost. Beyond this point, the additional cost of selling another cassette deck exceeds the additional revenue generated, and profits decrease.

By combining Figures 14.5 and 14.6 into Figure 14.7, you see that any unit for which marginal revenue exceeds marginal cost contributes to a firm's profits, and any unit for which MC exceeds MR subtracts from the firm's profits. The firm should therefore produce at the point where MR equals MC because this is the most profitable level of production.

This concept of marginal analysis falsely implies that pricing is a precise process. If revenue and cost remained at constant levels, then marketing managers could set prices for maximum profits. In practice, though, cost and revenue fluctuate constantly. The actions of competitors, the government, or other forces in the marketing environment can quickly diminish a producer's expected revenues. Thus marginal analysis is merely a model for setting prices to achieve maximum profitability. It offers little insight into the pricing of new products because their costs and revenues have not been established. Nevertheless, understanding the relationship between marginal cost and marginal revenue can certainly help marketing managers set prices of existing products, especially in competitive situations.

■ **breakeven point** the point at which the cost of making a product equals the revenue made from selling the product

Breakeven Analysis

The **breakeven point** is the point at which the cost of making a product equals the revenue made from selling the product. For instance, if an organi-

1 Price	2 Quantity Sold	3 Total Revenue (1) × (2)	4 Marginal Revenue	5 Marginal Cost (from Table 14.1)	6 Total Cost (from Table 14.1)	7 Profit (3) − (6)
$200	1	$ 200	$200	$ —	$ 170	$ 30
190	2	380	180	50	220	160
185	3	555	175	40	260	295
175	4	700	145	60	320	380
160*	**5**	**800**	**100**	**100**	**420**	**380**
155	6	930	130	140	560	370
145	7	1,015	85	180	740	275
130	8	1,040	25	220	960	80
115	9	1,035	−5	260	1,220	−185
100	10	1,000	−35	300	1,520	−520

*Boldface indicates best price-profit combination.

TABLE 14.2
Marginal Analysis (for production of cassette decks)

zation has total annual costs of $2 million and the same year it has revenues of $2 million, then it has broken even.

Figure 14.8 illustrates the relationships between costs, revenue, profits, and losses involved in determining the breakeven point. Knowing how many units must be sold in order to break even is important in determining the price. For example, consider a product priced at $200 per unit, with an average variable cost of $120 per unit and total fixed costs of $180,000. The breakeven point is calculated as follows:

$$\text{Breakeven point} = \frac{\text{total fixed costs}}{\text{unit price} - \text{average variable cost}}$$

$$= \frac{\$180,000}{\$200 - \$120}$$

$$= \frac{\$180,000}{\$80}$$

$$= 2,250 \text{ units}$$

To calculate the breakeven point in terms of dollar sales volume, the marketing manager multiplies the breakeven point in units by the price per unit. Thus, in the example above, the breakeven point in terms of dollar sales would be 2,250 (units) times $200, or $450,000. A firm would have to produce and sell 2,250 units at a price of $200 to begin making a profit.

If breakeven analysis is to be informative, a marketing manager should determine the breakeven point for each of several alternative prices. This enables the marketer to compare the impact of each price on total revenue, total costs, and the breakeven point. Although this comparative analysis does not indicate exactly what price to charge, it does help the marketer recognize what price alternatives are unacceptable.

FIGURE 14.7
Marginal Analysis

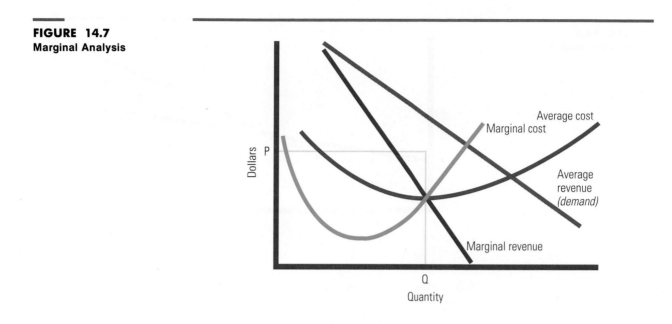

Although breakeven analysis is fairly simple and straightforward, it assumes that demand is basically inelastic and that the primary task in setting prices is to recover costs. Instead of focusing on the achievement of pricing objectives such as increasing market share or return on investment, breakeven analysis focuses only on how to break even. Hence, marketing managers can use this analysis to determine more accurately whether a product will at least achieve a breakeven volume.

EVALUATING COMPETITORS' PRICING BEHAVIOR

One of the major aspects of marketing strategy is a comprehensive examination of competitors' prices.[5] Even in an industry in which nonprice competition is prevalent, marketers still need information about competitors' prices to compete effectively. In some instances, an organization sets its prices slightly above or below competitors' prices to differentiate its products. Montblanc, the leader in the prestige pen market, charges $125 for its classic ballpoint pen. The firm uses advertising and quality guarantees to differentiate its pens from lower-priced competitors like Parker, Waterman, and Cross (see Figure 14.9).[6]

[5]Raphael Amit, Ian Domowitz, and Chaim Fershtman, "Thinking One Step Ahead: The Use of Conjectures in Competitor Analysis," *Strategic Management Journal,* September–October 1988, pp. 421–432.
[6]Joshua Levine, "Pen Wars," *Forbes,* January 6, 1992, pp. 88–89.

FIGURE 14.8
Breakeven Analysis

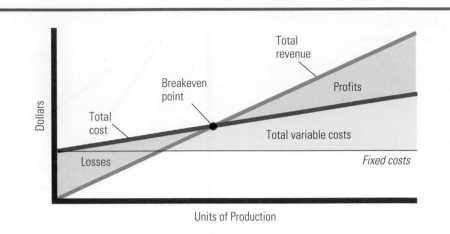

When one firm dominates an industry, it may set the tone for pricing decisions in the entire industry. De Beers Consolidated Mines, Ltd., which controls more than 80 percent of the world's diamond market, raised the prices of its diamonds by 13.5 percent.[7] Because of its industry leadership position, De Beers can raise prices with little concern about those charged by competitors. Marketing Close-up examines price decisions in the video game market, in which Nintendo has a 70 percent share.

Getting information about competitors' prices is not always easy, particularly in producer and reseller markets. Competitors' price lists are often closely guarded. Even when a business-to-business marketer does get a look at competitors' price lists, they may not be informative because the actual prices may be established through negotiation or other discounts may be applied. Customers and trade associations can also be a good source of competitor price information.

SELECTING A PRICING POLICY

■ **pricing policy** a plan or course of action for achieving pricing objectives

A **pricing policy** is a plan or course of action for achieving pricing objectives. Ford Motor Co. developed a price policy in which four moderately equipped versions of the Escort—a wagon, a sedan, a three-door hatchback, and a five-door hatchback—are priced at $9,999. The objective was to make buying an automobile less complicated.[8] Some have credited the success of General Motor's Saturn with its no-haggle, one-price policy.[9] Pricing policies are a significant ingredient in an overall marketing strategy because they determine the role of price in the marketing mix. They may relate to the introduction of new products, competitive or economic conditions, government regula-

[7]Andrea Stone, "De Beers Hikes Price of Ice 13.5%," *USA Today,* April 28, 1988, p. 1B.
[8]Neal Templin, "Ford Expands 'One-Price' Plan for Its Escorts," *Wall Street Journal,* March 12, 1992, pp. B1, B4.
[9]Arlena Sawyers, "No-haggle Pricing Going Full Throttle," *Advertising Age,* March 22, 1993, pp. S10, S28.

tions, or the realization of pricing objectives. More than one pricing policy may be employed to satisfy the needs of different market segments or to take advantage of particular opportunities. Pricing policies help marketers solve the practical problems of establishing prices. Some of the most common pricing policies are new product, promotional, psychological, and professional pricing.

New Product Pricing

The pricing of a new product is one of the most fundamental parts of the marketing mix. Price skimming and price penetration are typical pricing policies for new products.

■ **price skimming** a new-product pricing policy of setting the highest possible price that buyers will pay (to appeal to quality- and status-conscious consumers)

Price Skimming   **Price skimming** is setting the highest possible price that buyers will pay; it is a policy aimed at consumers who are concerned more about quality or status than about price. For instance, Simac's Gelatio automatic ice cream maker was introduced in department stores and gourmet cookware shops at a price of $450. By charging such a high price when ice cream makers normally cost around $50, Simac targeted its product at consumers who want the status of owning a high-priced, prestigious ice cream maker. Price skimming affords the most flexibility in pricing a new product because it is easier for a business to lower a high price than to raise a low price.

Price skimming has several advantages, particularly for products in the introductory stage of the life cycle. It can generate quick cash to help defray the costs associated with the product's research and development. A skimming price can also be used to keep demand in line with the firm's production

FIGURE 14.9
Pricing Behavior
Montblanc, the leader in the prestige pen market, uses advertisements such as this one to differentiate its high-priced pen from the competition.

Source: Courtesy Montblanc.

MARKETING CLOSE-UP

Nintendo, Sega Slash Prices

In May 1992, Nintendo Co. dropped the price of its Super NES system from $179.95 to $149.95. Sega Enterprises Ltd. reduced the price of its Genesis system from $149.95 to $129.95. Nintendo had already cut $20 from its introductory price of $199.95, and Sega had also cut $20 from its initial price of $179.95. The price cutting reflects sluggish growth in the $4 billion video game market. According to research conducted by Fairfield Research, a consumer-polling firm, about 37 percent of the families in the United States own a video game system. Basically, all families that want a video game already own one, so selling new systems means convincing consumers to upgrade their old one.

Nintendo dominates the industry with a 70 percent share of the market and generally sets the tone for price decisions. Sega has a 20 percent share of the market; the remaining 10 percent is shared by other firms. Nintendo did little price cutting for its first-generation system with an 8-bit chip. But after introducing its second-generation, 16-bit Super NES system, Nintendo found buyers were turned off by the $199.95 price. Sega, which beat Nintendo to mar-

ket with its 16-bit Genesis system, was outselling Nintendo in the 16-bit market. After the price reduction, Super NES began to outpace Genesis.

A month after dropping their prices, both companies reduced them again, this time to $99. Some experts say the systems are a real bargain at $99 (some stores put them on sale for $89). The battle for market share is critical because any expected growth in video game sales is in the 16-bit market. New sales also mean sales of game cartridges for the new system. Twelve million game systems and 60 million game cartridges were sold in 1991.

The price strategy seems to have worked. Many consumers found the $99 more affordable and bought a video game system, either for the first time or to replace an 8-bit system. Sales of games in 1992 climbed to about 17 million, game cartridges to 75 million.

Sources: Joseph Pereira, "Strategy of Slashing Prices Helps to Lift Video-Game Makers out of Sales Slump," *Wall Street Journal*, October 14, 1992, pp. B1, B8; Kate Fitzgerald, "Nintendo, Sega Slash Price of Videogames," *Advertising Age*, June 8, 1992, p. 44; and Joseph Pereira, "Nintendo, Sega Zap Prices As Video Game War Heats Up," *Wall Street Journal*, May 5, 1992, pp. B1, B4.

capabilities, which may be quite limited during the introductory stage. On the other hand, it takes longer to penetrate the market with a price-skimming policy. Price skimming also encourages competitors to enter the market.

price penetration
a new-product pricing policy of setting prices lower than prices of competing brands to gain access to a market and generate a larger unit sales volume

Price Penetration   **Price penetration** is setting a price lower than prices of competing brands to gain access to (penetrate) a market and generate a larger unit sales volume. Penetration pricing is sometimes used by organizations to gain a large market share quickly for a new product. This policy is less flexible than price skimming because it is more difficult to raise a penetration price than to lower a skimming price. Helene Curtis used penetration

FIGURE 14.10
Penetration Pricing
By advertising that Suave is for beautiful skin without paying an extravagant price, Helene Curtis attempts to penetrate the skin care market with lower prices.

Source: © Helene Curtis 1992.

Because you want beautiful skin without paying an extravagant price...

Suave introduces
a new line of facial care.

New Suave Facial Care. Now beautiful skin doesn't have to cost a fortune.

pricing to introduce the new line of skin care products shown in Figure 14.10.

Price penetration is an appropriate policy for products whose demand is highly elastic; in other words, consumers would purchase the product if it were priced at the penetration level, but not at a higher price. A penetration price may necessitate longer production runs, increasing production significantly and reducing the firm's per-unit production costs.

A penetration policy can also be advantageous when the marketing manager believes it would be easy for competitors to enter the market. Competitors may be reluctant to enter the market if an organization using a penetration price has already captured a large market. Moreover, when an organization has used a penetration price, the market may be less attractive to competitors because the lower per-unit price results in lower per-unit profits; this may cause competitors to perceive the market as not being particularly profitable.

Promotional Pricing

Price is often coordinated with another element of the marketing mix—promotion. The two variables are so interrelated that the pricing policy sometimes becomes promotion-oriented. Special-event pricing, price leading, and superficial discounting are three common types of promotional pricing.

■ **special-event pricing**
a form of promotional
pricing that involves coordinating price cuts with
advertising for seasonal or
special situations to increase
revenue or reduce costs

Special-Event Pricing   **Special-event pricing** involves coordinating price cuts with advertising for seasonal or special situations; its purpose is to increase revenue or reduce costs. For example, for the Fourth of July, retailers and consumer-goods producers often coordinate advertising and price discounts on products such as hot dogs, potato chips, soft drinks, beer, and charcoal. If an organization's pricing objective is survival, then special-event pricing can be used to increase cash flow. Special-event pricing requires coordination of production, scheduling, storage, and physical distribution to ensure that consumers can find the promoted products on store shelves. Whenever a company experiences a sales lag, it may launch a special sales event.

■ **price leader** a product
often sold below its usual
profit margin or even below
cost

Price Leaders   A product often sold below its usual profit margin or even below cost is called a **price leader.** Retailers sometimes use price leaders to attract customers to the store in the hope that sales of regularly purchased merchandise will rise and increase sales volume and profits. Convenience stores such as Southland Corporation's 7-Eleven often use this type of pricing for soft drinks and milk to attract consumers by giving them an impression of low prices.

■ **superficial discounting**
fictitous comparative pricing
in which a firm uses a deceptive markdown; sometimes
called "was-is pricing"

Superficial Discounting   **Superficial discounting** is false comparative pricing. An example is an advertisement declaring that a product "was regularly $259, is now $199" when in fact the product is normally priced at $199. Superficial discounting may be used by a retailer to give consumers the impression that a product is on sale. The Federal Trade Commission and the Better Business Bureau discourage this deceptive practice. When such discounts are genuine, they are acceptable, but a pricing policy that gives only the illusion of a discount is unethical and, in many states, illegal.

Psychological Pricing

■ **psychological pricing**
a pricing policy designed to
encourage purchases that are
based on emotional rather
than rational responses

Psychological pricing is designed to encourage purchases that are based on emotional rather than rational responses. It is used most often at the retail level and is seldom used for organizational products. The next sections discuss several psychological pricing policies, including prestige, odd-even, and customary pricing and price lining.

■ **prestige pricing** a psychological pricing policy
that sets prices artificially
high to imply a prestige or
quality image

Prestige Pricing   **Prestige pricing** involves setting prices artificially high to imply a prestigious or quality image. Prestige pricing is especially appropriate when consumers associate a higher price with higher quality. For this reason, perfumes, automobiles, liquor, jewelry, and even pharmaceutical products are often prestige-priced. La Giara olive oil, imported from Italy, is priced at $24 a litre, about three times the price of an ordinary bottle.[10] To be successful, prestige pricing must be supported by a strong brand image and a promotion program that reinforces this image. If the manufacturer of such a product significantly reduced its price, the price would then be inconsistent with the perceived prestigious or quality image of the product. The

[10]Joshua Levine, "Oil Snobs," *Forbes,* March 29, 1993, p. 93.

FIGURE 14.11
Odd-even Pricing
Many firms end prices with an odd number, assuming they will sell more. Kmart, for instance, prices it socks at $2.49 and $2.99.

Source: Courtesy Kmart Corporation. Photo: George Brenner.

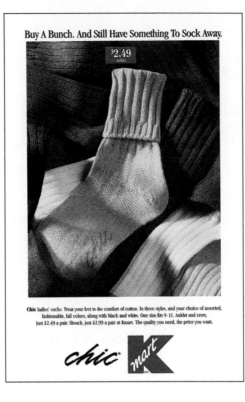

■ odd-even pricing
a psychological pricing policy of ending a price with a certain number in an effort to influence consumers' perceptions of the price or the product

■ customary pricing
a psychological pricing policy of setting prices on the basis of tradition

image of Chanel No. 5 perfume was damaged when discount chains like Perfumania reduced the price of a half-ounce bottle by $35.[11]

Odd-Even Pricing   **Odd-even pricing** is a policy of ending a price with a certain number in an effort to influence consumers' perceptions of the price of the product. Odd pricing assumes that consumers will buy more of a product at $9.99 than at $10 because they will perceive the product to be a bargain: It is less than $10. Some marketers believe that certain types of customers are more attracted by odd prices than by even ones. However, research has not supported the notion that odd prices produce greater sales. Nevertheless, odd prices are far more common today than even prices (see Figure 14.11).

A marketer might employ an even price in the hope that the consumer will perceive the product as being a high-quality, premium brand. A shirt maker, for example, may print on a premium shirt package a suggested retail price of $48 rather than $47.95. The even price of the shirt is used to reinforce its upscale image.

Customary Pricing   **Customary pricing** is a policy of setting prices on the basis of tradition. Economic conditions may result in fairly wide price

---

[11] Gretchen Morgenson, "Save $35," *Forbes,* March 16, 1992, pp. 70–71.

FIGURE 14.12
Demand Curve Illustrating
Price Lining

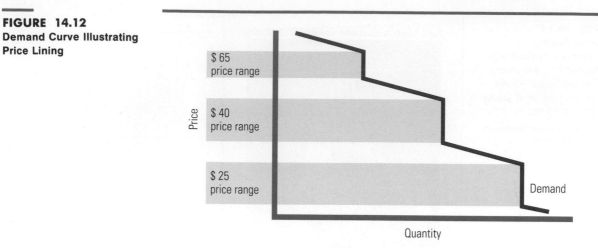

fluctuations, but some prices remain constant over a long period of time. Products such as chewing gum, fast food, magazines, and candy use this approach to pricing. In some cases, the size of the product is changed instead of the price. For years, the price of a candy bar was 5 cents. Rather than change the price, manufacturers changed the size of the nickel candy bar as the cost of its ingredients fluctuated. Obviously, the nickel candy bar is a thing of the past. Nonetheless, customary pricing is still used in this market.

Price Lining   The policy of setting a limited number of prices for selected lines or groups of merchandise is a form of psychological pricing known as **price lining.** A watchmaker may offer various styles of watches in one line for $25 and a more expensive line of watches for $40. Price lining eases consumers' decision making by holding one key variable constant in the final selection within a line or group.

The basic assumption underlying price lining is that the demand for various groups of products is inelastic. With price lining, the demand curve looks like a series of steps, as shown in Figure 14.12. If consumers perceive the prices to be attractive, they will concentrate their product search in a particular price range without responding to slight changes in price. Thus a men's clothing store that prices various lines of sports coats at $185, $135, and $85 assumes that reducing those prices to $180, $130, and $80, respectively, would not attract many more sales. A consumer who has already decided to buy a suit in the $135 price range would probably consider suits priced at $130 or even $140, but not suits priced in the $185 range.

■ **price lining** a psychological pricing policy of setting a limited number of prices for selected lines or groups of merchandise

■ **professional pricing** the pricing policy—practiced by doctors, lawyers, and others who have skills or experience in a particular field—in which a standard fee is charged for a particular service, regardless of the problems involved in providing that service

Professional Pricing

Doctors, lawyers, and others who have skills or experience in a particular field use **professional pricing,** the policy of charging a standard fee for a particular service, regardless of the problems involved in providing that service. For instance, some lawyers' standard fees are $500 for a house closing or $200 for a will.

Professionals have an ethical obligation not to take advantage of customers. For example, a person with a serious illness such as cancer may be willing to pay almost any amount for an operation or a treatment that will provide a cure or prolong life. In such circumstances, a doctor might be tempted to charge exorbitant fees but has the ethical obligation to charge fair prices rather than what the market will bear. Some health insurance companies pay only "usual and customary" fees for the services of doctors and dentists even when the charges exceed those levels. Lawyers for Fireman's Fund Insurance Co. investigate many of the firm's most expensive legal cases, on the lookout for lawyers who inflate bills or do unnecessary work. As a result, Fireman's Fund's legal expenses have declined, and several lawyers have been convicted of mail fraud and other crimes.[12] The pricing of professional services has also been subject to increased government scrutiny.[13] Point/Counterpoint takes a look at professional pricing.

CHOOSING A PRICING METHOD

■ **pricing method** a systematic procedure for setting prices on a regular basis

After deciding on a pricing policy or policies, a marketing manager must choose a **pricing method**—a systematic procedure for setting prices on a regular basis. The pricing method structures the calculation of the actual price. This section explains pricing methods based on demand, cost, and competition, and discusses some pricing methods used for organizational products.

Demand-oriented Pricing

■ **demand-oriented pricing** a pricing method based on the level of demand for a product

Demand-oriented pricing is based on the level of demand for a product. When demand for a product is strong, a high price is charged; when demand is weak, a low price is charged. This pricing method is also useful in using up idle capacity. Southern California Edison Co. charges lower prices for electricity during off-peak consumption periods.[14] Conversely, the demand for antique automobiles has escalated their value to as much as $75 million for certain models.

To use demand-oriented pricing, a marketer must first estimate the quantity of a product that consumers will demand at different prices. The marketer then chooses the price that generates the highest total revenue. Johnson & Johnson priced the cancer drug levamisole, used to treat colon cancer, at $1,250 to $1,500 for a year's supply. That's 100 times higher than the $14 price of an older veterinary version of the drug which had been used for

---

[12]Richard B. Schmitt, "An Insurers' Lawyer Sniffs Out Lawyers Inflating Their Bills," *Wall Street Journal*, July 21, 1992, pp. A1, A5.

[13]Ray O. Werner, "Marketing and the Supreme Court in Transition, 1982–1984," *Journal of Marketing*, Summer 1985, pp. 97–105.

[14]Gary A. Stern, Pamela Sorooshian, Richard S. Ridge, and Ronald K. Watts, "Reducing Household Electricity Consumption Peaks," *Sociology and Social Research*, July 1988, pp. 252–256.

POINT/COUNTERPOINT

Is Professional Pricing Ethical?

Pricing professional services is partly an emotional issue. Professional services often involve something close and personal to consumers—health, legal agreements, or financial matters. But consumers are usually at a disadvantage in evaluating those services. They often do not fully understand the nature of the services offered by physicians, lawyers, and other professionals, or the basis for pricing. It is therefore up to the individual professional to establish ethical prices.

Point Professionals such as doctors and lawyers who use professional pricing are bound by ethical codes in establishing their fees. These codes generally protect consumers from unreasonably high prices. In other words, professionals are ethically obligated not to charge unreasonably high or unfair rates. Additionally, the Supreme Court has ruled against medical professionals who fix prices by adhering to the same fee schedule.

In recent years, professionals also have begun to provide consumers with more information about prices. Many dentists, doctors, lawyers, and consultants now advertise the fees they charge for various services. Furthermore, professionals are open to discussing specific prices and payment options with patients or clients. Generally, price information can be obtained by calling the professional's office. In many cases, the new openness about fees has led to price competition among professionals, resulting in lower prices for consumers.

Counterpoint The demand for many professional services is price inelastic. A person with a serious medical problem has no choice but to pay for the needed treatment. Although professionals have an ethical obligation to establish fair prices, some don't. Routine office visits to physicians may cost as much as $50 or more for a few minutes of consulting time. Professionals who perform more complicated services may charge thousands of dollars for a few hours of their time.

One group that has come under fire for its fees is lawyers. In bankruptcy cases across the United States, many judges are trimming lawyers' fees. Sometimes law firms assign to a routine case two, three, or even four times the number of lawyers needed. The work may be performed by junior associates, but it is billed at the higher rates charged by senior associates. Clients are charged not only for their conversations with lawyers, but also for conversations between several lawyers. Hourly rates have run as high as $300; conference calls with four lawyers have resulted in fees of $660 an hour.

years. The demand for the product by colon cancer patients was high, of course. One renowned cancer expert at Mayo Clinic in Rochester, Minnesota, was highly critical of the high price.[15] The effectiveness of this pricing method clearly depends on the marketer's ability to accurately estimate demand.

[15] Marilyn Chase, "Doctor Assails J&J Price Tag on Cancer Drug," *Wall Street Journal*, May 20, 1992, pp. B1, B8.

Cost-oriented Pricing

■ **cost-oriented pricing** a pricing method in which price is determined by adding a dollar amount or percentage to the cost of the product to achieve the desired profit margin

In **cost-oriented pricing,** price is determined by adding a dollar amount or percentage to the cost of the product to achieve the desired profit margin. Cost-oriented pricing methods do not necessarily relate to specific pricing policies or objectives and do not consider supply and demand or the prices of competitors. They are, however, simple and easy to execute. Markup pricing and cost-plus pricing are two common cost-oriented pricing methods.

■ **markup pricing** a cost-oriented pricing method in which a predetermined percentage of the cost, called *markup,* is added to the cost of the product to determine the product's price

Markup Pricing   **Markup pricing** is a pricing method in which a predetermined percentage of the cost, called *markup,* is added to the cost of the product to determine the product's price. The markup may be expressed as a percentage of the cost or of the selling price. This method is common among retailers. Although the percentage markup in a retail store varies from one category of goods to another, the same percentage is often used to determine the price of items within a single product category (50 percent of cost for greeting cards, for example). In fact, the same or similar percentage markup may be uniform across an industry at the retail level. When most retailers use similar markups for the same product category, price competition is reduced.

Manufacturers and wholesalers may suggest standard markups for retailers that reflect expectations about operating costs, risks, and inventory turnovers. An average percentage markup on selling price may be as high as 150 percent or more for clothing and as low as 15 percent on some grocery items. The primary reason that retailers, who face numerous pricing decisions, use markup pricing is that it is convenient.

■ **cost-plus pricing** a cost-oriented pricing method in which the producer determines its costs and then adds a specified dollar amount or percentage of the cost to the selling price

Cost-Plus Pricing   **Cost-plus pricing** is a pricing method in which the producer (seller) determines its costs and then adds a specified dollar amount or percentage of the cost to the selling price. This method is appropriate when production costs are unpredictable or when production is a lengthy process, as is generally the case with construction projects. Cost-plus pricing is often used by construction and defense contractors that work for the government. This method may not be beneficial for the buyer because the seller may increase costs to obtain a larger profit margin. Cost-plus pricing is popular in times of rapid inflation, especially when the producer must use raw materials that are subject to price fluctuations.

Competition-oriented Pricing

■ **competition-oriented pricing** a pricing method in which an organization sets prices on the basis of its competitors' prices rather than its own costs and revenues

Competition-oriented pricing is a pricing method in which an organization sets prices on the basis of its competitors' prices rather than its own costs and revenues. This method is particularly appropriate in a market where price is the key variable of the marketing strategy and competing products are almost homogeneous. In such markets, some retailers tell consumers, "Shop around, then see us for the best deal in town," or "We'll beat anyone's price—guaranteed." Of course, businesses are obligated to honor such promises. Many firms in the telecommunications industry use this pricing method

FIGURE 14.13
Competition-Oriented Pricing
In the highly competitive, relatively homogeneous, telecommunications industry, firms such as GTE use competition-oriented pricing to increase market share.

Source: Courtesy GTE Company.

(see Figure 14.13). Competition-oriented pricing is simple to use and increases store traffic. This method is practical for a firm with a pricing objective to increase sales or market share. Competition- and cost-oriented pricing methods may be combined to determine the price levels necessary for a profit.

Pricing Organizational Products

Price decisions for organizational products are often different than price decisions for consumer products. Several methods exist for setting prices in organizational markets. The three most commonly used methods are administered, bid, and negotiated pricing.

Administered Pricing Under **administered pricing,** the seller determines the product's price (or prices), and the customer pays that designated price. Organizations using this method may implement a one-price policy in which all buyers pay the same price, or they may set a series of prices that are determined by one or more discounts.

In administered pricing, the seller posts list prices on a price sheet or in a catalogue. Quantity, cash, and trade discounts, if applicable, are then deducted from this price. Thus the actual, or net, price paid by an organizational customer is the list price minus all the applicable discounts. The seller may

■ **administered pricing**
a pricing method in which the seller determines the product's price and the customer pays that designated price

specify the price in terms of list price times a multiplier. For example, the price of an item might be quoted as "list price × .85"—indicating that the seller is discounting the product so that the customer can buy it at 85 percent of the list price. Adjusting the multiplier enables the seller to revise administered prices without having to issue new catalogues or price sheets.

■ bid pricing a pricing method in which the sellers submit sealed or open price proposals for the buyer's consideration

Bid Pricing   **Bid pricing** involves the submission of sellers' sealed or open price proposals for the buyer's consideration. The buyer notifies potential bidders (sellers) that they are to submit their bids by a certain date. Usually the lowest-bidding firm is awarded the contract, as long as the buyer believes that the firm is capable of supplying the specified products when and where needed. This approach is often used by construction companies seeking construction or repair contracts from state and local governments. In the open bidding approach, several sellers are asked to submit bids, which are made public. Sealed bids, by contrast, are known only to the buyer. In another bid pricing approach, called *negotiated bidding,* an organizational customer asks for bids from a number of sellers, evaluates the bids, and then negotiates the price and terms of sale with the most favorable bidders until a final transaction is completed or until negotiations are terminated with all sellers.

■ negotiated pricing a pricing method for organizational markets in which negotiations determine the final price even when list prices and discount structures are specified

Negotiated Pricing   For organizational markets, sellers must often engage in **negotiated pricing,** in which negotiations determine the final price paid by the organizational customer even when list prices and discount structures are specified. This type of pricing can be beneficial because it can foster discussions between seller and buyer regarding product specifications, applications, and perhaps product substitutions. The seller has an opportunity to provide technical assistance to the customer and perhaps sell a product that will better satisfy the customer's needs; of course, the final product choice might also be more profitable for the seller. The buyer benefits by gaining more information about the selection of products and terms of sale available, and may acquire a more suitable product at a lower price.

DETERMINING THE FINAL PRICE

The determination of a final price should be guided by pricing policies and methods. The final price should also be determined in accordance with well-planned pricing objectives and the needs and wants of the target market. Additionally, the marketing manager should evaluate demand, price elasticity, costs, competitive factors, and legal factors.

   Although a systematic approach to pricing is advocated, in practice, prices are often determined through trial and error rather than planning. The seller analyzes revenue and costs after the fact to determine whether a product has earned a profit. This approach to pricing is not recommended because it is imprecise and makes it more difficult to discern pricing errors.

In the absence of government-imposed price controls, pricing is a flexible and expedient means of fine tuning the marketing mix. Prices can be adjusted

quickly, in a matter of minutes or a few days in most cases. The other elements of the marketing mix lack this flexibility and freedom.

PRICING FOR GLOBAL MARKETS

The prices of domestic and foreign products usually differ. The foreign price may be higher because of the increased costs of transportation, supplies, taxes, tariffs, inflation, and other expenses necessary to adjust a firm's operations to international marketing. A firm may opt to change its basic pricing policy. A cost–plus approach to pricing products for international markets is probably the most common method used because of the great costs required to move products from the United States to a foreign country. Of course, our earlier discussion of pricing policies points out that understanding consumer demand and the competitive environment is a necessary step in selecting a price.

Exchange-rate fluctuations also have an impact on prices charged in foreign countries. The American dollar is no longer the standard for all transactions. As all major currencies float freely, the value of any money at a future date is uncertain; prices charged in different countries can change daily. Because of this risk, many firms insist on basing prices on their domestic currency; in so doing they pass the risk of foreign currency devaluation on to the buyer.

Firms may choose to establish lower prices in foreign markets. The sale of products in foreign markets at lower prices than those charged in the domestic country of origin is called **dumping.** Dumping is illegal in many countries if it reduces the competitiveness of domestic firms and workers. Japanese companies have been accused of dumping computer chips, television sets, and automobiles on the American market while charging Japanese customers high prices that include all research and development expenses. Zenith Electronics Corp. claims to have lost $500 million in profits over a five-year period as a result of the dumping of foreign television sets in the United States.[16]

■ **dumping** the sale of products in foreign markets at lower prices than those charged in the domestic country of origin

Discrepancies in prices between domestic and foreign countries have led to what is termed *gray markets,* in which foreign goods are brought into a country and sold at discount prices without the knowledge or consent of the manufacturer. In the mid-1980s, Americans traveling through Europe discovered that a Mercedes–Benz automobile that cost $24,000 in Los Angeles was priced at $12,000 in Munich. The result was an unofficial import business in European luxury goods. Today, many made-in-Japan products sell at lower prices overseas than in Japan. This has led to the "reimporting" of Japanese goods. Products such as cameras and cordless phones are purchased in the United States, taken back to Japan, and sold at discount prices.[17]

[16]Janet Novack, "It's like a Big Balloon," *Forbes,* July 20, 1992, p. 48.
[17]Larry Armstrong, William J. Holstein, and Alice Z. Cuneo, "Now, Japan Is Feeling the Heat from the Gray Market," *Business Week,* March 14, 1988, pp. 50–51.

SUMMARY

When determining prices, marketing managers must first estimate the demand for a product. A demand curve shows the quantity of products that consumers are willing to buy at different prices. For most products, there is an inverse relationship between price and quantity demanded: As the price of the product decreases, the demand increases, and vice versa. There is a more direct relationship for prestige products, however: Demand increases as price increases. Price elasticity of demand refers to the responsiveness of changes in quantity demanded to changes in price. With elastic demand, a change in price results in an opposite change in total revenue. If a change in price has a parallel impact on total revenue, demand is inelastic. When price changes have no impact on total revenue, demand is unitary.

Marketing managers must consider cost when determining prices. Fixed costs do not change when the number of units produced or sold changes; the average fixed cost is the fixed cost per unit produced. Variable costs vary with changes in the number of units produced or sold; the average variable cost is the variable cost per unit produced. The average total cost is the sum of the average fixed cost and the average variable cost. Marginal cost (MC) is the additional cost incurred when a firm produces one more unit of a product.

Marginal analysis means investigating what happens when an organization produces one more unit of a product. Marginal revenue (MR) is the change in total revenue that results from the sale of an additional unit, and average revenue (AR) is total revenue divided by quantity produced. A product earns the most profit at the point where MR equals MC.

The breakeven point is the point at which the cost of producing a product equals the revenue made from selling the product. To use breakeven analysis effectively, a marketer should determine the breakeven point for each of several alternative prices and compare the effects on total revenue, total costs, and the breakeven point for each price under consideration. Breakeven analysis does not tell marketers what price to charge for a product, but it does identify undesirable price alternatives.

A marketer needs information about competitors' prices to compete effectively. If a company employs price as a competitive tool, it can then price its brand below competing brands.

A pricing policy is a plan or course of action for achieving pricing objectives. Pricing policies for new products include price skimming (charging the highest possible price that buyers will pay, to appeal to quality- and status-conscious consumers) and price penetration (charging a price lower than prices of competitors, to gain access to a market and generate larger sales volume). Promotional pricing involves coordinating price with promotion. It includes special-event pricing, price leading, and superficial discounting. Psychological pricing is designed to encourage purchases based on emotional rather than rational responses. Examples include prestige, odd–even, and customary pricing, as well as price lining. Professional pricing is used by those with special skills or experience in a particular field.

A pricing method is a systematic procedure for setting prices on a regular basis. Demand-oriented pricing is based on the level of demand for the product. In cost-oriented pricing, price is determined by adding a dollar amount or percentage to the cost of the product. Two common cost-oriented pricing methods are markup and cost-plus pricing. Competition-oriented pricing occurs when an organization sets prices on the basis of competitors' prices. Competition-oriented pricing and cost-oriented pricing may be combined to achieve profitable price levels. In determining prices for organizational production, marketers use administered (list) prices, sealed or open bids, or negotiations.

The determination of a final price should be guided by pricing policies, methods, and objectives, as well as the needs of the target market. The marketing manager should also consider demand, price elasticity, costs, competitive factors, and legal factors. Price is a flexible and expedient means of fine tuning the marketing mix.

The prices of products sold domestically and those sold in foreign markets usually differ. Because of the costs necessary to market internationally, the foreign price may be higher than the domestic price. Firms may charge lower prices in foreign markets, but this practice, called dumping, is illegal in many countries if it reduces the competitiveness of domestic firms and workers.

KEY TERMS

demand curve
price elasticity of demand
elastic demand
inelastic demand
unitary demand
fixed cost
average fixed cost
variable cost
average variable cost
average total cost
total cost
marginal cost (MC)
marginal revenue (MR)
average revenue (AR)
breakeven point
pricing policy
price skimming
price penetration
special-event pricing

price leader
superficial discounting
psychological pricing
prestige pricing
odd-even pricing
customary pricing
price lining
professional pricing
pricing method
demand-oriented pricing
cost-oriented pricing
markup pricing
cost-plus pricing
competition-oriented pricing
administered pricing
bid pricing
negotiated pricing
dumping

QUESTIONS FOR DISCUSSION AND REVIEW

1. Explain why there is usually an inverse relationship between the price of a product and the quantity demanded.

2. Under what conditions does the quantity demanded increase when the price is increased? Give several examples of products for which this is the case.

3. What is price elasticity of demand? Define elastic, inelastic, and unitary demand. Give examples of products with each type of elasticity.

4. Distinguish between the various types of costs, including fixed, variable, total, and marginal.

5. At what point is profit maximized? Explain.

6. How do you calculate the number of products that must be sold to break even?

7. Why is it important for a firm to evaluate competitors' prices?

8. What is price skimming? Price penetration?

9. Discuss the three different types of promotional pricing, and give an example of each.

10. Compare demand-oriented and cost-oriented pricing.

11. What are the most common methods used to establish prices for organizational products? Give an example of how each would be used.

12. What are the major differences in determining prices of domestic and foreign products?

CASES

14.1 PROCTER & GAMBLE EXPERIMENTS WITH EVERYDAY LOW PRICING

Seven consumer goods firms, including Kraft, General Foods, Quaker Oats Co., and Colgate-Palmolive Co., are experimenting with pricing strategies that appear to achieve the same goals as everyday low pricing. But most of these firms deny they are initiating everyday low pricing strategies. Not to be confused with everyday low pricing by retailers like Wal-Mart Stores, the strategy used by manufacturers eliminates the varying prices they offer retailers as part of trade promotion deals. Procter & Gamble, however, did use everyday low pricing when it reduced the list prices on many of its best-selling brands.

The goal of Procter & Gamble's everyday low pricing strategy is to give better value to consumers who have suffered through a recession. But although the strategy is designed to give greater value to consumers, many retailers have openly protested. Claire D'Armour, vice president of corporate affairs at Big Y Foods, said, "We are not happy with P&G's everyday low pricing program. It takes away our flexibility as a retailer. Basically, P&G is saying we have one option—take it or leave it. We are therefore leaving it when we can."

Most warehouse clubs and mass merchandisers prefer everyday low pricing. On the other hand, many supermarket chains, including Jewel Food Stores, Vons Co., and Supermarket General's Pathmark, have publicly or privately expressed dissatisfaction to Procter & Gamble about its policy. Those retailers that operate with a strategy of "high-low" prices with frequent specials are particularly upset.

Procter & Gamble has felt the pressure but says it will not back down. The firm believes the program will benefit everyone—Procter & Gamble, retail customers, and consumers—because it results in lower operating costs and lower prices. In theory, the strategy frees up trade promotion dollars for additional promotional spending directed toward consumers. Procter & Gamble put the Tide and Cheer detergent brands under the everyday low pricing program; the entire laundry detergent line is now under the plan.

Most other major packaged goods marketers are watching Procter & Gamble and silently applauding its efforts. They also favor everyday low pricing as an alternative to expensive trade promotions, but do not have the resources to weather the potential backlash from retailers. Many companies are testing pricing programs with different names but all designed for the same reason, to reduce trade promotion spending and increase promotion to the final consumer. Meanwhile, the entire industry is hoping Procter & Gamble is successful.

Questions for Discussion

1. What is everyday low pricing, and why is there confusion surrounding this term?

2. Why has Procter & Gamble decided to use an everyday low pricing strategy?

3. Why do some retailers dislike everyday low pricing?

4. Why are most firms in the packaged-goods industries hoping that Procter & Gamble's pricing strategy is successful?

Based on information from Jennifer Lawrence, "Tide, Cheer Join P&G 'Value Pricing' Plan," *Advertising Age,* February 15, 1993, pp. 3, 59; Judann Dagnoli, "P&G Plays Pied Piper on Pricing," *Advertising Age,* March 9, 1992, p. 6; Julie Liesse, "Everyday Low Pricing by Any Other Name Attracting Converts," *Advertising Age,* April 27, 1992, p. 4; and Julie Liesse and Judann Dagnoli, "KGF Experiments," *Advertising Age,* February 24, 1992, pp. 1, 52.

14.2 PERSONAL COMPUTER PRICE WAR BENEFITS BUYERS

In the computer industry, the early 1990s will be known for a fierce and drastic price war involving most personal computer (PC) makers. In February 1992, Apple Computer, Inc. and Dell Computer Corp. cut prices by as much as 38 percent. Apple cut 10 percent from the price of its inexpensive Classics and 13 percent from the price of the PowerBook 100, its new notebook computer. Zenith Data Systems Corp. dropped prices on its desktop and portable models by up to 26 percent. Compaq dropped prices as much as 32 percent. Even IBM cut prices and introduced a new line of low-cost PCs.

Price cuts are not new in the PC industry. As new technologies are brought to the market, old ones drop in value. Historically, PC prices have dropped about 10 percent a year. But the price reductions of 25 percent in 1991 and 35 percent and higher in 1992 far exceeded the usual 10 percent and went beyond what anyone in the industry expected.

Prices began to fall in 1991 when newer, smaller firms like Dell Computer Corp., AST Research, and Zeos International starting to gain market share from the established, larger companies—IBM and Compaq Computer Corp. The U.S. PC market is quite fragmented. Apple's share is about 13 percent; IBM's is around 12 percent; the top twenty PC clone makers, including Compaq, Tandy, Zenith, AST, and Dell, hold about 41 percent; and hundreds of small and "no-name" PC makers together command the remaining 34 percent. The small companies, despite their size, gained market share by offering low prices, no-frills service, and mail-order distribution. They also helped push prices down across the industry. As an executive of a computer store chain put it, "Compaq and IBM know in the bottom of their hearts they have to stop losing market share. And the only way that's going to happen is cutting prices again."

Compaq set off a fierce round in the price war in June 1992 with its 32 percent price cut and the launch of the ProLinea line, priced under $1,000. Previously, Compaq had competed on its performance claims and kept prices under IBM's prices. But it failed to watch the smaller companies that began taking sales away with lower-priced PCs. To get prices back in line with the rest of the industry, Compaq brought out the ProLinea, its first product designed with manufacturing costs in mind. Compaq says its strategy has quickly shown results.

IBM introduced its low-priced PS/ValuePoint computers in October 1992. Priced in the $1,000 to $2,000 range, the machines are IBM's attempt to win customers who do not need the speed and high-quality graphics of the PS/2 and who pick the brand with the lowest price. IBM officials say they have previously not been successful at reaching that market, which comprises at least half of all PC buyers. "The name of the game is to hold market share," said Robert Corrigan, head of IBM's personal computer business, who called that philosophy a change for his company. Another change: IBM started selling directly to users through an 800 number and by mail.

The deep price cuts, the new products, and pent-up demand have contributed to a PC buying boom among consumers as well as traditional corporate customers. In a year, the median price of a top-of-the-line 486DX computer (based on Intel Corp.'s 80486 chip, which is desirable for handling the software written for the popular Microsoft Windows) dropped from $4,362 to $1,888. Less powerful PCs can be found for as little as $500. These prices make a PC viable for a broader market and bring in many new customers. The low prices and the many models geared for sale through mass merchandisers have helped make the home market the fastest-growing segment.

Whereas the PC price war benefits consumers, however, it hurts the smallest PC makers and is putting some out of business. The largest firms can better cope with narrowing profit margins and even losses. With the bigger companies becoming more competitive on price, many buyers of no-name computers are switching to brand names. Established computer companies like IBM, Compaq, Dell, and AST, since they design their own machines, have the advantage of using new technology as soon as it is introduced and immediately differentiating their products. Small firms making PC clones have to wait until they can buy new technology from component makers. To survive, the smallest companies are trying to get the best deals possible when buying component parts. Some are specializing in custom-made PCs and targeting high-end buyers. The bigger companies are also cutting costs. IBM and Compaq have laid off employees, and Compaq has renegotiated with key suppliers.

PC producers in Taiwan and Korea have been especially hurt by price cutting in the United States. They have often had to exceed U.S. manufacturers' price cuts because they have no name recognition. Having their production based in Asia also prevents them from responding quickly enough to the rapidly changing U.S. market. Korean PC exports dropped by more than 50 percent in one year. Korean PC producers are hurting from price cuts even in their own country; local prices have been generally three to five times higher than U.S. prices and have supported expanding sales overseas. Korean and Taiwanese manufacturers have had some success in Latin America and other parts of Asia, but have seen little success breaking into Japan, where U.S. companies have begun to make inroads in a market dominated by NEC Corp. Although Apple, Digital Equipment, Compaq, and IBM have cut prices in Japan to try to take market share from NEC, price cutting may not be effective in a market so different from that in the United States. In Japan, manufacturers in many sectors cooperate as much as they compete, the distribution system protects established companies, the home market is much smaller, and many Japanese buy first on service and function and second on price.

Price cutting has hit Europe, however, and buyers there are geared toward finding bargain PCs. Until recently, the market was much less saturated than in the United States and customers were willing to pay more—about 30 to 50 percent. But as customers are becoming more familiar with computers and new discount dealers and suppliers are emerging, Europeans are now shopping for low prices, and actual retail prices have dropped by as much as 40 percent. Now PC prices there are only about 10 percent higher than in the United States and, for U.S. firms, hardly cover the extra cost of doing business there.

Questions for Discussion

1. Which pricing method are the PC makers generally using? Explain.

2. What has been a major objective of the drastic price cutting by PC makers?

3. Why does a price war hurt the smaller computer companies much more than larger ones like Compaq and IBM?

4. Why is price viewed differently in different markets?

Based on information from Kyle Pope and David P. Hamilton, "U.S. Computer Firms, Extending PC Wars, Charge Into Japan," *Wall Street Journal,* March 31, 1993, pp. A1, A7; Catherine Arnst, "That 'Ho, Ho, Ho' Is Coming from Your Local PC Shop," *Business Week,* December 14, 1992, p. 96; Andrew Kupfer, "Who's Winning the PC Price Wars?" *Fortune,* September 21, 1992, pp. 80–82; John R. Wilke, "PC Giants' Price War Hurts Tiny Makers," *Wall Street Journal,* November 2, 1992, p. B1; Michael Williams and Masayoshi Kanabayashi, "Reaction Is Cool As PC Firms Export Price War to Japan," *Wall Street Journal,* November 11, 1992, p. B4; Michael W. Miller, "IBM Cuts Price of New PC Line to Battle Clones," *Wall Street Journal,* October 21, 1992, p. B1; Jeremy Mark and Damon Darlin, "Pricing Squeeze Threatens PC Firms in Korea, Taiwan," *Wall Street Journal,* August 28, 1992, p. B4; Kathy Rebello and Stephanie Anderson, "They're Slashing as Fast as They Can," *Business Week,* February 17, 1992, p. 40; and Jonathon B. Levine, "Everyone Loves a Bargain—Europeans Included," *Business Week,* Feburary 10, 1992, p. 118.

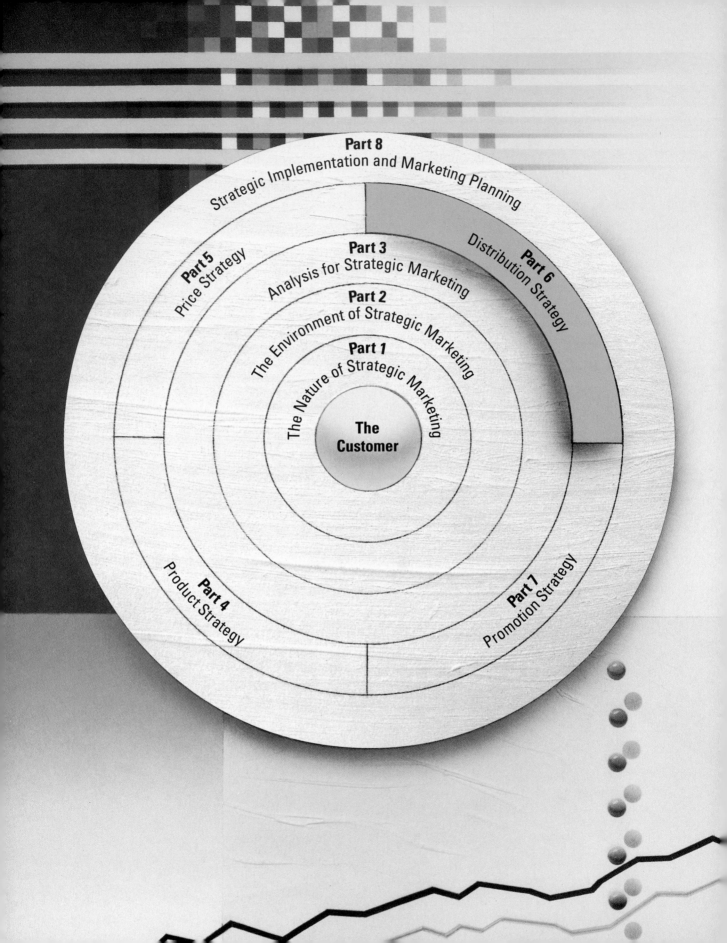

Part 8
Strategic Implementation and Marketing Planning

Part 5
Price Strategy

Part 3
Analysis for Strategic Marketing

Part 6
Distribution Strategy

Part 2
The Environment of Strategic Marketing

Part 1
The Nature of Strategic Marketing

The Customer

Part 4
Product Strategy

Part 7
Promotion Strategy

Distribution Strategy

Marketing Channels and Physical Distribution

OBJECTIVES

- *To describe the nature and structure of marketing channels.*

- *To identify the functions of marketing channels.*

- *To explain how marketing channels are coordinated through vertical or horizontal integration.*

- *To discuss marketing channel relationships, including the concepts of cooperation, conflict, leadership, and power.*

- *To explain the importance of physical distribution.*

- *To identify various physical distribution activities.*

At Helene Curtis's new distribution center in Chicago, you won't find order tickets, shipping tags, or, for that matter, many people. At the $32 million facility, computer-controlled fork lifts place packages on conveyors that read the bar codes and send products to their proper destinations. The center, which employs only 225 people, can handle over twice as much product as the six warehouses it replaced and has reduced Helene Curtis's distribution costs by 40 percent.

Along the entire marketing channel—from manufacturer to retail store—a high priority is being given to cutting the costs of distribution. Mervyn's, a chain of 247 moderately priced department stores, is completely redoing its distribution system. The company built four distribution centers and spent $80 million improving the distribution system. The average time merchandise spends moving between supplier and stores has been reduced from fourteen days to less than nine. As a result, sales have increased by 50 percent but inventory carrying costs have remained the same.

Distribution has become a high-tech business, and U.S. and foreign competition are squeezing profits and reducing the number of distributors. Since the 1960s, the cost of holding inventory has doubled, the cost of labor has jumped, and the labor pool has dwindled. Manufacturing customers are demanding more service as they adopt the just-in-time inventory approach. Quality is also important; slow, expensive, or defective deliveries result in dissatisfied customers.

The ways in which goods and services get to customers are changing as well. Large industrial producers are selling directly to customers. Foreign firms, competing on performance and price, are trying to gain a piece of the U.S. market through small distributing firms and catalogue companies. Warehouse clubs selling office furniture and other merchandise are luring small-business and manufacturing customers from traditional industrial distributors.

Lines blur between manufacturers and distributors as firms merge, grow, and diversify. Kennemetal Inc., a maker of carbide cutting tools, bought a leading general-line firm and a national mail-order catalogue distributor with four warehouses and now distributes a broad range of industrial products nationally. New super distributorships, such as Sun Distributors of Philadelphia, carry many and varied product lines. Cooperatives such as ID ONE, a group of thirty large independent distributors, buy and promote together to compete with superdistributors and national chains.

As management expert Peter Drucker says, "Changes in distributive channels may not matter much to GNP and macroeconomics. But they should be a major concern of every business and every industry."[1] ●

[1]Based on information from Rita Kosolka, "Distribution Revolution," *Forbes,* May 25, 1992, pp. 54–61; James Morgan, "Distribution in the 1990s," *Purchasing,* May 17, 1990, pp. 70–81; and Peter Drucker, "Manage by Walking Around—Outside," *Wall Street Journal,* May 11, 1990, p. B1.

Marketing channels provide the vital link with the customer. A firm can gain a competitive edge by providing products on a timely basis in the form desired by customers. And since distribution costs account for a sizable part of a product's cost—as much as 30 to 40 percent—most firms are looking for ways to trim distribution costs. This can be seen at stores like Sam's Club and Pace, where goods aren't even unpacked but simply put out on the floor and stacked to the ceiling. These cost savings are passed on to the customer. Those firms unable or unwilling to develop efficient marketing channels will have trouble competing and may find themselves out of business.

THE NATURE AND STRUCTURE OF MARKETING CHANNELS

■ **marketing channel (or channel of distribution)** a group of interrelated individuals or organizations that directs the flow of products to consumers

A **marketing channel** (sometimes called a **channel of distribution**) is a group of interrelated individuals or organizations that direct the flow of products to consumers.[2] Such a group or organization is called a **marketing intermediary** because it facilitates exchanges between producers, other intermediaries, and the final consumers of products. Because consumers are the focus of all marketing channel activities, satisfying their needs and desires is the most important concern of channel members, or marketing intermediaries. Wholesalers and retailers are classified as marketing intermediaries.

■ **marketing intermediary** an individual or organization that facilitates exchanges between producers, other intermediaries, and the final consumers of products

Marketing intermediaries can be divided into two major classifications: (1) merchants and (2) agents or brokers. A merchant assumes ownership of products and resells them for a profit. Agents and brokers do not purchase products outright but instead negotiate and expedite exchanges between buyers and sellers. For example, Comp-U-Card International is a broker, and retailer Neiman-Marcus is a merchant. In general, agents and brokers perform fewer marketing activities than do merchants.

Marketing channel members are critical to the success of any marketing endeavor because they specialize in facilitating exchanges. Marketing intermediaries reduce the number of sales contacts required for an exchange, thereby reducing the cost of distribution. Figure 15.1 shows that if six different buyers purchase the products of six different producers, thirty-six transactions will be required; each producer engages in an exchange with each buyer. If one marketing intermediary is used to facilitate the exchange, the number of transactions is reduced to twelve. Each producer engages in one exchange with the intermediary, and the intermediary engages in one exchange with each buyer. Reducing the number of transactions lowers the cost of the exchange.

[2]Louis W. Stern and Adel I. El-Ansary, *Marketing Channels,* 3rd ed. (Englewood Cliffs, N.J.: Prentice-Hall, 1988), p. 3.

FIGURE 15.1
Effect of Marketing Intermediaries on Number of Transactions in an Exchange

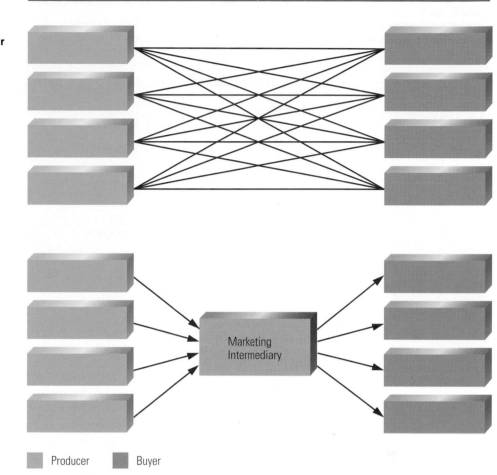

	Producer		Buyer

Because distribution is often the least flexible element of the marketing mix, marketing channel decisions are a key component of the marketing mix. In other words, once a marketing channel is established, it is difficult and costly to change it. Therefore, it is important to recognize the different types of marketing channels and the number of marketing intermediaries needed to serve various target markets.

Types of Channels

Products can be distributed *directly* from producer to consumer or *indirectly* through one or more marketing intermediaries. For instance, Pitney Bowes distributes its high-end fax machines (costing as much as $5,000) directly to corporate customers like Santa Fe Railway. Canon, Sharp, and other manufacturers distribute their cheaper (about $600) fax machines through electron-

Factor	Less Reliance on Intermediaries	More Reliance on Intermediaries
Consumer		
Size of purchase	Large	Small
Location	Concentrated	Spread out
Number	Many	Few
Special needs	Frequent	Infrequent
Producer's resources	Extensive	Limited
Product		
Perishability	High	Low
Cost or value	High	Low
Physical size	Large	Small
Technology	Complex	Simple
Competition	Weak	Strong
Alternative channels	None	Many
Laws	Relaxed	Strict

ics stores.[3] Selection of an appropriate channel depends on the consumer, the producer's resources, the product, the competition, the alternative channels available, and in some cases, the laws governing channel relationships. Table 15.1 illustrates how these factors influence the extent to which an organization relies on marketing intermediaries in selecting a marketing channel.

Recently, there has been a trend toward a greater presence of intermediaries in marketing channels. That is, we are seeing fewer direct channels. Several factors account for this trend.[4] First, the cost of selling directly to customers has risen very rapidly, making it even more economical to sell through resellers. For instance, retailers can sell the product lines of many manufacturers and thus reach a large number of customers more economically than can manufacturers. Second, many industries have concentrated on lowering inventory carrying costs by placing inventory when and where it is needed. Intermediaries such as wholesalers are able to react to demand better than producers can. Third, large distribution chains have grown in size in many industries, taking market share from smaller "mom and pop" distributors. Large chains like Kroger, for example, have all but eliminated the neighborhood grocery store. Finally, the development of computer applications for marketing channels has led to a growth in intermediaries. Computers have made it possible for intermediaries to perform their functions at major cost reductions.

[3]Graham Button, "Room at the Top," *Forbes,* January 20, 1992, p. 106.
[4]Frank V. Cespedes and E. Raymond Corey, "Managing Multiple Channels," *Business Horizons,* July–August 1990, pp. 67–77.

A marketing channel that is used for one product may not be suitable for another; the same channel used to distribute live Maine lobsters would not be used to distribute appliances. Likewise, one organization may select a different channel than the one used by competitors. L.L. Bean distributes clothing directly to consumers through catalogues, whereas Dillard's sells products through retail stores. A number of different channels are available for consumer and organizational products, as well as for products marketed in foreign countries.

Channels for Consumer Products Several typical marketing channels for consumer products are shown in Figure 15.2. In channel 1, the product moves directly from producer to consumers. Customers who purchase fruit and vegetables from a farmer's "truck stand" or pick their own fruit or vegetables are utilizing a direct marketing channel. Similarly, wineries that sell their wines directly to consumers (often visitors touring the winery) provide a direct marketing channel to consumers, although they may sell their wines through other channels as well. Most services are distributed through a direct channel because they are produced and consumed at the same time.

FIGURE 15.2
Marketing Channels for Consumer Products

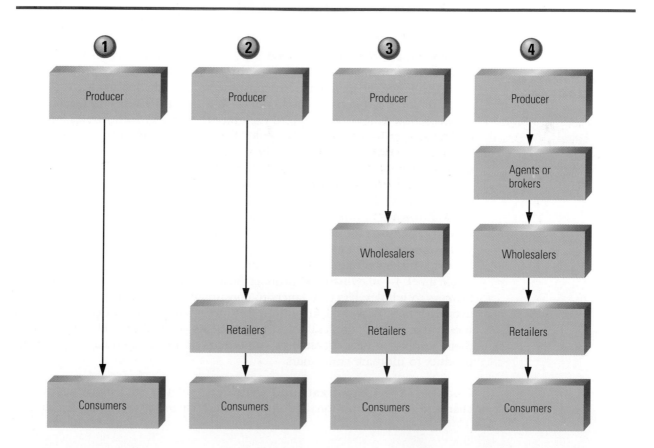

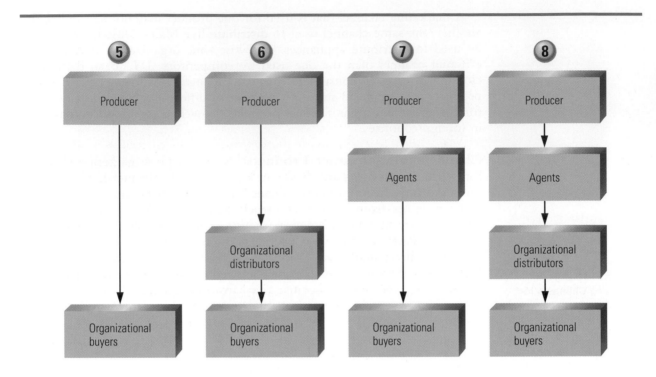

By contrast, channels 2, 3, and 4 represent indirect movement of goods or services from manufacturer to consumer. In channel 2, the product flows from the producer to retailers to consumers. This channel is often used for automobiles; most consumers do not wish to go to a factory in Michigan to purchase new Chevrolets; instead they buy them from authorized Chevrolet dealers that purchase the automobiles from General Motors. Using such a channel structure, large retailers like Kmart and Sears sell many products such as telephones and tires, which they buy directly from producers.

In channel 3, a product flows from the producer to wholesalers to retailers to consumers. This channel is used frequently for consumer products that are sold to large numbers of consumers through many retailers. A producer finds it easier to deal directly with a limited number of wholesalers rather than with thousands of retailers. For example, William Grant & Sons distributes its Scotch whiskey products globally through wholesalers and retailers.

Channel 4—in which the product flows from the producer to agents or brokers to wholesalers to retailers to consumers—is generally used for products with mass market distribution. Producers such as Iowa Beef Processors, Inc., often sell to wholesalers through agents or brokers. The wholesalers then supply the beef to retailers (supermarkets or restaurants) that sell the product to ultimate consumers.

Channels for Organizational Products   Figure 15.3 illustrates typical channels for organizational products. These channels are generally shorter than those for consumer products for many of the reasons outlined in Table 15.1. Channel 5, a direct channel of distribution, is often used for raw materials and expensive capital equipment. This is the most controllable channel; all marketing activities are conducted by the producer. The direct channel is especially useful when there are a small number of buyers with many special needs. If there are a large number of buyers, a direct channel can be very expensive.

Indirect distribution—achieved through channels 6, 7, or 8—may be more effective when there are larger numbers of buyers. Channel 6 is often used by heavy equipment manufacturers such as Caterpillar or John Deere. Although this channel results in some loss of control for the producer, it allows the producer to reach more buyers at a lower cost than does the direct channel.[5] For these reasons, this channel is very popular.

Channels 7 and 8 are appropriate when selling functions and information gathering are important. These channels are used to distribute agricultural products such as soybeans and fertilizer. Because organizational customers use products in the production of other products or for daily operations, retailers are rarely found in an organizational channel (even though organizational buyers may occasionally purchase products in retail stores). However, if an organizational buyer uses the organizational product as a component of a consumer product, then a new marketing channel is created. The final product may pass through wholesalers and retailers on its way to consumers. For example, when a consumer-goods manufacturer purchases fish for use in a frozen-dinner product, the fish itself follows an extended marketing channel—from commercial fishing company to agent to distributor to product manufacturer to wholesaler to retailer to final consumer.

■ **dual distribution** the use of two or more marketing channels to distribute the same product to the same target market

Dual Distribution   **Dual distribution** is the use of two or more marketing channels to distribute the same product to the same target market. By using dual distribution a firm can increase its products' availability to consumers. For instance, many companies like Neiman Marcus, General Nutrition Inc., Talbots, and Sundance sell their products through retail outlets as well as mail-order catalogues (see Figure 15.4). Likewise, Kirby vacuum cleaners and encyclopedias are sold through both direct channels (door-to-door) and retailers. Cooper Tire & Rubber distributes half its production through oil companies and retailers like Western Auto; the other half is sold through independent tire dealers.[6]

Dual distribution can be in violation of the Sherman Act if the arrangement results in restraint of trade. For instance, a petroleum producer may distribute gasoline through independent dealers as well as company-owned stations. However, gaining a competitive advantage by using company-owned stations to undercut the prices charged by independents is illegal.

[5]Thomas L. Powers, "Industrial Distribution Options: Trade-Offs to Consider," *Industrial Marketing Management,* 15, 1989, pp. 155–161.
[6]Alex Taylor, "Now Hear This, Jack Welch," *Fortune,* April 6, 1992, pp. 94–95.

FIGURE 15.4
Dual Distribution
Firms use dual distribution
hoping to increase product
availability to customers.
Sundance products, for
instance, are distributed
through two channels—
stores and catalogues.

Source: © 1993 Sundance Catalog
Company.

International Channels of Distribution   All products, including those sold across national boundaries, must be physically moved from the domestic producer to the consumer or organizational buyer. A firm marketing its products in other nations may decide to distribute products through existing marketing channels or to develop new international channels. The decision depends on the availability of both domestic and foreign channels that satisfy the distribution requirements. Japan has developed a complex called the Asia and Pacific Trade Center to facilitate direct access to retailers' purchasing agents by foreign suppliers. Retailers go directly to the center to make purchases from non-Japanese companies, which reduces costs and makes it easier for foreign firms to crack the Japanese market.[7]

Figure 15.5 illustrates the different organizations that may constitute an international marketing channel. Of course, numerous alternatives are available. Producers may choose to distribute directly to foreign consumers or to use one or more intermediaries. Cannondale Corp., based in Georgetown, Connecticut, specializes in high-performance mountain bikes and racing bikes. In an effort to move closer to the customer, Cannondale sells directly to about 260 Japanese dealers.[8] The choice depends on several factors: cost, market, coverage, and control. Cost is obviously an important factor; the expense of developing a separate foreign distribution system can be tremendous. The opening of retail stores in Europe, Canada, or Mexico can require large investments in facilities, research expenditures, and management costs. In addition, performing all the distribution functions may simply be too expensive for a company. The channel selected must ensure adequate, timely

---

[7]Jeffrey A. Tannenbaum, "A Japanese Complex May Aid Foreign Firms," *Wall Street Journal,* July 17, 1992, p. B1.
[8]Andrew Tanzer, "Just Get Out and Sell," *Forbes,* September 28, 1992, pp. 68–72.

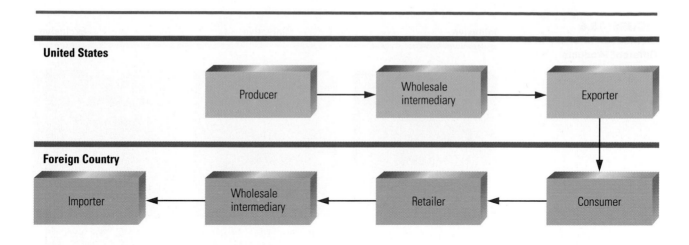

United States

Producer → Wholesale intermediary → Exporter

Foreign Country

Importer ← Wholesale intermediary ← Retailer ← Consumer

FIGURE 15.5
Example of an International Channel of Distribution for an American Firm

market coverage. Without sufficient distribution, a company may find it difficult to achieve desired sales. Control is another important consideration in the selection of an international channel. As more intermediaries become involved in the channel, a firm's ability to control price, promotion, and sales effort diminishes.

Distribution Intensity

■ **distribution intensity** the number of marketing intermediaries at each level of the marketing channel

When selecting a marketing channel, a firm must also determine the number of intermediaries needed to provide the best target market coverage. **Distribution intensity** is the number of marketing intermediaries at each level of the marketing channel. At the retail level, distribution intensity refers to the number of outlets that sell a particular product to consumers. Newspapers can be purchased from street vendors and at newspaper stands, convenience stores, grocery stores, and other outlets, but a stereo or computer can be purchased from only a few selected dealers. The product and the target market served often determine the distribution intensity. The three major levels of distribution intensity are intensive, selective, and exclusive distribution. Figure 15.6 compares the distribution intensity of different products.

■ **intensive distribution** distribution in which all available outlets are used for distributing a product

Intensive distribution means that all available outlets are used at each level of the channel to distribute a product. Convenience products such as bread, milk, canned goods, chewing gum, soft drinks, and newspapers receive intensive distribution. Some products, such as soft drinks and cigarettes, are available virtually everywhere through vending machines. Most consumer packaged products, such as detergents, soaps, and personal-care products, also rely on intensive distribution. These are generally less expensive products that are purchased frequently by a large number of consumers and require little shopping effort.

■ **selective distribution** distribution in which only some available outlets are chosen to distribute a product

Selective distribution uses only some available outlets to distribute a product. Shopping products and durable goods such as automobiles, stereos, and large household appliances usually fall into this category. Because such

FIGURE 15.6
Distribution Intensity of Different Products

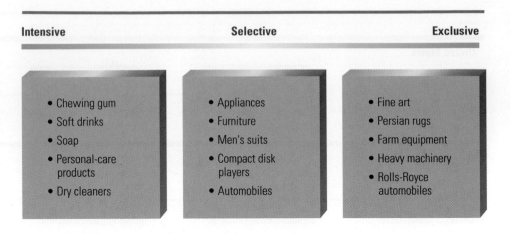

Intensive	Selective	Exclusive
• Chewing gum • Soft drinks • Soap • Personal-care products • Dry cleaners	• Appliances • Furniture • Men's suits • Compact disk players • Automobiles	• Fine art • Persian rugs • Farm equipment • Heavy machinery • Rolls-Royce automobiles

products are more expensive than convenience goods, consumers spend more time visiting several retail outlets to compare prices, designs, styles, and other features.

■ **exclusive distribution** distribution in which only one or very few outlets distribute a product

In **exclusive distribution,** a product is offered in only one or very few outlets within a relatively large geographic area. Organizations use exclusive distribution for products that are purchased rather infrequently, are consumed over a long period of time, or require service or information to fit them to buyers' needs. Private and business jets like the Gulfstream and Starship are sold on an exclusive basis. Some consumer products like luxury cars and custom-made jewelry are also distributed in this way.

FUNCTIONS OF MARKETING CHANNELS

As we state in Chapter 1, exchange is one of the primary means used to satisfy the needs of individuals and organizations. In our modern economy, we cannot produce everything required to satisfy our needs. One individual may have a vegetable garden in the back yard, and another person may make clothes. But unlike in primitive cultures, most of the things we need are produced by someone else and obtained through exchanges. As you recall, marketing activities are aimed at facilitating such exchanges, and distribution is critical because it enables firms to match their production capabilities to the needs of customers.

■ **sorting** the process through which the supply of goods and services produced by the manufacturer is matched with the assortment demanded by the consumer

Sorting is the process through which the supply of goods and services produced by the manufacturer is matched with the assortment demanded by the consumer.[9] An *assortment* is a combination of products created by the manufacturer or held by the consumer. Sorting is necessary because manufac-

---

[9]Stern and El-Ansary, p. 6.

turers generally produce a large quantity of a narrow assortment of products, whereas consumers typically demand a limited quantity of a broad assortment of products.

The sorting function consists of several activities, including sorting out, accumulation, allocation, and assorting.[10] *Sorting out* involves classifying heterogeneous supplies into relatively homogeneous groups. Products are classified by grade, color, or size. This function is especially common for raw materials and agricultural products. For instance, beef is graded as prime or choice. *Accumulation* is combining small groups of similar products into large groups of homogeneous products. Wholesalers accumulate a stock of goods for retailers, and retailers accumulate a stock of goods for consumers. *Allocation* is breaking down large, homogeneous stocks into smaller groups. A truckload of televisions is sold to retailers in smaller lots, who in turn sell single units to consumers. *Assorting* is combining products into collections or assortments that satisfy customer demand. Wholesalers develop product assortments for retailers, and retailers develop product assortments for consumers.

Marketing channel members perform many other functions: buying, carrying inventory, selling, transporting, financing, promoting, negotiating, conducting marketing research, and servicing. These functions, summarized in Table 15.2, enable products and information to flow from producers to consumers in a timely and efficient fashion. Channels also facilitate the flow of information and payments from consumers to producers. All of these functions must be performed through the marketing channel, although all channel members may not perform each function. For instance, General Motors may provide transportation, marketing research, and national advertising. Automobile dealers that sell GM cars carry inventory and perform buying, selling, financing, and servicing functions. Marketing functions are never eliminated, but are shifted backward or forward to reduce cost and improve efficiency. Veritas is a company that sells life insurance directly to consumers through the mail or by telephone, thus reducing distribution costs and eliminating the sales commission. The demand for fee-only life insurance is increasing and has many insurance companies scrambling to create their own no-commission policies.[11]

Marketing channels play a critical role in total quality programs. Quality expert Philip Crosby introduced a concept called *zero defects,* a performance standard that attempts to build quality into a product and eliminate costly errors.[12] Zero defects cannot be accomplished unless the right products get to the right customers when they want them.[13] Channels also link firms with the customer, *the* key to quality. Close to the Customer explores this link more closely.

[10]Wroe Alderson, *Marketing Behavior and Executive Action* (Homewood, Ill.: Irwin, 1957), pp. 201–202.
[11]Carolyn T. Geer, "Eliminating Middlemen," *Forbes,* March 2, 1992, pp. 92–93.
[12]Philip B. Crosby, *Quality Is Free* (New York: McGraw-Hill, 1979), pp. 200–201.
[13]Dennis J. Cahill, "It's Time for Santa, the Marketing Genius," *Marketing News,* December 7, 1992, p. 4.

TABLE 15.2
Functions of Marketing Channel Members

Function	Description
Buying	Purchasing a broad assortment of goods from producers or other channel members
Carrying inventory	Assuming the risks associated with purchasing and holding an inventory
Selling	Performing activities required to sell goods to consumers or other channel members
Transporting	Arranging for the shipment of goods
Financing	Providing funds required to cover the cost of channel activities
Promoting	Contributing to national and local advertising, and engaging in personal selling efforts
Negotiating	Attempting to determine the final price of goods
Marketing research	Providing information regarding the needs of customers
Servicing	Providing a variety of services, such as credit, delivery, and returns

COORDINATING MARKETING CHANNELS

The functions and efforts of channel members must be coordinated for the mutual benefit and efficient interaction of all parties involved, including the customer. This coordination is sometimes accomplished through the consensus of all channel members, in which case they voluntarily agree to perform those functions that are most beneficial to the entire channel. However, reaching a consensus of channel members, each with its own set of goals, is often quite difficult. For this reason, some marketing channels are organized and controlled by a single channel leader, which may be a producer, wholesaler, or retailer. The **channel leader** is responsible for guiding other channel members and coordinating their efforts to achieve channel objectives. The channel leader may establish channel policies and coordinate the development of the marketing mix. General Foods, for example, is a channel leader for some of the many products that it sells. Frequently, the channel member with the most financial resources and power is the channel leader.

Under the management of a channel leader, the various links or stages of the channel may be integrated either horizontally or vertically. Integration can stabilize supply, reduce costs, and increase coordination of channel members.

■ **channel leader** a channel member responsible for guiding other channel members and coordinating their efforts to achieve channel objectives and reduce conflicts

CLOSE TO THE CUSTOMER

Distribution At 7-Eleven

In 1985, Southland Corp., parent company of 7-Eleven, was the nation's largest retailer. With more than 7,500 7-Eleven stores, Southland's sales and profits were growing 10 to 15 percent each year and total sales had reached $8.5 billion. But Southland filed for bankruptcy protection in 1990. Ito-Yokado Co., a successful operator of 7-Eleven stores in Japan, invested $430 million in Southland in exchange for a 70 percent share of the company.

Today Ito-Yokado is pushing Southland to become more plugged into consumer trends. Toshifumi Suzuki, vice chairman of Southland's board, said of Southland executives, "They forgot what a convenience store is supposed to be." The plan is to refurbish 7-Eleven stores, offer many new products, and install a sophisticated inventory management system. Ito-Yokado executives believe that technology is the key to keeping track of customers. The company is putting the final touches on a $200 million system that monitors inventory and tracks customer preferences. Called Accelerated Inventory Management (AIM), the system is designed to cut inventories and give store managers prompt, accurate information on what customers are buying.

AIM is actually quite simple. Information about purchases is automatically stored in the computer.

Clerks even key in the approximate age and gender of customers to monitor buying patterns. Orders are transmitted instantly via satellite to distribution centers and manufacturers. Products that do not move are discontinued. The result is a bare-bones inventory that saves money. Shelf space is allocated to those products that local shoppers want.

When AIM is fully in place, each store will account for its entire inventory of about 2,400 items at least once a week. The new system is in the test stages, with the full-blown system linking stores and headquarters to be ready in 1996 or later. The system has been highly successful in Japan, where 7-Eleven is the largest convenience-store chain. Most U.S. stores are using a limited version of AIM. Slurpees and Big Gulps can still be found, but a wider range of products including fruits, vegetables, and fresh sandwiches has been added. By stocking the products customers want to buy, stores are already experiencing an increase in sales.

Sources: Wendy Zellner and Karen Lowry Miller, "A New Roll of the Dice at 7-Eleven," *Business Week,* October 26, 1992, pp. 100–101; Allen Liles, "Road to Long-Term Ruin," *Barron's,* January 27, 1992, p. 15; and Karen Lowry Miller, "Listening to Shoppers' Voices," *Business Week/Reinventing America,* 1992, p. 69.

Vertical Integration

■ **vertical integration**
the combining of two or more functions of a marketing channel under one management

Vertical integration occurs when one channel member acquires control of one or more other members of its marketing channel, usually by purchasing them. For instance, Willamette Industries generates plywood, wood products, and wood chips for its paper mills from the 1.2 million acres of timberland it owns in Oregon, Tennessee, the Carolinas, Louisiana, Arkansas, and

FIGURE 15.7
Types of Vertical
Marketing Systems

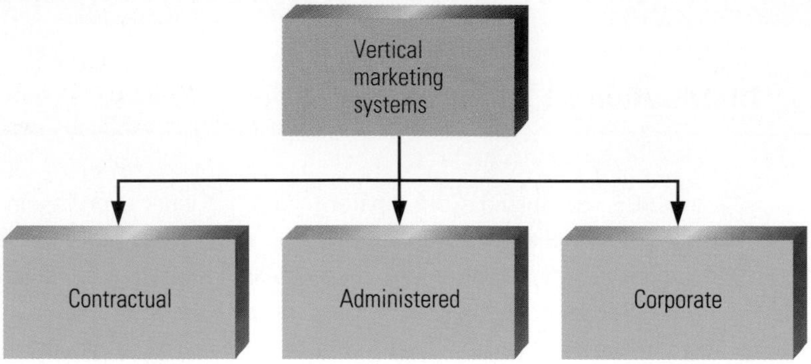

■ **vertical marketing system (VMS)** a marketing channel professionally managed and centrally controlled by a single marketing channel member

■ **corporate VMS** a marketing channel in which successive stages of the channel are united under one ownership

■ **administered VMS** a marketing channel in which channel members remain independent but informal coordination allows for effective interorganizational management

■ **contractual VMS** a marketing channel in which channel members are independent but have interorganizational relationships that are formalized through contracts or other legal agreements

■ **horizontal integration** the combining of firms at the same level of a marketing channel or the expansion of units (such as retail stores) at one level

Texas.[14] Recently, movie production companies like Twentieth Century-Fox Film Corp. began purchasing television stations to gain increased control over the outlets available for its products, movies, and television programs. Vertical integration eliminates the need for a marketing channel member to act as an independent organization.

Total vertical integration occurs when one organization controls all marketing channel functions, from manufacturing to servicing the final consumer. One company that uses this type of arrangement is Shell Oil, which owns oil wells, refineries, pipelines, terminals, and service stations.

A marketing channel that is professionally managed and centrally controlled by a single marketing channel member is a **vertical marketing system (VMS).** Vertical marketing systems improve distribution efficiency by combining the efforts of individual channel members.[15] As organizations have recognized their practicality, VMSs have increased in popularity. The three types of vertical marketing systems are shown in Figure 15.7.

In a **corporate VMS,** successive stages of a marketing channel are united under one ownership. Singer, for example, owns the retail outlets that sell its sewing machines, and Tandy owns the Radio Shack outlets that sell its products. Channel members in an **administered VMS** remain independent, but informal coordination allows for effective interorganizational management. Kellogg Co., Campbell Soup Company, and Kraft General Foods use administered channels. Channel members in a **contractual VMS** are also independent, but their interorganizational relationships are formalized through contracts or other legal agreements. Such legal agreements spell out the rights and obligations of each channel member. Franchise organizations such as McDonald's, shown in Figure 15.8, and KFC are contractual VMSs.

Horizontal Integration

Horizontal integration occurs when a channel member purchases firms at the same level of the marketing channel or expands the number of units (such

[14]John H. Taylor, "The Ducks Are Flying," *Forbes,* July 20, 1992, pp. 124–128.
[15]Stern and El-Ansary, p. 319.

as retail stores) at one level. For example, Allied Stores Corporation expanded its group of department-store chains by purchasing Federated Department Stores, which included the Rich's, Lazarus, Goldsmith's, Burdines, and Bloomingdale's department-store chains. Horizontal integration allows the combined organizations to achieve efficiencies and economies of scale in promotion, marketing research, purchasing, and the employment of specialists.

Horizontal integration is not always effective in improving distribution because organizations sometimes experience difficulty in coordinating the increased number of units. As a result, further marketing research and planning may be needed to manage large-scale operations. In addition, horizontal integration decreases organizational flexibility. Finally, the government has found some of these mergers to be in violation of the Sherman Act.

MANAGING CHANNEL RELATIONSHIPS

Each member of a marketing channel has a position with rights, obligations, and rewards; and each is subject to penalties for nonconformance. Moreover, each channel member has certain expectations of every other channel member. Retailers expect wholesalers to keep sufficient inventories on hand and to deliver goods on time. Wholesalers expect retailers to abide by the terms

FIGURE 15.8
Contractual VMS
McDonald's is a franchise, which is a contractual VMS. Owners of McDonald's franchises enter into a contractual agreement with the McDonald's organization which spells out the obligations of each party.

Source: McDonald's Corporation.

of payment contracts and to keep them informed about inventory levels. If the marketing channel is to operate effectively, channel members must cooperate with each other and keep conflict in check.

Channel Cooperation and Conflict

■ **channel cooperation**
a mutually helpful relationship in which channel members work together for the benefit of all members and the realization of overall channel objectives

■ **channel conflict** friction between marketing channel members, often resulting from role deviance or malfunction by one member

Channel cooperation occurs when channel members work together for their mutual benefit. Marketing channels cannot function without sustained cooperation. Cooperation is necessary if each channel member is to gain something from other members.[16] The realization of overall channel objectives and individual member objectives depends on cooperation. Unless a channel member can be replaced, the misconduct of one member can destroy the entire channel. Thus it is vital that policies be developed to ensure the welfare and survival of all indispensable channel members.

Channel conflict results from role deviance or malfunction, where one member does not conform to its expected role.[17] For example, wholesalers expect manufacturers to maintain product quality and production schedules, and expect retailers to market products effectively. In turn, retailers and producers expect wholesalers to provide coordination, functional services, and communication. If wholesalers, retailers, or producers fail to conform to other channel members' expectations, channel conflict results. By anticipating problems, marketing managers can make changes to resolve channel conflicts and improve cooperation.[18] For instance, the channel leader could explicitly spell out the responsibilities and performance levels expected of each channel member.

Conflicts between channel members are plaguing several industries. Large food producers pay supermarket chains millions of dollars to get shelf space for certain products. In the meat-packing industry, wholesalers rely on meat packers to cooperate by trimming the fat from cuts of meat. The amount of fat being left on meat by the packers has resulted in conflicts between the two parties, because wholesalers feel they are paying for too much fat. Leading computer companies are experiencing conflicts with producers of memory chips. Channel members must work to improve cooperation and reduce conflict to experience long-term satisfying relationships.

Resolving Channel Conflicts

When several individuals or organizations engage in a relationship, conflict is inevitable. This is certainly true for marketing channels. Nevertheless, many channel conflicts can be resolved through effective channel leadership.

---

[16] Wroe Alderson, *Dynamic Marketing Behavior* (Homewood, Ill.: Irwin, 1965), p. 239.
[17] Louis W. Stern and Ronald H. Gorman, "Conflict in Distribution Channels: An Exploration," in *Distribution Channels: Behavioral Dimensions,* ed. Louis W. Stern (Boston: Houghton Mifflin, 1969), p. 157.
[18] Kenneth G. Hardy and Allan J. Magrath, "Ten Ways for Manufacturers to Improve Distribution Management," *Business Horizons,* November–December 1988, pp. 65–69.

■ **channel power** the ability of one channel member to influence another member's marketing decision and goal achievement

The channel leader is able to reduce conflicts among channel members because it possesses channel power. **Channel power** is the ability of one channel member to influence another member's marketing decisions and goal achievement. Channel power enables a channel leader to influence overall channel performance. For example, it is becoming common for firms like Ford and Motorola—who won the Baldrige Award for quality—to require zero defects from their suppliers. This is power, and it influences channel performance. General Motors has announced a plan to choose as suppliers only those that can offer the highest quality at the lowest price. Even in-house parts-making operations will be cut if there is a more efficient outside supplier.[19]

Channel power is derived from the control of resources and services critical to other channel members. The channel member that controls resources on which other members depend is often the channel leader. For example, fertilizer dealers depend heavily on chemical manufacturers for many resources and services, including on-time product delivery, price information, employee training, legal assistance, and credit. As a result, the chemical manufacturer can influence dealers' decisions regarding budgets, size of product purchases, pricing, and advertising.[20] Power can increase conflict and reduce cooperation if one channel member uses coercion to influence others.[21] After Procter & Gamble purchased Crush International, it was expected that it would build the Crush brand beverages into market leaders. But even though P&G developed a new package and creative advertisements, the firm could not develop cooperative relationships with its middlemen—local bottlers across the United States. By using its power to force bottlers into supermarkets and to remove franchise guarantees, P&G alienated the bottlers; eventually it sold Crush International. In contrast, when IBM began making personal computers, it had no experience with computer dealers and retail sales, since it had always sold large mainframes through a direct channel. IBM reduced friction with new dealers and resellers such as Pulsar Data Systems by changing its sales compensation plans, sharing sales leads, and undertaking joint advertising (see Figure 15.9). The result was a fairly cooperative relationship with dealers.[22]

Producers such as IBM and Ford often act as channel leaders because of their economic clout. Retailers like Sears and Kmart—that derive power from high-volume sales and customer loyalty—may also be channel leaders. Finally, wholesalers can function as channel leaders, as does McKesson Corp. in the pharmaceutical industry.

---

[19] Zachary Schiller, David Woodruff, Kevin Kelly, and Michael Schroeder, "GM Tightens the Screws," *Business Week,* June 22, 1992, pp. 30–31.
[20] Steven J. Skinner, James H. Donnelly, Jr., and John M. Ivancevich, "Effects of Transactional Form on Environmental Linkages and Power-Dependence Relationships," *Academy of Management Journal,* September 1987, pp. 577–588.
[21] Steven J. Skinner, Jule B. Gassenheimer, and Scott W. Kelley, "Cooperation in Supplier-Dealer Networks," *Journal of Retailing,* Summer 1992, pp. 174–193.
[22] Allan J. Magrath, "The Hidden Clout of Marketing Middlemen," *Journal of Business Strategy,* March–April 1990, pp. 38–41.

FIGURE 15.9
Resolving Channel Conflicts
Channel conflict can be resolved through effective channel leadership. IBM works closely with resellers like Pulsar Data Systems to increase cooperation and reduce conflict.

Source: Courtesy of Pulsar Data Systems, Inc.

PHYSICAL DISTRIBUTION

■ **physical distribution**
the set of activities used in managing the flow of products from manufacturers to consumers and end users

Physical distribution is the set of activities used to manage the flow of products from manufacturers to consumers and end users.[23] Physical distribution activities can be conducted by any member of the channel. For instance, raw materials must be moved from their origin to the production facility; raw materials, parts, semifinished products, and finished products must be moved within the plant or to and from warehouses; and finished products must be moved to marketing intermediaries and on to the final consumer.

Physical distribution is becoming increasingly important as firms attempt to reduce costs and increase service. An organization can gain a competitive advantage through a well-designed physical distribution system. By getting products to the target market on a timely basis and in proper condition, a company can satisfy its customers and outsell its competitors. Also, a well-designed physical distribution system can decrease the total cost of distribution, although tradeoffs must be made to ensure efficient use of resources and customer satisfaction.

Total Distribution Cost

The major objective of physical distribution is to minimize costs and maximize service. Physical distribution managers attempt to reduce costs in all

[23] Donald J. Bowersax, M. Bixby Cooper, Douglas M. Lambert, and Donald A. Taylor, *Management in Marketing Channels* (New York: McGraw-Hill, 1980), p. 199.

areas, including transportation, order processing, and warehousing. However, reducing costs in one area may increase costs in another. For instance, it is sometimes less expensive to lease warehouse facilities than to own them. However, leasing could increase the cost of transportation because products would have to be transported from the factory to the leased warehouse instead of to an on-site warehouse. Many manufacturing firms develop partnerships or alliances with organizations that specialize in some physical distribution activity, such as transportation or warehousing. These partnerships dramatically improve the quality of customer service and reduce costs, because each organization is doing what it does best and most efficiently.[24]

By using a total cost approach, a firm views the physical distribution system as a whole, not as a series of unrelated activities. The firm tries to reduce the total distribution cost through an integrated approach to physical distribution. Instead of looking for the lowest possible transportation rates or warehousing costs, the organization balances the total costs of all activities against the level of service it wants to offer. The organization then adopts the combination of physical distribution activities that yields the lowest total cost but meets its customer service objectives.[25]

Cost Tradeoffs

To provide a specific level of service at the lowest possible cost, an organization must make cost tradeoffs in its distribution system to resolve conflicts about resource allocation. In other words, the higher costs of one activity must be offset by lower costs of another. For instance, catalogue retailers such as Spiegel, Inc., may wish to minimize the amount of time a customer has to wait to receive an order. This service objective, which requires carrying a large inventory, may conflict with the objective of minimizing inventory carrying costs. The company must then decide whether to trade higher inventory costs for better customer service to gain a competitive edge.

PHYSICAL DISTRIBUTION ACTIVITIES

The remainder of this chapter discusses the various activities involved in physical distribution. Figure 15.10 provides an overview of the activities involved in a physical distribution system.[26] These activities include developing customer service standards, selecting transportation modes, designing and operating warehouse facilities, designing an order processing system, physically handling the products, and establishing an inventory management and control system.

---

[24] Donald J. Bowersax, "The Strategic Benefits of Logistics Alliances," *Harvard Business Review,* July–August 1990, pp. 36–45.
[25] Brian S. Moskal, "Distribution: The Last Frontier," *Industry Week,* August 1, 1988, pp. 63–68.
[26] James R. Stock and Douglas M. Lambert, *Strategic Logistics Management,* 2nd ed. (Homewood, Ill.: Irwin, 1987), p. 42.

FIGURE 15.10
Physical Distribution Activities

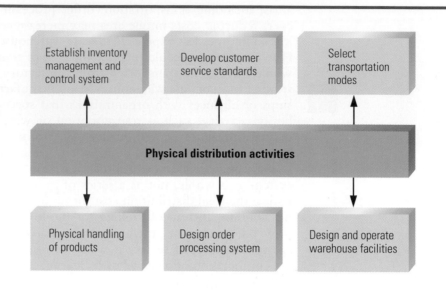

Developing Customer Service Standards

In accordance with the marketing concept, the design of a physical distribution system begins with consideration of customer needs. One survey found that improving customer service is a major priority in the distribution industry.[27] To this end, an organization must develop a set of service specifications. Each specification, called a **customer service standard,** identifies a specific and measurable goal appropriate to physical distribution. An example is "to process all customer orders within 72 hours." These standards influence other physical distribution activities such as transportation and warehousing. Customer service standards should be communicated to both customers and employees, and enforced by management. Service standards are critical in attracting and maintaining satisfied customers, and should therefore be tailored to customers' needs.

■ **customer service standard** a specification that identifies a specific and measurable goal appropriate to physical distribution

Customers may require many different services before, during, and after an exchange.[28] Before an exchange, a company needs to establish a good climate for service by offering fair prices and high-quality products. Additionally, a written statement that outlines the firm's service policy should be provided to customers. During the transaction of exchanges, reliable deliveries, sizable inventories, efficient order processing, and availability of emergency shipments may be desired by customers seeking a high level of service. After the transaction, installation, repairs and parts, warranties, answering customer complaints, and product packaging are critical elements of customer service. Failure to provide services may result in the loss of customers and possible legal action.

[27] Marge Meek, "Poll Shows Shift Toward Customer Service," *Chain-Store Age Executive,* May 1990, pp. 286–292.
[28] Ronald H. Ballou, *Business Logistics Management: Planning and Control,* 2nd ed. (Englewood Cliffs, N.J.: Prentice-Hall, 1985), p. 55.

Selecting Transportation Modes

Transportation is essential to all organizations because it makes products available to consumers when and where they want to purchase them. In fact, transportation represents one-third of all physical distribution costs.[29] A firm's ability to transport undamaged products to appropriate distributors in a timely fashion affects the firm's success in satisfying consumers' needs and wants. Thus transportation decisions should be weighed carefully and could serve as an important differentiating variable in a marketing strategy, as they do for air express company Federal Express. The selection of a transportation mode, or method, affects all aspects of the physical distribution system.

The five major transportation modes in the United States are railways, motor vehicles, inland waterways, pipelines, and airways. Table 15.3 illustrates typical transportation modes for various products.

Marketers consider many important factors in selecting a transportation mode. Obviously, cost is very important. Transit time (the total time a carrier possesses goods), reliability (dependability and consistency of service), capability (the ability to move specific kinds of products), and accessibility (the ability to move goods over a specific route) are also important. Although a truck can carry a replacement part for a computer system at a low cost, air freight may provide more reliable delivery. Other important considerations are security (safety) and traceability (the ease with which a shipment can be located). Table 15.4 ranks the transportation modes by various selection criteria.

Railways   Railways account for more than 36 percent of all transportation (see Table 15.3). Railways are used to carry relatively low value, bulky items for long distances. Products typically transported by rail include coal, sand, lumber, grain, and steel. Railways serve a fairly large number of locations at a reasonable cost, and delivery speed is generally adequate for the type of products that are transported. Railways have lost market share in recent years, especially to motor vehicles, because railways are less dependable and result in greater losses and damage.

Motor Vehicles   Motor vehicles account for nearly one-fourth of all transportation and continue to gain a greater share of the transportation market. They are the most flexible of all transportation modes because they can go nearly anywhere at any time and are fast and dependable. They are generally used to transport smaller shipments over shorter distances. Products shipped by motor vehicles include clothing, paper goods, livestock, food, and practically any other item. The major drawbacks to motor vehicles are that they are somewhat high in cost and low in fuel efficiency, and losses and damages can be significant. Increased hijacking in inner cities and between them also has caused concern. Because of their flexibility, trucks are often used along with some other mode of transportation such as railways or waterways.

---

[29] Cynthia Milsap, "Distribution Costs Fall—Rules Off," *Business Marketing,* February 1985 (report on study conducted for the National Council of Physical Distribution Management).

Mode	Ton-Miles* (billions)	Percent of Total Transportation (ton-miles)	Typical Products
Railways	1,071	37.5	Coal, grain, chemicals, lumber, automobiles, iron, steel, sand
Motor vehicles	735	25.8	Clothing, paper goods, computers, books, fresh fruit, livestock
Inland waterways	462	16.1	Petroleum, chemicals, iron ore, bauxite, grain
Pipelines	577	20.2	Oil, processed coal, natural gas, water, chemicals
Airways	11	0.4	Flowers, perishable food, emergency parts, overnight mail

*A ton-mile is the movement of 1 ton (2,000 pounds) of freight for the distance of 1 mile.

Source: *Statistical Abstract of the United States,* 1992, p. 600.

TABLE 15.3
Major Transportation Modes—and Percent Transportation by Mode

Inland Waterways   Inland waterways account for about 16 percent of all transportation. They are used to transport low-value, bulky products like coal, petroleum, and grain. Waterways represent the cheapest mode of transportation, are fuel-efficient, and involve low losses and damages. However, waterways are slow, less dependable than other modes, and limited in the number of locations served. They are often supplemented with motor or rail transportation.

Pipelines   Pipelines account for 22 percent of all transportation. Petroleum products and chemicals are most commonly transported via pipelines. Pipelines are generally owned by the firm or firms shipping the product. They offer uninterrupted movement at a relatively low cost, they are dependable and fuel-efficient, and they involve low losses and damages. Because pipelines are the slowest mode of transportation and very limited in the number of locations served, their use is limited.

Airways   Although airways account for less than 1 percent of all transportation, the importance of this transportation mode is growing. Perishable products, overnight packages, and emergency parts and supplies are frequently transported by air. As more and more firms conduct business in foreign countries, air transportation will be in greater demand. Airways offer the fastest delivery available (next to FAX) and are relatively dependable. Some type of motor vehicle pickup at the airport is usually required, which reduces the speed of delivery and increases the cost. The high cost of air transportation will continue to limit the range of products that can be shipped in this manner.

TABLE 15.4
Transportation Modes Ranked by Selection Criteria

	Water	Pipeline	Rail	Truck	Air
Lowest cost	1	2	3	4	5
Delivery speed	4	5	3	2	1
Number of locations served	4	5	2	1	3
Dependability	5	1	4	2	3
Range of products carried	3	5	1	2	4
Losses and damages	2	1	5	4	3
Fuel efficiency	2	1	3	4	5

1 = highest ranking

Sources: Donald J. Bowersax, David J. Closs, and Omar K. Helferich, *Logistical Management*, 3rd ed. (New York: Macmillan, 1986), p. 166; Carl M. Guelzo, *Introduction to Logistics Management* (Englewood Cliffs, N.J.: Prentice-Hall, 1986), p. 46; and Ronald H. Ballou, *Business Logistics Management: Planning and Control*, 2nd ed. (Englewood Cliffs, N.J.: Prentice-Hall, 1985), p. 194.

■ **intermodal transportation** transportation that combines two or more modes of transportation to obtain the benefits of the carriers involved

■ **freight forwarder** a transportation company that consolidates shipments from several organizations into efficient lot sizes

Coordinating Transportation Modes Marketing managers may have to integrate various modes of transportation to account for the strengths and weaknesses of alternative carriers. **Intermodal transportation** combines two or more modes of transportation in order to obtain the benefits the different carriers offer. Examples of intermodal transportation include piggyback (combining truck trailers and rail flatcars), fishyback (combining truck trailers and water carriers), and birdyback (combining truck trailers and air carriers). Because of the efficiency gains and savings, intermodal shipping is the fastest growing mode of transportation.[30] Intermodal transportation is important to firms conducting international business. For example, a truck trailer may be used to transport products from a factory to a rail center. At that point, the trailer may be placed on a flatcar and shipped piggyback to a port, then shipped fishyback to a foreign port.

Manufacturers may coordinate transportation modes themselves or may employ special transportation agencies. A **freight forwarder** is a transportation company that consolidates shipments from several organizations into efficient lot sizes. Consolidated shipments are practical for small loads (of less than 500 pounds) that would cost considerably more than full loads in railroad cars and trucks. A freight forwarder consolidates small loads from various shippers, purchases transport space from carriers, arranges for goods

[30]Daniel Machalaba, "Shippers Prepare to Jump on Rail-Truck Combinations," *Wall Street Journal*, December 29, 1992, p. B4.

to be delivered to buyers, and determines the most efficient means of transporting the goods. Freight forwarders provide a useful alternative for shipping goods to foreign markets. Their margin of profit is the difference between the less-than-carload rates they charge their customers and the lower carload rates they pay.

Transporting Hazardous Materials   A major challenge facing manufacturers, distributors, and transportation companies is the movement of hazardous materials. As the public grows increasingly concerned about the environment, firms face pressure to move hazardous materials safely and without incident. This task is quite complex considering the amount of hazardous materials shipped each day and the many regulations guiding these shipments. Marketing Close-up examines this issue in greater detail.

Designing and Operating Warehouse Facilities

■ **warehousing** the design and operation of storage facilities

Warehousing is the design and operation of storage facilities. Warehouses are often used by organizations for the storage of products until they are needed by channel members. In addition to storing goods, warehouses also perform other functions, such as sorting, marking, and assembling goods for shipment. Warehousing is an important marketing strategy decision that can reduce the costs of transportation and improve service by making products available when needed. Because maintaining or renting warehouse facilities is a significant cost of physical distribution, marketers must carefully weigh the type of facilities to use. Firms can use private or public warehouses, or a combination of both.

■ **private warehouse** a warehouse owned and operated by a company for the purpose of distributing its own products

Private Warehouses   A warehouse owned and operated by a company for the purpose of distributing its own products is a **private warehouse.** Private warehouses may be a distinct and separate operation of the firm, or they may be consolidated with other activities. When a firm purchases warehouse facilities, it is making a long-term commitment to a geographic location; private warehouses provide little flexibility in changing locations. Firms also face fixed costs for taxes, insurance, maintenance, and interest expenses. The largest users of private warehouses are retail chain stores.[31]

■ **distribution center** a large, centralized warehouse designed to facilitate the movement of goods in and out of storage as fast as possible

A **distribution center** is a large, centralized warehouse facility designed to facilitate the movement of goods in and out of storage as fast as possible.[32] Whereas more traditional warehouses hold goods for extended periods of time, the goal of a distribution center is to move products, not to hold them. Distribution centers are generally one-story buildings, which eliminates the

[31]James C. Johnson and Donald F. Wood, *Contemporary Physical Distribution & Logistics,* 2nd ed. (Tulsa, Okla.: Penwell, 1982), p. 356.
[32]Carl M. Guelzo, *Introduction to Logistics Management* (Englewood Cliffs, N.J.: Prentice-Hall, 1986), p. 102.

MARKETING CLOSE-UP

Shipping Hazardous Materials

Each day in the United States, 500,000 shipments of hazardous materials take place. Thousands of federal, state, and local regulations govern the movement of the more than 33,000 commodities classified as hazardous. In recent years, citizens' groups and the general public have expressed growing concerns about such shipments passing through their states. As a result, the job of moving hazardous materials safely and legally is becoming more difficult.

Firms involved in moving hazardous materials face increased regulations covering nearly every aspect, from the move itself to cleaning equipment afterward. Shippers of hazardous materials must comply with the Department of Transportation's HM-181 shipping rules, effective October 1, 1993. The rules cover how substances are classified, how shipping papers are completed, the type of packaging permitted, and emergency response requirements. These regulations apply regardless of the size of shipment, mode of transportation, destination, distance traveled, or value of the goods.

Under documentation rules, firms must provide emergency response information with every hazardous shipment. That includes information on potential hazards, first-aid measures, and instructions for those on the scene of an accident, plus a 24-hour telephone number for emergencies. Many chemical manufacturers already comply with these regulations, but other companies that move hazardous materials may face additional paperwork to meet the requirements.

It has become nearly impossible for manufacturers and transportation firms to keep up with all the regulations. In addition to Department of Transportation regulations, the International Maritime Dangerous Goods code regulates more than one thousand commodities classified as hazardous. Violators risk having shipments rejected by a carrier or turned back at a port, and also face criminal penalties in case of an accident. Many products covered by this code are not lethal chemicals but include cosmetics, adhesives, and garden supplies.

The Occupational Safety and Health Administration (OSHA) also focuses considerable attention on the proper handling and transportation of hazardous materials. OSHA requires that employers maintain complete and updated Material Safety Data Sheets, develop and implement a written hazardous communications program, and provide information and training on handling and transporting hazardous chemicals. Many experts on hazardous materials suggest, at a minimum, two simple steps to help shippers stay on top of changing regulations: (1) join the very best trade association in the area; and (2) designate at least one employee to become the firm's specialist in hazardous materials regulation.

Sources: Lawrence W. Bierlein, "How to Handle Hazmat Returns," *Traffic Management,* July 1992, p. 73; "Employer Compliance with OSHA," *Supervision,* August 1992, pp. 5–6; LeAnn Lodder, "Tough Laws Strand Cargo," *International Business,* July 1992, pp. 19–22; DOT's HM-181 Rule Means Major Changes in Hazardous Materials Shipment," *Environmental Manager,* June 1992, pp. 3–4, 12; and Peter Bradley, "Facing the Hazards of Moving Hazardous Materials," *Purchasing,* April 5, 1990, pp. 66–69.

need for elevators. Modern equipment such as computerized robots enables orders to be processed more rapidly. Distribution centers are located near major markets and transportation centers to minimize delivery time. Wal-Mart's stores are located within 600 miles of a distribution center. Supermarkets, department stores, convenience stores, and fast-food franchisers use distribution centers.

Public Warehouses   A **public warehouse** provides storage and related physical distribution facilities to organizations on a rental basis. These facilities may also offer services such as reshipping, filling orders, financing, displaying products, and coordinating shipments. Also, public warehouses can provide **bonded storage,** an arrangement in which imported or taxable products are not released to the owner until U.S. customs duties, taxes, or other fees have been paid by the owners of the products.[33] Bonded storage is common for liquor and tobacco products.

Present-day warehouses are expanding their services beyond the traditional function of providing storage space to include offering services for the distribution of goods. As a result of this new emphasis on services, warehouses are restructuring their prices. In addition, public warehouses are customizing their services for specific market segments rather than for several different industries.[34] Efficiency in materials handling techniques and the use of space, in the installation of computer systems, and in the holding of large inventories is further improving warehousing services.

Although the variable cost per unit is greater for a public warehouse than for a private one, a combination of private and public warehousing can provide flexibility in warehousing. A firm might designate a minimum storage area for private warehousing and store overflow inventories in public warehouses. For instance, a retailer might buy or lease private facilities on a long-term basis and utilize a nearby public warehouse to store seasonal or overflow inventories.

Designing the Order Processing System

The physical distribution process is activated by customer orders. **Order processing** is the receipt and transmission of sales order information. Efficient processing of orders can reduce the time required for delivery and thus increase customer satisfaction.

Order processing occurs in three major steps: order entry, handling, and delivery. The first step, *order entry,* begins when a customer or salesperson places an order by mail, telephone, or computer. *Order handling,* the second step, involves transmitting the order to the warehouse and the credit department. The warehouse verifies that the product is in stock, and the credit department checks prices, terms, and the customer's credit rating. If the

■ public warehouse a warehouse that provides storage and related physical distribution facilities and services to organizations on a rental basis

■ bonded storage an arrangement in which imported or taxable products are not released to the owner until U.S. customs duties, taxes, or other fees have been paid by the owners of the products

■ order processing the receipt and transmission of sales order information

---

[33]Johnson and Wood, p. 355.
[34]"Warehousing Trends: Service Moves to Center Stage," *Traffic Management,* October 1984, pp. 88–90.

credit rating is approved and the item is in stock, the order is filled; if the requested item is not in stock, a production order is sent to the factory. Finally, the order is packaged for shipping, and *order delivery,* the third step, is scheduled.

Order processing can be done manually for small-volume orders, but electronic processing has become common for most orders, particularly large-volume orders. Electronic order processing is especially desirable because it allows a firm to integrate order processing, production planning, inventory control, accounting, and transportation planning into an advanced information and communications system.[35]

Physical Handling of Products

■ **materials handling** the physical handling of products, in warehouse operations and in the transportation of products from manufacturers to distributors and ultimate consumers

Materials handling, the physical handling of products, is important both in efficient warehouse operations and in the transportation of products from the manufacturer to distributors and ultimate consumers. The characteristics of the product itself often determine how it will be handled. For example, bulk liquids and gases have unique characteristics that dictate how they must be stored in appropriate containers and transported through pipelines or in railroad or truck tanks.

■ **unit loading** the materials handling practice of grouping one or more boxes on a pallet or skid to permit efficient movement by mechanical means (such as fork lifts, trucks, or conveyor systems)

Materials handling techniques should expand the usable capacity of a warehouse, reduce the number of times a product is handled, improve service to customers, and increase customers' satisfaction with the product. Packaging, loading, and movement systems must be coordinated to minimize costs and maximize customer satisfaction. Computer networks like the one advertised in Figure 15.11 facilitate this task.

■ **containerization** the materials handling practice of consolidating many goods into a single container, sealed at the point of origin and opened at the destination

Materials handling techniques help improve efficiency in physical distribution. **Unit loading** is the practice of grouping one or more boxes on a pallet or skid to permit efficient movement by mechanical means such as fork lifts, trucks, or conveyor systems. **Containerization,** another technique, is the practice of consolidating many goods into a single container, sealed at the point of origin and opened at the destination. Containers are typically 8 feet wide, 8 feet high, and 10, 20, 25, or 40 feet long. Containerization improves security as well as efficiency because individual items are not handled in transit. Containerization also facilitates intermodal transportation by consolidating shipments for transportation by piggyback, fishyback, and birdyback. It has revolutionized physical distribution by augmenting the capabilities of transportation systems, enabling shippers to transport a wider range of cargoes quickly, reliably, and at stable costs.

Establishing Inventory Management and Control

■ **inventory management and control** the physical distribution activities that help marketers develop and maintain adequate assortments of products to satisfy target markets and meet customers' needs

Inventory management and control are physical distribution activities that help marketers develop and maintain adequate assortments of products to satisfy target markets and meet customers' needs. To achieve its profit goals,

[35]Stock and Lambert, p. 506.

FIGURE 15.11
Physical Handling of Products
RAM Mobile Data networks, such as the one used by Conrail, improve communication and coordination, increasing customer satisfaction with the product.

an organization must control the costs of obtaining and maintaining inventory. Inventory decisions affect physical distribution costs and the level of customer service provided. If, for example, a firm uses shelf space to store low-turnover products, it may lose money. Likewise, if it carries too few products in inventory, it may run out of a product. Such shortage of a product—called a **stockout**—could result in lower sales, a loss of customers, or brand switching.

■ **stockout** the condition that exists when a firm runs out of a product

A business should design its inventory system so that the number of products sold and the number of products in stock can be determined at specified checkpoints. This could involve tearing off a code number from each product sold so that the correct sizes, colors, and models can be tabulated and reordered. In many larger stores, such as Toys "R" Us and Wal-Mart, check-out terminals or cash registers are connected to central computer systems to allow instantaneous updating of inventory and sales records.

Businesses must have a systematic method of determining optimum reorder levels if they are to avoid stockouts and not tie up too much capital in inventory. The longer a product remains in stock, the greater the probability of obsolescence, theft, or damage. Nevertheless, the costs of carrying inventory must be balanced against the probability of stockouts. The amount of inventory needed to prevent a stockout, called **safety stock,** depends on the general level of demand. The amount of safety stock is independent of the amount that should be reordered for efficient order processing and transportation.

■ **safety stock** the amount of inventory needed to prevent a stockout

When reordering merchandise, an inventory manager faces tradeoffs between the cost of carrying a larger average inventory and the cost of carrying

a smaller one. A larger inventory ensures product availability and lowers order processing costs because orders are placed less frequently. A smaller inventory, on the other hand, lowers the overall cost of carrying inventory but raises order processing costs because reorders are more frequent.

To weigh the cost of carrying a larger average inventory (with infrequent orders) against the cost of processing many small orders, a model has been developed for the **economic order quantity (EOQ)**—the order size that minimizes the total cost of ordering and carrying inventory. The EOQ formula for the optimal order quantity is

$$EOQ = \sqrt{2DR/I}$$

where EOQ = optimum average order size (units)
D = total demand (units)
R = cost of processing an order
I = cost of maintaining one unit of inventory per year.[36]

For example, suppose the total demand for a manufacturer's refrigerators is 900 units a year, the cost of processing an order is $10, and the cost of maintaining a refrigerator in inventory is $20 a year. The optimum average order size is

$$\sqrt{2(900)(10)/20} = 30 \text{ units.}$$

The fundamental relationships underlying the widely used EOQ model form the basis of many inventory control systems. It is important to note, however, that the objective of minimizing total inventory cost must be balanced against maintaining the level of customer service (for example, product availability) that maximizes profits.

When establishing an inventory management and control system, it is important to try to balance all the conflicting objectives. Inventory management requires an effective communication system and a coordinated effort to ensure that the inventory control system supports the overall objectives of marketing and physical distribution. Several techniques have been used to improve inventory management and control, including just-in-time inventory and the 80/20 rule.

Just-in-time (JIT) inventory is a technique whereby the company maintains low inventory levels by ordering products more frequently and in smaller quantities, just at the time they are needed for production. Because the parts arrive just in time to be used, there should be zero parts inventory and no stock. Successful implementation of just-in-time inventory requires cooperative relationships among producers and suppliers.[37] Largely pioneered in Japan, just-in-time inventory is replacing EOQ in the United States. The results, when it is used properly, include better-quality products, quicker

■ economic order quantity (EOQ) the order size that minimizes the total cost of ordering and carrying inventory

■ just-in-time (JIT) inventory an inventory management technique whereby the company maintains low inventory levels by ordering products more frequently and in smaller quantities, just in time for production

---

[36] Frank S. McLaughlin and Robert C. Pickhardt, *Quantitative Techniques for Management Decisions* (Boston: Houghton Mifflin Company, 1978), pp. 104–119.
[37] Steve McDaniel, Joseph G. Ormsby, and Alicia B. Gresham, "The Effect of JIT on Distribution," *Industrial Marketing Management*, May 1992, pp. 145–149.

production time, and reduced operating costs, all of which increase competitiveness.[38]

Although just-in-time does have many benefits, it is not a cure-all. A smooth operating system is needed. Communication among managers as well as among suppliers, buyers, and their intermediaries is critical. One of the most important issues in the implementation of JIT is accurate demand forecasting. To make JIT work, a company must be able to predict needs very closely. This becomes even more important as suppliers need longer lead-times. Even if accurate predictions are possible, JIT makes little allowance for emergencies either within the company itself or with any of its suppliers. The system is only as strong as the weakest link in the supply chain. A problem with one supplier could hold up production, causing inefficiency as well as possible problems with customers waiting for products. In some cases the only way for a company to make JIT work is to have considerable clout with its suppliers and distributors.

■ **80/20 rule** a rule, based on the theory that 20 percent of a company's products account for 80 percent of its sales, that holds that fast-moving products generate a higher level of customer service than slow-moving products

The **80/20 rule** holds that fast-moving products generate a higher level of customer service than slow-moving products; it is based on the theory that 20 percent of a company's products account for 80 percent of its sales. Thus a company should keep an adequate supply of fast-moving products and a minimal supply of slower-moving products in inventory.

SUMMARY

A marketing channel, or channel of distribution, is a group of interrelated individuals or organizations that direct the flow of products to consumers. These marketing intermediaries may be classified as merchants (which assume ownership of products and resell them) or as brokers or agents (which act only as negotiators in marketing exchanges). Marketing channels are important to the success of any organization because they facilitate exchanges between buyers and sellers.

Products can be distributed directly from producer to consumer, or indirectly through one or more intermediaries. There are different marketing channels for consumer and organizational products. Consumer products may flow directly from producer to consumer or, more typically, indirectly through wholesalers, retailers, and agents or brokers. Organizational products are often distributed directly from producer to organizational buyer, but are also distributed indirectly through agents and organizational distributors. Dual distribution is the use of two or more marketing channels to distribute the same product to the same target market. Numerous alternatives are available for distributing products from a domestic producer to foreign consumers, either through existing marketing channels or through new international channels.

[38]Tom Murray, "Just-in-Time Isn't for Show—It Sells," *Sales & Marketing Management,* May 1990, pp. 62–67.

Distribution intensity is the number of marketing intermediaries at each level of the marketing channel. Intensive distribution makes products available in many outlets. Selective distribution involves fewer outlets than intensive distribution and is typically used for shopping products and durable goods. In exclusive distribution, a product is offered in only one or very few outlets.

One of the major functions performed by marketing channels is sorting, the process through which the supply of goods and services produced is matched with the assortment demanded. Sorting involves four activities: classifying heterogeneous supplies into homogeneous groups (sorting out); combining small groups of similar products into large groups of homogeneous products (accumulation); breaking down large, homogeneous stocks into smaller groups (allocation); and combining products into assortments that satisfy customer demand (assorting). Channel members also perform many other functions, including buying, carrying inventory, selling, transporting, financing, promoting, negotiating, conducting marketing research, and servicing.

Marketing channels must be coordinated for channel relationships to operate smoothly. The channel leader is responsible for coordinating efforts among channel members to reduce conflicts. Vertical integration occurs when an organization acquires control over one or more other members of its marketing channel. A vertical marketing system (VMS) is a marketing channel that is professionally managed and centrally controlled by a single marketing channel member; VMSs may be corporate, administered, or contractual. Horizontal integration occurs when a channel member purchases firms at the same level of the marketing channel or expands the number of organizations (such as retail stores) at one level.

Each marketing channel member has a position with rights, responsibilities, rewards for cooperation, and penalties for nonconformity. Channel cooperation occurs when channel members work together for the mutual benefit of all. When one member does not conform to its expected role, channel conflict results. Channel power is the ability of one channel member to influence another member's marketing decisions and goal achievement. Channel members must work together to improve cooperation and reduce conflict to experience long-term satisfying relationships.

Physical distribution includes the activities involved in managing the flow of products from manufacturers to consumers and end users. A well-designed physical distribution system is important because it can decrease the total cost of distribution. However, cost tradeoffs must be made to ensure customer satisfaction and efficient use of resources.

Physical distribution activities include developing customer service standards, selecting transportation modes, designing and operating warehouse facilities, order processing, materials handling, and inventory management and control.

To satisfy consumers' needs, an organization must develop customer service standards, which are specific and measurable goals appropriate to physical distribution. Service is critical in attracting and maintaining satisfied customers before, during, and after exchanges.

Selection of an appropriate mode of transportation is an important decision because it makes products available to consumers when and where they want to purchase them. The five major modes of transportation are railways, pipelines, motor vehicles, inland waterways, and airways. The selection of a transportation mode is based on cost, transit time, reliability, capability, accessibility, security, and traceability. Intermodal transportation combines two or more modes of transportation to exploit the benefits the different carriers offer. Freight forwarders are transportation companies that consolidate shipments from several organizations into efficient lot sizes.

Warehousing is the design and operation of storage facilities. Warehouses are used by organizations for the storage of products until they are needed by channel members. Warehouses also perform other functions, such as sorting, marking, and assembling goods for shipment. A warehouse owned and operated by a company for the purpose of distributing its own products is a private warehouse. A distribution center is a large, centralized warehouse designed to facilitate the movement of goods in and out of storage as fast as possible. Public warehouses provide storage, related facilities, and sometimes services to organizations on a rental basis. Although the variable cost per unit is greater for a public warehouse than for a private one, a combination of private and public warehousing can provide flexibility in warehousing.

Order processing involves the receipt and transmission of sales order information. The major stages in order processing include order entry, handling, and delivery. Order processing can be performed either manually or electronically.

Materials handling, the physical handling of products, is important both in efficient warehouse operations and in the transportation of products from the manufacturer to distributors and ultimate consumers. Packaging, loading, and movement systems must be coordinated to minimize costs and maximize customer satisfaction. Basic materials handling techniques include unit loading and containerization.

Inventory management and control are physical distribution activities that help marketers develop and maintain adequate assortments of products to satisfy target markets and meet customers' needs. Organizations need to determine efficient reorder points to minimize the possibility of stockouts (product shortages) and to prevent too much capital from being tied up in inventory. The economic order quantity (EOQ) is the optimum order size that minimizes the total cost of ordering and carrying inventory. Several techniques have been used to improve inventory management and control, including just-in-time inventory and the 80/20 rule.

KEY TERMS

marketing channel (or channel
  of distribution)
marketing intermediary
dual distribution

distribution intensity
intensive distribution
selective distribution
exclusive distribution

sorting	private warehouse
channel leader	distribution center
vertical integration	public warehouse
vertical marketing system (VMS)	bonded storage
corporate VMS	order processing
administered VMS	materials handling
contractual VMS	unit loading
horizontal integration	containerization
channel cooperation	inventory management and control
channel conflict	stockout
channel power	safety stock
physical distribution	economic order quantity (EOQ)
customer service standard	just-in-time (JIT) inventory
intermodal transportation	80/20 rule
freight forwarder	
warehousing	

QUESTIONS FOR DISCUSSION AND REVIEW

1. Define *marketing channel* and *marketing intermediary*. What is the fundamental difference between merchants and agents or brokers?

2. What factors should be considered when deciding how much to rely on intermediaries to distribute a product?

3. Describe the four types of marketing channels for consumer products. Give examples of products that are distributed through each of these different channels.

4. How do marketing channels for organizational products generally differ from marketing channels for consumer products?

5. Under what circumstances would a firm select a dual channel?

6. Discuss the different alternatives available to a firm selecting an international channel of distribution.

7. What is meant by *distribution intensity*? What are the various levels of distribution intensity?

8. Describe the functions of marketing intermediaries. Why are these functions necessary?

9. Discuss the three different types of vertical marketing systems.

10. Why is cooperation among channel members important? How can cooperation among channel members be improved?

11. What is physical distribution? What is the major objective of physical distribution?

12. What is a customer service standard? Why is it important?

13. What are some advantages and disadvantages of the five major transportation modes?

14. What are the advantages and disadvantages of private and public warehouses?

15. Why is efficient order processing critical? What steps can be taken to make sure that orders are processed smoothly?

16. How can efficient materials handling facilitate warehouse operations and transportation?

17. What factors should be considered when designing an inventory management and control system?

18. What techniques can be used by marketing managers to improve inventory control?

CASES

15.1 COMPAQ FIGHTS BACK

Compaq Computer Corporation, created in 1982, designs, manufactures, and markets its own line of computers for home and professional use. Even though it is relatively new to the personal computer (PC) market, Compaq is the largest manufacturer of IBM compatibles and thus is a major competitor of IBM, one of the market leaders. Compaq's sales doubled from 1986 to 1987, and net income tripled in 1988. This growth allowed the company to exceed $1 billion in annual sales in only five years, making it among the fastest-growing companies in history.

Part of Compaq's success can be traced to a very effective distribution network. One of its largest distributors was Businessland, Inc., the nation's largest computer retailer. Businessland accounted for 7 percent of Compaq's revenue; Compaq products made up 15 percent of Businessland's sales. Thus it came as a surprise to the industry when Compaq announced in April 1989 that it would no longer distribute through Businessland. In response to the decision, Businessland stock dropped almost 10 percent. Shortly after the announcement, industry analysts harshly criticized Compaq for the decision, saying that the break was the worst thing to happen to Compaq in a long time.

Maybe it was. In October 1991, CEO and cofounder Rod Canion announced the company's first-ever quarterly loss and the layoff of 1,700 employees, or 14 percent of the work force. Compaq had never before laid off an employee. Most industry observers attributed Compaq's problems to price, not distribution. Because of intense price wars, the firm's market share, revenues, and earnings had fallen faster than competitors'. Although Canion blamed Compaq's problems on the recession and hoped to ride it out, the chairman of the board, Benjamin Rosen, believed the company to be in "a crisis, almost a life-or-death situation." Canion was removed from his position.

Eckhard Pfeiffer, named CEO to replace Canion, restored the company to its lofty position nearly as quickly as it had fallen. In June 1992, Compaq announced an expanded line of PCs, including forty-five newer models, bringing to seventy-six the total number of models. The firm's across-the-board price cuts of up to 32 percent rocked the industry. The price of Compaq's high-quality machines was much closer to that of inferior clones. Third-quarter sales jumped 50 percent, to $1.1 billion, and earnings quadrupled to $72 million. The lower prices reduced gross profit margin 6 points, to 28 percent, but Compaq made up for the lower margins with volume. Compaq's share of the U.S. PC market was back to 5.1 percent in 1992 and was expected to reach 6.5 percent in 1993.

With new products and increased sales, Compaq is exploring new distribution alternatives. The firm more than doubled its worldwide outlets, to more than nine thousand, adding office supply discounters like Office Depot and Circuit City as well as computer stores. Plans are also under way to begin selling certain products through mail-order companies. Compaq is trying to gain market share in Japan, where it has about forty distributors, and has begun selling a machine with a Japanese-language operating system. In December 1992, Compaq also announced that it would begin selling some PCs by mail. Direct selling accounts for about 20 percent of U.S. PC sales. Rather than establish an internal operation, the computer maker will sell through five separate mail-order companies. Compaq is being careful not to cut out existing channels or create demand it cannot satisfy.

Although it is too soon to evaluate Compaq's new strategy, experts agree that the PC industry has changed forever. Products are expected to get better and cheaper and new products are expected to be introduced rapidly. Every distribution channel possible will be employed. Compaq and its competitors face a challenge. Said Compaq CEO Rosen, "We accept the challenge. There will never be a time when we can relax. We relaxed once, and don't ever want to go through that again. Prosperity is very dangerous."

Questions for Discussion

1. What makes distribution such a key component of Compaq's marketing mix?

2. Based on the available information, what are the possible reasons for Compaq's fall?

3. How do you evaluate Compaq's strategy to reduce prices and expand the distribution network, including mail-order sales? Are there any risks to these strategies?

Based on information from Peter Burrows, "Compaq: Turning the Tables on Dell?" *Business Week,* March 27, 1993, p. 87; Kyle Pope, "Compaq Is Hoping to Get Bigger by Thinking Smaller," *Wall Street Journal,* January 7, 1993, p. B4; David Kirkpatrick, "The Revolution at Compaq Computer," *Fortune,* December 14, 1992, pp. 80–88; Catherine Arnst, Stephanie Anderson Forest, Kathy Rebello, and Jonathon Levine, "Compaq: How It Made Its Impressive Move out of the Doldrums," *Business Week,* November 2, 1992, pp. 146–151; Michael Allen, "Compaq Plans to Begin Selling Some PCs by Mail," *Wall Street Journal,* December 9, 1992, p. B4; and James P. Miller and Karen Blumenthal, "Compaq Computer Drops Businessland as Distributor," *Wall Street Journal,* February 22, 1989, p. B1.

15.2   LUXOTTICA GROWS THROUGH VERTICAL INTEGRATION

Luxottica Group Spa of Italy is the world's largest maker and distributor of eyeglass frames. It has 28,000 customers, mostly small optical shops, and sells more than nine million pairs of frames a year, with nearly half bought by American consumers.

Luxottica emphasizes middle- and upper-end frames costing $70 or more and controls such expensive designer eyewear labels as Giorgio Armani, Yves St. Laurent, and Byblos. Fashion frames, costing $170 and up, represent 38 percent of Luxottica's sales—up from zero in 1987.

In the United States, Luxottica sells its frames through national eyewear chains such as LensCrafters and Pearle Vision Centers and also through opticians. The company's nondesigner frames, available in hundreds of styles and retailing for $40 to $120 a pair, are sold through Wal-Mart in the eyeglass centers it has set up in many stores. The lower-priced frames make up about 70 percent of Luxottica's revenues.

Italy's largest manufacturer, marketer, and distributor of eyeglass frames had simple beginnings. The firm is headquartered in Agordo, a small town in the Dolomite Alps of northern Italy. Founder and chairman Leonardo Del Vecchio, now Italy's top income earner, was sent at age 7 to an orphanage by his widowed mother, who could not support her five children during World War II. He worked his way through design school as an apprentice in a factory that made tooling and molds for such products as automobile logos, jewelry, and eyeglass frames. In 1958 at age 23, Del Vecchio used his savings to open a shop in Milan to make molds for plastic frames and bridges and other metal parts. In 1961, with the financial backing of two major customers, he moved his shop to Agordo and started Luxottica. In 1969 Del Vecchio began making eyeglass frames under his own brand name and a year later bought out his partners. A skilled craftsman, he realized that vertical integration in his industry could bring considerable profit. He says, "For ten years I sold parts. One day I say, 'I'm stupid. I'm sending parts to manufacturers. Why don't I industrialize this?'"

Del Vecchio therefore set to work eliminating intermediaries in production. Now besides making its frames, Luxottica designs its own machinery and makes its own tools, which gives it a three- to six-month lead-time over competitors. The company spends between $10 and $15 million a year on new machinery and another $3.5 million a year on research and development in such fields as plastics compounding and basic chemistry. Computers speed the design and manufacture of frames and help the company take designs from concept to market in sixty days. To take advantage of new trends in a fashion industry, Luxottica designers add more than a hundred new frame styles each year. The company's offerings of plastic and metal frames include about seven hundred styles.

Luxottica's integrated manufacturing lowered costs and increased quality. But it was Luxottica's distributors who greatly benefited from the manufacturer's increased efficiency because they controlled pricing to retailers. In response, Del Vecchio began buying out distributors.

Luxottica owns distributors in Germany and Canada and has a stake in all of its international distributors. To keep his company growing, Del Vecchio formed a joint venture with Japanese eyewear maker Charmant to distribute frames in Japan. Unlike most of its competitors, Luxottica owns its U.S. distribution company. This strong distribution system enables the Italian manufacturer to provide excellent service to all customers, not only the large optical chains but also opticians. Luxottica fills orders overnight, and in some cases within two hours. Delivery time, formerly days or weeks, was reduced after the company reorganized its U.S. sales staff and started equipping retail customers with computer software that checks Luxottica stock and places orders. Service has helped build strong loyalty among opticians, who rarely carry much inventory, and a good reputation among large customers. In annual vendor evaluations, LensCrafters has given Luxottica the highest overall rating among frame suppliers.

Luxottica's competitive edges have meant phenomenal growth and profitability in recent years. U.S. sales grew from $28 million to $143 million in the decade between 1982 and 1992. It is considered one of the better-performing growth stocks on the New York Stock Exchange. The company's profit margin is 13 percent on a worldwide net revenue of $44 million. To illustrate just how good that figure is, rival Safilo Group, which markets the Ralph Lauren Polo eyewear line, earns 8 percent on revenues of $197 million. In 1991, which Del Vecchio called "the worst year for our company," Luxottica increased sales and earnings about 20 percent.

Questions for Discussion

1. What gives Luxottica such a competitive edge over rivals?
2. Which marketing channel is used to distribute Luxottica frames to consumers?
3. Describe the distribution intensity of Luxottica products.
4. Would Luxottica's vertical integration give it an advantage or disadvantage in managing channel relationships? Why?

Based on information from Bill Saporito, "Cutting Out the Middleman," *Fortune,* April 6, 1992, p. 96; Katherine Weisman, "Piccolissima Cosa No More," *Forbes,* April 29, 1991, pp. 70, 72; Gene Marcial, "Italian Eyeglasses the U.S. Loves," *Business Week,* May 12, 1991, p. 91; and Stephen Kindel, "Frame Up," *Financial World,* January 2, 1991, pp. 58–59.

Wholesaling

OBJECTIVES

- *To explain the meaning and importance of wholesaling.*

- *To discuss the functions performed by wholesalers.*

- *To compare the different types of wholesalers.*

- *To determine the structure and functions of wholesaling in foreign countries.*

- *To identify organizations that facilitate wholesaling.*

- *To describe some current trends in wholesaling.*

OUTLINE

Functions of Wholesalers
  Serving Suppliers
  Serving Customers

Types of Wholesalers
  Merchant Wholesalers
  Brokers and Agents
  Manufacturers' Wholesalers

Wholesaling in Foreign Countries

Facilitating Organizations

Trends in Wholesaling

Asta Baskauskas and Margaret Kyle Petraits started their wholesaling company, Konceptual Design, in 1984 with less than $2,000 and little knowledge of wholesaling. Within six years they built their firm into a $1 million business that distributes top-of-the-line door hardware to designers, architects, and manufacturers.

Baskauskas was a former dental student, Petraits an interior designer. They faced many challenges in the traditionally male-dominated business of wholesaling, where distributorships often are handed down from father to son. Generally, wholesalers have little control over the quality, volume, and design of the products they represent. They must work out complex legal issues with manufacturers about how many wholesalers handle the products, how much of the product wholesalers must sell, when products will be delivered, and whether contracts will be renewed.

Baskauskas and Petraits took some wise first steps toward success. They chose the right product: high-quality doorknobs, latches, cabinet handles, and door plates made from brass, bronze, or even 24-carat gold plate. They initially chose as the manufacturer Vervloet-Faes, a Belgian, family-run company in business since 1905 that was looking for a U.S. distributor. Baldwin, a leading U.S. hardware manufacturer, was added in 1986.

Konceptual Design now represents about forty manufacturers, all carefully chosen. Baskauskas and Petraits did their homework to determine how each company has treated other wholesalers, what kind of advertising support it provides, and what its sales history has been—all valuable information for wholesalers.

Since service is often considered the core of distribution, Baskauskas and Petraits focus on providing customer service. Because Konceptual Design deals in expensive, high-quality items, customer expectations are high. The two owners advise architects and interior designers on which of the 45,000 different items will best suit their clients. They also handle special orders. Once they arranged for Vervloet-Faes to custom-make door handles for an air terminal for King Fahd of Saudi Arabia; Konceptual Design received a $100,000 order for 790 handles with the royal seal (two crossed swords and a palm tree). Baskauskas and Petraits work to ensure that their service to customers is not hampered by problems in the distribution channel. When the importer for one manufacturer failed to deliver orders on time or even return calls, they persuaded the manufacturer to find another importer.

As wholesalers, the two partners recognize that they are vulnerable because manufacturers can replace them. While building their business, they have tried to build in control by gaining exclusive distribution rights to product lines and by adding new lines. They entered an agreement with Vervloet-Faes to be its sole American distributor, which enhanced their influence with the Belgian manufacturer and allowed them to sign up other wholesalers—thus increasing sales and earnings. But even with this contract, Konceptual Design found that the Belgian manufacturer sold directly to customers and end-users in their territory. Enforcement of exclusive contracts, according to Baskauskas, is often impossible.

As Konceptual Design enters its second decade of business, it has established its own custom hardware manufacturing facility to maximize and control quality, volume, design, and service. Supplier relationships will continue to be maintained with manufacturers of component parts and accessories. This decision required a significant financial commitment, but Konceptual Design hopes to succeed both as a manufacturer and distributor.[1] ●

Wholesaling includes all the marketing activities of channel members that sell products to retailers and other organizational customers but not to ultimate consumers.[2] Basically, wholesalers purchase products and sell them directly to organizational customers, such as governments, restaurants, hospitals, supermarkets, and appliance stores, as well as to other wholesalers acting as intermediaries in the buying or selling of products.

■ **wholesaling** all the marketing activities of channel members that sell products to retailers and other organizational customers but not to ultimate consumers

Wholesaling is a major segment of the economy. Nearly 470,000 wholesaling establishments conduct business in the United States, with annual sales totaling over $2.5 trillion.[3] About 5,581,000 people are employed in wholesaling.[4]

FUNCTIONS OF WHOLESALERS

Wholesalers like Hercules Chemical Co., Inc., American Hospital Supply Co., and Malone & Hyde, Inc. (grocery products) perform many marketing functions—such as storage, transportation, and promotion—that are necessary to facilitate exchanges. Table 16.1 describes some of the major functions

[1] Based on information from correspondence with Asta Baskauskas, President, Konceptual Design Associates, Inc., April 27, 1993; "Architectural Digest Point of View: The Freedom to Create," *Architectural Digest,* November 1992; and David E. Gumpert, "They Can Get It for You Wholesale," *Working Woman,* August 1990, pp. 33–36, 97.
[2] Louis W. Stern and Adel I. El-Ansary, *Marketing Channels,* 3rd ed. (Englewood Cliffs, N.J.: Prentice-Hall, 1988), p. 101.
[3] *Statistical Abstract of the United States,* 1992, p. 771.
[4] *Statistical Abstract of the United States,* 1992, p. 771.

TABLE 16.1
Wholesaling Functions

Function	Description
Providing information and merchandising assistance	Supplying information about markets and products, and providing advisory services to assist customers in their sales efforts
Ordering	Anticipating customer needs and providing an assortment of required products
Negotiation	Serving as the purchasing agent for customers by negotiating supplies
Risk taking	Taking possession of products that can deteriorate and assuming responsibility for product performance
Promotion	Providing a sales force, advertising, sales promotion, and publicity
Handling and storage	Receiving, storing, stock keeping, order processing, packaging, shipping outgoing orders, and materials handling
Transportation	Arranging local and long-distance shipments
Ownership	Taking title to products and absorbing inventory-carrying costs
Financing and budgeting	Extending credit, borrowing, making capital investments, and forecasting cash flow
Protection and security	Safeguarding merchandise

of wholesalers. By performing these functions, wholesalers bridge the gap between production and consumption.[5] If a wholesaler does not perform these distribution functions, the manufacturer or another member of the marketing channel must; the functions have to be performed by someone. Topps Co., manufacturer of sports cards, has seen its accounts receivables rise steadily. The card-publishing business is risky because any sales to wholesalers can be returned to the manufacturer. Topps has to assume the risk while wholesalers wait to see how the cards sell before paying for them.[6]

Wholesalers perform marketing functions for organizations above and below them in the marketing channel. Above wholesalers in the channel are suppliers or producers, such as manufacturers; below wholesalers are retailers and consumers. For instance, wholesalers provide products to resellers below them in the marketing channel (see Figure 16.1).

---

[5] Stern and El-Ansary, p. 102.
[6] Roula Khalaf, "Card Glut," *Forbes,* December 21, 1992, p. 89.

FIGURE 16.1
Functions of Wholesalers
Wholesalers perform many different functions necessary to facilitate exchanges. One of the functions of food wholesalers is to provide fresh produce to supermarkets, which in turn sell to customers.

Source: Riser Foods Inc.

Serving Suppliers

Wholesalers function as an extension of a manufacturer's sales force by selling its products to retailers or other wholesalers. For instance, McKesson Corporation sells the pharmaceutical products of various producers to retailers. In addition, wholesalers may provide financial assistance. They may pay the costs of transporting goods, reduce a producer's inventory carrying costs by warehousing goods, and assume the losses from product deterioration or out-of-date merchandise and from buyers that turn out to be poor credit risks.

Wholesalers also provide other valuable services to suppliers. By anticipating customer needs and accumulating an assortment of required products, wholesalers allow suppliers to concentrate on product development. Wholesalers have an important resource needed by producers and retailers—the knowledge and understanding of particular markets. They make information available to suppliers about markets and products, and communicate supplier-sponsored promotional plans to other channel members. Tom Weisenbach, head of Mead Merchant's Michigan distribution operations, summed up the wholesaler's value to suppliers in this way: "We supply what the manufacturer often cannot. It may be quick local delivery. It may be credit. And it's almost always expertise on local markets they want to serve."[7]

[7]The Mead Corporation and Consolidated Subsidiaries, 1986 Annual Report, p. 5.

Although producers prefer more direct contact with retailers, it is simply not feasible in many situations. Wholesalers are located closer to retailers in the channel, a position which gives them a strategic advantage. Additionally, the cost of a single producer distributing its product directly to a large number of retailers would, in many instances, be prohibitive. Wholesalers, on the other hand, can spread their costs over many different products, and generally deal with fewer retailers. Therefore, producers often focus on the more easily controllable variables of the marketing mix—product, promotion, and price—and leave distribution to wholesalers, who can be more efficient and effective in implementing distribution.

Serving Customers

Wholesalers also provide many services for their customers, generally retailers or other wholesalers. Wholesalers specialize in understanding market conditions and in negotiating final purchases. They can therefore assist their retailer customers in the selection of inventory and spare them the task of finding and coordinating supply sources. Moreover, when a wholesaler handles purchases for several different retailer customers, the expenses can be shared by all the retailers. In addition, wholesalers generally offer retailers a wider range of products than manufacturers' salespeople can offer.

Because they buy in large quantities and deliver to customers in smaller quantities, wholesalers can perform physical distribution activities more efficiently than a producer or retailer. For instance, wholesalers can provide prompt and frequent delivery even when demand fluctuates. Their resources and capabilities allow them to provide the fastest delivery at the lowest cost. Furthermore, wholesalers make products available to customers at convenient locations when desired, which lets the wholesalers' suppliers and customers avoid risks associated with holding large product inventories.

TYPES OF WHOLESALERS

To meet the diverse needs of producers and retailers, many types of wholesalers have evolved. In addition, new types of institutions are constantly developing in response to producers and retail organizations that want to assume wholesaling functions. The specific classifications of wholesalers are not static; they shift as the distribution activities they perform change to meet the needs of a dynamic marketplace.

There are essentially three broad types of wholesaling institutions, based on the activities they perform: (1) merchant wholesalers, (2) brokers and agents, and (3) manufacturers' wholesalers. Figure 16.2 illustrates the various types of wholesalers discussed in the following sections, and Table 16.2 describes the functions of each.

■ **merchant wholesaler** a marketing intermediary that assumes both possession and ownership of goods as well as the risks associated with ownership

Merchant Wholesalers

A **merchant wholesaler** assumes both possession and ownership of goods as well as the risks associated with ownership. Generally, a merchant whole-

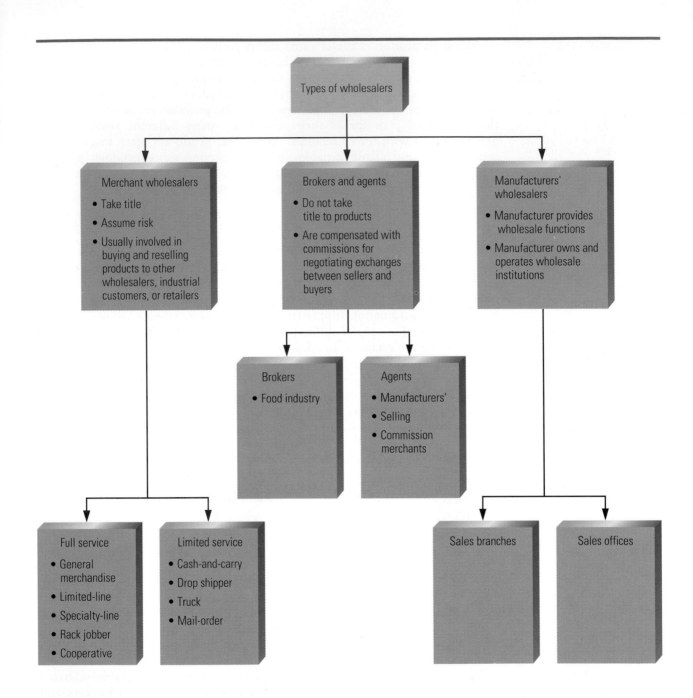

FIGURE 16.2
Types of Wholesalers

saler is involved in buying and reselling products to organizational or retail customers. The majority of wholesalers—nearly 391,000—fall into this category and account for 58 percent of the total sales volume of wholesalers.[8] As shown in Figure 16.2, there are two different types of merchant wholesalers, full-service and limited-service.

[8] *Census of Wholesale Trade*, 1987, pp. 1–3.

■ **full-service merchant wholesaler** a marketing intermediary that provides most services that wholesalers can perform

■ **general merchandise wholesaler** a full-service merchant wholesaler that carries a wide product mix

■ **limited-line wholesaler** a full-service merchant wholesaler that carries a narrow product mix of a few product lines

■ **specialty-line wholesaler** a full-service merchant wholesaler that carries a very limited variety of products

■ **rack jobber** a full-service merchant wholesaler that supplies display units and products, and performs purchasing and stocking functions for retailers

■ **cooperative** a full-service wholesaler that is owned and operated by the members

■ **limited-service merchant wholesaler** a marketing intermediary that assumes ownership of goods but specializes in only a few of the functions performed by wholesalers

■ **cash-and-carry wholesaler** a limited-service merchant wholesaler that performs most wholesaling functions except for delivery, financing, and promotional assistance

■ **drop shipper** a limited-service merchant wholesaler that performs most wholesaling functions and takes title of goods but does not physically possess, handle, or store products, or provide promotional assistance

Full-Service Merchant Wholesalers   A **full-service merchant wholesaler** provides most services that wholesalers can perform, including delivery, warehousing, credit, promotional assistance, and taking title of merchandise. The five types of full-service merchant wholesalers are general merchandise, limited-line, specialty-line, rack jobbers, and cooperatives (see Table 16.2).

A **general merchandise wholesaler** carries a very wide product mix, including such products as drugs, hardware, nonperishable foods, cosmetics, cleaning supplies, and tobacco. These wholesalers typically serve small department stores and "mom and pop" grocery stores.

A **limited-line wholesaler** carries a narrow product mix, usually only a few product lines. For instance, a limited-line wholesaler might specialize in lighting fixtures, oil-well drilling equipment, or chemicals for a specific industry.

A **specialty-line wholesaler** carries a very limited variety of products, usually only one product line or a few items within a product line. An example is a wholesaler which carries only expensive antique furniture. The customers of such specialty-line wholesalers are purchasing products for ultimate buyers that have specialized requirements.

A **rack jobber,** also called a service merchandiser, supplies display units as well as products, and also performs purchasing and stocking functions for retailers. A rack jobber sells on consignment—that is, the retailer does not have to pay for the merchandise until it is sold. Rack jobbers often specialize in magazines, housewares, hardware, pet products, nonprescription drugs, or cosmetics.

A **cooperative** is a full-service wholesaler that is owned and operated by the members (see Figure 16.3). Co-ops are especially popular in the agricultural industry, where they are established by farmers to buy fertilizer in large quantities and to get better prices for their harvest than they could by selling individually. The profits obtained by the co-op are divided among the members.

Limited-Service Merchant Wholesalers   A **limited-service merchant wholesaler** assumes ownership of goods but specializes in only a few of the functions performed by wholesalers. Table 16.2 summarizes the different services offered by limited-service wholesalers. Common limited-service wholesalers include cash-and-carry wholesalers, drop shippers, truck wholesalers, and mail-order wholesalers.

A **cash-and-carry wholesaler** performs most wholesaling functions except for delivery, financing, and promotional assistance. These wholesalers expect their customers (usually small businesses) to pay cash and to furnish transportation for their goods. Cash-and-carry wholesalers typically handle a limited line of products with a high turnover rate, such as groceries, construction materials, electrical supplies, or office supplies.

A **drop shipper,** sometimes called a desk jobber, performs most wholesaling functions and takes title of goods but does not physically possess, handle, or store products, or provide promotional assistance. A drop shipper takes orders from customers, purchases the desired goods from producers, and

Services provided	Merchant Wholesalers									Brokers and Agents				Manufacturers' Wholesalers	
	Full-service					Limited-service				Brokers	Agents				
	General merchandise	Limited-line	Specialty-line	Rack jobber	Cooperative	Cash-and-carry	Drop shipper	Truck	Mail-order	Food	Manufacturers'	Selling	Commission merchant	Sales branch	Sales office
Takes title of merchandise	Yes	Yes	Yes	Yes	Yes	Yes	Yes	Yes	Yes	No	No	No	No	Yes	Yes
Offers credit	Yes	Yes	Yes	Yes	Yes	No	Yes	No	Some	No	No	Yes	Some	Yes	Yes
Storage of goods	Yes	Yes	Yes	Yes	Yes	Yes	No	Yes	Yes	Some	Some	Yes	Yes	Yes	No
Delivery of goods	Yes	Yes	Yes	Yes	Yes	No	Yes	Yes	Yes	Some	Some	Yes	Yes	Yes	Yes
Long-term relationships with customers	Yes	Yes	Yes	Yes	Yes	Some	Some	Some	Some	Some	Yes	Yes	Yes	Yes	Yes
Assistance with promotion	Yes	Yes	Yes	Yes	Yes	No	No	Yes	No	Yes	Yes	Yes	No	Yes	Yes
Limited geographic territory	No	No	No	No	No	No	No	No	No	No	Yes	No	No	No	No

TABLE 16.2
Services Provided by Wholesalers

■ **truck wholesaler** a limited-service merchant wholesaler that delivers products directly to customers for on-the-spot inspection and selection but offers only limited services and requires cash purchases

■ **mail-order wholesaler** a limited-service merchant wholesaler that sells products to retail and organizational customers through a catalogue instead of a personal sales force

arranges for shipment of the goods to the customers. Thus drop shippers are primarily concerned with expediting exchanges through selling activities. They are most commonly used in transactions involving large-volume purchases that do not need to be sorted into groups of related products, such as coal and building materials.

A **truck wholesaler** delivers products directly to customers for on-the-spot inspection and selection but offers only limited services and requires cash purchases. Truck wholesalers often have regular routes and own and drive their own trucks. They play an important role in supplying small grocery stores with snacks, perishable items such as fruits and vegetables, and tobacco products.

A **mail-order wholesaler** sells products to retail and organizational customers through a catalogue instead of a personal sales force. Wholesale mail-order houses generally offer such products as jewelry, cosmetics, specialty foods, or automobile parts; they serve remote geographic areas where small retailers find mail-order purchasing convenient and efficient.

Brokers and Agents

Brokers and agents, the second major category of wholesalers, negotiate purchases for a commission but do not purchase products outright (see Table

FIGURE 16.3
Cooperative Wholesalers
Aalsmeer International Flower Market in the Netherlands, is a cooperative wholesaler of about 5,000 growers, and serves the global market for cut flowers and plants.

Source: © Clarke Weinberg/The Image Bank.

■ **functional middleman** a marketing intermediary— a broker or agent—that negotiates purchases for a commission but does not purchase products outright

■ **broker** a functional middleman whose primary function is to bring together buyers and sellers, generally on a temporary basis

■ **food broker** a marketing intermediary that sells food and general merchandise items to other wholesalers, grocery chains, institutional buyers, and food processors

16.2). There are far fewer brokers and agents, about 42,000, than merchant wholesalers. Brokers and agents account for 11 percent of the total sales volume of wholesalers.[9] A broker or agent is often referred to as a **functional middleman,** an intermediary who performs only a limited number of marketing functions, fewer than typical merchant wholesalers perform.

Brokers The primary function of a **broker** is to bring together buyers and sellers, generally on a temporary basis. Brokers do not own or physically handle products, and they are not involved in financing; thus they take almost no risks. They exist only to negotiate exchanges between buyers and sellers. The party that engages the broker's services pays the broker a commission, or brokerage fee.

Brokers generally specialize in a certain commodity, such as real estate, insurance, or groceries. A **food broker** markets food and general merchandise items to other wholesalers, grocery chains, institutional buyers, and food processors. Food brokers represent the manufacturer on a commission basis, do not take title or physical possession of the product, and normally do not represent competing accounts. The relationship can be terminated by either party on a 30-day notice or as determined by contract. For instance, Ralston Purina Company often markets its Chicken of the Sea tuna, Chex cereals, Eveready and Energizer batteries, and some Purina pet food products to retailers through food brokers as well as through direct sales forces.

[9]*Census of Wholesale Trade,* 1987, pp. 1–3.

■ **agent** a functional middleman who represents buyers or sellers on a permanent basis

■ **manufacturers' agent** a functional middleman who represents several different manufacturers and offers noncompeting, complementary product lines to customers

■ **selling agent** an independent middleman who markets a manufacturer's entire output or all of a specified product line

■ **commission merchant** an agent who receives goods on consignment from local sellers and negotiates sales in large central markets

■ **sales branch** a manufacturer-owned intermediary that sells products and provides support services for the manufacturer's sales force

Agents   Unlike a broker, an **agent** represents buyers or sellers on a permanent basis. The major types of agents are manufacturers' agents, selling agents, and commission merchants.

A **manufacturers' agent** represents several different manufacturers and offers noncompeting, complementary product lines to customers. The relationship between the agent and manufacturers is formalized by written agreements outlining territories, prices, order handling, and terms of sale relating to delivery, service, and warranties.

Most manufacturers' agents are small businesses with only a few employees. These agents are restricted to a particular territory, and the functions they perform for manufacturers are those that the manufacturers' own sales staffs would provide. Manufacturers' agents employ professional, highly skilled salespersons to contact potential buyers. A good, strong relationship with customers is the most important benefit manufacturers' agents can offer.

A **selling agent** is an independent middleman who markets a manufacturer's entire output or all of a specified product line. A selling agent usually handles sales for several producers and has full authority in the areas of price, promotion, and distribution. A selling agent generally provides more services than any other type of agent by assuming all the functions of the sales department and, sometimes, the marketing department.

Selling agents are often employed by small businesses and manufacturers whose seasonal production or limited resources make it difficult to maintain a marketing department. These agents most often distribute canned foods, household furnishings, clothing, and textiles.

A **commission merchant** is an agent who receives goods on consignment from local sellers and negotiates sales in large central markets. The agent takes possession of truckload quantities of commodities—such as agricultural, seafood, or furniture products—and transports them to a central market for sale. A commission agent specializes in obtaining the best price under market conditions and may have broad powers regarding prices and terms of sale. The agent's key functions are arranging delivery and providing transportation. After deducting a commission plus the expense of making the sale, the agent pays the remaining profits to the shipper.

Manufacturers' Wholesalers

Manufacturers' wholesalers are similar to merchant wholesalers but are owned and operated by manufacturers. There are about 36,000 manufacturers' wholesalers, accounting for 31 percent of total wholesale sales.[10] These manufacturer-owned intermediaries are either sales branches or sales offices (see Table 16.2).

A **sales branch** sells products and provides support services for the manufacturer's sales force. It offers credit, delivers goods, and gives promotional assistance, and also has facilities for storing and selling goods. Customers include other wholesalers, retailers, and industrial buyers. For example, AM International, Inc., a leading producer of graphics equipment and supplies,

---

[10]*Census of Wholesale Trade*, 1987, pp. 1–3.

POINT/COUNTERPOINT

Should Manufacturers Set Up Sales Branches and Sales Offices?

Manufacturers' wholesalers—sales branches and sales offices—offer one alternative to using a wholesaler. They thus are a form of vertical integration. By establishing sales branches and sales offices, manufacturers are responsible for the functions merchant wholesalers typically perform, such as storage, delivery, credit, assistance with promotion, and taking title to merchandise. Can a manufacturer perform these functions more efficiently than a wholesaler?

Point Developing their own sales branches and sales offices gives manufacturers greater control over the activities wholesalers normally perform. Manufacturers' sales branches and sales offices do not eliminate such functions; they simply integrate them into the manufacturers' operations. Through vertical integration, manufacturers can perform wholesale functions more effectively and more efficiently. Such vertical integration of wholesaling functions is becoming increasingly popular, especially among large manufacturers and retail firms.

Also wholesalers traditionally have not been aggressive marketers. Many are more concerned with storage, credit, and collection than with marketing strategy. Because of this emphasis, many wholesalers do not do a good job of marketing a manufacturer's products. Manufacturers' sales branches and sales offices enable manufacturers to assume some of the marketing activities and do a more aggressive job of marketing their products.

Counterpoint Establishing manufacturers' sales branches and sales offices is not always more efficient than dealing with a wholesaler. Although vertical integration may sound like a good idea, manufacturers may find it difficult to take on the functions of a wholesaler. Through division of labor, the manufacturer can specialize in production. Many manufacturers have attempted to take on wholesaling activities, only to see product quality fall. The wholesaler can be a channel partner and specialize in a number of distribution activities.

Wholesalers often are able to fill orders more quickly than are manufacturers. Since they are closer to local markets, wholesalers can identify users and their needs. Also, because a wholesaler represents several producers, it often can cover a territory at a lower cost than can a manufacturer's own sales force. Finally, the cost of establishing and maintaining sales branches and sales offices often discourages manufacturers from operating them.

■ **sales office** a manufacturer-owned intermediary that operates much like an agent

has sales branches in major cities around the world to handle the sales and service of its products.

A **sales office** operates much like an agent, but is owned by the manufacturer. Unlike a sales branch, a sales office does not carry inventory. In addition to selling the manufacturer's products, it may sell other products that complement the manufacturer's product line.

One of the major questions facing the manufacturer today is whether vertical integration—establishing its own sales offices, sales branches, and warehouse facilities—is more efficient than dealing with a wholesaler. Point/Counterpoint explores this issue.

TABLE 16.3
The Number of
Wholesalers in Selected
Countries

	Number of Wholesalers	Retailers per Wholesaler
Belgium	60,589	2.2
Brazil	46,000	19.3
Chile	561	2.0
Dominican Republic	589	19.0
El Salvador	396	3.6
Hungary	220	259.3
Kenya	2,277	1.8
Kuwait	2,819	4.9
Portugal	4,522	1.1
U.K.	108,392	2.1
Singapore	20,103	.8
Yugoslavia	1,413	58.4

Source: Statistical Yearbook 1985/86. Table 138, pp. 656–679. Copyright, United Nations 1988. Reproduced by permission. Retailers per wholesaler was calculated by dividing the number of retailers by the number of wholesalers for the same year.

WHOLESALING IN FOREIGN COUNTRIES

As we mention in Chapter 15, a variety of different channels can be used to distribute products from domestic to foreign markets. In each foreign country, there is a series of possible channel members that may be used to move products to foreign consumers; in some cases, a wholesale intermediary is part of this channel. Foreign merchant wholesalers will take title to products, whereas foreign agents will not. In many instances, wholesalers in foreign countries have exclusive distribution rights for a specific geographic area.[11]

The structure of wholesaling differs considerably from country to country. Table 16.3 shows the number of wholesalers and retailers in several countries. The number of wholesalers ranges from 220 in Hungary to more than 100,000 in the United Kingdom. The number of wholesalers is about the same in Chile and the Dominican Republic. But in Chile, a wholesaler will serve about two retailers, whereas a wholesaler in the Dominican Republic serves roughly nineteen retailers.

The functions performed by wholesalers also vary across countries. In some of the developing nations, wholesalers have very small operations. They carry a narrow product assortment, provide limited service and market coverage, and may demand credit. In some countries, wholesalers simply provide a warehouse function, taking orders from retailers and shipping desired quantities. In other countries, such as Japan, wholesalers share risk by performing other functions, such as financing, product development, and selling.

[11]Jean-Pierre Jeannet and Hubert D. Hennessey, *Global Marketing Strategies* (Boston: Houghton Mifflin Company, 1992), p. 389.

There has been a global trend toward vertical integration from the wholesale level back to manufacturing.[12] This means that large wholesalers are handling their own custom-made products. This is a major concern for many domestic firms who depend on foreign wholesalers to distribute their products. In some cases, marketers actually find the foreign markets blocked by large wholesalers. For instance, non-Indian firms find it difficult to distribute products to India because large wholesalers control many markets.

FACILITATING ORGANIZATIONS

- **facilitating organization** an organization that assists in the operation of the marketing channel but does not perform the negotiating function or sell products

In addition to the many types of wholesalers, other organizations also perform activities that facilitate channel functions. A **facilitating organization** assists in the operation of the channel but, unlike other types of channel members, does not perform the negotiating functions or sell products.[13] In some cases, a facilitating organization eliminates the need for a producer to use a wholesaling establishment. However, any of the functions that facilitating organizations perform can be assumed by other members of the channel (wholesalers, retailers, or producers).

Wholesalers and other channel members rely on facilitating organizations because these businesses "outside" the channel may perform various activities more efficiently and more effectively than channel members. Firms like Norfolk Southern, shown in Figure 16.4, perform essential services that add value and offer benefits that buyers want. Among the organizations that facilitate wholesaling functions are public warehouses, finance companies, transportation companies, and trade shows and trade marts.

As we describe in Chapter 15, a public warehouse is a storage facility operated on a rental basis. A manufacturer may decide to rent space in a warehouse instead of constructing its own facilities or utilizing the storage services of a merchant wholesaler. Public warehouses may also place orders, deliver products, collect accounts, and maintain display rooms where potential buyers can inspect products.

- **finance company** a company that loans marketing intermediaries (wholesalers or retailers) the money to pay for merchandise; the finance company owns the merchandise even though the intermediaries retain physical possession of it

Even though wholesalers or retailers retain physical possession of merchandise, it is sometimes owned by a **finance company** (or bank) that has loaned the intermediary the money to pay for the merchandise. Finance companies are often employed by automobile dealers; this practice is called *floor planning*. Floor planning allows dealers to maintain a large inventory of automobiles; when a vehicle is sold, the dealer may have to pay off the loan immediately.

- **transportation company** a rail, truck, air, or other carrier that helps manufacturers and retailers transport products without the aid of intermediaries

A **transportation company** (a rail, truck, air, or other carrier) helps manufacturers and retailers transport products without the aid of intermediaries. For example, J.B. Hunt Transport Services, a large trucking company, has developed agreements with several major railroad companies, including Santa Fe, Conrail, and Union Pacific. Through intermodal shipping, Hunt

---

[12] Philip R. Cateora, *International Marketing* (Homewood, Ill.: Irwin, 1990), p. 585.
[13] Bert Rosenbloom, *Marketing Channels: A Management View* (Hinsdale, Ill.: Dryden Press, 1987), p. 61.

FIGURE 16.4
Facilitating Organizations
Norfolk Southern is a facilitating organization that provides a variety of transportation modes.

Source: Courtesy Norfolk Southern Corporation. Created by J. Walter Thompson, USA.

is able to offer customers savings and rates that are fairly stable for several years. The company has also developed a new container that snaps onto the base of a Hunt truck, stacks on a railroad car, and carries 1,000 pounds more than ordinary containers.[14] Marketing Close-up shows how Norfolk Southern has succeeded by performing transportation services that offer value to customers.

Trade shows and trade marts assist in the selling and buying functions by allowing manufacturers or resellers to exhibit products to potential buyers. A **trade show** is a temporary exhibit typically held annually in a major city; it allows vendors to identify prospective customers and may thus eliminate the need for agents.[15] For instance, the Houston International Boat Show, a weeklong trade show held in January every year, provides a showcase for thousands of retailers, wholesalers, and manufacturers of boats and boating equipment, scuba equipment, recreational vehicles, and fishing and camping equipment. Jet Ski, Boston Whaler, Chris Craft, Evinrude, Hobie, Montgomery, Winnebago, and Coleman products are among those regularly represented at the Houston show. The advantages of trade shows include inexpensive person-to-person contact, information exchange between buyers and sellers, and a shorter sales cycle.[16] Table 16.4 lists the ten cities where trade shows are most often held.

■ **trade show** a temporary exhibit typically held annually in a major city to allow vendors to identify prospective customers

[14] Sally Solo, "Every Problem Is an Opportunity," *Fortune,* November 16, 1992, p. 93.
[15] Thomas V. Bonoma, "Get More out of Your Trade Shows," *Harvard Business Review,* January–February 1983, pp. 75–83.
[16] Edward A. Chapman, Jr., "Maximize Your Results with a Mission," *Marketing News,* August 20, 1990, p. 10.

MARKETING CLOSE-UP

Norfolk Southern Is Off and Running

For some companies, diversification is the key to survival. Not at Norfolk Southern Corp. Management at the Virginia-based railroad company believes that you should stick with the business that you know. This philosophy is paying off for Norfolk Southern. For the first nine months of 1992, earnings per share were $3.03, up 18 percent from the comparable 1991 period. Its net income was $430 million, up 12 percent, making Norfolk Southern one of the most profitable major companies in the transportation industry.

Norfolk Southern controls and owns all the common stock in two major operating railroads, Norfolk & Western RY (railway) and Southern RY Co. Between them, these railways cover more than 17,200 miles, mostly in the southeastern and midwestern U.S. and Ontario, Canada. Norfolk Southern also owns North American Van Lines, which provides moving and general freight services in the U.S. and Canada.

Although it is a very successful organization today, things haven't always gone well for Norfolk. As the company was getting its operations to run more smoothly, its coal and merchandising business slumped. In the early 1980s, Norfolk was losing much of its share of the railway market in the eastern United States. In addition to this, it failed in a $1.2 billion bid to take over Consolidated Rail Corporation (Conrail). But these setbacks did not force Norfolk Southern to cut its losses and diversify into other areas. The company worked out an agreement with Conrail and began to recapture much of the lost ground through competitive service. Eventually the coal industry made a recovery, and Norfolk was there to capture much of the market.

Today, Norfolk is working on getting more of the $100 billion intermodal traffic business—traffic that moves from road to railroad and back as easily as it moves from one railroad to another. It is developing a container called RoadRailer, a high-volume container that can operate easily on rail or on a highway. Norfolk is targeting this service at companies that use just-in-time inventory management systems.

Norfolk Southern has also made a commitment to improve quality in areas where customers have identified problems. Based on a comprehensive shipper survey that resulted in an overall satisfaction rating of just over 76 percent, Norfolk Southern started working to improve the areas where it was less than strong. The focus is on consistently meeting customer expectations and empowering employees to ensure creativity, innovation, and teamwork. Teams were established to address the following areas: customer expectations, service reliability, process re-evaluation and process engineering, elimination of billing errors, and improvement in the cost-pricing system.

Norfolk's singlemindedness makes the company profitable to do business with. A manufacturer's success can ride on whether or not it can supply undamaged goods on time. By using a facilitating company at the cutting edge of transportation development, firms can be sure they will be in on any new, cost-cutting technology that is developed. By missing such a development, a company could give a cost advantage to a competitor, an advantage that could make or break some markets.

Sources: Gus Welty, "Thoroughbred Quality: Off and Running," *Railway Age*, August 1992, pp. 83–88; "Norfolk Southern Announces Earnings," *PR Newswire*, October 28, 1992; Norfolk Southern Annual Report, 1991; and James Cook, "Tending the Base Business," *Forbes*, December 26, 1988, pp. 108–110.

TABLE 16.4
Top Ten Cities for
Trade Shows

City	Number of Major Annual Trade Shows
New York	29
Chicago	26
Dallas	19
Atlanta	18
Las Vegas	18
Anaheim	15
New Orleans	9
Los Angeles	8
Washington, D.C.	8
Louisville	6

Source: Reprinted by permission of *Sales & Marketing Management*. Copyright: Sales & Marketing Management, April 1988.

■ **trade mart** a permanent facility that firms can rent to exhibit products year-round

A **trade mart** is a permanent facility that firms can rent to exhibit products year-round. Trade marts are located in several major cities, including New York, Chicago, Atlanta, Dallas, and Los Angeles. At these marts, such products as computers and other office equipment, furniture, home decorating supplies, toys, clothing, and gift items are displayed and sold to wholesalers and retailers.

TRENDS IN WHOLESALING

The changing mix of activities performed by retailers and producers, as well as wholesalers' efforts to become more efficient, is blurring the distinction between channel members and will influence wholesaling in the future. New opportunities and hazards will result from the current trend toward larger retailers such as the Hypermarts of Wal-Mart Stores—which carry full lines of groceries, hardware, housewares, automotive parts, clothing, and appliances. The expanded product lines offered by these superstores will create new opportunities for wholesalers. A merchant grocery wholesaler, for instance, may decide to carry other low-cost, high-volume products that are sold in superstores. In France, hypermarkets that dominate the food retailing industry control the product mix, manufacturing schedules, and delivery schedules of their main suppliers.

However, some limited-function merchant wholesalers may no longer be needed. Truck wholesalers, which typically handle products purchased in limited quantities, may be eliminated as their functions are taken over by more efficient members of the marketing channel. The future of independent wholesalers, agents, and brokers depends on their ability to efficiently provide desired services for a carefully defined target market.

Some large retailers have begun to by-pass manufacturers' agents and to buy directly from producers. Lowe's Companies, Inc., the largest do-it-yourself building-supply retailer in the United States, and Builders Square, a home improvement chain, both buy directly from manufacturers. Some manufacturers claim that Wal-Mart has threatened to buy from other producers if it cannot buy directly from them. Given the tremendous marketing and financial clout of some of these large retailers, manufacturers' agents fear that direct selling may become a trend. For instance, in the U.S. hardware industry, new distributors such as Servistar are doing what three levels of wholesalers used to do, and 7-Eleven in Japan has eliminated five or six wholesale levels.[17] In the food industry, many large grocers are building their own supply networks and cutting out wholesalers like Super Foods.[18]

As competition intensifies, wholesale margins will continue to erode; profits shrunk 6 percent in 1991.[19] Wholesalers, in many cases, assume more functions from manufacturers in order to respond to increased competition.[20] In an effort to survive and prosper, wholesalers are relying on value-added services to expand margins and to strengthen relations with customers. They also are expanding aggressively into international markets; this trend is expected to continue with joint ventures and strategic alliances used to penetrate Europe and Asia.[21]

Acquisitions and mergers are also changing the shape of the wholesale industry. Wholesaling acquisitions and mergers are usually made to enter new markets or to strengthen a firm's position in existing markets.[22] This trend toward consolidation is expected to continue as firms realize these are useful growth strategies. In fact, between 1985 and 1990 the number of independent wholesalers decreased 11 percent.[23] Mergers help increase wholesalers' efficiency of operations and give them more leverage in dealing with suppliers and customers. Moreover, larger organizations can purchase sophisticated computer systems to facilitate customer orders and to coordinate inventory management and control and delivery. Consolidation is also being driven by large customers of wholesalers like Du Pont and Union Carbide who prefer to deal with a small number of large, reliable suppliers.

With a lackluster economy squeezing sales and with competition eroding margins in recent years, wholesalers have relied on technology to increase productivity and sales, or to maintain what sales they still have.[24] Most of the new technology is computer driven and includes on-line order entry systems, advanced inventory management systems, and automation of ware-

[17] Peter F. Drucker, "The Economy's Power Shift," *Wall Street Journal,* September 24, 1992, p. A16.
[18] Toddi Gutner, "Dinosaur?" *Forbes,* February 15, 1993, pp. 156–157.
[19] Joseph Weber, "It's 'Like Somebody Had Shot the Postman,'" *Business Week,* January 13, 1992, p. 82.
[20] Ronald D. Michman, "Managing Structural Change in Marketing Channels," *Journal of Consumer Marketing,* Fall 1990, pp. 33–42.
[21] Robert F. Lusch, Deborah S. Coykendall, and James M. Kenderdine, *Wholesaling in Transition: An Executive Chart Book* (Norman, Okla.: Distribution Research Program, University of Oklahoma, 1989), p. 21.
[22] Ibid., p. 20.
[23] "Mom and Pop Move out of Wholesaling," *Business Week,* January 9, 1989, p. 91.
[24] Weber, p. 82.

houses.[25] Union Pacific, a facilitating organization that provides transportation services, is the first railroad to install computer terminals in its locomotives. The efficiency and cost savings from the computer is generating new business.[26] List Hensley and Co., an Anheuser-Busch wholesaler, credits the contribution of computers for its success. Routing time for 85,000 cases has been reduced from three and a half hours to forty-five minutes.[27]

SUMMARY

Wholesaling includes all the marketing activities of channel members that sell to retailers and other organizational customers. More than 400,000 wholesaling establishments exist in the United States, with annual sales of nearly $2.5 trillion.

Wholesalers perform many services for suppliers and customers: supplying information and merchandising assistance, ordering, negotiating, taking risks, promotion, handling and storage, transportation, ownership, financing and budgeting, and protection and security. Although wholesalers can be eliminated from a marketing channel, their functions must be performed by manufacturers or other marketing channel members. Based on the functions they provide, wholesalers can be classified into three categories: merchant wholesalers, brokers and agents, and manufacturers' wholesalers.

Merchant wholesalers assume both possession and ownership of goods as well as the risks associated with ownership. Full-service merchant wholesalers provide most services that can be performed by wholesalers, including delivery, warehousing, credit, promotional assistance, and taking title of merchandise. General merchandise wholesalers, limited-line wholesalers, specialty-line wholesalers, rack jobbers, and cooperatives are full-service merchant wholesalers. Limited-service wholesalers assume ownership of goods but specialize in only a few of the services typically performed by wholesalers. Common limited-service wholesalers include cash-and-carry wholesalers, drop shippers, truck wholesalers, and mail-order wholesalers.

Brokers and agents are functional middlemen who negotiate purchases for a commission but do not purchase products outright. Brokers bring together buyers and sellers on a temporary basis. Food brokers market food and grocery products to wholesalers, retailers, and producers. Agents, representing buyers and sellers on a permanent basis, include manufacturers' agents, selling agents, and commission merchants.

---

[25] Lusch, Coykendall, and Kenderine, pp. 24–25.

[26] Daniel Machalaba, "Union Pacific's High-Tech Style Generates Business," *Wall Street Journal*, June 8, 1992, p. B5.

[27] Bob Deierlein, "Road Warriors: List Hensley and Company," *Beverage World*, November 1991, pp. 40, 42.

Manufacturers' wholesalers are similar to merchant wholesalers but are owned and operated by the manufacturer. These manufacturer-owned intermediaries include sales branches and sales offices. Sales branches may offer credit, store and deliver goods, and provide promotional assistance and other services. Sales offices, which do not carry inventory, operate much like agents.

The structure of wholesaling differs considerably from country to country. In some countries, wholesalers serve a large number of retailers. The functions performed by wholesalers also vary across countries; some perform only a limited number of functions, whereas others act as full-service merchant wholesalers. There has been a global trend toward vertical integration from the wholesale level back to the manufacturer, making it difficult for some firms to distribute their products in foreign markets.

Businesses that perform channel functions but do not sell products or negotiate exchanges are facilitating organizations. They include public warehouses, finance companies, transportation companies, and trade shows and trade marts. In some instances, these organizations eliminate the need for a wholesaling establishment.

The changing mix of activities performed by retailers and producers, as well as wholesalers' efforts to become more efficient, will influence wholesaling in the future. New opportunities should emerge for some wholesalers, and others may be eliminated. Some large retailers have begun to by-pass wholesalers and buy directly from producers. Many wholesalers will assume more functions from manufacturers to respond to this increased competition. The trend toward consolidation of wholesalers, through acquisitions and mergers, is expected to continue. Wholesalers will increasingly depend on technology to increase productivity and sales.

KEY TERMS

wholesaling
merchant wholesaler
full-service merchant
  wholesaler
general merchandise
  wholesaler
limited-line wholesaler
specialty-line wholesaler
rack jobber
cooperative
limited-service merchant
  wholesaler
cash-and-carry wholesaler
drop shipper
truck wholesaler
mail-order wholesaler

functional middleman
broker
food broker
agent
manufacturers' agent
selling agent
commission merchant
sales branch
sales office
facilitating organization
finance company
transportation company
trade show
trade mart

QUESTIONS FOR DISCUSSION AND REVIEW

1. What are some of the major functions provided by wholesalers?
2. How do wholesalers serve suppliers? Customers?
3. What is the difference between a full-service and a limited-service merchant wholesaler?
4. Why are brokers and agents sometimes called functional middlemen?
5. Under what conditions are brokers commonly employed? Agents?
6. What is a commission merchant?
7. Why are manufacturers' sales branches and sales offices classified as wholesalers?
8. How do the structure and functions of wholesaling differ from country to country?
9. Compare the different types of facilitating organizations and the functions they perform.
10. What is the difference between a trade show and a trade mart?
11. How will current trends in wholesaling influence future wholesaling activities?

C A S E S

16.1 McKESSON SERVES CUSTOMERS

McKesson Corporation is the nation's largest wholesaler of pharmaceuticals. The San Francisco–based firm is often cited for its innovative use of information technology to serve customers such as pharmacists and hospitals. But McKesson wasn't always a leader in information technology.

Until the mid-1970s, the distribution of drugs was somewhat inefficient. The nation's 30,000 independent pharmacies, 14,000 chain drug stores, and 7,600 hospitals spent hours filling out orders by hand. Then they would mail or telephone orders to wholesalers such as McKesson. This picture changed for McKesson when large drug store chains began putting many independent drug stores out of business. These small independents accounted for a large part of McKesson's sales, so the failure of smaller drug stores damaged McKesson's business. To protect itself, the wholesaler began to look for ways to help its customers succeed.

McKesson first examined the inefficient ordering system at its own warehouses. Orders were initiated when customers telephoned the warehouse. After recording an order by hand, workers in the warehouse would walk around alphabetically indexed shelves to fill the order, and eventually pack and ship it. The system was very slow, with turnaround on orders ranging from ten to fourteen days.

McKesson's solution to this problem was an order-entry system called Economost. McKesson supplied each customer store with a small data collection device powered by car batteries. Employees wheeled the devices around customers' stores in shopping carts, checking shelves for inventory and placing orders at the same time. This system cut turnaround time on orders to two or three days. Eventually, the original data collection device was replaced by a much smaller, hand-held electronic "wand" (now used in supermarkets to scan the bar codes on shelves).

Data collection through the Economost system show customers which items are moving slowly so they can replace them with better-selling ones. McKesson also relies on the system to suggest the best placement of products on pharmacy shelves. And the company is able to reduce turnaround time further by packing orders to coincide with the arrangement of customers' shelves.

McKesson began to search for other ways to use data collected through Economost. The system was eventually used to help each store set prices and design store layout to maximize profits. McKesson also relies on the system to provide accounting information such as balance sheets and income statements. In addition, Economost is used to warn consumers of harmful drug combinations by tracking prescription histories.

Through Economost, McKesson offers the independent drug stores many services that no single store could afford. As a result, drug stores can offer consumers lower prices and better service. This enables the drug stores to maintain their autonomy and fight off the big chains at the same time. The independent drug store owners are free to run their business, whereas managers of large chains have to answer to corporate headquarters and can be transferred at any time.

McKesson also benefits from the new system. Economost gives pharmacists an incentive to place orders with McKesson. The user fee McKesson charges drug stores covers the cost of developing the service. The system allowed McKesson to reduce its warehouses from 130 to 54, to eliminate five hundred clerical jobs, and to strengthen its customer base from twenty thousand customers averaging $4,000 worth of orders a month to fifteen thousand customers averaging $12,000 to $15,000 a month. And, by reducing the average number of shipments per customer from two per day to two per week, McKesson lowered its own inventory costs as well as those of its customers.

McKesson continues to develop new technologies to cut handling time and improve the quality of service. A warehouse management system called AcuMax makes use of hand-free, portable bar-code scanners to speed receipt, putaway, and shipment of orders. At its Spokane, Washington, distribution center, mispicks, which cost McKesson $80 each to correct, dropped by 72 percent just three weeks after the system was installed. The center requires only twelve order pickers to fill orders containing 600,000 items each month. Warehouse workers wear portable scanner and radio frequency data communication units which communicate directly with the main computer's inventory and accounts receivable program in less than two seconds. Workers also wear a scanner glove that is activated by pointing an index finger at the appropriate bar code. On their arms they wear small computer screens that display the customer order list, along with the exact shelf location of each item to be picked. McKesson plans to use AcuMax at many of its forty-five distribution centers.

Questions for Discussion

1. What functions do wholesalers like McKesson perform?

2. Why did McKesson feel a responsibility to help independent drug stores prosper?

3. How did McKesson use Economost to serve independent drug stores?

4. How does AcuMax improve efficiency and customer service?

Based on information from Gary Forger, "Better Data Cuts Handling Time at McKesson," *Modern Materials Handling,* August 1992, pp. 38–40; Alice LaPlante, "McKesson Cuts Costs with Wireless Scanner," *Infoworld,* May 25, 1992, p. 50; Gail Bronson, "Billion-Dollar Brainstorm," *Forbes,* October 19, 1987, p. 98; and Joan O'C. Hamilton and Catherine L. Harris, "For Drug Distributors, Information Is the Rx for Survival," *Business Week,* October 14, 1985, p. 116.

16.2 WHOLESALING TECHNOLOGY AT KAO

Kao Corporation is Japan's largest soap and cosmetics company and the sixth largest such company in the world, with annual sales exceeding $5 billion. According to James Abegglen, chairman of Gemini Consulting— Japan, no company can match the flexibility of Kao's distribution. Goods can be delivered within 24 hours to any of 280,000 shops, whose average order is only seven items. This capability is based on a world-class information system and a wholly owned network of wholesalers. This control enables Kao to get hot-selling items on store shelves faster and to keep smaller inventories than competitors.

The objective of Kao is to maximize the flexibility of the entire firm's response to demand. This requires not only flexible manufacturing, but an information system that links all aspects of the business: sales and shipping, production and purchasing, accounting, R&D, marketing, stores' cash registers, and sales representatives' hand-held computers.

Many firms in the United States and elsewhere rely on point-of-purchase data in determining production requirements. A manager generally receives information on the previous day's sales. At Kao, managers see daily sales, stock, and production figures. They can learn about a competitor's sale within a day and make necessary adjustments. When introducing a new product, information from 216 retailers is combined with a test-marketing program called the Echo System. This system uses focus group interviews and consumer responses through calls and letters to measure customer satisfaction faster than surveys do. Within two weeks of introduction, Kao knows if a product will be successful, who's buying it, whether the packaging is effective, and what needs to be changed. Response to the factory is immediate, and flexible manufacturing allows for instant changes.

The system at Kao basically eliminates the lag between a purchase and feedback about the purchase at the factory. This makes Kao less dependent on keeping finished-goods inventory. It also allows the firm to smooth out production levels and increase variety without increasing stock. In 1987, Kao made 498 products, and average inventory as a percent of sales was 9.2 percent. Today, Kao makes 564 products, and inventory is down to 8.6 percent.

Flexibility at Kao comes not only from manufacturing, but from information. A flexible factory is of little use if it cannot be exploited. Kao knows what's selling and can respond to this information very quickly at the factory.

Questions for Discussion

1. How does Kao stress flexibility?

2. Why is information and technology so important to Kao?

3. How does owning its wholesalers help Kao respond to customer demand more effectively than some manufacturing firms?

Based on information from Thomas A. Stewart, "Brace for Japan's Hot New Strategy," *Fortune,* September 21, 1992, pp. 62–74; Masayoshi Kanabayashi, "Japan's Top Soap Firm, Kao, Hopes to Clean Up Abroad," *Wall Street Journal,* December 17, 1992, p. B4; and "A Time For Mutual Respect And Understanding," *Fortune,* July 27, 1992, pp. S16–S17.

Retailing

The advent of the chain store in the 1920s was the beginning of the end for traditional department stores. Even though department stores have increased service, extended business hours, and upgraded their merchandise, they continue to lose market share to chains like Wal-Mart and Kmart, and more recently, to specialty stores like The Gap. Macy's filed bankruptcy in 1992 and, after reorganization, does not expect to show a significant gain in revenue until at least 1995. More and more, the huge discounters are ruling the marketplace.

Totes Inc. came up with a neat idea: slipper socks, a heavy pair of socks with rubbery treads to provide traction. Maybe they weren't the most fashionable, but a year after introducing them, Totes was selling 14 million pairs; Kmart and Wal-Mart alone accounted for 1.5 million pairs. But within two years, each of the discounters found suppliers that copied the slipper socks and sold them for less. Then they stopped carrying Totes and lowered the price of the slipper socks over 25 percent. This is what doing business with giant power retailers means. Can firms afford to do business with them? According to Ronald Best, the president of Totes, "You can't afford not to." In one category after another—toys, food, clothing, hardware, office supplies—large retailers are using sophisticated inventory management, intelligent selections, and competitive pricing to crowd out weaker stores.

Leading the charge are stores like Wal-Mart, Kmart, Toys 'R' Us, Circuit City, Home Depot, and Target, to name a few. Wal-Mart, for instance, is growing by 25 percent a year, and retailers as a whole are growing about 4 percent. Besides shopping at Wal-Mart, consumers are flocking to warehouse clubs and tightly focused "category killers," specialty stores which are taking over the sales of a wide range of products such as tires, toys, and appliances. The outcome is a shift in power from the giant manufacturers like Procter & Gamble to this growing circle of retail stores. More and more they are telling the largest manufacturers what to make, in what colors, sizes, and shapes, how much to ship, and when and how to ship it.

Consumers are also gaining clout as their buying habits change. They no longer divide retailers by the type of merchandise they carry since the same brands are available in a wide range of outlets. According to Wendy Liebmann, president of WSL Marketing in New York, "You used to go to the grocery store for food, to the drugstore for drugs, and to the department or discount store for clothes. That's just not true anymore." A study conducted by WSL found that the most popular places to shop for food in Tulsa, one of the nation's most representative test-market cities, are not grocery stores but food-drug combination stores. About 18 percent of all shopping trips in Tulsa are to discount stores like Wal-Mart, where women are as likely to buy groceries as clothes. Consumers, perceiving retail stores as interchangeable, now base selections primarily on price and convenience. Retailers must promote themselves as *brands* that fulfill clearly defined needs of consumers, something Wal-Mart has done through price, service, and convenience.[1] ●

As the opening feature illustrates, the face of retailing is changing. Consolidation is expected to continue in the years ahead. In the toy industry, just five retailers control over half the market.[2] That industry may provide a preview of what the future holds. In any event, retailers will continue to be a critical link in the marketing channel. They often are the only channel members that deal directly with consumers. Moreover, they are customers of producers and wholesalers. This dual role enables retailers to gain vital information from consumers and to provide insights to producers and wholesalers.

THE DEFINITION AND IMPORTANCE OF RETAILING

■ **retailing** the marketing activities involved in selling products to ultimate consumers for personal, family, or household use

Retailing includes all the marketing activities involved in selling products to ultimate consumers for personal, family, or household use. You probably purchase the products you use from various types of retailers—a grocery store, college bookstore, corner gas station, department store, or snack bar. Although most retailing activities take place in stores, retail exchanges also occur outside stores, through telephone contacts, vending machines, and mail-order catalogues.

Like wholesaling, retailing is a major sector of the U.S. economy. About 1,500,000 retailers provide a wide assortment of products to consumers, and employ approximately 20 million people.[3] Annual retail sales are nearly $2 trillion, up 5.1 percent from 1991.[4] The largest retailers in the United States are shown in Table 17.1.

Since retailers are positioned between producers (and wholesalers) and the ultimate consumers of products, they are close to the customer. Thus retailers serve as the producer's contact with the customer for the purposes of providing and gathering information and establishing the image of the product.

[1] Based on information from Zachary Schiller, Wendy Zellner, Ron Stodghill II, and Mark Maremont, "Clout!" *Business Week,* December 21, 1992, pp. 66–73; Jeffrey A. Trachtenberg, "Macy's Unveils Conservative Strategy for Future Profit," *Wall Street Journal,* November 6, 1992, p. B4; and Chip Walker, "Tulsa Shoppers: Ambassadors for America," *American Demographics,* January 1992, pp. 12–15.
[2] Schiller et al., pp. 66–73.
[3] *Statistical Abstract of the United States,* 1992, pp. 396, 760.
[4] Lucinda Harper, "Retail Sales Post 5.1% Increase For Last Year," *Wall Street Journal,* January 15, 1993, p. A2.

TABLE 17.1
The Top Ten U.S. Retailers

Rank	Name	Sales (in millions)
1	Wal–Mart	$43,887
2	Kmart	34,580
3	Sears, Roebuck	31,432
4	Kroger	21,350
5	American Stores	20,823
6	J.C. Penney	17,295
7	Dayton Hudson	16,115
8	Safeway Stores	15,119
9	A&P	11,591
10	May Co.	10,615

Source: "State of the Industry," *Chain Store Age Executive,* August 1992, p. 5a. Reprinted by permission of *Chain Store Age Executive* (August 1992). Copyright Lebhar-Friedman, Inc., 425 Park Avenue, New York, NY 10022.

Retailers also provide service for manufacturers and wholesalers. Retailers are the channel members that make products available where and when consumers want to purchase them. They obtain products from wholesalers and producers and offer them for sale in convenient and pleasant locations. They also maintain shopping hours that fit into the busy schedules of today's shoppers and in some cases provide delivery services. Finally, retailers assume risk by purchasing products and financing their product inventories. Pep Boys—Manny, Moe & Jack is an auto parts retailer that offers superior selection, price, and service to customers. For instance, Pep Boys stocks belts for 98 percent of all cars on the road, and unlike competitors, Pep Boys installs nearly everything it sells.[5] Table 17.2 summarizes the major functions of retailing.

■ **product assortment**
a collection of diverse products and competing brands

Most retailers develop a **product assortment**—a collection of diverse products and competing brands. Toys 'R' Us sells not only a wide assortment of toys and bicycles but also such products as infant furniture, clothing, and diapers. Some retailers offer fewer products and brands than others; members of vertically integrated marketing channels may in fact carry only one producer's products. Ann Taylor Stores carry only one brand of clothing.

TYPES OF RETAIL STORES

There are three major types of retail stores, shown in Figure 17.1: mass merchandisers, department stores, and specialty stores. Each type of retail store offers different product assortments according to the shopping preferences of its customers.

[5] Alex Taylor III, "How to Murder the Competition," *Fortune,* February 22, 1993, pp. 87–90.

Mass Merchandisers

■ **mass merchandiser**
a retail organization that
offers a wide but shallow
product mix, offers fewer
customer services than a department store, and appeals
to large heterogeneous target markets

A **mass merchandiser** is a retail organization that carries a wide but shallow product mix, offers fewer customer services than a department store, and appeals to large heterogeneous target markets. Mass merchandisers generally focus on lower prices, name-brand merchandise, high turnover, and large sales volumes. These stores are typically characterized by an image of efficiency and economy. As illustrated in Figure 17.1, mass merchandisers can be classified further as supermarkets, superstores, combination stores, hypermarkets, discount stores, warehouse showrooms, and warehouse/wholesale clubs.

■ **supermarket** a large,
self-service retailer that
stocks a wide assortment of
grocery products, as well as
some nonfood products

Supermarkets   A **supermarket** is a large, self-service retailer that stocks a wide assortment of grocery products, as well as some nonfood products. Most supermarkets carry limited lines of toys, cosmetics, housewares, and even some automotive supplies; many offer full-service pharmacies and check-cashing services. Consumers generally decide to shop at a Safeway, Winn-Dixie, Skaggs, A&P, Tianguis, or some other supermarket on the basis of prices, variety of products, selection and quality of produce, cleanliness, and convenience of location. Some supermarkets have also added

TABLE 17.2
Retailing Functions

Function	Description
Offering product assortments	Putting together a wide variety of products and brands from which customers can choose
Providing information	Providing information to consumers through advertising, in-store displays, and salespeople
Gathering information	Serving as the contact person in the flow of information (feedback, complaints, returns) from consumer to producer
Handling, storing, and assembling	Receiving merchandise, storing it, and, in some cases, assembling the product
Assuming risk	Paying for the merchandise before selling it to the consumer
Provide place, time, and possession utility	Making products available where and when consumers want to buy them, and providing a means of transferring ownership to the consumer

FIGURE 17.1
Types of Retailers

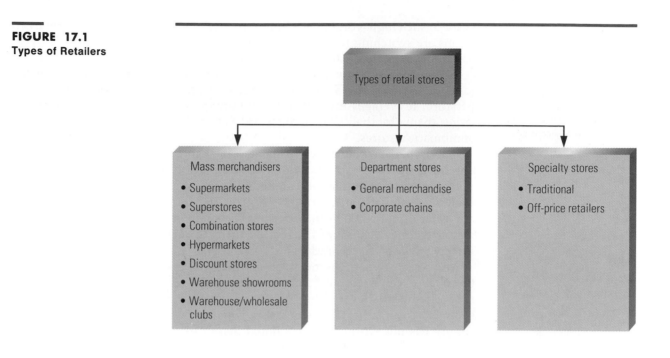

services such as delivery and extended hours. Supermarkets require efficient operations because their net profits after taxes are usually less than 1 percent of sales. For example, supermarkets like Kroger and Safeway have developed regional buying offices to keep close watch on demand. On the other hand, at A&P most purchasing is highly centralized, and has led to poor profit performance, one-third of 1 percent.[6]

The supermarket industry is undergoing some changes, driven by a consumer marketplace that continues to fragment. To reach customers more effectively, supermarkets are customizing to the neighborhood.[7] Many supermarkets now offer postage stamps, dry cleaning delivery, banking, prescriptions, and video rentals. By the end of the century, U.S. supermarkets will have a decidedly European, boutiquelike flavor.

Superstores, Combination Stores, and Hypermarkets   A **superstore** is a giant retail outlet that stocks most food and nonfood products ordinarily sold in a supermarket, as well as most products purchased on a routine basis, such as hardware, lawn and garden supplies, and small appliances. It is larger than a conventional supermarket—30,000 square feet compared to 18,000 square feet in a supermarket—and carries a wider assortment of merchandise. Superstores like the ones operated by Kroger and Safeway appeal to customers by emphasizing low prices and one-stop shopping. After losing market

■ **superstore** a giant retail outlet that stocks most food and nonfood products ordinarily sold in a supermarket, as well as most products purchased on a routine basis

[6]Matthew Schifrin and Toddi Gutner, "Too Sharp a Knife?" *Forbes,* March 1, 1993, pp. 44–45.
[7]Howard Schlossberg, "U.S. Supermarkets Likely to Take on European Flavor," *Marketing News,* January 6, 1992, p. 11.

share to such high-volume, low-margin, low-price stores, many supermarket chains are switching to this format. Kmart is also considering a plan to open 450 Super Kmarts in the next five years.[8]

■ **combination store** a mass merchandiser that is larger than a superstore and sells food and drugs in one store or two adjacent stores

A **combination store** sells food and drugs in one store or in two stores located side by side. This type of mass merchandiser is larger than a superstore. It averages more than 55,000 square feet of selling space, which is larger than a football field. Kroger and Super-X drug stores are examples of combination stores.

■ **hypermarket** a huge retail store that combines the one-stop supermarket and the discount store

The **hypermarket,** which originated in France, is a huge retail store that combines the one-stop supermarket and the discount store. A typical hypermarket stocks more than fifty thousand items, including groceries, clothing, building materials, and furniture. Some, such as Carrefour in Philadelphia, are as large as 330,000 square feet. Hypermarkets use advanced technology and operating techniques that enable them to increase sales volume and to offer very low priced products.

More than two thousand hypermarkets are operating in Europe, where they have been successful since the late 1960s. They have worked because they offer nearly everything in a single outlet and eliminate the need for shoppers to make several stops. But what seemed to be a can't-miss idea simply has not worked in the United States; many shoppers think they are too big and too remote.[9] Some of the most successful retailers, including Wal-Mart and Kmart, have tried hypermarkets in the United States. After building four Hypermarket U.S.A. stores, Wal-Mart abandoned the idea; Kmart stopped at three American Fare stores.[10] In Europe, most hypermarkets were built before shopping malls or big discount stores. In the United States, they entered a market packed with competing discount stores (with better selection), wholesale clubs (with better prices), and supermarkets and discounters (at better locations). The future of hypermarkets in the United States is clearly bleak.

■ **discount store** a self-service general merchandise retailer that offers brand-name products at low prices

Discount Stores   A self-service general merchandise retailer that offers brand-name products at low prices is called a **discount store.** Examples are Kmart, Wal-Mart, and Target stores. They carry a huge assortment of products—such as appliances, housewares, clothing, sports equipment, toys, and automotive supplies. Sometimes a food supermarket is operated as a department within a discount store. Many of the discounters are regional. Facing increased competition from other types of retailers, discount stores have improved store services, atmosphere, and location. As a result, some have raised their prices, blurring the distinction between discount stores and other types of retailers. The distinction is blurred further as discounters begin to offer more and more products previously sold in other retail outlets. In

[8]David Woodruff, Christopher Power, and Wendy Zellner, "Attention Kmart Shop . . . Hey, Where Is Everybody?" *Business Week,* January 18, 1993, p. 38.
[9]Kevin Kelly and Amy Dunkin, "Wal-Mart Gets Lost in the Vegetable Aisle," *Business Week,* May 28, 1990, p. 48.
[10]Laurie M. Grossman, "Hypermarkets: A Sure-Fire Hit Bombs," *Wall Street Journal,* June 25, 1992, p. B1.

FIGURE 17.2
Warehouse Showrooms
Warehouse showrooms like IKEA offer low prices but few services, as marketing functions are passed on to consumers.

Source: IKEA U.S., Inc.

response to price-conscious consumers, prestigious products like Chanel No. 5 perfume are increasingly sold at discount retailers such as the Cosmetic Center.[11]

 Discounters that sell primarily one type of product, like Toys 'R' Us, are known as *category killers.* These stores offer a tremendous selection and low prices. Rival discounters are adding to their stocks in an effort to combat category killers. Wal-Mart, Kmart, and Target stores, for instance, are stocking up on toys, forcing Toys 'R' Us to cut its prices.[12] *Single-price stores* are discounters that sell everything from shoes to shampoo for one price. Everything's $1, Simply 6, and Dollar Tree/Only One Dollar are examples of single-price stores that are rapidly opening across the country. The largest, One Price Clothing Stores, has annual sales exceeding $130 million.[13]

■ **warehouse showroom**
a large, high-volume, low-overhead retail store offering sizable, on-premise inventory but few services

Warehouse Showrooms The **warehouse showroom** is a large, high-volume, low-overhead retail store offering a sizable, on-premises inventory but few services (see Figure 17.2). It functions much like a discount store. A warehouse showroom can offer lower prices because it shifts some marketing functions to consumers, who must transport, finance, and perhaps store merchandise. Most consumers carry away their purchases in the manufacturers' cartons; at Food-4-Less supermarkets, customers even bag or box their own

[11] Gretchen Morgenson, "Save $35 on Chanel," *Forbes,* March 16, 1992, pp. 70–71.
[12] Mark Maremont and Greg Bowens, "Brawls in Toyland," *Business Week,* December 21, 1992, pp. 36–37.
[13] Christina Day, "Single-Price Stores' Formula for Success: Cheap Merchandise and a Lot of Clutter," *Wall Street Journal,* June 30, 1992, p. B1.

groceries. Although some supermarkets are using warehouse retailing, most warehouse showrooms are operated by large furniture retailers such as Wickes Furniture and Levitz Furniture Corporation.

■ **catalogue showroom**
a form of warehouse show-room where consumers select products from cata-logues that they've received in the mail or that are avail-able in the store

At a **catalogue showroom,** which is a form of warehouse showroom, consumers select products from catalogues that they've received in the mail or that are available in the store. Clerks fill orders from the warehouse area because the showroom's products are for display only and are stored out of buyers' reach. Products are sold in the manufacturers' cartons. Catalogue showrooms have low operating costs because their closed inventory rooms reduce shoplifting and display expenses. Catalogue showrooms like Service Merchandise and Best Products usually sell established brands and models that have little risk of being discontinued. The catalogue showroom is one of the fastest-growing areas of retailing.

■ **warehouse/wholesale club** a large-scale, mem-bers-only discount store that combines features of cash-and-carry wholesaling with discount retailing

Warehouse/Wholesale Clubs   The **warehouse/wholesale club,** the latest form of mass merchandiser, is a large-scale, members-only discount store that combines features of cash-and-carry wholesaling with discount retailing. Sometimes called buying clubs, these establishments carry a broad range of merchandise including appliances, housewares, hardware, clothing, food, and beverages. To keep prices down, warehouse or wholesale clubs carry shallow product lines—usually brand leaders—in a limited range of sizes and styles. Services are also kept to a minimum to keep prices low. Examples of these clubs include PACE Membership Warehouse, Costco, Price Club, and Sam's Wholesale Club (owned by Wal-Mart). Sam's leads the $28 billion club store market with over 33 percent of the market.[14]

Warehouse or wholesale clubs sell to businesses (small retailers usually account for over half of a warehouse club's sales) and individual consumers who are members. Membership fees are typically around $25. It is estimated that over 12 percent of all U.S. adults (21.7 million people) are club members.[15] In some instances, nonmembers are not required to pay a membership fee, but instead pay 5 to 10 percent more for purchases than do club members. A study conducted by Opinion Research Corp. reports that one shopper in five buys some groceries in club stores, which has a big impact on supermarket sales.[16] As their share of retail sales grow, and with over 600 warehouse clubs open in the United States, they are becoming the number-one challenge for conventional supermarkets.[17]

Department Stores

■ **department store**
a large retailer offering a wide product mix and or-ganized into separate depart-ments to facilitate service, marketing, and internal management

A **department store** is a large retailer offering a wide product mix and organized into separate departments to facilitate service, marketing, and internal management. A typical department store might have departments for

[14]Jennifer Lawrence, "For Openers, Sam's Club Has Personal Touch," *Advertising Age,* September 14, 1992, p. 22.
[15]James M. Degen, "Warehouse Clubs Move from Revolution to Evolution," *Marketing News,* August 3, 1992, p. 8.
[16]Richard Gibson, "Warehouse Clubs Have Big Impact on Grocers," *Wall Street Journal,* April 6, 1992, p. B1.
[17]Julie Liesse, "Welcome to the Club," *Advertising Age,* February 1, 1993, pp. 3, 5–6.

FIGURE 17.3
Department Stores
Bloomingdale's is a department store that offers a wide product mix and deep lines of apparel and cosmetics. Department stores typically feature personal atmosphere.

Source: © Andy Freeberg.

children's, women's, and men's apparel, as well as cosmetics, housewares and fine china, home furnishings, linens, dry goods, and perhaps even hardware, automotive supplies, recreation equipment, furniture, electronics, and appliances. Distinctive features of department stores include high levels of customer service and attractive atmosphere. Nordstrom, for example, is legendary for its customer service. The store earned the highest overall customer satisfaction rating in a survey of 70 U.S. department and discount stores, conducted by Frequency Marketing, a retail consulting firm in Milford, Ohio. The survey ranked stores on a variety of attributes, including price, convenience, and quality of merchandise.[18]

Typical department stores—such as Dillard's, Bloomingdale's, and Marshall Field's—obtain the majority of their sales from apparel and cosmetics. Department stores offer wide product mixes whose depth varies from store to store (see Figure 17.3). The unique feature of a department store, in comparison to other types of retailers, is that its total product includes personal assistance and a pleasant atmosphere. The department store is, in essence, a *shopping* store, where consumers can compare the price, quality, and service of a particular product with those of competing brands and at competing

[18]Cyndee Miller, "Nordstrom Is Tops in Survey," *Marketing News,* February 15, 1993, pp. 12–13.

stores. The terms of a department store's product warranty, satisfaction guarantee, or return policy may differ from those offered by other forms of retail stores.

General merchandise department stores attract customers by carrying a large number of product lines. For example, general merchandise department stores may carry sports equipment, automotive parts, insurance, and other services, such as hairstyling and opticians, in addition to traditional lines of clothing, tools, appliances, and so on. In some cases, these stores lease out space to other businesses that manage their own operations.

Because *corporate chain* department stores generate considerable sales volume, they have a great deal of control over the products they sell. Sears and J.C. Penney, for example, have been quite successful in integrating their marketing activities and acquiring ownership or control of other members of their marketing channels. In addition, consumer loyalty to these retailers and trust in their private store brands have made these retailers very powerful in channel leadership and competitive status.

The 1980s were a very tough time for department stores, as they lost market share to discounters, specialty stores, and mail-order catalogues. Several leaders, including Macy's and Federated, which owns A&S/Jordan Marsh, Bloomingdale's and Lazarus, reorganized under Chapter 11 bankruptcy protection. Department stores lost ground to discount stores not only on pricing but also on service. Although department stores may offer special customer service, so do some discount stores like Wal-Mart. But more important, discount stores expanded the definition of service to include efficiency in finding merchandise and speed in transactions.[19] Department stores may have more sales clerks, but they are valuable only if they can provide information about the merchandise or the location of products.

Department stores are responding by focusing on the customer. Some have learned that good service also means not running out of merchandise. Thus Federated had added in its chains an inventory- and sales-tracking system.[20] Department chains are also remodeling existing stores so that layouts are better suited to customer needs. Some are training employees to be more helpful to customers. Others are offering designer departments, restaurants, and optical shops. Many are trying to become more competitive on price. But consumers continue to have a perception that shopping at department stores automatically means paying higher prices.[21] Changing this perception may be the most difficult challenge facing department stores.

Specialty Stores

A **specialty store** differs from a mass merchandiser or department store in that it is smaller and offers a much narrower mix of products with deeper product lines. Such retailers—like clothiers Benetton, The Limited, and

■ **specialty store** a retail store that is smaller than a mass merchandiser or department store and offers a much narrower mix of products with deeper product lines

---

[19] Teri Agins, "Stores Try to Boost Service—But Cheaply," *Wall Street Journal,* December 16, 1992, pp. B1, B3.
[20] Laura Zinn, Dori Jones, and Walecia Konrad, "Federated's Slow Ride on the Up Escalator," *Business Week,* September 7, 1992, pp. 70–71.
[21] Gretchen Morgenson, "Business as Usual," *Forbes,* February 3, 1992, pp. 80–81.

FIGURE 17.4
Specialty Stores
Lady Foot Locker, a shoe specialty store, offers consumers a wide variety of women's casual footwear, such as Keds sneakers.

Source: Reprinted with permission from the Keds Corporation.

County Seat, shoe stores like Kinney Shoe Corp. and Lady Foot Locker (see Figure 17.4), and cosmetics stores like Crabtree and Evelyn—offer a limited number of product lines but a substantial assortment within each line. Other, independent specialty stores tend to be small businesses and include bookstores, florists, and bakery shops. Although these retailers may carry a few supporting product lines, they are still classified as specialty stores. The next sections discuss two types of specialty retailers, traditional specialty stores and off-price retailers.

■ **traditional specialty store** a specialty retailer that carries a narrow product mix with deep product lines

Traditional Specialty Stores   A **traditional specialty store,** sometimes called a limited-line retailer, carries a narrow product mix with deep product lines. Traditional specialty stores commonly sell jewelry, sporting goods, computers, or apparel. Allsports, Zales, The Gap, and Thornbury's Toys are examples of specialty stores. The Gap, with annual sales of $2.5 billion and earnings of $225 million, is the most popular and profitable specialty chain in America.[22]

Traditional specialty stores usually find it easier to compete on the basis of image rather than price with large department stores and mass merchandisers. By emphasizing and capitalizing on fashion, service, personnel, physical characteristics, atmosphere, location, and social class, specialty stores differentiate themselves and develop favorable consumer relationships. Italy's

[22]Russell Mitchell, "The Gap," *Business Week,* March 9, 1992, pp. 58–64.

Benetton found out the importance of image when controversial advertisements—with themes like AIDS and condoms—and the addition of more expensive sportswear were at odds with customers' image of the retailer. At one time Benetton had seven hundred stores in the United States, its largest market outside Europe. Today there are fewer than five hundred stores, as customers have been lured away by The Gap and Limited's Express, who offer more affordable merchandise.[23]

■ **off-price retailer** a specialty store that sells a limited line of name-brand and designer products below list price

Off-Price Retailers   An **off-price retailer** is a specialty store that sells a limited line of name-brand and designer products below list price. By purchasing manufacturers' seconds (slightly flawed merchandise) and overruns at below-wholesale prices, off-price retailers can charge 20 to 60 percent less than department stores. Most off-price retailers offer little service. Some feature central check-out counters, require cash payments, or have a policy of no merchandise returns or exchanges. Off-price retailing chains such as T.J. Maxx, Marshall's, and Hit or Miss are becoming increasingly popular. Filene's Basement, which sells designer clothes for 20 to 60 percent less than department stores, averages sales of $427 a square foot, about twice that of department stores.[24]

Notwithstanding its limitations, off-price retailing is expected to grow. Consumers are becoming increasingly attracted to discount prices, despite the limited service and less convenient locations. As consumers become even more fashion conscious, for instance, name-brand clothing at discount prices should draw more buyers.

RETAIL FRANCHISING

■ **retail franchising** a contractual agreement in which a supplier (the franchiser) grants a dealer (the franchisee) the right to sell the supplier's products in exchange for some type of consideration

Retail franchising is a contractual agreement in which a supplier (the *franchiser*) grants a dealer (the *franchisee*) the right to sell the supplier's products in exchange for some type of consideration. For instance, the franchiser may receive a percentage of the franchisee's revenues in exchange for furnishing marketing assistance, management training, or the building, equipment, and supplies. Many retail organizations, including Baskin-Robbins Inc., KFC (Kentucky Fried Chicken) Corp., and Hallmark Cards Inc., use franchise systems. The leading franchises are listed in Table 17.3.

Franchises are also becoming popular among professionals and service providers such as dentists, lawyers, real estate agents, and health clubs. Babies and children are the focus of many new franchises, like Baby Room U.S.A., which sells baby furniture, and A Choice Nanny, where franchisees learn to train nannies and place them with families for fees as high as $1,500. Mitsui Planning Co. of Japan is franchising pachinko, a cross between slot-machine

---

[23]Teri Agins, "Shrinkage of Stores and Customers in U.S. Causes Italy's Benetton to Alter Its Tactics," *Wall Street Journal,* June 24, 1992, pp. B1, B10.
[24]Shelley Neumeier, "Filene's Basement," *Fortune,* January 27, 1992, p. 87.

TABLE 17.3
Top Ten Franchises*

1. McDonald's
2. Subway Sandwiches and Salads
3. Dunkin' Donuts
4. Jani-King
5. Baskin-Robbins
6. ServiceMaster Cleaning Service
7. Chem-Dry Cleaning Service
8. Hardee's
9. Arby's
10. Domino's Pizza

*_Entrepreneur_ magazine ranks 500 franchise organizations by number of franchise outlets, start-up costs for franchise owners, number of years in business, and growth rate.

Source: Reprinted with permission from _Entrepreneur,_ January 1992, p. 129.

gambling and pinball. Even bungee jumping has been franchised; for $185,000, Air Boingo will set franchisees up with a 75-foot tower from which daring customers can jump.[25]

Basically, three types of franchising arrangements exist. In the oldest arrangement, a producer may franchise a number of stores to sell a particular brand of product. This method is used to sell Sherwin-Williams paints and most new General Motors, Chrysler, and Ford vehicles. An estimated 90 percent of all gasoline is sold through independent, franchised service stations.

In the second type of franchise agreement, a producer authorizes wholesalers to sell to retailers. This arrangement is typical in the soft-drink industry. Most national producers of soft-drink syrups—Coca-Cola, Dr Pepper, Pepsi-Cola, 7Up—franchise independent bottlers to sell their products to retailers.

In the third and most common franchise arrangement, a franchiser provides brand names, techniques, procedures, or other services rather than a complete product. Although the franchiser may perform some manufacturing and wholesaling functions, its principal contribution to franchisees is a carefully developed and controlled marketing strategy. Examples of this arrangement include Domino's Pizza, Wendy's International, Dairy Queen, Macco, Jiffy Lube Intl., and H&R Block.

Franchises have several advantages. The franchiser generally provides managerial guidance to the franchisee. In many cases, a franchiser offers a nationally known brand name and a proven product, as well as financial assistance. Franchises do have several drawbacks, however. A franchisee must pay an initial fee to the franchiser as part of the contractual agreement. A person who signs a franchise agreement also loses some control over the business, because the franchiser may want some control over items such as

[25]Jeffrey A. Tannenbaum, "Business Formats to Bungee Jumps, Franchising Spreads," _Wall Street Journal,_ April 13, 1992, p. B2.

the menu, the type of building, promotional activities, and so on. Finally, whereas some franchisers have developed excellent training programs, others provide little or no training or promise extensive training and do not deliver.

American franchises continue to increase their sales in both domestic and foreign markets. From 1980 to 1991 the number of franchises in the United States increased from 442,000 to 543,000.[26] Despite the recession, franchising experienced a phenomenal sales growth in 1991 of 6.1 percent, to over $750 billion.[27] Sales of goods and services reached over $750 billion. About 350 U.S. franchises operate more than 32,000 outlets in foreign countries, including the United Kingdom, West Germany, Japan, Mexico, France, Australia, Spain, and Russia.[28]

Despite the rapid growth of franchises, owning a franchise is getting tougher. For instance, the cost of starting a Hampton Inn is $2.3 million; a McDonald's, $363,000; and a Round Table Pizza, $322,000.[29] As a result, the profile of the typical franchise owner is changing. Whereas past franchisees started "mom and pop" operations with little or no business experience, today's franchise owners are more experienced businesspeople with proven management skills and adequate cash to invest.[30] Figure 17.5 shows an advertisement for Baskin Robbins franchises.

The growth of franchising has attracted many entrepreneurs with dreams of owning their own business; some have found they are buying a tough, low-paying job. For example, even though Subway has more than seven thousand franchises worldwide, a substantial number of them are losing money.[31] This illustrates an important point—the franchiser and the franchisee do not always have the same goals. The franchiser is interested in growth, since more outlets mean more fees. The franchisee, of course, is trying to make a profit. The result can be extreme conflict, especially when a new franchise outlet opens close to an existing store. While Taco Bell was boosting sales and profits by expanding its network more than 37 percent to 3,700 stores, many of the 320 franchisees saw sales fall. Franchisees for KFC and Burger King are facing similar problems with encroachment of new stores close to existing stores.[32]

 Complaints about franchising abuses are increasing; most complaints deal with investors not receiving sufficient information to make a decision.[33] To reduce problems in franchising, the International Franchise Association (IFA)

[26] *Statistical Abstract of the United States,* 1992, p. 770.
[27] Jennifer S. Stack and Joseph E. McKendrick, "Franchise Market Expands As Rest of Economy Slumps," *Marketing News,* July 6, 1992, p. 11.
[28] "Franchises Expected to Prosper in U.S. and Abroad in '88," *Marketing News,* May 23, 1988, p. 5.
[29] *USA Today,* February 11, 1988, p. 8B.
[30] Buck Brown, "New Owners of Franchises Belie Mom-and-Pop Image," *Wall Street Journal,* August 8, 1988, p. 13.
[31] Barbara Marsh, "Sandwich-Shop Chain Surges, but to Run One Can Take Heroic Effort," *Wall Street Journal,* September 16, 1992, pp. A1, A6.
[32] Amy Barrett, "Indigestion at Taco Bell," *Business Week,* December 14, 1992, pp. 66–67.
[33] Jeffrey A. Tannenbaum, "States Are Cutting Back on Enforcing Franchise Rules," *Wall Street Journal,* February 4, 1993, p. B2.

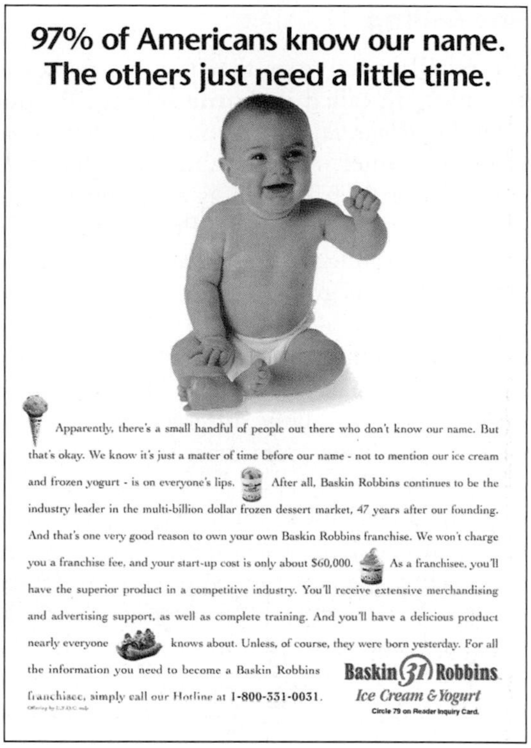

FIGURE 17.5
Retail Franchising
Baskin Robbins advertises to prospective investors a superior franchise for a start-up cost of $60,000, which includes extensive training and merchandising and advertising support.

Source: Baskin Robbins Ice Cream Co.

97% of Americans know our name. The others just need a little time.

has developed a new code of ethics for franchises. Unlike the previous code, the new one explicitly deals with major concerns such as encroachments on older franchisees by new ones within the same chain.[34] The code will succeed only if it is enforced, and the IFA vows to enforce it strongly. It is hoped that self-regulation will reduce the need for state and local governments, already facing budget constraints, to enforce franchising regulations. And continued abuses threaten the reputation of franchising and may turn away prospective investors.

NONSTORE RETAILING

■ **nonstore retailing** re-tailing activities that take place outside traditional store environments

Retailing activities that take place outside traditional store environments are referred to as **nonstore retailing.** Nonstore retailing is growing faster than in-store retailing; this growth is expected to continue in direct response to the shopping needs and time constraints of working couples. Various forms of nonstore retailing are in-home selling, direct marketing, and automatic vending.

[34]Jeffrey A. Tannenbaum, "Franchising Association Issues Its New Code of Ethics," *Wall Street Journal,* November 24, 1992, p. B2.

In-Home Selling

■ **in-home selling** nonstore retailing activities that
involve personal contacts
with consumers in their
homes

Nonstore retailing activities that involve personal contacts with consumers in their homes are called **in-home selling.** Products such as Fuller brushes, *World Book Encyclopedia,* and Avon cosmetics and fragrances are sold to consumers in their homes. Although in-home sellers traditionally used a random door-to-door approach known as *cold canvassing,* in-home sellers today employ a more efficient approach. Prospects are first contacted by phone or intercepted in shopping malls so that the salesperson can make appointments. The salesperson then goes to the prospects' homes to make sales presentations.

One variation of in-home selling is the home demonstration or party. One consumer hosts a "party" at which merchandise is displayed for a number of his or her friends. Many different products, ranging from Tupperware containers to decorative accessories to women's lingerie, are marketed in this manner.

Demographic changes in the United States over the last two decades have dramatically affected the in-home selling business. The growing ranks of women working outside the home means fewer household customers to reach and fewer salespeople (women were the traditional in-home sales representatives). In response, some in-home retailers have revised their strategies to sell products. Tupperware Company International is trying everything possible with Tupperware parties, offering them in offices and day-care centers, in parks, even in parking lots.[35] Marketing Close-up shows how Avon Products has changed its strategy to win back customers.

Direct Marketing

■ **direct marketing** nonstore retailing that uses nonpersonal media to introduce
products to consumers, who
then purchase the products
by mail or telephone

Direct marketing is nonstore retailing that uses nonpersonal media to introduce products to consumers, who then purchase the products by mail or telephone. To reach members of their target market, marketers often buy lists of potential customers that match the demographic profile of the target market. Often potential customers are contacted by telephone after they have been exposed to an advertisement. Business-to-business marketers report that direct marketing activities are receiving a greater percentage of their budgets.[36]

Direct marketing has grown into a huge industry, with yearly sales exceeding $200 billion.[37] Boosted by demographics and technology, the growth is expected to continue. More women continue to join the work force and thus have less time to shop. The senior segment is also growing and has more disposable income and less mobility. Through technology, orders can

[35] Laurie M. Grossman, "Families Have Changed but Tupperware Keeps Holding Its Parties," *Wall Street Journal,* July 21, 1992, pp. A1, A13.
[36] Carrie Goerne, "Business Marketers Find Increased Success As They Turn to Direct Mail," *Marketing News,* July 6, 1992, p. 3.
[37] Paul M. Barrett, "Law: Supreme Court Set to Rule in Tax Cases That Carry Big Consequences for States," *Wall Street Journal,* February 6, 1992, p. B6.

MARKETING CLOSE-UP

Avon . . . Still Calling?

For years the Avon lady was a fixture in American neighborhoods. Door-to-door selling built Avon Products into the world's largest manufacturer of beauty products. But, in the 1980s, as millions of women began to work outside the home, the cosmetics maker's pool of customers and sales representatives dwindled, and its sales faltered. By 1985, its profits were half what they had been in 1979.

Consumer research showed that many women thought Avon's make-up was "stodgy," its gift products overpriced, and its jewelry old-fashioned. So the company created a more contemporary line of jewelry, lowered the prices of its giftware to offer more items under $15, and expanded its lipstick and nail polish colors.

On the selling side, recruiting salespeople had become problematic, much as it had for other direct sellers like Mary Kay Cosmetics and Premark International's Tupperware division. To attract sales representatives and boost productivity, Avon improved incentive-compensation plans and offered free training programs for recruits. As a result, Avon's direct-sales business—which accounts for 70 percent of sales and 85 percent of operating profits—experienced a dramatic turnaround. Within a year sales rose 17 percent, to $2.9 billion, and profits jumped as much as 25 percent.

Today more than 450,000 sales representatives work for Avon and fill out some fifty thousand orders daily. Sales exceed $3.5 billion a year. Nonetheless, Avon estimates that at least ten million women in the United States who are interested in buying from Avon are not able to because no sales representative is calling. To win back some of these former customers and attract new ones, the company has begun mailing catalogues directly to potential customers nationwide. The move represents growing concern at Avon that its core market has matured. The growing number of working women means that fewer of them have time to meet with Avon representatives. Although Avon remains the nation's largest direct seller of beauty products, supermarkets and discount stores are stealing market share. Avon hopes that mail-order catalogues will help reach "stranded" customers.

The plan is to send catalogues to people who have moved or who no longer are active buyers. They can then order directly through the company or through a salesperson. Initial expectations are modest. Avon hopes catalogue sales will reach $25 million the first year. In the long run, Avon hopes to penetrate major cities and suburbs, the places where much of the female work force is absent at prime selling times. Avon is also increasing the use of 800 numbers in conjunction with this strategy.

Sources: Pat Sloan, "Avon Looks Beyond Direct Sales," *Advertising Age,* February 22, 1993, p. 32; Jeffrey A. Trachtenberg, "Catalogs Help Avon Get a Foot in the Door," *Wall Street Journal,* March 3, 1992, pp. B1, B3; "Automated Data Entry at Avon," *IMC Journal,* July–August 1992, pp. 26–27; "Direct Selling Cosmetics: Avon, Mary Kay Ahead," *Drug & Cosmetic Industry,* June 1992, pp. 46, 49; and Ronald Alsop, "Despite Doomsayers, Avon Is Still Calling," *Wall Street Journal,* March 1, 1988, p. 33.

be shipped in 24 hours, and databases allow more efficient niche marketing.[38] The following sections take a closer look at two forms of direct marketing, telemarketing and mail-order retailing.

Telemarketing   As its name implies, **telemarketing** uses telecommunications to reach prospective customers. In one form of telemarketing, **telephone retailing,** marketers sell goods or services by telephoning prospective customers whose names appear in the telephone directory (the cold canvass approach) or on a prescreened list. A popular method of developing telephone contacts is advertising that encourages consumers to initiate a call or to request information about placing an order. Although this type of nonstore retailing represents a small part of total retail sales, its use is growing.

Some observers believe that along with the growth in telemarketing has come an increase in the abuse of this form of direct marketing. Consumers complain that their privacy is being invaded by an increasing number of telephone calls and by the amount of information about them that is available to marketers. In some cases, customer lists are sold from one organization to another. Many firms compile customer lists containing an abundance of personal information, including income, buying habits, and the number and even names of family members; such information is sold without the customer's knowledge or consent. The continued use of personal information by third parties without the consent of the consumer jeopardizes the future of telemarketing.[39] The Federal Communications Commission is currently trying to prohibit businesses from using autodialers that are capable of calling thousands of customers and delivering prerecorded messages.[40]

Another form of telemarketing is home shopping. Cable and syndicated (noncable) television shopping networks offer viewers everything from fashions to appliances twenty-four hours a day. Hosts demonstrate the merchandise and buyers call toll-free numbers to place orders, which are delivered by mail. Home Shopping Network is the best known, but it is facing increased competition from other shopping networks, including Consumer Discount Network, QVC Network, and Cable Value Network. Home Shopping Network is counting on new technology which can handle twenty thousand phone calls a minute to secure its future.[41] Home shopping has quickly become a multibillion-dollar industry.

Mail-Order Retailing   The type of direct marketing in which sellers contact buyers through catalogues, direct mail, radio, television, magazines, or newspapers is called **mail-order retailing.** This impersonal form of retailing

■ **telemarketing** the use of telecommunications to reach prospective customers

■ **telephone retailing** a form of telemarketing in which marketers sell goods or services by telephoning prospective customers whose names appear in the telephone directory or on a prescreened list

■ **mail-order retailing** a type of direct marketing in which sellers contact buyers through catalogues, direct mail, radio, television, magazines, or newspapers

[38] Stanley H. Slom, "Direct Marketing Faces Hurdles," *Chain Store Age Executive,* September 1991, pp. 27–29.

[39] Linda F. Goldner, "Telemarketing and Privacy: Does the Customer Care?" *At Home with Consumers,* August 1992, pp. 2, 6.

[40] Mary Lu Carnevale, "Telemarketers Fight Banning of Autodialers," *Wall Street Journal,* January 20, 1993, pp. B1–B2.

[41] Johnnie L. Roberts and Mark Robichaux, "Diller Bets on Home Shopping Future," *Wall Street Journal,* December 14, 1992, pp. B1, B8.

FIGURE 17.6
Direct Marketing
Sellers market directly to buyers through mail-order retailing. Spiegel uses catalogue sales to market directly to consumers who value time and money.

Source: Courtesy Spiegel, Inc.

is essentially selling by description because customers generally do not see the actual product until they receive it in the mail. Companies like L.L. Bean and Lands' End make effective use of attractive catalogues and provide excellent service such as help with selections, monogramming, two-day delivery, or gift certificates. A wide assortment of products such as records, books, household goods, gifts, and clothing are sold to consumers through the mail. Companies target different markets. Lillian Vernon, for instance, appeals to the thrifty; Vernon's order size averages $38, compared with $130 for Sharper Image, $85 for Lands' End, and $60 for Crate & Barrel.[42] Placing mail orders by telephone is also becoming more common, because some companies make it possible for customers to place orders around the clock. Many large retailers such as Spiegel, shown in Figure 17.6, rely heavily on mail-order retailing.

Mail-order retailing is an efficient and convenient method of selling. Because mail-order houses do not incur the costs associated with personal selling and maintaining expensive stores, they can pass the savings along to consumers in the form of lower prices. Catalogues can also be developed for specific target markets. It was Sears' failure to target specific market segments that caused the firm to eliminate its catalogue, known as the Big Book, in

[42]Lisa Coleman, "I Went Out and Did It," *Forbes,* August 17, 1992, pp. 102–104.

1993.[43] Mail-order retailers are somewhat limited in the types of services they can provide because of their remoteness from consumers. Moreover, this method of retailing is more appropriate for specialty products than for convenience products. According to the Direct Marketing Association, U.S. households and businesses receive in excess of thirteen billion catalogues each year, with sales of approximately $30 billion.[44]

Business-to-business mail-order services are also experiencing tremendous growth. As organizations locate away from central areas, their salespeople find it increasingly difficult and costly to call on organizational customers. Additionally, it is quite expensive for a local supplier to stock products for the special needs of one or two customers. As a result, more and more firms are relying on catalogues to keep organizational customers up-to-date.

Automatic Vending

■ **automatic vending** an impersonal form of nonstore retailing in which money- or credit-card-operated machines provide products or services

Automatic vending is an impersonal form of nonstore retailing in which money- or credit-card-operated machines provide products or services. Convenience goods—cigarettes, chewing gum, newspapers, candy, sandwiches, beverages—are available in machines because consumers usually purchase them at the nearest available location. Consumers can also use vending machines to get air-travel insurance, perform banking transactions, or obtain entertainment in the form of video games, game tables, and juke boxes. Automatic vending machines are typically located in areas of heavy traffic—colleges, offices, hospitals, airports, public facilities—where they provide efficient and continuous service to consumers. Vending machines have advantages over stores because they do not require sales personnel or large space. However, these advantages are partly offset by the expense of frequent servicing and repair.

Automatic vending accounts for less than 2 percent of all retail sales. Although vending retail sales were relatively flat in the 1980s, sales may expand in the years ahead with the introduction of machines that accept dollar bills instead of coins and that dispense products like toothpaste, golf balls and tees, and breath mints. If consumers and retailers accept these innovative vending machines, they may be used to dispense motor oil at service stations, milk and bread at grocery stores, and some sporting equipment at golf courses and health centers.

 ## RETAILING IN FOREIGN COUNTRIES

The structure of retailing differs from country to country, just as the structure of wholesaling does. In Italy, retailing is dominated by specialty stores car-

[43] Cyndee Miller, "Sears Closes Book on Era; Competitors Hope to Improve on Success Stories," *Marketing News,* March 15, 1993, pp. 1–2.
[44] Carla Lazzareschi, "Catalogs Abandon Blanket Approach for Pinpoint," Lexington, Ky. *Herald-Leader,* March 24, 1992, p. A3.

TABLE 17.4
The Number of Retailers in Selected Countries

Country	Number of Retailers	Population per Retailer
Argentina	787,000	40
Ecuador	1,800	294
France	518,700	102
Hungary	63,700	157
Egypt	2,100	20,000
Iran	214,000	175
Indonesia	121,000	1,210
Italy	849,600	64
Japan	1,628,600	68
Nigeria	22,200	4,045
South Korea	673,600	63
Malaysia	96,000	142
Philippines	280,000	173
United Kingdom	345,000	162
West Germany	382,300	160

Source: *Euromonitor International Marketing Data and Statistics,* 15th edition, 1991; *European Marketing Data and Statistics,* 26th edition, 1991. Reprinted by permission of Euromonitor Publications, London.

rying narrow product lines. Retailers in Japan carry a wider variety of merchandise, but most act merely as brokers for large manufacturers.[45] Department stores in Japan that seemed invincible a few years ago are also being threatened by discount stores and factory outlets that are emerging nationwide for the first time.[46] New laws, however, are opening the door for large numbers of discount stores that offer much lower prices.[47] A firm marketing products in a foreign country must assess the structure and availability of foreign retailers in developing a marketing strategy.

Many foreign nations have large numbers of small retailers that offer limited services. As shown in Table 17.4, Argentina has 787,000 retailers, and South Korea has 673,600. Generally, smaller retailers in foreign countries are short on shelf and storage space. These retailers carry a narrow line of products and often experience stockouts. On the other hand, some countries have fewer retailers, but the population per retailer is extremely high. For instance, Egypt has twenty thousand people per retailer. It is nearly impossible for retailers to provide adequate service to this many people. To overcome the deficiencies in the structure and size of some foreign retailers, large firms like Sears and Kmart are expanding their operations around the world.

[45] Gale Eisenstodt, "In Step," *Forbes,* October 26, 1992, p. 50.
[46] Yumiko Ono, "Japanese Department Stores Fall from 1980s Heyday," *Wall Street Journal,* February 9, 1993, p. B4.
[47] Emily Thornton, ". . . And *Sayonara* to Mom-and-Pops," *Fortune,* November 30, 1992, pp. 13–16.

Many changes have been taking place in retailing throughout the world. Mass merchandisers such as supermarkets and discount houses can be found in both developed and underdeveloped countries. Automatic vending and mail-order retailing are also growing around the world. Although direct marketing is more developed in the United States, there is a trend toward direct marketing in many countries, including Germany, Japan, and France. Franchising is also growing globally, for the same reasons it has become popular in the United States. Many U.S. franchisers like KFC and McDonald's operate throughout the world.

There has also been growth in the number of international retailers, and this growth is expected to continue. As firms begin to realize that domestic growth potential is limited, they often turn their attention to foreign markets. Retailing firms from the United States, Canada, France, Japan, Germany, and other countries have established a global presence. IKEA (Swedish furniture store), the Body Shop (United Kingdom cosmetics firm), Benetton (Italian fashion chain), Aldi (German food retailer), and Pizza Hut (U.S. food retailer) are a few of the many successful international retailers (see Figure 17.7). L.L. Bean opened its first store outside New England, in Japan, but it won't be the last. The Tokyo store has been a huge success.[48] This trend toward international growth has been fueled by lower barriers to entry, improved communications, and the dramatic changes taking place in many countries, such as the reorganization of the former Soviet Union into several independent countries.

RETAIL STRATEGY CONSIDERATIONS

Retailers must consider several important factors when developing retail strategies. This section explains several factors that influence retail strategy decisions, including store location, store environment, scrambled merchandising, and the wheel of retailing.

Store Location

Store location is a critical strategic issue in retailing because it determines the trade area from which customers will be drawn. The *Wall Street Journal* located the largest U.S. outlets for twenty top brands. For most, the key to success was location.[49] Walgreen's, the largest drug store chain in the United States, attributes much of its success to store location. The locations, carefully selected to be convenient to consumers, generally are on a main street in a

---

[48]Colin Nickerson, "Far East Goes Down East," *Boston Sunday Globe,* February 28, 1993, pp. 1, 26.
[49]Richard Gibson, "Location, Luck, Service Can Make a Store Top Star," *Wall Street Journal,* February 1, 1993, p. B1.

FIGURE 17.7
International Retailing
The number of international retailers is on the rise. Body Shop is a British cosmetics firm with retail stores throughout the world.

Source: The Body Shop.

big city or suburb.[50] When selecting a location, retailers must consider the characteristics of the target market and the image of the firm. Most retailers prefer to locate stores where there is a high level of pedestrian traffic, as in a downtown shopping district or in a shopping mall. Gas station and convenience-store retailers prefer to locate where there is a high level of vehicular traffic. Other location considerations relate to the availability of parking and characteristics of the site, such as the surrounding area, the cost of the location, and the appearance of the building or lot being considered.

Retailers must also evaluate the characteristics of the types of stores in the area. Freestanding stores, an unplanned business district, or a planned shopping center all present different strategic marketing considerations.

Freestanding Store   A *freestanding store* is a building that stands by itself. This type of store generally gives the retailer greater flexibility and more room for expansion. Although these types of buildings generally have lower rents and lack close competition, freestanding retail stores cannot rely on other stores to help generate consumer traffic. Because of this limitation, the freestanding store is most commonly used by a large retailer, such as Toys 'R' Us, which can generate its own traffic. If no suitable building is available, a retailer may have one built. Freestanding stores also result in higher promotion costs for retailers.

Unplanned Business District   In an *unplanned business district,* stores are located in close proximity to one another without prior planning. Examples

[50]Ronald Henkoff, "A High-Tech Rx for Profits," *Fortune,* March 23, 1992, pp. 106–107.

of unplanned business districts include central business districts, secondary business districts, neighborhood business districts, and strips.

Central business districts are located in downtown areas of cities. Traditionally, this is where much of a city's business activity and shopping took place. Central business districts are usually served by mass transit, and in some cases rent can be fairly low. But with the movement of people—and more recently, of businesses—out of cities, many central business districts have become run-down and are not considered viable locations for retailers. Several cities, including Baltimore and Miami, have undertaken extensive urban renewal programs to bring life back to their central business districts.

A *secondary business district* is bounded by at least two major streets. It is typically smaller than a central business district, and serves a smaller trade area. Cities generally have several secondary business districts.

Neighborhood business districts are located in residential areas. This type of store location serves the convenience needs of a neighborhood by providing ready access to supermarkets, drug stores, and other smaller stores selling convenience and shopping goods.

A *strip* is a group or string of adjacent stores located along a major street or highway. The stores may carry similar product lines, but since strips are unplanned, many feature a wide variety of stores.

Planned Shopping Center   The final type of store location, the *planned shopping center,* is a coordinated, complementary mix of stores that is centrally planned, managed, and promoted to appeal to heterogeneous groups of consumers. The shopping center management ensures an environment that is comfortable and conveniently set up to serve consumers with a variety of needs. Parking facilities, landscaping, and special events create an overall atmosphere that attracts consumers. Planned shopping centers may be categorized as neighborhood shopping centers, community shopping centers, regional shopping centers, or power centers.

A *neighborhood shopping center* usually includes a grocery store, a drug store, specialty stores, a gas station, and fast-food restaurants. Such centers serve customers who live within ten to fifteen minutes away. Neighborhood centers offer shopping convenience for consumers and low operating costs for retailers. This type of location is susceptible to competitors because most purchases are based on convenience. If consumers can find a more convenient location or perhaps a newer facility, they may switch.

A *community shopping center* generally consists of one or two department stores, several specialty stores, and convenience stores. These centers serve a wider geographic area than do neighborhood centers, and consumers are willing to drive further distances to shop at them. Operating costs are low and the retailer can share promotions. In recent years, however, many community shopping centers have experienced high vacancy rates.

Regional shopping centers, commonly known as shopping malls, have large department stores, wide product mixes, and deep product lines. The large anchor department stores and variety of stores draw consumers from a wide radius. The cost of renting space in a regional shopping center is high, often limiting tenants to national chains. Minnesota's Mall of America, the nation's largest mall, has over four hundred stores, fourteen movie theaters, seven restaurants, five nightclubs, and a 97-acre theme park.[51] These huge malls, discount chains like Wal-Mart and Home Depot, and factory outlet malls that sell on the basis of price are posing a serious threat to older, traditional malls.[52] Some malls are responding by targeting fast-growing minority groups. The Tucson Mall in Arizona targets Hispanics, who as a group are growing five times faster than the general population; the South DeKalb Mall in Atlanta has repositioned itself as an Afrocentric retail center, aiming its marketing efforts at black consumers, whose spending power has grown nationally from $250 billion to $270 billion.[53]

Another type of planned shopping center is the *power center,* which is often located near a regional shopping center and contains as many as seven anchors such as discounters, large retailers, and superstores. With up to 500,000 square feet, a power center is designed to fill the gap between the community and the regional shopping center.

Malls and shopping centers are also searching for new locations. Many cities have experimented with urban malls and downtown shopping centers. The results have been fairly disappointing. Unfortunately, shoppers are reluctant to leave their homes in the suburbs, venture into urban areas, and pay for parking.[54] In retrospect, firms did not bring shopping to the customer. Rather, city officials thought that by turning downtown areas into malls similar to those found in the suburbs, they would bring people back into the cities. One concept which brings shopping to the customer is airport retailing, the subject of Close to the Customer.

Store Environment

Various psychological and social factors (discussed in Chapter 7) often influence what products consumers purchase and where they purchase them. When searching for a specific product, consumers usually go to one or more of several possible retail stores to compare brands, prices, quality, and service. Retailers therefore need to focus their marketing efforts on making the desired products available and on developing a marketing strategy that increases patronage. However, consumers do not always have a specific reason for going to a retailer; they may shop to escape boredom, to occupy time, to socialize, or to learn about something new. Consequently, retailers must develop a stimulating and interesting environment for shopping. A retail store's image and atmospherics are important aspects of consumer patronage.

[51]"Megamalls," *Better Homes and Gardens,* November 1992, pp. 213–220.
[52]Howard Rudnitsky, "Battle of the Malls," *Forbes,* March 30, 1992, pp. 46–47.
[53]Laurie M. Grossman, "After Demographic Shift, Atlanta Mall Restyles Itself as Black Shopping Center," *Wall Street Journal,* February 26, 1992, pp. B1, B5.
[54]Laurie M. Grossman, "Developed to Reinvigorate Downtowns, Many Urban Malls Are Disappointments," *Wall Street Journal,* November 16, 1992, pp. B1, B6.

CLOSE TO THE CUSTOMER

Airport Retailing

Airplane orders are at a record high, and new domestic airports are being built for the first time since 1974. According to the Federal Aviation Administration, passenger boardings on U.S. airlines will increase by 68 percent over the next decade. By the turn of the century, takeoffs and landings will increase by 29 percent. Without significant increase in airport capacity, more delays will occur, resulting in more time spent in airports by travelers.

The growth in air travel spells out greater opportunities for retailers to generate sales at airports. Well-known retailers are beginning to recognize this potential. Busy travelers will buy high-quality merchandise if they do not have to pay exorbitant prices for the convenience that airport shopping brings.

At Pittsburgh's airport, the newest in the United States, retailers have agreed to charge prices that are no higher than those at sister stores in suburban malls. Two dozen stores have opened in the airport's Air Mall, including The Nature Company, Body Shop, PGA Tour Shop, Tie Rack, Electronics Boutique, and Cartoon Cinema Classics. Some stores, the Body Shop for one, are reporting exceptional sales, but others, like Cartoon Cinema Classics, which sells stuffed toys and novelties, are finding business below expectations. Nonetheless, Pittsburgh's airport may start a trend in the United States that has already been apparent in European and Asian airports. The new Denver airport is planning for national and local merchants at each concourse.

Airport retailers have never been particularly interested in being customer-friendly. Focusing on operations, most airports still award one operator a contract to run all the concessions, which in effect reduces competition. But as the airline industry has suffered in general, airports are looking for ways to generate new revenues. One way, as the Pittsburgh airport is discovering, is to appeal to time-pressured but value-conscious travelers.

Not all airports are conducive to shopping. At Chicago's O'Hare, for instance, retailers would need a store in every terminal for maximum exposure. All passengers at Pittsburgh's airport must go through the Air Mall to get to any of the terminals. But millions of travelers pass through airports each year, many of them with incomes above $50,000 and with an hourlong layover between connections. These numbers are leading many industry observers to conclude that airports will find a way to bring retailers close to the customer.

Sources: Valerie Reitman, "Shops Take Off at Pittsburgh's Airport," *Wall Street Journal*, December 7, 1992, pp. B1–B2; Howard C. Gelbtuch, "Airport Retailing Is Taking Off," *Appraisal Journal*, April 1992, pp. 163–169; and Janet Porter, "UK Airports to Market Retailing Expertise in U.S.," *Journal of Commerce and Commercial*, July 30, 1991, p. 4A.

■ **image** the mental picture—both functional and psychological—that the consumer has of a retail store

Image   The mental picture—both functional and psychological—that the consumer has of a retail store is the store's **image.** A retail store must strive to develop an image that is appropriate for its target market. Some retailers use advertisements to create a prestigious image; other firms spend considerable sums for retail space, because a certain address carries prestige.

Both shopper characteristics and store characteristics influence a store's image. Shopper characteristics include demographics, lifestyle, perception, and behavior. Elderly consumers, for example, attach more importance than do younger consumers to whether the store has convenient parking and a rest area and whether it is close to other stores.[55] Factors such as clientele, location, promotional emphasis, integrity, convenience, economy, and the clarity and strength of the existing store image constitute store characteristics.[56] A retailer must understand the importance of these various characteristics in forming a store image. For example, the image of Ann Taylor suffered when the prices of its clothes were seen as too high for their quality. To restore its image, Ann Taylor introduced higher-quality, private label merchandise at lower prices.[57]

Atmospherics   The physical design of a store's space to appeal to consumers' emotions and to encourage them to buy is called **atmospherics.**[58] The physical aspects of department stores, restaurants, hotels, shops, and even service stations create atmospheres that might be perceived as warm, fresh, colorful, or depressing.

■ **atmospherics** the physical design of a store's space to appeal to consumers' emotions and to encourage them to buy

Atmospherics can be used in several ways when designing a store's space. One study found that color is important in attracting shoppers toward displays and providing certain aesthetic qualities that affect the image of the store and merchandise. Subjects in a furniture store, for example, were drawn to bright, warm colors such as yellow and red.[59] Casual Corner specialty stores use color schemes and seasonal displays to create an atmosphere that appeals to the working woman looking for a fashionable wardrobe.

Other atmospheric components are sound and smell. A retailer may be characterized by silence or soft music or even a noisy environment. Stores that have a distinct scent of perfume or smell of prepared food provide a unique atmosphere. The sweet aroma of baking pastries in a grocery store may stimulate spontaneous purchases of those goods.

Management must ensure that the retail store's atmosphere is consistent with the tastes of the target market. Thus a discount department store should try to create an atmosphere of practicality and frugality, and a high-fashion boutique should strive for an ambiance of style and novelty. Some retailers adapt the atmospherics of individual departments to appeal to different market segments. The "junior" department, discount basement, and hardware section may each have a unique atmosphere created through music and visual elements. Table 17.5 summarizes the various components of a restaurant's atmospherics.

[55] James R. Lumpkin and Robert E. Hite, "Retailers' Offerings and Elderly Consumers' Needs: Do Retailers Understand the Elderly?" *Journal of Business Research,* June 1988, pp. 313–326.
[56] Edgar R. Pessemier, "Store Image and Positioning," *Journal of Retailing,* Spring 1980, pp. 96–97.
[57] Teri Agins, "Ann Taylor Aims to Resew Torn Image," *Wall Street Journal,* September 14, 1992, pp. B1, B5.
[58] Philip Kotler, "Atmospherics as a Marketing Tool," *Journal of Retailing,* Winter 1973–1974, p. 50.
[59] Joseph A. Bellizzi and Ayn E. Crowley, "The Effects of Color in Store Design," *Journal of Retailing,* Spring 1983, pp. 21–25.

TABLE 17.5
Key Elements of
Restaurant Atmospherics

1. Appearance of exterior building and parking lot
2. Initial interior visual impression
3. Appearance and greeting of host or hostess
4. Lighting (bright—gregarious, casual to dim—intimate, romantic)
5. Carpeting (existence or nonexistence, type, thickness, color)
6. Wall decor and color scheme (type of wall covering, pictures, mirrors, greenery)
7. Music system (music type, tempo, loudness, sound quality)
8. Table arrangements
9. Air quality (odor, temperature, circulation)
10. Existence or nonexistence of a separated, nonsmoking area
11. General noise level (patrons' conversations, rattling dishes)
12. Number and appearance of other diners (dress, age, families with children)
13. Open appearance of a bar
14. Apparent attitude and friendliness of employees
15. Type and quality of furnishings
16. Use and type of place mats or table coverings, napkins, place settings
17. Interaction, if any, with owner, manager, or chef

Source: Ronald E. Milliman, "Restaurant Atmospherics," *Restaurants USA,* January 1988, pp. 22–23. Reprinted from the January 1988 issue of *Restaurants USA,* the monthly publication of the National Restaurant Association.

Scrambled Merchandising

■ **scrambled merchandising** the retailing strategy of adding unrelated products and product lines to an existing product mix

Scrambled merchandising is the retailing strategy of adding unrelated products and product lines—particularly fast-moving, high-volume items—to an existing product mix. This practice may be used to increase traffic, convert the store into a one-stop shopping center, generate higher profit margins, or stimulate impulse purchases. For instance, small kitchen appliances and watches are commonly scrambled by grocery stores.

Scrambled merchandising has several limitations. Retailers must deal with an additional group of marketing channel members and may lack expertise in buying, selling, and providing service for the scrambled products. Also, expanding into too many product areas may result in low turnover for some products. Finally, consumers may become confused about a store's image.

The Wheel of Retailing

■ **wheel of retailing**
a popular theory regarding the origin and evolution of retail stores

When attempting to make strategic decisions, retailers must be aware of the process through which retailers evolve and develop. One popular theory regarding the origin and evolution of retail stores is the **wheel of retailing,** illustrated in Figure 17.8. According to this hypothesis, new types of retailers typically enter the marketplace as low-status, low-margin, low-price operators, much like traditional discount stores (the *entry phase*). In the *trading-up phase,* retailers attempt to increase sales by improving facilities and adding product offerings and services, which in turn increase their investments and operating costs; these costs are passed on to consumers in the form of higher

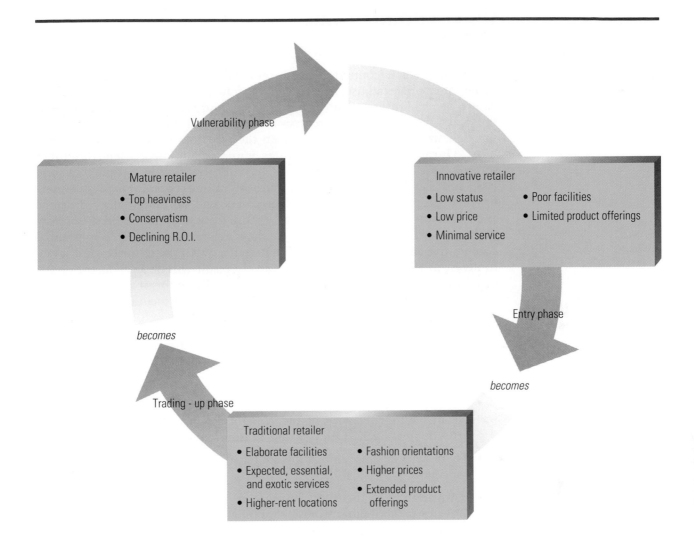

FIGURE 17.8
Wheel of Retailing

Source: Reprinted with the permission of Macmillan Publishing Company from *Retailing,* Fourth Edition by Dale M. Lewison. Copyright © 1991 by Macmillan Publishing Company.

prices. Finally, in the *vulnerable phase,* retailers mature as high-status, high-cost, high-price merchants, vulnerable to newer types of retailers entering the wheel of retailing.[60]

Supermarkets are going through the phases of the wheel of retailing. When they were introduced to shoppers in 1921, supermarkets offered lower food prices than the traditional general and specialty stores of the time, but only limited services. In time, they added a variety of new services, including delicatessens, free coffee, gourmet food sections, and children's areas with cartoon films. Today, supermarkets are being challenged by superstores and hypermarkets. These huge low-cost, low-price retailers offer consumers more product choices and lower prices than do traditional supermarkets.

[60]Dale M. Lewison, *Retailing,* 4th ed. (New York: Macmillan, 1991), pp. 72–73.

THE CHANGING RETAIL ENVIRONMENT

Successful retailers continuously monitor the dynamic retail environment to make appropriate adjustments in retail strategies. As we have noted, the nature of retailing has changed significantly and will continue to change in the years ahead. The retail recession of 1989 to 1991 was a major hurdle through which the industry passed on the way to a new retailing environment. During that period, the industry witnessed an unprecedented number of bankruptcies. Retail sales in the 1990s will grow slowly, people will shop less, and shoppers will be more purposeful and thus more destination-oriented than during the 1980s. Consumers will be more value-conscious and less status-conscious. They will be more loyal to specific stores. Successful stores will be more attentive to their target customers. A substantial competitive advantage will go to those retailers with the resources and savvy to invest in technology. In short, the likely result will be an industry dominated by a small number of large, technologically sophisticated firms.[61]

The general trends taking place in the United States include the following:

- Competition will remain extremely strong and the opportunities for expansion will be much reduced compared with those in the 1980s.

- There will be less growth in retail spending.

- Expansion opportunities will lie in acquisitions and mergers, the increasing diversity of the American consumer, and specific growth areas such as Florida and Washington state.

- There will be less innovation in terms of new store types and concepts.

- Innovation will focus on improving the profitability of existing stores, shopping stores, shopping centers, and distribution systems.

- The focus on existing stores and shopping centers will take two major forms—the application of information technology and systems to achieve greater efficiency and to cut costs, and smarter store-level marketing, employing electronic point-of-sale systems and consumer research.[62]

Technology is perhaps the most dynamic, rapidly changing area of retailing. Technology can be used to increase speed and efficiency and to help achieve overall retail objectives. In a survey of 256 retailers, Ernst & Young

[61] Ira Kalish, "After the Dust Settles: Retailing in the 1990s," *Chain Store Age Executive,* August 1992, pp. 10A–12A.
[62] David Rogers, "An Overview of American Retail Trends," *International Journal of Retail & Distribution Management,* 1991, pp. 3–12.

report several trends in retail technology. More retailers will rely on out-sourcing—contracting with other firms outside of the company—for a variety of technology functions, including operations systems. Technology will also be used to improve customer service by identifying merchandise that is on sale and by determining product availability from the warehouse or another store.[63] Strong systems will enable retailers to improve customer service by reducing transaction time, enhancing inventory replenishment, and freeing employees to concentrate on the needs of the customers rather than on paperwork. Technology will also allow stores to reduce costs, improve distribution efficiency, and engage in *micromarketing*—satisfying the needs of a diverse customer base.[64] Stores and merchandise will be differentiated to appeal to different consumer needs.

Retailers will continue to spend on automatic identification technologies like bar-code scanning.[65] These technologies have proven to be good investments by reducing transaction time and cashier error and by providing a valuable tool for inventory planning and control. Symbol Technologies of Bohemia, New York, is testing a new bar-code technology that can store about one hundred times more information than existing bar codes. When marketed, the new bar code will tell where the product came from, where it is supposed to go, and how it should be handled in transit.[66]

Retailers will be pressured to become more efficient as margins shrink. The retail consulting firm Management Horizons predicts that by the year 2000 retailers now accounting for half of all sales will disappear through bankruptcies, mergers, and other reorganizations.[67] As the consolidation of retailers continues, many are rethinking their distribution. Distribution centers are shrinking and cycle times are compressing. Many retailers are forming strategic alliances with vendors that aim at improving in-stock positions, shorting order times, and reducing inventories in the stores as well as in distribution centers. Relationships between retailers and vendors allow each party to share the inventory risk.[68] Retailers are also expected to add more store brands, which are already resulting in higher margins, attracting an increasing number of consumers, and providing a way for stores to differentiate themselves from competitors.[69]

Retailers face many challenges in the years ahead. Survival will be not only a matter of providing the goods and service that consumers want, but of providing them in an extremely competitive environment. The customer will truly be King. This means that successful retailers will have to invest in systems that speed transactions, reduce costs and therefore prices, and improve customer service.

[63] "Technology Trends in Retail: An Executive Overview," *Chain Store Age Executive*, October 1992, pp. 6–10.
[64] Kalish, pp. 10A–12A.
[65] Gary Robins, "Auto ID Update," *Stores*, June 1992, pp. 31–33.
[66] Mark Alpert, "Building a Better Bar Code," *Fortune*, June 15, 1992, p. 101.
[67] Schiller et al., pp. 66–73.
[68] "1992: A Pivotal Year?" *Chain Store Age Executive*, April 1992, pp. 6A–7A.
[69] "Retailers Hungry for Store Brands," *Advertising Age*, January 11, 1993, p. 20.

SUMMARY

Retailing includes all the marketing activities involved in selling products to ultimate consumers for personal, family, or household use. Most retailers try to develop product assortments—collections of diverse products and competing brands.

There are three major types of retail stores: mass merchandisers (supermarkets, superstores, combination stores, hypermarkets, discount stores, warehouse showrooms, catalogue showrooms, and warehouse/wholesale clubs); department stores (conventional, general merchandise, and corporate chains); and specialty stores (traditional and off-price retailers). The distinctions among types of retailers are based on the number and types of products and services they offer their customers.

Retail franchising is a contractual agreement in which a supplier (the franchiser) grants a dealer (the franchisee) the right to sell products in exchange for some type of consideration. A franchiser may authorize retailers or wholesalers to sell a product or may provide brand names, techniques, or other services rather than an actual product.

Nonstore retailing activities take place outside traditional store environments. Types of nonstore retailing are in-home selling, direct marketing (telemarketing or mail-order retailing), and automatic vending.

The structure of retailing differs from country to country. Some countries have a large number of retailers that offer limited services. Others have a small number of retailers serving many consumers. To overcome the deficiencies in the structure and size of some foreign retailers, many large firms are expanding their operations throughout the world. The growth in the number of international retailers is expected to continue.

Retailers must consider several factors when developing retail strategies. Store location is a critical issue because it determines the trade area from which customers will be drawn. The store's environment, another strategic factor, includes its image and atmospherics. Scrambled merchandising is the retailing strategy of adding unrelated products and product lines to an existing product mix. This practice may be used to enhance business in a number of ways. Finally, retailers must be aware of the theory of the wheel of retailing. According to this theory, new types of retailers usually enter the market as low-status, low-margin, low-price operators who eventually evolve into high-cost, high-price merchants, vulnerable to new institutions just entering the cycle.

The nature of retailing is changing significantly and will continue to change in the years ahead. Retail sales will grow slowly as people shop less. The future will likely see an industry dominated by a small number of large, technically sophisticated firms. Successful retailers will have the insight and resources to invest in systems that speed transactions, reduce costs and prices, and improve customer service.

KEY TERMS

retailing	nonstore retailing
product assortment	in-home selling
mass merchandiser	direct marketing
supermarket	telemarketing
superstore	telephone retailing
combination store	mail-order retailing
hypermarket	automatic vending
discount store	image
warehouse showroom	atmospherics
catalogue showroom	scrambled merchandising
warehouse/wholesale club	wheel of retailing
department store	
specialty store	
traditional specialty store	
off-price retailer	
retail franchising	

QUESTIONS FOR DISCUSSION AND REVIEW

1. Why are retailers so important in the marketing channel?

2. What is a mass merchandiser? Give examples of three different types of mass merchandisers.

3. What is the difference between a warehouse showroom and a warehouse club?

4. What makes department stores unique?

5. What is the difference between a traditional specialty store and an off-price retailer?

6. What is retail franchising? What are the major types of retail franchising? Give an example of each type.

7. How does nonstore retailing differ from traditional retailing?

8. How do you account for the popularity of direct marketing? Name some products that you recently purchased that involved direct marketing activities.

9. What are some of the ways in which retailing differs from country to country?

10. How is retailing changing throughout the world? Give an example of one of these changes that you have experienced.

11. What factors should be considered when selecting a store location?

12. What are the advantages and disadvantages of freestanding stores, unplanned business districts, and planned shopping centers?

13. Why are image and atmospherics so important to retail stores?

14. What is scrambled merchandising? Why would a firm use this practice?

15. What does the wheel of retailing suggest? Can you think of a case in which you observed the wheel of retailing turning?

16. Describe some of the future trends in retailing.

CASES

17.1 WAL-MART STORES' STRATEGY SUCCEEDS

Wal-Mart Stores was a well-kept secret for years. Except for stories about the wealth of founder Sam Walton, Wal-Mart received little attention. This low profile changed in 1988, when Wal-Mart was named in *Fortune* magazine's survey as the ninth most admired corporation in America. It ranked third among all corporations in 1993, and first among retailers. Now the largest, fastest-growing, and most profitable retailer in the world, Wal-Mart is getting attention.

Walton opened the first Wal-Mart in tiny Rogers, Arkansas, in 1962. His strategy was to focus on small towns. Conventional wisdom was that a discount store couldn't make it in a town smaller than fifty thousand. But Walton believed that national discounters were ignoring rural towns, and he found that small towns were an excellent niche. By offering good prices, a local discount store could keep people shopping at home instead of traveling several hours to a larger city. Walton's assumptions were correct. Wal-Mart has been growing at an average of more than 25 percent a year for over a decade. Roughly 365,000 people work in some 1,850 Wal-Mart stores, a 32 percent increase in only two years; new stores open weekly. The stores sell nearly $45 billion worth of merchandise annually, including clothing, small appliances, cosmetics, and more than fifty thousand other items.

Walton's location strategy was to build thirty or forty stores within 600 miles of a distribution center. After the stores were opened in rural towns, Wal-Mart would expand to nearby large metropolitan areas, such as Dallas, Kansas City, and St. Louis. When one geographic area reached its saturation point, Wal-Mart would expand into a new area. Wal-Mart uses eighteen distribution centers to serve stores in forty-four states. It orders directly from manufacturers and uses its own trucks for delivery. By using its own distribution system and quantity discounts, Wal-Mart realizes a tremendous cost savings, which it passes along to customers.

Wal-Mart's image and atmosphere are consistent with its pledge to give customer satisfaction. The physical facilities are plain, resembling a large warehouse. But the customer is number one. A sign reading "Satisfaction Guaranteed" hangs over the entrance to every store. Customers are often welcomed by an employee, called a "people greeter," eager to lend a helping hand. This customer orientation has enabled Wal-Mart to rely more on its reputation and word-of-mouth advertising. But as Wal-Mart moves into major urban markets and as competition among discount chains intensifies, it is spending more on advertising. The chain spent only $2.5 million on network television in 1990, $17.7 million in 1991, and more than $21.8 million in 1992.

Sam Walton died in 1992 at the age of 74, but his legacy lives on. He once said there is only one boss—the customer. That statement may best sum up his philosophy. A $1,650 investment in one hundred Wal-Mart stock shares in 1970, when they were made public, is worth $2.7 million today. Said Bernard Marcus, CEO of Home Depot, "He taught American business that the vast number of American people want value. He saw the future and he helped make the future, and I don't think retailing is ever going to go back."

Sam Walton's successor, David Glass, has big shoes to fill. But since he took over for Walton in 1988, sales have soared from $16 billion to $44 billion, passing sales of both Sears and Kmart. To continue growing, Glass plans to build more supercenters, 50 percent larger than typical Wal-Mart stores. Six supercenters have opened and fifteen others are under way. He also wants to make room in stores for wider aisles, rest benches, and other conveniences that will keep customers shopping longer. He is even testing foreign markets. Two stores are now owned in a joint venture in Mexico. Perhaps the greatest challenge facing Glass is the sheer size of Wal-Mart. Communicating with all the stores and employees will become increasingly difficult. Developing enough leaders to run the stores will not be easy either. And now that Wal-Mart is number one, competitors will be taking their best shots at the leader.

Questions for Discussion

1. What type of retail store is Wal-Mart?
2. What is Wal-Mart's location strategy?
3. What type of image and atmosphere has Wal-Mart created?
4. What challenges does Sam Walton's successor face?
5. According to the wheel of retailing, what will be the major threat to Wal-Mart in the future?

Based on information from Christy Fisher, "Wal-Mart Pours Ads into Net TV," *Advertising Age,* January 11, 1993, p. 3; Wendy Zellner, "O.K., So He's Not Sam Walton," *Business Week,* March 16, 1992, pp. 56–58; Bill Saporito, "What Sam Walton Taught America," *Fortune,* May 4, 1992, pp. 104–105; Jennifer Reese, "America's Most Admired Corporations," *Fortune,* February 8, 1993, pp. 44–48; and John Huey, "Wal-Mart: Will It Take Over the World?" *Fortune,* January 30, 1989, pp. 52–61.

17.2   IKEA CORNERS THE FURNITURE BUSINESS

With worldwide sales of $3.7 billion, Swedish-based IKEA (pronounced I *key* ah) is the largest furniture company in the world. From its beginnings as a mail-order retailer in Europe, IKEA has built a worldwide network of immense stores—there are ninety-five in twenty-three countries—that attract millions of customers with low prices, products with wide appeal, and a unique atmosphere and shopping experience.

IKEA's lure is its inexpensive, ready-to-assemble furniture, housewares, and accessories. The furnishings are generally of Scandinavian style, but IKEA also offers a limited line of more traditional items. One factor that has helped the retailer succeed is that it sells the same products in all of its stores. The furniture and decorative items are designed to appeal to consumers regardless of whether they live in Europe, Canada, the United States, Australia, Kuwait, or any of the other countries where outlets are located.

American shoppers welcomed IKEA immediately. When IKEA opened its first U.S. store in suburban Philadelphia, it was a grand event. A six-month media blitz and the mailing of one million catalogues helped draw roughly 130,000 people in the first four days. Sales for the first three months reached $8 million, $2 million higher than initial expectations. The two-story, six-acre store continues to pull in about 35,000 shoppers a week. Consumers responded similarly when the second IKEA opened in Elizabeth, New Jersey. On opening day, the New Jersey turnpike was backed up for nine miles. About 26,000 shoppers crowded into the store, and sales totaled over $1 million that day alone.

Behind IKEA is a simple marketing idea: Keep prices down and make shopping as pleasurable as possible. IKEA's merchandise is priced at 20 to 40 percent below competitors' offerings. The company targets consumers looking for value and willing to do some work themselves, such as serving themselves, transporting purchases, and assembling their furniture at home.

Each store, staffed by red-shirted information clerks, features stylish display rooms and a huge, self-service warehouse equipped with special shopping carts. At the front door, customers are given catalogues, tape measures, pens, and notepaper. They make their way along a well mapped out traffic pattern through the display rooms. The layout enables customers to look, obtain product information, and make purchase decisions without sales help. Signs remind customers that buying furniture unassembled means they pay lower prices and can take the items home. Shoppers pick up their purchases at a loading area and cart them home to assemble. Other important store features are a restaurant, a playroom, a nursery complete with baby sitters, and diaper-changing areas with complimentary diapers. These extras are designed to appeal to 25- to 44-year-old consumers, the group that buys most of the furniture in the United States.

One of IKEA's primary marketing tools is its annual catalogue, with photographs, product specifications, price list, description of the company, and pictures of its playroom and restaurant. IKEA guarantees prices for a year and holds only one sale a year, a strategy intended to increase the store's credibility. Bjorn Bayley, the president of IKEA North America, explains, "If you are always running sales, how does your customer know when he's getting a good price?"

Skillful site selection is another factor in the firm's worldwide success. IKEA scouts metropolitan areas for inexpensive land near major highways, a tactic that allows the company to target customers living up to ninety minutes away from a store. IKEA has stores in the Baltimore, Washington, D.C., Pittsburgh, New York City, and Los Angeles metropolitan areas. The company has focused recently on both U.S. coasts, with plans to establish eight of its huge stores in the New York and Los Angeles markets alone. Although IKEA offers mail-order service in Europe, American shoppers will have to continue to visit IKEA stores. Despite numerous requests from customers, the firm has no current plans to begin a mail-order business in the United States.

With its innovative concept and effective strategies, IKEA has been called "the new wave of retailing." The company opens about eight to ten new stores a year and plans to open as many as sixty U.S. outlets in the next two decades. The United States could become IKEA's largest overseas market by the year 2000. Sales from its seven American stores are around $250 million a year, and annual sales growth is expected to be about 30 percent.

Questions for Discussion

1. What type of retail store is IKEA? Explain.

2. Describe IKEA's strategy for store location, its image, and its atmospherics. How does each contribute to the company's success?

3. Considering current retail environment trends, do you think IKEA will experience continued success and growth in the United States?

4. Would you recommend that IKEA begin a mail-order business in the United States? What are some benefits and drawbacks it could experience?

Based on information from Steven Weinstein, "Masters of Their Universe: IKEA Furnishes More than Homes," *Progressive Grocer,* September 1992, pp. 95–98; Bill Saporito, "IKEA's Got 'Em Lining Up," *Fortune,* March 11, 1991, p. 72; Barbara Solomon, "A Swedish Company Corners the Business: Worldwide," *Management Review,* April 1991, pp. 10–13; Mary Krienke, "IKEA's Anders Moberg: NRF Honors Swedish Home Store President," *Stores,* January 1992, pp. 98–102; and Bill Kelley, "The New Wave from Europe," *Sales & Marketing Management,* November 1987, pp. 45–51.

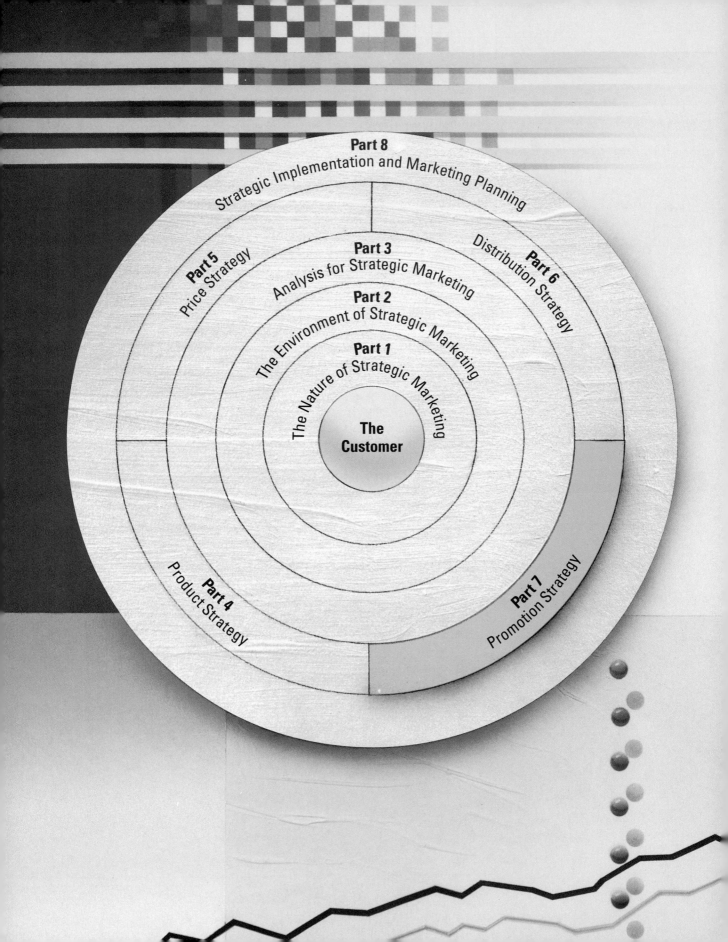

Part 8
Strategic Implementation and Marketing Planning

Part 5
Price Strategy

Part 3
Analysis for Strategic Marketing

Part 6
Distribution Strategy

Part 2
The Environment of Strategic Marketing

Part 1
The Nature of Strategic Marketing

The Customer

Part 4
Product Strategy

Part 7
Promotion Strategy

PART 7

Promotion Strategy

An Overview of Promotion

OBJECTIVES

- *To explain the meaning of promotion and its role in the marketing mix.*

- *To describe the communication process.*

- *To identify the major elements of the promotion mix and some of the factors that affect its composition.*

- *To discuss promotion in global markets.*

- *To identify the unique aspects of promotion for organizational products.*

- *To discuss the impact of promotion on society.*

OUTLINE

On January 20, 1993, William Jefferson Clinton was sworn in as the forty-second president of the United States. Virtually unknown to most Americans eighteen months earlier, the 46-year-old president sounded the note of generational transition in his inaugural address. Perhaps more than any president since John F. Kennedy, Clinton called on Americans to assume greater responsibility for their country's future. Outgoing president George Bush, who once seemed a lock to win a second term, watched stoically from his seat on the Capitol steps.

What was going through George Bush's mind as Bill Clinton took the oath of office? Perhaps he was recalling some of his triumphs during his twelve years in the White House, especially in regard to helping end the Cold War. Or maybe he was thinking about his failure to deal with the troubled economy. One thing is likely: George Bush was wondering about what might have been. Experts, given time to analyze the election, attributed Bush's defeat to his failure to run a positive campaign against Bill Clinton.

From the beginning, the Bush-Quayle advertising campaign ran into trouble. The first television commercial had to be withdrawn because it displayed the presidential seal. Federal law prohibits use of the seal in any way that suggests "sponsorship or approval." The campaign planners scrambled to retrieve the commercials, edit them, and send them back out to be aired. The subsequent television advertisements dealt primarily with Bill Clinton and questions about his character and likely performance. But those closest to both campaigns believed afterward that these negative advertisements backfired, failing to communicate Bush's message to the American people. Martin Puris, President Bush's top adman during the campaign, summed it up this way: "Any good communication, whether it's advertising or otherwise, needs a strong, focused direction to be good and relevant."

President Bush's campaign advertisements, in retrospect, were neither focused nor relevant to voters' concerns. According to Puris, the real issues were the president's accomplishments and his vision for the future. The Bush advertisements, however, included attacks on Clinton's character, experience, and record. One referred to a Clinton plan for a middle-class tax increase. But Clinton had never proposed such a tax. The Democrats had learned a valuable lesson in 1988—that negative advertising works best when it is not responded to effectively. Clinton's campaign team responded immediately to the tax increase advertisement and other negative advertisements; the immediate refutation made them backfire.

In contrast to President Bush's campaign, the Clinton-Gore campaign communicated its message of change loud and clear. The candidates and their advertisements did not waiver from that message, no matter how harsh the attacks from the other side. Millions of voters, one by one, became turned off by President Bush's seeming lack of touch with America's economic woes. In the end, Bush's image grew smaller and smaller, far removed from positive memories of the president as commander-in-chief of Operation Desert Storm.[1] ●

Effective communication is critical if marketing strategies are to be successful, whether in marketing a computer, a hospital, or a political candidate. Problems between families, friends, and even nations can often be attributed to communication failures. Likewise, communication breakdowns can have negative consequences for the marketing of goods, services, and ideas. As President Bush's own top adman put it, the president failed to communicate a clear message to the American people in 1992 and was not re-elected. Many organizations and individuals experience similar problems. Unfortunately, communication is often taken for granted, when in fact it is a very complex activity.[2] The failure to understand this complexity often leads to problems.

Marketers communicate messages about goods, services, ideas and causes, institutions, and people. This communication takes place through a variety of activities, including advertising, publicity, personal selling, and sales promotion. These activities are all part of promotion.

THE DEFINITION AND IMPORTANCE OF PROMOTION

■ **promotion** any communication activity used to inform, persuade, or remind the target market of an organization, its products, and its activities

Promotion refers to any communication activity used to inform, persuade, and remind the target market about an organization, its products, and its activities. Promotion can *directly* facilitate exchanges by communicating information about an organization's goods, services, and ideas to its target markets. For instance, Associated Air Freight, a mid-sized company that competes with larger express air services like Federal Express, directly promotes its services by having sales representatives personally call on executives

[1] Based on information from Steven W. Colford, "Bush Ad Team Slips Up Big in First TV Commercials," *Advertising Age,* August 10, 1992, pp. 1, 36; Lee Walczak, "George Bush Just Didn't Get It," *Business Week,* November 16, 1992, p. 40; Steven W. Colford, "Clinton Adman Says Bush Ad Backfired," *Advertising Age,* November 9, 1992, pp. 1, 42; and Steven Colford, "Bush Adman: 'My Most Frustrating Time,'" *Advertising Age,* November 9, 1992, pp. 1, 42.

[2] E.A. More and R.K. Laird, *Organizations in the Communication Age* (Sydney: Pergamon Press, 1985), p. 1.

of firms that rely on overnight shipping to convince them to give Associated Air Freight a try. Some companies use a flashier method, such as hot air balloons shaped like their products, to facilitate exchanges directly. Car dealers have used videotapes about their brands of cars to deliver personalized messages to prospects.[3]

Promotion can indirectly facilitate exchanges by communicating information about company activities and products to interest groups (such as environmental and consumer groups), current and potential investors, regulatory agencies, and society in general. Promotional activities can help a company justify its existence and maintain positive, healthy relationships with various groups in the marketing environment. For instance, chemical firms use promotion to communicate to the public and various environmental groups that they are acting with sensitivity toward the environment. After tragedies like the 1984 disaster in Bhopal, India—in which more than two thousand people were killed by poison gas that leaked from a Union Carbide plant—the promotional goal of these firms is to relieve health and environmental concerns before even stricter laws and penalties are imposed. The canners of Starkist, Chicken of the Sea, and Bumblebee tuna refused to purchase tuna caught in gill or drift nets, which also catch dolphins. To inform consumers about "dolphin safe" tuna, the companies released announcements to the media throughout the country and advertised on national television networks and in print. The environmental groups Greenpeace and Earth Island Institute recognized Chicken of the Sea and Starkist for their commitment.[4] Figure 18.1 shows how a firm uses promotion to indirectly facilitate exchanges.

Marketing managers may design a single promotional message for a specific target audience or communicate several different messages simultaneously, each targeted at a different group. For instance, Kodak targeted advertisements for its new Photo CD system at gadget fans with household incomes of at least $40,000. To reach this segment, Kodak advertised in such magazines as *Life, Gourmet,* and *Skiing,* and during television programs such as "L.A. Law" and "Late Night with David Letterman."[5] Kodak also developed another message about growth and profitability to be targeted at investors, and a third message about the company's good-will activities for society in general.

To make promotional efforts effective in communicating with consumers and the public, a firm must properly plan, implement, coordinate, and control all communications. First, the firm must obtain and use information from the marketing environment. The extent to which an organization can use promotion to maintain positive relationships with environmental forces depends largely on the quantity and quality of the information it acquires. To illustrate, to effectively communicate information to consumers that will

---

[3]Raymond Serafin, "Car Dealers Reach Prospects with Personalized Video Ads," *Advertising Age,* June 22, 1992, pp. 3, 38.
[4]Donna DeMayo, "Tuna Marketers Using Promotion to Ride the 'Dolphin Safe' Wave," *PROMO,* August 1990, pp. 24, 47.
[5]Joan E. Rigdon, "Kodak Focuses on Promotion of Photo CD," August 24, 1992, pp. B1, B8.

FIGURE 18.1

Facilitating Exchanges
Russell Athletic encourages young women to stay in school, to ensure not only their athletic career, but their future. The Stay in School campaign also illustrates that Russell Athletic is concerned about social issues.

Source: Courtesy of Russell Corporation.

persuade them to buy a particular product, marketers need data about these consumers and about the types of information they use when making purchase decisions for that type of product. Thus the collection (through marketing research) and use of data are critical in successfully communicating with selected markets.

To ensure effective communications with consumers and other groups, marketing managers must first understand the communication process.

THE COMMUNICATION PROCESS

The opening feature explained that President Bush failed to communicate a message that would persuade the American people to re-elect him. Likewise, many organizations fail to communicate effectively with their target audience. No matter how good the message, whether it is delivered in the best advertisement ever made, communication does not take place unless the audience receives the intended message.

■ **communication** the sharing of a common meaning

Communication can be defined as the sharing of a common meaning.[6] This sharing necessitates a transmission of information. In addition, the

---

[6]Terence A. Shimp and M. Wayne Delozier, *Promotion Management and Marketing Communication* (Hinsdale, Ill.: Dryden Press, 1986), pp. 25–26.

shared information must have a common meaning for the individuals involved. If you were to transmit a message in English to a person who understood only French, your meaning would not be understood. Communication can be described as a process in which a message is encoded and transmitted through a medium of transmission to a receiver who decodes it and then transmits some sort of response back to the source of the message (see Figure 18.2).

FIGURE 18.2
The Communication Process

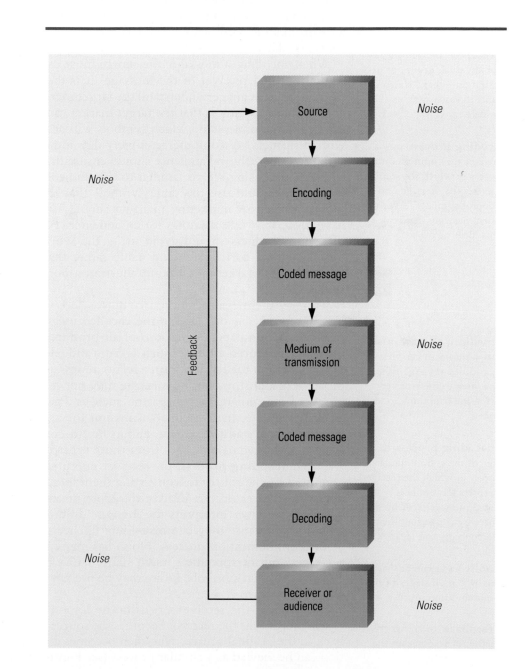

■ **source** a person, group, or organization that has a message to share with another person or group of persons

■ **message** an idea or experience that a source wants to share in the communication process

■ **receiver** the audience—an individual, group, or organization—that a source wants to reach with its message

■ **coding process** the phase of the communication process in which the source converts the message into a group of symbols, called a coded message, that represents ideas or concepts

■ **medium of transmission** a means of carrying the encoded message from the source to the receiver during the communication process

■ **decoding process** the stage of the communication process in which the receiver interprets the symbols (coded message) sent by the source by converting them into concepts and ideas

■ **noise** interference that affects any or all stages of the communication process

■ **feedback** the receiver's reaction or response to the source's message

As shown in Figure 18.2, communication begins with a **source**—a person, group, or organization that has a message to share with another person or group of persons. A **message** is an idea or experience that a source wants to share. A **receiver** (or audience) is the individual, group, or organization the source wants to reach with its message. For example, Giorgio Beverly Hills (the source) sent messages describing its new Red perfume to thousands of women (the receivers, or audience) through department-store promotions and advertisements in women's magazines.

To convey meaning, the source must *encode* the message, or convert it into groups of symbols—called a coded message—that represent ideas or concepts. This encoding is called the **coding process.**

When encoding a message, the source must use symbols that are familiar to the intended receiver of the message. It is therefore very important that the marketing manager understand the target market and present the message in language or symbols that the target market can grasp. Marketing research can be used to understand which symbols will be effective in communicating with customers. A computer company developing a sales presentation targeted at a nontechnical audience should ensure that its presentation is written and delivered using words familiar to that audience. In referring to concepts, the source should use the same symbols that the receiver uses to refer to those concepts. A marketing manager should avoid using symbols that can have more than one meaning for an audience. For instance, a manufacturer of copier products should avoid using the word *xerox* because it may be mistaken for a particular brand name rather than a generic term for copy machines. As Marketing Close-up illustrates, not all messages are written or spoken.

To relay the message, the source must select and use a **medium of transmission**—a means of carrying the encoded message from the source to the receiver. Ink on paper, vibrations of air produced by vocal cords, and electronically produced airwaves such as radio and television signals are examples of transmission media. If a source relays a message through an inappropriate medium of transmission, its message may not reach the right receivers. For instance, a health-related magazine such as *Prevention* would probably be an inappropriate medium of transmission for a cigarette manufacturer's or fast-food chain's advertisement, and its health-conscious audience would not be very receptive to messages from those types of marketers.

In the **decoding process,** the receiver interprets the symbols (coded message) sent by the source by converting them into concepts and ideas. Seldom does the receiver decode exactly the same meaning that a source encoded. When the receiver interprets the message differently from what the source intended, the cause may be **noise**—interference that affects any or all stages of the communication process. Noise has many sources, such as competing messages, misinterpretation, radio static, faulty printing, or use of ambiguous or unfamiliar symbols. Noise may be present at any point of the communication process.

Feedback is the receiver's reaction or response to the source's message. During feedback, the receiver becomes the source of a message that is directed back to the original source, who then becomes a receiver. Thus communication can be viewed as a circular process (see Figure 18.2). However, feedback

MARKETING CLOSE-UP

Nonverbal Communication in the Global Environment

When American firms conduct business in foreign countries, they often underestimate the significance of nonverbal communication. In some cultures, the verbal message is not as important as the nonverbal one. Managers accustomed to communicating through reports, contracts, and other written and verbal communication may be at a disadvantage in a foreign country. In Japan, for instance, considerable nonverbal communication is involved, including eye contact, facial expressions, and proxemics, or the physical and psychological space between people.

Time has different meanings in different countries. In the United States, a delay in responding to a communication is generally taken to mean that the issue is not important to the other party. The amount of time a person is kept waiting for a meeting indicates the importance of the person or subject. For instance, a salesperson kept waiting for several hours may get discouraged because this suggests that the purchasing manager is not interested in the product. But in some foreign countries, waiting is viewed much differently. In Latin America, the time a person is kept waiting means very little. In Japan, a lengthy delay of weeks or months does not mean the party has lost interest. Americans must have patience or risk a breakdown in communication. Giving a person a deadline in the Middle East is viewed as rude and demanding.

The connotations associated with greetings and body motions also vary across countries. Whereas it is traditional to shake hands in America, in India businessmen touch the palms of their hands and nod their heads in greeting. It is considered rude to shake hands with a woman in India. Kissing is considered offensive in India, and is not seen on television, in movies, or in public places. Bowing is the traditional form of greeting in Japan, where the culture puts an emphasis on showing respect, even for business cards. In Latin America a hearty embrace and friendly slap on the back are used for greeting. Arm gestures are used for emphasis in Latin America, the raised eyebrow means "yes" in the Middle East, and a forefinger to the nose means "me" in Japan.

Space also has different meanings throughout the world. In the United States, office size is an indicator of the relative status of an individual. Executives tend to have the largest corner office. As stature in the organization decreases, so does the size of the office. But the French locate offices according to activities and interests; the supervisor is usually found in the middle of subordinates to improve communication. And what is considered crowded in America is seen as spacious in Arab and Spanish cultures.

Finally, shapes, sizes, and colors convey different meanings. In Japan, pine bamboo or plum patterns are positive, as are muted shades. Cultural shapes such as the Buddha and combinations of black, dark gray, and white have negative overtones. Round or square shapes are acceptable in the Middle East, but symbols such as the six-pointed star or raised thumb are avoided. Europeans favor the colors of white and blue, whereas black generally has negative overtones. These differences have implications for dress, product and package design, and various forms of communication such as advertising.

Sources: Larry M. Hynson, Jr., "Doing Business with South Korea—Part II: Business Practices and Culture," *East Asian Executive Reports,* September 15, 1991, pp. 17–19; Evelyn Gilbert, "Japanese Pose Unique Challenge to U.S. Insurers," *National Underwriter,* July 22, 1991, pp. 4, 10–11; Arnold G. Abrams, "Body Language Speaks Louder than Words," *Life & Health Insurance Sales,* August 1992, pp. 10, 40; and James C. Simmons, "A Matter of Interpretation," *American Way,* April 1983, pp. 106–111.

may not take place immediately. For instance, a consumer-products manufacturer may advertise the benefits of a product (the message), but the consumer may not actually provide feedback until some time after receiving the source's message.

■ **channel capacity**
a limit on the volume of information that the communication process (or least efficient component thereof) can handle effectively

The communication process has a **channel capacity**, a limit on the volume of information that it can handle effectively. Channel capacity is determined by the least efficient component of the communication process. With verbal communications, there is a limit to how fast a source can speak and how much a receiver can decode. If a company develops an advertisement containing more than one message, the communication process may not be totally effective because the audience (receivers) may not be able to decode all the messages at the same time.

THE PROMOTION MIX

■ **promotion mix** the specific combination of four promotional methods—advertising, personal selling, sales promotion, and publicity—used by an organization for a specific product

Businesses use various promotional methods to communicate with individuals, groups, and organizations. Just as product, price, distribution, and promotion make up the *marketing mix,* so four components make up the promotion mix. The **promotion mix** is the specific combination of these four promotional methods—advertising, personal selling, sales promotion, and publicity—that an organization uses for a specific product.

The next sections present some general characteristics of each element of the promotion mix, investigate the primary factors that influence a company to use the various elements, and examine how promotion must be adapted for global markets. Chapters 19 and 20 analyze the promotion mix elements in more detail.

■ **integrated marketing communications** the application of various communication methods to accomplish marketing objectives

Recently, marketing firms have emphasized the need to coordinate various forms of persuasive communications. **Integrated marketing communications** is the application of various communication methods including advertising, sales promotion, public relations, direct marketing, and personal selling, to accomplish marketing objectives.[7] Each communication activity reinforces the other. In a survey of 100 marketing company executives, integrated marketing communications was rated as the most important factor that will influence marketing strategies in the next three to five years.[8] For promotions to be effective, each element of the promotion mix should reinforce the other through a well-planned—or integrated—communication program.

Promotion Mix Elements

The four major elements of the promotion mix are advertising, personal selling, sales promotion, and publicity. All four elements may be used to promote some products, but only two or three may be used for others.

[7]Regina Eisman, "Incentive Marketing: Building the Future," *Incentive,* June 1992, pp. 33–34, 100.
[8]Scott Hume, "Integrated Marketing: Who's in Charge Here?" *Advertising Age,* March 22, 1993, pp. 1, 52.

FIGURE 18.3
Promotion Mix Elements
Wrigley uses advertising to communicate its message to a target audience: smokers.

Source: Reprinted courtesy of the Wm. Wrigley Jr. Company.

■ **advertising** a paid form of nonpersonal communication about an organization, its products, or its activities that is transmitted through a mass medium to a target audience

Advertising   **Advertising** is a paid form of nonpersonal communication about an organization, its products, or its activities that is transmitted through a mass medium to a target audience (see Figure 18.3). The mass medium could be television, radio, newspapers, magazines, direct mail, signs on mass transit vehicles, outdoor displays, handbills, catalogues, or directories.

Advertising gives marketers the flexibility to reach an extremely large target audience or to focus on a smaller, precisely defined segment of the population. Some advertisements, for instance, are targeted at the growing Hispanic and Asian markets. Others are directed toward children, parents, senior citizens, or large portions of the population such as women or college students.

Advertising is an extremely cost-efficient promotional method because it can reach a large number of people at a low cost per person. For instance, the cost of a 30-second commercial during the 1993 Super Bowl was $850,000.[9] Since some 39 million American households watch the game each year, advertisers such as PepsiCo, Anheuser–Busch, Nike, and other companies believe the exposure their products receive from these advertisements

[9]Mark Landler, "Super Bowl '93: The Bodies Are Already Piled Up," *Business Week,* January 25, 1993, p. 65.

makes the costs worthwhile.[10] Advertising enables the user to transmit a message a number of times. In addition, the visibility that an organization gains from advertising can be used to enhance its public image.

Advertising has several drawbacks. Even though the cost per person reached may be low, the absolute dollar outlay can be extremely high. Organizations like Procter & Gamble, Coca-Cola, 3M, and IBM may spend millions of dollars to advertise a single product. These high costs can limit, and sometimes eliminate, advertising as an element of the promotion mix. Feedback from advertising is generally slow, if it occurs at all, and measurement of the effect of advertising on sales is difficult. Finally, advertising normally has less persuasive power over customers than other forms of promotion, such as personal selling.

Personal Selling   Face-to-face communication with potential buyers to inform them about and persuade them to buy an organization's product is called **personal selling**.[11] A real estate agent uses personal selling when he or she shows a house and tries to persuade the prospective home owner to purchase it. Because of its one-on-one nature, personal selling can be much more persuasive than advertising. In addition, personal-selling efforts generate immediate feedback, enabling the salesperson to adjust the message in response to customers' needs for information. However, because personal selling is communication with only one or a few individuals, it costs considerably more than advertising, which reaches a much larger audience.

Virtually everyone in the organization is involved in varying degrees in personal selling. From the president of a bank to the tellers, or from the CEO of a large manufacturing organization to the assembly-line workers, members of the organization must sell others both inside and outside on the organization's mission, people, and products. Although a salesperson may be responsible for making the actual calls on customers, other members of the organization must also be committed to sales. In Chapter 21, we examine how sales is also an internal function; leaders must sell others on the marketing goals of the organization.

Sales Promotion   **Sales promotion** is an activity or material that offers consumers, salespersons, or resellers a direct inducement for purchasing a product. This inducement, which adds value to or incentive for the product, might take the form of a coupon, sweepstakes, refund, demonstration, or display. As you can see in Figure 18.4, some firms even give away free samples as an inducement to purchase a product. The term *sales promotion* should not be confused with *promotion;* sales promotion is only one aspect of the larger area of promotion, which also includes advertising, personal selling, and publicity.

■ **personal selling** face-to-face communication with potential buyers to inform them about and persuade them to buy an organization's product

■ **sales promotion** an activity or material that offers consumers, salespersons, or resellers a direct inducement for purchasing a product

[10]Deidre A. Depke, "How to Spend $1 Million a Minute," *Business Week,* February 3, 1992, p. 34.
[11]Rolph E. Anderson, Joseph F. Hair, Jr., and Alan J. Bush, *Professional Sales Management* (New York: McGraw-Hill, 1988), p. 43.

FIGURE 18.4
Sales Promotion
Johnson & Johnson Vision Products, Inc. offers a free trial pair of SUREVUE® contact lenses, daily wear lenses you change every two weeks.

Source: Courtesy of Johnson and Johnson Vision Products, Inc.

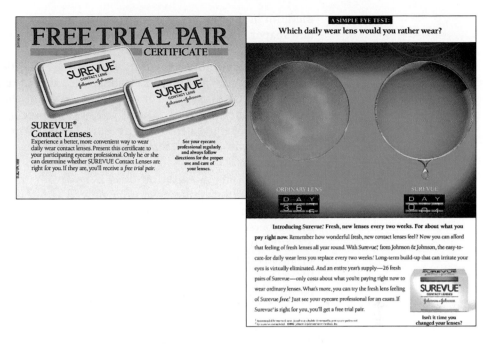

Sales promotion techniques are gaining popularity with consumers. For example, U.S. consumers increased their use of coupons by 14 percent in 1991, with resulting savings of $4 billion.[12] The trend continued in 1992, with an estimated 13 percent increase and a savings of $4.7 billion.[13] Manufacturers are reducing the expiration time for coupons to make them even more of a marketing weapon. Sweepstakes are also gaining favor. Although the value of a 50-cents-off coupon is known in advance, consumers like the idea that they could win a valuable prize such as a new car or a trip to Hawaii.

Organizations often make use of sales promotions to reinforce the effectiveness of other ingredients of the promotion mix, especially advertising and personal selling. Sales promotion can be used as the primary promotion vehicle, although such use is unusual. In contrast to advertising and personal selling, which are generally used on a continuous or cyclical basis, sales promotion devices get more irregular use. Often they are designed to produce immediate, short-term increases. For example, as the economy stagnated and consumer spending fell in the early 1990s, the use of health and beauty aid coupons rose 11.2 percent and the use of grocery-product coupons increased 2.6 percent.[14]

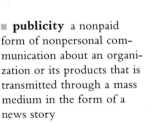

■ **publicity** a nonpaid form of nonpersonal communication about an organization or its products that is transmitted through a mass medium in the form of a news story

Publicity **Publicity** is a nonpaid form of nonpersonal communication about an organization or its products that is transmitted through a mass

[12]"Coupon Redemption up 14%," *Marketing News,* March 2, 1992, p. 1.
[13]Scott Hume, "Coupon Use Jumps 10% as Distribution Soars," *Advertising Age,* October 5, 1992, pp. 3, 44.
[14]Scott Hume, "Couponing Reaches Record Clip," *Advertising Age,* February 3, 1992, pp. 1, 41.

medium in the form of a news story. Examples of publicity include magazine, newspaper, radio, and television news stories about new retail stores or products, firms' personnel changes, or special activities. For instance, when Mattel held special promotions and events to mark the thirtieth anniversary of its Barbie doll, the celebrations (which included a celebrity-attended party in New York City) received much attention from the media. Publicity differs from the other elements of the promotion mix in that it does not directly facilitate exchanges. Instead, its purpose is to provide information to the general public and to create and maintain a favorable public image of the organization.

Although an organization does not pay for the transmission of publicity messages, publicity should not be viewed as *free* communication. Companies spend millions of dollars each year preparing news releases and encouraging media personnel to broadcast or print them. To perform these activities on a regular basis, an organization must hire employees, a public relations firm, or an advertising agency. In any case, the organization pays for the costs of these activities. Publicity must be planned and implemented so that it is compatible with, and supportive of, other elements in the promotion mix.

Factors Affecting the Composition of a Promotion Mix

Although a promotion mix can be composed of all four elements, a marketing manager may not use all four. Moreover, firms that market multiple product lines generally use different promotion mixes for each line or product. Many factors affect the composition of the promotion mix, including the organization's promotional objectives and policies, the organization's promotional budget, the characteristics of the target market, the characteristics of the product, and the cost and availability of promotional methods.

Promotional Objectives and Policies   The composition of an organizational promotion mix depends on its promotional objectives. Of course, the overall objective of promotion is for the receiver (target customer) to take some type of action: to buy a product, stop smoking, or make a donation to charity. But to achieve this primary objective, a firm may have what is sometimes referred to as a hierarchy of objectives. This hierarchy represents the response process the receiver may go through before taking action. One model of this response process is the AIDA model. The **AIDA model** maintains that the receiver goes through four successive stages: attention, interest, desire, and action.

The AIDA model in Figure 18.5 illustrates how an organization's promotion mix depends on its promotional objectives. For instance, if a firm's promotional objective is to make consumers aware of a new product, its promotion mix is likely to be heavily oriented toward advertising, sales promotion, and possibly publicity. If a nonprofit organization's promotional objective is to get a target market to take action by making donations, personal-selling efforts might be used to target potential donors and to facili-

■ **AIDA model** a model of the receiver's response process that maintains that a receiver goes through successive stages of attention, interest, desire, and action

FIGURE 18.5
The AIDA Model

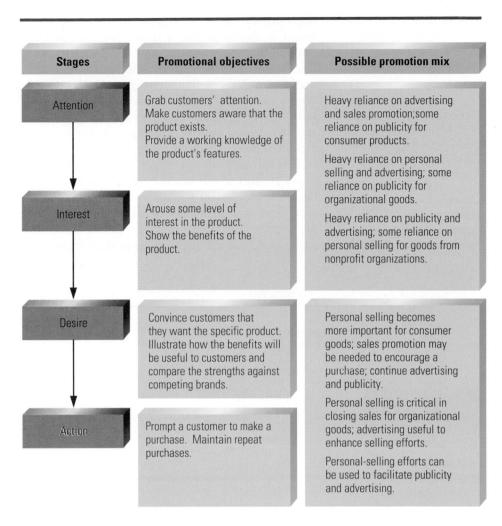

Stages	Promotional objectives	Possible promotion mix
Attention	Grab customers' attention. Make customers aware that the product exists. Provide a working knowledge of the product's features.	Heavy reliance on advertising and sales promotion;some reliance on publicity for consumer products. Heavy reliance on personal selling and advertising; some reliance on publicity for organizational goods. Heavy reliance on publicity and advertising; some reliance on personal selling for goods from nonprofit organizations.
Interest	Arouse some level of interest in the product. Show the benefits of the product.	
Desire	Convince customers that they want the specific product. Illustrate how the benefits will be useful to customers and compare the strengths against competing brands.	Personal selling becomes more important for consumer goods; sales promotion may be needed to encourage a purchase; continue advertising and publicity. Personal selling is critical in closing sales for organizational goods; advertising useful to enhance selling efforts. Personal-selling efforts can be used to facilitate publicity and advertising.
Action	Prompt a customer to make a purchase. Maintain repeat purchases.	

tate publicity and advertising efforts. To get audiences to overcome their apprehension about a movie that shows a great deal of pain and suffering, movie studios try to let audiences know that the movie explores other themes as well. In marketing the movie *Alive,* which recounts the 1972 crash of a chartered plane carrying an Uruguayan rugby team and how sixteen of the forty-five passengers survived seventy-two days in the Andes mountains by eating their dead teammates, the Walt Disney studio relied on advertisements and word-of-mouth to convince potential viewers of the merits of the movie.[15]

When deciding on the composition of a promotion mix, marketing managers must also decide whether to use a push policy or a pull policy. With a

[15] David J. Jefferson, "Somber Themes of Two New Films Test Merits of Studios' Marketing Strategies," *Wall Street Journal,* January 15, 1993, pp. B1, B2.

■ **push policy** promotion of a product only to the next member down in the marketing channel

■ **pull policy** promotion of a product directly to consumers to stimulate strong consumer demand

FIGURE 18.6
Comparison of Push and Pull Promotional Policies

push policy, the marketer promotes the product only to the next member down in the marketing channel (see Figure 18.6). In a consumer marketing channel with wholesalers and retailers, the producer focuses its promotion efforts on the wholesaler, who is the member below the producer in the marketing channel. Each channel member, in turn, promotes, or *pushes,* the product down through the marketing channel. Marketers employing a push policy generally focus on personal-selling efforts, although sales promotion and advertising may be used in conjunction with personal selling to push the products down through the channel.

By contrast, a business using a **pull policy** promotes its product directly to consumers to stimulate strong consumer demand for the product (refer to Figure 18.6). When consumers learn, through promotional activities, about a product that they believe will satisfy their needs and wants, they ask for the product in retail stores. To satisfy customers' demand, retailers in turn try to purchase the product from the producer or wholesalers. A pull policy

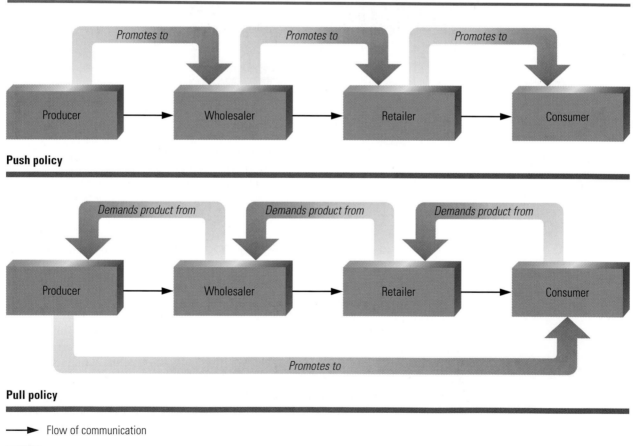

FIGURE 18.7
Pull Promotion Policy
Marion Merrell Dow advertises its nicotine patch to potential customers, even though the product is available by prescription only. This type of promotion policy stimulates strong demand for the product and encourages consumers to ask their doctor about it.

Source: Courtesy of Marion Merrell Dow, Inc.

"Ask your doctor about the Nicoderm patch."

Available by prescription only.

NICODERM®
[nicotine transdermal system]

is therefore intended to *pull* products down through the marketing channel by stimulating demand at the consumer level. To stimulate strong consumer demand, a marketer focuses promotional efforts on intensive advertising and, sometimes, on sales promotion. Many pharmaceutical companies use a pull policy, advertising directly to consumers and encouraging them to ask their doctors about certain prescription drugs (see Figure 18.7).

Some producers attempt to balance push and pull strategies. In other words, they use promotion to encourage retailers to stock the product (push strategy) and to induce customers to purchase the product (pull strategy). Today, a greater proportion of promotional dollars is spent on incentives aimed at wholesalers and retailers.[16] Close to the Customer explains how push and pull marketing led to a hit song for Billy Ray Cyrus.

Promotional Budget   The resources available limit how much an organization can spend on promotion. A company with a very small promotional budget will probably rely on personal selling because it is easier to measure a salesperson's contribution to sales than to measure the contribution of ad-

[16]Scott Hume, "Trade Promos Devour Half of All Marketing $," *Advertising Age,* April 13, 1992, pp. 3, 53.

CLOSE TO THE CUSTOMER

Pushing "Achy Breaky Heart"

You can tell my lips to tell my fingertips they won't be reachin' out for you no more, but don't tell my heart, my achy breakin' heart . . ." The Marcy Brothers thought the song would be a hit when they first heard it. So they put it on their 1991 album, recorded by Atlantic Records. Sid Marcy, father and manager of the Marcy Brothers, wanted Atlantic to release the track as a single, but record company officials said the song was too goofy.

The Marcy Brothers were right about the song, but it was Billy Ray Cyrus who made it a hit. Months after the brothers recorded the song, Cyrus began playing the song in nightclubs. He changed the line to "achy breaky heart" and recorded it himself. Unlike Atlantic, Cyrus's record label, Mercury, decided to push the song. Long before most people heard of Billy Ray Cyrus, a promotion team was at work. Mercury came up with an ingenious way to promote it after someone in a meeting proposed creating a new line dance based on Cyrus's stage moves. Mercury hired Nashville choreographer Melanie Greenwood to devise the dance, then made an instructional video and sent it to dance clubs.

Mercury sponsored dance contests in clubs, mostly out west. The dance caught on. When fans deluged radio stations with requests to play that achy breaky song, the stations had no choice but to comply. Mercury's decision to release the song as a single—an unusual step for a country song—and to put the single in record stores prompted pop radio stations to add "Achy Breaky Heart" to their play lists when they saw how well it was selling.

The song, written by Don Von Tress (who had never composed a hit record before), went to number one on the country charts and hit the top ten on the pop charts. Cyrus's first album, *Some Gave All,* became the number one pop album in the country even though it received poor reviews. *Entertainment Weekly* labeled Cyrus a "Dew Drop Inn regular who stumbled onto the big time." The big time indeed. Cyrus was written about in *Newsweek* and other publications and made the rounds of all the major talk shows.

The hit song is not much consolation for the Marcy Brothers, who say they would rather be rich than right. Some in Nashville have suggested that Cyrus's success was more the result of promotion than talent. Others, including music critic Robert Oermann, like Cyrus's first album because the music is fun. According to Oermann, "You can promote it to death, but you can't make people go out and put down $18 for a CD unless they want to."

Sources: Todd Pack, "Hit Depends on Who Pushes It, Not Just Who Plays It," Lexington, Ky. *Herald-Leader,* July 5, 1992, p. A12; Todd Pack, "Billy Ray Cyrus Has the Big Hit, but Marcy Brothers Sang It First," Lexington, Ky. *Herald-Leader,* July 5, 1992, p. A12; and "Leisure & Arts: Top Ten Singles/Albums," *Wall Street Journal,* September 8, 1992, p. A14.

vertising or publicity. To implement regional or national advertising and sales promotion activities, a business must have a considerable promotional budget.

Several methods are used to establish the promotional budget. Some firms, especially small firms with limited resources, simply *use all available funds*. This practice often results in an inadequate budget, because firms set the promotional budget only after meeting all other obligations and the budget is not related to the firm's promotional objectives. Many firms use the *percentage of sales* method; the promotional budget is based on a percentage of the previous year's sales or the next year's forecasted sales. This method is somewhat rigid, and can lead to overspending when sales are high and underspending when sales fall.

The *competition-matching* approach involves following the action of major competitors in establishing the promotional budget. This approach assumes that competitors are correct and that their decisions are also good for your firm. Another method for determining the promotional budget is the *objective and task* approach. This involves determining the tasks required to achieve the promotional objective and allocating the budget needed to perform these tasks. The objective and task approach is very effective because managers can accurately identify the tasks needed to accomplish the objectives. Because the budgeting decision is so difficult, some managers use an *arbitrary* approach and spend what they think is needed. However, setting a budget arbitrarily can be very dangerous, even for experienced managers.

Some organizations, especially small businesses, have a limited promotional budget. There are several inexpensive techniques these organizations can use and still stay within budget constraints, including networking with civic, business, and trade associations; cosponsoring a contest or event with another firm to share promotional costs; showcasing a business by sponsoring a Chamber of Commerce meeting at the place of business, such as a restaurant; having an employee who is an expert in a field write a newspaper column or give talks or workshops in this area of expertise; or, if the business is unique, persuading the local news media to do a feature story. Even though promotion is expensive, small organizations as well as larger ones can take advantage of low-cost promotion activities by being aggressive and creative.

Target Market Characteristics   Other factors that help determine the composition of a promotion mix are the characteristics of an organization's target market, such as size, geographic distribution, and demographics. If an organization's target market is quite small, its promotion mix will emphasize personal selling because this is an efficient means of communicating with small numbers of people. Conversely, when a target market includes millions of consumers, the promotion mix will probably stress advertising and sales promotion because these methods can reach large numbers of people at a low cost per person.

When a company's customers are concentrated in a small area, personal selling is more practical than when customers are dispersed across a vast geographic region. In the latter case, advertising may be a more efficient means of reaching numerous and widely dispersed customers.

Finally, demographic characteristics, such as age, income, social class, occupation, and education, may dictate the types of promotional techniques that a marketer selects. Whereas the over-65 age group may respond best to personal selling, the teenage market may be more receptive to advertising. Sales promotions such as coupons and refunds are important to lower- and middle-income families but make little difference to those with higher incomes.

Product Characteristics   The characteristics of the product affect the blend of elements in the promotion mix. Personal selling plays a major role in promoting organizational products, but advertising is used heavily to promote consumer goods. Consumer convenience products are generally promoted through national advertising and sales promotion; personal selling is used extensively for consumer durables such as home appliances, automobiles, and houses. Publicity is a component of the promotion mixes for both organizational and consumer goods.

Manufacturers of highly seasonal products, such as toys and Christmas, Thanksgiving, Valentine's Day, and July Fourth decorations and gifts, generally rely on advertising and, perhaps, sales promotion because off-season sales of these products are not sufficient to support an extensive year-round sales force. Toy producers have sales forces to sell to resellers, yet most depend heavily on advertisements to promote their products.

Service firms also rely heavily on advertising and personal selling to promote their products. As we mentioned earlier, personal selling is critical for services, because many times the salespeople represent the service. Sales promotion is somewhat more difficult to implement for services because of their intangible nature; however, premiums such as calendars and coffee mugs can be used to promote service providers like hospitals, dry cleaners, funeral homes, and so on. Service firms often rely more heavily on publicity than do firms marketing goods. Nonprofit organizations also rely heavily on publicity, as well as on advertising and personal selling, and not so much on sales promotion.

The price of a product also has an impact on the composition of the promotion mix. High-priced products like automobiles and major appliances require personal-selling efforts, as well as advertising, because consumers associate greater risk with the purchase of an expensive product and therefore expect information and advice from a knowledgeable salesperson. For this reason, most consumers would be reluctant to purchase an expensive refrigerator from a self-service establishment. On the other hand, advertising is more practical than personal selling at the retail level for low-priced convenience goods such as milk, flour, soft drinks, and newspapers. The profit margins on many of these items are too low to justify the use of salespeople, and most customers do not need, or even want, advice from sales personnel when making such routine purchases.

The composition of the promotion mix is also determined by the stage of the product life cycle. In the introduction stage of both organizational and consumer products, considerable advertising may be required to introduce potential consumers to the new product and encourage them to try it. For example, when Procter & Gamble introduced its new Tide With Bleach laundry detergent, advertising was critical in making consumers aware of the product's existence. Personal selling and sales promotion may also be advantageous during the introduction stage. Advertising is very important for convenience products in the growth and maturity stages. Organizational products, however, require a concentration of personal selling and some sales promotion efforts during these stages. For products in the decline stage, businesses usually curtail their promotional activities, particularly advertising. Promotional efforts in the decline stage focus instead on personal selling and sales promotion to gain a few more sales.

Distribution intensity is yet another factor that affects promotion mix decisions. Sales of products (typically convenience goods) marketed through intensive distribution depend heavily on advertising and sales promotion. Coupons, cash rebates, free samples, and other sales promotions can increase sales of many convenience products, including toiletries, cereals, frozen dinners, cake mixes, and coffee. Products marketed through selective distribution have widely varying promotion mixes. Exclusively distributed products, generally high-priced items, frequently necessitate more personal selling and less advertising.

Finally, the nature of the product affects the composition of the promotion mix. For instance, manufacturers of such personal-care items as hemorrhoid medications or feminine hygiene products rely primarily on advertising because consumers are embarrassed and reluctant to talk with salespersons about these products. Producers' advertising efforts may be enhanced by personal selling targeted at retailers carrying these products. Firms selling other personal-care remedies, such as drugs that stimulate hair growth for balding men, utilize advertising to consumers to supplement marketing programs to health care professionals, who prescribe such products for patients.

Cost and Availability of Promotional Methods   The costs of promotional methods are certainly important considerations when developing a promotion mix. National advertising and sales promotion efforts require large expenditures even though the cost per individual reached may be quite low. Because of budget constraints, many small businesses restrict their promotion mix to advertising through local newspapers, magazines, radio and television stations, and outdoor displays.

Availability of promotional techniques is another factor that marketers must explore when formulating a promotion mix. A company may discover that no available advertising media are effective in reaching a certain market. Finding an appropriate medium may be especially difficult when marketers try to advertise in foreign countries. Some media, such as television, are simply not available or not in widespread use. Other media that are available may be restricted in the types of advertisements they can run. For example, in Spain, marketers cannot advertise tobacco and alcohol products (with the

FIGURE 18.8
Adapting Promotion for Global Markets
This advertisement for Colgate toothpaste that runs in Switzerland says, "New Colgate Junior gobbles up the tooth decay monster."

Source: Colgate-Palmolive Company GmbH.

exception of beer and wine) on television; in Germany, marketers are prohibited from appealing to children in advertisements. In the United States, some state laws prohibit the use of certain types of sales promotion activities such as contests.

Adapting Promotion for Global Markets

Frequently, promotion must be modified because of language, legal, or cultural differences associated with the advertising copy (see Figure 18.8). For example, McDonald's developed advertisements directly aimed at Hispanics, showing three generations of a family that speaks both English and Spanish. McDonald's also has relied on strong community involvement to build its Hispanic following.[17] Table 18.1 lists some problems firms have encountered when promotion was not properly adapted for a foreign country. The Japanese use earthy humor to sell personal-care products that Americans promote discreetly. Casualness about bodily functions comes naturally in Japanese culture.

In addition, media decisions must be altered for foreign markets. Some countries, such as Sweden, do not have commercial television time available; in other countries, newspapers may not accept advertising. Television viewing habits and the circulation of magazines and newspapers vary greatly among countries and must be considered in the strategic adaptation of promotion.

Despite certain inherent risks that stem from cultural differences in interpretation, using the same advertisements in foreign countries does provide the efficiency of international standardization. Beverage companies often use the same message worldwide when advertising their products to create universal recognition of their products.

[17]David W. Helin, "When Slogans Go Wrong," *American Demographics,* February 1992, p. 14.

TABLE 18.1
Problems Caused by Improper Adaptation of Promotion for Foreign Markets

A firm introduced refrigerators into several Middle Eastern countries and included a photo of a well-stocked refrigerator interior—with a large ham on a central shelf!

Campbell's condensed soups didn't sell well in England because the Campbell's cans appeared small, compared to noncondensed English offerings.

Lever Brothers promised white teeth from its toothpaste but made the promise to Southeast Asians who hold discolored teeth to be a mark of prestige.

Chevrolet introduced its Nova automobile into South America without realizing that "no va" in Spanish means something like "won't go."

Baby food was introduced into several African nations with baby pictures on the labels. Potential consumers thought the jars contained ground-up babies.

Translators converted:
"Body by Fisher" into "Corpse by Fisher"
"Come Alive with Pepsi" into "Come Alive out of the Grave"
"Car Wash" into "Car Enema"

Source: Merle Crawford, *New Products Management,* 2nd ed. (Homewood, Ill.: Richard D. Irwin, 1987), p. 44. Reprinted by permission.

PROMOTION OF ORGANIZATIONAL PRODUCTS

Organizational products require different promotion mixes than those used for consumer products. Table 18.2 compares the promotional methods used for organizational and consumer products. Personal selling is very important, and more feasible, in organizational markets because they generally consist of fewer customers. Also, the technical features of many products (such as computers, farm equipment, and copier machines) sold through organizational markets are difficult to explain through nonpersonal forms of promotion. The high price of these products further limits the use of nonpersonal forms of promotion.

Business-to-business marketers rely on advertising much less than consumer-goods marketers, although they use advertising and sales promotion to support selling efforts. Advertising can generate product awareness and provide information to buyers about product features, helping sales personnel perform more effectively. However, advertisements for organizational products are usually less persuasive than those for consumer products. Also, because of the technical nature of many organizational products, advertisements must contain more detail about the product. Trade publications and direct mail are the main media used to advertise organizational products.

Element	Organizational Product	Consumer Product
Personal selling	Major emphasis on personal selling Critical in communicating technical product features Aimed at final consumer Follow-up is important	Much less emphasis on personal selling Generally aimed at intermediaries rather than final consumer Follow-up in person is less feasible
Advertising	Less emphasis on advertising Less persuasive Generally contains technical information Used to facilitate the personal-selling process and create product awareness Major media are trade publications, direct mail, and industry directories	Major emphasis on advertising More persuasive Contains less technical information Tends to be more entertaining Major media include television, radio, newspapers, magazines, and outdoor displays
Sales promotion	Significant part of promotion mix Heavy use of catalogues, trade shows, and trade allowances	Significant part of promotion mix Heavy use of coupons, contests, demonstrations, and displays
Publicity	Used to inform consumers and enhance the firm's image	Used to inform consumers and enhance the firm's image

TABLE 18.2
Comparison of Promotion Mix Elements for Organizational and Consumer Products

Sales promotion also plays an important role in promoting organizational products. Commonly used techniques include catalogues, trade shows, merchandise allowances, displays, and sales contests. Publicity is used by organizational marketers in the same manner that it is used by marketers of consumer products.

PROMOTION AND SOCIETY

Although the objective of promotion is to facilitate satisfying exchanges by communicating positive, persuasive information to a target market, promotion is one of the most highly criticized activities in marketing. Most of us would agree that it would be difficult to make informed purchase decisions without promotion activities. How would you know about the latest personal computers? Who would help you pick out a new suit and give advice on matching shirts and ties? Where would you go to test drive a car, and who would answer your questions? How would nonprofit organizations get their important messages across? Yet each of us at one time or another has probably questioned the value of promotion.

Perhaps the most fundamental criticism of promotion is that there is too much. Some sports fans have suggested that the Bud Bowl has received more attention than the Super Bowl. Although promotional activities can be beneficial to consumers, our highly competitive world has led many companies to increase promotional expenditures to record highs. Critics of promotion think that the result has had a negative impact on society.

First, some suggest that promotion is dishonest or unethical. Some critics believe that in the battle for the customer companies will say anything in their advertisements and through their salespeople to sell a product. The truth is that the Federal Trade Commission (FTC) uses several measures to protect consumers against false and deceptive promotion practices. Consumers must be provided all the information needed to make a decision, and a firm must be able to substantiate all claims made in its promotion messages. The FTC can issue a cease-and-desist order requiring a firm to stop using deceptive practices. Firms can also be required to run corrective advertisements or pay fines for deceptive promotion. Local agencies like the Better Business Bureau also work to combat deceptive promotion. Most companies try to adhere to the laws and regulations governing promotion activities. Foreign countries have similar regulations. Hungary's judicial Economic Competition Council fined Philip Morris $25,974 for illegal cigarette advertising. The firm's magazine advertisements were found to have broken Hungary's ban on advertisements that enhance consumption of tobacco products.[18]

Another criticism of promotion is that it leads to a materialistic society. Anyone who has argued with a 10-year-old about whether to buy brand-name athletic shoes would probably agree. Promotion, by its very nature, is persuasive. After seeing Michael Jordan dunk a basketball in an advertisement, most 10-year-olds will want a pair of Air Jordans. But marketing professionals argue that they cannot be responsible for family values; it is up to parents to make purchase decisions and communicate their beliefs to their children. We examine this issue in greater detail in the next chapter.

A third criticism of promotion is that it leads to higher prices; the cost of promotion is passed on to consumers and reflected in the product's price. But promotion allows firms to achieve economies of scale by increasing demand for their products. With higher demand, firms can mass-produce products and lower the per-unit cost, resulting in lower prices. In the case of professional pricing, promotion has actually stimulated price competition among dentists and lawyers.

Some critics have argued that promotion is in poor taste and encourages negative stereotypes. For example, erotic advertisements are used to sell products ranging from cosmetics to industrial tools. Some of these advertise-

---

[18]"Philip Morris Fined in Hungary," *Advertising Age,* November 9, 1992, p. 8.

ments portray stereotypical images of women that are neither realistic nor complimentary. Critics also cite billboards dotting the highway, the waste from excessive junk mail, and the invasion of privacy resulting from telephone solicitation. The truth is that what appeals to some people disturbs others. Whereas many consumers react favorably to an erotic advertisement, others are outraged. Stroh Brewery's Swedish Bikini Team advertisements featuring scantily clad young women were shelved after several groups responded negatively.[19] Likewise, some people may think a certain advertisement insults their intelligence, whereas others believe the advertisement helps them make a purchase decision. Firms have the responsibility to know their target market and develop promotion activities that are not viewed as in poor taste and that achieve promotional objectives.

A final criticism is that promotion can move people to buy products they do not need. Once again, it is difficult to resolve this criticism. As we discuss in Chapter 1, needs and wants differ, and many of our purchases fulfill *wants*. Thus, it could be argued that rational consumers do not buy products they do not want. On the other hand, many consumers find themselves questioning whether they really need a product once they get it home. Perhaps an aggressive salesperson convinced them they needed the product. Although promotion cannot force a person to buy a product, it is persuasive and certainly can be a strong factor in any purchase decision.

Promotion will always be controversial. Although some of the criticisms may be justified and others defended, it is up to each of us as consumers to decide if promotion has a negative impact on society. More importantly, it is the obligation of firms to develop promotion activities that meet the needs of the target market without having a negative impact on society. If customers or potential customers find a firm's promotional activities in poor taste, they will not buy the product and the firm will not achieve its promotional objectives.

SUMMARY

Promotion refers to the marketing activities used to communicate to a target market positive, persuasive information about an organization, its products, and its activities to directly or indirectly expedite exchanges. Promotion that directly expedites exchanges communicates information about an organization's goods, services, and ideas to its target markets. Promotion that indirectly facilitates exchanges communicates information about company activities and products to interest groups, current and potential investors, regulatory agencies, and society in general.

[19]Teri Agins, "Klein Jeans' Sexy Insert Didn't Increase Sales," *Wall Street Journal,* May 5, 1992, p. B1.

Communication can be defined as the sharing of a common meaning. Communication is a process in which a source encodes a message and transmits it through a medium of transmission to a receiver, who decodes it and then responds with feedback. In encoding its message, the source must use symbols familiar to and commonly used by the receiver to refer to the concepts or ideas being promoted. When the receiver interprets the message differently from what the source intended, the cause may be noise—interference at some point in the communication process. The communication process is limited by channel capacity, the volume of information that it can handle effectively.

The promotion mix includes four major elements: advertising, personal selling, sales promotion, and publicity. Advertising is paid nonpersonal communication about an organization, its products, or its activities transmitted through mass media. Personal selling is face-to-face communication with potential buyers. Sales promotion is an activity or material that offers consumers, salespersons, and dealers a direct inducement for purchasing a product. Publicity is a nonpaid form of nonpersonal communication about an organization or its products that is transmitted through a mass medium in the form of a news story.

Many factors affect the composition of the promotion mix, including the organization's objectives and policies, the organization's promotional budget, the characteristics of the target market, the characteristics of the product, and the cost and availability of promotional methods. An organization using a push policy promotes the product only to the next member down in the marketing channel. By contrast, a business using a pull policy promotes its product directly to consumers to stimulate strong consumer demand for the product.

Frequently, promotion must be modified for global markets because of language, legal, or cultural differences. Advertising copy may have to be changed because of differences that result from translation or because the advertisement is not appropriate for another culture. Media decisions may also have to be altered for foreign markets. However, some companies use the same advertisements in domestic and foreign countries because it provides the efficiency of international standardization.

Personal selling is the most important element of the promotion mix for organizational products, although advertising is used to supplement personal-selling efforts. Sales promotion and publicity are also important aspects of promotion for organizational products.

Promotion is one of the most highly criticized activities in marketing. Some of the common criticisms include the following: there is too much promotion; promotion is dishonest; promotion leads to a materialistic society; promotion leads to higher prices; promotion is in poor taste; and promotion moves people to buy things they do not need. The truth is that promotion is regulated and that firms using deceptive practices can be penalized. The true value or harm of promotional activities is often a matter of personal preference. If, however, promotion does not meet the needs of the target market, the firm will not achieve its promotion goals.

KEY TERMS

promotion
communication
source
message
receiver
coding process
medium of transmission
decoding process
noise
feedback
channel capacity

promotion mix
integrated marketing
    communications
advertising
personal selling
sales promotion
publicity
AIDA model
push policy
pull policy

QUESTIONS FOR DISCUSSION AND REVIEW

1. How can organizations use promotion to facilitate exchanges between buyers and sellers? Give an example of how promotion influenced you to purchase or adopt a good, a service, and an idea.

2. What is communication? What are the stages of the communication process? How can communication fail in the promotion of a product?

3. Why do firms vary in their use of the elements of the promotion mix?

4. What are some advantages of advertising? Some disadvantages?

5. What is the major strength of personal selling, compared with advertising?

6. Name some typical types of sales promotion and discuss the effectiveness of each.

7. In what ways does publicity differ from advertising? Is publicity always desirable for a company?

8. Describe the AIDA model. How does this model relate to promotional objectives?

9. Distinguish between a push policy and a pull policy. What promotional activities are generally used with each policy? Give a current example of a firm using a push policy and one using a pull policy.

10. How does the promotional budget influence the promotion mix?

11. How can an organization with resource constraints use promotion?

12. How do a product's characteristics affect the composition of the promotion mix? Give examples of various products and the promotion mix used for each.

13. What should international marketing firms be concerned with when adapting promotion to global markets?

14. Describe some major differences between promotion used for organizational products and promotion used in consumer markets. Why do these differences exist?

15. What are some common criticisms of promotion? Do you think these criticisms are valid? Why or why not?

CASES

18.1   SKI RESORTS TURN TO PROMOTION FOR A LIFT

On the U.S. ski slopes, business has been flat for more than a decade. Since 1980, 25 percent of U.S. ski resorts have closed. The industry's annual growth, 15 percent at its peak, is now about 3 percent. Vermont's Sugarbush Resort, for example, attracts 300,000 skiers a season, down from 425,000 a decade ago. What happened? Single, free-spending skiers of the baby boom generation married, had children, and started using their disposable income toward home and kids instead of expensive vacations. The recession and large number of layoffs of the early 1990s also took a toll on travel. Now the U.S. resorts are trying to get old skiers back and attract new ones with promotion geared toward families, non–jet setters, and foreign skiers.

Hoping to get children hooked on skiing and parents skiing longer, several resorts are remaking themselves as family destinations. Ski resorts think families are worth going after. A survey by a Boulder, Colorado, research firm showed that from 1991 to 1992 there was a 12 percent increase in the number of skiers who usually ski with family members. The number of children who ski has increased 18 percent since 1987, according to the United Ski Industries Association. Ski schools throughout the United States have experienced great demand for children's classes.

Ski resorts are adding family entertainment and marking off slopes where fast and reckless skiers are not welcome. Ski instructors are going to classes on how to teach children, and people trained in child psychology are managing children's centers at resorts. Vail and Beaver Creek in Colorado built children's ski areas resembling Indian villages or mining towns. Breckenridge Spa made its Kids' Castle four times larger. Alpine Meadows in California is doubling the space in its two children's centers. Snowmass in Colorado emphasizes its ski in/ski out lodging, which means easy access to the slopes for skiers with children. This feature helped Snowmass earn the rating of number one family resort by two ski magazines in 1992.

Smuggler's Notch Resort, near Burlington, Vermont, has promoted itself as a prime family spot. Its "Family Club Smuggler's Ski Week" package includes lodging, lift tickets, ski lessons, cross-country skiing, parties, ice skating, swimming, and tennis. The package costs a family of four from

$1,175 in early December to $1,995 over Washington's birthday week. For very small children, the resort has a petting zoo, a sliding hill, and a playground. Smuggler's offers nighttime sledding, family games each evening until 9 P.M., and a weekly torchlight parade and fireworks. To appeal to teenagers, who have a large influence over where a family goes to ski, the resort provides pizza parties, snow soccer, volleyball tournaments, and dances. Parents can enjoy nightly entertainment after 9 P.M., plus the weekly Parents' Night Out, while children get dinner, do crafts, and watch a movie until 10 P.M.

"Our slogan is fun for kids, freedom for parents," says Barbara Thomke, spokeswoman for the resort. Smuggler's array of facilities and activities geared to all ages has paid off for the resort: *Family Circle* magazine named it the country's top family ski area in 1991 and 1992. Families make up 80 percent of Smuggler's business.

Catering to families has its drawbacks, however. First, there is the perception of being easy. Although the resorts have tried to change that image, some hard-core skiers avoid any place that calls itself a family spot. Second is the problem of cost: Ski vacations are very expensive. To keep families coming, nearly all resorts are offering discount lift tickets for children; some, including Purgatory/Durango in southwest Colorado, let them ski free when they are with a paying adult.

In recent years resorts have increasingly promoted skiing to price-conscious skiers. Several offer discount lift tickets on slow days and coupon books for local skiers. Purgatory/Durango really stands out from other resorts. The resort targets everyday people who do not relate to the glamourous, wealthy image of the sport. Instead of showing perfect snow and beautiful people in the latest ski clothes, Purgatory advertisements show regular people in Polaroid camera shots and tell skiers they "don't have to be a celebrity to be treated like a star." One advertisement which ran in the four major ski magazines showed a slightly overweight local man dressed in an orange snowmobile suit and red hat and holding a pair of old, worn skis.

Other resorts are looking abroad for new skiers. For several years, Breckenridge Spa, an upscale lodge in Colorado, has been targeting foreign skiers, especially the British, who provide 40 percent of its revenues. The spa provides a currency exchange, British newspapers, and an afternoon tea with cucumber sandwiches and scones. Breckenridge executives find that compared with Americans, foreign visitors tend to stay two weeks rather than one and spend nearly twice as much—about $250 a day rather than $150. The resort hopes to increase its foreign business from the current 8 percent to 10 percent. Breckenridge has joined with Keystone, Copper Mountain, Arapahoe Basin, and other resorts to form a marketing consortium called Ski the Summit. The consortium began promoting to foreign skiers a few years ago. In trying to target German skiers, Ski the Summit invited one hundred German television and print reporters to ski the area during the 1992 season. U.S. resorts also are attempting to lure Japanese skiers. Hunter Mountain in New York offers a hillside sushi bar. Park City, Utah, has trail signs in Japanese.

Some industry experts question the long-term value of flashy promotional activities that may bring only one-time visitors to the slopes. Many ski resort marketers are trying to design their promotional mixes to keep customers coming back. At Sunday River Skiway in Bethel, Maine, president Leslie B. Otten conducts simple promotional programs with a clear aim: to turn first-time customers into lifetime buyers. Service begins in the parking lot, where attendants hand out maps and direct newcomers to an orientation center. For $33 a lesson, first-time skiers receive two hours on the slopes with an instruc-tor plus free use of skis, poles, and boots ($18 otherwise), a free lift ticket (worth $33), and the chance to sign up for two more lessons at the same rate. Students who complete three lessons get a coupon for a fourth day of free skiing. They also can buy poles, skis, and boots at the resort's cost.

Sunday River's learn-to-ski program doesn't make any money, but it does bring skiers back. Before the promotion started in 1985, only 20 percent of the resort's first-time visitors returned. Now more than 75 percent do. Gross revenues have increased from $6 million to $18.3 million. Otten uses other promotional methods to keep skiers coming back. He created a frequent-skier program which gives customers a free day of skiing after only five visits. Customers also receive mailings describing other special deals.

"We want to stay on top of mind," Otten says. "When we started here [in 1980] we tried to grow by stealing customers from other ski slopes by featuring lower prices, longer hours, or more services. That works for a while, but this is better."

Questions for Discussion

1. What promotion mix elements would ski resorts be most likely to use? Why?

2. What promotional objectives do you think U.S. ski resorts would have?

3. Could ski resorts direct some of their promotional messages to nonski-ers to try to reach this market? What would be some of the problems with this strategy?

4. Of what value would forming a marketing consortium be to a resort like Breckenridge?

Based on information from Mark Maremont, "Do Snowy Slopes Mean Dead Fish?" *Business Week,* March 15, 1993, p. 99; Marj Charlier, "U.S. Ski Resorts Stress Family Values," *Wall Street Journal,* November 20, 1992, pp. B1, B8; Sandra Atchison, Evan Schwartz, and Gregory Sandler, "At These Prices, Who Needs the Alps?" *Business Week,* February 10, 1992, p. 131; Paul B. Brown, "Return Engagements," *Inc.,* July 1990, pp. 99–100; and Mark Ivey, Corie Brown, and Alice Z. Cuneo, "Hi, I'm Goofy. Come Ski with Me," *Business Week,* February 15, 1988, pp. 58–60.

18.2   MERCEDES CHANGES ITS IMAGE

Mercedes-Benz of North America has long been renowned as the maker of one of the world's finest cars. The brand has been synonymous with quality. But after a hefty U.S. luxury tax, the dollar's weakness relative to the German mark, and the continuing recession caused sales to drop, Mercedes began to rethink its promotion strategy. In 1991, U.S. unit sales fell 24 percent to 58,869, a big drop compared with 1986 sales of 99,314 cars. At the same time, Nissan introduced Infiniti and Toyota introduced Lexus, luxury cars with lower price tags than Mercedes models. Now the goal of Mercedes-Benz is to convince U.S. consumers that its cars are still worth the price, even though they cost considerably more than others in the same class. The least expensive S-class model, the 300SE, is $69,400, and the top model, 600SEL, is $127,800.

One of the first priorities was to change Mercedes' image. For nearly twenty years, Mercedes had stuck with the same advertising slogan: "the best-engineered car in the world." Today's car buyers found this image aloof and intimidating. According to Marvin Sloves, head of the advertising agency with the $100 million Mercedes account, Mercedes needed to communicate a warmer and more approachable image to customers. The old image was so intimidating that, in the words of the chairman of the Mercedes National Dealer Council, "People would come into the showroom and ask, 'Is it okay if I sit in the car?'" Mercedes definitely had an image problem.

Sloves told Mercedes executives they needed a warmer and more approachable image. But he didn't want to count solely on a warmer image. Thus a new slogan was developed: "Sacrifice nothing." The new slogan was chosen to stress three themes, or what Mercedes people call core values: the car's history of pioneering safety features, its longevity, and its resale value. The message "sacrifice nothing" suggests subtly that competitors' cars are second best, that buying anything but a Mercedes would be a sacrifice. But the message is dignified and avoids mentioning specific ways Mercedes may be superior, such as by comparing the car's brakes or other features with those of competitors.

To convey its message to the target audience, Mercedes developed advertisements illustrating the new human touch. Television viewers saw a father toasting his daughter on her wedding day while giving her a new Mercedes, a young boy mesmerized by an old "gullwing" Mercedes, and a current owner's flashback to an accident she survived because she was driving a Mercedes—plus her explanation that she buys Mercedes to protect her children. In all cases, the company attempted to hit home the message of having the best. These advertisements represented a big shift from the stern values emphasizing engineering that were the mark of Mercedes for many years.

It will take some time to determine whether Mercedes succeeds in communicating the desired image to target customers. Initial results are positive. By mid-year 1992, sales stood at 39,593 cars, up nearly 20 percent from the same period the previous year.

Questions for Discussion

1. Why did Mercedes officials think they needed to change their product's image?

2. What message did Mercedes wish to communicate to the target audience?

3. How did Mercedes encode and transmit its message?

Based on information from Joshua Levine, "Mercedes with a Human Face," *Forbes,* September 14, 1992, pp. 474–476; Mark Landler, "Mercedes Finds Out How Much Is Too Much," *Business Week,* January 29, 1992, pp. 92–96; and Laura Bird, "Scali's New Mercedes Ads," *Wall Street Journal,* August 31, 1992, p. B6.

Advertising and Publicity

19

OBJECTIVES

● *To describe the role of advertising.*

● *To determine the various uses of advertising.*

● *To identify who is responsible for handling an organization's advertising program.*

● *To list the major steps in developing an advertising program.*

● *To discuss some of the challenges and considerations in international advertising.*

● *To identify the uses of publicity and the methods of dealing with unfavorable publicity.*

Like it or not, advertisements are everywhere: on the back of buses, on the sides of tractor trailers, under scoreboards at sporting events, and in rest rooms of restaurants, stores, and even planes. At supermarkets and drug stores, shoppers are bombarded with electric signs, closed-circuit radios playing commercials in aisles, and video recorders showing how to use products. At theaters and on videotapes, commercials sometimes crop up before the movie starts. It seems as though wherever there is a space, an advertisement is filling it.

Advertisers are constantly looking for new ways to get their messages to target audiences. Traditional media like television and magazines are especially cluttered. On the major networks (ABC, NBC, CBS), nonprogramming time per hour averages 12 minutes and 35 seconds; on five leading cable networks, 13 minutes and 50 seconds; on the Fox network, 14 minutes and 16 seconds; and on independent stations, 14 minutes, 33 seconds. ABC's "Full House" contains 15 minutes and 12 seconds of nonprogramming time in its hourlong broadcast. The 1993 Super Bowl (on NBC) lasted approximately 3 hours and 25 minutes. During this time, there were 24 breaks and 68 commercials. Increased television clutter has increased the extent to which viewers switch channels. Clutter is also evident in magazines in the form of heavy inserts, scent strips, gatefolds (fold-out advertisements attached to front or back covers), and "printaculars," spectacular print advertisements.

To break through the clutter, advertisers are using traditional media in new ways. Some billboards now sport elaborate lights and music. One for a southern California hospital featured a huge, inflatable heart with fans inside simulating beating motions. On television, both General Electric and Shearson Lehman Hutton have experimented with different sounds—buzzes, hums, and weird music—to catch the public's ear. Magazines feature pop-ups and computer chips that play Christmas carols.

Advertisers also are relying on alternative media, everything from matchbook covers to blimps. Although the use of nontraditional media represents a small part of total advertising dollars, it is growing fast. Americans spend billions of dollars each year to buy T-shirts that advertise consumer goods, movies, and political or social causes. Human billboards—people wearing huge popcorn bags—have handed out Smartfood cheese popcorn in Chicago. Jeep and Hardee's have advertised on Baltimore parking meters. Ski lifts carry lip balm and tanning lotion ads. Campbell Soup Company once put fish recipes calling for its soup on the back of Roman Catholic church bulletins during Lent. Do consumers really notice these advertisements? It's been estimated that although the average consumer is exposed to up to five thousand advertisements each day, he or she recalls only 1 percent of them. Nevertheless, to the enjoyment of some and the dismay of others, these unusual advertisements will continue to make their way into our lives.[1] ●

Advertising, in the form of signs, can be traced to Rome and the guilds of the Middle Ages. Paper was invented in China and the first paper mill built in Europe by 1275, both inventions paving the way not only for books but also for advertisements. The movable press, invented in 1440, led to the first forms of mass advertising, including newspaper advertisements, posters, and handbills. In 1704, the first advertisements in the American colonies appeared in the *Boston Newsletter*. The Industrial Revolution spurred the growth of advertising, and in 1841, Volney B. Palmer, a Philadelphia businessman, started the first advertising agency in the United States.

THE ROLE OF ADVERTISING

Today whether you're walking to school, driving a car, listening to the radio, or watching television, you cannot escape advertising. Recall that advertising is paid nonpersonal communication about an organization, its products, and its activities transmitted through a mass medium such as television, radio, newspapers, magazines, direct mail, or some type of outdoor display. Many organizations use advertising to reach a variety of target markets. In the United States alone, marketers spend some $130 billion each year on advertising.[2] Table 19.1 shows how much money the leading advertisers in the United States spend.

Business organizations are not the only users of advertising. Governments, churches, colleges and universities, civic groups, environmental groups, consumer rights organizations, and other nonbusiness organizations rely heavily on advertising to make the public aware of them, their causes, and their activities. Although this chapter focuses on advertising as it relates to business organizations, some concepts apply to other contexts as well. Figure 19.1 shows how nonprofit organizations also rely on advertising to communicate their messages.

[1] Based on information from Kevin Goldman, "Barrage of Ads in Super Bowl Blurs Messages," *Wall Street Journal,* February 3, 1993, p. B6; Joe Mandese, "Study Finds Shows with Worst Clutter," *Advertising Age,* February 17, 1992, pp. 3, 61; Richard Phalon, "Walking Billboards," *Forbes,* December 7, 1992, pp. 84–85; "Clutter Suffers Zap Attack," *Advertising Age,* March 30, 1992, p. 38; and Scott Hume, "Bounty in Most Unusual Places," *Advertising Age,* August 27, 1990, pp. S1–S14.
[2] Joanne Lipman, "As Industry Feels Spring of Hope, a Forecaster Cools His Optimism," *Wall Street Journal,* June 3, 1992, p. B5.

Because advertising is a highly visible activity in our society, it is often criticized for its prominent social role. Critics have complained that advertising makes people buy products they don't need, that it takes unfair advantage of children, and that it makes people too materialistic. Most advertisers recognize that advertising has been misused but argue that this is no longer the case. Even though advertising is regulated by national, state, and local government agencies and self-regulatory organizations such as the National Advertising Review Board, it continues to be the focus of much criticism. Point/Counterpoint explores advertising's social role.

THE USES OF ADVERTISING

Advertising is used to *inform, persuade,* and *remind*. Advertisements are used by individuals and organizations to inform a target market about a good, service, or idea, to persuade the target market to purchase the good or service or to adopt the idea, and to remind the target market that products are available to satisfy their needs and wants. Advertising can be used by individuals and organizations in a number of specific ways. Uses of advertising include promoting organizations and products, stimulating demand, reminding consumers about products and reinforcing their choices, countering advertising by competitors, supporting the sales force, and minimizing sales fluctuations.

Promoting Institutions and Products

■ **institutional advertising** advertising that promotes organizational images, ideas, or issues

Advertising that promotes organizational images, ideas, or issues rather than specific products or brands is called **institutional advertising.** Both profit and nonprofit organizations as well as individuals use institutional advertising. Advertising of political issues and political candidates is of this type.

TABLE 19.1
Annual Expenditures of Leading U.S. Advertisers

Rank	Company	Advertising Expenditures (in millions)
1	Procter & Gamble Co.	$2,149
2	Philip Morris Companies Inc.	2,046
3	General Motors Corp.	1,442
4	Sears, Roebuck and Co.	1,179
5	PepsiCo, Inc.	903
6	Grand Metropolitan	745
7	Johnson & Johnson	733
8	McDonald's Corp.	695
9	Ford Motor Co.	677
10	Eastman Kodak Co.	661

Source: *Advertising Age,* January 4, 1993, p. 16. Reprinted with permission.

FIGURE 19.1
Nonprofit Advertising
This advertisement from Red Cross communicates an important message to parents: make water safe with the Red Cross Water Safety Program.

Source: Courtesy The Advertising Council Inc.

A child can drown in just two inches of water. Make the water safe for your child with the Red Cross Water Safety Program. Call your local chapter. Little swimmers need a little help.

+ American Red Cross

Advocacy advertising is a type of institutional advertising used by organizations to communicate a position on an issue. Keene Corp., which years ago owned a subsidiary that made asbestos insulation products, ran advocacy advertisements attacking the way the courts and the legal profession have handled asbestos litigations.[3] After President Clinton accused the drug industry of taking excessive profits, the Pharmaceutical Manufacturing Association began a $500,000 advertising campaign proclaiming the benefits of prescription drugs to be worth the price.[4] Nonprofit organizations frequently use this type of advertising. For example, the American Cancer Society uses advertisements that advocate wearing sunscreen to help prevent skin cancer.

Most advertising is **product advertising,** which is used by business, government, and nonbusiness organizations to promote the uses, features, images, and benefits of their goods and services. Compaq Computer Corp. developed a new advertising campaign to change its image from that of a producer of high-quality, high-priced machines to a producer of lower-priced machines that are high quality.[5] Over $3.5 billion are spent each year to

■ **product advertising**
advertising used by business, government, and nonbusiness organizations to promote the uses, features, images, and benefits of their goods and services

[3]Wade Lambert, "Keene's Asbestos Fight Spreads Beyond Courts, onto Ad Pages," *Wall Street Journal,* June 29, 1992, p. B8.
[4]John Fairhall, "Drug Industry Takes Aim at Profiteering Allegations," *Lexington* (KY) *Herald-Leader,* March 8, 1993, pp. A1, A6.
[5]Joanne Lipman, "Compaq Pushing New Line, New Image," *Wall Street Journal,* June 2, 1992, p. B5.

POINT/COUNTERPOINT

Is Advertising Morally Defensible?

The debate probably started with the first advertisement, and probably will continue as long as advertisements are used. Is advertising a tool of communication or a detriment to society?

Point   Misuse has plagued advertising over the years. But the criticisms directed at advertising as a marketing tool and as a social influence are no longer justified. Of all the advertisements reviewed by the Federal Trade Commission in a typical year, 97 percent are found to be acceptable. As a result of increased legislation, intensified efforts of government regulatory agencies, and self-regulation, abuses of advertising are the exception, not the rule.

Advertising is a valuable communication tool in our society, without inherent qualities of good or evil. Advertising per se does not cause materialism, moral decline, or stereotyping. It rarely initiates trends or offers unconventional views; rather, it reflects attitudes and changes already present in society. If some advertisers deliberately mislead, the vast majority do not. They design advertisements and write copy carefully, and even include disclaimers so that advertisements will not be misconstrued. Ironically, some of the harshest critics of advertising use it to sell their books and their viewpoints.

Counterpoint   In spite of increased efforts to curb its misuse, advertising still has a negative impact on our society. At worst, advertising is untruthful; at best, it shows only the positive side of the sponsoring firm's product. In any case, there simply is too much advertising today, and this proliferation has an adverse effect on our society. Viewers, listeners, and readers are bombarded with too many advertisements, many of them in poor taste. Advertisements often use sex and even violence to sell products. Groups such as the National Organization for Women (NOW) have protested that many advertisements perpetuate stereotypes of women and ethnic groups.

Advertising holds far too much persuasive power to be considered a mere tool for communication. By promising greater sex appeal or some other unrealistic expectation, for example, advertisements manipulate people to buy products they do not need. And regardless of attempts at regulation, advertising continues to be riddled with unfair and deceptive practices, such as making promises that cannot be kept, providing incomplete information, making misleading comparisons, making a product look larger than it is, giving false testimonials, and using small-print qualifications.

■ **infomercial** a half-hour television commercial that generates telephone or mail responses for products or information

advertise automobiles, $1.4 billion for food advertising, and over $1 billion to advertise entertainment and media.[6]

A new form of product advertising gaining popularity is the infomercial. An **infomercial** is a half-hour television commercial that generates telephone or mail responses for products or information. They now run on at least 15 major cable networks, some reaching 55 million homes.[7] Popularized by

[6]R. Craig Endicott, "AT&T Tops Spending Despite Ford Rush," *Advertising Age,* May 11, 1992, p. 56.
[7]Timothy R. Hawthorne, "Infomercial Phone Response to Grow Dramatically," *Telemarketing Magazine,* August 1992, pp. 25–26.

Ross Perot during the 1992 presidential election, the infomercial industry is expected to reach $1 billion in revenue by 1993.[8] Once associated with gimmick marketing and get-rich-quick schemes, infomercials have recently been used by well-known firms including Volvo, Club Med, and General Motors. Infomercials generally take a talk-show or news format with information on goods, services, or ideas, as well as testimonials, celebrity endorsements, and opportunities for purchase or response through telephone or mail.[9]

Stimulating Demand

■ **pioneer advertising** advertising that tries to stimulate primary demand for a product by providing consumers with information about the product, its functions, uses, and where it can be purchased

■ **competitive advertising** advertising that builds selective demand for a specific brand by focusing on the uses, features, and value of the brand that benefit consumers and that may not be available in competing brands

■ **comparative advertising** a form of competitive advertising that contrasts two or more specified brands on the basis of one or more product features

Product advertising is often used to stimulate demand directly. When a business introduces an innovative or revolutionary new product, it tries to stimulate *primary demand*—that is, demand for a particular product category rather than for a specific brand. To spur primary demand for a new product, a company may use **pioneer advertising,** which informs consumers about the product, its functions, uses, and where it can be purchased. Pioneer advertising does *not* emphasize a brand name or compare brands because products in the introductory stage of the product life cycle usually have little or no competition. Industry and trade groups, such as The National Dairy Board, sometimes sponsor pioneer-type advertisements to stimulate demand for an existing product category. The American Egg Board used the advertisement in Figure 19.2 as part of a campaign to stimulate primary demand for eggs.

By contrast, **competitive advertising** focuses on the value, uses, and features of a brand that benefit consumers and that may not be available in competing brands. Competitive advertising is used to build *selective demand*—demand for a specific brand. For example, Wrigley attempted to stimulate selective demand for its Extra gum by advertising that chewing the gum was a natural way to help prevent tooth decay. The commercial was based on dental research showing that chewing gum helps produce and distribute more saliva, a natural defense against acids that contribute to tooth decay.[10]

Comparative advertising, a form of competitive advertising, contrasts two or more specified brands on the basis of one or more product features. This type of advertising is increasingly popular among producers of fast-food hamburgers, automobiles and trucks, credit cards, soft drinks, pain relievers, batteries, laundry detergents, and a multitude of other products (see Figure 19.3). Pontiac used comparative advertisements to claim that the Grand Am has a more powerful engine and better fuel economy than a Toyota Camry or Honda Accord, plus standard antilock brakes, and that it costs several

[8]Mark Landler, "The Infomercial Inches Toward Respectability," *Business Week,* May 4, 1992, p. 175.
[9]Howard Schlossberg, "Infomercial Industry Enjoys Strong Growth; Still Faces Some Hurdles," *Marketing News,* August 3, 1992, p. 13.
[10]Julie Liesse, "Chew on This: Wrigley's Extra Tackles Tooth Decay," *Advertising Age,* December 21, 1992, p. 30.

FIGURE 19.2
Stimulating Primary Demand
The American Egg Board uses advertisements such as this to stimulate primary demand for the "incredible, edible egg."

Source: American Egg Board.

NATURE'S MULTI-VITAMIN SOURCE.

thousand dollars less.[11] The 1988 Trademark Law Revision Act prohibits organizations using comparative advertising from misrepresenting the qualities or characteristics of the product.

Advertising can also stimulate demand by communicating to consumers information about additional uses for a product. Because consumers will buy only so much of a product for a specific purpose, marketers can stimulate demand only to a certain point. To spur demand beyond that point, they must either expand the market to include more people or develop and promote a larger number of uses for the product. If a marketer can successfully convince consumers to use the company products in more ways, sales will increase. For years, the advertisements of Kraft General Foods have included recipes that use a variety of Kraft products as ingredients.

Reminding and Reinforcing Consumers

Marketers sometimes use advertising to make consumers aware that an established brand is still around and that it has certain uses, characteristics, and benefits; this is known as **reminder advertising.** In the same vein, **reinforce-**

■ **reminder advertising** advertising used to make consumers aware that an established brand is still around and that it has certain uses, characteristics, and benefits

[11] Raymond Serafin and Cleveland Horton, "Comparison Ads Rev Up," *Advertising Age,* January 20, 1992, pp. 3, 53.

FIGURE 19.3
Comparative
Advertisement
Ragu uses a comparative advertisement to claim that its Super Mushroom sauce has as many mushrooms as those in the leading competitors' sauces combined.

Source: Courtesy of Van den Bergh Foods Company.

■ **reinforcement advertising** advertising used to assure current purchasers that they have made the right choice and to offer advice on how to get the most satisfaction from the product

ment advertising is used to assure current purchasers that they have made the right choice and to offer advice on how to get the most satisfaction from the product. Both reminder and reinforcement advertising are used to maintain market share for mature products.

Countering Advertising by Competitors

■ **defensive advertising** advertising used to offset or minimize the impact of a competitor's promotional program

Advertising used to offset or minimize the impact of a competitor's promotional program is referred to as **defensive advertising.** Although defensive advertising is not necessarily intended to increase sales or market share, it may thwart a competitor's efforts to cut into the advertiser's sales or market share. Defensive advertising is most often employed by firms in extremely competitive consumer-product markets, although it is occasionally used by nonbusiness organizations. For example, the Areba-Casriel Institute for Drug and Alcohol Abuse in New York City began advertising to counter advertising by other clinics in the increasingly competitive drug- and alcohol-rehabilitation field. The rehabilitation clinic had not advertised for more than twenty years; instead it relied on doctors' referrals and word-of-mouth recommendations to attract patients from Broadway, Wall Street, and the sports world.[12]

[12]Ronald Alsop, "Drug and Alcohol Clinics Vie for Patients," *Wall Street Journal,* November 14, 1988, p. B1.

Supporting the Sales Force

Advertising is used to support sales personnel by informing consumers about a product's uses, features, and benefits and urging them to contact local dealers or sales representatives. Examples of supporting media include trade magazine advertisements, direct mail, brochures, videos, and catalogues. This form of advertising is often designed to support personal-selling efforts for organizational products like insurance and for consumer durables such as automobiles and major household appliances. Advertising may also be used to help salespeople and retailers find prospective buyers. For instance, advertisements for tires, hardware, garden supplies, and other products on the Weather Channel and other national television networks may list local dealers of the products in the final seconds of the advertisements. Consumers interested in those brands then know where to find them in their area. In addition, print or television advertisements may suggest that a person can receive more information or a free gift by responding with a letter or a completed survey. Sales personnel can then contact the prospective buyers who respond.

Minimizing Sales Fluctuations

Finally, advertising may be used to minimize sales fluctuations that result from weather, holidays, or seasons. Advertisements promoting price reductions for snow tires, heaters, and winter coats can increase sales of those products during spring and summer months. Resorts and cruise ships often advertise reduced rates during the "off-season," and AT&T and GTE offer discounts to consumers using long-distance telephone lines during the night and on weekends when usage is low. Conversely, a business may refrain from advertising during peak sales periods to prevent overstimulation of sales to the point that the firm cannot satisfy all of the demand.

WHO IS RESPONSIBLE FOR THE ADVERTISING PROGRAM?

An advertising program may be handled by an individual or a few persons within the firm, an advertising department within the organization, or an independent advertising agency. In very small organizations, one or two employees are generally responsible for the advertising program. These persons rely on personnel at local newspapers and broadcast stations for services such as writing, artwork, and advice about scheduling media. Advances in computer technology (graphics and typography) now make it possible for small businesses to create fairly sophisticated advertisements on personal computers like the Apple Macintosh.

In larger businesses, the advertising program is typically the responsibility of an advertising department. This department may consist of a few persons with general advertising skills or a number of specialists, including writers, artists, media buyers, and technical production coordinators. A firm's adver-

TABLE 19.2
Top Ten Advertising Agencies

Agency	Annual Revenues (in millions)
1. WWP Group	$2,813
2. Interpublic Group of Cos.	1,989
3. Omnicom Group	1,807
4. Saatchi & Saatchi Co.	1,696
5. Dentsu	1,388
6. Young & Rubicam Inc.	1,072
7. Euro RSCG	951
8. Grey Advertising	735
9. Foote, Cone & Belding Communications	683
10. Hakuhodo	661

Source: *Advertising Age*, April 14, 1993, p. 1. Reprinted with permission.

tising department may employ the services of independent research organizations and free-lance specialists when their expertise is needed for a particular project.

Rather than develop their own advertisements, many organizations assign the job to an outside agency. An **advertising agency** is a business that specializes in creating advertisements for other organizations; many advertising agencies offer other promotion-related services such as assistance with publicity and sales promotions. The use of an agency may be helpful because of its experience and objectivity in advertising. Table 19.2 lists the ten largest advertising agencies worldwide.

■ **advertising agency**
a business that specializes in creating advertisements for other organizations and also offers other promotion-related services

When an organization employs the services of an advertising agency, the firm and the agency usually work together to develop the advertising program. How much each participates in the program's total development depends on the working relationship between the firm and the agency. Ordinarily a firm relies on the agency for ad writing, artwork, technical production, and formulation of the media plan. In return, organizations traditionally pay the advertising agency a 15 percent commission on media and production billings. However, many agencies have abolished the 15 percent fee at the request of their clients. Some agencies now charge a standard fee, others negotiate commission rates, and others tie their profits to a performance bonus. In any case, large advertising agencies face an uncertain future, as many clients are rebelling against 15 percent commissions and are doing more things for themselves, or turning to smaller agencies or other sources for ideas. For a campaign for its Black Top basketball shoes, Reebok used four different shops: Chiat/Day for advertising, a sales promotion agency to run local tournaments, a design firm for point-of-sale materials, and an outside media-buying agency.[13] In the past, an advertising agency would have handled all these functions.

[13]Joshua Levine, "Teaching Elephants to Dance," *Forbes*, March 15, 1993, pp. 100–102.

DEVELOPING THE ADVERTISING PROGRAM

The process of developing an advertising program, or campaign, involves several steps. Although the number and sequence of steps are not the same for every program, the major ones, shown in Figure 19.4, are (1) identifying the target market, (2) establishing the advertising objectives, (3) determining the advertising budget, (4) creating the advertising message, (5) developing the media plan, (6) launching the advertising program, and (7) measuring advertising effectiveness.

Identifying the Target Market

When developing the advertising program, advertisers must first identify the composition and needs of the target market because this is the group of people to whom they wish to communicate their message. All other decisions involved in the development of an advertising program are based on the target market, which must be precisely defined in the course of strategic marketing planning. When the target market has not been accurately identified, there is a greater chance that the advertising program will fail.

To understand the make-up and needs of the target market, marketers must have information concerning the location and geographic distribution of the target group; the distribution of age, sex, race, income, and education; and consumer attitudes regarding the purchase and use of both the advertiser's products and competing products. The exact kinds of information that an organization finds useful depends on the type of product being advertised, the characteristics of the target market, and the type and amount of competition.

An advertising program may be aimed at an entire target market or a single large segment of a market. Columbia Pictures targeted advertisements for *A League of Their Own,* a film about the All-American Girls Baseball

FIGURE 19.4
Major Steps in Developing an Advertising Program

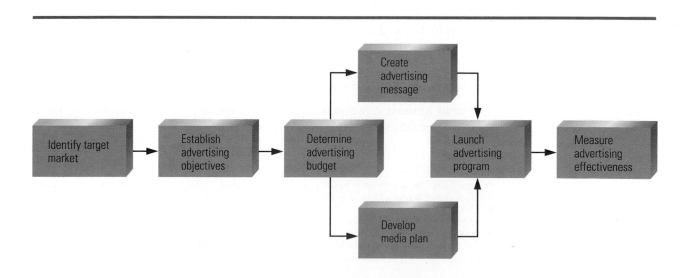
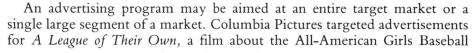

League in the 1940s, to baseball fans.[14] Johnson & Johnson aims advertisements for Baby Diaper Rash Relief at men, 80 percent of whom do some major grocery shopping every month.[15] Van Heusen, with a 9.9 percent share of the men's dress shirt market, passed rival Arrow, which has a 9.2 percent share. Since it is estimated that women purchase 60 to 70 percent of men's shirts, one of Van Heusen's strategies is to advertise directly to women. About half of Van Heusen's $8 million advertising budget is devoted to women's magazines like *Vogue* and *Glamour.*[16] Drug makers, which historically have marketed to doctors only, spend about $200 million a year to advertise about a dozen prescription drugs directly to consumers to encourage them to ask their doctors for a drug by name.[17] And many companies, including AT&T, Procter & Gamble, and Carnival Cruise Lines, target singles, who make up nearly 40 percent of the U.S. adult population, in advertisements for their goods and services.[18]

Establishing Advertising Objectives

■ **advertising objective**
a well-defined, measurable goal that specifies something that is to be accomplished through an advertising program

The next step in developing the advertising program is to consider the goals the firm hopes to achieve with the campaign. Each **advertising objective** should specify something that is to be accomplished through the advertising program. Advertising objectives should be stated in clear, precise, and measurable terms so that advertisers can evaluate whether or how well the objectives have been accomplished after the program has been launched. Consider the following objective: "The objective of our program is to increase average monthly sales from $50,000 to $75,000 within one year." This objective is clear, precise, specifies a time frame, and offers a current and a projected figure by which to measure success.

Like the previous example, advertising objectives are often stated in terms of sales. When this is the case, the objectives typically focus on raising absolute dollar sales, increasing sales by a certain percentage, or increasing the firm's market share. Objectives can also be stated in terms of communication. Some programs have as their objective increasing product or brand awareness, making consumers' attitudes more favorable, or increasing consumers' knowledge of a product's features or uses. A specific communication objective might be to raise product feature awareness from 0 to 50 percent in the target market within six months of introduction.

Determining the Advertising Budget

■ **advertising budget** the total amount of money that a marketer allocates for advertising for a specific time period

The total amount of money that a marketer allocates for advertising for a specific time period is the **advertising budget.** Many factors affect how much

[14]Marcy Magiera, "Hollywood Zeros In," *Advertising Age,* May 4, 1992, p. 18.
[15]Laura Zinn, "Real Men Buy Paper Towels, Too," *Business Week,* November 9, 1992, pp. 75–76.
[16]Teri Agins, "Women Help Van Heusen Collar Arrow," *Wall Street Journal,* May 22, 1992, pp. B1, B5.
[17]Joseph Weber and John Carey, "Drug Ads: A Prescription for Controversy," *Business Week,* January 18, 1993, pp. 58–60.
[18]Christy Fisher, "Census Data May Make Ads More Single-Minded," *Advertising Age,* July 20, 1992, p. 2.

TABLE 19.3
Advertising Expenditures as a Percent of Sales for Selected Industries (1992)

Industry	Advertising as a Percent of Sales
Agricultural production—crops	2.4
Air courier services	1.3
Beverages	8.5
Books	3.2
Computer terminals	4.3
Dolls and stuffed toys	15.5
Electronic housewares and fans	4.9
Games, toys (excluding dolls)	14.6
Grocery stores	1.3
Hotels, motels, tourist courts	3.2
Jewelry stores	3.2
Motion-picture theaters	3.2
Office furniture	1.1
Perfume, cosmetics	10.7
Phono records, audiotape, disks	11.9
Sausage, prepared meat	8.2
Sporting goods	3.4

Source: *Advertising Age,* July 13, 1992, p. 16. Reprinted with permission.

a firm allocates for advertising, including the geographic size of the market, the distribution of buyers within the market, the type of product advertised, and the firm's sales volume relative to competitors' sales volumes. Advertising budgets for organizational products tend to be quite small relative to the sales of the products. Consumer convenience goods generally necessitate large advertising expenditures.

Four approaches are commonly used to determine the amount of the advertising budget: the percent of sales, objective and task, competition-matching, and arbitrary approaches.

Percent of Sales Approach   A commonly used method of determining the advertising budget is the **percent of sales approach,** in which marketers multiply a firm's past sales, forecasted sales, or a combination of the two by a standard percentage of sales based on the company's traditional advertising expenditures and the industry's average. Table 19.3 provides some standard percentages of sales that are used by various industries. For example, a sporting goods firm might look at the data in Table 19.3 and then multiply its past year's sales ($5,000,000) by 3.4 percent (the average percent spent by other firms in its industry) to determine its advertising budget ($170,000). The major drawback to this approach is that it is based on the false assumption that sales create advertising, when, in fact, advertising generates sales. Using this approach, an organization that is experiencing declining sales would probably reduce the amount spent on advertising, which may, in fact,

■ **percent of sales approach** a common method of determining the advertising budget, in which marketers multiply a firm's past sales, forecasted sales, or a combination of the two by a standard percentage of sales based on the company's traditional advertising expenditures and the industry's average

cause a further decline in sales. Nonetheless, this technique has garnered widespread acceptance because it is easy to use and stabilizes a firm's market share within an industry.

Objective and Task Approach   The most rational approach to determining the amount of the advertising budget is the **objective and task approach,** in which marketers determine the objectives that a program is to achieve, identify the tasks required to accomplish them, and compute the cost of the tasks. This approach has one principal drawback: It is usually difficult to estimate the level of effort needed to achieve certain objectives. A frozen-dinner producer, for example, might find it extremely difficult to determine how much to increase national television advertising to boost a brand's market share from 5 to 15 percent. Because of this drawback, the objective and task approach is not widely used by advertisers.

Competition-Matching Approach   A third way to determine the advertising budget is the **competition-matching approach,** in which an organization matches major competitors' advertising appropriations in terms of absolute dollars or percentage of sales. Marketers who follow this approach are interested in the type and magnitude of their competitors' advertising. This technique should not be used exclusively because competitors probably have different advertising objectives and resources available for advertising. It may also be difficult to determine what competitors are budgeting for advertising.

Arbitrary Approach   A fourth method used to determine the advertising budget is the **arbitrary approach,** in which a high-level executive in the firm subjectively stipulates how much will be spent on advertising for a certain time period. Although this approach is certainly expedient, it often leads to underspending or overspending, as well as failure to achieve advertising objectives.

Determining the proper amount to spend on advertising activities is a critical decision. When too much money is allocated for advertising, financial resources that could be used elsewhere are squandered. Conversely, when not enough money is allocated, the advertising program cannot achieve its advertising and marketing objectives.

Creating the Advertising Message

Once the budget and objectives of an advertising program have been established, the advertiser must create the message it will communicate to the target market. The message depends on the **advertising platform,** which consists of the basic issues or selling features to be stressed in the advertising program; the platform usually highlights important characteristics that competitive products do not have. For instance, if a product has a unique safety feature that is important to consumers, the platform might be built on this base.

In addition to the advertising platform, advertisers must consider other factors when creating the advertising message. The content of the message

---

■ **objective and task approach** a rational method of determining the advertising budget, in which marketers define the objectives that a program is to achieve, identify the tasks required to accomplish them, and compute the costs of the tasks

■ **competition-matching approach** a method of determining the advertising budget, in which an organization matches major competitors' advertising appropriations in terms of absolute dollars or percentage of sales

■ **arbitrary approach** a method of determining the advertising budget, in which a high-level executive subjectively stipulates how much will be spent on advertising for a certain time period

■ **advertising platform** the basic issues or selling features to be stressed in an advertising program; usually highlights important features that competitive products do not have

FIGURE 19.5
Geographic Breakdown for
***Sports Illustrated* Regional**
Issues

Source: The following is reprinted courtesy of *Sports Illustrated* from the information contained in *Sports Illustrated's 1993 Rate Card*. Copyright © 1993 Time, Inc.

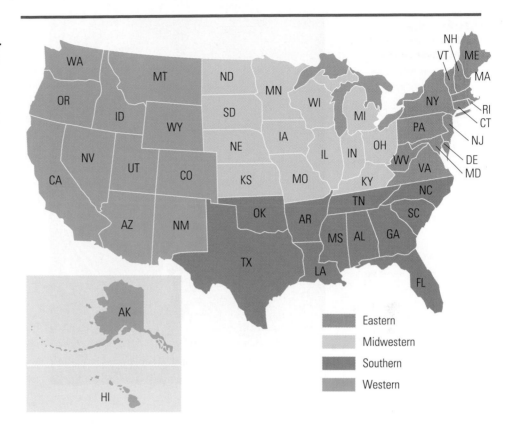

 is certainly shaped by the product's features, uses, and benefits. The characteristics of the target market—sex, age, education, race, income, occupation, and other attributes—influence both the content and form of the message. To ensure that the message is received and understood, an advertiser must use words, symbols, and illustrations that are meaningful, familiar, and attractive to those persons who make up the target market. For example, automobile advertisements are becoming more technical, with terms like *rack and pinion steering* and *double wishbone suspension*. But consumers may find it difficult to understand the meaning of these terms.

The content and form of the message are also dictated by the media used to relay the message. Outdoor displays (billboards, advertisements on buses and in subways) and short broadcast announcements require concise, simple messages, but magazine and newspaper advertisements can include more detail and longer explanations. Some types of media even provide geographic selectivity—that is, they create a precise message for a particular geographic section of the target market. Magazine publishers, for example, sometimes produce regional issues in which the advertisements and editorial content of copies distributed in one geographic area differ from those distributed in other areas. As shown in Figure 19.5, *Sports Illustrated* publishes four regional issues. A firm advertising in *Sports Illustrated* may vary its advertisements by region to appeal to the different demographic characteristics of each region.

FIGURE 19.6
The Basic Components of a Print Advertisement
Source: Oshkosh B'Gosh, Inc.

Body Copy

Illustration

Headline

Signature

Subheadline

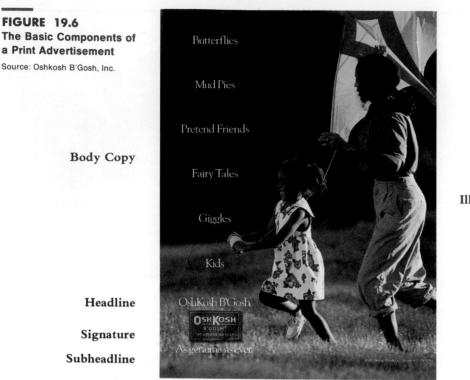

The basic components of a print advertising message are identified in Figure 19.6. The messages for most advertisements depend on the creative use of copy and artwork.

■ **copy** the verbal or written portion of an advertisement

Copy   The verbal or written portion of an advertisement is called **copy;** it includes headlines, subheadlines, body copy, and the signature (see Figure 19.6). The *headline* is critical because it may be the only part of the copy that people read. Its function is to grab the readers' attention and generate enough interest to make them want to read the rest of the advertisement. The *subheadline,* if included, ties the headline to the body copy and sometimes helps explain the headline. In most advertisements, the *body copy* consists of an introductory statement or paragraph, several explanatory paragraphs, and a closing paragraph. The body copy attempts to state the advantages and benefits of the advertised product, and suggests how the product can satisfy a reader's desire (or need) or solve a problem. The *signature* indicates the sponsor of the advertisement and may include the firm's trademark, name, and address in an attractive or distinctive manner.

Radio copy needs to be informal and conversational to attract an audience's attention because radio listeners generally are not paying full attention to messages relayed over the air. Since the radio message is so short-lived, radio copy should include only brief, well-known terms. For television copy, the audio material should balance the visual material; one should not overwhelm the other. Nonetheless, a television message should make maximum use of visual material.

■ **artwork** the graphic elements of an advertisement, including the illustration and layout

■ **illustration** a photograph, drawing, graph, chart, or table used in an advertisement

■ **layout** the physical arrangement of an advertisement's illustration(s), headline, and other copy elements

■ **media plan** a plan that establishes the specific media to be used in an advertising campaign and the dates and times that advertisements will appear

Artwork   **Artwork** consists of the graphic elements of an advertisement, including the illustration and layout (see Figure 19.6). The **illustration** may be a photograph, drawing, graph, chart, or table. It is used to grab the target market's attention, to induce the audience to read or listen to the copy, to communicate a message quickly, or to communicate an idea that is difficult to express verbally.

An advertisement's **layout** is the physical arrangement of its illustration(s), headline, and other copy elements. These elements of the advertisement in Figure 19.6 could have been arranged in a number of different ways. An advertisement's layout is the result of several stages of preparation and development, and it involves the input and exchange of ideas of everyone who takes part in developing the advertising program.

Developing the Media Plan

Americans watch television, listen to the radio, and read newspapers and magazines an average of eight hours and three minutes each day—as much as they sleep. Most of this time is devoted to television (three hours and forty-eight minutes) and radio (three hours and twenty-one minutes).[19] Vast sums of money are spent to advertise in the various media—newspapers, magazines, television, radio, outdoor displays, direct mail, and others (see Table 19.4). To obtain the greatest benefit from these media expenditures, advertisers must develop an effective **media plan,** which selects the specific media (particular newspapers, radio and television stations, and so on) to be used and the dates and times that advertisements will appear. The marketer or skilled media planner developing the media plan tries to communicate with the largest number of persons in the target market per dollar spent on media.

In developing the media plan, the planner must decide which kinds of media to use. The strengths and weaknesses of the major advertising media, shown in Table 19.5, influence this decision.

Newspapers   Newspapers make up the largest category of the advertising media. As shown in Table 19.4, spending for newspaper advertising exceeds $30 billion each year, with most of that amount purchased by local businesses. Firms can advertise in newspapers distributed locally, regionally, nationally, or internationally. Newspapers offer good coverage for firms of any size because there is at least one newspaper in every local market and many people read the newspaper every day. Newspapers are well suited for immediate needs since they can run advertisements with little lead-time. Advertisers can choose advertisements of any size, from a few lines in the classified section to full pages or separate supplements.

Because they reach diverse audiences, newspapers do not always allow advertisers to target their audience precisely. The life span of newspapers is very short because readers usually discard them quickly, but readers can clip or refer back to advertisements if they wish. The quality of the paper is

[19] "Top Cities for Watching, Listening, and Reading," *Fortune,* May 18, 1992, p. 18.

TABLE 19.4
Annual Advertising Media
Expenditures

Medium	Expenditure	
	Millions of Dollars	**Percent of Total**
Newspapers		
National	$ 3,602	2.7%
Local	27,135	20.7
Total	30,737	23.4
Magazines		
Weeklies	2,739	2.1
Women's	1,853	1.4
Monthlies	2,408	1.8
Total	7,000	5.3
Farm publications	231	0.2
Television		
Network	9,549	7.3
Cable (national)	1,685	1.3
Syndication	2,070	1.6
Spot (national)	7,551	5.8
Spot (local)	8,079	6.1
Cable (non-network)	475	0.3
Total	29,409	22.4
Radio		
Network	424	0.3
Spot (national)	1,505	1.2
Spot (local)	6,725	5.1
Total	8,654	6.6
Yellow Pages		
National	1,188	0.9
Local	8,132	6.2
Total	9,320	7.1
Direct mail	25,391	19.3
Business papers	3,090	2.4
Outdoor		
National	610	0.5
Local	421	0.3
Total	1,031	0.8
Miscellaneous		
National	12,124	9.2
Local	4,303	3.3
Total	16,427	12.5
Total		
National	76,020	57.9
Local	55,270	42.1
Grand total	$131,290	100.0%

Source: *Advertising Age*, May 3, 1993, p. 14. Reprinted with permission.

TABLE 19.5
**Strengths and Weaknesses
of Advertising Media**

Medium	Types	Strengths	Weaknesses
Newspapers	Daily Weekly Special	Accessible to almost everyone; national geographic flexibility; short lead-time; frequent publication; favorable for cooperative advertising; 'merchandising services	Not selective for socioeconomic groups; short life; limited reproduction capabilities; large advertising volume limits exposure to any one advertisement
Magazines	Consumer Business National Local Regional	Socioeconomic selectivity; good reproduction; long life; prestige; geographic selectivity when regional issues are available; read in leisurely manner	High absolute dollar cost; long lead-time
Television	Network Local CATV	Reaches large audience; low cost per exposure; uses audio and video; highly visible; high prestige; geographic and socioeconomic selectivity	High dollar cost; short life of message; size of audience not guaranteed; amount of prime timc limited
Radio	AM FM	Highly mobile; low-cost broadcast medium; message can be quickly changed; can reach a large audience; geographic selectivity; socioeconomic selectivity	Provides only audio message; has lost prestige; short life of message; listeners' attention limited because of other activities while listening
Direct mail	Letters Flyers Catalogues Samples Coupons Price lists	Little wasted circulation; highly selective; circulation controlled by advertiser; few distractions; personal; stimulates actions; use of novelty; relatively easy to measure performance; hidden from competitors	Expensive; no editorial matter to attract readers; considered junk mail by many; criticized as invasion of privacy
Outdoor displays	Painted buildings and vehicles Posters Billboards Electric spectaculars	Allows for repetition; low cost; message can be placed close to the point of sale; geographic selectivity; operable 24 hours a day	Message must be short and simple; no socioeconomic selectivity; seldom attracts readers' full attention; criticized for being traffic hazard and blight on countryside
Transit	Buses Taxicabs Subways	Low cost; frequency of message; "captive" audience; geographic selectivity	Limited audience; low impact; does not secure quick results

generally low and the use of color is limited. Generally, newspapers are the least willing of all media to negotiate price with advertisers.[20]

Magazines   The last decade has seen a dramatic increase in the number of magazines being published. Expenditures for magazine advertising also have grown in the last several years and now account for about 5 percent of total advertising volume. The top five magazines, by total advertising revenues, are *Parade, People, Time, Sports Illustrated,* and *TV Guide*.[21]

The sheer number and tremendous variety of magazines give advertisers the opportunity to target nearly any audience. Publications with huge circulations such as *Reader's Digest, Time,* and *Good Housekeeping* allow advertisers to reach huge general audiences. National magazines now can offer more local advertising by publishing several regional editions. Smaller, specialized magazines such as *Golf Digest, Apartment Life,* or *Cincinnati Magazine* reach more precise market segments.

Magazines offer the unique capability of high-quality color reproduction, a valuable asset in promoting many products. They also provide a more permanent message than do the other media since subscribers often keep their favorites in their homes or workplaces for weeks or months and pass them along to friends. Magazine advertisements are not suited for immediate messages; they take a long time to produce and may be outdated by printing time. Advertising in a widely circulated publication can be quite expensive.

Television   Another large medium, television accounts for approximately 22 percent of advertising expenditures. Advertisers spend in excess of $29 billion each year on television commercials (see Table 19.4). Automobile manufacturers alone spend a total of $2 billion to advertise their vehicles on television.

Perhaps television's greatest advantage is that it allows creative use of action, color, and sound to an extent not possible in any other medium. Television advertising also offers the capability of reaching vast audiences, since 98 percent of U.S. homes have at least one television set. Firms can advertise nationally on a major network, regionally through cable networks, or locally through local stations.

The major drawback of network television advertising is the high cost. A 30-second commercial can cost over $300,000 for broadcast during a popular show like "Murphy Brown."[22] To keep costs down, many advertisers now use 15-second ads with networks running more of these shorter ads during a commercial break. With so many aired during a program, television ads may not have much impact on viewers. At any rate, television ads have an extremely short life, which prompts creators to use special effects, unusual sounds, music, humor, and distinctive characters to encourage viewers to remember advertisements and products.

---

[20]Christy Fisher, "While Papers Say Prices Firm, Change on Horizon," *Advertising Age,* July 2, 1992, p. S-32.
[21]"Ad Age 300," *Advertising Age,* June 15, 1992, p. S-11.
[22]Joe Mandese, "Advertisers Vote for 'Murphy Brown,'" *Advertising Age,* September 7, 1992, pp. 3, 36.

Television advertisers face difficulty in determining the audience that actually sees the commercials. Viewers in public places like hotels, airports, restaurants, or stores are not counted. In homes, commercials play to empty rooms when viewers take breaks. Many viewers change channels when commercials begin, a habit called "zapping" that is made easier by today's remote controls and cable systems with over one hundred channels. Some rating systems estimate that zapping cuts a prime-time commercial's audience by 10 percent or more. According to Nielsen Media Research data, viewers are increasingly likely to change channels as advertising clutter grows. With a 10 percent increase in nonprogramming time, zapping jumps an average of 7 percent.[23] Empty rooms and zapping mean that television advertisers do not get the audience they pay for.

A new array of interactive media products will have a major impact on television advertising. Quantum, a 150-channel interactive pay-per-view cable service, allows subscribers to choose from a variety of movies at the times they want. As video-on-demand and other entertainment-oriented media grow in this decade, the range of broadcast media choices available to advertisers will grow wider. Traditional network television will risk losing audience and market share as advertisers follow consumers who either order videos with advertising at home or pay a premium to see movies without advertising.[24]

Radio   About 7 percent of all money spent on advertising goes for radio advertisements. Radio serves a large and varied audience (see Table 19.4). Homes in the United States have nearly 500 million radios. Because of the wide variety of programming catering to numerous interests, such as talk shows, all news, hard rock, classical, jazz, oldies, easy listening, or Spanish-language broadcasts, advertisers can easily pinpoint target audiences. Spending on radio advertising has grown significantly because of its relatively low cost and ability to reach precisely defined target audiences.[25]

Radio advertisements have the disadvantage of an extremely short life. Messages are limited because radio relies only on the sense of hearing. Listeners may keep radios turned on for background music or mere noise and end up ignoring the advertisements.

Direct Mail   As noted in Chapter 17, thousands of organizations send catalogues, advertisements, flyers, brochures, and fund-raising materials to homes, offices, or stores of target individuals. Over 19 percent of all advertising expenditures—more than $25 billion—goes for direct mail, the third largest advertising medium in the United States.

For direct mail to be effective, the material must reach the target group through up-to-date mailing lists. Advertisers can develop or purchase mailing lists that will reach nearly any target market imaginable, although selective mailing lists are expensive to buy. Direct mail's effectiveness is easily deter-

---

[23]"Clutter Suffers Zap Attack," *Advertising Age,* March 30, 1992, p. 38.
[24]Rachel Kaplan, "Video on Demand," *American Demographics,* June 1992, pp. 38–43.
[25]Joshua Levine, "Drive Time," *Forbes,* March 19, 1990, pp. 144–146.

mined through customers' orders or donations to fund-raising organizations. Even banks use direct mail. When targeting certain neighborhoods or high-income customers, some banks now mail catalogues explaining brokerage services, credit cards, and loans, along with applications, toll-free numbers, and even coupons for free checks. Traditionally considered one of the less expensive forms of advertising, direct mail is becoming more costly as postal rates rise. Many firms are trimming mailing lists to include only their best customers or prospects.

Outdoor Displays   Billboards, posters, and other outdoor displays account for about 1 percent of advertising expenditures. Outdoor displays are inexpensive and useful in high-traffic areas. Their main disadvantage is that only a brief message can be communicated. Many people criticize outdoor displays along highways and roads for detracting from the beauty of the natural scenery. In 1992, the federal government gave states two months to remove from areas along interstates and highways an estimated 114,000 outdoor displays that do not comply with the 1965 Highway Beautification Act.[26] These displays violate spacing, zoning, and other aspects of the law.

Transit   Another advertising medium is transit, both inside buses and subways and on taxis, buses, and commuter trains. Transit is a low-cost alternative and generally reaches a selective geographic market. The major drawback to this form of advertising is that it reaches a limited audience which does not include many professionals. Transit advertisements also are becoming cluttered and the audience is likely to be distracted.

Other Factors to Consider in Developing the Media Plan   In addition to choosing which medium to use, the planner must also select specific subclasses within each medium. For example, a dry soup maker such as Lipton or Knorr might decide to advertise on television and in magazines. Next, the marketer considers whether to use women's daytime, men's sports, family, late-night adult, or some other type of television programming and whether to use magazines geared to men, women, teenagers, or a general audience. Finally, having selected family television programs and women's and teenagers' magazines, the dry soup marketer must select the exact television stations and programs as well as the specific women's and teenagers' magazines to use.

Many other factors must be considered when devising a media plan. Media planners must analyze the location and demographic characteristics of consumers in the target market because different media appeal to particular demographic groups in particular locations. There are radio stations with programs designed for baby boomers, magazines for women in the 18-to-34 age group, newspapers for businesspeople, and television programs aimed at children. For instance, it would be futile for a vacuum cleaner marketer to

[26] Steven W. Colford, "Feds Set Fund to Ax Outdoor Boards," *Advertising Age,* March 16, 1992, pp. 1, 50.

advertise during Saturday morning cartoons because most children would neither be interested in nor have the buying power to purchase vacuum cleaners.

Media planners must also consider reach and frequency. *Reach* refers to the number of different people or households that are exposed to an advertisement during a certain period of time. For example, *TV Guide* has a paid circulation of about 15 million, *Woman's Day,* 4.5 million, and *Field & Stream,* 2 million.[27] However, media planners must realize that figures on reach can be misleading. Zapping can dramatically reduce the actual number of people that see a television advertisement. Likewise, readers may not see every advertisement in a magazine or may skip ad pages, especially when there is a high amount of clutter. *Frequency* is the number of times an advertisement reaches a person or household in the target market. This is important to media planners because it is a measure of the repetition that can be achieved through a certain media plan. Frequency is important when the advertising objective is to provide the target market with frequent reminders of the product. Frequency is highest for television, radio, and newspapers, and lowest for magazines, telephone directories, and outdoor advertisements.

Cost is another important consideration in developing a media plan. Advertisers attempt to obtain the best coverage possible for each dollar spent, but there is no accurate way to compare the cost and impact of a television commercial with the cost and impact of, say, a newspaper advertisement. For instance, a 30-second commercial on network television may run $300,000, whereas a national newspaper advertisement may be much less expensive. The television commercial, however, may have a greater impact on a larger number of people. Gerber Products Company uses direct mail advertising to reach new parents. Direct mail enables Gerber to provide a more personal message and to build trust with persons buying baby food and at the same time is more cost-effective.

Although the media used to relay an advertising message can shape the form and content of the message, it is also true that the content of the message can dictate the choice of media. Magazines, newspapers, and direct mail can be used more effectively than television or radio for advertisements that present numerous details or complex issues. Color, patterns, and textures are more effectively displayed in media that offer high-quality color reproduction, such as magazines or television. For example, Gatorade appears extremely flavorful and appealing in a full-color magazine advertisement, but it looks far less appealing in a black-and-white newspaper advertisement (see Figure 19.7).

Launching the Advertising Program

After creating the advertising message and developing the media plan, the marketer launches the advertising program. A successful launch requires a great deal of planning and coordination among the many people involved in

[27] "Ad Age 300," *Advertising Age,* June 15, 1992, p. S-2.

FIGURE 19.7
Color vs. Black and White Advertising
By showing new Gatorade in color, it looks flavorful and appealing, with a rich grape flavor. Shown in black and white, much is lost as the Gatorade appears flat.

Source: Reprinted with permission of The Quaker Oats Company.

■ **pretest** a test conducted before an advertising campaign begins to evaluate the effectiveness of one or more elements of the advertising message

■ **consumer panel** a group of actual or potential buyers of an advertised product who are asked to assess various dimensions of two or more advertisements

■ **inquiry** an examination of some element(s) of an advertising program conducted during the program to measure advertising effectiveness

the execution of the advertising campaign. Advertising agencies, research organizations, production companies, media firms, copywriters, photoengravers, and commercial artists are just a few of the people and organizations that may be involved in a program.

Detailed schedules must be prepared to ensure that various phases of the launch are carried out on time. Management must evaluate the quality of the work and take appropriate action when the work does not meet acceptable standards. In some instances, changes have to be made during the advertising campaign to make it more effective in meeting advertising objectives. For instance, a firm might substitute a different spokesperson, change the times at which an advertisement is run, or switch it to a different program.

Measuring Advertising Effectiveness

Measuring advertising effectiveness, the final step in the development of the advertising program, is a crucial activity. Advertising effectiveness can be measured before, during, and after the program launch.

Before the program begins, a **pretest** may be used to evaluate the effectiveness of one or more elements of the advertising message. To pretest an advertisement, marketers sometimes make use of a **consumer panel,** a group of actual or potential buyers of an advertised product who are asked to assess various dimensions of two or more advertisements. Focus-group interviews are also used to pretest an advertisement. Pretesting is based on the belief that actual consumers are more likely than advertisers to know what types of advertising will have the greatest impact on them.

During the advertising campaign, marketers typically use an **inquiry** to measure the advertising effectiveness of one or more of its elements. For instance, when an advertising program is first introduced, several advertisements may be run simultaneously, each containing a coupon or a form requesting information. The advertiser records the number of coupons or forms returned from each type of advertisement. If one of the advertisements generates a larger number of returned coupons, it is judged more effective than the others. In addition, advances in computer technology and physical measurement techniques now permit advertisers to measure who is paying attention to commercials and the strength of that attention, second by second, throughout a television commercial.

posttest measurement of advertising effectiveness after an advertising program

Measurement of advertising effectiveness after the campaign has begun is called a **posttest.** The type of posttest used depends on the advertising objectives. When advertising objectives are described in terms of communication—for instance, increasing awareness of or changing attitudes about a product or brand—then the posttest should measure whether these changes have indeed occurred.

For advertising objectives stated in terms of sales, a posttest should measure the change in sales or market share that can be attributed to the program. However, it is difficult to precisely measure changes in sales or market share that result from advertising. Factors independent of the advertising program, such as actions by competitors or government agencies and changes in economic conditions, consumer preferences, or even the weather, might augment or lessen a company's sales or market share. Historically, however, businesses with a higher relative advertising-to-sales ratio earn a higher return on investment and enjoy a larger market share.[28]

recognition test a posttest in which researchers show individual respondents actual advertisements and ask whether they recognize them

unaided recall test a posttest in which subjects are asked to remember advertisements that they have seen recently but are not given any clues to spur their memory

aided recall test a posttest in which respondents are asked to remember advertisements after being shown a list of products, brands, company names, or trademarks to jog their memories

In another type of posttest, marketers attempt to measure what consumers think or how much they remember about advertisements after they have been run. Video Storyboard Tests Inc. conducts an annual survey asking people simply to name outstanding advertisements; Pepsi and Energizer advertisements were number one and two, respectively, in the most recent survey.[29] With a **recognition test,** researchers show individual respondents actual advertisements and ask whether they recognize them. In an **unaided recall test,** subjects are asked to remember advertisements that they have seen recently but are not given any clues to spur their memory. The **aided recall test** is similar except that respondents are shown a list of products, brands, company names, or trademarks to jog their memories.

 ADVERTISING FOR GLOBAL MARKETS

As we note in Chapter 18, international marketers must often modify advertisements for foreign markets. One of the goals of advertising is to inform a target market about a good, service, or idea; therefore the symbols used by advertisers in the communication process must be familiar to and acceptable to the target. Additionally, since advertising is transmitted through a

---

[28] Sarah Stiansen, "Ogilvy Study: Advertising Works," *Adweek,* December 21, 1987, p. 12.
[29] Joanne Lipman, "Consumers' Favorite Commercials Tend to Feature Lower Prices or Cuddly Kids," *Wall Street Journal,* March 2, 1992, p. B1.

FIGURE 19.8
International Advertising
The Japanese firm Fuji developed this advertisement for its film to run in Germany.

Source: Campaign: Saatchi & Saatchi Advertising. Photo: Hubertus Hamm. Client: Fuji Photo Film, Germany.

mass medium, the availability and limitation of media in foreign markets have a significant impact on international advertising strategies. Figure 19.8 shows how a Japanese film company develops an advertisement run in Germany.

Challenges in International Advertising

Firms engaged in international marketing have discovered that developing a specific advertisement for every country carries tremendous costs. For example, to sell its products throughout the world, Coca-Cola has capitalized on a global marketing strategy that has resulted in a worldwide image for Coke. But it remains difficult for a company to successfully launch a global or standardized advertising campaign. Many firms view a standardized brand name as a necessity for a global campaign. Toyota, for instance, is pronounced the same way in all countries. But standardization also requires consistency in packaging, the competitive situation, brand awareness, and consumer attitudes. This is rarely the case, and many companies are forced to develop advertisements for foreign markets that are considerably different from those used at home. Nonetheless, the list of companies launching global advertising campaigns is growing rapidly. Propelling this trend is the proliferation of international media, especially satellite and cable-TV networks like Cable News Network International and British Sky Broadcasting.[30]

[30] Ken Wells, "Global Ad Campaigns, After Many Missteps, Finally Pay Dividends," *Wall Street Journal,* August 27, 1992, pp. A1, A8.

A major challenge for international advertisers is communicating with people in diverse cultures. One of the most common reasons for the failure of international marketers is that they do not understand the culture of the target market. As you recall from our discussion of the communication process, perception of the message may differ depending upon how receivers perceive the symbols used by the source. Some of the cultural barriers are very difficult, if not impossible, to overcome. Consequently, a company advertising in a foreign country must be familiar with the cultural beliefs of that country. For instance, Helene Curtis tailored advertisements for its hair care products in different ways. In Spain, middle-class women wash their hair infrequently, whereas British women frequently wash their hair. Japanese women, fearing a loss of protective oils, do not like to overwash their hair.[31] Companies can conduct research with foreign customers or use foreign distributors and advertising agencies to ensure that advertisements are consistent with the culture of the target market.

Language differences pose another challenge in international advertising. In most cases, meaning is lost in the literal translation from one language to another. This problem can be overcome by involving language experts or a foreign subsidiary or advertising agency in the translation. The low literacy rates in some countries and multiple languages or dialects used within a country are also barriers to international advertising. In these cases, it is important to communicate visually and verbally rather than through written language.

Government regulation that differs from country to country also presents a challenge to international advertising. For example, the advertising of cigarettes and tobacco products is strictly regulated in some countries.[32] In France, advertisements cannot show people smoking cigarettes, whereas cigarette advertising is permitted in Greece. Laws may restrict the amount of money that can be spent on advertising, the production of advertisements, the media used, the type of product advertised, the advertisement copy, and other aspects of the advertisement, such as making comparisons to competitors. Firms must be familiar with laws and regulations in foreign countries, and modify or develop advertisements that are acceptable.

Media Considerations

A variety of media alternatives are available to firms that advertise in the United States (see Table 19.5). However, many countries are still without commercial radio, and commercial television is unavailable to advertisers in some countries. Even when radio and television exist, government restrictions may prohibit advertising. Restrictions and limited availability may require international marketing firms to revise media plans.

Some segments of a foreign target market may be especially hard to reach with advertising. Ownership of televisions or radios and subscriptions to newspapers and magazines vary considerably throughout the world. Although advertisers may have access to these media, they may be limited

---

[31] "Haircare Creates a Parting of the Ways," *Financial Times,* September 7, 1989, p. 12.
[32] "Defending the Rights of Marlboro Man," *The Economist,* April 21, 1990, p. 84.

because they reach only a small number of people. Advertisers may therefore have to use a variety of media to reach a large part of a country's target population.

Cost is also an important factor in making media decisions. The cost of media varies widely from country to country. In countries where media space or time is limited and competition is strong, the cost can be very high. Media costs can also be high if firms have to use multiple media to reach the target market.

THE NATURE AND USES OF PUBLICITY

As defined in Chapter 18, *publicity* is nonpersonal communication about an organization or its products that is transmitted through a mass medium in the form of news but is not paid for by the organization. Publicity is part of a larger set of communication activities called **public relations,** which is designed to create and maintain a favorable image of an organization and may be paid or nonpaid. Publicity can be used to make people aware of a firm's products, brands, and activities; to maintain a certain level of positive public visibility; and to enhance a particular image, such as innovativeness or progressiveness. It can also be used to overcome a negative image. Superman generated a great deal of publicity when he was killed off by his editor at Time Warner's DC Comics in 1992, selling 3.5 million copies at $1.25 each— one of the best-selling comic books ever.[33] McDonald's benefited greatly from the publicity it received when President-elect Bill Clinton ended his morning jogs with his usual cup of decaf and a chat with other customers. Some industry experts estimate that this free publicity was worth millions of dollars to McDonald's.[34]

Publicity and advertising differ in several significant respects: (1) publicity is informative but not persuasive (advertising is typically both); (2) publicity messages are more subdued than advertising messages; (3) publicity releases do not identify sponsors; (4) publicity messages are not paid for by the organization; (5) publicity is usually included as part of a news program or print story; (6) publicity may have more credibility than advertising because it appears more objective; and (7) publicity messages are generally not repeated.

Several forms of publicity can be used by an organization. The **news release,** sometimes called a press release, is usually a single page of typewritten copy (containing fewer than three hundred words) about a newsworthy event; it is sent to news editors for possible publication. This is the most common form of publicity (see Figure 19.9). Table 19.6 lists some typical subjects of news releases.

■ **public relations**
communication activities designed to create and maintain a favorable image of an organization

■ **news release** a form of publicity that is usually a single page of typewritten copy about a newsworthy event and is sent to news editors for possible publication

---

[33] Laura Zinn, "It's a Bird, It's a Plane—It's a Resurrection," *Business Week,* April 12, 1993, p. 40.
[34] Scott Hume, "Clinton Serves McD's a PR Feast," *Advertising Age,* December 14, 1992, p. 6.

FIGURE 19.9
Example of a News Release

> **N E W S   R E L E A S E**
>
> **EG&G**
>
> **FOR IMMEDIATE RELEASE**
> 4 June 1993
>
> For further information contact:
> Deborah S. Lorenz, EG&G, Inc.
> Tel: (617) 431-4306
> NYSE symbol: EGG
> Philip Mottram, Wallac Oy
> Tel: 011 358 21 678335
>
> EG&G SIGNS AGREEMENT TO ACQUIRE FINLAND-BASED WALLAC GROUP
>
> Wellesley, Massachusetts and Turku, Finland ...EG&G, Inc. has
> signed today a definitive agreement to acquire as of June 10, 1993
> the capital stock of The Wallac Group (Wallac), a unit of Procordia AB.
> The purchase price is approximately U.S. $46 million.
>
> Headquartered in Turku, Finland, Wallac has 500 employees located
> in Scandinavia, the U.K. and the U.S. The company develops,
> manufactures and markets analytical and immunodiagnostic systems,
> instruments and reagents for clinical diagnostics, life-science
> research and environmental monitoring. Total 1992 sales equate
> to approximately U.S. $50 million.
>
> John M. Kucharski, Chairman of EG&G, Inc. commented, "The
> acquisition of Wallac will complement and enhance our analytical
> instruments and diagnostics systems capabilities."
>
> EG&G, Inc. is a Fortune 200 company with annual sales in excess
> of $2.7 billion. It designs and manufactures laboratory and
> field-test instruments and electronic and mechanical components
> for commercial customers worldwide. EG&G provides systems
> engineering, precision component manufacturing and test-site
> operating and management services to many government agencies and
> laboratories. It employs more than 30,000 people worldwide.
>
> **EG&G, Inc.,** Corporate Offices. 45 William Street, Wellesley, Massachusetts 02181 Tel: 617-237-5100 Fax 617-431-4255

■ **feature article** a form of publicity that is up to three thousand words in length and is usually prepared for a specific publication

■ **captioned photograph** a photograph with a brief description explaining the people or event pictured

■ **news conference** a meeting held for media representatives to announce major news events

■ **editorial film or tape** a film or tape distributed to broadcast stations or newspapers in the hope that its contents will be used in news stories

■ **sponsorship** providing support for and associating an organization's name with an event, program, or person

A **feature article** is longer than a news release, up to three thousand words, and is usually prepared for a specific publication. A **captioned photograph** is a photograph with a brief description explaining the people or event pictured. Captioned photographs are especially effective for illustrating a new or improved product with highly visible features. A **news conference** is a meeting held for media representatives so that organizations can announce major news events, such as new products and technologies; mergers, take-overs, or buyouts; and special events. Finally, an **editorial film or tape** may be distributed to broadcast stations or newspapers in the hope that its contents will be used in news stories.

Another form of publicity gaining use is **sponsorship**—providing support for and associating an organization's name with events, programs, or even people such as amateur athletes or teams. Besides publicity, sponsorship can involve advertising and sales promotion activities such as samples and contests. Thousands of firms sponsor sporting events, festivals of the arts, public radio and television programs, and public interest advertisements. At least four hundred large U.S. corporations have developed event-marketing departments with separate budgets; others hire consultants to take care of sponsorship for them. Small businesses often work with local government and

TABLE 19.6
Typical Subjects of News Releases

New products	Progress reports
Improved products	Acquisitions and mergers
Price changes	Company reorganizations
Organization anniversaries	Addition of new employees
Employee accomplishments	Community relations
Contributions to charity	

community organizations to sponsor events. Close to the Customer looks at how firms benefit by sponsoring sporting events.

Some large newspapers combine publicity and advertising. The *Los Angeles Times* was the first general-interest newspaper to include a "corporate news" section—advertising space filled with company news releases. This form of publicity differs from traditional publicity in that companies must pay for the space; however, the firms have more control over the content and timing of their releases. The major disadvantage is that readers may not want to read several columns of releases from different companies in a section labeled *advertisements*.

Creating a Publicity Program

Publicity is most effective when a firm creates and maintains a systematic, long-term program. If a firm hopes to have an effective publicity program, an individual, department, advertising agency, or public relations firm should be responsible for managing the program. A small-business owner can develop his or her own publicity program, perhaps with the help of a free-lance writer or consultant if needed. One important aspect of an effective publicity program is maintaining good working relationships with members of the media so that (1) they will be receptive to publicity messages provided by the organization, and (2) the publicity department or manager or small-business owner will understand the needs and requirements of the various media. Media personnel ignore many publicity messages because they are not newsworthy or are poorly written.

A firm should evaluate its publicity efforts. The effectiveness of a publicity campaign is usually measured in terms of media placements—the number of news releases, feature stories, and captioned photographs that are actually published or broadcast. Public relations firms make that information available to their clients. Organizations that do not use a public relations agency can hire clipping services—firms that clip news stories from newspapers and journals about an organization—to monitor print media to determine which releases are published, how often, and by whom. No such monitoring services are available to report instances of broadcast publicity. Organizations employing a public relations firm should judge it on both the quality of its work and the quality of service it provides.[35] Evaluating the quality of the

[35] Merrill Rose, "PR Firms Can't Control the Client, but They Can Still Deliver Quality," *Marketing News,* February 1, 1993, p. 4.

CLOSE TO THE CUSTOMER

Sponsoring Sporting Events

The last thing firms want to achieve through promotion is a low profile. Many sponsor various events to gain recognition, target specific segments, and increase sales with a "soft sell" that associates the product with something in which customers are very interested.

Sponsorship in the sporting field is expanding rapidly on both a national and international basis. More than 3,400 U.S. companies spend around $1.5 billion a year on national and local events. Some firms buy the right to name events after themselves, like the Coors International Bicycle Classic, the Sunkist Fiesta Bowl, the Mazda LPGA Championship in golf, and the Mazda Tennis Classic in women's tennis. Others contribute prize money in return for associating their names with events, such as the Ironman Triathlon in Hawaii, sponsored since 1981 by Anheuser-Busch, or the Iditarod sled-dog race in Alaska, financed by the bootmaker Timberland Co. Major sponsors paid about $10 million to associate their names, goods, and services with the 1992 Olympics. Most sponsors believe they are able to generate a great deal of publicity by associating their names with the Olympic ideal of excellence.

Motor sports have a high profile internationally, particularly in Japan, where they are popular with young people. The interest has increased with Japanese successes in world championships. Food-and-drink conglomerate Kibun sponsored the World Motorcycle Championships at Suzuka. Kibun kiosks sold a selection of the firm's products, and Kibun representatives served its new drink, launched at the event. In Japan, where labor is in short supply, the creation of a positive corporate image through sponsorship can be used to recruit top job prospects.

Stock-car racing has long been boosted by business. Procter & Gamble spends $5 million for a Tide car, a Crisco car, and a Folger's car, among others. There's even been an Underalls car—driver Sterling Marlin's Oldsmobile Delta 88—sponsored by Hanes Hosiery Inc. to appeal to women, who make up 43 percent of the stock-car racing audience. Each year at the Indianapolis 500, race sponsors hand out over $7 million in prize money, including awards for the oldest and youngest drivers. D.L. Clark Co., maker of the Slo Poke lollipop, sponsors the $5,000 Slo Poke award for the car with the slowest qualifying time. It might seem like a dubious distinction, but automobile racing is an expensive sport, so no one hesitates to accept the prize. And Clark gains significant publicity for its candy.

Some marketers are unsure that the expense of sponsorship, especially the high price tag for sports, pays off in sales. Volvo North America spends nearly $5 million a year to sponsor professional, college, and amateur tennis tournaments. Although the tennis program has increased the awareness of Volvo, how much more business it generates is difficult to measure. Despite the uncertain results, firms line up for the chance to link their names with big sports events.

Sources: David Beck, "Sponsorship the Japanese Way," *Management Accounting—London*, May 1992, pp. 40–41; Adam Shell, "Going for the Gold," *Public Relations Journal*, July 1992, pp. 16–20; Harris Collingwood, "And the Greasy Coveralls Prize Goes To . . . ," *Business Week*, May 25, 1992, p. 38; and Michael Oneal and Peter Finch, "Nothing Sells like Sports," *Business Week*, August 31, 1987, pp. 48–53.

work means asking questions such as how many media placements were obtained, how strong the writing was, or whether the event was conceived and executed with creativity and attention to detail. To determine quality of service, clients need to decide if the public relations agency knows the client's business (product, competition, industry), provides valuable data, diagnoses problems, makes recommendations, and helps implement them.

Handling Unfavorable Publicity

Sometimes organizations have to deal with unfavorable publicity surrounding an unsafe product, an accident, the actions of a dishonest employee, or some other negative event. Hamburger chain Jack in the Box faced a public disaster when a 2-year-old boy died of food poisoning after eating a meal bought there. The company took nearly a week to admit publicly its responsibility for as many as 300 non-fatal incidents of poisoning, and Jack in the Box president Robert Nugent attempted to deflect blame to state health authorities and the company that supplied the meat. Customers went to other burger chains by the numbers.[36] The effect of such negative publicity can be swift and dramatic. A single incident that results in unfavorable publicity can ruin a firm's image and destroy consumer attitudes that took years to build through promotional efforts. Wal-Mart's "Buy American" program was called into question when it became public knowledge that the retail giant imports tons of foreign products. Most retailers import foreign goods, but few profess as strong a policy on buying U.S.-made products than does Wal-Mart.[37] Although Wal-Mart's sales did not suffer, the firm became the focal point of unfavorable publicity.

Organizations should strive to avoid unfavorable publicity like that faced by Wal-Mart or at least to minimize the effects of such publicity when it does occur. Businesses can directly reduce incidents that might cause unfavorable publicity by implementing safety programs, inspections, and effective quality control procedures. Nonetheless, it is impossible to avoid all negative experiences. Thus firms must pre-establish policies and procedures for handling unfavorable publicity and news personnel when negative events do occur.

Rather than trying to discourage news coverage of negative events, in most cases organizations should try to expedite it; this leads to more accurate reporting of the facts. Wal-Mart CEO David Glass conceded that the firm buys considerable foreign goods, but said that it favors U.S. manufacturers that can meet its quality standards, even if their prices are up to 5 percent higher than those of foreign firms.[38] When news coverage is discouraged, rumors and inaccurate information may be passed on to consumers and the public, and an unfavorable event can easily turn into a scandal, tragedy, or even public panic.

[36] Ronald Grover, Dori Jones Young, and Laura Holson, "Boxed in at Jack in the Box," *Business Week,* February 15, 1993, p. 40.

[37] Wendy Zellner, "How True-Blue Is Wal-Mart's 'Buy American' Pledge?" *Business Week,* March 16, 1992, p. 58.

[38] Ibid., p. 58.

SUMMARY

Advertising is paid nonpersonal communication about an organization, its products, and its activities transmitted through mass media such as television, radio, newspapers, magazines, direct mail, and various types of outdoor displays. Advertising can be used by individuals and organizations in a number of ways: to promote organizations and products (institutional and product advertising); to stimulate demand and promote an increased number of uses for a product (pioneer, competitive, and comparative advertising); to remind consumers about products and reinforce their choices; to counter advertising by competitors; to support the sales force; and to minimize sales fluctuations.

An advertising program may be handled by an individual or a few persons within the firm, an advertising department within the organization, or an independent advertising agency. An advertising agency is a business that specializes in creating advertisements and other types of promotion for other organizations.

The development of an advertising program involves several steps; although the number and sequence of steps are not the same in every instance, they generally follow a similar pattern. Advertisers first consider the composition and needs of the target market. Next, they establish the objectives of the advertising program. Third, they determine the advertising budget. Then they create the message, develop the media plan, and launch the advertising campaign. Finally, the advertisers measure the effectiveness of the advertisements.

International marketers must often modify advertisements for foreign markets. In developing or modifying advertisements, firms face several challenges, including cultural differences, language barriers, and government regulations. In selecting media, international marketers should consider the availability of media, their ability to reach the target market, and the cost of reaching the target.

Publicity is nonpersonal communication about an organization or its products that is transmitted through a mass medium in the form of news but is not paid for by the organization. Publicity is part of the public relations function, which is designed to create and maintain a favorable image of an organization. Publicity messages are more informative and subdued than advertising, have more credibility, and are generally not repeated. Publicity may take the form of news releases, feature articles, captioned photographs, news conferences, editorial films and tapes, or sponsorship.

Publicity is most effective when a firm creates and maintains a systematic, long-term program. One important aspect of an effective publicity program is maintaining good working relationships with members of the media. The effectiveness of publicity is usually measured in terms of the number of news releases, feature stores, and captioned photographs that are actually published or broadcast.

An organization should avoid negative publicity by trying to reduce the occurrence of negative events. To lessen the impact of unfavorable publicity when it does occur, an organization should have pre-established policies and procedures for dealing with news personnel.

KEY TERMS

institutional advertising
product advertising
infomercial
pioneer advertising
competitive advertising
comparative advertising
reminder advertising
reinforcement advertising
defensive advertising
advertising agency
advertising objective
advertising budget
percent of sales approach
objective and task approach
competition-matching
  approach
arbitrary approach
advertising platform
copy
artwork

illustration
layout
media plan
pretest
consumer panel
inquiry
posttest
recognition test
unaided recall test
aided recall test
public relations
news release
feature article
captioned photograph
news conference
editorial film or tape
sponsorship

QUESTIONS FOR DISCUSSION AND REVIEW

1. What is institutional advertising? What type of organization would use it?

2. How can advertising be used to support sales personnel?

3. What is an advertising agency? Describe the relationship between the advertising agency and its clients.

4. What are the major steps in developing an advertising program?

5. Why is it important to identify the target market when developing an advertising program?

6. What is the difference between the objective and task approach and the percent of sales approach to setting the advertising budget?

7. What factors must be considered when developing a media plan?

8. What is the difference between reach and frequency? How are the two related?

9. Name and explain three different ways to measure advertising effectiveness.

10. What are the major challenges facing international advertisers? Do you think advertisements can be standardized for global markets?

11. When making media decisions, what are some of the factors that international marketers should consider?

12. What are the differences between publicity and advertising? How is publicity used?

13. What can a firm do when confronted with negative publicity?

C A S E S

19.1   NBC FACES PUBLIC RELATIONS CRISIS

T elevision viewers who watched the prime-time news magazine *Dateline NBC* on November 17, 1992, saw a dramatic fiery crash of a car and a pickup. The demonstration was part of a 15-minute segment called "Waiting to Explode?" that reviewed the safety record of General Motors' full-sized pickups sold from 1973 to 1987, which have dual fuel tanks placed on the outside of the truck frame. NBC noted internal GM reports implying that the "sidesaddle" tanks could explode and burn when the trucks were hit from the side, a charge made by consumer groups and product-liability lawyers in injury cases.

That 15-minute segment led to an unusual public battle between two prominent U.S. companies, GM and NBC—a battle eventually won by GM and causing extreme embarrassment for NBC. In response to the broadcast, GM sent a letter of complaint to NBC News calling the program unfair and asking for test data, and then began an investigation. GM officials became suspicious after examining the *Dateline NBC* show in slow motion. The one-minute videotape showed two crashes staged by an outside testing firm at a rural site in Indiana. The first, a 40 mph side-impact crash, did not result in fuel leakage or explosion; but the second, 30 mph crash crushed the pickup's fuel tank and lit the fuel into a ball of fire. NBC said the fuel was ignited by the headlight filament of the crash car. Previous GM tests had shown that the pickups should have withstood crashes at greater speeds without catching fire. After GM asked NBC several times to be allowed to inspect the trucks used in the test crashes, a *Dateline* producer told GM officials on January 4, 1993, that the trucks had been junked.

GM's investigation gained speed when Pete Pesterre, GM-pickup owner and editor of *Popular Hot Rodding* magazine, heard from an Indiana reader that a firefighter who videotaped the test crashes thought they were rigged. Pesterre located Brownsburg, Ind., fire chief Glen Bailey, Jr., and put GM in touch with him on January 15. The videotape, taken as standard procedure from a fire truck on the scene to assist with NBC's crash tests, showed the truck fire to be merely a 15-second flame. Analysis of that videotape and a second video, shot at the scene by an off-duty sheriff's deputy, clearly showed smoke coming from the bottom of the pickup before the impact.

Investigators for the carmaker checked 22 junkyards to find the test crash vehicles, two GM pickups and two Chevy Citations, then bought them for $400. A spent model rocket engine was found in the bed of the pickup burned in the crash. But the fuel tanks were missing. GM obtained a court order against the firm NBC hired to stage the crashes, the Indianapolis-based Institute for Safety Analysis, to prevent it from destroying the tanks, which were later found on a junk heap. The previous owner of the pickup told GM he had lost the gas cap and replaced it with a nonstandard one that he bent to fit.

Convinced the NBC crash tests were rigged, GM initiated a strong public relations campaign and a legal attack on NBC. On Monday, February 8, GM filed a defamation lawsuit against NBC. Then it held a two-hour news conference broadcast to news outlets and GM employees and dealers across the country. According to GM's chief lawyer Harold J. Pearce, "When you are fighting a case, you have the forum of court. But taken on by the media, I don't know of any other forum available than the public." Pearce made GM's case through videotapes, photographs, and eyewitness accounts. He claimed that model rocket engines detonated by remote control and an improper gas cap on a fuel tank caused the pickup fire during the test crash.

NBC executives were caught off guard by GM's dramatic public attack in the news conference. GM had sent some of its findings to the *Dateline* producer in January, but NBC News president Michael Gartner and NBC president Robert Wright only learned of the problem in a second letter, dated February 2. They believed NBC News was guilty only of careless journalism by failing to tell viewers that toy rocket engines—igniters—had been placed on the pickups. Only two days before the news conference, NBC stood by its *Dateline* report and claimed the igniters were irrelevant since experts concluded that headlight filament sparked the fire. The executive director of the Center for Auto Safety in Washington, D.C., defended NBC's use of the incendiary devices; he said igniters are used in test crashes so experts can determine if there is enough leaking fuel to start a fire. (Officials from the National Highway Traffic Safety Administration, however, said they do not use either igniters or flammable fuel to test fuel systems.)

NBC News executives and a safety consultant to the network accused GM of using the news conference to focus attention away from the real issue—safety of its trucks. Critics noted that the GM news conference came a week after an Atlanta jury found the carmaker guilty of negligence in the design of its pickups and awarded $105 million to the parents of a teenage boy killed when his pickup exploded in a crash with a drunken driver. GM lawyer Pearce denied that GM tried to divert attention from the verdict, which it would appeal. He said a court order restricted GM from discussing the case before the Atlanta verdict.

Faced with GM's lawsuit, increasing criticism from journalists, and the prospect of NBC affiliates losing advertising of local GM dealerships, NBC decided to settle with GM. At the end of the *Dateline NBC* show broadcast February 9, 1993, anchors Jane Pauley and Stone Philips read a long apology to viewers and to GM. They said NBC "does not dispute" that it used toy rocket engines as igniters in its staged crashes of GM trucks, that its report understated vehicle speed at impact, or that its report wrongly said a fuel tank ruptured. NBC agreed to reimburse GM about $2 million that it spent investigating the NBC report.

GM dropped the defamation suit and won a significant public relations victory. The company had long been remembered for its own 1966 public apology and $400,000 payment to consumer advocate Ralph Nader for investigating him after he attacked the Chevrolet Corvair for being unsafe.

NBC News was criticized by many U.S. executives as well as journalists. Some questioned the accuracy of prime-time TV magazines in general. But NBC's prompt apology persuaded many large advertisers to stay with the network. Even GM, after temporarily reassigning ads from NBC news shows to sports and entertainment programming, decided to maintain its $160 million ad budget with NBC; saying "We still have to sell cars," the marketing and advertising manager for North American Operations convinced top executives that halting the ads would hurt GM more than it would help. But the *Dateline* fiasco could affect renegotiations of GM's contract with NBC, which has slipped from first to last place in prime-time ratings among the three major networks.

NBC began an internal investigation. Said NBC News president Gartner, "If you make a mistake, you've got to stand up to it." He said he was still proud of the segment on GM trucks, except for the crash demonstration. "It was totally unnecessary in the larger scheme," he said. "It brought no new facts to this situation, but it brought into doubt the credibility of our operation." Unfortunately, NBC had to make another on-air apology only two weeks later for what it called "inadvertent" use of a video in a report claiming that overcutting timber in an Idaho forest was endangering fish. The video showed fish stunned for testing purposes and dead fish from another forest. On March 2, 1993, NBC News president Michael Gartner resigned.

Questions for Discussion

1. What was GM's objective in holding a news conference? Do you think the objective was achieved?

2. Were NBC's efforts effective in combatting negative publicity? Should NBC have done anything differently?

3. What is the result when a media organization loses credibility?

Based on information from Elizabeth Jensen, Douglas Lavin, and Neal Templin, "How GM One-Upped an Embarrassed NBC on Staged News Event," *Wall Street Journal,* February 11, 1993, pp. A1, A4; Douglas Lavin, "GM Accuses NBC of Rigging Test Crash of Pickup Truck on 'Dateline' Program," *Wall Street Journal,* February 10, 1993, pp. A3, A6; Joe Mandese, "GM Lawsuit Outguns NBC," *Advertising Age,* February 15, 1993, pp. 1, 58; "NBC Apologizes to GM for Rigging Crash," *Lexington* (KY) *Herald-Leader,* February 10, 1993, p. A3; Elizabeth Jensen, "Some Journalists Join GM in Criticizing NBC's Treatment of Truck-Crash Story," *Wall Street Journal,* February 10, 1993, pp. B1, B8; and "NBC News President Gartner Steps Down," *Lexington* (KY) *Herald-Leader,* March 3, 1993, p. A4.

19.2   CZECHOSLOVAK AIRLINES REVAMPS ITS IMAGE

Czechoslovak Airlines (CSA) is trying to transform itself into a private enterprise with legal assistance from the United States and the financial backing of Western partners. The problems faced by the former government-owned CSA include a lack of capital, sluggish markets, and a lack of experience in running for-profit enterprises. To begin to tackle these problems, CSA entered an agreement with J.P. Morgan and Co., making Morgan the airline's financial adviser.

CSA also suffers from its image as a dowdy Eastern European airline. That image may be the problem that poses the greatest obstacle to CSA. Eastern European airlines have long had a reputation of poor punctuality, an inferior safety record, and uncomfortable flights on old aircraft. In an effort to meet Western expectations for comfort, performance, and safety, CSA has purchased five Boeing 737s and may buy as many as ten more. The airline has also ordered two Airbus A310s. Eventually, CSA will remove all its Russian aircraft in favor of Western planes. The airline also upgraded its in-flight catering service to offer better and more varied meals.

CSA has allocated a $5 million advertising budget to develop a new image and a new advertising strategy. This strategy is to sell Prague as a hub to central Europe, a gateway to the Far East, and a destination in itself. The airline added seven destinations in 1992, for a total of fifty-three in Europe, the Mideast, the Far East, and the former Soviet Union.

CSA ran a $3.5 million domestic advertising campaign to reintroduce the carrier. The Mark/BBDO agency is handling the account. Newspaper and magazine advertisements were used to show Boeing airplanes with the theme "What airline is this?" Print advertisements run monthly in the United Kingdom in *The Economist*. Advertisements also appear in in-flight magazines and other publications in Germany. CSA kicked off its German campaign with a cocktail party in Berlin for travel agents at one of the biggest balls of the year. The airline was one of the sponsors of the ball. To play up its Prague base, CSA also sponsored the Prague Spring music concerts.

The breakup of Czechoslovakia into two nations, the Czech Republic and Slovakia, is not expected to change plans for CSA, 60 percent of which is owned by the Czech government. Air France and the European Bank for Reconstruction & Development in London have invested $60 million into CSA and own nearly 40 percent of the carrier. The alliance provides CSA with equity of $150 million, and some instant experience. Now CSA wants to establish the same type of image as its Western competitors.

Questions for Discussion

1. Why is it important for CSA to change its image?

2. How can advertising help CSA establish a new image?

3. Do you think purchasing new airplanes was a good move as CSA struggles to privatize? Explain.

4. How will CSA benefit from its alliance with Air France?

Based on information from Ann Marsh, "Czech Airline Wants Image of Western Competitors," *Advertising Age,* January 18, 1993, pp. I2, I29; Michael Mecham, "CSA Fleet of Western Transports Grows with Boeing 737 Deliveries," *Aviation Week & Space Technology,* July 13, 1992, p. 35; and Christopher P. Fotos, "Czechoslovakia Turns to U.S. Advisors to Help Privatize Carrier and Airports," *Aviation Week & Space Technology,* February 4, 1991, pp. 35, 41.

Personal Selling and Sales Promotion

OBJECTIVES

- To describe the nature and importance of personal selling.

- To describe the types of sales positions.

- To identify the steps in the personal-selling process.

- To determine the activities involved in managing the sales force.

- To explain how firms manage the international selling effort.

- To discuss sales promotion activities and their uses.

- To identify the types of sales promotion.

To retailers, selling once meant staying close to customers, knowing how your products could fill their needs and wants. Department stores like Sears were filled with knowledgeable, courteous salespeople. Suppliers like IBM developed deep, long-lasting relationships with industrial customers. In recent years, however, as competition has intensified and pressure has grown for short-term results, some companies have lost sight of their customers. At far too many companies, selling has been based on hustle and hype rather than customer service.

Now the focus is back on customers, as both consumers and businesses are moving to the firms that give them the most attention. From power plants to packaged-goods producers, companies are changing the way they sell to better serve their customers. They are accomplishing this by focusing on their most valuable resource—the customer. They are changing every aspect of sales: the way they sell, how they train and compensate the sales force, and how everyone, from the CEO to the designer to the engineer, is involved in selling. The customer, who was once king, is turning into a dictator. Consider:

- Home Depot's founder Bernard Marcus emphasizes ''smart selling'' and believes in endless training.
- Wal-Mart has demanded that it work directly with suppliers through partnerships. Wal-Mart deals face-to-face with suppliers like Procter & Gamble, Kraft, James River, and Black & Decker.
- Du Pont uses teams of sales representatives, technicians, and factory managers to solve customer problems and to create and sell new products.
- Nordstrom department stores have found that intense, personalized attention to customers pays off in growth and shopper loyalty.
- Toyota's Lexus line uses customer satisfaction as a key measure for compensating dealers.

In looking for a selling advantage, top companies practice smart selling. Several aspects of smart selling hold true for all businesses:

- Smart selling requires focusing the entire organization, from manufacturing to finance, on sales and customer service.

- Smart selling needs the involvement and attention of top management.
- Smart selling means building relationships with customers, not just getting the quick sale.
- Smart selling views salespeople as problem solvers, not just order takers.[1] ●

Today, many firms consider personal selling a critical element in their promotion mix. The days when "sales" conjured up images of Willie Loman from the play *Death of a Salesman* or Herb Tarlick from the television series "WKRP in Cincinnati" are coming to an end. The sales field now is more likely to be associated with the superior technical and communication skills of the companies described in the opening feature.

THE NATURE AND IMPORTANCE OF PERSONAL SELLING

As defined in Chapter 18, *personal selling* is face-to-face communication with potential buyers in an exchange situation.[2] Salespersons develop relationships with potential customers, identify their needs and match products to those needs, communicate information about product benefits and uses, and attempt to persuade prospective buyers to make a purchase. Personal selling is the most precise of the promotion mix elements because it enables marketers to focus their communication efforts on those buyers most likely to make a purchase decision. It also allows marketers to modify their messages to suit particular customers' information needs.

Most people believe that businesses spend more money on advertising than on any other element of the promotion mix. This is not true: U.S. firms spend more each year on personal selling than they spend on any other promotional method.[3] Personal selling is also the most costly component of the promotion mix. The average cost of making a sales call on an organizational customer is over $250, about $220 for service customers, and $210 for consumer-goods customers.[4] Approximately eleven million people are employed in sales jobs in the United States, compared with half a million in advertising.[5]

---

[1] Based on information from Christopher Power, Lisa Driscoll, and Earl Bohn, "Smart Selling," *Business Week,* August 3, 1992, pp. 46–48; Patricia Sellers, "How to Remake Your Sales Force," *Fortune,* May 4, 1992, pp. 98–103; and Arthur Bragg, "Getting Face-to-Face with Customers," *Sales & Marketing Management,* February 1991, pp. 44–48.

[2] Rolph E. Anderson, Joseph F. Hair, Jr., and Alan J. Bush, *Professional Sales Management* (New York: McGraw-Hill, 1988), p. 43.

[3] Carlton A. Pederson, Milburn D. Wright, and Barton A. Weitz, *Selling: Principles and Methods,* 9th ed. (Homewood, Ill.: Irwin, 1988), p. 11.

[4] "Hey, Where's My Survey of Selling Costs?" *Sales & Marketing Management,* March 1991, pp. 42–45.

[5] Lawrence B. Chonko and Ben M. Enis, *Professional Selling* (Boston: Allyn & Bacon, 1993), p. 2.

Since personal selling is so expensive, why do companies spend more on it than on advertising? Personal selling is more effective than advertising because salespeople can develop a unique message for each customer. Face-to-face selling allows salespeople to observe nonverbal behavior and respond accordingly. Adjustments in the communication message can be made instantly, whereas advertising is limited in how fast the message can be changed. Personal selling is truly adaptable, enabling the salesperson to change his or her behavior to fit the specific needs of the customer.

Personal selling plays an increasingly important role in the success of many firms today. Salespeople are often viewed as marketing consultants who diagnose customer needs and offer recommendations. As the critical link to buyers, salespeople are highly trained professionals who know the product and who can communicate their knowledge in a persuasive manner. This has not always been the case: Salespeople were once stereotyped as deceitful and lacking brains, talent, and sensitivity.[6] Some of these negative stereotypes still persist.[7] Point/Counterpoint examines this image.

TYPES OF SALES POSITIONS

Traditionally, salespeople have performed many functions, including prospecting for new customers, making presentations, taking orders, and serving customers. More recently, the role of the salesperson has been expanded in an effort to focus the entire company on its customers. Salespeople are customer advocates with detailed knowledge of their firm's products and their customers' needs. This knowledge helps them identify opportunities and resolve problems.

Traditional Sales Positions

■ **order taker** a type of salesperson who processes routine sales and reorders and maintains lasting, positive relationships with customers

Traditional sales positions can be divided into three broad categories: order takers, order getters, and support personnel. An **order taker** processes routine sales and reorders and maintains lasting, positive relationships with customers. A primary objective of this job is to make certain that customers have ample supplies where and when they are needed. In many businesses, *inside order takers* take orders by mail and telephone. Producers, wholesalers, and retailers have sales personnel who take orders from within the firm rather than from the field. For instance, the check-out clerk in a supermarket and the sales clerk in a department store are inside order takers. Order takers who travel to customers are referred to as *outside* (or *field*) *order takers*. Field order takers often develop special interdependent relationships with their

---

[6]Donald L. Thompson, "Stereotype of the Salesman," *Harvard Business Review,* January–February 1972, pp. 20–29.
[7]William A. Weeks and Darrel D. Muehling, "Students' Perceptions of Personal Selling," *Industrial Marketing Management,* May 1987, pp. 145–151.

POINT/COUNTERPOINT

Are Salespeople Shedding Their Negative Image?

Have you ever had a bad experience with a salesperson? Most consumers have. Some salespeople seem to be a little too pushy, some don't give you all the information you need, and some exaggerate claims to close a sale. A real estate agent, for example, may not tell a home buyer that a basement leaks because "she didn't ask." Unfortunately, such situations have given salespeople in general—even honest ones—a bad reputation. Salespeople are working hard to shed this negative image, but have they been successful?

Point   In sales, as in many situations, the improper actions of a few are what people remember most. Although many salespersons have been honest, hardworking individuals, some have been deceitful and seemed to bring out the worst in people. A negative image of salespeople has resulted. But this image is changing. Sales jobs now are viewed as challenging and rewarding, with a high degree of professionalism.

Why the change? As companies strive to meet the needs of customers, salespeople provide a vital link between the company and the final consumer. Recognizing this, many companies are working hard to improve this critical link to the customer. For instance, as differences in quality, style, and prices narrow between domestic and foreign car makers, automakers have realized that they can gain the competitive edge at their dealerships. So Detroit's Big Three are trying to upgrade their dealers and weed out undesirable ones. These firms, and many others, realize that successful salespeople help their customers solve problems, rather than pressure consumers into making an unwise purchase.

Counterpoint   Although many firms talk openly about the need to change the image of salespeople, the old stereotypes still exist. College students remain skeptical about entering the sales profession; some avoid it. Many consumers continue to associate salespeople with traits such as being pushy, obnoxious, and out of style. The sales profession is often viewed as door-to-door selling of household supplies and vacuum cleaners.

Salespeople run up against these negative stereotypes when they are out on the road calling on customers. Doors are still slammed in salespeople's faces. Some customers do their best to avoid salespeople, ducking behind corners and skipping meetings. Salespeople themselves recognize this problem, and many find it difficult to overcome these negative stereotypes. Even though salespeople themselves strive to shed their negative image and replace it with a positive one, selling remains an undervalued skill.

■ **order getter** a type of salesperson who seeks out new customers and tries to increase sales to present customers

customers. The salesperson counts on the customer to purchase a certain quantity of products from time to time; the customer expects the salesperson to take orders regularly and, sometimes, to deliver them.

An **order getter** seeks out new customers and tries to increase sales to present customers. An order getter engages in what is sometimes called *creative selling:* The salesperson tries to identify a potential buyer's needs and then presents information to help the buyer satisfy those needs. Some order getters are responsible solely for finding new buyers and persuading them to

■ **support personnel**
members of the sales staff
who facilitate exchanges but
are not usually involved in
selling products

■ **missionary salesper-
son** a support salesperson
employed by a manufacturer
to facilitate sales and offer
assistance to its own customers (wholesalers and
retailers)

■ **technical salesperson**
a support salesperson who
provides technical assistance
to the company's current
customers

■ **trade salesperson**
a type of salesperson who
takes orders in addition to
performing other support
functions and whose pri-
mary function is to help
customers promote the
producer's product

purchase a product. Other order getters concentrate on current customers, calling on individuals and organizations that have purchased products in the past.

Support personnel are not usually involved in selling products but rather are concerned with facilitating exchanges by identifying potential customers, educating them, establishing good will, and providing service after sales. Support personnel are involved primarily in the marketing of organizational products. The three most common types of support personnel are missionary, technical, and trade salespersons.

A **missionary salesperson** is employed by a manufacturer to facilitate sales and offer assistance to its own customers (wholesalers and retailers). For instance, a missionary salesperson for a medical supplies manufacturer may call on doctors and hospital administrators to provide information and persuade them to buy the manufacturer's products. If a call is effective, the organizations will order the products from the wholesalers that actually handle orders and sales of the producer's medical supplies.

A **technical salesperson** provides technical assistance to the company's current customers. He or she advises customers on product features and applications, system designs, and installation procedures. Because technical salespeople typically handle highly technical capital and accessory equipment and raw materials, they generally have degrees in one of the physical sciences or in engineering. Technical sales personnel are often used to promote organizational products such as computers, heavy equipment and machinery, steel, and chemicals.

Unlike other support personnel, a **trade salesperson** takes orders in addition to performing other support functions. The primary focus of this position is helping customers, especially retailers, promote the producer's product. A trade salesperson may be involved in setting up displays, restocking shelves, obtaining more shelf space, providing in-store demonstrations, and offering samples to store customers. For instance, a trade salesperson calling on a supermarket may rotate merchandise and pick up out-of-date or damaged goods. Food producers frequently employ trade salespersons.

Sales Positions in the Future

As we note in the opening feature, the nature of personal selling is changing. The major thrust of this change is focusing on the customer. Many firms are recognizing that the key element to improving quality is continual focus on the customer. As a result, salespeople are being asked to do a great deal more listening and questioning of the customer.[8] The resulting relationships between salespeople and their customers take many forms; salespeople may act as partners, consultants, advisors, or problem solvers. We will refer to this emerging trend in general as *smart selling*.

Successful selling in the 1990s and beyond will depend on a salesperson's ability to build a relationship with the customer. Additionally, successful

[8]Kerry Rottenberger and Richard Kern, "The Upside-Down Deming Principle," *Sales & Marketing Management,* June 1992, pp. 39–44.

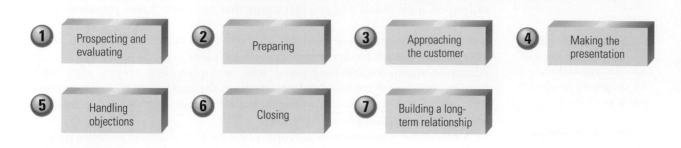

FIGURE 20.1
Steps in the Personal-Selling Process

salespeople will have to be willing to work with others to satisfy customer problems. Eastman Kodak has begun to evaluate its sales representatives on how well they coordinate with coworkers to help a customer.[9] Whereas salespeople were once viewed as somewhat independent and may have even had an incentive to compete with each other, they will not be operating solo in the future. Everyone from the product designers to the financial officers will be part of the selling team.[10]

This new type of sales position poses many challenges for sales managers. Experienced salespeople may not relate to a "team" approach to selling. But as customers find they have more and more quality products from which to choose, firms must focus their selling approaches on the customer. U.S. factories can now produce six million more cars and trucks a year than the public can buy. Even though the quality gap between U.S. and foreign producers has been virtually eliminated, Chrysler announced a "Customer One" program. The purpose of the program is to teach salespeople how to meet the needs of customers, as opposed to using the hard-sell approach typically employed by automobile dealers.[11]

Selling in the 1990s will mean convincing customers that a firm can give them the most value for the least money. This approach requires a sincere and concentrated focus on the customer. This successful salesperson will concentrate less on selling and more on contributing to the success of the customer.[12]

THE PERSONAL-SELLING PROCESS

Personal selling can be characterized as a process designed to provide customer satisfaction. The specific activities involved in the selling process vary among salespersons and selling situations. Although no two salespersons

[9]Patricia Sellers, "How to Remake Your Sales Force," *Fortune,* May 4, 1992, pp. 98–103.
[10]Christopher Power, Lisa Driscoll, and Earl Bohn, "Smart Selling," *Business Week,* August 3, 1992, pp. 46–48.
[11]Bradley A. Stertz, "For LH Models, Chrysler Maps New Way to Sell," *Wall Street Journal,* June 30, 1992, pp. B1–B2.
[12]Susan Caminiti, "Finding New Ways to Sell More," *Fortune,* July 27, 1992, pp. 100–102.

FIGURE 20.2
Prospecting
A critical first step of the selling process is to identify customers. Amtrak uses this advertisement and the promise of an 80-page travel guide to identify potential customers.

Source: National Railroad Passenger Corporation.

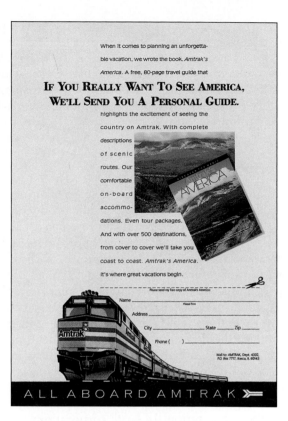

use identical selling techniques, salespeople move through the same general process as they sell products. This process consists of the seven steps shown in Figure 20.1: prospecting, preparing, approaching the customer, making the presentation, handling objections, closing, and building a long-term relationship with the customer. This final step—building long-term relationships with customers—is the objective of the personal-selling process.

Prospecting and Evaluating

■ **prospecting** developing a list of potential customers for personal-selling purposes

Prospecting involves developing a list of potential customers, or *prospects*. A salesperson identifies prospects from the company's sales records, other satisfied customers, trade shows, trade association directories, telephone directories, public records, newspaper announcements (of marriages, births, new product introductions, acquisitions, and so on), and other sources. The advertisement shown in Figure 20.2 is used to identify potential prospects. Sales personnel may also prospect by using advertisements that encourage interested persons to send in an information request form. The salesperson then contacts those people who have requested information. Insurance agents often prospect by regularly attending meetings of associations, clubs, or civic organizations.[13]

[13]"How Do I Prospect?" *Personal Selling Power,* March 1992, p. 52.

Once the salesperson has identified and developed a list of prospects, he or she evaluates whether each prospect has the buying power—ability, willingness, and authority—to buy the product. Based on this evaluation, some prospects may be deleted from the list. Others, judged as more acceptable, are ranked according to their potential. Companies use a variety of methods to qualify prospects, including questionnaires, marketing research, and face-to-face communication.

Preparing

Before approaching a prospect, a salesperson should examine information about that particular customer's specific product needs, current use of brands, feelings about available brands, and personal characteristics. Such information helps the salesperson select an appropriate approach and develop a sales presentation that precisely communicates with the prospect.

Preparation before the approach saves time for both the salesperson and the prospect and leads to a more effective interview. Without prior preparation, a salesperson may ask irrelevant or unnecessary questions, which not only waste time but can cause embarrassment. For instance, salespeople have mispronounced the names of potential customers, made appointments with the wrong people, and failed to bring necessary materials to meetings. Such blunders can terminate the sales effort.

One very important aspect of preparation, particularly in selling expensive items to large corporations, is to identify the key purchasing decision makers within the organization. In large corporations, many people have a voice in purchase decisions, and each person looks at the product from a different viewpoint. Although some salespeople may be more comfortable dealing with lower-level company executives, such as division managers, the product may ultimately be rejected by the president or vice president. Thus, when selling expensive capital and accessory equipment to large firms, salespeople should identify and target customers as high in the organization as possible, since they usually have the greatest authority to make decisions.

Approaching the Customer

The manner in which a salesperson initially contacts a potential customer is known as the **approach.** This step is critical because the prospect's first impression of the salesperson may be a lasting one.

Using referrals, a salesperson may approach the prospect and explain that an acquaintance, associate, or relative has suggested that the prospect might be interested in the product. Using another approach, the *cold canvass* method, a salesperson contacts potential customers without prior notification or consent. Finally, a salesperson may use a repeat contact approach; when making the contact, the salesperson mentions a previous meeting.

The approach used depends on the salesperson's preferences, the product being sold, the firm's resources, and the characteristics of the target market.

■ **approach** the manner in which a salesperson initially contacts a potential customer

Changing demographics of consumers have forced companies that used to rely on door-to-door selling to consider new methods of approaching the customer. With a growing number of women working outside the home, companies such as Fuller Brush and Avon can no longer depend exclusively on door-to-door sales to reach customers. Instead of knocking on doors, salespeople must approach customers by appointments, parties, and follow-ups to contacts made by mail or telephone.

Making the Presentation

In the sales presentation, the salesperson describes the product and its benefits, price, available options, and associated services (such as warranties and service contracts), and perhaps demonstrates the product. During the presentation, the salesperson must attract and maintain the prospect's attention. Having the prospect touch, hold, and actually use the product stimulates interest and desire for the product; it gets the prospect more involved with the product. The salesperson should also listen carefully to the prospect. Listening to the prospect's questions and comments and observing his or her responses gives the salesperson the best opportunity to ascertain the prospect's specific needs. The salesperson can then modify the presentation to suit the prospect's unique information needs.

Several approaches can be used when making a sales presentation, including the stimulus-response, need satisfaction, and formulated selling approaches.

Stimulus-Response Approach The **stimulus-response approach,** sometimes called the *canned sales approach,* is based on the belief that the customers will make a purchase if exposed to the right stimulus. Salespeople often use a standardized set of stimuli to produce the desired response—a sale. For instance, a life insurance salesperson might inject such stimuli as "financial security," "caring for your children," or "planning your future" into the sales presentation.

Need Satisfaction Approach The **need satisfaction approach** centers on the prospect's needs—the salesperson first tries to identify the needs of the buyer and then tailors the sales presentation to those needs. For instance, a real estate salesperson might ask home buyers how much they want to spend, how many bedrooms and bathrooms they need, how large a kitchen and living area they want, and whether they require a garage, fireplace, yard, and so on. The salesperson would then attempt to find and sell them a house that satisfies their particular needs. This selling approach is most consistent with the marketing concept.

Formulated Selling Approach With the **formulated selling approach,** the salesperson identifies the prospect's needs and then uses a formulated presentation that explains how the product can satisfy those needs. For instance, a salesperson in a computer retail store would attempt to identify a

■ **stimulus-response approach** a sales-presentation method based on the belief that customers will make a purchase if exposed to the right stimulus; sometimes called the canned sales approach

■ **need satisfaction approach** a sales-presentation method that centers on the prospect's needs—the salesperson first tries to identify the needs of the buyer and then tailors the sales presentation to those needs

■ **formulated selling approach** a sales-presentation method in which the salesperson identifies the prospect's needs and then uses a formulated presentation that explains how the product can satisfy those needs

customer's computing needs and then explain how a particular model fulfills them. The formulated presentation can be likened to the canned stimuli used in the stimulus-response approach.

Handling Objections

During the sales presentation, the salesperson must be prepared to handle objections to the product. Price is perhaps the most common objection, but customers also frequently object to service policies, product quality, the personality of the salesperson, and the reputation of the company itself. A well-prepared salesperson can generally overcome such objections.

One way of handling customers' objections is to anticipate and counter them before they are raised. However, this practice can be risky because the salesperson may mention some objections that the prospect had not thought of. Therefore, if possible, objections should be handled only when they are brought up. A good salesperson usually tries to elicit a prospect's objections so as to answer them. If objections are not vocalized, the salesperson cannot answer them, and they may keep the prospect from buying.

Closing

closing the stage in which the salesperson asks the prospect to actually buy the product(s)

The stage in which the salesperson asks the prospect to actually buy the product(s) is known as **closing.** During the presentation, the salesperson may use a *trial close* in which he or she asks questions that assume the prospect will purchase the product. The salesperson might ask the prospect about preferred models, sizes, or colors; financial terms; delivery and installation arrangements; or the quantity to be purchased. How the prospect reacts to these questions often indicates how close he or she is to actually making a purchase.

Salespeople often fail to ask questions that could bring a sales presentation to a close. Successful selling is often based on the ability to ask the right questions and engage customers in dialogue that promotes new thinking, comparisons, and perspectives. To ask better questions, salespeople should attempt to do the following: prepare questions before each presentation; use questions to strengthen their selling position; listen carefully as customers answer questions; and make sure questions reflect customers' needs, challenges, and priorities.[14]

A salesperson should attempt a trial close at several points during the presentation because the customer may be ready to buy. Attempts to close the sale may result in objections. Once they are expressed, however, the salesperson can answer the objections and attempt to close again. Salespeople should refrain from using deceptive techniques or pressuring prospects to close, because these tactics will result in dissatisfaction. For example, it may be effective to tell a potential customer that "another buyer was just looking at this car and is returning tonight with an offer." But a good salesperson knows that this kind of pressure does not help build a long-term relationship.

[14] "How to Ask Better Questions," *Personal Selling Power,* March 1992, p. 53.

A salesperson should not close until the prospect is ready to buy, understands the proposition or terms of the sale, and shows a high degree of interest.[15]

Building a Long-term Relationship

Following up a sale after a successful closing is important to building a long-term relationship. In this stage, the salesperson should contact the customer to learn what problems or questions may have arisen regarding the product and to provide or find immediate solutions for any problems. Activities such as these are crucial in securing future purchases. Salespeople should also keep in touch with buyers between purchases. Some salespeople follow up after a sale and then forget about customers. Contacting customers on a regular basis, if only to ask them if they are happy with the product, helps the salesperson to build a solid long-term relationship.

The changing nature of personal selling has given rise to *relationship selling,* in which sales activities are not focused only on making a sale. Salespeople are also expected to understand customers' needs, solve their problems, and adjust products and services to their changing needs.[16] Salespeople and other members of the organization may be involved in providing services such as maintenance or product modifications. Many firms with quality management programs, including Ford, Motorola, and Wal-Mart, have successfully established long-term relationships with suppliers and customers. In some instances, these relationships are formalized through partnerships. When customers are strongly committed to a selling organization because of the continuous service and benefits it provides, they are likely to stay in the relationship for a longer period of time.

Technology is also useful in building long-term relationships. If technology provides some unique benefit or services in the selling process, customers will be loyal to the firm that provides the benefit, not just to the product or salesperson. For instance, Frito-Lay uses a computer data network to help salespeople identify situations where supermarket managers can build profits by promoting more Frito-Lay products. With this computerized system, presentations to store managers can be created in just fifteen minutes, instead of the ten days they used to require. The time saved also enables salespeople to make more face-to-face calls.[17]

Relationship selling views selling as a long-term relationship between salesperson and customer. If both parties achieve their goals, the relationship should be successful and continue to prosper. As you can see in Table 20.1, there are many reasons that the selling process fails. By raising the level of professionalism in how they deal with the sales force, managers will see salespeople demonstrate the same standards with customers. Everyone in the organization must sell; managers should consider salespeople as customers and develop a plan for recruiting, training, and maintaining an effective sales force.

---

[15]"The Right Moment to Close," *Personal Selling Power,* March 1992, p. 54.
[16]Chonko and Enis, p. 35.
[17]Jack Falvey,"Selling to the Sales Force," *Sales & Marketing Management,* April 1992, pp. 12–14.

TABLE 20.1
Ten Ways to Lose a Sale

1. Not choosing prospects carefully
2. Using evasive or deceptive prospecting techniques
3. Talking too much and not asking questions
4. Being insincere
5. Focusing too much on the product and not on the customer
6. Lacking standards
7. Not being able to say or hear "no"
8. Using too much convincing and persuading
9. Lacking self-respect
10. Creating an adversarial relationship

Source: Reprinted by permission of *Sales & Marketing Management*. Copyright: December 1991.

MANAGING THE SALES FORCE

An organization's success often depends on the effectiveness of its salespeople because they are directly responsible for generating its sales revenue. The job of the sales manager is to sell the sales force. Effective sales management requires numerous decisions and activities in nine areas (shown in Figure 20.3): (1) establishing sales objectives, (2) determining the size of the sales force, (3) recruiting and selecting salespeople, (4) training salespeople, (5) compensating salespeople, (6) motivating salespeople, (7) establishing sales territories, (8) routing and scheduling salespeople, and (9) evaluating sales force performance.

Establishing Sales Objectives

Establishing sales objectives is a fundamental part of sales management. Sales objectives specify what the sales force as a whole and as individuals are expected to accomplish during a specified time period. Objectives provide direction and purpose and serve as performance standards for the evaluation and control of sales personnel. Thus sales goals should be stated in explicit, measurable terms and should stipulate the time period and geographic areas involved. Many firms are establishing objectives for customer satisfaction.

Sales objectives are usually established for the entire sales force and also for each salesperson. Objectives for the entire force are normally stated in terms of sales volume, market share, or profit. For instance, objectives for a textbook publisher's sales force might specify that it sell one million textbooks, increase market share for a particular text by 5 percent, or increase profits by 10 percent. Sales objectives for individual salespersons are more likely to be stated in terms of dollars or unit sales volume. Each textbook

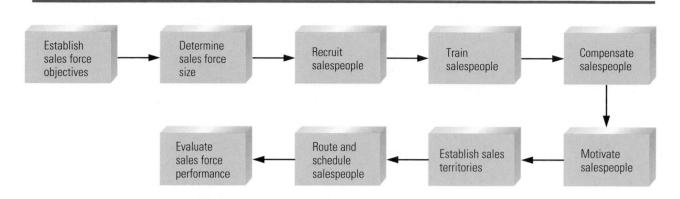

FIGURE 20.3
Sales Management Activities

salesperson, for example, might be expected to sell ten thousand books or $250,000 worth of books. Other individual sales objectives might be based on the average order size, the average number of calls per time period, and the ratio of orders to calls. Companies also are beginning to link sales objectives to other parts of the organization such as engineering or plant management.

Determining the Size of the Sales Force

Once the company has established sales objectives, it must decide how many salespersons are needed to achieve sales objectives and to promote its products. The size of the sales force is an important consideration because it affects the company's ability to generate sales and profits, as well as the compensation methods used, salespersons' morale, and overall sales force management. There are several methods for determining the optimal size of the sales force, including the equalized workload method and the incremental productivity method.

Equalized Workload Method In the **equalized workload method,** sales force size is dependent on the condition that every salesperson is assigned a more-or-less equal set of accounts in terms of the total amount of sales time and effort needed.[18] To apply this method, marketing managers must first divide customers into groups based on the size of purchases, and then calculate the number of sales calls required to satisfactorily service customer accounts in each group. To determine the sales force size, the marketing manager must then (1) multiply the number of customers in each group by the number of sales calls required annually to serve each group effectively, (2) add the results, and (3) divide this sum by the average number of calls made annually by each salesperson.

For example, consider a medical supply company that divides its customers into two groups: customers in group A have annual purchases exceeding

■ **equalized workload method** a method of determining the optimal size of the sales force in which the number of customers multiplied by the number of sales calls annually required to serve those customers effectively is divided by the average number of calls each salesperson makes annually

[18] Walter J. Talley, "How to Design Sales Territories," *Journal of Marketing,* January 1961, pp. 7–13; and Gilbert A. Churchill, Jr., Neil M. Ford, and Orville C. Walker, Jr., *Sales Force Management* (Homewood, Ill.: Irwin, 1981), pp. 160–167.

$25,000; customers in group B have purchases of less than $25,000. The company has 400 group A customers that each require 25 sales calls annually, and 700 group B customers that each require 14 sales calls annually. The firm's average salesperson makes 550 calls annually. In this case, sales force size is determined as follows:

$$\frac{400(25) + 700(14)}{500} = 36$$

The medical supply company therefore needs 36 salespersons.

This method has several drawbacks. It is difficult to approximate the number of sales calls required to service an account because, regardless of their standard purchase size, individual customers have different problems and needs. Additionally, a salesperson's workload depends not only on the number of sales calls but also on travel time between customers and on the amount of time spent with each customer. Nonetheless, many companies use this approach to establish sales force size.

■ incremental productivity method a method of determining the optimal size of the sales force in which the marketer continues to increase the size of the sales force as long as the resulting sales increases are greater than the additional selling costs that arise from employing more salespeople

Incremental Productivity Method   When using the **incremental productivity method,** a marketer continues to increase the size of the sales force as long as the resulting sales increases are greater than the additional increases in selling costs. The ideal sales force size allows the firm to obtain the greatest operating margin, which is the difference between total sales and total selling costs. In the hypothetical case shown in Table 20.2, as each of the first three salespersons is added to the sales force, the company experiences increases in sales and operating margin. The addition of a fourth salesperson, however, actually reduces the firm's operating margin. Thus the optimum sales force size of this company is three. The effectiveness of this method depends on the marketing or sales manager's ability to accurately estimate how much sales and selling costs will increase when a salesperson is added.

Recruiting and Selecting Salespeople

Recruiting and selecting is the process by which the sales manager develops a list of candidates for sales positions and chooses from among those candidates to staff the positions. Before beginning to recruit, the manager must develop a set of necessary qualifications that each applicant must satisfy to be considered. Applicants may be recruited from several sources: other departments within the firm, other firms, employment agencies, educational institutions, individuals recommended by current employees, and respondents to advertisements. The specific sources a sales manager uses depend on the type of salesperson required and the manager's experience with particular sources.

The process involved in selecting applicants to make up the sales force varies widely from one company to another. In some firms, the selection process consists of a single interview. In others, the process may include a written application, an initial interview, follow-up interviews, written and oral examinations, an evaluation of recommendations, and a physical examination. The selection procedure used should satisfy the company's needs for specific information about each potential salesperson.

Recruitment and selection of salespeople are not one-time decisions made in a vaccum. Markets and the marketing environment are dynamic, and an organization's objectives, resources, and marketing strategies must change accordingly. Additional salespersons with different skills may need to be hired to cover expanding or new markets. Also, management must ensure that, once hired, sales personnel perform in accordance with specified sales standards; corrective action may be necessary when a salesperson regularly fails to meet sales objectives. Thus recruiting and selecting the right mix of salespeople require continuous evaluation and decision making.

Training Salespeople

The next step in managing the sales force is training both new and experienced salespeople. Some organizations devote millions of dollars to training. As firms embrace relationship selling, they are rethinking the way they train salespeople. While high-pressure tactics are downplayed, salespeople are learning to become customer advocates with detailed knowledge of their product and their customers' businesses.

Sales training programs can be directed at the entire sales force or at a few individuals. They can be conducted by sales managers, other salespeople, or technical specialists from within the organization. There are also individuals and organizations that sell special sales training programs. Regardless of who manages the training program, several issues should be addressed, including the type of training, the location and timing, and the methods and materials to be used.

 Type of Training   Newly hired sales personnel generally require comprehensive training on personal-selling methods; the company's policies and procedures; and the company's products, including their benefits, applications, problems, services, warranties, packaging, sales terms, promotion, and distribution. Experienced personnel, on the other hand, need refresher courses for established products and training for new products, procedures, and selling techniques. Many companies, like Home Depot, view training as an endless process.

TABLE 20.2
Hypothetical Case Demonstrating the Incremental Productivity Method

Number of Salespeople	Total Selling Costs	Sales per Salesperson	Total Sales	Operating Margin
1	$ 20,000	$150,000	$150,000	$130,000
2	40,000	120,000	240,000	200,000
3	60,000	90,000	270,000	210,000
4	80,000	70,000	280,000	200,000
5	100,000	50,000	250,000	150,000

Location and Timing Training may occur daily, on the job, or during regular sales meetings. New employees in some organizations go through training programs before being assigned to a specific sales position. Other business organizations immediately put new recruits into the field, where they learn on the job and from other personnel. Training programs may last only a few days or as long as several years.

Training programs for experienced sales personnel are often held during slow sales periods. Such programs are usually brief but intense. Because training of experienced salespeople is typically an ongoing effort, the sales manager must determine the frequency, sequencing, and duration of these activities, and schedule them so as not to conflict with regular sales efforts.

Methods and Materials A sales training program may employ a variety of methods and materials, including lectures, films, texts, manuals, simulation exercises, programmed learning devices, audio- and videocassettes, demonstrations, case studies, and on-the-job training. The methods and materials used in a particular sales training program depend on the type and number of trainees, the program's content and complexity, the length of the training program, the size of the training budget, the location, the number of teachers, and teachers' preferences for specific methods and materials.

Compensating Salespeople

One of the goals in developing a personal-selling program is to attract, motivate, and retain a highly productive sales force. To accomplish that goal, the business must develop and implement a plan for compensating the sales force. The compensation plan should provide salespeople with an adequate degree of freedom, income, and incentive, yet allow sales management the necessary level of control. In addition, the sales compensation program should be flexible, fair, easy to administer, and easy to understand. To determine an acceptable level of compensation for each salesperson, the developer of the compensation program must consider the individual's value to the company, based on his or her tasks and responsibilities. The average annual compensation is $26,350 for a sales trainee, $38,631 for a mid-level salesperson, $57,819 for a top-level salesperson, and $65,352 for a sales supervisor.[19]

In general, sales compensation programs reimburse sales personnel for their selling expenses, offer a certain number of employee benefits, and provide an adequate income. To this end, a company may use one or more of three basic compensation methods: straight salary, straight commission, or a combination of salary and commission. Under a **straight salary compensation plan,** salespeople receive a specified amount of money per hour, week, month, or year. The salary remains the same until the salesperson is given a raise or a pay cut. This method of compensation is often used for persons selling agricultural chemicals. Compensation based solely on the amount of a person's sales in a given time period is known as a **straight commission**

■ **straight salary compensation plan** a plan by which salespeople are paid a specified amount of money per hour, week, month, or year

■ **straight commission compensation plan** a plan by which a salesperson's compensation is based solely on the amount of his or her sales in a given time period

[19]"Hey, Where's My Survey of Selling Costs?" *Sales & Marketing Management,* March 1991, pp. 42–45.

■ combination compensation plan a plan by which salespeople receive both a fixed salary and a commission based on sales volume

compensation plan. A commission may be based on a set percentage of sales or on a sliding scale having different percentage rates for each of several sales levels. The commission method is commonly used in the insurance industry. Under a **combination compensation plan,** salespeople receive both a fixed salary and a commission based on sales volume. An employee selling retail shopping products such as shoes and electronics may be paid on a combination compensation plan. Some plans now link compensation to long-term customer satisfaction.

Most firms use some form of the combination compensation plan. This method is popular because it provides both a specified level of financial security and some incentive to increase productivity. A straight salary is more practical for compensating new salespeople, and a straight commission is preferred if highly aggressive selling is required. When selecting a compensation method, sales management must consider the selling situation and select the plan most appropriate for the specific sales task. In addition, sales management should periodically review and evaluate the plan and make necessary adjustments to maintain its viability. Some firms, for instance, have found that commissions encourage salespeople to be attentive to the customer. On the other hand, some plans can backfire, such as Sears's combination plan at automobile service centers. After California officials accused Sears employees of systematically recommending unnecessary repairs, the retailer acknowledged that its compensation plan "created an environment where mistakes do occur."[20] Firms must be cautious to strike a proper balance between salary and commission.

Many companies offer salespeople another form of compensation known as a perquisite or "perk." The perks most commonly supplied to salespeople include telephone credit cards, company cars, corporate credit cards, and frequent flier programs. Others, used less often, include computers for use at home, health club memberships, and country club memberships.

Motivating Salespeople

To obtain high levels of productivity, a sales manager should develop a systematic approach for motivating salespersons. Motivating should not be considered an infrequent activity to be called upon only during periods of sales decline. To motivate salespeople, managers need to acknowledge and reward achievements and progress more than once a year.[21] Effective motivation of the sales force requires an organized set of activities performed continuously by the company's sales management.

One key to motivating sales personnel is to remember that they have personal needs and goals that they want to achieve. A sales manager must therefore attempt to create an organizational climate that allows sales personnel to satisfy personal needs and goals. Some firms hire consultants to help establish such a climate.

---

[20]Gregory A. Patterson, "Distressed Shoppers, Disaffected Workers Prompt Stores to Alter Sales Commissions," *Wall Street Journal,* July 1, 1992, pp. B1, B5.
[21]Ken Blanchard, "Reward Salespeople Creatively," *Personal Selling Power,* March 1992, p. 24.

Financial compensation is not the only means of motivating employees. Nonfinancial motivators—such as enjoyable working conditions, power and authority, job security, an opportunity to excel, and a voice in organizational affairs—can also be effective. Other methods of motivating the sales force include sales contests and similar tools that provide an opportunity to earn additional rewards. Some companies recognize achievements in creative or memorable ways, such as an appreciation luncheon, a personal call from the president of the company, or a small gift that relates to a salesperson's hobby or interests (see Figure 20.4).

Establishing Sales Territories

■ **sales territory** a geographic area for which one or more salespeople are responsible

The next step in sales force management involves establishing and assigning sales territories. A **sales territory** is a geographic area for which one or more salespeople are responsible. A sales territory can be a region of a country, a province, a state, or some other geographic breakdown, depending on the sales potential. Some firms have only a few salespeople who are assigned to an entire country, whereas others have hundreds of salespeople assigned to specifically defined geographic regions.

A company's sales territories are usually divided so that each has a similar sales potential or requires about the same amount of a salesperson's work. If territories are divided so that they have equal sales potentials, they will almost always be unequal in geographic size; salespersons assigned the larger territories will therefore have to work longer and harder to generate a certain sales

FIGURE 20.4
Motivating Salespeople
Texas Instruments advertises their products as premiums that can be used to motivate salespeople and improve productivity.

Source: © 1993 Texas Instruments Incorporated. Photo: Alex Stewart/The Image Bank.

volume. Conversely, when territories are divided so that they require equal amounts of work, sales potentials for those territories may vary and sales personnel who are partially or fully compensated through commissions will have unequal income potentials. As a result, rather than relying on a single approach, many sales managers try to balance territorial workloads and earning potentials by employing differential commission rates.

Routing and Scheduling Salespeople

Once the sales territories have been determined, someone must route and schedule sales calls in the field. These decisions depend on the sequence in which customers are visited; the exact roads or transportation (airline, train, or bus) schedules to be used; the number of calls to be made in a given period; and what time of day the calls will occur. Salespeople in some companies plan their own routes and schedules with little or no consultation with the sales manager. In other organizations, the routes and schedules are planned by the sales manager. Regardless of who is responsible for routing and scheduling, the major goals should be to maximize salespersons' selling time and to minimize the time and expenses spent on traveling and waiting.

The geographic size of a sales territory is an obvious factor in routing and scheduling decisions. Other considerations include the number and distribution of customers within the territory, the frequency and length of sales calls, the availability of roads and public transportation, and the location of the salesperson's home base in relation to customers' locations.

Evaluating Sales Force Performance

As the final step in sales force management, the sales manager must obtain certain information to evaluate the performance of the sales force. Useful sources of information include call reports, customer feedback, and invoices. *Call reports* specify which customers were called on and describe in detail the interaction with those clients. Customer feedback and sales invoices also provide an indication of a salesperson's activities and performance. In addition, traveling sales personnel must often file work schedules indicating where they plan to be during specific future time periods.

The performance of the sales force can be assessed in relation to the sales objectives. If an individual's sales objective was stated in terms of sales volume, then that person should be evaluated on the basis of the sales volume attained. Salespeople can be evaluated along several other dimensions, such as average number of calls per day, average sales per customer, number of new customer orders, average cost per call, average gross profit per customer, and actual sales relative to sales potential. The sales manager can evaluate a salesperson by comparing one or more of these dimensions with predetermined performance standards.

When the performance of the sales force is not up to standards, the sales manager must try to improve it. Corrective action may take the form of modifications in performance standards, extra sales training, or the application of other motivational methods. Sometimes comprehensive changes in the sales force are required.

MANAGING THE INTERNATIONAL SELLING EFFORT

Firms involved in international marketing also need to establish a sales force. Some firms employ foreign nationals to do the selling in a single country, whereas others organize an international sales force. In most cases, a firm will staff its sales force with foreign nationals directed by a foreign or domestic sales manager. When a company needs to deal directly with customers abroad, especially in the case of industrial goods, an international sales force is used.

Local Selling

■ **local selling** maintaining a sales force composed of locals from the country where a firm conducts business

Local selling is the maintenance of a sales force composed of locals from the country where a firm conducts business. Local selling has several major advantages. A local sales force knows the customs of the country and may be more effective in selling, at least initially. Other barriers, such as language and business etiquette, can be reduced or eliminated. The citizens and government of some countries also look favorably on foreign firms that create jobs for locals.

Despite its advantages, local selling poses several challenges to international firms. Recruiting qualified salespeople can be difficult in a country such as the United States, but even more difficult in some of the developing nations. The image of sales careers may also create problems for recruiters. As we said earlier, many salespeople are viewed as highly trained professionals in the United States, but in Europe sales is a less desirable occupation. Both of these factors make the search for talented salespeople more time consuming, but not impossible. Recruiting firms are also available in many countries to assist firms in locating salespeople with the desired qualifications.

Methods that are effective in compensating and motivating a sales force are also different from country to country. Not all cultures respond in the same way to commissions, bonuses, and other prizes. For instance, most U.S. firms rely on a combination compensation plan (commission plus bonus) and nonfinancial motivators such as enjoyable working conditions and the opportunity to excel. Japanese firms are more likely to use a straight salary compensation plan. An international firm must adhere to local customs in its plan for compensating and motivating salespeople.

The size of a local sales force depends upon the number of customers and the frequency of sales calls desired. In some countries, such as Japan or China, salespeople are expected to make several calls before attempting to close a sale. This means that the size of a sales force can differ considerably from country to country.

A major limitation of local selling has to do with language and culture. Although a local selling force speaks the language of local customers and understands the culture, it may have problems communicating with the corporate headquarters. For instance, a sales force composed of German nationals may have problems taking directions from a firm in the United States. Furthermore, it may not be able to deal with customers in neighboring European countries.

International Selling

International selling involves the travel of a firm's domestic sales force across national boundaries to meet directly with clients in a foreign country. International selling is a major commitment for a company and requires special skills. To be successful, a firm must overcome cultural barriers, differences in business practices, and reluctance from salespeople to accept a foreign assignment. Without a long-term commitment, firms find it difficult to succeed in international selling.

The international salesperson must deal with cultural diversity in the values and attitudes of foreign businesspeople. One of the critical obstacles salespeople face is finding the key decision maker in the customer company. This may be the purchasing agent, production manager, new products manager, other member of middle management, or any number of combinations of individuals. A successful international salesperson must be able to identify and communicate effectively with buying units that differ from country to country.

Purchase decisions may also take much longer than a salesperson is used to. International salespeople may encounter diverse business practices in various countries. Differences exist in how appointments are made, the number of people involved in the decision, and the number of meetings required before a decision is made. For example, visiting salespeople may be asked to attend banquets by the Chinese and get to know their hosts personally before negotiating a sale. As many as twenty or more individuals may be involved in the purchase, increasing the time it takes to make a decision.

International salespeople must also overcome the language barrier. If speaking the language of the customer is critical, sales territories must be assigned on the basis of language. In some cases, English may be spoken by most customers, and firms can use their existing salespeople. But even if customers speak English, they may prefer product information and sales brochures to be translated into their local language.

Firms involved in international marketing must select salespeople with the needed qualities and, in some instances, help them overcome any reluctance to accept a foreign assignment. As we said earlier, language skills may be one requirement. Additionally, international salespeople must be mature, patient, and knowledgeable on a variety of subjects. They will find themselves in situations where they are working alone, away from home, and confronted with new ideas and cultures. Negotiations are complicated because the participants come from different backgrounds. Misunderstandings and breakdowns in negotiations can occur unless salespeople have the skills needed to operate in an international environment.

Not all salespeople are eager to accept an international assignment. Whereas the travel may seem glamorous to some, others may not want to uproot their families. Many salespeople also fear that going to a foreign country for several years can adversely affect career advancement. The concern with relocating the family has generally been handled through special compensation packages that include housing allowances, school expenses for children, paid vacations, and a lucrative salary. The career advancement question can be addressed by eventually bringing salespeople home and promoting them for a job well done. Many individuals find international sales positions rewarding both financially and in terms of personal and professional growth.

THE NATURE AND USES OF SALES PROMOTION

As defined in Chapter 15, *sales promotion* is an activity or material that acts as a direct inducement (offering added value or incentive for a product) to consumers, salespersons, or resellers. It can take the form of a coupon, demonstration, display, refund, premium, or contest. Advertising, publicity, and personal selling are designed to communicate a message about a product, but sales promotion is used to generate an immediate sale. During the past decade, firms have been increasing the shift of marketing dollars from advertising to sales promotion, a trend that is expected to continue.[22] About 310 billion coupons were distributed in the United States in 1992, an increase of 6 percent from the previous year.[23] As media costs continue to rise, advertisers will seek new forms of promotion, and sales promotion will be one of the major alternatives.

Sales promotion offers many advantages over other types of promotion. Firms can attract customers quickly and, in some cases, encourage brand or store loyalty. Also, sales promotion can increase cooperation among channel members. For instance, a retail store may be more likely to cooperate with a manufacturer that provides point-of-purchase displays or coupons.

Sales promotion is not without limitations, however. In some instances, consumers become more interested in the sales promotion features—particularly coupons, contests, and trading stamps—than the products themselves. These consumers may not develop a strong brand loyalty and may switch products if a competitor runs an exciting promotion. In addition, too much promotion may signal product weaknesses to consumers. If a restaurant continually uses different sales promotion activities, such as two meals for the price of one, consumers may question the quality of the food.

Organizations have not always succeeded in their attempts to use sales promotion activities. Some objectives simply cannot be achieved with this type of activity or material. It cannot be used to compensate for a lack of advertising. Poor product quality or other marketing mix deficiencies cannot be overcome by sales promotion. Similarly, sales promotion cannot replace a highly trained sales force.

Sales promotion can be used to assist marketers in achieving a variety of objectives. A single sales promotion activity may be used for one or more reasons. Table 20.3 shows how sales promotion activities can be used to provide inducements to resellers, salespersons, and consumers.

[22]Scott Hume, "Trade Promos Devour Half of All Marketing," *Advertising Age,* April 13, 1992, pp. 3, 53.
[23]Scott Hume, "Coupons Set Record, but Pace Slows," *Advertising Age,* February 1, 1993, p. 25.

TYPES OF SALES PROMOTION

The many different types of sales promotion can be divided into two groups: those directed at resellers and those directed at final consumers. We also examine sales promotion methods used for international markets.

Sales Promotion Methods Directed at Resellers

Producers use sales promotion to encourage wholesalers and retailers to stock and promote their products. The methods used include free merchandise, merchandise allowances, buy-back allowances, buying allowances, dealer listings, dealer loaders, count and recount promotion, premium or push money, sales contests, and cooperative advertising.

Sometimes producers offer **free merchandise**—additional products at no charge—to resellers that purchase a stated quantity of the same or different products. A producer might offer ten free spiral notebooks to a retailer that agrees to purchase a hundred notebooks. To simplify handling and book-keeping, the producer would probably reduce the amount of the invoice by the cost of the ten notebooks. Occasionally, free merchandise is used as payment for allowances provided through other sales promotion methods.

A manufacturer's agreement to pay a reseller a specified amount of money in exchange for providing special promotional efforts, such as displays or advertising, is known as a **merchandise allowance.** For instance, Hill's Pet Products, Inc. might offer a merchandise allowance to pet stores that set up special displays to promote its Science Diet dog and cat foods. Merchandise allowances are best suited to high-volume, high-profit, easily handled products. One major drawback of offering merchandise allowances is that some retailers provide the promotional activities at only a minimally acceptable level just to obtain the allowances.

■ **free merchandise** a sales promotion method aimed at resellers whereby free merchandise is offered to resellers that purchase a stated quantity of the same or different products

■ **merchandise allowance** a sales promotion method aimed at resellers that consists of a manufacturer's agreement to pay resellers specified amounts of money in exchange for providing special promotional efforts, such as displays or advertising

TABLE 20.3
Objectives of Sales Promotion

Aimed at Resellers
To increase reseller inventories
To obtain displays and other support for products
To improve product distribution
To obtain more and better shelf space

Aimed at Salespersons
To motivate the sales force
To educate the sales force about product improvements
To stabilize a fluctuating sales pattern

Aimed at Consumers
To obtain the trial of a product
To introduce a new or improved product
To encourage repeat or greater usage by current users of a product
To bring more customers into retail stores
To increase the total number of users of an established product

■ **buy-back allowance**
a sum of money offered to a
reseller for each unit bought
after an initial deal is over

■ **buying allowance**
a certain amount of money
temporarily offered to resellers for purchasing specified
quantities of a product

■ **dealer listing** an advertisement that promotes a
product and identifies the
names and locations of participating retailers that carry
the product

■ **dealer loader** a gift provided to a retailer for purchasing a specified quantity
of merchandise

■ **count and recount promotion method** a sales
promotion method in which
a reseller is paid a specific
amount of money for each
product unit moved from its
warehouse in a given time
period

■ **premium** (or **push**)
money additional com-
pensation provided to salespeople to encourage them
to push a line of products

■ **sales contest** a competition designed to stimulate increased participation in sales
efforts by distributors, retailers, and sales personnel

A **buy-back allowance** is a sum of money offered to a reseller for each unit bought after an initial deal is over. The total amount of money that the reseller can receive is proportional to its purchases during the initial trade deal. Buy-back allowances therefore prompt cooperation during the initial sales promotion effort and encourage repurchases afterward. The main draw-back of this method is its high cost.

A **buying allowance** is a certain amount of money temporarily offered to resellers for purchasing specified quantities of a product; it is similar to a rebate. A soft-drink bottler, for example, might give retailers 25 cents for each case of soft drinks purchased. Buying allowances may be used to lower the price of a product temporarily, to encourage retailers to handle a new product, or to stimulate the purchase of an item in larger-than-normal quanti-ties. The buying allowance is easy to use and returns profits to resellers.

An advertisement that promotes a product and identifies the names and locations of participating retailers that carry the product is called a **dealer listing.** A national television advertisement for Michelin tires, for example, might list the dealers of Michelin tires in that television station's viewing area. Dealer listings encourage retailers to stock the product, bring more people into the retailers' stores, and encourage consumers to buy the product at participating retailers.

A gift provided to a retailer for purchasing a specified quantity of merchan-dise is referred to as a **dealer loader.** Dealer loaders in the form of important display components are often offered to encourage retailers to make spe-cial display efforts. For instance, a soft-drink producer might offer a grocery store a special permanent floor display in exchange for ordering a specified number of cases of soft drinks. Marketers use dealer loaders to obtain new distributors and to push larger quantities of goods.

In the **count and recount promotion method,** a reseller is paid a specific amount of money for each product unit moved from its warehouse in a given time period. The units of the product in the reseller's warehouse are counted at the start of the promotion and recounted at the end to calculate how many units have been moved from the warehouse. This method benefits a producer by reducing resellers' inventories, thus making resellers more likely to place new orders. However, this method may not appeal to resellers with small warehouses (or none at all) and is difficult to administer.

Additional compensation provided to salespeople to encourage them to push a line of products is called **premium** (or **push**) **money.** Premium money is most effective for those products for which personal selling is an important part of the marketing effort; it is not appropriate for promoting self-service products. This method can be quite expensive but does help a producer obtain commitment from the sales force.

A **sales contest** is a competition designed to stimulate increased participa-tion in sales efforts by distributors, retailers, and sales personnel. Sales con-tests can produce excellent results if they are not used so often that they reduce their impact on sales force motivation.[24]

---

[24] Marjorie J. Caballero, "A Comparative Study of Incentives in a Sales Force Contest," *Journal of Personal Selling & Sales Management,* May 1988, pp. 55–58.

To be effective in motivating the sales force, contests must be equitable for all salespersons involved. One advantage of contests is that they can stimulate participation at all levels of distribution. The primary disadvantages of sales contests are that the prizes are usually expensive, and the increased sales resulting from contests are generally short-lived.

cooperative advertising a producer's agreement to pay a certain amount of money toward a retailer's media costs for advertising the producer's products. Payments such as these provide retailers with additional funds for advertising. The amount paid by the producer is usually based on the quantities purchased by the retailer. To receive payment, the retailer must show proof that advertisements were run.

Trade shows, discussed in Chapter 16, can also be used by manufacturers to promote their products to resellers. Many firms exhibit their products at trade shows that are attended by wholesalers and retailers, where manufacturers' representatives can provide information, take orders, and identify potential customers.

Sales Promotion Methods Directed at Consumers

Sales promotion methods directed at consumers fall into three broad categories: those used by retailers, those used for established products, and those used for new products.

Sales Promotion Methods Used by Retailers   Retailers generally use sales promotion methods that increase sales of particular product items and increase consumer traffic within a particular establishment. The sales promotion methods commonly used by retailers include point-of-purchase materials, trading stamps, retailer coupons, and demonstrations.

A **point-of-purchase material** is a promotional item such as an outside sign, window or floor display, counter piece, or self-service carton used to encourage consumers to make a purchase. Point-of-purchase materials are designed to attract attention, inform customers, and encourage retailers to carry particular products. Displays in grocery stores have dramatically increased sales for a variety of products, including frozen dinners, laundry detergents, salty snacks, and soft drinks.[25]

Trading stamps are sales promotion items distributed by retailers to consumers in proportion to the amount of the consumers' purchases; consumers accumulate the stamps and redeem them for merchandise. Retailers such as service stations and supermarkets have traditionally used trading stamps to encourage consumers to patronize specific stores. Trading stamps can also increase sales of specific items when extra stamps are offered to purchasers of those items. This promotion method is attractive to consumers as long as it does not drive up the price of goods.

The popularity of trading stamps has been fading since the peak of the stamp craze in 1969. At that time, about three-fourths of all American

Margin definitions:

■ **cooperative advertising** a producer's agreement to pay a certain amount of money toward a retailer's media costs for advertising the producer's products

■ **point-of-purchase material** a promotional item such as an outside sign, window or floor display, counter piece, or self-service carton used to encourage consumers to make a purchase

■ **trading stamp** a sales promotion item distributed by retailers to consumers in proportion to the amount of the consumers' purchases (consumers save the stamps and redeem them for merchandise)

[25]Kathleen Deveny, "Displays Pay Off for Grocery Marketers," *Wall Street Journal,* October 15, 1992, pp. B1, B5.

grocery stores gave out stamps from more than four hundred stamp companies. Today, only about twenty stamp companies still exist.

■ **retailer coupon** usually a cents-off coupon distributed through advertisements or handouts and redeemable only at specific retail stores

A **retailer coupon** is usually a cents-off coupon that is distributed through advertisements or handouts and is redeemable only at specific retail stores. The use of retailer coupons is particularly beneficial when price is a primary motivation in consumers' purchasing behavior. Like trading stamps, retailer coupons are designed to encourage consumers to patronize particular stores; they may also be used to build sales volume for a specific brand. However, counteroffers by competing retailers can significantly reduce the effectiveness of retailer coupons. Some retailers honor competitors' coupons. Moreover, because of their emphasis on price, the use of coupons may weaken customer loyalty to a retailer. A recent survey found that there is near-universal use of coupons; 99 percent of American households redeem at least one coupon each year. This has led some experts to conclude that coupons may become less effective as more and more retailers offer them.[26]

Coupon fraud threatens the future of this sales promotion activity. It is estimated that companies pay out over $800 million a year in fraudulent claims, mostly to retailers.[27] They obtain coupons in bulk, not from shoppers buying products but from various other sources. Marketers are attempting to combat this practice by shortening the redemption period, designing coupons that are difficult to counterfeit, using technology to spot counterfeited coupons, and even hiring investigators to track down con artists illegally redeeming coupons.

■ **demonstration** a sales promotion method used by retailers on a temporary basis to encourage trial use and purchase of a product or to actually show how the product works

A **demonstration** of a product is often conducted on a temporary basis to encourage trial use and purchase of a product or to actually show how the product works. Because of the high labor costs associated with demonstrations, they are expensive to use. Nevertheless, they can be highly effective in promoting certain types of products, particularly kitchen appliances and food products in grocery stores.

Sales Promotion Methods for Established Products   Sales promotion techniques for established products are designed to provide additional value for customers purchasing the items. Cents-off offers, premiums, consumer sweepstakes, and consumer contests are typically used to promote established products.

■ **cents-off offer** a sales promotion device for established products whereby buyers deduct a certain amount (specified on the product's package or label) off the regular price of the product

A **cents-off offer,** on a product's package or label, allows buyers to deduct a specified amount from the regular price of the product. For instance, the label on a bottle of Fresh Start laundry detergent might say "$1.00 off retail price"; when the consumer purchases the detergent, the cashier automatically deducts one dollar from the price. This method encourages consumers to try the product, stimulates product sales, and promotes products in off-seasons. It is a popular method among producers because it is easy to control. However, it reduces the price for customers who would have bought the product at the regular price, and it requires special handling by retailers. In addition, frequent use of cents-off offers may cheapen a product's image.

---

[26] Scott Hume, "Coupons: Are They Too Popular?" *Advertising Age,* February 15, 1993, p. 32.
[27] Christopher Power, "Coupon Scams Are Clipping Companies," *Business Week,* June 15, 1992, pp. 110–111.

■ **premium** an item offered free or at a minimum cost as a bonus for purchasing a product

A **premium** is an item offered free or at a minimum cost as a bonus for purchasing a product (see Figure 20.5). It may be used to lure competitors' customers, introduce new sizes of established products, add variety to other promotional efforts, and stimulate loyalty. For example, gasoline stations frequently use premiums such as free soft drinks, glassware, and toy cars to increase sales. Premiums are usually distributed by retailers or through the mail, but they may also be placed on or in packages. To function effectively as an incentive to buy, the offered premium must be easily recognized and desired by consumers.

■ **consumer sweepstakes** a sales promotion device for established products in which consumers submit their names for inclusion in a drawing for prizes or cash

In a **consumer sweepstakes,** consumers submit their names for inclusion in a drawing for prizes or cash. A manufacturer may hold a sweepstakes to stimulate sales; sometimes it is teamed with another sales promotion method. One of the most popular and widely recognized consumer sweepstakes is offered by Publishers' Clearinghouse. Designed to increase sales of magazine subscriptions, this sweepstakes gives participants a chance to win $10 million. Marketing Close-up examines the use of consumer sweepstakes.

■ **consumer contest** a sales promotion device for established products in which individuals compete for prizes based on their analytical or creative skill or, sometimes, chance

In a **consumer contest,** individuals compete for prizes based on their analytical or creative skill or, sometimes, chance. For instance, consumers might be asked to find a specific item in a picture or to solve a puzzle. Grocery stores sometimes attempt to increase consumer traffic by offering Bingo-type games in which consumers collect game pieces each time they make a purchase, with the goal of filling in a game card to win cash or prizes. Contests may be used in conjunction with other sales promotion methods such as coupons. Consumer contests are used less often than are sweepstakes, which tend to attract a greater number of participants.

FIGURE 20.5
Promotion Methods Directed at Consumers
Maxell offers consumers various premiums, such as CDs, prerecorded tapes, and stereos, when they purchase Maxell blank audiotapes.

Source: Courtesy Maxell Corporation of America, Fairlawn, NJ.

MARKETING CLOSE-UP

Consumer Sweepstakes Produce Instant Winners

Dream vacations, new homes, cars, and Super Bowl tickets are just a few of the prizes being offered to consumers by companies sponsoring sweepstakes. According to Charles Visich, senior vice president of Southland Corp., "People are developing a pot-of-gold-at-the-end-of-the-rainbow mentality." State lotteries are partially responsible for creating this attitude. People find excitement in the possibility—as small as it may be—of becoming an "instant winner." With consumer interest so high, many firms are turning to sweepstakes.

Sweepstakes make sense to companies for several reasons. Consumers have become somewhat desensitized to small premiums, such as a coupon for 50 cents off or a $1 refund. The chance of a trip to Hawaii generates much more interest and excitement. Additionally, consumers who do not redeem coupons—only 4 percent of all supermarket coupons are ever redeemed—may enter sweepstakes. Some firms also find that sweepstakes are less expensive than other promotional methods, especially if only a few prizes are given away. The odds of winning some sweepstakes are one in a million. Since sweepstakes entry forms often require consumers to mail in their names and addresses, they provide an excellent way for firms to build databases.

Despite the growing popularity of sweepstakes, abuses by sponsors threaten the future of this promotion technique. For example, in 1988 a federal grand jury in Los Angeles indicted sweepstakes winner James Lee and marketing executives John Curtin III and Kevin Kissame and two of their relatives on mail fraud charges for rigging sweepstakes. Lee won a Mustang convertible in the Alpha Beta supermarket chain's sweepstakes, and a year later won a Chevrolet Corvette in a Taco Bell sweepstakes. Curtin and Kissame operate C&K Marketing of New Jersey, a firm that has conducted contests for many large firms, including PepsiCo and Procter & Gamble. They allegedly awarded three prizes to friends. C&K officials denied any wrongdoing.

Sweepstakes abuses are suspected to be widespread among some so-called charities. With names that can be confused with established charities, these organizations take in millions of dollars but give little to prize winners or to the causes they claim to represent. For example, three charities in New York (the American Heart Disease Prevention Foundation, the National Heart Research Fund, and the Center for Alternative Cancer Research) collected more than $10 million through sweepstakes, only 5 percent of which was spent on their programs. Such organizations send letters telling people they have won cash in a $5,000 charity sweepstakes. To claim the prize, recipients are encouraged to send a check for at least $5 made out to the charity. Most "winners" receive a prize of 10 cents. Federal officials and several states are cracking down on a number of organizations using bogus sweepstakes.

Many firms hope such abuses can be stopped. Sweepstakes have proved to be valuable promotional tools. Consumers like the idea of being instant winners, and most firms using sweepstakes believe they are effective. Because of the potential size of the prizes and the excitement of playing, sweepstakes have become a useful and frequently used promotional technique.

Sources: Scott Hume, "Sweepstakes Grow with Coupons," *Advertising Age*, December 7, 1992, p. 28; Rhonda L. Rundle, "A Crackdown on 'Charity' Sweepstakes," *Wall Street Journal*, March 6, 1989, p. B1; and Jeffrey A. Trachtenberg, "Sweepstakes Fever," *Forbes*, October 3, 1988, pp. 164–166.

Sales Promotion Methods for New Products

Three of the most common sales promotion techniques used to promote new products are manufacturers' coupons, money refunds, and free samples.

Much like a retailer coupon, a **manufacturer's coupon** is a cents-off certificate that allows consumers to purchase a specified product at a reduced price. A manufacturer's coupon, however, lets the consumer purchase the product from any retailer carrying the product. The "cents off" may be deducted from the purchase price or given as cash. Manufacturers' coupons are typically used to stimulate trial of new or established products. Such coupons may increase sales volume quickly, attract repeat purchasers, or introduce new package sizes or features. For the best results, coupons should be easy to recognize and should clearly state the offer and terms.

A **money refund** is a new product sales promotion method in which a consumer presents proof(s) of purchase to the manufacturer, which then reimburses the consumer the specified amount of money. Money refunds usually require multiple purchases of a product before the consumer can qualify for a refund. For example, a money refund may require a consumer to mail in five proofs of purchase, typically the Universal Product Code from the bottom or side of the package. This method, used primarily to promote trial use of a product, is relatively low in cost and has a limited impact on sales. Both M&M/Mars and Hershey Foods have offered cash refunds of one dollar for twenty wrappers submitted.[28]

A **free sample** is a sales promotion method used to encourage consumers to try a product for the first time, to increase sales volume in the early stages of a product's life cycle, or to obtain desirable distribution. For instance, a manufacturer might mail a small sample of a new shampoo to all consumers in its target market. When designing a free sample promotion, marketers should take into consideration factors such as the seasonality of the product, the characteristics of the market, and prior advertising. Free samples should not be used to promote mature products and slow-turnover products. New product sampling is growing; more effective giveaway programs with retailers have been developed at alternative locations like airports, theaters, and special events.[29]

manufacturer's coupon a sales promotion device for new products—a cents-off certificate that allows consumers to purchase a specified product at a reduced price from any retailer carrying the product

money refund a sales promotion method for new products in which the manufacturer mails the consumer a specified amount of money when proof of purchase is established

free sample a sales promotion method used to encourage consumers to try a product for the first time, to increase sales volume in the early stages of a product's life cycle, or to obtain desirable distribution

Sales Promotion Methods for International Markets

Many of the sales promotion methods used in the United States are also used by firms selling in foreign markets (see Figure 20.6). For example, the use of coupons is growing in countries throughout the world, especially the United Kingdom, Belgium, and Canada.[30] However, as in the case of advertising, sales promotion strategy must often be adapted to conditions in the foreign marketing environment. For example, premiums are frequently used

---

[28]"Hershey Hopes Refunds Will Knock Mars to the Moon," *Marketing News,* May 25, 1992, p. 5.
[29]Scott Hume, "Sampling Wins Over More Marketers," *Advertising Age,* July 27, 1992, p. 12.
[30]"Global Coupon Use Up; U.K., Belgium Tops in Europe," *Marketing News,* August 5, 1991, p. 5.

FIGURE 20.6
Promotion for International Markets
Promotions such as this coupon for Nestlé Slender are used in Spain and other countries, much as they are used in the United States.

Source: Courtesy of Nestlé S.A.

in the United States, but some countries have laws that prohibit the use of coupons or free gifts. Other countries restrict the amount of discounts that can be given to resellers. In many foreign markets, price reductions in the store are the most frequently used promotion tool.[31] Free samples, if permitted, are effective when introducing a product to a new market.

The portion of the promotion budget allocated to sales promotion may have to be increased in markets with media constraints. In some countries, sales promotion is the major element of the promotion mix because local conditions limit the use of advertising. In the absence of such constraints, sales promotions are used to supplement advertising and personal-selling efforts.

SUMMARY

Personal selling is face-to-face communication with potential buyers. There are three different types of traditional sales personnel. Order takers process routine sales and reorders and maintain lasting, positive relationships with customers. Order getters seek out new customers and try to increase sales

---

[31] Jean-Pierre Jeannet and Hubert D. Hennessey, *Global Marketing Strategies,* 2nd ed. (Boston: Houghton Mifflin, 1992), p. 491.

to present customers. Support personnel are not usually involved in selling products but rather are concerned with facilitating exchanges by identifying potential customers, educating them, establishing good will, and providing service after sales. The three types of support personnel are missionary, technical, and trade salespersons. Salespeople of the future will increasingly practice smart selling—building good relationships with customers.

Personal selling can be characterized as a process designed to provide customer satisfaction. The selling process consists of seven steps: prospecting for potential customers, preparing, approaching the customer, making the presentation, handling objections, closing, and building long-term relationships with customers.

Managing the sales force requires many decisions and activities in nine areas. These areas include (1) establishing sales objectives that specify what the sales force as a whole and as individuals are expected to accomplish during a specified time period; (2) determining the size of the sales force (using the equalized workload method or the incremental productivity method); (3) recruiting and selecting salespeople to staff sales positions; (4) training both new and experienced sales personnel; (5) compensating salespersons to motivate and retain them (using a straight salary, straight commission, or combination compensation plan); (6) motivating salespeople; (7) establishing sales territories; (8) routing and scheduling sales calls in the field; and (9) evaluating sales force performance.

Firms involved in international marketing also need to establish a sales force. Local selling is the maintenance of a sales force composed of foreign nationals from the country where a firm conducts business. Most firms staff their sales force with foreign nationals directed by a foreign or domestic sales manager. International selling involves the travel of a firm's sales force abroad to deal directly with customers in a foreign country. Firms using local selling or international selling must overcome cultural barriers and differences in business practices from country to country.

Sales promotion activities offer consumers, salespersons, and resellers direct inducements for purchasing a product. Sales promotion can be used by producers to encourage wholesalers and retailers to stock and promote their products. The methods used include free merchandise, merchandise allowances, buy-back allowances, buying allowances, dealer listings, dealer loaders, count and recount promotion, premium or push money, sales contests, cooperative advertising, and trade shows.

The sales promotion methods commonly used by retailers include point-of-purchase materials, trading stamps, retailer coupons, and demonstrations. Sales promotion techniques for established products consist of cents-off offers, premiums, consumer sweepstakes, and consumer contests. Three of the most common sales promotion techniques used to promote new products are manufacturers' coupons, money refunds, and free samples.

Many of the sales promotion methods used in the United States are also used by firms selling in foreign markets. The specific methods used must often be adapted to conditions in the foreign marketing environment. The percentage of the promotion budget allocated to personal selling may also have to be increased in markets with media constraints.

KEY TERMS

order taker
order getter
support personnel
missionary salesperson
technical salesperson
trade salesperson
prospecting
approach
stimulus-response approach
need satisfaction approach
formulated selling approach
closing
equalized workload method
incremental productivity
  method
straight salary compensation
  plan
straight commission
  compensation plan
combination compensation
  plan
sales territory
local selling

international selling
free merchandise
merchandise allowance
buy-back allowance
buying allowance
dealer listing
dealer loader
count and recount promotion
  method
premium (or push) money
sales contest
cooperative advertising
point-of-purchase material
trading stamp
retailer coupon
demonstration
cents-off offer
premium
consumer sweepstakes
consumer contest
manufacturer's coupon
money refund
free sample

QUESTIONS FOR DISCUSSION AND REVIEW

1. What is personal selling? What are the major differences between personal selling and advertising?

2. What is the major job of an order taker? An order getter?

3. Why is approaching the customer a critical step in the sales process?

4. What is the purpose of the sales presentation? How can it be accomplished?

5. What are the different ways in which sales objectives for individual salespersons are commonly stated? Give an example of each.

6. What are the major advantages and disadvantages of the equalized workload and incremental productivity methods for determining the size of the sales force?

7. What major issues should be addressed when developing a program to train salespeople?

8. What method of compensation would you prefer if you were a salesperson? Why?

9. What are the advantages of local selling? What are some of the challenges facing a firm using a local sales force in a foreign country?

10. Under what conditions should a firm establish an international sales force? What are the barriers to international selling?

11. What is sales promotion? What are the strengths and weaknesses of sales promotion?

12. What promotion methods are used to promote established products? New products? Why do the methods differ?

13. What adjustments must marketers make when adapting sales promotion to foreign markets?

CASES

20.1   SALES PROMOTION TO BOOST FAST-FOOD SALES

Competition is intense in the fast-food industry. Pizza is threatening the hamburger as the most popular type of fast food. Whereas McDonald's has 12,000 restaurants worldwide and annual sales of $18.8 billion, PepsiCo franchises Pizza Hut, KFC, and Taco Bell have 20,000 sites and worldwide sales of $13.8 billion. Burger King has 6,200 stores and worldwide sales of $6.1 billion, and is gaining on McDonald's. Burger King's share of the sandwich chain market has increased to 17 percent in 1990; McDonald's share dropped from 36 percent in 1990 to 33 percent. Many other chains, including Hardees, Wendy's International, and Long John Silver's, are battling for customers in the sluggish fast-food industry.

Customer traffic in fast-food restaurants has been leveling off for several years. In 1991, traffic rose 1.8 percent after rising 2.4 percent the previous year. Most of the growth, however, came at the expense of profits since a large percentage of fast-food transactions involved price reductions. In an effort to boost traffic without reducing prices, many chains turned to promotion.

In 1992, McDonald's spent over $30 million for tie-ins with "Batman Returns." For children, there were Batman Happy Meals. For teens and adults, McDonald's sold collector cups with scenes from the film and Batdisc lids that doubled as Frisbees. The Batman logo also appeared on food wrappers and bags.

Burger King continued as Disney's tie-in partner with the re-release of *Pinocchio,* a 52-year-old animated classic. Beach toys based on Pinocchio characters were offered through a Kids Club promotion. Burger King also promoted a 99-cent breakfast sandwich offer.

Although Wendy's does not have a movie partner, a "Summer of 99" sweepstakes was used to spotlight its 99-cent Super Value Menu. Customers were given the chance to win their choice of 99 prizes, including a 1992 Jeep Cherokee, 99 pounds of lobster, 99 minutes with country singer Randy Travis, and a 99-hour vacation in Fort Lauderdale. Entry forms were available in stores, and separate drawings were held for each prize.

Dunkin' Donuts, the major breakfast and lunch competitor to the full-menu chains, also started its largest promotion. The "Dunkin' Dough" rub-off card game offered $30 million in prizes. Among the prizes were $25,000 and $5,000 cash awards, Pontiac minivans, and American Airlines/Embassy Suites vacations. According to Ed Frechette, Dunkin' Donuts manager of sales promotion, "Consumers want to have a big prize to shoot for but also want to feel they can win *something*. A problem with some games in the past, like McDonald's Dick Tracy promotion [in 1990], is people didn't feel like they could win."

Questions for Discussion

1. Why do many fast-food chains rely heavily on sales promotion?

2. Compare the various tie-ins used to promote fast food.

3. What sales promotion method did Wendy's use?

4. Is there any advantage to Dunkin' Donuts' promotion strategy?

Based on information from Joshua Levine, "Look Who's Coming to Dinner," *Forbes,* March 1, 1993, pp. 104–105; Scott Hume, "Will Travelers Eat Up Summer Promotions?" *Advertising Age,* June 15, 1992, p. 29; Jim Levi, "Chipping Away at Burger Dominance," *Accountancy,* February 1992, pp. 84, 86; and Scott Hume, "Burger King Takes a Gamble with Ads," *Advertising Age,* November 5, 1992, pp. 1, 42.

20.2 BODY SHOP INTERNATIONAL THRIVES ON UNIQUE SELLING STYLE

Anita Roddick, who ran a restaurant and an eight-room hotel in her home-town of Littlehampton, England, was looking for something new to do. She came up with the idea of producing and selling shampoos, skin creams, and other body lotions made from fruit and vegetable oils rather than animal fats. Through marketing, she would capitalize on selling "natural" cosmetics to aging baby boomers—like herself—who generally distrust advertising and sales hype, demand product information, and are loyal to socially responsible companies.

With her idea and a $7,000 loan, Roddick hired a local chemist to develop animal-fat-free lotions. She opened her first shop in Brighton, and Body Shop International was born. Today more than seven hundred Body Shop stores operate around the world. Of the seventy-eight U.S. stores, sixty-four are franchised.

Body Shop does not advertise, but relies on in-store selling and promotion to communicate with customers. "Ninety-nine percent of *Fortune* 500 chief executives have never walked into a Body Shop," said Faith Popcorn, a consultant with Brain-Reserve, "yet this is what business will be like. And it is so contradictory to the way we are used to marketing."

Body Shop's strategy is to give the customers product information rather than a sales pitch. Salespeople are expected to develop a forthright relationship with customers, tell them about the history of lotions, and provide product information. Leaflets offer tips for skin care, and a manual containing product information is available in each store. Pamphlets scattered throughout stores also tell customers about Body Shop's recycling program, whereby customers can bring in used Body Shop bottles and get them refilled. Roddick also uses the stores to push Body Shop's social agenda, a variety of causes including "Save the Whales" and Amnesty International. With her long-running social campaign, Roddick intends for her company to demonstrate what she calls the new business consciousness.

Body Shop International prides itself on its knowledgeable staff. Courses in product ingredients teach salespeople about properties, structures, and sources of cosmetics. Employees are taught to serve the needs of customers who are culturally foreign. Training is also available to help franchises and partnership shop owners get involved in community projects. Work force training efforts are measured by employee attitude.

Roddick also displays slogans and messages around stores to motivate employees. One of her favorites is "If you think you're too small to have an impact, try going to bed with a mosquito." Even Body Shop trucks are used as rolling billboards for pithy slogans.

Not everyone is impressed with Body Shop's approach to selling products. The British press has become especially critical of Roddick and her husband. A London daily, the *Independent,* wrote: "They represent causes attractive to the liberal conscious. Yet this goodness is used, remorselessly, to sell vanity products. You wash your hair in global concern. And it is debatable whether the wizened peasants on the walls are dignified or patronized." Although there may be some debate about Body Shop's approach, most agree that selling in general will incorporate some aspects of it in the decade ahead.

Questions for Discussion

1. Do you think Body Shop uses relationship selling? Explain.

2. How does environmental consciousness fit into Body Shop's strategy?

3. How does the Body Shop train and motivate salespeople?

4. Do you think it is appropriate to use environmental concern in selling products?

Based on information from Philip Elmer-Dewitt, "Anita the Agitator," *Time,* January 25, 1993, pp. 52–54; Rahul Jacob, "What Selling Will Be Like in the '90s," *Fortune,* January 13, 1992, pp. 63–64; Jean Sherman Chatzky, "Changing the World," *Forbes,* March 2, 1992, pp. 83–87; and Barbara Dutton, "What Price Knowledge," *Manufacturing Systems,* August 1992, pp. T, E3.

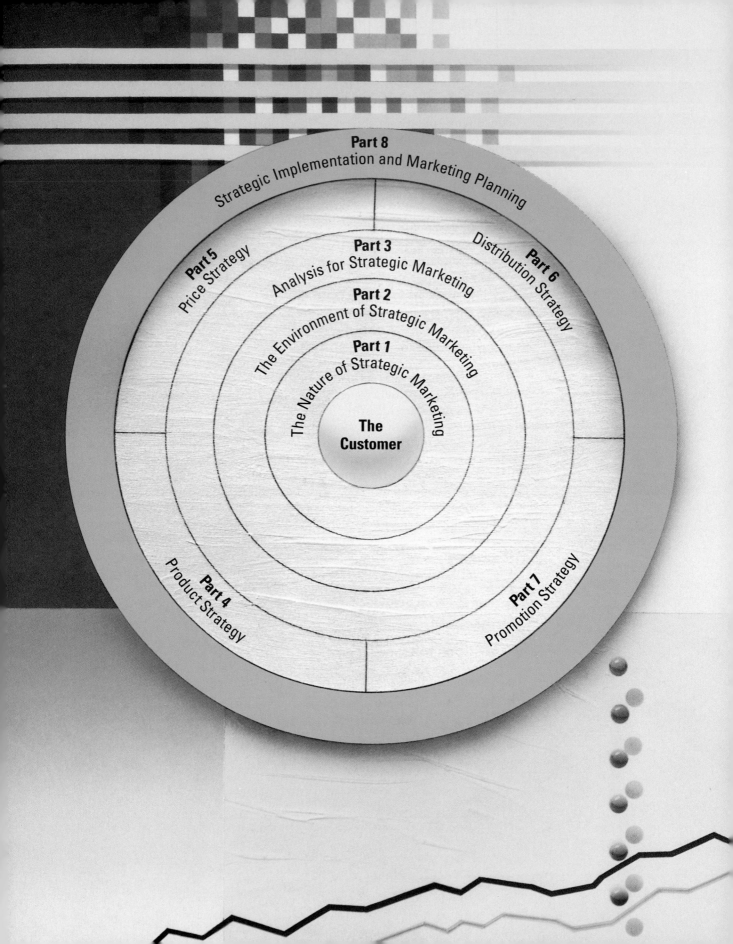

Part 8
Strategic Implementation and Marketing Planning

Part 5
Price Strategy

Part 3
Analysis for Strategic Marketing

Part 6
Distribution Strategy

Part 2
The Environment of Strategic Marketing

Part 1
The Nature of Strategic Marketing

The Customer

Part 4
Product Strategy

Part 7
Promotion Strategy

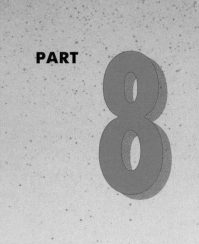

Strategic Implementation and Marketing Planning

PART

Organizing, Implementing, and Controlling Marketing Strategies

OBJECTIVES

- *To describe how a marketing department can be organized.*

- *To explain how marketing strategies are implemented.*

- *To discuss the concept of internal marketing.*

- *To determine the importance of controlling marketing strategies.*

- *To identify various methods of performance evaluation.*

After IBM unveiled its first computer in 1952, the company's profits rose yearly. But profits began to slide in 1985 when the U.S. computer industry went into a slump and the $50 billion company lost the technology lead it has yet to recover.

Then-CEO John Akers inherited the monumental task of recharging the company. At the same time he tried to keep one of the computer giant's best traditions—a full-employment policy. Most firms facing a decline in profits quickly laid off employees to slash costs and restore profits. But not IBM. Unlike many of its competitors, it did not fire a single employee. Instead, it redeployed its forces by sending thousands into sales jobs and early retirement.

Early retirement is often considered a risk because in many companies it results in the loss of important employees. But the risk paid off for IBM because 80 percent of the employees who left were in jobs IBM wanted to terminate. In addition, IBM lost a number of jobs through normal attrition. Attrition and early retirement together resulted in the loss of 39,000 employees between 1985 and 1987. About 9,400 persons took courses lasting up to eighteen months to train as sales agents and customer consultants as well as programmers. Another 45,000 employees completed less formal training—usually a few months or less—to fill jobs others had vacated. These measures enabled the company to cut costs without jeopardizing employee morale.

Akers also undertook the most significant reorganization of the company in thirty years, with the primary goal of improving IBM's products. Toward that end, Akers decentralized the firm's management structure by shifting decision-making power from a small group of top executives to six product and marketing groups. By delegating authority for new products and customer service to the managers of these groups, Akers hoped to eliminate the massive bureaucracy that hampered product development.

Seven years later, Akers stood at the podium during a hastily called meeting with security analysts and reporters as a legendary business era came to an end. Akers himself acknowledged that IBM was another huge company in big trouble. All the company stood for seemed lost: The future of the mainframe was in doubt, IBM's once-certain dividend was imperiled, and lay-offs were imminent. The problem Akers identified was the same he had recognized seven years earlier—a bulging, nonresponsive bureaucracy that stifled product development. IBM continued to depend on high-margin mainframe computers when computing power had become a desktop commodity, and to emphasize hardware when software and service now separated the winners from the losers.

After a $4.97 billion loss in 1992, the largest in U.S. corporate history, Akers resigned under pressure. IBM cut its quarterly dividend for the first time ever, by about 55 percent. As the search for a new leader began, the board made it clear that Akers's successor would be cold-blooded enough to make painful cuts in a company that had already eliminated 100,000 jobs, yet visionary enough to revive the world's largest computer firm. Akers had spent most of his tenure as CEO administering a series of unsuccessful reorganizations. The new leader will also have to make major organizational changes. If they do not work, IBM may not survive another seven years.[1] ●

hapter 1 states that marketing strategy involves selecting and analyzing a target market and developing a marketing mix for that market. But, as IBM and many other firms have learned, even the best-designed marketing strategies can fail without effective organization, implementation, and control. This chapter discusses the process of organizing, implementing, and controlling marketing strategies.

ORGANIZING THE MARKETING DEPARTMENT

■ **organizing** the structuring of a company to connect and coordinate resources and activities to achieve marketing objectives in an effective and efficient manner

■ **organizational structure** the framework of a marketing department that establishes the lines of authority and responsibility among marketing personnel, specifying who makes certain decisions and performs particular activities

The extent to which a firm's marketing management can plan and implement marketing strategies depends on how the marketing department is organized. **Organizing** involves the structuring of a company to connect and coordinate resources and activities to achieve marketing objectives in an effective and efficient manner. The **organizational structure** of a marketing department establishes the lines of authority and responsibility among marketing personnel, specifying who makes certain decisions and performs particular activities.[2] Designing a responsive and flexible organizational structure that is committed to quality and customer satisfaction is one of the most critical challenges facing marketing managers today. Yet there is obviously a gap between what managers say and do, a gap particularly evident when quality performance is linked with customer satisfaction.[3] Consider the following:

[1] Based on information from Carol J. Loomis, "King John Wears an Uneasy Crown," *Fortune,* January 11, 1993, pp. 44–48; Catherine Arnst and Joseph Weber, "IBM After Akers," *Business Week,* February 8, 1993, pp. 22–24; Michael W. Miller and Laurence Hooper, "Akers Quits at IBM Under Heavy Pressure; Dividend Is Slashed," *Wall Street Journal,* January 27, 1993; Geoff Lewis, Anne R. Field, John J. Keller, and John W. Verity, "Big Changes at Big Blue," *Business Week,* February 15, 1988, pp. 92–98; and Aaron Bernstein, "How IBM Cut 16,200 Employees—Without an Ax," *Business Week,* February 15, 1988, p. 98.
[2] James H. Donnelly, Jr., James L. Gibson, and John M. Ivancevich, *Fundamentals of Management,* 8th ed. (Homewood, Ill.: Irwin, 1992), p. 200.
[3] Jerry Bowles, "Is American Management Really Committed to Quality?" *Management Review,* April 1992, pp. 42–45.

- Eighteen percent of U.S. firms report that senior management evaluates quality performance less than once a year or not at all, compared with 2 percent of Japanese firms.

- Twenty-two percent of U.S. companies regularly translate customer expectations into the design of new products or services, compared with 58 percent of Japanese firms.

- Twenty-two percent of U.S. firms report that technology is of primary importance in meeting customer expectations, compared with 49 percent of Japanese firms.[4]

Many managers recognize that their organization is not responsive and flexible, able to move quickly when it must. These same managers often attribute the problem to people—departments that cannot get along, uncommitted or unmotivated employees, or the inability to develop quality products in a timely fashion. These are clear symptoms of problems with organizational structure.

The contribution of organizational structure to the performance of the organization is demonstrated each time a customer is satisfied. When customers are not satisfied, chances are great that the fault is with the organizational structure. Organizational structure provides an orderly arrangement among functions so that the marketing objectives can be accomplished effectively. Whereas the organizing function refers to the decisions managers make, the organizational structure reflects the outcomes of these decisions.

The result of structural problems can be disastrous for the organization. First, the organization becomes a collection of departments or independent groups pursuing their own goals rather than a coherent organization with a common goal. Second, the structure of the organization begins to dictate its strategy. This situation violates an important principle of management: Strategy should dictate structure. Finally, if structure is allowed to determine strategy, only strategies compatible with the existing organizational structure are acceptable. This approach severely limits the strategies that an organization can pursue effectively, especially efforts toward innovation and change.

General Motors illustrates how structural problems can damage an organization. In 1979, GM dominated the U.S. market for cars and light trucks with a 46 percent share; twelve years later its share fell below 35 percent. Although many factors have contributed to GM's problems—a drop in demand for large cars, obsolete factories, and poor quality, to name a few—these are all symptoms of a nonresponsive organizational structure, one that is failing. Efforts to change GM's structure have been hampered by a stubborn middle-management bureaucracy and an uncooperative United Auto Workers union. In addition to eliminating 74,000 jobs (including thousands of white-collar jobs) and twenty-one factories, experts believe that GM needs to restructure its entire organization to survive. Restructuring may include doing away with six separate operating divisions—Buick, Pontiac, Chevrolet, Oldsmobile, Cadillac, and Saturn—which is highly inefficient.[5]

[4] *International Quality Study* (American Quality Foundation and Ernst & Young, 1991), pp. 16–23.
[5] James Treece, "Doing It Right, Till the Last Whistle," *Business Week,* April 6, 1992, pp. 58–59.

Organizational structure must be consistent with the organization's marketing strategy. Strategic planning specifies *what* will be accomplished by *when;* organizational structure specifies *who* will accomplish what and *how* it will be accomplished. Many organizations, unfortunately, try to implement a new strategy with an obsolete organizational structure. The result becomes the failed "initiative of the month." For instance, a bank may recognize a need to be "more market driven" or "more quality conscious." The result is a new program for customer satisfaction or quality improvement. But a bank does not simply *become* quality conscious: rather, it must develop an organizational structure that results in the behaviors the strategy calls for. In developing an effective organizational structure, managers must delegate authority for performing tasks and organize the marketing department to establish task and authority relationships.

Delegating Authority

■ **authority** the organizationally sanctioned right to make a decision without the approval of a higher-ranking manager

In the process of organizing a marketing department, managers divide the work into specific tasks or activities and delegate authority to persons responsible for performing the tasks. **Authority** is the organizationally sanctioned right to make a decision without the approval of a higher-ranking manager.[6] For instance, once a sales manager is delegated authority to perform sales activities, he or she must make whatever decisions are necessary to carry out those activities.

■ **centralized organization** an organization in which top-level managers make most major decisions and delegate little decision-making authority to lower-level managers

■ **decentralized organization** an organization in which managers delegate decision-making authority as far down the chain of command as possible

Centralization and Decentralization   Delegating authority involves balancing the organization between two extremes—centralization and decentralization. In a **centralized organization,** top-level managers make most of the major decisions and delegate little decision-making authority *down* to lower-level managers. By contrast, in a **decentralized organization,** managers delegate decision-making authority as far down the chain of command as possible. At one extreme, *one* marketing manager makes *all* decisions; at the other extreme, *all* members of the marketing department make *all* decisions. In reality, most marketing departments fall somewhere in between these two extremes.

Several factors determine the extent to which an organization is centralized or decentralized. Generally, the more uncertain the marketing environment, the greater the tendency to decentralize. Recall from the opening example that IBM began to decentralize as the competitive and technological environment pressured the firm to make better products—and make them faster. History is another important factor; many firms centralize or decentralize according to what they have done in the past. More and more firms, however, are learning that they must make changes in their organizations to remain competitive. Organizations must also consider the nature of the decisions that are made. Costly and risky decisions place more pressure on the organization to centralize. Organizations like McDonald's and 3M use a centralized approach, as do many banks.

[6]Trudy Heller, "Changing Authority Patterns: A Cultural Perspective," *Academy of Management Review,* July 1985, pp. 488–495.

FIGURE 21.1
Decentralization
Motorola has become much more responsive since decentralizing, enabling the firm to introduce innovative products that exceed customer expectations.

Source: Ad courtesy of Motorola, Inc.

International organizations must weigh the tradeoffs between centralization and decentralization. On one hand, a centralized organization structure can be more efficient. Centralization allows the firm to keep records and most office personnel in one location, and to establish a pattern of initiatives and activities coming from headquarters. On the other hand, a decentralized organization structure is needed so the firm can respond quickly to the different foreign environments. Thus, for international firms to be successful, they must find a proper balance between centralization and decentralization.

Managers now have clear-cut guidelines for deciding whether to centralize or decentralize. Many successful firms remain centralized, and others are quite decentralized. The major concern is to delegate authority in such a way that the organization can achieve its marketing objectives.

Many firms are decentralizing, a trend that is expected to continue throughout the decade. Some, like Motorola, General Electric, United Parcel Service, and American Telephone & Telegraph, are thriving (see Figure 21.1).[7] Others are finding that decentralization has its drawbacks. KFC envisioned tastier foods and happier customers when it decentralized several years ago. But the firm's regional divisions failed to coordinate their efforts, and in so doing caused so much redundancy that the restructuring effort failed.[8] Aluminum Co. of America (Alcoa) found that customer rejections increased

[7]Christian Hill and Ken Yamada, "Motorola Illustrates How an Aged Giant Can Remain Vibrant," *Wall Street Journal,* December 9, 1992, pp. A1, A14.
[8]Gilbert Fuchsberg, "Decentralized Management Can Have Its Drawbacks," *Wall Street Journal,* December 9, 1992, pp. B1, B8.

and customer satisfaction decreased after the firm decentralized.[9] Other companies, including Levi Strauss, have experienced similar problems of overlapping functions and lack of coordination when they decentralized. Levi Strauss placed its order processing system under centralized control after retailers complained that they had to work with multiple divisions, each with its own procedures.[10] Marketing Close-up looks at Johnson & Johnson's decentralizing process.

In their book *In Search of Excellence,* Thomas Peters and Robert Waterman identify eight attributes that characterize the best-run companies in America.[11] Among the attributes of excellent firms is the fact that they are both centralized and decentralized. They delegate authority all the way to the shop floor, yet are fanatic about centralizing certain decisions they believe to be critical to the core value of the organization. For instance, 3M is recognized for encouraging engineers to *bootleg,* or borrow time, energy, and funds from other assignments to explore new product ideas. Yet a select group of engineers at 3M retains a relatively tight control over funding new product development projects. In essence, what Peters and Waterman are describing is the coexistence of steadfast centralized direction with adequate individual autonomy, a difficult balance for managers to strike. Some companies are decentralizing operations closest to the customer to remain responsive in the marketplace. Less visible internal functions such as personnel or order processing, as in the case of Levi Strauss, are centralized.

■ **empowerment** giving employees who are responsible for hands-on production, sales, or service activities the authority to make decisions or take action without prior approval

Empowerment   Some organizations have begun to empower workers to make decisions that typically have been made by superiors. **Empowerment** involves giving employees who are responsible for hands-on production, sales, or service activities the authority to make decisions or take action without prior approval.[12] For instance, a salesperson can negotiate price and other terms, or a ticket agent can give a customer a refund without calling the supervisor. Whereas decentralization refers to the delegation of authority to other *managers,* empowerment means that production, process control, and quality assessment become part of *everyone's* job and all individuals are given the ability and authority to take positive actions that will lead to high quality and performance. At Federal Express, for example, "all workers are routinely expected to take whatever initiative is required to fix problems and/or extend first-rate service to a customer."[13]

Empowerment is at the heart of any total quality management (TQM) program. It helps to accomplish many of the points advocated by leading quality experts. One of Philip Crosby's fourteen points is to define the type of training employees need in order to actively carry out their role in the

[9]Dana Milbank, "Restructured Alcoa Seeks to Juggle Cost and Quality," *Wall Street Journal,* August 24, 1992, p. B4.
[10]Fuchsberg, pp. B1, B8.
[11]Thomas J. Peters and Robert H. Waterman, Jr., *In Search of Excellence* (New York: Warner Books, 1982), pp. 15–16.
[12]Marshall Sashkin and Kenneth J. Kiser, *Total Quality Management* (Seabrook, Md.: Ducochon Press, 1991), p. 67.
[13]Tom Peters, *Thriving on Chaos* (New York: Knopf, 1988), p. 292.

MARKETING CLOSE-UP

Johnson & Johnson Decentralizes

Takeovers, mergers, and acquisitions dominated the business world during the 1980s, and financial restructuring was the name of the game. The 1990s are bringing a different kind of restructuring. Companies are trying to make their organizations more decentralized, to give employees more freedom, to foster creativity, and to eliminate the inefficiencies that have plagued many large firms. Although size is not the basic problem, it places a tremendous burden on managers. "The *Fortune* 500 is over," says management consultant Peter Drucker, meaning that large corporations will more and more divide their assets and resources into smaller, more efficient, and more independent businesses. IBM is organizing into more autonomous units, GM is eliminating 74,000-plus jobs and closing twenty-one factories, and AT&T is contracting out services like payroll, billing, and public relations.

A good example of a large organization with the best features of a small one is Johnson & Johnson. The company, with revenues of $12.4 billion, demonstrates the advantages of focus, flexibility, and speed. CEO Ralph Larson oversees 166 highly decentralized health care businesses ranging in size from $100,000 in annual sales to $1 billion. Larson expects the president of each company to act independently. Thus, instead of spending his time at his parent company's headquarters, Marvin Woodall, president of Johnson & Johnson Interventional Systems Co., manages his staff in a facility located an hour's drive away. If he needs to go to Europe to check on operations there, he doesn't ask a higher-up. Larson also decides whom to hire, what to produce, and whom to sell to. Ultimately, Larson and the other 165 presidents are accountable to executives at Johnson & Johnson corporate headquarters, which some presidents may visit only four times a year. A small 1.5 percent of Johnson & Johnson employees work at headquarters, which does not actually manage the numerous businesses but provides the capital and selects the people to run them.

One risk inherent in decentralization is duplication of function, which increases overhead. With its numerous businesses operating autonomously, Johnson & Johnson does have higher overhead than competitors: 41 percent of sales compared with 30 percent for more centralized Merck & Co. and 28 percent for Bristol-Myers Squibb Co. Sales functions are also duplicated, with Johnson & Johnson sales representatives from different units calling on large retailers like Wal-Mart and Kmart; retail giants often prefer to reduce the number of contacts from suppliers. To cut down on duplication, Larson has established employee teams called customer-support centers to work on site with retailers to simplify distribution and ordering. He has pushed the different companies to reduce duplication in payroll, purchasing, distribution, accounts payable, and other functions. Larson also pressures his managers to keep hiring from getting out of hand, another problem with decentralization.

In spite of some problems, decentralization has worked for Johnson & Johnson. The corporation has averaged annual profits of over 19 percent since 1980. In the face of intense global competition, decentralization may help firms to be focused and to encourage employee creativity and product development.

Sources: Joseph Weber, "A Big Company That Works," *Business Week*, May 4, 1992, pp. 124–132; Brian Dumaine, "Is Big Still Good?" *Fortune*, April 20, 1992, pp. 50–60; and Joseph Weber, "How J&J's Foresight Made Contact Lenses Pay," *Business Week*, May 4, 1992, p. 132.

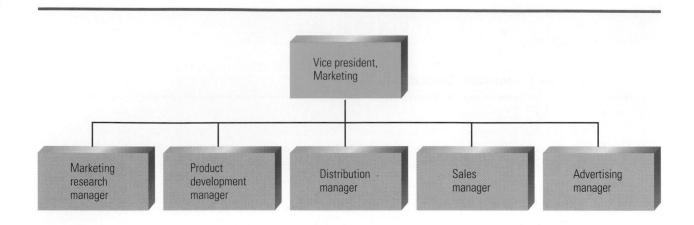

FIGURE 21.2
Example of a Functional Organization

quality improvement process.[14] W. Edwards Deming's points include removing barriers that rob workers of their right to pride of workmanship and making everyone responsible for the quality transformation.[15] The goal of employee empowerment is to stop trying to motivate workers with extrinsic incentives such as money and instead build a work environment that motivates them from within through intrinsic incentives such as pride in workmanship.[16] Empowerment is essential if employees are to make a total commitment to continuous quality improvement.

Approaches to Organizing the Marketing Department

Organizing a marketing department involves establishing its structure of *task* and *authority* relationships. Tasks are broken down into specific activities, assigned to individuals in various positions, and then put back together in units or departments headed by a manager. A marketing department can be organized according to functions, products, market segments, or some alternative form.

■ **functional organization** an organizational structure in which marketing departments are organized by general marketing functions such as marketing research, product development, distribution, sales, and advertising

Functional Organization   In a **functional organization,** marketing departments are organized by general marketing functions such as marketing research, product development, distribution, sales, and advertising (see Figure 21.2). The individuals who direct each of these functions report directly to the top-level marketing executive—usually the vice president of marketing. This structure is especially practical for small businesses with centralized marketing operations. In large firms, which tend to have decentralized marketing operations, a functional organization is less practical because of the number of people, activities, and products that must be coordinated.

[14]Philip B. Crosby, *Quality Is Free* (New York: Mentor, 1979), p. 238.
[15]W. Edwards Deming, *Out of the Crisis* (Boston: MIT Center for Advanced Study, 1986), pp. 23–24.
[16]V. Daniel Hunt, *Quality in America* (Homewood, Ill.: Business One Irwin, 1992), pp. 24–25.

Functional organization may be used by international firms with narrow product lines. Each functional manager has responsibility for one function throughout the world. The top-level marketing manager is generally based in the domestic country and has managers of that function in the various countries served. Functional organization is much less common in international companies than in domestic companies. It works best when the environment is fairly stable and tight control over processes and operations is desired.

■ **product-oriented organization** an organizational structure in which the marketing units are organized by product or product line, with a separate product manager taking full responsibility for the marketing of each specific product or line

Product-oriented Organization   In a **product-oriented organization,** the marketing units are organized by product or product line, with a separate product manager taking full responsibility for the marketing of each specific product or line. Businesses that offer many diverse products sometimes use this approach. In some cases, the product or product line may be a strategic business unit (SBU), discussed in Chapter 2. For example, American Brands, Inc., which offers financial services, tobacco products, hardware, office products, and golf and leisure products, is organized according to products. Other large organizations, like General Motors and Procter & Gamble, have used this approach. As shown in the hypothetical example in Figure 21.3, the product manager for the soap line has authority over the brand managers, who are lower in the organization hierarchy. The product manager may also draw on the resources of other staff members in the organization, such as the advertising or distribution manager. The product-oriented organization gives a firm the flexibility to develop special marketing mixes for different products. However, this type of organization can be expensive because each product has its own manager and, in some cases, assistant manager.

FIGURE 21.3
Example of a Product-Oriented Organization

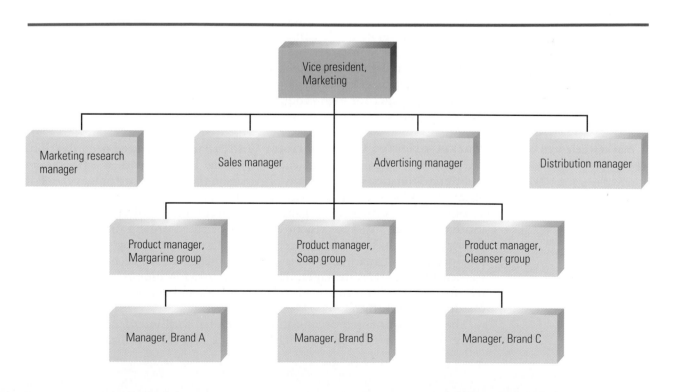

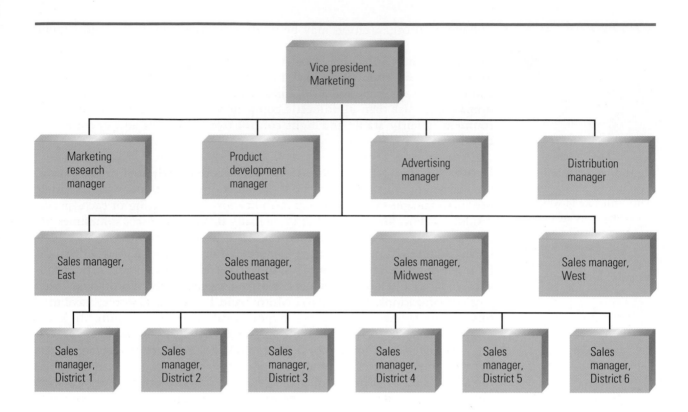

FIGURE 21.4
Example of a Market-Oriented Organization

The product-oriented organization is frequently used by international companies that have several unrelated product lines. This type of organization is especially useful in highly competitive international markets in which products are changing constantly because of technology. The major focus is on the product, and firms can quickly add or delete products as competitive conditions dictate. This type of organization is very expensive, because it requires a manager for each product and runs the risk of duplication of effort among divisions.

■ **market-oriented organization** an organizational structure in which the marketing department is structured on the basis of market segments, in addition to functions

Market-oriented Organization   With a **market-oriented organization,** the marketing department is structured on the basis of market segments, in addition to functions. Some firms organize on the basis of customer type. For instance, banks are typically organized on the basis of customer (consumer) accounts and commercial (organizational) accounts. Geographic regions are more commonly used to structure market-oriented organizations, as shown in Figure 21.4. In this case, the regional sales managers report directly to the vice president of marketing. District sales managers for each region report to their regional sales manager. This form of organization is especially effective for a firm whose customers' characteristics and needs vary greatly from one region to another.

The market-oriented organization is popular with international firms because they serve such diverse markets. This type of organization allows a company to respond to the local environment—to its culture, legal and political system, and economy. Some firms actually use a country-based organization, in which a separate organization is used for each country served. The market-oriented organization can be costly if a large staff is needed to integrate the activities of different departments or manage widely dispersed locations.

Alternative Forms of Organization Firms often organize on the basis of some combination of functions, products, or markets. Diverse product offerings may dictate that the marketing department be structured by products, but customers' characteristics may require a market-oriented organization. By combining organizational structures, a marketing department can develop and implement marketing strategies that both satisfy customers' needs and enable the organization to achieve its objectives.

International firms frequently combine organization forms because of the diversity in products offered and the markets served. Perhaps the most typical combination is product-oriented and market-oriented organization. This combination enables the firm to be responsive to two important dimensions, product and market.

■ **matrix organization**
a cross-functional organization overlay that creates multiple lines of authority and places people in teams to work on tasks for a finite period of time

One alternative design is the matrix organization, which, after more than thirty years of use, continues to elude definition. A **matrix organization** is a cross-functional organization overlay that creates multiple lines of authority and places people in teams to work on tasks for a finite period of time.[17] The functional departments are the foundation and a number of products or temporary departments are superimposed across the functional departments. The result, shown in Figure 21.5, is the existence of a dual, rather than singular, line of command. Although the matrix organization was first developed in the aerospace industry, it is now used in all types of organizations, both private and public.

As shown in Figure 21.5, individuals or teams in each cell report to two managers. For instance, someone working in marketing on product A would report to the vice president of marketing and product manager A. This arrangement is useful in speeding up the process of innovation, because the primary responsibility of each person is to help produce what the organization sells. The key is to free people from bureaucratic constraints by empowering them to create winning ideas and products while at the same time providing the structure needed to be successful.[18] Frigidaire Co., owned since 1986 by Electrolux, based in Sweden, uses a matrix organization that functions as a team and focuses attention on the consumer. The matrix organization has helped Frigidaire to become increasingly competitive, flexible, and market driven.[19]

---

[17]Robert C. Ford and Alan W. Randolph, "Cross-Functional Structures: A Review and Integration of Matrix Organization and Project Management," *Journal of Management,* June 1992, pp. 267–294.
[18]Martin K. Starr, "Accelerating Innovation," *Business Horizons,* July–August 1992, pp. 44–51.
[19]Richard Jaccoma, "Smart Moves in Hard Times," *Dealership Merchandising,* January 1992, pp. 164–167.

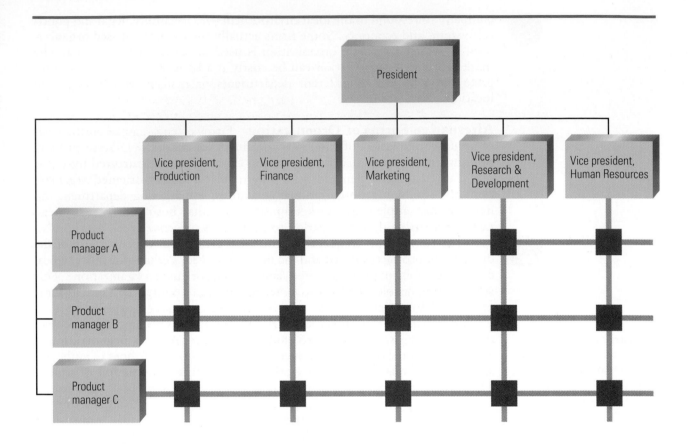

FIGURE 21.5
Example of a Matrix
Organization

■ **team** a group of employees who work closely to pursue common objectives

Teams play a major role in matrix organizations. A **team** is a group of employees who work closely together to pursue common objectives.[20] Some organizations become *team based,* using teams throughout the organization on a regular basis; others use teams more selectively. Some teams are directed by a manager, and others are self-managed. The idea behind self-managed work teams is for workers to become their own managers, a situation that increases reliance on their creative and intellectual capabilities and not only on their physical labor. At W.L. Gore & Associates, manufacturer of a wide range of electronic, medical, fabric, and industrial products, *associates*—this term is used instead of *employees*—work on self-directed teams without managers or bosses.[21] Regardless of which form is used, teams can move swiftly, flexibly, and effectively to produce innovative products. Team members learn one another's jobs and bring their ideas together, capitalizing on the creativity of the workers. When truly empowered, a team can change bored and demoralized *workers* into innovative and productive *partners*. Teams can be used for a variety of marketing activities, including personal selling, advertising, and product development.

[20] Charles Garfield, *Second to None* (Homewood, Ill.: Business One Irwin, 1992), p. 164.
[21] Frank Shippes and Charles C. Manz, "Employee Self-Management Without Formally Designated Teams: An Alternative Road to Empowerment," *Organizational Dynamics,* Winter 1992, pp. 48–61.

Matrix organizations have increased in popularity as organizations have decentralized and adopted quality programs. They are most appropriate when coordination is needed in complex and uncertain environments.[22] Matrix organizations lead to an efficient use of a specialized staff, offer timely response to a changing environment, enable technical specialists to interact with each other, free top-level management from day-to-day activities to spend more time planning, and provide opportunities for individual growth and development.[23] Since product or project groups are often employed with the matrix design, many organizations using teams adopt this form of organization because of its higher degree of flexibility and adaptability.

The matrix design has several drawbacks. For example, the matrix can lead to confusion because individuals or teams report to more than one superior. Several bosses may place conflicting demands on subordinates or struggle with each other for power, placing workers in a compromising position. In some cases, organizations may find that teams take longer to make decisions than individuals do. The matrix is also costly because additional managers and staff may be needed.[24] Dow Chemical adopted a matrix organization in the 1960s to promote internal communication. But instead of enhanced communication, Dow found that the matrix generated miles of red tape, scores of committees, and an even larger bureaucracy. Nonetheless, Dow continues to go with the matrix and credits it with many of the firm's successes.[25]

IMPLEMENTING MARKETING STRATEGIES

■ **implementing** putting marketing strategies into action

Organization provides the structure for marketing activities. Before exchanges can occur, however, marketing managers must implement the marketing program. **Implementing,** or putting marketing strategies into action, involves coordination of marketing activities, motivation of the personnel performing these activities, and proper communication flow within the marketing organization.

Coordination

To achieve marketing objectives, marketing managers must coordinate the activities of all who participate in the marketing program. Coordination requires that marketing managers work closely with managers in research and development, production, finance, accounting, and personnel to synchronize marketing activities with other functions of the firm. Without coor-

---

[22] Paul R. Lawrence, Harvey F. Kolodny, and Stanley M. Davis, "The Human Side of Matrix Organizations," *Organizational Dynamics,* September 1977, p. 4.
[23] Stanley M. Davis and Paul R. Lawrence, *Matrix* (Reading, Mass.: Addison-Wesley, 1977).
[24] Stanley M. Davis and Paul R. Lawrence, "Problems of Matrix Organizations," *Harvard Business Review,* May–June 1978, pp. 131–142.
[25] "Dow Draws Its Matrix Again—and Again, and Again," *The Economist,* August 5, 1989, pp. 55–56.

FIGURE 21.6
Coordination
It takes coordination between many different departments to develop products that meet customer expectations. Intergraph computer graphics system helps firms use an integrated product development approach.

Source: Compliments of Intergraph Corporation.

These Projects All Came Together Because Different Departments Could All Work Together.

Colgate-Palmolive uses an Intergraph system to create photorealistic models of new packaging concepts.   *Brown & Root used Intergraph's InRoads software to redesign this highway interchange in Orange County, California.*   *Puolimatka International of Turku, Finland used Intergraph's architecture and visualization software to design hotel interiors.*   *Using Intergraph's Engineering Modeling System, FASCO Industries (Consumer Products Division) reduces costly prototyping.*

These days, it takes groups of specialists to usher a product from its initial conception to its ultimate completion. And that assumes they're able to work together in a close, cooperative relationship to get the job done.

But consider the obstacles in their path.

Each group may be working with a different hardware system. Each may depend upon a different database. And to make matters worse,

the groups may be scattered, not just across the country, but over the entire globe.

And now you know why Intergraph computer graphics systems play such a key role in product development for so many of the world's best known companies.

No one promotes enterprise-wide integration as thoroughly as Intergraph. No one. You see, our workstations, systems software and

networking tools all work together. In addition, we offer the broadest portfolio of technical applications in the computer graphics industry. And Intergraph systems are compatible with a wide range of industry standards. So the investments our customers have made—both in time and money—are secure.

If your company could benefit from an integrated approach to product development—

one that helps you get to market faster with products that are both better designed and engineered—call us toll-free in the U.S. at **800-826-3515**. In Canada, call **403-250-6100**. We'll work together to make sure that your people can work together, too.

INTERGRAPH
Everywhere you look.

© 1991, Intergraph Corporation, Huntsville, AL 35894-0001. Intergraph is a registered trademark and Everywhere You Look is a trademark of Intergraph Corporation.

dination, the different departments may not be pursuing common objectives. For instance, the production department may be building new automobiles with larger engines when research conducted by the marketing department suggests that consumers want vehicles that are more fuel-efficient. A dramatic example of coordination is United Technologies' test facility. There, the efforts of the research, product development, and marketing departments are coordinated to create technologically advanced products that meet customers' present and future needs. As you can see in Figure 21.6, some firms market computer systems that help different departments work together.

Marketing managers can improve coordination by making each employee aware of how one job relates to others and how one person's actions contribute to the achievement of marketing objectives. Moreover, marketing managers must coordinate the marketing department's activities with the efforts of external organizations such as advertising agencies, wholesalers and retailers, researchers, and shippers.

Motivation

Motivating marketing personnel to perform effectively is another important element in implementing the marketing plan. Motivation can be viewed as a process involving three basic elements: an unsatisfied need, goal-directed behavior, and need satisfaction. The process begins with the unsatisfied physical, psychological, or social need. The unsatisfied need causes individuals to engage in some type of goal-directed behavior to satisfy the need. Achieving the goal satisfies the need and completes the motivation process.

Marketing managers can motivate employees to be more productive by identifying employees' goals and providing some means for employees to attain their individual goals as well as rewards for satisfactory performance. The plan for motivating personnel must be fair, must provide incentives, and must be understood by employees. In devising a plan for motivating employees, managers must remember that what represents a small reward or achievement of a minor goal for one employee may be the realization of a lifelong dream for someone else. Thus programs for motivating employees (often the responsibility of a human relations department) should allow for achievement of individual goals. Individual differences take on increased significance as the work force becomes more diverse. Motivation programs must be targeted at many different workers with a variety of aspirations and goals.

The degree to which a manager can motivate personnel can certainly influence the success of marketing efforts. Obviously, pay is an important motivator, but it is not the only motivator. Workers today are becoming increasingly concerned with job *quality*—the opportunity for personal growth and achievement. *Job enrichment* programs that give employees a sense of autonomy and control over their work, allow room for greater personal achievement and recognition, provide added challenges and responsibility, and promote individual advancement and growth are useful in motivating employees.[26] For example, salespeople's motivation is higher in jobs where they perform a variety of activities and can see the results of their work.[27]

Communication

Marketing managers cannot motivate personnel or coordinate their efforts without proper communication. Figure 21.7 illustrates a few possible communication flows. Communication with top-level executives keeps the marketing department aware of the company's overall objectives. It also provides guidance for the marketing department and directs how marketing activities are to be integrated with the activities of other departments. For instance, the vice president of marketing must work with the vice president of production to help design products that customers need and will want to buy. Top-level marketing executives must also communicate with marketing managers at the operations level, such as the sales, advertising, research, and distribution managers. Finally, managers at the operations level must communicate with each other and with those above and below them in the organizational hierarchy.

To foster communication among marketing managers, sales managers, sales personnel, and others, an information system should be instituted within the marketing department. The information system should support a variety of activities, such as planning, budgeting, sales analysis, performance evaluation, and report preparation. It should also facilitate communications with other departments in the organization and reduce unhealthy competition for resources among departments.

[26] Frederick Herzberg, "One More Time: How Do You Motivate Employees?" *Harvard Business Review,* January–February 1968, p. 53.
[27] Alan J. Dubinsky and Steven J. Skinner, "Impact of Job Characteristics on Retail Salespeople's Reactions to Their Jobs," *Journal of Retailing,* Summer 1984, pp. 35–62.

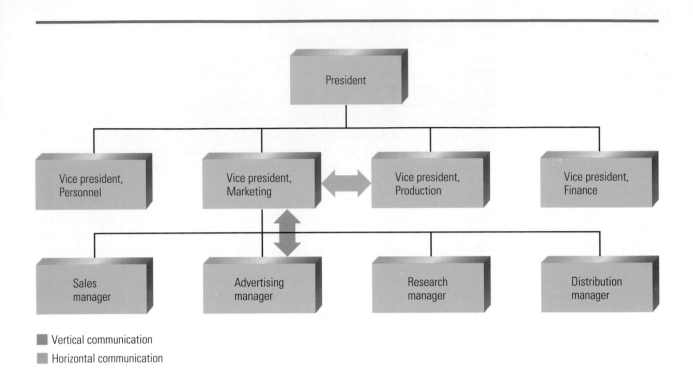

■ Vertical communication
■ Horizontal communication

FIGURE 21.7
Communication Flows

■ **internal marketing** the
process by which all mem-
bers of the organization
come to understand the values of the marketing system
and their role in implementing marketing strategies

INTERNAL MARKETING

Many of the marketing activities and ideas used to satisfy consumers can be
used *within* an organization to help implement the marketing program. **Internal marketing** is the process by which all members of the organization
(marketing and nonmarketing) come to understand the values of the marketing system and their role in implementing marketing strategies. Unless employees participate in implementing these strategies, quality cannot be "job
one" at Ford, the Maytag serviceperson cannot be the "loneliest person in
the world," and your local bank cannot be your "friendly" bank. Everyone—
from the assembly-line worker to the chief executive officer, from the teller
to the bank president—must perform his or her job effectively if marketing
strategies are to be implemented. Any one individual—an unfriendly receptionist, an incompetent technician, or an unmotivated salesperson—can reduce customer satisfaction.

Marketing strategies cannot be implemented without the cooperation of
employees. Thus internal marketing involves attracting, motivating, and retaining qualified internal customers (employees) by designing internal products (jobs) that satisfy employees' wants and needs.[28] The next sections discuss internal customers, internal products, and discretionary effort and peak
performance by employees.

[28]James H. Donnelly, Jr., Leonard L. Berry, and Thomas O. Thompson, *Marketing Financial
Services* (Homewood, Ill.: Dow Jones-Irwin, 1985), pp. 229–245.

Internal Customers

internal customer an employee in an organization

Just as organizations compete for external customers, so they also compete for the best internal customers. Each of an organization's employees is considered an **internal customer.** The first step toward customer satisfaction is to get employees to focus inward and satisfy internal customers. The extent to which a firm is successful in satisfying its internal customers will influence its ability to satisfy its external customers. An organization must sell its goods, services, or ideas to its employees before marketing these products to customers. Regardless of the job, every employee is a link in a chain of internal customers and suppliers that eventually leads to the external customer.[29] Stated another way, if the employees do not believe in the firm's products, how can customers be expected to believe in and purchase these same products? What would customers think about a restaurant if a waiter or waitress told them, "I never eat here"? When James Near became president of Wendy's, he learned that store managers were getting no respect from corporate headquarters and were passing their frustrations along to the crew. Feeling unappreciated, the crew made customers feel the same way. The customers cast their vote—for other restaurants.[30]

Many of the activities associated with marketing to external customers—market segmentation, marketing research, advertising, pricing, and so on—can be applied to an organization's internal customers. For instance, advertising can be used to communicate a firm's message to employees as well as to customers.[31] Figure 21.8 illustrates how an advertisement can be used to motivate employees to provide high-quality service.

Internal Products

internal product a job in an organization

A job is an **internal product** of an organization. If an organization expects to effectively implement its marketing program, it must develop internal products that are worth buying. People shop for jobs just as they shop for goods or services. People "buy" the jobs that are more attractive than available alternatives. The Public Agenda Foundation (a nonprofit research organization) reported that people want the following qualities in a job:

An environment in which workers are treated with respect

Interesting work

Recognition for good work

A chance to develop skills

An opportunity to work with people who listen to your ideas

A chance to think for yourself

A chance to see the end results of your work

[29] Chris Lee, "The Customer," *Training,* July 1991, pp. 21–26.
[30] James W. Near, "Wendy's Successful 'Mop Bucket Attitude,' " *Wall Street Journal,* April 27, 1992, p. A2.
[31] Franklin Acito and Jeffrey D. Ford, "How Advertising Affects Employees," *Business Horizons,* February 1980, pp. 53–59.

FIGURE 21.8
Internal Marketing
This advertisement from Southwest Airlines not only communicates to the external customer, it tells internal customers they are a critical part of the organization. It also tells employees that Southwest Airlines is a fun place to work.

Source: Courtesy Southwest Airlines.
Photo: Mark Hanauer.

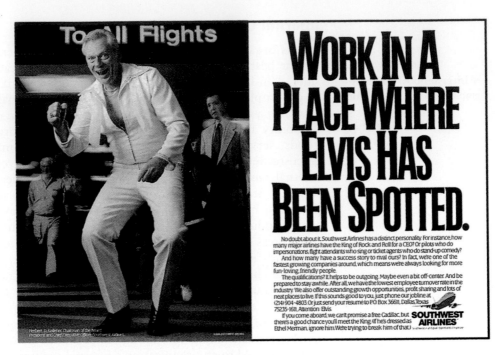

Efficient managers

Work that is not too easy

A feeling of being well-informed[32]

If organizations create jobs that satisfy employees' wants and desires, then employees' performance will improve.[33] Continuous improvement is a major aspect of total quality management programs.

Internal marketing continues after qualified internal customers have been recruited. The features of jobs (products) should be *remarketed*—that is, company values need to be perpetuated, superior performance recognized, and career growth opportunities made available. Internal customers, like valued external customers, must be given reasons for remaining with a firm. Employees must be continually reminded that they are valuable assets of the organization and must be provided with internal products that keep them with the firm. Close to the Customer illustrates how one firm understands the importance of internal marketing.

Discretionary Effort and Peak Performance

Successful internal marketing creates a company environment in which employees can achieve their true potential. **Discretionary effort** is the difference between the minimum amount of energy a worker must expend to keep

■ **discretionary effort**
the difference between the minimum amount of energy a worker must expend to keep from being penalized or reprimanded and the maximum amount of energy an employee can bring to a job

---

[32] Daniel Yankelovich and John Immerwahr, *Putting the Work Ethic to Work,* Public Agenda Foundation, New York, NY, 1983, p. 23. Reprinted by permission.
[33] W. Earl Sasser and Stephen P. Arbeit, "Selling Jobs in the Service Sector," *Business Horizons,* June 1976, pp. 61–65.

FIGURE 21.9
Graph Depicting
Discretionary Effort
and Peak Performance

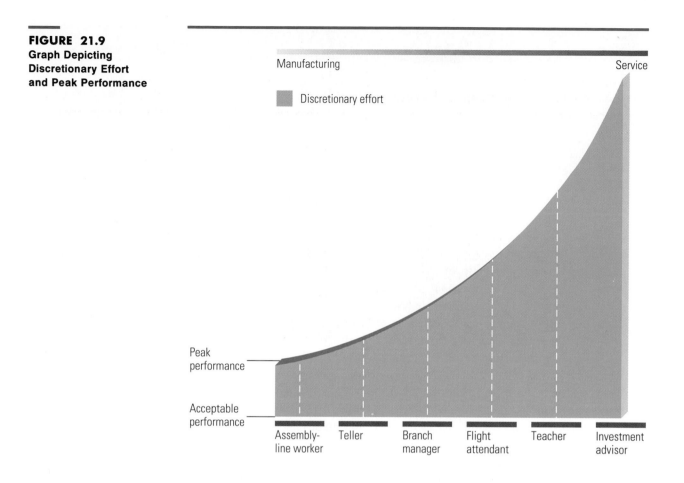

from being penalized or reprimanded and the maximum amount of energy an employee can bring to a job.[34] Discretionary effort is the difference between a flight attendant who does enough to get by and one who brings the maximum amount of labor and service to the job. The opportunity for discretionary effort varies according to the type of work different people perform (see Figure 21.9). For example, workers on an assembly line do not have the chance to bring a great deal of discretionary effort to the job because machines generally dictate the workers' output. In contrast, investment advisors have a much greater opportunity for discretionary effort in their profession.

Peak performance, the highest level of performance an employee can achieve, results when a worker surpasses acceptable performance by exerting discretionary effort.[35] As shown in Figure 21.9, service jobs allow for much more discretionary effort than do manufacturing jobs. As the number of service jobs continues to grow nationally, designing internal marketing activities to increase discretionary effort will become more important.

■ **peak performance** the highest level of performance an employee can achieve, which results when a worker surpasses acceptable performance by exerting discretionary effort

[34]James H. Donnelly, Jr., and Steven J. Skinner, *The New Banker: Developing Leadership in a Dynamic Era* (Homewood, Ill.: Dow Jones-Irwin, 1989), pp. 21–24.
[35]Ibid., pp. 21–24.

CLOSE TO THE CUSTOMER

Internal Marketing at Herman Miller

Herman Miller, Inc., is the design and engineering leader in the office furniture industry. In the 1960s, Herman Miller innovated the open office system. Consisting of shoulder-high "cubicles" that create a private atmosphere for their occupants, the open office system has become the standard in office design. In 1981, the American Institute of Architecture presented Herman Miller an award for its influence in office design. A chair made by Herman Miller is part of the permanent collection of the Museum of Modern Art in New York City. The firm's most recent innovation is its Relay line of office furniture, which features individual pieces that are light and movable. The purpose of Relay is to turn the office into a friendly environment in which furniture can be easily adjusted and changed around.

Founded by D. J. DePree in Zeeland, Michigan, in 1923, Herman Miller has always strived to be a design leader, not necessarily a market-share leader. (It is second in sales and profits to Steelcase.) To retain its reputation for designing innovative office products, Herman Miller spends roughly twice the industry average on research and design. The firm also strives to be a pleasant place to work. Herman Miller is innovative not only in its product line but also in its approach to its employees.

From the day that he started the company, D. J. DePree understood the importance of nurturing his employees' commitment to the mission of the organization. DePree's two sons, Hugh and Max, followed their father's example when it came their turn to run the business. Current chairman Max DePree states the company's mission as employees "attempting to share values, ideals, goals, respect for each person, the process of our work together." Recently named to the National Business Hall of Fame,

DePree believes that investing in employees always pays off.

This philosophy is evident in how the company treats its designers. To attract and retain talented people—such as Charles Eames, George Nelson, Gilbert Rohde, and Robert Propst—the company created a stimulating work environment (the "design yard") to make workers feel at home. Max DePree thinks it is critical not only to give employees the skills and motivation they need to be successful performers but also to enable them to enjoy their work. Then they will perform at their highest capabilities.

Jobs at Herman Miller are designed with the employee in mind. Manufacturing plants are brightly decorated, with artwork showing men and women at work. And long before participative management became popular, Herman Miller created "work teams," a bonus system that rewards employees who perform well. The latest job product is the "silver parachute." In the event of a hostile takeover, all plant workers who lose their jobs will receive big checks, just as the managers will.

Companies with good reputations have the competitive advantage of being able to attract the most talented workers, and Herman Miller has a good reputation. In *Fortune*'s annual survey of America's most admired corporations, Herman Miller has been number one for several years. Herman Miller recognizes that employees are customers and knows the advantage of staying close to "internal" customers.

Sources: Jennifer Reese, "America's Most Admired Corporations," *Fortune*, February 8, 1993, pp. 44–53; David Woodruff, "Office Furniture, As You Like It," *Business Week*, June 8, 1992, p. 61; "The National Business Hall of Fame," *Fortune*, March 23, 1992, pp. 112–119; Kenneth Labich, "Hot Company, Warm Culture," *Fortune*, February 27, 1989, pp. 74–78; and Dana Wechsler, "A Comeback in Cubicles," *Forbes*, March 21, 1988, pp. 54–56.

Naturally, most firms are interested in encouraging peak performance. But this is quite difficult because the key to peak performance—discretionary effort—is not easily controlled by managers. Sometimes teachers, lawyers, clerks, or construction workers are satisfied with acceptable performance, and their students, clients, and customers also accept it. According to a study conducted by the Public Agenda Foundation, only 23 percent of American workers believe they are working at full potential, and 44 percent say they do not put any more effort into their jobs than what is required.[36] But as the competition among firms grows more and more intense, organizations are learning, often the hard way, that acceptable performance is no longer enough. To convert a solid employee into an aggressive competitor, the organization must not only value better performance but also encourage a commitment to performance, year after year.[37]

The concept of internal marketing is also relevant for business-to-business marketers.[38] Many firms that market products to organizational customers realize the importance of service in their strategic marketing efforts. They also realize that customer satisfaction starts with employees. Internal marketing is useful in helping employees understand and accept the importance of interactions with organizational customers and their responsibility for the total quality performance of the firm. At Chaparral Steel, peak performance is encouraged by unleashing worker creativity. Workers receive a salary and bonus based on individual performance, company profits, and new skills learned. They forego punching a clock and set their own lunch hours and breaks. In return for freedom and trust, workers are expected to take the initiative needed to get the job done.[39]

CONTROLLING MARKETING STRATEGIES

■ **controlling** the process through which marketing performance is planned and evaluated

To achieve both marketing objectives and general organizational objectives, marketing managers must effectively control marketing efforts. **Controlling,** the process through which marketing performance is planned and evaluated, consists of three steps:

1. Establishing performance standards
2. Evaluating actual performance by comparing it with established standards
3. Taking corrective action to reduce discrepancies between desired and actual performance

The first step in the marketing control process entails planning what is to be accomplished. For purposes of control, these plans include statements that

---

[36] Yankelovich and Immerwahr, pp. 6–7.
[37] Andrall E. Pearson, "Tough-minded Ways to Get Innovative," *Harvard Business Review,* May–June 1988, pp. 99–106.
[38] M.P. Singh, "Services as a Marketing Strategy: A Case Study at Reliance Electric," *Industrial Marketing Management,* August 1990, pp. 193–199.
[39] Brian Dumaine, "Unleash Workers and Cut Costs," *Fortune,* May 18, 1992, p. 88.

■ **performance standard**
an expected level of performance against which actual
performance can be com-
pared

serve as performance standards. A **performance standard** is an expected
level of performance against which actual performance can be compared. For
example, a performance standard might require an increase in annual sales
of 10 percent or a monthly sales quota of $100,000. Performance standards
can be applied to budget amounts; in other words, a marketer might be
expected to achieve a certain objective without spending more than a given
amount of resources. Performance standards can also relate to product quality
or service.

The second step in controlling is evaluating whether actual performance
measures up to performance standards. Records of the actual performance of
both operations and management personnel are compared with performance
standards to ascertain whether and how much of a discrepancy exists. For
example, a sales manager compares a salesperson's actual sales with his or
her sales quota.

When there are significant negative discrepancies between actual performance and performance standards, managers should take corrective action, the
third step in the controlling process. At this point, marketing managers have
several options. They can take corrective actions to improve actual performance, to reduce or change the performance standard, or to do both. To
improve actual performance, the marketing manager may need to use better
methods of motivating personnel or more effective techniques for coordinating marketing efforts and communication with marketing personnel. However, the marketing manager may instead decide that the performance standards are unrealistic as written or that changes in the marketing environment
have made the performance standards unrealistic. For instance, a firm's annual sales quota may become unrealistic because of increased competition in
the market. In these instances, marketing managers may need to revise the
performance standards.

METHODS OF PERFORMANCE EVALUATION

Controlling marketing strategies requires assessing the effectiveness of the
strategies. The following sections describe three methods for evaluating the
performance of marketing strategies: sales analysis, marketing cost analysis,
and the marketing audit.

Sales Analysis

■ **sales analysis** a method
for controlling marketing
strategies whereby sales
figures are used to assess
an organization's current
performance

Sales analysis relies on sales figures to assess an organization's current performance. Sales analysis is probably the most common method of evaluation
because sales data are readily available in most organizations and because
such data provide some indication as to the target market's reactions to a
marketing mix. The fundamental unit of measurement in sales analysis is the
sales transaction—a customer order for a specified quantity of an organization's

product sold under specified terms by a particular salesperson or sales group on a certain date.

Current sales transaction data can certainly be used to monitor the impact of current marketing efforts. But that information alone is insufficient. To provide a useful basis for analysis, the current sales data must be compared with forecasted sales, industry sales, specific competitors' sales, or the costs incurred to achieve the sales volume. For instance, when the marketing manager knows that a firm's sales were forecasted to be $400,000 but actual sales were only $300,000, he or she is in a better position to gauge the effectiveness of the firm's marketing strategy.

Sales can be analyzed on the basis of dollar volume or market share. *Dollar volume sales analysis* is often used because the dollar is the common denominator of sales, costs, and profits. However, when analyzing sales on the basis of dollar volume, the analyst must factor in the effect of price increases and decreases on total sales figures. For example, if a firm experiences a 5 percent increase in sales volume over the previous year but has increased its prices by 5 percent during the current year, it has not experienced any increase in unit sales. Thus a marketing manager using dollar volume sales analysis must take the effects of such price changes into account.

Businesses can also look at market share in sales analyses. *Market-share analysis* allows a firm to compare its marketing strategy with competitors' strategies by appraising its market share—its product sales stated as a percentage of industry sales of that product. Market-share analysis can indicate whether sales changes have resulted from the firm's marketing strategy or from uncontrollable environmental forces. For instance, if a company's sales volume has declined but its share of the market is stable, the marketer can reasonably assume that industry sales have declined, probably because of some uncontrollable factor in the environment, and that this overall decline was reflected in the firm's sales. Conversely, if both the firm's sales and market share have declined, management should consider the possibility that the decline is the result of an ineffective or improperly implemented marketing strategy.

Marketing Cost Analysis

Sales analysis, although very important in evaluating the effectiveness of a marketing strategy, provides management with only part of the picture. To obtain a more complete picture, the firm must also scrutinize the marketing costs associated with using a given strategy to achieve a certain sales level. Using **marketing cost analysis,** the marketing manager breaks down and classifies costs to determine which are associated with specific marketing activities. By comparing the costs of previous marketing activities with the results achieved, marketers can more efficiently allocate the firm's marketing resources in the future. To evaluate the effectiveness of a current or recent marketing strategy, the manager compares its costs with the sales achieved. By identifying the areas in which a firm is experiencing high costs, marketing cost analysis can help businesses isolate profitable or unprofitable market segments or products.

■ **marketing cost analysis** a method for controlling marketing strategies whereby various costs are broken down and classified to determine which are associated with specific marketing activities

FIGURE 21.10
Marketing Cost Analysis
Andersen Consulting, a division of Arthur Andersen, offers cost analysis services that can help firms evaluate their performance.

Source: Reprinted with permission of Andersen Consulting.

Just don't expect it to roar.

In an effort to become swifter and more ferocious, many organizations may be tempted to make superficial changes. But this approach will rarely improve performance. Especially when information technology is part of the plan. Which is why Andersen Consulting

works with companies to link technology to the heart of their business. Their strategies, operations and human resources. Because these days, becoming a more aggressive competitor often means transforming the organization. And not just hopping on a technological bandwagon.

ANDERSEN CONSULTING
ARTHUR ANDERSEN & CO., S.C.
Where we go from here.

Marketing cost analysis should begin with an examination of accounting records. Accounting records generally classify costs on the basis of how the money was actually spent—on rent, salaries and wages, supplies, utilities, insurance, and so on. These are called *natural accounts* because they are listed by type of expenditure rather than by purpose. For instance, a rent account reporting annual expenditures of $100,000 does not indicate to the analyst whether the $100,000 was spent on the rental of production, storage, or sales facilities. Consequently, when analyzing marketing costs, marketing managers often reclassify some of the costs in natural accounts into *functional accounts,* which indicate the purpose of the expenditures. Common functional accounts include transportation, storage, order processing, selling, advertising, sales promotion, marketing research, and customer credit. As shown in Figure 21.10, accounting firms offer services that assist companies with this type of analysis.

In reclassifying the costs in natural accounts into functional accounts, the manager must consider three broad cost categories: direct costs, traceable common costs, and nontraceable common costs. A **direct cost** is directly attributable to the performance of a specific marketing activity. For example, the expense of television, magazine, and direct mail advertisements might be reported as the cost of selling a specific product. A **traceable common cost** can be attributed indirectly to a marketing function. For instance, the cost of hiring a support salesperson to answer customer questions and address

■ **direct cost** a cost that is directly attributable to the performance of a specific marketing activity

■ **traceable common cost** a cost that can be attributed indirectly to a marketing activity

■ **nontraceable common cost** a cost that cannot be ascribed to a specific marketing activity on the basis of any logical criterion and thus is assignable only on an arbitrary basis

■ **full-cost approach** an approach to determine marketing costs that includes direct costs, traceable common costs, and nontraceable common costs

■ **direct-cost approach** an approach to determining marketing costs that includes direct costs and traceable common costs but excludes nontraceable common costs

■ **marketing audit** a thorough, systematic, and objective review of an organization's marketing objectives, philosophy, strategies, organization, and performance

customer complaints through a toll-free number would be a traceable common cost allocated to the cost of selling a particular product or product line. A **nontraceable common cost,** however, cannot be ascribed to a specific marketing function on the basis of any logical criterion and thus is assignable only on an arbitrary basis. Examples of nontraceable common costs include interest, taxes, and the salaries of top management.

The extent to which the three categories of costs are considered in marketing cost analyses depends on whether the analyst uses a full-cost or direct-cost approach. With the **full-cost approach,** marketing cost analysis includes direct costs, traceable common costs, and nontraceable common costs. Supporters of the full-cost approach argue that all costs must be included in the analysis if an accurate profit picture is to be obtained. Opponents point out that, because nontraceable common costs are determined by arbitrary criteria, the full-cost approach does not yield actual costs. Using different criteria for nontraceable costs, the full-cost approach produces different results. Because of these inconsistencies, analysts may use the **direct-cost approach,** which includes direct costs and traceable common costs but excludes nontraceable common costs. Some critics of the direct-cost approach claim that it cannot be accurate because it omits one cost category.

The Marketing Audit

The final method of performance evaluation is the **marketing audit**—a thorough, systematic, and objective review of an organization's marketing objectives, philosophy, strategies, organization, and performance. The marketing audit highlights what activities the organization does well, helps pinpoint problems in executing marketing activities, and makes recommendations for improving the performance of these activities.[40] Marketing audits should be conducted regularly, perhaps annually or semiannually.

Table 21.1 lists many possible dimensions that analysts may examine in a marketing audit, including the marketing environment, the marketing strategy, the organization of the marketing department, the marketing information system, and productivity. A marketing audit may focus on all of a company's marketing activities or on only a few specific activities. The extent of the marketing audit depends on the costs involved, the target markets served, the composition of the marketing mix, and environmental conditions. The results of the audit may indicate that the organization should consider changing marketing strategies, focusing marketing efforts on a different market, altering the marketing mix, re-examining marketing opportunities, or taking some other action.

Marketing audits may be conducted by people within the organization or by outside consultants. A top-level marketing executive, a companywide auditing committee, or a manager from another department may serve as an internal marketing auditor. Although an audit by outside consultants is more expensive, organizations normally prefer to hire outside auditors because

[40] Philip Kotler, William Gregor, and William Rogers, "The Marketing Audit Comes of Age," *Sloan Management Review,* Winter 1977, pp. 25–43.

Part I. The Marketing Environment Audit

Macroenvironment

A. Economic-demographic
1. What does the company expect in the way of inflation, material short-ages, unemployment, and credit availability in the short run, intermediate run, and long run?
2. What effect will forecasted trends in the size, age distribution, and regional distribution of population have on the business?

B. Technological
1. What major changes are occurring in product technology? In process technology?
2. What are the major generic substitutes that might replace this product?

C. Political-legal
1. What are some of the laws being proposed that may affect marketing strategy?
2. What federal, state, and local agency actions should be watched? What is happening with pollution control, equal employment opportunity, product safety, advertising, price control, etc. that is relevant to marketing planning?

D. Cultural
1. What attitude is the public taking toward business and the types of products produced by the company?
2. What changes in consumer lifestyles and values have a bearing on the company's target markets and marketing methods?

E. Ecological
1. Will the cost and availability of natural resources directly affect the company?
2. Are there public concerns about the company's role in pollution and conservation? If so, what is the company's reaction?

Task Environment

A. Markets
1. What is happening to market size, growth, geographical distribution, and profits?
2. What are the major market segments and their expected rates of growth? Which are high opportunity and low opportunity segments?

B. Customers
1. How do current customers and prospects rate the company and its competitors on reputation, product quality, service, sales force, and price?
2. How do different classes of customers make their buying decisions?
3. What evolving needs and satisfactions are the buyers in the market seeking?

C. Competitors
1. Who are the major competitors? What are the objectives and strategies of each major competitor? What are their strengths and weaknesses? What are the sizes and trends in market share?
2. What trends can be foreseen in future competition and substitutes for this product?

D. Distribution and dealers
1. What are the main marketing channels bringing products to customers?

(continued)

2. What are the efficiency levels and growth potentials of the different channels?

E. Supplies

   1. What is the outlook for the availability of key resources used in production?

   2. What trends are occurring among suppliers in their patterns of selling?

F. Facilitators and marketing firms

   1. What is the outlook for the cost and availability of transportation services?

   2. What is the outlook for the cost and availability of warehousing facilities?

   3. What is the outlook for the cost and availability of financial resources?

   4. How effectively is the advertising agency performing? What trends are occurring in advertising agency services?

G. Publics

   1. What are the opportunity areas or problems for the company?

   2. How is the company effectively dealing with publics?

Part II. Marketing Strategy Audit

A. Business mission

   1. Is the business mission clearly focused with marketing terms and is it attainable?

B. Marketing objectives and goals

   1. Are the corporate objectives clearly stated? Do they lead logically to the marketing objectives?

   2. Are the marketing objectives stated clearly enough to guide marketing planning and subsequent performance measurement?

   3. Are the company's objectives appropriate, given the company's competitive position, resources, and opportunities? Is the appropriate strategic objective to build, hold, harvest, or terminate this business?

C. Strategy

   1. What is the core marketing strategy for achieving the objectives? Is it sound?

   2. Are the resources budgeted to accomplish the marketing objectives inadequate, adequate, or excessive?

   3. Are the marketing resources allocated optimally to prime market segments, territories, and products?

   4. Are the marketing resources allocated optimally to the major elements of the marketing mix, i.e., product quality, service, sales force, advertising, promotion, and distribution?

Part III. Marketing Organization Audit

A. Formal structure

   1. Is there a high-level marketing officer with adequate authority and responsibility over those company activities that affect customer satisfaction?

   2. Are the marketing responsibilities optimally structured along functional, product, end user, and territorial lines?

(continued)

B. Functional efficiency
   1. Are there good communication and working relations between marketing and sales?
   2. Is the product-management system working effectively? Are the product managers able to plan profits or only sales volume?
   3. Are there any groups in marketing that need more training, motivation, supervision, or evaluation?
C. Interface efficiency
   1. Are there any problems between marketing and manufacturing, R&D, purchasing, finance, accounting, and legal that need attention?

Part IV. Marketing Systems Audit

A. Marketing information system
   1. Is the marketing information system producing accurate, sufficient, and timely information about developments in the marketplace?
   2. Is marketing research being adequately used by company decision makers?
B. Marketing-planning system
   1. Is the marketing-planning system well conceived and effective?
   2. Is sales forecasting and market-potential measurements soundly carried out?
   3. Are sales quotas set on a proper basis?
C. Marketing control system
   1. Are the control procedures (monthly, quarterly, etc.) adequate to ensure that the annual-plan objectives are being achieved?
   2. Is provision made to analyze periodically the profitability of different products, markets, territories, and channels of distribution?
   3. Is provision made to examine and validate periodically various marketing costs?
D. New-product development system
   1. Is the company well organized to gather, generate, and screen new product ideas?
   2. Does the company do adequate concept research and business analysis before investing heavily in a new idea?
   3. Does the company carry out adequate product and market testing before launching a new product?

Part V. Marketing-Productivity Audit

A. Profitability analysis
   1. What is the profitability of the company's different products, served markets, territories, and channels of distribution?
   2. Should the company enter, expand, contract, or withdraw from any market segments, and what would be the short- and long-run profit consequences?
B. Cost-effectiveness analysis
   1. Do any marketing activities seem to have excessive costs? Are these costs valid? Can cost-reducing steps be taken?

(continued)

Part VI. Marketing Function Audits
A. Products
   1. What are the product line objectives? Are these objectives sound? Is the current product line meeting these objectives?
   2. Are there particular products that should be phased out?
   3. Are there new products that are worth adding?
   4. Are any products able to benefit from quality, feature, or style modifications?
B. Price
   1. What are the pricing objectives, policies, and methods? Are prices set on sound cost, demand, and competitive criteria?
   2. Do the customers see the company's prices as being in or out of line with the perceived value of its products?
   3. Does the company use price promotions effectively?
C. Distribution
   1. What are the distribution objectives and strategies?
   2. Is there adequate distribution and service?
   3. How effective are the following channel members: distributors, manufacturers' reps, brokers, agents, etc.?
   4. Should the company consider changing its distribution channels?
D. Advertising, sales promotion, and publicity
   1. What are the organization's advertising objectives? Are they sound?
   2. Is the right amount being spent on advertising? How is the budget determined?
   3. Are the ad themes and copy effective? What do customers and the public think about the advertising?
   4. Are the advertising media well chosen?
   5. Is the internal advertising staff adequate?
   6. Is the sales promotion budget adequate? Is there effective and sufficient use of sales promotion tools, such as samples, coupons, displays, and sales contests?
   7. Is the publicity budget adequate? Is the public relations staff competent and creative?
E. Sales force
   1. What are the organization's sales force objectives?
   2. Is the sales force large enough to accomplish the company's objectives?
   3. Is the sales force organized along the proper principle(s) of specialization (territory, market, product)? Are there enough (or too many) sales managers to guide the field sales reps?
   4. Does the sales compensation level and structure provide adequate incentive and reward?
   5. Does the sales force show high morale, ability, and effort?
   6. Are the procedures adequate for setting quotas and evaluating performance?
   7. How does the company's sales force compare to the sales force of competitors?

Source: Philip Kotler, *Marketing Management: Analysis, Planning, and Control*, 7/e, © 1991, pp. 726–728. Reprinted by permission of Prentice-Hall, Inc., Englewood Cliffs, N.J.

they usually have more experience, are more objective, and have more time to conduct the audit.

There is no specific method for conducting marketing audits, but firms should heed several general guidelines. A step-by-step plan should be developed and followed to ensure that the audit is methodical and objective. Auditors should carefully design audit questionnaires—the basis of most marketing audits—to ensure that the appropriate issues are covered. When conducting the audit, auditors should attempt to interview a diverse group of people from many parts of the company. They should start the audit process with the firm's top management and then move down through the organizational hierarchy. After completing the audit, auditors should report the results in a comprehensive written document.

Despite their benefits, marketing audits pose several problems. They can be expensive in terms of time and money. Choosing an auditor may be difficult because objective, qualified personnel may not be available. Also, marketing audits can be quite unsettling for employees who fear comprehensive evaluations, especially by outsiders.

SUMMARY

Organizing involves the structuring of a company to connect and coordinate resources and activities to achieve marketing objectives in an effective and efficient manner. Designing a responsive and flexible organizational structure that is committed to quality and customer satisfaction is a major challenge facing marketing managers. The organizational structure of a marketing department establishes the lines of authority and responsibility among marketing personnel, specifying who makes certain decisions and performs particular activities. Authority is the organizationally sanctioned right to make a decision without the approval of a higher-ranking manager. In a centralized organization, most of the decisions are made by top-level managers; in a decentralized organization, decision-making authority is delegated as far down the chain of command as possible. Empowerment, at the heart of total quality management (TQM) programs, involves giving employees authority to make decisions or take action without prior approval from supervisors. The marketing department can be organized on the basis of functions, products, markets, or other alternatives such as a combination of functions or a matrix organization.

Implementing means putting marketing strategies into action. Proper implementation of marketing plans depends on coordination of marketing activities, motivation of marketing personnel, and effective communication within the department.

Internal marketing is the process by which all members of the organization come to understand the values of the marketing system and their role in implementing marketing strategies. Internal marketing involves attracting, motivating, and retaining qualified internal customers (employees) by designing internal products (jobs) that satisfy employees' wants and needs. Discretionary effort is the difference between the minimum amount of energy a worker must expend to keep from being penalized or reprimanded and the maximum amount of energy an individual can bring to a job. Peak performance results when a worker surpasses acceptable performance by exerting discretionary effort. Internal marketing activities should encourage peak performance among employees.

The process through which marketing performance is planned and evaluated is controlling; it consists of establishing performance standards, evaluating actual performance by comparing it with established standards, and taking corrective action to reduce discrepancies between desired and actual performance. Performance standards are expected levels of performance against which actual performance can be compared.

Controlling requires evaluating the effectiveness of marketing strategies through sales analysis, marketing cost analysis, and marketing audits. Sales analysis relies on sales figures to assess an organization's current performance. Sales may be analyzed on the basis of dollar volume or market share.

Marketing cost analysis breaks down and classifies costs to determine which are associated with specific marketing activities. It frequently requires a reclassification of natural accounts into functional accounts on the basis of three broad cost categories: direct costs, traceable common costs, and nontraceable common costs. The full-cost approach to marketing cost analysis includes direct costs, traceable common costs, and nontraceable common costs; the direct-cost approach includes only direct costs and traceable common costs.

A marketing audit is a thorough, systematic, and objective review of an organization's marketing objectives, philosophy, strategies, organization, and performance. A marketing audit attempts to identify what activities a marketing department is doing well, to pinpoint problems in executing these activities, and to recommend ways to improve these marketing activities.

KEY TERMS

organizing
organizational structure
authority
centralized organization
decentralized organization
empowerment
functional organization
product-oriented organization
market-oriented organization
matrix organization
team
implementing
internal marketing
internal customer

internal product
discretionary effort
peak performance
controlling
performance standard
sales analysis
marketing cost analysis
direct cost
traceable common cost
nontraceable common cost
full-cost approach
direct-cost approach
marketing audit

QUESTIONS FOR DISCUSSION AND REVIEW

1. What is the difference between a centralized and a decentralized organization?

2. What factors determine the extent to which an organization is centralized or decentralized?

3. How can organizations empower employees? Why is empowerment an important aspect of quality and customer satisfaction?

4. How is the marketing department structured in a functional organization? In a product-oriented organization?

5. What types of companies would utilize a market-oriented organization to structure the marketing department?

6. Which type of organizational structure is best for international firms? When would a firm use the matrix organization?

7. How can marketing managers coordinate the different individuals involved in the marketing program?

8. What are some ways in which typical marketing activities can be used within an organization? Give an example of a firm that practices internal marketing.

9. Why should marketing managers be concerned with discretionary effort and peak performance?

10. Why is it important to control marketing strategies?

11. What is the difference between sales analysis and market-share analysis?

12. What are the three types of costs used in marketing cost analysis? Give an example of each type.

13. What is a marketing audit? What are some guidelines that firms should use when conducting a marketing audit?

CASES

21.1 3M ORGANIZES FOR INNOVATION

St. Paul-based 3M has become known as a master in the art of innovation. From the time 3M inventor Francis G. Okie came up with the idea of selling sandpaper as a replacement for razor blades in 1922, 3M has been willing to try new ideas. Okie's idea didn't work, although he continued to sand his own face. But several of his other ideas became big hits. For instance, Okie developed a waterproof sandpaper that produced a better exterior finish on cars and created less dust than other papers. It became the standard of the industry and 3M's first major success.

Originally known as Minnesota Mining & Manufacturing Co., 3M originated with a mistake. In 1902, five Minnesotans bought a piece of land on the shores of Lake Superior, planning to mine corundum, an abrasive used to make sandpaper. But the corundum in the mine turned out to be a low-grade ore, of no use. The company had to innovate or go out of business. First, 3M introduced a successful abrasive cloth for metal finishing. Then Okie hit it big with his Wetordry sandpaper.

Today, 3M markets more than sixty thousand products, ranging from popular Post-it Notes to heart-lung machines; over 25 percent of the sales came from products introduced in the last five years. Because of this success, 3M is cited year after year as one of the top manufacturing firms in the country. Representatives of many other companies have visited 3M headquarters looking for ideas.

One of the secrets to 3M's success is an organizational structure that encourages and rewards new product innovation. 3M is a highly decentralized organization. Employees have the authority and the freedom to pursue new products. For instance, Post-it Note inventor Art Fry took advantage of a 3M policy that allows scientists to spend 15 percent of their time on personal projects—a policy that encourages innovation. At 3M, the responsibility for developing new products is delegated to young scientists, referred to as "product champions." It is the job of the general managers—"executive champions"—to protect the product champions from corporate distractions.

The primary unit of support for product champions at 3M is the "venture team." When a scientist comes up with a new product idea, he or she recruits full-time members of a venture team from marketing, sales, manufacturing, finance, and technical departments. The team has the responsibility for designing the product and developing a production and marketing plan. As the project moves toward the market, everyone in the group is promoted. The product champion is allowed to manage the project as if it were his or her own business. If the team succeeds and the product becomes an independent department, each team member becomes a manager for that department and receives a promotion and an increase in pay. All members of the team are highly motivated because the system rewards the team and the individual.

To encourage innovation, divisions at 3M are kept small, each averaging $200 million in sales. Each of the more than forty divisions is seen as a separate company, with its own profit-and-loss statement. Within each division, employees are never far from the top or the bottom, and are expected to share knowledge and ideas with one another. By organizing in this manner, 3M prevents its employees from feeling what many other companies' employees do: that what they do doesn't matter. Rather, they feel that what they do is important.

To encourage product innovations, 3M initiated the 25 percent rule. Each division is required to generate 25 percent of its sales from products introduced in the past five years. Meeting this rule is crucial at 3M, and managers take it seriously. Bonuses are tied closely to this performance standard.

3M's $2 billion health care business is developing a wide range of products to protect health care workers and help organizations comply with Occupational Safety and Health Administration (OSHA) standards. Under its Managing Total Quality (MTQ) program, 3M works with health care facilities to assess their quality standards and implement more efficient practices. The firm helps a facility conduct an audit to analyze its current state of quality, trains people who train their health care workers to implement the quality program, and evaluates the state of quality after MTQ has been implemented.

There is perhaps no single factor that makes innovation work at 3M. The product champion, the executive champion, the venture team, and the MTQ program are at the center of the process. But they work because the organizational structure is highly supportive of innovation and allows scientists the freedom to fail or to succeed.

Questions for Discussion

1. How would you describe 3M's organizational structure?

2. Why is the venture team an important part of product innovation at 3M? How does 3M motivate members of venture teams?

3. What is the 25 percent rule?

4. Explain 3M's Managing Total Quality program.

Based on information from Ronald A. Mitsch, "R&D at 3M: Continuing to Play a Big Role," *Research-Technology Management,* September–October 1992, pp. 22–26; Donald E.L. Johnson, "3M Is Working with Health Care Facilities to Implement Its Managing Total Quality Process," *Health Industry Today,* August 1992, pp. 8–10; Russell Mitchell, "Masters of Innovation," *Business Week,* April 10, 1989; and "Lessons from a Successful Intrapreneur," *Journal of Business Strategy,* March–April 1988, pp. 20–24.

21.2 VOLVO INVESTS IN WORKERS

In 1974, Volvo AB dismantled the assembly line at its plant in Kalmar, Sweden. The line was replaced with a system in which cars are built by small, decentralized work teams that produce sections of cars. Volvo officials believe strongly that teams will improve quality and increase the pride employees take in their work. In fact, the Swedish automaker believes so strongly in teamwork that this system is also being put into place at the company's new plant in Uddevalla.

The Uddevalla plant was completed in 1990 to build Volvo's 740 and 940 models. By the end of 1991, the plant was producing about 22,000 cars annually; at full capacity the plant will employ one thousand workers and produce 40,000 cars. At the Uddevalla facility, self-managed teams of eight to ten members assemble complete cars from start to finish. Cars being assembled are not moved on a conveyor line from worker to worker but rather are assembled in a stationary position. A special device tilts the car as needed so that workers can perform their tasks. Each team has a high degree of autonomy and responsibility; it sets its own break times and vacation schedules and reassigns work when a team member is absent. Teams also participate in policy-making decisions and are responsible for a variety of tasks, including controlling quality planning, production, developing work procedures, servicing equipment, and ordering supplies.

Workers at the Uddevalla plant are paid for performance. Bonuses are paid for maintaining quality and productivity and for meeting weekly delivery targets. There are no supervisors or plant foremen; each of six "production workshops" houses 80 to 100 employees who are divided into assembly teams. Each assembly team has a coordinator, chosen on a rotating basis, who has direct contact with the managers. To make sure the system works, employees are provided with abundant information. Volvo also ensures that workers have an understanding of company history, tradition, and strategy. The free flow of information is encouraged, and workers have input on everything from assembly processes to new product innovations.

The new system at Uddevalla has not been totally successful. Although morale is up and absenteeism is down, productivity is not as high as at Volvo's plant in Ghent, Belgium, where building a car on the assembly line takes about half the time. Lennert Ericsson, president of the Metal Workers union at the Uddevalla plant, thinks the approach there will work: "I am convinced that our ways [teams] will be successful and competitive. Our next goal is to be better than Kalmar, and when we get to that, our goal will be to get to Ghent."

Volvo has invested heavily in training workers at the Uddevalla plant. First, employees attend a 16-week initiation course, part of a 16-month training program in which workers learn about automobile assembly. Workers are encouraged to share experiences with one another and exchange ideas.

Both the union and management feel confident that the new system will lead to a better organization. But it will take time. The system puts numerous demands on everyone and has met with some resistance. Like other automakers, Volvo hasn't escaped the worldwide slump in automobile sales. However, several experts pick Volvo as the company to invest in once the economy rebounds. Stock in the firm climbed from 35 in early 1991 to 60 about a year later, while shares of GM, Ford, and Chrysler were still down from their 1991 highs. Investment firm Bear Stearns thinks the Swedish automaker's profits will boom. In the meantime, in its effort to become the world's first truly global automobile producer, Volvo has developed alliances with French automaker Renault and Japan's Mitsubishi.

Questions for Discussion

1. Does Volvo practice internal marketing? Explain.
2. What types of internal products does Volvo offer its employees?
3. Why is empowerment important at Volvo's Uddevalla facility?
4. How does Volvo's approach to employees help the firm implement its marketing strategy?

Based on information from Charles Garfield, *Second to None* (Homewood, Ill.: Business One Irwin, 1992), pp. 165–168; "Safe, Staid Volvo May Soon Be Burning Rubber," *Business Week,* January 27, 1992, p. 27; and Stewart Toy, Mark Maremont, and John Rossant, "Gentlemen, Start Your Mergers," *Business Week,* May 25, 1992, pp. 43–44.

Developing the Marketing Plan

22

OBJECTIVES

- *To discuss the importance of planning in marketing.*

- *To analyze the elements of a marketing plan.*

- *To develop a sample marketing plan.*

OUTLINE

Throughout the text we have discussed many different organizations, some that achieved success and some that suffered failures. Organizations such as Wal-Mart, Airbus, 3M, Herman Miller, and the Jacksonville Symphony Orchestra have developed and implemented successful marketing strategies. Others, including General Motors, IBM, Czechoslovak Airlines, and Sears, struggle amidst intense competition.

In retrospect, we have witnessed many classic product failures. Perhaps one of the most widely cited failures is the Ford Edsel, a case where the desired image was not translated into tangible features. More recently, Ford's Lincoln-Mercury division's failure with the Merkur was attributed to product and distribution problems. Another product that failed to catch on as expected was the videodisc. Although it offered better sound and picture quality, along with lower prices, the videodisc did not provide the recording ability that consumers wanted and that the videocassette recorder provides. Coca-Cola changed the formula of the most popular soft drink in the world, forgetting about the huge baby boom generation which accounted for much of the Coke sales. Coca-Cola eventually decided to bring back the original formula, called Classic Coke. RJR Nabisco invested millions of dollars in Premier smokeless cigarettes, only to drop the product shortly after introduction; the cigarette neither satisfied smokers nor appeased antismokers.

The list of product failures could go on and on. What can we learn from such mistakes? According to research, 85 percent of new product failures result from faulty implementation of the marketing plan. What should a company expect from its marketing plan? A marketing plan does not guarantee success, but it does do the following: places customers at the center of the firm's marketing activities, differentiates the firm from the competition, ensures quality, communicates the firm's expertise and knowledge to customers, and provides a long-term orientation.[1] ●

[1] Based on information from John R. Graham, "What a Company Should Expect from Its Marketing Plan," *Marketing News,* February 15, 1993, pp. 7, 14; Robert H. Kent, "The Road to Progress," *Canadian Manager,* September 1990, pp. 20–23; "Missing the Market," *American Demographics,* December 1989, pp. 16–21; and Peter Waldman, "RJR Nabisco Abandons 'Smokeless' Cigarette," *Wall Street Journal,* March 1, 1989, p. B1.

hapter 1 presents the foundations of strategic marketing, and Chapter 2 introduces the concept of strategic marketing planning. The chapters that follow discuss the environment for strategic marketing, analysis for strategic marketing decisions, product strategy, price strategy, distribution strategy, and promotion strategy. In this, the final section of the book, we discuss the importance of organizing, implementing, and controlling marketing strategies. This chapter is somewhat different from previous ones in that it doesn't introduce any new terms. Rather, it contains the glue that holds all of the different aspects of marketing together—the marketing plan.

PLANNING IN MARKETING

The late president Dwight Eisenhower once observed, "Plans are nothing, planning is everything." We defined *strategic marketing planning* as the continuous process of developing and implementing marketing strategies to achieve specific marketing objectives, which in turn lead to the achievement of an organization's overall objectives. Thus strategic marketing planning enables marketing managers to look ahead and chart a course of action for the future. The work of planning is basically mental, and this is no doubt what Eisenhower was referring to. For a plan to succeed, sound strategic thinking must proceed by putting words down on paper.

Strategic marketing planning does not guarantee success. But without a plan, managerial decisions are likely to be haphazard and unfocused and may not produce desired results. For many years, the Steel Company of Canada (Stelco) failed to reach expected sales with its revolutionary Ardox nail. Stelco shipped the nails to industrial distributors by the boxcar, but did not know who were the final customers buying and using the nails.[2] One reason for many business failures is poor planning or no planning at all. Lack of planning or inadequate plans lead to serious problems, such as the following:

- A firm does not know who its customers are.
- A firm does not have adequate resources to sustain operations.
- A firm markets an inferior product.
- A firm selects a poor location.

There are many reasons why marketing managers must plan. Planning establishes marketing objectives and helps provide the coordination needed for achieving the objectives. Planning can also ensure that successful marketing strategies will be designed and, in cases where marketing strategies fail, can help explain why. Planning can also be used to determine who is respon-

[2] Andrew Gross, Peter Banting, Lindsay Meredith, and David Ford, *Business Marketing* (Boston: Houghton Mifflin, 1993), p. 5.

sible for what job, what resources are necessary to get the job done, and what opportunities or problems face the product.

Although the importance of marketing planning may seem obvious, managers in many organizations fail to develop adequate plans. Strategic marketing planning is costly, time consuming, and difficult. Proper planning requires agreement among people from different backgrounds as to approach, patience to wait for results, and a commitment to often new and unproven strategies. Developing a plan can also be risky for managers because plans involve setting objectives. If these objectives are not met, a manager's performance may be questioned. These may seem like good reasons for not planning, but organizations simply cannot afford to follow such a course. Intense global competition, customers who demand quality, and a constantly changing marketing environment put tremendous pressure on organizations to develop sound marketing plans. Close to the Customer examines Frito-Lay's marketing planning efforts.

Defining the Marketing Plan

As we note in Chapter 2, a *marketing plan* is a formally prepared and written document detailing the activities necessary to implement the marketing strategies. In other words, a marketing plan is much like a road map showing where we are now, where we want to go, and how we will get there. The logical progression of this road map is followed in the process of developing a marketing plan.

First, the organization must assess its current position. This alone is an enlightening experience. It forces the firm to examine both the changes and trends in the marketing environment, and the opportunities and threats facing the product for which the plan is being developed. Second, the firm must decide where it wants to go—its marketing objectives. This will dictate the direction of the organization for the term covering the plan. Recall from our earlier discussion that short-range plans cover a period of one year or less, medium-range plans two to five years, and long-range plans more than five years. Third, the firm must decide how it will achieve the marketing objectives. This step involves developing marketing strategies and programs and a plan for implementing and controlling these strategies.

Responsibility for the Marketing Plan

Generally, the responsibility for preparing the marketing plan lies with a top-level marketing executive. This person's title could be vice president for marketing, director of marketing, product manager, or brand manager. In a smaller company, it would be the owner or marketing manager. In some cases, consultants outside the organization who specialize in developing marketing plans are called upon to provide assistance. Consultants bring not only their expertise to the organization but also a more unbiased approach. One of the major obstacles to successful planning is motivating members of the organization to commit to the plan and, in some cases, to a new approach.

CLOSE TO THE CUSTOMER

Marketing Planning at Frito-Lay

It would appear that Frito-Lay has little to worry about. The division of PepsiCo is the top firm in the $9 billion U.S. salty-snack market, with a 45 percent share. But only a few years ago, consumers of Frito-Lay's munchies like Doritos and Tostitos switched brands in large numbers as the company raised prices, held marketing expenditures constant, and ignored competitors' sales promotions. Frito-Lay also allowed lapses in quality, such as too many broken chips in each bag. As a result, competitors began to nibble away at Frito-Lay's market share.

The biggest threat comes from Anheuser-Busch's Eagle Snacks, which introduced products at prices up to 20 percent lower than Frito-Lay's. Still unprofitable and with only 6 percent of the market, Eagle turned out chips that outperformed Frito-Lay's offerings in taste tests. This intense competition drove Frito-Lay's profit margins from 21.4 percent in 1990 to 18.9 percent the following year. Although Frito-Lay was in no danger of sinking, the company had reason for alarm.

PepsiCo Worldwide Foods brought in a new president and CEO, Roger A. Enrico, to boost profits and market share. Enrico, the former president and CEO of PepsiCo Worldwide Beverages, came armed with a new marketing plan: cut costs and use the savings to boost quality, lower prices, and develop new products and far better promotion. First he reformulated the Doritos brand, then introduced a new advertising campaign for Lay's and Ruffles potato chips. For both brands, the company changed the packaging, cut the salt content, and switched from soybean oil to cottonseed oil to improve flavor. Basketball stars Larry Bird and Kareem Abdul-Jabbar were signed on to promote Lay's potato chips in the product's first network television commercials in ten years. The "Ruffles Have Ridges" slogan was replaced with "Get Your Own Bag."

The revised marketing plan has brought results. According to Nielsen Marketing Research, Frito-Lay's share of the $4.2 billion supermarket salty-snack market increased more than 1 point, to 42.3 percent, in a year. Operating profits jumped 15 percent in the first half of 1992, and the company expected to earn $800 million on $4 billion in sales for 1992, a 13 percent gain over 1991 profits. Enrico would like to see profit gains in the range of 10 to 12 percent annually. It won't be easy. Eagle Snacks is also posting impressive gains of its own and plans to introduce new tortilla chips and pretzels. That's why, as Enrico knows, planning is a long-term effort.

Sources: Wendy Zellner, "Frito-Lay Is Munching on the Competition," *Business Week*, August 24, 1992, pp. 52–53; Patricia Sellers, "If It Ain't Broke, Fix It Anyway," *Fortune*, December 28, 1992, pp. 49–50; and Jennifer Lawrence, "Enrico Makes His Mark on Frito-Lay," *Advertising Age*, May 18, 1992, p. 26.

It is the responsibility of the marketing executive to overcome this obstacle. The development of the marketing plan hinges on commitment from those at the highest levels of the organization.[3]

Although the top-level marketing executive is responsible for the marketing plan, this does not imply that one person writes the plan. The person

[3]Dean C. Minderman, "7 Steps to Marketing Plan Success," *Credit Union Management*, April 1992, pp. 42–44.

responsible for the plan should solicit input from throughout the marketing organization. Assuming a functional organization, the vice president for marketing should consult with the managers of marketing research, product development, distribution, sales, and advertising. In turn, each of these managers may consult with other individuals. The vice president may also talk with the vice presidents of other functional areas as well as the president, to make sure the marketing plan is consistent with the overall plan of the corporation. Planning is a team effort, and input from all areas is critical.

ELEMENTS OF A MARKETING PLAN

There is no single best format to follow in developing marketing plans. Some plans are longer than others, and one organization rarely uses the same format as another. But all marketing plans should follow the logical progression we referred to earlier: Where are we now? Where do we want to go? How do we get there? Our concern is with the answers to these questions, not the format used to write the plan.

Table 22.1 presents the elements of a typical marketing plan. These are the same elements introduced in Chapter 2. Here we provide more detail under each element, reflecting the knowledge you have acquired during the course. In this section, we examine each of these elements of an integrated marketing plan in detail.

Executive Summary

The executive summary is a two- to three-page synopsis of the marketing plan. Although the executive summary appears first, it is actually the last part of the marketing plan to be written and perhaps the most difficult part to write. The purpose of the summary is to provide executives with a brief

TABLE 22.1
The Marketing Plan

I.	Executive Summary
II.	Current Marketing Situation
	A. The marketing environment
	B. Target market analysis
III.	Opportunities and Problems
	A. Major opportunities facing the product
	B. Major problems facing the product
IV.	Marketing Objectives
V.	Marketing Strategies
	A. Target market strategy
	B. Marketing mix strategy
VI.	Action Programs
	A. Activities and responsibilities
	B. Timetables and budgets
VII.	Controls
	A. Financial projections
	B. Monitoring procedures

overview of the highlights of the plan. Some executives may not be directly involved in the development of the plan or may not have time to read the entire document. For example, a brand manager may not have time to read the plans developed by other brand managers, but may want to read the executive summary. Likewise, the president or vice presidents of other functional areas may read the executive summary to keep informed about the firm's marketing activities.

The executive summary should include a short introduction and brief highlights of each element of the marketing plan. The summary should present the major opportunities and threats facing the product as well as the marketing strategies that will be used to capitalize on the opportunities. It is also important to include some information about budgets and timetables in the summary. Executives will be interested in the investment required to implement the plan, how long it will take, and anticipated sales and profits.

The executive summary is an important part of the marketing plan. It may be the only document that a top-level executive reads in deciding whether to support the plan. Thus the authors of the marketing plan have to strike a proper balance between providing enough information and providing far too much detail in the executive summary. The summary (and the entire plan) should be written in language that is familiar to the audience. By knowing the target audience, the marketing planners can develop an executive summary that meets the needs of the target. Not only executives but bankers, stockholders, and suppliers also may read the marketing plan.

Current Marketing Situation

The first step in developing a marketing plan is to analyze the current marketing situation for the product or brand covered by the plan. The purpose of a situation analysis is to determine the firm's current position. The results of this analysis will influence the latter stages of the marketing plan. Two aspects of the current marketing situation should be examined: the marketing environment and the consumer or organizational market.

The Marketing Environment   An analysis of the marketing environment is a major consideration in strategic marketing planning. The forces in the marketing environment directly or indirectly influence a firm's marketing activities. In developing a marketing plan, the marketer should include relevant background data on all aspects of the marketing environment. Table 22.2 presents the sample format for summarizing data about the marketing environment.

The data for analyzing the marketing environment come from both internal and external sources. Environmental scanning involves collecting data on a regular basis and adding the data to the marketing information system (MIS). Information is gathered through observation; review of business, trade, and government publications; and marketing research. If data are not readily available within the organization through the MIS, additional information will have to be collected. In many cases, this phase of developing the plan illustrates to organizations the benefit of an ongoing program for managing and organizing data gathered from inside and outside the organization.

Target Market Analysis Another aspect of the current marketing situation that must be examined is the market. The marketing plan should include a detailed analysis of current target markets, including product usage and consumer behavior. Once again, the purpose of this part of the plan is to determine where the firm is now. Table 22.3 lists the major factors that should be examined.

Table 22.3 is fairly comprehensive, and some of this information may not be needed, depending on the specific product. If an organization *knows* its target market, much of this information should be readily available. Johnson Publishing Co., for instance, sells several cosmetics lines, including Ebone, targeted at black women 18 to 30 years old, and Fashion Fair, targeted at older women.[4] In reality, most firms have demographic and sales data. Many firms do not have psychographic and product-related information and may have to conduct marketing research to obtain it.

Opportunities and Problems

This element of the marketing plan presents a detailed summary of opportunities and problems—both inside and outside the organization—facing the product that the plan deals with. Many of these opportunities and problems are derived from the analysis of the current marketing situation. For instance, a projected growth in the market may be an opportunity, whereas a projected decline may be a problem. Other issues may also surface that were not included in the situation analysis, such as production, research and development, personnel, or a corporatewide issue like a financial constraint.

Opportunities are the result of strengths or positive circumstances. A firm's human and financial resources, as well as its unique experiences and expertise, can be strengths or opportunities. Any other positive circumstance, such as market growth, a strong brand name, a patent or copyright, customer loyalty, or relationships with suppliers, should be considered an opportunity. Air Products & Chemicals found an opportunity by concentrating on new markets where competition is not so intense, such as the frozen-food and semiconductor industries for nitrogen, the space program for hydrogen, and rail, truck, and bus markets for methane fuel.[5] Problems, on the other hand, stem from weaknesses or negative circumstances. Problems can be the result of personnel limitations, financial constraints, government regulation, competition, and any other circumstance that has a negative impact on the firm's ability to implement its marketing strategy. The *Chicago Tribune* and many other newspapers have encountered problems with competition from television, changing lifestyles which have led to a fragmented market, and national newspapers like *USA Today*.[6] The advertisement in Figure 22.1 shows how a firm is taking advantage of an opportunity that results from a new product innovation.

Each opportunity and problem that is identified should be written in a clear, concise statement, and a rationale for the opportunity or the problem

---

[4]"Publisher Launches Cosmetics Line," *Marketing News,* January 15, 1993, p. 27.
[5]James Cook, "Futurology," *Forbes,* May 11, 1992, pp. 91–97.
[6]Christopher Palmeri, "Hometown Coverage," *Forbes,* February 15, 1993, pp. 48–50.

TABLE 22.2
Analysis of the Marketing Environment

Competition

Who are our major competitors?

_____

_____

_____

What are their strengths and weaknesses?

_____   _____

_____   _____

What are their objectives and strategies?

_____   _____

_____   _____

Who are our future competitors?

_____

_____

_____

Regulation and Politics

What laws exist or are being proposed that may affect our product?

_____

_____

What federal, state, and local agency actions should be watched?

_____

_____

What is the general political tone in the industry, and how does it influence our product?

_____

_____

Society

What is the attitude of society toward our product?

_____

_____

_____

(continued)

should be provided. The purpose of the rationale is to provide supporting data. For example, the rationale for the projected growth rate opportunity we mentioned might state exactly how much the market is growing, where it is growing, and so on. Table 22.4 provides a format for presenting opportunities and problems.

The identification of opportunities that can be exploited and problems that must be solved is extremely important. Although opportunities and problems

What social trends are occurring that have an impact on our product?

_____

_____

_____

Are any special interest groups likely to affect our plan?

_____

_____

_____

Economic Conditions

What is the buying power of consumers in current markets?

_____

_____

_____

What are the spending patterns of consumers in current markets?

_____

_____

_____

What is projected in terms of inflation, recession, and recovery, and how will this affect our product?

_____

_____

_____

Technology

What major changes are occurring in technology that influence our product?

_____

_____

_____

How is technology helping us? How is it hurting us?

_____

_____

_____

do not tell the marketing manager what to do, they identify the areas that must be addressed through marketing strategies. Unless a proper marketing strategy is developed, opportunities are not seized. Likewise, problems can be overcome only if they are addressed through marketing strategy.

It is also important to note that a problem, when handled properly, can be an opportunity. Many writers on the subject of positive thinking advocate the position that behind every problem is an opportunity. This may not be

TABLE 22.3
Target Market Analysis

Demographics
  Sex _____
  Age _____
  Income _____
  Occupation _____
  Education _____
  Household size _____
  Ethnic background _____
  Family life cycle _____
Geography
  Climate _____
  Terrain _____
  Market density _____
  Natural resources _____
Psychographics
  Personality _____
  Motives _____
  Lifestyle (VALS) _____
Product-related
  Usage (heavy versus light) _____
  Application _____
  Benefits _____
Organizational markets
  Geographic location _____
  Type of organization _____
  Size of customer _____
  Product use _____
Size of Market
  Market sales potential _____
  Current company sales _____
  Market share _____
  Projected market growth (decline) _____
  Company sales forecast _____

 true in all marketing situations, but it certainly is in some. Many U.S. firms have viewed foreign competitors as a problem while failing to develop their own international efforts. Other firms saw international opportunities as a great way to expand their business. Consumer dissatisfaction can lead to an opportunity if marketers rush in and rectify the problem, as Marketing Close-up illustrates.

Marketing Objectives

The next component of the marketing plan is the marketing objectives. The purpose of marketing objectives is to specify what is to be accomplished

FIGURE 22.1
Opportunities
The introduction of the electric car will mean both opportunities and problems for many firms. While gas sales may suffer, Southern California Edison is already promoting the advantages of electric cars.

Source: © 1993 David DiMicco.

through marketing activities; marketing objectives identify where the firm wants to go. They state the goals of the firm in terms of sales volume, market share, profit, or other objectives for the marketing plan. They should also be consistent with the overall objectives of the organization.

Marketing objectives should be written in clear, concise terms so that everyone involved in implementing marketing strategies knows exactly what he or she is trying to accomplish. They should also be realistic or attainable. Specifically, marketing objectives should state what is to be accomplished, how much is to be accomplished, and when it is to be accomplished. Objectives should be written in such a way that managers can measure later whether or not they have been reached. For instance, a marketing objective may be stated in the following manner: to increase sales (what is to be accomplished) by 10 percent (how much is to be accomplished) within one year (when it is to be accomplished). Table 22.5 provides a sample worksheet for determining marketing objectives.

Marketing planners must also decide how many objectives to establish and the extent to which they are prioritized. The number of objectives must be limited so that important areas are given adequate attention. If a firm has twenty marketing objectives, can it realistically pursue all of them with the same vigor? It may be more realistic to develop three or four key objectives. Another approach is to develop as many objectives as the marketing planners think are appropriate, and set priorities. For example, many marketing plans have failed because the major objective was to make a profit. Of course, a

TABLE 22.4
Opportunities and Problems

Opportunity _____
_____

Rationale _____
_____

Opportunity _____
_____

Rationale _____
_____

Opportunity _____
_____

Rationale _____
_____

Problem _____
_____

Rationale _____
_____

Problem _____
_____

Rationale _____
_____

Problem _____
_____

Rationale _____
_____

Problem _____
_____

Rationale _____
_____

MARKETING CLOSE-UP

Lever 2000 Capitalizes on Problem

Lever Bros. makes a variety of soaps, including Lifebuoy, Dove, Caress, Shield, and Lux. One of the problems the company faced was that each of its soaps was identified by a single characteristic, such as facial quality, deodorant properties, or gentleness. Consumers therefore thought they had to buy two or more brands of soap, perhaps Dove for the face, Lifebuoy for the male body, and Lux for the female body.

In response to this problem, Lever introduced a multipurpose family soap called Lever 2000, named for "2,000 body parts." The soap also appeals to both women and men through advertising and sampling; many households have become convinced they can get by with one brand of soap instead of two or more. Not only did Lever overcome its problem, but for the first time ever, overcame industry leader Procter & Gamble by capturing a 31.5 percent market share in the $1.6 billion soap market, compared with P&G's 30.5 percent share.

P&G still sells more bars of soap, but Lever's brands cost more. And with sales of $113 million in its first year on the market, Lever 2000 is expected to take more share from P&G. According to an analyst at Paine Weber, Lever surpassed all competitors. Lever 2000's triple function, as a moisturizer, deodorizer, and bacteria killer, plus a marketing blitz that sent samples to half of all U.S. households, proves people will buy new brands when they satisfy a need.

Lever will face more and perhaps tougher threats in the future. Dial has developed its own three-in-one soap called Spirit, which is available in most major markets. P&G is putting major resources behind its New Ivory Ultra Safe Skin Care Bar, another potential alternative to Lever 2000. If test marketing goes well, P&G will introduce New Ivory nationally in hopes of taking some of the suds out of Lever 2000 sales.

Sources: Valerie Reitman, "Buoyant Sales of Lever 2000 Soap Bring Sinking Sensations to Procter & Gamble," *Wall Street Journal,* March 3, 1992, pp. B1, B5; Christopher Power, "Everyone Is Bellying Up to this Bar," *Business Week,* January 27, 1992, p. 84; and Jennifer Lawrence and Pat Sloan, "P&G Plans Big New Ivory Push," *Advertising Age,* November 23, 1992, p. 12.

firm has to make a profit. But if quality and customer satisfaction are sacrificed for profit, the marketing plan is likely to fail. Experts say many companies are going too far in cutting service in efforts to cut costs. Cost cutting often involves laying off employees that are a critical link to customer satisfaction.[7] The achievement of one marketing objective, in this case product quality, may lead to the achievement of another objective, profit.

Marketing Strategies

Throughout the book, we emphasize that marketing strategy involves selecting and analyzing a target market, and then developing a marketing mix for

[7]Cyndee Miller, "In Their Efforts to Cut Costs, Companies Also Cut Service," *Marketing News,* January 15, 1993, pp. 9–10.

TABLE 22.5
Marketing Objectives

Type of Objective	_____
Objective	_____
Desired result	_____
Time frame	_____
Type of Objective	_____
Objective	_____
Desired result	_____
Time frame	_____
Type of Objective	_____
Objective	_____
Desired result	_____
Time frame	_____
Type of Objective	_____
Objective	_____
Desired result	_____
Time frame	_____

the target market. Marketing strategy dictates how a firm will reach its desired destination. Marketing strategies should be developed that take advantage of opportunities and avoid problems, resulting in the achievement of the marketing objectives. In this section, we discuss the part of the marketing plan that deals with marketing strategies, both target market strategy and marketing mix strategy.

Target Market Strategy The target market analysis section of the marketing plan provides details about the target market strategy. This section of the plan must address exactly at whom the organization will direct its marketing efforts and which approach it will use. For instance, a firm may decide to use a concentration approach to target women aged 34 to 45. Table 22.6 provides a sample format for presenting the target market strategy.

The target market should be clearly defined in terms of those bases used to identify the target, such as demographics, psychographics, geography, product-related elements, and so on. The specific approach used to select the target market—total market, concentration, or multisegment—should be detailed. Finally, a rationale should be provided for the chosen target market strategy.

Marketing Mix Strategy This part of the marketing strategies component of the plan describes how product, price, distribution, and promotion will be used to satisfy the target market. Each of the four elements of the marketing mix must be discussed. Here the plan should provide details explaining the strategy for each marketing mix variable, as well as a rationale. Table 22.7 presents an approach for writing this section of the marketing plan.

TABLE 22.6
Target Market Strategy

Description of Target Market or Markets

_____
_____
_____
_____
_____

Approach for Selecting Target Market

_____
_____
_____
_____
_____

Rationale

_____
_____
_____
_____

TABLE 22.7
Marketing Mix Strategy

Product Strategies

_____

Rationale

_____

Price Strategies

_____

Rationale

_____

Distribution Strategies

_____

Rationale

_____

Promotion Strategies

_____

Rationale

_____
_____

Marketing mix strategy is very important because, along with the target market strategy, it will determine a firm's competitive advantage. Unless the firm is doing something *better* than the competition—the product is of higher quality, the prices are lower, the distribution is faster, the promotion communicates better—it will have no competitive advantage. This will limit the effectiveness of the selected marketing strategies and reduce the likelihood that the firm will achieve its objectives. Even if the marketing strategies do result in a competitive advantage, competitors may reduce the effectiveness of those strategies by copying them. For instance, some airline companies have tried to increase business by cutting fares dramatically, but this price strategy has generally failed because other airline companies have simply lowered their fares as well. The best strategies are those that provide a competitive advantage and are very difficult for another firm to replicate. These strategies should be detailed in this section of the plan, with a timetable for implementation and financial implications in the following sections.

Action Programs

Action programs spell out the directives and responsibilities needed for implementing the marketing strategies. Action programs address several questions: What will be done? Who will do it? When will it be done? How much will it cost? Without an action program for accomplishment, it is very difficult for marketing strategies to be successfully implemented.

In Chapter 21, we learn that the organization of the marketing department establishes its structure of task and authority relationships. Tasks are broken down into specific activities, and each activity is assigned to an individual who is responsible for the completion of that activity. These activities relate directly to the marketing strategies. For example, an individual must be responsible for the activities that pertain to the promotion mix strategy—advertising, publicity, personal selling, and sales promotion. In the case of advertising, someone must be responsible for each specific activity performed, such as creating the message or developing the media plan. Each of these activities in turn relates to one of the marketing objectives. Table 22.8 provides a format for writing action programs.

As shown in Table 22.8, each activity performed should relate to one of the marketing objectives. One person should be assigned the responsibility for accomplishing each activity. This person must have sufficient authority to make the decisions necessary to complete the activity. A realistic completion date for each activity should be agreed upon and stated in the plan. All activities have to be coordinated, because the completion of one is often dependent upon the completion of another. Finally, a budget should be established for each activity to ensure that adequate funding is available to complete the activity on time.

Controls

The final section of the marketing plan includes the controls used to measure the results of the plan. Controls should be established to evaluate the plan

TABLE 22.8
Action Programs

Marketing Objective

Activities Performed	Person Responsible	Completion Date	Amount Budgeted

Marketing Objective

Activities Performed	Person Responsible	Completion Date	Amount Budgeted

on an ongoing basis and to take action to reduce discrepancies between desired and actual performance. Two major questions are addressed in this section of the plan: Are we achieving our objectives? What corrective actions should be taken? This section of the marketing plan generally contains financial projections and procedures for monitoring the plan.

Financial Projections   One tangible way to evaluate the marketing plan is to examine financial performance. For example, an increase in sales after the plan is implemented may provide evidence that the plan is working. At the very least, financial projections in the plan can be used as a benchmark for evaluating the plan. Table 22.9 shows the typical financial information projections found in marketing plans.

If the plan is for an existing product, the previous year's sales should be included. Again, this provides a starting point or benchmark to be used in evaluating financial performance. The plan should also include a sales forecast for the current period, whether it be a yearly, quarterly, or monthly projection. Cost estimates, including total fixed cost, total variable cost, and average variable cost, should also be included. Even though these are estimates, they are useful in controlling costs and ensuring that the firm is within budget. The sales and cost estimates can also be used to calculate a projected breakeven point and to project a profit or loss. A loss may be projected in some cases, depending on the product and the firm.

Once the marketing plan is implemented, the information contained in Table 22.9 is useful in monitoring financial performance. Firms should not wait for a long period of time before comparing actual performance to projected performance. Some firms establish procedures to monitor the results of the plan as soon as data are available, almost immediately. In this way, problems can be detected earlier and corrective action taken sooner.

Monitoring Procedures Information about a product's performance is of little value unless procedures are established to monitor objectives. The plan should identify who has specific responsibility for monitoring each objective and taking appropriate action when necessary. Each objective should be monitored at regular intervals. As we said earlier, some firms begin to monitor objectives as soon as possible, perhaps monthly, so that problems can be corrected immediately. Table 22.10 presents a format for monitoring objectives.

As you can see, each individual objective in the marketing plan (those objectives listed in Table 22.5) should be monitored. Procedures or performance standards must be established for monitoring objectives. If the objectives were stated properly—what is to be accomplished, how much is to be accomplished, and when it is to be accomplished—measuring actual performance against expected performance is straightforward. For example, if an objective is an annual increase in sales of 10 percent, actual sales can be used to monitor this objective and evaluate the result. One person in the organization should be responsible for monitoring ech objective and determining corrective action when actual performance does not measure up to the objective.

SAMPLE MARKETING PLAN

Carrie's Fresh Fruits & Vegetables
Abbreviated Marketing Plan

Table of Contents

I. Executive Summary

Carrie's Fresh Fruits & Vegetables opened its first store on Third Street in 1987. A second store was opened on Boston Road in 1989. The stores feature an open-market appearance and offer fresh fruits and vegetables in season; fruit salads; a limited selection of annual flowers in spring, summer, and fall;

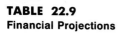

TABLE 22.9
Financial Projections

Previous year's sales _____

Current year's sales forecast _____

Cost estimates:

    Total fixed cost _____

    Total variable cost _____

    Average variable cost _____

Projected breakeven point _____

Projected profit (loss) _____

and pumpkins in the fall. Friendly and helpful staff, competitive prices, and a wide selection of fresh fruits and vegetables have made Carrie's a big hit. The success of the two stores has prompted Carrie Michel, the founder and owner, to consider expanding to a third location.

Carrie's major competitors are supermarket chains like Kroger and IGA, and other local fruit and produce distributors. The target market is individuals aged 18 and above, living within the city, who make food purchases for themselves or their families and want the freshest produce available. Major opportunities stem from Carrie's product selection, knowledgeable staff, and the trend toward a healthy environment. The major problems include limited parking at the current locations and convenience and price competition from the chains. Carrie's marketing mix strategy is to offer customers the widest selection of fresh fruits and vegetables at competitive prices, distributed through its present location and advertised in newspapers and on the radio.

Plans are to build a 10,000-square-foot market at a new location on Squires Road in the eastern section of the city, where many new housing subdivisions and apartment complexes have been built. A heavy concentration of potential customers lives in this area. Age, income, and other demographic characteristics of area residents suggest this would be a desirable location. A marketing

TABLE 22.10
Monitoring Procedures

Objective

_____

_____

_____

How will objective be monitored?

_____

_____

_____

Who is responsible for taking corrective action?

_____

plan has been developed that will ensure continued success of existing stores and future growth at existing and new locations.

II. Current Marketing Situation

A. Analysis of the Marketing Environment

Competition: Major competitors include supermarket chains like Kroger and IGA. Their strengths include location, number of stores, and customer loyalty. Other competitors are Harkins Fruit and Vegetables, a concept similar to Carrie's but with only one location near downtown, and the Farmers' Market, open during the summer months and featuring produce direct from farms. Increased competition is expected from warehouse clubs and large retailers like Wal-Mart.

Society: Society holds a favorable attitude toward fresh fruit and vegetables, since concerns about health have been growing for many years. Especially encouraging are well-publicized studies that have linked the consumption of fruits and vegetables to longevity, the reduction of cholesterol, and perhaps even immunity to certain cancers. Sales of fresh produce have risen steadily in recent years.

Economic Conditions: Despite the recession, purchases of fruit and vegetables have not fallen significantly. Compared to meats and processed foods, fresh fruit and vegetables are considerably less expensive. The encouraging economic picture can only mean increased sales.

B. Target Market Analysis

The target market for Carrie's is individuals aged 18 and up who make food purchases for themselves or for their families. Although most customers (60 percent) have a combined household income exceeding $40,000, all income levels are targeted. Customers come from a wide geographic area and include people in surrounding communities who work in the city. The majority of customers (80 percent) shop at the store closest to their residence. Specifically, consumers who want the freshest produce are targeted. Carrie's currently has a 17 percent market share, with annual sales of $1.2 million.

III. Opportunities and Problems

A. Major Opportunities

The major opportunity for Carrie's stems from its product selection, knowledgeable staff, and the trend toward healthy diets. Customers can get the freshest produce (often purchased from local growers), learn about preparation, obtain recipes, and receive excellent service. Fresh fruits and vegetables are available year-round, depending on what is in season, and at competitive prices.

B. Major Problems

The major problems facing Carrie's include limited parking at the two current locations and convenience and price competition from some of the chains. For instance, Kroger recently offered bananas on sale for 28 cents a pound, 30 cents cheaper than Carrie's price. The cost of produce has increased, making it more difficult to maintain current prices and service levels. New competitors such as superstores and warehouse clubs, which carry produce and compete on price, also pose a threat. Carrie's is at a disadvantage since as a specialty store it lacks the convenience of one-stop shopping; consumers who buy produce at Carrie's must also visit a supermarket or other store for groceries. And with only two locations, shoppers tend to come only once a week or less often.

IV. Marketing Objectives

1. To obtain a 20 percent market share within three years.
2. To increase sales by $100,000 within one year.
3. To offer the highest customer service in the industry.

V. Marketing Strategies

A. Target Market Strategy

Carrie's target market is any individual aged 18 or over who lives or works within the city and who prefers fresh fruit and vegetables.

B. Marketing Mix Strategy

Product: The widest selection of fresh fruit and vegetables in the city. Carrie's pledge will be to offer only the freshest produce year-round and the highest-quality service. The produce will be supplied by local growers as much as possible, and some of it will be organically grown, an important factor to many health-minded consumers. Carrie's offers the advantages of a farmers' market, but in permanent locations and with a guarantee of product quality. Carrie's allows customers to choose produce themselves, in any amount they wish, in contrast to prepacked produce at other stores. Products such as custom fruit baskets for gift giving should be considered.

Price: Prices will remain competitive, generally equal to or lower than those of competitors. Because of its fresh produce line, Carrie's has an image of charging higher prices than competitors. Customers must be informed that Carrie's prices are competitive. Current competitors' prices will be displayed whenever possible so that customers can compare.

Distribution: Carrie's will continue to distribute products through its two present locations and will open a third location in a different area of the city. The third location will increase sales significantly. The new store will also allow more volume purchasing to maintain price competitiveness and improve selection. Delivery should be considered, especially during holiday seasons. The feasibility of mail orders should also be examined. Parking continues to be the weakest link at the two existing stores. All locations will have an "open market" atmosphere and will be open from sunrise to sunset seven days a week.

Promotion: To maintain its image of quality and to further differentiate itself from competitors, Carrie's should direct a large proportion of its advertising budget toward newspaper and radio. Additionally, sales promotion strategies such as coupons, free samples, demonstrations of how to use unusual fruits or vegetables, recipe contests, and so forth must be developed in response to major competitors. Mailers should also be used to contact potential customers within five miles of each store. The advertising budget is currently five percent of sales. For the first year the new store is opened, it will be increased to eight percent to establish awareness. In subsequent years, a five percent advertising budget is anticipated.

VI. Action Programs

Carrie Michel and the two store managers are responsible for all marketing activities. Advertisements must be developed for radio within two months. Ongoing newspaper advertisements and sales promotion activities are the responsibility of the store managers. Carrie Michel is responsible for selecting the site of the new store within six months, with construction to begin in one year.

VII. Controls

The previous year's sales were $1,200,000, and the current year's sales forecast is $1,300,000. Total costs are estimated to be $1,150,000, with a projected profit of $150,000. Carrie Michel will be responsible for monitoring objectives.

SUMMARY

Strategic marketing planning is the continuous process of developing and implementing marketing strategies to achieve specific marketing objectives, which in turn lead to the achievement of the organization's overall objectives. Strategic marketing planning helps marketers look ahead and chart a course of action for the future. Even though marketing planning is important, managers in many organizations fail to develop adequate plans.

A marketing plan is a formally prepared and written document detailing the activities necessary to implement the marketing strategies. In developing a marketing plan, the organization must first assess its current position, then decide where it wants to go, and finally decide how it will get there. Generally, the top-level marketing executive is responsible for developing the marketing plan, with input from other members of the organization.

There is no single best way to develop a marketing plan. We present a plan that includes seven parts. The executive summary is a two- to three-page synopsis that provides a brief overview of the highlights of the plan. The current marketing situation provides an analysis of the marketing environment and the target market. Next, opportunities and problems facing the product are identified. Marketing objectives specify what is to be accomplished through marketing activities. The next component of the marketing plan, marketing strategies, dictates how a firm will achieve its marketing objectives. Then the action programs spell out the directives and responsibilities for implementing marketing strategies. The final section of the marketing plan includes the controls used to measure the results of the plan. Controls should be established to evaluate the plan on an ongoing basis, and to take action to reduce discrepancies between desired and actual performance.

QUESTIONS FOR DISCUSSION AND REVIEW

1. Why is planning important? What did Dwight Eisenhower mean when he said, "Plans are nothing, planning is everything"?

2. What types of problems are firms likely to encounter if they do not have a strategic marketing plan?

3. What is a marketing plan? What are the basic purposes of a marketing plan?

4. Who is responsible for the marketing plan?

5. List the elements of a typical marketing plan. Why are these necessary?

6. What is the purpose of the executive summary? How long should it be, and what should be in it?

7. Discuss the two aspects of the current marketing situation. Give some examples of the types of questions that are addressed in this part of the marketing plan.

8. Choose a product or firm you are familiar with and list three opportunities and three problems it faces.

9. Why should a firm establish marketing objectives? How should they be written?

10. What should the marketing strategy part of the plan include? What are some characteristics of the best strategies?

11. Explain why marketing plans must include action programs. What is likely to happen without them?

12. What is the difference between financial projections and monitoring procedures? Give an example of each.

C A S E S

22.1   PLANNING THE SATURN

Almost overnight, Saturn has become one of the most successful new brands in marketing history. Called the highest-quality American-made car, it has as few defects as Honda vehicles. Saturn is also amazingly successful at satisfying customers, trailing only Lexus and Infiniti. Saturn dealers across the country have faced the bittersweet predicament of looking at empty lots while the Spring Hill, Tennessee, factory could not keep up with orders. In July 1992, Saturn dealers sold 22,305 cars, an average of 115 each. This number exceeds even the most optimistic expectations and is twice the rate per Toyota dealer, the nearest competitor. Despite production restraints, Saturn sold 170,495 cars in model year 1992, a 236 percent increase over first-year sales.

But success did not come as easily as it may seem. General Motors used a sophisticated marketing plan and invested $5 billion in the project over nine years. (GM doesn't expect the Saturn to make a profit until the mid-1990s.) The major objective was to build a brand through a relentless focus on how customers relate to a product and the company that produces it. That focus resulted in an innovative, consumer-driven marketing strategy, making the Saturn different from any vehicle GM or Detroit has ever produced.

At the start, Saturn emphasized partnerships—with employees, suppliers, dealers, and eventually, customers. The result was the highest-quality car in the history of GM. Teams at the Spring Hill factory will not compromise quality. With their pay tied to quality targets, workers once staged a slowdown when a production increase resulted in more defects. Workers are empowered to stop the line if they see a problem and even to call suppliers immediately to talk about defective parts. A 14-member door team suggested rearranging machinery to improve quality and productivity. Says one of the team members: "You can trust the people you're working with. So if I come up with an idea, I won't be worked out of a job."

A great car isn't enough. Saturn managers needed to develop an innovative marketing plan to differentiate the brand from some forty competitors. GM developed the car as its answer to small imports and targeted it at buyers of Hyundai, Subaru, Volkswagen, and Mitsubishi vehicles. In positioning the automobile, Saturn managers relied not only on the vehicle itself, but also on image, perceptions, and the shopping/buying/owning experience. The marketing mix was developed to reinforce this strategy.

The product itself is on a quality level with competing imports. In addition, service is outstanding. The combination of quality product and high-level service has made Saturn owners some of the most satisfied among car buyers. Owners are called after a purchase and problems or complaints are fixed promptly. So far, complaints have been limited.

Saturn uses an aggressive price strategy. Prices start at $9,195, lower than most competing brands. This price is a fraction of what a Lexus or Infiniti costs, yet Saturn ranks among those brands in customer satisfaction. Prices are fixed through a no-haggle policy, and no rebates are offered.

GM believed distribution would have to be unique to truly change the way consumers view buying a car. Thus separate Saturn dealerships were established to sell and service only Saturns. All stores have the same name, "Saturn of (location)," to stress the Saturn brand instead of the dealer. Sales consultants are trained to listen to customers, treat them like intelligent people, and use a low-key approach to satisfying customer needs. They explain the no-haggle policy and even encourage potential customers to comparison-shop. This approach has created good will and an effective word-of-mouth endorsement from many buyers. Saturn buyers feel they are part of a special relationship.

Saturn also has used folksy, offbeat advertising to establish the car's image as unusual. Created by San Francisco's Hal Riney & Partners, the advertisements have focused on lifestyles of Saturn buyers and have been easy for consumers to relate to. The car itself takes a back seat to the customer and product themes important to baby boomers, such as safety and value. The advertisements have helped create an image of the friendliest, most-liked car company in America.

In time, Saturn may exert a great deal of influence on GM and the rest of the automobile industry. In a short period of time, its innovative marketing strategies have resulted in a car that buyers not only relate to, but purchase with enthusiasm and satisfaction.

Questions for Discussion

1. What is the major objective of GM's Saturn division?

2. Discuss how teams and empowerment are important at the Saturn factory in Spring Hill, Tennessee.

3. Summarize Saturn's strategic marketing plan. Does it bring the product close to the customer? Explain.

4. Did GM take a longer-than-normal time horizon in planning for the Saturn?

Based on information from David Woodruff, James B. Treece, Sunita Wadekar Bhargava, and Karen Lowry Miller, "Saturn," *Business Week,* August 17, 1992, pp. 86–91; Raymond Serafin, "The Saturn Story," *Advertising Age,* November 16, 1992, pp. 1, 13, 16; and David Woodruff, "May We Help You Kick the Tires?" *Business Week,* August 13, 1992, pp. 49–50.

22.2 GOODYEAR FIGHTS GLOBAL COMPETITION

After an invasion by foreign tire makers, only two U.S. companies remain, Goodyear Tire and Rubber Company and Cooper Tire. Starting in the late 1980s, Japan's Bridgestone/Firestone, France's Michelin, and Germany's General Tire expanded their market share and started taking over major U.S. tire manufacturers. A technological edge enabled the foreign firms to produce better tires. But in the last few years, Goodyear has rebounded with what CEO Stanley Gault describes as "complete marketing."

Gault came to Goodyear in April 1991 after the $11 billion company experienced its first loss in fifty-eight years. Foreign competitors were continuing to take market share, as Goodyear faced intense price competition. Gault established several objectives, including increasing market share.

A key to achieving this objective was to launch four new products to meet specific needs of consumers. One of the products is the Aquatred tire, which diverts water out from under the tire. The new tire had languished in Goodyear labs for nearly a decade, partly because of its odd looks. It has a large indentation in the center of the tread to channel water from under the tire. Using a public relations campaign targeted at the appropriate media, Goodyear obtained publicity which helped it sell 150,000 of the new tires before the first advertisements were run. *Consumer Reports* rated the Aquatred tops among touring tires. Goodyear sold one million Aquatreds in 1992.

Gault also opened new channels of distribution by signing up Sears, Wal-Mart, Kmart, and other chains where Americans were buying most of their tires. As a result, the number of outlets selling Goodyear tires increased by 3,100.

After the first year under Gault's plans, Goodyear's market share moved up half a point. But the move to sell tires through mass merchandisers alienated many independent Goodyear dealers. Some have started to carry rival brands such as Michelin and Bridgestone, and many others have added lower-priced private label brands. Some analysts predict the loss of business from dealers will erase one-third to one-half of the increase in tire sales attributed to the chains.

Questions for Discussion

1. What environmental factors led to changes in the tire industry?

2. How did Gault plan to achieve his marketing objective? Is his plan working?

3. How can Gault deal with the threat posed by independent Goodyear dealers?

Based on information from Erle Norton, "Last of the U.S. Tire Makers Ride Out Foreign Invasion," *Wall Street Journal,* February 4, 1993, p. B4; Peter Nulty, "The Bounce Is Back at Goodyear," *Fortune,* September 7, 1992, pp. 70–72; and Julie Liesse, "How Goodyear Rebounded," *Advertising Age,* October 19, 1992, p. 53.

Appendix A: Choosing a Career in Marketing

This book introduced some of the basic concepts of marketing. Believe it or not, you can use these same concepts to obtain the career you desire—by marketing yourself. Remember, the purpose of marketing activities is to facilitate satisfying exchanges, and a job is certainly an exchange situation. An organization has something of value to offer you—a career, pay, friends, and a means of using your skills. What do you have to offer an organization? The purpose of this appendix is to help you answer that question and to examine some opportunities in marketing.

SELECTING A CAREER THAT IS RIGHT FOR YOU

Perhaps the most important step in selecting a career is determining what is right for you. A person who likes to sell but doesn't like to travel will probably be unhappy as a traveling salesperson. There are a variety of jobs in marketing-related fields, and you have to match your interests and capabilities with their requirements. The formula for success is pretty simple: if you find a job doing what you like to do, your chances of succeeding are very good. The key to deciding what you want to do is to sort through your abilities, interests, and passions in life, and match them with an occupation.[1]

By attending college, you are already on your way to a successful career. Census Bureau data show that male college graduates earn 30 percent more than high school graduates; females, 40 percent more.[2]

Pay is not the only consideration in selecting a career, though it is often cited as one of the most important. Other considerations include location, job security, and opportunity for advancement.[3] If these and other factors are important to you, make sure that the organization you work for offers them.

What about a career in marketing? Surveys of college juniors show that only 3 to 5 percent of them plan on a career in marketing. But research has shown that as many as 35 percent of college graduates end up in marketing careers.[4] Why the big difference between intentions and behavior? There are several reasons. According to some estimates, roughly one-third of all people are employed in marketing-related jobs. And you do not have to be a market-

---

[1]Perri Capell, "How to decide what you really want to do," *Wall Street Journal's Managing Your Career,* Spring 1992, pp. 5–6.
[2]Gary Putka, "Benefit of B.A. Is Greater than Ever," *Wall Street Journal,* August 17, 1988, p. 21.
[3]"Ideal Careers," *Wall Street Journal,* April 7, 1988, p. 27.
[4]James Hansz, "Marketing: A Career Option," *Private Colleges,* 1987, pp. 99–102.

ing major to have a career in marketing. Students with degrees in advertising, psychology, and even statistics and engineering pursue marketing careers.

FINDING A JOB

It is primarily *your* responsibility to find a job. School placement services, parents, teachers, and friends can help, but you have to identify the job openings that match your career objectives. Many sources can be used to learn about job openings: state employment offices, civil service (government) announcements, classified ads, labor unions, professional associations, libraries, and employers themselves. Once you have identified the organizations and jobs you are interested in, you have to learn as much about them as you can. Then you have to set up a job interview.

Preparing a Résumé and Cover Letter

To be considered for a job, you must provide a good résumé. The résumé is your opportunity to sell yourself to prospective employers. It should summarize your objectives, qualifications, employment history, and educational background. Table A.1 presents the typical information found in a résumé. This information should be presented in a clear, concise, and positive manner. Remember, you are selling yourself, and the competition for the job could be intense.

A common error in résumés is the inclusion of too much information. Consider omitting the actual names of references and personal information such as religion, race, age, and weight. You want your résumé to be impressive, not unnecessarily long. The following guidelines should be helpful.

Limit the résumé to *one* page.
Avoid excessive detail.
Avoid the use of slang or professional jargon.

TABLE A.1
Contents of a Typical Résumé

Name, address, telephone number
Career objective (stated in specific terms)
Educational background—schools attended, degrees received, grade point averages
Work experiences related to chosen field
Qualifications—special skills, knowledge, honors or awards received, membership in organizations
Note stating that references are available on request

Use present tense for current activities, past tense for previous activities.

Do not make mistakes—spelling and grammatical errors reflect poorly on your qualifications.

Have a friend, parent, or teacher react to the résumé before it is printed.

Quality is important. Make sure the résumé has an attractive format and is typed or printed on good paper.

When contacting employers, you will need to include a cover letter of introduction with your résumé. A cover letter is very important because it may determine whether someone reads your résumé. In the first paragraph, tell exactly why you are writing the letter and how you heard about the opportunity or organization. The second paragraph should include one or two of your best qualifications. Try to set yourself apart from other job candidates. In the third paragraph, refer the reader to the enclosed résumé. The last paragraph should indicate where and when you can be reached to set up an interview. Keep it brief!

Acing the Interview

Interviews are another important aspect of job hunting. Whether it is held on campus or at a prospective employer's office, an interview is usually a series of questions and answers. Table A.2 lists some of the most commonly asked questions.

There are several steps you can take to ace an interview. Learn about the organization—its products or services, competition, current status or role in recent news events, and so on. Also, think about the specific type of job you want; be prepared to describe it to the interviewer(s). Be familiar with your own résumé, and practice answering questions.

Next, try to be well rested and ready on the day of the interview. Dress appropriately, arrive a few minutes before your appointment, relax, and remember to be yourself. During the interview, answer each question directly and concisely; your answers should convey a sense of cooperation and enthusiasm. In turn, feel free to ask any questions you might have about the position or organization. *Relevant* questions show that you are interested and well prepared.

A recent survey of over one thousand marketing recruiters identified several success requirements related to jobs for which they interviewed.[5] Overall, the most important qualification was oral communication skills. The other qualifications identified, in order of importance, were work ethics, initiative, ability to work well with others, planning and organizing skills, maturity, and ethical values. Thus, it is highly likely that in an interview, recruiters will attempt to determine the extent to which job candidates possess these skills. Anything candidates can do during the interview to demonstrate a proficiency for these skills is very important.

[5] Stephen W. McDaniel and J. Chris White, "The Quality of the Academic Preparation of Undergraduate Marketing Majors: An Assessment by Company Recruiters," *Marketing Education Review,* forthcoming.

TABLE A.2
Questions Asked in a
Typical Interview

In what type of position are you most interested?
Why are you interested in our company?
What jobs have you previously held?
Do you feel you received a good education?
What qualifications do you have that will make you successful?
What would you like for a salary?
What do you think determines success?
What type of boss do you prefer?
Tell me a story!
Did you do the best work you were capable of in college?
Why should we hire you?
What would you like to be doing in five years?
What is more important to you, the money or the type of job?
What accomplishment are you most proud of?
Are you willing to relocate?
What have you learned from your mistakes?

A short follow-up letter is a good idea after every interview. The letter should thank the employer for the interview and reaffirm your interest in the position. Be sure to write to the person who interviewed you.

CAREER ALTERNATIVES IN MARKETING

The career outlook in marketing is bright. Marketing is considered one of the best career paths for the 1990s.[6] The U.S. Bureau of Labor Statistics estimates that employment in marketing and sales will grow by 30 percent—from 12.6 to 16.3 million jobs—by the year 2000.[7] Many of these jobs will be in the area of sales, public relations, retailing, advertising, marketing research, product management, distribution management, and direct marketing.

Sales

There are more career opportunities in sales than in any other area of marketing. Personal selling involves informing customers and persuading them to buy products. Some selling positions focus more on providing information, while others emphasize locating potential customers and closing sales. Sales jobs can be careers in themselves or can lead to positions in management. Entry-level sales positions typically pay $15,000 to $30,000. Sales managers earn approximately $40,000 to $55,000, while national sales managers earn from $60,000 to $100,000. Sales compensation—often salary plus commis-

---

[6]John Stodden, "Ten Best Careers For the 90's," *Business Week Careers,* 1988, pp. 4–9.
[7]*Occupational Outline Handbook,* U.S. Department of Labor, 1988–1989, p. 12.

sion—sets no limit on the amount of money a person can make and therefore offers the greatest potential compensation.

Nearly all organizations sell. Sales positions can be found in a wide variety of organizations, including manufacturing, wholesaling, retailing, insurance, real estate, and many types of service businesses (banks, brokerage firms, travel agencies). Candidates for sales positions need good communication skills, self-discipline, and enthusiasm. Duties include, but are not limited to, contacting customers, developing new customers, taking orders, settling customer complaints, preparing sales reports, making presentations, and providing product feedback. Salespeople come from nearly any major.

Public Relations

Public relations programs help create the image or message of an organization and communicate it to the appropriate audiences. All types of firms—business, government, and nonprofit—employ public relations specialists. The starting salaries are sometimes $20,000 or less, but salaries can increase rapidly.

Written and oral communication skills are critical for success in a public relations job. A college education combined with writing experience is the best preparation for a public relations career. Generally, public relations companies do not provide extensive training for new personnel; most employees learn on the job.

Retailing

Although retailing careers often begin in retail sales, there is more to retailing than selling. Retail personnel manage the sales force and other personnel, select and order merchandise, and are responsible for promotional activities, inventory control, store security, and accounting. Large retail stores have a variety of positions, including department manager, buyer, and store manager. The starting salary for a department manager is $25,000 to $45,000; for a buyer, $25,000 to $45,000; and for a store manager, $25,000 and up. In some small retail stores, one manager may perform several different activities.

Today, many large retailers are looking to fill management positions with people who have a college education and a sincere interest in a retailing career. After being hired, these people are put through a formal training program and placed directly in retail management positions; they do not begin their careers as salesclerks. Such employees have a good opportunity for advancement to positions such as store manager, division manager, regional manager, or vice president of merchandising. A successful retailing career requires initiative, analytical ability, and decision-making ability.

Advertising

A wide variety of organizations employ advertising personnel. Although advertising agencies are the largest employers, many manufacturers, retail stores, banks, and even hospitals have advertising departments. Television and radio stations, newspapers, and magazines also employ advertising personnel. The entry-level salaries for account coordinators who assist account executives in handling advertising campaigns range from $15,000 to $20,000. An account manager earns from $40,000 to $70,000 annually.

Creativity, artistic talent, the ability to work with people, and strong communication abilities are just a few of the diverse skills needed for a successful career in advertising. Advertising personnel come from many different disciplines, including liberal arts, communications, journalism, advertising, and marketing.

Marketing Research

Many organizations offer challenging careers in marketing research—marketing research firms, advertising agencies, and business, government, and nonprofit organizations with marketing research departments. Researchers conduct industry research, advertising research, product and packaging research, new product testing, and test marketing. Researchers are involved in one or more stages of the research process, depending on the size of the organization conducting the research. The salary for a marketing research trainee ranges from $20,000 to $25,000; a marketing research director is paid $35,000 to $60,000.

Marketing research requires many different skills: statistics, data processing, psychology, and written and oral communications. Although some research positions require only a bachelor's degree, other specialized positions require a master's degree in marketing, statistics, or some related field.

Product Management

The product manager coordinates the activities required to market a product. Thus, a general knowledge of advertising, inventory control, marketing research, distribution methods, packaging, pricing, and selling is required. A product manager is responsible for the success (or failure) of a product and is paid well for this responsibility. The average salary range of a product manager is $35,000 to $60,000.

Most product managers have had college training in an area of business; many have earned a master's degree in business administration. Previous experience in sales and excellent communication skills are usually prerequisites for the position of product manager, which is a major step in the career path of top-level marketing executives.

Distribution Management

Distribution managers are responsible for the physical distribution of products within firms and through marketing channels. Distribution managers select transportation modes and the specific routes products will travel; they also prepare shipping documents, trace product shipments, maintain records, and monitor changes in distribution methods. Entry-level positions pay $20,000 to $25,000; distribution managers earn from $40,000 to $60,000.

Most employers prefer distribution managers who have fairly technical backgrounds in transportation, logistics, statistics, computer science, and operations management. Distribution management employs few people in comparison to other marketing-related fields and is not expected to experience dramatic growth in the near future.

Direct Marketing

Direct marketing—in which the seller uses one or more direct media (telephone, mail, print, or television)—is a rapidly growing field where people can advance quickly. Jobs in direct marketing include buyers (such as department store buyers who select goods for catalogue, telephone, or direct mail sales); catalogue managers; and order fulfillment managers. Salaries range from $15,000 to $30,000 for a person who solicits sales via the telephone, and from $20,000 to $40,000 for a catalogue manager.

Up to this point, direct-marketing entry-level positions have not required a great deal of education. Experience has been the most important quality that firms have looked for. Many employers recruit experienced individuals from other industries.

Appendix B: Financial Analysis in Marketing

This book presents the fundamentals of strategic marketing, but it does not discuss financial analysis. Marketers must understand the basics of financial analysis to make effective decisions. Therefore, this appendix examines three important areas of financial analysis—the income statement, performance ratios, and price calculations.

THE INCOME STATEMENT

The income statement shows a firm's sales, cost of goods sold, and operating expenses during a specific time period. An income statement also provides the net profit or loss of the firm for the given period. For example, a simplified income statement looks like this:

Net sales	$115,000
Cost of goods sold	24,000
Gross margin	$ 91,000
Expenses	64,000
Net income	$ 27,000

These figures come from a more complex income statement, shown in Table B.1. Net sales is gross sales less sales returns and allowances. Gross sales is the total amount of goods sold to customers during the year ended December 31, 1994. Sales returns are refunds for merchandise that is returned by customers; allowances are price reductions given to customers who keep the merchandise. For Aaron Enterprises, the net sales is calculated as follows:

Gross sales	$120,000
Sales returns and allowances	− 5,000
Net sales	$115,000

Cost of goods sold is the total cost of products that were sold during the given period. This figure is calculated by adding the beginning inventory and the net cost of delivered purchases, minus the ending inventory. The beginning inventory is the value of the firm's merchandise at the beginning of the period. Net cost of delivered purchases includes the cost of merchandise purchased (gross purchases) less any purchase discounts, plus the cost of obtaining merchandise (freight-in). The beginning inventory added to the net cost of delivered purchases is called the cost of goods available for sale. The ending inventory is the value of the stock on December 31, 1994. Because this amount was not sold, the cost of goods sold is calculated as follows:

Beginning inventory	$16,000
Net purchases (gross purchases − purchase discounts)	+ 29,000
Freight-in	+ 1,000
Cost of goods available for sale	$46,000
Ending inventory	− 22,000
Cost of goods sold	$24,000

Gross margin is the difference between net sales and the cost of goods sold. Gross margin represents the money that is left to pay all other expenses (after sales and costs) and to provide a return to the owners. Gross margin for Aaron Enterprises is $91,000.

TABLE B.1
Income Statement for a Retailer

Aaron Enterprises Income Statement For the Year Ended December 31, 1994			
Gross Sales			$120,000
Less: Sales returns and allowances			5,000
Net Sales			$115,000
Cost of Goods Sold			
Beginning inventory (at cost)		$16,000	
Gross purchases	$32,000		
Less: Purchase discounts	3,000		
Net purchases	$29,000		
Plus: Freight-in	1,000		
Net cost of delivered purchases		$30,000	
Cost of goods available for sale		$46,000	
Less: Ending inventory (at cost)		22,000	
Cost of goods sold			$ 24,000
Gross Margin			$ 91,000
Expenses			
Selling expenses			
Salaries and commissions	$17,000		
Promotion	14,000		
Delivery	1,000		
Total selling expenses		$32,000	
Administrative expenses			
Office salaries	$16,000		
Office supplies	2,000		
Miscellaneous	2,000		
Total administrative expenses		$20,000	
General expenses			
Rent	$ 7,000		
Utilities	3,000		
Miscellaneous	2,000		
Total general expenses		$12,000	
Total expenses			$ 64,000
Net Income			**$ 27,000**

Aaron Enterprises incurred several expenses in 1994. Selling expenses—salaries and commissions, promotion, and delivery—totaled $32,000. Administrative expenses for office salaries, office supplies, and miscellaneous items came to $20,000. General expenses, including rent and utilities, were $12,000. Thus, total expenses for the year were $64,000. Net income (gross margin − total expenses) for the year is $27,000.

PERFORMANCE RATIOS

The income statement can be used to derive several important performance ratios. These ratios are fairly simple to calculate and are useful in comparing the results of a current year with those of previous years. Because the ratios are expressed as percentages, they can also be used to compare one firm's performance with other firms in the industry.

Operating Ratios

Operating ratios express various items on the income statement as percentages of net sales.

Gross Margin Ratio   The gross margin ratio shows the percentage of each dollar available to cover operating expenses and achieve profit objectives. For Aaron Enterprises, the gross margin ratio is determined as follows:

$$\text{Gross margin ratio} = \frac{\text{gross margin}}{\text{net sales}} = \frac{\$\ 91,000}{\$115,000} = 79.1\%$$

Net Profit Ratio   The net profit ratio indicates the percentage of each sales dollar that is considered profit before payment of income taxes. The net profit ratio for Aaron Enterprises is calculated as follows:

$$\text{Net profit ratio} = \frac{\text{net profit}}{\text{net sales}} = \frac{\$\ 27,000}{\$115,000} = 23.5\%$$

Operating Expense Ratio   The operating expense ratio shows the percentage of each dollar needed to cover operating expenses. The operating expense ratio for Aaron Enterprises is calculated as follows:

$$\text{Operating expense ratio} = \frac{\text{total expenses}}{\text{net sales}} = \frac{\$\ 64,000}{\$115,000} = 55.6\%$$

Other Analytical Ratios

Several other ratios are useful in assessing a firm's performance.

Inventory Turnover Rate   The inventory turnover (stockturn) rate helps a business determine if it has an appropriate inventory level. This ratio indicates how many times an inventory is sold (turns over) during a given period.

This ratio can then be compared to other periods or industry standards. For Aaron Enterprises, the inventory turnover rate is computed on cost as follows:

$$\text{Inventory turnover rate} = \frac{\text{cost of goods sold}}{\text{average inventory at cost}}$$

$$\text{Average inventory at cost} = \frac{\text{beginning inventory} + \text{ending inventory}}{2}$$

$$= \frac{\$16,000 + \$22,000}{2}$$

$$= \$19,000$$

$$\text{Inventory turnover rate} = \frac{\$24,000}{\$19,000} = 1.3$$

Return on Investment   Return on investment (ROI) measures management's efficiency in generating income from the total amount invested in the firm. To calculate ROI, information from two different financial statements is needed. The income statement (Table B.1) provides the net income; the balance sheet, which states the firm's assets and liabilities, provides the figure for the total investment (assets) in the firm. Suppose the total investment in Aaron Enterprises is $100,000. ROI is calculated as follows:

$$\text{ROI} = \frac{\text{net income}}{\text{total investment}} = \frac{\$\ 27,000}{\$100,000} = 27\%$$

Another way to calculate ROI is to multiply the net income ratio by capital turnover. Capital turnover is a measure of net sales per dollar of investment; the ratio is figured by dividing net sales by total investment. The capital turnover ratio for Aaron Enterprises is

$$\text{Capital turnover} = \frac{\text{net sales}}{\text{total investment}} = \frac{\$115,000}{\$100,000} = 1.15$$

ROI is equal to capital turnover times the net income ratio. For Aaron Enterprises, this formula is:

$$\text{ROI} = (\text{capital turnover}) \times (\text{net income ratio})$$

or

$$\text{ROI} = \frac{\text{net sales}}{\text{total investment}} = \frac{\text{net income}}{\text{net sales}}$$

$$= \frac{\$115,000}{\$100,000} = \frac{\$\ 27,000}{\$115,000}$$

$$= (1.15)\,(23.5) = 27\%$$

PRICE CALCULATIONS

As discussed in Chapter 14, the marketing manager must choose a pricing method, a systematic procedure for setting prices on a regular basis. Two ratios that are useful for calculating selling prices and evaluating their effects are markups and markdowns.

Markups

Markup is the difference between the selling price and the actual cost of the item. The markup must cover the cost and contribute to profit. The markup ratio can be calculated in two ways, as a percentage of cost or as a percentage of selling price.

$$\text{Markup as percentage of cost} = \frac{\text{dollar markup}}{\text{cost}}$$

$$\text{Markup as percentage of selling price} = \frac{\text{dollar markup}}{\text{selling price}}$$

Suppose that an item costs $8 to make and the dollar markup is $2. The selling price would be $10.

$$\text{Markup percentage on cost} = \frac{\$\ 2}{\$\ 8} = 25\%$$

$$\text{Markup percentage on selling price} = \frac{\$\ 2}{\$10} = 20\%$$

Markup percentage on cost can be converted to markup percentage on selling price, and vice versa. The conversion formulas are

$$\begin{array}{l}\text{Markup percentage} \\ \text{on selling price}\end{array} = \frac{\text{markup percentage on cost}}{100\% + \text{markup percentage on cost}}$$

$$\begin{array}{l}\text{Markup percentage} \\ \text{on cost}\end{array} = \frac{\text{markup percentage on selling price}}{100\% - \text{markup percentage on selling price}}$$

For instance, if the markup percentage on cost is 50 percent, then the markup percentage on selling price is

$$\frac{50\%}{100\% + 50\%} = 33\frac{1}{3}\%$$

Suppose the markup percentage on selling price is 40 percent. Then the markup percentage on cost would be

$$\frac{40\%}{100\% - 40\%} = 66\frac{2}{3}\%$$

Markup percentage on selling price can be used to determine the selling price of a product, if the cost is known. For example, if an item costs $28 and the standard markup percentage on selling price is 45 percent, then the selling price equals markup plus cost.

Thus, if

100% of selling price (X) = 45% of selling price + cost

then

55% of selling price (X) = cost

Since cost equals $28,

$$0.55X = \$28$$

or

$$X = \frac{\$28}{.55}$$

Selling price = $50.91

The markup percentage on selling price could be converted to a cost basis as follows:

$$\frac{45\%}{100\% - 45\%} = 81.82\%$$

Then the selling price would be computed as follows:

Selling price = 81.82%(cost) + cost
= 81.82%($28) + $28
= $22.91 + $28
= $50.91

Markdowns

Markdowns are reductions on the original selling price of merchandise and are used to move damaged merchandise or inventory that has not sold. The markdown ratio (percentage) is computed as follows:

$$\text{Markdown percentage} = \frac{\text{dollar markdowns}}{\text{net sales in dollars}}$$

For instance, suppose that a firm sells five units of a product for $50 each. Five additional units remain in stock and have not sold for several months at the original price of $50. The firm therefore decides to lower the price by $10, from $50 to $40. If the five additional items sell at $40 each, then the overall markdown percentage would be calculated as follows:

$$\text{Markdown percentage} = \frac{5(\$10)}{5(\$50) + 5(\$40)} = \frac{\$50}{\$450} = 11.1\%$$

Glossary

accessory equipment equipment that is used in production or office activities but does not become part of the final physical product being manufactured

administered pricing an organizational pricing policy in which the seller determines the product's price (or prices) and the customer pays that designated price

administered VMS a marketing channel in which channel members remain independent but informal coordination allows for effective interorganizational management

advertising a paid form of nonpersonal communication about an organization, its products, or its activities that is transmitted through a mass medium to a target audience

advertising agency a business that specializes in creating advertisements for other organizations and also offers other promotion-related services

advertising budget the total amount of money that a marketer allocates for advertising for a specific time period

advertising objective a well-defined, measurable goal that specifies something that is to be accomplished through an advertising program

advertising platform the message of an advertising campaign, which consists of the basic issues or selling features to be stressed in the program and usually distinguishes important features that competitive products do not have

agent a functional middleman who represents buyers or sellers on a permanent basis

AIDA model a model of the receiver's response process that maintains that a receiver goes through successive stages of attention, interest, desire, and action

aided recall test a posttest in which respondents are asked to remember advertisements after being shown a list of products, brands, company names, or trademarks to jog their memories

allowance a concession in price offered by a seller to a buyer, usually to boost sales

approach the manner in which a salesperson initially contacts a potential customer

arbitrary approach a method of determining the advertising budget, in which a high-level executive subjectively stipulates how much will be spent on advertising for a certain time period

area sampling a variation of stratified sampling involving two stages: (1) dividing the population into geographic areas, such as blocks or census tracts, and (2) selecting units or individuals within the selected geographic areas for the random sample

artwork the graphic elements of an advertisement, including the illustration and layout

atmospherics the physical design of a store's space to appeal to consumers' emotions and encourage them to buy

attitude a person's overall feeling toward some object

attitude scale a method used to measure consumer attitudes; usually consists of a series of adjectives, phrases, or sentences about an object that subjects respond to, indicating the intensity of their feelings toward the object

authority the organizationally sanctioned right to make a decision without the approval of a higher-ranking manager

automatic vending an impersonal form of nonstore retailing in which money- or credit-card–operated machines provide products or services

average fixed cost the fixed cost per unit produced; calculated by dividing the total fixed costs by the number of units produced

average revenue (AR) the total revenue divided by the quantity produced

average total cost the sum of the average fixed cost and the average variable cost

average variable cost the variable cost per unit produced; calculated by dividing the total variable costs by the number of units produced

barter the trading of products

benchmarking the continuous process of measuring a firm's goods, practices, and services against those of its toughest competitors

benefit segmentation the division of a consumer market according to the benefits that customers want from the product

Better Business Bureau a local nongovernment regulatory agency (supported by local businesses) that settles problems between consumers and specific business firms and also acts to preserve good business practices in a community

bid pricing an organizational pricing method in which sellers submit sealed or open price proposals for the customer's consideration

bonded storage an arrangement in which imported or taxable products are not released to the owner until U.S. customs duties, taxes, or other fees have been paid by the owners of the products

Boston Consulting Group (BCG) approach a method developed by a management consulting company that evaluates strategic business units based on market growth rate and relative market share

brand a name, term, design, symbol, or any other feature that identifies one seller's good or service as distinct from those of other sellers

brand-extension branding a branding strategy of using an existing brand name as part of a brand for an improved or new product that is usually in the same product category as the existing brand

brand licensing a branding strategy in which a company allows approved manufacturers to use its trademark on other products for a licensing fee

brand manager a type of product manager who is responsible for a single brand

brand mark a symbol, design, or other element of a brand that cannot be spoken

brand name the part of a brand that can be verbalized; includes letters, words, and numbers, such as 7Up or Colgate

breakdown approach an approach for measuring company sales potential based on a general economic forecast for a specific time period and the market sales potential derived from it

breakeven point the point at which the cost of making a product equals the revenue made from selling the product

broker a functional middleman whose primary function is to bring together buyers and sellers, generally on a temporary basis

buildup approach an approach for measuring company sales potential based on projections of market sales potential for individual geographic areas

bundling the marketing of two or more services together as a single package for a special price

business analysis an assessment of a new product's potential profitability and its compatibility with the marketplace

business cycle a general pattern of fluctuations in the U.S. economy consisting of four phases: prosperity, recession, depression, and recovery

business-portfolio analysis evaluating an organization's current mix of products and businesses

business-to-business marketing marketing of products to organizations rather than to consumers

buy-back allowance a sum of money offered to a reseller for each unit bought after an initial deal is over

buying allowance a certain amount of money temporarily offered to resellers for purchasing specified quantities of a product

buying center all the individuals in an organization who participate in the purchase decision process, including users, influencers, buyers, deciders, and gatekeepers

buying power the ability to make purchases, which depends on the extent of one's personal resources (goods, services, financial holdings) and the state of the economy

buying power index (BPI) a weighted index that consists of population, effective buying income, and retail sales data

capital equipment the large tools and machines used in a production process

captioned photograph a photograph with a brief description explaining the people or event pictured

cash-and-carry wholesaler a limited-service wholesaler that performs most wholesaling functions except for delivery, financing, and promotional assistance

cash discount a price reduction that organizational marketers offer to buyers that make prompt or cash payments

catalogue showroom a form of warehouse showroom where consumers select products from catalogues that they've received in the mail or that are available in the store

centralized organization an organization in which top-level managers make most major decisions and delegate little decision-making authority to lower-level managers

cents-off offer a sales promotion device for established products whereby buyers deduct a certain amount (specified on the product's package or label) off the regular price of the product

channel capacity a limit on the volume of information that the communication process (or least efficient component thereof) can handle effectively

channel conflict friction between marketing channel members, often resulting from role deviance or malfunction by one member

channel cooperation a mutually helpful relationship in which channel members work together for the benefit of all members and the realization of overall channel objectives

channel leader a channel member responsible for guiding other channel members and coordinating their efforts to achieve channel objectives and reduce conflicts

channel power the ability of one channel member to influence another member's marketing decisions and goal achievement

closing the stage in which the salesperson asks the prospect to actually buy the products

codes of ethics organization rules and policies that provide members with formal guidelines for professional conduct

coding process the phase of the communication process in which the source converts the message into groups of symbols that represent ideas or concepts

cognitive dissonance the conflict buyers experience when they have doubts about a purchase, such as whether the product should have been purchased at all or whether a different brand or type of product should have been purchased

combination compensation plan a plan by which salespeople receive both a fixed salary and a commission based on sales volume

combination store a mass merchandiser that is larger than a superstore and sells food and drugs in one store or two adjacent stores

commercialization the full-scale manufacturing and marketing of a new product

commission merchant an agent who receives goods on consignment from local sellers and negotiates sales in large central markets

communication the sharing of a common meaning

company sales forecast the amount of a product a company actually expects to sell during a specific period at a specified level of marketing activities

company sales potential the amount of a product that an organization is likely to sell during a particular time period

comparative advertising a form of competitive advertising that contrasts two or more specified brands on the basis of one or more product features

competition firms that market similar or substitutable products in the same geographic area; in general, the rivalry among businesses for consumer dollars

competition-matching approach a method of determining the advertising budget, in which an organization matches major competitors' advertising appropriations in terms of absolute dollars or percentage of sales

competition-oriented pricing a pricing method in which an organization sets prices on the basis of its competitors' prices rather than its own costs and revenues

competitive advertising advertising that builds selective demand for a specific brand by focusing on the uses, features, and value of the brand that benefit consumers and may not be available in competing brands

component part a finished item or an item that needs little processing before becoming part of the physical product being manufactured

comprehensive spending patterns the relative proportions of household income allotted to annual expenditures for general classes of goods and services

concentration approach a market segmentation approach in which an organization directs its marketing effort toward a single market segment through a single marketing mix

concept testing presenting product concepts and benefits to potential customers in order to identify and eliminate poor product concepts

consumer behavior the actions and decision processes of people who purchase goods and services for personal consumption

consumer contest a sales promotion device for established products in which individuals compete for prizes based on their analytical or creative skill or, sometimes, chance

consumer decision making the five-stage process people go through when deciding what products to buy; includes problem recognition, information search, evaluation of alternatives, purchase decision, and postpurchase evaluation

consumer market purchasers or persons in their households who plan to consume or benefit from the purchased products and who do not buy products for the purpose of making a profit

consumer movement individuals and organizations that attempt to protect the rights of consumers

consumer panel a group of actual or potential buyers of an advertised product who are asked to assess various dimensions of two or more advertisements

consumer product a product purchased for personal and family consumption

consumer spending patterns the relative proportions of household money annually spent on certain kinds of goods and services

consumer sweepstakes a sales promotion device for established products in which consumers submit their names for inclusion in a drawing for prizes or cash

consumerism all the activities undertaken by independent individuals, groups, and organizations to protect their rights as consumers

containerization the materials handling practice of consolidating many goods into a single container, sealed at the point of origin and opened at the destination

contractual VMS a marketing channel in which channel members are independent but have interorganizational relationships that are formalized through contracts or other legal agreements

controlling the process through which marketing performance is planned and evaluated

convenience product a frequently purchased, inexpensive item that buyers spend little effort to find and purchase

convenience sampling a method of nonprobability sampling in which the researcher uses respondents who are readily available

cooperative a full-service wholesaler that is owned and operated by the members

cooperative advertising a producer's agreement to pay a certain amount of money toward a retailer's media costs for advertising the producer's products

copy the verbal or written portion of an advertisement

corporate VMS a marketing channel in which successive stages of the channel are united under one ownership

correlation method a technique of sales forecasting in which the forecaster tries to detect a relationship between past sales and one or more variables such as population, per capita income, or gross national product

cost-oriented pricing a pricing method in which price is determined by adding a dollar amount or percentage to the cost of the product to achieve the desired profit margin

cost-plus pricing a cost-oriented pricing method in which the producer determines its costs and then adds a specified dollar amount or percentage of the cost to the selling price

count and recount promotion method a sales promotion method in which a reseller is paid a specific amount of money for each product unit moved from its warehouse in a given time period

countertrading a form of international trade involving bartering agreements between two or more countries; allows nations with limited cash to participate in international trade

credit a buyer's ability to purchase something now and pay for it later

cultural diversity the differences that exist both within and between cultures

culture all the learned values, behaviors, and other meaningful symbols shared by a society

cumulative discount a quantity discount accumulated over a specified period of time

customary pricing a psychological pricing policy of setting prices on the basis of tradition

customer forecasting survey a technique of predicting sales by asking customers what types and quantities of products they intend to buy during a specific period

customer service standard a specification that identifies a specific and measurable goal appropriate to physical distribution

customs and entry procedures rules and procedures governing the inspection, documentation, and licensing of goods entering a country

cycle analysis an analysis that examines sales figures over a period of three to five years to determine whether sales fluctuate in a consistent, periodic manner

dealer listing an advertisement that promotes a product and identifies the names and locations of participating retailers that carry the product

dealer loader a gift provided to a retailer for purchasing a specified quantity of merchandise

decentralized organization an organization in which managers delegate decision-making authority as far down the chain of command as possible

decline stage the stage in the product life cycle in which sales fall rapidly and profits decrease

decoding process the stage of the communication process in which the receiver interprets the symbols sent by the source by converting them into concepts and ideas

defensive advertising advertising used to offset or minimize the impact of a competitor's promotional program

demand curve a graphic representation showing the quantity of products that consumers are willing to buy at different prices

demand-oriented pricing a pricing method based on the level of demand for a product

demarketing using marketing activities to reduce the demand for a product

demographic factor a personal characteristic—such as age, race, sex, income, education, marital status, family size, or occupation—that affects buying behavior

demonstration a sales promotion method used by retailers on a temporary basis to encourage trial use and purchase of a product or to actually show how the product works

department store a large retailer offering a wide product mix and organized into separate departments to facilitate service, marketing, and internal management

dependent variable in an experimental study, the variable that is contingent on, or affected by, the value of the independent variable

depression a phase of the business cycle in which unemployment is extremely high, income is very low, total disposable income is at a minimum, and consumers lack confidence in the economy

depth interview an interview in which the researcher tries to get the subject to talk freely about several subjects to create an informal atmosphere

derived demand organizational demand derived from consumer demand; a demand for products that arises because organizations purchase them to be used directly or indirectly in the production of goods and services to satisfy consumers' demand

descriptive study the type of study undertaken when marketers recognize that they must understand the characteristics of certain phenomena underlying a particular problem

direct cost a cost that is directly attributable to the performance of a specific marketing activity

direct-cost approach an approach to determining marketing costs in which cost analysis includes direct costs and traceable common costs but excludes nontraceable common costs

direct marketing nonstore retailing that uses nonpersonal media to introduce products to consumers, who then purchase the products by mail or telephone

direct ownership a long-term commitment to international marketing in which a business owns its foreign interests

discount store a self-service general merchandise retailer that offers brand-name products at low prices

discretionary effort the difference between the minimum amount of energy a worker must expend to keep from being penalized or reprimanded and the maximum amount of energy an employee can bring to a job

discretionary income disposable income left for

spending and saving after an individual has purchased basic necessities such as food, clothing, and shelter

disposable income after-tax income left for spending or saving

distinctive competencies an organization's skills and talents in areas such as production, finance, marketing, management, and resource (financial, human, technological, and material) utilization

distribution center a large, centralized warehouse designed to facilitate the movement of goods in and out of storage as fast as possible

distribution intensity the number of outlets in a trading area that sell a particular product

diversification a strategy of developing new products to sell in new markets

drop shipper a limited-service merchant wholesaler that performs most wholesaling functions and takes title of goods but does not physically possess, handle, or store products, or provide promotional assistance

dual distribution the use of two or more marketing channels to distribute the same product to the same target market

dumping the sale of products in foreign markets at lower prices than those charged in the domestic country of origin (when all costs are not allocated or when surplus products are sold)

early adopter a person who selects new products carefully and who may be viewed by persons in the early majority, late majority, and laggard categories as an opinion leader

early majority people who are deliberate and cautious about trying new products

ecology the study of the relationship between living things and their environment

economic conditions the various forces in the economy that influence organizations' abilities to compete and consumers' willingness and ability to purchase goods and services

economic order quantity (EOQ) the order size that minimizes the total cost of ordering and carrying inventory

editorial film/tape a film or tape distributed to broadcast stations or newspapers in the hope that its contents will be used in news stories

effective buying income (EBI) disposable income, including salaries, wages, dividends, interest, profits, and rents, less federal, state, and local taxes

80/20 rule a rule, based on the theory that 20 percent of a company's products account for 80 percent of its sales, that holds that fast-moving products generate a higher level of customer service than slow-moving products

elastic demand the type of demand for a product in which a change in price causes an opposite change in total revenue—that is, an increase in price decreases total revenue, and a decrease in price increases total revenue

embargo a government restriction that prohibits the import or export of certain goods

empowerment giving employees who are responsible for hands-on production, sales, or service activities the authority to make decisions or take action without prior approval

environmental analysis the process of assessing and interpreting the information gathered through environmental scanning

environmental scanning the process of collecting information concerning forces in the marketing environment

equalized workload method a method of determining the optimal size of the sales force in which the number of customers multiplied by the number of sales calls annually required to serve these customers effectively is divided by the average number of calls each salesperson makes annually

evoked set a group of brands from which the buyer can choose

exchange control a government restriction that limits how much profit a foreign-based firm can return to its home country

exclusive distribution only one or very few outlets distribute a product

executive judgment the intuition and experience of one or more company managers

experimental study a research study that investigates the relationship between different variables— the data collected proves or disproves that a particular variable X is the cause of the variable Y

experimentation research that controls those factors that are related to or may affect the variables under investigation so that the effects of the experimental variables may be measured

expert forecasting survey a technique of predicting sales that uses experts to help prepare the sales forecast

exploratory study the type of research conducted by marketers when more information is needed about a problem; a review of existing information on a topic or informal investigation of a problem

exporting the sale of products to a foreign country, which represents the lowest level of commitment to international marketing

extensive decision making the type of decision making a consumer uses when purchasing an unfamiliar expensive product or an infrequently bought item

facilitating organization an organization that assists in the operation of the marketing channel but does not perform the negotiating function or sell products

family packaging a packaging strategy of using similar packages or one major element of the design in the packaging of all products

feature article a form of publicity that is up to 3,000 words in length and is usually prepared for a specific publication

Federal Trade Commission (FTC) a federal regulatory agency with many administrative duties, whose basic function is "to prevent the free enterprise system from being stifled or fettered by monopoly or anticompetitive practices and to provide the direct protection of consumers from unfair or deceptive trade practices"

feedback the receiver's reaction or response to the source's message

field experiment an experimental study conducted in a natural setting that allows a marketer to obtain a more direct test of marketing decisions than does a laboratory setting

finance company a company that loans marketing intermediaries (wholesalers or retailers) the money to pay for merchandise; the finance company owns the merchandise even though the intermediaries retain physical possession of it

fixed cost a cost that does not change when the number of units produced or sold changes

F.O.B. (free-on-board) factory a price that excludes transportation charges and indicates a shipping point; F.O.B. factory is the price of merchandise at the factory, before it is loaded for shipment—therefore, the buyer must pay for shipping

food broker a marketing intermediary that sells food and other grocery products to other wholesalers, grocery chains, institutional buyers, and food processors

formulated selling approach a sales presentation method in which the salesperson identifies the prospect's needs and then uses a formulated presentation that explains how the product can satisfy those needs

free merchandise a sales promotion method aimed at resellers whereby free merchandise is offered to resellers that purchase a stated quantity of the same or different products

free samples a sales promotion method used to encourage consumers to try a product for the first time, to increase sales volume in the early stages of a product's life cycle, or to obtain desirable distribution

freight absorption pricing a form of pricing whereby organizations absorb all or part of their customers' actual shipment costs

freight forwarder a transportation company that consolidates shipments from several organizations into efficient lot sizes

full-cost approach an approach to determining marketing costs in which cost analysis includes direct costs, traceable common costs, and nontraceable common costs

full-service merchant wholesaler a marketing intermediary that provides most services that wholesalers can perform

functional middleman a marketing intermediary—a broker or agent—who expedites exchanges for a fee but does not purchase products outright

functional modification a change that affects a product's versatility, effectiveness, convenience, or safety; it usually requires that the product be redesigned

functional organization an organizational structure in which marketing departments are organized by general marketing functions such as marketing research, product development, distribution, sales, and advertising

general merchandise wholesaler a full-service merchant wholesaler that carries a very wide product mix

generic brand a brand that identifies only the product type (peanut butter, tomato sauce), but not the manufacturer or any other distinguishing information

geographic pricing a form of pricing that involves reductions for transportation and other costs associated with the physical distance between the buyer and the seller

global marketing the development of marketing strategies as if the entire world (or regions thereof) were one large market

good a tangible object, something that can be seen and touched

government organizations includes federal, state, county, and local governments

green marketing developing products and packages that are less harmful to the environment

gross domestic product (GDP) a measure of the purely domestic output of a country

gross national product (GNP) an overall measure of a nation's economic standing in terms of the value of all products produced by that nation for a given period of time

group interview an interview in which the researcher—through informal, unstructured questions—tries to generate discussion about one or several topics among six to twelve people

growth stage the product life cycle period in which sales rise rapidly and profits peak and then start to decline

heterogeneity the characteristic (of services) of inconsistency or variation in performance

heterogeneous market a market that consists of individuals with dissimilar product needs

horizontal integration the combining of firms at the same level of a marketing channel or the expansion of units (such as retail stores) at one level

humanistic philosophy a moral philosophy that focuses on individual rights and values

hypermarket a huge retail store that combines the one-stop supermarket and the discount store

hypothesis an educated guess or a conjectural statement that specifies how two or more variables are related

idea a philosophy, concept, or image

idea generation searching for new product ideas that will help firms achieve their objectives

idea marketing   using marketing activities to increase the acceptance of a social cause or social idea within a target market

idea screening   selecting ideas with the greatest potential for further development

illustration   a photograph, drawing, graph, chart or table used in an advertisement

image   the mental picture—both functional and psychological—that the consumer has of a retail store

implementing   putting marketing strategies into action

import tariff   a tax or duty levied against goods brought into a country

income   the amount of money a person or organization receives from wages, sales, rents, investments, pensions, and subsidy payments in a given period, usually one year

incremental productivity method   a method of determining the optimal size of the sales force in which the marketer continues to increase the size of the sales force as long as the additional sales increases are greater than the additional selling costs that arise from employing more salespeople

independent variable   the variable that is manipulated in an experimental study; a variable free from influence of, or not dependent on, other variables

individual branding   a branding strategy of using a different brand name for each product

industrial product   a product bought for use in the production of other products or in a business's operations

industrial service   an intangible product that many organizations require in their operations, such as financial, legal, or janitorial services

inelastic demand   a type of demand in which a price increase or decrease will not significantly affect the quantity demanded

information input   a sensation people receive through the sense of sight, taste, hearing, smell, or touch

infomercial   a half-hour television commercial that generates telephone or mail responses for products or information

infrastructure   the communications, transportation, and energy facilities that mobilize a nation

in-home selling   nonstore retailing activities that involve personal contacts with consumers in their homes

innovator   one of the first people to adopt a new product

inquiry   an examination of some elements of an advertising program conducted during the program to measure advertising effectiveness

inseparability   the characteristic (of services) of having simultaneous and indivisible production and consumption

institutional advertising   advertising that promotes organizational images, ideas, or issues

institutions   nonbusiness or nonprofit organizations that seek to advance nonbusiness goals; includes churches, hospitals, museums, universities, and charitable organizations

intangibility   the characteristic (of services) of not being capable of assessment by customers' sense of taste, touch, sight, smell, or hearing

integrated marketing communications   the application of various communication methods to accomplish marketing objectives

intensive distribution   all available outlets are used for distributing a product

intermodal transportation   transportation that combines two or more modes of transportation to obtain the benefits of the carriers involved

internal customer   an employee in an organization

internal marketing   the process by which all members of the organization come to understand the values of the marketing system and their role in implementing marketing strategies

internal product   a job in an organization

international marketing   the performance of marketing activities across national boundaries

international selling   travel of a firm's sales force across national boundaries to meet directly with clients in a foreign country

interpretation   the third step of the perceptual process in which people make sense out of information inputs

introduction stage   the stage in a product's life cycle when the product first appears in the marketplace, sales are zero, and profits are negative

inventory management and control   the physical distribution activities that help marketers develop and maintain adequate assortments of products to satisfy target markets and meet customers' needs

involvement   the degree of perceived relevance and personal interest a buyer has in a product or brand in a particular situation

joint demand   a type of organizational demand in which the sale of one product is dependent on the sale of another

joint venture   a partnership between a domestic firm and a foreign firm or government

judgment sampling   a method of nonprobability sampling in which the researcher hand-picks participants for the study

just-in-time inventory   an inventory management technique whereby the company maintains low inventory levels by ordering products more frequently and in smaller quantities, just in time for production

knowledge   the outcome of learning; consists of information stored in a person's memory

labeling   the display of important information on a product package

laboratory experiment an experimental study in which participants are invited to a central location to react or respond to experimental stimuli

laggard one of the last consumers to adopt a new product; they are oriented toward the past and suspicious of new products

late majority people who are quite skeptical of new products but eventually adopt them because of economic necessity or social pressure

layout the physical arrangement of an advertisement's illustration(s), headline, and other copy elements

learning changes in a person's behavior that are caused by information and experience

licensing an international marketing arrangement in which the licensee (a foreign company) pays the licensor (an international marketing firm) commissions or royalties for the right to use its name, products, patents, brands and trademarks, raw materials, production processes, or managerial and technical assistance

limited decision making the type of decision making employed for products that are purchased occasionally or when a buyer needs to acquire information about an unfamiliar brand in a familiar product category

limited-line wholesaler a full-service merchant wholesaler that carries a narrow product mix, usually only a few product lines

limited-service merchant wholesaler a marketing intermediary that assumes ownership of goods but specializes in only a few of the functions performed by wholesalers

line family branding a branding strategy in which an organization uses family branding only for products within a particular line rather than for all its products

local selling maintaining a sales force composed of locals from the country where a firm conducts business

mail-order retailing a type of direct marketing in which sellers contact buyers through catalogues, direct mail, radio, television, magazines, or newspapers

mail-order wholesaler a limited-service wholesaler that sells products to retail and organizational customers through a catalogue instead of a personal sales force

mail survey a survey in which questionnaires are sent to respondents, who are encouraged to complete and return them

manufacturer brand a brand developed and owned by its producer, who is usually involved with distribution, promotion, and to some extent pricing decisions for the brand

manufacturers' agent an independent middleman who represents several different manufacturers and offers noncompeting, complementary product lines to customers

manufacturer's coupon a sales promotion device for new products—cents-off certificate allows consumers to purchase a specified product at a reduced price from any retailer carrying the product

marginal cost (MC) the additional cost incurred when a firm produces one more unit of a product

marginal revenue (MR) the change in total revenue that results from the sale of an additional unit of a product

market a group of people who need and want a particular product, and have the buying power, willingness, and authority to purchase the product

market attractiveness–business position model a two-dimensional matrix that extends the Boston Consulting Group (BCG) approach to include market attractiveness and business strength

market density the number of potential customers within a unit of land area, such as a square mile

market development a strategy of increasing sales by introducing current products into new markets

market manager a person responsible for overseeing the marketing activities that serve a particular group or class of customers

market niche a small, unique part of a market segment

market opportunities opportunities that arise when the right combination of circumstances and timing allows an organization to take action to reach a particular market

market-oriented organization an organizational structure in which the marketing department is structured on the basis of market segments, in addition to functions

market penetration a strategy of increasing sales of existing products in current markets

market sales potential the amount of a product that specific customer groups are likely to purchase within a specified period at a specific level of industrywide marketing activity

market segment a group of individuals, groups, or organizations that share one or more characteristics that cause them to have relatively similar product needs

market segmentation the process of dividing a total market into groups of consumers who have relatively similar product needs

market test a means of forecasting the sales of new or existing products by making the product available to consumers in one or more test areas and measuring consumer purchases and responses to distribution, promotion, and price

marketing the process of planning and executing the conception, pricing, promotion, and distribution of ideas, goods, and services to create exchanges that satisfy individual and organizational objectives

marketing audit a thorough, systematic, and objective review of an organization's marketing objectives, philosophy, strategies, organization, and performance

marketing channel (channel of distribution) a group of interrelated individuals or organizations that direct the flow of products to consumers

marketing concept a management philosophy stating that an organization should strive to satisfy the needs of consumers through a coordinated set of activities that also allows the organization to achieve its objectives

marketing cost analysis a method for controlling marketing strategies whereby various costs are broken down and classified to determine which are associated with specific marketing activities

marketing databank files (often computerized) of routinely collected information and data acquired by an organization through marketing research

marketing environment all the forces outside an organization that directly or indirectly influence its marketing activities; includes competition, regulation, politics, society, economic conditions, and technology.

marketing era a customer-oriented period beginning in the early 1950s and continuing today in which businesses determine customer needs first and then develop products that satisfy those needs; the era that gave rise to the marketing concept

marketing ethics the moral evaluation of marketing activities and decisions as right or wrong, based on commonly accepted principles of behavior

marketing information system (MIS) the program for managing and organizing information gathered from inside and outside an organization

marketing intermediary an individual or organization that facilitates exchanges between producers, other intermediaries, and the final consumers of products

marketing management the process of planning, organizing, implementing, and controlling marketing strategies

marketing mix the combination of four elements: product, price, distribution, and promotion

marketing objective an objective that specifies what is to be accomplished through marketing activities

marketing plan a formally prepared and written document detailing the activities necessary to implement the marketing strategies

marketing research the collection, analysis, and interpretation of data for guiding marketing decisions

marketing strategy a plan for selecting and analyzing a target market and developing and maintaining a marketing mix that will satisfy this target market

markup pricing a cost-oriented pricing method in which a predetermined percentage of the cost, called *markup,* is added to the cost of the product to determine the product's price

mass merchandiser a large organization that offers fewer customer services than a department store and focuses on lower prices, name-brand merchandise, high turnover, and large sales volumes

materials handling the physical handling of products, in warehouse operations and in the transportation of products from manufacturers to distributors and ultimate consumers

matrix organization a cross-functional organization overlay that creates multiple lines of authority and places people in teams to work on tasks for a finite period of time

maturity stage the product life cycle period during which the sales curve peaks and begins to decline and profits continue to decline

mechanical observation device a camera, recorder, counting machine, or equipment that records physiological changes in individuals

media plan a plan that establishes the specific media to be used in an advertising campaign and the dates and times that advertisements will appear

medium of transmission a means of carrying the encoded message from the source to the receiver during the communication process

merchandise allowance a sales promotion method aimed at resellers that consists of a manufacturer's agreement to pay resellers specified amounts of money in exchange for providing special promotional efforts, such as displays or advertising

merchant wholesaler a marketing intermediary that assumes both possession and ownership of goods as well as the risks associated with ownership

message an idea or experience that a source wants to share in the communication process

missionary salesperson a support salesperson employed by a manufacturer to facilitate sales and offer assistance to its own customers (wholesalers and retailers)

modified rebuy purchase a type of organizational purchase in which a new-task purchase is changed the second or third time it is ordered or the requirements associated with a straight rebuy purchase are modified

money refund a sales promotion method for new products in which the manufacturer mails the consumer a specified amount of money when proof of purchase is established

monopolistic competition a market structure in which many firms are marketing a product, and each firm attempts to differentiate its product to convince consumers that its product is the one to buy

monopoly a market structure in which only one firm is marketing a product for which there are no close substitutes

moral philosophy a set of principles that dictates the right and moral way to behave

motivation research research that lets marketers analyze the major motives that influence consumer buying behavior

motive an internal energizing force or reason that moves a person toward a goal

multinational market group a group of two or more countries that agree to reduce trade and tariff barriers between one another

multisegment approach a market segmentation approach in which an organization directs its marketing efforts at two or more segments by developing a marketing mix for each segment

National Advertising Review Board (NARB) a self-regulatory agency, created by the Council of Better Business Bureaus and three advertising trade organizations, to screen national advertisements for honesty and process complaints about deceptive advertisements

need something that is required for basic human survival—water, food, shelter, or clothing

need satisfaction approach a sales-presentation method that centers on the prospect's needs—the salesperson first tries to identify the needs of the buyer and then tailors the sales presentation to those needs

negotiated pricing an organizational pricing policy in which negotiations determine the final price paid by the organizational customer even when list prices and discount structures are specified

new product a product that a specific organization has not marketed previously, although other organizations may offer similar products

new product development a six-phase process consisting of idea generation, idea screening, business analysis, product development, test marketing, and commercialization

new-task purchase a type of organizational purchase in which an organization is making an initial purchase of an item to be used to perform a new job or to solve a new problem

news conference a meeting held for media representatives to announce major news events

news release a form of publicity that is usually a single page of typewritten copy about a newsworthy event and is sent to news editors for possible publication

noise interference that affects any or all stages of the communication process

noncumulative discount a one-time price reduction based on the dollar amount of the order, number of units purchased, or product mix purchased

nonprice competition a policy in which a seller focuses on aspects other than price—such as distinctive product features, service, product quality, promotion, and packaging—to differentiate its products from competing brands

nonprofit marketing all marketing activities conducted by individuals or organizations to accomplish goals other than financial profit

nonstore retailing retailing activities that take place outside traditional store environments

nontraceable common cost a cost that cannot be ascribed to a specific marketing activity on the basis of any logical criterion and thus is assignable only on an arbitrary basis

objective and task approach a rational method for determining the advertising budget, in which marketers define the objectives that a program is to achieve, identify the tasks required to accomplish them, and compute the costs of the tasks

observation a method of collecting primary data in which researchers record the overt behavior of respondents, taking note of physical conditions and events

odd-even pricing a psychological pricing policy of ending a price with a certain number in an effort to influence consumers' perceptions of the price or the product

off-price retailer a specialty store that sells a limited line of name-brand and designer products below list price

oligopoly a market structure in which few firms are marketing a product and they control much of the supply of the product

opportunity a set of conditions that either limits unfavorable behavior or rewards favorable behavior

opportunity cost the value that a client or donor gives up in an exchange

order getter a type of salesperson who seeks out new customers and tries to increase sales to present customers

order processing the receipt and transmission of sales order information

order taker a type of salesperson who processes routine sales and reorders and maintains lasting, positive relationships with customers

organization marketing marketing effort designed to persuade members of a target market to identify with or become members of an organization

organizational buying behavior actions and decision processes of producers, resellers, and governments in deciding what products to buy

organizational market individuals or groups that purchase a specific kind of product for resale, direct use in the production of other products, or use in general daily operations

organizational mission a formal statement that states what management wants the organization to be and the guidelines for getting there

organizational objectives objectives that specify what the organization wants to accomplish

organizational strategy a plan that defines the means by which an organization will achieve its organizational objectives

organizational structure the framework of a marketing department that establishes the lines of authority and responsibility among marketing personnel, specifying who makes certain decisions and performs particular activities

organizing the structuring of a company to connect and coordinate resources and activities to achieve marketing objectives in an effective and efficient manner

overall family branding a branding strategy of giving all of a company's products the same name or part of the name

patronage motive a motive that influences where a person purchases products on a regular basis

peak performance the highest level of performance an employee can achieve, which results when a worker surpasses acceptable performance by exerting discretionary effort

percent of sales approach a common method of determining the advertising budget, in which marketers multiply a firm's past sales, forecasted sales, or a combination of the two by a standard percentage of sales based on the company's traditional advertising expenditures and the industry's average

perception the process through which people select, organize, and interpret information inputs and give them meaning

perceptual organization the second step of the perception process in which information inputs are organized and take on meaning

perfect competition an ideal market with a large number of sellers, no one of which can significantly influence the price or supply of the products

performance standard an expected level of performance against which actual performance can be compared

perishability the characteristic (of services) that service capacity unused in one time period cannot be stored for use in the future

person marketing the use of marketing activities to increase the visibility of and preference for an individual among a target market

personal factor a factor unique to a person that affects buying behavior

personal interview survey a face-to-face, one-on-one interview that is the most flexible method for collecting primary data

personal selling face-to-face communication with potential buyers to inform them about and persuade them to buy an organization's product

personality the total of all the traits, experiences, and behaviors that make up a person

physical distribution the set of activities used in managing the flow of products from manufacturers to consumers and end users

pioneer advertising advertising that tries to stimulate primary demand for a product by providing consumers with information about the product, its functions, uses, and where it can be purchased

place marketing marketing activities used to attract members of a target market to a particular area

point-of-purchase materials a promotional item such as an outside sign, window or floor display, counter piece, or self-service carton used to encourage consumers to make a purchase

politics the policies and goals of the government and its elected officials

pollution the contamination of water, air, and land

population all the elements, units, or individuals that are of interest to researchers for a specific study

Porter's Generic Strategy Model a model developed by Michael Porter which suggests that organizations should analyze their industry and then define a competitive niche using one of three generic strategies: cost leadership, differentiation, and focus

posttest measurement of advertising effectiveness after an advertising program

premium an item offered free or at a minimum cost as a bonus for purchasing a product

premium (push) money additional compensation provided to salespeople to encourage them to push a line of products

prestige pricing a psychological pricing policy that sets prices artificially high to imply a prestige or quality image

pretest a test conducted before an advertising campaign begins to evaluate the effectiveness of one or more elements of the advertising message

price the value placed on what is exchanged

price competition a policy whereby a firm focuses on price as a means of differentiating its products from others and attempts to match or beat its competitors' prices

price discrimination a policy of charging different prices to different groups of customers to give those paying less a competitive advantage

price elasticity of demand the relative responsiveness of changes in quantity demanded to changes in price

price leader a product often sold below its usual profit margin or even below cost

price lining a psychological pricing policy of setting a limited number of prices for selected lines or groups of merchandise

price penetration a new-product pricing policy of setting prices lower than prices of competing brands to gain access to a market and generate a larger unit sales volume

price skimming a new-product pricing policy of setting the highest possible price that buyers will pay (to appeal to quality- and status-conscious consumers)

pricing method a systematic procedure for setting prices on a regular basis

pricing objective a general goal that describes what an organization hopes to achieve through its pricing activities

pricing policy a plan or course of action for achieving pricing objectives

primary data data collected for a specific project

private distributor (private) brand a brand developed and owned by a reseller, such as a wholesaler or retailer

private warehouse a warehouse owned and operated by a company for the purpose of distributing its own products

problem definition the first step toward solving a marketing problem through a research study; involves identifying the nature and boundaries of a problem

process material material that is used directly in the production of other products but that, unlike a component part, is not readily distinguishable from the product

producers individuals and business organizations that purchase products to use in the production of other products or in their daily operations for the purpose of making a profit

product anything that satisfies a need or want and can be offered in an exchange

product adoption process the five-stage process that buyers go through in accepting a product; includes awareness, interest, evaluation, trial, and adoption

product advertising advertising used by business, government, and nonbusiness organizations to promote the uses, features, images, and benefits of their goods and services

product assortment a collection of diverse products and competing brands

product deletion the elimination of a product that no longer satisfies consumers or contributes to the achievement of organizational objectives

product development the phase in which a new product is moved from concept to test stage and other elements of the marketing mix (promotion, price, and distribution) are developed

product item a unique version of a product that is distinct from the organization's other products

product life cycle the course of product development, consisting of four stages: introduction, growth, maturity, and decline

product line a group of closely related products that are considered a unit because of marketing, technical, or end-use considerations

product line depth the number of products offered in a given product line

product manager a person responsible for managing a product, product line, or several distinct products that make up an interrelated group

product mix the total group of products offered by a firm, or all of the firm's product lines

product mix width the number of product lines offered by a firm

product modification the changing of one or more of a product's characteristics

product-oriented organization an organizational structure in which the marketing units are organized by product or product line, with a separate product manager taking full responsibility for the marketing of each specific product or line

product positioning a firm's decisions and activities aimed at shaping and maintaining a product concept in consumers' minds

product-specific spending patterns the relative proportions of annual household income spent on specific products within a general product class

production era the period of creating goods that began in the 1600s with the colonization of America and continued into the early part of the twentieth century

professional pricing the pricing policy—practiced by doctors, lawyers, and others who have skills or experience in a particular field—in which a standard fee is charged for a particular service, regardless of the problems involved in providing that service

Profit Impact of Market Strategy (PIMS) program a research program—developed by the Strategic Planning Institute (SPI), a nonprofit think tank—to assist member firms in analyzing marketing performance and formulating marketing strategies

projective technique a test in which subjects are asked to perform specific tasks for particular purposes while, in fact, they are being evaluated for other purposes

promotion the marketing activities used to communicate to a target market positive, persuasive information about an organization, its products, and its activities to directly or indirectly expedite exchanges

promotion mix the specific combination of four promotional methods—advertising, sales promotion, personal selling, and publicity—used by an organization for a specific product

prospecting developing a list of potential customers for personal selling purposes

prosperity a phase of the business cycle in which unemployment is low and the total national income is relatively high

psychological factor a force within an individual that affects purchasing behavior

psychological pricing a pricing policy designed to encourage purchases that are based on emotional rather than rational responses

public relations communication activities designed to create and maintain a favorable image of an organization

public warehouse a warehouse that provides storage and related physical distribution facilities and services to organizations on a rental basis

publicity a nonpaid form of nonpersonal communication about an organization or its products that is transmitted through a mass medium in the form of a news story

pull policy promotion of a product directly to consumers to stimulate strong consumer demand

push policy promotion of a product only to the next member down in the marketing channel

quality the totality of features and characteristics of a good or service that bears on the ability to satisfy stated or implied needs

quality modification a change that relates to a product's dependability and durability and usually involves an alteration in the materials or production process employed

quantity discount a price reduction that reflects the economy of purchasing in large quantities

quota a limit on the amount of a product that can leave or enter a country

quota sampling a form of nonprobability sampling in which the final choice of respondents is left to the researchers

rack jobber a full-service merchant wholesaler that supplies display units as well as products, and performs purchasing and stocking functions for retailers

random factor analysis an analysis that attributes irregular sales variations to random, nonrecurrent events such as regional power failures or natural disasters

random sampling basic probability sampling in which all units in a population have an equal or known chance of being selected

raw material a basic good that actually becomes part of a physical product

rebate a refund of part of the purchase price given by the seller to the buyer

receiver the audience—an individual, group, or organization—that a source wants to reach with its message

recession a phase of the business cycle in which total production, employment rates, income, and buying power decline

reciprocity an arrangement unique to organizational sales in which two organizations agree to buy from each other

recognition test a posttest in which researchers show individual respondents actual advertisements and ask whether they recognize them

recovery a transition phase in the business cycle during which the economy moves from recession to prosperity

reference group a group with whom an individual identifies to the extent that he or she takes on many of the values, attitudes, or behaviors of group members

regulation laws and regulatory agencies that influence the conduct of business

reinforcement advertising advertising used to assure current purchasers that they have made the right choice and to offer advice on how to get the most satisfaction from the product

reminder advertising advertising used to make consumers aware that an established brand is still around and that it has certain uses, characteristics, and benefits

research design the overall plan for conducting a research investigation

resellers intermediaries, such as wholesalers and retailers, that buy finished goods and resell them to make a profit

retail franchising a contractual agreement in which a supplier (the franchiser) grants a dealer (the franchisee) the right to sell the supplier's products in exchange for some type of consideration

retailer coupon usually a cents-off coupon distributed through advertisements or handouts and redeemable only at specific retail stores

retailing the marketing activities involved in selling products to ultimate consumers for personal, family, or household use

role a set of functions and activities that a person in a particular position is expected to perform

routine decision making the type of decision making a consumer uses when purchasing frequently purchased, low-cost items that do not require much thought

safety stock the amount of inventory needed to prevent a stockout

sales analysis a method for controlling marketing strategies whereby sales figures are used to assess an organization's current performance

sales branch a manufacturer-owned intermediary that sells products and provides support services for the manufacturer's sales force

sales contest a competition designed to stimulate increased participation in sales efforts by distributors, retailers, and sales personnel

sales era the period from the mid-1920s to the early 1950s during which businesses looked on sales as the major means of increasing profits

sales-force forecasting survey a technique of predicting sales by asking members of a firm's sales force to estimate the anticipated sales in their territories for a specified time period

sales office a manufacturer-owned intermediary that operates much like an agent

sales promotion an activity or material that offers consumers, salespersons, or resellers a direct inducement for purchasing a product

sales territory a geographic area for which one or more salespeople are responsible

sampling selecting a limited number of units to represent the characteristics of a total population

scrambled merchandising the retailing strategy of adding unrelated products and product lines to an existing product mix

seasonal analysis a technique in which the forecaster studies daily, weekly, or monthly sales figures to evaluate the degree to which seasonal factors such as climate and holiday activities influence the firm's sales

seasonal discount a price reduction offered to buyers that buy goods or services out of season

secondary data data from inside or outside an organization previously collected for some purpose other than the current investigation

segmentation base (or **variable**) a characteristic of individuals, groups, or organizations that marketing managers use to divide a total market into segments

selection the first step of the perception process in which people select some inputs and ignore others

selective distortion the changing or twisting of currently received information

selective distribution only some available outlets in an area are chosen to distribute a product

selective exposure the phenomenon of selecting some inputs (to be exposed to our awareness) and ignoring others because of the inability to be conscious of all inputs at one time

selective retention a phenomenon in which a person remembers information inputs that support personal feelings and beliefs and forgets inputs that do not

selling agent an independent middleman who markets a manufacturer's entire output or all of a specified product line

service an intangible product that often involves human or mechanical effort

service quality the conformance of service(s) to customer specifications and expectations

shopping product a product (such as an appliance, furniture, or clothing) that consumers are willing to spend more effort to plan for and purchase

situational factor a circumstance or condition that exists when a consumer is making a purchase decision

social audit the systematic examination of a firm's objectives, strategies, and performance of social responsibility activities

social class a relatively homogeneous and stable group of people with similar values, interests, lifestyles, and behaviors

social factor a force that other people exert on consumer behavior

social responsibility the conscious effort by an organization to maximize its positive impact and minimize its negative impact on society

societal marketing concept a management philosophy that considers the welfare of society as well as the interests of the firm and its customers

society all of the individuals that make up the human race and their characteristics and values

sorting the process through which the supply of goods and services produced by the manufacturer is matched with the assortment demanded by the consumer

source a person, group, or organization that has a message to share with another person or group of people

special-event pricing a form of promotional pricing that involves coordinating price cuts with advertising for seasonal or special situations to increase revenue or reduce costs

specialty-line wholesaler a full-service merchant wholesaler that carries a very limited variety of products—usually only one product line or a few items within a product line

specialty product a product with one or more unique characteristics that a large group of buyers is willing to spend considerable time and effort to purchase

specialty store a retail store that is smaller than a mass merchandiser or department store and offers a much narrower mix of products with deeper product lines

sponsorship providing support for and associating an organization's name with an event, program, or person

Standard Industrial Classification (SIC) system a system developed by the federal government to classify selected economic characteristics of industrial, commercial, financial, and service organizations

statistical interpretation analysis that focuses on what is average or what deviates from the average; analysis that shows how widely responses vary and how they are distributed in relation to the variable being measured

stimulus-response approach a sales-presentation method based on the belief that customers will make a purchase if exposed to the right stimulus; sometimes called the canned sales approach

stockout the condition that exists when a firm runs out of a product

straight commission compensation plan a plan by which a salesperson's compensation is based solely on the amount of his or her sales in a given time period

straight rebuy purchase a type of organizational purchase in which a buyer purchases the same products routinely under approximately the same terms of sale

straight salary compensation plan a plan by which salespeople are paid a specified amount of money per hour, week, month, or year

strategic alliance an agreement between two firms who pool their resources in a partnership more extensive than a joint venture; allows firms to gain access to new markets or technology

strategic business unit (SBU) a division, product line in a division, or other profit center within a parent company

strategic marketing planning the continuous process of developing and implementing marketing strategies to achieve marketing objectives, which in turn lead to the achievement of overall organizational objectives.

strategic window the often limited period of time during which market opportunities match the particular capabilities of a firm competing in a particular market

stratified sampling sampling in which researchers divide the population of interest into groups, according to a common characteristic or attribute, and then conduct a random sample within each group

style modification an alteration in taste, texture, sound, smell, or visual characteristics that affects the sensory appeal of a product

subculture   a subdivision of a culture in which people share similar attitudes, values, and actions that are different from those of the broader culture

superficial discounting   fictitious comparative pricing in which a firm uses a deceptive markdown; sometimes called "was-is pricing"

supermarket   a large, self-service retailer that stocks a wide and deep assortment of grocery products, as well as some nonfood products

superstore   a giant retail outlet that stocks most food and nonfood products ordinarily sold in a supermarket, as well as most products purchased on a routine basis

supply   something that does not become part of a finished product but does expedite production and operations

support personnel   members of the sales staff who facilitate exchanges but are not usually involved in selling products

survey   an interview conducted by mail, telephone, or in person to collect data

target market   a group of consumers at whom an organization directs its marketing efforts

team   a group of employees who work closely to pursue common objectives

technical salesperson   a support salesperson who provides technical assistance to the company's current customers

technology   the knowledge—often acquired from scientific research—of how to accomplish tasks and goals

technology transfer   the process by which an organization transforms new technologies into successful products

telemarketing   the use of a telephone as a tool to reach prospective customers

telephone retailing   a form of telemarketing in which marketers sell goods or services by telephoning prospective customers whose names appear in the telephone directory or on a prescreened list

telephone survey   a survey in which interviewers solicit respondents' answers to a questionnaire over the telephone and record their answers

test marketing   a trial launch of a product and its marketing mix in small regions chosen to represent the target market

time series analysis   a method in which the forecaster studies the firms' historical sales data to try to discover patterns in the firm's sales volume over time

total cost   the sum of total fixed costs and total variable costs

total market approach   a market segmentation approach in which a company develops a single marketing mix and directs it at the entire market for a particular product; also called undifferentiated approach

total quality management (TQM)   a management approach to long-term success through customer satisfaction, based on the participation of all members of an organization in improving processes, products, services, and the culture in which they work

traceable common cost   a cost that can be attributed indirectly to a marketing activity

trade (functional) discount   a reduction off the list price that a manufacturer gives to an intermediary for performing certain functions

trademark   a legal designation, registered with the U.S. Patent and Trademark Office, that gives the owner exclusive use of a brand name, brand mark, or part of a brand and prohibits others from using it

trade mart   a permanent facility that firms can rent to exhibit products year-round

trade salesperson   a type of salesperson who takes orders in addition to performing other support functions and whose primary function is to help customers promote the producer's product

trade show   a temporary exhibit typically held annually in a major city to allow vendors to identify prospective customers

trading company   a company that serves as a link between buyers and sellers in different countries

trading stamp   a sales promotion item distributed by retailers to consumers in proportion to the amount of the consumers' purchases (consumers save the stamps and redeem them for merchandise)

traditional specialty store   a specialty retailer that carries a narrow product mix with deep product lines

transportation company   a rail, truck, air, or other carrier that helps manufacturers and retailers transport products without the aid of intermediaries

trend analysis   an analysis that focuses on aggregate sales data, such as annual sales figures over a period of many years, to determine whether annual sales are generally rising, falling, or stable

truck wholesaler   a limited-service merchant wholesaler who delivers products directly to customers for on-the-spot inspection and selection but offers only limited services and requires cash purchases

unaided recall test   a posttest in which subjects are asked to remember advertisements that they have seen recently but are not given any clues to spur their memory

uniform geographic pricing   a form of pricing that results in a fixed average cost of transportation; sometimes referred to as postage-stamp pricing

unitary demand   the type of demand for a product in which the product's revenue does not vary with price changes

unit loading   the materials handling practice of grouping one or more boxes on a pallet or skid to permit efficient movement by mechanical means (such as fork lifts, trucks, or conveyor systems)

unsought product   a product purchased as a result of the sudden occurrence of a problem or in response to aggressive selling tactics that result in a sale that otherwise would not take place

utilitarian philosophy a moral philosophy that seeks the greatest satisfaction for the largest number of individuals

VALS (Values and Lifestyles) program a popular approach to consumer market segmentation that divides American lifestyles into nine categories: survivors, sustainers, belongers, emulators, achievers, I-am-me, experiential, societally conscious, and integrated

variable cost a cost that varies directly with changes in the number of units manufactured or sold

venture team an organizational unit responsible for creating entirely new products aimed at new markets

vertical integration the combining of two or more functions of a marketing channel under one management

vertical marketing system (VMS) a marketing channel professionally managed and centrally controlled by a single marketing channel member

want something that is desired but not required for basic survival

warehouse showroom a large, high-volume, low-overhead retail store offering sizable, on-premises inventory but few services

warehouse/wholesale club a large-scale members-only discount store that combines features of cash-and-carry wholesaling with discount retailing

warehousing the design and operation of storage facilities

warranty a document that stipulates what the manufacturer will do if a product does not work properly

wealth the accumulation of past income, natural resources, and financial resources

wheel of retailing a popular theory regarding the origin and evolution of retail stores

wholesaling all the marketing activities of channel members that sell products to retailers and other organizational customers but not to ultimate consumers

willingness to spend a disposition toward buying, which is influenced by a person's ability to buy, absolute and relative product prices, expected satisfaction from a product, and numerous psychological and social forces

zone prices a regional price that takes advantage of a uniform pricing system

(Credits continued from page iv)

Name and Organization Index

Subject Index

Railways, 497, 498 (table), 499 (table)
Random factor analysis, 206–7
Random sampling, 296
Rational decision making, 218
Raw materials, 318
Reach, 633
Reactive approach to environmental forces, 102–3
Reader's Digest, 630
Rebates, 435
Rebuy purchase
  modified, 260
  straight, 260
Recall test, to measure advertising effectiveness, 635
Receiver, 584
Recession, 96–97
  impact of, on retailing, 568
Reciprocity, 255
Recognition test, 635
Recovery, 96–97
Recruiting, salespeople, 664–65
Recycled products, 16
Reference groups, and consumer decision making, 226
Referrals, 658
Refund, 588
  money, 679
Regional shopping center, 562
Regression analysis, 207
Regulation, 79
  laws in, 79, 81
  regulatory agencies in, 81, 83–87
Regulatory agencies, 81
  federal, 83–85, 84 (table)
  local, 85
  nongovernmental, 85–87
  state, 85
Reinforcement advertising, 617–18
Relationship selling, 661, 665
Reliability, 282
Religion, and international marketing, 161
Reminder advertising, 617
Rent, 418
Repair items, 319
Repeat business, importance of, 11
Repositioning, 398–99, 399 (illus.)
Resellers
  in business-to-business marketing, 251–52
  sales promotion methods directed at, 673–75
Resource Conservation and Recovery Act (1984), 130
Retailer coupon, 676
Retailers, sales promotion methods used by, 675–76
Retail franchising, 550–53, 551 (table), 553 (illus.)
Retailing
  changing environment in, 568–69
  definition and importance, 540–41, 541 (table), 542 (table)
  in foreign countries, 558–60, 559 (table), 561 (illus.)
  franchising, 550–53, 551 (table), 553 (illus.)
  mail-order, 556–58
  nonstore, 553–58
  scrambled merchandising, 566
  store environment, 563–65
  store location, 560–63
  strategies in, 560–68
  telephone, 556
  wheel of, 566–67, 567 (illus.)
Retail stores, types of, 541–50, 543 (illus.), 545 (illus.), 547 (illus.), 549 (illus.)
Return on investment (ROI), pricing objectives based on, 424

Revenue
  average, 450
  marginal, 450
  total, 450
Robinson-Patman Act (1936), 78 (table), 79, 432, 435
Roles, and consumer decision making, 227–29
Roper Organization, 227
Routine decision making, 223
RUBS (rich urban bikers), 181
Run-out strategy, in product deletion, 406

Safety, right to, 128
Safety stock, 504
Sale
  role of advertising in minimizing fluctuations in, 619
  ways to lose, 662 (table)
Sales analysis, 710–11
Sales and Marketing Management
  Survey of Buying Power, 95, 288
  Survey of Industrial Purchasing Power, 268
Sales branch, 524–25
Sales contest, 674–75
Sales era, 13
Sales force
  compensating, 666–67
  determining size of, 663–64
  evaluating performance of, 669
  managing, 662–69, 663 (illus.)
  managing international, 670–72
  missionary, 655
  motivating, 667–68, 668 (illus.)
  recruiting and selecting, 664–65
  routing and scheduling, 669
  stereotype of, 653, 654
  supporting role of advertising in, 619
  technical, 655
  trade, 655
  training, 665–66
  types of, 653–56
Sales-force forecasting survey, 206
Sales forecasts, 205
  combination methods, 208
  correlation methods, 207
  executive judgment, 205
  market tests, 207–8
  surveys, 205–6
  time-series analysis, 206–7
Sales objectives, 425
  establishing, 662–63
Sales office, 525
Sales potential, 204–5
Sales promotion
  definition of, 672
  directed at consumers, 675–79
  directed at resellers, 673–75
  distinguishing between promotion and, 588
  for established products, 676–77
  in fast food sales, 683–84
  in international markets, 679–80, 680 (illus.)
  methods used by retailers, 675–76
  nature and uses of, 672
  for new products, 679
  objectives of, 672, 673 (table)
  and product life cycle, 597
  in promotion mix, 588–89, 589 (illus.)
  for services, 360–61
  types of, 673–80
Sales territories, establishing, 668–69
Sales transaction, 710–11
Sample-composition bias, in surveys, 291
Samples, free, 679
Sampling, 295–97
  area, 296–97
  in international marketing research, 301–2
  quota, 297

  random, 296
  stratified, 296
Scrambled merchandising, 566
Seasonal analysis, 206
Seasonal discounts, 435
Seasonal products and promotion mix, 596
Secondary business district, 562
Secondary data, 157, 286–87
  in international marketing research, 300–1
  obtaining, 287–89
  sources of, 288 (table)
Segmentation, *see* Market segmentation
Selection, and perception, 232
Selective demand, 616
Selective distortion, 233
Selective distribution, 485–86
Selective exposure, 232
Selective retention, 233
Self-regulatory programs, 86, 87
  effectiveness of, 86
Selling
  creative, 654
  international, 671–72
  in-home, 554
  local, 670
  personal, *see* Personal selling
Selling agent, 524
Semiconductor Industry Association (SIA), 88
Service(s), 350 (illus.)
  characteristics, 351, 353–55
  classifying, 355–58, 357 (illus.), 358 (illus.)
  as concern of organization buyer, 257–58
  definition of, 9–10, 314, 348–49, 548
  developing marketing strategies for, 358–63
  foreign competition in, 350, 351
  franchising of, 550–51
  heterogeneity of, 354–55
  industrial, 319 (illus.)
  inseparability of production and consumption, 353, 354 (illus.)
  intangibility of, 351 (illus.), 353
  perishability of, 354
  price strategy for, 361–62
  product strategy for, 359
  promotion strategy for, 359–61
  quality of, 363–67
Service businesses, marketing activities of, 10
Service firms, promotion mix used by, 596
Service provider
  goal of, in classifying services, 357–58
  skill of, in classifying services, 356–57
Service quality, 363–64
  criteria used to judge, 366 (table)
  improving, 364, 366–67
Sex, as segmentation base, 189
Shallow product lines, 546
Sherman Act (1890), 78 (table), 79, 135
  and dual distribution, 483
  and horizontal immigrations, 491
  and price fixing, 432
Shopping centers
  community, 562
  neighborhood, 562
  planned, 562
  regional, 562
Shopping mall intercept interview, 291–92
Shopping products, 316, 317 (illus.)
Showrooms
  catalogue, 546
  warehouse, 545–46
Signature, in advertising copy, 626
Single-price stores, 545
Situational factors, in consumer decision making, 240, 240 (illus.)
Smart selling, 655
Social audit, 136

Social classes, 225
  and consumer decision making, 225–26
  U.S., 228 (table)
Social factors
  in consumer decision making, 225–30
  in international marketing, 161
Social marketing, 10
Social responsibility, 124–25
  consumerism in, 127–29
  definition of, 124
  ecology, 129–32
  evaluating, 135 (illus.), 135–36
  green marketing, 16, 91, 132–35, 134
    (illus.), 332
  pyramid, 125 (illus.)
  societal expectations in, 126
Societal expectations, in social responsibility,
  126
Societal marketing concept, 15–17
Society, 88–89
  characteristics of, 89–90, 90 (illus.)
  definition of, 88
  and promotion, 600–2
  values of, 90–91, 92 (illus.)
Society of Competitive Intelligence Profes-
    sional (SCIP), 78
Soft-drink industry, franchising in, 551
Sorting, 486–87
Sorting out, 487
Source, 584
Soviet Union, and social responsibility,
  141–43
Special-event pricing, 458
Specialty-line wholesaler, 521
Specialty products, 316–17
Specialty stores, 548–50, 549 (illus.)
Spending patterns
  comprehensive, 96
  consumer, 92–95
  product-specific, 96
Sponsorship, 639–40, 641
Sports Illustrated, 412, 630
Staggers Rail Act (1980), 85 (table)
Stance toward environmental forces, 103
Standard & Poor's Register, 268
Standard Industrial Classification (SIC)
    system, 267–69
Standard in-process stock, 167
Standardized work, 167
Stars, 47
State regulatory agencies, 85
Statistical interpretation, 298
Status quo objectives, 424
Stereotypes
  role of advertising in, 615
  role of promotion in creation of, 601–2
  of salespeople, 653, 654
Stimulus-response approach, to sales presenta-
    tion, 659
  freestanding, 561
  types of retail, 541–50, 543 (illus.), 545
    (illus.), 547 (illus.), 549 (illus.)
Stockout, 504
Stores
  location of, 560–63
Straight commission compensation plan,
  666–67
Straight rebuy purchase, 260
Straight salary compensation plan, 666
Strategic alliance, 156
Strategic business unit (SBU), 45, 53, 697
Strategic marketing planning, 726
  for branding, 329–31
  defining organizational mission in, 37–41,
    43
  definition of, 37
  designing marketing strategies, 55–59

developing marketing plan, 60 (illus.),
  60–61, 61 (table)
developing organizational strategy, 44–54,
  45 (illus.), 46 (illus.), 48 (illus.), 49
  (illus.), 51 (illus.), 52 (illus.)
establishing marketing objectives, 54–55
establishing organizational objectives,
  43–44, 44 (table)
in retailing, 560–68
steps in, 37, 38 (illus.)
Strategic Planning Institute (SPI), 50
Strategic window, 43
Stratified sampling, 296
Strip, 562
Style modification, 402
Subculture, and consumer decision making,
  230
Subheadline, 626
Subliminal messages, influence of, on con-
  sumers, 234
Superficial discounting, 458
Supermarkets, 542–43, 567
Superstores, 543–44, 567
Suppliers, relationship between buyers and,
  266
Supplies, 318–19
Supportive services, for products, 337–38
Support personnel, 655
Survey of Buying Power, 95, 288
Survey of Industrial Purchasing Power, 268
Surveys
  mail, 289–91, 291 (table)
  personal interview, 291 (table), 292–93
  as source of primary data, 205–6, 289
  telephone, 291 (table), 291–92
Sweepstakes, 588

Takt-time, 167
Tampering, problem of, 331
Tangibility, concept of, 349
Targeting, in personal selling, 658
Target market(s), 19
  analysis of, in marketing plan, 731, 734
    (table)
  approaches for selecting, 200–4, 201 (illus.)
  characteristics of, and promotion mix,
    595–96
  identifying for advertising, 621–22
  in marketing plan, 738, 739 (table)
  marketing research in identifying, 383
  selecting and analyzing, 55, 57
Team approach to selling, 656
Teams
  role of in matrix organizations, 700
  venture, 384–85
Technical product, characteristics of, 339
Technical salesperson, 655
Technological environment, 165–66
Technology
  in building long-term relationships, 661
  definition of, 97
  in marketing environment, 97–100
  in retailing, 568–69
  in warehousing, 531–32
Technology transfer, 99
Telecommunications, 146
Telemarketing, 556
Telephone retailing, 556
Telephone solicitation, 372
Telephone survey, 291 (table), 291–92
Television, media plan for, 630–31
Television advertising, 372
Television copy, 626
Test marketing
  in new product development, 393–95
  in sales forecasting, 207–8

Textile Fiber Products Identification Act
    (1958)
Textile Labeling Laws, 80 (table)
Time, 630
Time series analysis, 206
Time utility, creating, 10–11
Toll, 418
Total cost, 449
  average, 449
Total distribution cost, 494–95
Total market approach, 201
Total quality management (TQM), 25–26,
    266, 694, 696
Total revenue, 450
Traceable common cost, 712
Trade deficit, 152–53
Trade discounts, 434
Trade-in allowances, 434–35
Trade magazines, 265
Trademark, 324
Trademark Act (1946), 327
Trademark Counterfeiting Act (1980), 78
    (table)
Trademark Law Revision Act (1988), 617
Trade mart, 530
Trade publications
  in business-to-business marketing, 599
  obtaining competition information in, 101
Trade salesperson, 655
Trade shows, 528, 675
  top ten cities for, 530 (table)
Trade surplus, 153
Trading companies, 154
Trading stamps, 675–76
Trading-up phase of retailing, 566
Traditional specialty store, 549–50
Training
  cross-cultural, 160
  for salespeople, 665–66
Transit advertisements, media plan for, 632
Transportation modes
  coordinating, 499–500
  selection, 497–500, 498 (table), 499 (table)
Transportation, U.S. department of, on ship-
    ping hazardous materials, 501
Transportation company, 527–28
Treaty of Rome, 168
Trend analysis, 206
Trial, in product adoption process, 396
Trial close, 660
Truck wholesaler, 522
Trusting patron, 236
TV Guide, 630, 633

Unaided recall test, 635
Undifferentiated approach, to target market
    selection, 201
Uniform geographic pricing, 433
Unitary demand, 446
United Nations, 132
  Conference on Environment and Develop-
    ment (UNCED), 111
Unit loading, 503
Universal Product Code (UPC), 336
  as proof of purchase, 679
Unplanned business district, 561–62
Unsought products, 317
USA Today, 731
U.S. News and World Report, 412
U.S.-Japanese free trade agreement, 170
Utilitarian philosophy, 117–18

Validity, in marketing research, 284
VALS (Values and Lifestyles) program, 194
Value shopper, 236